Development Econom

MW00339871

Development Economics: theory and practice provides students and practitioners with the perspectives and the tools they need to think analytically and critically about the current major economic development issues in the world.

Alain de Janvry and Elisabeth Sadoulet identify seven key dimensions of development: growth, poverty, vulnerability, inequality, basic needs, sustainability, and quality of life, and use them to structure the contents of the text. This book gives a historical perspective on the evolution of thought in development. It uses theory and empirical analysis to present readers with a full picture of how development works, how its successes and failures can be assessed, and how alternatives can be introduced. The authors demonstrate how diagnostics, design of programs and policies, and impact evaluation can be used to seek new solutions to the suffering and violence caused by development failures. This text is fully engaged with the most cutting-edge research in the field, and equips readers with analytical tools for the impact evaluation of development programs and policies, illustrated with numerous examples. It is underpinned throughout by a wealth of student-friendly features including case studies, quantitative problem sets, end-of-chapter questions, and extensive references.

This unique text aims at helping readers learn about development, think analytically about achievements and alternative options, and be prepared to compete on the development job market.

Alain de Janvry is Professor at the Department of Agricultural and Resource Economics, University of California, Berkeley, USA.

Elisabeth Sadoulet is Professor and Research Economist at the Department of Agricultural and Resource Economics, University of California, Berkeley, USA.

Development Economics

Theory and practice

Alain de Janvry and Elisabeth Sadoulet

Routledge
Taylor & Francis Group

LONDON AND NEW YORK

First published 2016
by Routledge
2 Park Square, Milton Park, Abingdon, Oxon OX14 4RN

and by Routledge
711 Third Avenue, New York, NY 10017

Routledge is an imprint of the Taylor & Francis Group, an informa business

Front cover image: A detail from the Diego Rivera mural, *La tierra dormida*, located at the Chapingo Autonomous University, Texcoco, State of Mexico, Mexico. Reproduction authorized by the National Institute of Fine Arts and Literature, 2015.

British Library Cataloguing in Publication Data
A catalogue record for this book is available from the British Library

Library of Congress Cataloging in Publication Data
De Janvry, Alain.
Development economics : theory and practice / Alain de Janvry and Elisabeth Sadoulet.
    pages cm
  1. Development economics. 2. Economic development. 3. Developing countries–Economic policy. 4. Developing countries–Social policy. I. Sadoulet, Elisabeth, 1945- II. Title.
HD82.D3765 2015   338.9–dc23
2015018633

ISBN: 978-1-138-88529-5 (hbk)
ISBN: 978-1-138-88531-8 (pbk)
ISBN: 978-1-315-71552-0 (ebk)

Typeset in Bembo
by Sunrise Setting Ltd, Paignton, UK

Contents

Figures

Tables

Preface

With 85 percent of the world's population living in developing countries, and half of humanity below the US$2.5/day international poverty line, defeating the "seven horsemen of underdevelopment"—lack of income growth, material poverty and hunger, vulnerability to shocks, inequality and inequity, low satisfaction of basic needs in health and education, lack of environmental sustainability, and an unsatisfactory quality of life—is one of today's most important world challenges. Over the last 60 years, since the emergence of development economics as a profession, we have seen stunning successes with selective dimensions of development—especially rapid income growth, reduction of extreme poverty, and rising satisfaction of basic needs—in some countries and for particular segments of their populations. But we have also seen continuing failures with other dimensions of development—especially vulnerability to shocks, rising inequality and inequity, and unsustainable development—and for many countries and social groups with almost all dimensions of development, with associated untenable human suffering, making the pursuit of success where it has as of yet been elusive particularly urgent.

As a profession seeking to promote economic development, we emerge from 60 years of thinking and practicing development economics with both pride and modesty. We have learned from experience that something can be done, and that what we design and implement can indeed succeed, but also that there are no magic recipes as to how to achieve development and that for too many places and people we have as of yet failed to uncover how to make development happen. The world of underdevelopment is simply too vast and heterogeneous for universal formulas to possibly exist: initial conditions are highly diverse, development objectives are multi-dimensional, implying the hard reality of trade-offs and the need for specific country choices, and constraints and opportunities are constantly changing. The history of development has much to teach us, but historical achievements are rarely directly transferable. The "big ideas" about development instruments that prevailed in the 1960s and 70s, using the state to overcome market failures, and in the 1980s and 90s, using the market to avoid state failures, have proven to be too blunt. New ideas for development are more needed than ever, but the quest for reinventing big ideas is a dead end. Clearly, market, state, and civil society all have roles to play for development to succeed, but specificity and balance in these roles needs to be imagined, designed, tried, and implemented for each particular time and place. As a consequence, learning what to know about development is less useful than learning how to think about it. "Thinking development" can then be applied to the practice of development at any particular place and time. Learning to think development and to translate development ideas into practice is thus the objective of this book. As we shall see, there are indeed many new and exciting ways of thinking development, and they can make a lot of difference for the successful practice of development.

In thinking development, we are equipped with history, current diagnostics, economic theory, causal empirical analyses of past experiences and current attempts, and practical experiences themselves. Bringing these together in a consistent body of thought and identifying effective instruments for development is the purpose of development economics. It aims to give us a set of tools and principles that we can apply to underdevelopment problems to seek to achieve economic development. Positive analysis—understanding why some countries and people are poor and others rich, why some are converging with the per capita income of rich countries and others not, through diagnostics and the identification of causal relations—helps us engage in normative analysis, proposing options as to what to do to make things different from how they are in poor countries, in a desirable direction in terms of their own development objectives, and in a feasible fashion for implementation. Options include countless dispersed bottom-up micro-level initiatives, capitalizing on what we can learn to make development work, and large-scale national policy initiatives, where the state effectively assumes its developmental functions. Development thus requires both thinking small and acting locally to seize multiple opportunities for improvements in wellbeing that are almost in everyone's reach, and thinking big and acting nationally and globally to promote growth and potentially take millions of people out of poverty through major technological and institutional innovations. This book focuses on how to bring rigor to the understanding of development, and on how to use our analytics to propose ways of transforming what we see into what we would like to see, thereby defeating the seven horsemen of underdevelopment in accordance with set priorities. This is an exciting purpose, requiring not only creative economic modeling and rigorous empirical analysis, but also offering countless opportunities to make a difference on an issue of immense importance.

The book is written for upper-division undergraduates in economics and for Master's students in public policy, development practice, or related fields of expertise. It consists of 22 chapters that can each be covered in one or two lectures. It delivers both breadth in offering a perspective on the origins and mechanisms of development, and depth in providing theoretical and empirical analytical techniques that development economists can take to the data and to the practice of development. The objective is to prepare students for jobs in international economic development, equipped with knowledge, experience, methods, and analytical techniques that should make them employable and high-performing. We consequently spend less time on ideological controversies and epistemological debates and more on looking at what works in helping professionals understand development and make it happen. Chapters are kept brief, with selected key messages proposed as entry points. Reasoning is as often as possible anchored in figures and formulas, econometric specifications are provided to show how to connect ideas to data, methods of impact analysis are used to establish causalities between events or interventions and outcomes, and plenty of results are provided, taken from the best studies available in the field. In reviewing these, students will be introduced to the main contributors to the literature, making them conversant with what the profession is currently doing and how it is impacting the practice of development. We thus hope that the book will not only be useful in helping students acquire the skills of a development economist and place themselves favorably on the job market, but also spark a passion for the subject and open opportunities to garner the many rewards that thinking and practicing development can bring to economists as concerned world citizens.

Acknowledgments

This book has been written over a long sequence of course offerings in development economics, principally at the upper-division undergraduate and Master's levels. These courses were offered for the Economics Department, the Department of Agricultural and Resource Economics, the Master's program in Public Policy, and the Master's program in Development Practice at the University of California, Berkeley. We also taught repeatedly using these materials in the Master's program in International Development and the program Gestion de Politique Economique at the CERDI (Centre d'Etudes et de Recherches sur le Développement International) in France. We deeply benefited from occasional co-teaching with distinguished colleagues, most particularly with David Roland-Holst, who wrote the initial draft of several of the chapters in the book and graciously allowed us to continue building on these chapters. This book would not have been started without his collaboration. We also co-taught with David Zilberman on the themes of natural-resource economics and common property resources. His classes were deeply influential and served as the basis for several of the chapters. On the history of development, we co-taught with Michael Watts from the Geography Department at the University of California, Berkeley for the Development Studies major. These were creative occasions from which we learned much and which gave us the basic structure of the history chapter.

We are fortunate to have had extraordinary teachers and colleagues in development economics from whom we have learned enormously over the years. They include George Kuznets, Albert Fishlow, and Pranab Bardhan at the University of California, Berkeley; Albert Hirschman at the Institute of Advanced Studies at Princeton University; T.W. Schultz at the University of Chicago; Vernon Ruttan at the University of Minnesota; Yujiro Hayami at FASID (Foundation for Advanced Studies on International Development) in Tokyo; Norman Collins at the University of California, Berkeley, and the Ford Foundation in Chile and India; Irma Adelman at the University of California, Berkeley; Erik Thorbecke at Cornell University; Patrick and Sylviane Guillaumont at the FERDI (Fondation pour les Études et Recherches sur le Développement International) in Clermont-Ferrand; François Bourguignon as chief economist at the World Bank; and Justin Lin, who succeeded him in that position.

From others, and without implicating them for possible mistakes and deficiencies, we learned much about the theory and the practice of development economics and this is reflected in the book. Martin Ravallion has been a source of inspiration while visiting on repeated occasions with the Development Economics Research Group at the World Bank. His seminal work on poverty and inequality, and also on the rigorous impact evaluation of development programs that he pioneered at the World Bank, has been highly influential. Jean-Jacques Dethier, at the World Bank and professor at Georgetown University, gave us access to his extensive writings on foreign aid and repeatedly came to lecture in our classes at Berkeley on this subject. We had the luck of working on the World Development Report on Agriculture at the World Bank with Derek Byerlee, one of the most knowledgeable academics and practitioners of agriculture in developing countries.

We also benefited a great deal from professional interactions with Michael Carter and the Basis Collaborative Research Support Program team; the extraordinarily creative J-PAL team headed by Esther Duflo, Abhijit Banerjee, and Rachel Gleenester, with their unique contributions to the introduction of field experiments in development-economic research; Edward Miguel, Paul Gertler, David Levine, and the CEGA team at the University of California, Berkeley; Gustavo Gordillo and Graziano da Silva at the FAO; colleagues on the Science Council of the CGIAR and on the High Level of Panel of Experts of the Committee on World Food Security; project managers at IFAD, USAID, and the World Bank; Blas Santos at the Kellogg Foundation; Finn Tarp at UNU-WIDER; Nora Lustig at Tulane University; and policy innovators such as Santiago Levy at the Inter-American Development Bank and José de Leon at *Progresa*.

We owe much as well to several colleagues who used the book for their own teaching and gave us useful feedback, to the many graduate student instructors who helped us run classes using drafts of the book, and to reviewers of several chapters. They contributed suggestions, criticisms, and, frequently, new materials. They include (in alphabetical order by their first name):

Alan Fuchs, economist at the World Bank
Andrew Dustan, professor at Vanderbilt University
Angeli Kirk, graduate student instructor at the University of California, Berkeley
Aprajit Mahajan, professor at the University of California, Berkeley
Bénédicte de la Brière, economist at the World Bank
Craig McIntosh, professor at the University of California, San Diego
Daley Kuzman, graduate student instructor at the University of California, Berkeley
Diana Lee, professor at Occidental College
Eduardo Montoya, graduate student instructor at the University of California, Berkeley
Frederico Finan, professor at the University of California, Berkeley
Gianmarco Leon, professor at the University Pompeu Fabra in Barcelona
Hideyuki Nakagawa, program officer at JICA
Jean-Philippe Platteau, professor at the University of Namur
Jeremy Magruder, professor at the University of California, Berkeley
Jing Cai, professor at the University of Michigan
Joseph Cummins, professor at the University of California, Riverside
Karen Macours, professor at the Paris School of Economics
Kelly Jones, research fellow at the International Food Policy Research Institute

Kenneth Lee, graduate student instructor at the University of California, Berkeley
Lourdes Rodriguez-Chamussy, economist at the World Bank
Marcel Fafchamps, professor at Stanford University
Maria Caridad Araujo, economist at the Inter-American Development Bank
Marieke Kleemans, professor at the University of Illinois at Urbana-Champaign
Matt Warning, professor at the University of Pudget Sound
Melissa Hidrobo, research fellow at the International Food Policy Research Institute
Peter Lanjouw, professor at the Free University of Amsterdam
Rinku Murgai, senior economist at the World Bank in India
Samuel Bazzi, professor at Boston University
Seth Garz, graduate student instructor at the University of California, Berkeley
Sikandra Christian, postdoctoral fellow at the Paris School of Economics
Stanislao Maldonado, professor at the University of Rosario in Colombia
Sylvan Herskowitz, graduate student instructor at the University of California, Berkeley
Tony Addison, deputy director of the United Nations University's World Institute for Development Economics Research (UNU-WIDER)

We are grateful for the able research assistance provided by Danamona Andrianarimanana and Eunice Kim in finalizing the manuscript.

We are deeply indebted to George Lobell, the chief editor at Sharpe Press, who was the first to invite us with a great deal of conviction to transform the successive drafts of this book into a final product. We are fortunate to have subsequently worked with excellent professional editors, particularly Laura Johnson at Routledge and Tim Hyde at Sunrise Setting.

The field of development economics is in rapid motion, with a large flow of exciting new contributions addressing a complex and changing world. This version of the book should be seen as a first installment that will be corrected, improved, and updated in the next two to three years. We consequently ask for your patience with the inevitable gaps and deficiencies you will notice in reading the book. We look forward to your comments and suggestions in preparing the next edition. We hope that you will find it as exciting to read and to teach with as we found it to write. It should be the starting point for fascinating classroom discussions, new research projects, and innovative initiatives in contributing to economic development. If it does this, it will have achieved its purpose.

Berkeley, September 22, 2015

Alain de Janvry and Elisabeth Sadoulet

Introduction

We discuss in this chapter the main dimensions and challenges of economic development, and the role of development economics in addressing them. This helps us understand why we should be interested in development economics. It also serves as background and justification for the outline of the book.

ECONOMIC DEVELOPMENT

A huge challenge: no less than 85 percent of the world's population

Achieving universal economic development is likely to be one of today's most important challenges for humanity. With 85 percent of the world's population living in developing countries, 58 percent of developing countries' population in poverty, and 26 percent in extreme poverty—some 1.6 billion people—the problem is of massive dimensions (these statistics are presented in Chapter 2). Differences in living standards are enormous between developing and industrialized countries, with a purchasing power parity (PPP) adjusted per capita income of only 15 percent in the former compared to the latter, and a minute 3 percent in the low-income developing countries. In spite of notable success stories, continued failure to achieve development for half of humanity not only has huge intrinsic welfare costs for that population but is also a lost opportunity for the population of the industrialized countries and poses serious threats to the survival of the entire human race. Achieving development should thus be an issue of concern not only to developing countries, but also to industrialized ones, and this not only on ethical grounds, but also for self-interest. Yet, as we will see in this book, achieving development is a highly complex issue to address, with causal determinants of development outcomes only partially understood, and approaches to success still largely to be discovered where development has as of yet failed to occur. Thus, while achieving universal development is easy to recognize as a fundamental objective for humanity at large, how to do this is still very much work in progress. It requires not only creativity and commitment, but also strong analytical skills in using the tools of development economics. The objective of this book is to help the reader acquire these skills and become an effective professional in contributing to the pursuit of development.

We show in Box I.1 the criteria we use in categorizing countries by level of economic development. Categories are largely based on the use of income to measure development.

BOX I.1 TERMINOLOGY USED IN CATEGORIZING COUNTRIES

The terminology we will be using in categorizing countries in terms of levels of development will vary according to the issues analyzed. It will broadly correspond to the following typology:

Developing countries, or less developed countries (LDCs)
Using per capita income, these countries are classified by the World Bank (2014) into the following groups:

- Low-income countries with Gross National Income per capita (GNIpc) ≤ $1,045 measured in US$ of 2013. In 2014, this category included 32 countries.
- Middle-income countries with GNIpc between $1,046 and ≤ $12,745. These are frequently divided into:

    - Lower-middle-income countries with GNIpc between $1,046 and ≤ $4,125. In 2014, this category included 33 countries.
    - Upper-middle-income countries with GNIpc between $4,126 and ≤ $12,745. In 2014, this category included 33 countries.

We also recognize the United Nations Capital Development Fund (UNCDF, 2014) classification of 48 Least Developed Countries that have not only low GNIpc, but also low basic-needs indicators and high economic vulnerability.

Developed countries, or more developed countries (MDCs), or industrialized countries
Using per capita income, they correspond to the high-income countries (with GNIpc at or above $12,746). In 2014, this category included 35 countries, and 27 of the countries in this group are members of the OECD (Organization for Economic Cooperation and Development).

A multidimensional concept: the "seven horsemen of underdevelopment"

Achieving development is about reaching a satisfactory level of human wellbeing, both on average and for everybody in a particular country. While easy to say, it is complex to achieve because wellbeing is multidimensional, with no single agreed-upon definition of what these dimensions are, and with inevitable trade-offs in achieving these dimensions. In this book, we characterize development under seven dimensions (presented in Chapter 1). Underdevelopment, the condition to be overcome by development, includes the following:

1. Low levels of national per capita income relative to the industrialized countries and insufficient income growth to allow convergence in per capita income toward that achieved in the industrialized countries.

2. Extensive material poverty accompanied by food insecurity and hunger.
3. Inequality in the distribution of income and inequity in chances to succeed.
4. Vulnerability to shocks and risk of falling into poverty and poverty traps.
5. Lack of satisfaction of basic needs in human development, most particularly health and education.
6. Rising natural-resource scarcity and environmental stress implying lack of inter-generational sustainability in access to and use of resources.
7. An unsatisfactory "quality of life" in a number of dimensions such as individual freedoms, human rights, capabilities (Sen, 1985), and happiness or life satisfaction.

These seven horsemen of underdevelopment, and how to characterize and defeat each one of them, as well as any chosen combination of them, will largely give us the structure and purpose of this book on development economics.

Trade-offs and national priorities: the need to choose

Because development—the achievement of individual and collective wellbeing—is so multidimensional, and countries are so heterogeneous and with limited resource endowments, there inevitably exist many trade-offs in outcome.[1] As a consequence, choices need to be made as to which aspects of development matter most for a particular society or social group. For some countries, income growth may be the single most important national objective. This is typically the case for the poorest countries. Accelerating GDP per capita (GDPpc) growth was thus the main objective for the early development economists in the 1950s and 1960s, and we recognize this as being China's main development objective. For other countries, poverty reduction may be the dominant concern. Countries and regions such as Sri Lanka, Kerala in India, and Cuba have made great progress in basic needs, reducing child mortality and promoting education, without high growth achievements. Realizing that growth does not easily trickle down to benefit the poor, most international development organizations took on poverty reduction as their main development objective starting in the mid 1970s. For the World Bank, development is defined as achieving "a world without poverty," the organization's motto. Combining labor-intensive growth with social-safety nets was the core strategy proposed by the landmark World Bank *World Development Report 1990: Poverty* (World Bank, 1990). Yet, for other countries, sharing more equally the benefits of growth and catering broadly to the population's basic needs may be a major policy objective, eventually at the cost of lower income growth. Broad-based inclusive development and social harmony are in this case put forward as priority achievements. This was the objective of the 2006 World Development Report on *Equity and Development* (World Bank, 2005). The Nordic countries (Denmark, Finland, Norway, and Sweden) are well known for their emphasis on egalitarianism, social cohesiveness, and democracy, with a large public sector for social protection and redistribution.

This multidimensionality of development, and existence of trade-offs in achieving the dimensions of development, implies that countries must carefully choose

3

for themselves their own priorities and make explicit the development objectives they pursue. This choice is hopefully made in a participatory fashion and broadly owned by the population, one of the functions of participatory processes and democratic forms of governance. In this perspective of multidimensionality, trade-offs and priorities, dispersed individuals or collectivities may seek to better their well-being under the loose guidance of the market, but an active role for the state is typically key in helping decide on overall development priorities and in coordinating agents when markets fail to guide development toward achieving the chosen priorities.

The primacy of growth: understanding selective convergence

Of all development objectives, income growth is likely the most important one as, without it, the other objectives—poverty reduction, reduced disparities, lesser vulnerability to shocks, satisfaction of basic needs, and achieving a satisfactory quality of life—are difficult if not impossible to achieve. Without growth, for example, reducing poverty has to be obtained by taking away from some to give to others, a redistribution difficult to achieve politically. With growth, some like Bhagwati and Panagariya (2013) argue that poverty reduction will necessarily follow through trickle-down effects, meaning that growth is both necessary and sufficient for poverty reduction. According to Dollar and Kraay (2002), cross-country data support the fact that "growth is good" for the poor because their per capita incomes rise on average by the same percentage as everyone else's in the economy. Others, like Drèze and Sen (2013), argue that growth is necessary but not sufficient, and that additional interventions are needed to make the poor benefit. But all agree on the necessity of growth. Drèze and Sen thus argue that pro-poor growth, under the guiding hand of the state, can be as effective for aggregate growth as market-led growth. Hence the tremendous importance given to understanding what makes growth happen, one of the most fundamental and yet paradoxically least understood subjects in development economics. In the last 60 years, growth performances among developing countries have clearly been highly unequal, with a subset of countries growing faster than the industrialized countries and thus catching up in per capita income, constituting the "convergence club" of emerging economies, while others are falling behind, diverging in per capita income (Lucas, 2000).

Debates have raged in attempting to explain the determinants of this selective convergence, especially the relative roles of four potential sources of growth, namely geography, institutions, policy, and culture. Contrasted positions are as follows:

1. *The role of geography and resource endowments*, a position championed by Diamond (1997) and Sachs and Warner (1999). Favorable geography includes a temperate climate, low exposure to endemic diseases such as malaria, abundant resource endowments, especially in land and soil quality, as well as in plant and animal species, a location away from the equator and tropical conditions, access to the sea, and a large domestic market size. Exporting natural resources can be an effective early source of growth according to the "vent for surplus" theory of Adam Smith.

Some forms of natural-resource abundance, especially oil and mineral resources, can however create a "resource curse" (or "paradox of plenty") that is detrimental to industrialization, sustainable growth, good governance, and social stability. When does resource abundance stop being an asset for growth and become instead an obstacle to growth? It can be due to real-exchange-rate appreciation diminishing the competitiveness of domestic agriculture and industry (see Chapter 10), volatile revenues associated with international market price fluctuations, government mismanagement of the resource, and conflict and corruption as resource rents are often easily appropriated (Collier, 2004). The curse can of course be managed, as shown by countries like Norway that combine abundant petroleum resources with sustained growth, egalitarianism, and democracy. Population is another resource endowment that matters for development, with excessively rapid population growth generally acting as a drain on savings, investment, and growth, and diminishing gains in GDPpc.

The geography hypothesis, however, fails to explain successful pre-colonial developments in tropical environments. This was the case of the Aztecs in Mexico, the Mayas in Mexico and Central America, and the Incas in Peru; the Ottoman Empire in the Middle East; and powerful kingdoms such as the Yoruba in Nigeria and the Kuba in the Democratic Republic of the Congo. Clearly, geography and resource endowments matter, but they are insufficient to explain lack of growth and inability to reduce poverty (Acemoglu and Robinson, 2012).

2. *The role of institutions*, a position championed by North (1990), Easterly and Levine (2003), Acemoglu and Robinson (2008 and 2012), and Besley and Persson (2011). Institutions relevant for development include, most particularly, the protection of property rights, the rule of law and the enforcement of contracts, inclusive political systems that hold in check the power of the elites and allow broad-based participation in political and economic activities, and government effectiveness in managing taxation and public expenditures. Ethnic fractionalization that leads to divisiveness and corruption can be part of the institutions detrimental to growth.

While democracy can be an effectively inclusive political system, a high degree of social divisions, such as the caste system in India, may make democracy-based collective action in the pursuit of long-term development priorities difficult, encouraging instead the dissipation of public revenues in populist subsidies and government handouts (Bardhan, 2012). Institutions are endogenous to development (i.e. they are both a determinant and an outcome of development), hence the particular challenge of showing the causal role of institutions in development. There may be a threshold to institutional development, below which countries will fall into failed states and poverty traps. Since there may be a role for foreign aid in achieving this threshold, helping countries escape poverty traps is a key issue in the debates on aid effectiveness (as we will see in Chapter 19).

Institutions are highly path-dependent in the sense that they tend to have considerable permanence, with long-term economic effects that continue to prevail long after they may have been reformed. Institutional reforms are thus key to development, but reforming economic institutions requires political reforms that give an emerging social group power to change the rules that prevail in a society—and

5

political reforms are hard to manage and predict, helping dysfunctional institutions eventually remain in place for a very long time, becoming the root cause of continued underdevelopment.

3. *The role of good policy*, a position best represented by the work of Frankel and Romer (1999) and Rodrik (2004). Important policies for growth include, in particular, trade and exchange-rate policy, policies in support of the business climate for private and foreign direct investment, fiscal and monetary policy, agricultural and industrial policy, policy toward sources of productivity growth (technological change, human skills), and social policy toward human development and the presence of social-safety nets. Bad policy includes excessive taxation, erratic policy reforms, and policy manipulation for rent-seeking to the benefit of a few and at the cost of lower overall growth. Like institutions, policies are endogenous to development, requiring careful identification strategies to demonstrate causality.

    Inability to make good policy can thus become another theory of underdevelopment. Developing countries are characterized by many market, state, and civil-society failures, and agents that could act on these failures are unable to devise good policy or strategic interventions. Instead, bad policy decisions are eventually made that reproduce underdevelopment, sometimes misguided by advice received from foreign donors. Examples are property rights that remain so ill defined as to prevent incentives to invest, attempts at central planning without the necessary information and implementation capacity, industrialization policies that run against comparative advantage, projects that turn into white elephants because they are not adapted to a country's capacity, and an inability to coordinate in achieving higher states of institutional development. However, as argued by Acemoglu and Robinson (2012), wrong policies as a cause of underdevelopment should not be blamed on ignorance, but on lack of interest on the part of ruling elites to implement policy reforms and on lack of political power for other groups to mobilize political coalitions to challenge them and introduce these reforms.

4. *The role of culture.* That culture matters for development was advocated long ago by German sociologist Max Weber (1864–1920) who argued that the Protestant ethic was key to thrift, hard work, and entrepreneurship in making the industrial revolution happen in England. For French political philosopher Alexis de Tocqueville (1805–59), high degrees of civic participation and social engagement were cultural traits key to understanding the strength of US democracy in the nineteenth century. More recently, the role of culture has been used to explain the ability to cooperate (Hayami, 2009, on the role of discipline for water management in rice-growing societies), the enforcement of contracts (Greif, 2006, on the enforcement of discipline by medieval traders over agents in distant transactions), the quality of governance (Putnam *et al.*, 1994, where the quality of performance of local governments is associated with the strength of civil society across regions of Italy), and trust in others (Platteau, 2000, with notions of generalized morality underlying trust and the enforcement of contracts), all of which are certainly important for development. Barro and McCleary (2003) used cross-country regressions to analyze the role of religious beliefs on growth. They found that stronger beliefs in heaven and hell are correlated with higher growth

rates (possibly acting as a disciplinary device), while church attendance (possibly more ritualistic) is associated with lower growth.

Cultural norms tend to have considerable inertia, with differences across nations persisting over the long run in spite of globalization. These cultural norms do indeed matter for development, but one has to be wary of causality for two reasons. The first is that cultural norms tend to be the long-term outcomes of particular institutional arrangements. Nunn and Wantchekon (2011), for example, showed that differences in levels of trust across regions of Africa can be traced back to the slave trade. Individuals whose ancestors were heavily raided by other native groups during the slave trade are found in opinion surveys to be less trusting today. The second is that development has been observed to occur under many different cultural contexts, implying that there is no superiority of one particular cultural norm over others for successful development.

These debates, that have opposed well known development economists, often in acrimonious confrontations, should evidently be resolved empirically, not ideologically. Personalization of rather extreme positions has not helped to find balance and common ground. There are, instead, obvious complementarities between these sources of growth that make them all relevant, if to different extents in different contexts, positing them as an issue of balance and coordination. Rigorous impact analyses should as much as possible be used to assess what matters for growth and convergence, turning the debate from one of personalities and ideologies to one of quality of analytics, a point effectively argued by Banerjee and Duflo (2011) that is central to the approach followed in this book. This has, however, been more easily done at the micro level, where we can implement identification strategies to deal with causality, and gain access to large data sets for statistical analysis, than at the macro level. Macro-level policies are more difficult to analyze statistically. Cross-country regressions are appealing and have been widely used, but they are difficult to identify rigorously (Bazzi and Clemens, 2012). Country case studies, such as Evans (1979) on Brazil and Gold (1986) on Taiwan, each offer rich unique experiences from which we can learn but not derive generalizable propositions.

State, market, and civil society: the iron triangle of development

In policy, there is a key debate about the relative roles of three channels of policy implementation that create a fundamental "iron triangle" of development: policies that act through the market and the private sector, policies where the state acts directly through its own implementation capacity, and policies that act through civil society. Some countries prefer to act directly through the power of the state—China, for example, with heavy reliance on state capitalism—while others prefer to promote the role of market forces—such as Chile, with extensive reliance on market liberalization and private-sector initiatives. Yet others give great importance to the role of civil-society organizations in participating in policy-making and in implementing policies—Japan, for instance, where agrarian communities have played a large role in supporting industrialization (the origin of the Toyota corporation) and in influencing political

7

decisions (the core supporters of the conservative Liberal Democratic Party, which has dominated politics almost continuously since 1955).

Achieving a balance between the roles of the state, the market, and civil society in development will be a recurrent theme in this book (Hayami, 2009; Karnani, 2011). Each performs a developmental role through different instruments (Figure I.1). The state acts through coercion, incentives, and partnerships; the market through competition and profit-seeking among largely private agents; and civil society through cooperation among members of organized groups. How to mobilize each instrument and avoid the corresponding state, market, and civil-society failures will thus call on vastly different policies. A key proposition here is that mobilizing the state, the market, and civil society for development has to be done not through laissez-faire but through coordination. While coordinating individual initiatives can be taken up by the private sector and civil society, the fundamental burden of coordinating the "iron triangle" falls on the state. In this perspective, the existence of an effective and accountable developmental state is one of the key factors for successful development, yet one of the most difficult conditions to achieve (Besley and Persson, 2011). This is because we know quite a lot about the role of the state in development from a functionalist perspective, but we know little about how to transform the state into one that will effectively assume these functions. Successful developmental states, such as China and Vietnam, are the products of their own particular histories, and these are hardly

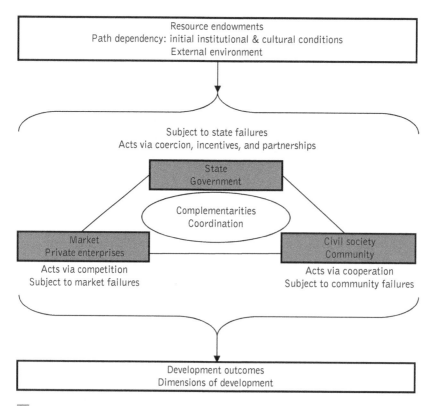

Figure I.1 *The "iron triangle" of development: state, market, and civil society*

replicable in other countries. Innovation is required to devise locally relevant solutions to the emergence and performance of a developmental state, one of the biggest challenges to successful development.

Changing ideas about the relative roles of the state, market, and civil society for development

Ideas about the relative roles of the state, the market, and civil society for development have been central to development economics and have been constantly changing (see Chapter 3). One can say that the industrial revolution in England (1750–1820) was largely market-driven, as described by the ideas of Adam Smith and the invisible hand. Growth during the "Western Experience" (1820–80), with industrial revolutions spreading from Belgium, France, and Germany to the US and Russia, and finally to Japan, was definitely state-led. Late industrializers needed protection against British industry. Growth during the "first globalization period," also called the "Age of Empire," with massive expansion of international trade and relatively free international migrations between 1880 (effectively starting in 1850) and 1914 was market-driven. The period of war and depression between 1914 and 1945, with the rise of protection in response to the Great Depression, the ideas of Keynes about the role of the state in economic recovery, the policies of the New Deal, and the rise of central planning in the Soviet Union, was state-driven. Industrialization in developing countries achieved by import substitution behind tariff protection or through export subsidies between World War Two and the debt crisis of 1982 was also state-driven, taking to the developing countries ideas derived from Keynes and the role of the state for catching up. The "second globalization period" in 1982–95, under policies promoted by the Washington Consensus in response to the debt crisis and the need for stabilization and adjustment policies, was market-driven. And rapid growth in the emerging economies and responses to the food, financial, and environmental crises since 1995 has definitely "brought the state back in" at the forefront of development in an effort to overcome market failures and coordinate and regulate private sector activity (Evans *et al.*, 1985). No doubt, state, market, and civil society all have roles to play that complement each other, but balance in these roles has swung like a pendulum across periods of development. The issue of determining the right balance in these roles for a particular country at a particular point in time has been the subject of major policy debates and differing positions to across schools of thought in development, a subject we will study in Chapter 3.

Market failures, state failures, and civil-society failures

Market, state, and civil society have essential roles to play in development, but each can fail in its functions (Figure I.1). Most recognized by theory are the multiple sources of market failure. They include public goods, externalities, economies of scale, imperfect competition, asymmetrical information (adverse selection/hidden information and moral hazard/hidden actions, creating, in particular, wealth-constrained capital markets that exclude the poor), coordination failures when there are multiple equilibriums, and high transactions costs (due, in particular, to ill defined or incomplete property rights, themselves a public good). Market failures can be self-correcting through, for example, private bargaining (conceptualized in the Coase theorem that we will discuss in Chapter 15), but most often will require state intervention (Stiglitz, 1989a). However, the state can also fail, a subject we will study in Chapter 21. Sources of state failure include limited administrative capacity, imperfect information, capture by rent-seekers and elites, corruption in achieving private gains at public expense, clientelism in using public resources to seek electoral support, and perverse incentives that distract the state from pursuing its social-planner role. Civil society and devolution of decision-making to local self-governance can make up for market and state failures, but civil society can also fail (Platteau and Abraham, 2002). Sources of civil-society failure include lack of transparency in decision-making at the community level, abuse of power by elders and local elites, and cooperation failures for reasons we will study in Chapter 16.

The "iron triangle" gives us a useful analytical framework to study the role of institutions in development: the state, the market (private sector), and civil society—three categories of institutions—each has important roles to play, and each has the potential to fail in fulfilling these roles. Of the three, any of the other two can partially compensate for the failures of each particular one, and can succeed in doing so, or not. Successful development thus requires an effective state, market, and civil society that each fulfills its functions (according to the chosen balance of roles to achieve the selected development objectives) and, as much as possible, compensates for what the others eventually fail to do.

The contexts in which development occurs

The contexts in which underdevelopment prevails, and development eventually occurs, are highly varied. Yet they have broad specifics that create differences with industrialized countries and with the textbook first-best environment of perfect markets where traditional Walrasian economics applies, and has been applied to industrialized countries. Hirschman (1981) thus called on the need to go beyond "mono-economics" in dealing with developing countries, to adapt economic reasoning to the context where development occurs. So what are some of the main aspects of context that call for different economic theories in development economics compared to traditional Walrasian economics? Here succinctly are some of the main features (some exogenous, but most endogenous to path-dependent underdevelopment) to be aware of:

1. Incomplete and weakly enforced property rights over resources, often characterized by open access or by common property without use rules. Weak property rights imply the risks of invasion or expropriation, limiting security of access to land and compromising investment.
2. Unfavorable agroecological and environmental contexts such as tropical, semi-arid, and mountainous, but also some highly favored regions, often with unexplored potential perhaps due to lack of public investment in infrastructure.
3. High population growth eroding per capita economic gains, and frequent high population density eventually creating Malthusian traps.

4. High transaction costs on markets due to lack of infrastructure, creating shallow local markets and forced autarky. Many countries are landlocked, making access to international markets highly costly.

5. Low levels of human capital in terms of literacy, educational achievements, and labor skills.

6. Poor health conditions compromising labor productivity and life expectancy. Pandemics such as HIV/AIDS have led to declining life expectancy in several countries. Exposure to specific communicable diseases such as malaria and tuberculosis increase mortality and reduce labor productivity.

7. Missing or wealth-biased markets for financial services resulting in the selective exclusion of the poor from potentially lucrative investment opportunities.

8. Exposure to uninsured risks, creating high vulnerability to shocks and the need to self-insure at a high cost and with imperfect protection against asset decapitalization and human suffering. Lack of social-assistance and social safety-net programs. Vulnerability to shocks implies a risk of non-sustainability of development achievements, including of incomes above the poverty line for a large share of the population (Guillaumont, 2009).

9. Weak governance capacity, characterized by lack of provision of public goods and services, corruption and extortion, and weak enforcement of contracts and regulation.

10. Frequent failed states and post-conflict societies, with exposure to unchecked violence, civil conflicts, population displacements, and the destruction of property.

11. High social and ethnic fragmentation, creating lack of trust in both private and public affairs.

12. Unfavorable business investment climates, with, in particular, lack of investment in public goods complementary to private investment, and many constraints on private investment.

13. Trade barriers and appreciated real exchange rates, discouraging foreign direct investment and international competitiveness.

14. Deep structural dualism, with a large informal sector characterized by involuntary self-employment and lack of social protection. Dualism often assumes a rural–urban dimension.

15. Cultural traits often characterized by social exclusion and discrimination, lack of trust, a culture of poverty and fatalism, masculinity and the downgrading of women, individualism, tolerance for the abuse of power, weak or absent social organizations, religious taboos and intolerance, etc. Note, obviously, that this does not have to be the case, and that many traditional societies are rich in social capital and informal institutions that create an asset for development.

16. High levels and incidence of poverty and hunger, inducing in turn high discount rates and high levels of risk aversion. Extensive rural poverty among smallholder farmers and landless agricultural workers is a major hurdle to growth. Rapid rural–urban migration leads to the accumulation of population in urban slums.

17. Environmental degradation and weak capacity to regulate externalities. Deep exposure to the impacts of climate change, water scarcity, and resource depletion, particularly among the poorest.

18. Lack of information and data on, for example, weather, agricultural production, local prices, incomes, value added by enterprises, etc. Available data are more often cross-sectional rather than time series and panels as needed to track progress over time.

Note that none of these contextual features are the exclusive privilege of developing countries. They are almost all also found, to some extent, in industrialized countries. However, their coexistence and extensiveness is definitely a characteristic of developing countries. In line with Hirschman, development economics needs to adapt to these specifics for economics to be relevant for development.

How do poor people behave?

To design potentially effective anti-poverty development policies and programs, we need to understand why do poor people do what they do, a point stressed by Banerjee and Duflo (2011) and by Karlan and Appel (2011) in their recent books. An initial premise is that the poor follow the same general patterns of human behavior as the rest of humanity. Indeed, any of us could be poor according to the randomness of birth (Rawls, 1971). However, the contexts and circumstances under which the poor decide what to do are markedly different from the ones where the non-poor operate, and the consequences of the decisions they make can be much more serious for survival, meaning that even identical behavioral motives will typically lead to very different decisions and outcomes. The framework we will use to think of how poor people behave and how their decisions can be affected by policies and programs is represented in Figure I.2.

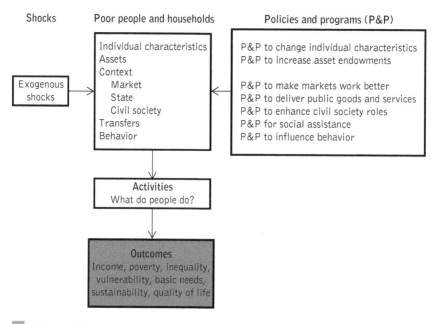

Figure I.2 *How poor people behave and the role of policies and programs in development*

Outcomes are the product of five determinants of the activities people engage in: individual characteristics (such as age, gender, ethnicity, and social-class background); asset endowments in six forms of capital (natural, physical, financial, human, social, and moral); the quality of the context where the assets are used to engage in activities that generate development outcomes (most particularly income growth) as characterized by the market (such as effective demand, competition, and transactions costs), the state (such as public goods, regulations, and potential partnerships), and civil society (such as trust and solidarity); transfers that can induce and complement autonomous incomes (such as benefits from social-protection and social-assistance programs); and behavior with its irrationalities, spontaneities, temptations, contradictions, informational deficits, and poor-specific cultural constraints (Rabin, 1998; Kahneman, 2011). Individual characteristics are largely given, but policies and programs (P&P in Figure I.2) can be targeted at the other four determinants of outcomes—assets, context, transfers, and behavior—giving us a convenient way of categorizing interventions and what they can be expected to achieve. It is important to see that there are both complementarities and trade-offs in the use of policies and programs to affect particular development outcomes. Piecemeal policies and programs initiatives in a second-best context where there are pervasive market, state, and civil-society failures will consequently always be hazardous in terms of desired outcomes, a subject we will explore in Chapter 21. Poverty can derive from a wide variety of causes, including low asset endowments (for example in land, education, and health), an unfavorable context (such as lack of infrastructure, missing or inaccessible financial services, and a high unemployment rate), lack of access to transfers (such as missing social-safety nets and social exclusion), and perverse behavior (such as time inconsistency in decision-making and high levels of risk aversion). Successful anti-poverty programs will need to address each and every one of these possible pitfalls.

Alternative current interpretations of what induces development

The field of development economics is one of sharp and highly personalized controversies as to what causes underdevelopment and what could be done to unleash development, in particular through foreign aid. Some of the most notable current positions (explored in Chapter 19) that we will consider are the following:

1. *Jeffrey Sachs*. In his book *The End of Poverty* Sachs (2005) argues that state planning is important to achieve coordination in reaching better outcomes among multiple equilibriums, that a few simple reforms and technologies can make a big difference (most importantly the following seven instruments: chemical fertilizers and improved seeds, insecticide-treated bed nets, improved water sources, diversification into cash crops, school feeding programs, deworming of children, mobile phones and energy-saving stoves), that subsidies can be effective in inducing the adoption of new technologies, that a big push in foreign aid can shift a country from a low to a high development equilibrium, and that donor coordination in pursuing implementation of the UN's Millennium Development Goals is essential and can succeed. He believes that rich countries' foreign assistance is held back by

lack of understanding and of political will. He has been a vocal advocate of foreign aid, frequently accompanied in his promotional campaigns by popular personalities such as U2 rock star Bono and actress Angelina Jolie.

2. *William Easterly.* In his book *The White Man's Burden* Easterly (2006) is skeptical about the roles of governments and public foreign-aid programs, and suggests instead working with NGOs at the level of small projects, experimenting with and seeking to uncover what works. This perspective stresses the key role of rigorous impact evaluation of alternative options for the "seekers" to determine what works and what does not.

3. *Paul Collier.* In his book *The Bottom Billion* Collier (2007) stresses the primacy of peace and security to give development a chance, the importance of good governance that can be improved through foreign aid, and the use of a broad set of orthodox policy instruments such as trade and performing markets. Focus is on the use of traditional economic instruments with the potential of benefiting the poorest billion people.

4. *Daron Acemoglu and James Robinson.* In their work on "root causes," Acemoglu and Robinson (2008) emphasize the role of basic institutions such as property rights, governance to hold in check the power of the elites and politicians, and the rule of law. In their more recent book, *Why Nations Fail* (Acemoglu and Robinson, 2012), they emphasize the importance of inclusiveness in both economic and political institutions for sustained growth. Inclusive economic institutions enforce property rights, create a level playing field among citizens, and encourage investments in new technologies and skills across all people. Inclusive political institutions distribute political power widely but achieve enough political centralization to enforce law and order, secure property rights, and sustain an inclusive market economy. Extractive institutions, unlike inclusive institutions, concentrate economic and political power and opportunities in the hands of a few. In a "reversal of fortune" caused by institutional determinism, formerly rich colonies with extractive institutions have become today's underdeveloped nations (such as India, Ghana, and Peru), in contrast with formerly poor colonies with inclusive institutions that have now become developed nations (such as the US, Canada, New Zealand, and Australia) (Acemoglu *et al.*, 2002). Consistently with their model, they express doubt about China's ability to sustain rapid economic growth if it does not evolve toward a more inclusive form of governance.

5. *Abhijit Banerjee and Esther Duflo.* In their book *Poor Economics* Banerjee and Duflo (2011) stress the need to understand the behavior of the poor in providing them with better options that can work for them, and the need to meticulously experiment using RCTs (randomized control trials) to explore different ways of doing things in order to find out what works. Their emphasis is more on micro-level programs and projects than on government-level policies because they are more amenable to rigorous impact analyses and because there exist many cost-effective opportunities to improve the welfare of the poor at that level. This perspective on behavior and experimentation has been pursued further—especially in the field of microfinance and the role of commitment devices to help people help themselves—by Karlan and Appel (2011) in their book *More Than Good Intentions.*

6. *Dani Rodrik.* In his book *One Economics, Many Recipes* Rodrik (2007) argues that there is not just one single recipe for growth, but that each country needs to identify its own main binding constraints in comprehensive "growth diagnostics" and define correspondingly specific solutions. In particular, it is important for a country to define its own industrial and trade policy, making use if need be of unorthodox policy instruments such as trade protection, subsidies, and public ownership of enterprises. For this, countries must adopt creative and experimental approaches to institutional reforms as opposed to following blueprint lists of reforms advocated for all countries, as for example under the Washington Consensus. The Chinese industrialization strategy, with extensive presence of public firms and the use of piloting to test out new policies, is cited as an important illustration of the growth-diagnostic approach.

7. *Aneel Karnani.* In his book *Fighting Poverty Together* Karnani (2011) argues that what the poor desire most is not self-employment in the informal sector backed by microfinance loans, but a steady job in the formal sector with expectations of future income gains. Thus the key to fighting poverty is to promote the competitiveness of, and employment creation in, small and medium enterprises. In achieving this, the private sector (through advice), the state (through the investment climate), and civil society (through oversight over the state) all have complementary roles to play. Governments also have an important responsibility in helping the poor acquire the human capital necessary to find employment in the modern sector.

There is much to learn from each of these positions, including avoiding falling into overly simplistic interpretations of what can help achieve development. In this book, we take the position that development is basically an issue of complementarities and of effective coordination between the three fundamental institutions of development: the state and the government, the market and the private sector, and civil society and the community. Each has roles to play that are complementary to those of the others (but can also partially substitute when the others fail to perform), acts through specific instruments (respectively coercion, partnerships, and incentives for the state, competition and profits for the market, and cooperation and oversight for civil society), and has its own sources of failures. While different weights can be given to state, market, and civil society in a development program, these roles need careful balance and coordination. Achieving this balance and coordination is the essence of successful development. For this, impact evaluation of alternative approaches is essential. Rigorous impact evaluation calls on the identification of causalities, with a variety of methods available for this purpose, including RCTs (as advocated for example by Glennerster and Takavarasha, 2013), but also going beyond this toward natural experiments and statistical identification techniques (see Chapter 4).

Positive analysis of development: diagnostics and causalities

From a positive standpoint, heterogeneity in time and space means that development diagnostics, and the causal determinants of development outcomes, have to be constantly established and re-established. This is because the context where development unfolds is always changing. Some of the major emerging contextual features are economic, political, environmental, and cultural globalization; the development of integrated commodity value chains at a world scale; the rapid pace of technological and institutional innovations; rising resource scarcity, most particularly of water and land; and environmental stress such as global climate change. Hence there are no permanent regularities that can characterize development. It is consequently more important to learn how to conduct development diagnostics and how to establish causalities via modeling and empiricism than to attempt to memorize recipes and blueprints that will most likely lag reality. While history is of fundamental importance as a source of inspiration in decision-making, and in understanding the origins of the current state of affairs across nations (what we call path-dependency), the context in which industrialized countries achieved their development is long gone. Development has to be constantly described anew and reinvented. For this, positive analysis is needed, consisting of quantitative and qualitative diagnostics and the identification of causal relations.

Normative analysis of development: learning from others, discovering solutions

From a normative standpoint, heterogeneity and changing conditions imply that there are no silver bullets to achieve development. Some countries have been successful at achieving development, while others have not, but there is no single way in which these successes or failures have been achieved (Rodrik, 2004). The most successful current growth performers, with China in the lead, have in fact followed distinctly heterodox policy packages, with, for example, lack of complete property rights over land, a large public-enterprise sector, heavy market interventions (in particular, through exchange-rate controls), severely constrained financial markets, restricted labor movements between rural and urban areas, and non-democratic forms of governance (Lin, 2011). Heterodoxy is in part necessary because the context in which development happens is always changing. New approaches need to be constantly designed, experimented with, assessed for impact, and improved upon. Successful approaches must be scaled up and sustained to help reduce underdevelopment. Because of the multiple trade-offs in the dimensions of development and the need to adapt to changing circumstances, a "development project" is an intensely personal, social, and national undertaking, taking on many forms and shapes, often totally different from projects that have served other nations well at other times. As such, development is a deeply ideological project (a personal and collective choice), and it must not be assessed outside its particular ideological context. Development is problematic because we do not have blueprints and proven recipes with which to prognosticate, but this is also what makes the field so creative and exciting. As economists, development economics gives us a set of concepts and tools to help us think development toward the design, implementation, assessment, and potential improvement of potentially effective solutions.

The causal revolution in economic development

In development economics, beyond the legitimate satisfaction of curiosity and the pure accumulation of knowledge, the purpose of positive analysis is to support normative

prescriptions, namely the design of project alternatives and of policy recommendations to improve on development outcomes. This is because, by definition of underdevelopment, we do not like what we see and want to change it. What we need for
this is the rigorous identification of causal relations, whereby a development outcome
Y is causally related to exogenous determinants X that fall into two categories

$$Y = f(X_1, X_2),$$

where X_1 are uncontrolled variables such as weather, the world economic context,
past events, and current initial conditions, and X_2 are policy instruments such as
taxes and tariffs, public investment, technology, and transfers (see Chapter 8). To use
such a relationship in making policy recommendations, we need to make sure that
there are neither endogeneities in X_2 nor omitted variables correlated to X_2, both
of which would create biases in assigning the causality of X_2 to Y. Failing to control
for endogeneity and omitted variable biases implies that the observed relationship
between X_2 and Y reveals partial correlation, not causality. If so, the coefficients
attached to them in predicting Y are influenced not only by what else is in the
regression equation, but also by many factors that are not. The presumed relation
between X_2 and Y cannot be used to make policy recommendations. Establishing
causality is extraordinarily difficult, and indeed all too rare in the development
literature (Ravallion, 2009b).

Some determinants of Y are unambiguously exogenous, such as weather shocks.
Using properly executed RCTs is a way of establishing causality. In some cases, natural
experiments can be found that replicate what would have been achieved via RCT.
This is the case with lottery assignments, boundary conditions such as a poverty line,
and program roll-outs in time and space where the participation order is not correlated
with outcomes. Cross-sectional determinants are rarely satisfactory, unless right-hand-
side variables suspected of endogeneity can be instrumented by exogenous variables
that meet the exclusion criterion (i.e. predict the instrumented variable without any
other direct or indirect effect on the outcome variable). Cross-country panel regressions have been widely used at the macro-policy level, but remain questionable in
establishing causality by using lagged variables for statistical identification (Lindauer
and Pritchett, 2002; Rodrik, 2012). These and other techniques to establish causality
will be explored in Chapter 4.

It is the purpose of good identification in econometrics and of careful impact analysis
to establish causality. We should, however, be aware that much of what is published in
development economics as "determinants" and subsequently used to make project
and policy recommendations is not causal. Part of the profession is still hardly aware
of the distinction. Only the top journals in the field guarantee their readers that causality has been established. Carefully separating the causal from the correlational is a
precondition to engaging in credible quantitative analysis for policy purposes. In this
book, we will make every effort to rely only on empirical results where causality has
been credibly established, or accordingly warn the reader. Because it is so important, we
will in each case point out what identification strategy has been used. Unfortunately,
for many development issues we are not yet at the stage where causal results are available,

and for some they will never be because of the nature of the problem. This all too frequently leaves us with the difficult dilemma for policy advice of having to choose between rigorous but limited research results and using experience and correlational results with a grain of salt.

Big game, small game in choosing development strategies

The big game for poverty reduction is to focus on achieving rapid growth in low-skill labor-intensive activities in medium and large enterprises, complemented by the provision of social-safety nets. This is the strategy that was proposed by the *World Development Report 1990* (World Bank, 1990) on poverty, an important milestone in development thinking. It was effectively implemented by China once it started the structural transformation of its economy away from agriculture. South Africa has also pursued this with some success. The small game is for poor people to become successful entrepreneurs in informal-sector micro-enterprises, a strategy championed by NGOs and microfinance institutions, and to gradually lift themselves out of poverty. The development profession has been fascinated with the small game, often in association with NGOs or directly as academic exercises in development. It has pragmatically focused on bottom-up local approaches because they offer many opportunities for poverty reduction, while larger state-based opportunities may be out of reach (Banerjee and Duflo, 2011). A word of caution, however, is not to lose sight of the big game, as advocated for instance by Ravallion (2012) and Rosenzweig (2012). Most poor people are indeed unlikely to become successful entrepreneurs (even most of the non-poor tend to fail as entrepreneurs), but, with proper training, they can be effective workers and employees in initially low-skill jobs. The big game can benefit from experimenting and learning at the level of the small game, with an eventually successful transition from small to big as lessons are internalized in larger programs and policy reforms. But small game and transition must be clearly distinguished, and managed as such so that one feeds into the other (de Janvry, 2013).

Keys to success with the big game—the high road to poverty reduction via employment creation for low-skill workers in formal-sector medium and large firms—are the following (see Karnani, 2011):

1. A supportive investment climate, especially one offering policy credibility and public goods in support of private investment. This requires a "facilitating state," inducing continuous private-sector technological and industrial upgrading based on comparative advantages, and nudging the private sector through "smart" subsidies and protection to create incentives to invest and internalize the information externalities created by first-mover firms (see Lin, 2009, for China, and Chapter 9).
2. Employment creation in medium- and large-scale enterprises, requiring the state to carefully "pick winners"—potentially successful labor-intensive enterprises—through subsidies or public–private partnership opportunities.
3. Investment in labor skills among the poor—in particular, in health for a productive labor force and in education and training for employable skills.

Success with the big game also requires a "structural transformation" from an agrarian economy toward remunerative urban employment. The following are the conditions for success (see Chapter 18):

1. Support for competitive smallholder agriculture as a path-dependent reality: this is where poor people are located and this is what they are doing, especially in Africa. For this, China offers a useful lesson to Africa with the household-responsibility system: poverty reduction was initially achieved principally through productivity growth in smallholder agriculture, with both market-based incentives and extensive public support (Ravallion, 2009a).
2. Modernization and diversification of smallholder agriculture as a transition toward land concentration and urban employment with extensive rural–urban migration.
3. Support for the informal sector (both urban and in the rural non-farm economy) as a holding pattern for labor absorption until formal employment is sufficiently available, and as a nursery for potentially successful medium-sized enterprises.
4. Social-safety nets that support risk-taking and boost future productive capacity, such as conditional cash transfers for education and health, and workfare programs for local productive capacity.

The need to think development

Because of these constantly changing and idiosyncratic dimensions of development, it is more useful for us as economists to learn how to "think development"—i.e. how to use what development economics can help us understand and do—rather than to learn about development processes and outcomes—i.e. big ideas in development and presumed universal blueprints (what Rodrik (2007) calls "presumptive approaches") that may have worked at a particular time and place. This is why this book is about development economics (like Ray, 1998) rather than economic development (like Todaro and Smith, 2012). Most particularly, it is about learning how to conduct descriptive diagnostics, identify causalities based on modeling and empiricism, design programs and policies to address development deficiencies and implementation opportunities from the chosen development perspective, and assess outcomes for results-based management. Diagnostics, causalities, design, implementation, experimentation, and assessment is our agenda in learning to think development.

DEVELOPMENT ECONOMICS

Tasks of development economics

Thinking economic development is something that can be learned. It consists in using the conceptual and statistical tools of economic analysis to address the major economic development problems of our time. Tools include economic concepts such as economies of scale, asymmetrical information, market failures, induced institutional and technological innovations, multiple equilibriums and the role of coordination across economic agents, game theory, risk management and risk coping in enterprise and household strategies, bargaining outcomes in intra-household decision-making, collective action in managing common property resources and lobbying, and commitment devices in policy-making. Tools also include what has been learned in psychology and economics about how people decide on what they do, as applied to the conditions under which the poor live (Banerjee and Duflo, 2011). The problems to be addressed with these tools are the seven horsemen of underdevelopment, which must be defeated according to a country's priorities. Learning to think development is thus acquiring expertise in effectively applying the theoretical and empirical instruments of economics to salient development issues in order to: (1) diagnose problems, (2) establish causalities using modeling and identification in quantitative analysis, (3) design approaches such as policies and programs that can improve development outcomes according to the selected priorities, (4) think of implementation in term of political feasibility and administrative capacity, and (5) assess outcomes for results-based management. Programs and policy instruments are the same as in the rest of economics, as argued by Krugman (1994), but the questions addressed and the objectives sought are specific to development economics.

Development economics as a distinct field of economics

There are four building blocks to thinking development. The first is a good mastery of the concepts and instruments of economic analysis that matter in addressing development issues. These are learned in intermediate micro, macro, and econometric courses, but they will be sharpened in this book as they are adapted to the issues addressed in development. The second is a good knowledge of current development issues so we are aware of the facts that need interpretations and interventions. Daily reading of the press, and weekly exposure to magazines such as *The Economist* are important for this purpose. The third is a perspective on the history of development so we do not miss the opportunity of learning from past experiences and do not need to reinvent the wheel as we face issues that have been addressed previously, while at the same time exercising caution in extracting relevance from the past to deal with current development issues. And the fourth is the willingness to think development by conducting detailed diagnostics, establishing rigorous causal analyses of development outcomes via modeling and empirical analysis, experimenting with new approaches, learning from successes and failures, and helping promote and scale up what has been learned and seems to work.

Toward a "new development economics"

Development economics as a field of economics is not new (this will be explored in Chapter 3). As a body of thought to manage catching up in per capita income with the more advanced industrialized economies, it started as "political economy" with the thinkers behind the Western experience (from France in 1820 to Japan in 1880) and the Asian miracles (the "gang of four" in the 1950s and 1960s, composed of Taiwan, South Korea, Hong Kong, and Singapore). As an academic discipline, it started with the "Pioneers in Development" in the 1940s and 1950s (Meier, 1985). These economists were influenced by reconstruction after World War Two under the Marshall Plan and by crisis management under Keynesian economics. Including economists such as Rosenstein-Rodan (1943), Lewis (1955), Myrdal (1957), and Hirschman (1958), they focused their attention on the acceleration of growth in developing countries. Subsequently, in the 1960s, as growth was accelerating, development economists became concerned with the growing income gaps across nations and the failures of trickle-down effects from growth in eradicating poverty. They included economists such as Walt Rostow, Hollis Chenery, Raul Prebisch, Hans Singer, and Irma Adelman. They were strongly committed to advising on policy, with bold ideas about the role of the state in managing catching up and reducing poverty. But the field of development economics was seen by mainstream economists as somewhat of an eccentric exercise, with broad integrative efforts across sub-disciplines of economics and with other disciplines in the social sciences, but with a lack of theoretical rigor due in part to the vastness of the subject and weak empiricism due to the lack of databases.

In recent years, as development economics found its way into all major economics departments, it experienced a revolution. This was due to four important factors:

1. *Advances in economic theory* relevant to development issues such as endogenous growth, multiple equilibriums, imperfect information, market failures, contract theory, political economy of governance, induced technological and institutional innovations, behavioral economics applied to poverty, and collective action. Relevant advances have been more in micro- than in macroeconomics, perhaps because new data have become more extensively available at that level, because development economists have enthusiastically gone to the field to run local experiments, and because there is a lot of low-hanging fruit, i.e. opportunities to intervene in local development and achieve significant and rapid poverty reduction.

2. *Convergence in policy concerns* between developed- and developing-country contexts. It was for some time thought that concern with issues of market failures and dysfunctional institutions was the privilege and the defining feature of development economics. With the emergence of the New Institutional Economics as a mainstream field, it became obvious that these market and institutional failures are just as relevant to developed as to developing countries, even if less blatantly observed. Thus mainstream economists such as Stiglitz (1989b) turned to the developing world in search of "experiments in pathology" to more clearly observe the consequences of failures, with the debate on sharecropping in contract theory a good illustration. In so doing, mainstream economists discovered unsuspected value in the study of development economics and this helped make room for it in economic curricula.

3. *Availability of extensive databases*, such as the Living Standards Measurement Surveys (LSMS) for household income and expenditures (Deaton, 1997), the Development and Health Surveys (DHS) for demographic variables, partial release of individual records from population censuses (IPUMS: Integrated Public Use Microdata Series), access to administrative data from major public programs,

21

sometimes as a consequence of "right to know" legislation, as in Mexico, greater data sharing between researchers through publication requirements in major journals, and greater data accessibility through the internet, including collection of mega data on such phenomena as weather, geography, communications, and night-time light.

4. *Systematic efforts at results-based program management,* with use of experimental methods and government and donor demands for rigor in impact analyses to identify causalities, measure returns, and improve on existing program and policy designs. This has created a booming market for economic expertise applied to development policies and programs.

What we see today is indeed remarkable for development economics, with not only most economics departments at major universities hosting a field in development economics, but also top rated general-interest economic journals publishing development papers, and large numbers of talented young faculty members and students enthusiastically addressing development issues as their main professional concerns.

Selecting take-home messages

Economic development, the subject addressed by development economics, is huge. It concerns progress for the world and humanity in defeating the seven horsemen of underdevelopment. It will be a lifetime project for those of you who get passionate about it and commit to seeing it succeed. This book can only be a modest introduction to a vast ongoing undertaking. To do this, it concentrates on what is most important: learn how to think development and acquire expertise about the practice of development. It thus focuses on analytical tools applied to development problems more than on descriptions of facts. Chapters on each aspect of development are kept brief with the idea that excessively long reading assignments for students are self-defeating: they simply do not get done. Extensive references to sources are provided, allowing for further reading. The book makes choices within each chapter, offering as a starting point a set of key take-home messages that are correspondingly developed in the chapter. These messages serve to make explicit the choices made for each subject and to provide a learning device so issues of first-order importance are not overlooked in reading.

Development as problem solving

Because there are no magic bullets to solve the underdevelopment problem, and each country has its own idiosyncratic priorities, opportunities, and constraints, development economics is all about problem solving. How best to design a policy or program to address a particular development issue? How to design the impact evaluation of a development experience to identify causality between intervention and outcomes? Design and identification are two fundamental skills that development economists must acquire. To help the reader acquire these skills, we present throughout the book a set of case studies of design and identification, and quantitative exercises to be solved.

This allows readers to get acquainted with specific development experiences, learn how they have been addressed through policy and program design and implementation, and see how they have been evaluated through a particular research strategy.

WHY SHOULD WE BE INTERESTED IN DEVELOPMENT ECONOMICS?

As we embark on the study of development economics, a bit of introspection is useful in asking ourselves why we are doing this. Development economics is both positive and normative: it consists in attempts to explain development, and the lack thereof, and to analyze and propose approaches—new ideas, programs, and policies—that can improve development performance. The normative component of development economics is unusually important among branches of economics: most of us will commit to the subject not driven simply by curiosity but because we do not like what we see (i.e. development outcomes such as economic stagnation, poverty and hunger, vulnerability to devastating shocks, rising inequalities and lack of fairness in opportunities, lack of satisfaction of the most basic human needs in education and health, environmentally unsustainable development paths, the collapse of livelihoods due to mismanagement of the environment, and shockingly low qualities of life) and want to do something about it. If so, we need to be clear about this as it will help us to be motivated. We can think of seven non-exclusive motives to be interested in the subject:

A job in a booming field. There is a huge and expanding job market in international economic development, driven by the immensity of the subject. It is located in universities and think-tanks teaching and researching development; in international development agencies, NGOs, and philanthropic foundations practicing and advocating development; in business firms investing in developing countries (foreign direct investment by multinational corporations, "fortune at the bottom of the pyramid" (Prahalad, 2005) with firms seeking large markets among poor consumers, and corporate social responsibility for firms to do good in terms of human welfare at the same time as doing well in terms of profits), and in private service agencies with expertise in development (consultants, for-profit providers of expertise and services). Because it is motivated by the desire for change, development economics is uniquely oriented at policy advice and problem solving, with a large effective demand for its services. It can consequently be highly profitable to invest in acquiring the skills of development economics in order to find a job in international economic development.

An intellectual interest, with much to discover. As a 60-year-old profession, we still have a very incomplete understanding of the behavioral and institutional processes involved in development. This includes issues such as human and social behavior under the hardship of poverty (Bertrand *et al.*, 2004); state, private enterprise, and civil-society responses to market failures; designing institutions that can perform at early stages of development, social organizations for different geographical contexts, and forms of governance when fiscal and administrative capacities are weak; and understanding the logic of what motivates people and governments in other societies. International development is indeed a curiosity and a rich adventure, both intellectually and emotionally. This creates a powerful intrinsic motivation for the study of development economics.

A distinct field of economics. Even if the tools of the development economist are largely the same as those of other economists, development economics is, as suggested by Hirschman (1981), quite distinct as a field of economics. It is uniquely integrative as the many dimensions of economics have to be brought together and related to other disciplines in order to diagnose and advise comprehensively. Development economists thus require both depth in the tools of their trade and breadth in the multiple dimensions of the development problem, both across fields of economics and across disciplines not only in the social sciences but also beyond. Recently, development has become a source of unique, large databases, particularly on households, firms, communities, nations, and natural resources. Many prominent labor- and industrial-organization economists (with Jean-Jacques Laffont at the Toulouse School of Economics a good example) have turned to development, where they can pursue highly relevant issues by adapting the tools they used in the industrialized-country context. It is also an opportunity to design and implement experiments that could often not be conducted elsewhere, with due respect for the protection of human subjects. Engaging in RCTs has thus become a rapidly expanding and action-related way of rigorously researching development problems (see, for example, the fieldwork done by Innovations for Poverty Action (IPA) at www.poverty-action.org/).

A social self-interest. In a globalized world, industrialized countries cannot ignore the underdevelopment problem because development and underdevelopment are inextricably interconnected. This occurs through such processes as market development and trade, competition over scarce resources such as petroleum and land, international migration and illegal entries, health pandemics, cross-boundary pollution, environmental stress and loss of biodiversity, global terrorism, and the propagation of ideas. Reducing underdevelopment is thus in the best long-term interest of industrialized countries' citizens, providing a powerful rationale for foreign-aid expenditures, as long as they are effectively used for development.

An adventure. We are all curious about distant places, other civilizations, and exotic discoveries, and we all soul search about our place in the wider world. International development is unique for this as it includes traveling, visiting, understanding others, exchanging experiences, and marveling at analogies and differences. Data collection in villages in Yemen or the slums of Mumbai is a unique opportunity to see people and places in a purposeful fashion. A peace-corps experience is often as valuable an experience in self-discovery as it is in directly helping host communities. The field of international development is unusually rewarding in providing an opportunity to discover both how the rest of humanity lives and thinks and how we fit in the broader order.

An act of solidarity and altruism. It is indeed shocking to us to see on our television screens the sufferings of emaciated children dying of hunger while we sit comfortably at home, especially if we think, rightly, that this does not have to be the case. We also see remarkable examples of what well designed and well implemented interventions can do, with no limits to imagination, from small local start-ups exploring innovative ideas to big policy reforms. Being interested in development is thus motivated by an urge to contribute to the wellbeing of others, particularly the poorest of the poor, perhaps with a Rawlsian rationale according to which "it could have been me" (Rawls, 1971), using the tools of research, advocacy, engagement in development programs, policy design and advice, and the quest for a more effective use of foreign aid and philanthropy.

A moral responsibility at a planetary scale. Following McNamara's (1973) lead, the World Bank seeks to achieve "a world free of poverty," its motto as posted on the wall of its headquarters' great hall. Yet we started this introductory chapter observing that 58 percent of developing countries' population lives in poverty. The Bill and Melinda Gates Foundation (2015) justifies its work in international development on the premise that "every life has equal value." Yet there are huge inequities across lives in the chances of achieving equal levels of wellbeing. If we believe that the world can indeed be free of poverty and that every life has equal value, and put our beliefs into practice, then we have to assume responsibility for world development, wherever it fails to happen and can be made to happen.

BOOK OUTLINE

This book was developed in the classroom over many years of teaching upper-division undergraduates in economics and Masters in public policy, international health, and development practice at the University of California at Berkeley. Its focus is pragmatic: to prepare students to use development economics to understand what makes underdevelopment happen and what helps development succeed. It focuses on analytical techniques at a level that corresponds to an upper-division introduction to micro- and macroeconomics. It avoids calculus, but makes extensive use of geometric presentations and arithmetic formulas. It uses econometrics, but at a level that economics and public-policy majors dominate and is largely self-contained. The objective is to prepare graduating seniors and Masters to enter the job market in international economic development. For that reason, it stresses what works, both to diagnose underdevelopment and to formulate and experiment with new approaches to development. It brings to the classroom not only long years of research in development economics, but also fieldwork and collaboration with governments, international development agencies, and NGOs across all regions of the world. The book is designed to endow students with analytical skills in economic development and to promote a passion for what the field can offer to others and to oneself. The book outline is as follows:

Chapter 1. What is development? Issues and indicators
Chapter 2. The state of development
Chapter 3. History of thought in development economics
Chapter 4. Impact evaluation of development policies and programs
Chapter 5. Poverty and vulnerability analysis
Chapter 6. Inequality and inequity
Chapter 7. International trade and industrialization strategies
Chapter 8. Explaining economic growth: the macro level
Chapter 9. Endogenous economic growth
Chapter 10. International finance and development
Chapter 11. Population and development

This collection of chapters includes more than can typically be taught in a one-semester course, implying that every instructor needs to make choices as to which chapters to cover. In a typical 15-week semester with some 26 effective courses, a selection of 18 to 19 chapters is usually the maximum possible.

NOTE

1 Note that it is often said that "poverty is multidimensional" (see, for example, Donaldson and Duflo, 2013). In this book, we keep the word poverty for the monetary shortfall to reach an income or consumption poverty line. We say instead that wellbeing and development are multidimensional, with poverty as one of the dimensions of development.

REFERENCES

Acemoglu, Daron, and James Robinson. 2008. "The Role of Institutions in Growth and Development." Washington, DC: World Bank on behalf of the Commission on Growth and Development, Working Paper No. 10.

Acemoglu, Daron, and James Robinson. 2012. *Why Nations Fail*. New York: Crown Business.

Acemoglu, Daron, Simon Johnson, and James Robinson. 2002. "Reversal of Fortune: Geography and Institutions in the Making of the Modern World Income Distribution." *Quarterly Journal of Economics* 117(4): 1231–94.

Banerjee, Abhijit, and Esther Duflo. 2011. *Poor Economics: A Radical Rethinking of the Way to Fight Global Poverty*. New York: Public Affairs.

Bardhan, Pranab. 2012. "Development Economics: New Directions, New Pitfalls." Working paper, Department of Economics, University of California at Berkeley.

Barro, Robert, and Rachel McCleary. 2003. "Religion and Economic Growth across Countries." *American Sociological Review* 68(5): 760–81.

Bazzi, Samuel, and Michael Clemens. 2012. "Blunt Instruments: Avoiding Common Pitfalls in Identifying the Causes of Economic Growth." *American Economic Journal: Macroeconomics* 5(2): 152–86.

Bertrand, Marianne, Sendhil Mullainathan, and Eldar Shafir. 2004. "A Behavioral-economics View of Poverty." *American Economic Review* 94(2): 419–23.

Besley, Timothy, and Torsten Persson. 2011. *Pillars of Prosperity: The Political Economics of Development Clusters*. Princeton, NJ: Princeton University Press.

Bhagwati, Jagdish, and Arvind Panagariya. 2013. *Why Growth Matters: How Economic Growth in India Reduced Poverty and the Lessons for Other Developing Countries*. New York: Public Affairs.

Bill and Melinda Gates Foundation. 2015. "Foundation Fact Sheet." http://www.gatesfoundation.org/Who-We-Are/General-Information/Foundation-Factsheet.

Collier, Paul. 2004. "Natural Resources, Development, and Conflict: Channels of Causation and Policy Interventions." World Bank: Annual World Bank Conference on Development Economics.

Collier, Paul. 2007. *The Bottom Billion*: Why the Poorest Countries are Failing and What Can Be Done About It. Oxford: Oxford University Press.

de Janvry, Alain. 2013. Book review of *More than Good Intentions: How a New Economics Is Helping Solve Global Poverty* by Dean Karlan and Jacob Appel. *Economic Development and Cultural Change* 61(2): 465–9.

Deaton, Angus. 1997. *The Analysis of Household Surveys: A Microeconometric Approach to Development Policy*. Baltimore: Johns Hopkins University Press.

Diamond, Jared. 1997. *Guns, Germs, and Steel: The Fates of Human Societies*. New York: W.W. Norton and Co.

Dollar, David, and Aart Kraay. 2002. "Growth is Good for the Poor." *Journal of Economic Growth* 7(3): 195–225.

Donaldson, David, and Esther Duflo. 2013. "Will Growth Eradicate Poverty?" MIT OpenCourseWare, Lecture Notes in Development Economics, Microeconomic issues and policy models. http://dspace.mit.edu/bitstream/handle/1721.1/77095/14-73-fall-2009/contents/lecture-notes/MIT14_73F09_lec02.pdf (accessed 2015).

Drèze, Jean, and Amartya Sen. 2013. *An Uncertain Glory: India and its Contradictions*. Princeton, NJ: Princeton University Press.

Easterly, William. 2006. *The White Man's Burden*. New York: Penguin Press.

Easterly, William, and Ruth Levine. 2003. "Tropics, Germs, and Crops: How Endowments Influence Economic Development." *Journal of Monetary Economics* 50(1): 3–39.

Evans, Peter, Dietrich Rueschemeyer, and Theda Skocpol, eds. 1985. *Bringing the State Back In: New Perspectives on the State as Institution and Social Actor*. New York: Cambridge University Press.

Evans, Peter. 1979. *Dependent Development: The Alliance of Multinational State and Local Capital in Brazil*. Princeton, NJ: Princeton University Press.

Frankel, Jeffrey, and David Romer. 1999. "Does Trade Cause Growth?" *American Economic Review* 89(3): 379–99.

Glennerster, Rachel, and Kudzai Takavarasha. 2013. *Running Randomized Evaluations—A Practical Guide*. Princeton, NJ: Princeton University Press.

Gold, Thomas. 1986. *State and Society in the Taiwan Miracle*. New York: Sharpe Publishers.

Greif, Avner. 2006. *Institutions and the Path to the Modern Economy: Lessons from Medieval Trade*. New York: Cambridge University Press.

Guillaumont, Patrick. 2009. "An Economic Vulnerability Index: Its Design and Use for International Development Policy." *Oxford Development Studies* 37(3): 193–228.

Hayami, Yujiro. 2009. "Social Capital, Human Capital, and the Community Mechanism: Toward a Conceptual Framework for Economists." *Journal of Development Studies* 45(1): 96–123.

Hirschman, Albert. 1958. *The Strategy of Economic Development*. New Haven, CT: Yale University Press.

Hirschman, Albert. 1981. "The Rise and Decline of Development Economics." In *Essays in Trespassing: Economics to Politics and Beyond*. Cambridge: Cambridge University Press.

Kahneman, Daniel. 2011. *Thinking, Fast and Slow*. New York: Farrar, Straus and Giroux.

Karlan, Dean, and Jacob Appel. 2011. *More than Good Intentions: How a New Economics Is Helping to Solve Global Poverty*. New York: Penguin Books.

Karnani, Aneel. 2011. *Fighting Poverty Together: Rethinking Strategies for Business, Governments, and Civil Society to Reduce Poverty*. New York: Palgrave Macmillan.

Krugman, Paul. 1994. "The Fall and Rise of Development Economics." http://web.mit.edu/krugman/www/dishpan.html (accessed 2015).

Lewis, W.A. 1955. *The Theory of Economic Growth*. London: Allen and Unwin.

Lin, Justin Yifu. 2009. *Economic Development and Transition: Thought, Strategy, and Viability*. New York: Cambridge University Press.

Lin, Justin Yifu. 2011. *Demystifying the Chinese Economy*. New York: Cambridge University Press.

Lindauer, David, and Lant Pritchett. 2002. "What's the Big Idea? The Third Generation of Policies for Economic Growth." *Economía* 3(1): 1–39.

Lucas, Robert. 2000. "Some Macroeconomics for the Twenty-first Century." *Journal of Economic Perspectives* 14(1): 159–68.

McNamara, Robert. 1973. "The Nairobi Speech: Address to the Board of Governors." Washington, DC: World Bank Group Archives.

Meier, Gerald. 1985. *Pioneers in Development*. Oxford: Oxford University Press.

Myrdal, Gunnar. 1957. *Economic Theory and Under-developed Regions*. London: Duckworth.

North, Douglass. 1990. *Institutions, Institutional Change, and Economic Performance*. New York: Cambridge University Press.

Nunn, Nathan, and Leonard Wantchekon. 2011. "The Slave Trade and the Origins of Mistrust in Africa." *American Economic Review* 101(7): 3221–52.

Platteau, Jean-Philippe, and Anita Abraham. 2002. "Participatory Development in the Presence of Endogenous Community Imperfections." *Journal of Development Studies* 39(2): 104–36.

Platteau, Jean-Philippe. 2000. *Institutions, Social Norms, and Economic Development*. Amsterdam: Harwood Academic Publishers.

Prahalad, C.K. 2005. *The Fortune at the Bottom of the Pyramid: Eradicating Poverty through Profits; Enabling Dignity and Choice through Markets*. Upper Saddle River, NJ: Pearson Education.

Putnam, Robert, Roberto Leonardi, and Rafaella Nanetti. 1994. *Making Democracy Work: Civic Traditions in Modern Italy*. Princeton, NJ: Princeton University Press.

Rabin, Matthew. 1998. "Psychology and Economics." *Journal of Economic Literature* 36(1): 11–46.

Ravallion, Martin. 2009a. "Are There Lessons for Africa from China's Success Against Poverty?" *World Development* 37(2): 303–13.

Ravallion, Martin. 2009b. "Evaluation in the Practice of Development." *World Bank Research Observer* 24(1): 29–53.

Ravallion, Martin. 2012. "*Fighting Poverty One Experiment at a Time: A Review of Abhijit Banerjee and Esther Duflo's Poor Economics: A Radical Rethinking of the Way to Fight Global Poverty*." *Journal of Economic Literature* 50(1): 103–14.

Rawls, John. 1971. *A Theory of Justice*. Cambridge, MA: Harvard University Press.

Ray, Debraj. 1998. *Development Economics*. Princeton, NJ: Princeton University Press.

Rodrik, Dani. 2004. "Rethinking Economic Growth in Developing Countries." The Luca d'Agliano Lecture for 2004. http://citeseerx.ist.psu.edu/viewdoc/summary?doi=10.1.1.465.4079 (accessed 2015).

Rodrik, Dani. 2007. *One Economics, Many Recipes: Globalization, Institutions, and Economic Growth*. Princeton, NJ: Princeton University Press.

Rodrik, Dani. 2012. "Why We Learn Nothing from Regressing Economic Growth on Policies." *Seoul Journal of Economics* 25(2): 137–51.

Rosenstein-Rodan, Paul. 1943. "Problems of Industrialization of Eastern and South-Eastern Europe." *Economic Journal* 53(210/211): 202–11.

Rosenzweig, Mark. 2012. "Thinking Small: A Review of Abhijit Banerjee and Esther Duflo's *Poor Economics: A Radical Rethinking of the Way to Fight Global Poverty*." *Journal of Economic Literature* 50(1): 115–27.

Sachs, Jeffrey, and Andrew Warner. 1999. "The Big Push, Natural Resource Booms, and Growth." *Journal of Development Economics* 59(1): 43–76.

Sachs, Jeffrey. 2005. *The End of Poverty: Economic Possibilities for Our Time*. New York: Penguin Press.

Sen, Amartya. 1985. *Commodities and Capabilities*. Amsterdam: North-Holland.

Stiglitz, Joseph. 1989a. *The Economic Role of the State*. New York: Wiley-Blackwell.

Stiglitz, Joseph. 1989b. "Markets, Market Failures, and Development." *American Economic Review* 79(2): 197–203.

Todaro, Michael, and Stephen Smith. 2012. *Economic Development*. Boston: Addison-Wesley.

UNCDF. 2014. "Least Developed Countries." www.uncdf.org/en/least-developed-countries (accessed 2015).

World Bank. 1990. *World Development Report 1990: Poverty*. Washington, DC.

World Bank. 2005. *World Development Report 2006: Equity and Development*. Washington, DC.

World Bank. 2014. *World Development Report 2014: Risk and Opportunity, Managing Risk for Development*. Washington, DC.

What is development?

Indicators and issues

TAKE-HOME MESSAGES FOR CHAPTER 1

1. Development is about human wellbeing, and wellbeing is a multidimensional concept with inevitable trade-offs. Hence, there is not one single definition of development that everybody can agree upon. Any development diagnostic (positive analysis) and development program (normative analysis) must clearly specify the definition of development that is being used, and this is a personal and social ideological choice.

2. We recognize seven dimensions of development that together tend to encompass what is typically considered to be development: income and income growth, poverty reduction and food security, reduced inequality and inequity, lesser vulnerability to shocks, improved satisfaction of basic human needs in health and education, sustainability in resource use, and a broadly defined satisfactory quality of life. These seven dimensions can all be measured and monitored using corresponding indicators.

3. Besides the primacy of income growth as the main instrument needed to achieve development, there is broad agreement, as expressed in the United Nations Millennium Development Goals, that three dimensions are essential in making progress toward development: poverty reduction, meeting basic needs, and striving toward environmental sustainability. Other dimensions of development have less consensus support.

4. There is considerable unevenness across countries and over time in progress along the dimensions of development—in particular, regarding convergence toward the per capita incomes of industrialized countries. A role of development economics is to explain why performances are so uneven and to determine what can be done to improve the situation in accordance with country development objectives.

5. A key empirical issue is whether income growth helps achieve the other dimensions of development, from equality to happiness. Results with cross-country regressions, while generally plagued with endogeneity problems, tend to show that income growth is only a weak determinant of progress in overall development, suggesting the need for more direct interventions, such as social-protection programs and the targeted delivery of public goods to meet basic human needs.

6. The multidimensionality of development and the heterogeneity of country conditions and priorities imply that, to more effectively pursue development, a country-specific

vision of development needs to be determined, comprehensive development diagnostics performed, priorities established and trade-offs recognized, and a development strategy formulated, assigning in particular specific roles to the market, the state, and civil society in achieving development.

7. This chapter gives an overview of the course, explaining the logic of the subsequent analyses. As such, it introduces many concepts that will be more thoroughly developed in the corresponding chapters.

SEVEN DIMENSIONS OF DEVELOPMENT

Development is about the enhancement of human wellbeing. Wellbeing is a multidimensional concept implying priorities and trade-offs, with the consequence that defining development is a national and personal choice reflecting the social needs and aspirations of the corresponding individual, group, class, or nation.

Few would disagree with the generic statement that "development" is preferable to "underdevelopment." At the same time, there is considerable disagreement across individuals and nations as to what is meant by development, and, once agreed on what it is, how it is to be achieved. Development is one thing for some and another for others. Some put achieving a rapid rate of economic growth as the main objective. This characterizes countries like postwar Japan and China, which pursued neo-mercantilist models with low-priced exports driving economic growth. In their debate on how to reduce poverty in India, Bhagwati and Panagariya (2013) argue that the main instrument is more rapid economic growth, facilitated by further trade liberalization and an improved investment climate, notably in terms of labor laws and land ownership. Others give a great deal of importance to maintaining low inequality. This is the case in the Nordic countries and Japan in the more recent period, heavily taxing high incomes to level out social inequalities through transfers. The World Bank's (2005) *World Development Report 2006* made the case that lowering inequality is a factor not only of reduced poverty, but also, in the long run, accelerated economic growth. Others place a great deal of importance on securing access to basic needs for all, with comprehensive coverage of publicly provided health, education, and pension services. This perspective on the role of the state in delivering a universal minimum basic-needs coverage applies to much of continental Europe and Canada. Sen and Drèze (2013) argue that large public investments in health, education, and other dimensions of social welfare for the poor would not only be effective at reducing poverty in India, but would also mobilize a badly neglected source of growth.

We thus start the study of development with a paradox. We agree on the desirability of a state of affairs—development—but we have difficulty agreeing on defining exactly what it is. This is because development is multidimensional. While there may be situations where we achieve gains simultaneously in all the dimensions of development, in most cases there will be trade-offs, implying the need to establish social priorities. The dimensions of development and their relative importance are in the end a social and a personal choice, i.e. an ideological and moral statement (with ideology defined, in the Free Dictionary, as "the body of ideas reflecting the social needs and aspirations of an individual, group, class, or culture; a set of doctrines or beliefs that form the basis of a political, economic, or other system").

So, when talking about development and making judgments about it, it is important to be clear as to what we mean. Without this, debates about development are more often than not about irreconcilable ideological differences regarding the definition of development, rather than useful propositions about how to achieve a particular development agenda. However, one has to recognize that there is no development without ideology, simply because there are so many dimensions to wellbeing and trade-offs involved in both which dimensions to prioritize and how to achieve progress in them.

A good starting point to look for dimensions of development on which there is broad agreement is the Millennium Development Goals (MDGs)—a set of objectives defined by the UN in 2000 to be met in 2015 and formally endorsed by all 191 UN member states (World Bank, 2009). The MDGs are listed in Box 1.1. The goals and the associated indicators enable comparison of the state of development across countries and provide yardsticks to monitor progress over time. While they inevitably simplify the reality of development to just a few dimensions, and may consequently bias the development priorities of governments that want to achieve recognizable measures of progress according to the MDGs, they help reveal broad international agreement on what constitutes some of the fundamental aspects of development. An example of bias is, for instance, reducing by half the incidence of extreme poverty (defined as people with consumption inferior to PPP (purchasing power parity) $1/day) in Goal 1, which may be achieved at the cost of neglecting the poorest of the poor, who are more difficult to take out of poverty, even though they are the ones suffering most from it. Another potential bias is the emphasis, in Goal 2, on universal primary education, which may be achieved at the cost of reduced investment in higher education when the latter may be essential to support entrepreneurship, leadership, and higher economic growth.

BOX 1.1 THE MILLENNIUM DEVELOPMENT GOALS

Goal 1: Eradicate extreme poverty and hunger: halve between 1990 and 2015 the proportion of people whose income is less than PPP$1/day as well as the proportion of people who suffer from hunger.

Goal 2: Achieve universal primary education: ensure that all boys and girls complete a full course of primary schooling.

Goal 3: Promote gender equality and empower women: eliminate gender disparity in primary and secondary education.

Goal 4: Reduce child mortality: reduce by two thirds the under-five mortality rate between 1990 and 2015.

Goal 5: Improve maternal health: reduce by a quarter the maternal mortality ratio between 1990 and 2015; achieve universal access to reproductive health.

Goal 6: Combat HIV/AIDS (Human Immune Deficiency Virus/Acquired Immune Deficiency Syndrome), malaria, and other diseases: halt by 2015 and begin to reverse the spread of HIV/AIDS, and the incidence of malaria and other major diseases.

Goal 7: Ensure environmental sustainability: integrate the principles of sustainable development into country policies and programs; halve by 2015 the proportion of people without sustainable access to safe drinking water and basic sanitation; achieve, by 2020, a significant improvement in the lives of at least 100 million slum dwellers.

Goal 8: Develop a global partnership for development: develop an open, rule-based, predictable and non-discriminatory trading and financial system; increase foreign aid to the least developed countries; reduce debt to levels sustainable in the long term.

Source: http://mdgs.un.org/unsd/mdg/Host.aspx?Content=Data/snapshots.htm (accessed 2015).

As can be seen in Table 1.1, progress toward meeting MDG 1 on reducing by half the proportion of people in extreme poverty (defined as below $1.25 rather than $1 since 2008) is on track for the developing regions overall. The global poverty rate that was 46.7 percent in 1990 had been reduced to 22 percent by 2010, meeting the goal five years ahead of schedule. Three quarters of the reduction in the number of poor (700 million people) during these 20 years occurred in China. However, as can

Table 1.1 *Progress toward MDG 1 on poverty as of 2010*

MDG 1 Poverty	1990	2010	MDG met
Developing regions	46.7	22	Yes
Northern Africa	5.2	1.4	Yes
Sub-Saharan Africa	56.5	48.4	No
Latin America and the Caribbean	12.2	5.5	Yes
Caribbean	24.9	28.1	No
Latin America	11.7	4.5	Yes
Eastern Asia (includes China)	60.2	11.6	Yes
Southern Asia including India	51.5	29.7	No
Southern Asia excluding India	52	21.5	Yes
Southeast Asia	45.3	14.3	Yes
Western Asia	5.1	3.6	No
Oceania	42	35	No
Caucasus and Central Asia	9.8	3.5	Yes
Least developed countries (LDCs)	64.6	46.2	No

Proportion of population living below $1.25 purchasing power parity (PPP) income per day (%).
Source: http://mdgs.un.org/unsd/mdg/Host.aspx?Content=Data/Trends.htm.

Table 1.2 *Progress toward MDG 1 on hunger as of 2013*

MDG 1 Hunger	1990–2	2011–13	MDG met
Developing regions	23.6	14.3	No
Northern Africa	<5	<5	Unclear
Sub-Saharan Africa	32.7	24.8	No
Latin America & the Caribbean	14.7	7.9	No
Caribbean	27.6	19.3	No
Latin America	13.8	7.1	Close
Eastern Asia	22.2	11.4	Close
Eastern Asia excluding China	9.9	11.3	No
Southern Asia	25.7	16.8	No
Southern Asia excluding India	26.3	16.4	No
Southeast Asia	31.1	10.7	Yes
Western Asia	6.6	9.8	No
Oceania	13.5	12.1	No
Caucasus and Central Asia	14.4	7	Yes
Least developed countries (LDCs)	38.6	29	No

Proportion of population below minimum level of dietary energy consumption (%).
Source: http://mdgs.un.org/unsd/mdg/Host.aspx?Content=Data/Trends.htm.

be seen in the table, progress is not on track in all regions of the world. While it will easily be met in Eastern Asia (including China), Northern Africa, Latin America, and South Asia when it excludes India, it will not be met in Sub-Saharan Africa, South Asia when it includes India, Western Asia, the Caribbean, and Oceania.

It is notable that progress toward achieving food security and eliminating hunger is much more difficult to achieve than reducing extreme monetary poverty, an issue we will address in Chapter 18. As can be seen in Table 1.2, the MDG 1 on hunger will largely fail. Only in Latin America excluding the Caribbean and in East Asia including China is it likely to be met.

Of the other MDGs (see Table 1.3), eliminating gender disparity in primary education (MDG 3) is on track, as well as halving the proportion of the population without sustainable access to safe drinking water (part of MDG 7). Those that are notably failing are achieving universal primary education (MDG 2), reducing infant (MDG 4) and maternal (MDG 5) mortality, and halving the proportion of people without sustainable access to basic sanitation (part of MDG 7).

The concepts enumerated in the MDGs help us draw a list of some of the dimensions of development on which there is broad agreement. In correspondence with the MDGs, we propose to work with the following seven dimensions of development, our seven horsemen of underdevelopment (by analogy with the biblical Four Horsemen of the Apocalypse: namely, conquest, war, famine, and death) mentioned in the Introduction:

1. Income and income growth (MDG 1).
2. Poverty and hunger (MDG 1).
3. Inequality and inequity (MDG 3).

Table 1.3 *Progress toward other MDGs in developing regions*

MDG		1990	2012
Goals attained			
MDG 3A	Eliminate gender disparity in primary education (% ratio females/ males between 97 and 103)	86	97
MDG 7C	Halve the proportion of the population without sustainable access to drinking water (%)	30	13
Goals failing			
MDG 2A	Achieve universal primary education (%)	80	90
MDG 4A	Reduce by $\frac{2}{3}$ the under 5 mortality rate (deaths per 1000 live births)	99	53
MDG 5A	Reduce by $\frac{3}{4}$ the maternal mortality rate (deaths per 100,000 live births, women 15–49)	430	230

Source: UN. 2014. The Millennium Development Goals Report. New York.
http://mdgs.un.org/unsd/mdg/Resources/Static/Products/Progress2014/English2014.pdf.

4. Vulnerability (implicit in MDG 1 since vulnerability to income shocks is a major source of poverty—it is, however, notable that vulnerability to shocks and poverty was a great absence in the MDGs).
5. Basic needs in education and health (MDGs 2, 4, 5, and 6), and in sanitation and housing (MDG 7).
6. Environmental sustainability (MDG 7).
7. Quality of life: empowerment (MDG 3) and a long list of other features associated with capabilities and happiness, serving also as an open-ended category for what is not included in the previous six dimensions of development.

Note that MDG 8 on global partnership for development is an instrument more than an objective and, for this reason, does not appear in the retained seven dimensions of development, even though it features heavily in the development strategies of successful countries.

Clearly, the MDGs indicate broad agreement about the importance of three goals: poverty/income/growth, basic needs in health and education, and environmental sustainability. The other goals—greater equality and equity, reduced vulnerability, and improved quality of life—are recognized but not given the same salience, and hence are likely to be more unevenly stressed across country programs, with a greater role for country preferences. In recent years, the issue of equality and equity has gained increasing recognition with important books such as Stiglitz (2012) and Piketty (2014), as well as the new World Bank priorities of not only reducing extreme poverty, but also promoting shared prosperity worldwide.

As we are getting close to the 2015 MDG end date, the UN has already organized consultative processes to define the post-2015 Development Agenda. Two major decisions have already been taken. One is to integrate the old MDGs with the Rio Sustainable Development Goals (defined in Agenda 21 of the United Nations

Conference on Environment and Development (UNCED, 1992) held in Rio de Janeiro in June 1992). This will give greater weight to environmental issues—in particular, to those related to climate change. It also shifts the emphasis from focusing only on goals (results) to focusing also on means (processes). The other major decision is to make the agenda universal: namely, applying it to all countries and citizens—not just to developing countries—especially in addressing the sustainable-development dimension. While consultations are still ongoing, several reports have been released suggesting what the Agenda is likely to include (UN DESA, 2013). Here are a few that are telling of the forthcoming priority dimensions of development:

1. Growth has been effective in taking nearly 1 billion people out of extreme poverty (defined as per capita consumption below PPP$1.25/day) in the 1990–2010 MDG period. Now, the remaining 1.2 billion extreme poor are located in two types of country. The first is emerging countries such as China and India, where growth has been successful, but where large numbers still remain excluded. For these poor, the issue of social inclusion into the growth process will be the key issue. The second is poor countries with failing states and post-conflict conditions, where growth will be harder to achieve, especially Sub-Saharan Africa, Haiti, Yemen, etc. It is estimated that, by 2030, half of the world's extreme poor will be in these countries. Due to state failures, delivering aid in these countries will have to be done largely outside the public sector, relying on specialized ad hoc institutions such as social-development funds or NGOs. Efforts will need to be made to improve governance and to promote growth and organize social-safety nets under conditions of weak governance.

2. Growth will not be sufficient to reduce extreme poverty as the remaining poor are further removed from the poverty line compared to the poor that were taken out of poverty under the MDGs. This will require more emphasis on effective social programs, urban as opposed to rural poverty, and income-generation capacity by the ultra poor themselves that may require specifically targeted transfers to develop this capacity.

3. Greater focus should be given to vulnerability to shocks as recurrent food, financial, and climatic crises are a major source of new poor. Securing peace and stability is essential to avoid not only the high social costs of insecurity, but also the periodic destruction of assets and the corresponding income setbacks.

4. Achieving sustainable growth in the context of climate change and global competition over scarce resources will require that the new goals address not only the policies pursued by developing countries, but also by industrialized countries.

5. Effective use of aid and delivery of social protection require good governance. Hence more emphasis will be given to improving the developmental capacity of the state.

6. Finally, political stability and improved governance require participation of the middle class, including those who recently moved out of poverty. Hence, the new goals need to focus not only on the poor and the continuing reduction of poverty, but also on the non-poor and their roles in the development process.

In what follows, we review in turn each of the seven dimensions of development, discussing in each case the corresponding indicators for measurement. Most of the dimensions are the object of subsequent specific chapters and will be comprehensively developed later. In this chapter we develop only what is not presented in the corresponding specialized chapters.

INCOME AND INCOME GROWTH

The first and most broadly agreed upon dimension of development is the level and growth of per capita income. The World Bank defines the "more developed countries" (MDCs) as countries with levels of per capita gross national income (GNIpc) in excess of $12,745 in 2013 (World Bank, *World Development Indicators*). Income is what gives a household the monetary capacity to consume, invest, or save. For this reason, as stressed by Nobel Prize winner Robert Lucas (1988), income growth has to be a key instrument to achieve higher wellbeing. Without growth, raising the wellbeing of selected segments of the population, e.g. the poor, would have to be done through taxation and redistribution, i.e. at the cost of others. This approach to poverty reduction is clearly politically more difficult to achieve than attempting to reduce poverty through pro-poor growth, i.e. growth that directly contributes to raising the incomes of the poor. Governments and development agencies thus focus on growth as the key instrument to achieve development. For the World Bank, for instance, income growth is the necessary condition to reduce poverty, either directly through income generation by the poor or through taxation and redistribution of some of the benefits of growth toward them. Hollis Chenery, World Bank Vice-President for Development Policy from 1972 to 1982, thus championed the concept of "redistribution with growth" as the preferred approach to poverty reduction (Chenery *et al.*, 1974). What indicators could we use to characterize income and income growth?

At the national level, income is measured as Gross National Product (GNP). GNP is the sum of Gross Domestic Product (GDP), which is the aggregate of value-added by all firms in the country, and of net factor incomes from abroad (under the form of repatriated profits and remittances sent by migrants). In value-added, we include production for home consumption, which is important in developing countries with a large subsistence agricultural sector. This production has to be valued at its opportunity cost, i.e. at the price that would have to be paid if the goods produced for home consumption had to be bought on the market. Services are particularly difficult to measure. We typically do not have a quantity of the service, only a value (the value of banking services, say), which raises the issue of the implicit price used in this valuation.

To give an average measure of wellbeing, GDP can be divided by population size, giving us GDP per capita (GDPpc) or income per capita—a broadly used indicator in making development comparisons across time or across countries. Growth in GDPpc is a good measure of progress over time in average income. On the expenditure side,

$$GDP = C + I + G + (X - M)$$

is the sum of consumption (C), investment (I), government expenditures (G), and net exports (exports (X) minus imports (M)). GNI, referred to above to measure income in the World Bank's country classification, is for all practical purposes equal to GNP except for the adjustment of subtracting depreciation and indirect business taxes.

Calculating change over time: compound annual growth rates

The average annual growth rate, g, is a useful way of describing the growth performance of a variable y (such as GDPpc) across a given number of years T. How do we measure g from an initial value y_0 in year 0 and a final value y_T in year T?

Growth rate computed between two dates

If an initial value y_0 is compounded at the annual growth rate g for T years, the terminal value is:

$$y_T = y_0(1+g)^T.$$

Alternatively, solving this equation for g, the growth rate that has transformed y_0 into y_T over T years of compounded growth is:

$$g = (y_T/y_0)^{1/T}-1.$$

The average annual growth rate in percentage terms over the period is thus calculated as:

$$g = 100\left[\left(\frac{y_T}{y_0}\right)^{\frac{1}{T}} - 1\right],$$

which is easily entered as a formula in an Excel spreadsheet.

Growth rate computed over the whole period

When we have a continuous time series of annual data, the average annual growth rate should not be calculated using only the initial and terminal years, as above, but as the fitted log linear trend across the whole time series.

To see this, we start from the same definition of the growth rate $y_t = y_0(1+g)^t$ and take the log transformation denoted ln:

$$\ln y_t = \ln y_0 + \ln(1 + g)t.$$

Let $\ln y_0 = \alpha$ and $\ln(1 + g) = \beta$. Recalling that $\ln(1 + g) \approx g$ for small values of g (where $\approx$ means approximately equal), we can interpret the coefficient β as g in the following regression equation,

$$\ln y_t = \alpha + \beta t + \varepsilon_t,$$

where t indexes years. β is the average annual growth rate over the time period:

$$\beta = \frac{d \ln y}{dt} = \frac{dy / y}{dt} = \textit{Rate of change in y per year} = \textit{Average annual growth rate} = g.$$

In Excel, this is obtained by applying the following formula to the time series running from an initial y to a final y:

$$g = 100 * [LOGEST \ (Intial \ y: Final \ y) - 1],$$

where the *LOGEST* function estimates the exponential curve that best fits the data series. g is the average annual growth rate in percentage terms.

Comparisons over time: the need to adjust for inflation

If prices change, comparisons of GDPpc over time may reflect rising monetary incomes and prices, i.e. "money illusion," as opposed to real gains in wellbeing. To compare wellbeing over time, we need to deflate current (nominal) income by a price index, typically the consumer price index (CPI) for income or the GDP deflator for GDP. With a CPI equal to 100 in the base year:

Real GDPpc measured in prices of the base year = 100 * Nominal GDPpc/CPI.

GDPpc is then compared over time as measured in the base-year currency value. An example for Brazil is given in Table 1.4. Over the 2000–13 period, there was successful nominal GDP growth (11.5 percent/year), but also high inflation (8 percent/year) and some population growth (1.1 percent/year). What was the resulting real GDPpc growth?

To measure growth in real GDPpc, we can use the following approximate formula:

Real GDPpc growth = Nominal GDPpc growth – Rate of growth of CPI.

Table 1.4 *Comparing GDPpc over time for Brazil*

Brazil	Units	GDPpc 2000	GDPpc 2013	Average annual growth %
Nominal GDP	Million current Reales	1179482	4844820	11.5
Population	Million	174.5	200.4	1.1
GDP deflator	2000 = 100	100	270.7	8.0
Nominal GDPpc	Reales	6759	24180	10.3
Real GDPpc	Reales of 2000	6759	8931	2.2

Source: World Bank, *World Development Indicators.*

The rate of growth of the CPI (or GDP deflator) is the rate of inflation. In Table 1.4, taking inflation into account, the average annual growth rate in real GDPpc—a true measure of wellbeing—is only 2.2 percent compared to 10.3 percent in nominal GDPpc growth and 11.5 percent in nominal GDP growth. Using nominal as opposed to real figures to measure changes in wellbeing would be quite misleading.

Time to double at a given growth rate: the 70 years rule

Taking logarithms in the growth equation $y_T = y_0 (1+g)^T$, a useful approximation to the growth formula is:

$$\ln y_T = \ln y_0 + T \ln(1+g) \approx \ln y_0 + T g,$$

using the same approximation formula for g as above. This allows solving for T, the time needed to go from y_0 to y_T at a growth rate of g. Here are two examples where this calculation of T is useful.

Example 1: What is the number of years T needed to double y?

$$T = \frac{\ln 2y - \ln y}{g} = \frac{\ln 2}{g}.$$

Remember that $\ln 2 = 0.7$. Then if $g = 10$ percent, $T = 7$ years. Time to double has also conveniently been called the "70 years rule." This is because $\ln 2 = 0.7$. Hence the number of years to double is 70 years divided by the percent growth rate. If the growth rate is 10 percent, time to double is $70/10 = 7$ years. If 1 percent, it is 70 years.

Example 2: What is the time needed to get out of poverty for a given initial level of income y_0, a given poverty line z (defined as an income threshold to be out of poverty—see Chapter 5), and a given growth rate g in income?

$$T = \frac{\ln z - \ln y_0}{g}$$

If $z = 100$, $y_0 = 50$, and $g = 2$ percent, then $T = 35$ years. By contrast, if $g = 10$ percent, then $T = 7$ years. This is a useful formula to measure the importance of growth in helping erase a given initial poverty gap.

Comparisons across countries: the need to bring income figures into a single currency

Comparing income across countries requires measuring it in the same monetary unit, i.e. the same national currency. There are two options for this. The first is to use the official exchange rate that tells us how many local currency units (LCU) are needed to acquire 1US$. The other is to use an exchange rate that reflects the purchasing power of the local currency relative to the US dollar, taking into account price differences across countries, called the Purchasing Power Parity exchange rate (PPPe). The first is easier to calculate, but the second gives a more accurate measure of wellbeing if prices are significantly different across the countries compared.

Comparisons at the official exchange rate

Define the official exchange rate as e = number of LCU/US\$1. Thus e is the price of the US dollar for a foreign national—a Mexican citizen, say. In August 2010, the official exchange rate for the Mexican peso was 12.8 pesos/US\$. This is the number of pesos the Mexican citizen needs to pay to acquire one US\$. Levels of GDPpc can be compared across countries by transforming the GDPpc measured in LCU into GDPpc measured in US\$ at the official exchange rate. This is done by dividing GDPpc measured in LCU by the exchange rate:

$$GDPpc^{\$} = \frac{1}{e} GDPpc^{LCU}.$$

The problem with this approach is that movements in the exchange rate will create changes in $GDPpc^{\$}$ even if there has been no change in $GDPpc^{LCU}$. For instance, a devaluation of the official exchange rate from 6 pesos/US\$ to 12 pesos/US\$ will halve $GDPpc^{\$}$ in Mexico measured in dollar terms even though there has been no immediate change in the country's average level of wellbeing. Conversely, countries that maintain an overvalued official exchange rate—say, at 6 pesos/US\$ instead of 12 pesos/US\$—will appear better off than they really are when GDPpc is measured in dollar terms. For this reason, we would like to use an exchange rate that reflects some equilibrium value. This is the "equilibrium exchange rate" that is sustainable in terms of inflows and outflows of dollars into and out of the country. We will see in Chapter 10 how this exchange rate is defined and measured.

Comparisons at the PPP-adjusted exchange rate

There are typically large differences in prices across countries, so \$1 may buy more in, say, India, than it does in the US. For example, you could buy a haircut in India for \$1 that is of the same quality as you get for \$10 in the US. To account for price differences in comparing GDPpc across countries as a measure of wellbeing, we thus need to adjust for the relative purchasing power of currencies—and the adjustment can make a big difference in assessing relative levels of wellbeing.

To make cross-country comparisons of GDPpc that reflect relative wellbeing while prices differ, we can define an exchange rate that adjusts for the purchasing power of a dollar in the two countries. This is the PPPe, defined as the number of LCUs required to buy the same amount of goods and services (of equal quality) as US\$1 in the US. In this case, GDPpc measured in US\$ with the same purchasing power as in the US is:

$$PPP\ adjusted\ GDPpc^{\$} = \frac{1}{PPPe} GDPpc^{LCU}.$$

The PPP index is calculated for a particular basket of goods. If we want to compare poverty across countries using the PPPe, we would need to use the consumption basket of the poor, or of people around the poverty line. This is, however, typically not done, meaning that the PPP adjustment is only approximate for the comparison of interest.

The importance of the PPP adjustment to GDPpc can be visualized in the following two figures.

In Figure 1.1, the horizontal axis measures the rank of each country in GDPpc in 2011. The vertical axis measures the country's PPPe relative to its official exchange rate. The horizontal line at 1 is, by definition, the PPPe relative to the official e for the US. PPPe is below the official exchange rate, e, in most countries with a GDP inferior to that of the US. Consequently, as can be seen in Figure 1.2, in low-income countries, $PPPGDPpc^{\$} > GDPpc^{\$}$, i.e. GDPpc in dollars measured at the PPPe (the wiggly line), is higher than GDPpc in dollars measured at e (the smoother line). In India, for example, PPP GDPpc was $2,149 compared to a GDPpc of $450. In the US, $PPPGDPpc^{\$} = GDPpc^{\$}$ by construction, equal to $30,600 in that same year. In high-income countries such as Japan and Germany, $PPPGDPpc^{\$} < GDPpc^{\$}$. In Japan, for example, PPPGDPpc was $24,041 compared to a GDPpc at the nominal exchange rate equal to $32,230. Taking into account price differences, which tend to be lower in poorer countries for a same-quality product or service, thus tends to reduce differences in wellbeing when measured as GDPpc.

Genuine Progress Indicator (GPI): accounting for non-marketed services

Measuring a country's income should take into account the value of all goods and services, including those that are not transacted in the market (Nordhaus, 2000). On

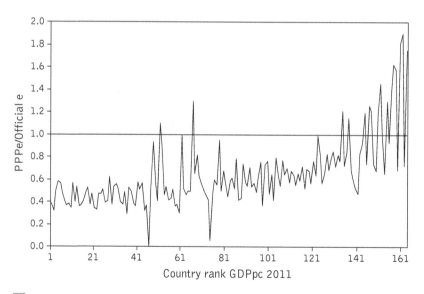

Figure 1.1 *PPP vs. official exchange rate across countries, 2011*

Source: World Bank, *World Development Indicators.*

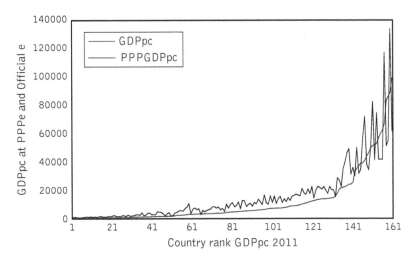

Figure 1.2 *GDPpc at PPP vs. at official exchange rate across countries, 2011*

Source: World Bank, *World Development Indicators.*

the positive side, this would include unpaid work, such as childcare provided at home by a parent and the production of so-called "z-goods" performed by a household member. A z-good is a home-produced good or service such as preparing meals out of purchased ingredients, fetching water and firewood, and maintaining the home. These can be extremely time consuming to produce, with a high opportunity cost on the amount of time left for wage earning or the production of marketable activities. This is particularly important to fully account for the genuine contribution of women to national income as a large part of their work typically consists in unpaid services. On the negative side, negative externalities, such as the costs of crime and social breakdown and of environmental damage, should also be taken into account in measuring a country's income. A GPI that includes these concepts would be:

GPI = GDP + Value of unpaid work − Costs of crime and social breakdown − Cost of environmental damage.

The GPI is not widely used as it can be given different definitions by different users and is demanding to measure. Yet what is interesting is that for the US GPI < GDP and the gap between the two is rising over time. This indicates that GDP growth increasingly overstates genuine growth in economic progress due to mounting unrecognized costs.

Stiglitz *et al.* (2009), in a report to the Commission on the Measurement of Economic Performance and Social Progress, pushed further the critique of GDPpc as a measure of economic performance and social progress. As an average measure, GDPpc overlooks the potential role of economic inequality on individual income. A better measure of individual wellbeing would then be *median* as opposed to average

43

income. If inequality rises sufficiently, most people could become worse off even though average income is increasing. Looking at the US for the 1984–2006 period, average income rose by 43 percent while median income only rose by 15 percent due to rising inequality. In the 2000–6 period, average income rose while median income actually fell.

Because GDP measures flows (current production) as opposed to stocks, it also fails to reflect sustainability in economic progress. Current GDP may be achieved at the cost of depletion of wealth, compromising future production. Assessing sustainability thus requires looking at stocks of capital (natural, physical, human, social) and how each of these is passed on to future generations. Because there are many missing markets for components of these stocks of capital, it is impossible to construct an aggregate monetary indicator. Stiglitz *et al.* (2009) thus recommend using a monetary aggregate only for items for which reasonable valuation techniques exist, such as physical capital, human capital, and some of the natural resources. For the rest, separate indicators of stocks should be used to monitor sustainability, including physical indicators of proximity to dangerous levels of environmental damage such as those associated with climate change and the depletion of world fisheries stocks.

Development issues with income and income growth

While there is broad agreement that income and income growth are fundamental for development, explaining growth remains one of the most difficult and weakest aspects of development theory. This will be explored in Chapters 8 and 9. A key issue will be to understand why the GDPpc of some countries is converging with that of the industrialized countries, while it is diverging for others. Besides explaining aggregate growth and income convergence between less and more developed countries, it is important to understand: (1) what makes growth more or less "pro-poor," i.e. effective for poverty reduction; (2) what the role of spillover effects is across firms in inducing productivity growth, and the consequent role of clusters of economic activity in industrialization strategies; (3) under what conditions rising wages become an engine of growth in creating domestic effective demand, thus reconciling growth and equity—a key policy debate in China today—as it attempts to move beyond export-led "neo-mercantilism," where wages are just a cost on growth; (4) whether more equality and less poverty can themselves be sources of growth; and (5) whether the process of income generation in itself can be a source of wellbeing (so-called "process utility") as opposed to a cost, i.e. whether work itself can be a source of happiness.

POVERTY AND HUNGER

Chapter 5 is devoted to the issues of conceptualizing, measuring, explaining, and reducing poverty, so we only introduce the subject here as a dimension of development.

Measuring poverty

The first MDG concerns the reduction of extreme poverty and hunger. This choice clearly signals broad agreement that reducing poverty is central to development. Agreement on the importance of poverty reduction also implies agreement on the centrality of growth: growth can make poverty reduction Pareto optimum (i.e. with no losers, though after compensation, if necessary) and hence more politically feasible than poverty reduction via income redistribution, particularly in countries where poverty is a mass phenomenon. It is no surprise, then, that for the World Bank, whose motto is "A world without poverty," enhancing pro-poor economic growth is a major concern. In its 1990 report titled *Poverty*, the World Bank (1990) called attention to the importance of labor-intensive growth, since employment is the main mechanism through which the poor, whose main asset is themselves, can derive incomes from growth.

Measuring poverty requires:

1. Choosing an indicator of wellbeing, in this case either income or consumption per capita. This is typically measured as the per capita expenditures in a household because we do not have data on individual consumption.
2. Comparing this indicator to a threshold—a particular poverty line. A household will be categorized as poor if its per capita income or consumption falls below the poverty line.

Once we know how to characterize poverty, we can develop indicators to measure it. The most widely used poverty indicator is the headcount ratio (also called incidence of poverty), measured as the percentage of people in the population with income or consumption below a chosen poverty line. Thus any statement about the extent of poverty has to be carefully qualified by a statement about the specific poverty line that has been used. Measuring poverty is important to target poverty interventions, track progress with MDG 1, and evaluate the impact of anti-poverty policies and programs. A major policy instrument for poverty reduction is the country-level Poverty Reduction Strategy Paper (PRSP), which involves both a comprehensive diagnostic of poverty (a so-called poverty assessment) and specification of a comprehensive strategy to attack poverty. We will analyze these issues in detail in Chapter 5—in particular, how to conduct a poverty assessment, an exercise in much demand. In what follows, we assess where we are at with poverty reduction at a world scale, and enumerate the development issues that need to be addressed regarding the poverty-reduction objective.

Progress in poverty reduction across the world

According to the latest global poverty data, available in 2014, in spite of rapid economic growth and the stunning success of some countries in reducing poverty, poverty remains staggeringly high in developing countries. Some 1.2 billion people are living on less than PPP-adjusted $1.25/day, representing 21 percent of the population in developing countries (Table 1.5). These are the world's extreme poor.

Table 1.5 World poverty using a $1.25/day poverty line, 1981 to 2010

Region	Poverty headcount ratio at $1.25/day poverty line (percentage)		Change in headcount ratio (% points)	Number of poor (million)		Change in number of poor (million)	% distribution of LDC poor	% distribution of LDC population	Population
	1981	2010	1981–2010	1981	2010	1981–2010	2010	2010	2010
East Asia and Pacific	77	12	−65	1097	251	−846	20.7	34.1	2010.44
China	84	12	−72	835	156	−680	12.8	20.8	1224.62
E. Europe and Central Asia	2	1	−1	8	3	−5	0.3	8.1	477.06
Latin America and Caribbean	12	5	−7	42	30	−13	2.4	9.9	583.89
Middle East and North Africa	10	2	−7	16	8	−9	0.7	5.6	331.26
South Asia	61	31	−30	568	507	−62	41.8	27.7	1633.15
India	60	33	−27	429	400	−29	33.0	22.7	1338.3
Sub-Saharan Africa	51	48	−3	205	414	209	34.1	14.5	853.57
Total developing countries (LDC)	52	21	−32	1938	1212	−726	100	100	5889.37

Sources: For poverty, World Bank, *PovcalNet*; World Bank, *World Development Indicators*.

The percentage of people in extreme poverty fell from 52 percent in 1981, and 42 percent in 1990, to 21 percent in 2010 so that the world, as a whole, has already met the MDG 1 of halving the 1990 poverty rate by 2015. The total number of poor declined between 1981 and 2010 from 1.9 to 1.2 billion, with most of the decline coming from China. Most of the developing countries' extreme poor are now located in South Asia (42 percent), Sub-Saharan Africa (34 percent), and East Asia (21 percent). Only in Sub-Saharan Africa is the absolute number of poor still increasing (from 205 million in 1981 to more than double that figure, 414 million, in 2010), while it has remained essentially unchanged at nearly 400 million in India. It is notable that the only significant success in reducing the number of poor has been in East Asia, and mainly in China, where 678 million people have moved out of extreme poverty in 29 years. Also notable is that an estimated 78 percent of the world's extreme poor are rural and 63 percent are engaged in agriculture—a fact that is generally ignored because urban poverty is much more visible and better represented politically than rural poverty (World Bank, 2007a). Taking the remaining 1.2 billion extreme poor out of poverty will be harder than reducing the number of poor under the MDG. Today's poor are increasingly concentrated in low-income countries, (mainly composed of 26 Sub-Saharan countries, together with Afghanistan, Haiti, Myanmar, Nepal, and Bangladesh) with weaker governance than the middle-income countries that have been so successful at poverty reduction in the last 29 years. It is estimated that more than half of the world's extreme poor will be in these countries by 2030. As poverty is increasingly located in "hard" places—with open conflicts, post-conflict conditions, and failed states—this will make the task of using foreign aid for poverty reduction particularly challenging. New approaches will need to be designed, experimented with, and evaluated.

Economic growth has been the main instrument to reduce poverty. But not all growths are equally effective for poverty reduction. And the poverty-reducing value of growth can be enhanced by the implementation of anti-poverty programs. There has consequently been considerable interest in finding out how to make growth more pro-poor. What is meant by pro-poor growth has itself been the subject of controversy. For the United Nations Development Program (UNDP), growth is pro-poor if it benefits the poor more than the non-poor (Kakwani et al., 2004). But growth does not have to be pro-poor in the UNDP sense to reduce poverty. Growth in China was not pro-poor because inequality increased, implying that it benefited the non-poor more than the poor. However, it was exceptionally poverty reducing because it was so high and so sustained, and disproportionately benefited the rural areas where most of the poor were located. Between 1981 and 2005, growth took more than 300 million (mainly rural) people out of poverty through the household-responsibility system that assigned individual land plots to smallholder farmers and through market liberalization that created incentives for productivity growth in small-scale agriculture. In this way, as argued by Ravallion and Chen (2007), growth can be pro-poor if it significantly reduces poverty, even if the non-poor benefit more from growth than the poor: that is, even if inequality increases. Pro-poor growth when inequality falls has been called "relative pro-poor growth;" and pro-poor growth when inequality rises has been called "absolute pro-poor growth."

47

The important policy issue in using growth for poverty reduction will thus be how to increase the elasticity of poverty reduction with respect to income growth, defined as:

$$E = \frac{\%\ change\ in\ poverty\ headcount\ ratio}{\%\ change\ in\ mean\ per\ capita\ income\ or\ consumption},$$

which measures the percentage change in the poverty rate associated with a 1 percent growth in income or consumption (Bourguignon, 2003). For a sample of 67 developing and transition economies, Ravallion and Chen (1997) find that E, for a headcount ratio calculated with a PPP-adjusted \$1/day poverty line, is around -3. This means that a 1 percent increase in mean income or consumption expenditures reduces the share of people living in poverty by 3 percent. In surveying results on estimates of E, the *World Development Report 2000/01* (World Bank, 2000) finds considerable heterogeneity across countries, with values ranging from -1.5 to -5.

What are the policy instruments that can be used to raise E? Bourguignon (2003) shows that greater equality in the distribution of income (at given mean income) increases the poverty-reducing value of growth, with an elasticity ranging from -1.5 in very unequal countries to -6 in very equal countries. In this sense, even if no intrinsic value is attached to greater equality as a dimension of development, it can be an effective instrument for poverty reduction when initial inequality is high. This raises the very important issue of the relationship between growth, inequality, and poverty that will be extensively studied in Chapters 5 and 6. The Chinese success in reducing poverty could thus have been even greater had inequality not increased at the given rate of growth (Ravallion and Chen, 2007). But then, growth may have been lower had inequality been prevented from rising through constraints on entrepreneurship or through taxation for redistribution. There may thus exist a trade-off between reducing poverty through greater growth (with higher inequality) and through lower inequality (with potentially lower short run growth)—an important issue to be discussed in analyzing the relationship between growth, inequality, and poverty.

Development issues relating to poverty

With poverty reduction the main objective of international economic development, as expressed in the MDG 1, there are a number of issues in the development–poverty relationship that will be of concern to us. Some of the most important are the following:

1. Is it better to think about poverty in absolute terms (i.e. the monetary value of per capita consumption relative to a monetary poverty line) or in relative terms (i.e. where does an individual's per capita consumption fit relative to that of others)?
2. Behavior, at given asset endowments and in a given context where the assets are used, clearly affects poverty; but does poverty in turn affect behavior and growth? If the poor behave in ways that are specific to them, i.e. if there is a "poor economics" as proposed by Banerjee and Duflo (2011), then their behavior needs

to be understood in order to design potentially effective anti-poverty policies and programs.

3. Ravallion (2012) shows that lower poverty can itself be a source of growth, possibly implying that high poverty as an initial condition can stifle a country's income-generation capacity and its likelihood of convergence in GDPpc toward high-income countries.

4. Poverty is not only chronic, but also for many transitory, associated with exposure to specific uninsured shocks (Dercon, 2002). In turn, transitory poverty may become a source of chronic poverty if the poor fall into poverty traps or have difficulty recapitalizing their level of productive assets. Putting into place social-assistance programs to reduce vulnerability to shocks may thus be a very effective long-term anti-poverty strategy.

5. What are the pathways out of poverty, and what are the policy instruments that can be used to make these pathways more effective? Most importantly, what are the relative roles of income growth (creating employment and investment opportunities for the poor) vs. income transfers (through accurately targeted social-assistance programs and social-safety nets) in reducing poverty?

INEQUALITY AND INEQUITY

Even though inequality does not appear explicitly among the MDGs, reducing it figures prominently among development objectives for many countries. Reducing rapidly rising disparities is a major political concern in emerging economies such as China and South Africa because of the political tensions they create. In addition, reducing inequality through social programs, as in Brazil, can become an additional source of growth. The *World Development Report 2006* (World Bank, 2005) analyzed the importance of inequity as both a source of future inequalities and a policy concern. The subjects of inequality and inequity are analyzed in detail in Chapter 6.

Measuring inequality and inequity

Inequality is an ex-post concept, describing how aggregate income is distributed across a population after income has been achieved. It can be measured as the share of aggregate income held by the top *X* percent of the population relative to the share of aggregate income held by the bottom *Y* percent. For instance, the share of the richest 20 percent relative to the share of the poorest 40 percent takes on the following values: India: 1.7; Japan: 2.4; US: 2.9; Senegal: 5.3; Brazil: 9.1. As this shows, inequality varies widely across countries. We will see other measures of inequality such as the Gini coefficient in Chapter 6.

By contrast to equality, equity is an ex-ante concept: it measures the degree of equality in opportunities to generate future income or to achieve other development objectives such as education and health. Equity could be measured by the relative probability of achieving a high-school education for two children born in different countries or social classes. For Sen (1985), equity is equality in the distribution of

49

"capabilities," i.e. what people can do or their opportunity set, which is largely determined by their asset endowments and the context in which these assets are used. Inequities among individuals tend to be related to differences in the socio-economic status of their parents, gender, race and ethnicity, rural vs. urban contexts, etc. Social networks, including kinship networks, are important instruments through which inequities are reproduced. This is how inheritance is transferred and job referrals are obtained. Affirmative action is a set of policy interventions designed to redress inequities. These policies do more than erase discrimination and level the playing field (i.e. they do more than implement the concept of a republican state, as in the French ideal, through which everybody is provided with equal access to public goods and services): they give positive advantages to some who are handicapped by their social origins in achieving equal future outcomes.

Why be concerned with inequality in development?

In as much as there is agreement on the importance of poverty reduction for development, why should we be concerned with equality and equity? Since there is broad agreement that growth is the main engine for poverty reduction, a powerful argument in favor of concerns with equality and equity would be that they are instruments for faster growth. This is the line of thinking followed in the *World Development Report 2006* (World Bank, 2005). But, then, what are the channels through which greater equality could be a potential determinant of faster growth?

There are two arguments against equality helping promote growth. The first is the observation made by Keynes that the aggregate rate of saving tends to rise with greater inequality because the rich save a higher share of their additional income than the poor (have a higher marginal propensity to save), while the poor consume a higher share of theirs compared to the rich (have a higher marginal propensity to consume). For Keynes in the 1930s, in the context of an underconsumption crisis, restoring growth by boosting consumer demand required redistributing income toward the poor—an approach successfully implemented through the New Deal policies. In this case, greater equality and higher growth are complementary, a fortunate win–win. In developing countries, however, the issue is generally the exact opposite: it is lack of savings and investment, not lack of consumer demand, that tends to act as a constraint on growth, implying that greater inequality would be favorable to growth.

Note that this position on the role of inequality as a source of growth is compatible with the arguments of supply-side economics proposed by Nobel Prize-winner Robert Mundell. According to this argument, based on Say's Law, "supply creates its own demand." Hence the issue with growth is to increase investment, not to be concerned, as Keynesians are, with demand creation. According to Mundell, low tax rates on income and capital gains are favorable to private investment and growth. Higher inequality is compatible with higher savings and investment. Benefits for others are achieved through trickle-down effects, with a "rising tide lifting all boats." And growth induced by tax cuts may in turn increase overall tax revenues. This position was key to Ronald Reagan's tax cuts and to the doctrines of Reaganomics in the US and Thatcherism in the UK.

There are, however, counter-arguments. Supply-side economics was criticized by Keynesians such as Krugman (2009) as erroneous and supported by the personal interests of the wealthy. Detailed micro-studies of poor behavior have shown that the poor also can save if they have access to safe and remunerative savings instruments (Collins *et al.*, 2009). In addition, the demand for non-tradable goods (goods that are not freely traded; we will see a rigorous definition in Chapter 7) may be important to stimulate the emergence of domestic industry when there are economies of scale in production (Adelman, 1984). Domestic market size will increase with income redistribution—for instance, via redistributive land reform. And domestic savings may not be so important for growth as there are other sources of liquidity for investment such as commercial loans, foreign direct investment, and overseas development assistance.

The second argument against equality helping to promote growth is that a certain degree of inequality creates incentives for entrepreneurs to take risks, which is in turn good for growth. However, incentives can also decline when inequality becomes excessive. Inside the firm, for instance, it may discourage teamwork and effort, and induce sabotage (Rabin, 1993). There would then exist an inverted U curve between inequality and incentives to take risks and work hard, with some inequality creating incentives, and too much inequality disincentives.

Arguments in favor of lower inequality promoting growth include increasing access to education across the population; increasing the share of the population with ownership of collateralizable assets that provide access to loans; reducing the public expenditure costs of social-control and welfare programs; boosting solidarity and cooperation that can be powerful instruments for growth, particularly when coordination is important to move to a higher level of equilibrium; and shifting demands by the median voter away from taxation for redistribution and toward pro-growth policies. Sharply rising inequalities in industrialized countries (the We Are the 99 Percent or Occupy Wall Street movements) have brought this issue into political debates in these countries as well. As argued by Stiglitz (2012), rising inequality allows political capture by the rich, with policy targeted at rent-seeking to their benefit and regressive redistribution through subsidies and public goods becoming a drain on growth. We will explore these arguments and seek empirical evidence for them in Chapter 6. Much of the recent empirical-growth literature has supported the existence of a positive relation between greater equality and growth (World Bank, 2005).

There are, of course, other reasons to prefer a more egalitarian society beyond its role as an instrument for growth. They include political participation and democracy, as well as congeniality, which are dimensions of development that we will discover in looking at quality of life.

Growth, poverty, and inequality: the development triangle

Growth, poverty, and inequality are related through a "development triangle." Each is influenced by the others and can be an instrument to affect the others. Of the five channels that link them, as represented in Figure 1.3, some are better established than others. They are as follows: (1) "Growth is good" to reduce poverty (Dollar and Kraay, 2001), particularly growth in agriculture on which most poor people depend for their

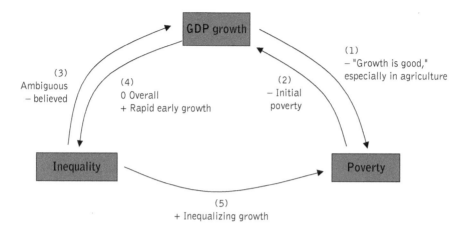

Figure 1.3 *The development triangle: five channels linking growth, poverty, and inequality*

living. (2) A lower initial incidence of poverty is likely to favor higher growth, a regularity recently identified by Ravallion (2012). (3) As seen above, inequality acts on growth through multiple channels, making the net effect ambiguous, but is generally believed by development agencies to stifle growth beyond a certain level. (4) Growth may overall be neutral for inequality, but rapid early growth, as in Vietnam and China, is strongly associated with rising disparities. And (5) greater inequality enhances poverty at a given income level, while poverty reduction may or may not reduce inequality. We will apply this development triangle to specific country case studies in Chapter 6. For the moment, it signals that the corresponding development outcomes cannot be addressed independently of each other.

VULNERABILITY TO SHOCKS

Here, again, we can think of reducing vulnerability to shocks as having intrinsic value as a dimension of development: living a life of insecurity due to exposure to uninsured risks such as illness, death of a family member, crop failure, or civil conflict, is certainly detrimental to wellbeing. Indeed, exposure to uninsured shocks has been shown to be one of the main causes of poverty. Dercon (2008) observed that poverty increased by 50 percent in Ethiopia with the severe drought of 2002–4. Exposure to early-life rainfall shocks can have long-term consequences. Maccini and Yang (2009) find that, in Indonesia, women with a 20 percent higher early-life rainfall relative to normal local rainfall are less likely to report poor health as adults, attain greater height, have better school achievements, and ultimately live in households with higher asset endowments. Reducing vulnerability to shocks can thus be a powerful instrument to reduce the emergence of new poor. The observation has frequently been made that successful anti-poverty programs reduce the number of poor in the short run, but that exposure to shocks for the non-poor can cancel the long-term program impact on the number of poor. Shocks create new poor from among the vulnerable non-poor that reconstitute the stock of chronic poor (Krishna *et al.*, 2004). In Uganda, 42 percent of the poor observed in the period 1979–2004 had fallen into poverty during that period (Krishna, 2012).

We can define vulnerability to poverty for the non-poor as the probability of falling into poverty as a consequence of exposure to shocks. Vulnerability to poverty for the non-poor thus contributes to increasing the future incidence of poverty. For a poor person, vulnerability to shocks would be the probability that future incomes are lower than current income as a consequence of shocks, increasing the depth of poverty. Food insecurity, or vulnerability to hunger, would similarly be defined as the probability that food consumption falls below a minimum consumption standard (the calorie equivalent of a poverty line). For those already below this threshold, food insecurity would be the probability of a decline in food consumption due to exposure to shocks.

Risk aversion

Exposure to uninsured risks and risk aversion contribute to reproducing poverty. The marginal utility of income rises as income falls. Consequently, in terms of utility, the poor are more vulnerable than the non-poor to a decline in income: a shock that reduces income by a given amount has more impact on their wellbeing than the same income loss for the non-poor. Thus the poor will have a higher level of risk aversion in their economic behavior, limiting their options and expected income gains. The cost of this higher risk aversion in terms of expected income is conceptualized in Figure 1.4. Here, we see the set of possible projects a farmer can choose from in a risk–return framework: a higher expected profit $E(\Pi)$ project is matched with a higher risk measured as the variance of profit $V(\Pi)$ along the profit-possibility frontier. The utility function of the risk-neutral farmer is flat, allowing him to select the

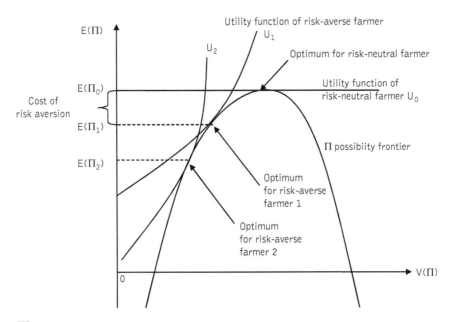

Figure 1.4 Cost of risk aversion and risk premium for a risk-averse farmer

project with the highest possible expected profit. The more risk aversion a farmer has, the steeper the utility function in the risk–return framework. As a consequence, the cost of risk aversion in terms of expected profits rises with risk aversion from farmer 1 with utility function U_1 to farmer 2 with utility function U_2. Uninsured risks thus create a perverse dynamic of poverty: the poor are more risk averse, they choose less risky projects with lower expected profits, and as a consequence they fall further behind in income relative to others. Reducing exposure to shocks, reducing the consequences on welfare of a given shock, and providing insurance against the consequences of shocks are thus fundamental aspects of development policy.

Safety-first

An extreme form of risk aversion associated with high levels of poverty is safety-first (Lipton, 1968): it requires that the probability that any single income event falls below a survival threshold be very small—say, not more that 5 percent (i.e. on average less than once in 20 years). Safety-first is a form of risk aversion that will restrict risk-taking much more than agreeing on a reduction in expected income in exchange for risk reduction. Here, it is not the average risk that the household wants reduced, but, rather, that in every single year exposure to risk be small, imposing a much more stringent constraint on initiatives that can be taken to escape poverty. If the threshold below which income cannot fall under safety-first is survival, and there are no opportunities to smooth consumption across annual events (through either self-insurance via food stocks or borrowing from friends and moneylenders, or through mutual insurance via solidarity among neighbors), then safety-first would be an expected pattern of behavior among the very poor, severely restricting their income opportunities.

Sources of risks

Risks to which the poor are exposed come from a staggering variety of sources. They include:

- Natural disasters: droughts, floods, heatwaves, hurricanes, pest invasions, earthquakes, and mudslides. With climate change, exposure to weather shocks is rising. Because the poor are close to nature (75 percent of the world poor are rural) and mainly dependent on agriculture (including livestock, fisheries, and forestry) for their livelihoods, they are more exposed than the non-poor to natural disasters.
- Health shocks: illness, accidents, epidemics, death of a parent.
- Social disasters: theft, assault, civil war, extortion.
- Economic shocks: international prices shocks (rising prices for food and energy under the food crisis; falling coffee prices for producers), unemployment, inflation, recession, bank failures.
- Political events: policy changes, discontinuation of social programs (electoral cycles, fiscal austerity).
- Environmental damages: air pollution from forest fires, emissions from neighboring firms.

Reducing risk and reducing the consequences for wellbeing of exposure to risk will be a major policy challenge.

Globalization and risk

An important area of debate that separates pro- and anti-trade advocates is whether globalization is increasing food insecurity due to greater price volatility in international markets (e.g. grain-price spikes in 2008 and 2011 and higher variance in the monthly spot prices of staple foods). Through globalization, a country finds itself exposed to new sources of risk originating in distant parts of the world. At the same time, international market prices—for instance, for staple foods—are more stable than domestic prices due to greater diversification of sources of supply. Open-economy prices are likely more stable than closed-economy prices as international demand is more price elastic. During the 2008 world food crisis, some countries would not have been exposed to price shocks had their goods remained non-tradable, but most countries would have had larger shocks. Keeping the world market open—for instance, by resisting export bans and higher export taxes when prices rise—is thus important for the welfare of the world poor. For a food-dependent country, a key policy issue is determining the optimal balance between trade openness and food self-sufficiency, a policy debate with strong ideological overtones that we will explore in Chapter 18.

Types of risk

In terms of the way risks can be managed by individuals, institutions, and policy, it is important to distinguish between two types of risk: covariate and idiosyncratic.

1. Covariate risks can be nationwide, region-wide, or community-wide when they affect all households in a nation, region, or community. These risks cannot be insured at the corresponding geographical level (country, region, locality) as all households are affected by the same shock at the same time. Broader cross-regional insurance schemes are needed, through, in particular, formal insurance and reinsurance across geographical units. That is, each insurer has local information to reduce adverse selection and moral hazard in selecting clients, but can subsequently trade insurance contracts to diversify its own portfolio across regions. Facilitating these trades is the function of global re-insurance companies such as Swiss Re and Munich Re.

2. Idiosyncratic risks affect specific individuals or households. They are easier to insure locally as not all households will be hit by the same shock at the same time. They include illness and death (but not due to a major plague) and individual accidents and misfortunes. In this case, mutual insurance across kin or neighbors who know each other well, enabling them to avoid adverse selection and moral hazard, can help manage these types of risk (Scott, 1977). The degree to which such mutual insurance is practiced has been a subject of intense empirical scrutiny following the lead of Townsend (1994). In his study of Indian villages, he

finds that, while full insurance does not obtain, households do insure each other to a considerable extent. Empirically, mutual insurance is verified by the fact that individual consumption levels would not be influenced by contemporaneous income shocks, after controlling for village average consumption. In other words, individual positive and negative shocks are shared through redistribution, with the result that individual consumption levels (though at different levels due to different wealth positions) all vary with the village average level.

Risks of irreversibility

A key issue concerning vulnerability to poverty is whether exposure to a short-run shock could push people who were, on average, above the poverty line (non-poor and transitory poor) into chronic and persistent poverty, where their incomes are now, on average (chronic poor) or always (persistent poor) below the poverty line. If this can happen, it suggests that some short-term shocks can create long-term irreversibilities, preventing households from bouncing back out of the bad shock. There are many causes for such irreversibilities, the most notable of which are:

1. Children taken out of school when parents are hit by a shock (as parents need the contribution of child labor to cope with the shock or to save on school costs) who never return to school. Using ICRISAT's (the International Crops Research Institute for the Semi-Arid Tropics) India panel data for rural households, Jacoby and Skoufias (1997) show how income shocks in a context of financial-market failures result in a decline in school attendance. Jensen (2000) and Beegle et al. (2006) show that agricultural shocks increase child labor and reduce school attainment in Côte d'Ivoire and Tanzania respectively. This can be prevented. Access to credit in Tanzania helps protect children from these shocks and keep them at school. Conditional cash transfers in Mexico help parents keep their children at school (de Janvry et al., 2006).
2. Reduced consumption and malnutrition during a shock, particularly during the final pre-natal months and the first three years of life, leading to altered physical development and stunting, with no possible recuperation of normal growth and development (see Hoddinott (2006) for Zimbabwe).
3. Fire sales of productive assets such as bullocks, plows, and land, making recapitalization very slow if not impossible (see Antman and McKenzie (2007) for Mexico).
4. Relocation to refugee camps as a consequence of crop failure, with difficulty in returning home as land and assets left behind are typically appropriated by others.
5. Homelessness, caused by short-run incapacity to pay rent, where physical appearance and newly acquired habits make it difficult to compete for jobs (even for which the individual would be qualified) and to re-enter the labor force.

If short-run shocks (i.e. exposure to uninsured risks) can have such long-term consequences, providing social-safety nets to the vulnerable non-poor and poor is an important policy instrument for poverty reduction that has been much misunderstood and underused. In this perspective, social protection can be not only a welfare-enhancing instrument, but also an instrument for sustained growth and productivity gains. Insuring incomes and assets from exposure to short-run shocks thus deserves greater attention, when many poor countries have no formal social-safety-net programs. Many innovations have recently been made to the provision of social assistance—in particular, through a "twin-track approach" that provides immediate relief from poverty through cash or food transfers, while ensuring improved long-term incomes through, for example, education and the provision of local public goods to prevent the recurrence of poverty. Conditional Cash Transfer programs such as *Oportunidades* in Mexico and *Bolsa Família* in Brazil, productive safety nets as introduced in Ethiopia and Yemen, and the Mahatma Gandhi National Rural Employment Guarantee Act in India are part of this new wave of social-assistance programs. We will develop these issues in Chapter 14.

Means of reducing vulnerability to shocks

So what are the instruments available to a household that wants to protect itself from exposure to risk? Households want to achieve consumption smoothing: they can bear fluctuating incomes (especially if this is associated with higher expected incomes) but would like consumption to be smooth so that all of the household gets fed all of the time, the definition of food security. As shown in Figure 1.5, there are three categories of action that can be used for this purpose.

Risk reduction consists in pursuing actions that help reduce the probability and severity of a shock. Education reduces exposure to unemployment shocks, preventive medicine such as vaccinations reduces exposure to health shocks, investment in irrigation reduces exposure to drought shocks and floods, and drought-tolerant new plant varieties reduce yield losses when extreme climatic events occur. Risk reduction helps protect income from shock exposure.

Risk management (ex-ante relative to shocks) consists in actions that help decrease the impact on income of a future shock. They include:

1. *Self-insurance* by choosing activities that are low yield and low risk (such as cultivating traditional crops that are resilient to weather shocks); diversifying the portfolio of income-earning activities toward activities with low correlations in net incomes; accumulating precautionary savings such as food stocks; investing

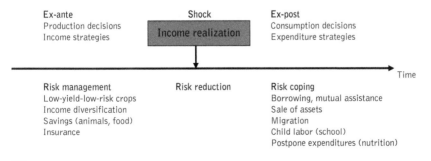

Figure 1.5 *Responses to income shocks: risk management and risk coping*

in liquid assets that can be rapidly sold such as animals, as opposed to fixed assets such as farm equipment (Rosenzweig and Wolpin, 1993). It is important to recognize that none of these strategies are free: risk management through self-insurance is costly as it implies sacrificing expected income to reduce the variance of income. Risk management through self-insurance can consequently be a powerful contributor to the reproduction of poverty, stressing the importance of access to insurance as an instrument to reduce poverty.

2. *Mutual insurance* by investing in social-network membership, such as patron–client relationships and community solidarity. This can be pursued in stable agrarian communities, where people share information and social capital, thus helping to avoid moral hazard and adverse selection in insurance relationships. These sources of insurance can only cover non-covariate shocks at the community level. They are also limited by the extent of the commitment that individuals have to honor sharing when others have been exposed to a large negative shock (Ligon *et al.*, 2002).

3. *Formal insurance.* While formal insurance is rarely available to smallholders, new index-based weather-insurance contracts offer the promise of availability (Carter, 2012). Until now, however, they have failed to be adopted on a large scale without heavy subsidies, an issue we will address in Chapter 13.

Risk coping (ex-post relative to shocks) consists in pursuing actions that help relieve the impact of an income shock on essential consumption (Dercon, 2002). They include postponing consumption of non-essential goods, reducing school and health expenditures, sending children to work, selling assets, taking emergency loans, receiving transfers and social assistance, and migrating to an urban slum or a refugee camp. As observed among pastoralists in Northern Kenya by Janzen and Carter (2013), poor households will tend to smooth assets (protect herd size) by destabilizing consumption when hit by a shock, while better-off households will smooth consumption by destabilizing assets (sell heads of livestock).

Like risk management, risk coping through one's own means is costly as it leads to the decapitalization of assets, rising indebtedness, and social obligations of future reciprocity. If risk coping does not help the household get out of poverty when hit by an adverse shock, that household may find itself permanently among the chronic poor. Effective social-assistance programs are here essential to help prevent irreversibilities whereby exposure to uninsured short-run shocks can become sources of long-term poverty.

Risk coping and risk management are related. Better risk coping allows for less risk management, and, as a consequence, for more risks in income generation to achieve higher expected incomes. A credible social-safety net, such as guaranteed employment in India as a constitutional right, which offers better risk coping opportunities, should lead to higher risk-taking. Flood-tolerant rice varieties induce farmers to invest more in fertilizers, achieving higher yields not only in flood years (better risk coping) but also in good years (reduced risk management through self-insurance) (Emerick *et al.*, 2015).

We conclude by observing that vulnerability to short-run shocks that can push a household into long-term, and sometimes intergenerational, poverty is an increasingly important aspect of the fight against poverty, which will require better understanding and greater policy attention. As we have seen, while absent from the MDGs, resilience to vulnerability is an important part of the post-2015 sustainable-development objectives. How to reduce, cope with, and manage vulnerability to shocks is developed in Chapters 5 and 14.

BASIC NEEDS: HUMAN DEVELOPMENT

Low and stagnant income, poverty, inequality/inequity, and vulnerability—our first four underdevelopment horsemen—are all monetary dimensions of development. The importance of human development as a development objective was stressed by Paul Streeten (1994) and by the UNDP in its annual *Human Development Report*, starting in 1990 (UNDP, 2015). For them, "people are the real wealth of a nation" (UNDP, 2010), not accumulated capital. They made a major contribution to development objectives by stressing the role of non-monetary aspects of wellbeing and significantly broadening the dimensions of development.

The concept of basic needs

Basic needs are multidimensional

As can be seen from the MDGs, there is broad agreement that meeting basic human needs is an important dimension of development. The MDGs refer to basic needs such as health, education, sanitation, and housing. The UNDP includes in its Human Development Index (HDI) various indicators of health and education. Meeting basic needs is clearly a development objective as they are important intrinsic dimensions of wellbeing. Wellbeing is significantly enhanced by the consumption of health and education. But basic needs are also important instruments of development as they help raise the productivity of labor, make institutions work better, support citizen engagement, and allow more democratic forms of governance. However, which categories of basic need matter most (better health, more education, or improved nutrition?), and, correspondingly, how to weight the relative components of basic needs in constructing a basic-needs indicator, have been controversial subjects. Unless one situation is better than another in all dimensions of basic needs and can thus be declared superior, comparing levels of satisfaction of basic needs across situations (e.g. across countries or over time for a given country) when there are trade-offs in the dimensions of basic needs is arbitrary as it depends on the choice of weights, on which it is unlikely that there will be agreement.

Basic needs as public goods

Basic needs are qualitatively different from the other dimensions of development that we have discussed. Income, poverty, inequality, and vulnerability all relate to monetary income that ultimately determines command over market goods. This income can be earned and spent individually or collectively, and the corresponding indicators of development can be measured in monetary units. For example, the percentage of the population in poverty or hunger is determined by comparing two monetary measures, y (per capita consumption expenditures) and z (a poverty line). Basic needs are qualitatively different because they include a large component of public goods—and, because of this, their provision is subjected to extensive market failures, generally due to large positive externalities, which imply that private provision is inferior to the social optimum. Consequently, the satisfaction of basic needs requires state participation, collective action, or altruism. Provision can come from government agencies and programs, but also from community-based organizations (CBOs), non-governmental organizations (NGOs), businesses (through corporate social responsibility (CSR) programs), churches, and philanthropic institutions (frequently organized as foundations).

Dimensions of basic needs

Basic needs can be measured in terms of achievements (ex-post) or of access to the sources of basic needs (ex-ante). The most important indicators of basic needs are:

Health

Ex-post	Life expectancy at birth, overall and for males and females.
	Infant mortality rate (e.g. under five years' old).
	Maternal mortality rate.
	Incidence of HIV/AIDS and other communicable diseases.
Ex-ante	Access to health services (number of doctors per person, distance to a health post) and quality of health services (e.g. quacks vs. licensed doctors among health providers).
	Access to safe water and sanitation.

Education

Ex-post	Net enrollment ratio in primary and secondary school.
	Dropout rate, grade-repetition rate, and grade-retention rate.
	School attainment: completed years of education.
	Literacy rate.
	Scores in standardized tests.
Ex-ante	Availability of schools: distance, cost, class size.
	Quality of education: teacher absenteeism and qualifications, school resources.

Nutrition

Ex-post	Prevalence of malnutrition and hunger: low birth weight; low height-for-age (stunting) and low weight-for-age (wasting).
	Micronutrient deficiencies (hidden hunger): iron (anemia), zinc (morbidity), iodine (mental impairment), and vitamin A (blindness).
Ex-ante	Existence of school feeding programs.
	Access to bio-fortification programs.

Indicators of basic needs

Because basic needs are multidimensional, there is a multiplicity of indicators of basic needs. The most important five are listed below.

Child health: z-scores (World Health Organization (WHO))

In statistics, a z-score is a standardized indicator defined as $z = (x-\mu)/\sigma$, where x is a raw score such as the height or weight of an individual, μ the mean raw score in the population, and σ the standard deviation of the raw score in the population. The z-score is thus the distance between the raw score of the individual and the population mean measured in units of standard deviation. If x follows a normal distribution, a z-score of -2 means that this child is among the 2.3 percent children with the lowest x. In health, the mean and standard deviations used are those of a US reference population characterized by the National Center for Health Statistics. The idea of using the US as the reference population is justified by the recognized fact that all children under the age of 24 months have the same growth potential, whatever their particular ethnic origin. There are two z-scores used to characterize the health status of a child population:

Height-for-age ratio. A child will be characterized as moderately *stunted* when his height-for-age z-score is between -2 and -3, and severely stunted with a z-score less than -3. Stunting reflects chronic malnutrition, i.e. long-term exposure to malnutrition and ill health. It is an endemic characteristic not a short-term indicator. The relevant indicator for a particular population is the percentage of children of a given age and gender who have a z-score of -2 or less. If this percentage is in excess of 2.3 percent (the norm in the reference population), then the population is said to have a higher than expected prevalence of stunting. For children under five years' old, the percentage of children with a height-for-age z-score of -2 or less, i.e. who are stunted, is 23 percent in Ecuador, Botswana, and South Africa, and 26 percent in Ghana.

Weight-for-height ratio. A child will be characterized as moderately *wasted* when his weight-for-height z-score is between −2 and −3, and severely wasted with a z-score less than −3. Because weight responds quickly to nutritional status and ill health

Table 1.6 *Prevalence of under-5 child malnutrition in Ecuador*

Prevalence of under-5 child malnutrition in Ecuador (%)

	Stunted	Wasted
Male	24.0	1.7
Females	22.1	1.7
Indigenous	46.6	2.8
Mestizo	21.1	1.6
White	18.6	1.5
Urban	16.9	1.8
Rural	30.6	1.6
Sierra	31.9	1.4
Coast	15.6	1.8
Poor	27.6	1.9
Non-poor	16.5	1.4
Total	23.1	1.7
Reference population	2.3	2.3

Source: World Bank (2007b).

(e.g. loss of weight due to diarrhea), it offers a short-run indicator of health. It is a convenient measure to characterize the welfare benefits of program interventions such as water sanitation, with spectacularly quick results in reducing child wasting. It was used for example as the outcome measure in studies of the health impact on children of water-sanitation programs in Argentina (Galiani *et al.*, 2005) and Senegal (Bassole and Arcand, 2006), showing in both cases highly positive results. In Ecuador, the percentage of children under five years' old characterized as wasted is 1.7 percent, which is less than the 2.3 percent in the reference population (Table 1.6). Thus, while chronic malnutrition resulting in stunting is a serious problem in Ecuador, low weight potentially resulting in wasting is not.

Z-scores can be calculated for particular subsets of the population to obtain a detailed social and geographical mapping of the incidence of malnutrition. Table 1.6 shows that stunting in Ecuador is mainly associated with boys, indigenous populations, rural inhabitants, the Sierra, and the poor. These figures are extremely high, in spite of the fact that Ecuador is a middle-income country.

Global burden of disease (WHO)

The Global Burden of Disease (GBD) measures the gap between the current health status of a population and the ideal situation, where everyone lives into old age, free of disease and disability. It is measured in disability-adjusted life years (DALY), where one DALY is one lost year of healthy life due to premature mortality or to ill health and/or disability. DALYs are measured by the WHO for 130 causes of mortality and ill health categorized into three groups: communicable diseases, non-communicable diseases, and injuries.

As shown in Figure 1.6, DALYs are measured using the following formula:

$$DALY = YLL + YLD,$$

where YLL = years of life lost due to early death relative to ideal life expectancy at birth, taken as the Japanese life expectancy, the longest in the world, equal to 83 years. YLD = years of life lost due to ill health and disability. Each year under a particular disease or disability is assigned a weight that gives the corresponding fraction to a

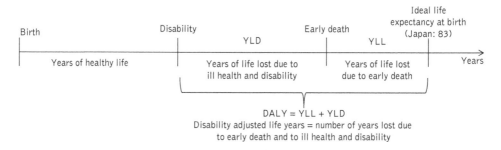

Figure 1.6 *Global burden of disease measured as DALY: disability-adjusted life years*

healthy year. If a disability incapacitates you at 50 percent of a healthy life, then the corresponding YLD is half the number of years lived suffering this disability.

GBD = The share of DALY in the ideal life expectancy.

The incidence of the GBD between premature death and disability reveals different health statuses across regions (WHO, 2014). For instance, in Africa, 77 percent of the GBD is due to premature death and 23 percent to disability. By contrast, in China and Latin America, only 56 percent of the GBD is due to premature death, while 44 percent is due to disability.

Malnutrition: food insecurity (Food and Agriculture Organization (FAO))

The prevalence of hunger is the equivalent for malnutrition of the headcount ratio for poverty. The nutritional norm used by the FAO as equivalent to the poverty line is 2,800 calories/person/day for adult men and 2,000 calories/person/day for adult women. The prevalence of hunger is the percentage of the population below this nutritional norm. For example, the prevalence of hunger is 75 percent in Somalia and 31 percent in Nicaragua. The FAO estimated that 819 million people suffered from chronic hunger worldwide in 2003–5, representing an increase of 23 million from 796 million in 1990–2. With the incidence of the food and financial crises, this number rose to 1 billion in 2009, its highest number ever.

The depth of hunger is measured as the distance to the nutritional norm for the hungry. For a country, it is the average calorie deficit of the undernourished relative to the nutritional norm. For example, the depth of hunger is 490 calories/person/day in Somalia and 300 in Nicaragua.

Human Development Index (UNDP)

The Human Development Index (HDI) is the most celebrated basic-needs index. It was developed by the UNDP to complement the measurements of poverty calculated by the World Bank using monetary measures of income or expenditures and their transformation into poverty, inequality, and vulnerability indicators. The HDI combines indicators of health, education, and PPP-adjusted per capita income into a single index as an average with equal one-third weights:

$$HDI_k = \frac{1}{3} \sum_{i=1}^{3} \frac{H_{ik} - H_{i\min}}{H_{i\max} - H_{i\min}} \text{ for country } k, \text{ were:}$$

H_1 = health: life expectancy at birth (ranging from 39 years in Sierra Leone to 80 years in Japan); H_2 = educational attainment index, a weighted average of two indicators— the adult literacy rate with a weight of two thirds (ranging from 15 percent in Niger to 99.8 percent in the Russian Federation) and the primary, secondary, and tertiary gross enrollment ratio with a weight of one third (ranging from 15 percent in Niger to 113 percent in Australia); and H_3 = PPP-adjusted per capita income (ranging from $458 in Sierra Leone to $29,605 in the US).

As an example, the maximum life expectancy across nations is 80 years (Japan). The minimum life expectancy is 39 (Sierra Leone). Singapore's life expectancy is 77.3 years and China's is 70.1 years. The H_1 indexes for Singapore and China are then respectively equal to:

$$H_{1,Singapore} = \frac{77.3 - 39}{80 - 39} = 0.93, \ H_{1,China} = \frac{70.1 - 39}{80 - 39} = 0.76.$$

In Singapore, the remaining life-expectancy gap is thus only 7 percent of the maximum gap. In China it is 24 percent of the maximum gap.

The HDI is useful but arbitrary. One can wonder, for instance, why include per capita income in the HDI instead of keeping it as a pure basic-needs indicator. It is also obvious that the one-third weighting scheme does not derive from any particular theory of basic needs. For this reason, a country's HDI rank is more meaningful than the absolute value of the index. However, countries would have different HDI rankings had other weights been used. Nevertheless, comparing a country's HDI rank to its GDPpc rank is quite revealing. We see countries with high HDI rank and low GDPpc rank (such as Cuba, Vietnam, and other former socialist countries) as well as the reverse, countries with high GDPpc rank and low HDI rank (such as Brazil and the Latin American countries in general). While Figure 1.7 shows that countries converge to fairly uniform levels of HDI as income rises, a striking observation is the very wide disparities in HDI that exist across countries at low levels of GDPpc. It is clear that development is indeed a social and political choice: countries can decide which dimensions of development to emphasize. Poor countries can, to a significant extent, give themselves high or low HDIs. Pairs of countries like South Africa and Ecuador, and Botswana and Chile, have similar PPP-adjusted GDPpc, yet the first in each pair

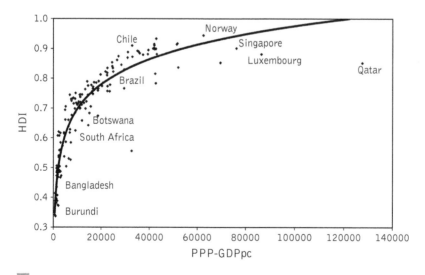

Figure 1.7 HDI and PPP-GDPpc, 2013

Source: World Bank, World Development Indicators.

has a low HDI compared to the second. A country's choice of development priorities has an important role to play in determining the observed HDI outcomes.

In 2010, the UNDP redefined the HDI as a multiplicative instead of an additive composite of health, education, and income, implying imperfect substitution among these dimensions of basic needs instead of perfect substitution with the additive index:

$$HDI_k = \prod_{i=1}^{3} \left(\frac{H_{ik} - H_{i,\min}}{H_{i,\max} - H_{i,\min}} \right)^{\frac{1}{3}}, \text{ with:}$$

H_1 = health measured as life expectancy at birth; H_2 = education measured as the geometric average of mean years of schooling for adults and expected years of schooling for school age children

$$H_2 = \sqrt{(meanschooling) * (expectedschooling)}; \text{ and}$$
$$H_3 = \ln(PPPGNI_{pc}).$$

While this geometric (multiplicative) mean is more meaningful than the previous arithmetic (additive) mean in limiting substitution possibilities across dimensions of basic needs, it retains the same arbitrariness in choice of weights for the components of the index.

The Acute Multidimensional Poverty Index (MPI)

Alkire and Santos (2010) recently proposed an improvement over the HDI called the MPI, the Multidimensional Poverty Index (Table 1.7). Like the HDI, it uses three

Table 1.7 Dimensions of the Acute Multidimensional Poverty Index

Dimension	Indicator (weight)	Poverty threshold
Health	Child mortality (1/6)	Any child has died in the family
	Nutrition (1/6)	Any adult or child is malnourished
Education	Years of schooling (1/6)	No household member has completed 5 years of schooling
	Child enrollment (1/6)	Any school-age child not attending school up to class 8
Living standards	Access to electricity (1/18)	No electricity
	Drinking water (1/18)	No access to safe drinking water within 30 minutes' walk round trip
	Sanitation (1/18)	Sanitation facility not improved or shared with other households
	Flooring (1/18)	Dirt, sand, or dung floor
	Cooking fuel (1/18)	Uses dung, wood, or charcoal
	Assets (1/18)	Does not own more than one of radio, TV, phone, bike, motorbike, refrigerator. No car or truck

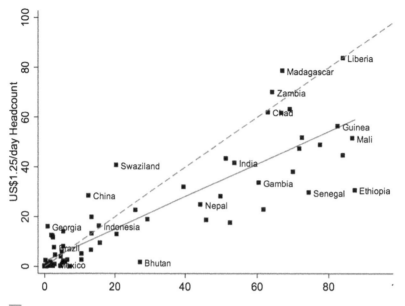

Figure 1.8 *Scatter plot of MPI vs. $1.25/day headcount ratio (upper line is the 45⁰ diagonal, lower line is a regression fit)*

Sources: World Bank, *World Development Indicators*; Alkire and Santos (2010).

dimensions of poverty: health, education, and standard of living, with equal weights. Within each category, indicators for individual households are compared to a threshold: two indicators for health (child mortality and nutrition), two for education (years of schooling and child enrollment), and six for standard of living (access to electricity, drinking water, sanitation, flooring, cooking fuel, and assets). The third category is thus more appropriate than PPP-GDPpc as used in the HDI as it characterizes, in part, access to public goods. The threshold for each indicator is given in Table 1.7. A household is declared "poor" if it is below threshold in at least 30 percent of these indicators. At the national level, the MPI is the percentage of the population declared "poor." While choice of indicators and weights remains arbitrary, it is interesting to observe that some countries have high MPI rates compared to their monetary poverty rate (percent of the population below $1.25/day) such as India, while other countries have a relatively low MPI rate compared to their poverty rate such as Tanzania (Figure 1.8). In Africa, most of the poverty comes from monetary poverty, while in India most comes from deprivation in health and education, i.e. public-goods poverty. The regression line located below the 45⁰ line in Figure 1.8 suggests that, across countries, progress in MPI reduction is harder to achieve than progress in monetary-poverty reduction. Globally, it indicates that it is harder to improve the social aspects of wellbeing than monetary poverty. This is reflected in the MDGs, where MDG 1 on monetary poverty is globally met, while the goals of cutting child mortality by two thirds and maternal mortality by three quarters are far from being met. Goals on sanitation and education will also be missed.

SUSTAINABILITY IN THE USE OF NATURAL RESOURCES

Concepts of sustainability

Should development be concerned with the wellbeing of more than the current generation? There is a powerful biological motivation in parents to care for the wellbeing of their living descendants—children, grandchildren, and increasingly greatgrandchildren as life expectancy extends. But what about concerns beyond two or three generations? What about generations unborn during our lifespan? And should parents be concerned with the wellbeing of future descendants other than their own progeny or immediate kinship, i.e. beyond reproduction of their own genes? The human race is distinct from animal species in its ability to imagine futures and develop empathy for generations unborn and for a larger social group, if not from the whole of humanity. This may be motivated by altruism, but also by common interest in the survival of "spaceship earth" (Boulding, 1966) with its limited stocks of land, oxygen, water, and other resources. This brings us to the concept of "sustainability" as a dimension of development.

Following the Brundtland Commission (World Commission on Environment and Development, 1987), sustainability is defined as the concern with intergenerational equity: that the wellbeing of future generations should not be inferior to that of the current generation as a consequence of the current generation's behavior toward the use of natural resources and the environment. This is easy to say in general terms, but hard to define specifically and very hard to implement. Hard to define because the wellbeing derived from natural resources by future generations can include many dimensions, implying again an ideological choice, such as the income derived from the resource, the option value of using the resource at a future date (i.e. deriving utility from maintaining the right to use the resource in the future), the existence value of the resource (i.e. deriving utility from knowing that the resource still exists), the valuation of a non-marketed resource (i.e. deriving utility from the use of resources that have no market and hence no price), and the stock of the resource (i.e. deriving utility from the present value of the future use of resources held in stock). Achieving sustainability in resource use will clearly be different depending on the definition of wellbeing we use.

We can differentiate between two types of sustainability that are differentially difficult to achieve: strong and weak (Daly, 1999).

Strong sustainability requires maintenance over time of the natural resource itself or of the flow of services from the natural resource as its functions cannot be duplicated by manufactured capital. This is the case with old growth forests or open-sea-catch fisheries.

Weak sustainability requires maintenance over time of the income stream derived from the natural resource, including the possibility of deriving it from manufactured goods and services that can substitute for the natural resource. Soil fertility can thus be depleted now if it can be replaced by the use of fertilizers and improved seeds to maintain yields. Income derived from a natural resource that is being depleted (deforestation) can be invested in new sources of income that do not require the resource (industry).

Hence with this dimension of development, as with the overall concept of development, we need to carefully specify "sustainability of what" if we are concerned with intergenerational equity.

The concept of sustainability is particularly difficult to implement in policy-making for a very simple reason: future generations are not here today to bid on markets for conservation of the resource to allow for their own future use. Sustainability is thus par excellence a value statement, a vision of people and society, and a very strong moral and ideological choice. As can be seen with the cost to deal with climate change—a clear intergenerational issue related to resource use—not all governments are willing to endorse the sustainability objective. International negotiations to reduce carbon emissions at the source of climate change that will affect future generations have to this day largely failed. The Kyoto Agreement to limit emissions only included the industrialized counties, and not even the US, then the world's largest polluter. No wonder that sustainability is a dimension of development on which there is considerable disagreement, particularly in terms of time horizon (how many generations in the future?) and social scope (concern with the future wellbeing of the immediate family, kinship clan, nation, or humanity). It also has the unique feature that it cannot be achieved without the active participation of industrialized countries as the main source of emissions and also the main bearer of the cost of preserving biodiversity as a global public good. The post-2015 Sustainable Development Goals, if they include concerns with sustainability, will thus have to include both industrialized and developing countries, as opposed to the MDGs.

Sustainable development goes beyond the use of natural resources. It concerns any issue of intergenerational equity related to the transmission of the stocks of assets that determine wellbeing. Stiglitz *et al.* (2009: 11) defined it as follows: "Whether levels of well-being can be sustained over time depends on whether stocks of capital that matter for our lives (natural, physical, human, social) are passed on to future generations." The accumulation of debt by this generation that will have to be paid by subsequent generations is an important aspect of lack of sustainability. It is a major element in the current debate over high levels of public debt. It of course depends on why public debt has been incurred. If public debt supports investment and growth, future generations may benefit. If, however, public debt largely supports current consumption by this generation, with no growth effect of the type expected by Keynesians, then it clearly fails to meet the sustainability criterion in development.

Issues of sustainability and development

In this book, we will devote considerable attention to issues of sustainability in the management of natural resources (Chapter 15) and the ability of local communities to manage natural resources effectively when they are held as common property (Chapter 16). The first issue looks at the role of governance in compensating for market failures to internalize externalities, and at whether private parties can internalize externalities in bargained second-best arrangements when governments fail. A key issue throughout the reasoning on the sustainable management of natural resources is the allocation of property rights to overcome the tragedy of the commons associated with open-access resources. Property rights can be assigned individually or in common property, raising the questions of whether communities can cooperate in managing common property resources (CPR) and what the determinants of successful cooperation are. There is also the issue of inter-temporal valuation of resources through the discount rate. Discounting is partially determined by the opportunity cost of capital, but also by behavioral traits such as procrastination that create inter-temporal inconsistencies and may have a powerful impact on the way natural resources will be used and depleted.

QUALITY OF LIFE

If development is about wellbeing, are there additional dimensions of development to the six analyzed above (namely, income growth, escape from poverty, equality and equity, security, basic needs in education and health, and environmental sustainability)? Clearly, there are, but they become more diffuse in public opinion and more controversial. We need for this a broad, open-ended seventh category that allows us to insert many dimensions of wellbeing that we know matter, even if they are not universally agreed upon. We will call them quality of life. We rely for this on Sen's (1985) capabilities approach and on Easterly's (1999) classification of the dimensions of quality of life beyond the six already identified.

Sen's capabilities approach

For Sen (1985), development is a process of expanding freedoms. Greater freedoms derive from the enhancement of "capabilities," defined as the choices that a person makes among "functionings" that could be achieved, and the freedoms he or she has in exercising such choices. Functionings are what people can be or do: being educated, healthy, well nourished, and self-confident. Functionings are in turn determined by "entitlements," defined as the set of alternative commodities and services that a person can command in a society using the totality of rights and opportunities that he or she faces. Entitlements, then, depend on factors such as availability of public goods, personal characteristics, asset endowments, social norms, climate and environmental conditions, and individual differences in relative deprivation. Sen's heralded contribution to the understanding of development based on the concepts of *entitlements*, *functionings*, *capabilities*, and *freedoms* was to broaden the definition of development beyond simple measures of income, consumption, and wealth to include important issues of freedom and choice (Sen, 2000). In this perspective, progressing toward development fundamentally consists in attacking the sources of capability deprivation and in expanding the set of capabilities.

Easterly's indicators of quality of life

In an attempt at characterizing quality of life at the country level, Easterly (1999) used 81 indicators beyond income. These included the categories considered above such as education, health, and inequality, as well as important categories for achieving a higher quality of life:

- *Individual rights and democracy*. This includes indicators such as: freedom from expropriation, government not breaking contracts, bureaucratic quality, rule of law, freedom from corruption, civil liberties, human-rights rating, percentage of children working, political rights, and independence of politics from the military. Similarly, Frey and Stutzer (2000) have stressed the importance of democracy as a determinant of happiness—and Narayan, in her study *Voices of the Poor* (2000), revealed through interviews with tens of thousands of people the importance of rights and liberties in their wellbeing. Contrasting India and China, Sen (2000) evidenced the role of democracy and freedoms as an instrument in preventing famines.

■ *Political stability and peace.* Indicators used by Easterly here include: frequency of cabinet changes, deaths from political violence, strikes, assassinations, coups, revolutions, riots, deaths from war, racial tensions, and separatist movements. Collier (2007) stressed peace and security as the number one demand that populations place on their leaders. Since the state has monopoly over institutionalized violence, this is indeed a key public good in securing quality of life.

■ *Absence of "bads"* such as fraud, terrorism, robberies, rapes, drug crimes, various dimensions of environmental pollution, and suicides.

The list can be long and is open ended. It again makes the point that development is about wellbeing, and that wellbeing is a multidimensional concept, with the need to make priorities and to recognize the existence of trade-offs in development achievements.

DEVELOPMENT GOES BEYOND INCOME, BUT CAN INCOME GROWTH DELIVER DEVELOPMENT?

We have seen that income growth is a key dimension of development, but that development goes beyond income. However, even in a multidimensional perspective, an important question is whether income growth will deliver the other dimensions of development. We have seen that income growth—for example, in China—has been the main cause of poverty reduction. Dollar *et al.* (2013), using 118 countries over four decades, show that 75 percent of the growth in income of the bottom 20 percent is due to overall economic growth. It is also the case that vulnerability to poverty declines as per capita income rises: the further above the poverty line you are in normal times, the less likely it is that a bad year will take you below the poverty line. Finally, we have seen convergence in national levels of basic needs as income per capita rises (Figure 1.7), but with considerable heterogeneity in the satisfaction of basic needs across countries with an equal level of GDPpc when still at low-income levels.

It is, however, precisely dissatisfaction with the way growth delivers development that led development economists in the 1960s and 70s such as Thorbecke (1966), Adelman and Morris (1973), Sen (1983), Streeten (1994), and the UNDP staff to look beyond simple income growth as the source of development. This raised the issue of the quality of growth, which, as we have seen above, can increase the elasticity of poverty reduction with respect to income growth. Questioning the quality of growth means that one is concerned with the process through which growth is achieved, not only the quantity of growth. The process could, for example, be the degree of low-skill labor intensity in manufacturing, production of food by smallholder farmers as opposed to large commercial farms, small and medium firms as opposed to large enterprises, and greener growth as opposed to heavy polluting and non-renewable resource-intensive growth. Questioning the quality of growth also raises the issue that some dimensions of development may simply not be delivered by higher-income achievements. One such controversy has been whether higher income is itself a source of greater happiness.

It is well known that the relationship between income and happiness is complex and tenuous. In recent years, economists have devoted considerable attention to uncovering the determinants of happiness (Frey and Stutzer, 2001). Governments where democracy does not prevail, such as China today and Brazil when it was under military dictatorship, tend to be quite concerned that rapid income growth also delivers happiness to secure acceptance of the regime and political stability. The Gallup World Poll (Gallup, 2015) asks people to rate their level of life satisfaction (happiness) on a scale of 1 (dissatisfied) to 10 (satisfied) by asking the question: "All things considered, how satisfied are you with your life as a whole these days?"

While it is now well recognized that increasing income may not contribute to higher levels of happiness in industrialized countries, constituting the so-called "Easterlin paradox" (Easterlin, 1974; and see Clark *et al.*, 2008), there is strong empirical evidence supporting the fact that rising GDPpc in developing countries does increase happiness (Deaton, 2008). Overall, at levels of income below PPP-adjusted $10,000 (corresponding to countries like Brazil and Mexico), people become happier when income rises. But this also depends on how income gains have been achieved. Being employed to earn income may be more important for happiness than getting an equivalent unemployment compensation. Easterlin (2013) suggests that full employment and comprehensive social-safety nets are the most important sources of gains in happiness, not economic growth. We know from psychological studies that wellbeing is more than money and material rewards ("money does not buy happiness"). Lottery winners are briefly happy and excited about monetary gains, but soon report not being any happier than they were before they won the lottery as they get used to being wealthier. Kahneman *et al.* (2006) blame this on a "focusing illusion," which causes people to exaggerate the expected impact of additional income on happiness. Happiness research shows that social trust and the quality of personal relations with others become more important than material rewards once survival is secured—and also that higher inequality has a negative effect on happiness (Graham and Felton, 2006).

Deaton (2013) has revisited the issue of the role of income on happiness. He still maintains that, cross-sectionally, income raises happiness up to PPP-adjusted $10,000 but not beyond. However, he shows that a given percentage gain in income continues to raise happiness at all income levels. In other words, while the marginal contribution of an additional dollar becomes insignificant beyond the $10,000 threshold, a 4 percent increase in income continues to increase happiness linearly by one point on the Gallup life-satisfaction scale at all income levels. While this result is important in maintaining the role of money as a meaningful source of happiness at all income levels, it also confirms that other factors become increasingly important in contributing to happiness beyond income as income rises.

Establishing an econometric relationship between income and indicators of quality of life remains, however, marred with estimation problems. Cross-country regressions of the type:

$$L_{it} = \alpha + \beta y_{it} + \varepsilon_{it},$$

where L is a quality of life indicator in country i in year t, and y is the log of per capita income (i.e. GDPpc), show a strong relation between per capita income and quality of life. A positive β means that higher income improves quality of life. However, this result has little credibility due to spurious correlations: both income and quality of life are affected by many other variables not included in the regression.

Cross-country panel analysis improves on this by introducing year and country fixed effects in equations such as:

$$L_{it} = \lambda_t + \mu_i + \beta y_{it} + \varepsilon_{it},$$

where λ and μ are year and country fixed effects respectively. The surprising result found by Easterly (1999) is that, while the cross-section relationship between income and quality of life is strong (32 out of the 81 indicators of quality of life have a significantly positive β), it tends to vanish once country fixed effects are introduced (only 10 out of the 81 indicators maintain a positive relation). This means that the relationship holds across but not within countries.

If the relation is estimated in terms of income growth and improvements in quality of life (i.e. estimated in the change between two successive periods), namely:

$$L_{it} - L_{it-1} = \lambda_t - \lambda_{t-1} + \beta(y_{it} - y_{it-1}) + \varepsilon_{it} - \varepsilon_{it-1},$$

only 6 out of 69 indicators of quality of life are affected by country growth.

This weak role of growth in explaining quality-of-life improvements may be due to the existence of longer lags in the relation between income growth and quality of life. Alternatively, the result suggests that country fixed factors (such as resource endowments, access to the sea, ethnic fragmentation, social infrastructure, climate, and the legal system) are important determinants of quality of life. More interestingly, since many of the indicators of quality of life are public goods, the result suggests that the rise in GDPpc does not easily translate into increased public goods. Clearly, policy interventions are needed in order to make growth more effective in enhancing the quality of life in a particular country.

CONCLUSION: DEVELOPMENT IS MULTIDIMENSIONAL, SO CAN WE AGREE ON WHAT IT IS?

The concept of development we use here has been broadened beyond monetary income or expenditures (i.e. beyond per capita income or consumption and its various transformations into poverty, inequality/inequity, and vulnerability) to include basic human needs, sustainability, and the multiple dimensions of wellbeing. There is clearly no possible agreement on an optimum weighting scheme of the dimension of development to create a universal development index. Avoiding the death of a child cannot be weighted against the deprivations of having a dirt floor, cooking with wood, or not having a radio, TV, telephone, bike, or car (Ravallion, 2011). Aspects of development that matter most depend on the heterogeneity of situations, personal choices, and moral and ideological differences. The HDI and MPI weightings of the dimensions of basic needs are legitimate but arbitrary, and a broader index covering the multiple dimensions of development would clearly be worthless.

There is, evidently, the possibility of agreement under the particular circumstance when one situation (a time period, a country) is better than another in all possible dimensions of development. In this case, choice of weights would be inconsequential in ranking the development level of one situation vs. the other. The ranking of situations in the dimension of development would be robust, i.e. unchanged by the choice of weights, but this is the exception rather than the norm. In the norm, trade-offs exist. In this case, the best option is probably to use an array of indicators, without attempting to weight the relative importance of the criteria reflected by these indicators, and to describe the trade-offs across indicators, a position endorsed by Ravallion (2011).

The concept of development does not have to be so undefined, however, because there is in fact broad agreement that some dimensions of development matter more than others. As indicated by Sen (1983), there is strong agreement that development must deliver income growth, poverty reduction, basic-needs satisfaction, and the reduction of vulnerability. Agreement on the other dimensions of development may be weaker, such as on the importance of equality/equity, sustainability, and particular aspects of the quality of life. The MDGs, as an expression of broad international consensus, focused attention on poverty, inequality, basic needs, sustainability, and empowerment. With these two positions on development—Sen and the MDGs—we are not far from our seven dimensions of development. Yet any attempt at weighting the dimensions of development is futile as it is bound to meet with strong disagreement. Trade-offs need to be recognized. Explicit choices in the face of trade-offs are essential. It is reflected in personal and social choice. There is consequently no development without morals and ideology. In the practice of development, making these choices is both necessary and desirable. At all levels, what is important is that these choices be well informed, broadly participatory, deeply owned, clearly recognized, and allow the right to and respect of dissensions and minority positions.

CONCEPTS SEEN IN THIS CHAPTER

Ideology
Millennium Development Goals (MDGs)
Seven dimensions of development
GDPpc: nominal, real, in US$ at nominal exchange rate, growth rate, time to double or 70 years rule

PPP exchange rate and GDPpc at the PPP exchange rate

Genuine Progress Indicator (GPI)

Basic needs: Human Development Index (HDI)

Acute Multidimensional Poverty Index

z-scores: height-for-age (stunting) and weight-for-age (wasting)

Global Burden of Disease (GBD) and DALYs

Malnutrition and food insecurity

Vulnerability to poverty

Poverty traps

Non-poor, transient poor, chronic poor, persistent poor

Risk aversion

Safety-first

Risk management and risk coping

Quality of life and happiness

Easterlin happiness paradox

Pareto optimality in policy outcome

Sen's capabilities and functionings

REVIEW QUESTIONS: WHAT IS DEVELOPMENT? INDICATORS AND ISSUES

1. Development is a multidimensional concept. What are seven dimensions that would enter into a definition of development? How do they correspond to the MDGs?

2. Measures of income and growth: define GDP and PPP-adjusted GDP. In poor countries, is PPP-GDPpc larger or smaller than GDPpc measured at the nominal exchange rate? Why? How to adjust GDPpc for inflation? For a given growth rate of income, how to measure the number of years it will take for income to double?

3. Measures of basic needs and social welfare: define the HDI. How useful is it in characterizing the state of basic needs? Define the z-scores and give an interpretation.

4. Define a DALY. How is this concept useful in characterizing the disease burden of a population?

5. What is meant by vulnerability and by poverty traps? What is meant by risk management and risk coping?

6. What are the dimensions of development on which there is broad agreement, and the dimensions on which there is much less agreement? Explain why.

REFERENCES

Adelman, Irma. 1984. "Beyond Export-Led Growth." *World Development* 12(9): 937–49.

Adelman, Irma, and Cynthia Taft Morris. 1973. *Economic Growth and Social Equity in Developing Countries.* Stanford, CA: Stanford University Press.

Alkire, Sabina, and Maria Emma Santos. 2010. "Acute Multidimensional Poverty: A New Index for Developing Countries." Working Paper 38, Oxford Department of International Development, Oxford University.

Antman, Francisca, and David McKenzie. 2007. "Poverty Traps and Nonlinear Income Dynamics with Measurement Error and Individual Heterogeneity." *Journal of Development Studies* 43(6): 1057–83.

Banerjee, Abhijit, and Esther Duflo. 2011. *Poor Economics: A Radical Rethinking of the Way to Fight Global Poverty.* New York: Public Affairs.

Bassole, Léandre, and Jean-Louis Arcand. 2006. "Does Community Driven Development Work? Evidence from Senegal." Clermont-Ferrand: CERDI Working Papers 200606.

Beegle, Kathleen, Rajeev Dehejia, and Roberta Gatti. 2006. "Child Labor and Agricultural Shocks." *Journal of Development Economics* 81(1): 80–96.

Bhagwati, Jagdish, and Arvind Panagariya. 2013. *Why Growth Matters: How Economic Growth in India Reduced Poverty and the Lessons for Other Developing Countries.* New York: Public Affairs.

Boulding, Kenneth. 1966. "The Economics of the Coming Spaceship Earth." In H. Jarrett (ed.), *Environmental Quality in a Growing Economy,* 3–14. Baltimore: Resources for the Future/Johns Hopkins University Press.

Bourguignon, François. 2003. "The Growth Elasticity of Poverty Reduction: Explaining Heterogeneity across Countries and Time Periods." In T. Eicher and S. Turnovsky (eds.), *Inequality and Growth: Theory and Policy Implications,* 3–36. CESifo Seminar Series. Cambridge, MA: MIT.

Carter, Michael. 2012. "Designed for Development Impact: Next Generation Approaches to Index Insurance for Smallholder Farmers." Working paper, Department of Agricultural and Resource Economics, University of California at Davis.

Chenery, Hollis, Montek Ahluwalia, Clive Bell, John Duloy, and Richard Jolly (eds.) 1974. *Redistribution with Growth.* New York: Oxford University Press.

Clark, A., P. Frijters, and M. Shields. 2008. "Relative Income, Happiness, and Utility: An Explanation for the Easterlin Paradox and Other Puzzles." *Journal of Economic Literature* 46(1): 95–144.

Collier, Paul. 2007. *The Bottom Billion.* Oxford: Oxford University Press.

Collins, Daryl, Jonathan Morduch, Stuart Rutherford, and Orlanda Ruthven. 2009. *Portfolios of the Poor: How the World's Poor Live on $2 Day.* Princeton, NJ: Princeton University Press.

Daly, Herman. 1999. *Ecological Economics and the Ecology of Economics.* Cambridge, MA: Elgar Publishers.

de Janvry, Alain, Frederico Finan, Elisabeth Sadoulet, and Renos Vakis. 2006. "Can Conditional Cash Transfer Programs Serve as Safety Nets in Keeping Children at School and from Working When Exposed to Shocks?" *Journal of Development Economics* 79(2): 349–73.

Deaton, Angus. 2008. "Income, Health, and Well-being around the World: Evidence from the Gallup World Poll." *Journal of Economic Perspectives* 22(2): 53–72.

Deaton, Angus. 2013. *The Great Escape: Health, Wealth, and the Origins of Inequality.* Princeton, NJ: Princeton University Press.

Dercon, Stefan. 2002. "Income Risk, Coping Strategies, and Safety Nets." *World Bank Research Observer* 17(2): 141–66.

Dercon, Stefan. 2008. "Fate and Fear: Risk and its Consequences in Africa." *Journal of African Economies* 17(2): 97–127.

Dollar, David, and Aart Kraay. 2001. "Growth is Good for the Poor." Washington, DC: World Bank Policy Research Working Paper No. 2587.

Dollar, David, Tatjana Kleineberg, and Aart Kraay. 2013. "Growth Still Is Good for the Poor." Washington, DC: World Bank Policy Research Working Paper No. 6568.

Easterlin, Richard. 1974. "Does Economic Growth Improve the Human Lot? Some Empirical Evidence." In P. David and M. Reder (eds.), *Nations and Households in Economic Growth*, 89–125. New York: Academic Press.

Easterlin, Richard. 2013. "Happiness, Growth, and Public Policy." *Economic Inquiry* 52(1): 1–15.

Easterly, William. 1999. "Life During Growth." *Journal of Economic Growth* 4(3): 239–76.

Emerick, Kyle, Alain de Janvry, Elisabeth Sadoulet and Manzoor Dar. 2015. "Technological Innovations, Downside Risk, and the Modernization of Agriculture." Working paper, Department of Agricultural and Resource Economics, University of California at Berkeley.

Frey, Bruno, and Alois Stutzer. 2000. "Happiness Prospers in Democracy." *Journal of Happiness Studies* 1(1): 79–102.

Frey, Bruno, and Alois Stutzer. 2001. *Happiness and Economics*. Princeton, NJ: Princeton University Press.

Galiani, Sebastian, Paul Gertler, and Ernesto Schargrodsky. 2005. "Water for Life: The Impact of the Privatization of Water Services on Child Mortality." *Journal of Political Economy* 113(1): 83–120.

Gallup. 2015. *The Gallup World Poll*. www.gallup.com/services/170945/world-poll.aspx (accessed 2015).

Graham, C., and A. Felton. 2006. "Inequality and Happiness: Insights from Latin America." *Journal of Economic Inequality* 4(1): 107–22.

Hoddinott, John. 2006. "Shocks and Their Consequences across and within Households in Rural Zimbabwe." *Journal of Development Studies* 42(2): 301–21.

Jacoby, Hanan, and Emmanuel Skoufias. 1997. "Risk, Financial Markets, and Human Capital in a Developing Country." *Review of Economic Studies* 64 (3): 311–35.

Janzen, Sarah, and Michael Carter. 2013. "The Impact of Microinsurance on Asset Accumulation and Human Capital Investments: Evidence from a Drought in Kenya." Working paper, Department of Agricultural and Resource Economics, University of California at Davis.

Jensen, Robert. 2000. "Agricultural Volatility and Investments in Children." *American Economic Review* 90(2): 399–404.

Kahneman, Daniel, Alan Krueger, David Schkade, Norbert Schwarz, and Arthur Stone. 2006. "Would You Be Happier if You Were Richer? A Focusing Illusion." *Science* 312(5782): 1908–10.

Kakwani, Nanak, Marcelo Neri, and Hyun Son. 2004. "Pro-poor Growth: Concepts and Measurement with Country Case Studies." Brasilia: UNDP, International Poverty Centre.

Krishna, Anirudh. 2012. "Who Became Poor, Who Escaped Poverty, and Why? Developing and Using a Retrospective Methodology in Five Countries." *Journal of Policy Analysis and Management* 29(2): 351–72.

Krishna, Anirudh, Patti Kristjanson, Maren Radeny, and Wilson Nindo. 2004. "Escaping Poverty and Becoming Poor in 20 Kenyan Villages." *Journal of Human Development* 5(2): 211–26.

Krugman, Paul. 2009. *The Return of Depression Economics and the Crisis of 2008*. New York: W.W. Norton and Co.

Ligon, Ethan, Jonathan Thomas, and Tim Worrall. 2002. "Informal Insurance Arrangements with Limited Commitment: Theory and Evidence from Village Economies." *The Review of Economic Studies* 69(1): 209–44.

Lipton, Michael. 1968. "The Theory of the Optimizing Peasant." *Journal of Development Studies* 4(3): 26–50.

Lucas, Robert. 1988. "On the Mechanics of Economic Development." *Journal of Monetary Economics* 33(1): 3–42.

Maccini, Sharon, and Dean Yang. 2009. "Under the Weather: Health, Schooling, and Economic Consequences of Early-life Rainfall." *American Economic Review* 99(3): 1006–26.

Narayan, Deepa with Raj Patel, Kai Schafft, Anne Rademacher, and Sarah Koch-Schulte. 2000. *Voices of the Poor: Can Anyone Hear Us?* New York: Oxford University Press.

Nordhaus, William. 2000. "New Dimensions in National Economic Accounting." *American Economic Review* 90(2): 259–63.

Piketty, Thomas. 2014. *Capital in the Twenty-first Century*. Cambridge, MA: Harvard University Press.

Rabin, Matthew. 1993. "Incorporating Fairness into Game Theory and Economics." *American Economic Review* 83(5): 1281–302.

Ravallion, Martin. 2011. "On Multidimensional Indices of Poverty." *Journal of Economic Inequality* 9(2): 235–48.

Ravallion, Martin. 2012. "Why Don't We See Poverty Convergence?" *American Economic Review* 102(1): 504–23.

Ravallion, Martin, and Shaohua Chen. 1997. "What Can New Survey Data Tell Us about Recent Changes in Distribution and Poverty?" *World Bank Economic Review* 11(2): 357–82.

Ravallion, Martin, and Shaohua Chen. 2007. "China's (Uneven) Progress against Poverty." *Journal of Development Economics* 82(1): 1–42.

Rosenzweig, Mark, and Kenneth Wolpin. 1993. "Credit Market Constraints, Consumption Smoothing, and the Accumulation of Durable Production Assets in Low-Income Countries: Investment in Bullocks in India." *Journal of Political Economy* 101(2): 223–44.

Scott, James. 1977. *The Moral Economy of the Peasant: Rebellion and Subsistence in Southeast Asia*. New Haven, CT: Yale University Press.

Sen, Amartya. 1983. "Development: Which Way Now?" *Economic Journal* 93(December): 745–62.

Sen, Amartya. 1985. *Commodities and Capabilities*. Amsterdam: North-Holland.

Sen, Amartya. 2000. *Development as Freedom*. New York: Anchor Books.

Sen, Amartya, and Jean Drèze. 2013. *An Uncertain Glory: India and its Contradictions*. Princeton University Press.

Stiglitz, Joseph. 2012. *The Price of Inequality*. New York: W.W. Norton and Co.

Stiglitz, Joseph, Amartya Sen, and Jean-Paul Fitoussi. 2009. *Report by the Commission on the Measurement of Economic Performance and Social Progress Sustainability*. Paris: French Government.

Streeten, Paul. 1994. "Human Development: Means and Ends." *American Economic Review* 84(2): 232–7.

Thorbecke, Eric and Irma Adelman. 1966. *The Theory and Design of Economic Development*. Baltimore: Johns Hopkins University Press.

Townsend, Robert. 1994. "Risk and Insurance in Village India." *Econometrica* 62(3): 539–91.

UN DESA (United Nations Department of Economic and Social Affairs). 2013. "Realizing the Future We Want for All." www.un.org/en/development/desa/policy/untaskteam_undf/report.shtml (accessed 2015).

UNCED (United Nations Conference on Environment and Development). 1992. *Agenda 21*. http://sustainabledevelopment.un.org/content/documents/Agenda21.pdf (accessed 2015).

UNDP (United Nations Development Program). 2010. "The Real Wealth of a Nation? Its People." New York. www.one.org/us/2010/11/04/the-real-wealth-of-a-nation-its-people/ (accessed 2015).

UNDP. 2015. "Human Development Reports." New York. http://hdr.undp.org/en.

WHO. 2014. www.who.int/gho/mortality_burden_disease/daly_rates/en/. Geneva: World Health Organization (accessed 2015).

World Bank. 1990. *Poverty*. Oxford: Oxford University Press.

World Bank. 2000. *Attacking Poverty. Word Development Report 2000/01*. Oxford: Oxford University Press.

World Bank. 2005. *Equity and Development. World Development Report 2006*. Washington, DC.

World Bank. 2007a. *Agriculture for Development. World Development Report 2008*. Washington, DC.

World Bank. 2007b. *Nutritional Failure in Ecuador: Causes, Consequences, and Solutions*. Washington, DC.

World Bank. 2009. http://web.worldbank.org/WBSITE/EXTERNAL/EXTDEC/EXTGLOBAL MONITOR/EXTGLOMONREP2009/ (accessed 2015).

World Bank. PovcalNet. http://iresearch.worldbank.org/PovcalNet/index.htm (accessed 2015).

World Bank. *World Development Indicators*. http://data.worldbank.org/indicator (accessed 2015).

World Commission on Environment and Development. 1987. *Our Common Future*. New York: Oxford University Press.

Chapter 2

The state of development

TAKE HOME MESSAGES FOR CHAPTER 2

1. There has been success in development. Many middle-income countries, particularly in East Asia and more recently in South Asia, have grown rapidly, sharply reducing world extreme poverty and creating a large world middle class. However, there are still huge gaps in per capita incomes between high-income OECD (PPP$41,389 per capita in 2013), middle-income (PPP$6,974), and low-income (PPP$1,754) countries.

2. World income polarization is enormous, with high-income countries accounting for 18 percent of world population and controlling 67 percent of world income, while low- and middle-income countries account for 82 percent of world population and only control 33 percent of world income.

3. Convergence in per capita incomes with high-income countries is highly selective, only happening for a small "convergence club," but including some of the most populous developing countries.

4. With selective convergence, international inequality in the distribution of income has increased across countries but fallen across individuals due to the sharp increases in income among the large Chinese and Indian populations. Intra-country inequality has also been on the rise in most industrialized and developing countries, contributing to widespread political tensions, and making the issue of inequality a priority development issue.

5. Most of the world's poverty and hunger is located in South Asia and Sub-Saharan Africa, and the number of poor is rising in these regions. Only China has been successful in sharply reducing the number of poor, taking some 694 million people out of poverty in the last 29 years.

6. There has been rapid convergence in health and educational achievements among middle- and high-income countries, but levels of life expectancy remain highly unequal among low-income countries, with both high and low achievers at a similar level of GDPpc, indicating that satisfaction of basic needs is not only driven by income, but also by social choice.

7. While the US is by far the world's largest source of greenhouse gas emissions on a per capita basis, since 2007 China has become a larger source of CO_2 emissions than the US due to the sheer size of its economy.

8.   There were steady gains in democratic freedoms until the end of the Cold War in 1989, but gains have leveled off since then. By contrast, there has been a sharp decline in the number of armed conflicts since the end of the Cold War, mainly due to the successful termination of ongoing conflicts.

We characterize in this chapter the state of development in 2013 using the seven dimensions of development identified in Chapter 1. What we shall see is a great deal of unevenness in progress toward development, with remarkable successes from which to learn, telling us that achieving development is indeed far from hopeless, and also many failures, showing us how difficult it is to improve wellbeing for the "bottom billion" of extreme poor (Collier, 2007).

INCOME GROWTH AND THE CONVERGENCE CLUB

We have seen that wellbeing is first and foremost measured in terms of real per capita income. By this standard, as can be seen in Figure 2.1, the stunning success in GDPpc growth was located in East Asia and the Pacific, led by China, where per capita income increased by 18 times since 1965, while it increased by only 2.8 times

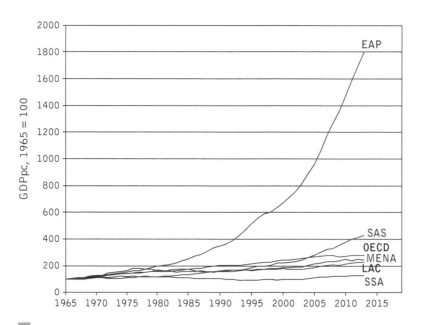

Figure 2.1 *GDPpc by region 1965–2013 at constant US$, 1965 = 100*

EAP = East Asia and the Pacific, SAS = South Asia, OECD = Countries of the Organization for Economic Cooperation and Development, MENA = Middle East and North Africa, LAC = Latin America and the Caribbean, SSA = Sub-Saharan Africa.

Source: World Bank, *World Development Indicators.*

in the OECD countries. South Asia also performed better than the OECD countries, with income increasing by 4.3 times, and growth accelerating sharply after 2000. All other regions have had long-run income growth inferior to that of the OECD countries: in 50 years, GDPpc increased by 2.5 times in the Middle East and North Africa, 2.3 times in Latin America and the Caribbean, and only 1.3 times in Sub-Saharan Africa. We thus see the emergence of a "convergence club" (Lucas, 1990) of regions—East Asia and the Pacific and South Asia—with GDPpc rising faster than in the high-income OECD countries and catching up with them, while the other regions of the world are lagging and falling further behind in per capita income. The main deficit in per capita income growth is clearly located in Sub-Saharan Africa, which, consequently, deserves most attention in this respect. Clearly, developing regions are split into two subgroups on the basis of the convergence criterion. Thinking development as a homogenous phenomenon would thus be clearly wrong. Instead, heterogeneity in income growth is what prevails among developing countries.

The data in Table 2.1 characterize the current state of world development in terms of population and income across regions. There are five dominant regularities that stand out in the table: (1) the permanence of huge gaps in per capita income across countries; (2) high polarization, with a small share of world population controlling a large majority of world income; (3) a high population tax in Africa and South Asia in translating GDP growth into per capita income growth; (4) selective convergence in per capita income, with a few developing countries catching up with high-income countries and many lagging behind; and (5) a considerable degree of instability in per capita income growth (not shown in the table).

Huge income gaps remain

Average per capita income in the high-income OECD countries was, in 2013, $42,809 compared to $4,809 in the middle-income countries, and $677 in the low-income countries. In PPP-adjusted dollars, these figures are $41,389 for the high-income countries, $6,974 for the middle-income countries, and $1,754 for the low-income countries. In the middle-income countries, PPP-adjusted per capita income is thus only 17 percent of that in the high-income countries. In the low-income countries, it is a meager 4 percent of income in the high-income countries. Even in China, where growth has been exceptionally rapid for the last 23 years (10.1 percent/year), per capita income measured in US$ at the official exchange rate was only 12.8 percent of that in the US in 2013, and 22.4 percent when measured in PPP-adjusted US$ (Table 2.2). For India, income was 2.8 percent of that in the US measured at the official exchange rate and 10.2 percent when measured in PPP-adjusted US$. Successful growth and income convergence in these countries should thus not be mistaken for the fact that huge income gaps remain.

A highly polarized world

Another way of looking at the development problem is to compare the concentrations of population and of income between high-income and low- and middle-income

Table 2.1 State of the world in 2013, by income levels and regions

Geographical area	Population million 2013	% of world population 2013	Population growth 2013	GDPpc US$ 2013	GDPpc PPP$ 2013	% of world GDP 2013	GDPpc growth 1980–2013
World	7125	100	1.2	10514	14293	100	1.5
Low- and middle-income countries	5818	81.7	1.3	4208	8505	32.7	2.8
High-income countries	1306	18.3	0.5	38634	40187	67.4	1.9
Low-income countries	849	11.9	2.2	677	1754	0.8	1.0
Lower middle-income countries	2561	35.9	1.5	2044	5999	7.0	2.5
Upper middle-income countries	2409	33.8	0.8	7746	13577	24.9	3.3
High-income OECD countries	1054	14.8	0.5	42809	41389	60.2	1.9
Low- and middle-income countries							
East Asia and the Pacific	2006	28.2	0.7	5690	10791	15.2	7.1
Eastern Europe and Central Asia	272	3.8	0.7	7287	13975	2.6	1.6
South Asia	1671	23.5	1.3	1409	5005	3.1	3.9
Middle East and North Africa	345	4.8	1.7	4313	11872	2.0	1.4
Latin America and the Caribbean	588	8.3	1.1	9617	14510	7.5	1.1
Sub-Saharan Africa	936	13.1	2.7	1700	3304	2.1	0.3

Source: World Bank, World Development Indicators.

Table 2.2 *State of the world in 2013: China, India, and the US*

	Population million	% of world population	Population growth	GDPpc US$	GDPpc PPP$	% of world GDP	GDPpc growth
Geographical area	2013	2013	2013	2013	2013	2013	1980– 2013
China	1357	19.1	0.5	6807	11904	12.3	10.1
India	1252	17.6	1.2	1499	5410	2.5	6.2
US	316	4.4	0.7	53143	53143	22.4	2.9

Source: World Bank, *World Development Indicators.*

countries. The figure is stunning, revealing a highly polarized world: high-income countries control 67 percent of world income with only 18 percent of world population. By contrast, middle- and low-income countries have 82 percent of world population, with only 33 percent of world income. The US controls 22.4 percent of world GDP with only 4.4 percent of world population. By contrast, China controls 12.3 percent of world GDP with 19.1 percent of world population, while, for India, the corresponding figures are 2.5 percent for income and 17.6 percent for population.

Another way of thinking about global income disparities is of a world of 7 billion people with an approximate 1-5-1 billion population distribution between low-income, middle-income, and high-income countries. The first is the "bottom billion" that lives in the low-income countries (Collier, 2007). The world income split corresponding to this population distribution is 1-32-67, a clearly hugely polarized distribution. Rounding up these figures gives us a stunning, easy-to-remember image: 1-5-1 in population controls 1-30-70 in income, resulting in 1-6-70 relative per capita incomes matching the 1-5-1 population split.

A high population tax on income growth in Africa and South Asia

GDP growth may be high, but high population growth can tax away a large share of that growth in terms of per capita income. Using the identity:

$$\dot{GDPpc} = \dot{GDP} - \dot{Pop},$$

where a dot on a variable represents growth rate, the population tax is the percentage loss in GDP growth due to population growth:

$$\frac{\dot{GDP} - \dot{GDPpc}}{\dot{GDP}} = \frac{\dot{Pop}}{\dot{GDP}}.$$

This can be seen in Table 2.3 and Figure 2.2 for the period 2000–13. In Sub-Saharan Africa, 55 percent of GDP growth, which reached a respectable 4.9 percent/year during the period, is taxed away by a correspondingly high rate of population growth (equal to 2.7 percent/year). Latin America and the Caribbean had growth in GDPpc comparable to that of Africa during the period (1.9 percent), even though GDP growth was only 3.2 percent/year. This is because of a low rate of population growth, equal to only 1.3 percent/year, and, correspondingly, a population tax of only 39 percent. Population growth is also rather high in South Asia (1.5 percent/year), but GDP

Table 2.3 GDP growth and population tax, 2000–13

| Regions | Average annual growth rates 2000–13 | | | Population tax |
	GDPpc	Population	GDP	(Pop growth/GDP growth)
ECA	4.0	0.5	4.5	10.2
EAP	7.7	0.8	8.6	9.3
SA	4.9	1.5	6.5	23.0
LAC	1.9	1.3	3.2	39.2
MENA	2.2	1.7	3.9	43.9
SSA	2.1	2.7	4.9	55.1
World	1.5	1.2	2.7	44.9

Source: World Bank, *World Development Indicators.*

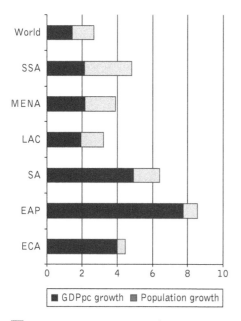

Figure 2.2 GDP growth and population tax, 2000–13

Source: World Bank, *World Development Indicators.*

growth has been very rapid over that period (6.5 percent/year), resulting in a population tax of only 23 percent. East Asia and the Pacific combine the advantages of both very high GDP growth (8.6 percent/year) and low population growth (0.8 percent/year), with, as a consequence, a population tax only equal to 9 percent. With virtually no population growth in Europe and Central Asia (0.5 percent/year), the population tax is 10 percent and nearly all GDP growth (4.5 percent/year) translates into per capita income growth (4 percent/year). Clearly, population growth is important for the growth in per capita income. We will return to an analysis of the determinants of fertility and the implications of population growth for development in Chapter 11.

Selective income convergence

Over the 1980–2013 period, convergence in per capita income was confined to East Asia and the Pacific and South Asia. As can be seen in Table 2.1, GDPpc growth in high-income countries was 1.9 percent (the benchmark for convergence over the period) and it was exceeded or equaled by growth in these two regions, where it was 7.1 percent in East Asia and the Pacific and 3.9 percent in South Asia. Divergence characterized the other three regions: Middle East and North Africa (1.4 percent), Latin America and the Caribbean (1.1 percent), and, especially, Sub-Saharan Africa (0.3 percent). In 2000–8, however, growth was strong in the developing countries, and all regions had a GDPpc growth in excess of that of the high-income countries, including Sub-Saharan Africa, one of the fastest-growing regions in the world during that time. Convergence is thus not hopeless: it can be done, but it is exposed to considerable instability, especially in Latin America and Africa, with good and bad periods for reasons that need to be understood.

Figure 2.3 represents country-level convergence or divergence with the US over the period 1960 to 2013 for countries with complete GDPpc data series in the World Bank's *World Development Indicators*. The horizontal axis classifies countries by their GDPpc in 1960 relative to GDPpc in the US. The US thus has a value of 1. Denmark, Norway, and Luxemburg had GDPpc above the US. On the vertical axis is the average annual growth rate in GDPpc for each country over the period. This is one of the most familiar figures in the growth literature, known as the "convergence triangle" plot. This is because the country labels in the scatter plot form a triangle, showing much more variation in growth rates among the initially poorer than richer countries. The horizontal line in the figure is at 2.1, the growth performance of the US for the period. All countries in the scatter graph with their labels above the line converged; those below diverged.

The top ten convergers and divergers in Figure 2.3 are identified in Table 2.4. Most of the divergers are in Sub-Saharan Africa. It is remarkable that in 1960 some of the top convergers had very low levels of GDPpc compared to the US. GDPpc was only 1 percent of that in the US in China and India, and 2 percent in Botswana, Indonesia, and Sri Lanka. In the 1960s, these countries were often considered as "basket cases" for achieving growth. It also shows that success in converging is geographically widespread, including not only countries in East Asia (China, Korea, Singapore, Malaysia, Indonesia), but also in South Asia (Sri Lanka, India), Sub-Saharan

Africa (Botswana), and Latin America (Belize). This presents a hopeful picture. Success can be achieved even if you are poor and wherever you are located. It shows how much difference can good institutions and good policy make for poor countries in joining the convergence club.

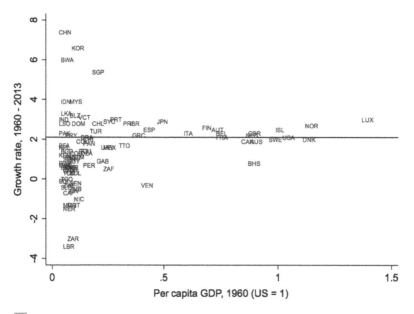

Figure 2.3 *The convergence triangle plot, 1960–2013*

Source: World Bank, *World Development Indicators.*

Table 2.4 *Top ten convergers and divergers, 1960–2013*

Top ten divergers			Top ten convergers		
Country	*GDPpc 1960 US = 1*	*GDPpc growth rate 1960–2013*	*Country*	*GDPpc 1960 US = 1*	*GDPpc growth rate 1960–2013*
Liberia	0.03	−3.4	China	0.01	7.4
Congo, DR	0.05	−3.0	Korea, Rep	0.07	6.6
Niger	0.03	−1.5	Botswana	0.02	6.0
Mauritania	0.05	−1.3	Singapore	0.16	5.4
Madagascar	0.03	−1.3	Malaysia	0.06	3.9
Nicaragua	0.08	−1.0	Indonesia	0.02	3.9
Central African Rep	0.03	−0.7	Sri Lanka	0.02	3.3
Cote d'Ivoire	0.06	−0.6	Belize	0.06	3.2
Zambia	0.06	−0.5	India	0.01	3.0
Sierra Leone	0.02	−0.4	Dominican Rep	0.07	2.8

Source: World Bank, *World Development Indicators.*

Convergence was quite different in the 2000–10 period, with high growth in Sub-Saharan Africa and low growth in the US. You can use the data in the *World Development Indicators* (online) to draw the convergence triangle for that period.

Growth instability

Income growth can be quite erratic, as affected by a variety of crises, more recently the "triple crisis" (Addison *et al.*, 2010): finance, food, and climate change. Poor African countries are in particular highly exposed to weather fluctuations. As a consequence, GDPpc growth can be quite unstable, adding an element of vulnerability to the welfare cost of low growth. This can be seen in Figure 2.4a that compares annual GDPpc growth in the US with that of Zimbabwe. The coefficient of variation (equal to the standard deviation divided by the average) of GDPpc growth was equal to 1.1 for the U.S. and −7 for Zimbabwe over the 1975–2013 period. Growth fluctuations relative to average growth were thus seven times larger in Zimbabwe than in the US. And, as the lower panel figure shows, this growth instability in Zimbabwe is highly correlated to annual fluctuations in rainfall, making it very hard to control.

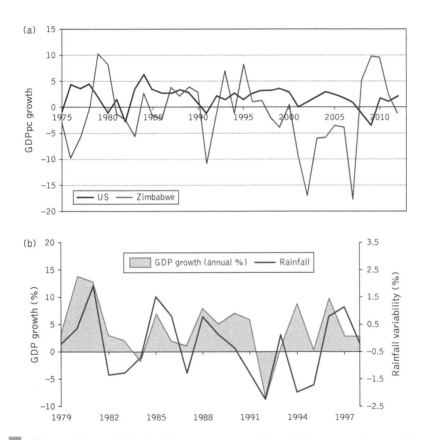

Figure 2.4 *Instability in GDPpc growth in the US and Zimbabwe 1975–2013 (a), and correlation with rainfall in Zimbabwe (b)*

Source: World Bank, *World Development Indicators;* World Bank, 2007.

POVERTY AND HUNGER

Poverty

In 2010, as we saw in Chapter 1, 58 percent of the population in developing countries lived in poverty on less than PPP-adjusted \$2.50/day and 21 percent in extreme poverty on less than PPP-adjusted \$1.25/day. Table 2.5 gives a characterization of the extreme-poverty headcount ratio (the percentage of the population in poverty) and of the malnourishment (hunger) headcount ratio by regions.

What this shows is that the highest extreme-poverty rates are in Sub-Saharan Africa (48 percent), followed by South Asia (31 percent), with 33 percent in India. Because it has both a large population and a high poverty rate, South Asia harbors 42 percent of the total number of poor in developing countries. Next, 34 percent are located in Sub-Saharan Africa because the poverty rate there is so high even though it only has 14 percent of the developing world's population. While East Asia has 34 percent of developing-world population, a low poverty rate (12 percent) implies that it only has 21 percent of the world poor.

Hunger (malnourishment) tracks extreme poverty fairly closely, but not exactly. As can be seen in Table 2.5, the world share of hungry people is higher than the share of poor people in East Asia and especially China, Latin America, and the Middle East and North Africa. Access to food is thus not only a matter of income, but also of the price of food and existence of social programs providing targeted access to food for the poor; and these regions fare poorly in this respect. It is also a household choice in allocating consumption expenditures, with often deceptively low progress in nutrition in spite of eventually rapid income growth.

Figure 2.5 describes progress in reducing poverty across regions of the world. In terms of headcount ratios, we see stunning progress in East Asia (mainly China, where the headcount ration declined from 84 percent in 1981 to only 12 percent in 2010), and some progress in all regions. Even in Africa, after increasing from 51 percent in 1981 to 58 percent in 1996, the poverty rate declined over the subsequent 14 years to 48 percent in 2010. There has thus been recent progress in reducing the incidence of poverty, even in Sub-Saharan Africa.

However, progress is more elusive when looking at the number of poor. This is because the poverty rate (defined as the ratio of the number of poor to the size of the population) can fall while the number of poor increases: all it takes is an increase in the number of poor that does not exceed population growth.

Figure 2.6 shows the number of extreme poor by region, with an index equal to 100 in 1981. In East Asia, the number of poor fell between 1981 and 2010 to only 23 percent of what it was at the beginning of the period. In China, the number of poor in 2010 was only 17 percent of what it was in 1981. The numbers were 835 million in 1981 and 141 million in 2010, implying that 694 million Chinese got out of poverty in the intervening 29 years, an unparalleled event in the history of humanity. The number of poor more than doubled in Sub-Saharan Africa, and declined only modestly in South Asia, and especially in India.

In 2010, the numbers of extreme poor were 245 million in East Asia (141 in China), 2 in Europe and Central Asia, 31 in Latin America, 8 in the Middle East and

Table 2.5 Poverty and hunger in developing countries by regions, 2010

Regions	Population % by region	Poverty headcount (%) $1.25/day	% of world poor	Malnourishment headcount (%)	% of world malnourished	Total population (million)	Malnourished population (million)	Number of poor $1.25/day
	2010	2010	2010	2008–10	2008–10	2000	2008–10	2010
East Asia and Pacific	34	12	21	8	22	2010.44	169.1	251
China	21	12	13	13	20	1224.62	158.1	156
Europe and Central Asia	8	1	0	0	1	477.06	7	3
Latin America and Caribbean	10	5	2	9	6	583.89	50.3	30
Middle East and North Africa	6	2	1	7	3	331.26	23.5	8
South Asia	28	31	42	19	40	1633.15	309.9	507
India	23	33	33	17	29	1338.3	228.6	400
Sub-Saharan Africa	14	48	34	26	28	853.57	221.6	414
Total developing countries	100	21	100	13	100	5889.37	781.4	1212

Sources: World Bank, World Development Indicators; FAO, 2014.

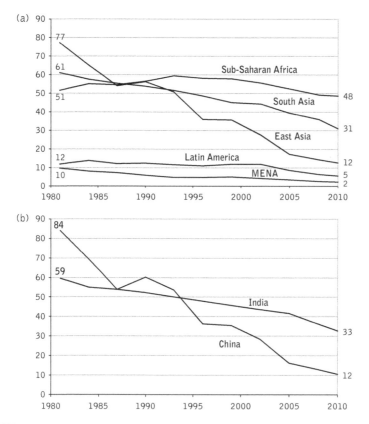

Figure 2.5 *Headcount ratios at $1.25/day by region (a), China, and India (b), 1981–2010*

Source: World Bank, *World Development Indicators.*

North Africa, 499 in South Asia (394 in India), and 419 in Sub-Saharan Africa, with a total of 1.2 billion.

As can be seen in Figure 2.7, rural poverty (at the $1.25 extreme-poverty line) has declined, but the rural headcount ratio, which was double the urban ratio in 1988 (54 percent vs. 27 percent), still remains nearly double in 2008 (34 percent vs. 18 percent) (IFAD, 2011). Most of the decline has been due to East Asia. In Sub-Saharan Africa, the rural headcount ratio rose from 51.7 to 61.6 percent over the period. In South Asia, it declined modestly from 55.9 to 45.2 percent. At a world scale, rural poverty, which accounted for 80 percent of world poverty in 1988, still accounts for 72 percent in 2008. The number of extreme rural poor remains in excess of 1 billion. Hence any attempt at reducing world poverty must first and foremost focus on the rural sector, one reason why the performance of agriculture is so important for poverty reduction in the developing world (World Bank, 2007). Even if world population is becoming urbanized (it accounted for 43 percent of developing-world population in 2008), with 800 million people moving from rural areas to cities over the last 50 years, and migration is part of the solution to rural poverty, rural populations must be prepared to migrate successfully out of poverty instead of transposing

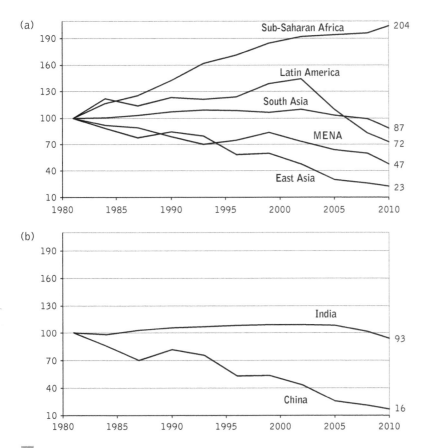

Figure 2.6 *Number of poor at $1.25/day by region (a), China, and India (b), 1981–2010 (1981 = 100)*

Source: World Bank, *World Development Indicators.*

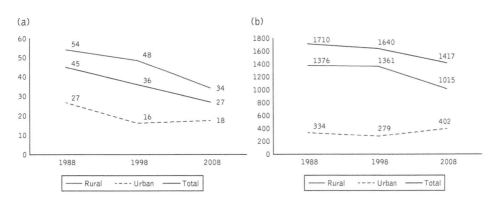

Figure 2.7 *Rural, urban, and total extreme poverty headcount ratios (a) and number of extreme poor in the developing world in million (b)*

Source: IFAD, 2011.

poverty from the rural to the urban population. This requires investing in their human capital, while rural education has typically lagged far behind urban achievements. The number of urban poor increased from 334 to 402 million over the 1988–2008 period. The rapid rise of urban slums testifies to this lack of preparedness of rural people when they reach urban labor markets (see Chapter 12).

Food security and hunger

Food crises are not new. There was a spike in the price of food in 1974 following Russia's invasion of Afghanistan and the US embargo on food exports. Food prices exploded again in 2007–8. This time prices were driven by diversion of corn supply to the production of biofuels (induced by the sharp rise in energy prices), bad weather affecting harvests, low international food reserves, speculation on commodity markets, and embargoes on food exports implemented by large countries such as India to keep their domestic prices low. Food prices, including rice, wheat, and corn, more than doubled in nominal terms between 2000 and 2008 (Figure 2.8), and achieved another peak in 2011. These staples still provide half of the calories for the world's poor majority, and the social implications of these price increases have been socially and politically disastrous.

While poverty is measured directly using household-survey data, hunger (malnourishment) is calculated by the FAO in its annual *State of Food Insecurity in the World* report in an indirect way at the country level. It starts from per capita food availability (measured as production + imports − exports + net change in stocks) and from estimated consumption taking into account income inequality. The difference is used to predict

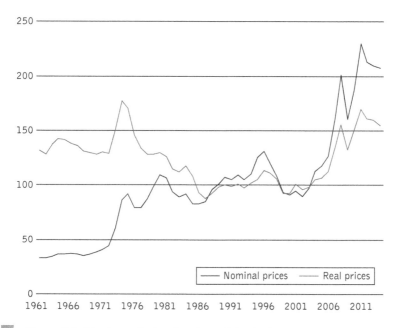

Figure 2.8 *Rise in nominal and real world food prices, 1961–2014, with 1998–2000 = 100*

Source: FAO, 2014.

the number of malnourished and the gap in food availability to eliminate hunger. Strong assumptions need to be made in this calculation, and past estimates have frequently been revised. A disadvantage of the approach is that it does not give an individual profile of the hungry in the way we can characterize the poor. The FAO's indirect approach compensates by providing an annual estimate of hunger that would not be available on the basis of household-survey data.

As can be seen in Figure 2.9, success in reducing world poverty was not matched by a corresponding decline in world hunger. The number of extreme poor declined from 1.9 billion in 1990 to 1.1 billion in 2010. By contrast, the number of undernourished in the developing world was 994 million in 1990–2 and still 791 million in 2012–14 (FAO, 2014). The hunger rate only fell from 23.4 percent in 1990–2 to 13.5 percent in 2012–14, failing to meet the MDG 1 on hunger. In Africa, the number of hungry increased from 182 million in 1990–2 to 227 in 2012–14, and the

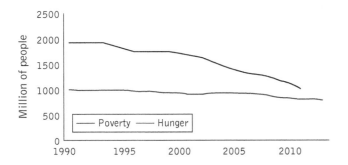

Figure 2.9 *Number of extreme poor (black line) and hungry (blue line) in million, 1990–2013*

Sources: World Bank, PovcalNet (poverty); FAO, 2014 (hunger).

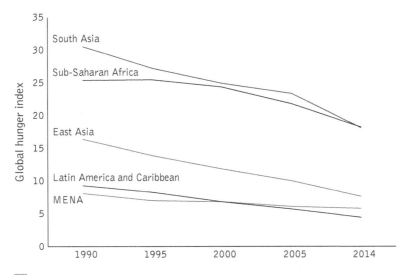

Figure 2.10 *Global Hunger Index by region, 1990–2014*

Source: IFPRI, 2014.

hunger rate only fell from 27.7 percent to 20.5 percent. It is important to understand why it is so difficult to achieve food security, when we seem to have a better understanding of how to reduce poverty. This is an issue that will be addressed in Chapter 18.

The International Food Policy Research Institute (IFPRI) constructs a Global Hunger Index for developing countries and countries in transition that combines three equally weighted indicators: undernourishment (the proportion of the population with insufficient calorie intake), child underweight (the proportion of children under five affected by wasting, stunting, or both), and child mortality (mortality rate of children under five). The index varies between 0, the best possible score, and 100, the worst possible score. For the world, the index declined from 20.6 in 1990 to 12.5 in 2014 (IFPRI, 2014). Regional contrasts are interesting (Figure 2.10). They show that South Asia remains the region with the most critical hunger status, closely followed by Sub-Saharan Africa. Major progress has been made in East and South East Asia, converging to low hunger scores comparable to those for the Middle East and North Africa and for Latin America and the Caribbean.

INEQUALITY

Inequality differs greatly across countries (Table 2.6). It is measured by the Gini coefficient that ranges from 0 for perfect equality to 100 for maximum inequality (it will be defined more precisely in Chapter 6). Inequality tends to be highest in Latin America (55 in Brazil, 59 in Honduras). It is somewhat lower in Sub-Saharan Africa (34 in Ethiopia, 40 in Senegal, 49 in Nigeria, 51 in Rwanda), and much lower in

Table 2.6 Gini coefficients in different countries, around 2010

2008–11	Country	PPP-GDPpc	Gini	Income share lowest 20%	Income share highest 20%	Kuznets ratio 20/20
Africa	Ethiopia	1041	34	8.0	41.9	5.3
	Rwanda	1242	51	5.2	56.8	11.0
	Nigeria	5048	49	4.4	54.0	12.2
	Senegal	2140	40	6.1	46.9	7.7
	South Africa	11426	63	2.7	68.2	25.3
East Asia	China	9053	42	4.7	47.5	10.0
South Asia	Bangladesh	2093	32	8.9	41.4	4.7
	Pakistan	4139	30	9.6	40.0	4.2
	India	4549	34	3.7	42.8	11.6
Latin America	Peru	9724	49	3.8	53.1	13.9
	Brazil	13773	55	0.8	58.8	74.4
	Mexico	14726	47	4.8	53.2	11.0
	Honduras	4188	59	1.8	61.9	35.0
South East Asia	Vietnam	4400	36	7.4	43.4	5.9
	Indonesia	7872	37	7.7	44.1	5.7
	Thailand	12575	40	6.7	47.2	7.1

Source: World Bank, World Development Indicators.

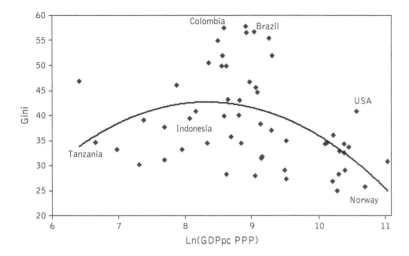

Figure 2.11 *The Kuznets-inverted U hypothesis*

Source: World Bank, *World Development Indicators.*

South Asia (30 in Pakistan, 32 in Bangladesh, 34 in India). It is also low in South East Asia (36 in Vietnam, 37 in Indonesia, 40 in Thailand). South Africa, with its history of apartheid, is an anomaly with a Gini of 63.

The Kuznets-inverted U curve

These inequality measures create an interesting cross-country regularity called the "Kuznets-inverted U," visualized in Figure 2.11: inequality is lower at low and high levels of GDPpc, and highest at the middle levels of GDPpc, precisely where the Latin American countries are located. As we will see in Chapter 6, this regularity is not causal in the sense that a rising GDPpc would be first inequalizing and then equalizing, but useful to describe the state of inequality across countries. It is an example of cross-country regression inviting fallacious policy implications, because causality does not prevail. As a consequence, it would be wrong to expect that simply accelerating growth to raise the level of GDPpc would necessarily, at some stage, deliver a decline in income inequality.

Inequality over time

Over time, few countries have seen a decline in the level of inequality, especially when growth has been rapid. In China, very rapid economic growth has been associated with rising inequality. Rising inequality has reduced the poverty-reduction value of growth. However, because growth has been so rapid, it has had a large impact in reducing poverty in spite of rising inequality (Figure 2.12). In Brazil, where inequality has always been among the highest in the world (as can be seen in Figure 2.11), there was a steady decline in the Gini coefficient between 1989 and 2006. This has in part been attributed to social safety-net programs, such as *Bolsa Família*, which have effectively

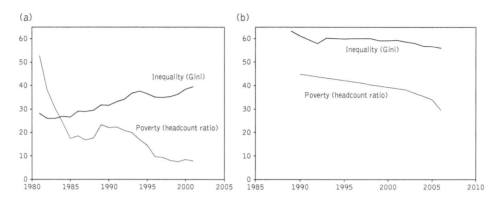

Figure 2.12 *Poverty and inequality in China (a) and Brazil (b)*

Sources: Ravallion and Chen (2007) for China; Paes de Barros (2007) for Brazil.

targeted the poor in transferring a cash allowance to them, and to progress in access to education (Ravallion, 2010). Several other Latin American countries with strong income-transfer programs also saw a decline in inequality in 2000–6—in particular, Ecuador, Bolivia, and Chile—while it increased in Costa Rica, Nicaragua, and Honduras, countries with weaker social programs (Calva and Lustig, 2010).

Is the international distribution of income becoming more or less unequal?

If convergence of countries' GDPpc were universal, the world distribution of income across countries would become more equal. We have seen that universal convergence does not hold, and that there is instead a convergence club (Lucas, 1990), with some countries successfully converging and many others diverging relative to the GDPpc of high-income countries. It then becomes an empirical question as to whether the international distribution of income is becoming more or less unequal.

The international distribution of income can be measured at two levels (Bourguignon and Morrison, 2002): at that of countries (concept 1 in Figure 2.13) and at that of individuals by weighting countries by their population size (concept 2 in Figure 2.13). The result shows an interesting contrast. Selective convergence implies that the world distribution of income across countries (concept 1) has become more unequal, with a Gini coefficient rising from 47 in 1952 to 56 in 2006 (Milanovic, 2009). However, members of the convergence club happen to include some of the world's most populous countries, especially China and more recently India. As a consequence, convergence has helped raise the income of many of the poorest people in the world. Weighted by population size (concept 2), international inequality in GDPpc has, consequently, steadily fallen, particularly after 1990.

We thus conclude this analysis of the state of the world in terms of inequality with the following three observations:

1. Inequality has increased within many countries, such as China, but it has also recently fallen in some countries such as Brazil and a few other Latin American

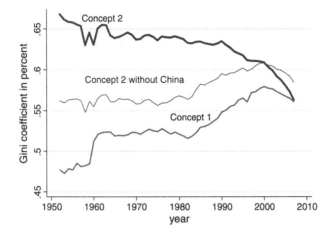

Figure 2.13 *Inter-country and international inequality*

Concept 1 = Inter-country inequality (unweighted by population size)
Concept 2 = International inequality (weighted by population size)

Source: Milanovic, 2009.

countries (more on this in Chapter 6). A heuristic observation would be that pure growth is inequalizing (e.g. China, Vietnam), especially when rapid, but that social programs can be used to counteract this effect and achieve greater equality with growth (e.g. Brazil). Market and state can thus lead to different outcomes in the growth–inequality relation according to their respective roles in an economy.

2. International inequality in GDPpc across countries unweighted by population size has increased quite sharply, except in the 2000s. This corresponds to the information we found on convergence. There has been selective convergence over the long run, implying rising inequality. However, developing countries had successful growth in the 2000s before the food and fiscal crises in 2008, allowing convergence for all regions of the developing world, Sub-Saharan Africa included, and implying a decline in world inequality.

3. Because convergence benefited some very large, initially poor countries, particularly China and India, international inequality with countries weighted by population size has declined steadily, accelerating in the last 20 years with rising growth in India. This decline in inequality at a world scale has led to a fundamentally important phenomenon: the rise of a world middle class, with its own particular capabilities, ideological bents, and policy demands.

The rise of a world middle class and of the relatively poor

We can look at how the intra-country distribution of income aggregates across countries into the world distribution of income, and how it changed between 1970 and 2000. This is seen in Figure 2.14 taken from Sala-i-Martin (2006). We can see how the world became richer over this 30-year period, with a falling share of world population below the $1/day poverty line (vertical line). We can also see how income inequality

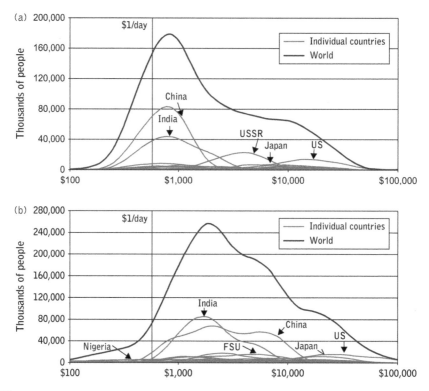

Figure 2.14 *The world distribution of income and individual country distributions in 1970 (a) and 2000 (b)*

Source: Sala-i-Martin, 2006.

has increased in China and India, with the frequency distributions of income flattening out. While in 1970 most of world inequality came from inter-country differences in levels of income, by 2000 intra-country inequality was playing a very large role in aggregate world inequality. Finally, if we define middle class as being in the $1,000 to $10,000 income range, we see how the promise of entering the middle class (an interesting way of characterizing success in development) has effectively been met for a majority of the Chinese and Indian populations.

Success in reducing absolute poverty has increased the middle class by millions, but also the ranks of the relatively poor (Ravallion, 2012). The decline in absolute poverty is measured by the percentage of people below the absolute international poverty line of $1.25/day in PPP-adjusted dollars. However, countries also use their own poverty line in counting their poor, and periodically revise their poverty line upward as average income rises. In 2011, China, for example, doubled its poverty line from 90cents/day to $1.80 in constant 2005 purchasing power. This rising poverty line as GDPpc rises gives a concept of "weakly relative poverty," a poverty count that takes into account average income in a country. Under this criterion, for two people with the same real income living in two countries with different GDPpc, the one in the richer country will feel relatively worse off. As absolute poverty falls with rising GDPpc, and national poverty lines are adjusted upward, the number of relatively poor can increase, suggesting a rise in relative deprivation. This is what Ravallion documents using data for the 1981–2008 period across more than 100 countries. Using this criterion, the number of absolutely poor (with a PPP $1.25 a day poverty line) declined from 1.9 billion in 1981 to 1.3 billion in 2008 (and the poverty rate fell from 52 percent to 22 percent). However, the number of relatively poor rose from 0.5 billion in 1981 to 1.4 billion in 2008. In 2008, poverty thus consisted of 48 percent of absolutely poor people and 52 percent of relatively poor people. In fighting absolute and relative poverty, then, the world still faces a double challenge: addressing absolute poverty for 1.2 billion people and addressing relative poverty (i.e. social exclusion) for 1.4 billion people.

BASIC HUMAN NEEDS

We defined basic needs principally in terms of health and education. What we see is a strong convergence in health and education across countries, in part because these indicators of wellbeing are bounded upward, in contrast to income, which can grow exponentially. Hence it is easier to register progress for those lagging behind than for those already at a high level of satisfaction of basic needs. However, catching up has also been selective across dimensions of basic needs and across regions. As can be seen in Table 2.7, catching up has been strong in life expectancy at birth and in secondary-school enrollment in the developing countries of East Asia and the Pacific, Europe and Central Asia, and Latin America and the Caribbean, but less so in infant-mortality rates. MDG 4 is to reduce by two thirds the under-five mortality rate in 1990–2015.

Table 2.7 *Gaps in the satisfaction of basic needs across regions and relative to the OECD countries, 2012*

Regions	Life expectancy at birth (years)	Infant mortality rate (per 1,000 live births)	School enrollment secondary (% gross)	Urban population (% of total)	Population growth (annual %)
EAP (developing)	73.8	17.2	82.9	49.6	0.7
ECA (developing)	72.3	19.1	93.3	60.2	0.7
LAC (developing)	74.5	16.3	88.1	79.0	1.2
MENA (developing)	71.4	21.4	80.7	59.5	1.7
SA	66.6	46.6	63.1	31.4	1.3
SSA	56.4	63.8	41.2	36.8	2.7
High income: OECD	80.7	4.4	101.0	80.8	0.3

Note: Developing means that only low- and middle-income countries of the corresponding region are included. In South Asia and Sub-Saharan Africa, all countries are developing.

Source: World Bank, *World Development Indicators.*

Only 17 countries had met this target by 2010 and an additional 23 countries are expected to meet the goal by 2015, leaving 101 countries missing the target.

Even for basic needs, where there has been strong catching up, large gaps remain in Sub-Saharan Africa and South Asia. Life expectancy in Sub-Saharan Africa is only two thirds that in the OECD countries. Secondary-school enrollment in Sub-Saharan Africa is one third that in the OECD countries and just over half that in South Asia.

The process of selective catching up in life expectancy at birth compared to income can be seen in Figure 2.15 for 1980 and 2012. While income disparities remain large between Latin America and the Caribbean, Middle East and North Africa, and East Asia relative to the OECD countries (measured on the horizontal axis in constant

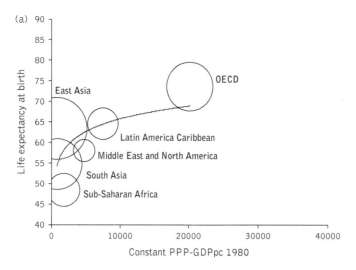

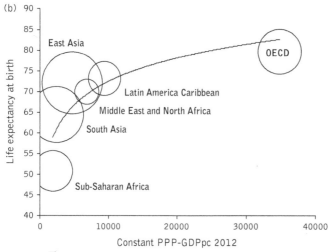

Figure 2.15 *Selective catching up in life expectancy at birth across regions, 1980 (a) and 2012 (b). Size of bubbles is proportional to population*

Source: World Bank, *World Development Indicators.*

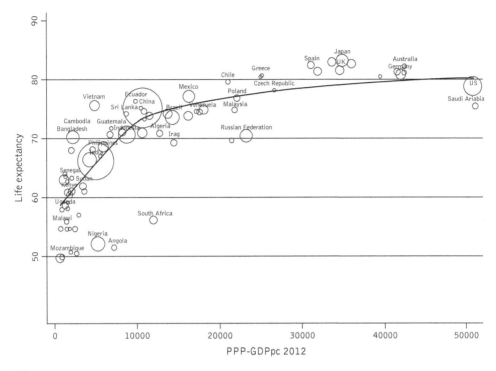

Figure 2.16 *Life expectancy by countries, 2000*

Bubble size is proportional to population.

Source: World Bank, *World Development Indicators.*

PPP-GDPpc in 1980 and 2012), these regions have reached levels of life expectancy at birth (vertical axis) that are getting close to those of the OECD countries, with only South Asia and Sub-Saharan Africa lagging behind.

This catching up is also seen in the sharp kink in the non-parametric fit between PPP-GDPpc and life expectancy at birth in Figure 2.16. While life expectancy rises sharply with income to a level of PPP$12,000, it reaches levels in China, Brazil, Mexico, Venezuela, Chile, and Malaysia that are not so different from those in the US once this threshold has been reached.

There are, however, considerable disparities in levels of life expectancy across low- and lower-middle-income countries. Countries like Mozambique and Bangladesh, Nigeria and Vietnam, Angola and Sri Lanka, and South Africa and China have similar levels of per capita income, yet vastly different levels of satisfaction of basic needs—high in the first member of each pair and low in the second. This shows that meeting basic needs is not only determined by income (what you can afford), but also, importantly, by policy priorities in funding public goods (what you choose to achieve as a development project). This reminds us once again that development is not just a process of income growth, but also a choice as to which dimensions of development you choose to achieve as a particular society. Even poor countries can achieve high levels of basic needs if this is a choice they decide to make (Hans Rosling (2007) makes a lively presentation on TED (Technology, Entertainment and Design) of basic-needs statistics across time and countries using bubble graphs. We suggest that you watch his presentation, "New Insights on Poverty," appreciating in which countries the satisfaction of basic needs has converged and in which it has lagged behind.)

SUSTAINABILITY IN RESOURCE USE

We have seen that economic growth is the cornerstone of development, promising not only higher levels of wellbeing through higher consumption levels, but also facilitating the reduction of poverty, inequality, and vulnerability. Through taxation, it also facilitates the provision of health and education as public goods, even if there exists a wide margin for social choice, as we have just seen. Yet growth may not be sustainable due to two consequences of growth itself: increasing resource scarcity, in particular of energy, minerals, water, and land; and growth externalities such as emissions and climate change. Today, we may envy the prosperity yielded to some by growth, yet more than 5.6 billion people can only aspire to it. What would actually happen in terms of resource scarcity and pollution if the "other 80 percent" attained OECD living standards? Three prominent threats to sustainability are climate change, energy demand, and deforestation. We shall see in each case that the risks faced by least developed countries are especially serious because of their vulnerability to these threats.

GHG emissions and climate change

Evidence increasingly indicates that greenhouse-gas (GHG) emissions are contributing to climate change, with rising temperatures and unstable rainfall patterns. This has far-reaching implications for the world's crop yields, water storage in glaciers, the sea level, extinction of species, and a rising incidence of storms, forest fires, droughts, floods, and heat waves (Stern, 2006). GHG emissions originate disproportionately in industrialized countries (the so-called Annex I countries in the Kyoto Agreement). With 20 percent of world population, they contribute 46 percent of world emissions. By contrast, the non-Annex I countries, with 80 percent of world population, contribute 54 percent. As can be seen in Table 2.8, in 2010, the US, with 4.5 percent of world population, contributes 16.7 percent of global GHG. On a per capita basis, a person in an industrialized country contributes four times more than a person in the "other 80 percent." The US is by far the largest polluter on a per capita basis. A person in the US contributes 13 times more to global GHG than a person in South Asia, and 23 times more than a person in Africa.

While, on a per capita basis, the US emit 20,583kg per person per year, while China emits only 3,862kg per person, the sheer size of the Chinese population implies that China, by 2007, had become a larger contributor to global CO_2 emissions than the US (Figure 2.17). This creates a huge new policy dilemma for international agreements on climate change. While China makes a large and rising contribution to global emissions, it is still a poor country that has not yet enjoyed the benefits of industrialization in terms of rising per capita incomes. In addition, climate change is not caused by the current flow of emissions, but by the accumulated stock in the atmosphere.

Table 2.8 *Regional distribution of per capita greenhouse gas emissions, 2010*

Regions	GHG (tons per capita)	% of global GHG	% of world population
Canada	15.6	1.5	0.5
East Asia and Pacific (all income levels)	5.5	34.8	32.0
Europe and Central Asia (all income levels)	7.9	20.2	12.9
Latin America and Caribbean (all income levels)	3.0	5.1	8.6
Middle East and North Africa (all income levels)	5.9	6.5	5.5
South Asia	1.4	6.6	23.3
Sub-Saharan Africa (all income levels)	0.8	2.0	12.6
US	18.7	16.7	4.5
World	5.0	100	100

Source: World Bank, *World Development Indicators.*

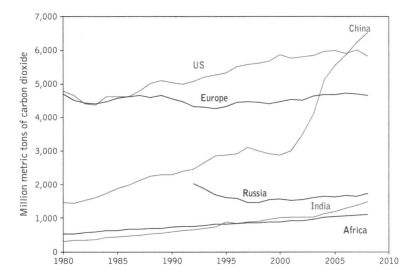

Figure 2.17 *Contributions to global CO$_2$ emissions, 1980–2008*

Source: US Energy Information Administration, online.

In Figure 2.17, this is the area under each curve, since the beginning of industrialization. Clearly, most of the contributions to climate change came from industrialized countries, not China and the other emerging economies. Hence these countries have been demanding in international agreements that industrialized countries be the ones bearing the brunt of the necessary reductions in global emissions. We will analyze in Chapter 15 what this implies for the design of a comprehensive new climate treaty that would go beyond the Kyoto agreement (extended to seven years beyond January 2013 and mostly including only industrialized countries) in introducing a world cap-and-trade system for emissions that includes developing countries.

Energy sustainability

As can be seen in Figure 2.18, energy consumption tracks closely rising per capita income. The large bubble in the uppermost north-east corner is the US, while the two very large bubbles near the south-west corner are India and China (left and right respectively). In light of current energy-market conditions, the impact on international prices of the latter two bubbles rising toward the first would be huge, unless new sources of energy are developed in due time.

Higher prices for resources will have two economic impacts: incentives for productivity gains and rationing of scarcity. Economic incentives can be expected to trigger innovations that make more productive use of existing resources, like the Green Revolution, which dramatically increased agricultural yields and food security in Asia and Latin America (but not Sub-Saharan Africa) in the context of famines in the 1960s and 1970s. Greater fuel efficiency, renewable energy innovations, and recycling are all rational and technologically progressive responses to rising energy prices. The innovation process not only helped overcome scarcity in the past, but helped trigger new waves of prosperity in knowledge-intensive industries. The timing of this outcome relative to rising energy demand is, however, a huge gamble. Recent years have seen considerable price volatility on energy markets, indicating that this process of adaptation to rising demand is far from smooth.

We see rationing happening in many developing countries where energy supply is inferior to demand at prevailing prices. Electricity stoppages are frequent and

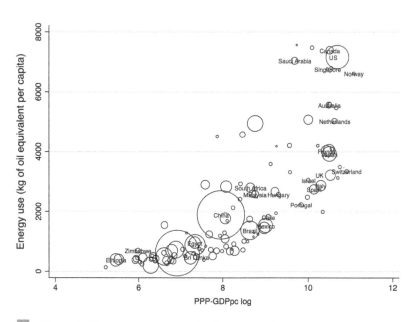

Figure 2.18 *Energy use per capita, by country, income, and population, 2005*

Bubble diameter is proportional to country population.

Source: IEA, *Statistics* (energy-use data); World Bank, *World Development Indicators* (income and population data).

Table 2.9 *Average annual rate of change in forest area (sq km), 1990–9, 2000–11, and 1990–2011*

Regions	1990–9	2000–11	1990–2011
East Asia and Pacific	−0.17	0.37	0.13
Latin America and Caribbean	−0.50	−0.46	−0.49
South Asia	−0.01	0.25	0.16
Sub-Saharan Africa	−0.57	−0.50	−0.53

Source: World Bank, World Development Indicators.

unpredictable in places like India and the Dominican Republic, creating huge efficiency losses. Non-price management of energy distribution implies looking at non-market mechanisms such as quotas and random cuts. It also implies looking at risk management (such as investing in autonomous electricity generators) and risk-coping mechanisms that curtail enterprise competitiveness.

Deforestation

A final consequence of growth has been rapid and accelerating deforestation in many developing regions (Table 2.9). In East Asia and the Pacific and South Asia, the deforestation trend has recently been reversed. In China, efforts at reforestation have been made through a large payment-for-environmental-service program, the Sloping Land Conversion Program, that pays farmers to retire steeply sloped lands from agriculture and reforest them (analyzed in Chapter 15). In Latin America and the Caribbean and Sub-Saharan Africa, deforestation continues unabated under the pressure of expansion of the agricultural frontier. Agricultural growth through area expansion thus runs into sustainability problems, with associated contributions to climate change, loss of biodiversity, and soil erosion in watersheds.

QUALITY OF LIFE

Quality of life is multidimensional. We focus on four indicators to get some sense of how it is progressing across nations and over time: happiness, quality of governance, democratic freedoms, and incidence of conflicts and violence.

Happiness

The *World Happiness Report*, led by Helliwell *et al.* (2010) proposes a Gross National Happiness (GNH) index based on nine categories equally weighted and 33 indicators distributed across these nine categories as follows:

1. Psychological wellbeing (including a measure of life satisfaction collected by the Gallup World Poll that asks respondents to evaluate the quality of their lives on a scale of 0 to 10, positive and negative emotions, spirituality)

2. Good health (self-reported health, healthy days, disability, mental health)
3. Time use (work, sleep)
4. Education (literacy, schooling, knowledge, values)
5. Cultural diversity and resilience (native language, cultural participation, artisan skills, conduct)
6. Good governance (political participation, services, governance performance, fundamental rights)
7. Community vitality (donation, safety, community relationships, family)
8. Ecological diversity and resilience (wildlife damage, urban issues, responsibility toward the environment, ecological issues)
9. Living standards (household per capita income, assets, housing)

Results for 2010 classify the following 10 countries at the top of subjective happiness: Iceland, New Zealand, Denmark, the Netherlands, Ireland, Singapore, Malaysia, Norway, Tanzania, and Sweden. The results show that developing countries such as Malaysia and Tanzania can eventually display high levels of happiness. The 10 countries with the lowest scores are Ethiopia, Romania, Iraq, Ukraine, Russia, Zambia, Albania, Zimbabwe, Moldova, and Bulgaria. This suggests that not only low income but also the stress and disruption of transition economies can create un-happiness. A detailed analysis of determinants of happiness for Bhutan shows that the most important contributing categories are good health (14 percent), community vitality (12 percent), ecological diversity and resilience (12 percent), and psychological wellbeing (12 percent), rather than living standards (income), education, and quality of governance. We can conclude that income is important for happiness at low levels of income, but that at higher levels of income, relative income, social trust, quality of work, freedom of choice, and political participation are more important than additional income, thus confirming the Easterlin paradox (1974), discussed in Chapter 1.

In characterizing quality of life, another useful source of information is the World Values Survey conducted by the Institute for Social Research at the University of Michigan, which gives information about values and cultural changes in societies all over the world. Information is available at www.worldvaluessurvey.org/ (accessed 2015).

Quality of governance and failed states

The World Bank's (2011) *Worldwide Governance Indicators* reports on six broad dimensions of governance for over 200 countries over the period 1996–2010 (information is available at http://info.worldbank.org/governance/wgi/index.aspx#home (accessed 2015)). The six dimensions of governance are:

1. *Voice and accountability*, which captures perceptions of the extent to which a country's citizens are able to participate in selecting their government, as well as freedom of expression, freedom of association, and the existence of a free media.

2. *Political stability and absence of violence*, which measures perceptions of the likelihood that a government will be destabilized or overthrown by unconstitutional or violent means, including domestic violence and terrorism.
3. *Government effectiveness*, which captures perceptions of the quality of public services, the quality of a civil service and the degree of its independence from political pressures, the quality of policy formulation and implementation, and the credibility of a government's commitment to such policies.
4. *Regulatory quality*, which captures perceptions of a government's ability to formulate and implement sound policies and regulations that permit and promote private-sector development.
5. *Rule of law*, which captures perceptions of the extent to which agents have confidence in and abide by the rules of society, and in particular the quality of contract enforcement, property rights, the police, and the courts, as well as the likelihood of crime and violence.
6. *Control of corruption*, which captures perceptions of the extent to which public power is exercised for private gain, including both petty and grand forms of corruption, as well as "capture" of the state by elites and private interests.

These indicators allow the characterization of countries with failed states. Common characteristics of failed states include:

- A central government so weak or ineffective that it has little practical control over much of its territory;
- non-provision of public services;
- widespread corruption and criminality;
- refugees and involuntary movement of populations;
- a sharp economic decline.

Failed states are characterized by the Fund for Peace (2012) on the basis of social, economic, and political indicators that inform these features. In 2011, there were 20 countries listed as failed states: namely, Somalia, Chad, Sudan, the Democratic Republic of the Congo, Haiti, Zimbabwe, Afghanistan, Central African Republic, Iraq, Côte d'Ivoire, Guinea, Pakistan, Yemen, Nigeria, Niger, Kenya, Burundi, Guinea-Bissau, Myanmar, and Ethiopia. For some countries, these are chronic features, while they are transitory for others. Chronic failed states require an approach to development that focuses on state reconstruction and, in the immediate future, relies less on state roles and more on international assistance, the private sector, and domestic civil society, especially NGOs.

Democratic freedoms

The Freedom House (2012), an NGO supported by the US federal government, publishes an Index of Country Democratic Freedoms including civil liberties and political rights. Based on this information, countries are classified as free, partly free, and not free. Figure 2.19 shows the evolution of the percentage of countries in each category. It documents the remarkable progress of democracy, with the "free" category rising from 30 to 45 percent of all countries over the 1972–2012 period. At the same

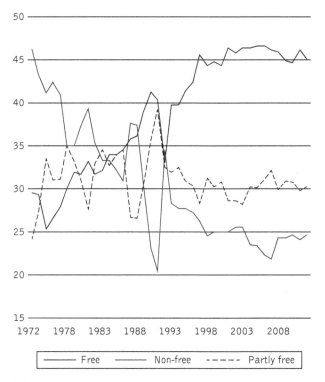

Figure 2.19 *Index of Country Democratic Freedoms: percentage distribution of countries among free, non-free, and partly free categories, 1973–2012*

Source: Freedom House (2012).

time, countries labeled as "not free" fell from 46 to 25 percent. Yet it is also notable that democratic gains have stagnated in the decade following the fall of the Berlin Wall in 1989.

Progress is also uneven across regions. In Sub-Saharan Africa, only 20 percent of countries were qualified as free in 2013, and this percentage, which increased from 6 percent in 1983 to 23 percent in 2003, has subsequently declined. In the Middle East and North Africa, only 6 percent of countries were characterized as free in 2013, while 66 percent remained non-free.

Incidence of armed conflicts and violence

Armed conflict, defined as an event exceeding 25 battle-related deaths in a year and involving a state government as at least one of the warring parties, is recognized as a major cause of underdevelopment and of regression in levels of development achieved (Collier, 2006). It is notable that there has been a significant decline in the last 15 years in both the number of armed conflicts and the number of casualties in such conflicts. As can be seen in Figure 2.20, the major turning point was in 1991–2 following the end of the Cold War. Today, there are few inter-state conflicts and most conflicts are

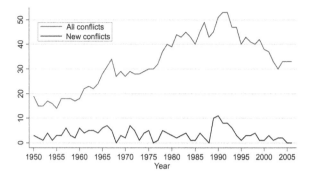

Figure 2.20 *Number of armed conflicts: all and new, 1950–2006*

Source: Buhaug *et al.*, 2007. Based on data from the Center for the Study of Civil War, PRIO.

intra-state, numbering some 32 in 2006. There are few new conflicts, and the observed decline in the number of conflicts originates in the successful termination of ongoing conflicts. Conflicts are mainly located in the geographical axis running from the Caucasus to the Philippines through the Middle East and the Indian subcontinent, and in the Great Lakes and the Horn of Africa. According to the International Peace Research Institute (PRIO), the increase in conflict termination has been associated with the end of the Cold War, the expansion of peacekeeping operations by the UN, and the role of the International Court of Justice in The Hague (Buhaug *et al.*, 2007).

The long-term decline in violence as a world phenomenon has been noted by psychologist Steven Pinker (2011) in his much heralded book, *The Better Angels of Our Nature: Why Violence has Declined.* Violence is associated with military conflict, homicides, genocides, and torture, as well as the abusive treatment of children, homosexuals, racial and ethnic minorities, and animals. According to Pinker, the decline in violence is associated with historical forces, most particularly (1) the rise of the modern nation state and judiciary with its effective monopoly on the use of legitimate force (the definition of the state, according to Max Weber); (2) the rise in long-distance trade, which makes other people more valuable as partners; (3) an increasing respect for the interests and values of women; (4) the rise of literacy, mobility, and mass media, which help people take into account and embrace the perspectives of others; and (5) the rising role of knowledge and rationality in human affairs. These historical forces are driven by a shift in balance between "inner demons" and "better angels," two opposite sets of psychological forces in people's behavioral determinants. Inner demons that push people toward violence include tendencies toward predation, dominance, revenge, sadism, and ideology, while better angels guide people toward cooperation and altruism include empathy, self-control, moral norms, and reason. In Pinker's optimistic view of humanity, people's basic impulses are not Hobbesian (that is, according to English philosopher Thomas Hobbes, 1588–1679, who advocated the need for a strong central authority to avoid human proclivity to discord and conflict) tendencies toward hatred and destruction, but inner propensities toward cooperation and altruism that are gradually emerging and guiding world affairs.

109

CONCLUSION

We have seen in this chapter a set of descriptive statistics about the state of development in the world. They give us a useful diagnostic of the current situation with development and how it has evolved over time. But these are just descriptive statistics, without pretense to causation. They do not tell us why we see what we see, nor what could be done to improve on the current situation if we do not like what we see. For this, we need theories and estimations of causal econometric relations. These are what we will look at in subsequent chapters in order to design and implement policy interventions to improve on the state of development.

CONCEPTS SEEN IN THIS CHAPTER

Poverty headcount ratio vs. number of poor
Strong convergence and selective convergence in GDPpc
GDP growth and population tax
Malnourishment/hunger headcount ratio
Global Hunger Index
Gini coefficient
Kuznets-inverted U curve
Inequality across countries (inter-country inequality) and across households (international inequality)
Weakly relative poverty
Payment for environmental services
Gross National Happiness Index
Worldwide governance indicator
Failed state
Index of Country Democratic Freedoms
"Inner demons" and "better angels" in explaining violence

REVIEW QUESTIONS: THE STATE OF DEVELOPMENT 2015

1. What is the meaning of economic convergence and to what extent have we observed it in recent decades? Is there a "convergence club" and who are some of the members and non-members?
2. Discuss the global prevalence of poverty: levels and changes. Where is it located by region and sector of economic activity? What are the main successes and failures? What can be said about the rate of poverty and the number of poor in Sub-Saharan Africa?
3. Economies have mostly been growing for the last two decades, but what has happened to global inequality? Discuss changes in inequality in terms of countries and of households.
4. Has there been convergence in basic needs? Is there more convergence in basic needs than there is in GDPpc? Why?

REFERENCES

Addison, Tony, Channing Arndt, and Finn Tarp. 2010. "The Triple Crisis and the Global Aid Architecture." Helsinki: UNU-WIDER Working Paper No. 2010/01.

Bourguignon, Francois, and Christian Morrison. 2002. "Inequality among World Citizens: 1820–1992." *American Economic Review* 92(4): 727–44.

Buhaug, Halvard, Scott Gates, Håvard Hegre, and Håvard Strand. 2007. "Global Trends in Armed Conflict." Centre for the Study of Civil War, International Peace Research Institute (PRIO), Oslo.

Collier, Paul. 2006. "War and Military Spending in Developing Countries and Their Consequences for Development." *Economics of Peace and Security Journal* 1(1): 10–13.

Collier, Paul. 2007. *The Bottom Billion: Why the Poorest Countries are Failing and What Can Be Done About It.* Oxford: Oxford University Press.

Easterlin, Richard. 1974. "Does Economic Growth Improve the Human Lot? Some Empirical Evidence." In P. David, and M. Reder (eds.), *Nations and Households in Economic Growth.* New York: Academic Press.

FAO. 2014. *The State of Food Insecurity in the World 2014.* Rome: FAO.

Freedom House. 2012. www.freetheworld.com/datasets_efw.html (accessed 2015).

Fund for Peace. 2012. http://global.fundforpeace.org/ (accessed 2015).

Helliwell, John, Richard Layard, and Jeffrey Sachs. 2010. *World Happiness Report.* Columbia University: The Earth Institute.

IEA (International Energy Agency). *Statistics.* www.iea.org/statistics/ (accessed 2015).

IFAD (International Fund for Agricultural Development). 2011. *Rural Poverty Report 2011.* Rome: International Fund for Agricultural Development.

IFPRI (International Food Policy Research Institute). 2014. *Global Hunger Index: The Challenge of Hidden Hunger.* Washington, DC: IFPRI.

López-Calva, Luis Felipe, and Nora Lustig. 2010. *Declining Inequality in Latin America: A Decade of Progress.* Washington, DC: Brookings Institution Press and UNDP.

Lucas, Robert. 1990. "Why Doesn't Capital Flow from Rich to Poor Countries?" *American Economic Review* 80(2): 92–6.

Milanovic, Branko. 2009. "Global Inequality Recalculated: The Effect of New 2005 PPP Estimates on Global Inequality." Washington, DC: World Bank, Research Department.

Paes de Barros, Ricardo. 2007. "The Recent Decline in Income Inequality in Brazil and Its Consequences on Poverty." Rio de Janeiro: IPEA.

Pinker, Steven. 2011. *The Better Angels of Our Nature: Why Violence has Declined.* New York: Viking.

Ravallion, Martin. 2010. "A Comparative Perspective on Poverty Reduction in Brazil, China, and India." *World Bank Research Observer* 26(1): 71–104.

Ravallion, Martin. 2012. "A Relative Question." *Finance and Development* (December): 40–3.

Ravallion, Martin, and Shaohua Chen. 2007. "China's (Uneven) Progress against Poverty." *Journal of Development Economics* 82(1): 1–42.

Rosling, Hans. 2007. "New Insights on Poverty." www.ted.com/speakers/hans_rosling.html (accessed 2015).

Sala-i-Martin, Xavier. 2006. "The World Distribution of Income: Falling Poverty and . . . Convergence, Period." *Quarterly Journal of Economics* 61(2): 351–97.

Stern, Nicholas. 2006. *Stern Review Report on the Economics of Climate Change*. London: Her Majesty's Treasury.

US Energy Information Administration. www.eia.gov/ (accessed 2015).

World Bank. 2007. *Agriculture for Development: World Development Report 2008*. Washington, DC.

World Bank. 2011. *Worldwide Governance Indicators*. http://info.worldbank.org/governance/wgi/index.aspx#home (accessed 2015).

World Bank. *PovcalNet*. http://iresearch.worldbank.org/PovcalNet/index.htm (accessed 2015).

World Bank. *World Development Indicators*. http://data.worldbank.org/indicator (accessed 2015).

Chapter 3

History of thought in development economics

TAKE-HOME MESSAGES FOR CHAPTER 3

1. History matters in understanding today's patterns of development and underdevelopment: there is a strong path dependency in crafting today's economic capacities and institutions that affect development outcomes.

2. While most of the determinants of development outcomes are internal to countries, development and underdevelopment are linked as part of an overall historical process that has both winners and losers. Progress for some countries has been achieved at the expense of setbacks for others, enhancing international income inequalities. This applies most particularly to extractive colonial relations and to the slave trade.

3. Development requires a balance between the roles of the market, the state, and civil society. Yet different schools of thought have given different relative importance to these institutions, especially market and state, in pursuing development outcomes, offering an informative way of contrasting these schools of thought.

4. Schools of thought can only be understood by reference to the specific historical context in which they emerged and in which they intended to act. Starting with a periodization of history is thus essential to establish the domain of application of each school and its corresponding logic.

5. On that basis, eight major schools of thought can be recognized, each with a corresponding historical period. They are: the mercantilists (precursors to the industrial revolution), classical political economy (the British experience), relative economic backwardness and modernization theory (the Western experience), globalization and comparative advantage (the age of empire), New Deal economics and central planning (war and depression), development economics (the Asian experience), the Washington Consensus (age of globalization), and open-economy industrialization (second-generation reforms).

6. In development economics, some of the lasting contributions are the ideas of the need for a Big Push (Rosenstein-Rodan) or a Critical Minimum Effort (Leibenstein) in investment due to economies of scale in modern industry, and whether this coordinated investment effort requires balanced (Nurkse) or unbalanced (Hirschman's linkage effects) growth. Also lasting are the ideas of redistribution with growth (Chenery)

or redistribution before growth (Adelman) to achieve egalitarian growth. In all cases, these approaches to development require the strong guiding hand of the state.

7. In the current post-Washington Consensus period, key ideas are: (1) recognition of the need for more country-specific approaches to the role of the state—in particular, in shaping up the business climate and investing in people and social protection; (2) a rediscovery of the role of institutions and the political economy of development; and (3) a more complex view of the links between poverty and growth.

INTRODUCTION: WHY HISTORY MATTERS

History matters in understanding current patterns of development and underdevelopment across countries. For example, underdevelopment in Sub-Saharan Africa today cannot be understood without reference to the massive extraction of slaves and the division of Africa by European colonial powers at the 1884 Berlin Conference, imposing country boundaries that often had little or no correspondence with prior societies and ethnic territories. The disruption was massive. Some 18 million slaves were exported from Africa during the 400 years of the slave trade. By 1900, 90 percent of Africa had fallen under European control (Landes, 1999).

In studying the role of path dependency in explaining current levels of development, Nunn (2008b) asks the question: can African countries' current levels of GDPpc be at least partially explained by their history of slavery? The data he uses are slave-shipping records and historical documents recording slaves' ethnicities for 52 countries. They measure the number of slaves exported from a country between the years 1400 and 1900. The magnitude across countries is quite heterogeneous, with exported slaves reaching 3.6 million in Angola, 2 million in Nigeria, 1.6 million in Ghana, and 1.4 million in Ethiopia. Results show that there is still a strong negative cross-country relationship between the number of slaves exported (normalized by land area) and current economic performance measured by GDPpc as of 2000. As can be seen in Figure 3.1, the African countries that are the poorest today are those from which the most slaves were exported per unit of area. To make sure that the relation is causal, instrumental variables are used, predicting the number of slaves exported using the sailing distances from each country to the nearest locations of demand for slave labor. Another verification of causality is that countries from which more slaves were exported were the richest at the time, not the poorest as they are today. Ethnic fractionalization and weakened institutions of governance created by the procurement of slaves through internal warfare, raiding, and kidnapping that resulted in subsequent state collapse and ethnic divisions are the causal channels between slave exports and underdevelopment. Because slaves were typically captured in violent raids with the participation of agents from neighboring tribes, the slave trade also affected the level of trust that prevails today among relatives, neighbors, co-ethnics, and local governments, adding another channel of causation between slavery and current economic performance. In a follow-up study, Nunn and Wantchekon (2011) find that current levels of trust, as measured in Afrobarometer

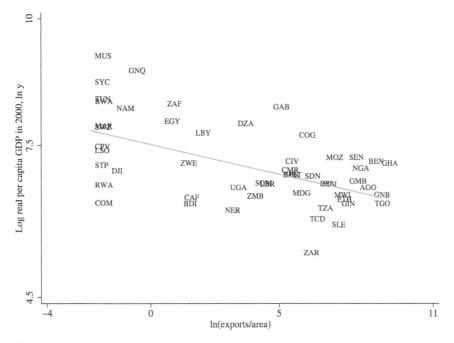

Figure 3.1 Path dependency in current levels of development in Africa

Relationship between log slave exports normalized by land area, ln(exports/area), and log real per capita GDP in 2000, ln y.

Source: Nunn, 2008b.

opinion polls, are systematically lower where respondents' ancestors were more heavily affected by the slave trade.

In another study that shows the importance of path dependency, Bockstette *et al.* (2003) analyze whether the degree of "state antiquity," i.e. countries that have had a stronger state over the long period starting in 1AD, have achieved faster economic growth and reached a higher level of GDPpc in the twentieth century. A country's national index of state antiquity at time t is measured as:

$$state\ antiquity_t = \sum_{t=0}^{39} \frac{q_{1t} * q_{2t} * q_{3t}}{(1+\delta)^t} \Bigg/ \sum_{t=0}^{39} \frac{1}{(1+\delta)^t},$$

where q_1 measures whether the government was organized above the tribal level, q_2 whether the ruling authority was local as opposed to foreign, q_3 whether the ruling authority controlled at least 50 percent of the current national territory vs. less, and δ is a discount rate. These indicators are each measured over a series of forty 50-year periods stretching over two millennia. The index is highest for China, with a value of 1, and lowest for Mauritania, with a value of 0.07. While results cannot claim causality because there may be omitted variables correlated with state antiquity that affect today's performance, they suggest that the long-term historical strength of the state significantly increases a country's economic growth performance over the period

115

1960 to 1995, accounting for half of the difference in growth rates between countries like China and Mauritania.

Not only does the history of institutions matter for today's development performance, but the history of ideas does too. The history of thought in development economics tells us why particular interpretations of underdevelopment were proposed and how they translated into policies that may still affect development outcomes today. The history of institutions and the history of thought are thus inextricably related: events shaped thought and thought shaped policy. We can say that thought in development economics that matters for modern development started with mercantilism and the first colonial period (the age of discovery) around 1500—so we need to cover 500 years of history of development and underdevelopment to help us understand what we see today, clearly a major challenge in a brief chapter. But details matter less than the logic of the evolution of thought in relation to events and ideology. This is what we present here.

BASIC PRINCIPLES IN ANALYZING THE HISTORY OF THOUGHT IN DEVELOPMENT ECONOMICS

We follow four principles in analyzing the history of thought in development economics.

1. *Development and underdevelopment are linked.*
   Development and underdevelopment are part of a **single world-scale process**. It would be a serious error to analyze underdevelopment as separate from development because countries have been linked through such events and processes as the slave trade, colonialism and the carving of empires, resource extraction with unequal benefits from trade and often unabated plunder, unequal protection benefiting advanced countries and undermining industrial advances in fragile economies such as India and China (Chang, 2002), the international transmission of price shocks and economic crises, foreign direct investment and the repatriation of profits, international migration and flows of remittances, geopolitics such as the spread of the Cold War, the diffusion of technological and institutional innovations, and the global impact of emissions resulting in climate change. The link between development and underdevelopment has played an important role in the spectacular emergence of new centers of economic growth such as the four tigers (Taiwan, South Korea, Singapore, and Hong Kong) following World War Two and more recently the rise of economic powerhouses such as Brazil, Russia, India, China, and South Africa, the so-called BRICS. It has also played a big role in holding countries back—for example, in shoring up corrupt and dictatorial regimes for geopolitical purposes in countries such as the Democratic Republic of the Congo and Nicaragua. Ideas have been derived from these experiences that have in turn affected the development strategies of other countries. The role of interdependencies in blaming the underdevelopment of some on the development of others may have been overdone by some schools of thought such as Dependency Theory (see, for example, the critique by Cardoso, 1977), but they clearly play a role that is central to understanding development.

116

2. *Schools of thought in development economics have both positive and normative intents.*
    A school of thought is anchored in positive analysis to provide it with an **explanation** of development achievements, or lack thereof: income growth, poverty, inequality, vulnerability, the satisfaction of basic human needs, sustainability, and various aspects of the quality of life. As we saw in Chapter 1, development is multidimensional, with important trade-offs in achievements. Which dimensions of development a particular school of thought chooses to stress in its diagnosis is an ideological choice. It is from this diagnosis that a school of thought proposes **a political project** that will be endorsed by a specific group of people for the purpose of altering the chosen dimensions of development. This normative statement is consequently deeply ideological. It will inevitably favor some segments of the population more than others, sometimes to the detriment of others. Because they are ideological projects, many schools of thought have emerged in contradiction to other schools of thought, such as Dependency Theory, which emerged in contradiction to the thinking of modernization theory underpinning the Western experience, or the Washington Consensus that emerged in contradiction to Development Economics after the failures of the debt crisis. Schools of thought are deeply rooted in the social conflicts of the historical periods in which they emerge and are applied. It is a huge and frequent mistake to critically assess schools of thought out of context, thereby constructing a paper tiger all too easy to belittle and dismiss.

3. *We place schools of thought in eight major periods of history starting in 1500.*
    They are the following (see the summary in Table 3.1):

    1500 to 1700: the precursors of the Industrial Revolution, consisting mainly of the mercantilists (1500 to 1750) in the context of colonial expansion and the age of discovery;
    1700 to 1820: the British experience, running from the agricultural revolution starting in 1700 to the industrial revolution over the 1750–1820 period;
    1820 to 1880: the Western experience, consisting of the spread of classical industrial revolutions from Belgium, France, and Germany, following the end of the Napoleonic wars in 1820, to the US and Russia in mid century, and finally Japan in 1880;
    1880 (effectively starting in 1850) to 1914: the age of empire, with globalization of economic relations, free trade, large international movements of both capital and labor, and a second phase of colonial expansion;
    1914 to 1945: war and depression, beginning with the Great War of 1914–18 and the end of *la belle époque*, leading to depression, protectionism, Soviet central planning, the responses of the New Deal, and World War Two;
    1945 to 1982: the "glorious years" of development economics and the Asian experience, with rapid economic growth fueled by import substitution, export-oriented industrialization, and the related economic take-offs of the four tigers—and several new tigers—and decolonization of Sub-Saharan Africa, a period that ends with the debt crisis that starts with Mexico in 1982;
    1982 to 1997: the age of globalization, with massive expansion of trade and international capital movements, open-economy industrialization with the

Table 3.1 Summary of periodization of history and schools of thought in development economics

1. Historical period	2. Main historical events	3. Schools of thought	4. Main objectives and instruments	5. Legacy	6. Ends with	7. Discussion
1. 1500 to 1700: The Precursors	Trade and colonialism. "Age of discovery"	Mercantilists	Wealth accumulation via trade and plunder (India, LAC)	State for growth: protection of trade monopolies	Agricultural revolution (physiocrats)	Trade for wealth. Monopolistic routes. Welfare of merchants and state. Colonies for plunder or settlement: reversals of fortune
2. 1700 to 1820: The British Experience	Agriculture and industrial revolution in England	Classical political economy	Industrial growth	Agriculture for industry. Trade and colonialism for capital accumulation	Rise of competitors	Conditions for the industrial revolution: labor, capital, technology, market, state. Why not China? Role of market
3. 1820 to 1880: The Western Experience	Agriculture and industrial revolutions in the "Western" sequence	Relative economic backwardness (REB)	Industrial growth for catching up. Industrialization imperative for militarism	Agriculture for industry (North–South). State intervention for growth: protection, substitutes	Complexity of techniques. Free trade (UK)	World development map: temperate and tropical. Role of substitutes. Role of state
4. 1880 (1850) to 1914: The Age of Empire	Globalization. Free trade. International capital and labor movements	Globalization and comparative advantage	Trade for efficiency (outward growth)	Market for growth	World War One	Ricardo and Manchester Doctrine. Repeal of Corn Laws. Trade, FDI, migration: role of market
5. 1914 to 1945: War and Depression	World War One, the Great Depression, and World War Two	Protectionism and the New Deal for recovery. Soviet experience and central planning	Keynesian policies. State for recovery (Western world) and industrialization (Soviet)	Role of a strong state for development	End of World War Two	State to overcome market failures and address poverty

Table 3.1 continued

1. Historical period	2. Main historical events	3. Schools of thought	4. Main objectives and instruments	5. Legacy	6. Ends with	7. Discussion
6. 1945 to 1982: The "Glorious Years" of Development and the Asian Experience	Growth to reconstruct and promote own industry (inward). Asian Experience (NICS). Decolonization of Africa	Development Economics. Growth-with-equity. Dependency Theory	1950s & 60s: Growth. Import substitution and export-oriented industrialization. 70: Poverty and equity	50s, 60s: State for growth (protect and subsidize). 70s: State for poverty and equality	Debt crisis and state excesses	From Western to Asian experience. 50s–60s: state for growth. 70s: state for basic needs. Role of agriculture (Green Revolution)
7. 1982 to 1997: The Age of Globalization	Macro-balances, globalization, Chinese experience. Transition out of central planning	Washington Consensus. Stabilization and adjustment	Macrofundamentals. Liberalize (trade and finance), privatize, descale the state	Role of market and FDI for open-economy industrialization	Stabilization and adjustment with failures to deliver growth. Asian financial crisis	From state (ISI, Basic Needs) to market. From planning to market
8. 1997 to today: Post-Washington Consensus	Growth and MDG failures (India, LAC). Africa lagging	Endogenous growth. Open economy industrialization. New institutional economics. Sustainable growth. New political economy. Impact analysis	Role of the state for private investment. Role of integrated value chains for efficiency. Role of civil society organizations for voice	State for second-generation reforms: asset redistribution, public goods, sustainability, social assistance	Successful but limited convergence. Energy and food crises. Global climate change	From market (Washington Consensus) to state-market complementarity (post-Washington Consensus)

acceleration of growth in China, and transitions out of central planning following the fall of the Berlin Wall in 1990, ending with the 1997 Asian crisis;

1997 to today: the post-Washington Consensus, with "second-generation reforms," following critiques of globalization and development failures under the Washington Consensus, particularly in Sub-Saharan Africa.

4. *Relative roles of state, market, and civil society.*

As we have seen (Figure I.1), development requires a balance between the complementary roles of the market (and private-sector firms), the state (and government), and civil society (and its various organizations). Different schools of thought assign a differentially important role to each component of this trinity. Schools of thought can thus in part be characterized by the relative importance they attach to market and state in their normative development strategies, with civil society performing a relatively secondary role compared to those of market and state. We will discover an important pendulum in the relative roles of state and market as schools of thought succeed each other over the course of history. In what follows, each school of thought is broadly characterized as follows:

i. historical context;
ii. definition of development endorsed by the school and its corresponding objectives;
iii. positive analysis of development—theories and interpretations;
iv. normative analysis of development—policies and strategies, with specific relative prescriptive roles for market and state;
v. outcomes and performance—successes and failures;
vi. intellectual legacy—lessons learned for economic development.

SELECTED SCHOOLS OF THOUGHT IN DEVELOPMENT

The precursors (1500–1700): mercantilists and colonial plunder

Mercantilism dominated economic thought for the pursuit of development in the long period from 1500 to 1750 (Cipolla, 1996). The mercantilists believed that the accumulation of bullion (gold and silver) was the basis of the wealth and power of nations. Bullion was accumulated via international trade, seen as a zero-sum game between competing merchants. The state had an active role to play in helping national merchants accumulate wealth under protectionism (import tariffs), granting monopolistic positions to specific trading companies (exclusive trade routes), and protecting trade routes via military and naval power. Until 1688, the East India Company had a government-enforced monopoly over trade with Asia. The most important imports to Britain were textiles from India. Mercantilist thought as a doctrine was driven by the interests of the merchants who benefited from trade and of the government that benefited from collecting tariffs and taxes on merchants as well as bribes in exchange for continued monopoly power. This was against the wellbeing of workers and farmers who were expected to remain at subsistence level to minimize production costs and enhance national competitiveness (hence the neo-mercantilist label frequently assigned to China's current development strategy). As trade insured demand for the product of national manufactures, neither was there any concern for the welfare of consumers as a source of effective demand. Mercantilism was driven by the rent-seeking interests of merchants and governments.

Mercantilist trade also consisted in exploration and colonialism (the age of discovery), profits from the slave trade, and the plunder of metals in India and Latin America, leading to the accumulation of capital that could subsequently be invested in the industrial revolution (Landes, 1999). The colonial experience was to have very different impacts across colonized countries depending on whether they were **colonies of extraction** (with high population density and riches to be taxed or plundered) or **colonies of settlement** (with low population density and good climate for European settlers). Only colonies of settlement gave themselves inclusive institutions, with strongly protected property rights, limits to the power of the elites, and the broad participation of the population in entrepreneurship and investment. The subsequent differential growth performance led to an eventual "reversal of fortune": the initially richer colonies of extraction (India, Latin America) would subsequently lag in growth behind the initially poorer colonies of settlement (US, Canada, Australia, New Zealand) (Acemoglu *et al.*, 2002). This reversal of fortune, based on exogenous conditions (presumed to be favorable health conditions) that led to the selective emergence of good institutions and their reproduction over time through path dependency, was used to emphasize the role of inclusive institutions as a key determinant of successful long-term development.

The role of institutions in economic development was also analyzed by Sokoloff and Engerman (2000). The logic of their arguments is that a country's factor endowments and the degree of inequality in the distribution of these endowments determine the choice of institution (Figure 3.2a). Endowments include land availability and soil quality, wealth, human capital, and political power. Institutions could be large slave-based plantations or family farming. In Cuba, soil quality defined comparative advantage in sugar and coffee with economies of scale in production, leading to the option of large plantations and slave labor, and high levels of economic inequality. In the US, soil quality privileged grains that led to the choice of family farms and an egalitarian distribution of wealth. The choice of institution is thus important for the level of

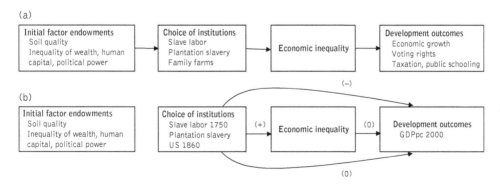

Figure 3.2 *Engerman–Sokoloff hypothesis (a) and Nunn's (2008a) test (b)*

economic inequality. Current development outcomes, including economic growth, political systems (voting rights), and public policy (taxation, availability of public schooling) are determined by economic inequality—basically, the slave plantation (unequal) vs. the family farm (egalitarian) dichotomy.

Causalities are difficult to establish. Nunn (2008a) took the Engerman–Sokoloff hypothesis about the relation between slave labor, large plantation slavery, economic inequality, and current GDPpc to the data (Figure 3.2b). He used data on slavery both for former colonies in 1750 and US states in 1860 and found that the hypothesized negative relation between slave labor and development is maintained, as well as the positive relation between slavery and high inequality. However, there is no empirical support for a direct role for large plantation slavery on development outcomes, nor for economic equality on development. Institutions are not exogenous to development outcomes, and need some type of instrumentation, a challenge taken up by Acemoglu *et al.* (2001) in their work on the role of institutions in development. We analyze in Chapter 4 how an instrumental variable approach has been used to establish this causality between good institutions and development.

Alsan (2015) gives empirical support to the Sokoloff and Engerman (2000) on the role of geographical endowments in shaping institutions and affecting economic development. She looks at the role of the tsetse fly, which thrives in the humid tropics of Africa. The fly causes sleeping sickness in humans and is deadly to animals. She constructs a "tsetse suitability index" to measure exposure to the insect across space. She shows that in areas of high tsetse suitability there were 23 percent fewer domesticated animals and 6 percent less use of the plow in farming in the pre-colonial period. Farming without the help of animals was much less productive, resulting in more reliance on foraging, more scattered populations and a lower population density, and less centralized states. This helps explains the observation that Sub-Saharan Africa is land abundant with a low population density. This pattern persists today, with lower levels of economic development in areas with a higher tsetse-suitability index.

There are two major intellectual legacies for thought in development economics from this period of mercantilism and colonial expansion. The first is the importance of state protection for the success of emerging economic interests, a policy instrument that was to be key for latecomer countries seeking to catch up with more advanced nations. The second is the importance of institutions for development, with inclusive institutions and a centralized state authority leading to sustained growth in per capita income, while extractive institutions resulted in unstable political regimes with infighting over the appropriation of rents and poor growth performance (Acemoglu and Robinson, 2012).

The British experience (1700–1820): classical political economy and the agricultural and industrial revolution

How do we explain the main quantum leap in the world history of economic development: namely, the industrial revolution in Britain in the period from 1750 to 1820? In terms of economic thought, this British experience is associated with the classical liberal political economists: Adam Smith (praising the role of individual incentives and of the market in coordinating individual initiatives toward the social good), Thomas Malthus (stressing the role of population growth in maintaining wages at subsistence level, and of land rents in creating an expanding domestic market for industrial goods when workers' wages were at subsistence level), and David Ricardo (developing the concept of comparative advantage in trade, leading to the Manchester doctrine, advocating free trade and the repeal of the protectionist Corn Laws). The primary role of the market in development, supported by a facilitating state, was a common thread in their ideas. Following the reasoning of economic historian Paul Bairoch (1973), five complementary conditions were met in Britain that allowed the industrial revolution to occur: availability of labor, capital, technology, markets, and natural protection.

1. *Labor: role of the agricultural revolution* (1700–50)
   The agricultural revolution consisted in a major increase in land and labor productivity in farming that was the product of both technological and institutional innovations. Technology contributed new crops and new rotations (including the famous Norfolk rotation: turnips–barley–clover–wheat), raising production on a limited amount of land (saving land) and freeing labor from agriculture for employment in industry. It also led to the accumulation of capital by landlords, in the form of higher land rents, which could be invested in industry. Institutional change consisted in the enclosure movement that prevented peasants from accessing landlords' fields after harvest to graze their animals, forcing many impoverished rural households to migrate to the city, and providing cheap labor for industrial employment. The enclosure movement also enabled clover planting instead of leaving fields fallow, which in turn supported sheep husbandry and the production of wool for the textile industry. A legacy of this experience for development is the key role of productivity gains in agriculture to provide cheap food and cheap labor for industry, "agriculture on the road to industrialization," to quote Mellor (1998). Indeed, most industrial revolutions were preceded by agricultural revolutions by some 50 years—a powerful historical regularity (Bairoch, 1993).

2. *Capital: role of mercantilism and colonialism*
   In addition to the accumulation of rents by landlords, enhanced by the agricultural revolution, profits from mercantilism and colonialism could be invested in industry. They were the source of "primitive accumulation" of capital in nascent industries. This capital was, of course, not neutral on the colonies of extraction from which profits were derived. The massive disruption of these countries' social order and of indigenous institutions in the wake of the slave trade (Nunn, 2008b) and colonial plunder (Acemoglu *et al.*, 2002) was to be an important negative consequence of this source of capital for British industry.

3. *Technology: role of property rights*
   The first industrial revolution was based on technological advances in manufacturing that increased labor productivity. The introduction of property rights that protected innovators was important in stimulating these advances. This led to the introduction of the steam engine as a source of power for motion on factory

floors, the spinning jenny, the power loom, and the use of coal for iron smelting. Introduction of the division of labor and repetitive tasks in production chains (as famously described in Adam Smith's pin factory) allowed the replacement of skilled artisans organized in manufactures with cheaper low-skill workers organized in factories (Toynbee, 1968). Innovations in transportation followed, with the building of canals, steam trains, and steamboats. A distinctive feature of the technological advances of this first industrial revolution is that they could easily be copied by other entrepreneurs because the tools of the emerging industries did not require capital goods that were themselves the product of industry. Rather, capital goods could be directly produced by local blacksmiths and carpenters. In terms of intellectual legacy, these conditions for early industrialization were quite different from the conditions that prevail for late industrializers, where capital goods have to be acquired from the product of already established industries in industrialized countries.

4. *Market: the creation of effective demand*
   Industry needs markets to sell products and transform goods into profits. Markets can be found externally (through trade, selling in colonies) and in the consumption of rents by landlords (since, according to Malthus, labor would always be at subsistence level due to demographic growth) and of profits by industrialists (Ricardo's growth model with cheap labor and rich industrialists not only investing but also consuming the products of modern industry). In this first industrial revolution, then, rising wages were not important for the expansion of a domestic market—and the harsh living conditions of the working class and extensive poverty in spite of hard work have been widely documented. This is an important intellectual legacy from the British industrial experience: expanding markets in trade and investment, and in the consumption of profits and rents, rather than in domestic consumer demand boosted by rising wages, was an important precedent in support of Asia's neo-mercantilist approach.

5. *Natural protection: role of a facilitating state*
   As the first industrialized country, Britain did not need to protect itself from competing modern industries in other parts of the world. Natural protection, not free trade, was thus the regime under which industry initially emerged in Britain. It was only after industry had been firmly established that Britain shifted, in 1846, under the Manchester doctrine, to free trade in food (with repeal of the Corn Laws) and in industrial goods (Chang, 2002). The state had other roles to play in supporting industrialization. It was important in limiting the arbitrary power of elites (in England, the Glorious Revolution of 1688 limited the power of the king, and the Declaration of Rights in 1689 shifted power to parliament, creating more inclusive political institutions without weakening the power of the state), in securing property rights and the rule of law, reforming finance to provide access to capital for industry (with creation of the Bank of England in 1694), and expanding the tax base to provide public goods (Acemoglu and Robinson, 2012). As indicated by Adam Smith in 1755, an effective state for the development of common interests is one that can manage taxation, enforce contracts, and organize public spending (Besley and Persson, 2011).

The intellectual legacy here is: (1) the role of the market and trade based on comparative advantage as the engine of development once competitiveness has been achieved, and (2) the role of inclusive economic institutions under the guidance of a centralized state, guaranteeing an appealing investment climate. A major historical puzzle is why it was not China that was first to achieve the industrial revolution, given that it was at the time far ahead of Britain in many aspects of technology and public administration. This question has fascinated historians, who have given several answers.

According to Justin Lin (1995), the Chinese state was tightly organized to administer the emperor's affairs: to manage major public works such as irrigation and to levy taxes, leaving little room for innovation and budding entrepreneurs. This was in contrast with the bourgeoisie in Britain (the people of the "bourg," the cities), who were not subjected to the same rigid feudal controls as were peasants in the countryside, giving them freedom to invest in new ventures and seek gains in social status through the accumulation of wealth. In China, the best talents were carefully screened from the mass of the population and trained to staff the bureaucracy, creating a highly capable bureaucratic state but stifling entrepreneurship in civil society. This bureaucracy was good at mass diffusion of innovations once they had occurred—for instance, in irrigated rice cultivation—but left little space for competition and innovation in the way the loose European social structure created room for merchants and manufacturers to invest their profits and rents in industry.

Jared Diamond (1997) provides another interpretation, which also relies on the suffocating role of a centralized bureaucratic state. According to him, power in China was too tightly centralized in the hands of a single person, the emperor, who could arbitrarily decide to close the country off from the world and hence stifle innovation. In Europe, by contrast, there were too many independent states for the entire continent to make this mistake collectively, not to mention the growing political power of some classes in England since the time of the Magna Carta in 1215, and the Glorious Revolution in 1688 that severely limited the arbitrary power of the monarch.

The Western experience (1820–80): "relative economic backwardness" and modernization theory

Economic development is all about catching up: how do countries that are currently lagging (at that time, the whole world relative to Britain) manage to increase investment and accelerate growth to converge their GDPpc with that of more advanced countries? The international diffusion of the industrial revolution, referred to as the Western experience, that started with Belgium and France in 1820 and ended with Japan in 1880, was the most extraordinary period of catching up, with "relative economic backwardness," in Harvard historian Alexander Gerschenkron's term (1962), providing a powerful stimulus to emulate the British experience and rapidly industrialize. Industrialization in Belgium and France followed the end of the Napoleonic wars; Germany (acquiring the capacity to produce modern weapons through Bismarck's industrialization for militarism), Austria, and Sweden followed in the 1850s; Spain, Italy, and Russia (following the abolition of serfdom that freed labor for industry) in the 1860s; then the US in 1865, following the Civil War that introduced trade protection for Northern industry, in opposition to the free-trade policy favored by Southern agriculture, and ended slavery, thus freeing labor for the industrial North; and finally Japan, which, with the end of the feudal Tokugawa regime and restoration of the Meiji emperor in 1880, acquired the industrial capacity to protect itself militarily from the colonial ambitions of Western powers. This extraordinary sequence clearly delineated the West, including Japan (no further industrial take-offs were to happen until the emergence of the NICs (the newly industrialized countries), consisting of Taiwan, South Korea, Singapore, and Hong Kong, after World War Two, the so-called four tigers, or gang of four). How did it happen?

Gerschenkron (1962) analyzed how countries could find "substitutes" for the conditions of Britain's industrial revolution in order to fight relative economic backwardness. He finds that some of the notable determinants of success in industrializing were as follows.

1. *Diffusion of the agricultural revolution and labor availability*
   As Bairoch (1973) observed, all Western industrial revolutions were preceded by an agricultural revolution some 50 years previously, as in Britain. These agricultural revolutions were based on technological and institutional changes. The technological feature was the diffusion to similar temperate zones of the land-saving agricultural technologies that had largely been innovated in Holland (as a response to high population pressure, fueled by mercantilist prosperity, on very scarce land) and adopted in England as part of its agricultural revolution. Diffusion often occurred through the international migration of European farmers settling in colonies with broad expanses of available land and favorable health conditions,

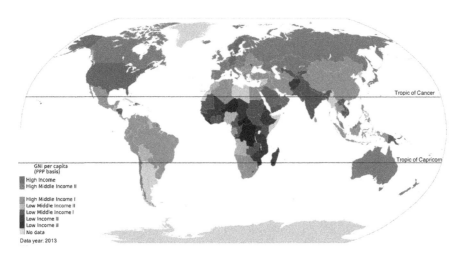

Figure 3.3 *Correspondence between temperate zones and income per person: low-income countries are mainly located in the tropics, while high-income countries are located in northern and southern temperate zones*

Source: World Bank, 2013.

126

the so-called "settler" colonies described in Acemoglu *et al.* (2001). This created a remarkable and fundamental path-dependent regularity for development: it confined the Western experience to temperate zones in the northern and southern hemispheres, drawing the map for what was to emerge as the "North" (more precisely, temperate regions in both hemispheres, including Argentina, Uruguay, Chile, Australia, New Zealand, and South Africa) vs. "South" (tropical and semi-arid regions across all continents) dichotomy between industrialized and developing worlds, a division that can still be recognized today in the world map of per capita income (Figure 3.3). On this map, low-income countries largely lie between the tropics of Cancer and Capricorn, while high-income countries are in temperate zones. Institutional changes included the development of new social classes in agriculture (a landlords–farmers–workers class structure, as in Britain) with either smallholder farming (France with tenant farmers, the US with homestead settlers) or large-scale agriculture (Eastern Europe with traditional aristocratic landlords and formerly bonded labor, transforming into farmer-entrepreneurs with wage labor). As in the case of the agricultural revolution in Britain, gains in agricultural productivity allowed the freeing of labor for industry and the availability of low-priced food, keeping nominal wages in industry low.

2. *Role of colonialism and banks for capital accumulation*
   With a second era of colonialism starting in 1800, colonies were important for market expansion and massive international migration of labor and land settlement. But the repatriation of profits was less determinant of capital accumulation in industry. Banks could now provide a substitute source of capital for investment relative to what had been achieved via "primitive accumulation" in the first colonial period. This was particularly the case in Germany, where banks financed the accumulation of capital in industry and profits earned in colonies had only a minor role to play.

3. *Role of technology and the advantage of backwardness in leapfrogging*
   The simplicity of techniques in these early industrial revolutions meant that capital goods could still largely be produced with the tools of the carpenter and the blacksmith, not as products of modern industry (as would be the case later on, in the so-called second industrial revolution, when developing countries would undertake industrialization by import substitution or export subsidies). Continuity of investment in the transition from artisans to industrialists was thus important for successful industrialization. In this perspective, it is fundamental to note that none of the countries that industrialized under the Western experience had suffered from extractive colonialism (as did India or Latin America), which would have disrupted the continuity of techniques with destruction of the capacity of artisans to produce capital goods for industry. With artisans in place, latecomers could derive an "advantage from backwardness," leapfrogging straight into the use of modern technologies and institutions developed elsewhere by simply copying them, as opposed to having to innovate for themselves. As explained by Lin (2012), this effective management of the advantage of backwardness for leapfrogging was key to the rapid industrialization of China.

4. *Role of rising wages for the expansion of domestic markets*

   External markets could be found through the gradual expansion of free trade after the 1850s, with the decolonization of Latin America and emergence of the "first liberal period" and massive globalization of the world economies. But the expansion of effective demand was principally found in rising wages. Large-scale labor migrations into colonies of settlement and rising labor productivity contributed to the rise of domestic wages and the expansion of demand for the products of industry. This created a virtuous circle of rising labor productivity, expanding domestic markets based on expenditure from wage incomes, and rising prosperity for workers with a consequent decline in poverty, a process that we referred to as "social articulation" (de Janvry and Sadoulet, 1983), a growth–poverty logic sharply contrasted with neo-mercantilist growth models based on cheap labor and exports. There is here a powerful intellectual legacy in the role of rising wages for market expansion as an effective way of achieving pro-poorness in growth.

5. *Role of the state and industrial protection*

   The desire to converge acted as a powerful "industrialization imperative," particularly when motivated by militaristic objectives, as in Germany and Japan, where industry offered the promise of access to the modern tools of warfare (Cipolla, 1996). At that time, only in Britain, where industrialization was securely established, could free trade be introduced, following the teachings of Ricardo and the Manchester doctrine. Shifting to free trade was a key move by Britain to capitalize on its historical advance, which allowed her to dominate the world economy until World War Two. For other countries, protection was needed to industrialize because of British industrial competition. In the US, protection was a major motivation for the North in the Civil War, while the agricultural South preferred free trade. Japan industrialized as a closed economy, with strong state intervention to tax agriculture and directly invest in industry. The intellectual legacy here is the key role of an active centralized state with inclusive institutions in managing the policy context for successful industrialization and catching up (Acemoglu and Robinson, 2012).

The first liberal period and the age of empire (1880–1914)

As the Western experience came to an end, and Britain dominated the world economy, ruling the seas and capitalizing through free trade on its large industrial advance, there was a remarkable period of 35 years of peace and prosperity. It saw a massive expansion of world trade, of international capital movement, and of relatively unimpeded international labor movement. It has been called the "first liberal period"—the first massive economic globalization—by Eric Hobsbawm (1989) in his book *The Age of Empire*. The now independent Latin American countries—those that were victorious in wars of independence under Simón Bolívar in Venezuela (1821) and José de San Martin in Argentina (1816), Peru (1823), and Bolivia (1824)—could engage in world trade. It greatly benefited some of them such as Argentina and Uruguay that could place their agricultural goods (cereals, meats, and wool) on the British market in exchange for imports of industrial goods. But it also meant that infant industry was unable to emerge and compete due to lack of protection. Much of the rest of the non-Western world was in a second period of colonialism, with spheres of influence sealed by various military alliances, and rising competition for Britain from Germany and the US. This extraordinary period of market expansion and prosperity, referred to as *la belle époque* in Europe, came to an end with World War One, induced in part by rising colonial competition and the fragility of alliances that could propagate local conflicts, as occurred accidentally in the Balkans, into a world conflagration, the first great war.

War and depression (1914–45)

The crash of 1929 has been attributed, among other things, to: (1) the burst of a speculative bubble on the stock market fueled by easy access to credit with lack of regulation of the banking sector; (2) a highly unequal distribution of income that led to underconsumption relative to productive capacity; and (3) countries trying to protect themselves by relying on "beggar-thy-neighbor" policies such as restricting imports through tariffs and quotas or by competitive devaluation of their nominal exchange rates (to make imports more expensive and their exports more competitive) in order to cure domestic depression and unemployment (Galbraith, 1961). In terms of thought in development economics, this period was important as it established the role of the state in managing the economy through Keynesian policies and the interventions of the New Deal. Early development economics that followed World War Two was deeply influenced by Keynesian thought transposed to the conditions of developing countries.

The World War One period also saw the 1917 Russian Revolution, a result of worker and peasant discontent in a context of rapid industrial growth, massive poverty and inequalities, the very high social costs of war, and poor governance under Tsar Nicholas II. Expropriation of land and capital for state ownership under Lenin and the Bolsheviks, and centrally planning the allocation of resources to productive sectors, initially allowed rapid growth and extensive coverage of basic needs. The intellectual legacy of this experience was to introduce a new role for the state in economic development, assuming many of the allocative functions typically reserved for the market. It became appealing to many developing countries, ranging from India and Egypt to a number of the emerging post-colonial nations of Africa, forming the so-called "Third World" countries, aligned with neither communism nor capitalism. In this context, public ownership of productive assets was extensive and allocation through central planning was important in setting priorities for public investment.

The "glorious years" of development and the Asian experience (1945–82)

The early period (1950s and 1960s): emphasis on industrialization and GDP growth

As the world emerged from World War Two, developing countries in the mid 1940s had to search for new development strategies to sustain growth. The breakup of colonial empires during and after World War Two had created newly independent countries such as India, Pakistan, the Philippines, Indonesia, Syria, and Lebanon that were looking for strategies to achieve rapid industrialization. The old order, based on a global division of labor, whereby industrialized countries exported manufactured goods and

129

developing countries specialized in agriculture and raw material exports, was no longer functional because the industrialized countries were in crisis following the destructions of the war. More inward-looking development strategies were now needed. Accelerating growth based on industrialization to meet demand in domestic markets became the central objective. A massive investment in industry—a big push—was needed because of economies of scale. To achieve this, developing countries had to intervene to protect or subsidize their infant industries until these economies of scale and learning-by-doing could be achieved, lowering average production costs to the point where emerging industries could be competitive in an open economy. These were the strategies of import-substitution industrialization (ISI) and export-oriented industrialization (EOI), the first relying on trade protection for selected sectors of industry and the second on subsidies to selected firms (we will analyze these in detail in Chapter 8). The state was also central in supporting a massive investment effort in infrastructure and in basic industries. Foreign aid was often important in providing access to the foreign exchange needed to import capital goods.

How these investments were to be made was a subject of controversy among the first generation of development economists, the so-called "pioneers in development" (Meier, 1985), including famous names like Paul Rosenstein-Rodan, Harvey Leibenstein, Ragnar Nurkse, Albert Hirschman, Raúl Prebisch, Hans Singer, and Gunnar Myrdal. For Rosenstein-Rodan (1943), a simultaneous coordinated investment effort in many industries was necessary in order for the wages paid in each industry to create effective demand for all of them. Because there are economies of scale in production, due mainly to large fixed costs that have to be incurred to start production, each firm has to achieve a minimum scale. No firm can start producing if other firms do not. Rosenstein-Rodan's example was that of a shoe factory, with a minimum scale to achieve profitability, and which can only sell its shoes if enough other industries pay wages that create effective demand for shoes. This was Rosenstein-Rodan's (1943) theory of the Big Push and Leibenstein's (1957) idea of the need to achieve a Critical Minimum Effort—hence the need for government intervention, using public policy to create the minimum investment effort.

This Big Push may require "balanced growth" across sectors (Nurkse, 1952), i.e. investment in every sector of the economy at the same time. The idea was that there are economies of scale in industry and complementarities among industries, either on the production side through technological spillovers or on the demand side in creating effective demand for industrial goods. The need for a sectorally balanced approach was challenged by Hirschman (1958), who suggested that a more efficient way of using public investment to promote growth when there are economies of scale is to pursue "unbalanced growth," focusing scarce investments on a few sectors with large forward and backward linkages with other sectors.

These pioneers in development have been labeled "structuralists" because their vision of a developing economy in the early post-World War Two period was characterized by a great deal of inflexibility in the allocation of resources (Dethier, 2009). This was due to their belief in fixed proportions and indivisibilities in technology (as opposed to smooth neoclassical substitutions), inelasticities in the supply and demand of goods, services, and factors, low responses to economic incentives such as relative price signals, and binding constraints on investment such as savings and balance-of-payments in two-gap models (we will study these in Chapter 8). Because of these inflexibilities the pioneers had little faith in the role of the price system, hence the market being seen as failing to provide the right incentives. They preferred instead pervasive state controls, with comprehensive central planning of inputs, outputs, and investment activity, public investment in large-scale projects in basic industries, and heavy protection via direct controls (such as licensing) and high import-tariff barriers. These pioneering structuralist ideas were not lost by the development profession; they were subsequently formalized in a more flexible neoclassical context by economists (often referred to as "monetarists" in contrast to structuralists) such as Murphy *et al.* (1989) for the role of the Big Push and Krugman (1992) for the role of forward and backward linkages.

The Harrod–Domar (Domar, 1957) model (see Chapter 8) provided the theoretical background for how growth was to be obtained under structuralist conditions: save, seek the most productive technology in terms of output per unit of capital, accumulate capital in industry, and grow toward an industrial take-off. With urban-based industry the priority, agriculture was to be squeezed for a financial surplus (through forced deliveries, cheap food policies, and direct taxation, as we will see in Chapter 18) that could be invested in industry. The expectation was that, with surplus labor in agriculture (Lewis, 1954), no particular effort was needed to increase the productivity of labor in agriculture to feed urban workers. While labor migrated toward urban-based industry, those who remained in agriculture could maintain production and insure continued access to cheap food and low nominal wages for urban workers.

With massive famines in India in the mid 1960s, the presumption that agriculture could be taken for granted while focusing on industrial investment was proven wrong. This led to the dual-economy framework, where technological change in agriculture was seen as necessary to raise labor productivity in order to compensate for the loss of labor associated with rural–urban migration and to keep food prices low (Lele and Mellor, 1981). This so-called Green Revolution restored the historical role that agriculture had played in the British and Western experiences, as evidenced by Bairoch (1973). Green Revolutions succeeded in Asia and Latin America, supporting industrialization, but failed to occur in Sub-Saharan Africa, with its more difficult tropical conditions, stifling an industrial take-off. Another major change in thought was the importance of accessing foreign exchange to import capital goods for modern industry, as capital goods could no longer be produced with the tools of the blacksmith and the carpenter as in the British and Western experiences. Here again, this meant focusing on agriculture as a source of foreign-exchange earnings, and also calling on foreign direct investment, foreign loans, and foreign aid as sources of foreign exchange to relax the two-gap constraints on industrial investment: domestic savings for investment, and foreign exchange to maintain the balance of payments while importing capital goods and intermediate products for industry. As Africa was gaining independence from the European powers in the early 1960s, defining growth strategies that could help these new nations catch up rapidly became a central concern for their governments and the development profession.

Another influential perspective on growth, this time historical as opposed to the theoretical perspective of Harrod–Domar, was provided by Rostow's (1960) modernization theory. It used the history of the modernization of Western nations to derive a sequence of evolutionary stages that all countries were presumed to travel through in order to

131

achieve sustained economic growth. The perspective stressed the importance of free trade and participation in the world economy as driving factors behind modernization. The five stages were as follows:

1. *Traditional society*: The economy is dominated by peasant agriculture organized in a rigid and relatively static feudal system.
2. *Preconditions for take-off (the agricultural revolution)*: The main change is an increase in agricultural productivity, allowing the generation of a financial surplus in agriculture that can be invested in industry, with government playing a major role in extracting and investing part of this surplus in infrastructure and human capital.
3. *Take-off (the industrial revolution)*: A major increase in investment in industry and the emergence of an institutional framework to mobilize loanable funds and expand trade. A class of domestic entrepreneurs emerges that drives the industrialization process. The series of take-offs witnessed by Rostow basically corresponds to the Western experience described above, hence the Western-centric perspective of his theory— the assumption that it provides the model for the rest of the world to emulate.
4. *Drive to maturity (the structural transformation)*: This is sustained by continued investment in industry and structural transformation of the economy away from agriculture. As industry grows faster than agriculture, the share of agriculture in both employment and GDP steadily declines.
5. *Age of high mass consumption (industrialized country)*: Sustained by rising wages, consumer demand drives growth, and society can expand leisure and luxury-goods consumption.

This theory is not without serious criticisms. It is less a theory than a classification of stages of progress toward industrialization. Causal relations between policy instruments and growth outcomes are missing; and reversals of fortune, resulting in regression across stages not predicted in the sequence, are always possible and have indeed been observed (Fishlow, 1965). Neither is it clear whether this Western model of modernization observed in the nineteenth century applied to the conditions faced by countries that wanted to industrialize in the twentieth century.

The development objectives, development theories, and development policies and programs characterizing this early period are summarized in Table 3.2 (see, similarly, the review of doctrines in development economics starting in 1950 by Thorbecke, 2006).

From growth to development: the emergence of development economics (1970–82)

A major shift in thought in development economics occurred in the 1970s. While growth had been extraordinarily successful in much of East Asia and Latin America, poverty continued unabated, with high unemployment, rising inequality, excessively rapid rural–urban migration, and expanding urban slums. Contradicting the pioneers' expectations, the benefits of growth were not trickling down to the poor sufficiently rapidly to reduce poverty and avoid rising inequality, in particular through employment and wage effects (Little *et al.*, 1970). For development economics, the central question thus became whether growth could be made more pro-poor. For the first time, it

Table 3.2 *Development economics in the 1950s and 1960s*

Development objectives	Development theories	Development policies and programs
GDP growth	Structuralism and central planning	Capital accumulation for growth
Industrialization	Market failures	ISI and EOI
	Big Push and Critical Minimum Effort	Big public infrastructure projects
	Balanced vs. unbalanced growth	
	Sectoral coordination and linkages	Green Revolution
	Harrod–Domar growth model	
	Rostow stages of growth and take-off	
	Two-gap models: savings and foreign exchange	
	Dual-economy models: role of agriculture	

became evident that growth was necessary but not sufficient for poverty reduction; that growth could not be the only objective for economic development; and that development had to be multidimensional, including poverty, inequality, and access to basic human needs in health and education. McNamara (1973), then president of the World Bank, gave a celebrated speech at the 1973 annual meeting, in Nairobi, where he redefined the mission of the World Bank as the eradication of poverty.

Important schools of thought emerged to address these concerns. One was the "redistribution with growth" approach of Chenery *et al.* (1974) at the World Bank, which proposed to reduce poverty by redistributing part of the income gains from growth to the poor via taxation. Another, deriving lessons from success in achieving both growth and inequality reduction in the Asian NICs, was Adelman's (1978) "redistribution before growth," which advocated massive redistributive land reform and educational campaigns before growth (that would increase the return to the land and individually held human capital assets) in order to make the subsequent growth more equitable and effective for poverty reduction. This was inspired by the implementation of such policies in Taiwan and South Korea under US occupation following World War Two. Strategies of "agriculture-development-led industrialization" were also important, whereby domestic industry could be driven by the demand for non-tradable goods originating in rising incomes in agriculture based on technological change in that sector: the aforementioned Green Revolution (Adelman, 1984; Mellor, 1998). Priority was also given to development approaches that would both promote low-skill labor-intensive growth (as advocated by the International Labor Office) and satisfy basic needs in education and health (as advocated by the UNDP). The first part of this strategy was to create opportunities for the poor, the second to increase the capacity of the poor to take advantage of these opportunities. This two-pronged strategy was central to the World Bank's 1990 *Poverty* report (World Bank, 1990).

The body of thought referred to as Dependency Theory was similarly motivated by the failures of growth to reduce poverty in an interdependent world economy

133

Table 3.3 *Development economics in the 1970–82 period*

Development objectives	Development theories	Development policies and programs
GDP growth	Redistribution with growth	Asset redistribution
Poverty reduction	Redistribution before growth	Investment in human capital
Income distribution	Employment strategies	ISI, EOI, up to delinking
Basic needs	Integrated rural development	Support for informal sector
	Agriculture-development-led industrialization (ADLI)	Rural development
	Dependency Theory	

with highly unequal participants characterized as belonging to "center and periphery" (Frank, 1967). According to the theory, resources are extracted from the periphery to the benefit of the center through trade with "unequal exchange" (Emmanuel, 1972). The theory was developed as a counter-position to Rostow's modernization theory, which strongly advocated the benefits of globalization. It introduced a more radical set of policy interventions, including delinking from international trade (seen as a source of highly unequal gains and poverty reproduction), prohibition of foreign direct investment, and massive asset redistribution toward greater state ownership, inspired in part by the Soviet and Chinese experiences.

The intellectual legacy of this period was fundamental for development economics: it stressed the multidimensionality of the development objective, the importance of the state for growth and catching up (in ISI and EOI strategies, all the way to Dependency Theory's delinking), the importance of making growth qualitatively more effective for poverty reduction (through employment creation, support for smallholder farming in integrated rural development programs, and for competitive small and medium enterprises), and also the importance of a direct role for the state in delivering public goods for basic needs and providing social-safety nets.

This period of remarkable growth and the search for ways of achieving pro-poor growth was, in a sense, the golden age of development economics. It came to an end with the debt crisis when Mexico defaulted in 1982, followed by similar defaults in most other developing countries. This happened because debt had been accumulated under conditions of easy borrowing (due to excess bank liquidity, in particular following the oil shock of the mid 1970s) and because of a sudden rise in interest rates, due to US monetary policy, and recession in industrialized countries.

The development objectives, development theories, and development policies and programs characterizing this early period are summarized in Table 3.3.

The age of globalization (1982–97): Washington Consensus, stabilization, and adjustment

With growth compromised by the debt crisis, and recession contributing massively to the rise of poverty, priority had to be given again, as in the 1950s, to accelerating growth. Since much of the blame for the economic crisis was attributed to excessive state intervention (inefficient ISI policies associated with continued protectionism, large fiscal deficits associated with permissive subsidies under EOI policies, and excessive public debts), the solution was not to be found in new roles for the state, but in returning to greater roles for the market. Stabilization policies had to be put into place to restore both external (balance of payments) and internal (inflation, balanced budgets) equilibriums. Structural adjustment had to be sought to avoid the conditions that had led to the crisis. This was the set of policy reforms advanced by the Washington Consensus (Williamson, 1990), broadly endorsed by the International Monetary Fund, the World Bank, and Washington think tanks such as the Institute for International Economics. It implied a return to liberalism (a second liberal period, as under the age of empire) and a move toward renewed globalization. The main policy dimensions of the Washington Consensus were the following:

1. *Fiscal discipline*: balanced budgets, tax reforms, public-spending priorities other than subsidies.
2. *Financial liberalization*: deregulation of the banking sector, competitive exchange rates.
3. *Trade liberalization* for goods and services.
4. *Deregulation* of foreign direct investment.
5. *Privatization* of public enterprises.

The reforms—to reduce the role of the state in economic affairs, to increase reliance on market forces, to give the economy a greater outward orientation, and to increase private ownership—were mainly at the macro level, seeking to restore balance in the economy's macro fundamentals, with little concern for sectoral impacts (for instance, on agriculture) and for the institutional reforms needed to secure supply responses in the real sectors. The reforms consisted principally of austerity measures, with a heavy cost for development, resulting in what has been called the "lost development decade" (Easterly, 2001). They are to be assessed in terms of the historical context in which they occurred: not as a development model but as a crisis response in dealing with the cumulative consequences of unsustainable disequilibria.

It became quickly evident that the stabilization and adjustment policies of the Washington Consensus had two major shortcomings. One was that they were too socially costly to be politically sustainable; the other was that they were more effective at restoring macroeconomic balances than at inducing economic growth, particularly in Africa. The first led to responses such as UNICEF's "Adjustment with a Human Face" (Cornia *et al.*, 1987), which called for more attention to be paid to meeting basic human needs in the context of implementing adjustment policies, due in part to the irreversibilities that deprivations in health and education imposed on children. Fiscal austerity needed to be seconded by strong social-safety nets to avoid these irreversibilities. The other was the call for second-generation reforms, which would cater to the needs of private entrepreneurs in responding to the new economic conditions set in place by structural adjustment (Stiglitz, 2002). Lags in private-sector responses could indeed have high costs in terms of foregone

135

Table 3.4 *Development economics in the 1982–97 period*

Development objectives	Development theories	Development policies and programs
Back to primacy of growth	Washington Consensus, neo-liberalism	Globalization and outward orientation
Stabilization and adjustment		Privatization
Increased reliance on markets	Government failures	Market deregulation, liberalization
Descaling the role of the state	Getting prices right	Induce private-sector investment, FDI
Macroeconomic fundamentals		

economic growth and rising poverty. The Asian financial crises of the mid 1990s were a costly awakening to the fact that the incomplete reforms of the Washington Consensus could not sustain growth. Difficulties with transitions out of central planning in Eastern Europe and Central Asia, following the fall of the Berlin Wall, also suggested that new approaches were needed. This opened the road to several new schools of thought that drive much thinking in development economics today, but that basically have two components in common: the return of the role of the state in economic development, and greater pragmatism in the design of development strategies.

The development objectives, development theories, and development policies and programs characterizing this period are summarized in Table 3.4.

Post-Washington Consensus second-generation reforms: growth diagnostics and institution building (1997–today)

The new approaches restored the role of the state in development, but through different instruments to those used in the "glorious years," and by clearly complementing the role of the market. They also gave greater importance to the role of civil-society organizations in decentralization, the delivery of local public goods, the provision of social-safety nets, and the sustainable management of the environment. And they reset the focus of development on its multidimensionality: not only restoring growth following the debt crisis and difficult transitions out of central planning, but also reducing poverty and inequality, delivering basic needs, addressing vulnerability to shocks, and, importantly, achieving a more sustainable use of natural resources. These objectives were enshrined in the MDGs. There was also greater recognition that one approach will not work everywhere—as opposed to simply "getting the prices right" under the Washington Consensus—because initial conditions are so different across countries. As a consequence, Lindauer and Pritchett (2002) note that this marks the end of "big ideas" in development economics. To the contrary, country diagnostics are necessary to identify the most binding constraints on growth and to define country-specific growth strategies (Hausman *et al.*, 2006). Putting in place the right institutions is essential, as well as addressing the political economy of policy reforms. And the link between growth and poverty is

136

Table 3.5 *Development economics in the 1997–today period*

Development objectives	Development theories	Development policies and programs
MDGs. Back to poverty	End of big ideas; country specificity, trade-offs	Pro-poor growth, equity for growth
	Growth diagnostics, binding constraints	
Reduce vulnerability	Microeconomic foundations of development	Open-economy industrialization
	Poor economics	Neo-mercantilist model
Growth–poverty–inequality nexus	Endogenous growth and multiple equilibria	Business climate for private investment
Good governance and institution building	New Institutional Economics	Investment in people and empowerment
	New Political Economy	
Sustainable development	State–market–civil-society complementarities	Social-safety nets and CCT
	Agriculture for development	Impact evaluation, results-based foreign aid

seen as a more complex two-way relation, where poverty reduction is not only the product of growth, but also a potential source of growth. The schools of thought that emerged to meet the challenges of development economics beyond the Washington Consensus are the focus of this book. The following are some of the main theories and approaches to development (see Table 3.5):

1. *Endogenous growth*
   Growth tends to beget growth, leaving many countries behind, but also allowing countries such as China, India, and Vietnam to catch up and converge in per capita income with the industrialized countries. According to the endogenous growth theory (see Chapter 9), this is because there are economies of scale in capital accumulation and spillovers across firms from investment in research and development occurring in particular in geographical clusters of economic activity (Romer, 1990). There are also spillovers across individuals created by investments in human capital such as education and training. Because these positive externalities (spillovers) are important for growth, the state needs to intervene to compensate for individual and firm underinvestment in sources of growth such as education and training, and research and development. The state also has a fundamental role to play in putting into place what will be an appealing business climate for private investment: infrastructure, the rule of law, secure property rights, the provision of public goods and services, etc. (World Bank, 2012). The state must also invest in people and empower them, particularly poor people who might otherwise be excluded, through education, health, social protection, and institutions to promote their voice and participation (Dethier, 2009). And the state needs to assume strong regulatory functions to prevent corruption, assist conflict resolution, enforce the rule of law, and regulate competition. In endogenous

137

growth, the state thus finds itself again as a key actor in development. Successful endogenous growth needs a strong activist state.

2. *Open economy industrialization*

The stunning growth successes of countries as large as China and as small as Mauritius, where foreign direct investment and producing for the export market play a key role, suggest new growth and development strategies where globalization and multinational corporations become an asset for growth, not a liability as seen by Dependency Theory (we will study this in Chapter 7). Key here is an investment climate and a semi-skilled and willing labor force that is attractive to foreign investment. In this neo-mercantilist model, labor is a cost and low wages help a country to compete in the international market, since wages are not necessary to create effective demand for the products of industry as in the closed-economy model of the Big Push. While foreign firms may sometimes be sweatshops with harsh working conditions and low wages—as, for example, in the apparel sector in Bangladesh—working conditions and wages in these firms are usually better than in domestic firms (Aitken *et al.*, 1996). Importantly, they may also create linkages with domestic firms, helping a domestic industrial sector and entrepreneurial class emerge and gradually assume the momentum of industrialization and growth, as in China (Rodrik, 2006).

3. *New institutional economics*

Resource endowments (land, minerals) and geography (e.g. access to the sea, good harbors) are important for growth (Sachs, 2005), but so are institutions (Acemoglu *et al.*, 2004). Institutions are the rules that codify how people relate to each other (see Chapter 20). They are social products, and consequently both an endogenous outcome and a determinant of development. Understanding institutions, from governance to firms and local organizations, is thus fundamental. Good institutions reduce transactions costs on markets, spread risks, and contain adverse selection and moral hazard in human interactions. New institutions are needed to make markets work better, and to provide alternatives to markets (e.g. contracts, organizations, microfinance institutions, social networks) when markets fail. Institutional innovations are thus fundamental for second-generation reforms (Stiglitz, 2002) to go beyond the Washington Consensus and seek both greater supply responses to market incentives and potentially greater pro-poor effects in economic growth.

Important contributions have been made by Acemoglu *et al.* (2001) to show empirically that institutions matter for long-term economic performance. They use the histories of 32 former colonies to show that institutions protecting against the risk of expropriation (strength of property rights) were a determinant of 1995 levels of PPP-adjusted GDPpc. Because there could be reverse causality between income and institutions they use an instrumental variable approach, whereby potential settler mortality in colonial times predicts current institutions (this is analyzed in detail in Chapter 4). The logic of the argument is as follows:

i. Potential settler mortality, an exogenous feature due to exposure to weather-determined health hazards such as malaria, determined whether or not colonies had European settlements.

ii. European settlements led to the early introduction of European-type institutions protective of property rights, as opposed to extractive institutions in other colonies.

iii. With the path-dependent persistence of institutions, as shown by Bockstette *et al.* (2003), good early institutions predict the presence of better current institutions.

iv. Predicted (instrumented) better current institutions, as measured by the average level of protection against expropriation risk over the 1985–95 period, explain higher GDPpc in 1995.

The approach is ingenious and the paper has had a major impact on the profession, providing empirical support for a widely shared belief: namely, that institutions do matter for economic growth. We discuss in Chapter 4 questions that have been raised about the validity of the method used to establish the causal role of institutions.

4. *New political economy*

State interventions are needed when markets fail (due in particular to public goods, externalities, economies of scale, imperfect information, and undesirable social outcomes). Public reforms are also needed when governments fail (due to corruption and to rent-seeking, allowing the appropriation of rents at a social cost), and these reforms may be the result of civil-society demands. Public programs are needed to support community initiatives such as community-driven development and to provide social-safety nets (such as guaranteed-employment programs). Many policy interventions go awry because the state is captured by special interests, or is used for clientelistic purposes by politicians and bureaucrats (see Chapter 21). And policy reforms and programs need to be politically feasible to be implemented. Making policy recommendations without a corresponding political-economy analysis is meaningless. Understanding the political economy of development, both positive and normative, has to be center stage for new approaches to development. Important efforts have thus been made in post-Washington Consensus development economics to understand how the state can be made to assume its developmental functions effectively (Besley and Persson, 2011).

5. *Sustainable growth*

With enormous population pressure on world resources, and large external effects of economic activities on the environment—with consequences such as water pollution and global climate change—reconciling growth and sustainability has become an inescapable dimension of development (see Chapter 15). In most situations, it is the poor who are the main victims of environmental changes, making environmental sustainability a key dimension of development. This has opened a new frontier in development economics concerned with property rights for proper incentives, devolution of control over resources to local communities and their capacity to cooperate in assuming this function, investment in green technologies, and the introduction of markets for environmental services as part of international agreements to deal with climate change. Here, again, the market (private actors), state, and civil society have new roles to play that require close coordination.

139

6. *Impact evaluation for accountability and learning*

We cannot design new policies and programs if we cannot assess causalities. How much of observed outcomes (growth, poverty, basic needs) is due to specific development initiatives (policies and programs) and how much is due to spurious correlations (for example, fertilizer was subsidized in Malawi, but the observed favorable outcomes may have been due to good rainfall that year, not to the subsidies). A whole new approach to development (presented in Chapter 4) tries to establish causalities so we can learn and improve on what is being done, helping to design better programs and better policies. Results-based management of public and international aid programs has become a key requirement to justify budgets. This can be done by randomizing interventions or by seeking "natural experiments" that allow for the establishment of counterfactuals (controls) against which individuals or institutions can be compared (Banerjee and Duflo, 2009). Monitoring and evaluation, and impact analysis, are thus needed not only for accountability in public and donor spending, but also for experimenting and piloting lessons to be internalized in redesigning and improving the approaches that have been tried.

7. *Agriculture for development*

In the classical development paradigm of the 1970s (e.g. Adelman, 1984; Mellor, 1998), agricultural growth was seen as a key instrument for industrialization and for the structural transformation of the economy (with a declining share of labor employed in agriculture and a declining share of GDP originating in agriculture) as the economy was diversifying away from agriculture. But agriculture has many functions to perform in support of the multidimensionality of development (see Chapter 1), including contributions not only to growth, but also to the reduction of poverty and hunger, the narrowing of rural–urban income disparities, the reduction in vulnerability and food insecurity, and the delivery of environmental services. In this new paradigm, agriculture is broadly used for development (as opposed to more narrowly for industrialization), with trade-offs in outcomes that require priority setting and policy interventions (see Chapter 18). In this perspective, made all the more urgent by recurrent food crises associated with rising volatility in food prices, global recession, and climate change, agriculture comes back as a priority instrument in development agendas. This is particularly relevant for Sub-Saharan Africa, where agriculture must be the main engine of economic growth and where most of the rural poor depend on agriculture for their livelihoods.

THE DIGITAL REVOLUTION AND THE FUTURE OF CONVERGENCE

During the 1990s, there was remarkable convergence toward the GDPpc of the OECD countries for a large number of developing countries, creating a convergence club of emerging-market economies (Sachs and Warner, 1995). Primary among these have been Taiwan, South Korea, Hong Kong, Singapore, China, India, Indonesia, Brazil, Mexico, and South Africa. During the 2000s, this convergence club expanded in part because growth decelerated in the OECD countries, but also because it accelerated sharply in Sub-Saharan Africa, propelled by the demand for

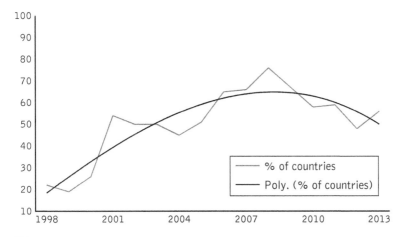

Figure 3.4 *Size of the convergence club, 1998–2013*

Measured as the percentage of the total number of developing countries with a growth rate in GDPpc exceeding that of the US in the corresponding year.

Source: World Bank, *World Development Indicators.*

mineral products originating in emerging economies. Following the 2008 crisis, this club has been shrinking. As can be seen in Figure 3.4, the percentage of developing countries converging in GDPpc with the US rose from 20 percent in 1998 to a peak of 76 percent in 2008, declining to 50 percent in 2012–13.

This decline may be due to the consequences of the 2008–9 Great Recession affecting growth in the OECD and, indirectly, demand for manufacturing exports from emerging economies, in turn reducing demand for raw materials from the African economies. But it may be due to something much more structural that is redefining the opportunity to join the convergence club on the basis of industrialization under the current Third Industrial Revolution—the digital revolution. According to Rodrik (2013a), this is creating "premature de-industrialization" in the developing countries.

Previous industrial revolutions displaced labor, but also created new employment opportunities, in particular for low-skill labor in the mechanized factory system to replace typically more skilled artisans organized in manufactures. Globalization offered emerging economies opportunities to industrialize based on access to foreign markets, foreign finance, and foreign direct investment. Rapid industrialization based on cheap low-skill labor has been the engine of convergence for these economies. Manufacturing is particularly good for convergence because it achieves unconditional convergence in labor productivity through technological transfers (Rodrik, 2013b). As growth induced a rise in wages (as in China's coastal provinces), the converging economies could switch to more demanding industrial products—from textiles to home appliances and then to automobiles. This in turn created the opportunity for other countries or interior provinces in China endowed with cheap labor to pursue rapid low-labor-skills industrialization. Is this now coming to an end?

The Digital Revolution is creating a situation in which there is a sharp reduction in the cost of capital goods associated with computing power, web-based communications,

141

and automation and robotics in production. This is resulting in a decline in demand for large numbers of low-skill workers, an increase in demand for a small number of high-skill workers, displacement of manufacturing back to countries with high-skill labor, and an increase in the share of capital in the total product. The consequence is a large pool of underemployed unskilled labor at a world scale, a fall in real wages for unskilled labor, and sharply rising inequality in the distribution of income, what might be called the Piketty (2014) phenomenon. Opportunities to join the convergence club based on low-skill industrialization to meet foreign demand (the neo-mercantilist model) is becoming harder for those that are still converging, such as Bangladesh, and a declining option for those, such as Sub-Saharan Africa, that are waiting to join the bandwagon of industrializers based on foreign direct investment, foreign capital, and foreign demand.

The implication is that developing countries may have to switch to another growth strategy. With fewer options offered by exports, foreign finance, and direct foreign investment, more attention has to be given to the growth of the domestic market. This can, for a while, rely on public-works programs and a construction boom, as occurred in China, but ultimately it requires rising real wages and greater attention paid to reducing income inequality as part of a more inclusive growth strategy. As a point of comparison, household final consumption only accounted for 35 percent of GDP in China in 2012, when it represented 60 percent in India, 63 percent in Brazil, 66 percent in Mexico, and 68 percent in the US (World Bank, *World Development Indicators*). In this household-consumption-driven growth strategy, labor income is no longer just a cost on capital, but a source of effective demand. The development of education and skills, the promotion of entrepreneurship, and the provision of social-safety nets become fundamental instruments for sustained growth.

CONCLUSION

Development is an ongoing process, with many trade-offs in the dimensions of development achieved. History matters because there is a strong path dependency in the current determinants of growth and development. Learning from history and from the different schools of thought that have prevailed in the process of economic development as issues emerged is thus important. It informs us about what can be done and about what should be avoided. Particularly revealing in the sequence of schools of thought that we have reviewed is the relative importance of the roles of the market and the state in development—an ongoing debate. But the history of thought in development economics has to be read carefully, with due concern for the changing contexts in which it unfolded and for the motivations behind what was attempted by each particular school of thought. As we look forward in an increasingly globalized world with powerful integrated value chains, major technological and institutional innovations, and global climate change, new approaches need to be devised, experimented with, appraised, and scaled up. History matters and much can be learned from the past, but pragmatism and innovation in devising new approaches will be the key to successful development in a brand new world. While path dependency strongly influences what a country can do for development at one point in time (a position endorsed by for example Acemoglu *et al.*, 2004), there is also considerable room for policy initiatives and the introduction of new programs to alter the course of future development (a position endorsed by, for example, Banerjee and Duflo (2009) and Rodrik (2006)).

CONCEPTS SEEN IN THIS CHAPTER

Path dependency

Market failure and role of the state

Mercantilism and neo-mercantilist model

Agricultural and industrial revolutions

Relative economic backwardness

Advantage from backwardness (leapfrogging)

Development economics

Big Push and Critical Minimum Effort

Import-substitution industrialization (ISI)

Export-oriented industrialization (EOI)

Open-economy industrialization (OEI)

Balanced vs. unbalanced growth

Inter-sectoral linkages

Economic dualism

Two-gap models

Stages of growth and economic take-off

Trickle-down effect

Redistribution with growth

Redistribution before growth

Washington Consensus

Stabilization and structural-adjustment policies

Endogenous growth

New Institutional Economics

Structural transformation

Digital revolution

REVIEW QUESTIONS: HISTORY OF DEVELOPMENT AND HISTORY OF THOUGHT IN DEVELOPMENT ECONOMICS

The five major schools of thought in development economics are: classical political economy (the British experience), relative economic backwardness (the Western experience), development economics (the Asian experience), the Washington Consensus, and the post-Washington Consensus.

1. Place each school in its general historical context.
2. What is the main objective and policy proposition of each school?
3. What is the perceived relative importance of the state and the market in each school?

REFERENCES

Acemoglu, Daron, and James Robinson. 2012. *Why Nations Fail: The Origins of Power, Prosperity, and Poverty*. New York: Crown Business.

Acemoglu, Daron, Simon Johnson, and James Robinson. 2001. "The Colonial Origins of Comparative Development." *American Economic Review* 91(5): 1369–401.

Acemoglu, Daron, Simon Johnson, and James Robinson. 2002. "Reversal of Fortune: Geography and Institutions in the Making of the Modern World Income Distribution." *Quarterly Journal of Economics* 117(4): 1231–94.

Acemoglu, Daron, Simon Johnson, and James Robinson. 2004. "Institutions as the Fundamental Cause of Long-Run Growth." In Philippe Aghion and Steven N. Durlauf, (eds.), *Handbook of Economic Growth*, 386–472. Amsterdam: Elsevier.

Adelman, Irma. 1978. *Redistribution Before Growth: A Strategy for Developing Countries*. The Hague: Martinus Nijhof Editions.

Adelman, Irma. 1984. "Beyond Export-led Growth." *World Development* 12(9): 937–49.

Aitken, Brian, Ann Harrison, and Robert Lipsey. 1996. "Wages and Foreign Ownership: A Comparative Study of Mexico, Venezuela, and the United States." *Journal of International Economics* 40(3–4): 345–71.

Alsan, Marcella. 2015. "The Effect of The TseTse Fly on African Development." *American Economic Review* 105(1): 382–410.

Bairoch, Paul. 1973. "Agriculture and the Industrial Revolution, 1700–1914." In Carlo Cipolla (ed.), *The Fontana Economic History of Europe: The Industrial Revolution,* Vol. 3, 452–506. London: Collins/Fontana Books.

Bairoch, Paul. 1993. *Economics and World History: Myths and Paradoxes*. Chicago: University of Chicago Press.

Banerjee, Abhijit, and Esther Duflo. 2009. "The Experimental Approach to Development Economics." *Annual Review of Economics* 1(1): 151–78.

Besley, Timothy, and Torsten Persson. 2011. *Pillars of Prosperity: The Political Economics of Development Clusters*. Princeton, NJ: Princeton University Press.

Bockstette, Valerie, Areendam Chanda, and Louis Putterman. 2003. "States and Markets: The Advantage of an Early Start." *Journal of Economic Growth* 7(4): 347–69.

Cardoso, Fernando Henrique. 1977. "The Consumption of Dependency Theory in the United States." *Latin American Research Review* 12(3): 7–24.

Chang, Ha-Joon. 2002. *Kicking Away the Ladder: Development Strategy in Historical Perspective*. New York: Anthem Press.

Chenery, Hollis, Montek Ahluwalia, Clive Bell, John Duloy, and Richard Jolly (eds.). 1974. *Redistribution with Growth*. New York: Oxford University Press.

Cipolla, Carlo. 1996. *Guns, Sails, and Empires: Technological Innovation and European Expansion, 1400–1700*. New York: Barnes and Noble.

Cornia, Giovanni Andrea, Richard Jolly, and Frances Stewart. 1987. *Adjustment with a Human Face*. Oxford: Oxford University Press.

de Janvry, Alain, and Elisabeth Sadoulet. 1983. "Social Articulation as a Condition for Equitable Growth." *Journal of Development Economics* 13(3): 275–303.

Dethier, Jean-Jacques. 2009. "World Bank Policy Research: A Historical Overview." Washington, DC: World Bank Policy Research Working Paper 5000.

Diamond, Jared. 1997. *Guns, Germs, and Steel: The Fates of Human Societies.* New York: W.W. Norton and Co.

Domar, Evsey. 1957. *Essays in the Theory of Economic Growth.* Oxford: Oxford University Press.

Easterly, William. 2001. "The Lost Decades: Developing Countries' Stagnation in Spite of Policy Reform 1980–1998." *Journal of Economic Growth* 6(2): 135–57.

Emmanuel, Arghiri. 1972. *Unequal Exchange.* New York: Monthly Review Press.

Fishlow, Albert. 1965. "Empty Economic Stages?" *Economic Journal* 75(297): 112–25.

Frank, Andre Gunder. 1967. *Capitalism and Underdevelopment in Latin America.* New York: Monthly Review Press.

Galbraith, John Kenneth. 1961. *The Great Crash, 1929.* New York: Houghton Mifflin Harcourt Publishing Company.

Gerschenkron, Alexander. 1962. *Economic Backwardness in Historical Perspective.* Cambridge, MA: Harvard University Press.

Hausman, Ricardo, Dani Rodrik, and Andrés Velasco. 2006. "Getting the Diagnosis Right: A New Approach to Economic Reform." *Finance and Development* 43(1): 12–15.

Hirschman, Albert. 1958. *The Strategy of Economic Development.* New Haven, CT: Yale University Press.

Hobsbawm, Eric. 1989. *The Age of Empire 1875–1914.* New York: Vintage Books.

Krugman, Paul. 1992. "Toward a Counter-counterrevolution in Development Theory." *World Bank Economic Review* Supplement (Proceedings of the Annual Bank Conference on Development Economics): 15–38.

Landes, David. 1999. *The Wealth and Poverty of Nations: Why Some are So Rich and Some So Poor.* New York: W.W. Norton and Co.

Leibenstein, Harvey. 1957. *Economic Backwardness and Economic Growth.* New York: Wiley.

Lele, Uma, and John Mellor. 1981. "Technological Change, Distributive Bias, and Labor Transfers in a Two Sector Economy." *Oxford Economic Papers* 33(3): 426–41.

Lewis, Arthur. 1954. "Economic Development with Unlimited Supplies of Labor." *The Manchester School of Economic and Social Studies* 22(2): 139–91.

Lin, Justin Yifu. 1995. "The Needham Puzzle: Why the Industrial Revolution Did Not Originate in China." *Economic Development and Cultural Change* 43(2): 269–92.

Lin, Justin Yifu. 2012. *Demystifying the Chinese Economy.* New York: Cambridge University Press.

Lindauer, David, and Lant Pritchett. 2002. "What's the Big Idea? The Third Generation of Policies for Economic Growth." *Economía* 3(1) Fall: 1–39.

Little, Ian, Tibor Scitovsky, and Maurice Scott. 1970. *Industry and Trade in Some Developing Countries.* Oxford: Oxford University Press.

McNamara, Robert. 1973. "The Nairobi Speech: Address to the Board of Governors." Washington, DC: World Bank Group Archives.

Meier, Gerald. 1985. *Pioneers in Development.* Oxford: Oxford University Press.

Mellor, John. 1998. "Agriculture on the Road to Industrialization." In Carl Eicher and John Staatz (eds.), *International Agricultural Development,* 136–54. Baltimore: Johns Hopkins University Press.

Murphy, Kevin, Andrei Shleifer, and Robert Vishny. 1989. "Industrialization and the Big Push." *Journal of Political Economy* 97(5): 1003–26.

Nunn, Nathan. 2008a. "Slavery, Inequality, and Economic Development in the Americas: An Examination of the Engerman–Sokoloff Hypothesis." In E. Helpman (ed.), *Institutions and Economic Performance,* 148–80. Cambridge, MA: Harvard University Press.

Nunn, Nathan. 2008b. "The Long-term Effects of Africa's Slave Trades." *Quarterly Journal of Economics* 123(1): 139–76.

Nunn, Nathan, and Leonard Wantchekon. 2011. "The Slave Trade and the Origins of Mistrust in Africa." *American Economic Review* 101(7): 3221–52.

Nurkse, Ragnar. 1952. *Problems of Capital Formation in Underdeveloped Countries.* New York: Oxford University Press.

Piketty, Thomas. 2014. *Capital in the Twenty-First Century.* Cambridge, MA: Harvard University Press.

Rodrik, Dani. 2006. "Industrial Development: Stylized Facts, and Policies." Working paper, John F. Kennedy School of Government, Harvard University.

Rodrik, Dani. 2013a. "The Past, Present, and Future of Economic Growth." Working Paper 1. Munich: Global Citizen Foundation.

Rodrik, Dani. 2013b. "Unconditional Convergence in Manufacturing." *Quarterly Journal of Economics* 128(1): 165–204.

Romer, Paul. 1990. "Endogenous Technological Change." *Journal of Political Economy* 98(5, part 2): S71–102.

Rosenstein-Rodan, Paul. 1943. "Problems of Industrialization of Eastern and South-Eastern Europe." *Economic Journal* 53(210): 202–11.

Rostow, W.W. 1960. *The Stages of Economic Growth: A Non-communist Manifesto.* Cambridge, MA: Cambridge University Press.

Sachs, Jeffrey. 2005. *The End of Poverty: Economic Possibilities for Our Time.* New York: Penguin Press.

Sachs, Jeffrey, and Andrew Warner. 1995. "Economic Convergence and Economic Policies." In W. Brainard and G. Perry (eds.), *Brookings Papers on Economic Activity* 1, 1–95. Washington, DC: Brookings Institution.

Sokoloff, Kenneth, and Stanley Engerman. 2000. "History Lessons: Institutions, Factor Endowments, and Paths of Development in the New World." *Journal of Economic Perspectives* 14(3): 217–32.

Stiglitz, Joseph. 2002. *Globalization and Its Discontents.* New York: W.W. Norton and Co.

Thorbecke, Erik. 2006. "The Evolution of the Development Doctrine, 1950–2005." Helsinki: WIDER Research Paper No.155.

Toynbee, Arnold. 1968. *The Industrial Revolution.* Boston: Beacon Press.

Williamson, John. 1990. *Latin American Adjustment: How Much Has Happened?* Washington, DC: Institute for International Economics.

World Bank. 1990. *World Development Report 1990: Poverty.* New York: Oxford University Press.

World Bank. 2012. *Investment Climate Assessment Reports.* http://go.worldbank.org/VROL4C2IH0 (accessed 2015).

World Bank. 2013. "GNI Per Capita PPP." http://data.worldbank.org/indicator/NY.GNP.PCAP.PP.CD/countries?display=map (accessed 2015).

World Bank. *World Development Indicators.* http://data.worldbank.org/indicator (accessed 2015).

Chapter 4

Impact evaluation of development policies and programs

TAKE-HOME MESSAGES FOR CHAPTER 4

1. Impact evaluation seeks to establish causality between an intervention and the resulting outcomes, and to quantify the magnitude of the changes in outcomes that can be attributed to the intervention.

2. Impact evaluation is useful for three objectives: achieving accountability in development expenditures, establishing what works and help improve on the design and implementation of policies and programs, and, if possible, deriving generic lessons for other development initiatives.

3. The key issue in measuring impact is to establish a counterfactual against which the changes in outcomes induced by the intervention can be measured. The counterfactual should measure what would have happened to the beneficiaries in the absence of the intervention.

4. The most common methods of impact analysis include randomized control trials (RCTs), propensity score matching, difference-in-differences, roll-outs, discontinuity designs, event analysis, and instrumental variables. The validity and usefulness of each method depends on the way the program is implemented and the data that can be made available. It is thus critically important to carefully review the underlying assumptions to insure the validity of a method before using it.

5. Use of these methods has helped bring a level of rigor to development economics that was often missing. However, they only apply to well defined and relatively narrow questions in a given context for which answers have strong internal validity but a priori no external validity beyond this particular context.

6. Quantitative impact evaluation methods are usefully complemented by qualitative appraisals that help suggest hypotheses for data collection and analysis, and causal channels for the relationships estimated in quantitative analyses.

7. At the macro level, the impact of policy reforms is frequently assessed using cross-country regressions. It is, however, difficult with this approach to meet the exogeneity requirement for a causal estimation of the role of policy on development outcomes such as growth.

HOW DO WE KNOW WHAT WORKS FOR DEVELOPMENT?

Every year, governments and donors spend billions of dollars on development initiatives (Easterly, 2006). In 2012, the total OECD overseas development assistance budget to developing countries was US$151billion (OECD, 2014). Many more development initiatives go unfunded for lack of resources—so it is important to know what was achieved as a consequence of investing in a particular development project. What deserves to be scaled up and what should be abandoned? How can current designs be improved? The main difficulty in answering these questions, and thus in learning how to do better development based on the results obtained, is not so much in measuring benefits and costs as in assigning causality. How do we know that a particular result (benefit) is truly the outcome of a particular policy or project intervention (cost) and not of spurious correlation with other events such as good weather or overall economic growth, or of hidden characteristics of the project's participants such as their differential level of entrepreneurship? The emerging field of impact evaluation in economic development aims to answer questions of causality. Credible impact evaluation is in high demand to determine accountability in development expenditures and to practice "results-based management" for better development interventions. In this chapter, we review the different methods that are used in impact evaluation and illustrate applications of these methods to various development interventions.

EVALUATION SYSTEMS

A development intervention consists in a policy reform or in a project leading to results (Figure 4.1). The intervention itself consists in inputs (typically an investment expenditure, a technological innovation, or an institutional innovation) to specific activities leading to outputs. In *Oportunidades*, a conditional cash transfer (CCT) program in Mexico which pays eligible mothers to send their children to school, the inputs are the offers of conditional payments, the activities the implementation of payments with verification that conditionalities have been met, and the outputs the program uptake in terms of number of beneficiaries. The objective of the intervention is to achieve a number of outcomes (results). Some are intermediate such as increased educational achievements (enrollment, grade achieved, quality of learning); others are final outcomes corresponding to the goals of the intervention, such as better employment, higher incomes, and less poverty. Intermediate outcomes tend to be short-run while final outcomes are typically long-run.

Every project is subjected to different forms of monitoring and evaluation. Impact evaluation is only one of them, and the more rarely performed because it is more demanding in skills and resources. Typical forms of evaluations include the following:

Figure 4.1 Project sequence

1. *Ex-ante project appraisal.* This involves attempts at measuring expected costs and benefits, and internal rates of return, of proposed projects (Squire and van der Tak, 1975). Evaluation is done at market prices for the project itself (financial evaluation, using the market interest rate for discounting) and at social (shadow) prices using a social discount rate and internalizing the externalities created by the project to measure the social value of the project (economic analysis).
2. *Programmatic evaluation: the logframe approach.* The logical-framework (logframe) approach developed by USAID in 1969 uses indicators to describe inputs, activities, outputs, and outcomes. It evaluates achievements by assessing the state of progress against the planned inputs, activities, outputs, and outcomes at given times (intermediate and final) as specified in the original project design. It is largely a systematic reporting methodology used to track progress according to plan.
3. *Comprehensive expenditure review.* This type of review is implemented by accountants to track the use of financial resources in a public project. It helps to observe and explain inconsistencies between actual and planned expenditures.
4. *Impact analysis.* This is the most demanding form of evaluation as it attempts to assign causality to specific interventions for observed changes in selected indicators of outcomes. The basic challenge is to establish how the beneficiaries of an intervention would have fared in absence of the intervention: the counterfactual situation. The impact is measured by the difference between the observed outcome and the counterfactual outcome.

OBJECTIVES AND OVERVIEW OF IMPACT EVALUATION

Impact evaluation of public programs is often required by law. This is the case in Mexico, where all programs that use federal resources are expected to report impacts on a bi-annual basis to the executive and the legislative bodies. An independent evaluation unit, CONEVAL (the National Council for the Evaluation of Social Development Policy), has been set up for this purpose. It is also required in the US following the 1993 Government Performance and Results Act, fully implemented from 1997. Philanthropic organizations such as the Bill & Melinda Gates Foundation and international organizations such as the World Bank are also committed to impact evaluations of their projects. The International Initiative for Impact Evaluation (referred to as 3ie) is a broad coalition of development organizations set up to pursue the impact evaluation of development projects. Impact evaluations have three main objectives:

1. *Accountability.* The accountability objective is to assess ex-post the value of a program to justify its costs. Impact methods are needed so that benefits due to spurious correlates—for example, high yields due to good weather, or contributions made by other interventions that occurred at the same time and place—are not assigned to the program. Impact assessment for accountability is important to enable program financers (donors, governments, international organizations) to know what was obtained that can be attributed to the money spent. The ex-post cost–benefit calculation for a project requires the measurement of benefits, which should be obtained through impact analysis. This work is typically done by presumed impartial external evaluators.

2. *Results-based management.* The objective here is to use the results of the impact evaluation to make adjustments to the program (provide feedback), ranging from continuation with minor adjustments to major changes, redesign, and eventual cancellation. Experimentation and evaluation should be directed at key features of the program with as yet untested designs. The objective is to learn from experience. Stakeholders should ideally participate in the evaluation, and the implementing agency should have incentives to learn from both successes and failures. Impact assessment for results-based management is important for program managers and should be part of the pilot phase of any large program.

3. *Generic lessons for the profession.* Results from the evaluation may have something generic to teach the development profession at large. In this case, results from the evaluation, if freely available, are an international public good. Indeed, many programs around the world such as CCT and community-driven development (CDD) are designed by analogy with programs that have been shown to be worthwhile by rigorous impact evaluations at the pilot stage or in other countries. Rigorous impact evaluations of *Progresa/Oportunidades*, the Mexican CCT program, have certainly contributed both to the permanence of the program across presidential political cycles and the adoption of the approach in many countries across the world (Levy, 2006). Deriving generic lessons from a particular impact evaluation requires cautious assessment of the external validity (domain of application) of the results obtained, as discussed below.

CHALLENGES OF IMPACT EVALUATION

The main difficulty in impact analysis is establishing causality between an intervention X and an outcome Y, as we saw in Figure 4.1. Say that we observe a correlation between X and Y. There are four reasons why this correlation may exist, only one of which implies causality between X and Y:

- Causality: $X \rightarrow Y$, where the arrow means "causes." In this case, correlation is indeed due to X causing Y.
- Reverse causality: $Y \rightarrow X$. In this case, correlation is due to Y causing X.
- Simultaneity: $X \rightarrow Y$ and $Y \rightarrow X$. Here, X and Y are correlated because they are jointly determined.
- Spurious correlation/omitted variable bias. In this case, correlation is due to the fact that there exists a third variable Z such that $Z \rightarrow X$ and $Z \rightarrow Y$. X and Y are correlated because they are both affected by Z.

The art of impact analysis is to find methodologies that statistically establish the first reason for an observed correlation—namely, true causality—while ruling out any of the other three reasons. Erroneous causalities may come from biased *program placement* or from *self-selection* of treated units that create spurious correlations with other variables that influence the observed outcomes.

An example of bias coming from program placement is when health facilities are located in the neighborhoods where they are most needed, i.e. where there are more unattended health issues. Health interventions across locations are then positively correlated with the incidence of bad health: they appear to be the cause of bad health, when the correlation is in fact due to reverse causality. An example of bias coming from self-selection is when we attempt to measure the effect of micro-credit by observing that women who use micro-credit achieve higher incomes than those who do not. This may, however, be due to spurious correlation as it is likely that it is the most entrepreneurial women who achieve better business outcomes and who self-select in taking loans to do business; hence we cannot disentangle what is due to their entrepreneurship and what is due to the loan by comparing their business outcomes with those of non-borrowers. Entrepreneurship (Z) creates a spurious correlation between participation (X) and outcome (Y). In this case, the omitted variable bias (the role of entrepreneurship) exaggerates the value of participation on the observed outcome; in other cases, it can mitigate it. An example of simultaneity is the amount of credit received by a client and her repayment performance: growth in loan size is a function of performance, itself a function among other factors of the amount to be repaid; hence, it cannot be said that the observed loan received causes the observed repayment performance. We need to make use of evaluation techniques (also called identification strategies) that will help us distinguish strict causality from spurious correlations, reverse causality, and simultaneity.

Techniques for impact evaluation

Suppose that we have a sample of units (individuals. households, firms, etc.) drawn randomly from a large population. We are interested in the effect of their participation in a program (P) on an outcome (Y) such as schooling, consumption, profits, etc. Let us call $Y_i(1)$ the outcome for unit i with the program, and $Y_i(0)$ the outcome for the same unit without the program. The impact or causal effect δ_i of the program for this unit is:

$$\delta_i = Y_i(1) - Y_i(0).$$

Of course, we can never observe for a given unit both $Y_i(1)$ and $Y_i(0)$, we only observe $Y_i(1)$ for the program beneficiaries and $Y_i(0)$ for those that did not participate in the program; therefore it is impossible to measure the impact of a program on one particular unit.

Impact evaluation is a statistical approach, meaning that we do not attempt to define the impact of the program on one particular unit but the average impact in the population from which we had drawn the sample, δ. Because the average of the difference in outcomes is equal to the difference in averages, we can write this:

$$\delta = E(Y_i(1) - Y_i(0)) = E(Y_i(1)) - E(Y_i(0)),$$

where the symbol $E(.)$ denotes expectation (or average) in the population. So now the challenge is to find a way to estimate these two averages. If we are only interested in the population of participants in the program, $E(Y_i(1))$ can be estimated with the average of the Y_i of the beneficiaries—and we would now need to find a way to estimate what would have been their average outcomes had they not benefited from the program. This is what is called the counterfactual outcome. Using the average outcome among the non-beneficiaries in general does not work because non-beneficiaries are most often different from beneficiaries in many dimensions, including the outcome of interest. Finding a credible counterfactual is not easy. All the methods that we discuss below resort to finding non-beneficiaries that are as similar to beneficiaries as possible, except for the fact that they did not benefit from the intervention. These people form a group to which the group of beneficiaries is compared. These methods therefore require observation of many units (villages, firms, households, or individuals) in both the beneficiary and the comparison groups.

There exists a range of techniques for impact analysis. Which technique applies best for which evaluation is part science and part imagination and practice—call it the art of impact evaluation. Each case is different, and the impact-evaluation strategy to be used needs to be correspondingly designed. We discuss and subsequently develop seven of the most commonly used methods:

1. *Experimental design with randomization* to construct treatment (T) and control (C) groups. This is the randomized-control-trial (RCT) approach (Duflo *et al.*, 2008). It is often regarded as the "gold standard" of impact analysis since randomization is the most accurate way of splitting a large population into two statistically identical treatment and control groups. Impact can then be measured by simple differences in observed outcomes between the T and C groups, and tested for statistical significance relative to zero. It should be done when relevant and feasible, but it is not always adequate and possible (Deaton, 2010).

2. *Matching methods* where a C group is constructed ex-post relative to an intervention, having similar observable characteristics that affect the outcome of interest. The main method in this category is the propensity score matching (PSM) approach. The underlying assumption is that if members of the T and C groups are identical in terms of observable variables then they may also be identical in terms of the non-observable variables that can affect outcomes. In this case, the only source of difference in outcome would be due to the program.

3. *Difference-in-differences technique*, so called diff-in-diffs, where, under certain assumptions, the *change* in the before and after outcomes for treated units can be compared to the *change* in outcome for non-treated units over the same period, serving as control. The underlying assumption for the validity of the method is that the two groups would have been on "parallel trends" were it not for the intervention so that the difference in changes in outcome between T and C during the intervention is not due to a fundamental differential dynamic between them.

4. *Roll-out of a program and panel analysis*. This is a generalization of the difference-in-differences technique that applies to cases where units are progressively incorporated into a program in a staggered roll-out. The underlying assumption is that there are no other changes in the context or in the behavior of the units that can affect the outcome of interest and that are correlated with but not due to incorporation into the program. By observing all the units throughout the whole period of incorporation, one can estimate the impact of becoming a beneficiary.

5. *Regression discontinuity designs (RDD)* when eligibility is given by a threshold (e.g. being below the poverty line for a subsidy) and we use as a counterfactual individuals that are just above (*C*) as opposed to just below (*T*) the poverty line. The assumption is that cases just below and above the threshold are identical in all aspects other than being treated or not. This allows measuring a local average treatment effect (LATE) around the threshold value of the qualification criterion.

6. *Event analysis.* This method is used to analyze the impact of an event that occurred at a very precise point in time and induced a quasi-immediate response in the outcome of interest so quick that it is unlikely that the observed change could have been induced by other events. An example is the announcement of the unexpected death of a political leader on share prices. The impact is simply measured by comparing the change in outcome for different units (firms or sectors of production, for example) that are differentially related to the event.

7. *Instrumental variables (IV) approach* to control for non-causal correlations. This method is applied when participation in the program is endogenous (either as a choice by the beneficiaries or a placement by the program managers) but there exists an external exogenous factor that influenced the uptake of the program but is not otherwise correlated with the outcome. The IV method then measures the impact of the program on those beneficiaries that have joined the program because of this external factor. This is another type of LATE, where "local" applies to this subgroup of beneficiaries.

The methods described in (2) to (6) above are often designated as "quasi-experimental." They consist in defining a comparison group of non-beneficiaries that is as good as would have been obtained through randomization for the purpose of measuring impact. Qualitative methods such as interviews and case studies are very useful complements, but not substitutes, to quantitative impact analysis. Properly used, qualitative methods help formulate hypotheses to be tested quantitatively and provide interpretations of what may be the underlying causal channels in observed impacts. They are also useful for uncovering the rationality and inner interpretations of why people (such as the poor) and institutions (such as governments) do what they do, which quantitative impact analysis will not tell us.

EXPERIMENTAL DESIGN—RCT

When feasible, randomization is the most rigorous approach to construct a treatment and a control group from among an eligible population (Duflo, 2006; Banerjee and Duflo, 2009). This is because randomization over a sufficiently large number of units creates statistically identical treatment and control groups. If randomization is properly done, and the samples are large enough, the two groups should not have any statistically different features that could create correlations between treatment and outcomes that are not due to the treatment. Impact can then be measured by simple difference in the outcome variable between treatment and control groups. Obtaining the statistical property derived from large numbers is easier if the randomization can be done at the individual level rather than at the village or the institutional (e.g. school, microfinance

153

institution, cooperative, local government) level; but practical or ethical considerations do not always allow randomization at the lowest level.

As in medical trials, the ethics of randomization has to be carefully assessed. The basic principle of ethical randomization is that a group of people can be denied the intervention to serve as control, but we cannot: (1) actively hurt them, (2) mislead them or give them wrong information, or (3) make them worse off than they would otherwise be without the experiment. As for participants, they must be offered the freedom not to participate and to withdraw from participation at any time if they so desire. In any research university, these procedures are closely supervised by a Committee for the Protection of Human Subjects. There is a long tradition in using randomized trials ethically in medicine and pharmaceuticals that is now being applied to social experiments.

A typical case where randomization is fairly easy to implement is when a budget-constrained organization plans an intervention in a sample of villages or schools. An RCT requires that the organization selects more candidate villages or schools than the number in which it would be willing to intervene and then randomly selects from among these units the sub-sample that will receive the intervention. Another case where randomization should be feasible is when the program intends to reach a very large population but the target population cannot be treated all at once because of budgetary or administrative constraints; thus the program needs to be deployed gradually. The fairest way of deciding who will be treated first is to draw lots under public oversight. Those with delayed treatment serve as the control group for the treated.

Figure 4.2 shows how the evaluation of the CCT *Progresa* was designed. Implementation of *Progresa* all over rural Mexico was planned to take about 2 years from mid 1998 until mid 2000. The starting point for the construction of the evaluation sample was the random selection of 506 communities from all of the communities eligible for the program in seven states of Mexico. These communities were then randomly allocated to the program in the first wave in May 1998 (320 communities) or in the last wave in 2000 (186 communities). A year and a half later, in January 2000, all the communities were incorporated in the treatment as the program was by then covering the whole country.

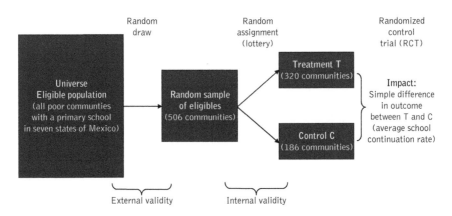

Figure 4.2 *RCT with application to* Progresa, Mexico

With randomization, the measure of impact, called the average treatment effect, can be obtained by **simple difference** in the average outcome between treatment and control groups:

$$ATE = \underbrace{\bar{Y}_T}_{\substack{\text{average outcome} \\ \text{in treatment group}}} - \underbrace{\bar{Y}_C}_{\substack{\text{average outcome} \\ \text{in control group}}},$$

where $\bar{Y}_T$ is the average outcome for individuals in group T, and $\bar{Y}_C$ the average outcome for individuals in group C. The statistical test of this difference is a t-test for means or a Chi^2 for percentages. This simple difference can also be measured for subgroups of treated and control individuals to evaluate the heterogeneity of program effects.

The validity of the randomization can be verified by checking that there are on average no statistically significant differences between households (or individuals) in the treatment and control groups based on observable characteristics. For this, we typically do statistical tests of differences of means for as many relevant observable characteristics (that are unaffected by the program) of the two groups as possible. If we work at a 5 percent precision level, not more than 5 percent of these differences should be significantly different from zero. If there is a baseline survey collected before the program is implemented, this verification can include the main outcome or variables related to it.

An important question when using RCTs is the external validity of the results, i.e. to what extent do the results apply to populations beyond the sample used in the analysis. In the particular case of the *Progresa* RCT, the result applies to the original population from which the sample has been drawn, i.e. all villages from the seven states of Mexico, but to no other populations. External validity thus does not extend to other Mexican states. For this, we need to replicate the experiment in these other states, and start to learn how results systematically differ as characteristics of the populations change. Once we have enough replicas of the experiment across different populations, we can start predicting the measured outcome as a function of population characteristics.

Examples of RCT studies

There are by now many studies using RCTs to address precise development questions. Here are some examples.

What is the benefit from de-worming school children in rural Kenya? (Miguel and Kremer, 2004)

Without treatment, over 90 percent of rural school children in Kenya were infected with worms. De-worming with pills is cheap, but is not done by individual parents because there are strong externalities across children: a treated child is soon re-infected by others who have not been treated. This is a case where the positive externality associated with treatment leads to private underinvestment and justifies coordinated public intervention at the school level. But what is the benefit from putting public money into de-worming interventions at the school level? This was addressed through RCT by randomizing 75 primary schools with over 30,000 children of ages 6 to 18 into three arms:

T1 school treated in 1998 and 1999;
T2 school not treated in 1998 and treated in 1999;
C school not treated in 1998 or 1999.

The staggering of treatment allows the measurement of the magnitude of spillover effects between treated and non-treated schools within a certain distance. Results show that treatment reduces school absenteeism by 7.5 percentage points, or one quarter of the initial absentee level, but does not have an observable effect on test scores within two years after treatment. The latter may be due to increased congestion in the classroom, low quality of classroom teaching, or the need for longer time lags between treatment and observable outcomes. Treatment also has externalities on neighboring schools, reducing absenteeism on average by 2 percentage points in non-treated schools in a radius of up to 6km. These reductions in absenteeism amount to an increase of 0.14 years of schooling on average in the area. Because the cost of de-worming is only US$0.49 per child per year, the authors conclude that de-worming is a very cheap way of increasing schooling, costing 0.49/0.14= $3.50 per additional year of schooling. These results have helped boost de-worming campaigns across Africa as cost-effective interventions to improve school achievements, such as the Deworm the World Initiative that has reached 37 million children across 27 countries.

Impact of Progresa *on school continuation rates* (de Janvry and Sadoulet, 2006)

With the *T* and *C* villages selected as indicated above, all poor households from the villages assigned to *T* were offered the CCT.[1] A key outcome, the continuation rate, is the percentage of school children currently enrolled who will enroll at school the year after. Impact is measured as the difference in average continuation rates between children in poor households in the *T* and *C* villages. Results in Table 4.1 show that the program had no statistically significant impact on enrollment in primary school (98 percent among *T* children compared to 97 percent among *C* children). Most children go to school and there is no need to waste program resources paying mothers for this. The program is, by contrast, quite effective in inducing greater enrollment in secondary school. There we see that enrollment among *T* children was 75.9 percent compared to enrollment among *C* children of 63.6 percent, a statistically significant gain in enrollment of 12.3 percentage points, or of 19.3 percent over *C* enrollment. Note that, in spite of the CCT offer, 24.1 percent of children in the *T* communities still drop out at time of entry into secondary school. This indicates that the program was effective for 12.3 percent of children but insufficient to address the reasons that make another 24.1 percent of the children drop out. Other interventions, either on

Table 4.1 *School continuation rates by grade,* Progresa *program, Mexico*

School continuation rate by grade (%)	Treatment group	Control group	Difference (% points)	Statistical significance
Primary school	98	97	1	No
Entry into secondary school	75.9	63.6	12.3	Yes

Source: de Janvry and Sadoulet, 2006.

the demand side (larger transfers, individual counseling) or supply side (better quality of schools, reduced teacher absenteeism) would be needed to entice these children to enter secondary school.

Does repayment frequency affect default in microfinance lending? (Field and Pande, 2008)

The question addressed in this study is whether the weekly repayment that is so frequently requested by microfinance lenders is essential to monitor clients and ensure high repayment rates. The experiment randomly assigned clients to a weekly (control) or monthly (treatment) repayment schedule and found no significant effect of repayment schedule on client loan delinquency or default. These findings suggest that a less frequent repayment schedule can allow microfinance institutions to significantly lower their transaction costs without increasing client default. Experiments of this type are typical of those that contribute to results-based program management as described above.

Other RCT experiments

1. *Do people who learn that they are HIV positive change their sexual behavior?* In a randomized experiment in Malawi, people who have been tested for HIV were randomly selected to be paid to be informed about the result of their test. Only 34 percent pick up the result without an incentive, the cash incentive doubling that number (Thornton, 2008). Results show that people who learn that they are HIV positive are three times more likely to purchase condoms to reduce the chance of infecting others.
2. *What is the impact on poor people of access to microfinance loans?* New branches were randomly opened by a microfinance lender in 52 of 104 neighborhoods of Hyderabad, India (Banerjee *et al.*, 2015). Results three years later showed almost no effect on the lifestyles of poor people, including healthcare and education, but suggested potential future gains as access to credit in treatment areas helped pre-existing businesses increase investment and achieve higher profits.
3. *How important is it to know the expected return from education in making schooling decisions?* In the Dominican Republic, Jensen (2010) observed that perceived expected returns to secondary schooling are very low for most students relative

to true returns measured with earnings data. In an experiment, students in a randomly selected subset of schools were provided with information on the expected gains in earnings from secondary education. Relative to the control group, informed students on average completed 0.2 more years of schooling over the next four years. The effect was larger among non-poor students, with 0.33 more years of schooling, while there was no effect on the poorest students. An interpretation suggested by qualitative observations is that poor students, in spite of being informed, remain constrained by poverty and credit constraints in their ability to attend school.

4. *How effective is providing textbooks in raising test scores?* In an RCT experiment in Kenya, 25 of 100 schools were randomly selected to receive official government textbooks (Glewwe *et al.*, 2009). Contrary to expectations, results show that textbooks did not increase average test scores. Only students with high pre-test scores benefited, suggesting that the textbooks were ill suited for the typical student with difficulty in reading in English, which is not their mother tongue.

5. *Does improving management practices help increase productivity in large firms in India?* This RCT conducted by Bloom *et al.* (2013) provides evidence on the importance of management practices in large textile firms in India. Thirty-eight large firms were randomly selected to receive diagnostic consulting during the first month, followed by four months of intensive support for the implementation of the consultations' recommendations. The control plants received only one month of diagnostic consulting. The study showed that adopting these management practices raised productivity by 17 percent in the first year through improved quality and efficiency and reduced inventory, and within three years led to the opening of more production plants. The reason why the firms receiving intensive support had not previously adopted these profitable management practices was lack of information and lack of competitive pressures.

Natural experiments with randomization

It is possible to find natural experiments that mimic an RCT. This is the case when treatment selection has been based on a random allocation or a lottery system. Finding such cases has the advantage over an RCT that the experiment may be large-scale and that it may have occurred a long time ago, allowing the observation of long-term impacts. The difficulties are in ascertaining ex-post that allocation was truly random, and in finding data that characterize outcomes for both beneficiaries and non-beneficiaries. Some examples are as follows.

1. *Does gender affect governance in India?* In India, starting in 1993, one third of village council (*gram panchayat*) heads was reserved for women, and the third of villages reserved for female election was randomly selected. This provides a randomized policy experiment to assess whether the types of public good provided by the *panchayat* is affected by the gender of the council head. Results obtained by Chattopadhyay and Duflo (2004) for 265 village councils in West Bengal and Rajasthan show that it does. Where women relative to men demand more

investment in public goods such as drinking water, *panchayat*s with a woman head delivered differentially more gender-biased goods. In this context, a politician's gender did influence policy decisions. Note that a repeat of the study by Ban and Rao (2008) failed to find such difference in India's southern states. This illustrates the issue of external validity of results that we look at again in the next example.

2. *How does the Hajj affect attitude with respect to non-Muslims?* For logical and safety reasons, Saudi Arabia, which hosts the annual Hajj pilgrimage to Mecca, has established quotas for the number of Hajj visas available for each major Islamic country. Pakistan handles this restriction with a lottery for applicants. Using the 2006 lottery that awarded visas to less than 60 percent of the applicants, Clingingsmith *et al.* (2009) compare successful and unsuccessful applicants after the event. They find that participation in the Hajj increases belief in equality and harmony among different Muslim groups, as well as tolerance with respect to non-Muslims. The sample for this analysis was randomly drawn from the complete list of applicants and the survey took place by phone five to eight months after the Hajj. Unsurprisingly, a large number of applicants could not be reached, and only 63 percent of the attempted interviews were completed. More worrisome is that this attrition from the initial balanced sample is higher for the successful than for the unsuccessful pilgrims. In cases like this, the balance of characteristics has to be checked again after attrition, and robustness checks must be performed against concerns about selection.

3. *Does school quality affect student performance?* Many school districts have adopted an open enrollment system where students apply for admission to particular schools, and successful applications are drawn randomly. This provides a natural experiment with randomization of student allocation across schools which can be used to test the role of school quality on educational performance. Lai *et al.* (2011) used this to assess the role of middle-school quality on educational performance in Beijing. Results show that school quality (measured by school dummy variables called fixed effects) is a strong determinant of student performance. These fixed effects are in turn highly correlated with teacher qualifications as measured by official rankings, indicating what matters in determining school quality.

4. *Are subsidies to secondary education cost-effective?* Vouchers covering about half of the cost of attending private secondary school were allocated by lottery to 125,000 students in Colombia under the PACES program (Programa de Ampliación de Cobertura de la Educación Segundaria) (Angrist *et al.*, 2002). Lottery winners were found to be 10 percent more likely to complete 8th grade and with higher scores on standardized tests. Impacts were larger for girls than for boys. Because there were irregularities in implementation the authors used the win or loss status of students rather than whether they used a voucher. In cases like this, what is measured is not the average treatment effect of the voucher but what is called the intention-to-treat (ITT) effect of the voucher. Angrist *et al.* conclude that the social cost of the subsidies was less than the private benefits, and that demand–side subsidies to secondary education are thus cost-effective.

159

Estimating behavioral parameters so as to simulate the outcomes of alternative program designs

An important limitation of simple impact analyses is their "black-box" nature: they provide a measure of the impact of a very specific program in the way it was implemented, but cannot tell us for example why people responded the way they did, nor how they would have responded had the level of subsidy been different. Consider the evaluation of *Progresa*. While we can measure the effect of the large conditional cash transfer that was offered to the household, we cannot infer from this experiment whether a higher continuation rate into secondary school would have been achieved with a higher transfer. In order to be able to improve the design of the program, we would need a complete scheme of responses to different levels of subsidy, or the elasticity of response to the subsidy level. An example of such an approach is given in Cai *et al.* (2012) for weather-insurance contracts offered to rice farmers in China.

Some potential problems with randomized experiments

While an RCT may be the cleanest way of organizing an impact evaluation, several difficulties may arise. Deaton (2010) gives a critical review of the value of RCTs in economic development, including the following difficulties:

1. *Hawthorne effect.* A randomization bias may be created if subjects change their behavior because they know they are being studied (Landsberger, 1958). Participants may pay more attention to what they are doing because they know it is being observed, or they may interpret what is being investigated and adjust their responses to try to please the experimenter. In this case, the observed outcome does not represent the outcome that would have been observed in the absence of the treatment intervention. This in turn compromises the external validity of the experiment.
2. *John Henry effect.* Control households may work harder to compensate for not being treated and keep up with the treated. This biases the measure of impact toward underestimation.
3. *Contamination or spillover effects.* This happens when some of the controls that were randomly excluded from treatment are able to receive the treatment, or, conversely, if some members randomly selected for the treatment do not receive it. To avoid this, treatment and control need to be kept sufficiently separate, making similarity between the two groups also more difficult to achieve.
4. *Dropout or attrition effects.* Some members of the treatment group may drop out of the experiment before completing the program. This is often the case for experiments that last for a long time. In this case, there is a selection effect since randomization was done on the offer of treatment or at the outset of the experiment, not on whether individuals completed the treatment. Selection in dropping out may create bias if those who drop out are different in terms of the measured outcome from those who continue the experiment.
5. *Pioneer and partial equilibrium effects.* Most RCTs are run for short periods of time, typically two to three years, and experiments tend to be small. Early "pioneer"

effects of an experiment may be quite different from later effects, sometimes in the opposite direction. This is because learning effects may take some time. Short-term investment may draw down welfare but deliver future gains. General equilibrium effects on prices will occur once the treatment becomes widespread—for instance, via diffusion of an innovation. Learning and diffusion effects may cancel early gains. Results from a short-term and localized experiment should thus be interpreted with a great deal of caution as to what they mean for broader and sustainable development.

Power calculation: what is the minimum sample size needed to detect the impact of a program?

The impact evaluation of a program is a test of the following hypothesis:

H_0 (null hypothesis)—the program has no impact;
H_1 (alternative hypothesis against which H_0 is tested)—the program has an impact.

Hypothesis testing can only reject a hypothesis. Hence rejecting H_0 will lead us to conclude that the program had an impact. When testing whether a program had an impact, two errors can be committed: a Type I error is committed when the evaluation concludes that the program had an impact when in reality it did not; a Type II error is committed when the evaluation cannot detect an impact that occurred. Control over the size of Type I errors is obtained by choosing a significance level for the test of the null hypothesis that there is no impact. If we set the significance level at, say, 5 percent then there is only a 5 percent chance that we mistakenly conclude that there is an impact when there is none. Control over Type II errors depends critically on the size of the sample used for the experiment. The power of the test of an impact evaluation is the probability that it will detect a difference between T and C groups when one exists. An 80 percent power of the test is a common choice; it means that the sample size is chosen to find an impact in 80 percent of the cases where one has occurred. Gertler *et al.* (2011) describe the power-calculation method that allows definition of the minimum sample size necessary to detect the expected impact of a program.

Measuring spillover effects

We saw above that spillover effects can pollute counterfactuals and bias the measurement of impacts of a treatment. However, spillover effects are usually desirable outcomes of an intervention as they create multiplier effects on costly treatments. For example, are non-beneficiary households of *Progresa* CCTs (because they are above the poverty line) more likely to send their children to school in treated communities? Bobonis and Finan (2009) find that there are such peer effects. The enrollment decisions of beneficiary children influence the enrollment decisions of program-ineligible children, particularly when it is the poorer households in the community who sent their children to school. This suggests that targeted policies can have large multiplier effects. As such, we are very much interested in measuring the spillover effects of an intervention.

Spillover effects are typically measured by isolating control communities from treatment communities, and by varying the intensity of treatment within the treated communities. The larger the number of individuals treated in a community, controlling for size, the larger the external effect on others should be, allowing us to measure a multiplier effect, eventually with non-linear returns. Baird *et al.* (2014) developed a design method for RCTs in order to rigorously measure spillover effects. It consists in first randomizing the intensity of treatment within communities and then randomly assigning individual treatment conditional on this cluster-level intensity. They show how to adjust power calculations to this methodology and to calculate average treatment effects.

Conclusion on RCTs

Randomization is generally the preferred approach if it can be organized ahead of the intervention. It works better for simple and well defined interventions where benefits are at the individual level—we can have many observations and outcomes of interest are sufficiently short-term that we can observe them in a survey a few years after the intervention. Verification of the validity of the randomization requires checking the balance across treatment and control groups of all the characteristics not affected by the program. This information is typically obtained in a baseline survey implemented prior to the intervention. Thus, while the RCT impact evaluation does not need a baseline survey, such a survey is useful to assess the validity of the randomization.

Several limitations of the RCT approach should be kept in mind when choosing from methods to achieve identification (Ravallion, 2012). They include the possibility that the experiment influences the behavior not only of the treatment, but also of the control group, that there is selection in people considering the offer of participating in the treatment, that the RCT does not track general equilibrium effects—for example, on prices that may affect impact—and that withholding treatment can sometimes harm members of the control group (Barrett and Carter, 2010). Thus even if it is the generally preferred approach, an RCT is not free of its own risks and limitations.

MATCHING METHOD TO CONSTRUCT CONTROL GROUPS: PROPENSITY SCORE MATCHING

Randomization is not always possible, in particular for events that have already occurred and whose impact we would like to measure ex-post *facto*—and donors and governments frequently ask for an impact evaluation of a program that has already been implemented. One available option is propensity score matching (PSM). This matching method consists of selecting as a control group non-participants that are comparable to participants in a large number of *observable* essential characteristics.

The key assumption for the validity of the method is that the *unobserved* characteristics are sufficiently similar across the treated (*T*) and control (*C*) groups not to create spurious correlations between treatment and outcome of the type we described above. It means that, once we control for all the observable characteristics of participants, participation in the program is not correlated with any other determinant of the outcome. The method applies best to programs that have only covered part of the potential population of beneficiaries, where selection was based on criteria completely independent of the potential impact of the program, and where personal choice had little to do with participation.

The necessary data consist in a sample of participants (usually from a special survey designed for the program's evaluation) and a large sample of non-participants (usually from some other large existing survey, such as a Living Standards Measurement Study for households) from which one can pick the comparison group. Both surveys must include information on variables X that are important determinants of program participation and outcomes.

A PSM method is used to construct a control group (C) that can be compared to the treated group (T). The steps to implement the procedure are as follows:

1. Select a very large number of variables X that help predict program participation. Use both T and non-participant samples to estimate the probability of participation $p(X)$ as a function of the variables X.
2. Instead of matching individuals on all the Xs, which is difficult to do when there are many of them, match them on the basis of a similar estimated probability of participation $p(X)$ (their propensity score). For each participant i to the program find the closest matches $m(i)$ among non-participants, i.e. the non-participant(s) with the closest predicted value of probability of participation to participant i. It is critically important that these propensity scores are very close (e.g. do not differ by more than 1/1000) and hence to start with a very large number of potential counterfactuals are required to find at least one close match for each participant.
3. The impact of the program is the average difference in outcomes between each treated individual and his/her matched control. Because this is a matched sample that corresponds to the treated group it is called treatment on the treated (ToT). It does not tell us what would have been the impact for non-beneficiaries that do not resemble the beneficiaries.

$$ToT = \frac{1}{N_T} \sum_{i \in T} \left(Y_i - Y_{m(i)} \right),$$

where N_T is the number of beneficiaries in the T group, Y_i the outcome for treated individual i, and $Y_{m(i)}$ the outcome for the individual matched to i. There are many variations to this method—for instance, using the average of several matches, or many matches that are weighted according to how "close" they are to the treated person in their propensity scores (Imbens and Wooldridge, 2009).

Examples of PSM studies

1. *Argentina's workfare program Trabajar (Jalan and Ravallion, 2003a).* In 1997, in the context of a serious unemployment crisis that affected 18 percent of the labor force, the government of Argentina introduced a workfare program, Trabajar. Beneficiaries were self-selected in response to a low wage offer to encourage the participation of the poor only. There was no baseline survey and no randomization scheme. Impact evaluation thus had to be based on the ex-post construction of a control group.

163

This was done by PSM, combining a large national sample survey with a survey of participants that used the same questionnaire and was carried out at the same date some four months after initiation of the program. Households from the area where the program was not offered (*C* in Figure 4.3) were matched to participants (*T*). The underlying feature that justified the use of PSM was that the implementation of the workfare program in a specific locality depended on circumstances at the local level that were not correlated with the cause and consequences of unemployment, and that unless there were some obvious difficulties that could be captured by observable characteristics (such as distance, physical conditions, etc.), the program was sufficiently attractive that all eligible persons would participate in the program if offered the chance, eliminating the problem of self-selection. Results show that participants achieved a gain in income equal to about half the prevailing gross wage, and that the program was well targeted, with some 80 percent of participants coming from the poorest quintile of the population.

2. *Does piped water reduce diarrhea for children in rural India? (Jalan and Ravallion, 2003b).* Jalan and Ravallion used PSM to match households with and without piped water in a cross-sectional survey for rural India implemented in 1993–4 with 33,000 households from 1765 villages in 16 states. The survey collected data on the education and health status of 9,000 households with piped water and 24,000 without. The probability of having access to water given household characteristics was estimated using a logit model. Matches were then made between closely valued treatment and control households using a tolerance limit of 0.001.

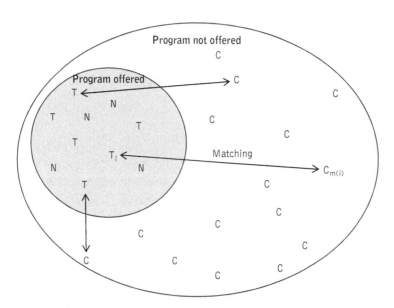

T = Households which were offered the program and chose to participate
N = Households which were offered the program and chose not to participate
C = Households which were not offered the program = potential controls

Figure 4.3 *PSM for impact evaluation of Trabajar*

The interesting result is that piped water contributes to reducing the prevalence and duration of diarrhea among children under five in observationally identical households. However, health gains largely bypass children in poor families, particularly where the female member is uneducated, suggesting that infrastructure needs to be complemented with promotion of health knowledge and income-poverty reduction to be effective in reducing child diarrhea.

Conclusion on PSM

PSM can be a useful technique, often because we have no choice of other methods in conducting ex-post the impact evaluation of a program, but it can also be misused because the underlying assumptions are strong, namely that the T and C groups do not differ in unobservable characteristics that affect program outcomes. It should, for instance, not be applied to the study of a program that has been broadly offered to the population and where there has been self-selection in participation. In this case, it is quite likely that participants differ from non-participants on unobserved characteristics correlated with the outcome, even after controlling for observables. Many studies have used PSM in this context, when the method is in fact unable to control for hidden determinants of participation that bias the results. Similarly, the method cannot be used to estimate the impact of programs that have been purposefully placed in particular areas to achieve impact, because these areas have been selected on the basis of characteristics that may influence the outcome of interest.

DIFFERENCE-IN-DIFFERENCES METHOD

An alternative approach to measuring the impact of a program is to start from the change over time observed in the outcome variable y among beneficiaries. This change cannot be interpreted as policy impact, of course, because many other things that may have affected the outcome have changed during the same period. One way to take these "natural changes" into account is to compute the change over time observed among non-beneficiaries during the same period. Subtracting the change observed over time among non-beneficiaries from that observed among beneficiaries produces the difference-in-differences estimate of the impact of the program.

The validity of this method depends on a crucial assumption: that in the absence of the program the *change* in the outcome variable among beneficiaries would have been identical to that among non-beneficiaries. This can be seen in Figure 4.4, where the change in y that occurred in the control group is applied as the no-intervention counterfactual to the treatment group. This assumption is often given the name "parallel trends" between the control and the treatment without intervention. While this crucial assumption cannot be verified, one should at least ensure that this was the case, for example, in a period prior to the program, i.e. verifying that the changes were "parallel" prior to the intervention, as shown in Figure 4.4.

The minimum data needed are observations before and after implementation of the program, for both the treatment group and the comparison group. Hence we need both a baseline survey before the program and a follow-up (evaluation) survey after the

165

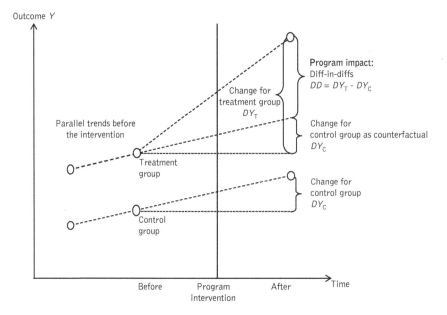

Figure 4.4 *Difference-in-differences method*

program. In addition, observations of the same treatment and control group for at least two periods before implementation of the program are necessary to support the parallel-trend assumption, unless convincing alternative tests in support of the validity of the counterfactual trends are provided, as mentioned in the conclusion section.

The average treatment effect is computed as:

$$ATE = (\bar{Y}_{T1} - \bar{Y}_{T0}) - (\bar{Y}_{C1} - \bar{Y}_{C0}),$$

where $\bar{Y}_{T0}$ and $\bar{Y}_{T1}$ are the average outcomes before and after the program intervention for the treated group, and $\bar{Y}_{C0}$ and $\bar{Y}_{C1}$ for the control group. In the ATE expression, the change in the outcome variable for the control group $(\bar{Y}_{C1} - \bar{Y}_{C0})$ represents changes due to the natural trend and all other events, and the change for the treatment group $(\bar{Y}_{T1} - \bar{Y}_{T0})$ represents the change in outcome due to the natural trend, all other events, and the program intervention.

Examples of use of the diff-in-diffs approach

Impact of a school-construction program on educational achievements and wage earnings

In this study, Duflo (2001) analyzes the impact of a large school-construction program that took place in Indonesia using resources from the oil boom, with 61,000 new primary schools built in the period 1974–8. What was the impact of school construction on educational achievements (years of education) and later on wages earned? A clever idea is to use the 1995 population census and to look at the educational and wage achievements of two different cohorts of people: the cohort of people who were of school age before the program and could not benefit from the program, and the cohort of people who attained school age after the program and could fully benefit from the program. People who were of school age during the program would only partially benefit and are not considered in the analysis. The "before" cohort is defined by the older group that was 12–17 years' old in 1974, the "after" cohort by the younger group that was 2–6 years' old in 1974. The contrast between the control and the treatment comes from the variation in program intensity across districts. The school-construction program was high intensity in some regions but low intensity in others. This allows for a difference-in-differences set-up similar to the generic methodology in Figure 4.4. The parallel-trends verification is made by comparing the educational achievements of two cohorts that attended primary school prior to the program: those who were aged 12–17 in 1974 and those 18–24 in 1974. Table 4.2 reports the means of years of education for the different cohorts by treatment and control region. This allows for the calculation of difference-in-differences for both pre-program changes (verifying the parallel-trends assumption) and for before–after program implementation.

Figure 4.5 shows verification of pre-intervention parallel trends in changes in years of education and how the program intervention modified these trends. Impact is measured by difference-in-differences for the y outcomes (years of education) as follows:

$$Dy_T - Dy_C = (8.49 - 8.02) - (9.76 - 9.40) = 0.47 - 0.36 = 0.11 \text{ years of education.}$$

Note that there was a larger gain for the T group even though they started with a lower initial level of years of education, i.e. the school-construction program had a placement bias toward districts with low educational achievements. Using the two cohorts that went to school prior to the construction project allows verification that the evolution of years of education was similar in what became the T and C regions,

Table 4.2 *Mean years of education by age cohort and level of intensity of school-construction program*

	Years of education		
	Level of program intensity in region of birth		Difference
	Low (C)	High (T)	(T–C)
Six years before (18–24 in 1974)	9.12	7.70	−1.42
Before (12–17 in 1974)	9.40	8.02	−1.38
After (2–6 in 1974)	9.76	8.49	−1.27
Pre-program changes	0.28	0.32	0.04
Before–after changes	0.36	0.47	0.11

Source: Duflo, 2001.

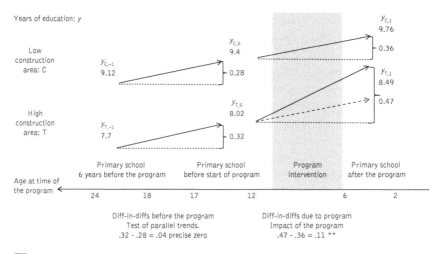

Figure 4.5 *Impact of school construction program on years of education and verification of parallel-trends hypothesis*

with increases of 0.32 and 0.28 years of education respectively. These are not significantly different from each other (a 0.04 difference-in-differences). Computing a similar difference-in-differences for wages, Duflo finds that the long-term impact of the school-construction programs is a 2.6 percent increase in wages for those that benefited from it. The difference between the number of schools constructed per 1,000 children in high- and low-program regions is 0.90. We can thus conclude that for every one school constructed per 1,000 children, the impact on education was an increase of $0.11/0.90 = 0.12$ years of education, leading to an increase in wages of $2.6/0.90 = 2.9$ percent. Based on this outcome, the economic return to investment in education is estimated at between 6.8 and 10.6 percent, a level well in excess of the cost of money for social-investment programs.

Impact of malaria-eradication campaigns on labor productivity

A similar approach was used by Bleakley (2010) to analyze the impact of the malaria-eradication campaigns in the US (circa 1920) and in Brazil, Colombia, and Mexico (circa 1955) on adult income according to the extent of childhood exposure to the eradication campaign. Childhood exposure to malaria depresses subsequent labor productivity and occupational income. Bleakley compared the incomes of the child cohorts (0–18 years old) born during and after the eradication campaigns with those of the preceding generation, and in both malaria-infested areas (in which the campaign should make a difference) and in non-malaria-infested areas (where the difference is simply due to the underlying trend in income). As shown in Figure 4.6a, child exposure to the eradication campaign varies from 0 for children already older than 18 when the campaign started to 1 for children born after initiation of the campaign.

The campaign to eradicate malaria in Brazil took place in the mid 1950s. Each dot in Figure 4.6b represents the coefficient from a regression of (log) income of adult men on the pre-campaign level of malaria mortality in the state where they were

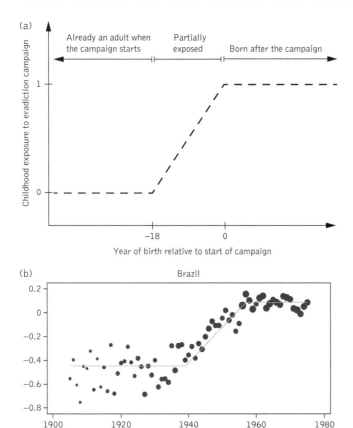

Figure 4.6 *Childhood exposure to eradication campaign (a) and impact of pre-campaign level of malaria mortality on adult occupational income in percentage points (b). In Brazil, the campaign occurred during the 1950s*

Source: Bleakley, 2010.

born. It shows that for all cohorts born before 1940, which were fully exposed to malaria when children, there is a strong negative correlation between the level of malaria and their future income as an adult. Adults born in areas with maximum intensity of malaria had on average an income 40 percent lower than those born in an area without malaria. For cohorts born after 1957, the year when the eradication campaign was over, the negative relationship between pre-campaign malaria and income is no longer present. Cohorts born between these two dates had intermediate levels of childhood exposure to the campaign, and the effect is negative, with a magnitude that decreases for later birth years.

Impact of issuing land/property titles to urban squatters in Lima (Field, 2007)

Does acquiring a formal ownership title induce homeowners to significantly increase house renovations? A nationwide titling program for urban squatters was launched in 1995 in Peru. Halfway through the program, in 2000, a survey was conducted with

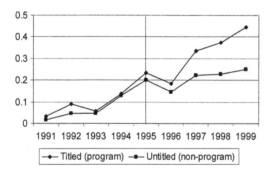

Figure 4.7 *Annual number of housing renovations (vertical axis) for those with and without titles in Lima*

Source: Field, 2007.

retrospective questions on all improvements made to the house since 1991, both in areas where the program had been implemented and in areas selected for implementation but not yet reached by the program. Assuming that the order in which the program was introduced was unrelated to the individual home-improvement pattern, impact can be measured by comparing annual improvements with and without the program.

Figure 4.7 shows time trends in the number of housing renovations per year between 1991 and 1999 among households living in neighborhoods that participated in the titling program and households in non-program neighborhoods. The vertical dotted line corresponds to the onset of the titling program in 1995. The graph indicates that there was no difference in renovations between the *T* and *C* groups before the program, and that there was a clear divergence in the rate of investment coinciding with the year in which the titling program began. The diff-in-diffs estimated impact is based on the comparison of investment made in 1994–5 and 1999–2000. The analysis also found that titling had a significant effect on labor-market participation—working more in the labor market and less at home—and in substituting adult for child labor. This was attributed to tenure security freeing labor from having to guard the house against invasion by others. By contrast, there was little impact on access to credit, a presumed potential main gain from a formal title.

Conclusion on the diff-in-diffs approach

The diff-in-diffs method has been extensively used to analyze the impact of policies with both macro- and microeconomic data. Macro data consist in panels of countries or states within a country. The main issue is that policies such as educational reforms are not introduced independently of contextual changes; they may be introduced across states in a federal country when there is a local need or demand for them, or in conjunction with other policies. This creates a typical "omitted variable bias," where the panel analysis will assign to the policy reform the impact of all other events and policies that happened at the same time in the treated areas. There is no test that can prove the absence of omitted variable bias. Only a convincing argument and robustness checks to the incorporation of other policy or contextual variables can dismiss suspicion that spurious correlation is creating the result. Similar issues arise with microeconomic studies, where participation in a program is correlated with other changes in behavior. Again, a good understanding of what motivated the decision and robustness checks to the incorporation of potential spurious correlates are the way to build the results' credibility.

The validity of the approach can be subjected to robustness checks, beyond the test of parallel trends before the intervention. These include falsification tests, which consist in verifying that outcomes that could not be affected by the program are indeed moving together both before and after the start of the intervention in the T and C groups, i.e. with no impact of the treatment.

The diff-in-diffs methodology can also be combined with other impact evaluation methods such as PSM. Matching based on observed baseline characteristics can be done before applying a diff-in-diffs methodology within each subgroup of matched units. The diff-in-diffs controls for unobserved characteristics that are constant across time between the two groups.

GENERALIZATION OF THE DIFF-IN-DIFFS APPROACH: ROLL-OUTS WITH PANEL DATA

There are many cases of programs or policies that use a roll-out with staggered entry, which may provide a way to define proper counterfactuals. The different units enter the treatment at different points in time. In Figure 4.8, unit 1 is treated at time t_1, unit 2 at time t_2, unit 3 at time t_3, etc. The idea is that the units that have not yet been treated at time t may serve as the control group for the units that are being treated at time t. The impact that we are trying to capture is the change in outcome (here a decline, say, in poverty) measured on the vertical axis that seems to happen whenever a unit is being treated. It is therefore necessary to have data on all units over the whole period of the roll-out, and the impact is estimated with what is called fixed-effects estimation with panel data (see Appendix 4.1).

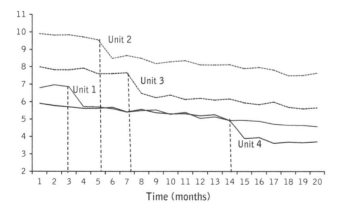

Figure 4.8 *Roll-out of a program with staggered entry. Months on the horizontal axis, outcome indicator on the vertical axis*

The key assumption for the validity of the method is similar to that for the diff-in-diffs: there are no other changes in the context or the unit's behavior that are correlated with the entry into the program and may affect the outcome of interest. Two important cases may occur that do not verify this assumption. The first is when entry into the treatment is correlated with the trend in outcome of the unit. To see this, consider the case where the program incorporates first the units with the steepest trend in performance and later those with flatter trends. The treated units will have a steeper decline than the non-treated, simply by selection, and hence this could appear as an effect of the treatment. The second is when the program incorporates each year in which the units had a bad shock (a short-term increase in their outcome in Figure 4.8). The year after incorporation, much of what we may measure as impact could simply be natural recovery. This is the so-called "Ashenfelter dip." Ashenfelter (1978) noted that the mean earnings of participants in employment and training programs generally declines during the period just prior to participation. This phenomenon has since been observed for participants in many other employment and training programs. Whatever the reason, this clearly leads to an overestimation of the earnings benefit of these programs.

Thus two verifications need to be done prior to using the panel method: (1) that the trends observed for the different units prior to the program are not correlated with the time at which they will be treated in the future; and (2) that there is no unusual level of outcome in the periods just before entry into the treatment.

Panel data are also used to analyze country-level policy interventions and relationships between macroeconomic variables—trying to establish, for example, the causal effect of trade liberalization on growth, corruption on growth, or growth on inequality, etc. The units of analysis are the countries, and observations are taken over several years, constituting panel data. While these analyses ask big questions of importance for development, they raise some particular econometric issues that we develop in Appendix 4.2.

Examples of the roll-out approach include:

1. *Privatization of local water companies in Argentina (Galiani et al., 2005).*
   Does privatization of water delivery improve the quality of water services? Local water companies in Argentina were gradually privatized, providing a case of staggered entry of municipalities into the program, with variation in ownership of water provision across time and space in municipalities. The data are on a panel of municipalities observed before and after privatization.

   Results show that child mortality fell by 8 percent in the municipalities that privatized their water services and that the effect was largest (26 percent) in the poorest areas. Robustness was verified by adding control variables that vary across both municipalities and time such as real GDP per capita, the unemployment rate, and public spending per capita. Another convincing robustness check, using the falsification-test approach, is to show that these results only apply when the cause of death is related to water quality (infectious and parasitic diseases), not for death from congenital anomalies or respiratory diseases. This confirms that the phenomenon is not related to a general improvement in child health care.

2. *Staggered entry of the branches of a microfinance institution (MFI) into a credit bureau.*
   Does introduction of a credit bureau improve the repayment performance of borrowers and the screening ability of micro lenders? This study combined a natural experiment, the staggered entry of branches of a large MFI in Guatemala into a credit bureau, with an RCT to inform borrowers from the MFI branches about the implications of a credit bureau for their future ability to borrow (de Janvry *et al.*, 2010). A credit bureau makes available to all lenders information about the debt level and the repayment performance of any client with any particular participating lender. Information that was previously private to one lender thus becomes public to all lenders, which should increase incentives for clients to repay their loans and help lenders screen candidates for loans more effectively. But does it do so, and for whom does it work best? This pairing of natural and randomized experiments allows for the identification of how new information enters on the supply and the demand sides of the market. Results indicate that the credit bureau generated large efficiency gains for lenders in helping credit agents screen applicants for loans more effectively, and that these gains were augmented when borrowers understood the rules of the game. However, the credit bureau rewarded good borrowers but penalized weaker ones. This was especially the case for women with ultimately good repayment performance but typically more erratic month-to-month repayment behavior. When this was recorded in the credit bureau, it reduced their access to loans and increased economic differentiation across genders.

3. *Roll-out of telephone towers and market performance for fishermen in Kerala.*
   Jensen (2007) gives a superb illustration of the use of a roll-out design to estimate the role of information on market performance. He studied the impact of the introduction of cell phones on fish-price dispersion, fish waste, profits, and prices paid by consumers at 15 landing sites (one every 15 km or so) along the coast of Kerala in India. Travel time means that each fisherman only has time to bring his catch to one market, and there is no storage. As phone towers were being built across regions and over periods of time (between 1997 and 2001), fishermen in covered areas could call/SMS ahead while still at sea to determine which market to go to. He observed for a five-year period (1996–2001, starting one year before the roll-out of phone towers) the weekly prices of sardines on these markets. The identification strategy is given by the roll-out, allowing a panel specification of outcomes across three regions and over four periods (period 0 before the introduction of towers, and periods 1, 2, 3 for the roll-out of towers). Descriptive statistics in Figures 4.9a and 4.9b show that the introduction of towers led to the rapid adoption of cell phones by fishermen (4.9a), and that price volatility was sharply reduced as cell phone use spread (4.9b). Results show that: (1) there was a sharp reduction in price dispersion. The coefficient of variation of prices (standard deviation over mean) fell from 60–70 percent before cell phones to 15 percent after. Prices thus converge to the law of one price, where prices do not differ across two markets by more than the cost of transportation between them. (2) There was waste reduction. (3) Profits for fishermen increased by 8 percent. (4) Prices for consumers declined by 4 percent and the consumer surplus increased

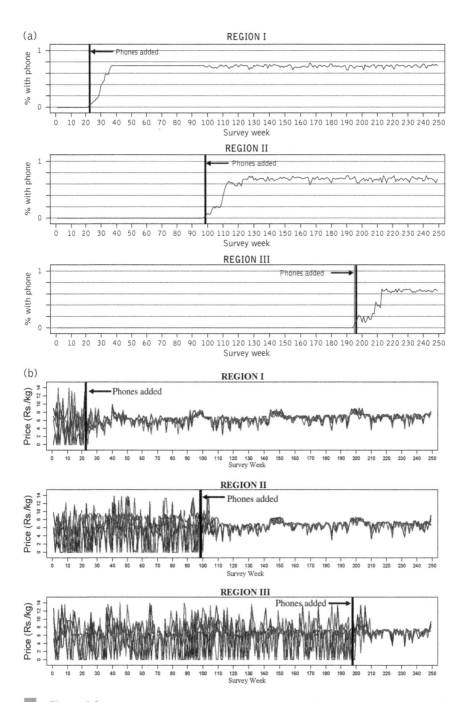

Figure 4.9 *Impact of introduction of phone towers on adoption of cell phones (a) and fish-price dispersion (b) in Kerala*

Source: Jensen (2007).

by 6 percent. Information on prices across markets, allowing fishermen to increase their hedging, thus helps markets work better and creates welfare gains for both producers and consumers. This result shows that information technology can create significant benefits for poor people.

Conclusion on roll-out and panel data

Just like in the case of the diff-in-diffs, this is a method with potentially vast application, notably to analyze the impact of large-scale policy or program initiatives that have been implemented in a staggered fashion. The main problem is that most policies are rolled out for a specific purpose and with rules that may be correlated with their expected impact. This is why it is crucial to thoroughly understand the process of the roll-out, and then to verify that prior to the program, trends in the different units of observation were similar or at least unrelated to the program, and that the program was not implemented in response to shocks to the outcome of interest. Furthermore, there is always the risk that other changes in the context or other policies affecting the outcome have taken place simultaneously with the program/policy. This is in fact almost always the case. One needs to perform robustness checks by adding these other factors as control variables in the panel regression and verifying that the estimated impact remains roughly the same.

REGRESSION DISCONTINUITY DESIGNS (RDD)

When eligibility for a treatment is determined by meeting a threshold value (such as a poverty line, an age limit, a geographical boundary, or a score in a standardized test), we can compare the outcome variable for observations just below and just above the threshold after the program has been implemented. The expectation is that people just below and just above the threshold are identical in all observable and non-observable characteristics and conditions, except for program participation. In this case, we measure a LATE that is valid around the threshold. The key assumption for the validity of the method is that the outcome would be a continuous function of the indicator used for eligibility around the threshold if it were not for the program.

A test in support of the validity of the approach is that there are no discontinuities around the threshold for relevant variables other than the treatment and the outcome variables. One can also verify that there was no such discontinuity in the outcome of interest in a period prior to the implementation of the program. The discontinuity should only appear with implementation of the intervention.

The advantage of the method is that there exist many programs that have boundary conditions in defining eligible populations. The limitation of this technique is that the impact is strictly measured only around the threshold. If we use the poverty line, comparing outcomes for people just below and above the line only helps assess the impact of the program on the marginally poor, not on the extreme poor, even though the extreme poor may be of greatest interest to the program. Examples of discontinuity designs are as follows.

Sharp discontinuity: impact of a large anti-poverty CCT program in Uruguay on political support for the government (Manacorda et al., 2011)

Do CCTs buy political support? In April 2005, a newly elected center-left government in Uruguay launched a CCT program in response to a major economic crisis, and the program lasted until December 2007. Program eligibility was determined by a poverty index (a predicted income score based on a large number of pre-treatment covariates) and only households with scores below a predetermined threshold were eligible. Households on each side of the threshold are essentially similar, but those just below received the transfer while those just above did not (Figure 4.10a). In Figure 4.10b, we observe that beneficiary households just below

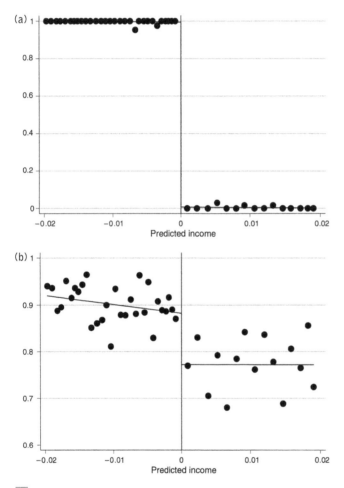

Figure 4.10 *RDD: cash transfers and political support: program eligibility and participation (a); program eligibility and political support for the government (b). Vertical axes = percentage of households that receive the transfer (a) and that express their support for the current government relative to the previous (b)*

Source: Manacorda et al., 2011.

the threshold of eligibility are more likely to favor the current government relative to those just above. The impact of the program on government support is measured by the jump in support at the threshold, as we assume that since households on each side are essentially identical they would have the same opinion were it not for the program. The estimate shows that beneficiaries are about 13 percentage points more likely to support the government compared to non-beneficiaries around the poverty threshold.

To support the validity of the design, Manacorda *et al.* (2011) apply exactly the same analysis to the various household pre-treatment characteristics that are correlated with program eligibility such as household per capita income, average years of education, size, average age, gender, years of education, and whether the person had voted at the previous election. They do not find discontinuity in any of them.

Fuzzy discontinuity: the Chinese transfer program for counties in poverty (Meng, 2013)

In some circumstances, implementation of the program has been less rigorous than that required by the discontinuity rule, and some units below the thresholds have not been incorporated in the program while others above the thresholds have been (Figure 4.11). This was the case, for example, with the Chinese 8–7 plan, a large transfer program supporting productive investment in about 600 counties in poverty implemented over the period 1994–2004. Provided that there is a large jump in the percentage of beneficiaries at the threshold, the RD approach can still be implemented, with an adaptation for the fuzziness of the discontinuity. The analysis shows that the program resulted in a substantial gain in rural income for the treated counties.

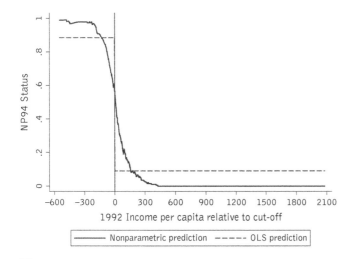

Figure 4.11 *Fuzzy discontinuity in program placement, Chinese 8–7 plan. Fraction of countries that were designated as poor on the vertical axis*

Source: Meng, 2013.

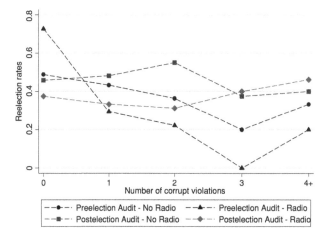

Figure 4.12 *Impact of corruption levels on incumbent mayors' re-election rates*

Source: Ferraz and Finan, 2008.

Impact of exposing corrupt politicians on electoral accountability

In 2003, Brazil's federal government introduced a system of random audits aimed at exposing corrupt practices in the use of federal funds received by municipalities. Information from these audits was disseminated to the general public. Ferraz and Finan (2008) used an RDD to assess whether audits held before the municipal elections of 2004 had an impact on electoral outcomes for incumbent mayors compared to audits held after the election in municipalities with the same levels of reported corruption. The results in Figure 4.12 indicate that audits released before the election had a significant impact on incumbents' electoral performance. These effects were more pronounced in municipalities where a local radio station broadcasted the information. The implication is that a better-informed electorate can impose greater electoral accountability on local politicians.

Conclusion on RDDs

When properly implemented and analyzed, RDDs yield an estimate of the local treatment effect that can be almost as good as a randomized experiment in measuring a treatment effect. Note that this treatment effect is a LATE, as it only applies to the units close to the threshold—and the method can only be implemented when there is a high density of units around the threshold, i.e. enough power to estimate the impact.

EVENT ANALYSIS AND EVENT-SEVERITY ANALYSIS

In general, if there is a one-time event that affects all units of analysis (households, firms, municipalities)—for example, a national policy reform—we cannot identify its impact. This is because we do not have a counterfactual for this particular event. Many things may have occurred at the same time as the reform and we cannot separate the impact of the reform from that of the other occurrences. For example, a change in fertilizer prices due to a one-time RER appreciation may affect yields, but the weather may have been good that year, contributing to the observed higher yields. We cannot attribute the observed change in the outcome of interest to the event under study.

There is however a special case where this can be done. This is when the event is concentrated in time and has a well defined and large short-run effect, the implication being that any observed change in outcome could hardly be attributed to anything else. In this case, we can simply take the change in outcome between just after and just before the event as the measure of impact. This has been applied to a study of the importance of political connections in the market valuation of the economic success of firms. The sudden death of an influential or corrupt leader can affect the share prices of firms linked to this particular politician or political party. Efficient stock markets will internalize new information in firm values almost instantly. News about Indonesian President Suharto's failing health were found by Fisman (2001) to affect the stock price of firms connected to him. The degree of connection of a firm to Suharto allows an event-severity analysis, with a higher connection expected to lead to larger price shocks. Results show that investors estimated that the value of firms with a political connection to Suharto would drop by 20 percent if he died, with the size of the price shock related to the degree of Suharto dependency.

Guidolin and La Ferrara (2007) analyzed the impact on the market value of diamond-mining firms of the sudden death of long-time rebel leader Jonas Savimbi in 2002 in Angola, ending four years of civil war. The news that war had ended led to a sharp fall in the share price of these firms. This event analysis revealed that international stock markets perceived peace as bad news for the companies that had established their operations in Angola in a context where mining revenues had been important to finance the war.

INSTRUMENTAL VARIABLES ESTIMATION: CONTROLLING FOR UNOBSERVABLES WITHOUT A COMPARISON GROUP

When participation in a program is endogenous, either because of self-selection or program placement, non-participants cannot in general be used as a comparison group for participants. However, if there is an external exogenous factor that influenced the uptake of the program but is not otherwise correlated with the outcome, one can identify the impact of the program with the instrumental variables (IV) estimation method (Figure 4.13). This external factor, called "instrument," is used to predict participation in the program. Different units will thus have a different predicted probability of participation because of the external factor. The impact on the program is then measured by comparing the outcomes of subgroups with different predicted probabilities of participation. By only using the predicted participation in the program, and not the actual participation, one avoids the possible spurious influence of the unobservables in estimating the impact of the program. The IV approach provides a LATE in the sense that it measures the impact of the program on the subgroup whose participation has been enhanced by the instrument.

179

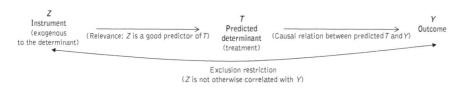

Figure 4.13 *Instrumental variables approach to causal analysis*

The conditions for the validity of this statistical method are quite demanding. The instrument must be a good predictor of the treatment (relevance) and not be correlated to the outcome through another channel (exclusion restriction). It should not influence the outcome, either directly or indirectly through another channel; it should not be influenced by the outcome; and it should not be influenced by a factor that influences the outcome. Showing that the instrument is a strong predictor of the treatment is easily done by computing the simple correlation between the instrument and the treatment; but it is impossible to test for the exclusion restriction. All we can hope for is to maintain the assumption by appealing to solid economic reasoning or introspection.

This instrumental variables estimation method is widely used to establish the causal effect of a continuous variable (such as growth, the quality of an institution, the level of education, etc.) beyond what we have narrowly defined as a program, as described in the first two examples below. A particularly interesting use of the method is to combine it with an RCT on the instrument itself. When eligibility for the program is universal, for example, but uptake is not high, one can randomly select units to receive a promotion or encouragement to participate in the program. It is a valid instrument for the uptake itself as it affects uptake (if the promotion is effective) and, by virtue of the randomization, is uncorrelated with anything that matters.

1. *Is growth failure a cause of civil conflicts?* To measure the impact of economic growth in African countries on the likelihood of civil conflict, Miguel *et al.* (2004) instrument growth by rainfall variation. The presumption is that rainfall, a clearly exogenous event, favors growth but does not directly affect the incidence of conflict. The weather instrument meets the relevance condition because rain-fed agriculture is important for African growth. However, the exclusion restriction requires that weather shocks do not directly affect civil conflict, which may be challenged by recent results on the direct impact of climate on conflict by Hsiang *et al.* (2013). The authors of the 2004 study find that a weather-induced 5-percentage-point decline in growth increases the likelihood of conflict by one half the following year. They also find that the impact of income shocks on civil conflict is not significantly different in African countries with a wide range of institutional, political, social, and economic characteristics.

2. *Are "good" institutions a source of growth?* To explain the role of institutions on income per capita, Acemoglu *et al.* (2001) used differences in mortality rates among European settlers some 500 years earlier to instrument current institutions. The presumption is that where mortality was high and Europeans could not

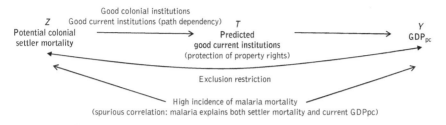

Figure 4.14 *Instrumental variables and risk of spurious correlation*

settle they introduced extractive institutions, in contrast to where they could settle and introduced inclusive institutions (secure property rights, protection from abuse of power by elites and politicians, and broadly egalitarian opportunities) prone to economic growth. The validity of the instrumentation requires that the exclusion restriction be met: settler mortality does not directly predict GDPpc. As can be seen in Figure 4.14, this is thrown into doubt if, as shown by Gallup and Sachs (2001), mortality and GDPpc are both explained by the persistent effect of malaria on mortality and growth.

3. *Do investments in school infrastructure improve educational outcome?* In 1991, the Bolivian Social Investment Fund funded small-scale investment in education, health, and water infrastructure. While the offer was universal, within some criteria of eligibility, this program was demand-driven in that communities had to apply, and not all eligible communities took up the program. As part of the evaluation of the program, communities in one area were randomly selected to receive active promotion of the program, with information and visits from the program staff. This promotion was then used as an instrument for uptake of the program by the communities. Results found that education investments succeeded in improving the quality of school infrastructure and material but not the educational outcome except for a small decrease in dropout rate (Newman *et al.*, 2002).

Randomized promotion (also called an encouragement design) is a useful strategy for evaluating the impact of voluntary programs, and of programs with universal eligibility, as it does not interfere with the program and does not impose exclusion. It has, however, limitations. First, the promotion needs to be effective to substantially change the uptake of the program. Second, as with any instrumental variables method, it estimates the impact of the program on the communities that were induced to sign up with the program by the promotion, and these may be quite different from the communities that signed on even without promotion, or those that did not even respond to the promotion.

Conclusion on the instrumental variables approach

The method of instrumental variables allows for the estimation of the impact of a treatment when the treatment is endogenous. To be valid, however, the instrumental variable must not only be correlated with the treatment but also be uncorrelated with any factor that influences the outcome of interest. It is therefore extremely difficult to find a valid instrument.

We should not forget that the instrumented causal variable only explains the outcome in terms of its variation due to the instrument. If, for example, we instrument rural–urban migration with weather shocks in the rural area, then the migration that explains the outcome (e.g. the prevailing urban wage) is only the migration induced by the bad weather shock (called push migration) as opposed to the more normal pull migration induced by superior earning opportunities in the urban environment.

MAKING IMPACT EVALUATION MORE USEFUL FOR POLICY PURPOSES

A great deal of attention is given in impact evaluation to internal validity. This consists in showing that the control group has been properly chosen against the treatment group within the selected population of eligible control individuals, households, institutions, or communities. But usefulness for policy purposes requires that results also achieve some reasonable level of external validity with respect to the broader population of eligible individuals, households, institutions, or communities. Establishing the external validity of an impact can be obtained by replicating the experiment over different selections of eligibles, by estimating behavioral parameters (e.g. elasticities), by exploiting heterogeneity in impact, or by planning experimentation across a variety of contexts. Cai *et al.* (2015), for example, establish the validity of demand for insurance over different market conditions by estimating the full demand function over a range of prices. The role of municipality characteristics on the impact of Bolsa Escola can be established by measuring a separate impact for each municipality, and correlating estimated impacts with municipal characteristics to establish external validity across municipalities (de Janvry *et al.*, 2012). Facilitating the replication of experiments over a broad set of contexts to establish the external validity of policy interventions was one of the reasons for creating the Innovation for Policy Action (IPA) that is currently operating in more than 30 countries (Karlan and Appel, 2011).

REGISTERING A PRE-ANALYSIS PLAN

One source of bias in empirical research is selective reporting by the researcher of favorable results while ignoring negative results, a process referred to as "data mining," or "cherry picking," that has long plagued econometric analysis. This leads to an excess of false positive results, namely of positive results that cannot subsequently be replicated. It also leads to report results that apply positively to a subset of the population identified by data mining, without reporting that they do not hold or hold contrarily in other subsets. To avoid this, many sources of social-science research funding now require the filing of a pre-analysis plan (PAP), something that has long been in place for medical and pharmaceutical research. By law in the US, all clinical trials have to be pre-registered. In this pre-analysis plan, researchers must indicate how the data will be collected and analyzed in advance of their seeing the data (Miguel *et al.*, 2014). This is now increasingly demanded for RCTs in the social sciences due to their analogy with clinical research.

To limit bias in reported results, the PAP must specify how the data will be collected and used to test hypotheses, and be deposited in a hypothesis registry. PAP registries exist with the American Economic Association Randomized Control Trial Registry, the Jameel Poverty Action Lab (J-PAL), EGAP (Experiments in Governance and Politics), and 3ie (International Initiative for Impact Evaluation). The PAP is not publicly available, but must be released by the researcher at the time of the presentation of the results.

Casey *et al.* (2012) give the example of the evaluation of a CDD program in Sierra Leone, the GoBifo supported by the World Bank. It was implemented as an RCT with 118 treatment and 118 control villages, and had the purpose of not only delivering local public goods, but also making local institutions more democratic and egalitarian. The CDD did this by imposing requirements for the participation of marginalized groups and women to the allocation of program resources. The authors' PAP specified which measures of involvement of marginalized groups in collective action were to be used to test this hypothesis. In the data, there were 334 measures of key outcomes that could have been used to test the hypothesis of impact on local institutions. Among these, seven could have been picked to make it look as though the program strengthened local institutions, and another six to make it look as though it weakened institutions. By confining themselves to the PAP (in other words, by tying their hand when it came to data mining and cherry picking), the authors found a positive short-run effect on local public goods such as schools and latrines, but no evidence of sustained impacts on collective action, participatory decision-making, or the involvement of marginalized groups. Cherry picking, on the other hand, could have demonstrated the strengthening or weakening of local institutions. This result runs contrary to conventional wisdom in the development community on the value of the CDD approach in catalyzing collective action and democratizing local decision-making. The result suggests that CDDs in fact do not alter traditional local structures of authority that can regain control over decision-making beyond allocation of program resources.

The PAP approach has both benefits and costs for research. The main benefit is the avoidance of data mining and bias in reporting. Elaborating the PAP also helps researchers to specify their experiment more effectively: the sample to be used, the data to be collected, the hypotheses and models to be tested, the treatment equation to be estimated, the procedure to be used to deal with survey attrition, the robustness tests to be run, etc. This helps improve the design of the questionnaire and avoids omitting variables that will subsequently be key to the analysis. If a hypothesis is specified as a one-sided test, it increases the power of the test for a given database. The pre-analysis also facilitates a quicker move into data analysis.

The costs of the PAP may be to limit the analysis to that which can be anticipated at the time of designing the experiment, reducing subsequent surprises and discoveries revealed by the data. For this reason, a PAP is more adequate for confirmatory than for exploratory research. The PAP as such does not reduce the number of false hypotheses produced and taken to the data—and it does not increase the robustness of results that need more data to be collected and more results to be replicated (Coffman and Niederle, 2014). For this reason, use of a PAP must be carefully weighted between benefits and costs. While generally useful for RCTs that are implemented to test well defined hypotheses, it should not be imposed by donors on all research projects.

QUALITATIVE METHODS

Qualitative methods complement quantitative methods in assessing impact (Kanbur, 2001). Qualitative methods can help researchers gain insights from beneficiaries and program administrators on what works and does not work in a project, and why. For example, they can help understand the reasons why qualifying individuals participate and, especially, do not participate in a program, and they can help identify the perceived effects of different interventions. These analyses, however, also need to be designed in a way that brings forward the contrast between beneficiaries and non beneficiaries. Narayan's *Voices of the Poor* (2000), with information collected in extensive interviews and focus groups on some 40,000 poor (and non-poor) people, gives us insights into the nature and determinants of poverty that can be influenced by personal or political interests. Ideally, voices of the poor should be contrasted with voices of the no-longer poor so the experience of those who escaped from poverty can be contrasted with those who remained in poverty. Qualitative methods thus need design to inform us about presumed causal determinants of observed outcomes.

Qualitative methods can be used before quantitative analysis, preferably before a survey is conducted. They are useful for formulating hypotheses for the quantitative relationships, for defining the information that needs to be collected in a survey, and for identifying the main dimensions of heterogeneity of impact. After the quantitative analysis or, preferably, during it, they can assess the plausibility of the results and help to interpret them—especially the presumed channels through which impact has occurred—and refine the hypotheses.

CONCEPTS SEEN IN THIS CHAPTER

Counterfactual

Treatment and control groups

Randomized control trial (RCT)

Internal and external validity

Power of the test

Hawthorne and John Henry effects

Spillover effects

Average Treatment Effect (ATE)

Intention to Treat (ITT)

Propensity score matching (PSM)

Common support

Average Treatment Effect on the Treated (ToT)

Difference–in–differences (diff-in-diffs)

Test of parallel trends

Staggered entry and panel analysis

Regression discontinuity designs (RDD)

Local Average Treatment Effect (LATE)

Sharp and fuzzy discontinuities

Event analysis

Instrumental variables approach (IV)

Exclusion restriction in using instrumental variables

Robustness checks

Falsification tests

Qualitative methods

REVIEW QUESTIONS: IMPACT EVALUATION AND DEVELOPMENT INTERVENTIONS

1. What is a counterfactual? Why do we need a counterfactual to do an impact analysis of a development intervention?
2. Why is a randomized control trial often considered to be the most rigorous approach to impact evaluation? In this case, how is the counterfactual defined? How is impact measured?
3. Propensity score matching is often used when no baseline survey was done. How is the counterfactual defined? What are some of the caveats of the approach?
4. Difference–in–differences is the most widely used method. Give an example. How do we reassure ourselves that the counterfactual is adequate?
5. The roll-out of a program opens an opportunity for estimating its impact. What are the conditions for the validity of this method? What tests are done to support the validity of the method?
6. Discontinuity designs are often sought in natural experiments. How is the counterfactual defined? Give an example. What are some of the limitations of the approach?
7. When can you use the instrumental variables estimation method? What are the conditions for the validity of the instrument?

NOTE

1 The *Progresa* CCT is described in Chapter 14.

REFERENCES

Acemoglu, Daron, Simon Johnson, and James Robinson. 2001. "The Colonial Origins of Comparative Development: An Empirical Investigation." *American Economic Review* 91(5): 1369–401.

Angrist, Joshua, Eric Bettinger, Erik Bloom, Elizabeth King, and Michael Kremer. 2002. "Vouchers for Private Schooling in Colombia: Evidence from a Randomized Natural Experiment." *American Economic Review* 92(5): 1535–58.

Arellano, Manuel, and Stephen Bond. 1991. "Some Tests of Specification for Panel Data: Monte Carlo Evidence and an Application to Employment Equations." *Review of Economic Studies* 58(2): 277–97.

Ashenfelter, Orley. 1978. "Estimating the Effect of Training Programs on Earnings." *Review of Economics and Statistics* 60(1): 47–57.

Baird, Sarah, Aislinn Bohren, Craig McIntosh, and Berk Özler. 2014. "Designing Experiments to Measure Spillover Effects." Washington, DC: World Bank Policy Research Working Paper No. 6824.

Ban, Radu, and Vijayendra Rao. 2008. "Tokenism or Agency? The Impact of Women's Reservations on Village Democracies in South India." *Economic Development and Cultural Change* 56(3): 501–30.

Banerjee, Abhijit, and Esther Duflo. 2009. "The Experimental Approach to Development Economics." *Annual Review of Economics* 1(1): 151–178.

Banerjee, Abhijit, Esther Duflo, Rachel Glennerster, and Cynthia Kinnan. 2015. "The Miracle of Microfinance? Evidence From a Randomized Evaluation." *American Economic Journal: Applied Economics* 7(1): 22–53.

Barrett, Christopher, and Michael Carter. 2010. "The Power and Pitfalls of Experiments in Development Economics: Some Non-random Reflection." *Applied Economic Perspectives and Policy* 32(4): 515–48.

Barro, Robert. 1991. "Economic Growth in a Cross Section of Countries." *Quarterly Journal of Economics* 106(2): 407–43.

Barro, Robert. 1996. "Determinants of Economic Growth: A Cross-Country Empirical Study." Cambridge, MA: NBER Working Paper No. 5698.

Barro, Robert, and Rachel McCleary. 2003. "Religion and Economic Growth." *American Sociological Review* 68: 760–81.

Bazzi, Samuel, and Michael Clemens. 2012. "Blunt Instruments: Avoiding Common Pitfalls in Identifying the Causes of Economic Growth." *American Economic Journal: Macroeconomics* 5(2): 152–86.

Bleakley, Hoyt. 2010. "Malaria Eradication in the Americas: A Retrospective Analysis of Childhood Exposure." *American Economic Journal: Applied Economics* 2(2): 1–45.

Bloom, Nicholas, Benn Eifert, Aprajit Mahajan, David McKenzie, and John Roberts. 2013. "Does Management Matter? Evidence from India." *Quarterly Journal of Economics* 128(1): 1–51.

Bobonis, Gustavo, and Frederico Finan. 2009. "Neighborhood Peer Effects in Secondary School Enrollment Decisions." *Review of Economics and Statistics* 91(4): 695–716.

Burke, Paul, and Andrew Leigh. 2010. "Do Output Contractions Trigger Democratic Change?" *American Economic Journal: Macroeconomics* 2(4): 124–57.

186

Burnside, Craig, and David Dollar. 2000. "Aid, Policies, and Growth." *American Economic Review* 90(4): 847–68.

Cai, Jing, Alain de Janvry, and Elisabeth Sadoulet. 2015. "Social Networks and the Decision to Insure." *American Economic Journal: Applied Economics* 7(2):81–108.

Casey, Katherine, Rachel Glennerster, and Edward Miguel. 2012. "Reshaping Institutions: Evidence on Aid Impacts Using a Pre-Analysis Plan." *Quarterly Journal of Economics* 127(4): 1755–812.

Chattopadhyay, Raghabendra, and Esther Duflo. 2004. "Women as Policy Makers: Evidence from a Randomized Policy Experiment in India." *Econometrica* 72(5): 1409–43.

Ciccone, Antonio, and Marek Jarocinski. 2010. "Determinants of Economic Growth: Will Data Tell?" *American Economic Journal: Macroeconomics* 2(4): 222–46.

Clingingsmith, David, Asim Ijaz Khwaja, and Michael Kremer, Harvard. 2009. "Estimating the Impact of the Hajj: Religion and Tolerance in Islam's Global Gathering." *Quarterly Journal of Economics*, 124(3): 1133–70.

Coffman, Lucas, and Muriel Niederle. 2014. "Pre-Analysis Plans are Not the Solution. Replications Might Be." Working paper, Economics Department, Ohio State University.

Deaton, Angus. 2010. "Instruments, Randomization, and Learning about Development." *Journal of Economic Literature* 48(2): 424–55.

de Janvry, Alain, and Elisabeth Sadoulet. 2006. "Making Conditional Cash Transfers More Efficient: Designing for Maximum Effect of the Conditionality." *World Bank Economic Review* 20(1): 1–29.

de Janvry, Alain, Craig McIntosh, and Elisabeth Sadoulet. 2010. "The Supply- and Demand-Side Impacts of Credit Market Information." *Journal of Development Economics* 93(2): 173–88.

de Janvry, Alain, Frederico Finan, Elisabeth Sadoulet. 2012. "Local Electoral Incentives and Decentralized Program Performance." *Review of Economics and Statistics* 94(3): 672–85.

Duflo, Esther. 2001. "Schooling and Labor Market Consequences of School Construction in Indonesia: Evidence from an Unusual Policy Experiment." *American Economic Review* 91(4): 795–813.

Duflo, Esther. 2006. "Field Experiments in Development Economics." In Richard Blundell, Whitney Newey, Torsten Persson (eds.), *Advances in Economics and Econometrics: Theory and Applications, Ninth World Congress*, Vol. 2(42): 322–348. Cambridge: Cambridge University Press. (See also BREAD Policy Paper No. 002, 2005).

Duflo, Esther, Rachel Glennerster, and Michael Kremer. 2008. "Using Randomization in Development Economics Research: A Toolkit." In T. Paul Schultz and John Strauss (eds.), *Handbook of Development Economics* Vol. 4: 3895–962. Amsterdam: Elsevier.

Easterly, William. 2006. *The White Man's Burden: Why the West's Efforts to Aid the Rest Have Done So Much Ill and So Little Good.* New York: Penguin Press.

Ferraz, Claudio, and Frederico Finan. 2008. "Exposing Corrupt Politicians: The Effect of Brazil's Publicly Released Audits on Electoral Outcomes." *Quarterly Journal of Economics* 123(2): 703–45.

Field, Erica. 2007. "Entitled to Work: Urban Tenure Security and Labor Supply in Peru." *Quarterly Journal of Economics* 4(122): 1561–1602.

Field, Erica, and Rohini Pande. 2008 "Repayment Frequency and Default in Micro-Finance: Evidence from India." *Journal of European Economic Association Papers and Proceeding* 6(2-3): 501–9.

Fischer, Stanley. 1993. "The Role of Macroeconomic Factors in Growth." Cambridge, MA: NBER Working Paper No. 4565.

Fisman, Raymond. 2001. "Estimating the Value of Political Connections." *American Economic Review* 91(4): 1095–102.

Galiani, Sebastian, Paul Gertler, and Ernesto Schargrodsky. 2005. "Water for Life: The Impact of the Privatization of Water Services on Child Mortality." *Journal of Political Economy* 113(1): 83–120.

Gallup, John, and Jeffrey Sachs. 2001. "The Economic Burden of Malaria." *American Journal of Tropical Medicine and Hygiene* 64(1 Suppl): 85–96.

Gertler, Paul, Sebastian Martinez, Patrick Premand, Laura Rawlings, and Christel Vermeersch. 2011. *Impact Evaluation in Practice.* Washington, DC: World Bank.

Glewwe, Paul, Michael Kremer, and Sylvie Moulin. 2009. "Many Children Left Behind? Textbooks and Test Scores in Kenya." *American Economic Journal: Applied Economics* 1(1): 112–35.

Guidolin, Massimo, and Eliana La Ferrara. 2007. "Diamonds Are Forever, Wars Are Not: Is Conflict Bad for Private Firms?" *American Economic Review* 97(5): 1978–93.

Hsiang, Solomon, Marshall Burke, and Edward Miguel. 2013. "Quantifying the Influence of Climate on Human Conflict." *Science* 341: 1212.

Imbens, Guido, and Jeffrey Wooldridge. 2009. "Recent Developments in the Econometrics of Program Evaluation." *Journal of Economic Literature* 47(1): 5–86.

Jalan, Jyotsna, and Martin Ravallion. 2003a. "Estimating the Benefit Incidence of an Antipoverty Program by Propensity-Score Matching." *Journal of Business and Economic Statistics* 21(1): 19–30.

Jalan, Jyotsna, and Martin Ravallion. 2003b. "Does Piped Water Reduce Diarrhea for Children in Rural India?" *Journal of Econometrics* 112(1): 153–73.

Jensen, Robert. 2007. "The Digital Provide: Information (Technology), Market Performance and Welfare in the South Indian Fisheries Sector." *Quarterly Journal of Economics* 122(3): 879–924.

Jensen, Robert. 2010. "The (Perceived) Returns to Education and the Demand for Schooling." *Quarterly Journal of Economics* 125(2): 515–48.

Kanbur, Ravi. 2001. "Q-SQUARED? A Commentary on Qualitative and Quantitative Poverty Appraisal." Conference held at Department of Economics, Cornell University.

Karlan, Dean, and Jacob Appel. 2011. *More than Good Intentions: How a New Economics is Helping to Solve Global Poverty.* New York: Dutton.

Khwaja, Asim Ijaz, and Atif Mian. 2008. "Tracing the Impact of Bank Liquidity Shocks: Evidence from an Emerging Market." *American Economic Review* 98(4): 1413–42.

Lai, Fang, Elisabeth Sadoulet, and Alain de Janvry. 2011. "The Contributions of School Quality and Teacher Qualifications to Student Performance: Evidence from a Natural Experiment in Beijing Middle Schools." *Journal of Human Resources* 46(1): 123–53.

Landsberger, Henry. 1958. *Hawthorne Revisited.* Ithaca, NY: Cornell University Press.

Levine, Ross, and David Renelt. 1992. "A Sensitivity Analysis of Cross-Country Growth Regressions." *American Economic Review* 82(4): 942–63.

Levy, Santiago. 2006. *Progress Against Poverty: Sustaining Mexico's Progresa-Oportunidades Program.* Washington, DC: Brookings Institution Press.

Manacorda, Marco, Edward Miguel, and Andrea Vigorito. 2011. "Government Transfers and Political Support." *American Economic Journal: Applied Economics* 3(3): 1–28.

Mauro, Paolo. 1995. "Corruption and Growth." *Quarterly Journal of Economics* 110(3): 681–712.

Meng, Lingsheng. 2013. "Evaluating China's Poverty Alleviation Program: A Regression Discontinuity Approach." Working paper, Department of Economics, School of Economics and Management, Tsinghua University.

Miguel, E., C. Camerer, K. Casey, J. Cohen, K. M. Esterling, A. Gerber, R. Glennerster, D. P. Green, M. Humphreys, G. Imbens, D. Laitin, T. Madon, L. Nelson, B. A. Nosek, M. Petersen, R. Sedlmayr, J. P. Simmons, U. Simonsohn, and M. Van der Laan. 2014. "Promoting Transparency in Social Science Research." *Science* 10.1126/ science.1245317.

Miguel, Edward, and Michael Kremer. 2004. "Worms: Identifying Impacts on Education and Health in the Presence of Treatment Externalities." *Econometrica* 72(1): 159–217.

Miguel, Edward, Shanker Satyanath, and Ernest Sergenti. 2004. "Economic Shocks and Civil Conflict: An Instrumental Variables Approach." *Journal of Political Economy* 112(4): 725–53.

Narayan, Deepa. 2000. *Voices of the Poor: Can Anyone Hear Us?* New York: Oxford University Press.

Newman, J., M. Pradhan, L. B. Rawlings, G. Ridder, R. Coa, J. L. Evia, (2002). "An Impact Evaluation of Education, Health, and Water Supply Investments by the Bolivian Social Investment Fund." *World Bank Economic Review*, vol. 16(2): 241–74.

Nunn, Nathan. 2008. "The Long-term Effects of Africa's Slave Trades." *Quarterly Journal of Economics* 123(1): 139–76.

O'Neill, Donal. 1995. "Education and Income Growth: Implications for Cross-Country Inequality." *Journal of Political Economy* 103(6): 1289–301.

OECD. 2014. International Development Statistics (IDS) online databases. http://www.oecd.org/dac/stats/idsonline.htm (accessed 2015).

Ravallion, Martin. 2012. "Fighting Poverty One Experiment at a Time: *Poor Economics: A Radical Rethinking of the Way to Fight Global Poverty*: Review Essay." *Journal of Economic Literature* 50(1): 103–14.

Rodrik, Dani, 2012. "Why We Learn Nothing from Regressing Economic Growth on Policies." *Seoul Journal of Economics* 25(2): 137–51.

Sachs, Jeffrey, and Andrew Warner. 1995. "Economic Reform and the Process of Global Integration." *Brookings Papers on Economic Activity* 1: 1–118.

Squire, Lyn, and Herman van der Tak. 1975. *Economic Analysis of Projects*. Baltimore: Johns Hopkins University Press.

Thornton, Rebecca. 2008. "The Demand for, and Impact of, Learning HIV Status." *American Economic Review* 98(5): 1829–63.

Topalova, Petia, and Amit Khandelwal. 2011. "Trade Liberalization and Firm Productivity: The Case of India." *Review of Economics and Statistics* 93(3): 995–1009.

Wacziarg, Romain, and Karen Horn Welch. 2008. "Trade Liberalization and Growth: New Evidence." *World Bank Economic Review* 22(2): 187–231.

Econometrics of impact analysis

In this appendix, we outline the econometric analysis to be pursued in using each of the impact methods reviewed in the chapter.

RANDOMIZATION

Let y_i = outcome variable for individual i, $T_i = 1$ if i is in the treatment group, $T_i = 0$ if i is in the control group. Using regression analysis, we estimate:

$$y_i = \alpha + \delta T_i + \varepsilon_i.$$

The randomization insures that $E(\varepsilon_i | T_i = 1) = E(\varepsilon_i | T_i = 0)$ which is the condition for $\hat{\delta}$ to be an unbiased estimator of the impact. This is an average treatment effect (ATE).

We check the validity of the randomization by testing the equality of means of characteristics Z between the T and C groups. This is done by a test of difference in means or a regression similar to that above. Validity of the randomization is established if not more than 5 percent of the differences are significantly different from zero at the 5 percent significance level.

We can use observable covariates Z to add precision to the estimation and to verify, as a robustness check, that $\hat{\delta}$ is invariant to the introduction of covariates in the regression:

$$y_i = \alpha + \delta T_i + Z_i\beta + \varepsilon_i$$

We can also measure heterogeneity of the program effect for individuals with specific characteristics z (such as gender, age, education, socio-economic status, etc.) by interacting these characteristics with the treatment variable. We now estimate:

$$y_i = \alpha + \delta T_i + Z_i\beta + \gamma z_i + \phi T_i z_i + \varepsilon_i$$

In this equation, the estimated impact on individuals with characteristics z_i is $\hat{\delta} + \hat{\phi} z_i$.

PROPENSITY SCORE MATCHING

1. Get representative and comparable data on participants and non-participants, possibly from two different surveys using identical questionnaires and collected

roughly at the same time. The survey must include all variables X that are important determinants of both program participation and outcomes.

2. Estimate the probability p of program participation as a function of observable characteristics X (using a logit or other discrete choice model):

$p(X) = \Pr(T \mid X)$.

3. Use the estimated coefficients to generate the predicted value $\hat{p}(X_i)$, called the propensity score, for each member i of the treatment and comparison groups.

4. Matching: for each participant i, find the non-participant j with closest value of the propensity score $\hat{p}(X_j) \approx \hat{p}(X_i)$ where $\approx$ means approximately equal. To make this more effective:

■ Restrict the samples to ensure *common support*, i.e. only keep the range of values for the propensity score that includes both participants and non-participants, as shown in Figure 4.A1. With a large area of common support you can be confident that participants and non-participants are quite similar, and hence that the matching on observables is indeed credible.

■ Determine a *tolerance limit*: How different can matched control observations be? E.g., only match observations that have a difference $\left| \hat{p}(X_i) - \hat{p}(X_j) \right| < 0.001$

5. Once matches have been made, the difference in outcome between each participant and its match is the estimated gain due to the program for that observation. Calculate the mean of these individual gains to obtain the average overall gain for

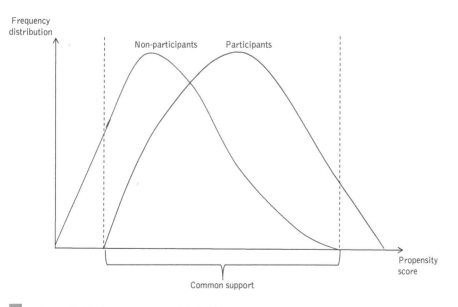

Figure 4.A1 *Common support in PSM*

participants. This is the Average Treatment Effect on the Treated (ToT) since it is measured on a representative sample of participants.

DIFFERENCE-IN-DIFFERENCES

To measure impact as a difference-in-differences effect in a regression framework, let: $After_i = 0$ if observation i is from the base line survey, $After_i = 1$ if it is from the follow-up survey, $T_i = 1$ if observation i is in the treatment group, $T_i = 0$ if it is in the comparison group.

The impact δ is estimated by regressing y on T, $After$, and the product T $After$:

$$y_i = \alpha + \beta T_i + \gamma After_i + \delta T_i After_i + \varepsilon_i.$$

We can verify that:

$$\bar{y}_{T1} = \alpha + \beta + \gamma + \delta$$
$$\bar{y}_{T0} = \alpha + \beta$$
$$\bar{y}_{C1} = \alpha + \gamma$$
$$\bar{y}_{C0} = \alpha$$

Hence, the difference in differences is:

$$(\bar{y}_{T1} - \bar{y}_{T0}) - (\bar{y}_{C1} - \bar{y}_{C0}) = \delta,$$

which measures the Average Treatment Effect (ATE).

The validity of the method is based on the assumption that the change observed in the comparison group is a good counterfactual for the change observed in the treatment group. To support this assumption, one needs to verify that these two groups changed similarly in the period prior to the program (this is sometimes referred to as the parallel-trends verification). This is done by estimating the same equation as above with two observations prior to the treatment and verifying that δ is not significantly different from 0 and small (i.e. a precise zero).

STAGGERED ENTRY WITH PANEL DATA: ROLL-OUT OF A PROGRAM

This is a generalization of the difference-in-differences method to a succession of time periods with staggered entry of units into the program. In a panel regression framework, the estimated equation is:

$$y_{it} = \delta T_{it} + \mu_i + \gamma_t + \varepsilon_{it},$$

where:

μ_i are fixed effects for each unit i (to account for cross-sectional differences in the level of outcome y);

γ_t are time-fixed effects for each period t (to account for changes over time common to all units); and

T_{it} is the treatment variable, equal to 1 after the unit has entered the program, and 0 before.

Support for the validity of the assumption of identical changes over time in treated and untreated units is given by showing that:

- The pre-program trends are not correlated with the order of entry in the program.

This can be tested by a regression such as:

$$(y_{it} - y_{it-1}) = \alpha + \beta Entry_i + \gamma_t + \varepsilon_{it},$$

where $Entry_i$ is the time period at which unit i entered the program, applied to all the periods prior to the first entry into the program.

- Entry into the program is not associated with a lagged performance. This is done by adding one variable into the panel equation:

$$y_{it} = \delta T_{it} + \beta L_{it} + \mu_i + \gamma_t + \varepsilon_{it},$$

where L_{it} is equal to 1 for the time period just before unit i entered the program.

- Adding other variables X_{it} that may have an influence on the outcome y, and verifying that the estimated value of δ is robust to this addition in:

$$y_{it} = \delta T_{it} + X_{it}\beta + \mu_i + \gamma_t + \varepsilon_{it}.$$

REGRESSION DISCONTINUITY

Let I be the indicator on which the eligibility threshold is defined, with the critical value for eligibility set at 0. We can estimate the impact δ with the equation:

$$y_i = \alpha + \delta T_i + f_1(I_i) + (I_i > 0) f_2(I_i) + \varepsilon_i,$$

where $f_1(I_i)$ and $f_1(I_i)$ are polynomials in the indicator that are different before and after the threshold. δ is a LATE since the internal validity of the measured impact is only over a small interval around the threshold.

There is sometimes fuzzy discontinuity in that the eligibility rule is not strictly enforced, with some people participating on the wrong side of the threshold and vice versa. In this case, participation needs to be predicted using the rules of program eligibility as predictors, in an instrumental variable estimation.

Support for the validity of the assumption that the outcome variable would be continuous over the threshold is provided by estimating the same equation for variables that are not affected by the program, and verifying that δ is not significantly different from 0 and small (i.e. a precise zero).

EVENT ANALYSIS

Say that you consider an event E that took place at a precisely defined time, which for simplicity we note t. The event analysis will use a measure of the change in outcome Δy_i for unit i between time $t - \eta$ and $t + \eta$, i.e. over a short window of time around the event. Each unit (firm, household, etc.) is characterized by an intensity of relationship/dependency to the event z_i. The impact of the event is simply estimated by regressing Δy_i on z_i:

$$\Delta y_i = \alpha + \delta z_i + \varepsilon_i.$$

The underlying assumption for the validity of the method is that there are no unobservable factors (included in ε_i) that are correlated with the degree of dependency on the event and can explain the differential changes in outcome over such a short time period. Essentially, what is assumed here is that while each unit may have received some shocks within that very narrow window of time that explain a rapid change in outcome, these have no reason to be correlated with the degree of dependency to the event unless they are due to the event.

The main test to support the validity is to repeat the same analysis over other small windows of time before the event, and verify that the estimated coefficients are precise zero, suggesting that the estimated impact does not capture a fundamental difference in the dynamic behavior of the units. This is very similar to the diff-in-diffs method, although done over a very short window around a dramatic event.

INSTRUMENTAL VARIABLES ESTIMATION

Starting from the initial model to be estimated:

$$y = \alpha + \delta T + X\beta + \varepsilon,$$

where y denotes the outcome of interest, T the treatment variable (which can be discrete or continuous), X observable factors that explain y, and ε the error term that contains all the unobservable factors that influence y. A key condition for the OLS to deliver an unbiased estimator for δ is that ε be uncorrelated with T and X. When this is not the case, we can still use this equation to estimate δ provided we can find an instrument z for T. The instrument is a variable that is correlated with T, but uncorrelated with ε. We can thus think of estimating a simple regression:

$$T = \lambda + \pi z + X\gamma + v$$

and predict $\hat{T} = \hat{\lambda} + \hat{\pi} z + X\hat{\gamma}$ (that is, we have one such value for each observation). By construction, the prediction $\hat{T}$ is uncorrelated with ε. We can then run the initial regression using $\hat{T}$ instead of T.

$$y = \alpha + \delta \hat{T} + X\beta + \varepsilon,$$

where the error term ε is now uncorrelated with $\hat{T}$ and X.

Note that if the omitted variable problem was serious, the estimated parameter with this method can be quite different from that estimated with the OLS. However, if the instrument is weak (does not correlate strongly with T) or imperfectly uncorrelated with ε, then the IV estimation can be worse than OLS. If we find several instruments, the analysis can be strengthened by using them jointly.

Caveats with the IV approach:

■ It is very difficult to find an instrument that meets the two conditions of relevance and exclusion. The IV method that appears as a panacea because it is so easy to conceptualize will rarely resist scrutiny. An example is the Acemoglu *et al.* (2001) IV strategy that looked initially pretty ingenious, but was subsequently heavily criticized.

■ A statistical test of over–identification (OID) restrictions is to show that if one instrument is valid, others may be valid as well. It does not, however, give us a test of the validity of the first instrument.

■ Lagged variables are not good instruments (as in the Arellano and Bond (1991) method frequently used in cross–country regressions, discussed below) if there are lagged omitted variables that have persistent effects.

■ The best source to find an instrument is a theory as to why it may be valid, not statistical validation.

Macro-level impact evaluation
The rise and fall of cross-country regressions

THE TEMPTATIONS OF CROSS-COUNTRY REGRESSIONS

We have seen how to estimate a causal relation between X and Y at the micro level. The units of analysis were typically students, teachers, households, classrooms, firms, villages, branches of a microfinance institution, and municipalities. Many important development questions are raised at country level, particularly regarding policy interventions. For this, the unit of analysis is the country, and the empirical analysis would be cross-country, seeking to estimate how a country-level X causally explains a country-level outcome Y, frequently GDP or GDP growth. There has indeed been a very large field of macro-level development-economics research using cross-country regressions. This is tempting as we now have many online databases that give us cross-country data over time. Well known data sets for cross-country analysis include the Summers-Heston data set (the Penn World Table: www.pwt.econ.upenn.edu) and the World Bank's *World Development Indicators*, which we use extensively in this book.

It is then possible to ask a whole set of big questions about the determinants of development outcomes. Some of the well known studies that attempted to answer the following questions:

- Does trade liberalization affect economic growth? Sachs and Warner (1995), Wacziarg and Welch (2008).
- Does investment in education lead to higher economic growth? Barro (1991, a paper with more than 10,000 citations), Barro (1996, a paper with more than 3,000 citations), O'Neill (1995).
- Does corruption affect growth? Mauro (1995), Barro (1996).
- Does foreign aid affect growth? Burnside and Dollar (2000).
- Does inflation affect growth? Fischer (1993).
- Does religion affect growth? Barro and McCleary (2003).

We can of course replace growth by any of the other development outcomes (poverty, inequality, vulnerability, basic needs, sustainability, quality of life) and run the regressions again. Regressions can also be run with inequality as the X and poverty as the Y, etc., and all possible combinations, a large source of papers indeed. An example is the Kuznets inverted-U curve that we studied in Chapter 6 that relates inequality to GDPpc level.

Some of the big X variables are exogenous shocks such as weather events, but most are national policies or institutions, as listed above. Clearly, these causalities could not be studied at the micro level. If they hold at a world scale, they are the ultimate achievement in external validity. No wonder that cross-country regressions have generated so much enthusiasm and continue to be so present in many economics journals. But are they statistically valid? The big issue is exogeneity of the X determinants—and the big answer is that they most often are not, casting doubt on the validity of the policy implications derived from the analysis.

ECONOMETRIC ISSUES IN CROSS-COUNTRY REGRESSIONS

Cross-country cross-sectional regressions

The basic cross-country regression is written as follows:

$$\left(\frac{GDP_i^{new} - GDP_i^{old}}{GDP_i^{old}} \right) = \alpha + \beta GDP_i^{old} + \delta X_i + Z_i \gamma + \varepsilon_i,$$

where i is the country index, GDP_i^{old} a base period level of GDP, GDP_i^{new} the current level of GDP, X the policy variable of interest (such as trade liberalization, education, etc.), and Z other country indicators. δ is the effect of changing one unit of X on the growth rate. There are two difficulties with this specification:

1. The relationship is often fragile as the regression is influenced by a few outlying country data points and by the control variables arbitrarily included in the regressions. Results will often change by adding or removing a control variable (Levine and Renelt, 1992) and also by removing or adding specific countries (Ciccone and Jarocinski, 2010). It is important here to plot the data so we see the role of particular country data points in influencing the estimated fit. They will show whether the regression is driven by a few outlying country cases, while the majority of countries may show no particular pattern.
2. There is a correlation between X_i and ε_i that violates the exogeneity condition to obtain unbiased estimates of δ. This can be due to three reasons:

   ■ Omitted variables that are correlated with the right-hand-side variables. For example, school enrollment as a determinant of GDP growth is correlated with unobservables such as the population's entrepreneurship or drive to succeed that affect both enrollment and growth. This omitted-variable bias is typical of cross-sectional regressions.
   ■ Reverse causality or simultaneity as GDP growth and X affect each other. For example, education induces growth, but higher growth induces more school enrollment. The same can be said about health.
   ■ Policies are fundamentally endogenous choices (Rodrik, 2012). Governments choose optimal policies based on their desire to affect development outcomes.

197

As a consequence, the outcome induces the policy response as much as the policy response affects the outcome. In addition, governments choose optimal policies based on country-specific unobservable characteristics such as market imperfections, corruption, and state capacity. As a consequence, policy levels are correlated with these unobservables, a problem that cannot be fixed by adding more control variables Z to the equation.

Cross-country panel data

Typically, we now have more than a cross section of country data and have instead long panels of cross-country data. If we have many years of data and X_i varies over time, we can introduce time (γ_t) and country (μ_i) fixed effects in the regression equation as follows:

$$\left(\frac{GDP_{it} - GDP_{it-1}}{GDP_{it-1}}\right) = \mu_i + \gamma_t + \beta GDP_{it-1} + \delta X_{it} + Z_{it}\gamma + \varepsilon_{it}.$$

This specification solves the problem of fixed observable and unobservable differences between countries as we are effectively using changes in X_i to explain changes in growth *within* each country. But changes in X_i over time are not random, especially if they are policies. We are thus left with the same issue as with pure cross-country data, except now with a correlation between change in X_{it} and change in ε_{it} that violates the condition for an unbiased estimation of δ.

Using instrumental variables

In their attempt at solving the endogeneity problem in cross-country regressions, researchers have frequently used an instrumental variables approach at the level of macro phenomena. An example is the work by Acemoglu *et al.* (2001) on the role of institutions for growth. Working with cross-country data, they explain growth by the quality of contemporary governance, which itself is of course endogenous and therefore instrumented by European settlers' mortality (the argument is that the disease burden in colonial times affected the type of institutions settlers created, which in turn has affected contemporary institutions). Other commonly used instruments for the quality of governance and institutions are the origin of the country's legal system (French, British, and others), legal ethno-linguistic fractionalization, and distance from the Equator. Another example is Nunn's (2008) study, in which geographical features such as proximity to good shipping corridors in Africa affected the intensity of slavery, which in turn reduces current growth performance in a cross-country regression. The problem is that the same instruments have also been used to explain trade, foreign aid, development of the financial sector, corruption, inequality in land distribution, inflation, and other determinants of growth. This violates the exclusion restriction, a critical condition for the validity of the instrument, according to which the instrument must not directly influence growth through a channel other than the cause it is instrumenting. Papers like Acemoglu *et al.* (2001) have thus been questioned for using an instrumentation that does meet the exclusion restriction (see Chapter 3).

In cross-country panel data, the country fixed effect controls for much of the omitted variable bias, but it is much harder to find good instruments because they have to be exogenous and vary over time—so none of the historic events can be used. In recent studies, the most popular instruments have been population, rainfall, and world market prices. Burke and Leigh (2010) wanted to know if economic contractions induce democratic change. They instrumented economic contractions by rainfall and world commodity prices, two exogenous phenomena, and found that lower growth raises the probability of democratic change. Miguel *et al.* (2004) asked whether lack of GDP growth is a cause of civil conflict in Africa. Using cross-country regressions for 41 African countries over the 1981–99 period, they instrumented economic growth with rainfall variation, showing that negative growth shocks are strong predictors of civil conflict.

In all cases, the main question that needs to be asked is whether there may be other channels through which the instrument may influence the outcome of interest (growth, democratic change, civil conflicts)—and, if so, we should incorporate or control for these channels and verify that the results are robust for the choice of instrument. Instrumentation at this level is not easy and needs to be carefully justified, yet it may be feasible based on a good understanding of the phenomena studied.

State-of-the-art statistical identification

Recent advances in econometrics (Arellano and Bond, 1991) have proposed to (1) specify the cross-country regression in differences in the variables rather than levels, (2) use lagged differences of the dependent variable as regressor ($\Delta y_{it-1} = y_{it-1} - y_{it-2}$), (3) instrument change variables Δy_{it-1} and ΔX_{it} with their lagged values Δy_{it-2} and ΔX_{it-1}, and (4) use new estimation techniques (the Generalized Method of Moments). The lags help deal with simultaneity issues, but they do not solve the endogeneity problem that come from lagged omitted variables that have persistent effects. The problem of identification of causality between X and Y thus remains largely unresolved.

We thus conclude that, even with state-of-the-art statistical methods, it is difficult to secure exogeneity of X or ΔX in cross-country regressions. Endogeneity, especially spurious correlation, is a deep conceptual issue unlikely to be fixed by making the model more complex.

MACRO-LEVEL IMPACT EVALUATION: WHAT CAN BE DONE?

Cross-country regressions, even with panel data, instrumental variables, and state-of-the-art statistical identification techniques may not meet current demands for the rigorous identification of causalities needed to make policy recommendations. Yet we need to progress with identification of causalities at the macro level. What are the options? Here are two that have been used.

1. *Careful use of instrumental and statistical methods (Bazzi and Clemens, 2012).* The choice of instruments should be anchored in theory that includes the main other determinants of growth (or any other macro phenomenon of interest). Econometric techniques should be used to check the validity and strength of the instruments.

2. *A macro–micro approach.* Identification of causalities in cross-country growth equations is clearly difficult. It does not mean, however, that the correlates measured in these regressions are fallacious. A complementary approach is to use the apparently robust results from cross-country regressions to generate hypotheses that can be taken to the microdata, where they can be subjected to rigorous testing through natural or controlled experiments. For example, the cross-country result between trade liberalization and growth can be taken to microdata. Topalova and Khandelwal (2011) used the rapid occurrence of trade liberalization in India to measure its impact on firm productivity as an "event analysis," where it would be unlikely that other factors intervened during the short period. The cross-country result between liquidity shocks and growth can similarly be tested using micro-level natural experiments. Khwaja and Mian (2008) used the differential liquidity shocks induced by a surprise nuclear test in Pakistan in 1998 on all lenders and loans. They find that liquidity shocks affected investment in small firms, but that large firms were able to use their clout to get the funds they needed. This gives a different perspective on the role of micro-level impact studies as helping to garner cumulative evidence on the causal validity of macro phenomena suggested by cross-country regressions.

Chapter 5

Poverty and vulnerability analysis

TAKE-HOME MESSAGES FOR CHAPTER 5

1. Measuring poverty is essential to identify the poor, understand who they are, design and target anti-poverty interventions, and monitor and evaluate the performance of these interventions.

2. Any statement about poverty is relative to the choice of a poverty line. Poverty lines can be nutrition-based, international, relative, weakly relative, and subjective. The key is to be explicit and consistent about the choice of such a line in making statements about poverty.

3. The P^α indicators are the most commonly used measures of chronic poverty, specializing in the headcount ratio, the depth of poverty, and the severity of poverty indices for $\alpha = 0, 1$, and 2 respectively.

4. Vulnerability to unexpected shocks such as bad harvests, job loss, and illness is an important source of new poor, potentially leading to irreversibility and poverty traps. Vulnerability to poverty is typically more widespread than poverty itself. Measuring vulnerability to poverty requires both a poverty line and a vulnerability threshold. It is difficult to do, as it requires predicting future income or consumption. Yet measuring vulnerability is essential for designing policies and programs to prevent poverty in the future. Reducing vulnerability to poverty requires safety-net policies that differ from the policies used to combat chronic poverty.

5. Interventions to reduce poverty include: (1) pro-poor income growth, with emphasis on increased access to assets for the poor and improved opportunities and productivity in their use of the assets, and (2) introduction of social-safety nets and social-assistance programs for the poor. New approaches such as conditional cash transfers and productive safety nets combine short-run transfers with longer-run income generation.

6. Understanding how the poor live and why they do what they do is essential for designing poverty-reduction interventions. The behavior of the poor is in many aspects similar to that of the non-poor except for the context in which it applies and the stakes for survival.

Reducing poverty and hunger, as stated in the first MDG, is likely to be the most widely shared development objective. Hunger, with emaciated children shown stunned or dying on our television screens, is simply repulsive. Few can remain indifferent. Vulnerability to shocks—a tsunami, a drought, a flood, a pandemic, a civil war—similarly arouses broad compassion of the Rawlsian "it could be me" type (Rawls, 1971). It is also a major source of new poor. Reducing vulnerability to shocks and the associated irreversibilities in health, education, and asset endowments is thus a major instrument for poverty reduction—and reducing vulnerability to poverty may have more than intrinsic value for the poor if maintaining a share of the population in poverty is inefficient, reducing growth and imposing a social cost shared by all (Ravallion, 2012). As with all aspects of development, we need to address poverty through both positive and normative analyses. How do we characterize and explain poverty through diagnostics and identification of causal determinants? What can be done to reduce poverty using well designed and targeted policies and programs?

In order to answer these two questions we need to progress in a logical sequence of nine steps:

- First, we need to agree on the choice of a monetary indicator of wellbeing (y) that can be used to characterize poverty.
- Second, we need to agree on a threshold level (z) for this indicator, called a poverty line, below which the poor will be found.
- Third, using household survey data, we can identify the households with $y < z$ and obtain a description of the poor. Who are they? Where are they located? What do they do?
- Fourth, we can develop a number of poverty indicators that will help us measure various aspects of poverty. How prevalent is it in the population? How deep is it relative to the poverty line? How unequal is wellbeing among the poor?
- Fifth, we can distinguish among the poor between those who are chronic poor and those who are transitory poor, calling on different types of policy instrument to deal with each type of poverty. We can also characterize what we mean by vulnerability to poverty.
- Sixth, we can look at special aspects of poverty such as its intra-household incidence by gender and age, its intergenerational transmission, and mobility in and out of poverty from year to year or before and after an intervention.
- Seventh, we can construct poverty maps to visualize the geographical location of different aspects of poverty and overlay these maps with factors that we may think are determinants of poverty (such as agro-ecological quality of the environment, distance to a city, population density, etc.), consequences of poverty (such as crime and disease), and instruments to reduce poverty (such as social expenditures).
- Eighth, we can measure the effectiveness of economic growth in reducing poverty, and the role of different qualities of growth such as its sectoral origin—agriculture in particular—and its labor and skill intensity. We can also measure the impact on poverty of social programs aimed at the reduction of chronic poverty and of vulnerability to shocks.

■ Finally, ninth, we can ask, "how do the poor live?" and "why do they do what they do?" This is essential for the design of anti-poverty programs if they are to be effective. We will take on the design and implementation of such programs in Chapter 14.

As we shall see, there exists considerable expertise in characterizing, measuring, and analyzing poverty. By contrast, we are poorly equipped to explain poverty, particularly the rigorous establishment of causal determinants. We are also quite weak at understanding what works and does not work to reduce poverty, particularly in helping take large numbers of people out of poverty. While central to development economics, understanding and reducing poverty remain major challenges that limit our ability to act decisively on this major scourge of humanity.

The World Bank, donors, and national governments engage in periodic poverty assessments, in particular to help countries develop Poverty Reduction Strategy Papers (PRSPs) (World Bank, 2009b). PRSPs are needed to define effective poverty-reduction strategies and for heavily indebted poor countries (HIPC) to qualify for debt relief. Conducting poverty assessments requires a number of well defined skills and techniques. This chapter proposes to give the reader the knowledge and instruments needed to conduct such assessments.[1]

CHARACTERIZE WELFARE: CHOICE OF AN INDICATOR OF WELLBEING

What indicator (*y*) to use to measure wellbeing? Income vs. consumption

There are two monetary indicators we could use to measure an individual's level of wellbeing at a particular point of time: income per capita or consumption expenditure per capita. While the most intuitive may be income, it is in fact better to use consumption. There are several reasons for this. One is that consumption is closer to wellbeing as it creates utility, while income *per se* does not. Income is a means and not an end. The other is that individuals will attempt to smooth consumption across years when income fluctuates (Figure 5.1a). Temporarily low and high incomes would thus give an erroneous characterization of wellbeing. Consumption is also smoothed

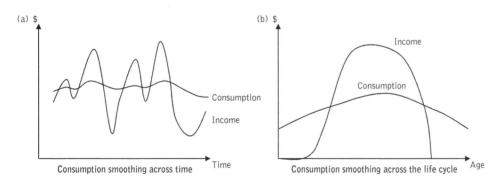

Figure 5.1 *Use of income or consumption to measure wellbeing*

across the life cycle, exceeding income in youth, falling behind income at working age, and exceeding income again in old age (Figure 5.1b). Consumption is also relatively easier to measure as there are many sources of income that are quite difficult to capture, such as the return to assets, transfers across households, income earned abroad, and remittances received from migrants—and much of the labor income in developing countries is earned in the informal sector where it is unrecorded. Finally, people may misreport their income for their own benefit, spending on items that their spouse may not approve of such as a new vehicle or fancy dinners for the family (Ashraf, 2009). The aggregate effect of this can be very large in terms of recorded income and mismeasurement of poverty.

There are, however, specific difficulties in using consumption as a welfare indicator that we must be aware of. They include:

1. Information on consumption expenditures is generally not available for individuals but for households. This is because the household is the unit of decision-making for purchases of consumer goods and for the production of so-called z-goods (home-produced consumption goods, such as creating meals out of purchased food ingredients (Lancaster, 1966)). It is very difficult to observe how consumption is distributed across individual members within a household. For that reason, surveys characterize consumption at the household level.

2. There are large errors in measuring consumption. Think how you would answer questions about how much you spent on food during the last week, on services such as utilities or rents during the last month, and on durable goods during the last year. Such recalls can only be approximate. If the survey is conducted with the husband he might under-report his private consumption of tobacco, alcohol, and gambling. Extrapolating responses from week to year or month to year may be erroneous if there is strong seasonality such as a "hungry" season and a "productive" season like in many tropical countries. Households are sometimes asked to record their daily expenditures in diaries (this is done by China's National Bureau of Statistics), but this quickly becomes tedious for them, and attrition rates are not random: people with high opportunity costs tend to drop out of the sample first, creating a bias in how representative the data from diaries are of the population.

3. Consumption expenditures vary with tastes. It is consequently difficult to use them to make inter-personal comparisons of wellbeing, something we need to do in measuring poverty. For example, some people do not spend money on alcohol and tobacco, not because they cannot afford them, but because they simply do not like them.

4. How to measure expenditure on durable goods? In principle, we should measure the service provided by the durable good over the period of time, namely its depreciation at the current price, plus the opportunity cost of the money tied up in the value of the asset. This requires information on the price of the asset, its useful lifespan, a depreciation rate, and the opportunity cost of capital.

5. Finally, households are differentially able to smooth consumption, in particular by wealth level and social position that determine their capacity to save and to access loans. This creates differences in consumption across households by ability to smooth, with more low and high measurements among those less able to smooth.

Adjusting *y* for a number of factors

In order to use the information on consumption expenditures as an indicator of well-being, we need to make the following adjustments:

1. For changes in prices for comparisons over time. For this, we need to use a deflator such as the Consumer Price Index (CPI) to calculate real expenditures. There are, however, controversies as to whose consumption is characterized by the composition of the CPI—for instance, should we be using a CPI for households around the poverty line in measuring poverty? Small differences in the choice of a CPI can make large differences in the measurements of poverty, leading to famous controversies such as "the great India poverty debate" (Deaton and Kozel, 2005).
2. For spatial price differences for country/regional comparisons. For this, we need to use a PPP-adjusted exchange rate for comparisons across countries and CPIs that are specific to regions or to urban–rural differences for comparisons across regions (Deaton, 1997).
3. Many commodities consumed are home-produced, including food and z-goods. They need to be valued in monetary terms to be added to purchased commodities, but at what price? In principle, it should be at their opportunity cost: the purchase price for commodities that would have been bought had they not been home produced (for net-buyer households); the sale price for commodities that would have been sold had they not been consumed (for net-seller households). In practice, for each commodity we tend to use the average price for transactions on the closest local market.
4. We need to account for the imputed value of public goods and services received by the household (e.g. free or subsidized health care, school lunches, public education). Failing to include these in y can lead to large mistakes in assessing changes in wellbeing. For example, poverty fell in Ghana according to the World Bank Poverty Assessment during the period of structural adjustment, while it rose according to local NGOs. The NGO assessment was due to a sharp decline in access to public goods associated with austerity policies that had not been measured in the expenditure indicator used in the World Bank assessment (Kanbur, 2001).

These are just some of the adjustments that need to be made in calculating per capita consumption expenditure. They show that many decisions need to be made in elaborating consumption statistics, and that they can make a very large difference in the final measurements. Making these decisions transparent is important, as is their careful consideration by users of the consumption statistics.

Household vs. individual wellbeing

We said that consumption expenditure is measured at the household level. However, a given expenditure for a household of ten creates less wellbeing than for a household of two. Wellbeing is individual, measured by per capita consumption. How do we do this?

1. Per capita consumption is measured using *adult equivalence scales*, to take into account differences in demographic composition for comparisons across households (Deaton, 1997). This consists in giving consumption weights to household members according to their gender and age that correspond to their relative consumption levels. For example, the OECD gives a weight of 1 to adult males, 0.7 to adult females, and lower weights to children according to their ages with an average of 0.5. The gender and age-adjusted family size in adult equivalence scale $n*$ is then:

$$n^* = \sum_k w_k n_k,$$

where n_k is the number of household members in category k and w_k the consumption weight of demographic category k. The OECD scale to calculate the number of adult equivalents (AE) in a household is:

number of AE = 1 + 0.7 (number of adults − 1) + 0.5 number of children.

A household with two adults and two children would thus have an AE equal to 2.7. The poverty assessments using the World Bank's Living Standards Measurement Survey (LSMS) frequently use the following scale:

number of AE = number of adults above 17 + 0.5 number of children 13 to 17 + 0.3 number of children 7 to 12 + 0.2 number of children 0 to 6.

These weights are really empirical questions, and do not need to be arbitrary. As suggested by Deaton (1997), they can be established by regressing household consumption on its number of members by gender and age.

2. Per capita consumption should also allow for the existence of *economies of scale* in consumption for household-level public goods (housing, durable goods, heating, electricity) vs. private goods (food, child education). In this case, a public good is one that is non-excludable and non-rival for household members. This adjustment is done as follows. Say that total household consumption is: $y = C_f + p_h C_h$, where:

C_f = consumption expenditure on private goods f such as food,
C_h = consumption expenditure on household-level public goods h such as housing, and
p_h = price of housing (with food price as numéraire, $p_f = 1$).

Per capita consumption is then: $y_{pc} = \dfrac{C_f}{n^*} + p_h \dfrac{C_h}{n^{*\beta}}$, where:

n^* = number of adult equivalent household members, and
β = degree of "privateness" of the good, with $\beta = 0$ for a pure public good such as housing and $\beta = 1$ for a pure private good such as food.

206

Hence per capita expenditure in the household is $y_{pc} = (C_f + p_h C_h) / n^*$ if there are only private goods, and $y_{pc} = (C_f / n^*) + p_h C_h$ if C_h is a pure public good. This adjustment can obviously make a big difference to the measure of per capita consumption, especially if there are large differences in the importance of household-level public goods across households.

Specific types of poverty: hunger

Poverty takes on specific forms, such as hunger. In this case, y would be measured as daily per capita caloric intake, and compared to the daily minimum energy requirement for that category of individuals. The UN's Food and Agriculture Organization defines the minimum on average as 1,800kg calories per day, with requirements adjusted by a person's age, gender, and activity level. Other forms of nutritional deficits can be measured—for instance, for proteins or specific types of micronutrient, referred to as "hidden hunger."

Data availability

Measuring poverty is data intensive, particularly if we want to have measurements over time and across many geographical settings. Significant progress has been made in recent years in making publicly available large databases that can be used to measure poverty. They allow us to characterize poverty and to test many hypotheses about correlates or determinants of poverty, as well as the impact on poverty of specific programs and policy reforms. Some of the most important data sources are:

1. *Living Standards Measurement Survey (LSMS).* They can be cross-sectional, repeated surveys, or panel data. Information on their availability is posted by the World Bank at http://go.worldbank.org/WKOXNZV3X0.
2. *Household income and expenditure surveys.* Examples include the NSS data for India, ENIGH data for Mexico, PNAD data for Brazil, SUSENAS household surveys for Indonesia, ENCOVI data for Guatemala, the Vietnam Longitudinal Survey (VLS), etc.
3. *Population censuses (with 5–10 percent release of individual records).* They sometimes have information on self-reported income, as in Brazil; more often they give correlates of income such as quality of housing and ownership of durable goods, as in Mexico. Population census data are available through IPUMS (Integrated Public Use Microdata Series) at the University of Minnesota (http://usa.ipums.org/usa/).
4. *Demographic and Health Surveys (DHS) implemented by ICF International and funded by USAID.* They give data on housing, assets owned, and durable goods, but not on consumption expenditures or income. See: http://www.measuredhs.com/aboutsurveys/dhs/start.cfm.
5. *Employment and wage surveys.* They are collected by labor ministries and report on individual incomes and access to public services as well as unemployment and wages. They have the interesting feature of being constructed as rotating panels, typically following an individual over six quarters before replacement.

SEPARATING THE POOR FROM THE NON-POOR: CHOOSING A POVERTY LINE (Z)

Deciding who is poor and non-poor based on knowledge of y for individuals in a particular population requires choosing a threshold level z of y that can be called a "poverty line." This is quite difficult because there is no agreement on the definition of poverty, nor on what would be a threshold for a given poverty concept. Is poverty absolute? Is it relative to others so it changes with the average level of y in a country? Clearly, z for a poor US citizen cannot be the same as for a poor Zambian. For the first, z would allow for a car; for the second, a pair of shoes. As a consequence, a country-level z typically rises with the country's GDPpc. It is important to note the following:

■ Any statement about poverty is relative to the choice of a poverty line; there is no possible absolute statement about poverty. A statement about poverty must be explicit about the poverty line to which it refers.
■ Because there is no agreement on a single poverty line, it is often best to use several clearly defined alternative poverty lines.
■ Consistency should be maintained in the definition of a poverty line when comparisons are made across time, geography, or subsets of a population.

The most commonly used definitions of a poverty line are discussed below.

Nutrition-based poverty line

A common metric for humanity is our daily calorie intake. The recommended minimum can then be used to establish a universal poverty line. In Figure 5.2, the calorie-expenditure function relates calories purchased to a level of food expenditure. There are decreasing returns because consumers buy increasingly expensive sources of calories as expenditure rises: beans and corn at the lower end, poultry and meat at the upper. Figure 5.2 also shows the Engel curve: it traces the level of food expenditure as income (or total expenditure) rises. At very low levels of income, most expenditure is on food. As income rises, the share of expenditure on food decreases. Our definitions are:

■ Extreme poverty line or indigence or absolute poverty line: z_{abs} = monetary cost of the recommended minimum calorie intake (2000 ca/day/adult). In Mexico, this poverty line is called "food poverty."
■ Normal poverty line: z = expenditure level necessary to consume the recommended minimum calorie intake of 2000 ca/day/adult, along with non-food expenditures normally associated with that level of food expenditure.

In poor countries, z will be twice z_{abs} if the food budget share of the poor is 50 percent. In the US, z is three times z_{abs}, but raising it to seven times is currently under discussion as the food budget share of the poor is only about 15 percent.

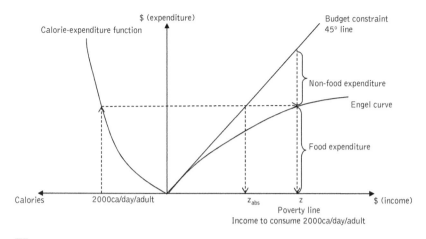

Figure 5.2 *Nutrition-based poverty line*

International poverty line

This is the poverty line used for international comparisons by the World Bank in the *World Development Indicators*. It was set at $1/day for extreme poverty and at $2/day for poverty, measured in PPP dollars. Recently (see Chapter 2), these poverty lines were raised to PPP$1.25/day and PPP$2.5/day respectively, basically because the old $1/day measure is now lower than that any single country uses as its own poverty line. The reason for choosing $1.25 is that it is the poverty line currently used by the 15 poorest countries with such data.

Relative poverty line

Poverty is not only an absolute, but also a relative concept. People feel poor in relation to the consumption levels of others, perhaps the average or median expenditure in their corresponding reference group. This is the concept of relative deprivation: people attach value to their income or consumption in relation to the mean in their country or community of residence. The relative poverty line can also be interpreted as the cost of social inclusion: it is the level of expenditure necessary to participate with dignity in customary social and economic activities. A relative poverty line is commonly used in Europe to make poverty statements. In this case, z is a fixed share k of mean expenditure $\bar{y}$ in the population: $z = k\bar{y}$. For example, Atkinson (1995) uses $k = 0.5$ for poverty and $k = 0.33$ for extreme poverty. Poverty will then be a measure affected by inequality: it remains constant if inequality does not change and all incomes go up by the same percentage, and it would fall with the two previous absolute poverty lines. It can increase if mean expenditure remains constant but inequality in the distribution of income rises.

Weakly relative poverty line

There is an alternative option to the stark contrast between an absolute poverty line (either nutrition-based or international), which is favored for poor countries, and a

209

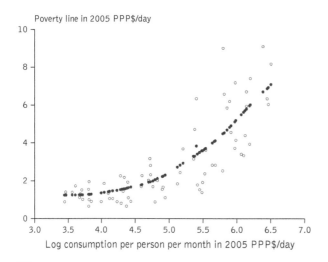

Poverty line in 2005 PPP$/day

Log consumption per person per month in 2005 PPP$/day

Figure 5.3 *National poverty lines rise with countries' mean consumption*

Source: Ravallion and Chen, 2011.

relative poverty line, which is favored for rich countries, especially in Europe. This is the "weakly relative poverty line" proposed by Ravallion and Chen (2011). It is based on the observation that countries periodically raise their own poverty line as GDPpc rises. This is to take into account the fact that the concept of poverty has a dimension of relative deprivation. As can be seen in Figure 5.3, taken from Ravallion and Chen (2011), the poorest 20 countries in the world have an absolute poverty line in the order of PPP$1.25/day. As income rises, so does the poverty line, but not in a regular fashion. It is set for instance at $24/day in the US ($23,830 a year for a family of four, with 2.7 adult equivalents) and $43/day in Luxembourg. By contrast with the strict relative poverty line that is set as a fraction of mean or median income or consumption (call it the "strongly relative poverty line"), the weakly relative poverty line rises with average income but only after it exceeds the absolute poverty threshold and not in a strictly proportional relation to mean or median income. This poverty measure, while loosely defined because country adjustments cannot be predicted, has the advantage of giving a measure of poverty that accounts for both absolute and relative poverty. To make cross-country comparisons we use the predicted national poverty line per person per day in PPP$ for the given level of PPP-adjusted GDPpc. As we saw in Chapter 2, while world absolute poverty fell from 1.9 billion people in 1981 to 1.3 billion in 2008 using the PPP$1.25/day criterion, world relative poverty in excess of absolute poverty rose from 0.5 billion in 1981 to 1.4 billion in 2008. Total absolute and relative poverty thus rose from 2.4 billion in 1981 to 2.7 billion in 2008.

Subjective poverty line

Finally, we can say that poverty is not only an absolute or a relative standard, but, importantly, a perception. In this case, we can ask households, "what expenditure do you consider to be absolutely minimal?" and compare this with their actual expenditure

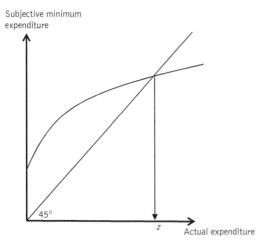

Subjective minimum
expenditure

45°

z

Actual expenditure

Figure 5.4 *The intersection of the subjective minimum curve and the 45° line defines the subjective poverty line*

as shown in Figure 5.4. Those with an actual expenditure inferior to the stated sub-jective minimum would be considered to be in poverty, i.e. people above the 45° line in Figure 5.4. Like all subjective statements (for instance, in contingency valuation where people are asked about a willingness to pay for an object or a service), this measure suffers from a framing effect: it very much depends on how the question is asked. While logically appealing, such measures must be used with caution because we have imperfect control over framing when data are collected by multiple enumerators.

DESCRIBE POVERTY: POVERTY PROFILE AND CORRELATES OF POVERTY

Poverty profile

Say that we have a household survey such as an LSMS that gives us the per capita expenditure level y_i, $i = 1, \ldots, n$ for each of the n members of a representative sample of the population. We can rank these n individuals by increasing level of expenditure, from the poorest to the richest. We also have a poverty line z. If we compare y_i to z, we find that q individuals have $y_i < z$, i.e., are in poverty.

These data allow us to draw in Figure 5.5 a very useful representation of poverty in the population: the poverty profile. The horizontal axis is the population from 1 to n ranked by expenditure level; the vertical axis is their corresponding y_i. The horizontal line is the poverty line at z.

There are two useful observations to make of the poverty profile. The first is that it tends to be quite flat precisely where it crosses the poverty line because we have a lot of people with similar income levels around z. This implies that small changes in the level of the poverty line will have large implications for the level of poverty q. This stresses again the importance of (and sensitivity to) the choice of a poverty line on any particular poverty statement. The second is that there is a lot more information about poverty in a poverty profile than simply the number of people q below z: we can also

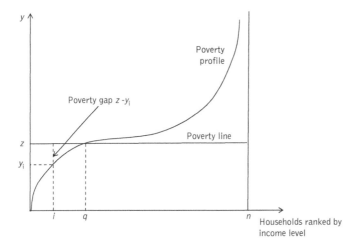

Figure 5.5 *Poverty profile*

read the *poverty gap* $z - y_i$ for each poor person $i < q$. This is an important piece of information: it tells us how much expenditure the individual needs to get out of poverty. The aggregate poverty gap is the amount that would have to be transferred to each of the poor ($i = 1, ..., q$) to eliminate poverty if we knew exactly their actual y_i. The sum of these transfers over the poor is the minimum welfare budget that we need to have to implement cash transfers that eliminate poverty under perfect information about current levels of y.

Correlates of poverty. Who are the poor? Where do they live? What do they do? How do they live?

With people classified below and above the poverty line, we can also look at the average characteristics of poor vs. non-poor individuals or households. These are very useful descriptive statistics to diagnose poverty and to help target anti-poverty interventions. The variables we use are those found in the LSMS or household surveys. They typically give us information on the following aspects of the population:

■ Characteristics of individuals in the household: age, gender, race, ethnicity, education, and health status.
■ Demographic characteristics of the household: gender of head, size, and dependency ratio (number of children and elders per working-age adult).
■ Asset position: land, livestock, tools, and social capital.
■ Activities: sector of economic activity, crops sold, type of employment.
■ Location: rural/urban, region, neighborhood.
■ Access to public services: electricity, piped water, health facility, school, social-assistance programs.
■ Access to market and private services: distance to market, road infrastructure, access to financial services.

We can use typical LSMS household-survey data to look at the differences in means (using a t-test) or percentages (using a Chi^2 test) in the characteristics and circumstances of the poor vs. non-poor. This gives us a useful profile of poverty. This is done for Ecuador in Table 5.1. We see that the poor are younger, have less education, and larger families than the non-poor. They are disproportionately self-employed, in agriculture and in the informal sector. The non-poor have by contrast more secondary and especially higher education. They work more in the formal private sector, the public sector, and the service sector. They are more likely to be employers. They have much greater access to public services such as water, electricity, and sewage. And they have on average an income 3.7 times larger than the poor.

Another way of looking at the correlates of poverty is to use a regression analysis where the dependent variable is the log of household per capita consumption, and the right-hand-side variables are the households' characteristics and circumstances. These variables are not causal because they may be determined jointly with consumption.

Table 5.1 *Characteristics and circumstances of the poor and non-poor in Ecuador, and tests of differences in means or in percentages*

Ecuador, 2000	Poor	Non-poor
Household characteristics		
Age of household head	46.4	49.4***
Number of members	5.5***	3.9
Education of household head		
Primary or no education (%)	63.1***	38.1
Secondary (%)	32.2	36.6*
Higher education (%)	4.6	25.3***
Sector of employment		
Informal sector (%)	80.4***	55.8
Formal private sector (%)	16.4	31***
Public sector (%)	3.1	13.2***
Sector of activity		
Primary (agriculture)	56.9***	26.4
Industrial	15.3	15.2
Services	27.8	58.4***
Occupational category		
Self-employed	67.1***	42.9
Worker	22.5	26.2
Employer	10.4	30.9***
Annual income	137.3	509.4***
Access to public services		
Water	43.5	70.7***
Electricity	54	85.1***
Sewage	26.3	60.9***

Significantly larger at the *** 1% confidence level, ** 5% level, * 10% level.

Source: World Bank, 2004.

Table 5.2 *Correlates of consumption in Nicaragua: 1998, 2001, and 2005.*
Estimates significant at the 5 percent level are shown in bold.
Omitted dummy categories correspond to a household in the
Rural Central region with a head who is unemployed and has
no education

Dependent variable: log of household per capita consumption

	1998	2001	2005
Region			
Urban Pacific	**−0.28**	**−0.19**	−0.2
Rural Pacific	−0.27	**−0.11**	**−0.15**
Urban Central	**−0.22**	**−0.16**	**−0.15**
Urban Atlantic	−0.03	0.03	0.07
Rural Atlantic	−0.3	−0.04	−0.03
Household head			
Female	−0.03	−0.03	−0.01
Under age 35	**−0.13**	**−0.13**	−0.09
Primary education	**0.14**	**0.14**	**0.17**
Secondary education	0.37	**0.37**	**0.36**
More than sec. education	0.86	**0.82**	**0.87**
Not in labor force	0.07	0.09	0.1
Household head sector			
Agriculture	0.09	0.08	0.06
Mining	0.08	−0.04	−0.08
Manufacturing	0.02	0.04	0.03
Gas, electricity, water	0.08	0.11	0.1
Construction	0.04	0.01	0
Commerce	**0.17**	**0.18**	**0.18**
Transport	**0.3**	**0.27**	**0.17**
Financial services	0.22	**0.24**	0.14
Community services	0.04	0.02	0
Household services			
Piped water	**0.17**	**0.18**	**0.19**
Electricity	**0.22**	**0.23**	**0.21**
Paved road	**0.22**	**0.19**	**0.11**
Household composition			
# infants (under 5)	**−0.17**	**−0.15**	**−0.16**
# children (5–14)	**−0.14**	**−0.14**	**−0.14**
# adults	−0.05	−0.06	−0.07
# seniors	**−0.1**	**−0.04**	−0.06
Constant	**9.34**	**9.1**	**9.1**
Number of observations	3827	4165	6856
R−squared	0.56	0.57	0.55

Source: World Bank, *Nicaragua Poverty Assessment,* 2008.

We call this a descriptive regression. Estimated coefficients are partial correlations, meaning that they will change as we change the other variables in the equation. In spite of the lack of causality, estimated coefficients are useful descriptive statistics to help us understand what correlates with income. Statistical tests tell us if the corresponding partial correlation is significantly different from zero. For Nicaragua, using the 1998, 2001, and 2005 LSMS, we observe that several variables are strongly correlated with per capita consumption (Table 5.2). The estimated coefficients give us the percentage gains or losses in income associated with each right-hand-side variable compared to the base category at given level of all the other variables. Here, the base category is a household in the Rural Central region, with an unemployed head and no education. In 1998, a household in the Urban Pacific region had 28 percent less per capita consumption than a household with the same characteristics living in the Rural Central region. In 2005, a household with a household head with primary education had 17 percent more per capita consumption compared to the base category (no education), 36 percent if it had secondary education, and 87 percent if it had more than secondary education. Clearly, education has a high pay-off in terms of consumption achievements. Households with a head who works in the commerce or transport sector have 18 percent and 17 percent more per capita consumption respectively. Households with one more under 5 infant have 16 percent less per capita consumption, and 14 percent if they have one more child in the 5–14 age category. And there is a very strong association between better access to household services—piped water, electricity, and paved roads—and higher per capita consumption, as high as 19 percent more for piped water and 21 percent for electricity.

We also see that across years, the correlates of consumption have remained remarkably stable.

MEASURING POVERTY: CHOOSING A POVERTY INDICATOR

Now that poverty has been described, we would like to summarize the information contained in the poverty profile with a few scalars that are easy to measure and communicate. A profile is nice to look at, but hard to describe in words. This is why we need indicators.

Choice of a poverty indicator: axiomatics

All poverty indicators are based on the distribution of income or consumption y truncated at z. A poverty index's generally desirable properties are:

- Monotonocity (Sen, 1976): a decrease in y of a poor person should increase the poverty index.
- Transfer (Sen, 1976): a transfer of y from poor to less poor should increase the index.
- Transfer sensitivity: the rise in the index declines as the y transfer from poor to less poor is taken from richer poor.

A poverty index's specifically desirable properties are:

- Population symmetry: if two identical populations are pooled, the index should not change.
- Proportion of poor: if the share of poor increases, the index should increase.
- Focus (Sen, 1976): the index is independent of the y level of people above z.
- Decomposability: if the poverty of a subgroup increases, the index increases.

There are two commonly used categories of poverty indicators: the P_α class and the average exit time from poverty for a population.

Members of the P_α class: incidence, depth, and severity of poverty

Foster *et al.* (1984) proposed a general class of poverty indicators, the P_α class, also known as FGT, defined as:

$$P_\alpha = \frac{1}{n} \sum_{i=1}^{q} \left(\frac{z - y_i}{z} \right)^\alpha.$$

Dividing the poverty gap, measured in local currency units (LCU), by the poverty line, also in LCU, makes it into a unit-free number. The index specifies three indicators according to the value given to the scalar α:

1) If $\alpha = 0$, $P_0 = q/n$. This is the *headcount* ratio, or *incidence of poverty*, or *poverty rate*. It measures the share of people who are poor in the population. It is the simplest and most commonly used poverty indicator.

   P_0 does not satisfy the monotonicity and transfer axioms. It does not tell us how poor the poor are. Yet it is the most widely used poverty index.

2) If $\alpha = 1$, $P_1 = \dfrac{\sum_{i=1}^{q} (z - y_i)}{nz}$.

   This is the *poverty gap index* or the *depth of poverty*, where:

   $\sum_{i=1}^{q} (z - y_i)$ is the total expenditure deficit of the poor, or total poverty gap. It measures the cost of eliminating poverty with perfect targeting (i.e. if we knew exactly the expenditure level y_i of every poor person); and

   nz is the cost of eliminating poverty without targeting (i.e. if we had no information on the expenditure level of anyone in the population and consequently had to give z to each person to make sure that no one is left in poverty).

Hence P_1 is the ratio of the targeted to the untargeted budget needed to eliminate poverty. Alternatively, $100 (1-P_1)$ is the percentage saving in the poverty budget due to ability to target the poor.

   P_1 satisfies the monotonicity and transfer axioms. It does not measure inequality among the poor.

3) If $\alpha = 2$, $P_2 = \dfrac{1}{n}\displaystyle\sum_1^q \left(\dfrac{z - y_i}{z}\right)^2$.

This is the *severity of poverty* index. It weights the poverty gap as a square, giving greater weight to expenditure deficits further away from the poverty line. In this sense, P_2 is sensitive to the distribution of expenditures among the poor. A population with a greater share of extreme poor among the poor will have a higher P_2, even if it has the same P_0 and P_1 as another population.

P_2 satisfies the monotonicity and transfer axioms. It measures inequality among the poor.

As a numerical example, consider a population with four individuals with $y_i = \{7, 3, 4, 8\}$ and a poverty line $z = 5$. Calculate P_0, P_1, and P_2:

$P_0 = 2/4 = 0.5$

$P_1 = 3/20 = 0.15$

$P_2 = 5/100 = 0.05$.

Note that α can be interpreted as a policymaker's measure of aversion to poverty. The higher α is, the more concern there is with people further away from the poverty line. At the limit, if α reaches infinity, the policymaker becomes Rawlsian, where the only concern is with the welfare of the poorest individual in society. Using α to measure the policymaker's poverty aversion thus represents the extent to which the welfare of the poorest of the poor is given priority in assessing aggregate poverty.

As illustrations of how poverty indicators describe changes in the poverty profile between two situations, consider the following three cases.

1. In Figure 5.6, the poverty profile shifts to the left between situations 1 and 2. In this case, undoubtedly P_0, P_1, and P_2 are all lower in 2 than they were in 1.
2. In Figure 5.7, the two poverty profiles intersect at q, but shift to the left below the poverty line. In this case, P_0 remains constant between 1 and 2, but both P_1 and P_2 are lower in 2 than they were in 1.
3. In Figure 5.8, the two poverty profiles intersect below the poverty line, but area A is equal to area B. In this case, P_0 and P_1 remain constant between 1 and 2, but P_2 is lower in 2 than it was in 1.

As a policy application, consider the following question: how should a country target a given welfare budget in order to minimize P_0, P_1, or P_2? Figure 5.9 illustrates the answers. To minimize P_0, it should start spending on the least poor (where the poverty profile crosses the poverty line) until budget B is exhausted. For P_2, it should start spending on the poorest until budget A is exhausted. But there is no rule for P_1 as a dollar-of-poverty gap is the same across all poor. Note that the first MDG stresses reducing P_0. It can consequently create a policy bias in poverty-reduction programs, giving priority to the least poor among the poor, the opposite of what would have happened had the first MDG stressed reducing P_2.

217

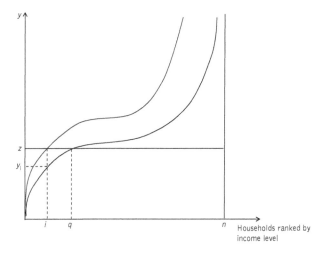

Figure 5.6 *Decline in P_0, P_1, and P_2 between 1 (dark line) and 2 (blue line)*

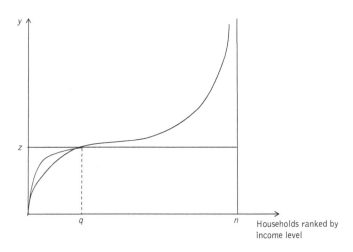

Figure 5.7 *Constant P_0 with declines in P_1 and P_2 between 1 (dark line) and 2 (blue line)*

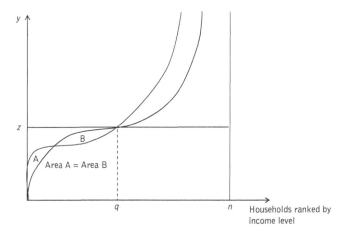

Figure 5.8 *Constant P_0 and P_1 with a decline in P_2 between 1 (dark line) and 2 (blue line)*

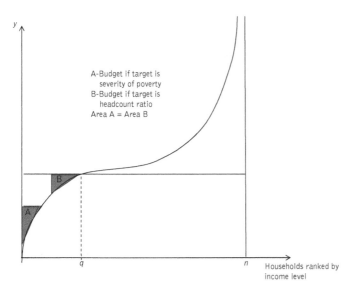

y

A-Budget if target is
  severity of poverty
B-Budget if target is
  headcount ratio
Area A = Area B

B

A

q

n

Households ranked by
income level

Figure 5.9 *Budget allocation to minimize P_0 (area B) and to minimize P_2 (area A)*

Table 5.3 *Poverty in Madagascar by socio-economic group, 1994*

Socio-economic group	P_0	Rank	P_1	Rank	P_2	Rank
Small farmers	81.6	1	41	1	24.6	1
Large farmers	77	2	34.6	2	19	2
Unskilled workers	62.7	3	25.5	4	14	5
Herders/fishermen	61.4	4	27.9	3	16.1	3
Retirees/handicapped	50.6	5	23.6	5	14.1	4

Source: Coudouel *et al.,* 2002.

P_0, P_1, and P_2 are differentially informative about poverty, and thus complement each other. Consider the measurements of these three indicators in Table 5.3 for population subgroups in Madagascar. They show that unskilled workers are at higher risk of being in poverty ($P_0 = 62.7$) compared to herders and fishermen ($P_0 = 61.4$). However, their poverty is less deep and less severe ($P_1 = 25.5$, $P_2 = 14$) than it is for herders and fishermen ($P_1 = 27.9$, $P_2 = 16.1$). Hence targeting interventions to reduce the incidence of poverty, or the severity of poverty, will lead us to prioritize different subgroups of the population.

Average exit time from poverty

Another useful, easily interpreted poverty indicator is the number of years t that it would take to eliminate poverty at a given growth rate in per capita expenditure (Morduch, 1998). Consider the following question: what is the number of years t_i needed by a poor woman i with current expenditure y_i to reach the poverty line z if her expenditure grows at the annual rate g? In discrete time, it would be given by the

219

solution to $y_i(1+g)^{t_i} = z$. Hence, taking logarithms and approximating $\ln(1+g)$ by g, the exit time out of poverty is:

$$t_i = \frac{\ln z - \ln y_i}{g}.$$

If, for instance, this poor woman's current expenditure level is $y_i = 500$ and $z = 1,000$, and her income grows at the rate of 2 percent per year, it will take her 35 years to escape poverty. For the whole population of poor, the average exit time is:

$$T_g = \frac{1}{N}\sum_{i=1}^{N} t_i.$$

The T_g indicator is decomposable into population-weighted subsets of the population of poor. Like P_2, it is sensitive to the distribution of income among the poor. As opposed to P_2, it is measured in meaningful units, namely years. However, it requires a statement about a growth rate g that we may want to avoid.

Robustness of a poverty profile over a range of z: poverty comparisons without a poverty line

A major inconvenience of poverty statements is that they are conditional on the choice of a poverty line. There may be situations, however, where we can compare poverty across two situations A and B without concern for the choice of a poverty line. This would be the case if the poverty profile of B lies above (or below) that of A at all levels of y as in the Figure 5.10a. In this case, we say that there is first-order stochastic dominance. The headcount ratio is unambiguously lower in B than in A, whatever the poverty line. If this is the case, irrespective of the poverty line z, then $P_0^A > P_0^B$, $P_1^A > P_1^B$, and $P_2^A > P_2^B$. We say that poverty comparisons are robust to the choice of a poverty line. This would not be the case if poverty profiles cross between

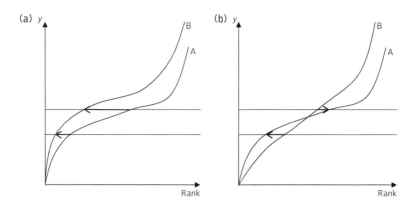

Figure 5.10 *Robustness of a poverty profile to choice of a poverty line: robust (a) and not robust (b)*

220

two alternative poverty lines as in Figure 5.10b. In this case, poverty may have declined or increased according to the chosen poverty line.

We may not be sure about the exact value of the poverty line, but be confident that it is between a lower limit $\underline{z}$ and an upper limit $\overline{z}$, i.e. that

$$\underline{z} < z < \overline{z}.$$

In this case, all that is needed to make a poverty statement irrespective of the precise choice of a poverty line is that the poverty profiles do not cross within the range $[\underline{z}, \overline{z}]$.

Comparing population subgroups: the relative risk of being poor

When comparing poverty across population subgroups, a useful statement is the relative risk of being poor in each subgroup. If P_0^u is the urban poverty rate and P_0^r the rural poverty rate, the relative risk of poverty for the rural vs. the urban population is:

$$(P_0^u - P_0^r)/P_0^u.$$

For Madagascar, where $P_0^r = 0.77$ and $P_0^u = 0.47$, this would be $(0.77 - 0.47)/0.47 = 0.64$. We can then say that a rural inhabitant is, on average, 64 percent more likely to be poor than an urban inhabitant.

Decomposition of P_α by population subgroups: contributions to poverty

We often would like to know how much different population subgroups contribute to total poverty measured by a P (or a T) indicator. Let $j = 1, \dots, k$ be k exclusive population subgroups, each with a population n_j and poverty index P_α^j. A convenient feature of the P indicators is that we can write:

$$P_\alpha = \sum_{j=1}^{k} m_j P_\alpha^j, \text{ where } m_j = \frac{n_j}{n} \text{ is the population share of subgroup } j.$$

P indicators have the desirable property of being additively decomposable. Dividing by P_α and multiplying by 100 for percentages, we can calculate the percentage contribution of group j to the total poverty index as $100 * m_j P_\alpha^j / P_\alpha$.

Decomposition of the change in P_α between two periods of time

When we observe P_α at two points in time, say 0 and t, for k population subgroups, we would like to know how much of the aggregate change in the poverty indicator came from changes in poverty within each group, and how much came from the changing importance of the groups in the population. To do this, we decompose the change in the indicator ΔP_α into three terms:[2]

$$\Delta P_\alpha = P_{\alpha t} - P_{\alpha 0} = \sum_{j=1}^{k} \Delta \left(m_j P_\alpha^j \right) = \sum_{j=1}^{k} m_{j0} \Delta P_\alpha^j + \sum_{j=1}^{k} P_{\alpha 0}^j \Delta m_j + \sum_{j=1}^{k} \Delta m_j \Delta P_\alpha^j,$$

where:
first term = changes in poverty internal to each group;
second term = changes in the relative size of each group; and
third term = cross effects.

Example 1: the changing composition of poverty in Guatemala

Using the LSMS for 2000 and 2006, Table 5.4 characterizes changes in poverty in Guatemala for the whole country and across population subgroups by area, ethnicity, and gender of the household head (World Bank, 2009a). Poverty rates are higher among rural, indigenous, and male-headed households. Between 2000 and 2006, the poverty rate declined overall and in all groups. However, as the population became increasingly urbanized, the contribution to poverty of non-indigenous and female-headed households increased. We can thus say that poverty in Guatemala is becoming increasingly urbanized, non-indigenous, and feminized.

Example 2: impact of the debt crisis on the structure of poverty in Buenos Aires

Consider in Table 5.5 poverty in Buenos Aires before (1980) and after (1989) the debt crisis that occurred in 1985 (Morley, 1995). The headcount ratio increased from 6 percent to 22 percent. Decomposing the population in subgroups by educational level shows that large increases in the headcount ratio occurred among people with middle levels of education. Indeed, looking at how the percentage distribution of poverty changed, we see that the contribution to poverty of illiterates declined from 40 to 12 percent, while that of grade-school and high-school subgroups increased from 51 to 70 percent and from 12 to 16 percent respectively. For the high-school subgroup, this was due to both an increasing population share from 23 to 27 percent (as education continued to progress) and a rising headcount ratio from 0.03 to 0.13.

Table 5.4 *Poverty patterns in Guatemala, 2000 and 2006*

	Headcount ratio		Population share		Contribution to poverty	
	2000	2006	2000	2006	2000	2006
Total Guatemala	56.2	51	100	100	100	100
By area						
Urban	27.1	30.0	38.6	48.1	18.6	28.3
Rural	74.5	70.5	61.4	51.9	81.4	71.7
By ethnicity						
Non-indigenous	41.4	36.2	57.4	62.4	42.3	44.3
Indigenous	76.2	75.7	42.6	37.6	57.8	55.8
By gender of household head						
Male	57.6	53.4	85.3	81.2	87.4	85.0
Female	47.9	40.8	14.7	18.8	12.5	15.0

Source: World Bank, 2009a.

Table 5.5 *Impact of the debt crisis by educational level, Buenos Aires*

Educational levels	Headcount ratio		Population share		Contribution to poverty	
	1980	1989	1980	1989	1980	1989
Illiterate	0.34	0.51	7	5	40	12
Grade school	0.05	0.27	61	57	51	70
High school	0.03	0.13	23	27	12	16
University	0.01	0.04	9	11	2	2
Total	0.06	0.22	100	100	100	100

Source: Morley, 1995.

This confirms the assertion that vulnerability to the debt crisis created a class of new poor among educated people who lost their jobs in formal sectors of employment, both private industry and government, which previously had low poverty rates.

DYNAMICS OF POVERTY AND VULNERABILITY: TRANSITORY AND CHRONIC POVERTY

Types of poor

Poverty is a dynamic condition and we may observe high mobility in and out of it: some people fall into poverty, some escape from poverty, and others are forever trapped in poverty. For this reason, the overall poverty rate may be misleading: we may have had no change in P_0 over a certain period of time and yet many people may have moved into and out of poverty during the period. It is useful therefore to distinguish between three categories of poor in terms of the dynamics of poverty:

1. *Transitory poor/temporary poor:* people with an average income $\bar{y}$ above z, but who are sometimes in poverty. They have a low (but non-zero) vulnerability to poverty in that there is a low likelihood they will experience poverty in a particular year during the period of observation.
2. *Chronic poor:* people who are on average below z, but who are sometimes out of poverty. They have a high vulnerability to poverty as they are highly likely to experience poverty in a particular year during the period of observation.
3. *Persistent poor:* people who are always below z. They have maximum vulnerability to poverty as their likelihood of being in poverty in a particular year is equal to one.

Adding the never poor, households can be distributed across four categories, as in Figure 5.11, where we see the poverty line z and the average expenditure $\bar{y}_i$ over a particular period of time for a household i in each category. Expenditure is subject to shocks, with the result that there can be considerable mobility in and out of poverty.

223

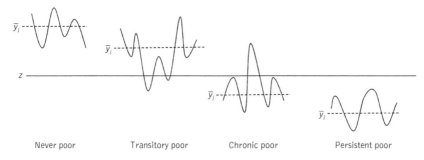

Figure 5.11 *Never poor and three categories of poor: transitory, chronic, and persistent*

An example of the importance of transitory poverty in characterizing overall poverty is given by Jalan and Ravallion (2000) for rural southwest China. Over the period 1985–90, the percentage of households that belonged to the four categories were:

Never poor   41 percent
Transitory poor   36 percent
Chronic poor   18 percent
Persistent poor   5 percent

The headcount ratio over the period would thus have been 23 percent, i.e. the percentage of households in chronic and persistent poverty with an average income below the poverty line. However, accounting for transitory poverty, as many as 59 percent of the households would have been in poverty during the period. It is typical to find that the number of transitory poor (non-poor people who are vulnerable to falling into poverty) is much larger than the number of chronic and persistent poor. The number of persistent poor (5 percent) is notably very small compared to the number of people who can stochastically cycle into and out of poverty (54 percent).

Vulnerability to poverty

Defining vulnerability to poverty

Poverty as measured by $y_{it} < z$ for a household i at time t (now) and summarized for a population by the P_α indicator is an ex-post concept. It measures who is currently poor and can help us assess how effective past anti-poverty programs have been and who benefited from them. But governments and development agencies are also interested in knowing what impacts their current or proposed interventions will have on future poverty. For this we need to identify who the future poor may be, both from among the currently poor and the non-poor—namely, which are the households that are vulnerable to poverty. Vulnerability to poverty is thus an ex-ante concept, while poverty is an ex-post outcome. We will say that a household is vulnerable to poverty if it has a high probability of being poor in the next year. To analyze a population's

224

vulnerability to poverty we need to identify the determinants of future consumption, estimate a particular household's vulnerability to poverty, and devise policy interventions that can reduce vulnerability to poverty.

With y_{it} per capita consumption of household i at time t, and z the poverty line, an indicator of vulnerability to poverty v_{it} for this household would be its ex-ante probability of being in poverty:

$$v_{it} = \Pr(y_{i,t+1} < z).$$

We can say that a household is vulnerable to poverty if, at time t, the probability of being poor in the next period $t + 1$ is greater than an arbitrary threshold α:

$$v_{it} > \alpha$$

Highly vulnerable: households with $\Pr(y_{t+1} < z) \geq 50$ percent. They have more than a one in two chance of being poor in the next period.

Moderately vulnerable: households with $\Pr(y_{t+1} < z) \geq P_0$ and <50 percent, where P_0 is the current poverty rate that measures the average probability of being poor. This says that this household has less than a 50 percent chance of being in poverty in the next period, and hence is not highly vulnerable, but is more likely than a randomly drawn household of being poor in the next period.

Not vulnerable: households with $\Pr(y_{t+1} < z) < P_0$.

Note that to characterize vulnerability to poverty we need to use two thresholds: one for poverty (the poverty line z) and one for risk (the probability threshold α). Any statement about vulnerability, such as about the percentage of the population vulnerable to poverty, must carefully state which are the z and α thresholds used in making the statement.

Measuring vulnerability to poverty

Measuring the vulnerability to poverty of a particular household requires predicting its future consumption, which is clearly more difficult than observing whether the household is currently in poverty or not. It requires identifying the determinants of y_{it} and using them to predict future $y_{i,t+1}$.

We do this by estimating a consumption equation where y_{it} is a function of a set of determinants $X_{i,t-1}$ either constant over time or from previous years. This will typically include the following four categories of variables:

■ Household characteristics such as gender, ethnicity, and caste.
■ Household asset endowments: natural capital (land), human capital (demographic structure, education, skills, health), physical capital (tools, equipment), financial capital (liquid assets such as money, jewelry, and small animals), and social capital (network membership, social status).

225

- Context in which the assets are used: agro-ecological conditions, market access and conditions, institutions (availability of financial services, membership of organizations), common and public goods, policies.
- Transfers: access to social-safety nets, remittances.

The estimated equation is for example:

$$\text{Ln } y_{it} = \alpha + \beta X_{i,t-1} + \varepsilon_{it}.$$

Using the estimated parameters and the observed values X_{it}, we can get estimates of both the household's expected level of per capita consumption in the next period, $E(y_{i,t+1})$, and its variance σ. Given the model, the predicted income follows a lognormal, and for a poverty line z, we then have a prediction of the probability that the household will be in poverty, $Pr(y_{i,t+1} < z)$, as in Figure 5.12. It is measured by the area under the frequency distribution of y and below the poverty line. This area can be compared to α to assess whether the household is vulnerable to poverty or not. As can be seen in Figure 5.12, vulnerability to poverty can increase with (1) a higher poverty line, (2) falling expected consumption, and (3) rising variability of consumption.

Note that bad data, i.e. data with a lot of measurement errors, will inflate estimates of σ, exaggerating the estimated risk of falling into poverty. Less frequent data will underestimate vulnerability to poverty as they will miss a lot of short-term entries into and exits from poverty. Note also that we can study vulnerability to hunger in exactly the same way, using for y an indicator of nutrition and for z a nutritional threshold below which there is hunger.

An often used simple definition of vulnerability is that a household is vulnerable if its income is not much higher than the poverty line. The World Bank, for instance, reported poverty and vulnerability in Latin America and the Caribbean by using a poverty line of PPP\$4/day and a vulnerability line of PPP\$10/day. The vulnerable

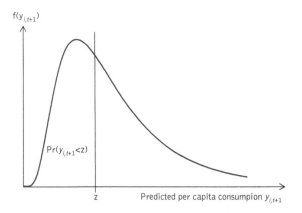

Figure 5.12 *Estimated vulnerability to poverty for a household*

226

population is then people with a PPP$ daily expenditure between 4 and 10. Using this definition, the poverty rate in 2010 was 30 percent, while the vulnerability rate was 35 percent. They also find that while the poverty rate declined from 45 percent to 30 percent between 1995 and 2010, the vulnerability rate increased from 30 to 35 percent—so vulnerability has not only exceeded poverty, but has also been rising while poverty has been falling. This observation is symptomatic of the emergence of a lower-middle class that has escaped poverty but remains vulnerable to shocks that could drive them back into poverty. Addressing vulnerability to poverty is thus an increasingly important component of an anti-poverty strategy. As we saw in Chapter 1, while vulnerability to poverty was not a concern of the MDGs, it is an important consideration for the post-2015 Sustainable Development Goals.

Types of shock

Shocks that affect a household's expenditure level, and hence its vulnerability to poverty, can be classified into four types (Dercon, 2001):

1. *Shocks to its assets*: illness or accident affecting capacity to work, loss of animals, land expropriation, loss of value of financial assets.
2. *Shocks to the context in which it uses its assets to generate income*: drought and flood, fall in producer prices, rise in consumer prices, unemployment, civil war.
3. *Shocks to the context in which it transforms its income into consumption*: rising food prices, market disintegration.
4. *Shocks to transfers*: loss of access to a safety net, economic crisis at the destination of migration affecting remittances.

These shocks can be idiosyncratic (illness) or covariate (drought and flood, recession, policy changes, political cycles). Idiosyncratic shocks can be insured locally (e.g. through mutual insurance) but not covariate shocks.

Identifying the causes of vulnerability is essential for designing anti-poverty strategies that can reduce vulnerability to poverty. Yet because we need panel data to do this analysis, and such data are still rare in developing countries, rigorous studies of the causes of vulnerability are few. We discuss here some of the available studies.

Several recent empirical analyses have shown that exposure to short-run shocks can have long term consequences that affect the likelihood of being in poverty. Using panel data for rural Pakistan collected by the International Food Policy Research Institute, Alderman *et al.* (2006) show that exposure of preschool children to nutritional shocks can have long-term consequences on their school enrollment. Nutritional shocks are measured by a child's height-for-age z score (stunting), as instrumented (predicted) by exogenous price shocks for major food commodities at age five. Using the 2000 Indonesia Family Life Survey, Maccini and Yang (2009) find that better rainfall (an exogenous positive shock) in a woman's birth year affects her adult achievements in many dimensions of wellbeing. A 20 percent higher rainfall relative to the local norm implies being 0.6 cm taller, completing 0.22 more schooling grades, and living in households with higher asset endowments. The channel of causation

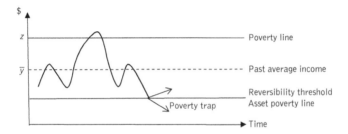

Figure 5.13 *Shock and poverty trap when crossing the asset-poverty line*

proposed by the authors runs from early-life rainfall to better infant health, higher educational attainment, and, finally, higher adult socio-economic status.

Similarly, exposure to a negative shock can create irreversibilities. This is the case when a short-run shock transforms transient poor into chronic or permanent poor. This happens when the shock leads to asset decapitalization, e.g. the sale of productive assets, taking children out of school, exposing infants to malnutrition during the critical first thousand days of existence, and becoming homeless and losing the capacity to get a job. Irreversibilities can thus create poverty traps if households cannot escape poverty in a multiple equilibrium framework (as we will see in Chapter 9), or quasi-poverty traps if they need very long periods of time to accumulate sufficient assets to move out of poverty (Antman and McKenzie, 2007).

To understand the idea of a poverty trap, we can introduce the concept of an asset (or income) threshold for reversibility, i.e. an asset-poverty line (Figure 5.13). Below this threshold, a household becomes captive to poverty, often referred to as entering a vicious circle of poverty. For pastoralists in Northern Kenya, according to Carter and Barrett (2006), this may be the minimum herd size below which profitable management through transhumance in the dry season is no longer possible. In classical models of farm-household behavior, such as Eswaran and Kotwal's (1986), this is represented by a minimum threshold of capital endowment necessary to enter into or remain in farming (as we will see in Chapter 22).

Policy instruments to combat persistent and chronic poverty: cargo nets and safety nets

Reducing persistent and chronic poverty requires raising the average level of expenditure. This can be done by improving the household's asset position, the quality of the context in which it uses its assets to generate income and transforms income into consumption, and/or increasing permanent transfers. These have been called cargo-net instruments that can lift average income (Carter and Barrett, 2006). A key component of cargo-net policies is overall economic growth that improves the context in which the assets are used, in particular by creating new and better employment and investment opportunities for the poor.

Reducing transitory poverty can be achieved not only by raising the average level of expenditure, but also by reducing exposure to risk, better risk management, and improved access to risk-coping instruments. Risk management to avoid transitory poverty includes accumulating precautionary savings (often in the form of liquid productive assets such as animals) that can be dis-saved when needed, and participation in formal or informal insurance schemes. Risk coping to avoid transitory poverty includes access to rapid-disbursement credit and to social-assistance programs. These have been referred to as safety-net (as opposed to cargo-net) instruments that can place a floor on expenditures so households do not fall below the poverty line. The safety net can be for income and expenditures, but also, importantly, on assets to avoid decapitalization and preserve future income-earning capacity. A low-cost one-time intervention in response to a shock can thus have long-term benefits, with huge cost savings in terms of future poverty. Here are some examples (that we will analyze in Chapter 14):

The Mahatma Gandhi National Rural Employment Guarantee Scheme (India)
Emergency health coverage (Indonesia)
Emergency scholarship program (South Korea)
The Index-based Livestock Insurance Scheme (Mongolia)
Rapid inclusion in a CCT program (Chile)
Workfare programs in community projects to provide quick relief from poverty via targeted wage earnings and to improve the longer-term local food-production capacity via local public goods such as water-management infrastructure (Ethiopia and Yemen)

What is important to remember here is that different causes of poverty require different policy instruments. In their study of poverty in rural China, Jalan and Ravallion (2000) find that health and education help reduce chronic poverty, but that they have no influence on transitory poverty. While a great deal of attention has been given to combating chronic poverty, not enough attention has been given to protecting the vulnerable non-poor from falling into poverty. Low-cost, well targeted interventions can have huge long-term benefits if they can help prevent the transitory poor from becoming the new permanent poor.

Dynamics of poverty: entry and exit

With poverty being a dynamic state of nature, we can categorize in Table 5.6 the households in a particular population into four categories in terms of the probability of their entering into poverty and exiting from it. From a policy standpoint, the critical categories are those with a high probability of entry and a low probability of exit. We can then look at the characteristics of the individuals who belong to each of these four categories to establish how to target the most critical of them. This was done, for example, in Poland in 1993–6 in the context of the transition from a centrally planned to a market economy (Okrasa, 1999). The key variables characterizing individuals are demography (age of household head, education, type of household, gender, marital status), location (rural, large town), employment sector (public, private), socio-economic status (employees, farmers, self-employed, welfare recipients, pensioners),

Table 5.6 *Entry and exit from poverty, Poland 1993–6*

Poland, 1993–6		Probability of exit from poverty	
		High	Low
Probability of entry into poverty	High	**High poverty mobility** Single Married without children Has savings account Participates in transfer network	**High poverty persistence** Low education Married with many children Disabled Employed in public sector Welfare recipient
	Low	**Low poverty persistence** University degree Single Employee Self-employed Pensioner	**Low poverty mobility** Widowed Divorced Indebted Farmer

Source: Okrasa, 1999.

financial assets (savings account), access to transfers (private, public), and access to social benefits (family allowances, unemployment benefits). What we see is that critically vulnerable individuals, with a high probability of entry into poverty and a low probability of exit, are more likely to be those with low education, many children, disabilities, employment in the public sector, and recipient of welfare transfers.

OTHER ASPECTS OF POVERTY

Economic mobility: upward and downward

Transition matrices, where population is classified by expenditure quintiles in an initial and a terminal period, allow us to track economic mobility over time. If the period of observation is long enough, this allows the measurement of long-term changes in poverty status. Indicators of mobility are for example:

- The percentage of households that remain in the same expenditure category (lack of mobility).
- The percentage of households that move up or down by one or more quintiles (degrees of mobility).

In Vietnam, the economy grew at 8 percent/year between 1993 and 1998. How did this affect the poor and the non-poor? This can be seen in the transition matrix for poverty between these two years in Table 5.7. The Vietnam LSMS are panel data so we can track the poverty status of each individual in 1993 and 1998. Of the 56 percent poor in 1993, 27 percent (about half) had escaped poverty in 1998, a remarkable

Table 5.7 *Transition matrix for poverty in Vietnam, 1993 and 1998*

	Poor in 1998	Not poor in 1998	Poverty rate in 1993
Poor in 1993	0.29	0.27	0.56
Not poor in 1993	0.05	0.39	
Poverty rate in 1998	0.34		

Source: Glewwe *et al.*, 2002.

achievement. Of the 44 percent non-poor, 39 percent were still non-poor in 1998, but 5 percent (i.e. 11 percent of them) had fallen into poverty, indicating that the period was not smooth sailing for all, in spite of rapid growth and a successful decline in the poverty rate from 56 percent to 34 percent.

Intergenerational transmission of poverty: the inheritance of poverty

Children born to poor parents are much more likely to be poor themselves as they will likely receive low education and inferior health care from their parents, both of which are assets that are powerful determinants of future incomes. This is a key aspect of inequity (that we will analyze in Chapter 6). CCT programs such as *Oportunidades* in Mexico, *Bolsa Família* in Brazil, and many others across the world pay poor mothers to send their children to school. These transfers pursue a twin-track approach: a short-run reduction in poverty through the cash transfers, and a long-term reduction in poverty by breaking its intergenerational inheritance, predicting that better educated children, through enforcement of the conditionality on school attendance, will be less poor. Because these programs are relatively recent, we still have little evidence of whether beneficiaries' positive educational achievements translate into long-term reduced inheritance of poverty, although a recent five-year follow-up of *Oportunidades* beneficiaries by Behrman *et al.* (2011), based on the RCT design of the initial intervention, shows positive results. The authors find that beneficiaries have higher schooling achievements (i.e. get higher grades), work less as young adults as they postpone entry into the labor force, work more when older, and shift employment from agriculture to non-agricultural activities.

Intra-household poverty: role of gender in poverty

Even though it has been found that some degree of altruism prevails in the allocation of food across members of a household, consumption is nevertheless unequally distributed (Pitt *et al.*, 1990). Male and earning members of the household are typically given priority, particularly in terms of who eats first. Both the higher average level and the smaller variance in calories consumed by men relative to women reflect in part the greater participation by men in activities in which productivity is sensitive to health status. As a consequence, women and girls tend to consume less than their equitable share when food is scarce. Household-level measures of poverty that do not take into account intra-household disparities underestimate the true extent of individual-level poverty, perhaps by as much as 25 percent (Haddad and Kanbur, 1989).

THE GEOGRAPHY OF POVERTY: POVERTY MAPS

Constructing a poverty map

Poverty maps are useful in helping visualize the geographical location of poverty. They can be overlaid with other maps such as population density, agro-ecological quality, distance to major agglomerations, and fiscal expenditures on welfare programs to observe the correspondence of these variables with poverty. The most commonly used methodology to construct a poverty map consists in combining household-survey data, that provides information on income or consumption, with household-level population census data that do not give such information but provide information on variables that are correlated with income (Elbers *et al.*, 2003). The objective is to get an income or consumption prediction for every household in the country. The approach follows three steps.

Step 1. Use household survey data (e.g. an LSMS or a household income and expenditure survey) to estimate a predictive equation of the per capita expenditure level y_i of an individual i with characteristics X_i. The X_i are individual-level correlates of poverty that are available in both the household survey (called intensive data) and the population census data (called extensive data). They include individual characteristics (such as age, gender, education, and professional activities), household characteristics (such as family size and dependency ratio), and variables that characterize the context in which the household is located (such as rural or urban, population density, and employment structure).

Step 2. Use population census information on every individual in the country to predict individual expenditure levels using the predictive function estimated with the household survey. Note that this requires accessing census data on individuals, which is often highly restricted and constitutionally protected. These expenditure predictions are then averaged over individuals in "small areas" (e.g. census tracts or municipalities) to reduce the variance of the prediction. This gives per capita expenditure predictions for population groups (e.g. of no less than 5,000 individuals to ensure reasonable accuracy and yet provide sufficiently fine-grain poverty maps). Calculate the desired poverty indicators such as members of the P_α class for each small area.

Step 3. Map the poverty indicators for each small area using Geographical Information System techniques.

As an example, to construct a map of the headcount ratio P_0 in small areas, in the first step we estimate:

$y = f(X)$ using the information on y and X in a household survey.

In the second step we use the estimated function (denoted by $\hat{f}$) to predict y (denoted by $\hat{y}$) for every individual in the population:

$\hat{y} = \hat{f}(X)$ using the same X in the population census.

232

We then use the $\hat{y}$ in each small region to calculate the corresponding P_0. And we construct a map with a color scheme representing the levels of P_0 in each small area in the country.

Using a poverty map for policy analysis: poverty rate vs. poverty density

The poverty map for Vietnam in Figure 5.14 shows that headcount ratios (left panel) tend to increase with distance from markets. For example, areas with the highest incidence of poverty are located far away from Hanoi in the north. By contrast, the poverty density, which measures the number of poor people in a location per unit of area (right panel), shows that the majority of the poor live in close proximity to or within urban areas. Hence the map reveals that most of the poor are not in remote areas, but right next to where the non-poor are located. Focusing on poverty rates as opposed to poverty density would thus lead to very different poverty-reduction strategies. Focusing on poverty density would consist in building opportunities incrementally, starting from urban areas, rather than trying to promote opportunities in remote areas

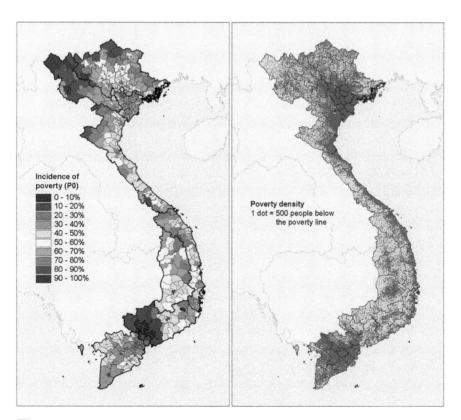

Figure 5.14 *Mapping the incidence and density of poverty in Vietnam*

Source: Minot *et al.*, 2003.

233

to reduce poverty rates where they are the highest. Similar maps can be used to visualize the geography of other dimensions of development such as children's z-scores (Fujii, 2010).

REDUCING POVERTY: THE RELATIVE ROLES OF INCOME GROWTH AND SOCIAL PROGRAMS

In China, rapid growth has been the main instrument in reducing poverty, in spite of rising inequality. In Brazil, social programs have played an important complementary role to growth (Ravallion, 2009). In general, growth is expected to be the main instrument to reduce poverty, but how effective is it for this purpose? How much does aggregate income growth effectively trickle down to the poor? This is measured by the elasticity E of income of the poor with respect to aggregate income, or of income of the poor relative to income of the rich. If E is larger than one, growth is pro-poor in the UN Development Program sense of benefiting the poor more than the average population or the rich (Kakwani and Pernia, 2000). For E to be larger than one, the poor have to gain proportionally more from growth than the rich, meaning that inequality has to fall. What is the available empirical evidence on the size of E, and what are the policy instruments that can be used to increase E?

"Growth is good": $E = 1$

Using cross-country regressions for 92 countries with at least two observations (allowing us to measure growth in each episode between two observations), each no less than five years apart, Dollar and Kraay (2002) found that E tends overall to be equal to one. This means that the percentage changes in the income of the poorest quintile (y) and of the overall population (Y) are equal, namely: $(\Delta y / y)_{poor} = (\Delta y / y)_{overall}$, with zero average impact on inequality for that partition of the population. They use this result to conclude that "growth is good" for the poor, with the policy implication that accelerating growth is the most effective and easily implemented instrument for poverty reduction, and that not too much should be expected from income-redistribution policies for poverty reduction.

This result has been highly influential on the primacy given to growth by international organizations such as the World Bank and the IMF in their poverty-reduction strategies. While controversial, this result has been generally upheld in the many subsequent critical assessments of the study. However, the robust overall result hides considerable heterogeneity across countries (Ravallion, 2001). Indeed, many countries have been able to achieve highly pro-poor growth with $E > 2$, while many others have experienced highly inequalizing growth with $E < 0.5$. In their data, Dollar and Kraay find that 20 percent of the growth episodes observed had $E > 2$, 30 percent between 1 and 2, 18 percent between 0.5 and 1, and 32 percent < 0.5. It is thus important to look at heterogeneity, beyond averages.

In Brazil, over the 1981–2005 period, growth aided by social programs to reduce inequality resulted in an elasticity of poverty with respect to income of –4.3, compared to an effect of –0.8 in China, where growth was the main policy objective, inequality increased, and social programs were lacking. In India, where both growth and social programs were used to reduce poverty, the elasticity was only −0.4, basically because growth was not low-skill labor-intensive and social programs were generally poorly targeted, with extensive leakage of benefits to the non-poor (Ravallion, 2009). The implication is that we need to learn which mechanisms achieve pro-poor growth and where it has occurred, so inequality reduction can be used as an additional instrument to growth in attacking poverty, particularly for countries where economic growth is modest and initial inequality very high. This will be addressed in Chapter 6.

E depends on the quality of growth

Can we do better than $E = 1$? It depends on the "quality" of growth. Squire and Walton, in the 1990 World Development Report titled *Poverty* (World Bank, 1990), suggested that poverty reduction requires labor-intensive growth complemented by targeted transfers and safety nets. Datt and Ravallion (1998) find that, in India, growth in agriculture was the most poverty reducing among economic sectors. This is not surprising given the fact that most of the poor are rural and that most of them depend on agriculture for their livelihoods. Using a cross-country panel regression, Ligon and Sadoulet (2007) find that GDP growth originating in agriculture is two to three times more effective in raising the income of households with the 50 percent lowest expenditure levels compared to GDP growth originating in the rest of the economy. This is shown in Figure 5.15, where the five poorest expenditure deciles in the population achieved larger expenditure gains when GDP growth originates in agriculture rather than non-agriculture.

Growth can thus be made more pro-poor. Focusing public investments in sectors with larger E is an instrument. This elasticity can be raised by increasing the asset position of the poor, improving the context in which they use their assets, and providing

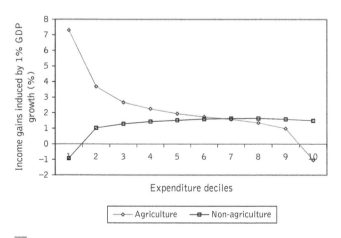

Figure 5.15 *GDP growth originating in agriculture is more effective in raising the expenditure of the poor than growth originating in non-agriculture*

Source: Ligon and Sadoulet, 2007.

235

them with safety nets so they can take more entrepreneurial or labor-market risks. Poverty reduction also requires targeted interventions since not all poor are able to benefit from growth through employment and investment opportunities—and vulnerable non-poor households are exposed to shocks that could take them into poverty. Social-assistance programs should thus be an integral component of pro-poor growth, with such programs financed by revenues derived from growth through taxation. In this fashion, growth is made more pro-poor both by creating opportunities for the poor to participate more in growth through employment and self-employment, and by providing social-safety net programs linked to growth performance.

Reduced inequality can contribute to poverty reduction

If between two periods there has been not only income growth, but also a reduction in inequality, the observed decline in poverty originates both in a growth and a distribution effect (Bourguignon, 2003). This is visualized in Figure 5.16. The transformation of the initial distribution of income (on a logarithmic scale) into the final distribution shows first a growth effect (a pure shift to the right in the distribution of income without change in its shape) followed by a change in the shape of the distribution (with less dispersion around the mean, showing reduced inequality) at constant mean. The poverty rate (headcount ratio) is the area under the curve and to the left of the poverty line. We can see that the total decline in poverty is due to two effects: a (larger) growth effect and a (smaller) distribution effect.

This effect of income growth ($\dot{y}$) and inequality growth ($\dot{G}$) on growth in the poverty rate ($\dot{P}_0$) can be approximated with the following additive formula:

$$\dot{P}_0 = E_p^y \dot{y} + E_p^G \dot{G} + \text{Residual},$$

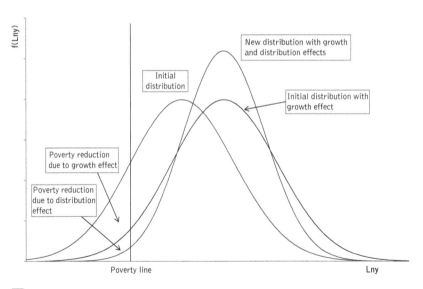

Figure 5.16 *Decomposition of change in the poverty rate into growth and distribution effects*

where E_p^y is the income elasticity of poverty and E_p^G the inequality elasticity of poverty. These elasticities can be estimated econometrically with cross-country data on growth spells in the following equation:

$$\dot{P}_0 = \beta_1 + \beta_2 \dot{y} + \beta_3 \dot{y} G + \beta_4 \dot{y} \frac{z}{\mu} + \beta_5 \dot{G} + \beta_6 \dot{G} G + \beta_7 \dot{G} \frac{z}{\mu} + \varepsilon,$$

where G is the initial inequality, z the poverty line, μ initial average income, and ε a residual term. The income and inequality elasticities of poverty deriving from this equation are respectively:

$$E_p^y = \beta_2 + \beta_3 G + \beta_4 \frac{z}{\mu}$$

$$E_p^G = \beta_5 + \beta_6 G + \beta_7 \frac{z}{\mu}.$$

Fosu (2014) calculated these for 80 countries in the world and 18 Sub-Saharan countries where there had been poverty reduction over the period since the early 1990s when growth accelerated. Table 5.8 shows that there was an 8.4 percent annual decline in poverty in all countries and 3.4 percent in Sub-Saharan Africa, a good performance for Sub-Saharan Africa compared to previous periods when the poverty rate had been rising. Across all countries, growth explained 76.5 of the decline in poverty and reduced inequality 10.4 percent. In Sub-Saharan Africa, by contrast, reduced inequality made no contribution to poverty reduction, and possibly the reverse. The decline in poverty all came from growth. Yet growth was also less effective in reducing poverty in Sub-Saharan Africa than it was in all countries, implying a lower elasticity of poverty with respect to growth than globally. The policy implication is that growth is essential for poverty reduction but that greater attention should be given both to making growth more pro-poor and using reduced inequality as a source of poverty reduction.

Datt and Ravallion (1992) proposed an exact decomposition of the observed change in P between two periods (0, 1) into a component due to average income growth and a component due to change in inequality. Let P (that can be P_0, P_1, or P_2) be written as a function of the poverty line z, mean income μ, and the distribution of per capita income f:

Table 5.8 *Roles of growth and distribution in poverty reduction: all countries and Sub-Saharan Africa*

	Observed growth in poverty rate	% role of income growth	% role of equality growth	% role of residual term	Total effect
All countries	−8.4	76.5	10.4	13.1	100
Sub-Saharan Africa	−3.1	67.7	−4.8	37.1	100

Source: Based on data in Fosu, 2014.

$P(z/\mu, f)$.

The discrete change in poverty between two periods (0, 1)

$$\Delta P = P(z/\mu_1, f_1) - P(z/\mu_0, f_0),$$

can be decomposed into:

$$\frac{1}{2}\left[P(z / \mu_1, f_1) - P(z / \mu_0, f_1) + P(z / \mu_1, f_0) - P(z / \mu_0, f_0)\right]$$

$$+ \frac{1}{2}\left[P(z / \mu_0, f_1) - P(z / \mu_0, f_0) + P(z / \mu_1, f_1) - P(z / \mu_1, f_0)\right]$$

In this decomposition, the first term (the growth component) measures the change in P due to a change in mean income with no change in distribution; the second term (the redistribution component) measures the effect of a change in distribution with no change in mean income.

How this is done in practice is as follows. For a given poverty line z:

1. Use income data at time 0 for the population below the poverty line z to calculate $P(\mu_0, f_0)$.
2. Use the same income data at time 0 multiplied by μ_1/μ_0 to calculate $P(\mu_1, f_0)$.
3. Use income data at time 1 for the population below the poverty line z to calculate $P(\mu_1, f_1)$.
4. Use the same income data at time 1 multiplied by μ_0/μ_1 to calculate $P(\mu_0, f_1)$.

For India, Datt and Ravallion (1992) find that the growth effect largely dominates over the redistribution effect (Table 5.9). In India, the redistribution effect helped

Table 5.9 *Growth and distribution components of changes in poverty*

Country	Period	Change in P_0	Growth component	Distribution component	Source
Brazil	1981–1988	0	−4.5	4.5	World Bank (2006)
Brazil	1998–2004	−2.9	0.9	−3.7	World Bank (2006)
China rural	1996–2001	−1.5	−2.2	0.4	World Bank (2006)
China urban	1996–2002	−3.2	−6.9	6	World Bank (2006)
Madagascar	1993–2001	14.7	13.6	3.3	World Bank (2006)
Nigeria	1996–2003	−6.9	−3.6	−2.3	World Bank (2006)
Pakistan	1998–2002	3.7	−5.7	9.4	World Bank (2006)
Peru	1996–2002	3.7	−5.7	9.4	World Bank (2006)
Ivory Coast	1985–1988	15.9	16.9	−0.1	Grootaert (1995)
India rural	1977–1988	−15.9	−9.7	−6.1	Datt and Ravallion (1992)
India urban	1977–1989	−7.1	−7.9	−0.2	Datt and Ravallion (1992)

Source: Datt and Ravallion, 1992.

further reduce poverty, implying that growth was pro-poor. In Brazil, for the 1981–8 period before the introduction of social programs, the redistribution effect erased the growth component, with a zero net poverty effect. Similar decompositions for other developing countries have generally found that the growth effect dominates over the redistribution effect, but that reducing inequality can nevertheless be an important contributor to poverty reduction. Social programs that help reduce inequalities—for example, Brazil's successful *Bolsa Família* and Zero Hunger programs, starting in 2001—can thus be important poverty-reduction instruments, complementing the potential effectiveness of growth. For the 1998–2004 period the redistribution component helped reduce poverty, while growth itself was not particularly poverty reducing.

HOW DO THE EXTREME POOR LIVE?

The extreme poor are people who live on less than PPP$1.25/day. We by now have a large number of household surveys (such as the publicly available LSMS and DHS) that give us a detailed characterization of how poor people manage their lives, organize their households, earn their incomes, spend their money, relate to markets, and access public goods (Banerjee and Duflo, 2007). These data, complemented by RCTs, have been interpreted psychologically and economically for new insights about how the poor decide on what they do. They have been explored in recent books by Collins *et al.* (2009), Banerjee and Duflo (2011), and Karlan and Appel (2011). Observing the economic lives of the poor compared to those of the non-poor throws up several surprises. While the fundamental determinants of behavior are basically the same for the poor as for the non-poor—they have the same desires, psychological weaknesses, and inconsistencies—the context and the stakes in their making decisions are very different.

An important common theme is the considerable heterogeneity of behavioral patterns. Hence one has to be careful not to resort to clichés, and instead look carefully at the data. In spite of heterogeneity, there are some frequently observed regularities.

1. *Extended household structure.* The poor tend to live in larger households, with many children but also many adults, often married, who remain attached to the household, resulting in extended, multi-generational households. We will see in Chapter 11 that children have valuable income and protection functions for their poor parents, which explains large families, and that extended families can be effective in managing risks and achieving economies of scale in consumption.

2. *Multiple sources of income.* The poor tend to have multiple sources of income (engaging in what is sometimes called pluriactivity) instead of specializing in one activity. Small farmers will typically derive some 50 percent of their household income from off-farm employment and self-employment in the rural non-farm economy (analyzed in Chapter 22). Diversification of sources of income is in part due to lack of opportunities (e.g. lack of sufficient access to land to be a full-time farmer, lack of full-time employment in a formal-sector job), but it is also part of risk-management strategies, where diversification helps stabilize income flows, if at a cost in terms of expected incomes.

3. *Second-best entrepreneurship.* The poor tend to be workers in the informal sector or self-employed micro-entrepreneurs, also in the informal sector, instead of being formally employed. Self-employment (e.g. as a subsistence farmer, a street vendor, or a garbage collector) is in general not their first-best option, but a strategy to cope with un- and underemployment in the formal sector. A large segment of this employment and entrepreneurship in the informal sector is thus counter-cyclical to formal-sector wage-earning employment opportunities. This will be explored in Chapter 12.

4. *Underconsumption of staple foods.* The poor tend to underspend on calorie-rich staple foods, even if their calorie intakes are low; and they occasionally spend on expensive tasty foods and relatively luxurious consumer goods (tobacco, alcohol) and entertainments (festivals, weddings, funerals, and religious rituals). A long-term behavioral puzzle for economists has been why the income elasticity of calorie intake is so low among the poor, contributing to the reproduction of malnutrition and hunger, especially among children, even when income rises—for example, with introduction of the cultivation of cash crops (this will be discussed in Chapter 18).

5. *Low investment in health and education.* The poor tend to underinvest in their children's health and education, even when these investments are economically profitable. There is notable underinvestment in preventive health expenditures such as insecticide-treated bed nets and vaccination. Under high subsidies, demand is positive, but the price elasticity of demand is high as soon as prices are positive, with demand frequently becoming zero before price reaches market value. This may be because gains are far away in the future (as seen today with high discount rates due to capital-market failures and poverty), in part due to their own lack of information about the benefits of these investments, and in part due to resignation to being sick and illiterate, which is associated with the "culture of poverty." This is analyzed in Chapter 17.

6. *Lack of formal savings, borrowing, and insurance.* The poor tend to under-save in formal savings accounts and not to have access to formal loans and forms of insurance due to selective market failures. Lack of savings is partially due to difficulty in holding on to savings in the face of family and community pressures to share with others in dire need. Saving, borrowing, and risk reduction are all very important, but as a consequence are mainly done through often highly inefficient informal mechanisms such as food reserves and animals for precautionary savings, and money lenders for borrowing (Collins *et al.*, 2009). This is analyzed in Chapter 13.

7. *Temptation and procrastination.* Like the rest of the population, the poor often lack self-control, spending on temptation goods and postponing decisions. However, these temptations tend to have higher costs for their health and nutrition than in the case of the non-poor. Decisions postponed due to procrastination (for instance, purchasing fertilizers after harvest when they have cash in hand, as observed by Duflo *et al.*, 2011) are not a distinct behavior, but they have severe consequences on wellbeing for the poor. This is analyzed in Chapter 22.

8. *Migration.* The poor tend to engage in short-term migration instead of more costly and more risky longer-term and permanent migration. It is notable, in

Indian villages, how little permanent migration there is, in part due to lack of a national civil-registration system that allows people to be recognized in areas other than their own, in part due to local social relations that provide support and insurance that are lost when moving to an anonymous urban context. The recent introduction of a Unique Identification (UID) number for India's 1.2 billion people, with 600 million UIDs already assigned by 2015, may facilitate rural–urban migration for the poor. This is analyzed in Chapters 12 and 14.

9. *Underuse of public services.* The poor tend to have limited access to public services, and these services tend to be of low quality. However, the poor also tend to underuse the public services to which they have access (Sen-type entitlements), especially in health and education. Some of the most effective social-safety net programs, such as the *Chile Solidario*, consist not in creating new services, but in helping the poor know their rights in order to access what is already in place. Access to social services and to social safety-net programs is explored in Chapter 14.

10. *Lack of risk management.* The poor are risk-averse, at a heavy cost to their expected incomes, but tend to undermanage risks ex-ante, often unrealistically wishing for the best and counting on the benevolence of others. Early-warning systems for incoming droughts tend to be underused by pastoralists, with adverse consequences when drought strikes (Lybbert *et al.*, 2007). Index-based weather-insurance schemes, while potentially effective in addressing standard adverse selection and moral-hazard problems in insurance, thus tend to have very low uptake without heavy subsidies. This is explored in Chapter 13.

11. *Adverse risk coping.* The poor tend to cope with shocks with short-run responses that have long-term, often irreversible consequences. These include reducing food consumption for young children, postponing health expenditures, not seeking medical treatment, taking children out of school, and selling productive assets. These adjustments tend to bear more on women than on men, and on girls than on boys. This was explored earlier in this chapter.

12. *Precarious asset ownership.* The poor own very few assets, and their asset ownership is frequently informal and precarious, reducing the productive value of the assets they control—for instance, as forms of collateral to access financial services (De Soto, 2000). However, most of the rural poor, who constitute the vast majority of the world poor, have access to some land on which they can produce part of their subsistence needs. Use of these limited assets tends to be extensive, achieving low yields, with large opportunities for picking the low-hanging fruit of productivity gains. Use of land for production for home consumption in achieving food security is explored in Chapter 18.

13. *A heavy burden of decision-making.* Banerjee and Duflo (2011) note that poor people need make decisions on many issues that are taken for granted by people in developed countries. They need to worry about water quality, food safety, personal security, securing savings, and coping with health shocks, when these services are largely predetermined for citizens in rich countries. In addition, these decisions often have to be made with incomplete access to information, information that is sometimes incorrect, and with low capacity to make use of the information

241

available, resulting in erroneous choices or simply in no decisions. The lives of the poor could thus be improved just by simplifying the many decisions they need to make—for instance, by providing safe tap water or access to a minimum safety net when adversity strikes.

In conclusion, understanding how the poor live and how they decide is fundamental in designing programs to improve their wellbeing. Indeed, these programs all have to be incentive compatible with what the poor do for themselves as individuals and collectively, given the constraints and opportunities under which they operate. What is striking is that there exists much low-hanging fruit, with room for improvement of the lot of the poor.

ARE THERE BEHAVIORAL POVERTY TRAPS?

Can poverty induce patterns of behavior that contribute to reproducing poverty? If it can, then there could be behavioral poverty traps. There is a long history of this reasoning in explaining the stubborn persistence of poverty, and recent empirical evidence has given it credence (Figure 5.17).

The most famous argument in favor of behavioral poverty traps was proposed by the anthropologist Oscar Lewis (1959) in his study of a culture of poverty among five families in Mexico. According to Lewis, fatalism and resignation to the fact of being poor was an important aspect of their culture. The poor felt excluded and marginalized, undermining their will to organize to overcome poverty—and the culture of poverty is learned by the youth and reproduced from generation to generation. The theory has been criticized for blaming the victim, providing the rich with an apology for the existence of poverty.

Behavioral responses to poverty can also create poverty traps. Using both laboratory and natural experiments, Mullainathan and Shafir (2013) showed that scarcity of money, food, sleep, security, and other immediate needs creates cognitive impairments, forcing the mind to concentrate on solving the immediate problem at hand at the cost of less attention given to other issues and to the long-term consequences of decisions taken in a "scarcity trap." According to them, "scarcity captures the mind" and limits the availability of brain bandwidth to address other issues, reducing ability to perform in tests and tasks, narrowing perspective on the future, and reducing

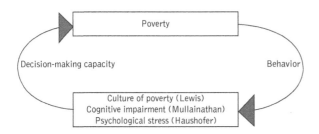

Figure 5.17 *Are there behavioral poverty traps?*

self-control. As a consequence, many decisions are ill taken, with eventually severe long-term consequences that contribute to the reproduction of poverty, creating poverty traps. The poor need help to help themselves in taking a broader and longer-term perspective on their condition—for instance, providing them with more regularity in work, with more options for setting deadlines for saving, and more opportunities to raise their eyeline beyond the focus on immediate survival, principally by reducing exposure to scarcity.

Psychological and neurological factors also play a role. It is well established in psychology that poverty contributes to afflictions such as depression, stress, an inability to focus on issues beyond immediate survival, low self-esteem, loss of self-control, fatalism, and myopia. The psychology of poverty thus translates into a mindset that affects the ability to think of the future (affecting savings and investments), effort and persistence, employability, interpersonal relations (on and off the job), social networks, and many other outcomes. This in turn reproduces poverty. Poverty thus becomes endogenous to poverty in a typically vicious circle of reinforcement.

The role of psychological stress in decision-making has been tested in both laboratory and field experiments. In a natural experiment, Mani *et al.* (2013) studied the impact of financial stress on decision-making in the pre-harvest period (when it is high) vs. the post-harvest period (when it is lower) among sugar cane farmers in Tamil Nadu. They measured analytical capacity using Raven's Progressive Matrices to test for fluid intelligence, and numeric Stroop tasks to test for cognitive control. They found that performance is significantly worsened by financial stress, comparable to the impact of severe alcoholism on decision-making, roughly equal to the loss of 13 IQ points. An individual's stress level can be objectively measured by their level of cortisol, a steroid hormone produced by the brain. High levels of cortisol have been shown in clinical trials to affect decision-making, in particular increasing focus on short-term responses. In a set of recent studies, Chemin et al. (2013) and Haushofer and Shapiro (2013) have shown that poverty contributes to high cortisol levels. Using cortisol tests, Chemin *et al.* found that, in Kenya, low rainfall raises stress levels among farmers but not among non-farmers. Haushofer and Shapiro (2013) used an RCT to show that a large positive cash transfer to poor rural Kenyans reduces stress/cortisol levels and improves psychological perceptions of wellbeing. While this is a recent field of study, available evidence suggests that the psychological stress associated with poverty can have strong neurobiological consequences that affect behavior and create poverty traps. High cortisol levels can be treated by pharmaceutical drugs and therapy, but mainly by addressing the cause of psychological stress.

CONCEPTS SEEN IN THIS CHAPTER

Adult equivalent scales
Household-level public goods
Hidden hunger

Poverty line: nutrition-based, international, relative, weakly relative, and subjective
Poverty profile
Poverty gap
FGT indexes: P_0 (headcount), P_1 (depth), and P_2 (severity)
Decomposition of P index
Exit time from poverty
Determinants of poverty
Chronic vs. transitory poverty
Vulnerability to poverty
Irreversibilities
Poverty trap
Intergenerational transfer of poverty
Intra-household poverty
Twin-track approach to social assistance
Poverty map
Temptation goods

REVIEW QUESTIONS: POVERTY AND VULNERABILITY ANALYSIS

1. Poverty: give four alternative definitions of a poverty line.
2. Define the adult equivalence scale. Explain why it is important to correct for demographic composition and economies of scale at household level when making wellbeing comparisons.
3. Graph an income profile and a poverty line: what do they show?
4. Define (give formula), name, and give an interpretation of the P_α index and its specialization into: P_0, P_1, and P_2. Show an example of a change in P_1 and P_2 for a constant P_0. How do we calculate the aggregate P_0 from the P_0 for subgroups of the population? How do we calculate the contribution that each group makes to total poverty? Can the number of poor increase if P_0 is falling?
5. Anti-poverty interventions. How would you explain the main determinants of poverty? What are some of the corresponding policy instruments?
6. How do you define chronic and transitory poverty?
7. How do you define vulnerability to poverty? How do you define risk management and risk coping? What are some of the instruments that households can use to manage risk and to cope with risk?

NOTES

1   Useful general references on the measurement and analysis of poverty are Haughton and Khandker (2009), Ravallion (1996), and the World Bank's Poverty Net website (World Bank, 2009b).
2   We use here the property that $\Delta XY = Y\Delta X + X\Delta Y + \Delta X\Delta Y$ where $X = m$ and $Y = P_\alpha$.

REFERENCES

Alderman, Harold, John Hoddinott, and Bill Kinsey. 2006. "Long Term Consequences of Early Childhood Malnutrition." *Oxford Economic Papers* 58(3): 450–74.

Antman, Francisca, and David McKenzie. 2007. "Poverty Traps and Nonlinear Income Dynamics with Measurement Error and Individual Heterogeneity." *Journal of Development Studies* 43(6): 1057–83.

Ashraf, Nava. 2009. "Spousal Control and Household Decision-Making: An Experimental Study in the Philippines." *American Economic Review* 99(4): 1245–77.

Atkinson, Anthony. 1995. *Incomes and the Welfare State: Essays on Britain and Europe.* Cambridge University Press.

Banerjee, Abhijit, and Esther Duflo. 2007. "The Economic Lives of the Poor." *Journal of Economic Perspectives* 21(1): 141–67.

Banerjee, Abhijit, and Esther Duflo. 2011. *Poor Economics: A Radical Rethinking of the Way to Fight Global Poverty.* New York: Public Affairs.

Behrman, Jere, Susan Parker, and Petra Todd. 2011. "Do Conditional Cash Transfers for Schooling Generate Lasting Benefits? A Five-Year Follow-up of PROGRESA/ Oportunidades." *Journal of Human Resources* 46(1): 93–122.

Bourguignon, François. 2003. "The Growth Elasticity of Poverty Reduction: Explaining Heterogeneity across Countries and Time Periods." In T. Eicher and S. Turnovsky (eds.), *Inequality and Growth: Theory and Policy Implications,* 3–26. Cambridge, MA: MIT Press.

Carter, Michael, and Christopher Barrett. 2006. "The Economics of Poverty Traps and Persistent Poverty: An Asset-Based Approach." *Journal of Development Studies* 42(2): 178–99.

Chemin, Matthieu, Joost de Laat, and Johannes Haushofer. 2013. "Negative Rainfall Shocks Increase Levels of the Stress Hormone Cortisol Among Poor Farmers in Kenya." Abdul Latif Jameel Poverty Action Lab, MIT, Cambridge, MA.

Collins, Daryl, Jonathan Morduch, Stuart Rutherford, and Orlanda Ruthven. 2009. *Portfolios of the Poor: How the World's Poor Live on $2 a Day.* Princeton, NJ: Princeton University Press.

Coudouel, Aline, Jesko Hentschel, and Quentin Wodon. 2002. "Poverty Measurement and Analysis." In Jeni Klugman (ed.), A *Sourcebook for Poverty Reduction Strategies.* Washington, DC: World Bank.

Datt, Gaurav, and Martin Ravallion. 1992. "Growth and Redistribution Components of Changes in Poverty Measures: A Decomposition with Applications to Brazil and India in the 1980s." *Journal of Development Economics* 38(2): 275–95.

Datt, Gaurav, and Martin Ravallion. 1998. "Farm Productivity and Rural Poverty in India." *Journal of Development Studies* 34(4): 62–85.

Deaton, Angus. 1997. *The Analysis of Household Surveys: A Microeconometric Approach to Development Policy.* Johns Hopkins University Press.

Deaton, Angus, and Valerie Kozel. 2005. "Data and Dogma: The Great Indian Poverty Debate." *World Bank Research Observer* 20(2): 177–99.

Dercon, Stefan. 2001. "Assessing Vulnerability to Poverty." Working paper, Department of Economics, Oxford University.

De Soto, Hernando. 2000. *The Mystery of Capital: Why Capitalism Triumphs in the West and Fails Everywhere Else.* New York: Basic Books.

Dollar, David, and Aart Kraay. 2002. "Growth is Good for the Poor." *Journal of Economic Growth* 7(3): 195–225.

Duflo, Esther, Michael Kremer, and Jonathan Robinson. 2011. "Nudging Farmers to Use Fertilizer: Theory and Experimental Evidence from Kenya." *American Economic Review* 101(6): 2350–90.

Elbers, Chris, Jean Lanjouw, and Peter Lanjouw. 2003. "Micro-Level Estimation of Poverty and Inequality." *Econometrica* 71(1): 355–64.

Eswaran, Mukesh, and Ashok Kotwal. 1986. "Access to Capital and Agrarian Production Organization." *Economic Journal* 96(382): 482–98.

Foster, James, Joel Greer, and Erik Thorbecke. 1984. "A Class of Decomposable Poverty Measures." *Econometrica* 52(3): 761–6.

Fosu, Augustin. 2014. "Growth, Inequality, and Poverty in Sub-Saharan Africa: Recent Progress in a Global Context." Working Paper 2014–17, Centre for the Study of African Economies, Oxford University.

Fujii, Tomoki. 2010. "Micro-Level Estimation of Child Under-nutrition Indicators in Cambodia." *World Bank Economic Review* 24(3): 520–53.

Glewwe, Paul, Hassan Zaman, and Michele Gragnolati. 2002. "Who Gained from Vietnam's Boom in the 1990s?" *Economic Development and Cultural Change* 50(4): 773–92.

Haddad, Lawrence, and Ravi Kanbur. 1989. "How Serious is the Neglect of Intra-Household Inequality? (What Difference Does it Make to the Measurement and Decomposition of Inequality and Poverty?)." Warwick University, Development Economics Research Centre.

Haughton, Jonathan, and Shahidur Khandker. 2009. *Handbook on Poverty and Inequality.* Washington, DC: World Bank.

Haushofer, Johannes, and Jeremy Shapiro. 2013. "Household Response to Income Changes: Evidence from an Unconditional Cash Transfer Program in Kenya." Abdul Latif Jameel Poverty Action Lab, MIT, Cambridge, MA.

Jalan, Jyotsna, and Martin Ravallion. 2000. "Determinants of Transient and Chronic Poverty: Evidence from Rural China." *Journal of Development Studies* 36(6): 82–99.

Kakwani, Nanak, and Ernesto Pernia. 2000. "What is Pro-poor Growth?" *Asian Development Review* 16(1): 1–22.

Kanbur, Ravi. 2001. "Economic Policy, Distribution and Poverty: The Nature of Disagreements" *World Development* 29(6): 1083–94.

Karlan, Dean, and Jacob Appel. 2011. *More than Good Intentions: How a New Economics Is Helping to Solve Global Poverty.* New York: Dutton.

Lancaster, Kelvin. 1966. "A New Approach to Consumer Theory." *Journal of Political Economy* 74(2): 132–57.

Lewis, Oscar. 1959. *Five Families: Mexican Case Studies in the Culture of Poverty.* New York: Basic Books.

Ligon, Ethan, and Elisabeth Sadoulet. 2007. "Estimating the Effects of Aggregate Agricultural Growth on the Distribution of Expenditures." Background paper for the *World Development Report 2008.* Washington, DC: World Bank.

Lybbert, Travis, Christopher Barrett, John McPeak, and Winnie Luseno. 2007. "Bayesian Herders: Updating of Rainfall Beliefs in Response to External Forecasts." *World Development* 35(3): 480–97.

Maccini, Sharon, and Dean Yang. 2009. "Under the Weather: Health, Schooling, and Economic Consequences of Early-life Rainfall." *American Economic Review* 99(3): 1006–26.

Mani, Anandi, Sendhil Mullainathan, Eldar Shafir, and Jiaying Zhao. 2013. "Poverty Impedes Cognitive Function." *Science* 341: 976–80.

Minot, Nicholas, Bob Baulch, and Michael Epprecht. 2003. "Poverty and Inequality in Vietnam: Spatial Patterns and Geographic Determinants." Washington, DC: International Food Policy Research Institute.

Morduch, Jonathan. 1998. "Growth, Poverty, and Average Exit Time." *Economics Letters* 58: 385–90.

Morley, Samuel. 1995. *Poverty and Inequality in Latin America: The Impact of Adjustment and Recovery in the 1980s.* Baltimore: Johns Hopkins University Press.

Mullainathan, Sendhil, and Eldar Shafir. 2013. *Scarcity: Why Having Too Little Means So Much.* New York: Times Books.

Okrasa, Wlodzimierz. 1999. "The Dynamics of Poverty and the Effectiveness of Poland's Safety Net (1993–96)." Washington, DC: World Bank Policy Research Working Paper No. 2221.

Pitt, Mark, Mark Rosenzweig, and Md Nazmul Hassan. 1990. "Productivity, Health, and Inequality in the Intra-household Distribution of Food in Low-Income Countries." *American Economic Review* 80(5): 1139–56.

Ravallion, Martin, 1996. "Issues in Measuring and Modeling Poverty." *Economic Journal* 106(438): 1328–43.

Ravallion, Martin. 2001. "Growth, Inequality, and Poverty: Looking Beyond Averages." *World Development* 29(11): 1803–15.

Ravallion, Martin. 2009. "A Comparative Perspective on Poverty Reduction in Brazil, China, and India." Washington, DC: World Bank Policy Research Working Paper No. 5080.

Ravallion, Martin. 2012. "Why Don't We See Poverty Convergence?" *American Economic Review* 102(1): 504–23.

Ravallion, Martin, and Shaohua Chen. 2011. "Weakly Relative Poverty." *Review of Economics and Statistics* 93(4): 1251–61.

Rawls, John. 1971. *A Theory of Justice.* Cambridge, MA: Harvard University Press.

Sen, Amartya. 1976. "Poverty: An Ordinal Approach to Measurement." *Econometrica* 44(2): 219–31.

World Bank. 1990. *World Development Report 1990: Poverty.* Washington, DC.

World Bank. 2004. *Ecuador Poverty Assessment.* Washington, DC: World Bank Report No. 27061-EC.

World Bank. 2008. *Nicaragua Poverty Assessment.* Washington, DC: World Bank Report No. 39736-NI.

World Bank. 2009a. *Guatemala Poverty Assessment.* Washington, DC: World Bank Report No. 43920-GT.

World Bank. 2009b. *PovertyNet.* http://povertynet.org/ (accessed 2015).

World Bank. *World Development Indicators.* http://data.worldbank.org/indicator (accessed 2015).

Inequality and inequity

TAKE-HOME MESSAGES FOR CHAPTER 6

1. Inequality is an absolute concept that does not require definition of a threshold such as the poverty line. Measuring inequality requires information about per capita expenditures for the entire population, not just for individuals below the poverty line, as in measuring poverty.

2. To represent inequality, the equivalent to the poverty profile in representing poverty is the Lorenz curve that maps the cumulative percentage of total income against the cumulative percentage of total population ranked by increasing per capita income.

3. The most popular inequality indicator is the Gini coefficient, which ranges from 0 for perfect equality to 1 for perfect inequality. As opposed to the P_α poverty indicators, the Gini coefficient cannot be decomposed by population subgroups; it can be decomposed by sources of income. The Theil inequality index can be decomposed by population subgroups into the sum of within-group and between-group inequality.

4. While inequality has until recently been given little attention in development compared to poverty, it has become a major issue for reasons of both efficiency and welfare. High inequality is generally thought to reduce economic growth in the long term, making greater equality potentially both intrinsic to wellbeing and instrumental to sustained growth. However, there may exist short-term trade-offs between growth and equality.

5. According to Stiglitz and Fukuyama, high inequality can become a source of inefficiency if it allows the rich to capture the political system and use it for rent-seeking. Piketty similarly finds that the "forces of divergence" in the distribution of income to the benefit of the very rich lie in the capture of political power by the interests of capital.

6. Inequality is unlikely to be reduced simply by higher levels of GDPpc, following the Kuznets inverted-U curve, or by higher levels of economic growth, meaning that specific policies to reduce inequality must be introduced if reducing inequality is a policy objective.

7. Lower inequality helps growth make a larger contribution to poverty reduction. If pro-poor growth is inequality reducing, it unambiguously reduces poverty. However,

inequalizing growth can also reduce poverty, as it did in China and Vietnam, if it is sufficiently high that the growth effect overcomes the inequalizing effect on the income
of the poor.

8. Equity can be intrinsic and instrumental to development, but the case for increasing
equity has as yet received insufficient attention and the policy initiatives to achieve it
are less sharply drawn than those for reducing poverty and inequality when the latter
two are high.

9. Inclusive growth stresses the process through which growth is achieved, in particular
by providing productive employment opportunities to all that want to work in order
to create a feeling of belonging instead of alienation and frustration, particularly for
the youth.

By contrast to poverty, inequality is not measured relative to an arbitrary threshold: it
does not require specification of a poverty line. However, it is more demanding in
terms of data as it requires information on the income or expenditure level not just
of the poor but of all individuals in the population.[1]

DESCRIBING AND MEASURING INEQUALITY

Describing inequality: the Lorenz curve

By analogy with the poverty profile, a graphic representation of inequality is given
by the Lorenz curve (Figure 6.1). It is constructed using the per capita expenditure
(or income) levels for a representative sample of the population for which we want
to measure inequality, the inhabitants of a particular country, say. We first rank individuals from the poorest to the richest. We then represent the cumulative percentage of the population on the horizontal axis, and the corresponding cumulative
percentage of expenditures on the vertical axis. The plot we obtain is the Lorenz
curve. It gives us for example what percentage of total expenditure is spent by the
5 percent poorest, the 10 percent poorest, etc., until 100 percent of total expenditure has been accounted for. We can construct a Lorenz curve to characterize inequality in the distribution of other variables of interest such as income, land,
education, and livestock.

If income (or expenditure) were perfectly equally distributed among members of
the population, the Lorenz curve would be the 45-degree line. If it were maximally
unequally distributed, with all income held by just one person, the Lorenz curve
would be the outer edge of the 100x100 box. The further away the Lorenz curve is
from the 45-degree line, the more unequal is the distribution of income.

Note that if two Lorenz curves do not cross, inequality is unequivocally higher
with the one further away from the 45-degree line. But Lorenz curves can cross, in
which case simple visual inspection may not be enough and we will need to use a
specific scalar indicator to ascertain inequality.

Cumulative % of total expenditure

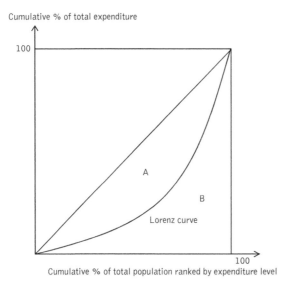

Cumulative % of total population ranked by expenditure level

Figure 6.1 *The Lorenz curve*

Measuring inequality

Define: n = number of persons in the population,

r_i = expenditure (or income) rank of person i, $1 \leq r_i \leq n$,

y_i = expenditure of person i,

μ = average expenditure in the population,

σ = standard deviation of expenditure,

Y = total expenditure of the population.

Note the following four inequality indicators:

1. *The coefficient of variation:* $CV = \dfrac{\sigma}{\mu}$

   The CV measures inequality as the standard deviation of expenditure per unit of average expenditure. It has the advantage of being unit-free and of being additively decomposable across subgroups of the population.

2. *The Gini coefficient:* $G = \dfrac{A}{A+B} = \dfrac{2}{n\mu}\text{cov}(y, r)$, $0 \leq G \leq 1$.

   In Figure 6.1, the Gini coefficient G is the ratio of area A, between the 45-degree line and the Lorenz curve, to area $A+B$, where B is the area between the Lorenz curve and the outer box. It runs between 0 (complete equality) and 1 (maximum inequality). Empirically, a useful way of measuring the Gini coefficient is to calculate the covariance between income (y) and rank (r) across observations, and multiply it by $2/n\mu$.

250

With households ranked from lowest to highest y, y_r is the income of the household with rank r between 1 and n. The Gini coefficient can be calculated as:

$$G = \frac{2\sum\limits_{r=1}^{n} ry_r}{n\sum\limits_{r=1}^{n} y_r} - \frac{n+1}{n}.$$

If, for example, incomes in a population of four are $y_r = \{1, 2, 3, 6\}$, then the Gini coefficient is:

$$\frac{2[1(1) + 2(2) + 3(3) + 4(6)]}{4(12)} - \frac{5}{4} = 0.33.$$

The Gini coefficient is the most frequently used measure of inequality. It has the inconvenience that two Lorenz curves that cross may have the same Gini. It is also better at characterizing differences in the distribution of income in the middle of the distribution than at the extremes. It has the further inconvenience of not being additively decomposable across subgroups of the population (unlike P_α indicators).

Examples of Gini coefficients for selected countries are given in Table 6.1. They show that the Gini coefficient (expressed in percentage terms) can be

Table 6.1 Gini coefficients, income shares, and Kuznets ratios, 2008–11

Country	PPP-GDPpc	Gini	Income share lowest 20%	Income share highest 20%	Kuznets ratio 20/20
South Africa	11426	63	2.7	68.2	25.3
Honduras	4188	59	1.8	61.9	34.4
Brazil	13773	55	0.8	58.8	73.5
Rwanda	1242	51	5.2	56.8	10.9
Nigeria	5048	49	4.4	54.0	12.3
Peru	9724	49	3.8	53.1	14.0
Mexico	14726	47	4.8	53.2	11.1
China	9053	42	4.7	47.5	10.1
Senegal	2140	40	6.1	46.9	7.7
Thailand	12575	40	6.7	47.2	7.0
Indonesia	7872	37	7.7	44.1	5.7
Vietnam	4400	36	7.4	43.4	5.9
Ethiopia	1041	34	8.0	41.9	5.2
India	4549	34	3.7	42.8	11.6
Bangladesh	2093	32	8.9	41.4	4.7
Pakistan	4139	30	9.6	40.0	4.2

Source: World Bank, World Development Indicators.

low in both very poor countries such as Bangladesh (32) and Ethiopia (34) and very rich countries such as Norway (26, not in the table). It tends to be highest in Latin American countries (e.g. 55 in Brazil, 47 in Mexico), which are mainly middle-income countries.

3. *The Theil entropy index:* $T = \sum_{i=1}^{n} \frac{y_i}{Y} \ln\left(\frac{n y_i}{Y}\right).$

This index runs from 0 (perfect equality) to $\ln(n)$ (maximum inequality). It is often used because it is additively decomposable across population subgroups (see below), a convenient feature when we want to measure how much each population group contributes to total inequality. It has the inconvenience that it cannot be used if there are negative incomes in the population because logs are then undefined.

4. *Income shares and Kuznets ratios*

A versatile indicator of income inequality is income shares: for example, what is the share of total income held by the richest 20 percent of the population (Table 6.1). This would be 68 percent in South Africa, 62 percent in Honduras, and 59 percent in Brazil. The chosen population percentage (here the top 20 percent) depends on the purpose of the analysis. For the 99 percent Occupy Wall Street Movement in the US, it would be the share of total income held by the top 1 percent. We can also use ratios of income shares, called Kuznets ratios: for example, the ratio of the percentage of total income held by the richest 20 percent to the percentage of total income held by the poorest 20 percent. This indicator is useful for characterizing what happens at the extremes in the distribution of income. The ratio would be about 4 in Norway (not in the table) and 74 in Brazil. It is notable that the inequality ranks across countries are not the same across the Gini, the income share of the top 20 percent, and the Kuznets 20/20 ratio. South Africa dominates in terms of Gini (63) and share of the top 20 percent (68), but not in terms of the Kuznets 20/20 (25). Brazil dominates with the Kuznets 20/20 (74), but not with the Gini (55) and the share of the top 20 percent (59). This suggests the usefulness of using several indicators of inequality to better characterize the shape of the Lorenz curve.

As can be seen in Figure 6.2, Lorenz curves can cross, as illustrated for China and the Philippines in 2010. Inequality rankings then depend on the indicator used. The Philippines are more unequal than China according to the Gini coefficient (43.0 in the Philippines vs. 42.1 in China), the income share of the richest 10 percent (33.6 percent in the Philippines vs. 30 percent in China), and the top 10 percent/bottom 40 percent Kuznets ratio (2.2 in the Philippines vs. 2.1 in China). By contrast, China is more unequal than the Philippines according to the income share of the poorest 20 percent (4.7 percent in China vs. 6 percent for the Philippines) and the top 10 percent/bottom 20 percent Kuznets ratio (6.4 in China vs. 5.6 in the Philippines).

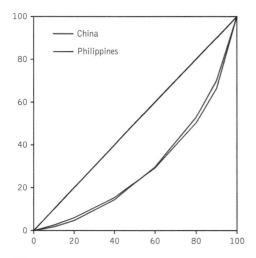

Figure 6.2 *Lorenz curves can cross: China and the Philippines, 2010*

In general, it is useful to use several inequality indicators as they each characterize inequality in a different part of the distribution of income—in particular the Kuznets ratios for the extremes of the income distribution and the Gini coefficient for the middle of the distribution.

DECOMPOSING INEQUALITY

Decomposition of Theil entropy index by population subgroups

The Gini coefficient cannot be decomposed additively by population subgroups. For this we have to use the Theil entropy index *T*. Decomposition across *k* subgroups of the population ($j = 1, ..., k$), would be:

$$T = \underbrace{\sum_{j=1}^{k} y_j T_j}_{\text{within–group inequality}} + \underbrace{\sum_{j=1}^{k} y_j \ln\left(\frac{y_j}{m_j}\right)}_{\text{between–group inequality}},$$

where y_j is the income share of group *j*, m_j is the population share of that group, and T_j is the Theil entropy index for group *j*. This tells us how much of total inequality is due to within-group as opposed to between-group inequality. If most of the inequality is across geographical regions, for example, then the focus of policy to reduce aggregate inequality should be regional development to reduce disparities across regions. In China and Vietnam, most of the inequality is across regions. In Latin America, by contrast, most of the inequality is within regions. In Ecuador, for instance, intra-municipality inequality accounts for as much as 86 percent of total inequality (Elbers *et al.*, 2003). This implies that inequality needs to be addressed at the local level if total inequality is to be reduced.

Decomposition of the Gini coefficient by sources of income

The Gini coefficient can be decomposed by sources of income (Adams, 1991). Say that there are $k = 1,\ldots,K$ sources of income, each contributing y_{ik} to the total income y_i of household i, with $\sum_k y_{ik} = y_i$.

Define:

mean income in the population $= \mu$

mean income from source $k = \mu_k$

weight of the income source in mean income $= \mu_k/\mu = w_k$

within source household rank $= r_k$

overall household income rank $= r$

relative correlations $= R_k = \text{cov}(y_k, r)/\text{cov}(y_k, r_k)$

overall Gini $= G$

Gini of income source $= G_k$

The decomposition of the total Gini is given by $G = \sum_k w_k R_k G_k$.

Hence the share of income source k in total inequality is equal to $w_k R_k G_k/G$.

For rural Egypt (Table 6.2), remittances from abroad are a minor source of income, accounting for only 9.6 percent of the total. This is the weight of the income source, w_k, for remittances. However, receiving remittances is highly corre-lated with the household's overall income rank (meaning that they are more frequent among the richer), and remittances are unequally distributed across house-holds (as few of them have the luck of receiving remittances from migrants), with a Gini of 0.93. As a consequence, remittances account for as much as 27.3 percent of total inequality, much more than their income share. The opposite applies to non-agricultural sources of income for rural households. They represent a much larger 32.6 percent of total income, but have a lower correlation with rank (they make a lesser contribution to the income of the richer) and have a lower Gini coefficient (0.68) (as they are much more broadly accessible) than remittances. As a result, non-agricultural incomes only account for 11.7 percent of total inequality, much less than their income share.

Table 6.2 Decomposition of overall income inequality in rural Egypt

Rural Egypt	Agriculture	Non-agriculture	Remittances	Total
Weight of income source (%) w_k	57.8	32.6	9.6	100
Relative correlations R_k	0.63	0.16	0.92	1
Gini of income source G_k	0.51	0.68	0.93	0.30
Relative Gini G_k/G	1.69	2.25	3.09	1.00
Share of income source in total Gini (%)	61.0	11.7	27.3	100

Source: Adams, 1991.

RELATIONSHIP BETWEEN LEVEL OF INCOME (GDPpc) AND INEQUALITY: EMPIRICAL EVIDENCE ON THE KUZNETS INVERTED-U CURVE

How do we explain inequality? In the 1950s, Simon Kuznets (1955) formulated an interesting hypothesis about the relationship between per capita income and inequality across countries. It is now called the Kuznets inverted-U curve between inequality and GDPpc, according to which inequality first rises and then falls as income per capita rises.

This relationship has become both a well known and controversial regularity in development economics. To establish this relationship, Kuznets used cross-country data, (you can find cross-country data online at World Bank's *World Development Indicators*). Plotting these data for 2007 between PPP-adjusted LnGDPpc and the Gini coefficient indeed gives an inverted-U relationship as shown in Figure 6.3.

The equation to be estimated to test this hypothesis is:

$$s_i = \alpha + \beta y_i + \gamma y_i^2 + \varepsilon_i,$$

where s_i is the Gini coefficient or the income share of the upper income group in country i (say the top 20 percent), and y_i is lnGDPpc in country i. An inverted-U relationship implies that $\beta > 0$ and $\gamma < 0$. If this is estimated for the income share of the lowest 20 percent or 40 percent, the estimated coefficients would be $\beta < 0$ and $\gamma > 0$, implying an upright U. A measure of inequality that takes the ratio of the income share of the top 20 percent to the income share of the bottom 20 or 40 percent would show the Kuznets inverted-U curve of rising and then falling inequality.

Robinson (1976) proposed a simple explanation for the Kuznets inverted-U. Say that the economy is divided into two sectors, agriculture and industry, with relatively egalitarian income distribution within each sector, but a different mean income

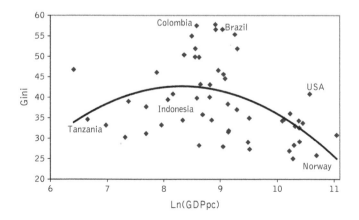

Figure 6.3 *The Kuznets inverted-U hypothesis*

Source: World Bank, *World Development Indicators*.

across them. The simple statistical artifact of the population shifting from one sector to the other—namely, the well established structural transformation of the economy as GDPpc rises—would imply rising inequality followed by falling inequality.

Why has this relationship aroused so much interest in the profession? If true, the rise in inequality at low levels of income would be considered "normal." Indeed, we know that inequality has been rising very rapidly in countries such as China, India, and Vietnam that are experiencing explosive growth at low levels of GDPpc. According to the Kuznets curve, GDPpc needs to reach a critical level of the order of PPP\$4,000 (ln of 4,000 = 8.3 in Figure 6.3) for inequality to start falling. The policy implication is powerful: there is no need to introduce particular policies to contain the rise of inequality, especially if these policies have an opportunity cost in terms of growth, as a higher level of GDPpc will itself subsequently take care of inequality. In fact, it is better to concentrate on accelerating growth, and be patient with inequality. This result had a powerful influence on the pioneers of development who, in the 1950s and 1960s, focused their attention on growth rather than on income distribution. But does the Kuznets inverted-U really hold true? Is there a causal relationship between GDPpc and inequality? The answer is no.

Kuznets and many of his followers used cross-country data to establish the GDPpc–inequality relationship. Cross-country data show that inequality is highest in Latin America (middle-income countries), followed by Africa and South Asia (low-income countries), South East Asia (upper-middle-income countries), and finally the OECD high-income countries. This in itself describes an inverted-U curve. But this is purely cross-sectional and cannot claim causality: GDPpc and inequality are jointly determined by complex growth processes, and there are omitted variables in the regression that could also explain the observed inequality level. Clearly, Africa will not become Latin America, and Latin America will not become South East Asia as GDPpc rises. It is not because the inverted-U holds across countries that it will hold for a particular country as its income rises.

The many empirical studies that have used cross-section data confirm the Kuznets hypothesis, basically due to the Latin America effect at middle-income level (see, for example, Ahluwalia (1976) using 60 countries). Studies that have used cross-country panel data to establish whether this relation holds not between but within countries have in general rejected the hypothesis. Deininger and Squire (1998) introduced country fixed effects in a cross-country panel. The equation they estimate is:

$$s_{it} = \alpha + \beta \, y_{it} + \gamma \, (1/y_{it}) + \delta_i + \varepsilon_{it},$$

where the δ_i are country fixed effects, and where $\beta < 0$ and $\gamma < 0$ if the Kuznets inverted-U hypothesis holds true. Results show that while the Kuznets effect holds cross-sectionally, it vanishes when country fixed effects are introduced, meaning that it does not hold within countries. For the few countries with sufficient data to estimate a separate regression, only in 10 percent of them do we find evidence of a Kuznets inverted-U.

There are cases such as Taiwan, South Korea, and Indonesia where "equalizing growth" has been observed. In countries like Brazil, inequality rose and fell as GDPpc increased, but the decline has not been due to growth alone, but to social policies introduced by the Cardoso and da Silva governments to reduce inequality. Hence we cannot simply wait for income growth to reduce inequality. If there is a concern with inequality, special policy interventions are needed to reduce it such as Brazil's ambitious social programs.

THE ALVAREDO–ATKINSON–PIKETTY–SAEZ CRITIQUE

Using a century of data for the period 1913 to 2012, Alvaredo *et al.* (2014) show that inequality in the US and in many other countries, both industrialized (the UK, Canada, and Australia) and developing (Argentina, Colombia, Indonesia, India, China, and South Africa), followed a pattern inverse to the Kuznets inverted-U curve. The measure of inequality they use is the income share of the top 1 percent or 10 percent in the distribution of income. They find that the pattern for the 100-year period was U-shaped (Figure 6.4). In the US, the share controlled by the top 1 percent in 1928 was 24 percent, which fell to 9 percent in 1970 and rose again to 24 percent in 2007 (and 23 percent in 2012 after the shock of the financial crisis). For the top 10 percent, it was 50 percent in 1928, 33 percent in 1970, and back to 50 percent in 2007 and 2012.

Rising inequality is concentrating income at the very top of the distribution of income, and the share of the ultra rich continues to rise at a world scale. In 2014, 211,000 individuals, representing only 0.004 percent of world population, owned 13 percent of world wealth, equal to about twice US GDP. These individuals are about equally distributed between the US, Europe, and Asia.

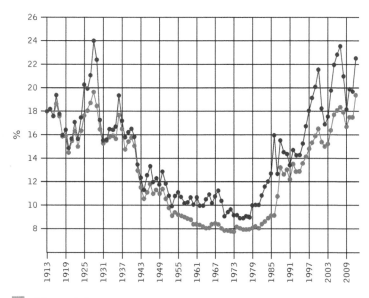

Figure 6.4 *Top 1 percent income share in the US, 1913–2012. Upper curve includes capital gains; lower curve excludes capital gains*

Source: Alvaredo *et al.*, 2014.

In a book that sold more than a million copies, *Capital in the Twenty-First Century*, Piketty (2014) identifies the "forces of divergence" in the distribution of income currently at play. He relies on the functional (as opposed to the personal) distribution of income—namely, how income is distributed across the different factors of production: labor of different skills, capital (dividends, capital gains, interest payments, profits from private business), and land (rents). Most capital is owned by the richest few, translating the functional into the personal distribution of income. For example, rich CEOs own a lot of stock options, making a functional distribution of income that favors the return to capital, contributing to rising inequality in the personal distribution of income. The rule Piketty proposes is that inequality will rise when $r > g$, where r is the rate of return on capital while g is the growth rate of GDP. By contrast, inequality falls when $r < g$, implying that the growth rate of labor income is higher than the growth rate of GDP. Data show that, in the post-World War One period, i.e. the period of the Great Depression, progressive tax policies associated with Keynes and the New Deal, inflation eating away real savings, minimum-wage laws, and friendly policies toward labor unions kept the rate of return on capital below the growth rate of the economy. Since 1970, by contrast, the return to capital has risen sharply, while wages have stagnated. The sharp upturn in inequality was associated with the Reagan–Thatcher conservative counter-revolution in the 1980s, with greatly reduced progressive taxation, restraints on the growth of government expenditures, and sharp attacks on union power. The capture of political power by the interests of capital, not market forces such as globalization or technological change, was thus the main "force of divergence." Piketty predicts that, unless tax laws on both income and wealth are sharply revised, this trend of increasing inequality will continue. However, managing the political economy of a "progressive counter-revolution" is not discussed in his book.

IMPACT OF GDPpc GROWTH ON POVERTY AND INEQUALITY

Is growth good for poverty reduction and how does it affect inequality? Does initial inequality affect the poverty-reduction value of growth? This has been analyzed econometrically in a number of cross-country regressions. Results help build the quantitative relationships in the growth–inequality–poverty development triangle.

Growth and poverty

We know that income growth tends to be a powerful instrument for poverty reduction (recall Figure 5.16 giving a decomposition of change in the poverty rate into growth and distribution effects). This is seen using a cross-country regression in Figure 6.5, where an increase in a country's per capita consumption or income y (measured as the change in the log of y between two successive surveys) reduces the poverty rate P_0 (measured as the change in the log of the headcount ratio between the same two successive surveys), while a decline increases poverty. The regression coefficient in a log–log relation is an elasticity of -2.38, meaning that a 1 percent increase in average income decreases the poverty rate by 2.38 percent,

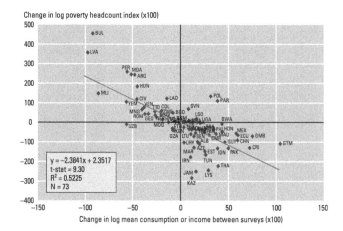

Figure 6.5 *Relation between change in income and change in the poverty headcount ratio*

Source: World Bank, 2005a.

a powerful effect. Because the regression is in change in *y* over change in P_0, it has the advantage of controlling for all country fixed factors, giving it some causal credibility. With a t-statistic of 9.3, this elasticity is significantly different from zero. Growth is obviously good for poverty reduction, but there is a lot of country heterogeneity around the average relation.

Growth and inequality

What can we expect growth to do to inequality? If, according to Dollar and Kraay (2001), growth has an elasticity (*E*) of 1 between the income of the poorest quintile (*y*) and the average income for the whole population (*Y*), as we saw in Chapter 5, then growth should be neutral on inequality. This elasticity is:

$$E = \frac{\Delta y / y}{\Delta Y / Y} = 1.$$

It means that, percentage-wise, growth benefits the poor as much as it does the rest of the population. It of course does not mean that the poor benefit from growth as much as the rich do in absolute terms. Say that, initially, *y* = 10 for the poor and *Y* = 100 for the whole population, then, with *E* = 1, the poor get one tenth of the benefits of growth, their initial share. However, income distribution remains unaffected.

That growth has on average no impact on inequality is verified empirically in Figure 6.6. Here, the change in the Gini index (measured as the change in log Gini between two surveys) is regressed on growth in per capita consumption or income *y* (measured as the change in the log of *y* between two successive surveys). The elasticity is almost zero with a t-statistic of 0.5, indicating that it is not significantly different from zero. On average, growth is neutral on inequality. However, we can also see a

259

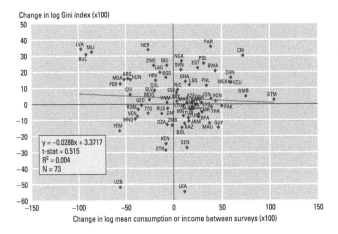

Figure 6.6 *Relation between change in income and change in inequality*

Source: World Bank, 2005a.

considerable dispersion in country observations around this non–significant relation. It shows, for example, that countries like China (CHI in Figure 6.6) have had inequalizing growth, while countries like Mauritius (MAU) have had equalizing growth.

Quality of growth in terms of initial inequality

Why is growth eventually inequalizing or equalizing for a same growth performance? A candidate explanation is that a lower initial inequality can help countries achieve more poverty reduction per percentage point of income growth. This is verified empirically in Figure 6.7. Here, the elasticity of poverty reduction with respect to income is:

$$E = \frac{dP_0 \, / \, P_0}{dY \, / \, Y},$$

meaning that it should be negative if growth reduces poverty. In Figure 6.7, this elasticity is regressed on the initial level of inequality. Results show that the elasticity is larger (more negative) the lower the initial Gini index. The regression coefficient is 13.8, meaning that a 0.1 point increase in the initial Gini index increases the elasticity by 1.38. A higher inequality in the initial distribution of income implies that subsequent growth has less capacity to reduce poverty, and this is with a t-statistic of 2.45, indicating that it is significantly different from zero. Hence the quality of growth for poverty reduction depends on the initial level of inequality.

Pro-poor growth

If $E = 1$ with a 10 to 1 initial income ratio between rich and poor, the poor have gained 1 and the rich have gained 10, clearly not a pro-poor outcome. The UN

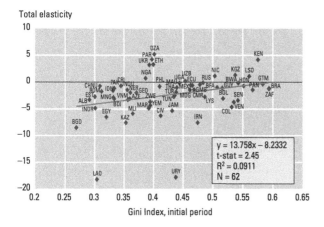

Figure 6.7 *The poverty reduction value of lower inequality*

Source: World Bank, 2005a.

Development Program (UNDP) (Zepeda, 2004) consequently defines pro-poor growth as growth with an elasticity greater than 1: namely, a pattern of growth where inequality falls. However, growth can benefit the poor if it reduces the poverty rate in spite of rising inequality. This was the case for China where inequality rose between 1980 and 2001, but the poverty headcount ratio fell from 64 to 17 percent (Ravallion and Chen, 2007) simply because growth was so high. In Vietnam, similarly, following the Doi Moi (trade-liberalization) policies initiated in 1986 that created a "socialist market-oriented economy," GDPpc grew by 37 percent between 1993 and 1996, the Gini coefficient increased from 31 to 35, but the poverty headcount ratio fell from 58 to 37 (Haughton and Khandker, 2009). Clearly, in both cases, growth would have been even more pro-poor had inequality not increased. Hence the change in inequality does matter in determining how pro-poor growth is going to be.

How pro-poor has growth been? The Growth Incidence Curve

To assess whether an observed past growth episode has been pro-poor or not, Ravallion and Chen (2003) proposed to visualize the whole distribution of income growth across the initial distribution of per capita incomes by quantiles in a population. This is the Growth Incidence Curve, or GIC. (Quantiles can also be deciles or percentiles.) If income growth has been higher for the low quantiles, then the GIC slopes downward, inequality declines, and growth was pro-poor, benefiting the poor more than the rich; if the opposite, the GIC slopes upward and growth was inequalizing. This is illustrated in Figure 6.8 for China, taken from Ravallion and Chen. For the overall period 1990–9, all income groups gained: the poverty rate thus fell whatever the choice of poverty line (Figure 6.8a). There is "first-order dominance in poverty." However, the GIC was positively sloped and inequality rose. Growth was absolutely pro-poor in the sense that the poor gained, but not relatively pro-poor in

261

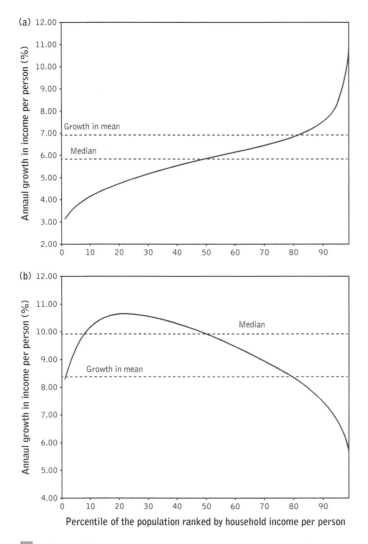

Figure 6.8 *Growth incidence curve for China, 1990–9 (a) and 1993–6 (b)*

Source: Ravallion and Chen, 2003.

the UNDP (Kakwani, 1997) sense that it benefited the poor more than the rich. Looking at specific sub-periods within this time interval, 1993–6 turns out to be one where the poor gained more than the rich (Figure 6.8b). This particular period was thus pro-poor both in the sense that the poor gained and that they gained more than the rich, achieving UNDP-type relative pro-poor growth.

To distinguish between the Kakwani-UNDP and Ravallion and Chen-World Bank interpretations of pro-poor growth we used the term "absolute pro-poor growth" for growth that reduces poverty, even if the rich benefit more than the poor and inequality increases (Ravallion and Chen, 2003), e.g. China's recent growth; and we use the term "relative pro-poor growth" for growth that benefits the poor more than the rich, i.e. poverty declines as well as inequality (Kakwani, 1997), e.g. Brazil's recent growth.

IMPACT OF INEQUALITY ON GROWTH: NINE CAUSAL CHANNELS

Is inequality bad or good for growth? If it is bad, then we have a functionalist case against inequality: reducing it would help accelerate growth, with the associated benefits for poverty reduction. If it is good, then we have to deal with a difficult policy trade-off: do we prefer more equality or more growth, with one having an opportunity cost for the other? There is no simple answer, and the relation may be non-linear in the sense that some inequality may be good for growth while too much inequality may not be. It may also be the case that inequality is good for growth in the short run (as in China today as it pursues a neo-mercantilist growth strategy based on exports and cheap labor), but that it is detrimental to sustaining growth in the long run (if it needs to turn inward to find effective demand in rising wages, what we call social articulation). In this case, what would be the optimum level of inequality to maximize growth in both the short and the long run? This is one the most passionate debates in development economics, with huge policy implications. What is the evidence? Empirical results are mixed, with a negative relationship found by Perotti (1996), a zero relationship by Barro (2000), and a positive relationship for the short and medium term by Forbes (2000).

Using cross-country data for 67 countries and measuring the average annual GDPpc growth rate for the period 1960–85, Perotti (1996) finds that higher inequality is associated with lower income growth. A one-standard-deviation increase in inequality induces 0.6-percentage-point lower GDPpc growth. Exploring four channels through which this may occur, he finds that three seem to be important: (1) higher inequality increases the fertility rate and reduces the rate of per capita income growth; (2) higher inequality lowers investment in education and reduces the rate of growth; and (3) higher inequality increases socio-political instability and reduces the rate of growth. There is, by contrast, no evidence that higher inequality induces demands for redistributive policies and a heavier fiscal burden (as argued by Persson and Tabellini (1994), see below) that could reduce income growth.

This result has been challenged by Forbes (2000), who repeats the Perotti study using better inequality measurements and panel-data estimation methods instead of cross-sectional estimation. She measures growth for 45 countries over successive 5-year periods during 1966–95. She finds that inequality increases growth in the short and medium run, but leaves unexplored the channels through which this occurs.

There are nine channels through which inequality may affect growth.

Aggregate rate of savings and growth

Inequality is good for growth if it increases the aggregate rate of savings, and hence the rate of investment, capital accumulation, and growth. This is the behavioral observation famously made by Keynes: the marginal propensity to save (MPS) increases with the level of income. This is shown in Figure 6.9a, where MPS is

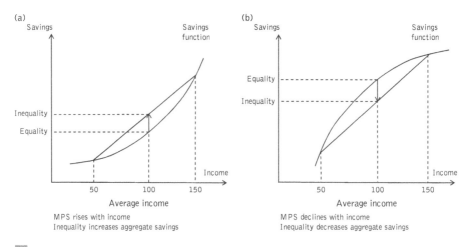

Figure 6.9 *Impact of inequality on per capita savings*

the slope of the savings function. Average income (100) is the same with equality (two individuals with 100 each) and with inequality (two individuals with 50 and 150 each). However, the average of the savings by two individuals with incomes 50 and 150 is higher than that of two individuals with 100 each. Hence greater inequality leads to a greater aggregate level of saving and to higher investment in physical capital. This would be good for poor countries, where saving to support investment is always in short supply and may be the binding constraint on growth, as we will see in the Harrod-Domar growth model (see Chapter 8). But recent empirical evidence shows that poor people can have high rates of savings, in particular because they have high levels of risk aversion and the need to self-insure requires them to hold large amounts of precautionary savings such as animals and food stocks. In this case, the MPS declines as income rises. This is shown in the right panel of Figure 6.9. In this case, average saving is lower with more inequality. If the poor have access to safe and profitable savings instruments, such as formal financial services, they could save in ways that make capital available for investment. More equality is then good for savings, investment, and growth.

In China, incomes are still low, but the personal rate of savings is 38 percent, in part motivated by precaution due to lack of insurance and social-security coverage. However, Keynes has a point in that the extreme poor cannot afford to both save and survive. In addition, the savings held by the poor are often not held in money (for example, when they are in grains or animals) and not available to others for investment in productive projects. As a consequence, higher inequality may be good for growth, at least in very poor countries.

Market failures linking asset concentration and total factor productivity

If there are market failures, the first welfare theorem according to which market outcomes are efficient independently of how the assets are distributed no longer holds: equality (asset distribution) is related to efficiency (growth). This is the famous non-separability theorem, which is so important for development economics as many markets fail in the developing economy, and efficiency could be improved by redistribution of the assets toward those who make relatively more efficient use of them (Bardhan, 1996). What the theorem says is that the degree of equality in asset ownership affects the growth rate of the economy. But how?

Inequality in the distribution of the assets will be bad for growth if there is an inverse relation between asset concentration (e.g. farm size or wealth) and productivity (e.g. yields, TFP, or profits), as in Figure 6.10. In this case, asset redistribution (e.g. land reform) can increase both equality and efficiency. This inverse relation can come from labor-market failures: family labor working on small farms is cheaper than hired labor working on large farms. This is because family labor has no recruitment costs and is motivated to work hard by being the residual claimant on the gains from effort. By contrast, wage labor on large farms is more expensive as it incurs transaction costs in hiring and supervising. As a consequence, there will be more labor per hectare on small farms and higher yields if farming is labor intensive, creating the inverse relation.

Note, however, that the negative relationship may turn into a positive one. There may be economies of scale in production due to use of technology with fixed factors. Capital-market failures may imply the existence of a positive relationship between asset concentration and productivity if larger farmers have more access to credit per hectare. In this case, if farming is capital intensive, the inverse relation (due to labor-market failure) can be cancelled by a second market failure (capital-market failure). Larger farmers may also have more access to politically allocated inputs such as subsidized fertilizers. With a positive relation, equality gains in asset distribution are obtained at the cost of an efficiency loss, a tough policy choice to handle, making the political economy of redistributive land reform much harder to achieve. Advocates of redistributive land reform toward family farming such as Lipton (2009) have thus typically held that the inverse relation does prevail or that it can be made to hold.

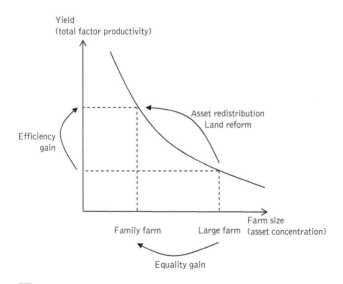

Figure 6.10 Equality gain in asset distribution and efficiency gain: the inverse relation

In using the relation between farm size and TFP to design policy, we need to make sure that the observed relation is causal. The inverse relation may, for example, be created by spurious correlation with land quality if smaller farms are on better land. A positive relation may not be causal either if better farmers have accumulated more land or if sharecropping contracts on small farms create disincentives to effort (as we will see in Chapter 20).

For Galor and Tsiddon (1997), the role of inequality as a source of growth may have a technological basis. They suggest that a concentration of high-ability workers in technologically advanced sectors is how growth acceleration initially takes place. Mobility of high-ability workers across sectors is thus good for growth at the same time as it is a source of increasing inequality.

Social and political instability

Inequality can have direct costs on disposable-income growth if it induces crime and political instability. The costs are police protection and eventual loss and destruction of assets. In this view, inequality has an opportunity cost for growth, with South Africa as a vivid example. Demombynes and Özler (2005) find that inequality leads to crime: burglary rates are 20–30 percent higher in police-station jurisdictions that are the wealthiest among their neighbors, suggesting that criminals travel to neighborhoods where the expected returns from burglary are the highest. Crime, defined as the sum of losses due to theft, security costs, and protection payments, is an important negative element of the investment climate for private firms (World Bank, 2004).

Political economy of voting patterns and fiscal policy

If high income inequality combines with democracy, the median voter will be relatively poor as median income is well below mean income, as shown in Figure 6.11. A relatively poorer median voter, who by constitutional law carries the election, will demand higher taxation in order to benefit from income-redistribution policies. Expectation of redistributive taxation on incremental earnings (as opposed to an equal lump-sum tax) has been shown by Persson and Tabellini (1994) to discourage savings and investment, thus slowing down economic growth. This may, however, not be the case if the fiscal expenditures demanded by the median voter are growth-enhancing public goods. Saint-Paul and Verdier (1993) explore an alternative where increased fiscal revenues are invested in public education, contributing to an acceleration of growth. At this stage, the proposition is theoretical, without rigorous empirical support.

The pessimistic view of the impact of inequality on economic outcomes through the political process was most comprehensively argued by Stiglitz (2012) in his recent book *The Price of Inequality*. Instead of using the theory of the median voter, as Persson and Tabellini do, he uses the theory of rent-seeking (that we will review in Chapter 21). Stiglitz's argument is that concentrated economic power (inequality) leads to concentrated political power and, through rent-seeking, to changes in market and political rules favoring the top 1 percent in the distribution of income. This

266

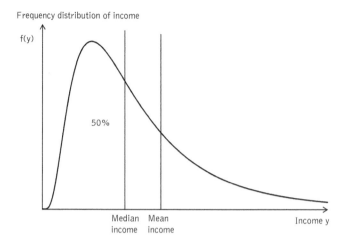

Frequency distribution of income

f(y)

50%

Median income Mean income Income y

Figure 6.11 *Median-voter model with vote determined by income position*

includes reduced public expenditures on education and health (while the rich use high-quality private healthcare and education), underfunding of social programs such as unemployment insurance and food stamps, deregulation of sectors of economic activity that favor the upper class (most particularly the financial sector), and a tax code that benefits the wealthy. Like in the theory of rent-seeking, these private gains are achieved at a social cost, with negative outcomes on both efficiency (growth, economic stability) and equity (poverty, the reproduction of inequality). In this perspective, summarized in Figure 6.12, government intervention is necessary to hold rent-seeking in check and reduce inequality. This has successfully occurred in two previous periods of US history, where sharply rising inequality induced economic crises: the Gilded Age of the robber barons' monopolies in the 1880s that was followed by the introduction of anti-trust reforms in the Progressive Era; and the Roaring 20s and the Great Depression that were followed by the progressive social policies of the New Deal. But will this happen again in response to the Great Recession of 2008–9? Will the Occupy Wall Street movement and the *indignados* of Spain have the power to mobilize the state in favor of restoring greater equality and equity? Stiglitz is pessimistic about the taste for reform (the loss of "audacity of hope," to use President Obama's terminology) to deal with the crisis of 2008–9 and frustrated at political deadlock in the legislative canceling the ability of government to implement change toward the reduction of economic inequality and the restoration of equity. In his perspective, the state has a key role to play in holding inequalities in check for the sake of both growth and equity. Politics, and the avoidance of political capture, is essential for successful development. How to do this, however, is not clearly spelled out in Stiglitz's book.

In his recent book, *Political Order and Political Decay*, Fukuyama (2014) goes beyond Stiglitz in exploring how political capture, itself the result of sharply rising economic inequality, has led to institutional decay and compromised growth. To be effective, a liberal democracy needs a strong state, and this in turn is based on two pillars: political

267

Figure 6.12 *The price of inequality, according to Stiglitz (2012)*

accountability and the rule of law. During the first half of the twentieth century, industrialization allowed new actors to emerge with no interest in the old clientelist system and prone to supporting a strong state. This strong state introduced the policies of the New Deal and achieved successful recovery and growth. As inequality rose after 1970, political capture by economic elites undermined these two pillars of liberal democracies, leading to loss of trust in the state, loss of state authority, and loss of public resources. The challenge of social democracies is to be able to reform themselves internally to preserve enough equality of opportunity and combat institutional decay. Whether this can be done is still largely unanswered.

Access to financial capital

Capital markets are imperfect. Because of asymmetrical information between lender and borrower and the associated risk of default for the lender, these markets are wealth-constrained: collateral is needed to access credit (Banerjee and Newman, 1993; Boucher *et al.*, 2008). Hence those without collateral—most of the poor—are locked out of the credit market. With higher inequality in asset ownership, for a given stock of assets, more people do not have collateralizable assets, and many good investment projects that could be pursued by poor entrepreneurs are left unfinanced. As a result, investment suffers and inequality reduces growth. If wealth determines access to credit and credit is the source of investment and additional wealth, then there is a natural process of wealth concentration. This vicious circle of rising wealth inequality and increasing exclusion can only be broken down by public interventions redistributing collateralizable assets or delinking access to credit from wealth ownership serving as collateral. The latter is the microfinance revolution that we will study in Chapter 13.

Aggregate investment in human capital

Inequality reduces investment in human capital because poor people will be constrained in investing in education. They cannot afford to postpone earning income, and thus forego investment in education with longer-term returns (see Chapter 17). They are also constrained in borrowing to invest in education due to lack of collateral, as we have just seen (Galor and Zeira, 1993). As a consequence, rising inequality decreases aggregate investment in education while it increases aggregate investment in physical capital through the Keynesian effect of a rising MPS. If growth is in part driven by human capital, inequality is detrimental to growth—and as growth is more capital intensive, it in turn limits employment and further increases the level of inequality. Here again, inequality begets more inequality through underinvestment in education.

Inequality and incentives

While some inequality is important to provide incentives for effort, investment, and risk-taking, high levels of inequality create feelings of unfairness that can reduce incentives to work and induce sabotage and crime such as the destruction of property (Rabin, 1998). Inequality also makes acceptance of reforms that require austerity more difficult to obtain, as in Hirschman and Rothschild's (1973) "tunnel effect," an analogy in which you accept your fate if everyone is stuck in a traffic jam in a tunnel, but you lose patience with your condition if cars in lanes other than yours start moving forward. Inequality diminishes willingness to cooperate. Disincentives to cooperation in the workplace and to support policy reforms, both of which are correlated with inequality, are thus detrimental to growth.

Inequality and domestic market size

Domestic industry needs to find markets for its products. For tradable goods these can be export markets (what has been called the neo-mercantilist model). They have been very effective for China and Brazil during the years of rapidly expanding international trade. But when a financial crisis hits these markets, as was the case with the global financial crisis of 2007–8, expanding domestic markets become essential to sustain economic growth, not only for the growth of non-tradable industrial goods and services, but for industry under import-substitution industrialization strategies, as the average cost of producing tradable goods needs to be reduced through domestic-market economies of scale before they become competitive on the international market (we will analyze this in Chapter 7). The expansion of domestic markets can be achieved by reducing inequality. This is what Latin American countries tried to do through land reform in the 1960s, a policy promoted by President Kennedy and the Organization of American States at the 1961 Punta del Este Conference in Uruguay. More recently, Brazil has been quite effective at reducing income inequality through the promotion of primary and secondary education, and through *Bolsa Família*, its massive CCT program (UNDP, 2009).

Inequality can also be reproduced through the composition of effective demand that originates in a particular pattern of inequality. With high inequality, there will be more demand for luxury goods (durable goods, cars, etc.) that tend to be more capital-intensive and skilled-labor-intensive in production. As a consequence, the functional distribution of income favors capital and skilled labor over unskilled labor. With capital and skills concentrated in the hands of a minority, this reinforces inequality in the personal distribution of income, unleashing a perverse pattern of inequality feeding on more inequality. The counter-proposition is a more equal distribution of income that increases the demand for wage goods. If these are more unskilled-labor-intensive (food, simple industrial products produced in small firms, etc.) than luxury goods, they favor unskilled labor employment and wages, and hence a more egalitarian distribution of income. In this case, labeled "social articulation" (de Janvry and Sadoulet, 1983; Murphy *et al.*, 1989), growth unleashes a virtuous cycle where equality begets more equality. Initial conditions (for example, in the way land and education were initially distributed in Taiwan and South Korea before industrialization started), and structural reforms that redistribute assets such as land and homogenize access to education, are important for unleashing such a virtuous growth cycle (Adelman and Robinson, 1978).

Inequality and institutional quality

Finally, inequality can reduce the efficiency of institutions such as firms/farms and cooperatives. The more egalitarian colonies of settlement—such as the US, with its Homestead Act for land allocation, and Canada and Australia, with their similar acts— had highly dynamic family farm-based agricultures that have been heralded as the most efficient way of organizing agricultural production. Inequality can pervert institutional quality, too, such as the operation of producer cooperatives. Banerjee *et al.* (2001) studied 100 sugar-producer cooperatives in the state of Maharashtra, India. The cooperatives sell the sugar produced by their members, and pay them a price per kilogram of sugar that must, by law, be the same for all members. There are, however, divergent interests among members according to farm size: small farmers prefer the cooperative to give them higher prices while large farmers, who control the cooperative's budget, prefer lower prices. Higher retained earnings, as a consequence of lower prices, are invested in construction and other projects from which they derive direct rents. Higher inequality gives greater political power to the larger farmers over management of the cooperative. Lower prices in turn lead to lower investment and slower production growth. As a consequence, higher inequality has both efficiency and equity costs for the performance of the institution. In this case, by lowering institutional quality, higher inequality leads to lower growth. The role of inclusive (more egalitarian) as opposed to extractive (more unequal) institutions on growth has been analyzed historically by Acemoglu and Robinson (2012). Their thesis is that inclusive political and economic institutions are a necessary condition for sustained long-term economic growth.

CAN GREATER EQUALITY BE A SOURCE OF EFFICIENCY GAINS?

If markets are perfect, the Separability Theorem in welfare economics holds: asset ownership does not affect efficiency in resource use. Factors of production are efficiently allocated according to their relative prices (equating the value of marginal product of each factor to its price), and inputs can be acquired by entrepreneurs in markets irrespective of their ownership. Who owns what affects the distribution of income but not efficiency. In other words, the size of the pie (the economy) is unaffected by how the pie is cut (income distribution). Applied to land, for instance, and assuming that there are no economies of scale in production, the Separability Theorem implies that asset concentration (farm size) does not affect total factor productivity (yield). Redistributing land across farms of different sizes—for example, from large to small under a redistributive land-reform program—would have no impact on efficiency. The equity gain is obtained at no opportunity cost in terms of efficiency. But is this true when there are market failures?

If there are market failures, efficiency is affected by asset ownership (Bardhan, 1996). There are indeed plenty of cases of market failures in developing countries. (1) Capital is cheaper for individuals or firms who own collateralizable assets. The capital market is wealth-constrained. Wealthier individuals will have access to cheaper capital, favoring larger firms. (2) Self-employed labor (becoming the residual claimant on effort) is cheaper than hired labor as it avoids search and supervision costs. (3) Insurance may not be available, implying that poor entrepreneurs who are more risk-averse will have to self-insure by sacrificing expected income for lower risk. They may not be able to adopt higher-yielding but more risky seed varieties that larger farmers with access to insurance or with more capacity to self-insure can adopt. (4) Access to land-rental contracts may be available to farmers who belong to the same social circles as large landowners, while landless workers may lack referrals or be seen by landlords as more risky in case of conflict (Macours *et al.*, 2010). Asset position and social class thus determine access to land. (5) Finally, educational achievements are very much determined by parents' economic status. This is because poor parents cannot borrow against their children's future incomes, preventing them from accessing the liquidity needed to send their children to school. Additionally, discrimination based on gender, caste, religion, ethnicity, race, and various stereotypes will diminish the return from investing in education, affecting school achievements.

With many markets failing, the issue of asset distribution as a potential source of efficiency gains is all the more important for developing countries. This can be seen in Figure 6.13, where we consider land productivity (yield), as a measure of efficiency, against farm size (asset concentration), as a measure of equity. In all cases, we assume that there are no economies of scale; differences come from market failures. In Figure 6.13a, there are no market failures. Efficiency and equity are not related: separability holds. How assets are distributed does not affect yield, nor, as a result, economic growth. By contrast, Figure 6.13b shows an inverse relation between productivity and farm size. This occurs when the only market failure is for labor, farming is labor-intensive, and labor is cheaper on small farms, where it is a residual claimant, than on larger farms, which use wage labor. In this case, asset redistribution toward smaller farms (equity) has an efficiency gain. Equity is efficient. Redistributive land reform from large to small farms is win–win in terms of efficiency and equity. Finally, in Figure 6.13c farming is capital-intensive and risky, and there are market failures on the capital and insurance markets with the result that capital is cheaper and insurance more accessible for larger farmers. The inverse productivity–farm-size relationship has turned positive. Equity comes at an opportunity cost: a redistributive land reform from large to small farmers improves equity but reduces efficiency. Under these conditions, such redistribution is more politically difficult to implement as land concentration breeds productivity gains.

Clearly, there are no general rules, and empirical evidence on the inequality–growth relation is mixed (Banerjee and Duflo, 2003). What prevails in a particular

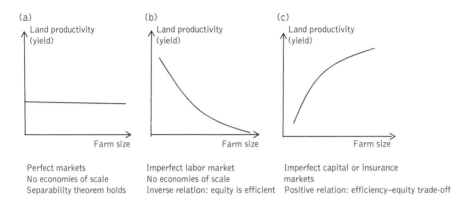

(a)

Land productivity (yield)

Farm size

Perfect markets
No economies of scale
Separability theorem holds

(b)

Land productivity (yield)

Farm size

Imperfect labor market
No economies of scale
Inverse relation: equity is efficient

(c)

Land productivity (yield)

Farm size

Imperfect capital or insurance markets
Positive relation: efficiency–equity trade-off

Figure 6.13 *The efficiency–equity relation*

situation is a complex combination of these various market failures. In the latter two cases, non-separability holds, but the efficiency–equity relationship depends on the particular prevailing conditions. However, the important policy implication is that equity gains do not always have to be achieved at an efficiency cost. Opportunities can be found— for example, in labor-intensive farming, or if we use microfinance to decouple access to credit from collateral ownership—where equity gains can be efficient. This is the message that the World Development Report (WDR) on *Equity and Development* (World Bank, 2005a) wants to convey.

If the positive relation between farm size and land productivity comes from market failures and biases in access to public goods between large and small farms, then policy interventions can be used to level the playing field across farms and restore the inverse relation (Carter and Barham, 1996). This is where such development initiatives as microfinance, micro-insurance, and public-extension systems have a role to play.

WHAT ROLES FOR ETHNIC FRACTIONALIZATION AND GENETIC DIVERSITY?

Ethnic fractionalization

Some countries, especially in Sub-Saharan Africa, were created by colonial powers, in particular at the Berlin Conference of 1884, where Africa was shared among European nations, with little regard for its ethnic composition. This happened in part because so little was known at the time about the social structure of Africa. As a consequence, these countries frequently have a high degree of ethnic fractionalization, meaning that many ethnic groups co-exist within the country. Is this one of the contributing factors to today's low institutional and policy quality, and poor growth performance? The issue was first addressed by Easterly and Levine (1997). To indicate fractionalization they used the Hirschman–Herfindhal index, defined as:

$$F = \sum_{i=1}^{k} n_i (1 - n_i),$$

where there are k ethnic groups and n_i is the share of the population belonging to group i. This means that each individual in group i has the probability $(1 - n_i)$ of meeting someone from a different group. Considering all individuals in a group, the index measures the probability that two randomly selected individuals in a country belong to different groups. Groups defined on an ethnic, linguistic, caste, and religious basis are of interest, and whether greater fractionalization impacts on a country's economic performance. The issue is addressed through cross-country regressions where outcome variables can be quality of policy (literacy rate, infant mortality, infrastructure), quality of institutions (corruption, level of financial development, political freedoms), and income growth. Results obtained by Easterly and Levine show that greater ethnic and linguistic fractionalizations tend to encourage the emergence of lower-quality policies and institutions, typically associated with growth performance, but that they only have a weak correlation with growth. According to their results, religious fractionalizations don't matter.

In a follow up article, Posner (2004) shows that a stronger correlation between fractionalization and growth is obtained when ethnic groups are limited to those engaged in political competition for the country's economic policies. He restricts the analysis to Politically Relevant Ethnic Groups, and shows that fractionalization among these groups has a significant negative correlation with a country's income growth.

These results have to be treated with caution. Causality is not established, in part because self-declared ethnic membership can be an endogenous choice driven by the quest for advantage (Rao and Ban, 2007). Politically relevant ethnic groups are clearly motivated by the expectation of policy and institutional gains. As is often the case, without some natural experiment that provides identification causality is poorly established by simple statistical means in cross-country regressions. As a consequence, the debate on fractionalization and growth is far from closed. In a study of the emergence of efficiency-enhancing producer organizations in Burkina Faso, Bernard et al. (2010) found that greater village-level ethnic diversity prevents social conservatism from opposing these organizations in case they undermine solidarity in support of local social-safety nets. In this case, diversity is good for efficiency-enhancing social change.

Genetic diversity

Ethnic fractionalization is in part based on genetic diversity. Ashraf and Galor's (2013) Out of Africa hypothesis shows that spatial variation in genetic diversity declines with the migratory distance between the locus of *Homo sapiens*' emergence in Africa tens of thousands of years ago and current population settlements across the globe. They observe that genetic diversity is very high among African populations, declines with distance among Asian and European populations, and is quite low among Native American populations—and they find that there is an optimum level of genetic diversity in relation to many development outcomes. For example, Ashraf et al. (2014) show that there is an inverted-U relation between genetic diversity and economic achievements as measured by per capita nighttime light intensity, suggesting the existence of an optimum degree of diversity; and Arbath et al. (2014) show that ethnic diversity, affecting ethnic fractionalization, has been associated with a greater frequency of civil conflict in the last half century. Their interpretation is that genetic diversity undermines trust and cooperation, increases income inequality, and reduces investment in public goods. If many current development outcomes are shown to have their roots in factors that were determined a very long time ago, as far back as the dawn of humanity, then initial conditions continue to matter.

WHAT ROLE FOR EQUITY IN DEVELOPMENT?

The WDR 2006 (World Bank, 2005a) addressed the issue of *Equity and Development*, an important dimension of development previously neglected. It is not clear, however, that the policy implications of addressing equity bring in much that was not there before in the pursuit of development.

Equity is defined as equality of opportunity for success: it is an ex-ante concept relative to outcomes. Equity requires level playing fields so development outcomes for individuals depend only on their levels of effort and on luck, not on particular circumstances such as their individual characteristics, asset endowments, and the contexts in which the assets they have are used. The WDR 2006 documents the fact that there are massive inequities attached to gender, race, caste, place of birth, parental education, paternal occupation, and parental socio-economic status.

According to Roemer (2012), the traditional utilitarian "equality approach" to development consists in equalizing outcomes such as income, wages, and life expectancy. By contrast, an "equal opportunity approach" to development equalizes outcomes only at equal levels of effort. It requires equalizing the role of circumstances on outcomes at given effort. Alternatively, it requires eliminating inequalities that are due to circumstances for which persons should not be held responsible as they are beyond their control.

But why should policy be concerned with equity in development? There are two reasons: one intrinsic, the other instrumental.

The intrinsic value of equity is the broadly shared feeling that egregious disparities of opportunity violate a sense of fairness, particularly when the individuals affected can do little about them. For Rawls (1971), this can derive from a self-serving concern that if we do not know where we will fit in the distribution of opportunities, due to what he called the "veil of ignorance," we should a priori prefer a more egalitarian distribution of opportunities. Political philosophies, international human-rights declarations, and leading religions are all concerned with equity— and achieving a certain level of equity should be an important dimension of well-being, i.e. of development, as defined in Chapter 1. This has been the objective of affirmative-action policies: redressing inequities by equalizing chances of success, generally by creating the positive advantages necessary to compensate for unequal initial circumstances (Roemer, 1998). The general intrinsic value of equity is easy to establish, then; but how much equity to seek is evidently a deep ideological choice, especially if equity may have an opportunity cost for the other dimensions of development, most particularly short-run economic growth.

The instrumental value of equity, as argued by the WDR 2006, is that higher levels of equity can be efficient, resulting in long-run higher levels of economic growth.

This is of course much harder to establish. How efficient is equity? Are there more cost-effective sources of growth than equity? Can too much equity be inefficient? If it is efficient in the long run, when does the long run start? The WDR provides two examples to make the case for the efficiency value of equity. One is when there are market failures, and greater equality in the distribution of assets (the inverse relation between asset distribution and total factor productivity that we have seen in Figure 6.13) is a source of productivity gains. Asset redistribution (e.g. land reform) becomes a source of both increased equity and growth. The other derives from the work of Acemoglu *et al.* (2002), seen in Chapter 3, who argue that more egalitarian land-settlement patterns (e.g. the Homestead Act in the US) led to more inclusive political and economic institutions, which in turn induced more long-term growth, resulting in the "reversal of fortune" between initially richer colonies of extraction and initially poorer colonies of settlement. These are telling examples, and the issue is greatly important, but the research agenda to relate equity to growth is clearly unfinished.

There are policy implications to increase equity at both the domestic and the international level. At the domestic level, they include greater investment in human capacities, more equitable access to justice, land, and infrastructure, and greater fairness in market relations, especially financial and labor markets. At the international level, they include more open global markets for goods and labor (migration opportunities), and increased levels of foreign aid. While motivated by equity gains, these policies are, in the end, not qualitatively very different from what would be done to reduce poverty, vulnerability, and inequality. If these policies are in deficit, then simply increasing them should contribute to equity. And this may be the first-order-of-importance issue for development. The quantitative targeting of these policies will, however, be different with an equity rather than an equality concern as they must compensate for initial handicaps to achieve equality of outcomes.

INCLUSIVE GROWTH

Equity is an ex-ante concept; equality an ex-post concept. But does the process of growth itself carry welfare implications? We see today high levels of alienation, disenfranchisement, and conflict that are not necessarily related to inequity and inequality. Rebellious youth—think of Islamic State fighters in the Middle East, who are joined by thousands from industrialized countries—may have had initially equal chances, and are most frequently not in poverty, yet feel excluded to the point of seeking redress via armed rebellion. Inclusive growth is thus an important criterion in terms of social welfare. It does not require pro-poor growth in the *relative*/UNDP sense, whereby growth would reduce inequality. This can be obtained ex-post through income transfers that would not create inclusion. Pro-poor growth in the *absolute*/Ravallion–Chen sense is thus sufficient. Growth has to be poverty-reducing. What counts is the *process* through which growth is obtained, as opposed to ex-ante equity and ex-post equality. Importantly, it has to do with giving people an opportunity to contribute to and benefit from economic growth. The main form through which this obtains is *productive employment* as the means of increasing income. It is well recognized that employment confers not only income but also social status, respect, and a sense of purpose, competence, and efficacy (Clark and Oswald, 1994). And the current employment status of an individual should have potential for future income growth, either in the actual job or by finding another job in the same or another sector. It thus implies the possibility of labor-productivity growth to lift the wages of the employed and the returns to self-employment. For this, skills development is essential. Inclusive growth is thus a process, with a long-term perspective. Achieving it requires more than growth, as pursued, for example, through the Hausmann *et al.* (2005) diagnostic framework of growth that focuses on relaxing the most binding constraints to higher growth. The framework needs to be extended to identify not only constraints to growth, but also constraints to all willing individuals to contribute and benefit from growth (Ianchovichina and Lundström, 2009). It also requires more than the World Bank's objective of "shared prosperity" (Kim, 2014) that can be achieved through transfers.

Empirical studies have shown that unemployment is a source of unhappiness that cannot be compensated for by income transfers (Carroll, 2007). Crost (2011) uses a diff-in-diffs approach to show that Germany's subsidized employment program for the unemployed maintains a level of happiness superior to compensation lost through unemployment benefits. Panel data allow testing for parallel trends in happiness before the event of unemployment, and participation to subsidized employment.

Youth frustration with high levels of unemployment, meaningless jobs in terms of fulfillment and future development, and transfers that may keep people above the poverty line but does not eliminate dissatisfaction with their lifestyles, are today central issues to development. Violent youth responses such as the Islamic State and Boko Haram are symptoms of failed inclusive growth. How to achieve inclusive growth is a huge challenge that needs to be addressed as it is key to long-term sustained growth in wellbeing and to social stability, even if there may exist short-term trade-offs between the pace of growth and the process of growth.

CONCLUSION: THE GROWTH–INEQUALITY–POVERTY DEVELOPMENT TRIANGLE

We have seen that income growth, poverty, and inequality are three fundamental dimensions of development (Chapter 1). Together they constitute a development triangle, where each dimension interacts with the other two. The information we use to construct this triangle is the initial levels of income, poverty, and inequality, and the growth in income, poverty, and inequality. What we have learned about these interactions in the last chapter and this is summarized in Figure 6.14.

Effect of growth on inequality

Consider first the relation between growth and inequality (relation (1) in Figure 6.14). We have seen that the relation between income level and inequality as described by the Kuznets inverted-U is descriptively solid across countries but causally ambiguous. Cross-country econometric studies done by Deininger and Squire (1998) and Easterly (1999) find that there is no systematic impact of growth on income distribution as

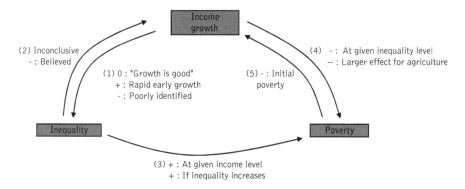

Figure 6.14 *The development triangle between growth, inequality, and poverty*

soon as country fixed effects are introduced in cross-country regressions. The Dollar and Kraay (2001) result—the elasticity of GDPpc growth on the income of the poor is equal to one—supports the proposition that there is, on average, no overall impact of growth on inequality. Because growth's impact on the distribution of income is neutral (the income of the poor rises proportionately to the income of the rich when aggregate income rises), Dollar and Kraay declare growth "good for the poor." Bourguignon (2004) claims that a long-term negative relation should exist, with growth reducing inequality, but that it has been econometrically difficult to establish. An example of a reason for a negative relation is that income growth helps reduce fertility and average family size, and increases investment in education. Identification is difficult because there is too much specificity across countries as to how this relation holds: it is affected by widely differing initial conditions and by highly specific policy interventions. It may also be the case that, in countries like Brazil, there has not been enough growth to have a visible impact on reduced inequality—and it is also likely that, as confirmed by case studies, rapid early growth (for example, in China and Vietnam) has been strongly inequalizing. Deaton (2013) thus makes the argument that incomplete escape from poverty and disease has been a major source of rising inequalities.

This suggests that an overall relation between growth and inequality has not been identified, meaning a straight pro-growth strategy will not be effective *per se* in reducing high levels of inequality. We have seen, however, in Chapter 5 that there is considerable heterogeneity across countries in the elasticity of poverty with respect to income growth. Heterogeneity suggests that there is considerable scope for policy innovation in making growth more pro-poor in the UNDP sense of falling inequality.

Effect of inequality on growth

Turning to relation (2) in Figure 6.14, we saw in Chapter 1 that inequality can have positive or negative impacts on growth through different channels. On the positive side, this involves an increase in the aggregate rate of saving, enhancing investment and growth. On the negative side, this involves the role of credit-market failures, whereby the poor lack collateral to access credit. This implies that wealth inequality reduces investment by the poor in productive projects, education, and insurance, at a cost to growth. Persson and Tabellini (1994) made the political argument that higher inequality pushes the median voter into demanding more redistributive policies, and hence higher tax rates that deter investment. Social conflict induced by inequality can also impose a cost on investment through higher security expenditures and the deterrence of violence. And inequality may reduce market size for import-substitution industrialization strategies, compromising investment when there are economies of scale in production. Not surprisingly, different authors have obtained conflicting empirical results. Forbes (2000) found a positive cross-country relation between inequality and growth, Alesina and Rodrik (1994) a negative relation, and Ravallion and Chen (2007) no relation for China over the 1981–2001 period of rapid growth. With so many channels at play, it is important to look specifically at particular countries and periods where specific channels of influence may have been present. The inequality–growth relation is empirically inconclusive. There remain, however, widespread beliefs in the development profession that reducing inequalities can, in the long run, be growth-promoting (World Bank, 2005a). It is also clear that there are many policy instruments that can be used to make reduced inequality a source of growth. Asset redistribution—for example, through land reform—can help reduce credit-market failures. "Smart" income redistribution through, for example, CCTs such as *Oportunidades* in Mexico and *Bolsa Família* in Brazil, can help improve the formation of human capital. In this perspective, social protection not only reduces inequality, but can be a source of efficiency gains, a theme developed in Chapter 14.

Effects of growth and redistribution on poverty

There is no ambiguity in relation (3) between inequality and poverty. At a given level of GDPpc, less inequality is poverty-reducing. There is, similarly, no ambiguity in relation (4) between growth and poverty: at a given level of inequality, a higher GDPpc reduces poverty. These two effects reinforce each other in reducing poverty. We saw in Chapter 5 that Datt and Ravallion (1992) give us an additive decomposition of the growth in the poverty rate $(\dot{P}_0)$ into a component due to income growth $(\dot{y})$ and a component due to growth in inequality $(\dot{G})$. The magnitude of these two effects on poverty depends on the corresponding elasticities of poverty with respect to income (E_P^y) and to inequality (E_P^G), according to the formula:

$$\dot{P}_0 = E_P^y \dot{y} + E_P^G \dot{G} + \text{Residual}.$$

The size of these elasticities determines the "quality" of growth and redistribution for poverty reduction. As we have seen, growth has been weakly poverty-reducing in Sub-Saharan Africa compared to the rest of the world (Fosu, 2015). Growth originating in agriculture tends to be particularly effective for poverty reduction as shown through cross-country data (Ligon and Sadoulet, 2007) and for India (Datt and Ravallion, 1998) and China (Ravallion and Chen, 2007). From a policy standpoint, it tells us that growth is essential but that it can be made more pro-poor through policy interventions, and that inequality reduction can be a fundamental instrument for poverty reduction, all the more so if it can also contribute to growth.

Effect of initial poverty on growth

Ravallion (2012) has recently advanced the proposition that initially high levels of poverty are growth-reducing in relation (5) in Figure 6.14. The channels through which this is happening (less poverty implying more middle-class entrepreneurship on the supply side and greater market size on the demand side) are still to be established, suggesting an interesting research agenda.

CONCEPTS SEEN IN THIS CHAPTER

Lorenz curve
Gini coefficient
Theil entropy index
Kuznets ratios
Kuznets inverted-U hypothesis
Personal and functional distribution of income
Growth Incidence Curve
Absolute and relative pro-poor growth
Links between inequality and growth, equalizing growth
Separability theorem between efficiency and equity
Collateralizable assets
Self-employment and residual claimancy
Inverse relation between yield and farm size
Ethnic fractionalization
Hirschman–Herfindhal index
Inequity and affirmative action
Inclusive growth
Development triangle: growth–inequality–poverty

REVIEW QUESTIONS: INEQUALITY AND INEQUITY

1. Define the Lorenz curve, the Gini coefficient, and Kuznets income ratios. How can there be the same Gini for two different Lorenz curves?
2. Explain the Kuznets inverted-U curve, and why it cannot be used for economic policy.
3. If we construct a triangle between growth, poverty, and inequality, what are the relations that hold empirically between these outcomes, and in which direction?
4. What are the different ways in which inequality can affect economic growth?
5. What is meant by equity and how does it differ from equality? How do you reduce inequity as opposed to inequality?

NOTE

1   A useful reference on inequality measures is the World Bank's (2005b) *Poverty Manual*.

REFERENCES

Acemoglu, Daron, Simon Johnson, and James Robinson. 2002. "Reversal of Fortune: Geography and Institutions in the Making of the Modern World Income Distribution." *Quarterly Journal of Economics* 117(4): 1231–94.

Acemoglu, Daron, and James Robinson. 2012. *Why Nations Fail: The Origins of Power, Prosperity, and Poverty.* New York: Crown Business.

Adams, Richard. 1991. *The Effects of International Remittances on Poverty, Inequality, and Development in Rural Egypt.* Washington, DC: International Food Policy Research Institute Research Report No. 86.

Adelman, Irma, and Sherman Robinson. 1978. *Income Distribution Policy in Developing Countries: A Case Study of Korea.* Stanford: Stanford University Press.

Ahluwalia, Montek. 1976. "Inequality, Poverty, and Development." *Journal of Development Economics* 3(4): 307–42.

Alesina, Alberto, and Dani Rodrik. 1994. "Distributive Politics and Economic Growth." *Quarterly Journal of Economics* 109(2): 465–90.

Alvaredo, Facundo, Anthony Atkinson, Thomas Piketty, and Emmanuel Saez. 2014. The World Top Incomes Database. http://topincomes.g-mond.parisschoolofeconomics.eu/ (accessed 2015).

Arbath, Cemal, Quamrul Ashraf, and Oded Galor. 2014. "The Nature of Civil Conflict." Department of Economics, Brown University.

Ashraf, Quamrul, and Oded Galor. 2013. "The Out of Africa Hypothesis, Human Genetic Diversity, and Comparative Economic Development." *American Economic Review* 103: 1–46.

Ashraf, Quamrul, Oded Galor, and Marc Klemp. 2014. "The Out of Africa Hypothesis of Comparative Development Reflected in Nighttime Light Intensity." Department of Economics, Brown University.

Banerjee, Abhijit, and Andrew Newman. 1993. "Occupational Choice and the Process of Development." *Journal of Political Economy* 101(2): 274–98.

Banerjee, Abhijit, and Esther Duflo. 2003. "Inequality and Growth: What Can the Data Say?" *Journal of Economic Growth* 8(3): 267–99.

Banerjee, Abhijit, Dilip Mookherjee, Kaivan Munshi, and Debraj Ray. 2001. "Inequality, Control Rights, and Rent Seeking: Sugar Cooperatives in Maharashtra." *Journal of Political Economy* 109(1): 138–90

Bardhan, Pranab. 1996. "Efficiency, Equity, and Poverty Alleviation: Policy Issues in Less Developed Countries." *Economic Journal* 106(September): 1344–56.

Barro, Robert. 2000. "Inequality and Growth in a Panel of Countries." *Journal of Economic Growth* 5(1): 5–32.

Bernard, Tanguy, Alain de Janvry, and Elisabeth Sadoulet. 2010. "When Does Community Conservatism Constrain Village Organizations?" *Economic Development and Cultural Change* 58(4): 609–41.

Boucher, Stephen, Michael Carter, and Catherine Guirkinger. 2008. "Risk Rationing and Wealth Effects in Credit Markets: Theory and Implications for Agricultural Development." *American Journal of Agricultural Economics* 90(2): 409–23.

Bourguignon, François. 2004. "The Poverty–Growth–Inequality Triangle." Washington, DC: World Bank.

Carroll, Nick. 2007. "Unemployment and Psychological Well-Being." *Economic Record* 83(262): 287–302.

Carter, Michael, and Bradford Barham. 1996. "Level Playing Fields and Laissez Faire: Post-Liberal Development Strategies in Inegalitarian Agrarian Economies." *World Development* 24(7): 1133–50.

Clark, Andrew, and Andrew Oswald. 1994. "Unhappiness and Unemployment." *Economic Journal* 104(424): 648–59.

Crost, Benjamin. 2011. "The Effect of Subsidized Employment on Happiness." Working paper, Department of Agricultural and Consumer Economics, University of Illinois at Urbana-Champaign.

Datt, Gaurav, and Martin Ravallion. 1992. "Growth and Redistribution Components of Changes in Poverty Measures: A Decomposition with Applications to Brazil and India in the 1980s." *Journal of Development Economics* 38(2): 275–95.

Datt, Gaurav, and Martin Ravallion. 1998. "Farm Productivity and Rural Poverty in India." *Journal of Development Studies* 34(4): 62–85.

Deaton, Angus. 2013. *The Great Escape: Health, Wealth, and the Origins of Inequality.* Princeton, NJ: Princeton University Press.

Deininger, Klaus, and Lyn Squire. 1998. "New Ways of Looking at Old Issues: Inequality and Growth." *Journal of Development Economics* 57(2): 259–87

de Janvry, Alain, and Elisabeth Sadoulet. 1983. "Social Articulation as a Condition for Equitable Growth." *Journal of Development Economics* 13: 275–303.

Demombynes, Gabriel, and Berk Özler. 2005. "Crime and Local Inequality in South Africa." *Journal of Development Economics* 76(2): 265–92.

Dollar, David, and Aart Kraay. 2001. "Growth is Good for the Poor." Washington, DC: World Bank Policy Research Working Paper No. 2587.

Easterly, William. 1999. "Life during Growth." *Journal of Economic Growth* 4(3): 239–76

Easterly, William, and Ross Levine, 1997. "Africa's Growth Tragedy: Policies and Ethnic Divisions." *Quarterly Journal of Economics* 112(4): 1203–50.

Elbers, Chris, Peter Lanjouw, Johan Mistiaen, Berk Özler, and Kenneth Simler. 2003. "Are Neighbours Equal? Estimating Local Inequality in Three Developing Countries." Working Paper Series. Helsinki: World Institute for Development Economic Research (UNU-WIDER).

Forbes, Kristin. 2000. "A Reassessment of the Relationship between Inequality and Growth." *American Economic Review* 90(4): 869–87.

Fosu, Augustin. 2015. "Growth, Inequality and Poverty in Sub-Saharan Africa: Recent Progress in a Global Context." *Oxford Development Studies* 43(1): 44–59.

Fukuyama, Francis. 2014. *Political Order and Political Decay: From the Industrial Revolution to the Globalization of Democracy.* New York: Farrar, Staus and Giroux.

Galor, Oded, and Joseph Zeira. 1993. "Income Distribution and Macroeconomics." *Review of Economic Studies* 60(1): 35–52.

Galor, Oded, and Daniel Tsiddon. 1997. "Technological Progress, Mobility, and Economic Growth." *American Economic Review* 87(3): 363–82.

Haughton, Jonathan, and Shahidur Khandker. 2009. *Handbook on Poverty and Inequality.* Washington, DC: World Bank. http://documents.worldbank.org/curated/en/2009/01/10522315/handbook-poverty-inequality (accessed 2015).

Hausmann, Ricardo, Dani Rodrik, and Andrés Velasco. 2005. *Growth Diagnostics.* Working paper, John F. Kennedy School of Government, Harvard University.

Hirschman, Albert, and Michael Rothschild. 1973. "The Changing Tolerance for Income Inequality in the Course of Economic Growth." *Quarterly Journal of Economics* 87(4): 544–66.

Ianchovichina, Elena, and Susanna Lundström. 2009. "What Is Inclusive Growth?" Economic Policy and Debt Department (PRMED). Washington, DC: World Bank.

Kakwani, Nanak. 1997. "Growth Rates of Per-capita Income and Aggregate Welfare: An International Comparison." *Review of Economics and Statistics* 79(2): 201–11.

Kim, Jim Yong. 2014. "Shared Prosperity: A Goal to Reduce Inequality." *The Korea Herald*, October 29. http://www.koreaherald.com/view.php?ud=20141029000656 (accessed 2015).

Kuznets, Simon. 1955. "Economic Growth and Income Inequality." *American Economic Review* 45(1): l–28.

Ligon, Ethan, and Elisabeth Sadoulet. 2007. "Estimating the Effects of Aggregate Agricultural Growth on the Distribution of Expenditures." Working paper, Department of Agricultural and Resource Economics, University of California at Berkeley.

Lipton, Michael. 2009. *Land Reform in Developing Countries*. Abingdon: Routledge.

Macours, Karen, Alain de Janvry, and Elisabeth Sadoulet. 2010. "Insecurity of Property Rights and Matching in the Tenancy Market." *European Economic Review* 54(7): 880–99.

Murphy, Kevin, Andrei Shleifer, and Robert Vishny. 1989. "Income Distribution, Market Size, and Industrialization." *Quarterly Journal of Economics* 104(3): 537–64.

Perotti, Roberto. 1996. "Growth, Income Distribution, and Democracy: What the Data Say." *Journal of Economic Growth* 1(2): 149–87.

Persson, Torsten, and Guido Tabellini. 1994. "Is Inequality Harmful for Growth?" *American Economic Review* 84(3): 600–21.

Piketty, Thomas. 2014. *Capital in the Twenty-First Century*. Cambridge, MA: Harvard University Press.

Posner, Daniel. 2004. "Measuring Ethnic Fractionalization in Africa." *American Journal of Political Science* 48(4): 849–63.

Rabin, Matthew. 1998. "Psychology and Economics." *Journal of Economic Literature* 36(March): 11–46.

Rao, Vijayendra, and Radu Ban. 2007. "The Political Construction of Caste in South India." Development Research Group. Washington, DC: World Bank.

Ravallion, Martin. 2012. "Why Don't We See Poverty Convergence?" *American Economic Review* 102(1): 504–23.

Ravallion, Martin, and Shaohua Chen. 2003. "Measuring Pro-poor Growth." *Economics Letters* 78(1): 93–9.

Ravallion, Martin, and Shaohua Chen. 2007. "China's (Uneven) Progress against Poverty." *Journal of Development Economics* 82(1): 1–42.

Rawls, John. 1971. *A Theory of Justice*. Cambridge, MA: Harvard University Press.

Robinson, Sherman. 1976. "A Note on the U-hypothesis Relating Income Inequality and Economic Development." *American Economic Review* 66(3): 437–40.

Roemer, John. 1998. *Equality of Opportunity*. Cambridge, MA: Harvard University Press.

Roemer, John. 2012. "Economic Development as Opportunity Equalization." Working paper, Department of Economics, Yale University.

Saint-Paul, Gilles, and Thierry Verdier. 1993. "Education, Democracy, and Growth." *Journal of Development Economics* 42(2): 399–407.

Stiglitz, Joseph. 2012. *The Price of Inequality*. New York: W.W. Norton and Co.

UNDP. 2009. "Social Protection in Latin America: Brazil, Chile, and Mexico." Interview Series. Brasilia: International Policy Centre for Inclusive Growth.

World Bank. 2004. World Development Report 2005: *A Better Investment Climate for Everyone.* Washington, DC.

World Bank. 2005a. World Development Report 2006: *Equity and Development.* Washington, DC.

World Bank. 2005b. *Poverty Manual.* http://siteresources.worldbank.org/PGLP/Resources/PovertyManual.pdf (accessed 2015).

World Bank. *World Development Indicators.* http://data.worldbank.org/indicator (accessed 2015).

Zepeda, Eduardo. 2004. ''Pro-poor Growth: What Is It?'' International Poverty Center One Pager Number 1, UNDP.

International trade and industrialization strategies

TAKE-HOME MESSAGES FOR CHAPTER 7

1. Comparative advantage in trade can originate in country differences in resource endowments, in ways of organizing production, and/or in policies. Trade based on comparative advantage is a source of static and dynamic efficiency gains for participating countries that are enhanced by specialization. Trade should thus be good for growth, even though empirical results show a great deal of heterogeneity in impact associated with the presence of complementary policies.

2. The benefits from trade are unequally distributed across participating countries and between producers, consumers, and government, with both winners and losers. As a consequence, any move toward trade liberalization is a controversial political proposition, and aggregate efficiency gains may be lost to concerns about distribution.

3. The domestic price of a tradable good is affected by both trade and exchange-rate policies. Trade indicators characterize nominal, effective, and real protection. Taxation of agricultural exportables, that used to be quite high in developing countries in the early 1980s, has declined substantially over the last 25 years.

4. Latecomer countries can achieve international competitiveness when there are economies of scale in production through import-substitution industrialization (ISI), export-oriented industrialization (EOI), and open-economy industrialization (OEI) policies, each with their own particular conditions for success. Careful choice of an industrialization strategy is thus a key component of development policy.

5. The impact of trade liberalization on poverty reduction is ambiguous. In the short run, trade affects the prices of products and factors, and whether the poor benefit or not from these changes depends on which sectors they produce in and which products they consume. In the longer run, the impact on poverty is through the reallocation of labor across sectors as countries specialize and trade. In some cases, labor-productivity gains may be associated with labor-saving technological change and demand for higher labor skills, with no resulting gains in the labor earnings of the poor.

6. When there are environmental costs in production that are not internalized in private costs, trade opening creates gains from both trade and environmental effects. For an importing country with no environmental regulation, imports help reduce

domestic pollution. For an unregulated exporting country, trade creates net social gains but also large environmental costs. Because the unregulated exporting country acquires unfair trade advantages and can serve as a pollution haven for the world, industrialized countries demand the harmonization of environmental standards across trading countries. This is in turn problematic as the developing countries could have the right to focus on growth while postponing environmental controls, in the same way as the now industrialized countries did.

We explore in this chapter the role of trade in development strategies. To do this, we need to first understand why countries trade, who gains and loses from trade, what the policy instruments are that can be used to promote trade, and how trade affects both efficiency in the use of resources and the distribution of income. We then analyze how trade instruments can be used to design industrialization strategies, each of which has particular advantages and risks.

TRADE OPENNESS

A key aspect of the process of globalization has been the rapid rise in the importance of trade in GDP. Trade openness for country i in year t is measured as the share of trade in GDP, namely:

$$(X_{it} + M_{it})/GDP_{it},$$

where X is exports and M imports. The role of exports in creating effective demand for GDP can also be measured as the share of exports in GDP. Figure 7.1 shows that trade openness increased from 1967 to 2013 in all regions, indicating that trade (Figure 7.1a) and exports (Figure 7.1b) have grown faster than GDP. It shows, too, that it is in middle-income countries that the rise of trade openness and of the share of exports in GDP have been greatest. Until 1985, it was high-income OECD countries that were the most export-oriented, with exports accounting for 18 percent of GDP. After 1985, the share of exports in GDP became highest in middle-income countries, reaching 34 percent in 2006, before the shocks of the food and financial crises brought it down to 27 percent in 2009, rising again to 30 percent in 2012. In low-income countries, the importance of trade has also increased, keeping pace with growth of trade in the OECD countries, particularly in the last two decades.

Growth in exports has been spectacular in many middle-income countries. In China, exports grew by 18 percent/year between 1992 and 2008, and in India by 14 percent. They grew by more than 8 percent annually in Brazil, Korea, Mexico, Argentina, Indonesia, South Africa, Thailand, Egypt, Colombia, Malaysia, the Philippines, and Chile. Trade that was dominated by flows among high-income countries in the 1980s (accounting for 80 percent of all trade in 1985) is now dominated

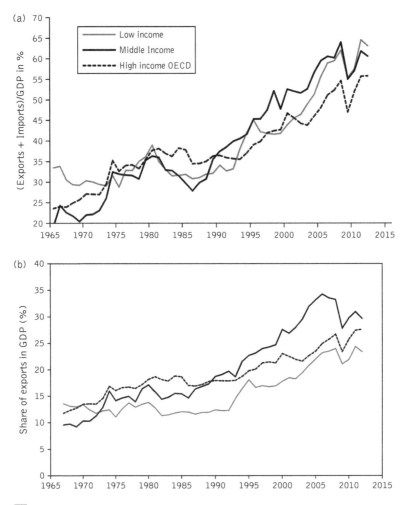

Figure 7.1 *Trade openness (a) and share of exports in GDP (b) by country category, 1967–2012*

Source: World Bank, *World Development Indicators.*

by North–South, South–North, and South–South trade. The share of exports from low-income countries to other low-income and middle-income countries rose from 24 percent in 1994 to 42 percent in 2008.

Today, China accounts for 20 percent of all manufactured goods imported by the US, mainly labor-intensive products, contributing to the decline in the price of many consumer goods. This share exceeds 30 percent in apparel, textiles, furniture, leather goods, electrical appliances, and jewelry. This has created gains for consumers, but at the cost of employment losses and declining wages in sectors competing with Chinese imports, as we will see later in the Autor *et al.* (2013) study of the "China syndrome."

Sachs and Warner (1995) constructed a dummy variable (i.e. a variable only taking the values of 0 and 1) for openness based on five individual dummies for specific trade-related policies. A country was classified as open if it did not display any of the following characteristics:

1. Average tariff rates of 40 percent of more.
2. Non-tariff barriers covering 40 percent or more of trade.
3. A black-market exchange rate lower by 20 percent or more than the official exchange rate.
4. A state monopoly on major exports.
5. A centrally planned socialist economic system.

This index was measured by Wacziarg and Welch (2008) for 141 countries over the period 1960 to 2000. Results in Figure 7.2 show that there was a major increase in trade openness starting in 1985. In 2000, 73 percent of the countries in the world, representing 47 percent of world population, were open to international trade. The authors relate the timing of being open (which they call trade liberalization) to indicators of economic performance such as trade openness, physical-capital investment, and growth in GDPpc, contrasting their levels before and after liberalization. They find that, on average across all countries, trade liberalization was associated with large increases in these indicators, concluding that trade liberalization does indeed matter for economic performance.

Previously non-traded services have seen a recent sharp increase in trade. These include banking, insurance, telecommunications, retailing, transportation, and professional services such as accounting, auditing, and international law. Borchert et al. (2014) show that trade in services remains restricted, however, and that restrictive trade policies are detrimental to investment flows in services and to trade in services. In particular, restrictions on foreign acquisitions, discrimination in licensing,

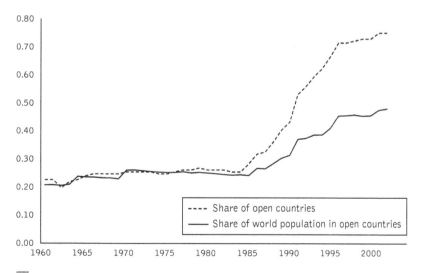

Figure 7.2 *Trade openness according to the Sachs and Warner criterion, 141 countries*

Source: Wacziarg and Welch, 2008.

restrictions on the repatriation of earnings, and lack of legal recourse all have a significant and sizable negative effect on the expected value of sectoral foreign investment into service sectors.

In India, trade liberalization came rapidly in the context of the 1991 balance-of-payments crisis and imposition by the IMF of conditionalities attached to structural-adjustment loans that mandated trade liberalization. This sudden exogenous trade-policy shock was analyzed by Topalova and Khandelwal (2011) to measure how reductions in trade protection induced higher levels of productivity in manufacturing firms. They found that tariff reductions increased competition and caused firms to increase their efficiency. Reduced import tariffs provided firms with more and cheaper access to imported inputs. Increased competition and access to modern inputs boosted firm-level productivity, particularly in import-competing industries, in industries not subject to excessive domestic regulation, and among domestic firms. Their study was thus able to exploit an exogenous trade shock as an events analysis to establish a causal link between trade liberalization and firm productivity.

GAINS FROM TRADE: WHY COUNTRIES TRADE, BUT NOT EVERYONE GAINS

When prices differ between countries by more than transaction costs, private traders can profit from exporting and importing. While this is the most basic impetus for trade, there is a more universal argument for international specialization based on aggregate efficiency. In principle, the world as a whole could benefit if each country specialized according to its relative efficiency, subject to the assumptions from the microeconomic theory of perfect competition. Just like Adam Smith's argument for microeconomic specialization in using the market to exchange, there could be aggregate benefits to an international division of labor and trade if this arises from real differences in efficiency.

While there are many practical obstacles to realizing such efficiency gains, let alone distributing its benefits, it is worth examining the potential gain from trade since we see many examples of trade-induced prosperity around the world. We consider two economic units: the Home economy (H) and all other countries pooled into the Rest of the World (W). We consider two goods: Food (F) and manufacturing (M).

The Home economy in Figure 7.3 has its own autarky prices (p_M^H, p_F^H), but it faces world prices (p_M^W, p_F^W) for both goods. The domestic price of M is relatively cheaper than in the world market, and the domestic price of F relatively more expensive. Think of China as an illustration. With trade, the country could gain from exporting M and importing F. From its initial domestic production point (S_M, S_F), the Home country then has an implied budget set determined by the international value of its output. This is depicted by what is called the Trading Possibility Line (TPL), defined by:

$$\text{TPL} : p_M^W M + p_F^W F = p_M^W S_M^H + p_F^W S_F^H = Y^H$$

where Y^H denotes national income at world prices. Thus Home can "purchase" any combination of goods (M, F) satisfying the national income-constraint TPL.

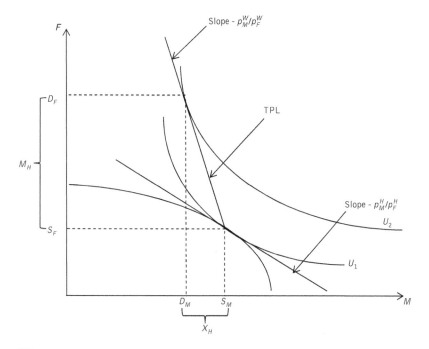

Figure 7.3 *Static gains from trade for the Home economy*

According to the example, its optimal choice would be (D_M, D_F), which achieves higher utility $(U_2 > U_1)$ than the initial autarky point (S_M, S_F). To reach this point, Home must export Manufactures in the amount $X_H = S_M^H - D_M^H$ and import Food in the amount $M_H = D_F^H - S_F^H$. By following comparative advantage, this country's consumption possibilities can extend beyond its production possibilities, achieving higher national utility by engaging in trade.

A parallel narrative can be developed for the Rest of the World, which plays a symmetric role in this simplified two-country story. As intuition would dictate, this block of countries can gain by exporting the food needed by Home and importing its Manufactures. In the process of reconciling these two pairs of demand and supply schedules, the world relative prices are achieved and trade is in equilibrium.

By these relatively simple mechanisms, goods and services move between countries with differing comparative advantages. Within the countries, however, other adjustments can take place. In particular, countries can be expected to exploit comparative advantage further by specializing: namely, by moving resources away from import-competing sectors (with falling relative price under trade) to expand export-competing ones (with rising relative price under trade). Of course, this brings domestic stakeholder groups into at least partial conflict, indicating that gains from trade are not equally distributed as some sectors expand with trade liberalization while others contract.

Specialization to derive further benefits from trade is illustrated in Figure 7.4. Home further exploits its comparative advantage by expanding the production of Manufactures (which increases from S_M^1 to S_M^2) at the expense of domestic Food

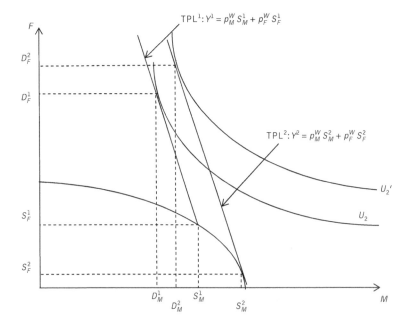

Figure 7.4 *Further gains from specialization*

production (which falls from S_F^1 to S_F^2). This process directly increases national income, from $Y^1 = p_M^W S_M^1 + p_F^W S_F^1$ to $Y^2 = p_M^W S_M^2 + p_F^W S_F^2$.

The results of this process for trade and national income can be summarized in three inequalities. Growth of income:

$$Y^1 = p_M^W S_M^1 + p_F^W S_F^1 < p_M^W S_M^2 + p_F^W S_F^2 = Y^2, \text{income gain.}$$

Growth of trade:

$$X_M^1 = S_M^1 - D_M^1 < S_M^2 - D_M^2 = X_M^2, \text{increased exports of } M.$$

$$M_F^1 = D_F^1 - S_F^1 < D_F^2 - S_F^2 = M_F^2, \text{increased imports of } F.$$

To achieve the observed specialization, resources must be shifted from the falling-price sector (Food) to the rising-price sector (Manufacturing). This price differential is what stimulates increased resource demand in Manufacturing, bidding labor away from Food. When these adjustments have run their course, employment is higher in Manufacturing and lower in Food, but wages are higher in both sectors since there is only one labor market. These observations reflect another fundamental insight of trade theory.

To measure the efficiency and distributive effects of trade liberalization between two countries we consider trade from a traditional supply and demand perspective, and evaluate welfare in terms of Consumer and Producer Surplus. Looking at Food

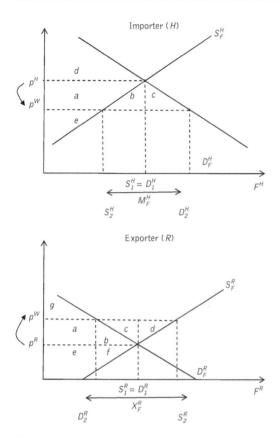

Figure 7.5 *Domestic gains and losses from trade in food*

this time, we depict in Figure 7.5 both the importing (H) and exporting country (R). Here, illustratively, H would be China and R Brazil.

We calculate in Table 7.1 the consumer and producer surplus to characterize the welfare gains or losses for consumers, producers, and the nation as a whole from moving from autarky to trade.

This analysis shows that trade can be a contentious issue in both countries due to its redistributive implications. Although both nations gain in the aggregate (Net Social Gain or surplus (NSG) > 0), consumers do so at the expense of producers in the importing country (H), and the other way round in the exporting country (R). Hence in both countries there are aggregate efficiency gains, but also winners and losers from trading Food. An example would be trade in corn between the US (R) and Guatemala (H) under CAFTA (the Central America Free Trade Agreement). The US has comparative advantage in corn and will export, while Guatemala will import. Both countries gain overall, but farmers lose in Guatemala, while consumers gain. This explains the strong resistance of corn producers to the CAFTA agreement, while urban interests were in favor.

Because trade liberalization creates positive NSG with winners and losers, taxes and transfers can be used to compensate the losers and achieve Pareto optimality after

291

Table 7.1 *Welfare gains and losses from trade for consumers, producers, and the nation*

	Importer (H)			Exporter (R)		
	Consumer surplus	*Producer surplus*	*Net social gain*	*Consumer surplus*	*Producer surplus*	*Net social gain*
Surpluses under autarky	d	$a + e$		$a + b + g$	$e + f$	
Surpluses under trade	$a + b + c + d$	e		g	$a + b + c + d + e + f$	
Gains from trade	$a + b + c$	$- a$	$b + c$	$- (a + b)$	$a + b + c + d$	$c + d$
Sign of gains from trade	$+$	$-$	$+$	$-$	$+$	$+$

compensation. Pareto optimality means that there will be no losers from the reform after compensation has been paid. In Table 7.1, consumers can be taxed of (a) in Home to compensate producers for their losses, and producers can be taxed of ($a + b$) in Rest of World to compensate consumers for their losses. In both cases, gainers still gain after tax because $NSG > 0$. In principle, a Pareto-optimum reform should be politically feasible.

The big question for losers is whether compensation will effectively be paid after trade liberalization has occurred. There is a difficult *time consistency* problem to be addressed here because liberalization will occur before the gains from liberalization have effectively materialized (Fernández and Rodrik, 1991). Compensation cannot be paid (or be set aside in escrow) before the trade reform has occurred. To make the trade reform politically feasible the government needs a *commitment device* that guarantees losers that they will be compensated for their losses through a tax on winners. As we will see later when we address the political economy of policy (Chapter 21), a key difficulty in implementing policies that have a time-consistency problem is the pervasive lack of credible commitment devices available to governments. Indeed, many good reforms that can create NSGs remain unfulfilled because a credible commitment to pay compensation to achieve Pareto optimality cannot be made.

It should also be clear that, while both countries gain from trade, these gains can be unequal. There is no reason in Table 7.1 for ($b + c$) in the importing country H to be equal to ($c + d$) in the exporting country R. There is also an issue of the differential capacity of countries to capture the gains from specialization shown in Figure 7.4, particularly when the trade agreement is between an industrialized and a developing country, as is the case with many of the recent bilateral agreements such as NAFTA (between Canada, the US, and Mexico) and CAFTA (between the US, Central American states, and the Dominican Republic). This is in part due to the unequal capacity of the countries to adjust their production patterns to the new terms of trade and specialize to maximize gains. Trade has thus been denounced as resulting in "unequal exchange." Stiglitz and Charlton (2005) have called for the need to complement trade agreements with "behind the border" assistance for developing countries to help them adapt their production structures to their comparative advantages in trade so there can be "Fair Trade for All." Aid-for-trade would help trade become a more effective instrument to promote development.

Another difficulty for poor countries in gaining from trade is that they may face systematically higher export costs than rich countries. Waugh (2010) has developed a model of trade frictions between rich and poor countries. He finds that to reconcile observed bilateral trade volumes and price data with the predictions of his model the trade frictions between rich and poor countries must be systematically asymmetric, with poor countries facing much higher export costs relative to rich countries, significantly reducing their exports. He argues that these trade frictions are sufficiently important to contribute to standards of living that are 30 times higher in rich than in poor countries. However, the source of poor countries' high costs, calculated as a residual in Waugh's model, isn't clear, meaning that the channels involved will need to be identified to provide a basis for policy recommendations.

A source of tension in opening a country to trade is the differential skills components of the goods traded. If trade is between low skill goods exported by a developing country (such as apparel in China) and high skill goods exported by an industrialized country (such as electronic products in the US), then trade will induce a decline in low-skill wages in the industrialized country relative to high-skill wages, and an increase in low-skill wages in the developing country relative to high-skill wages.

This result is known as the Stolper–Samuelson theorem: a rise in the relative price of a good due to trade opening (here, the low-skill good in China and the high-skill good in the US) will lead to a rise in the return to the factor used most intensively in the production of the good, and, conversely, to a fall in the return to the other factor.

For this reason, low-skill workers in the industrialized country who anticipate this relative decline in purchasing power may strongly resist trade agreements. Trade agreements may contribute to rising inequality in wages to the detriment of low-skill workers, as has been the case in the US for the most recent decades of increasing globalization. In the developing country, by contrast, trade expansion should be effective not only for poverty reduction (income gains for low-skill workers), but also contribute to a decline in income disparity between high- and low-skill workers. But for this to happen complementary reforms may be needed, as we discuss below in asking the question: is trade good for poverty reduction?

ABSOLUTE, COMPARATIVE, AND COMPETITIVE ADVANTAGE

According to Ricardo (1817), two countries—North and South, say—will gain from trading in two commodities—food and textiles, say—even though one—South, say—may have absolute advantage in both. Absolute advantage is having a lower unit cost of production in both goods. Consider two countries with the same resource endowments. Factors are perfectly mobile across sectors and fully immobile across countries. If all resources were allocated to the production of only one good, production levels achieved in tons would be as in Table 7.2, panel A.

Table 7.2 Absolute and comparative advantage in trade

A. Production and consumption in North and South without trade and all resources allocated to production of one good

	Food	Textiles	Opportunity cost of food in tons of textiles	Opportunity cost of textiles in tons of food
North	100	100	1	1
South	400	200	0.5	2
Total	500	300		

B. Production and consumption in North and South without trade, with equal allocation to sectors

	Food	Textiles
North	50	50
South	200	100
Total	250	150

C. Production after trade

	Food	Textiles
North	0	100
South	300	50
Total	300	150

D. Consumption after trade

	Food	Textiles
North	75	50
South	225	100
Total	300	150

E. Gains from trade

	Food	Textiles
North	25	0
South	25	0
Total	50	0

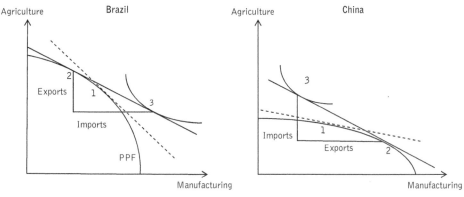

Brazil: PPF shows comparative advantage in agriculture
China: PPF shows comparative advantage in manufacturing
Dotted line: domestic terms of trade under autarky
1: production and consumption under autarky
Full line: international terms of trade
With trade, relative price of manufacturing to agricultural goods falls in Brazil and rises in China
Trade: Brazil exports agriculture and imports manufacturing goods; reverse in China
2: production with trade
3: consumption with trade

Figure 7.6 *Factor endowments, comparative advantage, and trade*

This shows that South has absolute advantage over North in both goods as it can produce more (400 food or 200 textiles) vs. South (100 food or 100 textiles) with the same resource endowment. Under this condition, is there a reason for trade? Yes, because South has an opportunity cost in producing food in terms of forgone textile production that is only 0.5 compared to 1 in North. North has an opportunity cost of producing clothes in forgone food production that is 1 compared to 2 in South. The two countries have different comparative advantages, North in textiles and South in food, that make trade mutually beneficial. As opposed to absolute advantage, comparative advantage is having a lower opportunity cost in production than the other country. In this case, there will be gains from trade for both countries.

In Panel B, production and consumption before trade are determined by an arbitrary 50 percent allocation of production capacity to each sector. The domestic terms of trade in North are 1, and 0.5 in South. If the international terms of trade are within this range, say 2/3, countries will gain from trading, with production as in Panel C and consumption in Panel D. North exports 50 of textiles and imports 75 of food. Gains from trade are shown in Panel E, with both countries gaining from greater specialization in production based on comparative advantage and achieving higher consumption levels in food.

The logic of comparative advantage and trade between Brazil and China is illustrated in Figure 7.6. The PPF (production-possibility frontier) for Brazil shows that factor endowments give it comparative advantage in agriculture, while the PPF for China shows that factor endowments give it comparative advantage in manufacturing. Before trade, production and consumption are at 1 in both countries. Opening to trade will displace production to 2 and consumption to 3. Brazil specializes in

295

agriculture, exports agricultural products, and imports manufactured goods. China specializes in manufacturing goods, exports manufactures and imports food. Both countries gain from trade as utility at 3 is higher than it was under autarky at 1.

These are the lessons from the theory of trade based on comparative advantages:

1. A country should export the commodities that use its relatively abundant factors, and import the commodities that use its relatively scarce factors.
2. Labor-abundant countries export labor for capital through trade in commodities, while factors are internationally immobile.
3. Trade in products leads to eventual factor-price equalization. This is the Stopler–Samuelson theorem.
4. These results hold under the assumption that markets are perfectly competitive, with all externalities internalized (see below for an analysis of the gains from trade when environmental externalities are not internalized).
5. Gains from trade are not necessarily equal across countries. They depend on international terms of trade.
6. No mechanisms are in place to ensure that losers in the world market will be compensated by winners. Within a country, losers can be compensated by winners through taxes and transfers if the government has the political will to do so.

Ricardo's theory of comparative advantage, developed in its current version by Heckscher and Ohlin as the basis on which to specialize and trade, is a static concept based on countries' differences in factor endowments. The risk, however, is that countries will specialize in sectors with little potential for future productivity growth, providing no guidance for the design of a long-term industrialization strategy. This led Michael Porter (1985) to propose instead the concept of *competitive advantage*. Here, a country achieves competitiveness in trade not only through resource advantage, but also capabilities advantage derived from superior labor skills, technology, and reputation. Capabilities advantage includes patents and trademarks, proprietary know-how, and reputation, all of which can be established irrespective of resource endowments. Competitive advantage can also be acquired through international factor mobility as in an open-economy industrialization (OEI) strategy (see below), where foreign direct investment (FDI) is the vehicle for acquiring capital, skills, and the embedded determinants of competitiveness. The interest of competitive advantage for development policy is that it opens the door to strategic planning about how to achieve industrialization based on endogenous advantages that can be purposefully invested in and acquired.

TRADE POLICY AND INDICATORS OF PROTECTION

To characterize a country's trade policy, we need a certain number of indicators that can tell us how "free" it is, or how distorted away from free trade through various trade interventions. Consider the following definitions:

$p^\$$ = world market price in foreign currency (US$);
p^b = border price in local currency units (LCU);

p^d = domestic price in LCU;
e = nominal exchange rate in LCU/$;
Tradable good (T) = good, the price of which is determined by the border price and by trade and exchange rate policies;
Non-tradable good (NT) = good, the price of which is determined by equality between supply and demand on the domestic market.

The price of a tradable good is: $p^d = p^b(1 + t), p^b = ep^\$$, where:

$t = t_M$ = import tariff rate;
$t = -t_E$ = export tax rate;
$t = s$ = domestic producer subsidy (+) or tax (−) rate.

These concepts are illustrated in Table 7.3. In this example, the international price is \$100/metric ton (MT). The official exchange rate is 40 rupees/\$, so the border price in local currency is 4,000 RS/MT. If there is an import tariff of 30 percent, then the domestic price in local currency is 5,200 RS/MT. The price is thus affected by both the exchange-rate policy that sets e, and the trade policy that sets t_M. These two policy instruments can complement or substitute for each other.

There are two indicators typically used to characterize the degree of protection of a particular commodity. They are the nominal and the effective protection coefficients, defined as follows:

Nominal protection coefficient = NPC

$$NPC = \frac{p^d}{p^b} = 1 + t$$

If $NPC > 1$, producers are protected, consumers (users) are dis-protected (taxed).
If $NPC < 1$, producers are dis-protected (taxed), consumers (users) are protected.

Table 7.3 *International, border, and domestic prices as affected by exchange-rate and trade policies*

Domestic price		Trade policy	Border price	Exchange rate	World market price
		Tariffs taxes subsidies		Nominal exchange rate	
Formula	$p^d = p^b (1 + t_M)$	t_M, t_E, s	$p^b = ep^\$$	e	$p^\$$
Example	4000*1.3 = 5200 RS/MT	$t_M = 0.3$	40*100 = 4000 RS/MT	$e = 40$RS/\$	100\$/MT

Nominal protection can also be measured as a rate, the nominal rate of protection (NRP):

$$NRP = \frac{p^d - p^b}{p^b},$$

which will then be > 0 if producers are protected and < 0 if taxed. This is also called the nominal rate of assistance (NRA) when direct output subsidies are added to the domestic price.

Recent NRA measures by Anderson (2008) show that while taxation of agricultural exportables was quite high in the 1960s to mid 1980s (typically 30 percent, see Krueger *et al.*, 1988), it has now been reduced to zero as a consequence of extensive trade liberalization (Figure 7.7). Importables remain protected (typically 20 percent) by import tariffs, usually to favor domestic producers from a national food-security perspective. Overall, between exportables and importables, agriculture now benefits

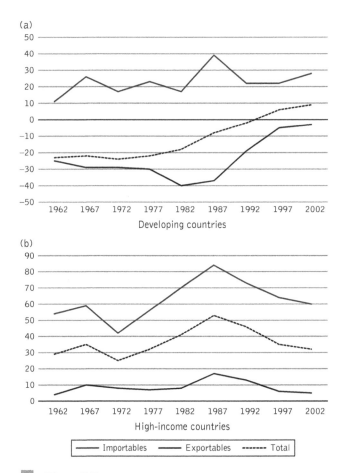

Figure 7.7 *Nominal protection of agriculture in developing (a) and high-income (b) countries, 1962–2002*

Source: Anderson, 2008.

from protection as opposed to taxation in the previous period. In high-income countries, protection has been the norm, and it has not changed significantly over the period analyzed.

Effective protection coefficient = EPC

The effective protection coefficient takes into account the impact of trade and exchange-rate policies not only on the product side, but also on the cost of intermediate inputs used in production.
Define:

p = price = unit value of output;
c = cost of intermediate goods used in production per unit of output (purchased inputs from other industries).
VA = value added = cost of primary factors such as labor, land, and financial capital per unit of output.

$p = c + VA$. Hence: $VA = p - c$. The effective protection coefficient is:

$$EPC = \frac{VA^d}{VA^b} = \frac{p^d - c^d}{p^b - c^b}.$$

If $EPC > 1$, producers are protected, consumers (users) are disprotected (taxed).
If $EPC < 1$, producers are disprotected (taxed), consumers (users) are protected.

Note that EPC is a better measure of protection than NPC since a product may be protected but, if inputs are also protected, the effective protection is less than the nominal protection.

Real protection

The domestic price of imported goods or of import substitutes is:

$$p^d = ep^\$ (1 + t_M).$$

The domestic price of exported goods is:

$$p^d = ep^\$ (1 - t_E).$$

We see from this that we can protect tradable goods through exchange-rate policies and/or trade policies. For example, a devaluation (or depreciation) of the exchange rate raises e and increases the price of tradable goods. Similarly, an increase in import tariffs or a decline in export taxes will increase the domestic price of tradable goods.

We can develop an indicator of protection, the real protection coefficient (RPC), that tells us how much of protection comes from exchange rate distortion (EDist) and how much from trade distortions (NPC). Let e^* be the equilibrium exchange rate (i.e. the level at which e should be in equilibrium, as we will see in Chapter 10) and $pb^* = e^* p^\$$ the border price at the equilibrium exchange rate. The RPC is:

$$RPC = \frac{p^d}{p^{b^*}} = \frac{ep^\$(1+t)}{e^* p^\$} = \frac{e}{e^*}(1+t) = EDist.NPC,$$

the product of the indicators of exchange-rate and trade-policy interventions. Between the mid 1960s and the mid 1980s, when exportable agriculture was heavily taxed, as seen in Figure 7.7, most of the taxation came from an overvalued (low) exchange rate (EDist) as opposed to heavy export taxes (NPC).

Exchange-rate and trade policies can be substitutes or complements for protecting a commodity. For example, when there is a devaluation of the exchange rate in Argentina, the country typically raises export taxes on agriculture to lower the domestic price of food, thus redistributing income from agriculture (that benefits from the devaluation) to the urban sector (that benefits from the export tax). Similarly, the world food crisis has induced the Argentine government to raise export taxes on agriculture in order to protect consumers and redistribute income from farmers (considered wealthy overall as farms can be very large) to the rest of society (poverty is mainly urban), creating huge political discontent among farmers.

Trade creation and trade diversion

When a free-trade agreement or a customs union is created, exporters to countries in the agreement/union may find themselves displaced by exporters from within the union. Take the example of lamb imported by the UK from New Zealand, the most efficient producer in the world. When the UK joined the European Union, tariffs and non-tariff barriers were imposed on New Zealand imports, and France, a higher-cost producer but within the EU, became the new source of imports for the UK. Trade was *diverted* away from the more efficient producer, New Zealand, and trade was *created* for France. The efficiency gain of a free-trade agreement or customs union is thus the net effect of trade creation and diversion. In the short run, the efficiency loss from trade diversion will be larger than the efficiency gain from trade creation. In the longer run, a reason for enacting the agreement/union may be to seek productivity gains in the new source of exports, resulting in net efficiency gains.

USING TRADE POLICY FOR DEVELOPMENT: TARIFFS AND SUBSIDIES

Given the significance of trade for growth, domestic income distribution, and risk management, it is not surprising that trade policy is a major instrument for development. Indeed, most countries have entire ministries devoted to trade and trade policy, particularly in developing countries where trade provides important opportunities for growth, technology transfers, and public revenues. Because of their authority over national borders, governments can exert significant direct influence on trade, and they can also exert pervasive influence on trade incentives and trade-related behavior though other policies.

Import tariffs: protecting sectors

One of the most common trade policies is import protection, where governments take measures to limit foreign competition in domestic markets. Imports can be restricted by many kinds of administrative measures such as safety standards (e.g. sanitary and phytosanitary standards for food imports), trade preferences that admit goods from some countries but not from others, quantity restrictions, and, the most common method, tariffs, also called *ad valorem* import taxes. As one might suppose, these measures restrict market opportunities in order to serve some national policy agenda, including consumer safety, protection of domestic firms and/or jobs, food security, and geopolitical goals. Tariffs may also be introduced in response to lobbying, from employers or workers who want to restrict competition from foreign firms to protect profits or jobs.

The efficiency and redistributive effects of an import tariff are analyzed in Figure 7.8, using the tools of consumer and producer surplus in welfare economics. Assume that imports are perfect substitutes for the domestic good and that the importing country is small, so changes in imports do not affect the world price ($p^\$$). In this case, application of a tariff t yields a domestic price $p^d = ep^\$ (1 + t)$, and the detailed welfare effects are as described in Figure 7.8 and Table 7.4. The import tariff benefits producers, hurts consumers, benefits government through tariff revenues, and creates a net social loss relative to free trade. The inefficiency cost is measured by areas $(b + d)$. The redistributive gains to the benefit of producers and government have a sharp cost both for consumers and for society at large.

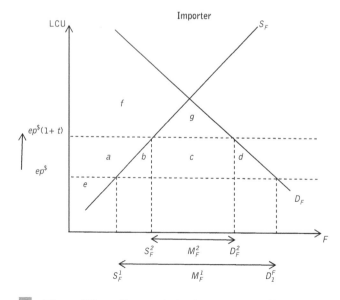

Figure 7.8 *Welfare analysis of an import tariff*

Table 7.4 Gains and losses from an import tariff for consumers, producers, and the nation

	Exporter			
	Consumer surplus	Producer surplus	Government budget	Net social gain
Free trade	$a + b + c + d + f + g$	e	0	
Import tariff	$f + g$	$a + e$	c	
Net effect	$-(a + b + c + d)$	a	c	$-(b + d)$
Sign of effect	$-$	$+$	$+$	$-$

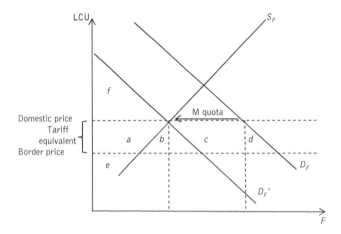

Figure 7.9 Welfare analysis of an import quota

Protection may be obtained by imposing an *import quota* as opposed to an import tariff (Figure 7.9). In this case, domestic demand is shifted to the left from D_F to D_F' by the amount of the import quota. The domestic price falls relative to autarky (where domestic supply equals domestic demand for food), but remains above the border price. This price gap over the border price can be interpreted as a tariff equivalent or an implicit tariff. The welfare analysis of an import quota is then exactly the same as that of a tariff in Table 7.4; the only difference is that an import quota does not generate government revenue (c in Figure 7.8) but instead rent (c in Figure 7.9) for the importers who were granted the import quota. If this import quota is auctioned competitively among importers, government can transform the importers' rent into government revenue. Quotas are, however, much more difficult to manage than tariffs since they require the specification of import quantities of all goods in the protected sector as opposed to a single tariff over prices in the protected sector. Import quotas also invite corruption (to acquire import licenses) and smuggling (to benefit from the high domestic price). Tariffication of quotas is thus one of the first reforms required for membership of the World Trade Organization. It is subsequently easier to legislate the descaling of tariffs than the reduction of quotas.

Example: protection of the sugar sector in the US

Consider the case of US import quotas on sugar.

> US domestic production = 6.3 million tons
> Import quotas = 2.1 million tons (25 percent of domestic supply)
> p^d = 466 \$/ton
> p^b = 280 \$/ton
> Implicit tariff = *NPC* equivalent = 1.66 (i.e. 66 percent nominal protection)
> ΔPS = \$1066 million for 12,000 workers = \$90,000 per job
> ΔCS = −\$1647 million for 275 million consumers = \$6 per consumer
> Rent to foreigners = \$396 million
> Efficiency loss = \$185 million

The import quota on sugar thus implies large redistributive gains for producers (and their workers), a small cost per capita for consumers, and a small efficiency loss relative to the magnitude of the distributional effects. Hence it is clear that political demands for the sugar quota are motivated by the large gains for US farmers that will not be opposed by consumers as the corresponding per capita tax is sufficiently small to remain unnoticed by each of them.

Production subsidies: "picking winners"

Another common trade policy to promote the competitiveness of firms with export potential involves subsidizing potential "winners" (Figure 7.10 and Table 7.5). These subsidies typically come in the form of state-subsidized credit, financial guarantees, technological assistance acquired from abroad, subsidies to R&D, and trade fairs to promote the firms on the international market (Wade, 1990). The subsidies improve the competitiveness of the selected firms and help them gain scale to become competitive without subsidy. Production subsidies to potential winners have been extensively used in the export-oriented industrialization (EOI) strategy, analyzed below. While potentially beneficial in the long term, the short-term effect of an export subsidy is to create a gain for the subsidized firms at a cost to government, but at no loss to consumers and with a smaller distortion at the national level than created by a protective tariff. As can be seen in Figure 7.10, the NSG is −*b* with a production subsidy, instead of −(*b* + *d*) with an import tariff. It is thus less disruptive of overall efficiency. However, it implies a cost to government equal to (*a* + *b*) instead of a revenue equal to *c*. It also requires that government pick winners without making mistakes and without falling into cronyism and corruption.

DYNAMIC GAINS FROM TRADE: IMPORT-SUBSTITUTION INDUSTRIALIZATION AS A POLICY GAMBLE

An import-substitution industrialization (ISI) strategy is a dynamic gamble that can have a high development pay-off if it succeeds, but which can also fail. It was followed by many countries that wanted to protect themselves from competition from more

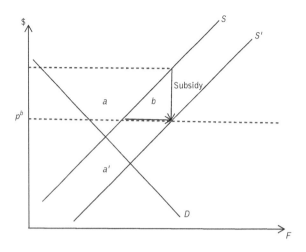

Figure 7.10 *Welfare analysis of a production subsidy in support of EOI*

Table 7.5 *Gains and losses from a production subsidy to stimulate exports under EOI*

	Exporter			
	Consumer surplus	Producer surplus	Government budget	Net social gain
Net effect	0	$a' = a$	$-(a + b)$	$- b$
Sign of effect	0	+	−	−

advanced countries in order to industrialize. The sequence of moves is described in Figure 7.11, and consists of the following four steps:

1. Before ISI with trade (Figure 7.11a). The terms of trade between agriculture and industry for the country with free trade is the ratio of their border prices p_A/p_I. Production is at A and consumption at C.
2. Introduction of a protective tariff t_M on industry under ISI (Figure 7.11a). The terms of trade for the country become $p_A/p_I(1+t_M)$. Production is now at B and consumption at E.
3. The dynamic gamble is that industrial protection will induce investment and technological change in industry, shifting the production-possibility frontier (PPF) upward toward industry (Figure 7.11b). Now, production is at F and consumption at H.
4. Returning to free trade under ISTE (import substitute then export), production will be at A′ and consumption at C′. This is a huge gain compared to the starting point at C thanks to progress in industrialization under temporary protective tariffs.

304

(a)

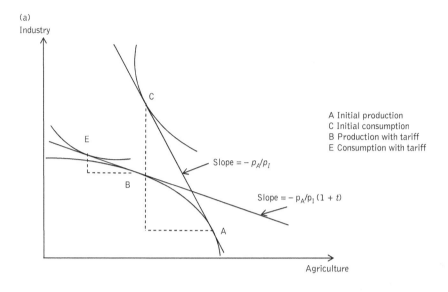

(b)

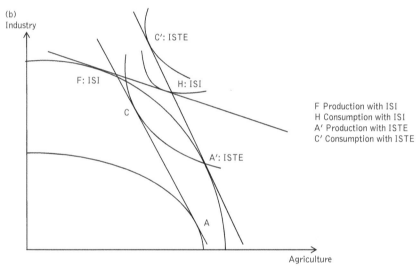

Figure 7.11 *ISI strategy as a gamble*

The strategy can, however, fail, and it has critics such as Justin Lin (2009) as well as advocates such as Dany Rodrik (2004). It will fail if the PPF does not shift upward toward industry as expected in step 3. It can also fail if the country never returns to free trade as expected in step 4 under the pressure of vested interests in the protected industry, remaining at H instead of shifting to C′. Most countries started their industrialization under ISI, including the Asian tigers, and Latin America after World War Two. However, it was more successful for the first group of countries than the second, where political opposition to a return to free trade was often quite strong under the populist governments in power during the 1945–82 period, when ISI was pursued.

TRADE AND INDUSTRIALIZATION STRATEGIES: HOW TO CHOOSE?

When there are large economies of scale in industrial production (that typically come from fixed costs that need to be spread over large volumes of output, or from learning-by-doing associated with the level of output), latecomer countries face a major obstacle in competing with more developed countries' (MDCs) firms with already established economies of scale that set the international market price. This is the *infant industry* dilemma: the latecomer could have lower average production costs (AC) than MDCs' incumbent firms, but it needs to achieve scale to reach this lower average cost. This is true not only in high-technology sectors, but even for mundane products like modern textiles. How can this be achieved? Governments can consider three alternative industrialization strategies:

1. ISI. Protect sectors of industry until they become internationally competitive and then open the country to free trade (this is the ISTE strategy).
2. EOI. Open the economy and subsidize selected firms (pick winners) until they become competitive.
3. OEI. Open the economy, create an appealing investment climate, and call on FDI to bring in firms already at a scale that makes them internationally competitive.

The differences between these three approaches are summarized in Figure 7.12. The world price $p^\$$ is determined by the AC of established international competitors (AC_{MDC}), the incumbent firms, at their current level of output. This price constitutes the reference average cost for domestic firms to achieve competitiveness on the international market.

ISI (Import-substitution industrialization)

Under ISI, import tariffs are imposed to raise the domestic price to the level of the infant industry's AC. This allows the LDC firm to start producing for the domestic market. As output increases, AC falls, eventually to a point where the firm is

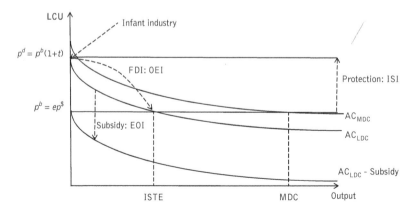

Figure 7.12 *Industrialization strategies compared: ISI, EOI, and OEI*

competitive on the international market and protection can be removed (ISTE). The advantage of this approach is that it does not require a public budget; on the contrary, it generates revenues for government on competitive imports. These revenues can be invested to provide public goods important for the competitiveness of domestic industry. ISI also has the advantage that firms can learn to compete on the domestic market, where quality requirements are far less than on the export market. And it does not require the government to select specific firms, only to decide on protection for broad sectors of industry.

A difficulty for small countries is that ISI requires a large domestic market in which firms can achieve economies of scale sufficient to become internationally competitive at ISTE. With high inequality and concentrated assets, this may be difficult to achieve even in large countries. This is one of the reasons why Latin American countries pursued redistributive policies such as land reform that could help enlarge domestic effective demand for industrial goods. Another difficulty is that protection creates powerful sectoral lobbies of employers and workers (e.g. Peronism in Argentina at the peak of ISI was supported by both the employers' unions (CGE, the General Confederation of Employers) and the workers' unions (CGT, the General Confederation of Workers)) that will ally to militate against removal of protection. The risk is that, once introduced, protective tariffs will be politically very difficult to remove. Successful implementation requires credibility on the part of government that protection is only temporary, and will soon be decreased following a pre-announced schedule. Yet, as we will see in Chapter 21, governments lack instruments to make credible policy commitments. In South Korea, protection was granted but with a credible announcement that it would only be for five years (Amsden, 1989). In most other places, credibility was lacking, as producers knew that they could capture government over the interests of consumers once their economic positions had been established.

The ISI strategy was widely implemented in Latin America from the depression of the 1930s until the debt crisis of 1982. It was advocated by influential economists of the time such as Raúl Prebisch in Argentina and Hans Singer and Celso Furtado in Brazil. In their view, an important reason to industrialize was the belief that the international terms of trade between primary products and manufactured goods would deteriorate over time, a long-run trend known as the Singer–Prebisch thesis. This prediction did not hold true, as witnessed by the rising relative prices of petroleum resources and mineral products such as copper (Baer, 1972). If the terms of trade deteriorate, countries should move away from primary exports such as agriculture and mining, and industrialize on their own.

ISI was to be pursued first for consumer-goods sectors and later on for the intermediate and capital-goods sectors. It indeed helped to create domestic industries, but protection proved all too difficult to remove, blocking evolution toward successful export industries and reproducing over time high-cost industries paid for by consumers in the form of high domestic prices. In addition, industrializing to substitute for imports does not a priori guide investment toward the country's comparative-advantage sectors. As a consequence, the industry being built behind protective tariffs may never achieve competitiveness in an open economy (Lin, 2009). Finally, as we will see in detail in Chapter 10, countries under ISI maintain appreciated exchange rates

307

(low official exchange rates e) as a consequence of reduced import demand (importers' lower demand for dollars due to import tariffs lowering the domestic price of dollars) and to cheapen imports of capital goods for industry. However, a low exchange rate penalizes agricultural exports, which are typically the source of the foreign-exchange revenues needed to import capital goods for industry. As a consequence, agriculture stagnates, inducing recurrent foreign-exchange crises that can severely limit the capacity of industry to import the capital goods it needs. This conflict between agriculture and industry under ISI, and the resulting economic instability and political confrontations between farmers and industrialists, has been conceptualized as the "theory of sectoral clashes" (Mamalakis, 1969).

EOI (Export-oriented industrialization)

The EOI strategy consists in subsidizing firms (as opposed to protecting sectors of industry under ISI) that have the potential to achieve competitiveness on the international market. The advantage of the approach is that it can be narrowly targeted to these potential winners, and it does not require trade distortions under the form of tariffs that negatively affect domestic consumers and introduce a large net social loss (Amsden, 1989). It can work for small countries that do not have a large domestic market, but there are four difficulties that must be tackled to make it succeed.

The first is that it is costly for government: where will the subsidies come from? Any fiscal expenditure has an opportunity cost—for example, in providing health, education, and infrastructure to the population. In South Korea and Taiwan, where EOI was successfully applied after 1945, subsidies came in large part from foreign aid, but this is not easily replicable today.

The second difficulty is the need for firms to be directly competitive on the international market (with subsidies) with the ability to achieve quality and reputation to create demand for their products. There is no protected learning on the domestic market as under ISI.

The third difficulty is the risk of corruption in government when choosing which firms to subsidize. The state needs autonomy in assigning and removing subsidies, but it also needs access to detailed information on firms, requiring the kind of embeddedness (close, often personal, relations) that can easily lead to corruption and loss of autonomy. This dilemma of "embedded autonomy" was explored by Peter Evans (1995) for Korea, Brazil, and India. The strategy was successfully used in Japan, e.g. in the 1950s and 1960s to promote its steel industry, and in East Asia, initially with apparel firms, followed by home-appliance and electronics firms. But it also contributed to the 1997 Asian financial crisis, where cronyism in subsidizing firms that did not need subsidies or could not achieve competitiveness even after being subsidized implied continued high fiscal costs and the continued existence of inefficient firms.

Finally, firm-level subsidies, as opposed to sector-level tariffs, are more exposed to rent-seeking pressures, making their subsequent removal more difficult than that of tariffs. According to Rodrik (1995), this is because a tariff is essentially a public good to all producers of import substitutes in the protected sector of industry. Because they only derive a small part of the benefits of lobbying, individual producers will tend to freeride on lobbying rather than invest significant resources in sustained political influence. In the case of producer subsidies, by contrast, firms are individually targeted and prone to client relationships between entrepreneurs and regulators. They will be more inclined to invest in lobbying to attempt to reproduce the subsidy even once competitiveness has been achieved. Tariffs are thus more distortive (as seen in Figure 7.8), but less prone to lobbying; subsidies are less distortive (as seen in Figure 7.10), but more prone to lobbying. A forward-looking government concerned with keeping lobbying in check to move toward trade liberalization once industrialization has been achieved may well prefer the more distortive tariff instrument.

Effective use of subsidies has always been difficult and controversial in policy-making. To be effective, a subsidy needs to be "smart" in meeting the following three generic conditions:

- It does not create perverse behavioral responses by the recipient, such as disincentives to perform (reduce average costs).
- It does not displace sustainable ways of solving the problem, but, on the contrary, encourages them (firms remaining competitive without subsidies).
- It does not become permanent, creating dependency and a continuing drain on resources that have an opportunity cost. The policy-maker wants beneficiaries to "graduate" out of the need for the subsidy.

To achieve this, EOI requires a carefully announced and credible schedule of declining subsidies to help establish industrial capacity and "push" firms down the average-cost curve to the point where they can be autonomously competitive.

OEI (Open-economy industrialization)

The OEI strategy is very attractive as it does not require a long phase of learning, as is the case with ISI and EOI, until firms reach the scale at which they can be competitive without protection or subsidies. Here, the gamble is that putting into place the proper investment climate in an open-economy setting will attract foreign direct investment (FDI) from firms that have already established expertise elsewhere and achieved the scale to be competitive. A good investment climate includes political stability, infrastructure, rule of law, secure property rights, a disciplined and semi-skilled labor force, good macroeconomic fundamentals, and commitment to an open trade and finance regime. The International Finance Corporation and the World Bank (IFC/WB, 2012) publish annually an "ease of doing business" index that ranks countries from 1 to 183. For each country the ranking is calculated as the average of the percentile rankings on each of the ten topics included in the index: starting a business, dealing with construction permits, registering property, getting credit, protecting investors, paying taxes, trading across borders, enforcing contracts, resolving insolvency, and getting electricity.

OEI was successfully implemented in countries ranging from tiny Mauritius to large China. A drawback of the approach is that foreign firms are not a substitute for domestic industry in terms of long-run industrialization. In this sense, as argued by Rodrik (2004), OEI is not a substitute for an industrialization strategy: it creates industries, but not necessarily a domestic industrial class. China's skillfully promoted domestic firms in sub-contracting with and eventually taking over from foreign firms after a period of learning, helping the country develop its own entrepreneurial class and industry. This was not the case with Mexico (before NAFTA) and the Dominican Republic, where FDI occurs in industrialized zones (also called *maquilas* and enclave industries) using domestic labor but with few linkages with domestic firms.

Note that these contrasted strategies have often been used sequentially, as in Taiwan and South Korea, starting with ISI, following up with EOI, and increasingly relying on OEI. Different countries will use these strategies according to their domestic-market size (key for ISI), fiscal resources (key for EOI), and international appeal (key for OEI). The conditions for success and the risks of failure of each strategy are summarized in Table 7.6.

IS TRADE GOOD FOR GROWTH?

Theory tells us that trade openness is good for growth. Freer trade should provide incentives for investment and technological change, open access to new ideas and innovations, help achieve economies of scale previously limited by small domestic markets, break monopoly power on domestic markets and increase competition, and limit rent-seeking activities that benefit from trade restrictions. Empirical evidence is, however, mixed, suggesting that the link between trade and growth may be mediated by specific country characteristics and complementary policies. Results from cross-country regressions usually show that trade liberalization, as measured by trade shares, is associated with growth. Well known studies include those of Edwards (1997), Frankel and Romer (1999), and Dollar and Kraay (2001). However, rising trade shares are notably endogenous and typically associated with other policy interventions. As suggested by Rodriguez and Rodrik (2001), the introduction of trade policy measures rather than trade shares should be used to characterize trade liberalization. Doing this, Harrison (1996) and Irwin and Terviö (2002) find a significant negative effect of trade on economic growth, while Vamvakidis (2002) still finds a positive relation. These mixed results may be interpreted as giving support to Stiglitz and Charlton's (2005) proposition that trade policy is necessary but not sufficient to induce growth. They argue that it must be complemented with behind-the-border policies such as investment in human capital, labor regulations, and infrastructure to transform trade liberalization into economic growth.

While the effect of trade on growth is thus uncertain, trade has been recognized to increase productivity in manufacturing firms. This has been attributed to access to cheaper imported intermediate inputs and to increased competition from imports, resulting in the elimination of inefficient firms. We have seen this in Topalova and Khandelwal's study (2011) of trade liberalization in India. Tybout and Westbrook found similar results (1995) with trade liberalization in Mexico in the 1984–90 period, when many inefficient firms went bankrupt. These large productivity gains, however, will not translate into aggregate GDP growth on their own.

Table 7.6 ISI, EOI, and OEI compared

Industrialization strategies	Policy instruments	Conditions for success	Advantages	Disadvantages and risks
ISI: Import-substitution industrialization	Protective tariffs on infant sectors of industry	Large domestic market to achieve scale and learning-by-doing	Creates public revenues. No need for government budget	High welfare cost on consumers and high net social loss
	Appreciated (low) exchange rate for cheap imports of capital goods. Asset redistribution (land reform) to reduce inequality and expand domestic market size	Responsive shift in PPF biased toward industry		Will the country have the capacity to import needed raw materials and intermediate goods, especially with appreciated exchange rate discouraging exports (e.g., agriculture)? Foreign exchange shortages will create sectoral clashes and stop-and-go crises with periodic exchange rate devaluation
		Credible policy commitment that protection is only temporary		Political opposition of employers and workers in ISI industries to removing tariffs: ISTE can fail as protection is reproduced. ISI guided by domestic demand but not by comparative advantage. ISTE may result in non-competitive industrialization

Table 7.6 continued

Industrialization strategies	Policy instruments	Conditions for success	Advantages	Disadvantages and risks
EOI: Export-oriented industrialization	Production subsidies to firms	Budget for costly subsidies (need export revenues from agriculture or mining, loans from international banks, foreign aid)	No cost on consumers and smaller net social loss from distortions	Firms must be able to enter world market with subsidies from the beginning (especially if small domestic market)
	"Pick the winners": firms expected to achieve international competitiveness	Good non-venal bureaucracy: capacity to pick the winners w/o corruption and cronyism	Less rent-seeking pressures by sectors than by firms (Rodrik, 1995): ISI more distortive but less capture	Firms need to establish reputation, quality recognition, trade fairs
		Credible schedule to decrease and remove subsidies		
OEI: Open-economy industrialization	Investment climate to attract FDI and MNC	Good investment climate: stable government, rule of law, property rights, infrastructure	Potential for quick success	Does not create national industry and local entrepreneurs (except if linkages with foreign firms exist and learning effects occur)
		Commitment to open trade policy (role of WTO membership). Stable exchange rate and free movements of capital		Not a substitute for a domestic industrial policy
		Skilled and reliable labor force		

IS TRADE GOOD FOR POVERTY REDUCTION?

The same ambiguous result applies to the potential role of trade in reducing poverty. There are basically two channels through which trade liberalization can benefit the poor, one static and the other dynamic.

The static response is due to product and factor-price changes taking resources and technology as given (see Figure 7.3). The product-price effect on poverty occurs when the poor derive their incomes from sectors that have comparative advantage and will benefit from higher prices with trade. This is in general the case when comparative advantage is derived from the production of goods making use of unskilled labor. Examples are the apparel industry in Bangladesh and tradable agricultural sectors such as coffee and cocoa in Côte d'Ivoire. If the poor are workers in these sectors, or small-holder net-sellers of their goods, they will benefit. The factor-price effect is explained by the Stopler–Samuelson theorem: trade changes relative factor prices in favor of the more abundant factor. If poverty is due to an abundance of unskilled labor, trade will increase unskilled labor's wages and reduce poverty. In a famous multi-country study of the impact of trade liberalization on employment, Krueger (1983) used this proposition to argue that trade reforms should benefit the poor.

The dynamic response is the reallocation of labor across sectors in response to the change in the terms of trade, helping countries specialize in response to trade (see Figure 7.4). For this, labor must move out of contracting sectors and shift to expanding ones. Yet empirical studies suggest that labor mobility is typically limited by barriers to the entry and exit of firms and to the hiring and firing of workers (Harrison, 2006). As trade exposes domestic firms to foreign competition, they may respond by increasing the use of temporary and informal labor, with worse employment conditions (Goldberg and Pavnik, 2003). Trade may also stimulate expansion of natural-resource exports that are not labor-intensive. This is the case with the export boom in Sub-Saharan Africa that is driven by mineral and petroleum exports, leaving many young people unemployed and frustrated with social exclusion, as in Nigeria today. Finally, trade may favor industries using mechanization and semi-skilled labor such as the car industry in Mexico, creating a backlash against the poor with unskilled labor (Harrison and Hanson, 1999). NAFTA had very strong positive results on Mexico's balance of trade with the US, and led to sharp increases in manufacturing-labor productivity at the same time as real wages fell (Shaiken, 2014). The rising gap between productivity and wages is reminiscent of the neo-mercantilist model based on cheap labor for the export sector at the cost of domestic purchasing power and slow growth of production for the domestic market. Shaiken attributes this inability of Mexican workers to share in labor productivity gains to lack of labor rights in the export sector to form independent unions that can exert pressure to maintain a link between productivity and wages. It results in what he calls "high-productivity poverty." In China, where poverty has been massively reduced, it is not clear how much of this has been due to trade. Poverty was reduced before trade liberalization as a consequence of the decollectivization of agriculture, the household-responsibility system in farming, and domestic market liberalization.

Empirical studies give conflicting evidence on the trade–poverty relation, as expected with so many competing channels at play. In her vast study of country cases, Krueger (1983) finds that exporting sectors were indeed labor-intensive, but that the employment effects of trade liberalization were limited and that benefits did not trickle down to the poor. Subsequent studies that explicitly address the poverty-reduction value of trade liberalization such as Beck *et al.* (2005) and Dollar and Kraay (2001) found no effect. Others such as Guillaumont Jeanneney and Kpodar (2011) found that trade could in fact increase poverty. An interesting result obtained by Agénor (2004) is the existence of a Kuznets inverted-U relation between globalization and poverty: first, trade opening leads to contraction of the import-competing sectors, increasing poverty, to be followed in a second stage by expansion of the export-oriented sectors that can reduce poverty.

Autor *et al.* (2013) analyze the impact of imports from China on the US labor market. They identify causality by using an instrumental variable approach, where the growth in US imports from China is predicted by the growth in Chinese exports to other high-income countries, reflecting changes in supply conditions in China, exogenous to labor-market conditions in the US and thus meeting the exclusion restriction. They isolate the impact on the labor market by focusing on regional economies (counties) with manufacturing industries that compete with Chinese imports. For example, Raleigh in North Carolina competes with Chinese furniture imports, while Fresno in California specializes in fruit and vegetables that are not exposed to Chinese competition. They develop on that basis an index of "exposure" to Chinese imports. They find that the negative effects of exposure for US workers have been large. They attribute 25 percent of the decline in US manufacturing employment during the 1990–2007 period to imports from China. Import competition also decreased labor-force participation, lowered wages on local labor markets, and induced a rise in uptake in unemployment and disability transfer benefits. Reductions in earnings are regressive as they are concentrated among workers with lower initial wages and weaker attachment to the labor force. Consumer gains have thus been paid for by declines in labor incomes and the shift of the burden of displacement to public transfers. High-wage workers are better able to cope with import competition. This phenomenon of consumer gains at the cost of income losses for low-wage workers is what Robert Reich (2008) has analyzed under the label of "supercapitalism."

The policy implication is that, as for growth, the poverty-reduction benefits of trade do not accrue automatically, and that complementary policy reforms are needed to make trade liberalization into an effective instrument for poverty reduction. This is especially important in supporting the reallocation of resources toward sectors with newly acquired comparative advantages and in helping the poor participate in these sectors as workers or entrepreneurs. Reallocating resources requires policies to improve the investment climate (Newfarmer and Sztajerowska, 2012), reduce abuse of market power, and develop financial markets (Le Goff and Singh, 2013); and increasing the poor's participation requires policies to develop labor skills, support entrepreneurship, and establish social-safety nets to encourage risk-taking (Karnani, 2011).

TRADE AND THE ENVIRONMENT

The dilemma of differing environmental standards

Countries that trade have different levels of domestic regulation of the environmental effects of production. Some have strict policies to internalize negative pollution externalities. Others either do not have these policies in place or do not enforce them. This creates conflicts among countries as differential regulation of environmental externalities can create unfair advantages in trade. Developing countries with weak environmental regulation can easily be accused of serving as production havens for polluting activities for exports. In many cases, pollution spills across borders or into the global environment (such as chlorofluorocarbons that destroy the ozone layer, SO_2 that contributes to acid rain, and CO_2 that causes climate change). Trade agreements have typically been concerned with *product* specifications (price policies, subsidies, quantity restrictions, dumping, food-safety standards) and not with *process* specifications (environmental and labor conditions). With increased globalization, this is now changing. The NAFTA trade agreement between Canada, the US, and Mexico had environmental and labor side agreements to regulate process in addition to product. This is pushing countries to harmonize their environmental and labor policies for the sake of fairer trade. It is well known that environmental policies become more stringent with rising per capita income. Forcing developing countries to have stricter environmental policies because they trade may not correspond to their domestic policy priorities. Requiring harmonized environmental standards can be unfair to them, limiting their opportunities to grow, as today's industrialized countries did not face strict environmental regulations when they were at similar levels of GDPpc.

Limiting developing countries' access to more developed countries' markets because they have environmental standards that correspond to their own priorities can be seen as disguised protectionism. At the same time, free trade can induce poor countries' governments to lower their environmental standards as a way of increasing their competitiveness in exporting to industrialized countries, inducing a race to the bottom in environmental protection. This creates a huge policy dilemma. At the same time, trade agreements are one of the few instruments that can serve as a disciplinary device for countries that do not have the will to improve their environmental standards.

Impact of environmental regulation on import and exports

We consider the case where there is a negative externality in production and where the polluter does not have property rights over pollution. He can then be liable for the polluter-pays principle and be subjected to a tax to reconcile the private cost of production (where he externalizes pollution costs on others) with the social cost of production (where the externality is internalized as a private cost, through taxation, for instance). This will be analyzed in detail in Chapter 15. We follow here the implications of opening the country to trade when it will be either a net importer or a net exporter of the polluting good, and when production decisions are based on either private costs (with a negative externality) or on social costs (when the externality is internalized through taxation).

Gains from trade for a net importer

Opening the country to trade in Figure 7.13 will transform it into an importing country since the border price ($ep^\$$) is inferior to the domestic price under autarky. Net social gains (NSGs) from trade with production decisions at private costs in Table 7.7 are equal to 1 + 2, and these gains are completely captured in the form of consumer surplus. Trade without environmental regulation eliminates part of domestic pollution because production is reduced from q_A to q_P by imports. NSG from reduced pollution are equal to 3 + 5. Pollution remains on reduced domestic production. The importing country with no environmental regulation thus has a double gain from trade opening: strict gains from trade and environmental gains from reduced production of the polluting product.

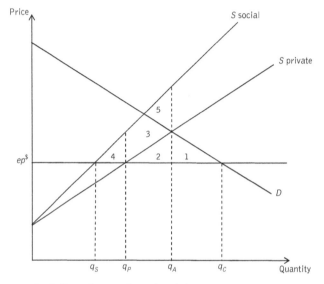

q_A Production and consumption under autarky
q_C Consumption under trade
q_P Production under trade at private costs (without environmental regulation)
q_S Production under trade at social costs (with environmental regulation)
$q_C - q_P$ Imports without environmental regulation
$q_C - q_S$ Imports with environmental regulation

Figure 7.13 *Gains from trade for an importing country with and without environmental regulation*

Table 7.7 *Gains from trade for an importing country with and without environmental regulation*

	Production based on	
	Private costs	Social costs
NSG from trade	1 + 2	1 + 2 + 3 + 4
NSG from change in pollution	3 + 5	0
Aggregate NSG	1 + 2 + 3 + 5	1 + 2 + 3 + 4

If the country introduces environmental regulation under the form of a polluter-pays tax, the country internalizes the environmental externality, and production decisions are taken at social costs. NSG from trade are larger (equal to 1 + 2 + 3 + 4) since the country produces less (at q_S instead of q_P), and imports are larger due to the environmental regulation. All gains are captured by consumers. There are, however, no further environmental gains to be had from trade opening.

Gains from trade for a net exporter

With the border price above the domestic price under autarky, the country in Figure 7.14 will be a net exporter when it opens to trade. Without environmental regulation, there are large gains from trade, equal to 1 + 2 + 3 + 4, that are entirely captured by producers (Table 7.8). Production increases from q_A to q_P, and exports are $q_P - q_C$. There are, however, large social costs associated with the increase in pollution, equal to − 1 − 5. The country gains in exports by not internalizing pollution costs, but pays a heavy price in welfare losses due to pollution. The aggregate NSG from these two effects is ambiguous. Acting as a pollution haven, this export-driven-growth strategy pays a heavy price in unabated pollution costs. You can think of China and its neo-mercantilist growth strategy as an illustration.

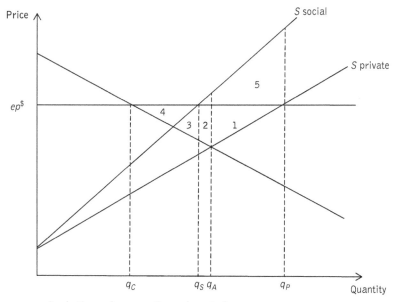

q_A Production and consumption under autarky
q_C Consumption under trade
q_P Production under trade at private costs (without environmental regulation)
q_S Production under trade at social costs (with environmental regulation)
$q_P - q_C$ Exports without environmental regulation
$q_S - q_C$ Exports with environmental regulation

Figure 7.14 *Gains from trade for an exporting country with and without environmental regulation*

Table 7.8 Gains from trade for an exporting country with and without environmental regulation

	Production based on	
	Private costs	Social costs
NSG from trade	1 + 2 + 3 + 4	4
NSG from change in pollution	- 1 - 5	0
Aggregate NSG	2 + 3 + 4 - 5	4

Introducing environmental regulation will reduce domestic production to q_S. Gains from trade are thus sharply reduced, with production still above what it would be with environmental regulation and no trade. This small gain from trade is, however, now unambiguously positive.

The struggle over harmonized environmental standards in trade

Countries have different environmental standards according to their levels of GDPpc. Poor countries have priorities other than reducing pollution: they want accelerated growth and convergence in income. Demand for environmental amenities is income elastic and rises sharply with income. As a consequence, trade patterns are affected, to the disadvantage of the exporter with tight environmental standards. If externalities are trans-boundary or globalized, trade disadvantages are complemented by environmental costs from the unregulated exporter. In addition, firms are encouraged to move to countries with less environmental regulation. This creates environmental gains in rich countries as pollution-intensive firms leave and environmental costs in the poor host country. Jobs are also lost in environmentally regulated countries, unleashing political pressures to reduce environmental standards.

There are, as a consequence, demands in industrialized countries to harmonize environmental standards across trading nations; but harmonization will mean that regulations are too strict for developing countries relative to their optimum policy, and too lax for developed countries relative to their own optimum. This creates a huge policy dilemma, which to date, in the failure to extend the Kyoto Protocol to both developed and developing countries, has not been resolved. The solution in the NAFTA side agreement on the environment was to let each country set its own environmental standards, but establish a tripartite commission charged with verifying that each country's standards are effectively enforced. This was based on the observation that the main difference in internalizing externalities across countries was due less to differences in legislation than to differences in law enforcement. While a convenient way of gaining time, this leaves unresolved the longer-term problem of harmonization of environmental standards.

Trade, environment, and development agendas can easily find themselves on a collision course (Brainard and Sorkin, 2009), and urgent post-Kyoto negotiations are needed to coordinate the world trading system with development and environmental concerns. Important challenges in these negotiations include the following (de Melo and Mathys, 2010):

1. Given the importance of trade for development, it is essential to accommodate environmental concerns while maintaining a trading system as open as possible to guarantee the gains from trade, including market access, technology transfers, and international capital movements to the benefit of developing countries.
2. A major contribution of the Kyoto Protocol was the introduction of a global Carbon Credit Trading System (CCTS), together with the Clean Development Mechanism (CDM) (see Chapter 15). This effectively separates where abatement takes place from who bears the cost of abatement. This mechanism helps reduce pollution havens and serves as an instrument to transfer funds and technology to developing countries.
3. Trade in environmental goods and services should be liberalized to the benefit of all. Trade in these goods (ethanol, solar panels) and services are currently subject to high tariff and non-tariff barriers.
4. Finally, the World Trade Organization will have to decide whether imposing import taxes on polluting goods violates free-trade rules. Taxes can be on goods that pollute locally at the point of consumption such as cars; or on goods such as aluminium that pollute where they are produced. This major decision is still pending.

TRADE AND FOOD SECURITY

Governments are deeply concerned with achieving food security for their citizens. An open-trade regime is generally believed to reduce the price variability of staple foods on domestic markets because prices are more stable on the international market. This is simply because demand is more elastic on the international market and production shocks average out over many dispersed areas contributing to aggregate supply. This has been true in general, but recent price spikes on the world market (in 1973–4 and again in 2006–7) have shown that the world market can be the source of price instability. This has brought to the fore the question of food security and how best to achieve it.

Two broad strategies can be pursued to improve a country's food security. One is food self-sufficiency, where food availability derives from national resources. The other is food self-reliance, where trade is used to access part of the food consumed, in particular by eventually exporting non-food cash crops in exchange for the import of staple foods to complement domestic supply. In both cases, the accumulation of food stocks can be used to stabilize prices. When using trade for self-reliance, variable tariffs, taxes, and subsidies can also be used to stabilize domestic prices. We review here how both food stocks and trade interventions can be used to stabilize grain prices.

Price-band buffer-stocks programs

The theory of storage and food-price stabilization was developed by Williams and Wright (1991). Demand for food for consumption is highly inelastic, especially in

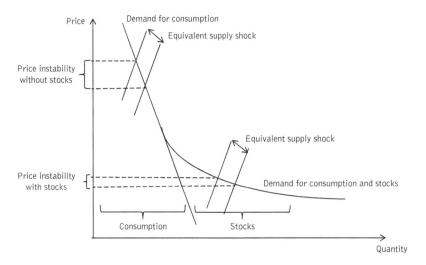

Figure 7.15 *Price stabilization with food stocks*

poor countries. As a consequence, small movements in supply lead to large fluctuations in prices. Food stocks can, however, be accumulated to make demand for food more elastic. Private traders will accumulate stocks if the current price of a stored unit can be expected to rise at a rate that covers the cost of storage and the interest rate on the value of the unit stored. Competitive traders will thus engage in inter-temporal arbitrage in the expectation of deriving a profit by buying at low prices and selling at high prices. This is seen in Figure 7.15, where stocks accumulation at low prices makes demand more elastic. When stocks exist, equivalent supply shocks create much smaller price fluctuations. Use of public food stocks tends, however, to be limited by lack of information on existing private stocks and by vested interests in either holding high levels of stocks to favor producers (as in India) or not accumulating stocks due to their fiscal costs (as in most of the world in the decade prior to the 2006–7 food crisis). Implementation typically follows a policy announcement that prices will be maintained within a predetermined price band. Efficiency gains to society as a whole are dwarfed by redistributive gains and losses between producers and consumers, making the political economy of public stocks management particularly exposed to capture.

Trade instruments to manage price volatility

Prices can also be maintained within price bands through trade instruments. To protect its consumers from price spikes, an exporting country can impose export taxes, export quotas, or outright export bans when prices rise above the band, and use tax revenues to subsidize producers when prices fall below the band. During the 2006–7 food crisis, 33 countries imposed export restrictions to prevent rising international market prices from transferring to the domestic market. India banned rice exports to Bangladesh. While helpful to stabilize domestic prices in India, export restrictions increase price volatility on the international market—in Bangladesh in this particular case.

320

To protect its producers, an importing country can impose import tariffs when prices fall, and use tariff revenues to subsidize consumers when prices rise. Egypt and Tunisia did this to keep domestic prices low during the food crisis. Chile has also relied extensively on variable tariffs to stabilize domestic prices within a pre-announced price band. As shown by Gouel and Jean (2015), the most effective food-price-stabilization strategy for a country would consist in an optimum combination of storage and trade policies.

Again, the difficulty is in implementation. The setting of price bands is exposed to political debate. Support prices tend to divorce producer responses from long-run changes in international prices—and the large redistributive effects are an invitation to lack of transparency in policy-making and to rent-seeking to achieve political capture (Wright and Prakash, 2011). It is important, too, to recall that reduced fluctuations on domestic markets are achieved at the cost of increased volatility on the world market, where poorer, food-dependent countries may be severely hurt. Social-safety nets targeted at the poorest people can be used to decrease reliance on public stocks and trade interventions to stabilize prices, an issue we will study in Chapter 14.

DECLINE OF THE WTO AND THREATS TO MULTILATERALISM

The WTO was created in 1995 to codify the world trade system under a common set of rules and help weaker countries gain competitiveness in the world market. It now has 159 member countries that participate in decision-making on a highly democratic basis: one country, one vote, irrespective of size and per capita income. Democratic ideals can, however, become a source of paralysis. The WTO started to decline in 2003 when the US at the Cancun meeting refused West African countries' demand to reduce its cotton subsidies. The 2001 Doha round of multilateral agreements has been stalled. Efforts to jump-start the Doha trade negotiations at the 2013 Bali Ministerial Meeting of the WTO only resulted in minor trade-facilitation arrangements on customs barriers and non-tariff measures. The US, EU, and Japan are resisting the reduction of agricultural-trade barriers that would benefit many developing countries with comparative advantage in agriculture. This is especially serious for these developing counties as agriculture is their main road to industrialization (see Chapter 18). Trade liberalization in industry has benefited countries such as China enormously, contributing to the massive decline in poverty over the last ten years; but it has also accelerated the deindustrialization of industrialized countries, faced with competition from low-labor-cost countries. The WTO's three-speed process of trade liberalization, according to which rich countries would reduce tariffs and subsidies faster than emerging countries, while poor countries were exempted, is now being resisted by the US and EU due to the extreme competitiveness of the emerging countries, while Brazil and India want to continue to benefit from this advantage.

The decline of multilateralism has been met with the proliferation of regional and bilateral free-trade agreements (FTAs), currently numbering 379. This is resulting in a fragmentation of the global trading system, favoring the most powerful trading partners, especially the US, EU, and China, while hurting excluded countries. The US is negotiating mega regional FTAs outside the WTO framework: the Trans-Pacific

321

Partnership (TPP) with eleven countries in the Asia–Pacific region (Australia, Brunei Darussalam, Canada, Chile, Japan, Malaysia, Mexico, New Zealand, Peru, Singapore, and Vietnam) and the Trans-Atlantic Trade and Investment Partnership (TTIP) with the EU. These agreements could have major trade-diversion effects on excluded countries such as Brazil, China, and India. Negotiations are also being pursued among 50 countries on trade liberalization in services, and this is being done outside the WTO framework.

Fragmentation of the global trading system and unequal gains in bilateral trade agreements are a source of both global inefficiencies and inequities. Overcoming this situation requires reactivating the WTO process (Evenett and Jara, 2014). Existing preferential trade agreements need to be brought into the WTO multilateral framework. WTO trade agreements need go beyond trade issues to include respect for social rights, environmental protection, regulation on export embargos, and control over exchange-rate manipulation, designed to gain trade advantage (see Chapter 10). The incredible success of trade in support of productivity growth and, frequently, poverty reduction that has prevailed since the fall of the Berlin Wall is now under serious threat. Only a return to guided multilateralism under the leadership of the WTO will place all participants on a level playing field and help the least advantaged countries achieve competitiveness and derive gains from trade.

CONCEPTS IN THIS CHAPTER

Trade openness

Comparative advantage

Absolute advantage

Competitive advantage

Gains from specialization

Singer–Prebish thesis on international terms of trade

Time-consistency problem in achieving Pareto optimality after compensation

Commitment device

Behind-the-border assistance and aid-for-trade

Stolper–Samuelson theorem

Heckscher and Ohlin theory of comparative advantage

Michael Porter's competitive advantage

Trade creation and trade diversion of bilateral free-trade agreements

Industrialization strategies: ISI vs. EOI vs. OEI

Border price, domestic price

Import tariff, export tax

Production and export subsidy

Tradable good vs. non-tradable good

Trade policy indicators: NPC, EPC, NRA, real protection

Trade creation and trade diversion

Producer surplus, consumer surplus, net social gain (or deadweight loss)

Welfare effects of a tariff, a production subsidy

ISI as a gamble
Infant industry
Picking winners for subsidy
Firm-level subsidies more exposed to lobbying than industry-level tariffs
"Smart" subsidies
Good investment climate
Harmonization of environmental standards
Environmental side agreements
Self-sufficiency and self-reliance
Elasticity of demand with food stocks
Price bands
Variable tariffs and taxes
WTO and multilateralism
Regional and bilateral free-trade agreements

REVIEW QUESTIONS: INTERNATIONAL TRADE AND INDUSTRIALIZATION STRATEGIES

1. Explain why countries trade with a simple economic model. How are efficiency gains achieved? Why are there usually redistributive gains and losses? Give examples.
2. Can trade liberalization be made Pareto optimum after compensation? Why do you need a commitment device to make this credible?
3. Define the world market price, the border price, and the domestic price. How do a country's exchange-rate policy and trade policy affect the domestic price? Define the nominal protection coefficient: what does it mean?
4. Show the effects on consumer surplus, producer surplus, government costs or revenues, and the net social gain associated with an import tariff and a production subsidy.
5. Contrast the three industrialization strategies: ISI, EOI, and OEI. Explain what each strategy consists in and its advantages and inconvenient.
6. Why is ISI a strategy that can fail and what can be done to increase the chances of success?

REFERENCES

Agénor, Pierre-Richard. 2004. "Does Globalization Hurt the Poor?" *International Economics and Economic Policy* 1(1): 21–51.

Amsden, Alice. 1989. *Asia's Next Giant: South Korea and Late Industrialization.* New York: Oxford University Press.

Anderson, Kim. 2008. "Policies Affecting Agricultural Incentives in Developing Countries." Working paper, School of Economics, University of Adelaide.

Autor, David, David Dorn, and Gordon Hanson. 2013. "The China Syndrome: Local Labor Market Effects of Import Competition in the United States." *American Economic Review* 103(6): 2121–68.

Baer, Werner. 1972. "Import Substitution and Industrialization in Latin America: Experiences and Interpretations." *Latin American Research Review* 7(Spring): 9–122.

Beck, Thorsten, Aslı Demirgüç-Kunt, and Ross Levine. 2005. "Finance, Inequality, and the Poor: Cross-country Evidence." *Journal of Economic Growth* 10(3): 199–229.

Borchert, Ingo, Batshur Gootiiz and Aaditya Mattoo. 2014. "Policy Barriers to International Trade in Services: Evidence from a New Database." *World Bank Economic Review* 28(1): 162–88.

Brainard, Lael, and Isaac Sorkin. 2009. *Climate Change, Trade and Competitiveness: Is a Collision Inevitable?* Washington, DC: Brookings Trade Forum 2008/2009.

De Melo, Jaime, and Nicole Mathys. 2010. *Trade and Climate Change: The Challenges Ahead.* Clermont-Ferrand, France: FERDI.

Dollar, David, and Aart Kraay. 2001. "Trade, Growth, and Poverty." Washington, DC: World Bank Policy Research Department Working Paper No. 2615.

Edwards, Sebastian. 1997. "Trade Policy, Growth, and Income Distribution." *American Economic Review* 87(2): 205–10.

Evans, Peter. 1995. *Embedded Autonomy: States and Industrial Transformation.* Princeton, NJ: Princeton University Press.

Evenett, Simon, and Alejandro Jara (eds.). 2014. *Building on Bali: A Work Program for the WTO.* London: Centre for Economic Policy Research.

Fernández, Raquel, and Dani Rodrik. 1991. "Resistance to Reform: Status Quo Bias in the Presence of Individual-Specific Uncertainty." *American Economic Review* 81(5): 1146–55.

Frankel, Jeffrey, and David Romer. 1999. "Does Trade Cause Growth?" *American Economic Review* 89(3): 379–99.

Goldberg, Pinelopi, and Nina Pavnik. 2003. "The Response of the Informal Sector to Trade Liberalization." *Journal of Development Economics* 72(2): 463–96.

Gouel, Christophe, and Sébastien Jean. 2015. "Optimal Food Price Stabilization in a Small Open Developing Country." *World Bank Economic Review* 29(1): 72–101.

Guillaumont Jeanneney, Sylviane, and Kangni Kpodar. 2011. "Financial Development and Poverty Reduction: Can There Be a Benefit without a Cost?" *Journal of Development Studies* 47(1): 143–63.

Harrison, Ann. 1996. "Openness and Growth: A Time-series, Cross-country Analysis for Developing Countries." *Journal of Development Economics* 48(2): 419–47.

Harrison, Ann (ed.). 2006. *Globalization and Poverty.* Chicago: University of Chicago Press for NBER.

Harrison, Ann, and Gordon Hanson. 1999. "Who Gains from Trade Reform? Some Remaining Puzzles." *Journal of Development Economics* 59(1): 125–54.

IFC/WB. 2012. "Doing Business." Washington, DC: International Finance Corporation and World Bank. http://www.doingbusiness.org/rankings (accessed 2015).

Irwin, Douglas, and Marko Terviö. 2002. "Does Trade Raise Income? Evidence from the Twentieth Century." *Journal of International Economics* 58(1): 1–18.

Karnani, Aneel. 2011. *Fighting Poverty Together: Rethinking Strategies for Business, Governments, and Civil Society to Reduce Poverty.* New York: Palgrave Macmillan.

Krueger, Anne. 1983. *Trade and Employment in Developing Countries. Volume 3: Synthesis and Conclusions.* Chicago: University of Chicago Press.

Krueger, Anne, Maurice Schiff, and Alberto Valdés. 1988. "Measuring the Impact of Sector-specific and Economy-wide Policies on Agricultural Incentives in LDCs." *World Bank Economic Review* 2(3): 255–72.

Le Goff, Maëlan, and Raju Singh. 2013. "Does Trade Reduce Poverty? A View from Africa." Washington, DC: World Bank Policy Research Working Paper No. 6327.

Lin, Justin Yifu. 2009. *Economic Development and Transition: Thought, Strategy, and Viability.* Cambridge, MA: Cambridge University Press.

Mamalakis, Markos. 1969. "The Theory of Sectoral Clashes." *Latin American Research Review* 4(3): 9–46.

Newfarmer, Richard, and Monika Sztajerowska. 2012. "Trade and Employment in a Fast-changing World." In D. Lippoldt (ed.), *Policy Priorities for International Trade and Jobs,* 7–74. Paris: OECD.

Porter, Michael. 1985. *Competitive Advantage.* New York: Free Press.

Reich, Robert. 2008. *Supercapitalism: The Transformation of Business, Democracy, and Everyday Life.* New York: Vintage Books

Ricardo, David. 1817. *On the Principles of Political Economy and Taxation.* Indianapolis: Liberty Fund Books.

Rodriguez, Francisco, and Dani Rodrik. 2001. "Trade Policy and Economic Growth: A Skeptics Guide to the Cross-national Evidence." In B. Bernanke and K. Rogoff (eds.), *NBER Macroeconomics Annual 2000* Vol 15: 261–325. Cambridge, MA: MIT Press.

Rodrik, Dani. 1995. "Political Economy of Trade Policy." In G. Grossman and K. Rogoff (eds.), *Handbook of International Economics,* Vol. 3, 1457–94. Amsterdam: Elsevier Science B.V.

Rodrik, Dani. 2004. "Industrial Policy for the Twenty-First Century." Working Paper Series rwp04–047, John F. Kennedy School of Government, Harvard University.

Sachs, Jeffrey, and Andrew Warner. 1995. "Economic Reform and the Process of Global Integration." *Brookings Papers on Economic Activity* 1: 1–118.

Shaiken, Harley. 2014. "The NAFTA Paradox." *Berkeley Review of Latin American Studies* Spring: 36–43.

Stiglitz, Joseph, and Andrew Charlton. 2005. *Fair Trade for All: How Trade Can Promote Development.* New York: Oxford University Press.

Topalova, Petia, and Amit Khandelwal. 2011. "Trade Liberalization and Firm Productivity: The Case of India." *Review of Economics and Statistics* 93(3): 995–1009.

Tybout, James, and Daniel Westbrook. 1995. "Trade Liberalization and Dimensions of Efficiency Change in Mexican Manufacturing Industries." *Journal of International Economics* 39(August): 53–78.

Vamvakidis, Athanasios. 2002. "How Robust is the Growth-openness Connection? Historical Evidence." *Journal of Economic Growth* 7(1): 57–80.

Wacziarg, Romain, and Karen Horn Welch. 2008. "Trade Liberalization and Growth: New Evidence." *World Bank Economic Review* 22(2): 187–231.

Wade, Robert. 1990. *Governing the Market.* Princeton, NJ: Princeton University Press.

Waugh, Michael. 2010. "International Trade and Income Differences." *American Economic Review* 100(5): 2093–124.

Williams, Jeffrey, and Brian Wright. 1991. *Storage and Commodity Markets.* New York: Cambridge University Press.

World Bank. *World Development Indicators.* http://data.worldbank.org/indicator (accessed 2015).

Wright, Brian, and Adam Prakash. 2011. "The Fallacy of Price Interventions: A Note on Price Bands and Managed Tariffs." In Adam Prakash (ed.), *Safeguarding Food Security in Volatile Global Markets,* 241–52. Rome: FAO.

Chapter 8

Explaining economic growth

The macro level

TAKE-HOME MESSAGES FOR CHAPTER 8

1. GDPpc growth is the cornerstone of development. Yet it is one of the most difficult economic outcomes to explain and predict, with many competing theories, but also many different potentially effective strategies to accelerate growth.

2. The standard growth model is based on a structural form with five key parameters: the rate of population growth, the rate of saving, the rate of depreciation of capital, the rate of technological change, and the parameters of the production function. The effect of the rate of population growth on the growth of per capita income is ambiguous.

3. The Harrod–Domar model identifies the rate of saving and the choice of technique (the incremental capital-output ratio, or ICOR) as the two determinants of a country's growth rate. By contrast, the Solow model focuses on the relative roles of technological change and factor deepening in explaining growth, leaving, however, technology, which is the main determinant of long-term growth in per capita income, unexplained by the model. Predictions of universal convergence in per capita income, as technology is considered to be an international public good, are also questionable.

4. The technologies available as an international public good for developing countries may not be best for their current factor-price ratio. However, in accordance with Solow, they can help these countries leapfrog toward the use of advanced technologies.

5. Dual-economy models stress the importance of labor transfers out of agriculture and of cheap food to keep nominal industrial wages low for growth in employment in industry. In the Lewis classical model, there is surplus labor in agriculture and labor transfers have zero opportunity cost for food production. In the Jorgenson neoclassical model, there is full employment, and productivity growth in agriculture is necessary for labor transfers without rising food prices. In the Lele–Mellor model, there is surplus labor in agriculture, but productivity growth in agriculture is necessary to keep industrial wages low.

6. Other models such as ADLI (agriculture demand-led industrialization), sectoral linkages, and competitive advantages based on institutional capacity explain why investing in agriculture is important for industrialization as a source of effective demand of multiplier effects and of foreign-exchange earnings.

THE GROWTH PUZZLE

We have seen that economic growth is the cornerstone on which economic development is built (Chapter 1). We have also seen that growth performances across nations have been highly unequal, with some developing countries converging in per capita income with industrialized countries while others have been lagging behind, leading to the concept of conditional convergence (Chapter 2). And we have seen that finding ways to catch up with industrialized countries has been a primary objective in the long history of thought in development economics (Chapter 3). Yet our ability to explain economic growth, a central purpose of economics as a science, is highly deficient, leaving us with what has been called the "mystery of economic growth" (Helpman, 2004) and the "elusive quest for growth" (Easterly, 2002).

What we know is that output growth basically depends on two determinants: (1) factor accumulation (labor, capital, materials, land) and the way these factors are combined in production for a given technology, as represented by the production function; and (2) gains in factor productivity deriving from how technology, institutions, and factor quality change over time. However, what drives factor accumulation and especially gains in factor productivity remains highly contentious. Different models offer different explanations with different policy implications for what to do to accelerate growth. The truth is that each of these models offers particular insights into the growth process under particular circumstances, without exhausting potential explanations. For that reason, there are lessons to be derived from each of the main models that have been proposed to explain growth.

With growth, as with the other dimensions of economic development, we are interested in both the positive analysis of growth (what explains economic growth) and its normative analysis (what can be done to accelerate growth). To answer these questions, economists use economic models and take these models to the data for estimation, simulation, and predictions.

In the quest to explain income growth, we will meet two families of models: classical and neoclassical growth models with exogenous technological change (treated in this chapter), and endogenous-growth models with technological change an outcome of economic decision-making (Chapter 9). In both families of models, technological change plays a key role in explaining growth, yet with very different outcomes and policy implications. The first family of models predicts income convergence across countries, while the second predicts conditional convergence or no convergence at all. The verdict on the validity of one family of models or the other thus requires empirical verification.

GENERIC MODELING OF INCOME GROWTH

Structure of economic models

An economic model is a simplification of reality that captures a complex process to explain an outcome, here economic growth. Because it has to be a simplification of reality, a model is always "reductionist," i.e. it omits details and has a large *ceteris paribus*

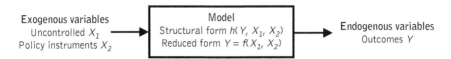

Figure 8.1 *Structural and reduced forms of an economic model*

clause, whereby other economic processes beyond the one under study are held constant. The model will be useful or not depending on the realism of the assumptions made about the processes at work and the capacity to replicate observed growth and predict future growth. Hence all models need to be carefully assessed in terms of the validity of their assumptions relative to the field of application in which we would like the model to hold (its internal validity), and in terms of whether their predicted outcomes match reality.

As shown in Figure 8.1, a model includes exogenous variables (X) that fall into two categories: uncontrolled variables such as weather, the world economic context, and past events (X_1); and policy instruments such as taxes and tariffs, public investment, technology, new institutions, and transfers (X_2). It includes endogenous variables that represent the outcomes of interest (Y). And it includes a set of technological, institutional, and behavioral functions that relate Y, X_1, and X_2. These functions can be written in structural form as $h(Y, X_1, X_2)$, representing the assumptions of the model. They can also be written in reduced form as the solution to the model: namely, $Y = f(X_1, X_2)$, where f also derives from h.

In positive analysis, the first purpose of models is to check the logical structure of the reasoning and derive unexpected predictions; and the second is to estimate the parameters in the h and f functions. The first purpose is important because it is when a model is fully constructed that we know that the logic of the reasoning is complete and rigorous. Theory and theoretical derivations thus play a fundamental role in securing rigor in economic reasoning and in tracking the implications of the assumptions made. The second purpose is important in taking ideas to the data, enabling links between theory and empiricism. The model helps us formulate the equations that we want to estimate to either test the validity of the model or use it for normative purposes. Since there are many competing equations we could take to the data, having an economic model from which these equations derive helps us know exactly what it is that we are estimating.

In normative analysis, models are used for two purposes: policy simulations and predictions.

Policy simulations have the purpose of answering the following questions:

How does a change in X_2 lead to a change in Y for given h and X_1?
How does a change in h lead to a change in Y for given X_1 and X_2?

Predictions, or forecasts, have the purpose of answering the following question:

For a future X_{t+1}, what is the corresponding predicted Y_{t+1} for given h?

Theoretical rigor, a link to empiricism, simulation, and prediction are thus the four purposes of modeling in economics.

Generic structure of a growth model

The generic structure of a per capita income growth model is as follows.

Initial conditions at time t

Say that output is a function of capital, labor, technology, and a way of organizing production. This can be represented as follows.

Initial factor endowments: K_t (stock of capital), L_t (labor force).
Initial total factor productivity (TFP): A_t (technology).
Initial income (or output level): $Y_t = f(A_t, K_t, L_t)$, where Y_t is aggregate income and f is the production function that transforms technology, capital, and labor into output.

Growth process

Say that income growth originates in three sources: growth in the labor force accompanying population growth, growth in the stock of capital as part of income is saved and invested, and growth in TFP representing technological change.

1. *Demographic behavior:* $\Delta P/P = \Delta L/L = \dot{L}$ is the rate of population (P) and labor force (L) growth. A dot on top of a variable indicates the rate of growth of that variable. Here the rate of labor-force participation in the population is constant as there is full employment. As a consequence, the rate of labor-force growth is equal to the rate of population growth. This rate of population growth n may be a function of initial income Y_t. The population-growth equation is thus $L_{t+1} = L_t(1 + n)$.
2. *Savings behavior:* $S_t = sY_t$, where s is the rate of savings out of income Y and S is total savings. With $Y_t = C_t + S_t$, what is not saved is consumed and does not help capital accumulation. Hence we assume that the market exists and that prices play no role.
3. *Investment behavior:* all savings are invested. This is the budget constraint on investment: $I_t = S_t$, where I is investment.
   The change in the stock of capital is then: $\Delta K_t = I_t - \delta K_t$, where δ is the rate of depreciation of capital. The stock of capital at $t+1$ is thus $K_{t+1} = K_t - \delta K_t + I_t$.
4. *Gains in TFP:* at $t+1$, the new level of TFP is A_{t+1}, which can be exogenous (as in the neoclassical growth model) or endogenous (as in the endogenous-growth model, through a process to be defined). The rate of technological change is λ, with $A_{t+1} = A_t(1 + \lambda)$. The structural form of the model thus includes five parameters: n, s, δ, λ, and $f(.)$.

329

New conditions at time t+1 (reduced form of the model)

At time $t+1$, the new levels of factor endowments due to savings and investment and to growth in the labor force are:

$$K_{t+1} = K_t + \Delta K_t$$
$$L_{t+1} = L_t + \Delta L_t.$$

The new level of income (output) is consequently: $Y_{t+1} = f(A_{t+1}, K_{t+1}, L_{t+1})$.

The new level of per capita income is: $y_{t+1} = Y_{t+1}/L_{t+1}$.

Hence we learn from the model that aggregate income growth $(Y_{t+1} - Y_t)/Y_t$ depends:

  positively on the rate of savings s;
  negatively on the rate of depreciation of capital δ;
  positively on the rate of labor-force (population) growth n;
  positively on the rate of technological change λ.

The rate of change in per capita income, $(y_{t+1} - y_t)/y_t$ depends on population growth in an ambiguous fashion: positively in providing more labor, which is good for aggregate income growth, and negatively in contributing more people with a claim on total income, lowering per capita income.

  This generic growth model is summarized in Figure 8.2.

CAPITAL ACCUMULATION FOR GROWTH: THE HARROD–DOMAR MODEL

The Harrod–Domar model was developed in the 1930s and 1940s following the Great Depression and used extensively in the 1950s, the early years of development economics, when the main objective of development was to accelerate GDP growth

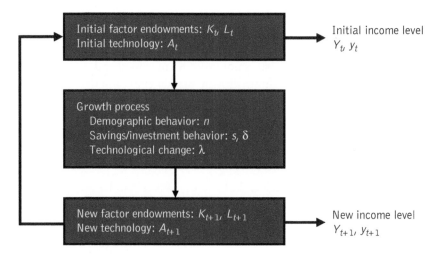

Figure 8.2 *Generic growth model*

(Chapter 3). Its purpose is to show how capital accumulation sustains growth, and how savings and technology determine capital accumulation (Domar, 1957). For this, the model makes five strong simplifying assumptions:

1. The economy is closed to trade and foreign direct investment. Hence all investment has to come from domestic savings.
2. Capital and labor are used in fixed proportions in production. Hence there are no substitution possibilities among inputs.
3. Capital is the limiting factor to output growth, not labor. Labor is in unlimited supply. Hence population growth and labor availability are not issues.
4. There are constant returns to scale for each factor. Hence the return to capital at the margin is always the same, whatever the level of the stock of capital.
5. Technology (the production function) is such that a fixed quantity of additional capital (ΔK) gives us a fixed proportional increase in output (ΔY), where the proportionality factor is $k = \Delta K/\Delta Y = \text{ICOR}$, or the incremental capital output ratio, an assumed simple technological specification. This is a Leontief fixed-proportions technology, where there are no decreasing marginal returns in the relation between capital and output, as opposed to the standard neoclassical decreasing-marginal-product specification that we will see in the Solow model below. The higher the ICOR, the less productive the technology is, i.e. we will need more additional capital per unit of increment of output ($\Delta Y = 1$). Hence the ICOR is the inverse of the marginal productivity of capital.

The structural form of the model consists in three equations:

1. *An aggregate production function*: $\Delta Y = (1/k)\Delta K$, obtained from the definition of the ICOR.
2. *A savings function*: $S = sY$, where S is aggregate savings and s is the rate of savings out of national income Y.
3. *An investment function*, where the demand for investment (I) is equal to available savings (S): $I \equiv \Delta K = S$. Investment (I) increases the stock of capital (ΔK).

These three equations can be solved for the reduced form of the model, where the endogenous outcome of interest is the rate of economic growth defined as:

$$\dot{Y} = \frac{\Delta Y}{Y}.$$

Hence using equation (1) to replace ΔY, equation (3) to replace ΔK, and equation (2) to replace S, we obtain:

$$\dot{Y} = \frac{\Delta Y}{Y} = \frac{1}{k}\frac{\Delta K}{Y} = \frac{1}{k}\frac{S}{Y} = \frac{s}{k}.$$

The interpretation of this result is that the growth rate of the economy ($\dot{Y}$) increases with the rate of savings (s) and decreases with the ICOR (k), a simple but highly suggestive result for the design of growth policies.

Note that if there is depreciation of capital, as in the generic growth model above, then part of investment is absorbed by the need to replace depreciated capital. The investment function then becomes:

$$I \equiv \Delta K + \delta K = S,$$

where δ is the rate of depreciation of capital. The growth rate of the economy is then reduced by δ as follows:

$$\dot{Y} = \frac{s}{k} - \delta.$$

There can now be zero or even negative growth if the rate of savings is insufficient for s/k to exceed the rate of depreciation of capital.

We can also calculate the rate of growth in per capita income, where P is population and n the rate of population growth. Per capita income is $y = Y/P$ and the rate of growth of per capita income is:

$$\dot{y} = \dot{Y} - \dot{P} = \frac{s}{k} - (\delta + n).$$

Growth in per capita income is thus enhanced by the rate of saving and the productivity of capital, and reduced by the rate of depreciation of capital and the rate of population growth. There can be zero per capita income growth (a Malthusian trap) if the rate of population growth is in excess of $(s/k) - \delta$.

It is easy to get information on the ICOR. The World Bank's *World Development Indicators* available online give data for every country and year on:

gross fixed capital formation as a percentage of GDP = $\Delta K/Y$;
GDP annual growth in percentage = $\Delta Y/Y$.

The ratio of the two is the ICOR.

Table 8.1 gives the ICOR for India, South Africa, China, and Brazil using this formula. They show that India and South Africa use low productivity technology, with ICORs of 6.7 and 6.3, respectively, compared to China and Brazil that use more productive technology with ICORs of 4.2 and 3.7, respectively. This means, ultimately, that India needs almost twice as much additional capital per unit of additional GDP as Brazil does.

The policy implications for accelerating growth are clear from the solution of the model: raise the rate of saving (i.e. promote savings through stronger financial institutions) and lower the ICOR (i.e. increase the marginal productivity of capital through better technology). Domestic saving can also be complemented by foreign aid transfers, provided they are used for investment. With growth driven by capital accumulation, savings (domestic and foreign) and technology are the answers to growth. Even with international capital movements and foreign direct investment, the model remains relevant because domestic savings are indeed the main source of investment. Using data for the OECD economies during the period 1960–74, Feldstein and

Table 8.1 *Growth according to the Harrod–Domar model*

2008 Country Name	Gross fixed capital formation (% of GDP)	GDP growth (annual %)	ICOR
India	32.9	4.9	6.7
South Africa	22.6	3.6	6.3
China	40.8	9.6	4.2
Brazil	19.1	5.2	3.7

Source: World Bank, World Development Indicators.

Horioka (1980) showed that net capital flows are small relative to investment, i.e., that there exists an almost perfect correlation between domestic savings and investment.

Because it is both easy to use and suggestive of policy instruments that can accelerate growth, the Harrod–Domar has been one of the most influential models in the early years of development economics. Here are three important uses of the model.

Foreign aid and the Big Push

Say that foreign aid is attributed as a share f of Y and that it is fully added to domestic savings. Total savings would then be $sY + fY$ and the growth rate of the economy equal to $\dot{Y} = (s + f)/k$. In poor countries, the rate of foreign aid can easily be 20 percent for a 10 percent rate of savings. With an ICOR of 4, the rate of growth would jump from 2.5 percent to 7.5 percent, an important contribution to implementation of the Big Push. Alternatively, foreign aid can be seen as financing the gap between necessary savings $s*$ and domestic savings s to achieve a desired rate of per capita income growth $\dot{y}*$. The financing gap provided by foreign aid is then $f = s* - s$. This has provided a powerful rationale for the role of foreign aid in achieving per capita income growth and income convergence, the main objective of foreign aid in the 1950s, as we will see in Chapter 19.

Two-gap model

A popular extension of the Harrod–Domar model in the 1960s in Latin America was the idea that there are two kinds of capital goods used in production, some of domestic origin (e.g. buildings) financed by domestic savings and some of foreign origin (e.g. imported intermediate goods and machinery) that must be paid for with foreign savings. If the two forms of capital are in fixed proportion, then one or the other type of saving will always be binding—the one that is most in deficit. This is the two-gap model (Chenery and Bruno, 1962). Foreign aid that increases foreign savings can thus be quite effective in enhancing growth if there is a deficit of foreign exchange but enough domestic savings. On the other hand, foreign aid will not be useful for growth if there is a deficit of domestic savings but enough foreign exchange to acquire the necessary imported capital goods.

333

Two-sector Soviet model

Centrally planned economies, like the Soviet Union, but also Egypt and India (with an economist such as Prasanta Chandra Mahalanobis, the key architect of India's Second Five Year Plan), looked at the economy as composed of two sectors: a capital-goods sector and a consumption-goods sector. Capital goods are used to produce more capital goods and also consumption goods. If the objective of the plan is to maximize long-term production of consumer goods, the way to do this is to post-pone consumption to invest heavily in the capital-goods sector. Under central planning, priority was given to allocating available domestic savings to heavy industry, while imposing austerity on consumers on behalf of faster future income growth. The problem with this "capital fundamentalism" was increased inefficiencies in the capital-goods industries, postponing forever the emergence of the desired consumer-goods sector. The Harrod–Domar model was thus both used and misused, but was extraordinarily influential between 1930 and 1960.

The model and its various extensions (discussed in Easterly, 2002) have useful insights for how growth is achieved and how it can be accelerated; but it is too simplistic to be useful for policy-making in today's more globalized and more tech-nologically complex world. In particular, it does not allow for a decreasing marginal product of capital ($MPK = 1/k$), for substitutions in production between capital and labor, and for technological change, which we know are important for growth. The Solow model tries to compensate for these deficiencies.

PRODUCTIVITY GROWTH AND FACTOR DEEPENING: GROWTH ACCOUNTING IN THE SOLOW MODEL

The Solow (1957) model builds on the Harrod–Domar model in seeking to explain growth, but adds several neoclassical features to the rigid technological specification. It recognizes that there is a decreasing marginal product to each factor of production and possible substitutions between labor and capital in production. Some countries will choose a more labor-intensive growth path with a low capital/labor ratio because labor is cheap relative to capital, while others will choose a more capital-intensive growth path with a high capital/labor ratio because labor is expensive relative to capital. The model also captures a major lesson learned from data analysis after World War Two: namely, that TFP gains played a very important role in contributing to observed output growth. This means that output growth can come from two sources: factor deepening (more labor and/or more capital used in production according to factor proportions) and TFP growth. TFP is thus the part of output Y that cannot be explained by factors of production such as labor and capital. TFP growth can origi-nate in technological change (more productive techniques), in institutional change (better ways of organizing production), or in improvements in the quality of factors of production such as labor (education, health, skills) and capital (more productive machines, new seeds in agriculture). The model maintains the Harrod–Domar assumption of constant returns to scale for both factors combined, but with decreas-ing returns for each factor separately.

334

Considering the case in which TFP growth shifts the production function upward (so-called Hicks neutral technological change because it does not favor one factor over another), the aggregate production function for the economy can be written as $Y = Af(K, L)$, where Y is national income, A TFP, K capital, and L labor. f is a typical neoclassical production function with decreasing returns to the deepening of each factor separately, i.e. the marginal contribution of each factor to output growth declines as use of the factor increases. Because f is assumed to have constant returns to scale, the production function can also be written as: $Y/L = Af(K/L)$ or $y = Af(k)$, where $y = Y/L$ is the productivity of labor (or income per capita since L is also population) and $k = K/L$ is capital intensity, or the stock of capital per worker. This allows a two-dimensional representation of the production function as in Figure 8.3.

In the structural form of the model, the economy uses labor and capital to maximize profit given the prices of the product ($p = 1$), of labor (w, the wage), and of capital (r, the interest rate). Given this profit-maximizing behavior, the production function f, and product and factor prices, the reduced form of the model gives the growth rate of output $\dot{Y}$ to be equal to:

$$\dot{Y} = \frac{\Delta Y}{Y} = \frac{\Delta A}{A} + w_K \frac{\Delta K}{K} + w_L \frac{\Delta L}{L},$$

where $w_K = rK/Y$ is the share of capital in total income and $w_L = wL/Y$ is the share of labor in total income. $\Delta A/A$ is the rate of technical change, or TFP growth, and $\Delta K/K$, $\Delta L/L$ are the rates of factor accumulation or factor deepening. This is Solow's well known and useful growth accounting formula.

If we observe, as in Figure 8.3, the economy at two points in time, we know $\Delta Y/Y$, $\Delta K/K$, $\Delta L/L$, w_K, and w_L. We can use the difference to measure the role of TFP, called the unexplained residual, in accounting for the observed growth. Specifically, the rate of TFP growth $\Delta A/A$ is given by:

$$\frac{\Delta A}{A} = \frac{\Delta Y}{Y} - w_K \frac{\Delta K}{K} - w_L \frac{\Delta L}{L}.$$

This is of course a bit of a risky measurement of the role of A in growth as any underestimation of $\Delta K/K$, $\Delta L/L$ during the period will lead to an inflated measure of $\Delta A/A$. Still, this is an amazingly simple way of obtaining quantitative information on a fundamental source of economic growth: namely, the rate of TFP growth—we can call it technological change, for simplicity. Early measurements by Solow (1957) for the US over the 1910–50 period suggested that $\Delta A/A$ could have accounted for as much as 88 percent of observed GDPpc growth. No wonder that it called the attention of the economics profession to the role technological change could play in accelerating growth, a potentially cheaper option than factor deepening. This large measurement was likely excessive, in part due to missed components of capital accumulation such as military expenditures during this critical period, accounted for by the unexplained residual.

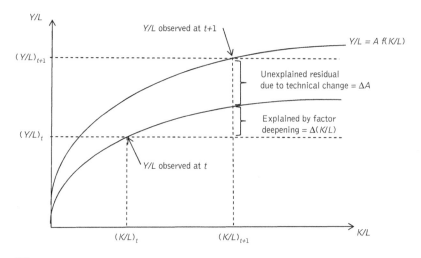

Figure 8.3 *Factor deepening and productivity growth in the Solow model*

Recent measurements for Hong Kong, Singapore, South Korea, and Taiwan, the four Asian NICs, over the period 1966–90, when they experienced rapid GDP growth, shows that productivity growth may not have been as large as estimated by Solow for the US, but that it did matter and in some countries more than in others (Young, 1995). The results in Table 8.2 tell us what were the sources of growth for these countries that were at the heart of the "Asian miracle."

Contrary to expectations, we see that the Asian miracle was not due so much to technological change as it was to Harrod–Domar-type factor deepening, in particular of capital in Hong Kong (explaining 41 percent of observed growth) and Singapore (explaining 65 percent of observed growth). Labor deepening was the main source of observed growth in South Korea (44 percent of observed growth) and Taiwan (40 percent of observed growth). The unexplained residual, technological change, contributed a respectable 31 percent of observed output growth in Hong Kong and 24 percent in Taiwan. The surprise, however, is that factor accumulation mattered so much. It raises the troubling question of how growth will be sustained in the long run given that there are decreasing returns to factor deepening in the neoclassical production function.

What are the long-term growth predictions of the Solow model? A rigorous derivation of these results is given in Appendix 8.1. The key results are these.

1. Because of decreasing returns to factor deepening, the model converges to a steady state (y^*, k^*), where capital per worker and labor productivity (income per capita) stop growing. This implies that, at the steady state, national income Y^* grows at the same rate as the labor force L: namely, at the rate of population growth. Ultimately, all countries converge to y^*: there is worldwide convergence in income per capita.
2. As shown in the Appendix, the level of per capita income at the steady state increases with the rate of savings, TFP, and the share of capital in national income. It decreases with the rate of depreciation of capital and the rate of population growth.

Table 8.2 *Sources of growth for the Asian NICs according to the Solow model*

1966–90	Share of labor	Growth labor	Share of capital	Growth capital	Residual TFP	Observed GDP growth
	w_L	$100*\Delta L/L$	w_K	$100*\Delta K/K$	$100*\Delta A/A$	$100*\Delta Y/Y$
Hong Kong	0.63	3.20%	0.37	8.00%	2.30%	7.30%
Share of observed growth		28%		41%	31%	100%
Singapore	0.51	5.70%	0.49	11.50%	0.20%	8.70%
Share of observed growth		33%		65%	2%	100%
South Korea	0.7	6.40%	0.3	13.70%	1.70%	10.30%
Share of observed growth		44%		40%	16%	100%
Taiwan	0.74	4.90%	0.26	12.30%	2.10%	8.90%
Share of observed growth		40%		36%	24%	100%

Source: Young, 1995.

3. Growth in per capita income only happens in the process of convergence to the steady state, where it will stop. This growth slows down as the economy gets closer to the steady state due to decreasing returns to factor deepening. Hence initially poorer countries that start with a lower level of *k* grow faster than richer countries with an initially higher level of *k*. There is convergence: income per capita grows faster in poorer than in richer countries.

4. While growth is thus transitional toward the steady state, displacement of the steady state helps sustain growth in per capita income. The only source of long-term displacement of the steady state is TFP growth—technological change. This is the model's most important prediction. Solow assumes that technology is an international public good to which all countries have equal access and equal absorptive capacity in using it. As a consequence, all countries are using the same production function, and any upward shift in the production function due to technological innovations will propagate equally across all countries. Under this scenario, long-term growth in per capita income is only due to technological change. Since it is by assumption the same in all countries, there will be universal long-term income convergence between LDC and MDC. A happy scenario. But is it credible? As always with economic modeling, it depends on the validity of the assumptions made.

There are three main problems with the assumptions and the predictions of the Solow model.

Exogenous technological change

The first problem is that the model is in a sense incomplete because it gives a major role to TFP as a source of sustained growth, yet TFP growth itself is not explained by the model. All the model does is tell us how TFP growth is transformed into income growth, without telling us how we could increase TFP growth. For this we would need a class of models able to explain where technological progress comes from, which will be the objective of the "endogenous growth models" (Romer, 1990) analyzed in Chapter 9, in contrast to the "exogenous growth models" proposed by Harrod–Domar (role of the ICOR) and Solow (role of TFP), where technology is an international public good, equally available to all countries.

Solow is correct, however, regarding access to technology as an international public good for the "backward" countries, which is part of the "advantage of backwardness" noted by Gerschenkron (1962). In his analysis, the greater the backwardness of a country, the greater the possibility of relying on borrowed rather than endogenous technologies. These countries can borrow technology as an international public good, at least until they have improved their technology to the point of needing to innovate for themselves and start to invest in costly research and development. Lin (2012) thus observes that the success of the four Asian tigers (Taiwan, South Korea, Hong Kong, and Singapore) in the 1960s, and of China until today, is that they were all very good at technological borrowing and industrial upgrading (i.e. at using imported technologies to switch to more profitable production processes, products, and value chains, thus technologically leapfrogging). Technological borrowing could be done through imitation, using reverse engineering, or through foreign direct investment. Think, for example, how important reverse engineering of the German Leica camera was for Japan in starting its own very successful camera sector in the postwar period.

Adopting existing technologies from industrialized countries is, however, not that simple. It requires the capacity to select, import, and eventually adapt these technologies to the context that prevails in the backward country. This requires infrastructure, education, a reliable legal system, an inviting investment climate, and a domestic market of sufficient size, all of which in the case of the Asian tigers and China needed strong, proactive state support to enhance their absorptive capacity. Hence even if technology is an international public good, it may diffuse unequally across developing countries according to their own capacities to adopt and adapt.

It is also interesting to consider the type of technology that can be accessed by a backward country (LDC) as an international public good given scientific progress applied to technological innovations in industrialized countries (MDCs). Consider in Figure 8.4 the concept of an innovation possibility frontier (IPF), the envelope of all possible unit isoquants in the factor space between capital (K) and labor (L), which, as science goes, is a true international public good (Hayami and Ruttan, 1971). With scientific progress, the IPF drifts toward the origin, from its former level when the MDC was using labor-intensive technology at point 1 in Figure 8.4 to its current level where the MDC is using capital-intensive technology at 2 in accordance with its new factor-price ratio, where capital has become cheaper and labor more expensive than at 1. Because the generation of particular technologies within the IPF is costly, the MDC only explores the area of the current IPF that corresponds to its current factor-price ratio, $(p_L/p_K)^{MDC}$. The LDC would like technology 3 that is not available from the MDC and needs to be generated by the LDC itself, at a cost that it cannot afford. This creates a dilemma for the LDC in seeking to import international technology as an international public good: it can use either the old technology at 1, which corresponds to its current factor-price ratio, or the MDC's modern technology at 2, which does not correspond to its relative factor prices. In the end, it should use the current MDC technology since it is less costly for the LDC than 1. It can be used with minor adjustments at 4 that correspond to the LDC price ratio, but it is inferior for the LDC relative to the non-existent technology at 3. Gerschenkron's "advantage of backwardness" in providing access to technology as an international public good, as in the Solow model, does exist, even if it does not deliver to the LDC the optimum technology in terms of cost minimization given the state of international science. In accordance with Lin's policy recommendation, the LDC can leapfrog from 1 to 4 by shopping for technology in the international economy.

Universal convergence

The second problem with the Solow model is that the predicted universal convergence in per capita income is not empirically supported. According to Solow, countries with the same rate of saving, rate of population growth, rate of depreciation of capital, and rate of technological change should ultimately achieve the same level of per capita

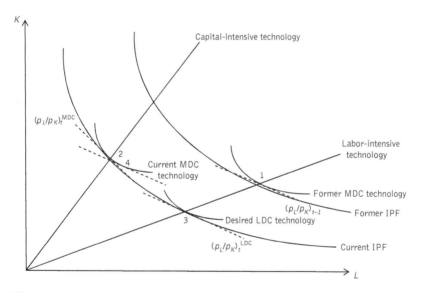

Figure 8.4 *IPF and the availability of technology as an international public good. The dashed lines are average unit cost functions and their slopes are equal to the factor-price ratios of labor to capital. Hence the average unit cost is larger at 1 than at 4, and at 4 than at 3*

income, whatever the initial level of per capita income. Baumol (1986) was the first to show that there was convergence for 16 rich countries over the period 1870 to 1979. In each case, the regression to test for convergence is:

$$GDPpc_{it} = \alpha + \beta GDPpc_{i,1870} + \varepsilon_{it},$$

where $(GDPpc)_{it}$ is per capita income in country i and year t, and $(GDPpc)_{i,1870}$ is the initial-year per capita income in country i. If there is convergence, the estimated β is negative: countries with a lower initial level of per capita income grow faster, converging in per capita income with countries with a higher initial level of per capita income.

Convergence was empirically verified across the US for the period 1960–84, across the six founding countries of the EU over the period 1950–85, and for the Asian tigers and China. However, it is not verifiable for a larger sample of initially heterogeneous countries. Using a sample of 36 countries with data for nearly 200 years, Easterly and Levine (2001) showed that dispersion in per capita income between the initially richer group and the initially poorer group widened from 6 to 1 to 70 to 1. Pritchett (1997) also finds that the income gap between richest and poorest countries increased five times between 1870 and 1990. As we saw in reviewing the state of development in Chapter 2, convergence is selective: some countries do converge while many others lag behind. This is a difference that the Solow model is unable to explain.

International labor and capital movements

Finally, if the Solow model were right, we should see no desire for labor migration from LDCs to MDCs since the marginal product of labor should be higher in LDCs still lagging in factor deepening. This is contradicted by the facts. An estimated 160 million, or 69 percent of all international migrants, now live in high-income countries, and 73 percent of all international migrants come from low- and middle-income countries (ECOSOC, 2013). Similarly, we should see MDC capital anxiously flowing to LDCs in search of higher rewards. Again, this is not what we see, particularly in Africa. This has been called the Lucas paradox (Lucas, 1990), for which two main explanations have been proposed. One is that there are frictions to capital mobility toward LDCs, preserving a large gap between MPK_{LDC} and MPK_{MDC}, with the former vastly larger than the second at equilibrium, perhaps in the order of 4 to 1. The other is that there are large price differences to the disadvantage of LDCs (Hsieh and Klenow, 2007). Prices of investment goods are higher in LDCs due to low efficiency in producing investment goods such as machinery and equipment, and low efficiency in producing exportables that can be traded for investment goods. Additionally, prices of consumption goods are lower, especially of non-tradable goods, which are an important share of output.

The result is that the Solow model is interesting in bringing out the relative roles of technological change and factor deepening in explaining growth, and useful in providing us with a growth-accounting methodology still applicable today, as in the

Young study of the Asian tigers. However, the aggregate-growth story leaves much to be explained and has implications that do not match well established empirical regularities. Yet, in spite of these criticisms, the Solow model has been and remains the workhorse of modern growth modeling and earned its author the 1987 Nobel Prize in economics.

THE ROLE OF AGRICULTURE IN GROWTH: STRUCTURAL TRANSFORMATION

History tells us that productivity gains in agriculture—the agricultural revolution—have been a precondition for successful industrialization (Chapter 3). To take this into account, growth models need to work with a sectoral disaggregation that allows us to conceptualize the role that agriculture plays in facilitating industrialization and aggregate income growth.

There is a well known regularity in the way the sectoral structure of an economy changes as income rises. It is called the "structural transformation" (Kuznets, 1966; Chenery and Taylor, 1968). It describes how the shares of agriculture, industry, and services, in both total employment and GDP, change as GDPpc rises. Following this regularity, the share of agriculture declines in both employment and GDP, with a lower share for agriculture in GDP than for agriculture in employment, signaling lower labor incomes in agriculture than in the rest of the economy (Figure 8.5) (Timmer, 1988). This is consistent with the observation we made in Chapter 5 that most of the poor in low-income countries are associated with agriculture and located in the rural sector.

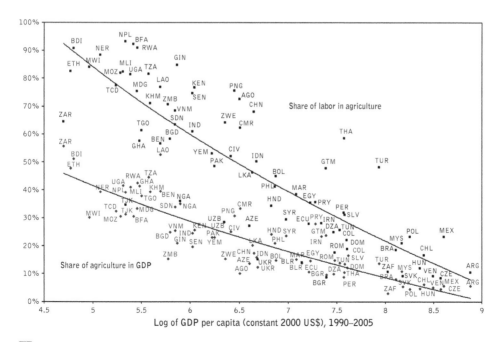

Figure 8.5 *Structural transformation across countries*

Source: World Bank, 2007.

This observation is purely descriptive, and not causal: lowering the employment and GDP shares of agriculture will not induce a higher GDPpc. In fact, in Sub-Saharan Africa, we see rapidly declining shares of agriculture in employment associated with rural–urban migration without an increase in GDPpc (Figure 8.6a). This contrasts with Asia, where the declining share of agriculture in employment was associated with rapid growth in GDPpc (Figure 8.6b). The contrast suggests something important about growth, and the potential role of agriculture in growth.

In Asia, with a successful structural transformation, the share of agriculture in employment declined because employment growth was occurring faster in the rest of the economy. This suggests an interesting potential role for agriculture in economic growth: successful agricultural growth accelerates growth in other sectors of

(a)   Structural transformation in Sub-Saharan Africa

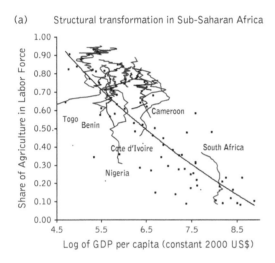

(b)   Structural transformation in Asia

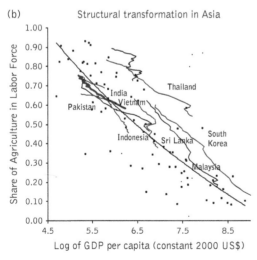

Figure 8.6 *The structural transformation in Sub-Saharan Africa (a) and Asia (b) in the 1960–2005 period*

Source: de Janvry and Sadoulet, 2010.

the economy. If these sectors grow faster than agriculture, the share of agriculture declines in both total employment and GDP. This decline is then a measure of success of the role of agriculture in development, not of failure: agriculture declines as a share of the economy because it helps the rest of the economy accelerate its growth, exceeding that of agriculture itself. For agriculture, the mission accomplished in contributing to aggregate growth is a relative decline in its share of GDP and employment, an outcome that can easily be misunderstood. The dual-economy models that are presented in the next section conceptualize this process, interpreting how growth in agriculture contributes to triggering growth in the other sectors of the economy.

THE ROLE OF AGRICULTURE IN GROWTH: DUAL-ECONOMY MODELS

The basic model

The key question addressed by dual-economy models is how agriculture can help industrial growth, inducing structural change in the economy and redefining its importance relative to industry in GDP and in employment. To answer this question, we construct a model that has two sectors: agriculture and industry. Following the insights of Lewis (1954), who received the Nobel Prize in 1979 for his work, there is a fundamental asymmetry between these two sectors, which he refers to as "dualism." Agriculture uses land and labor in production, and output can also increase through TFP growth. By contrast, industry uses capital and labor in production, and TFP also affects output. Hence capital accumulation only happens in industry, and the two sectors are related through the labor market. The labor market in industry is competitive: employers must attract workers by offering them their opportunity cost in agriculture plus their migration cost. Agriculture can then contribute to industrial growth through two effects: it can release labor for industrial employment and/or it can lower the price of food to lower the nominal wage and the cost of labor for industry, thus favoring employment in industry. In both cases, rising employment in industry in response to investment and capital accumulation is what drives economic growth.

We use the following notations:

Y agricultural output, with a production function:

$Y = tf(\text{smaller of } A \text{ and } A^+, \text{Land})$

t	technological change (TFP) in agriculture
A	labor force in agriculture
A^+	maximum agricultural labor usefully employed, i.e. with a non-zero marginal product of labor
$A - A^+$	surplus labor in agriculture, i.e. labor in agriculture with zero marginal product in agricultural production
M	industrial (manufacturing) employment
Pop	total labor force (proportional to population) $= A + M$

343

$\overline{w}'_A$ fixed subsistence wage in agriculture (real wage)

p_Y price of the agricultural good

$w_A = p_Y \overline{w}'_A$ nominal wage in agriculture

w_M nominal wage in industry

Δ rural–urban migration cost, hence the labor market is in equilibrium when:

$$w_M = w_A + \Delta.$$

The agricultural production function can be represented as in Figure 8.7.

Labor in agriculture is productively employed up to A^+. Beyond this level, called the Lewis turning point, labor is in surplus: it has a zero marginal product and can consequently be removed from agriculture at no opportunity cost in terms of level of agricultural output. There is a transition between full employment where $MP_L = w$ and surplus labor where $MP_L = 0$. This is referred to as disguised unemployment, where the marginal product of labor is positive, but less than w when full employment would prevail. We focus on the case of surplus labor, and briefly discuss the transition separately.

Three competing dual-economy models

There are three alternative formulations of dual-economy models depending on whether or not there is surplus labor, hidden unemployment, or full employment in agriculture, and whether productivity gains in agriculture help reduce the cost of labor for industry through a lower nominal wage. We review these three models in turn.

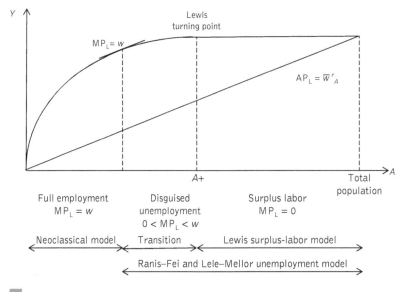

Figure 8.7 *Agricultural production function with surplus labor, disguised unemployment, and full employment*

Model 1: dual-economy model with surplus labor—the Lewis classical model

Arthur Lewis assumed that there is surplus labor in agriculture. Surplus labor means that there is more labor than necessary in agriculture to achieve the current level of production. This implies that some unemployed or underemployed workers can be removed from agriculture without decreasing the production of food at current technology. Surplus labor also means that there is a labor-market failure in agriculture in the sense that the wage is not determined by employment. Lewis assumes that there is a fixed real wage $\bar{w}'_A$ that corresponds to the subsistence needs of the agricultural population. As shown in Figure 8.7, it can be interpreted as the return to labor obtained by sharing equally the product of agriculture among the whole population.

With surplus labor, $A > A^+$. Employment in agriculture is to the right of the Lewis turning point in Figure 8.7. The nominal wage in agriculture is the fixed real wage times the price of food: $w_A = p_Y \bar{w}'_A$. Because the two sectors are related through the labor market, the wage paid in industry must be equal to the agricultural wage plus the migration cost Δ, $w_M = w_A + \Delta$. What does this tell us about the role of agriculture for industrial growth? In fact, agriculture has no active role: investment can occur in industry, increasing industrial employment and pulling labor out of agriculture; but agricultural output and the price of food remain unchanged for as long as there is surplus labor in agriculture and those left behind in agriculture can reorganize to maintain the same level of agricultural output when some agricultural workers leave. A lower real wage in agriculture (i.e. more poverty in agriculture) would of course lower the nominal wage in industry and favor growth, but this sad reality is not an interesting policy implication. A higher rate of population growth will reproduce surplus labor, postponing the stage when surplus labor will disappear at the Lewis turning point and, with the labor-market failure thus eliminated, the time when wages will rise with industrial employment. Population growth is thus a source of continued poverty for workers, in spite of eventually rapid industrial growth, which is determined by capital accumulation in industry, as in the Harrod–Domar model, or by TFP growth in industry, as in the Solow model.

The main lesson from the Lewis model is that agriculture can serve as a reservoir of surplus labor for a long time, especially if there is population growth, and that for as long as surplus labor exists growth can occur rapidly through investment in industry. The role of agriculture is passive, providing food and labor to industry without the need to invest in agriculture. The model thus justified neglecting agriculture and legitimized a strong "urban bias" (Lipton, 1977) in development policies. In addition, in this development strategy, growth occurs without creating benefits for workers, as wages are not responsive to employment creation in industry due to surplus labor. Labor is just a cost on growth (like in the neo-mercantilist model), never a benefit in creating effective demand for industry (as in the Big Push model seen in Chapter 3). Growth under surplus labor is inequalizing, with rising income accruing to capital as opposed to labor, which remains paid at subsistence level. The key policy lesson is that investment in industry is the engine of growth, like in the

Harrod–Domar model, and that foreign aid can be very effective for growth in providing capital for investment in industry.

There have been quite a few tests of the surplus-labor hypothesis. A celebrated natural experiment was used by T.W. Schultz (1964). In 1918–19, an influenza epidemic in India exogenously and sharply reduced labor availability in agriculture. Surplus labor would mean that agricultural output was not affected. He found that agricultural output declined by 8 percent, concluding that there was no surplus labor. The test was criticized by Sen (1967), who argued that output could fall even with surplus labor because those left behind could not gain access in the short run to the private lands of those killed by the epidemic. Further tests have reported the fact that the marginal product of labor in traditional agriculture is very low, providing support for the surplus-labor hypothesis.

Model 2: dual-economy model with full employment—the Jorgenson neoclassical model

So what happens to the role of agriculture once surplus labor has been removed, and full employment has been achieved? The economy is now to the left of the Lewis turning point and beyond the transition phase between the two models in Figure 8.7. The marginal product of labor in agriculture has risen to the level of the wage in industry, adjusted for migration cost. The dual-economy model with full employment was developed by Jorgenson (1967) and is referred to as neoclassical because the labor market can now be assumed to work, with the wage determined by equating the supply and demand for labor. Under this condition, $w_M = w_A + \Delta$. Workers can no longer be removed from agriculture without lowering agricultural output. If agricultural output falls, food prices will rise, nominal wages will increase, and there will be a break in industrial investment and growth.

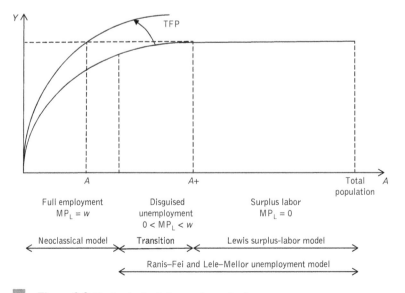

Figure 8.8 *Technological change in agriculture*

Looking at the agricultural production function, the policy solution is clear: we need technological change in agriculture to maintain agricultural output with less labor in agriculture than before. As can be seen in Figure 8.8, with TFP gains shifting the production function upward, agricultural output can be maintained in spite of employment in agriculture declining to A. Rising employment and growth can proceed in industry. Productivity growth in agriculture (the agricultural revolution and, more recently, the Green Revolution) is needed to make labor available to industry (the industrial revolution) without agricultural output falling, as this would put upward pressure on food prices and hence on the nominal wage. The key link is releasing labor from agriculture for industrial employment without an increase in the price of food and wages. Otherwise, increased labor costs would gradually drive the economy into stagnation, the so-called "Ricardian trap" (Hayami, 2001). This is an appealing model as it explains the well known historical regularity analyzed in Chapter 3, that productivity growth in agriculture is necessary for successful industrialization. But is labor scarcity really the limiting factor to industrial growth in today's developing economies? With the pervasiveness of surplus labor or low labor productivity in agriculture and unemployment in the urban sector epitomized by extensive urban slums, this does not appear to be the case.

As can be seen in Figure 8.7, there is a transition from surplus labor, where the Lewis model applies, to full employment, where the neoclassical model applies, through a phase where the MP_L in agriculture is greater than zero (end of surplus labor) but has not yet reached a level equal to the industrial wage (full employment). This is the phase of "disguised unemployment." Even though there is no full employment, labor cannot be removed from agriculture without a fall in agricultural output. In this transition, the price of food rises due to scarcity and as a consequence the nominal wage in industry must rise to preserve the real wage. Higher labor costs are detrimental to profits in industry and as a consequence to investment. This presages the importance of introducing technological change in agriculture to maintain agricultural output in the face of increasing labor scarcity and to protect industrial investment from the disincentive of rising food prices.

Model 3: dual-economy model with unemployment and a role for agriculture—the Ranis–Fei and Lele–Mellor models

We know that there is a huge employment problem in developing countries that have high population growth rates and a flood of young people entering the labor market every year—no less than 4 million in India and 1 million in Bangladesh (World Bank, 2007). In Africa, we have a vision of excessively rapid rural–urban migration and expanding urban slums, a phenomenon that will be analyzed in Chapter 12. These observations make the Lewis labor-market-failure assumption appealing, as opposed to Jorgenson's full employment that would fit better the labor-market conditions of industrialized countries. At the same time, we know that agriculture has an important role to play in providing cheap food and thus preventing the rise in the nominal cost of labor, which would be detrimental to industrial employment and growth. Indeed, a major interpretation of the slow growth of industry in Sub-Saharan Africa is that labor costs are too high, due in particular to the high price of food, as a Green Revolution of sufficient scale has failed to occur there.

Lower food prices also mean that real wages can increase, helping reduce poverty, while nominal wages can fall, cheapening labor for industry, a win–win combination that requires technological change in agriculture. This is seen in the real-wage formula $\bar{w}_A^r = w_A{\downarrow}/p_Y{\downarrow}$, where the real wage can rise or remain constant while both the price of food p_Y and the nominal wage w_A are falling. With a fixed real wage under surplus labor or hidden unemployment (see Chapter 12), the reasoning is then as follows. With TFP gains in agriculture, the price of food and the nominal wage can fall while keeping the real wage constant. Lower nominal-wage costs for industry would induce more investment in industry, and aggregate growth. This reasoning was proposed by Ranis and Fei (1961) and also by Lele and Mellor (1981) in their interpretations of the dual economy. The key role of productivity growth in agriculture (the agricultural revolution) for industrialization is thus via the price of food and its role in the determination of the nominal wage cost for industrial employers. This assumes that food is not tradable, or imperfectly so, in the sense that TFP and factor deepening in domestic agriculture determine the domestic price of food. This is only partially true when there is international trade, although many of the most important staple food items remain largely non-tradable because they correspond to local tastes and are not traded (such as cassava and banana plantain in Sub-Saharan Africa), are perishable and costly to transport, or there are huge transaction costs insulating domestic markets (e.g. in landlocked African countries with poor infrastructure).

China is a good illustration of industrialization under the dual-economy model with surplus labor and rapid productivity growth in agriculture (Young, 2003). The dismantling of the commune system and the household-responsibility system that allocated land to farm households created incentives for rapid productivity growth in agriculture. Market reforms gave farmers the freedom to sell surplus food on the domestic market as a national non-tradable. This helped keep the price of food and nominal wages for industry low while labor was rapidly drawn toward industrial employment. Because urban migration was restricted through the Hukou labor-registration system, industry (in the form of township enterprises) went to rural towns in search of cheap labor. Agriculture could thus successfully fulfill its archetype role for industrialization: offer abundant labor that could be removed from agriculture with no decline in agricultural output thanks to technological change, and provide cheap food to keep labor costs low and incentives to invest in industry high.

THE ROLE OF AGRICULTURE IN GROWTH: OTHER MODELS

There are other reasons why investing in agriculture may be an important source of growth. This could be investing to raise TFP growth, or starting to invest in agriculture, making capital a factor of production in agriculture as it is in industry, thus transcending the dual-economy simplification. Four reasons to invest in agriculture for GDP growth at early stages of development have been invoked.

Agriculture as a growth sector

The first reason to invest in agriculture as a source of growth is mechanical: since agriculture is a large sector in poor countries (typically 30 to 50 percent of GDP at early stages of structural transformation, as we have seen in Figure 8.5 on structural transformation), growth in that sector has a high weight in aggregate growth, justifying public investment in agriculture. If we can get agriculture to grow faster, it will simply be reflected in higher GDP growth. Gollin *et al.* (2002) analyzed the growth experiences of 62 developing countries over the period 1960–90. They found that growth in agricultural productivity was important in explaining aggregate growth in GDP per worker. Specifically, the direct contribution of agriculture to GDP growth accounted for 54 percent of observed growth. Through the release of labor for employment in the other sectors of the economy, agricultural productivity gains accounted indirectly for another 29 percent of GDP growth. Non-agricultural growth, independent of the direct and indirect contributions of agriculture, accounted only for the remaining 17 percent.

Inter-sectoral linkages and growth-multiplier effects

The second reason to invest in agriculture is because agriculture has large growth-multiplier effects on other sectors of the economy. These growth effects occur through forward and backward inter-sectoral linkages, initially analyzed by Hirschman (1958) to design his "unbalanced growth" strategy, where investments are targeted at sectors with strong linkages (Chapter 3). Forward linkage effects occur when agricultural outputs are used as inputs in non-agricultural production such as agro-processing and processed-food marketing. Backward linkage effects occur through the demand from agriculture for intermediate inputs such as fertilizers and marketing services that can be produced domestically. In China, for instance, over the 1980–2001 period, $1 of value-added growth in agriculture is estimated to have induced $1 of growth in non-agriculture, while $1 of growth in non-agriculture only induced $0.18 of growth in agriculture (World Bank, 2007). For Africa, measurements tend to agree on the existence of agricultural-growth multipliers of the order of 1.3 to 1.5, meaning that $1 of value-added in agriculture generates an additional 30 to 50 cents of value-added in non-agriculture (Christiaensen *et al.*, 2011). In this perspective, investing in agriculture at early stages of development is seen as effective targeting of scarce investment funds. It works particularly well in relatively closed economies because trade dampens the growth-linkage effects of agricultural growth: exports can compete with forward linkage effects and imports with backward linkage effects.

Consumption linkages

The third reason is that initial stages of industrialization tend to be oriented toward the production of non-tradable industrial goods such as those in agro-industry (processed foods, beer), low-quality plastic (buckets, toys), and metal goods (roofing, transport carts, bicycles). The market for these goods will expand with incomes earned by farmers.

349

A rapidly growing agriculture, fueled by productivity growth, thus creates expanding markets for industry through local effective demand. The limiting factor to industrialization is thus seen to be demand as opposed to productivity growth or factor deepening. This is Mellor's (1998) "Agriculture on the Road to Industrialization," and Adelman's (1984) "agriculture demand-led industrialization," or ADLI. The role of effective demand creation for local industry is verified by the fact that a good harvest, as, for example, in India following a favorable monsoon, is typically followed by a boom in local industry: "when agriculture performs, everything performs," as the saying goes. Using Social Accounting Matrices (SAM) for 27 countries, Vogel (1994) examined the strength of the linkages between agriculture and the rest of the economy at different stages of economic development. He finds that backward and consumption linkages are strong at early stages and that demand created by rising rural incomes accounts for 70 percent of these linkages. Forward linkages become important at later stages when agro-industry and food processing start to emerge. This approach to industrialization through productivity gains in agriculture and consumption linkages— typical of SAM multiplier models—is appealing, but it assumes that there are no constraints on the supply side of industry (i.e. that there is excess capacity in production) in responding to market opportunities, a short-term possibility at best.

Competitive advantage

Finally, thinking, for instance, of Sub-Saharan Africa, the fourth reason is the idea that agriculture and agro-industry are sources of comparative and competitive advantage for these economies not offered by modern industry and services. This is based on three observations (Eifert *et al.*, 2005).

The first is that Africa has factor endowments rich in natural resources and in unskilled or semi-skilled labor, giving it comparative advantage in primary products (agriculture, mining, and petroleum) and agro-industry. Mining and petroleum exports have in the last 15 years helped many African economies be among the fastest-growing in the world. But agriculture is more labor-intensive and offers the exceptional opportunity of being very effective for poverty reduction due to its smallholder structure.

The second is that high indirect costs for doing business are less limiting on agriculture and agro-industry than they are on more sophisticated branches of manufacturing (as pursued in China) or high-tech tradable services (as pursued in India). Evidence of these costs is obtained from the *Investment Climate Assessments* (World Bank, 2008). They show that African manufactures have difficulty competing internationally due to poor transport infrastructure, unreliable sources of power, lack of telecommunications, and the high cost of security. They also lack the legal and financial services and the regulatory institutions needed to compete with many middle-income developing countries where these institutions are better established.

The third is the importance of economies of scale and of spillover effects in clusters of economic activity (see Chapter 9). They make entry for newcomers difficult, calling for a Big Push approach to industrial investment. Clusters exist in agro-industry—for instance, horticultural exports in Kenya and Senegal and cut flowers in Ethiopia— but rarely in other sectors of manufacturing.

The conclusion of this fourth argument in support of agriculture as an engine of growth is that opportunities exist to pursue this approach in Sub-Saharan Africa, and that labor-intensive agro-industry can offer a road to learning and achieving scale toward diversified manufacturing. Resource-abundant countries like Chile, Malaysia, Australia, and the US relied on resource-processing industries in their early stages of industrialization. Current high prices on international food and agriculture markets further reinforce the proposition that investing in agriculture and agro-industry as a source of growth, both for exports and import substitution, can be good business for aggregate growth and pro-poor income generation (see Chapter 18).

CONCEPTS SEEN IN THIS CHAPTER

ICOR
Harrod–Domar growth rate of an economy
Financing gap and role of foreign aid for growth
Total Factor Productivity (TFP) growth
Factor deepening
Solow growth accounting formula and the unexplained residual
Solow steady state ($y*$, $k*$) and transition growth
Technological change (TFP growth) as an international public good
Advantage of backwardness
Innovation possibility frontier (IPF)
Technological leapfrogging
Structural transformation of the economy
Dual economy or dualism
Surplus labor
Classical dual-economy model (Lewis)
Lewis turning point
Neoclassical dual-economy model (Jorgenson)
Ranis–Fei and Lele–Mellor dual-economy model with surplus labor and food prices
Role of technological change in agriculture for growth
Forward and backward linkages
Consumption linkages
ADLI (agriculture demand-led industrialization)

REVIEW QUESTIONS. EXPLAINING ECONOMIC GROWTH: THE MACRO LEVEL

1. The Harrod–Domar growth model: define the ICOR. How is the rate of economic growth determined in the Harrod–Domar model? What are the model's policy recommendations to accelerate growth?

2. The Solow growth model: how does the model specify the role of productivity growth vs. factor deepening in explaining output growth? How do you use the model to measure the role of technological change (TFP growth) in explaining part of the observed growth rate?

3. Why does the Solow model predict convergence in GDPpc between LDCs and MDCs? Are the assumptions used to reach this result credible? Does the prediction fit the facts?

4. Dual-economy models
    4.1. Lewis classical dual-economy model with surplus labor.
    4.2. Jorgenson neoclassical dual-economy model with full employment.
    4.3. Lele–Mellor mixed dual economy with unemployment and a role for agriculture.

For each model: what are the assumptions? What are the policy recommendations to accelerate growth?

REFERENCES

Adelman, Irma. 1984. "Beyond Export-led Growth." *World Development* 12(9): 937–49.

Baumol, William. 1986. "Productivity Growth, Convergence, and Welfare: What the Long-run Data Show." *American Economic Review* 76(5): 1072–85.

Chenery, Hollis, and Michael Bruno. 1962. "Development Alternatives in an Open Economy: The Case of Israel." *Economic Journal* 72(285): 79–103.

Chenery, Hollis, and Lance Taylor. 1968. "Development Patterns: Among Countries and Over Time." *Review of Economics and Statistics* 50(3): 391–416.

Christiaensen, Luc, Lionel Demery, and Jesper Kühl. 2011. "The (Evolving) Role of Agriculture in Poverty Reduction—An Empirical Perspective." *Journal of Development Economics* 96(2): 239–54.

de Janvry, Alain, and Elisabeth Sadoulet. 2010. "Agriculture for Development in Africa: Business-as-Usual or New Departure." *Journal of African Economics* 19(supplement 2): ii7–ii39.

Domar, Evsey. 1957. *Essays in the Theory of Economic Growth.* Oxford: Oxford University Press.

Easterly, William. 2002. *The Elusive Quest for Growth.* Cambridge, MA: MIT Press.

Easterly, William, and Ross Levine. 2001. "What Have We Learned from a Decade of Empirical Research on Growth? It's Not Factor Accumulation: Stylized Facts and Growth Models." *World Bank Economic Review* 15(2): 177–219.

ECOSOC (Department of Economic and Social Affairs). 2013. *International Migrant Stock: By Destination and Origin.* New York: UN, Population Division.

Eifert, Benn, Alan Gelb, and Vijaya Ramachandran. 2005. "Business Environment and Comparative Advantage in Africa: Evidence from the Investment Climate Data." Washington, DC: Center for Global Development Working Paper No. 56.

Feldstein, Martin, and Charles Horioka. 1980. "Domestic Saving and International Capital Flows." *Economic Journal* 90(356): 314–29.

Gerschenkron, Alexander. 1962. *Economic Backwardness in Historical Perspective: A Book of Essays.* Cambridge, MA: Harvard University Press.

Gollin, Douglas, Stephen Parente, and Richard Rogerson. 2002. "The Role of Agriculture in Development." *American Economic Review* 92(2): 160–4.

Hayami, Yujiro. 2001. *Development Economics: From Poverty to the Wealth of Nations*. New York: Oxford University Press.

Hayami, Yujiro, and Vernon Ruttan. 1971. *Agricultural Development: An International Perspective*. Baltimore: Johns Hopkins University Press.

Helpman, Elhanan. 2004. *The Mystery of Economic Growth*. Cambridge, MA: Harvard University Press.

Hirschman, Albert. 1958. *The Strategy of Economic Development*. New Haven, CT: Yale University Press.

Hsieh, Chang-Tai, and Peter Klenow. 2007. "Relative Prices and Relative Prosperity." *American Economic Review* 97(3): 562–85.

Jorgenson, Dale. 1967. "Surplus Agricultural Labor and the Development of a Dual Economy." *Oxford Economic Papers* 19(3): 288–312.

Kuznets, Simon. 1966. *Modern Economic Growth*. New Haven, CT: Yale University Press.

Lele, Uma, and John Mellor. 1981. "Technological Change, Distributive Bias, and Labor Transfers in a Two Sector Economy." *Oxford Economic Papers* 33(3): 426–41.

Lewis, Arthur. 1954. "Economic Development with Unlimited Supplies of Labor." *The Manchester School* 22(2): 139–91.

Lin, Justin Yifu. 2012. *Demystifying the Chinese Economy*. New York: Cambridge University Press.

Lipton, Michael. 1977. *Why Poor People Stay Poor: Urban Bias in World Development*. Cambridge, MA: Harvard University Press.

Lucas, Robert. 1990. "Why Doesn't Capital Flow from Rich to Poor Countries?" *American Economic Review* 80(2): 92–6.

Mellor, John. 1998. "Agriculture on the Road to Industrialization." In Carl Eicher and John Staatz (eds.), *International Agricultural Development*, 136–54. Baltimore: Johns Hopkins University Press.

Pritchett, Lant. 1997. "Divergence, Big Time." *Journal of Economic Perspectives* 11(3): 3–17.

Ranis, Gus, and John Fei. 1961. "A Theory of Economic Development." *American Economic Review* 51(4): 533–65.

Romer, Paul. 1990. "Endogenous Technological Change." *Journal of Political Economy* 98(5): S71–102.

Schultz, Theodore W. 1964. *Transforming Traditional Agriculture*. New Haven, CT: Yale University Press.

Sen, Amartya. 1967. "Surplus Labor in India: A Critique of Schultz's Statistical Test." *Economic Journal* 77(305): 154–61.

Solow, Robert. 1957. "Technical Change and the Aggregate Production Function." *Review of Economics and Statistics* 39(3): 312–20.

Timmer, Peter. 1988. "The Agricultural Transformation." In H. Chenery and T. N. Srinivasan (eds.), *Handbook of Development Economics*. Vol. 1, 275–303. Amsterdam: North Holland.

Vogel, Steve. 1994. "Structural Changes in Agriculture: Production Linkages in Agricultural Demand-led Industrialization." *Oxford Economic Papers* New Series 46(1): 136–56.

World Bank. 2007. *World Development Report 2008: Agriculture for Development*. Washington, DC.

World Bank. 2008. *Investment Climate Assessments.* Washington, DC.

World Bank. *World Development Indicators.* http://data.worldbank.org/indicator (accessed 2015).

Young, Alwyn. 1995. "The Tyranny of Numbers: Confronting the Statistical Realities of the East Asian Growth Experience." *Quarterly Journal of Economics* 110(3): 641–80.

Young, Alwyn. 2003. "Gold into Base Metals: Productivity Growth in the People's Republic of China during the Reform Period." *Journal of Political Economy* 111(1): 1220–61.

Solution to the Solow growth model

We give here a rigorous presentation of the Solow model and a derivation of its growth implications.

Consider a Cobb–Douglas production function for national income: $Y = AK^\alpha L^{1-\alpha}$ with constant returns to scale. Y is national income, K the stock of capital, and L the labor force with full employment. Because of constant returns to scale (the sum of the exponents to capital and labor in the Cobb–Douglas production function is equal to one), it can be written as: $Y/L = A(K/L)^\alpha$, where labor productivity Y/L is a function of capital intensity K/L, i.e. of the stock of capital per worker. Or, in lower-case notation, $y = Ak^\alpha$ with $y = Y/L$, $k = K/L$.

Using the savings–investment equation from the generic growth model:

$$S = sY = I \equiv \Delta K + \delta K_t = K_{t+1} - K_t + \delta K_t,$$

where s is the rate of savings and δ the rate of depreciation of capital. Hence the stock of capital in period $t + 1$ is:

$$K_{t+1} = (1 - \delta)K_t + sY_t,$$

or, in terms of capital intensity, $(K_{t+1}/L_t) = (1 - \delta)(K_t/L_t) + s(Y_t/L_t)$. The rate of population growth is n, i.e., $L_{t+1} = L_t(1+n)$. Replacing:

$$(K_{t+1}/L_{t+1})(1 + n) = (1 - \delta)(K_t/L_t) + s(Y_t/L_t) \text{ or, in lower-case notation,}$$

$$k_{t+1}(1 + n) = (1 - \delta)k_t + sy_t.$$

Hence the change in the stock of capital per worker is:

$$\Delta k = k_{t+1} - k_t = sy_t - (n + \delta)k_t.$$

We thus see that if savings is larger than depreciation and the erosion of capital per worker due to population growth, i.e. $sy_t > (n + \delta)k_t$, the stock of capital per worker and output per worker are growing. By contrast, if $sy_t < (n + \delta)k_t$, they are shrinking. This implies that the model predicts the existence of a steady state level $(k*, y*)$ where the amount of capital per worker does not change over time, and,

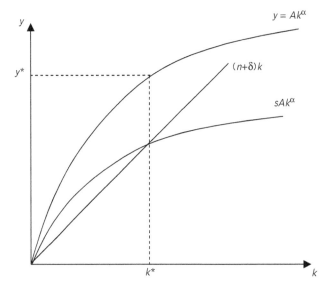

Figure 8.A1 *Steady-state solution (k*, y*) of the Solow growth model*

correspondingly, neither does the productivity of labor. For economies that start with a $k < k*$, there is growth to reach the steady state, what is called "transition growth," but all economies stop growing once they have reached the steady state $(k*, y*)$. The steady state is thus obtained for $\Delta k = 0$, i.e., when $sy_t = sAk^\alpha = (n + \delta)k$.

This steady state is seen in Figure 8.A1 as the intersection $(k*, y*)$ between the straight line $(n + \delta)k$ and the concave function sAk^α, where curvature comes from the decreasing marginal productivity of capital per worker in the Cobb–Douglas production function.

The following are properties of this solution:

1. At the steady state, k and y are, by definition, constant at $k*$ and $y*$. Population grows at the rate n, the savings rate is s, and the depreciation rate is δ, while capital intensity and labor productivity are constant. With $y = Y/L = y*$ constant,

$$Y = y * L, \text{ and } \frac{dY}{Y} = \dot{Y} = y * \frac{dL}{L} = y * n.$$

As a consequence, the growth of national income at the steady state is only a function of the population (labor force) growth rate n. It is not affected by the rate of saving nor by the depreciation rate.

2. Countries converge to the steady state through growth that will be faster the further away they started from the steady state. This is the "transition growth path" to steady state. With

$$\Delta k = sAk^\alpha - (n + \delta)k,$$

the growth rate in k is:

$$\frac{\Delta k}{k} = \dot{k} = sAk^{\alpha-1} - (n + \delta).$$

This convergence to zero growth at the steady state is represented in Figure 8.A2. It shows that the growth rate of capital, and hence of national income α, is larger the further the country is below the steady state level. Initially poorer countries thus grow faster than initially wealthier countries. This is how income convergence is achieved.

3. The level at which the steady state is achieved varies as follows: it increases with the rate of savings s, TFPA, and the share of capital in national income, all of which shift the concave function in Figure 8.A1 upward, and hence also the $(y*, k*)$ intersection; and it decreases with the rate of depreciation of capital δ (that shifts the concave function downward) and with the rate of population growth n (that shifts the straight line upward in Figure 8.A1, and hence brings the intersection $(y*, k*)$ downward).

4. TFPA shifts the steady state upward in Figure 8.A3. It consequently induces more growth as it places the economies further away from the steady state, inducing more "transition growth."

5. The rate of saving increases per capita income at the steady state. Two countries, 1 and 2, with identical A, n, and δ will have a ratio of per capita income equal to:

$$\frac{y_1}{y_2} = \left(\frac{s_1}{s_2}\right)^{\frac{\alpha}{1-\alpha}}.$$

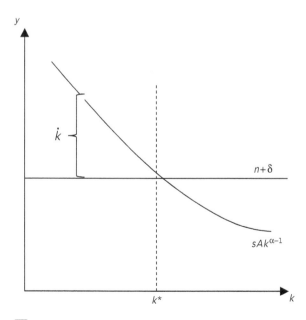

Figure 8.A2 *Rate of convergence to the steady state*

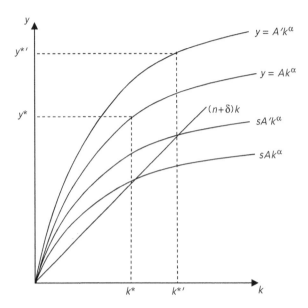

Figure 8.A3 *Role of TFP growth in inducing more transition growth*

Hence the country with the higher rate of saving has the higher per capita income. This can be used to explain why countries with high rates of saving such as in East Asia achieve higher levels of income at the steady state.

Endogenous economic growth

TAKE-HOME MESSAGES FOR CHAPTER 9

1. Neoclassical growth theory identifies the rate of technological progress as the primary driver of long-term economic growth, but offers few insights about what determines it. The Solow prediction on universal convergence in per capita income levels across countries is at odds with observed facts on selective convergence. The theory of endogenous economic growth addresses these issues.

2. One of the biggest challenges to induce investment and achieve successful growth is coordination across firms to exploit production complementarities and reach a high-level investment equilibrium.

3. Endogenous growth theories aim at explaining the origins of productivity gains by constructing models where firms invest in knowledge, making productivity growth endogenous.

4. The main result of endogenous growth is the existence of increasing returns to scale in aggregate output. This implies divergence in growth rates of per capita income across countries.

5. Because investment in research creates positive spillover effects across firms, the state is called upon to intervene to internalize positive externalities and induce the socially optimal level of investment in research. Spillover effects are enhanced by the proximity of firms in economic clusters, implying that firm location can be an important determinant of productivity growth.

6. To keep up with technological opportunities, a country should constantly pursue technological upgrading consistent with comparative advantage. The "new structural economics" identifies the role of the state in managing this process.

7. Innovation is a complex process, with a key role for behavior in terms of entrepreneurship, the formation of expectations, and learning both by doing and from others.

EXPLAINING GROWTH

Lessons from exogenous growth

The classical and neoclassical growth models proposed respectively by Harrod–Domar and Solow identify technology as a major determinant of aggregate economic growth: a low ICOR (a high marginal productivity of capital) in Harrod–Domar, and a high rate of TFP growth in Solow. Yet these models are incomplete since they do not explain where technology comes from nor how the flow of new technologies can be enhanced. In the dual-economy models, we saw greater specificity in the agriculture–industry interactions and the importance of TFP growth in agriculture for successful industrialization, but technological progress in agriculture remains equally exogenous. Clearly, if we are to give such great importance to technology in explaining growth, we need to have theories that are more explicit at explaining how technology is produced, adopted, and diffused. This is what we look at in this chapter. This includes issues of coordination of investment across sectors, increasing returns to scale when technology generation is endogenous, limited access to international technology when there are intellectual property rights, and the role of policy in promoting the generation, adoption, and diffusion of technology.

In recent years, new thinking has emerged to address the issue of the role of technology in growth. The objectives of these advances have been to:

- *Endogenize technological change*, i.e. explain in particular the origins of the Solow residual that determines the long-run rate of growth in the economy since there are decreasing marginal products to factor deepening.
- *Explain conditional economic convergence* across countries due to uneven technological progress, as opposed to the Solow model's prediction of universal convergence.
- *Explain why the availability and use of technology differ* across countries (as opposed to Solow's diffusion of technology as an unimpeded international public good), creating a "technological divide," and in particular the role of intellectual property rights (IPR) in stimulating investment in research and limiting access to technology.
- *Explain the role of the state in promoting technological innovations*. Market failures (positive externalities, spillover effects) and coordination failures in investment across firms call for a role for the state in public investment in sources of growth such as R&D, education, and infrastructure.

Conditional convergence and the role of policy

There have been multiple attempts at testing empirically the predictions of the Solow model on convergence in per capita income levels. If there is convergence, then the initial level of income should negatively affect the rate of growth of the economy toward the common steady state: countries with initially lower levels of per capita income y should grow faster than countries with initially higher levels of y. This can be tested in a cross-country regression framework between the growth rate in income $\dot{y}$ and the initial level of income y as follows:

$$\dot{y}_{i,(t,t+T)} = \alpha + \beta y_{it} + \varepsilon_{it},$$

where i is country, t is year, and ε an error term uncorrelated with y. $\dot{y}_{i,(t,t+T)}$ is country i's growth rate in per capita income measured over T years starting with year t. y_{it} is per capita income in base year t, the beginning of the period over which growth is measured. If there is convergence, then the regression coefficient β should be negative. If convergence is conditional on a set of initial (presumed exogenous) country characteristics X_{it}, then the equation to be estimated is:

$$\dot{y}_{i,(t,t+T)} = \alpha + \beta y_{it} + \gamma X_{it} + \varepsilon_{it}.$$

A negative estimated β will indicate that there is convergence once you control for the factors X that also influence growth. Finding out the X variables that allow you to reveal convergence is thus a weighty policy question that has motivated a large number of cross-country studies.

Conditional convergence

Following an earlier analysis by Barro (1991), Mankiw *et al.* (1992) used cross-country growth regressions to test the convergence hypothesis that derives from the Solow model. Using a sample of 22 OECD countries, they find that there has been convergence in per capita income over the period 1960–85, validating Solow. However, when the sample is extended to 75 countries including developing countries, β is no longer significantly different from zero and income convergence disappears, contradicting Solow. As we saw in Chapter 8, the Solow model suggests that the X variables in the income-growth equation should include the savings rate and the rate of population growth (a good example of how modeling is used to specify the econometric relation to be taken to the data). Mankiw *et al.* find that β becomes negative and significant when these variables are included in the growth regression. They also find that the explanatory power of the Solow income-growth equation is significantly increased by adding to the X variables the country's investment in human capital, an empirical discovery that will be key to formulation of the endogenous-growth model (see below). The "extended" Solow model thus includes the following X_{it} variables:

> the savings rate (with a positive effect on growth);
> the rate of population growth (with a negative effect);
> the rate of secondary education (with a positive effect).

This model predicts convergence, conditional on these additional variables. With this extension, the estimated rate of convergence toward the stationary-state per capita income is 2 percent per year, meaning that half of the per capita income gap between the stationary-state level and the initial level would be achieved in 35 years (using the "70 years rule" we saw in Chapter 1). In other words, if countries' savings rates, population-growth rates, and rates of schooling did not differ, then we would observe a tendency for per capita income in poor countries to grow faster than in rich ones. In this framework the force of convergence (the negative relationship between initial level of GDPpc and growth) is universal but other determinants of growth can enhance or impede it. This is the idea of conditional convergence.

Table 9.1 *Convergence in open but not in closed economies*

Average annual growth rate in per capita income (%)	Open countries	Closed countries
Rich countries	2.29	0.74
Poor countries	4.49	0.69

Source: Sachs and Warner, 1995.

Role of policy

Sachs and Warner (1995) showed that the strength of convergence itself could depend on the policy context, leading to heterogenous selective convergence. They looked at 111 countries with growth measured by the annual rate of change in per capita income over the 1970–89 period. They looked for the role of economic policies, particularly trade (degree of openness), rate of secondary education, rate of investment, and rate of inflation. Their main emphasis was on the role of trade openness. As shown in Table 9.1, they found that income grew faster in open rather than in closed economies, both rich and poor, but more so in the latter.

These results also show that there was no convergence among economies that were closed in the base period, but that there was strong convergence among economies that were open. Here, open is defined by several indicators including tariff barriers inferior to 40 percent, no state monopoly in exports, and an exchange-rate premium on the parallel market for foreign currency of less than 20 percent.

This and other studies provide reasonable empirical evidence that "good" policies are important for growth, and that rich countries tend to have better policies than most poor countries. Good policies include macro (low inflation), trade (high openness measured as (exports + imports)/GDP), fiscal (a low fiscal deficit), and monetary (no major overvaluation of the exchange rate) policies. The studies suffer, however, from a serious endogeneity problem in interpreting determinants as causal, as analyzed in Chapter 4. Policies are not country characteristics, but endogenous choices made by country governments that need to be explained in a theory of growth and eventual convergence. Why do some countries have better policies than others? And, in particular, can poor countries have good policies that will enable them to converge? This is a key question for convergence that needs to be answered. Endogenous growth is a step in that direction.

THE COORDINATION PROBLEM IN GROWTH

The multi-industry investment game

Because investment takes place in firms in different economic sectors that complement each other, the conditions for economic growth require solving a complex coordination problem. To appreciate this, consider the case of three sectors that were central to the industrial revolution in the US: coal, steel, and railroads.[1] Assume that

Coal		Railroad Invest Steel				Railroad Withhold investment Steel	
		Invest	Withhold			Invest	Withhold
	Invest	50, 50, 50	−100, 0, −100		Invest	−100, −100,0	−100, 0, 0
	Withhold	0, −100, −100	0, 0, −100		Withhold	0, −100, 0	0, 0, 0

Figure 9.1 *The multi-industry investment game*

		Steel	
		Invest	Withhold
Coal	Invest	50, 50	−100, 0
	Withhold	0, −100	0, 0

Figure 9.2 *Investment coordination game with two industries*

each industry is composed of one firm, with identical costs, prices, and capacity. There is a fixed investment cost of 100 LCU (local currency units) which is wasted if any of the other industries do not invest. The pay-off for each industry, if the other two invest, is 50 LCU. In this case, the three industries are engaged in an investment game with pay-offs indicated in Figure 9.1.

Each industry must choose between investing and withholding investment based on what it expects the other two industries to do. There are two strategic Nash equilibria[2] for this game: three-way mutual investment with pay-offs (50, 50, 50) for the coal, steel, and railroad industries respectively, or no investment with pay-offs (0, 0, 0). In any other situation, at least one party will opt out of investment, driving the solution to the no-investment equilibrium.

This game is a coordination (or assurance) game. To learn how to solve it, consider for simplicity the case where there are only two industries, Coal and Steel, with the pay-off matrix shown in Figure 9.2 extracted from Figure 9.1.

Finding the solution is as follows. Coal must decide whether to invest or not. It looks at Steel. If Steel invests, Coal gets 50 by investing and 0 by withholding. It will choose to invest. On the other hand, if Steel withholds, it loses 100 by investing and breaks even at 0 by withholding. It will choose to withhold. We now consider what Steel will decide. It looks at Coal. If Coal invests, Steel gets 50 by investing and 0 by withholding. It will choose to invest. If Coal withholds, it loses 100 by investing and breaks even at 0 by withholding. It will choose to withhold. The solution is thus that both industries always prefer to do the same thing as the other. The solution is either (invest, invest) or (withhold, withhold). This is a coordination game. If the two industries can coordinate by consulting with each other before playing the game, they will choose the (50, 50) option over the (0, 0) option, i.e. they both prefer to invest. The multi-industry investment game in Figure 9.1 is an extension of this same reasoning to three players. The (50, 50, 50) solution will be preferred by all partners over the (0, 0, 0) solution if they can coordinate.

This game reveals essential complexities of the economic-growth process. Four of the issues we discuss in this chapter are represented here.

The first and most important of these is *strategic interaction* or *interdependence* of investment decisions. Traditional growth models view investment as savings-driven, or decentralized and guided by some invisible hand representing countless independent firm decisions. In the multi-industry set-up analyzed here, none of the three firms can make a profit unless the other two do, and thus none will commit to investment unless the others do. Hence coordination in decision-making regarding investment by each industry is crucial for success. But how is coordination achieved?

The second issue is the importance of *information* and *expectations formation*. Since firms rarely move simultaneously, real investors must consider the risk of choosing their strategy without knowing exactly what or when the others will decide. Clearly, successful entrepreneurship requires not only good information, but also intuition and insight, what Keynes called "animal spirits."

The third issue is the *dichotomy of outcomes*, in this example between what are sometimes called low- and high-level equilibria—full industrialization or no industrialization—with no middle ground. With multiple equilibria, it is no surprise that industrialization will not be a smooth continuous process, but typically marked by leaps and bounds.

The fourth issue is the existence of *spillovers* or *network externalities* between economic activities, each of which relies on the viability of others for goods and services essential to its own survival. As a consequence, clustering of economic activity with better access to information and local spillover effects across firms and sectors may be essential, as, for instance, in Silicon Valley in California or the Wenzhou cluster in the Zhejiang province of China.

This coordination game is revealing of what may drive growth, a world already quite different from the ones represented in the classical and neoclassical growth models. If it is indeed important, we need to understand how coordination is achieved.

The role of coordination: multiple equilibria in development

From a development-policy perspective, achieving coordination is key for growth. Clearly, an economy has higher growth potential if complementary investments can be facilitated, while low-level equilibrium threatens stagnation. We shall see that many physical and institutional features of developing countries undermine the potential for private coordination, making the need for public-sector facilitation all the greater. Unfortunately, public institutions can be weak in both coordination capacity and in mobilizing the financial resources that may be needed to provide incentives and overcome coordination barriers. We thus uncover a fundamental dilemma of growth in developing countries: the role of the state in coordinating and mobilizing resources is all the more important precisely where it is weakest. The importance of fixing governance for growth will thus be a key lesson from endogenous-growth theories, an issue we will address in Chapter 21.

A general example of the coordination problem is given in Figure 9.3, which depicts the strategic investment decision by an individual firm *i* subject to its expectations

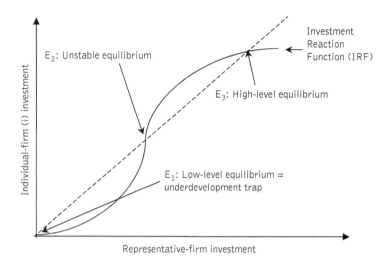

Figure 9.3 *Multiple equilibria: the investment-coordination problem*

about investment levels by the other firms in the industry. We assume that multiple firm commitments are necessary for success because of industry linkages, so this firm will not invest if it expects no investment by the other firms. Thus its Investment Reaction Function (IRF) begins at the origin, which is the same low-level equilibrium $(0, 0)$ that we saw in the multi-industry investment game above. This represents the investment stagnation or underdevelopment trap in which a developing country may find itself. Even when they expect others to begin investing, individual firms will under-commit (IRF below the 45° diagonal) because they are risk-averse and want more familiarity with the market and profitability conditions. At representative firm investment levels below E_2, this tendency to under-commit keeps the economy in the underdevelopment trap $(0, 0)$ at E_1. If, by contrast, individual firms expect other firms to invest above the E_2 threshold, there would be a sea change in their expectations, motivating over commitment and driving collective investment to the high-level equilibrium E_3, allowing economic growth to occur. Call E_1 underdevelopment, and E_3 development, from the perspective of investment, and we have a suggestive theory of growth and development that has been widely used.

Obviously, growth-oriented developmental states aspire to the latter outcome, but many in the developing world may be trapped in the former. This theory of multiple equilibria, with the need to call on *coordination* to move from the low- to the high-level equilibrium, as opposed to reliance on market forces, is a central proposition in endogenous-growth theories. This Big Push (coordinated investment effort) idea is not new (see Murphy *et al.*, 1989; Bardhan, 1995). It had been central to development theories since the very beginning of development economics with the contributions of pioneers such as Rosenstein-Rodan (1943), Leibenstein (1957), and Hirschman (1958), discussed in Chapter 3. The difference between the low- and high-level development outcomes is, importantly, due to a combination of structural and behavioral factors with a potentially crucial role for the state as a coordinating agent, if it can acquire the capacity to do that. This model is extremely revealing in showing that not only do markets matter for growth, but also that non-market institutions able to solve the coordination problem have a crucial role to play.

STRUCTURAL DETERMINANTS OF GROWTH

As we have seen, many economic realities in developing countries do not conform to the assumptions of perfectly competitive markets. The most tangible departures from the perfect-competition model have to do with: (1) the role of investment in knowledge, and the increasing returns that these investment create, (2) the agglomeration of firms in geographical clusters to benefit from spillover effects, and (3) the "new structural economics" with continuous technological upgrading. We address each of these issues in turn.

Endogenous-growth theory: investing in knowledge and increasing returns

We have seen that the Solow growth model relies on technological change as the only source of long-term growth in per capita income, yet takes technological change to be exogenous. The theory of endogenous growth proposed by Romer (1990) extends the Solow model by introducing a mechanism that explains the origin of technological change, i.e. it makes the A factor in the Solow model an endogenous outcome. In this model, firms invest in sources of productivity growth, seeking extra profits. Hence technology is not an international public good freely available to all in a perfectly competitive global economy, as in the Solow model, but the costly outcome of firms investing in research and employing labor in research activities to try to capture monopoly profits protected by patents. In addition, research is a cumulative process, and the growth of knowledge associated with a given level of employment in research activities is proportional to the stock of knowledge already available in the country, creating economies of scale.

At country level, a part L_Y of the total labor force L is employed in the production sector, where it generates the output Y, and the other part L_A is employed in the research sector, where it generates TFP A, with $L = L_A + L_Y$.

In the Solow model, the production function was:

$$Y = Af(K, L) = AK^{\alpha} L^{1-\alpha},$$

where f has constant returns to scale: doubling K and L would double output Y, while each factor (holding the other factor constant) has a decreasing marginal product. Technological change is Hicks neutral on factor use as it is multiplicative of the production function, shifting upward the production function without affecting the relative marginal productivity of factors at a given K/L ratio.

In the Romer model, the production function is:

$$Y = f(K, A(L_A)L_Y) = K^{\alpha}(A(L_A)L_Y)^{1-\alpha}.$$

Technological change is Hicks labor saving in that it increases the marginal productivity of L_Y relative to that of capital at a given K/L ratio. The labor input in the production function is now AL_Y, the product of the accumulated stock of knowledge A and productive labor L_Y. TFPA is thus formulated as a "labor augmenting" technological change. As a consequence, if A grows because more L_A is applied to the generation of A, then f displays increasing returns to scale. The gain in productivity ΔA coming from technology and other improvements in knowledge is assumed to be proportional to the level of productivity A already achieved:

$$\Delta A = A\delta L_A,$$

where δ is a technical coefficient that relates employment in research to the research outcome. This means that the increase in A for a given L_A rises with the past stock of knowledge A. This is the main assumption of the model and it has drastic implications for convergence and for access to sources of productivity growth for developing countries. The growth perspective is much bleaker for the developing countries than in the Solow world of perfect markets and unimpeded access to technology. The features of the two models are compared in Table 9.2.

First, if there are increasing returns to scale, this rules out convergence. As knowledge generates more knowledge, advanced countries that already have a higher stock of knowledge grow faster than developing economies. The contrasted predictions of the Solow and endogenous-growth models for international labor flows are shown in Figure 9.4. As a rule, labor (and similarly capital) should flow from low-value-marginal-product-of-labor (VMP$_L$) countries to high VMP$_L$ countries since VMP$_L$ = wage. According to Solow (Figure 9.4a), with decreasing returns labor would move from MDCs to LDCs, where marginal returns are still very high, and induce convergence. As we know, this is not what we observe (Lucas, 1988). According to endogenous growth (Figure 9.4b), with labor-augmenting technological change creating increasing returns to scale, labor should move from LDCs to MDCs, accelerating divergence. While this is restricted by controls on international labor migration, this is indeed what we know labor does and would like to do more.

Second, because knowledge is protected by IPR, which are necessary to create incentives for firms to invest in research and derive profits from their investments, it

Table 9.2 *Solow and endogenous-growth models compared*

Model structure	Solow model	Endogenous-growth model
Production function	$Y = Af(K, L)$	$Y = f(K, A(L_A)L_Y)$
Technological change ΔA	Hicks neutral, exogenous	Labor-saving, endogenous
Origin of technological change	International public good	Firm investment of L_Y in R&D
Market structure	Perfect competition	Monopoly power (patents)
Returns to scale	Constant	Increasing due to $\Delta A = A\delta L_A$
Model predictions		
Income growth across countries	Convergence	Divergence
Predicted international labor flows	From MDCs to LDCs	From LDCs to MDCs

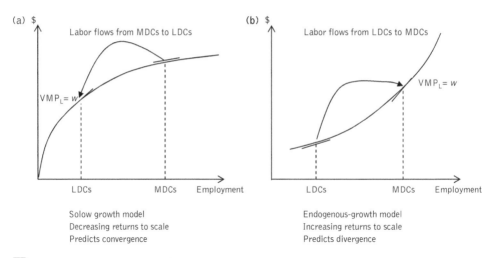

Figure 9.4 *Contrasted predictions of the Solow (a) and endogenous-growth (b) models for international labor flows*

is a private instead of a public good, at least for as long as patent protection lasts, typically 20 years. As a result, technological advances are trapped in the MDC setting where they originated.

Jones and Romer (2010) provide evidence of the importance of TFP as a source of growth. Figure 9.5 shows that there exists a close cross-country relation between TFP and GDPpc. TFP is calculated as a labor-augmenting technological change, as in the Romer model above. Country TFP and GDPpc are measured relative to the US, which thus has coordinates of 1 on the two axes of Figure 9.5.

The endogenous-growth model may, however, be too pessimistic about reality. As we saw in Chapter 2, many initially low per capita income countries have successfully converged in GDPpc with the industrialized countries. While frontier technology is privately costly, accessing technology that has become generic after 20 years is free for latecomers, allowing technological leapfrogging, even with a lag relative to the potential first best, as we saw in Chapter 8. OEI strategies provide a mechanism to access frontier technology as foreign direct investment brings knowledge developed in other countries—and, in many cases, IPR are not enforced in developing countries (witness the extensive counterfeiting of brands) or special licensing is granted with the idea that markets are segmented (as, for example, for some pharmaceutical products), opening the possibility of widespread imitation with no research costs.

The model shows that productivity gains accelerate as knowledge begets more knowledge. What the model does not tell us, however, is how rich countries became rich: namely, how did they start acquiring the knowledge advantage that they now have? We need to understand the genesis of industrialization—endogenous growth can then tell us how the process will accelerate based on increasing returns to scale once unequal initial conditions have been established. In that sense, the Romer endogenous-growth model falls short of providing us with a theory of development for initiating growth. It is better as a growth model for today's industrialized countries, and was indeed developed for this purpose.

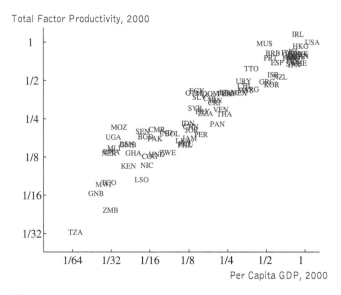

Figure 9.5 *Cross-country relation between GDPpc and TFP, 2000. GDPpc and TFP relative to USA*

Source: Jones and Romer, 2010.

A third, very important implication of the model is that productivity growth has large spillover effects across firms, as firms benefit from others' research discoveries. As a consequence, no firm completely internalizes the benefit of its own investment in research in spite of IPR. This calls for government intervention, as individual firms will tend to underinvest in research relative to the social optimum. Endogenous growth thus brings into the story not only market failures associated with the search for monopoly profits protected by IPR, but also market failures associated with positive externalities in research. This calls for a role for the state to induce higher levels of investment in research through grants or public-sector research in order to compensate for the positive externalities created by each firm.

The policy implications of this growth model are important, but quite different for MDCs and LDCs. Because markets do not accurately price the value of innovation in firms' products, and there is generally no market for the externalities created, a competitive market will underinvest in activities of this kind. This has two immediate implications: on the one hand, technology leaders must invest in R&D as a public good in order to sustain their leadership; on the other, followers have a strong incentive to freeride on existing innovations. Latecomer industrial economies like China can capture R&D benefits at a substantial discount by adopting existing MDC technologies, which in many cases are home-delivered by FDI, thus leapfrogging over the technological stages that MDC firms had to go through, a huge advantage to achieve rapid convergence.

In this perspective, LDCs' resource-cost advantages—low wages, cheap natural resources, etc.—are essentially bartered for relatively scarce advanced technology. These technologies, in addition to producing high-quality goods, confer a variety of positive learning externalities for domestic entrepreneurs, including advanced skills, international supply-chain integration, and attendant global-production, marketing, and quality standards. In this context, governments may have a strong incentive to facilitate international partnerships to capture more extensive learning opportunities for domestic entrepreneurs. This is how the OEI strategy that we analyzed in Chapter 7 can serve to not only industrialize but also as an industrialization strategy to promote the emergence of a domestic entrepreneurial class.

The role of geographical clusters of firms: spillover effects across firms

This is another important implication of endogenous-growth theory. Given spillover effects across firms, location can be an important determinant of productivity growth. When related firms operate in proximity to one another, forming geographical clusters of economic activity, spillovers are more likely to occur, conferring network externalities that can accelerate average growth rates relative to firms operating in isolation (Porter, 1998). This localized networking offers firms increased market access, local labor pools with specialized skills, joint-use infrastructure, and shared community resources. It is well known that competitors set up next to each other when they want to capture a larger market share. Nicholas Kaldor, the UK economist, observed that medieval cities had streets that specialized in particular crafts. Two of the most famous modern examples of clusters are the industrial districts in the Po Valley in Italy (Piore and Sable, 1990) and Silicon Valley in California. The Wenzhou cluster in the Zhejiang province of China is also famous for its concentration of entrepreneurs. It is the origin of 25 percent of the shoes and 50 percent of the eyeglasses and cigarette lighters produced in China, a success due to proximity of hundreds of firms in the same industry, which benefit from spillovers in market discovery (Strauss *et al.*, 2009). Other clusters in China specialize in socks, buttons, lighting appliances, and pumps. The recognized advantages of these industrial clusters or agglomeration economies are: (1) information spillovers, (2) the division and specialization of labor among enterprises producing parts, components, and final products, and (3) the development of skilled labor markets (Otsuka and Sonobe, 2009). However, a disadvantage for individual entrepreneurs is the high rate of imitation that rapidly erases rents for innovators. This of course creates strong incentives for the leading firms to keep innovating to remain ahead of close competitors. One can easily see how clusters of economic activity are an instrument both of growth and of economic divergence.

The new structural economics: technological upgrading

The "new structural economics" proposed by Justin Lin (2011) is an open-economy growth strategy based on the continuous industrial and technological upgrading of an economy, consistent with its changing comparative advantages. Upgrading means that the country continuously needs to reconsider and anticipate which industries should form its leading sector, and which technologies these sectors should be using. The leading sector could be agro-industry, textiles, home appliances, electronics, the car and aircraft industries, etc. It is likely that these will be used sequentially as the leading sector as countries learn and factor-price ratios change toward more costly labor and cheaper capital. Technology may be more or less capital intensive. Industrial and technological upgrading thus needs a dynamic private sector that will invest the most appropriate technology in the leading sector. However, this will not occur as a product of market forces (laissez-faire) alone; an effective facilitating state is needed for two reasons, both associated with market failures. The first is that there are positive information externalities associated with investing in economic innovations (upgraded sectors and technologies). As a consequence, the first mover has a disadvantage that needs to be compensated for by government subsidies to avoid underinvestment. The facilitating state should thus provide "smart nudges" to the firms that lead the upgrading. The second is that there are coordination failures in moving up the industrial and technological ladder in accordance with comparative advantage. It is necessary to adjust the country's endowments such as human capital, infrastructure, business environment, and legal institutions so they support the proposed industrial and technological upgrading. This requires complex coordination that only a facilitating state can provide. Backwardness is an advantage as it helps the country use technologies and introduce industries already developed in more advanced countries. This upgrading in turn redefines the country's competitive advantage that builds on its comparative advantage.

Smart nudging through protection and subsidies in line with the country's current comparative advantage is different from ISI, which ignores comparative advantage. It is also different from investing in capital-intensive heavy industries (the Soviet two-sector model implemented in India and Egypt in the 1960s) or in advanced sectors (the computer industry in Brazil, the aircraft industry in Indonesia) that ignore current relative-price ratios (cheap labor, expensive capital) and defy comparative advantage. According to Lin, these policies created the basis for rent-seeking in maintaining protection and subsidies as opposed to establishing competitive firms in an open-economy context.

Critics of the new structural economics have noted that it is heavily reliant on the capacity of the state, while lacking a theory of the state as to how to achieve this capacity. In addition, the sectors that may lose from state-led upgrading need to be compensated, as sunken capital does not have the flexibility to be reallocated to the emerging competitive sectors. Finally, social assistance is needed to help shelter those who are vulnerable to the restructuring, both to provide incentives for change and to avoid rising poverty. The new structural economics is appealing and matches the growth strategy followed by China, but it is incomplete in how it can be applied to countries with weak state capacity and weak social-safety nets.

Toward a unified growth theory

Galor (2011) recently proposed an extension of the endogenous-growth model into a unified growth theory that takes into account the long-term interactions between demographic forces, technological progress, human-capital formation, and selective convergence. He starts from the Malthusian trap, where lack of technological progress in agriculture holds the population in check, the economy is stagnant, and workers

371

are at subsistence level. This is the condition that has prevailed over the long run for humanity. The social cost of stagnation, however, induces a search for technological progress to escape from the Malthusian trap. Initial technological progress creates a demand for investment in human capital: namely, education, skills, and health. Increased demand for human capital shifts the demand for children from quantity to quality. Decreasing fertility rates are the engine for a demographic transformation, with falling birth rates catching up with falling death rates and resulting in lower rates of population growth. This in turn helps accelerate the rate of TFP growth, as in endogenous-growth theory. Sustained growth in successful countries creates a convergence club. Rising inequality across countries is the outcome, with large segments of world population converging in per capita income with the advanced countries, and others left behind in poverty in stagnant countries.

BEHAVIORAL DETERMINANTS OF GROWTH

The production, availability, and use of technology are significantly influenced by structural considerations, but, ultimately, it is human behavior that determines innovation, adoption, and diffusion. At all levels of technology development and use, differences in behavior—depending on characteristics that vary with place and social context—help explain technological disparities and their attendant growth effects. We look at three aspects of behavior that affect investment and growth: entrepreneurship, the formation of expectations, and the process of learning.

Entrepreneurship

Entrepreneurship, widely stressed in the endogenous-growth literature that derives from the classical writings of Schumpeter (1961), is an important behavioral trait for successful growth (Aghion and Howitt, 1997). Entrepreneurship is defined as self-employment instead of wage employment, an initiative that will lead to enterprise start-ups, contributing to economic growth if it succeeds. According to Schumpeter, the entrepreneur is a coordinator of production, an innovator, the creator of new firms. In a developing-country context, however, where open unemployment is not possible due to lack of social protection programs (such as unemployment insurance), self-employment has two motivations: one is "entrepreneurship by necessity," as an alternative to unemployment, typically in the informal sector; the other is "entrepreneurship by opportunity," driven by profit-seeking, typically in the formal sector. We thus expect the existence of a U-curve between self-employment and GDPpc, which will be high at low levels of GDPpc when self-employment serves for subsistence, decline as more formal employment becomes more extensively available, and rise as opportunities for profit-driven entrepreneurship become more widespread.

An individual will choose entrepreneurship over wage employment if the return from the former is larger than that from the latter (Naudé, 2014). This can be written as:

$$pA\theta f(L) + \eta - wL - K > wL + \mu,$$

where p is the price of the product, A is TFP, θ is entrepreneurial ability, $f(.)$ the production function in the firm created by the entrepreneur, L labor allocated to entrepreneurial activities or wage work, η non-pecuniary benefits from entrepreneurship, w the wage in employment, K start-up costs, and μ other benefits derived from wage employment. This simple choice equation allows us to determine the policies that will help promote entrepreneurship, which can be regrouped into three categories.

The first is entrepreneurial ability θ. This is a trait of character that is particularly difficult to understand and to induce, associated with risk-taking, self-confidence, and the belief that success can reward effort. Education, for instance, has an ambiguous role in entrepreneurship. A higher level of education increases the expected return from entrepreneurship, in particular as it helps to address market failures. However, it also raises the wage in employment, which in turn decreases entrepreneurship. Highly educated people may thus prefer wage employment to self-employment. Wealth may increase entrepreneurship by reducing exposure to credit-market failures (Banerjee and Newman, 1993). Greater wealth inequality may then increase the rate of start-ups when start-up costs (K) are high and a venture-capital market is not developed.

The second is the role of *non-pecuniary benefits* from entrepreneurship represented by η. The culture of risk-taking vs. that of secure employment is important here, as is the social acceptance of failure. Policies can be put in place to protect individuals from failure (such as bankruptcy laws and social-safety nets) and induce risk-taking. Finally, policies can also be put in place to reduce the socially perverse allocation of entrepreneurial activity to monopoly power, rent-seeking, tax evasion, and predatory activities. This will be explored in Chapter 21. Social networks are important in supporting entrepreneurship. They include family, friends, community, and ethnic groups. In the Chinese context, the social environment of family and community networks seems to have been important in explaining who are the successful entrepreneurs (Djankov *et al.*, 2006). For Japan, Hayami (1996) has shown how the rural community was the cradle of the just-in-time manufacturing system successfully introduced by Toyota, allowing cost savings by minimizing inventories. This discipline in respecting contracts for the quality and timing of delivery of component parts to the Toyota factory by a large number of small and medium enterprises was made possible by the strong relations of cooperation and trust developed among community members over centuries of joint efforts in irrigated rice farming. Culture and ethics thus play an important role in fomenting entrepreneurship.

The third category is the role of the economic, political, and legal *context* in which potential entrepreneurs behave, represented by p, K, and A. This includes the "investment climate" with features such as property rights, contract-enforcement mechanisms, access to financial institutions, financial stability, and reasonable regulatory burdens on enterprise start-ups. The World Bank's *Doing Business* project (2015) provides indicators of business regulations and the protection of property rights for local firms in 189 economies and selected cities at the subnational level. De Soto (2002) has stressed the constraints on entrepreneurship imposed in Peru by bureaucratic start-up costs and regulatory burdens on new enterprises. Clusters of economic activity have an important role to play in providing favorable contexts for start-ups (Besley and Persson, 2011).

An interesting question about entrepreneurship in the developing-country context is why there are so many small firms, as opposed to medium to large ones. Banerjee and Duflo (2007) explore answers including entrepreneurship by necessity, family ownership, low education, capital constraints due to credit-market imperfections, high-risk conditions, lack of infrastructure preventing economies of scale, and benefits from informality. The latter include tax and regulation avoidance, and non-payment of social benefits to workers, in particular when non-contributory social-assistance programs substitute for contributory social protection, as argued by Levy (2008) for Mexico.

Expectations

As we saw with the multi-industry investment game, expectations about the behavior of others can strongly influence individual investment decisions. When one is confident about the market potential for the development or use of a technology, one is more likely to move forward, accepting risks in anticipation of likely rewards. To a significant extent, expectations of this kind can be self-fulfilling, as early innovators/adopters raise the expectations of others regarding the potential of technology. Recent advances in macroeconomic theory (following the dismal failure to predict the 2007–8 financial crisis with traditional macro models based on market efficiency and agent rationality) have shown that investment cycles and bubbles respond to animal spirits, herd effects, irrational exuberance, collective gloom, and other powerful psychological forces, which are difficult to predict and yet have tremendous importance in determining willingness to spend and invest (Akerlof and Shiller, 2009). Technology's social dimension can make it highly contagious. For example, mobile phones are partly phones, but also audio and email devices, virtual companions, security devices, and fashion accessories. How expectations are determined and how they influence behavior remains incompletely understood. The assumption of pure rationality in the formation of expectations under the rational-expectations hypothesis (Sargent, 1987), so fashionable before the entry of psychology in economics and the 2007–8 macro failure, is insufficient to explain such basic decisions as consumption, saving, and investment, even at the aggregate level. This interface between psychology, social behavior, and economics is a fascinating field of study making rapid progress (Rabin, 1998), with important applications in development economics.

Learning

Because technological change is by definition about what is new, learning plays an essential role in innovation, adoption, and diffusion. We can expect societies with effective bureaucratic systems, greater homogeneity, and higher levels of technical literacy to be rapid adopters of technological innovations. This has been a historical advantage for China, with its highly effective bureaucracy and its extensive communication system supporting the rapid and exhaustive diffusion of innovations (Lin, 1995).

Learning can follow different paths. We saw in Chapter 8 that average costs can be reduced through "learning by doing," where simply doing more of the same thing over a longer period of time improves performance. This is where one's own accumulated experience matters; but learning can also be derived from others through the diffusion of information in social networks and imitation. This is "learning from others," and it is where membership of more informed networks can confer significant advantages (Foster and Rosenzweig, 1995). Conley and Udry (2001), for instance, show how information about a profitable new crop such as pineapples in Ghana circulates through social networks. When these networks are gender-based, as in Ghana, and men are the innovators, women farmers may find themselves excluded from opportunities to learn from others. Cai *et al.* (2015) show how in China information about a new weather-insurance product for rice circulates through village social networks. Farmers are willing to share what they know, but not necessarily what they do, even though others would like to know this to make their own choices. This is because they are concerned with the risk of losing face if it turns out that they made the wrong decision. If social networks are useful to share knowledge and help learning, then distributing information to people who are central to networks—people well connected to others and well trusted by others—is a way of organizing diffusion campaigns for technological or institutional innovations (see Beaman *et al.*, 2014).

CONCLUSION

We conclude this chapter on endogenous-growth theory with the results of a review by Jones and Romer (2010) of the major empirical facts about the nature and the determinants of growth in the recent period. They highlighted six dominant regularities.

First, there has been an extraordinary rise in the extent of the market via globalization, with increased worldwide flows of goods (trade), ideas (innovations), finance (FDI), and people (migration). Hence the international market and the globalization of exchanges have had a fundamental role to play in countries' growth performances since World War Two.

Second, seen from the long-term perspective of the last 500 years, there has been a sharp overall acceleration of growth in population and in GDPpc.

Third, there exist large differences in GDPpc growth rates across countries, which increase with distance from the technology frontier, showing the importance of institutions and institutional change for growth. In other words, disparities in growth performance across countries are largest at low levels of GDPpc and decline as GDPpc rises. Institutional change plays a key role in successfully joining the convergence club (Acemoglu and Robinson, 2012).

Fourth, there are large income and TFP differences across countries, with high TFP associated with high GDPpc. Differences in measured inputs (factor deepening) explain less than half of the enormous cross-country differences in GDPpc. TFP differences (differences in the role of ideas and innovations for growth) are strongly affected by institutional choices.

Fifth, there has been a rapid increase in human capital per worker in successfully growing countries. Growth is thus not only based on investment and physical–capital accumulation (as in the Harrod–Domar model), but also on human capital.

Sixth, there is surprisingly long-run stability in relative wages for skilled and unskilled workers. The rising quantity of human capital relative to unskilled labor has not been matched by a sustained decline in its relative price, showing its increasing value for growth. Hence growth is increasingly dependent on the accumulation of human capital (the source of ideas), and the rapid accumulation of human capital has met the demand for this source of growth.

CONCEPTS SEEN IN THIS CHAPTER

Conditional convergence
Extended Solow model
Multi-industry investment game and coordination
Multiple equilibria and coordination
Endogenous growth
Growth spillovers
Economic clusters
Big Push
New structural economics
Industrial and technological upgrading
Learning by doing and learning from others
Social networks
Entrepreneurship by necessity and by opportunity

REVIEW QUESTIONS: ENDOGENOUS ECONOMIC GROWTH

1. How does endogenous growth intend to go beyond exogenous growth (the Solow model)?
2. Explain the coordination problem across economic sectors (multi-industry investment game). Show how this relates to jumping from one equilibrium to another when there are multiple equilibriums.
3. How does the Romer model explain the endogeneity of productivity growth and what does it imply for convergence?
4. Why are there agglomeration spillovers, creating benefits for clusters of economic activity? Give examples.
5. How does the international transmission of technology occur according to endogenous-growth theory, and how does this differ from the Solow model?
6. Discuss how government can play a constructive role in overcoming obstacles to industrialization based on the contributions of endogenous-growth theories.

376

NOTES

1 We owe this example to Bruce Wydick (2008), whose book is an excellent introduction to applications of game theory in development economics.
2 A Nash equilibrium is a set of strategies which are individually optimal for each agent, subject to the others' best responses.

REFERENCES

Acemoglu, Daron, and James Robinson. 2012. *Why Nations Fail: The Origins of Power, Prosperity, and Poverty.* New York: Crown Business.

Aghion, Philippe, and Peter Howitt. 1997. *Endogenous Growth Theory.* Cambridge, MA: MIT Press.

Akerlof, George, and Robert Shiller. 2009. *Animal Spirits: How Human Psychology Drives the Economy, and Why It Matters for Global Capitalism.* Princeton: Princeton University Press.

Banerjee, Abhijit, and Andrew Newman. 1993. "Occupational Choice and the Process of Development." *Journal of Political Economy* 101(2): 274–98.

Banerjee, Abhijit, and Esther Duflo. 2007. "The Economic Lives of the Poor." *Journal of Economic Perspectives* 21(1): 141–67.

Bardhan, Pranab. 1995. "The Contributions of Endogenous Growth Theory to the Analysis of Development Problems: An Assessment." In J. Behrman and T.N. Srinivasan (eds.), *Handbook of Development Economics,* Vol. 3, Part 2: 2983–98. Amsterdam: Elsevier Science B.V.

Barro, Robert. 1991. "Economic Growth in a Cross Section of Countries." *Quarterly Journal of Economics* 106(2): 407–43.

Beaman, Lori, Ariel Ben Yishay, Jeremy Magruder, and Mushfiq Mobarak. 2014. "Can Network Theory-based Targeting Increase Technology Adoption?" Working paper, Yale School of Management.

Besley, Timothy, and Torsten Persson. 2011. *Pillars of Prosperity: The Political Economics of Development Clusters.* Princeton: Princeton University Press.

Cai, Jing, Alain de Janvry, and Elisabeth Sadoulet. 2015. "Social Networks and the Decision to Insure." *American Economic Journal: Applied Economics* 72(2): 81–108.

Conley, Timothy, and Christopher Udry. 2001. "Social Learning through Networks: The Adoption of New Agricultural Technologies in Ghana." *American Journal of Agricultural Economics* 83(3): 668–73.

De Soto, Hernando. 2002. *The Other Path: The Economic Answer to Terrorism.* New York: Basic Books.

Djankov, Simeon, Yingyi Qian, Gérard Roland, and Ekaterina Zhuravskaya. 2006. "Who Are China's Entrepreneurs?" *American Economic Review* 96(2): 348–52.

Foster, Andrew, and Mark Rosenzweig. 1995. "Learning by Doing and Learning from Others: Human Capital and Technical Change in Agriculture." *Journal of Political Economy* 103(6): 1176–1209.

Galor, Oded. 2011. *Unified Growth Theory.* Princeton: Princeton University Press.

377

Hayami, Yujiro. 1996. "The Peasant in Economic Modernization." *American Journal of Agricultural Economics* 78(5): 1157–67.

Hirschman, Albert. 1958. *The Strategy of Economic Development.* New Haven, CT: Yale University Press.

Jones, Charles, and Paul Romer. 2010. "The New Kaldor Facts: Ideas, Institutions, Population, and Human Capital." *American Economic Journal: Macroeconomics* 2(1): 224–45.

Leibenstein, Harry. 1957. *Economic Backwardness and Economic Growth.* New York: Wiley.

Levy, Santiago. 2008. *Good Intentions, Bad Outcomes.* Washington, DC: Brookings Institution Press.

Lin, Justin Yifu, 1995. "The Needham Puzzle: Why the Industrial Revolution Did Not Originate in China." *Economic Development and Cultural Change* 43(2): 269–92.

Lin, Justin Yifu, 2011. "New Structural Economics: A Framework for Rethinking Development." *World Bank Research Observer* 26(2): 193–221.

Lucas, Robert. 1988. "On the Mechanics of Economic Development." *Journal of Monetary Economics* 22(1): 3–42.

Mankiw, Gregory, David Romer, and David Weil. 1992. "A Contribution to the Empirics of Economic Growth." *Quarterly Journal of Economics* 107(2): 407–37.

Murphy, Kevin, Andrei Shleifer, and Robert Vishny. 1989. "Industrialization and the Big Push." *Journal of Political Economy* 97(5): 1003–26.

Naudé, Wim. 2014. "Entrepreneurship in Economic Development: Theory, Evidence, and Policy." In B. Currie-Alder, R. Kanbur, D. Malone and R. Medhorn (eds.), *International Development: Ideas, Experience, and Prospects.* Oxford: Oxford University Press.

Otsuka, Keijiro, and Tetsushi Sonobe. 2009. "The Community Mechanism of Contract Enforcement: What Are the Differences between Rural Communities and Industrial Clusters?" Tokyo: Foundation for Advanced Studies on International Development.

Piore, Michael, and Charles Sable. 1990. *The Second Industrial Divide.* New York: Basic Books.

Porter, Michael. 1998. "Clusters and the New Economics of Competition." Harvard Business Review 76(6): 77–90.

Rabin, Matthew. 1998. "Psychology and Economics." *Journal of Economic Literature* 36(1): 11–46.

Romer, Paul. 1990. "Endogenous Technological Change." *Journal of Political Economy* 98(5): S71–102.

Rosenstein-Rodan, Paul. 1943. "Problems of Industrialization of Eastern and South-Eastern Europe." *Economic Journal* 53(210): 202–11.

Sachs, Jeffrey, and Andrew Warner. 1995. "Economic Reform and the Process of Global Integration." *Brookings Papers on Economic Activity* July: 1–118.

Sargent, Thomas. 1987. "Rational Expectations." *The New Palgrave: A Dictionary of Economics* 4: 76–9.

Schumpeter, J.A. 1961. *The Theory of Economic Development.* New York: Oxford University Press.

Strauss, John, Edward Qian, Minggao Shen, Dong Liu, Mahdi Majbouri, Qi Sun, Qianfan Ying, and Yi Zhu. 2009. "Private Sector Industrialization in China: Evidence from Wenzhou." Working paper, Department of Economics, University of Southern California, Los Angeles.

World Bank. 2015. *Doing Business.* www.doingbusiness.org/ (accessed 2015).

Wydick, Bruce. 2008. *Games in Economic Development.* New York: Cambridge University Press.

International finance and development

TAKE-HOME MESSAGES FOR CHAPTER 10

1. One of the main links between international financial flows and the domestic economy is through the exchange rate. The exchange rate appreciates (the domestic currency gains strength) when it goes down as measured in LCU/$ and depreciates when it goes up.
2. Exchange-rate regimes can be floating, fixed, or dollarized. Each regime can only achieve two of three policy goals: exchange-rate stability, exchange-rate autonomy, and foreign-exchange accessibility.
3. The real exchange rate (RER) is the ratio of the price of tradable to the price of non-tradable goods. It has a strong impact on real balances in the economy. An appreciation of the RER shifts domestic production from tradable (typically agriculture and industry) to non-tradable goods (typically services), consumption and input use from non-tradable to tradable, and increases imports and reduces exports, thus shrinking the balance of trade.
4. In accordance with China's neo-mercantilist growth strategy, the Chinese yuan is held highly depreciated, favoring Chinese exports and penalizing imports. Maintaining the depreciated yuan requires investing a large share of foreign-currency earnings in US treasury bonds, balancing the US's large trade deficit.
5. Three events that affect the stability of the RER are ISI (appreciation), the Dutch disease (appreciation), and a speculative attack on domestic currency (depreciation). Policy instruments are available to mitigate each of these, but they can fail.

EXCHANGE RATES AND DEVELOPMENT

Exchange rates play an important role in international trade and finance because they determine the international value of domestic resources. Classical trade theory suggests that only relative prices matter, i.e. that comparative advantage comes from relative domestic resource costs and does not depend on the nominal comparison of the value of currencies. If we lived in a simple global barter economy, this would be true—only physical goods would circulate between countries, converted to local currency prices on arrival. This was more likely in ancient trade, but the desire to carry purchasing power (financial capital) across borders is also very old.

Today, international capital markets operate completely in tandem with international flows of goods and services. Countries like the US can run large deficits in their balance of current accounts (imports and exports) only because they have compensating large surpluses in their balance of financial accounts (financial-asset flows). Others like China do just the opposite, running large surpluses in their balance of current accounts which are absorbed by large deficits in their balance of financial accounts. Demand for currency-conversion services now totals billions of dollars a day in the spot market and trillions in the foreign-exchange derivatives markets. The scale of these activities means that macroeconomic policy, in developed and developing countries alike, must include consideration of international financial flows. Speculative attacks on a country's currency can have devastating effects on its real economy. On the other hand, a large capital inflow can be a welcome bonanza, but also a curse—the Dutch disease—if it temporarily upsets relative prices in the domestic market, bankrupting sectors of economic activity that may have long-term comparative advantage. In this chapter, we provide a general overview of international finance issues as they are relevant to LDC economies. The two main categories of interest are exchange rates and foreign direct investment. We discuss exchange rates and how they link the real and financial realms of an economy.

COUNTRY CURRENCIES

There are three categories of country in terms of the currency of use (Guillaumont Jeanneney, 2011). The first is countries with their own specific national currencies—India uses the rupee, and Mexico the peso—managed autonomously by their own central banks. The second is countries that share a currency with several other countries in a monetary union. The European Monetary Union is the wealthiest such union, with 17 countries out of 27 EU members sharing the Euro, which is managed by a single central bank, the European Central Bank. Other monetary unions are the West African Economic and Monetary Union (UEMOA) that groups eight countries (with the CFA as the shared currency), the Central Africa Economic and Monetary Community with six countries, and the Caribbean Monetary Union with eight island nations. The third category is countries that use a foreign currency, either as their single currency or combined with a domestic currency. Integral dollarization applies in Ecuador, El Salvador, Panama, and Zimbabwe. Integral use of the Euro applies in the Balkan nations of Montenegro and Kosovo. Other countries use a combination of the US dollar and a domestic currency, with individuals choosing which currency to hold and use for transactions. In this case, there will be a fixed exchange rate between the dollar and the domestic currency. The share of bank deposits held in dollars can vary widely across countries. In 2000, they ranged from 92 percent in Bolivia and Cambodia to 66 percent in Peru, 46 percent in Hong Kong, and less than 1 percent in Guatemala and Bangladesh (De Nicoló et al., 2003).

Currencies have different degrees of marketability. A currency can be fully convertible into other currencies at the going nominal exchange rate with no restrictions. The US dollar is an example of a fully convertible currency. In other cases, convertibility is restricted—for example, allowed for current operations (sale and purchase of goods, payment to production factors, gifts and transfers) but not for capital movements (purchase or sale of non-financial assets) so that international investments are controlled but not domestic trade transactions. Convertibility may also be more restricted for residents of a country than for non-residents. The Indian rupee is an example of a partially convertible currency. When countries are members of a currency union, there is full convertibility within the union, but convertibility may be restricted externally, as is the case with the West African CFA zone. Finally, a currency is non-convertible if it is not tradable on international foreign-exchange markets nor convertible by individuals and companies for domestic trade. Some countries allow the export and trade of their currencies externally. This is usually the case with industrialized countries' currencies. In developing countries, trading bills outside the country is in general forbidden.

DEFINITIONS: NOMINAL, REAL, AND REAL EFFECTIVE EXCHANGE RATES

There are two ways of looking at exchange rates: as a financial index of relative currency prices (the nominal exchange rate) or as a real index of the prices of relative commodity bundles (the real exchange rate).

Nominal exchange rate

The nominal or official exchange rate between a local currency and a foreign currency is defined as:

e = current price of a dollar (or unit of another foreign currency) in terms of local currency = *(Number of Local Currency Units)/(Foreign Currency Unit)* = *LCUs/FCU,*

e.g. 14.7 pesos/US$ for Mexico in January 2015. Hence e is simply the price of the "buck" in Mexico, i.e. the pesos you need to pay to buy a "buck" when you are there. This value is ultimately determined by a combination of market forces and government, mainly central-bank, interventions. When the nominal exchange rate e declines in currency markets due to a change in the balance between supply and demand of dollars (with supply increasing more than demand), this is termed *appreciation* of the domestic currency relative to the foreign currency. When this decline happens because the government decides to lower the nominal or official exchange rate, it is termed *re-valuation*. In both cases, the local currency—say, the Mexican peso—gains value as Mexicans need fewer LCUs to buy a dollar. In practical terms, the government can achieve this by one or both of two interventions. The country could outlaw currency exchange at other rates and/or the central bank could sell

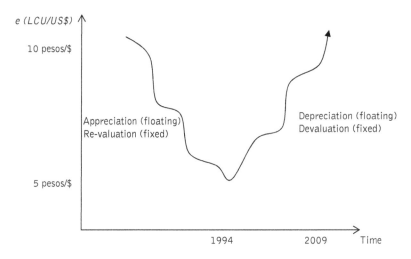

Figure 10.1 *Movements of the nominal/official exchange rate*

foreign exchange in markets, increasing the supply of foreign currency and driving down its price (*e*). Conversely, the nominal exchange rate *e* can rise, in which case the domestic currency *depreciates* if it happens as a consequence of dollar demand increasing more than supply, or it can be set higher by central-bank intervention, which is called a *devaluation* of the exchange rate.

These movements are heuristically represented in Figure 10.1. In the case of either a re-valuation or a devaluation, the legal and financial capacity of the government to set the exchange rate will be tested by black markets for exchange controls and by speculators for central-bank intervention. As intuition would suggest, developing-country governments are at a disadvantage in both cases due to limited enforcement capacity and limited foreign-currency reserves. Yet because foreign exchange is so important in the real economy, exchange-rate policy is a fundamental force for growth and stability. In the case of an appreciation or a depreciation, the drivers are shifts in the demand and supply of dollars on the domestic market. Here again, the government will be tested by speculators and unexpected shocks on commodity markets.

To summarize these definitions:

e = LCUs/US$ = nominal or official exchange rate

appreciation or *re-valuation*: *e* decreases as need fewer LCUs per US$ (the LCU gains strength relative to the dollar)
depreciation or *devaluation*: *e* increases as need more LCUs per US$ (the LCU loses strength relative to the dollar).

Real exchange rate

While the nominal exchange rate represents the relative price of the currencies of two countries, the real exchange rate (RER) measures the relative price of goods and services in the two countries. The real exchange rate of the Mexican peso with respect to the US dollar is a ratio of prices in the US over prices in Mexico. Both of these prices need to be measured in the same currency, so clearly the RER will be influenced by the nominal exchange rate. There are two common expressions for the RER.

One is called the internal RER, defined as:

$$RER = \frac{P_T}{P_{NT}}.$$

The numerator P_T is the border price for tradable goods. The denominator P_{NT} is the price of non-tradable goods. Both are measured in LCU.

The other is called the external RER defined as:

$$RER = \frac{eWPI^\$}{CPI^{LCU}}.$$

Here, the foreign price is measured by the Wholesale Price Index (WPI) in the US converted in LCU at the nominal exchange rate. The domestic price is measured by the Consumer Price Index (CPI).

The first definition is more theoretical and used for conceptual reasoning. The second is more empirical, with the corresponding data easily found in World Bank and IMF statistics.

Note that there is a relation between the RER and the PPP-adjusted nominal exchange rate that we saw in Chapter 1. If all goods were tradable and traded without policy interventions, and if foreign and domestic residents purchased identical baskets of goods, PPP would hold for the exchange rate and the GDP deflators (price levels) of the two countries. The real exchange rate would then always be equal to 1.

Tradable and non-tradable goods are defined by the rules of price formation for each type of good as follows.

Tradable good (T)

This is a good with a domestic price determined by e and an international price as an export or import substitute, $p^\$$. Hence the domestic price of an imported tradable good with a tariff t_M is $p^d = ep^\$ (1 + t_M)$ and with an export tax t_E is $p^d = ep^\$ (1 - t_E)$. The market for a tradable good is quantity adjusted through the level of imports or exports at the border price, as shown in Figure 10.2.

Non-tradable good (NT)

This is a good with a domestic price determined by equality between supply and demand on the domestic market. If exports or imports are fixed quantities, such as an import quota, the good remains a non-tradable because its price is still set by equality between supply and demand after trade shifts these functions. Hence there can be (exogenous) trade of non-tradable goods as shown in Figure 10.3.

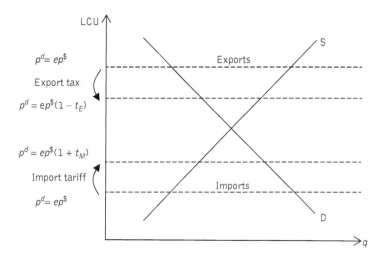

Figure 10.2 *Market equilibrium for a tradable good (quantity adjustment only)*

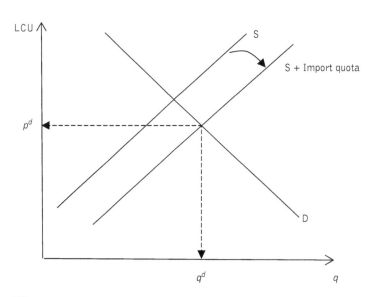

Figure 10.3 *Market equilibrium for a non-tradable good (price and quantity adjustments)*

Note carefully that tradable and non-tradable goods are not types of good, but types of rule of price formation. The same good can be tradable in a country and non-tradable in another where trade is quantity restricted. Services used to be mostly non-tradable, but have become increasingly so, in particular with internet trading and international travel—for example, for health services in foreign hospitals. The same is true for perishable goods, such as grapes and cut flowers—the internationalization of value chains has made them into tradable goods. Some services like construction remain largely non-tradable.

Although goods/services markets can be subject to intervention, we say that a currency *appreciates in real terms* when the RER decreases and that it *depreciates in real terms* when the RER increases.

Real effective exchange rate

The real effective exchange rate (REER) is a measure of the relative strength of a currency for imports and exports that takes into account both the country's exchange rate and trade policies. It includes the RER and the effects of tariffs t_M and import subsidies s_M on imports and of taxes t_E and export subsidies s_E on exports as follows:

REER for imports: $REER_M = RER\ (1 + t_M - s_M)$
REER for exports: $REER_E = RER\ (1 - t_E + s_E)$.

EXCHANGE-RATE REGIMES

From a purely financial perspective, the nominal exchange rate is an important policy variable as it is the price at which currencies are transacted. The fundamentals of comparative advantage, resource allocation, and real economic growth, however, are more strongly driven by the real exchange rate. Because they have important similarities and differences for economic policy, it is important to understand both. As usual, economists look for insights about economic variables in the concept of market equilibrium. For the nominal exchange rate, the market equilibrium is the LCU price of foreign currency that equilibrates supply and demand for currency conversion in existing markets. The main markets are the spot market, i.e. conversion today (within 48 hours), and the forward market, i.e. conversion at a fixed day in the future. Like a daily stock price, the nominal rate has trend, seasonal, cyclical, and random components, making it only partially indicative of underlying economic fundamentals.

It is important to recognize that nominal exchange rates can reflect a combination of economic fundamentals and policy preferences. In particular, governments can intervene on the demand or supply sides of markets for any currency, distorting more fundamental valuation signals from private market forces. Recognition of this complication leads to a threefold classification of exchange-rate regimes: flexible (floating and imperfectly floating), fixed (pegged and crawling pegged), and dollarized (fully dollarized and currency board). They each have their advantages and inconveniences, which we discuss below (Dornbusch, 2001; Reinhart and Rogoff, 2004).

Flexible (floating) exchange rate

Adjustment by market-driven appreciation or depreciation of the nominal exchange rate obtained by equalizing unfettered private supply and demand for foreign currency. This is depicted in Figure 10.4, where the supply of US$ can come from a multiplicity of sources including export earnings, FDI, foreign portfolio investment (FPI), remittances from migrants, foreign aid, new debt, and the sale of US$ reserves by the central bank. The demand for US$ is for imports, profit repatriation by foreign firms,

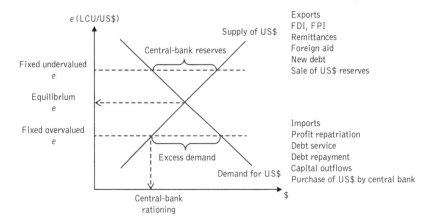

Figure 10.4 *Supply and demand of dollars by holders of domestic currency*

debt service, debt repayment, capital outflows, and the purchase of US$ by the central bank. Equality of supply and demand for dollars determines the country's equilibrium (floating) nominal exchange rate. This floating exchange rate can be affected by the central bank through the management of foreign-currency reserves. We will describe this as an imperfectly floating exchange rate.

Fixed (pegged) exchange rate with capital controls

When the exchange rate is fixed by the central bank, there will be excess demand for dollars when the exchange rate is overvalued. This is typically the case in Latin America and the Caribbean, where there is differential inflation with respect to the US$, with adjustments in the exchange rate lagging upward movement in all other prices, leading to overvaluation. There will be an excess supply of dollars when it is undervalued (as in China), as shown in Figure 10.4. In the first case, the central bank must ration access to dollars, issuing permits and leaving excess demand uncovered. In the second case, the central bank must buy and export dollars, purchasing, for instance, US treasury bonds, as China does. The central bank thus has to intervene in the foreign-exchange market either by selling or buying foreign currency in order for the equality between the supply and demand of foreign currency to occur at an exchange rate close to the official fixed exchange rate, or by rationing access to dollars if this is not sufficient.

Depreciation can create domestic inflation as it stimulates exports, while appreciation can reduce export competitiveness. Countries may intervene to arrest or at least slow these tendencies to limit domestic adjustment costs. To intervene *against depreciation* (associated with an increase in demand for dollars to D^{Dep} in Figure 10.5), the central bank will buy domestic currency (and hence sell dollars, shifting the supply of dollars to the right) to keep its value from falling too fast, contributing to import-price inflation. The central bank's ability to sustain this depends on its foreign-currency reserves, which in most developing countries are limited. This kind of policy

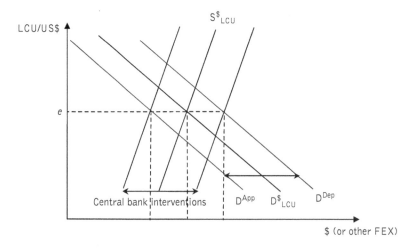

Figure 10.5 *Central bank interventions to stabilize the exchange rate*

is often pursued by governments that are highly dependent on imports of politically sensitive commodities such as energy and food (Broda, 2001). Intervening to avoid depreciation of the national currency helps mitigate upward pressures in the prices of these key imported commodities.

On the other side of the market, an export-oriented country might intervene *against appreciation* (associated with a decline in demand for dollars in Figure 10.5, shifting the demand for dollars to D^{App}) to keep prices of its goods competitive in foreign markets. This is done by having the central bank absorb incoming dollars (shifting the supply of dollars to the left) with new domestic money or near-money (bonds). This strategy is termed "neo-mercantilism" and is pursued by many successful Asian export economies, Japan for a long time and China more recently.

In both cases, the timing and scope of interventions depends on the central bank's goals and resources. LDCs defending currencies against depreciation generally have limited dollar reserves. Neo-mercantilist countries defending currencies against appreciation have the opposite problem: large reserve accumulation that can antagonize trading partners by overvaluing their exports and limiting market access. China, for example, had accumulated dollar reserves in excess of $3 trillion by 2012.

With fixed exchange rates, one reason why currencies tend to appreciate is differential inflation, i.e. more inflation in the country than there is in the US. As a result, the price of non-tradables (the domestic CPI) rises faster than the price of tradables (the US WPI). Unless the country devalues its currency, appreciation will hurt exports and favor imports, leading to a deficit in the balance of trade. In fixed exchange rate regimes, with countries hesitant to devalue their currency in order not to signal weakness to foreign investors, this has been a classical reason why countries have had a tendency to have overvalued currencies. To avoid this phenomenon, many countries use a crawling-peg approach to exchange-rate fixing, whereby the exchange rate is indexed from the price of domestic goods.

387

While there has been a tendency for countries to move from pegged (fixed) to floating exchange rates, most countries have in fact returned to exchange regimes intermediate between fully floating and fully pegged (Fisher, 2001). They maintain limited flexibility by exercising control over international capital movements to limit exchange-rate fluctuations.

Dollarization (currency board)

When exchange rates become chronically unstable, some countries turn to dollarization or a currency board, which guarantees convertibility of the LCU into US$ by fixing $e = k\text{LCU/US\$}$, where $k=1$ means literal dollarization (as, for example, in Panama, Ecuador, and in Argentina until 2001), i.e. one unit of the LCU is worth 1US$. Official dollarization occurs when the country adopts the US dollar as legal tender (e.g. Panama). A strategy like this may seem attractive to achieve price stability, but it is politically unpalatable and creates structural risks because it means that the country no longer has an exchange-rate policy that it can use to adjust the domestic price of tradable goods. The currency board is prevented from holding domestic assets, which can restrain inflation and fiscal deficits, but also limits monetary policy.

If there is differential inflation in the country relative to the US dollar, the country cannot devalue its currency. The only way of avoiding overvaluation is by cooling down the economy to reduce inflation. Lack of an exchange-rate policy to deal with differential inflation can thus be very costly to the real economy. This was the case in Argentina, which, after years of dollarization, was prompted to abandon it after repeated recessions to control for inflation.

Exchange-rate policy and trade-offs

Figure 10.6 illustrates the challenge facing the central bank with regard to the choice of an exchange-rate regime (Krugman and Obstfeld, 2008). Each policy goal in the triangle indicates a desirable feature of an exchange-rate regime: exchange-rate stability, foreign-exchange accessibility, and exchange-rate autonomy. However, each exchange-rate regime only achieves a subset of the policy objectives. Since only one regime can be implemented at a time, there are difficult policy trade-offs.

Specifically, what Figure 10.6 shows is that each exchange-rate regime only achieve two of the three policy goals: a floating exchange rate delivers exchange-rate autonomy and foreign-exchange accessibility, but at the cost of eventual exchange-rate instability; a fixed exchange rate (achieved by controlling accessibility of foreign exchange, in particular central-bank rationing when there is overvaluation, as we saw in Figure 10.4) delivers exchange-rate autonomy and exchange-rate stability, but at the cost of constrained accessibility of foreign exchange; finally, dollarization of the exchange rate (use of a currency board) delivers exchange-rate stability and foreign-exchange accessibility, but at the cost of loss of autonomy of the country's exchange-rate policy. Hence there is no panacea, and each nominal

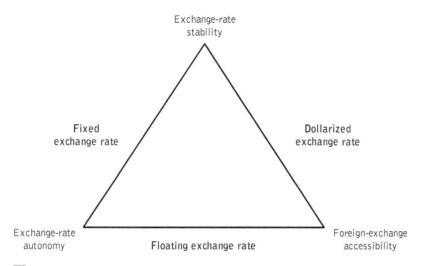

Figure 10.6 *The exchange-rate-policy triangle*

exchange-rate regime has particular advantages, but is also exposed to undesirable consequences.

Equilibrium exchange rate

The equilibrium level of the nominal exchange rate is determined by equality between the supply of dollars and the demand for dollars in the country, thus achieving balance-of-payments equilibrium. This equilibrium is sustainable when the supply and demand of dollars can be maintained (instead of, for example, a supply of dollars based on high levels of debt, temporary aid inflows, or a short-term export boom). Factors that affect dollar supply are export earnings (that depend on the prices of exported goods and the volume of exports) and foreign capital inflows (aid, debt, interest rate). Factors that affect dollar demand are import expenditures (that depend on import prices and volumes), capital flight, and foreign capital outflows (debt service). Import tariffs restrict imports and hence the demand for dollars, as, for example, under ISI policies analyzed below. In calculating the equilibrium exchange rate we need to identify the elements of this supply and demand that are sustainable in the medium term.

Two methods to estimate the equilibrium exchange rate are the PPP equilibrium exchange rate approach and the permanent-fundamentals approach.

The PPP equilibrium exchange rate

An important determinant of exchange-rate movements should be the difference between the domestic rate of inflation and inflation rates in the rest of the world. If domestic inflation exceeds inflation abroad, then, other things being equal, the currency will tend to appreciate. The PPP theory asserts that this effect should be the main explanation for exchange-rate movements. Correspondingly, one can define

389

the PPP equilibrium exchange rate in any year in relation to a base-year equilibrium exchange rate as:

$$e^*(PPP) = e_0^* \frac{P^d/P_0^d}{P^\$/P_0^\$},$$

where $P_0^d, P_0^\$, e_0^*$ are the domestic price index, the foreign price index, and the equilibrium exchange rate in the base year. By choosing a base year in which the official nominal exchange rate e_0 was at an equilibrium level, this expression can be used to compute a time series of equilibrium exchange rates. The choice of the base year is, however, the tricky part of this approach. One usually chooses a year in which the balance of payments was roughly in equilibrium or at an acceptable long-term disequilibrium value, and for which this equilibrium was not obtained by exceptional constraints imposed on imports, exports, or capital movements. All necessary data on exchange-rate and price indices are available in the IMF's *International Financial Statistics*.

The fundamentals approach

Edwards (1989) proposes that the RER is, in equilibrium, determined by the fundamentals of the economy. Fundamentals include the country's trade regime measured by trade openness (the share of exports and imports in GDP), the financial regime measured by financial openness (the ratio of the official to the black-market exchange rate), and the terms of trade, real income, and capital inflows (remittance transfers, capital inflows, and foreign aid). The regression equation is:

$$RER_t = f(Fundamentals_t) + \varepsilon_t,$$

and the equilibrium exchange rate at a particular time t is the value of the RER predicted by this equation.

IMPACT OF A CHANGE IN THE RER ON REAL BALANCES

If the RER appreciates, P_T/P_{NT} falls (think of a typical Latin American country with dollar inflows due to agricultural and mining exports, or with differential inflation and a fixed nominal exchange rate). This change in relative prices in turn affects production, consumption, input use, and exports and imports. The changes (represented by arrows) in the real economy induced by appreciation are shown in Table 10.1.

Incidence analysis of RER appreciation identifies the winners as the producers of non-tradable goods, the consumers of tradable goods, and the suppliers of tradable inputs (foreign sellers, importers). The losers are the producers of tradable goods, the consumers of non-tradable goods, and the suppliers of non-tradable inputs (labor, natural resources). Thus the poor will be among the losers if they happen to produce tradable goods (e.g. coffee and cocoa) and consume non-tradable goods (e.g. cassava and banana plantain). This would be the case for the poor in East and Central African countries.

Table 10.1 *Real-balances implications of RER appreciation*

	Change induced by appreciation
Impact on the production structure (Q_T, Q_{NT})	$Q_T \rightarrow Q_{NT}$
Impact on the consumption structure (C_T, C_{NT})	$C_T \leftarrow C_{NT}$
Impact on the structure of input use	$X_T \leftarrow X_{NT}$
Impact on imports (M) and exports (E)	$M \uparrow, E \downarrow$
Impact on the balance of trade $= E - M$	$BofT \downarrow\downarrow$

Note that China maintains a depreciated RER, with, as a consequence, opposite effects on its real economy from those described in Table 10.1, in particular a large positive effect on its balance of trade that is the source of international capital exports to the US. Because it favors Chinese exports to the US, and penalizes US exports to China, this depreciated-real-exchange-rate policy is attracting a lot of attention from the US government, particularly when there is a high rate of unemployment at home and elections are close. The US government puts pressure on the Chinese government to appreciate its currency as it would like to increase US exports to China as an instrument of employment creation.

What this analysis of real balances tells us is that a country's exchange-rate policy can have a significant influence on its economic structure and growth performance. Relying on primary exports as a source of growth (such as copper exports from Chile and Peru, petroleum exports from Venezuela and Nigeria, and mineral exports from the Democratic Republic of Congo and Botswana) will chronically appreciate a country's RER. As a consequence, it will have a hard time developing its tradable sectors of industry and agriculture. In Chile, successful copper exports are always in competition with successful fruit exports as they appreciate the currency and make Chilean fruits less competitive on the world market. The mineral export boom, driven by Chinese demand, that successfully accelerated African countries' growth in the 2000–8 and 2010–12 periods is favorable neither to industrialization nor to the development of their agricultural exports. In that sense, the "easy" growth that originates in mineral- and energy-product exports makes it harder to pursue long-term industrialization and agricultural strategies. It is part of the "resource curse" that materializes through appreciation of the RER.

Another case that illustrates the difficulty of developing with an appreciated currency is that of the African countries in the CFA zone that is pegged to the Euro. This includes all the former French colonies from Senegal to Madagascar. The advantage of the CFA for these countries is to have a currency that is officially traded in international financial markets. This is good for their financial and commercial operations. The disadvantage is that the Euro is too strong (appreciated) for these countries, making their exports uncompetitive. When the CFA was devalued in 1994, exports temporarily boomed; but renewed appreciation soon cancelled this temporary advantage. The Euro may in turn gain strength relative to the US dollar, creating a double source of RER appreciation for the CFA countries when dealing with the rest of the world, where trade is in US dollars.

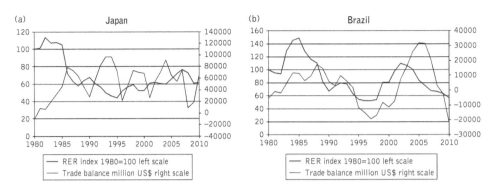

Figure 10.7 *Real exchange rate and trade balance: Japan (a) and Brazil (b), 1980–2010*

Source: World Bank, *World Development Indicators.*

An empirical validation of the impact of the exchange rate on the real side of the economy is Asikoglu and Uctum's (1992) analysis of Turkey. They find that the real depreciation of the exchange rate pursued during the 1979–88 period induced an important shift in the composition of output toward tradables, an impressive growth of exports, and has been an essential component of the successful overall growth of the economy.

Figure 10.7's comparison of the real exchange rates and trade balances of Japan and Brazil illustrates the contrast between a growing surplus in the trade balance in Japan (a), inducing a decline in the real exchange rate, and fluctuations in the real exchange rate, inducing corresponding fluctuations in the trade balance in Brazil (b). In the first, causality runs from balance-of-trade surpluses to RER appreciation, while in the second it runs from RER depreciation to rising balance-of-trade surpluses.

Consequences of an exchange-rate devaluation

Countries with an overvalued exchange rate will periodically need to devalue their currency, in particular as induced by a balance-of-trade crisis in which they run out of foreign exchange to support essential imports of food, capital, and intermediate goods. Devaluation will induce changes in real balances, which are the opposite of those in Table 10.1. There are additional consequences of an exchange-rate devaluation, as follows (Edwards, 1989):

■ The price of tradable goods rises. This will induce domestic inflation, especially when tradables are an important component of the CPI. Inability to control inflation will lead to renewed appreciation of the currency, and the need for future devaluations. While modest inflation may be good for growth, as prices need to reflect improvement in the quality of goods, more than modest inflation is detrimental to growth because of the uncertainty it creates on expected returns from investment. Inflation is, in addition, notably detrimental to the real incomes of the poor (Easterly and Fisher, 2001).

- Whether the economy will benefit or not from devaluation depends on: (1) whether increases in border prices are transmitted to producers of tradable goods, as opposed to being absorbed by intermediaries, and (2) whether producers have the capacity to respond to price incentives through higher levels of production. When producers are smallholder farmers and small and medium enterprises, the elasticity of supply response may be low, resulting in more inflation and less growth.

- Where FDI flows to tradable sectors, FDI should increase. Where it flows to non-tradable sectors, FDI should decrease. In China, many foreign enterprises have invested to service the domestic market with non-tradables such as national telecommunications. These enterprises will not be particularly interested in putting political pressure on China to appreciate/revalue its currency as it will decrease the demand for C_{NT}. This creates a discrepancy between the US government's interest in appreciation to create jobs in the US, and US firms' interest in lucrative investments in the Chinese market for non-tradable goods.

- Fiscal revenues and expenditures will typically increase as poor countries raise most of their fiscal revenues by taxing the tradable sector, while spending fiscal revenues on non-tradable services, principally public-sector employment. An exchange-rate devaluation will thus help finance and lead to social-assistance programs.

- In the short run, growth may be reduced as there is a fall in effective demand and a fall in the production of non-tradable goods. In the medium and longer run, however, devaluation should stimulate the production of the tradable sectors, and induce economic growth. The 1994 devaluation of the CFA in Sub-Saharan Africa led to a boost in exports and growth.

- The impact on poverty depends on the sources of income of the poor in relation to the tradables sector. The poor in tradable sectors will gain—typically smallholder farmers producing cash crops for the international market. The urban poor may, however, be more engaged in the non-tradables sector, and lose from devaluation. Inflation may also contribute to a loss in their real income. Increased fiscal revenues are a potential source of compensation, i.e. they can be used to increase social-assistance programs such as workfare and cash transfers. Fiscal revenues can also be raised by taxing the short-term gains from devaluation of export agriculture.

- Speculators who guess the timing of the devaluation, or have insider information about it through corrupt practices, can benefit substantially. All they have to do is shift their assets to dollars the day before the devaluation, and back into local currency the day after, capturing a wealth gain as large as the devaluation, short of transaction costs. This was not an unusual practice in making fortunes in Latin America in the years when large devaluations were recurrent.

THREE EXAMPLES OF EXCHANGE-RATE SHOCKS

To better understand how exchange rates and capital flows can affect domestic economic conditions, we analyze three cases of exchange-rate shocks, arising from trade policy, current-account imbalances, and capital-account destabilization. In each case,

393

we examine how the exchange rate is affected, the implications for the real side of the economy, and potential government policy responses.

ISI policies and import tariffs on industry

Figure 10.8 illustrates how a policy restricting imports, like a tariff or a quota, induces an appreciation of the exchange rate with implications for other sectors of the economy. Because import demand falls, so does the demand for foreign currency by domestic currency holders. This leftward shift in demand for dollars lowers the value of the nominal exchange rate e, which will appreciate the RER if the terms of trade remain constant. For the protected industry, the tariff t_M raises the domestic price as the positive effect of protection exceeds the negative effect of appreciation:

$$p^d = ep^\$(1 + t_M).$$

However, for all the non-protected tradable sectors, the RER appreciation lowers the domestic price since, for them,

$$p^d = ep^\$,$$

which is damaging to their competitiveness. If the protected sector uses imported capital goods, this RER appreciation becomes another source of advantage. This was at the heart of the ISI strategy in protecting sectors through trade policy (import tariffs on the sector producing the good to be import-substituted) and exchange-rate policy (exchange-rate appreciation cheapening the cost of imported capital goods).

While disprotection via appreciation does not matter for capital goods that are not produced in the country (and that the country has no ambition of producing at this stage of its industrialization program), agriculture and other tradable-goods sectors will suffer in this context. If ISI is sustained over time and is to succeed, then complementary investments will be needed to promote productivity growth and lower average costs in these sectors, particularly if they are important for foreign-exchange earnings, such as agricultural exports. Argentina, for instance, relied on agricultural exports for foreign-exchange earnings that were necessary to import raw materials and intermediate inputs for its nascent industry. By creating disincentives to invest in agriculture, RER appreciation periodically induced agricultural export crises, compromising foreign-exchange earnings for the country, and slowing down the process of ISI (Mamalakis, 1971). This sectoral policy conflict between agricultural exports and ISI resulted in "stop–go cycles" for ISI, with the need to periodically devalue the currency to restore agricultural growth and exports, redistribute income toward the rural sector, and boost foreign-exchange earnings as needed by industry itself.

RER appreciation is not only detrimental to the non-protected tradable sectors, it also cheapens capital goods and hence increases the capital intensity of the emerging industrial sectors (as measured by their capital/labor ratios), reducing employment and the share of labor in the benefits of growth. ISI policies, through RER appreciation, thus tend to make growth more regressive and less pro-poor.

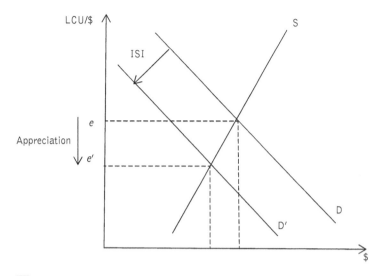

Figure 10.8 *Impact of ISI on the exchange rate*

In conclusion, ISI has the following effects through a combination of trade and exchange-rate policies:

- Protection through tariffs of the selected sectors of industry, the objective of the industrialization strategy. For these sectors, trade protection is greater than dis-protection via RER appreciation, and they are the real winners of the strategy.
- Disprotection of all non-protected tradable sectors through appreciation of the RER. Most damaged is agriculture, putting at risk rural livelihoods and foreign-exchange earnings if agriculture is an important source of exports.
- Imported capital goods are cheapened by appreciation, providing another incentive to invest in industry; but industry then tends to be capital-intensive. Workers in the ISI industries benefit, but employment is limited by capital intensity, lowering wages overall. This creates a privileged formal labor sector in the ISI industries, typically represented by powerful labor unions that will militate for continued protection, and a large informal sector of the unemployed, contributing to inequality.
- The main policy implication is that ISI is most effective when it is short and moves as soon as possible to ISTE to avoid continued RER appreciation. The other is that it is important to maintain the competitiveness of investments in productivity growth in the non-protected tradable sectors in the face of temporary appreciation.

Dutch disease, or the nefarious implications of a temporary export boom

The theory of comparative advantage tells us that countries should specialize, moving domestic resources from activities with relatively low international returns to those with higher returns. When all goods are tradable, this is a natural process leading to higher domestic and global efficiency. When some goods are non-tradable, however, export booms and the large net foreign-exchange inflows they create can seriously distort the domestic economy. For example, North Sea oil and gas discoveries caused huge foreign-currency flows into Norway and Holland (hence the name "Dutch disease"); spikes in copper prices cause large foreign currency flows into Chile, Peru, and Zambia; coffee-price booms do the same for Central America and Rwanda; and rapid increases of foreign aid to countries favored by donors as a consequence of a political event can have the same effect. As shown in Figure 10.9, the increased inflow of foreign currency shifts the domestic supply of dollars to the right, appreciating the RER. The consequences of this appreciation on the real economy were described in Table 10.1. They imply reduced competitiveness of the traditional export or import-competing sectors (particularly agriculture and industry), which go into decline. In addition to this structural distortion, booms can promote unsustainable borrowing and speculative inflows of hot money.

The problem of a Dutch disease is not the boom: everybody likes to have one, particularly politicians with short-term tenures. The problem is when the boom ends: the country will then find itself decapitalized in its essential tradable sectors, agriculture and industry, with the associated losses of employment and GDP. Petroleum has for this reason been called a "resource curse," even "the devil's excrement" (*The Economist*, 2003). Because these temporary booms can be so detrimental to a country's long-term welfare, governments may want to introduce a set of policies to mitigate the effects of a non-sustainable boom in foreign currency inflows so they do not create the "disease" (Corden and Neary, 1982; Van Wijnbergen, 1984).

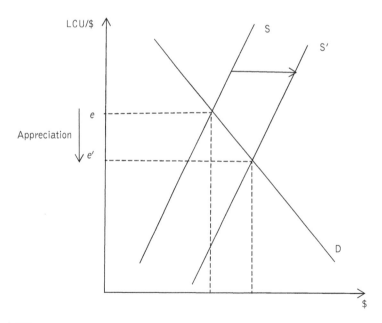

Figure 10.9 *Impact of a temporary export boom on the exchange rate: the Dutch disease*

Policy remedies to counteract the effects of a Dutch disease include the following:

1. Sterilize part of the dollar earnings by depositing them in a foreign account or buying US treasury bonds instead of repatriating them. This is hard to sustain politically beyond the short run. It requires a strong government that has the authority to postpone consumption. Cameroon and Chad have been trying to do this with their oil revenues, and it is what China does with its trade surplus, allowing it to maintain a depreciated RER in spite of its huge foreign-exchange earnings.

2. Invest abroad. This was done by Japan in South East Asia, by Taiwan in China, and by Mexico in Central America. This allows the re-export of dollars earned to avoid appreciation of the RER.

3. If the foreign-exchange boom is due to FDI/FPI, impose a Tobin tax on foreign-capital movements to reduce inflows, or require that a percentage of the FDI be deposited at the central bank. This was done by Chile during its growth boom in the 1970s and early 1980s to cool appreciation of the peso that was detrimental to the competitiveness of its agricultural exports.

4. Increase the productivity of the tradable-goods sectors, especially agriculture, to compensate for falling domestic prices and thus maintain their competitiveness. This requires technical change or institutional innovations that are sources of productivity growth. Public revenues earned from the booming sector (public ownership of the petroleum sector in Mexico, the tax on foreign mine earnings in Peru and Chile) can be invested in infrastructure and in research and development that will boost the competitiveness of the tradable sectors.

5. Avoid short-term booms, e.g. avoid large increases in foreign aid or in foreign debt. Given the expected subsequent social costs of the Dutch disease, this is what Lustig (2000) has called "socially responsible macroeconomics." But it is of course politically difficult to resist the temptation of the short-run benefits of an economic boom, particularly with short-term electoral cycles.

Speculative attacks

Every financial crisis (in Mexico, Brazil, South East Asia, Russia, and more recently Greece) pits currency traders against central-bank authorities, who want to neutralize contagion by limiting domestic asset depreciation. If traders think that the central bank is not credible in its intention or ability to defend a currency against devaluation, they will launch a speculative attack, buying dollars at the current exchange rate to induce a devaluation that will increase the value of their dollar holdings. In Figure 10.10, the speculative attack shifts the demand for dollars to the right, putting pressure on the central bank to devalue the currency (fixed exchange rate) or let the currency depreciate (floating exchange rate). Imagine, for example, that you are buying dollars at 5 pesos/US$ on Friday; then there is a devaluation on Monday morning that raises (devalues) the exchange rate from 5 to 10 pesos/US$, and you can sell your dollar holdings at 1US$ for 10 pesos, effectively doubling the value of your peso

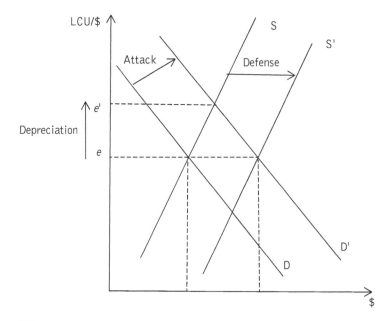

Figure 10.10 *Impact of a speculative attack on the exchange rate*

wealth over the weekend. This involves (usually highly leveraged) trading against the currency, hoping that the central bank will sell a lot of dollars cheaply (at the current low exchange rate) before capitulating. The exchange rate will then rise quickly, allowing the traders a windfall profit. The stakes in this battle are much higher than the traders' potential profits, however, because of the effect of credibility on capital flight and investor confidence. Exchange-rate devaluation is devastating for a country's OEI strategy: foreign investors who brought their money into the country at 5 pesos to the dollar will now have to pay 10 pesos to repatriate one dollar of profits, a bad signal in attracting FDI. For that reason, countries will make every effort to defeat the speculative attack. The intervention, unfortunately, can be very expensive, meaning that LDC monetary authorities have limited capacity to defend the currency. Defensive interventions can be on the supply side or on the demand side.

What prompts the expectation of devaluation that motivates a speculative attack?

1. *Inconsistent macroeconomic policies.* This would be the case if the government borrows abroad to fund large budget deficits (e.g. in the 1983 debt crisis) and appears to be unable to service the borrowing. It would also be the case if there is domestic inflation due to money creation by the government to finance its budget deficit. Differential inflation creates appreciation that will become unsustainable, requiring devaluation.
2. *Sudden shifts in expectations about the sustainability of macroeconomic policies.* This includes the belief that the government will not be willing to raise interest

rates or borrow from abroad to defend the currency, perhaps because there are incoming elections or there is a new government in power. It may also happen if there is a sharp drop in tax revenues, or a drop in capital inflows such as remittances from abroad and foreign aid. Contagion can spread across similar countries, too, with difficulty in signaling to speculators that the same may happen in others.

Statistics indicating the causes of potential devaluations include a high debt-to-export ratio, a debt exceeding some 90 percent of GDP (the current US level, while Greece is at 130 percent), and a high debt-to-reserves ratio. These indicators are informed by rating agencies such as Moody's Corporation and Standard & Poor's. They let governments know whether they may be at risk of a speculative attack on their currency, something that can happen any time speculators see a profit to be made via currency devaluation. Fortunes have been made by people such as George Soros, who were able to predict the timing of impending devaluations.

Supply-side policies to counter a speculative attack

As the demand for dollars increases while the speculative attack progresses, shifting D to D', the central bank can avoid a depreciation of the RER by increasing the supply of dollars on the domestic market, shifting the supply from S to S' in Figure 10.9. Where will these dollars come from?

1. The country's central bank sells its dollar reserves to meet the increased demand. This is the easiest policy, but it is limited by the size of the foreign-currency reserves held by the central bank.
2. Increase domestic interest rates to attract foreign capital. The risk is that high interest rates will slow down investment and bankrupt domestic firms, creating a recession. Hence policy-makers face a tough choice between devaluation and recession. A devaluation will deter future FDI as it undermines confidence in the stability of the domestic currency; a recession will create unemployment and discontent.
3. Borrow from abroad—for example, from the IMF by obtaining a balance-of-payments loan, or from the US Treasury, as Mexico did in 1994 under the Clinton administration. Helping countries fend off speculative attacks by making them dollar loans is the main reason for the IMF's existence. But the size of the loan will be limited by a poor "investment climate," and the lender will attach severe conditionalities, including strict fiscal discipline, which is socially costly and politically dangerous. IMF loans are thus both essential to a country unable to meet its dollar payments, and highly disliked for their social costs. Greece today is a painful illustration of the social costs of austerity imposed by external lenders in qualifying for the loan.
5. The US Federal Reserve Bank cooperates with the country under attack by buying LCUs. When Mexico faces a speculative attack, for example, the US sells

dollars to Mexicans and buys pesos in exchange for dollars, increasing its peso reserves—a friendly gesture. While "a friend in need is a friend indeed," this is limited by the extent of cross-country solidarity and mutual interests.

The different policy instruments available on the supply side of the market for dollars are all limited, and countering the speculative attack may fail, resulting in devaluation.

Demand-side policies to deter speculative attacks
(making devaluation impossible)

This is where dollarization, or introduction of a currency board, as in Argentina, can serve as the ultimate recourse. The central bank pegs the local currency to the US dollar, making devaluation impossible; but if there is a sustained run on the dollar, this will require a huge recession (with unemployment, falling consumption, and falling demand for imports) in order to decrease dollar demand through contraction of the real economy, as devaluation is no longer a policy option. However, it has merit as a short-run measure and was effectively used by a number of countries with a currency under speculative attack such as Ecuador and Israel. The mistake that Argentina made was to maintain dollarization beyond its use as a short-run instrument, depriving the country of a foreign-exchange policy and imposing high social costs in containing inflation through years of rigorous fiscal austerity.

CONCEPTS SEEN IN THIS CHAPTER

Tradable and non-tradable goods
Flexible (floating) and fixed (pegged) exchange rates
Nominal and real (RER) exchange rates
Internal vs. external definition of the RER
Appreciation vs. depreciation of the RER
Exchange-rate devaluation
Exchange-rate policy triangle
Equilibrium exchange rate
PPP-equilibrium exchange rate
Fundamental determinants of the equilibrium exchange rate
Import tariffs and RER appreciation
Stop–go cycles under ISI due to RER appreciation
Dutch disease and RER appreciation
Foreign-exchange sterilization
Speculative attack and the risk of depreciation
The devaluation vs. recession dilemma
IMF conditionalities
Dollarization to prevent devaluation

REVIEW QUESTIONS: INTERNATIONAL FINANCE AND DEVELOPMENT

1. Define and explain the difference between:
   tradable (T) and non-tradable (NT) goods
   nominal and real exchange rates (RER)
   appreciation and depreciation of the RER
2. Identify three determinants of supply and three of demand for foreign exchange.
3. How does the real exchange rate influence the real side of the economy: production of T and NT goods, consumption of T and NT goods, use of T and NT inputs, exports, imports, and the balance of trade? Take as an example the case of a depreciation of the RER in China.
4. Why does ISI contribute to an appreciation of the RER and why is this bad for agriculture?
5. What is the Dutch disease, how does it come about, what are its implications for the economy, and what policy instruments can be used to prevent it from happening?
6. What can the central bank do when there is a speculative attack on the domestic currency? Why do we talk about a devaluation vs. recession dilemma when using the interest rate to counter a speculative attack?

REFERENCES

Asikoglu, Yaman, and Merih Uctum. 1992. "A Critical Evaluation of Exchange Rate Policy in Turkey." *World Development* 20(10): 1501–14.

Broda, C. 2001. "Coping with Terms of Trade Shocks: Pegs vs. Floats." *American Economic Review* 91(2): 376–80.

Corden, N., and J. Neary. 1982. "Booming Sector and De-industrialization in a Small Open Economy." *Economic Journal* 92(368): 825–48.

De Nicoló, G., P. Honohan, and A. Ize. 2003. "Dollarization of the Banking System: Good or Bad?" Washington, DC: World Bank Policy Research Working Paper No. 3116.

Dornbusch, R. 2001. "Fewer Monies, Better Monies: Discussion on Exchange Rates and the Choice of Monetary-policy Regimes." *The American Economic Review* 91(2): 238–42.

Easterly, William, and Stanley Fisher. 2001. "Inflation and the Poor." *Journal of Money, Credit, and Banking* 33(2): 160–78.

The Economist. 2003. "The Devil's Excrement: Is Oil Wealth a Blessing or a Curse?" May 24.

Edwards, Sebastian. 1989. *Real Exchange Rates, Devaluation, and Adjustment*. Cambridge, MA: MIT Press.

Fisher, Stanley. 2001. "Exchange Rate Regimes: Is the Bipolar View Correct?" *Journal of Economic Perspectives* 15(2): 3–24.

Guillaumont Jeanneney, Sylviane. 2011. *Régimes et Stratégies de Change dans les Pays en Développement*. Clermont-Ferrand: CERDI.

International Monetary Fund. *International Financial Statistics*. http://elibrary-data.imf.org/finddatareports.aspx?d=33061&e=169393 (accessed 2015).

Krugman, Paul, and Maurice Obstfeld. 2008. *International Economics: Theory and Policy*. New York: Harper Collins.

401

Lustig, Nora. 2000. "Crises and the Poor: Socially Responsible Macroeconomics." Washington, DC: Inter-American Development Bank, Sustainable Development Department, Poverty and Inequality Advisory Unit Working Paper No. 108.

Mamalakis, Markos 1971. "The Theory of Sectoral Clashes and Coalitions Revisited." *Latin American Research Review* 6(3): 89–126.

Reinhart, C.M., and Kenneth Rogoff. 2004. "The Modern History of Exchange Rate Arrangements: A Reinterpretation." *Quarterly Journal of Economics* 119(1): 1–48.

Van Wijnbergen, S. 1984. "The Dutch Disease: A Disease after All." *Economic Journal* 94(373): 41–55.

World Bank. *World Development Indicators.* http://data.worldbank.org/indicator (accessed 2015).

Population and development

TAKE-HOME MESSAGES FOR CHAPTER 11

1. Total world population reached the 7 billion mark in 2011 and is predicted to stabilize somewhere between 9 billion in 2045 and 12 billion in 2100. Currently, 82 percent of world population lives in the developing world (low- and middle-income countries) and 92 percent of world population growth originates in these countries

2. Population growth is a major issue in international development. It is generally considered to be excessive in developing countries with negative consequences for GDPpc, the provision of basic needs, and environmental sustainability.

3. The demographic transition is an upsurge in population growth associated with death rates falling ahead of birth rates, until birth rates also decline to catch up with death rates, allowing the population to stabilize again after a major quantitative jump.

4. The demographic dividend is a one-time opportunity for a low dependency ratio, permitting high rates of labor-force participation and high rates of savings, both favorable to growth.

5. The determinants of total fertility rates (TFR) are associated with the economic advantages provided by children to parents as sources of income, insurance, and satisfaction. As parents' income rises, the income and insurance functions of children decline, reducing the demand for children. The satisfaction motive in the demand for children shifts from quantity to quality, implying a price effect that also contributes to reducing demand.

6. Supply-side contraception programs help reduce the gap between the actual number of children and the desired number.

7. Population policies to reduce fertility rates aim at reconciling private and social gains from family size. They can focus on the supply side and/or on the demand side for contraception. If there are positive social externalities from higher TFR, pro-natalist policies can be used to boost family size. If there are negative externalities, family-planning policies can deter large families.

8. Gender preference to the advantage of boys, especially in Asia, implies both large numbers of missing women and sibling rivalry to the detriment of girls' welfare.

Population growth is both an asset and a liability for development. It is an asset in that a growing population is a source of youthful labor, social-security contributions, and expanding markets. At the household level, children are sources of income and protection for their parents. Poor people typically prefer to have larger numbers of children as both a choice and a necessity. But they are also a liability. From a simple arithmetical standpoint, population growth subtracts from GDP growth in determining growth in per capita income. It also tends to be a source of declining land per capita, food insecurity, environmental degradation, congestion externalities, and urban blight, as well as a drain on public goods and services. There are both positive and normative questions associated with population growth. Positive questions include: what are the determinants of fertility behavior? Why do countries go through a demographic transition with a phase of exploding population growth? Why is there a decline in population growth as per capita income rises? How do countries benefit from a one-time demographic dividend as fertility declines while the share of elderly people in the population is still relatively low? Normative questions include: how can we reduce population growth if it is deemed excessive? If contraception is the main instrument to reduce fertility, when is it more important to focus on the supply side and when on the demand side of contraception?

Our thesis in this chapter is that children fulfill three functions for parents: they are sources of income, protection, and satisfaction. The transition from high to low fertility—the demographic transition—is associated with children losing their income and protection functions for parents, maintaining their universal satisfaction function increasingly through quality as opposed to quantity. Understanding the determinants of fertility is key to designing population policy. With world population reaching 7 billion in 2011 and expected to peak somewhere between 9 billion in 2045 and 12 billion in 2100, population policy is a key, yet much neglected, aspect of international economic development.

DEFINITIONS: DEMOGRAPHIC CONCEPTS

We start with the definition of a number of concepts used in demographic analysis. The corresponding 2012 data for selected countries ranked by PPP-adjusted GDPpc are presented in Table 11.1.

The *crude birth rate* (b) of a population is the number of live births per 1,000 people per year. In 2012, it was 49.8 in Niger, 37.1 in Sierra Leone, 35.5 in Kenya, 33.5 in Ethiopia, 18.8 in Mexico, 15.1 in Brazil, 12.6 in the US, 12.1 in China, and 8.2 in Japan.

The *crude death rate* (d) of a population is the number of deaths per 1,000 people per year. In 2012, it was 17.4 in Sierra Leone, 11.2 in Niger, 8.5 in Kenya, 7.8 in Ethiopia, 7.2 in China, 6.4 in Brazil, 4.5 in Mexico, 8.1 in the US, and 10.0 in Japan.

Note that the birth and death rates of a population depend on the age structure of that population. If the percentage of young people is very high, as would be the case in a low-income country, the aggregate death rate can be lower in the low-income country (such as Ethiopia, with a crude death rate of 7.8) than in a high-income country (such as Japan, with a crude death rate of 10.0), even though the death rate is higher in each age group than in the high-income country.

404

Table 11.1 _Demographic indicators, selected countries, 2012_

Country	PPP-GDPpc (2012 US$)	Crude birth rate (per 1,000 people)	Crude death rate (per 1,000 people)	Infant-mortality rate (per 1,000 live births)	Life expectancy at birth (years)	Total fertility rate (births per woman)
Niger	899	49.8	11.2	61.6	58.0	7.6
Ethiopia	1240	33.5	7.8	46.2	63.0	4.6
Sierra Leone	1610	37.1	17.4	109.6	45.3	4.8
Kenya	2189	35.5	8.5	48.8	61.1	4.5
India	5138	20.7	7.9	42.9	66.2	2.5
Nigeria	5535	41.5	13.5	76.6	52.1	6.0
Guatemala	7107	31.4	5.3	26.6	71.7	3.8
China	10945	12.1	7.2	11.7	75.2	1.7
Brazil	14574	15.1	6.4	12.9	73.6	1.8
Mexico	16178	18.8	4.5	13.1	77.1	2.2
Japan	35315	8.2	10.0	2.2	83.1	1.4
US	51755	12.6	8.1	6.1	78.7	1.9

Source: World Bank, _World Development Indicators._

The *annual rate of natural increase* of a population (r) is the difference between the birth rate and the death rate: $r = b - d$. Based on the above statistics, in 2012 it was 3.9 percent in Niger, 2.7 in Kenya, 2.6 in Ethiopia, 2.0 in Sierra Leone, 1.4 in Mexico, 0.9 in Brazil, 0.5 in China and the US and −0.2 in Japan.

The *annual natural increase in population* is rN, where N is population size at the beginning of the year. Each year, 84.3 million people are added to world population, 82.6 in the less developed countries and 1.7 in the more developed countries. Ninety-eight percent of world population growth is thus located in the LDCs. The observed increase in population takes into account net migration and for that reason differs from the natural increase in population.

Other useful indicators of fertility are the following. For deaths:

■ The *infant mortality rate* is the number of deaths of children less than a year old per 1,000 live births. In 2012, it was 109.6 in Sierra Leone, 76.6 in Nigeria, 46.2 in Ethiopia, 42.9 in India, 13.1 in Mexico, 6.1 in the US, and 2.2 in Japan.

■ *Life expectancy at birth.* In 2012, it was 45 in Sierra Leone, 63 in Ethiopia, 74 in Brazil, 77 in Mexico, 79 in the US, and 83 in Japan. The US had the highest life expectancy in the world in the 1950s, but has by now fallen to 34th, ranking below Chile, Costa Rica, and Cuba. Life expectancy is higher for women (86.4 in Japan, 81.2 in the US) than for men (79.9 in Japan, 76.4 in the US), but there has been a tendency toward convergence among genders in the last decade.

For births:

■ The *total fertility rate* (TFR) is the average number of children that will be born to a woman in a population during her reproductive years (15 to 49). In 2012, it was 7.6 in Niger, the highest in the world, 6.0 in Nigeria, 4.8 in Sierra Leone, 4.6 in Ethiopia, 2.5 in India, and 2.2 in Mexico. For the world, in 2012, the TFR was 2.4.

■ The *replacement fertility rate* for zero growth of a population is 2.1. Any population with a TFR inferior to 2.1 and no net immigration is declining in size.

■ In industrialized countries, the TFR is in most cases below replacement level. It is 1.9 in the US (1.8 for white women and 2.4 for Hispanic women), below 1.5 in most European countries (1.4 in Italy and Germany, 1.3 in Spain, with France's 2.0 above the others), and 1.4 in Japan. High-income countries such as South Korea (1.3), Singapore (1.3), and Taiwan (1.1) are also way below replacement rate. Brazil, as a middle-income country, has a TFR of 1.8. China, with its one-child policy, is a unique low-income country with a TFR of 1.7, largely below replacement rate.

Age–gender *population pyramids* are an effective way of visualizing population growth as affected by birth and death rates and other events. The pyramid gives the number of people by gender and age group. Figure 11.1 shows the contrast between four population pyramids in 2012, with population rapidly growing in Kenya, slowing down in China, stagnant in the US, and shrinking in Japan. The corresponding demographic indicators are given in Table 11.2.

406

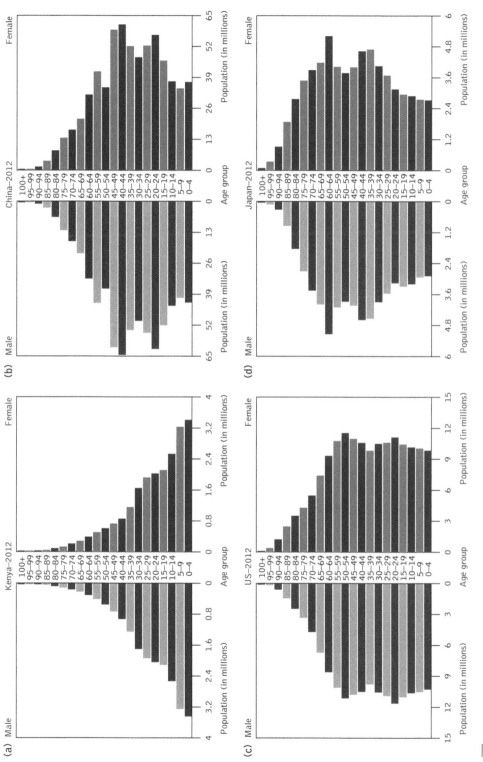

Figure 11.1 *Population pyramids by age and gender for Kenya (a), China (b), the US (c), and Japan (d), 2012*

Source: US Census Bureau, *International Programs.*

Table 11.2 *Population dependency ratios for Kenya, China, the US, and Japan, 2012*

	Kenya	China	US	Japan
Total population (million)	42.0	1343.2	313.9	127.4
Youth 0–14 (million)	18.3	233.2	61.1	17.2
Elderly 65+ (million)	1.2	122.3	43.1	30.4
Working-age population (million)	22.6	987.8	209.6	79.8
Youth-dependency ratio	0.81	0.24	0.29	0.22
Elderly-dependency ratio	0.05	0.12	0.21	0.38
Total dependency ratio	0.86	0.36	0.50	0.60

Source: US Census Bureau, *International Programs.*

A pyramid with a wide base and a narrow top, as in Kenya, characterizes a population with a high birth rate and a high death rate. As conditions improve, the birth rate declines and the base of the pyramid shrinks, as in China. When life expectancy rises, the population pyramid becomes more like a tower, as in the US. Finally, the pyramid starts reversing, with the most numerous age group rising from 0–4 in Kenya to 60–4 in Japan.

Countries with high population growth rates have high *dependency ratios*. The dependency ratio is the ratio of non-working-age to working-age population. The non-working-age population is defined as people 0–14 years' old for the youth and people 65 years' old and above for the elderly. The *youth-dependency ratio* is the number of people 0–14 relative to the number of people 15 to 64. In countries with rapidly growing populations, about a quarter of the population can be 14 years' old or under (e.g. 25 percent in Algeria). This places a high burden on the working-age population. The *elderly-dependency ratio* is the number of people 65 years' old and above relative to the number of people 15 to 64. In slow-growing populations with long life expectancy, the elderly-dependency ratio increases, placing a new burden on the working-age population. In Japan, 22 percent of the population is 65 years old or more.

The total dependency ratio can be high either because there are many young people or because there are many old people, both relative to the number of working adults. The dependency ratio will thus be lowest when the population growth rate is declining while there are still few elderly people to support. This transition creates a one-time opportunity for a low dependency ratio, with the possibility of high rates of labor-force participation and savings called the demographic dividend. This demographic dividend was important in helping Taiwan and South Korea achieve high rates of savings and high rates of growth in the postwar period, when they had their economic booms (Lee and Mason, 2006). As Table 11.2 shows, among the four countries compared, China is the one with the highest demographic dividend (a total dependency ratio of 0.36) compared to Kenya (0.86), the US (0.5), and Japan (0.6). In Mexico, as can be seen in Figure 11.2a, the demographic dividend will be greatest in 2022. The total dependency ratio will fall from 92 percent in 1980 to 51 percent in 2022, and rise

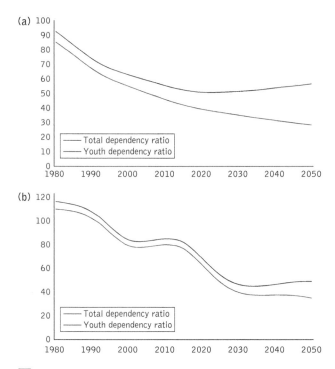

Figure 11.2 *The demographic dividend in Mexico (a) and Kenya (b), 1980 to 2050. The elderly-dependency ratio is the difference between the total and youth-dependency ratios*

Source: US Census Bureau, *International Programs.*

to 57 percent in 2050 as the population ages. In this case, an important determinant of the demographic transition is aging of the population. In Kenya (b), the demographic dividend will be greatest in 2035. The total dependency ratio will fall from 113 percent in 1980, to 44 percent in 2035, and rise to 48 percent in 2050. In this case, most of the action comes from the decline in the youth-dependency ratio. As Sub-Saharan Africa countries enter a phase of demographic dividends, an important question is whether this one-time opportunity to raise savings will be used to support an industrial take-off, as it was in East Asia.

These contrasting statistics on TFR and age structure illustrate the world-population dilemma. Population growth is generally considered to be excessive in poor countries, and too low in rich countries. The issue could be resolved by international migration, with the poor countries exporting surplus population to the rich ones for mutual benefit. However, as we will see in Chapter 12, international migration, which was unrestricted in the 1850–1914 period, the age of empire, is now severely restricted. We have a situation in which surplus labor accumulates in poor countries, with the associated dramas of low investment in human capital, unemployment, and poverty, while labor shortages occur in rich countries and productive labor is in deficit to support an aging population.

Table 11.3 Population growth rates and years to double

	Population growth rate (%)					Number of years to double				
	1970	1980	1990	2000	2010	1970	1980	1990	2000	2010
World	2.1	1.7	1.7	1.3	1.2	33	40	40	53	59
By income level										
Low-income	2.6	2.5	2.7	2.4	2.2	27	28	26	29	32
Middle-income	2.5	2.0	1.9	1.4	1.2	28	35	37	50	60
High-income	0.9	0.8	0.7	0.5	0.6	76	85	94	136	114
By region										
Sub-Saharan Africa	2.6	2.9	2.8	2.7	2.7	27	24	25	26	26
Middle East and North Africa	2.7	3.2	3.4	1.9	2.0	25	22	20	36	35
South Asia	2.3	2.4	2.2	1.8	1.3	30	29	31	39	51
Latin America and the Caribbean	2.5	2.2	1.9	1.5	1.1	27	31	37	47	61
East Asia and the Pacific	2.6	1.5	1.5	1.0	0.7	27	47	46	73	104

Note: The number of years to double is equal to ln2/r where r is the annual growth rate.

Source: World Bank, *World Development Indicators.*

Table 11.4 Distribution of world population, 2013

	Total population (billion)	Share of total population (%)	Population growth (annual %)	Years to double	Share of total population growth (%)
World	7.12	100	1.2	60	100
Low-income	0.85	11.9	2.2	31	23.1
Middle-income	4.97	69.8	1.1	61	69.0
High-income non-OECD	0.25	3.5	0.7	98	2.2
High-income OECD	1.05	14.8	0.5	149	6.0

Source: World Bank, *World Development Indicators.*

SOME DATA FOR WORLD POPULATION

Total world population reached the 7 billion mark in 2011, and was 7.12 billion in 2013. The current prediction for the level at which world population is likely to stabilize is somewhere between 9 billion in 2045 and 12 billion in 2100. There has been a rapid decline in the rate of population growth at a world scale, from 2.1 percent/year in 1970 to 1.2 percent/year in 2010, and this decline has started to occur in low-income countries as well, where it fell from 2.6 percent to 2.2 percent over the same period (Table 11.3).

We can appreciate the decline in the population growth rate by using the number of years needed to double population size. It is measured as ln2/r, where r is the population growth rate (see Chapter 1). At a world scale, it rose from 33 years in 1970 to 59 years in 2010. It is lowest in Sub-Saharan Africa, where it is 26 years, and highest in East Asia and the Pacific, where it is 104 years. In spite of this decline, population growth remains a huge problem on a world scale as total population is still expected to increase by a minimum of 2 billion, nearly an extra 30 percent on an already crowded planet, before it stabilizes. Predicted population growth implies that food production will have to increase by 60 percent over the next 30 years. As we will see in Chapter 18, this is an enormous challenge in a world where unused land is very limited and climate change is threatening the sustainability even of existing yields.

Listed below are other important aspects of world population.

1. Eighty-two percent of world population lives in the *developing world* (low- and middle-income countries), and 92 percent of world population growth originates in these countries (Table 11.4). The world-population problem is fundamentally associated with developing countries and, very importantly, as we will see, with poverty in these countries. Projected to 2050 (Figure 11.3a), world population will be 9.4 billion, with 1.3 billion people in high-income countries and 8.1 billion in developing countries, 86 percent of the total. The future regional distribution of world population is also stunning (Figure 11.3b). Population in East Asia will peak in 2025 at 1.63 billion and subsequently decline to 1.51 billion. By contrast, high fertility will drive total population to 3.32 billion in South Asia and 1.81 billion in Sub-Saharan Africa, two regions where poverty is also extreme. In 2050, 1.81 billion of world population will be located in the least developed countries, with the highest rate of population growth.

2. World population is rapidly becoming *urbanized*. The world rate of urban population growth is 2.8 percent, and 50 percent of world population was urban by the end of 2008. In Latin America, the urban population share is already 73 percent. While world population is becoming urbanized, world poverty remains predominantly rural.

3. There are many *mega-cities* in the low- and middle-income countries. Examples include Mexico City (18.1 million inhabitants), Mumbai (18), Sao Paulo (17.7),

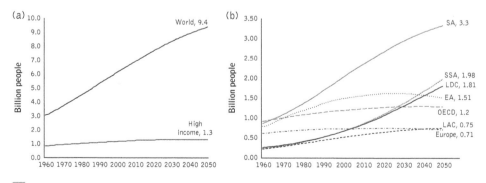

Figure 11.3 *Distribution of world population between world and high-income countries (a) and by regions (b), 1960–2050. In (a), developing countries' population is the difference between the two curves*

Source: US Census Bureau, *International Programs*.

Shanghai (14.2), Lagos (13.5), and Calcutta (12.9). The rate of population growth tends to fall sharply with displacement of the population from the rural to the urban environment. The nature of poverty is also different in the urban than it is in the rural environment, calling on different types of anti-poverty intervention. In general, anti-poverty programs such as CCTs have been more successful in the rural than in the urban environment, as we will see in Chapter 14.

4. The *incidence of AIDS* in Sub-Saharan Africa has had a huge toll on the population, with an estimated 7 million deaths since the beginning of the pandemics. In 2013, HIV prevalence was as high as 27 percent in Swaziland, 15 percent in Zimbabwe, 19 percent in South Africa, and 13 percent in Zambia. Largely because of AIDS, life expectancy at birth has fallen from a high of 59 years in 1990 to a low of 46 in 2004 in Swaziland, from 61 in 1985 to 43 in 2002 in Zimbabwe, from 62 in 1992 to 52 in 2005 in South Africa, and from 51 in 1978 to 41 in 1998 in Zambia (World Bank, *World Development Indicators*). AIDS has a high economic cost as deaths are concentrated among working-age adults. It increases the dependency ratio, leaving grandparents and the community in charge of orphans. In some villages in Zambia, as many as 30–40 percent of the children are orphans.

HISTORY OF WORLD POPULATION AND DEMOGRAPHIC TRANSITION

Three demographic revolutions

World population has gone through three demographic revolutions, each with huge spurts in population size.

During the *Neolithic period*, some 10,000 years BC, associated with agriculture displacing hunting and gathering as the main source of food (Diamond, 1997). It is estimated that world population was around 1 million.

During the *agricultural and industrial revolutions* in today's industrialized countries, during the 1700–1880 period. World population reached 1 billion in 1800.

When the *health revolution* reached developing countries from the 1940s, following the introduction of DDT to control malaria, polio vaccines, and antibiotics such as penicillin. By 1950, world population was 2.5 billion.

The demographic transition

The demographic transition is a one-time population explosion that occurs as death rates fall ahead of birth rates. It comes to an end when birth rates also decline, eventually converging with death rates. This is illustrated in Figure 11.4 for industrialized (Figure 11.4a) and developing (Figure 11.4b) countries. In industrialized countries, the demographic transition has been completed, with low birth and death rates, and a correspondingly low population growth rate. In developing countries, the transition is still in progress, with a low death rate and a high birth rate, and a high population growth rate. As these two figures show, most population growth today comes from developing countries. The challenge in overcoming the population explosion in these countries is to reduce the birth rate, as death rates have already started to decline with the diffusion of the health revolution.

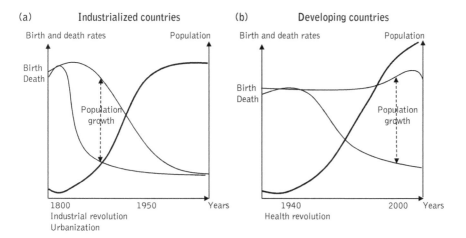

Figure 11.4 *The demographic transition in industrialized (a) and developing (b) countries. Birth and death rates in thin lines; total population in heavy line*

Drawn on the basis of historical regularities.

CAUSES OF POPULATION GROWTH

What explains population growth? For Malthus, population growth was held in check by food availability. For modern demographers, population growth can be explained by the calculus of economic advantage made by a couple deciding how many children to have. The ability to not exceed this number in turn depends on the availability of contraception.

Malthus: the dismal economics of hunger

For Reverend Thomas Malthus, who in 1798 wrote *An Essay on the Principle of Population*, the "passion between the sexes" always pushes population growth ahead of growth in food supply. As a consequence, population growth is held in check not by demographic restraint but by food scarcity and famines. This is because population grows at a geometric (multiplicative) rate while food availability (measured in number of people that can be fed) grows at an arithmetic (additive) rate, as shown in Figure 11.5. Whenever the population growth rate exceeds the food availability growth rate, people die due to "gigantic inevitable famines, wars, epidemics, pestilence, and plagues," in Malthus' own words. There is a stable equilibrium, where the growth in food availability determines the growth of population.

The Malthusian position on the inevitability of starvation as population runs against the limits of food availability has persisted. Paul Ehrlich (1968), in his book *The Population Bomb*, predicted the inevitability of "famines of unbelievable proportions," with "hundreds of millions of people starving to death" in the 1970s and 1980s due to overpopulation. For Ehrlich, the policy implication was not technological, but the need to rapidly bring world population under control, reducing the growth rate to zero or turning it negative. He suggested that foreign aid to countries such as India,

413

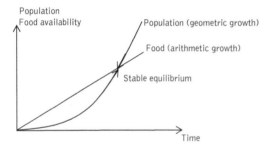

Figure 11.5 *Malthusian population equilibrium: the dismal economics of hunger*

with insufficient programs to limit population growth, should be canceled, as any economic gain would be eliminated by population growth.

Other modern neo-Malthusian positions include the report of the Club of Rome, *The Limits to Growth* (Meadows *et al.*, 1972), which predicted exponential growth in population, industrialization, and pollution, with slow growth in food production. Using a world growth model, the Club of Rome expected petroleum resources to be exhausted by 1992 and iron by 2065. Even with successful exploration for energy and minerals, growth would come to an end by 2070.

Malthusian predictions have been criticized, and proven wrong by events. Fertility has declined due to changes in the logic of family size and the availability of contraception, and there has been much technological change in food production, allowing food availability to grow exponentially. Although world population continues to grow, and tensions still exist in food supply keeping pace with population, food is no longer a global constraint on population. The Green Revolution averted mass famines in India at the time of Ehrlich's predictions. Sen (1981) showed that the Bengal famine of 1943, in which 3 million people died, was not due to lack of food relative to population, but people's lack of access to available food. Poverty, rising food prices, and inadequate food-distribution systems were to blame rather than population explosion and absolute food scarcity. Sen argued that countries with democratic forms of governance and a free press have never suffered from extended famines. Thus, while local famines and resource scarcity (for example, in Rwanda, where land scarcity likely contributed to genocide) can be induced by population growth, markets (with prices signaling scarcity and inducing response) and states (though public goods and social protection) are likely to help avert neo-Malthusian doom through technological and institutional innovations.

Growth theory has also been used to explain how an economy can shift away from a Malthusian world, where income per capita is held stagnant by population growth, to a Solow world, where population can grow without implying a decline in per capita income. Hansen and Prescott (2002) propose a model with two technologies: a Malthus technology, where output is a function of technology, land, labor, and capital, and a Solow technology, where output is a function of technology, labor, and capital, but not of land. If land is in fixed amount, and population growth responds to income (as in Malthus), then population growth will bring down wages and increase land rents, two regularities observed in the pre-industrial world—in England before 1800, say. Once

TFP has become sufficiently important, the Solow technology becomes more profitable than the Malthus technology. Decreasing returns to labor (with fixed land) are replaced by constant returns to scale, as in the Solow production function. Labor productivity can now increase even with population growth. Population growth is no longer a factor of stagnant real wages. The key to the story is that technological progress started to occur in the Malthusian world, allowing labor productivity to rise and making the Solow world superior. Rising labor productivity gives value to investment in education, and can induce a demographic transition due to the fact that children are no longer important productive assets for subsistence production (Rosenzweig and Evenson, 1977), and the quality of children is more important than the quantity (Galor and Weil, 2000).

Determinants of decline in fertility

The decline in the TFR can come from an increase in the age of marriage or from a decline in marital fertility. The latter is the most important. To reason economically about how incentives can affect fertility rates, three preconditions must hold.

1. *Fertility outcomes are subject to willful choice.* When they engage in sexual behavior, people know the implications for family size.
2. *Fertility decisions are determined by the calculus of advantage (utility maximization).* Economic gains and costs are rationalized into fertility decisions. Social norms associated with fertility patterns provide guidelines for fertility decisions. In other words, this calculus does not have to be made each time when it matters, it is ingrained in culturally accepted fertility norms, even though there may exist long lags in the adjustment of these norms to changes in economic context (Easterlin, 1967). Large families may be associated with social status, and this may persist for a long time after the economic rationality for large families has declined.
3. *Some methods of fertility control are available, ranging from inefficient to more efficient.* This allows a couple calculating economic advantage in fertility decisions to adjust the actual number of children they will have to the desired number since desired family size is overall less than actual family size without fertility control. Lack of access to more efficient methods of fertility control implies that the actual number of children may exceed the desired number.

Calculus of economic advantage

In deciding how many children to have, parents consider three types of benefit: income, insurance, and satisfaction.

1. *A child is a source of income.* Children are assets that can provide services to parents at home and in fields and factories. Child labor brings wage earnings to the household. Because there are rearing and maintenance costs before benefits are accrued, a child will be a valuable asset to have if:

PV benefits (services, income) > PV costs (rearing, feeding), where PV is present value calculated at the discount rate that characterizes this particular household.

2. *A child is a source of insurance.* A large number of children allows a household to diversify its sources of income for risk management, receive transfers from children for risk coping following a shock, provide physical protection to parents, and offer them old-age protection.

The protection function of children implies that parents will want to have children to care for them when they are old. The risk that children will die determines how many children parents should have to make sure that at least one of them will be there to help. Say that $\bar{P}$ is the desired probability of having at least one child to look after you at old age—for example, 95 percent. Let q be the probability that a child will die (or will be unable or unwilling to assist you in your old age). If you have one child, the probability that he will be there to help at old age is $P = 1 - q$. If you have two children, the probability that at least one will be there to help is $P = 1 - q^2$. The optimum number of children n to have to achieve your protection objective $\bar{P}$ is thus given by $\bar{P} = 1 - q^n$. Solving for n gives $n = \ln(1 - \bar{P})/\ln q$. Numerical examples are given in Table 11.5. If $\bar{P} = 0.95$ and the death rate of children is $1/2$, then $n = 4$. If the death rate falls to 0.3, then you only need 2 children. Reduced mortality thus allows parents to meet their protection objective with a smaller number of children. If social protection increases and the protection objective from children falls to 0.9, then you only need 3 children instead of 4 with a 50 percent mortality rate.

Other factors can affect the desired number of children parents must have to secure their protection objective. q, the probability that a child will not support you (not be there, not be willing, or not be able), can fall with the child's income. This explains why people in richer countries need fewer children to secure protection, and why people in poorer countries need more. q can rise with the loss of a child's sense of responsibility toward parents. If social change or migration implies a loss of family values toward aging parents, then parents need to have more children to achieve their protection objective. Parents may not be able to predict future declines in child mortality, implying permanence of large families for protection—larger than needed.

$\bar{P}$ can also change, affecting n. If parents are more risk-averse, perhaps because they are poorer, their target $\bar{P}$ rises, and so does n. If parents' own mortality risk

Table 11.5 *Desired number of children to achieve a protection objective*

Protection objective $\bar{P}$	Probability of disappearance of a child q	Desired number of children n
0.95	0.5	4
0.95	0.3	2
0.95	0.1	1
0.9	0.5	3
0.9	0.3	2
0.9	0.1	1

declines, longer life expectancy can raise $\bar{P}$. And if other sources of protection become available, such as public social-assistance programs, $\bar{P}$ falls, and so does the required number of children.

3. *A child is a source of satisfaction.* Children have been compared to "durable consumer goods" (Blake, 1968). They provide utility to parents in many different ways, and compete in the household's budget constraint with other goods and services. There are important trade-offs between quantity and quality of children, with a choice to be made between a larger number of less-educated children and a smaller number of better-educated ones.

Increased investment in the quality of children may come from longer life expectancy, which increases the present value of returns from education. This was studied by Jayachandran and Lleras-Muney (2009) in Sri Lanka in the 1946–53 period, when there was a rapid decline in the maternal mortality rate (MMR) due to greater availability of health care and improved transportation to hospitals for delivery. At that time the TFR was 5 and the lifetime risk of a woman dying in childbirth was 9 percent. The MMR declined from 1.8 per 100 live births to 0.5, implying an increase in life expectancy at age 15 of 4.1 percent. Investment in the human capital of girls was thus significantly increased. Since boys were not affected by this change, they serve as a control for the increase in life expectancy for girls. The authors use a triple-diff erence approach by district (only some benefi ted by the health improvements), time (before and after the MMR decline), and gender (girls as treatment vs. boys as control). The girls considered treated were aged 2–11 in 1946, i.e. those whose educational achievement could have been affected by the gain in life expectancy. Results show that for every additional year of life expectancy girl literacy increased by 2 percent and years of education by 3 percent.

TFR hypotheses: price and income effects

The TFR is determined by the demand for children. How does this demand vary with income? The empirical regularity we observe is that the TFR declines as income rises. An inferior good is a good consumed less as consumer income rises. Bologna, frozen dinners, and canned goods are the classical examples. Does this mean that children are inferior goods? Hopefully not.

The answer to this puzzle was provided by Gary Becker (1981). It comes from a price effect as income rises: better-off parents prefer higher quality and hence more costly children (in terms of health, education, access to material goods, asset endowments, etc.), implying that observed demand declines with income through the price (cost) effect. An important component of the price effect is the rise in the opportunity cost of parents' time spent raising children as income rises. In Figure 11.6, we see that an income effect increases the demand for children. Children are normal goods. However, the rise in the price of children associated with quality reduces the magnitude of this income effect (Figure 11.7a). Additionally, there may be a change in tastes, whereby the consumption of other goods is increasingly preferred to having more children. This further reduces the demand for children (Figure 11.7c). Finally, the

417

price of consumer goods typically falls with technical progress and trade opening, further contributing to a decline in the demand for children (Figure 11.7b). The net effect of rising income (positive), the rising price of children, changing tastes, and falling prices for consumer goods (all negative) may well be a decline in the demand for children as income rises.

This net effect is illustrated in Figure 11.8. The demand for children increases as a function of income. Children are normal goods. However, as income rises, so do the price

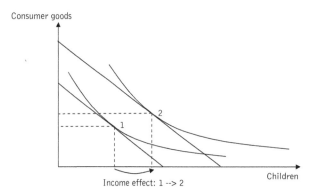

Figure 11. 6 *Income effect on the demand for children*

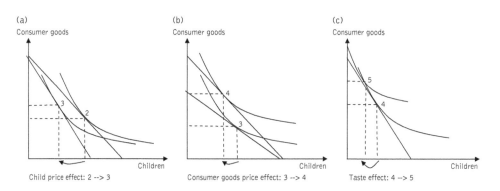

Figure 11.7 *Child-price (a), consumer-good-price (b), and taste (c) effects on the demand for children*

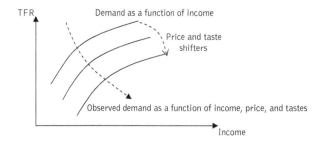

Figure 11.8 *Children as normal goods*

418

of children and the taste for child quality, shifting the income function downward. If this price and taste effect is sufficiently large, the net effect is a declining observed demand for children, making them look like inferior goods.

We can now return to the regularity of the demographic transition described in Figure 11.4 and ask what was the main determinant of the fall in birth rates that triggered the transitions? There are two main potential determinants: rising incomes that induce a change in fertility decisions, following the Becker hypothesis of a price effect coming from the opportunity cost of raising children, and change in the demand for children from quantity to quality that rises with income.

Galor (2010) shows that demographic transitions occurred across Western European countries at the same time, starting in 1870, even though they had very different levels of per capita income. By then, England was much richer than France and Germany, yet all had sharply declining birth rates. What was common to all countries was technological progress that increased the demand for human capital. This in turn shifted the demand for children from quantity to quality. The result was a decline in fertility rates and demographic transitions. According to Galor, the impact of technological change on the demand for child quality was the key determinant of fertility declines and transitions to sustained growth, not income effects.

In the current period, the observed demand for children also shifts downward with the availability of contraception. This is because the availability of contraceptive devices reduces unwanted fertility. As supply-side contraception programs in Bangladesh have demonstrated, this shift in demand induced by supply-side availability of cheap and safe contraception can have a large effect on TFR even as income remains low. In Bangladesh, the TFR fell from 6.3 in 1975 to 3.4 in 1994, largely as a consequence of increased availability of contraception (Kanti, 1997). This is illustrated in Figure 11.9, where supply-side programs shift downward the demand for children from actual number (without contraception) to desired number (with contraception), lowering the TFR. Demand-side programs in turn allow to travel along the downward-sloping desired demand as GDPpc rises.

Does the supply side matter? Across countries, we can observe in Figure 11.10 a strong negative relation between availability of contraception and TFR. This would

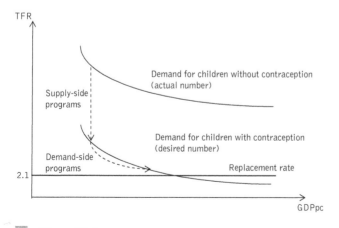

Figure 11.9 *Effects on TFR of supply-side and demand-side contraception programs*

suggest that supply-side policies are important in bringing down the fertility rate. However, this is just a correlation, with no implication about causality between contraceptive prevalence and TFR. This is because causality can run on the supply side (availability of contraception brings down the TFR, as seen in Bangladesh) as well as on the demand side (demand for low TFR induces the plentiful availability of contraception, as in Western Europe). There is also spurious correlation with many determinants of access to contraception and fertility such as per capita income, education, and the degree of urbanization of the population. Reading causality into Figure 11.10 would simply be wrong. We need to rely on RCTs or on natural experiments with the roll-out of contraceptive devices over time and space to resolve the causality problem.

Miller (2010) used the roll-out of the PROFAMILIA family-planning program in Colombia as a natural experiment to identify the role of the supply side of contraception on fertility. He found that family-planning services were responsible for only 10 percent of the decline in fertility during Colombia's demographic transition. Most of the action on TFR was thus on the demand side. Availability of family-planning services was, however, important in helping young women postpone marriage and achieve substantially higher levels of education and participation in the labor force. Using the roll-out of the Green Revolution in India as another natural experiment, Rosenzweig (1990) also found that availability of family-planning programs to reduce the cost of fertility control made only a small contribution to the decline in fertility compared to demand-side effects.

Another source of doubt about the role of the supply side in bringing down the TFR is that the European countries achieved their demographic transitions without

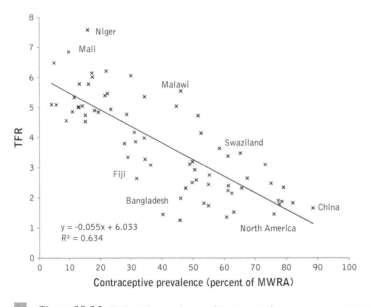

Figure 11.10 TFR and prevalence of contraceptive use across countries, 2012–14. MWRA is married women of reproductive ages

Source: World Bank, World Development Indicators.

420

access to modern contraceptive methods. Demand for low fertility and use of traditional methods may thus suffice. However, this may be at a considerable utility cost in meeting the desired demand for children, and achieving the necessary cultural change may take a long time, both of which would be reduced by availability of contraception. But this experience also suggests that the demand-side may, overall, be the main determinant of a decline in TFR.

We can conceptualize how changes in the determinants of desired demand for children lead to a demographic transition. We argued that children are sources of income, insurance, and satisfaction for parents. These three determinants of desired demand change as income rises and as other transformations occur such as urbanization, rising economic opportunities for women and their empowerment in fertility decisions, and the rising role of education in securing a child's future success. A demographic transition would then be associated with the following changes in the functions of children:

children lose their function as a source of income for parents;
children lose their function as a source of insurance for parents;
children never lose their function as a source of satisfaction for parents, but quality of children is increasingly valued over quantity, leading to a decline in TFR through a price and taste effect.

These three negative effects on the demand for children induce a decline in birth rates and a demographic transition, where low birth rates finally catch up with low death rates. We explore these three effects below.

Economic determinants of desired total fertility: Summary

In the following, we summarize and attach signs to the variables that can be expected to determine the importance of the three functions fulfilled by children that affect the desired TFR. There exists a large empirical literature that relates TFR across households to determinants of fertility behavior, classified here between satisfaction (Table 11.6), income (Table 11.7), and insurance (Table 11.8).

Table 11.6 *Satisfaction function of children*

Sign on TFR Determinants

+	Parents' income (children are not an inferior good) = income effect (Blake, 1968)
−	Child quality (which increases with income) = direct price effect (Becker, 1981)
−	Consumption of other goods and services (which increases with income) that compete with expenditure on children = cross-price effect
−	Opportunity cost of parents' time (which increases with income, and also with opportunities for women to work, female education, and urbanization) = price effect
+	Culture of large families (machismo, religious values). Cultural norms reflect both the current and past economic value of children, creating a path-dependency effect (Easterlin, 1967). People may lag in processing information on the decline in death rates that would lead them to have fewer children.

Table 11.7 *Income function of children*

Sign on TFR *Determinants*

+	Opportunities for child labor: on-farm work, employment in rug and brick factories, absence of child-labor laws, culture of child labor (Basu and Van, 1998), no compulsory education laws or lack of enforcement
+	Easy substitution of parents' labor by child labor: children as suppliers of z-goods (fetching water and firewood), herding animals, care of younger siblings by older girl
+	Direction of intergenerational income transfers from young to old: remittances, intra-household transfers, care of elderly parents (Lee, 1990)
+	Children used to compensate for market failures in credit (for example, through remittances), provide parents with residual claimant labor (which is cheaper and more trusted than hired labor that requires supervision, Wydick (1999))
−	Autonomous income gains (randomized cash transfers to young girls in Malawi) lower fertility rates (Baird *et al.*, 2011)
−	Technological change (roll-out of the Green Revolution in agriculture) increases the return to investment in human capital. This induces more investment in schooling (quality effect) and lowers fertility (Rosenzweig, 1990)
−	Farm size, mechanization, use of enclosed fields for grazing animals, private-property rights (instead of community allocation of land according to need) reduce the income function of children.

Table 11.8 *Insurance function of children*

Sign on TFR *Determinants*

+	Threats of violence and expropriation: children help protect against physical insecurity, against expropriation from slum dwellings without property rights
+	Children compensate for market failures in insurance and for deficits in access to social safety-net programs
−	Access to social-security programs (contributory pensions), access to insurance services (flexible credit, health and life insurance), and access to social-assistance programs (non-contributory pensions, social-safety nets). Increased security of property rights (Field, 2003).

POPULATION POLICY

We now turn to normative analysis: how can population policy be designed to affect the TFR? This depends on whether the current level of population growth is seen by policy-makers as a positive or a negative factor in their development program. As seen in Figure 11.11, parents decide on their optimum number of children by equating the private marginal cost (slope of the private-cost function) and the private marginal benefit (slope of the benefit function) of a child. If there are no externalities to childbearing (i.e. all cost and benefit implications of this additional person are either borne by the parents or transmitted to society through markets), the private optimum fertility decision coincides with the social optimum. If there are positive externalities from having children, the socially optimum family size is larger than the private choice. If there are negative externalities, it is lower. The first case calls for policies to increase the TFR, the second to decrease it (Lee, 1990). We consider each set of policies in turn.

Policies to increase the TFR

These are necessary when the social benefits of more children exceed private benefits. Many Western European countries have introduced pro-birth policies to induce parents to have larger families.

Reasons why a higher TFR may be seen as socially desirable include the need for a faster-growing labor force to sustain a higher GDP growth rate when there are restrictions on international migration, empty or underused geographical areas that can be settled (e.g. the Brazilian Amazon under the military regimes), the cost of spreading public goods such as infrastructure (e.g. in the Democratic Republic of the Congo, with vast empty spaces that are highly costly to connect), more soldiers and economies of scale in defense expenditures, an increase in domestic market size, and pressures on social security, with pay-as-you-go becoming increasingly costly due to population aging (as in Western Europe and the US). Intergenerational transfers through public expenditures on health, education, and pensions create large positive externalities in industrialized countries.

Policy instruments are designed to create private incentives for parents to have more children. They are a way to internalize in parents' choices the positive externalities that an additional child generates. They include cash transfers to large families such as family allowances in Western Europe, and other rewards such as larger families paying lower prices for public services. Another effective way of inducing parents to have more children is the provision of public or subsidized child-care facilities to help balance work and family life.

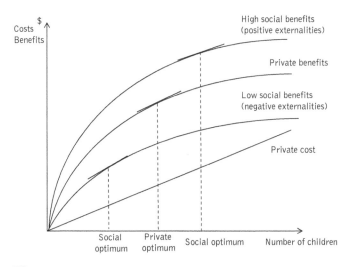

Figure 11.11 *Private and social benefits and fertility decisions*

Policies to decrease the TFR

These are necessary when the social benefits of more children are inferior to private benefits. An additional child creates a gain for the parents but a negative social externality. Family-planning programs are a response to this situation, both increasing the supply side of contraception and reducing the desired demand for children.

Reasons why a lower TFR may be socially desirable include the following:

- A high population growth rate reduces per capita income gains from GDP growth through the population tax we saw in Chapter 2.
- Large reservoirs of rural surplus labor contribute to continued poverty in spite of industrialization and growth. Population growth postpones the Lewis turning point in the classical dual-economy model we saw in Chapter 8. Real wages will not start rising with growth until surplus labor has been eliminated.
- High youth dependency ratios result in low savings rates, postponing the growth benefits of a demographic dividend discussed earlier in this chapter.
- It is difficult to meet the public-goods needs of a rapidly growing population in health, education, infrastructure, and housing.
- There are congestion externalities in urban environments such as overcrowded slums and traffic jams (we will discuss this in Chapter 12).
- Environmental stress associated with population density leads to lower growth and high negative externalities on wellbeing such as air and water pollution (we will discuss this in Chapter 15).

As we saw in Figure 11.9, policies to decrease fertility can focus on both the supply and the demand sides of fertility decisions. We consider them in turn.

Supply-side population policies

These consist in increasing the availability of contraception and reducing its price if there is a gap between actual and desired fertility. This is the approach that was effectively pursued in Bangladesh. The justification for a subsidy for family-planning services is that there are positive social externalities from smaller family sizes. Targeting the subsidies to the poor is justified further by their liquidity constraint in accessing contraception.

Pritchett (1994) analyzes empirically whether the TFR across countries can be explained by the gap between actual and desired fertility (that can be reduced by increased availability of family-planning services) or simply by desired fertility. He finds that unwanted fertility plays only a minor role, and that fertility desires explain 90 percent of observed differences in fertility outcomes. The correlation between contraceptive prevalence and the TFR observed in Figure 11.10 may not run causally from contraception to the TFR, but from desire for low fertility inducing a supply of contraceptive services. Thus reducing fertility first requires a reduction in fertility desires (demand side), and only then a reduction in unwanted fertility (supply side).

424

Demand-side population policies

These consist in inducing households to decrease their desired number of children. There are three main instruments for this.

The first is to decrease poverty (Mamdani, 1972). This is because rising incomes decrease demand for the income and security functions of children, and shift the satisfaction function of children from quantity to quality. Based on this logic, anti-poverty programs create the side benefit of potentially reducing the TFR. Using an RCT approach, Baird *et al.* (2011) find that conditional cash transfers reduce fertility through the channels of extended schooling, reduce teenage pregnancy, and postpone marriage.

The second instrument is to increase the effective price of children by offering parents a trade-off with other benefits. One option is to offer a higher quality–quantity trade-off in raising children. This derives from greater opportunities for parents to invest in the quality of their children—for instance, through access to higher-quality education. Another option is better health services, which extend children's life expectancy, reducing the demand for larger numbers and increasing the value of investing in child education (Jayachandran and Lleras-Muney, 2009).

Female education, changes in women's reproductive rights, and increased employment opportunities for women also have powerful effects on fertility decisions. Many of these benefits come with urbanization. In all cases, they raise the opportunity cost of child-rearing. Using distance to a university as a determinant of access to education, Currie and Moretti (2003) find that better-educated women tend to have better-cared-for babies. Using a natural experiment in India, where a large Indian textile firm changed workers' contracts from fixed-term to daily employment, Sivasankaran (2014) found that the longer duration of employment under fixed-term contracts had the effect of delaying marriage and reduced desired fertility.

Finally, improved social services such as social protection and social assistance can reduce the demand for children in their insurance function.

The role of culture in shaping the demand for fertility

Changing parents' perception of the benefits of smaller families can also influence fertility demand. The TFR declined rapidly in Brazil—from 6.3 in 1960 to 1.9 by 2010—with very little government intervention. Preferences for smaller families developed thanks in part to declines in child mortality and changes in women's opportunities. However, culture also played a role. The popularity of television soap operas (*telenovelas*) featuring families with only two children seems to have helped change fertility desires. To show this, La Ferrara *et al.* (2012) used as an identification strategy differences in the timing of entry of Rede Globo—the network with a monopoly on *telenovelas*—into different regional markets. Using population-census data for the period 1970–91, they found that women living in areas covered by the Rede Globo signal had significantly lower fertility. They also found that the effect was strongest for women of lower socio-economic status and for women in the central and late phases of their fertility cycle, consistent with the decision to stop having children.

425

Mini-dramas for radio, television, and movies were used in Bangladesh to appeal to and change opinions of male audiences regarding family planning, including a soap opera that was written specifically to glamorize the role of family-planning outreach workers (Manoff, 1997). The Bangladeshi family-planning program was a resounding success, reducing the TFR from 6.3 in 1970 to 2.7 in 2007. Though the program included significant supply-side interventions, including many new clinics and thousands of outreach workers, the role of media in changing fertility desires was indispensable.

Demand can also be affected by a change in intra-household bargaining between wife and husband over the use of contraception. Ashraf *et al.* (2014) used an RCT in Zambia to test the usefulness of involving men in decision-making regarding the use of contraception. They contrasted a treatment where both husband and wife are offered access to injectable hormonal contraception with one where the offer is made to the woman alone (this form of contraception is observable only to the woman). They found that involving men reduced demand for contraception by 19 percent and increased the likelihood of giving birth by 27 percent. Allowing only women access to concealable contraception is thus a better approach to reducing fertility. They found, however, that this had a long-term cost for household harmony, with more mistrust and tension, and lower women's happiness and health as a psychological cost of making contraceptives concealable. Giving some control to men over contraceptive decisions may thus lessen marital tensions created by the moral hazard of unobservable contraceptive methods.

Reconciling social objectives and private rationalities

One of the most difficult aspects of population policy to lower the TFR is aligning social optimality and private desires. In some countries, this has been done coercively (Sinding, 2007). In 1979, China, with the largest population in the world, imposed the one-child policy enforced by social sanctions such as monetary fines, job loss, and loss of access to public services. As coercion is relaxed, with couples allowed to have two children if one parent was an only child, it appears that the high cost of children, with an extraordinary premium on quality, may not result in a return to larger families. India under Indira Gandhi also used coercion, in 1976, with loss of access to public services for larger families and forced sterilization of the poor beyond a threshold family size. This policy was violently opposed and could not be sustained. In Indonesia under Suharto, couples refusing to comply with family planning and birth limits faced restrictions on access to micro-credit, loss of education subsidies for civil servants, and even forced migration to rural areas.

Most countries are seeking to reduce the gap between actual and desired number children through more effective supply-side policies and incentives on the demand side. Increased availability of contraception can be quite effective if the gap is large. Bangladesh was successful in reducing demand without a change in income. Most importantly, countries that want to reduce the TFR are seeking to reduce the desired number of children. Income and price effects, as well as changes in the culture of large families and information on reduced child mortality, offer a broad range of policy instruments for this purpose. In the late 1970s and early 1980s, Bangladeshi women received cash payments as reimbursements for sterilization procedures, an approach that has, however, been criticized in the context of extreme poverty limiting a woman's actual wishes.

A stalled fertility transition in Sub-Saharan Africa?

In 1950, there were two Europeans for every African. If present trends continue, there will be two Africans for every European by 2050. The TFRs of African countries and those of other countries when they were at the same stage of fertility transition (such as Asian and Latin American countries during the 1970s) are comparable, but the recent pace of fertility decline is slower. Many African countries seem to have stalled, with TFRs stuck at 5. The reason for the stall may be twofold: (1) Africans have a larger ideal family size than was observed in other countries at this stage of transition, and (2) unmet needs for contraception remain high. It is likely that both demand-side interventions to change the ideal family size and supply-side interventions to increase the availability of contraceptives will be necessary for the African fertility transition to progress (Bongaarts and Casterline, 2013).

OTHER ISSUES IN POPULATION AND DEVELOPMENT

The debate on "missing women"

The ratio of men to women is expected to be about equal to 1. It is in fact a little higher for boys, reaching 1.05, but this is compensated by a slightly higher infant-mortality rate for boys, bringing the natural sex ratio to about 1. In Western countries, the ratio of men to women is 1. In recent history, this has not been the case in several Asian countries. The ratio is 1.07 in China, 1.08 in India, and 1.11 in Pakistan. This deficit of girls has been attributed to the recent availability of ultrasound diagnostics that help reveal the sex of the child before birth. A preference for boys, enhanced in China by the one-child policy, induces abortions that select against girls. Excess mortality of young girls can also be due to purposeful neglect. A preference for boys is associated with the differential role that boys are expected to play in earning income and receiving inheritance, while girls need to be provided with expensive marriage dowries. Sen (1992) estimated that there are some 60–100 million "missing women" in Asian countries. Bardhan (1974) finds rationality for selective girl neglect by comparing North and South India. The imbalance in sex ratios is high in the North, but small in the South. In the North, wheat is mechanized and requires largely heavy manual labor provided by males; in the South, rice is transplanted and harvested manually and is female-labor intensive. This difference creates better employment and earning opportunities for women in the South, suggesting missing women are not a result of biological factors but of adverse economic incentives ingrained in cultural norms.

Missing women may create an unexpected incentive effect, affecting economic growth. Wei and Zhang (2011) argued that fierce competition among men in the marriage market has been a powerful incentive for effort, risk-taking, saving, and investment. They used an instrumental variable approach to households' demographic status by exploring regional variations in the financial penalties for violating official birth quotas and in the proportion of the local population that is legally exempted from the family-planning policy. According to them, imbalance in the sex ratio may have added as much as 2 percent to China's annual GDP growth.

Sibling rivalry

If parents face constraints in the time or financial resources available to them to spend on their children's education and health, and if there is a preference for boys, then the demographic composition of the household will affect investment in human capital for each child (Morduch, 2000). At any given number of siblings, the investment in human capital will increase with the percentage of sisters a child has, both boy and girl. Boys compete with other boys for resources, and girls compete with boys. As a consequence, both genders benefit from having fewer boys in the family. The best environment for human-capital investment in girls is a family with girls only. For investment in boys, it is a family with sisters only.

Note that if there are positive spillover effects from boy consumption, then a girl may benefit from having a brother. This would be the case for the consumption of household public goods, as opposed to private goods. Vaccination may be such a case, where taking a boy to be vaccinated may increase a sister's likelihood of being vaccinated as well (Jones, 2014).

There is also an interesting family-size effect on girls (G) when there is a preference for boys (B). Couples will stop having children once they have had a boy, but continue to have more until they have one. Family compositions will then be: B, GB, GGB, GGGB, etc. This implies that girls will be in larger households than boys. If child welfare declines with family size, then a preference for boys implies that girls have on average less access to household resources than boys.

These examples show that demographic composition matters for child-welfare outcomes in ways that are easy to observe empirically and important.

CONCEPTS SEEN IN THIS CHAPTER

Crude birth and death rates
Population growth rate
Total fertility rate (TFR)
Life expectancy at birth
Doubling time
Population pyramid
Demographic dividend
Pay-as-you-go in social security
Demographic transition
Malthusian population trap
Income function of children

Insurance function of children

Satisfaction function of children

Becker quantity–quality trade-off in the demand for children

Population policy: supply side vs. demand side

Boy preference and missing women

Sibling rivalry

REVIEW QUESTIONS: POPULATION AND DEVELOPMENT

1. Define the total fertility rate (TFR).
2. Explain the phenomenon of a "demographic transition." How does it help explain rapid population growth in particular historical periods?
3. Explain the phenomenon of the "demographic dividend." How does it come about and what potential advantages does it offer for growth?
4. Determinants of fertility behavior: how do the income, insurance, and satisfaction functions of children explain the TFR? How do these roles change through the demographic transition?
5. What are the relative roles of supply of contraception and demand for children in determining observed TFRs?
6. How does Becker explain the demand for children? Are children inferior goods? How do price effects come about? Explain the quantity–quality trade-off in the demand for children and how this affects the TFR.
7. If population growth is judged excessive, what can be done to reduce it? Distinguish between supply-side and demand-side interventions.

REFERENCES

Ashraf, Nava, Erica Field, and Jean Lee. 2014. "Household Bargaining and Excess Fertility: An Experimental Study in Zambia." *American Economic Review* 104(7): 2210–37.

Baird, Sarah, Craig McIntosh, and Berk Özler. 2011. "Cash or Condition? Evidence from a Cash Transfer Experiment." *Quarterly Journal of Economics* 126(4): 1709–53.

Bardhan, Pranab. 1974. "On Life and Death Questions." *Economic and Political Weekly* 9(32–4): 1293–304.

Basu, Kaushik, and Pham Hoang Van. 1998. "The Economics of Child Labor." *The American Economic Review* 88(3): 412–27.

Becker, Gary. 1981. *A Treatise on the Family.* Cambridge, MA: Harvard University Press.

Blake, Judith. 1968. "Are Babies Consumer Durables?" *Population Studies* 22(March): 5–25.

Bongaarts, John, and John Casterline. 2013. "Fertility Transition: Is Sub-Saharan Africa Different?" *Population and Development Review* 38(s1): 153–68.

Currie, Janet, and Enrico Moretti. 2003. "Mother's Education and the Intergenerational Transmission of Human Capital: Evidence from College Openings." *Quarterly Journal of Economics* 118(4): 1495–532.

Diamond, Jared. 1997. *Guns, Germs, and Steel: The Fates of Human Societies.* New York: W.W. Norton and Co.

Easterlin, Richard. 1967. "Population Growth and Economic Development." *The Annals of the American Academy of Political and Social Science* 369(1): 98–108.

Ehrlich, Paul. 1968. *The Population Bomb.* New York: Ballantine Books.

Field, Erica. 2003. "Fertility Responses to Urban Land Titling Programs: The Roles of Ownership Security and the Distribution of Household Assets." Working paper, Department of Economics, Duke University.

Galor, Oded. 2010. "The Demographic Transition: Causes and Consequences."*Cliometrica* 6(1): 1–28.

Galor, Oded, and David Weil. 2000."Population, Technology, and Growth: From Malthusian Stagnation to the Demographic Transition and Beyond." *American Economic Review* 90(4): 806–28.

Hansen, Gary, and Edward Prescott. 2002."Malthus to Solow." *American Economic Review* 92(4): 1205–17.

Jayachandran, Seema, and Adriana Lleras-Muney. 2009. "Life Expectancy and Human Capital Investments: Evidence from Maternal Mortality Declines." *Quarterly Journal of Economics* 124(1): 349–97.

Jones, Kelly. 2014. "Growing Up Together: Cohort Composition and Child Investment." *Demography* 51(1): 229–55.

Kanti, Paul. 1997. "Changes in Reproductive Behavior in Bangladesh." *Geographical Review* 87(1): 100–4.

La Ferrara, Eliana, Alberto Chong, and Suzanne Duryea. 2012."Soap Operas and Fertility: Evidence from Brazil."*American Economic Journal: Applied Economics* 4(4): 1–31.

Lee, Ronald. 1990. "Population Policy and Externalities." *Annals of the American Academy of Political and Social Science* 510(July): 17–32.

Lee, Ronald, and Andrew Mason. 2006. "What is the Demographic Dividend?" *Finance and Development* 43(3): 16–17.

Mamdani, Mahmood. 1972. *The Myth of Population Control Family, Caste, and Class in an Indian Village.* New York: Monthly Review Press.

Manoff, Richard. 1997. "Getting Your Message Out with Social Marketing."*American Journal of Tropical Medicine and Hygiene* 57(3): 260–5.

Meadows, Donella, Dennis Meadows, Jørgen Randers, and William Behrens. 1972. *The Limits to Growth.* New York: Universe Books.

Miller, Grant. 2010. "Contraception as Development? New Evidence from Family Planning in Colombia." *Economic Journal* 120(545): 709–36.

Morduch, Jonathan. 2000. "Sibling Rivalry in Africa." *American Economic Review* 90(2): 405–9.

Pritchett, Lant. 1994. "Desired Fertility and the Impact of Population Policies." *Population and Development Review* 20(1): 1–55.

Rosenzweig, Mark. 1990. "Population Growth and Human Capital Investments: Theory and Evidence." *Journal of Political Economy* 98(5): S38–S70.

Rosenzweig, Mark, and Robert Evenson. 1977."Fertility, Schooling, and the Economic Contribution of Children in Rural India: An Econometric Analysis." *Econometrica* 45(5): 1065–79.

Sen, Amartya. 1981. *Poverty and Famines: An Essay on Entitlements and Deprivation*. Oxford: Clarendon Press.

Sen, Amartya. 1992. "Missing Women: Social Inequality Outweighs Women's Survival in Asia and North Africa." *British Medical Journal* 304(March): 587–8.

Sinding, Steven. 2007. "Overview and Perspective." In Warren Robinson and John Ross (eds.), *The Global Family Planning Revolution: Three Decades of Population Policies and Programs*, 1–12. Washington, DC: World Bank.

Sivasankaran, Anitha. 2014. "Work and Women's Marriage, Fertility, and Empowerment: Evidence from Textile Mill Employment in India." Working paper, Department of Economics, Harvard University.

US Census Bureau. *International Programs*. www.census.gov/population/international/index.html (accessed 2015).

Wei, Shang-Jin, and Xiaobo Zhang. 2011. "The Competitive Saving Motive: Evidence from Rising Sex Ratios and Savings Rates in China." *Journal of Political Economy* 119(3): 511–64.

World Bank. *World Development Indicators*. http://data.worldbank.org/indicator (accessed 2015).

Wydick, Bruce. 1999. "The Impact of Credit Access on the Use of Child Labor in Household Enterprises: Evidence from Guatemala." *Economic Development and Cultural Change* 4(4): 853–69.

Labor and migration

TAKE-HOME MESSAGES FOR CHAPTER 12

1. Developing countries' labor markets are typically highly dualistic, with a formal sector offering wages above the full-employment equilibrium, and surplus labor accumulating in the informal sector with low wages and harsh work conditions.

2. Rural–urban migration is an integral component of the structural transformation of an economy that accompanies GDPpc growth.

3. Influx of rural immigrants, pushed into urban labor markets by different factors such as bad weather shocks or attracted by higher income and accessibility of public goods ("lights of the city") can crowd out local residents in the formal sector and push them into informal employment.

4. The Harris–Todaro model explains domestic migration in the context of labor-market failure. High urban formal-sector wages induce migration of individuals until unemployment is sufficient to lower the expected wage to the level of the current wage in emitting rural areas. Migration can thus continue to occur even with very high levels of urban unemployment.

5. Migration decisions are generally part of a household strategy, where the migrant is expected to send remittances back to the emitting household. This requires an understanding of migrants' motivations for remitting, ranging from altruism to trade.

6. The "new economics of migration" looks at migration as a way for a household to overcome local market failures in credit and insurance, allowing it to make better use of its resources through the remittances received.

7. Migration has both benefits and costs for the emitting community, the emitting country, and the recipient countries. They need to be carefully understood and managed to optimize the social benefits from migration and remittances.

With generally rapid population growth and insufficient new jobs, developing countries are facing a huge employment problem. Because labor is the main asset that poor people have, creating opportunities for them to use this asset productively is the main instrument for poverty reduction. It is no surprise, then, that providing employment opportunities in remunerative activities, elevating the skill level the labor force, and pacing migration between rural origins and urban destinations to avoid the expansion of urban slums are major development issues. In this chapter, we first look at the logic of employment in the formal and informal sectors. We then look at two bodies of theory that aim to explain why people migrate: one when the decision to migrate is taken at the individual level, the other when it is taken at the household level. We consider international migration and look at its impact on the communities and countries from which migrants come, as well as on the receiving countries.

LABOR AND EMPLOYMENT

The employment problem in developing and industrialized countries

The employment problem takes different forms in different countries. In developing countries, few people can afford to be openly unemployed. Because there is typically no formal social assistance provided to the unemployed, everyone able to work has to generate a living in some way, with different degrees of success. This is the role of the informal sector, where entry is easy, labor productivity is low, labor regulations such as paying the legal minimum wage and respecting work-safety codes are absent or not respected, taxes are not paid, social benefits are absent, and value-added is generally not counted in GDP (though it is often guesstimated). Informal-sector employment can range from self-employment shoe-shining, selling lottery tickets on the sidewalk, and garbage recycling to employment in sweatshops, where working conditions are harsh, pay is low, there are no social benefits, and workers' rights are not recognized. Because entry to the informal sector is easy, it provides a survival strategy for unskilled workers and new urban migrants. A large informal sector, sprawling urban slums, lack of public services for slum dwellers, and high congestion externalities are symptomatic of a developing country's urban environment. It is important in this context to induce more firms to enter into the formal sector, allowing them access to formal financial institutions and public support (Levy, 2008) and their workers better conditions.

The labor problem in industrialized countries is different. In continental Europe, employment conditions tend to be rigid, union power is high, and social benefits comfortable. The problem is a relatively high rate of unemployment as employers are careful about hiring new workers that are expensive and that they will have a hard time dismissing should they want to. In the US, by contrast, employment is more flexible, union power generally weak, and social benefits limited. Jobs are often available on a part-time basis, with few if any social benefits. As a consequence, the labor problem has historically been less one of employment than of remunerative wages and social protection for unskilled labor. Over the last 25 years, real wages for unskilled labor have been falling steadily, and disparities between skilled and unskilled workers have been rising, contributing to the rise in inequality. At the end of 2014, the unemployment rate was 5.6 percent in the US compared to 10.4 percent in France, 13.4 percent in Italy, 23.7 percent in Spain, and 25.8 percent in Greece (Trading Economics, online). The labor problem in continental Europe has been one of creating more jobs, while in the US it has been one of creating better jobs.

433

Indicators of unemployment

Given the fact that there is little open unemployment in developing countries due to lack of unemployment insurance and other formal social-safety nets, there is a bigger underemployment than unemployment problem. Characterizing employment requires indicators that include but go beyond open unemployment. As an illustration, the employment problem in Colombia in the 1970s has been characterized by the International Labor Office (ILO) as follows:

1. *Open unemployment*: defined as people "actively seeking work," measured at 5 percent.
2. *Hidden unemployment*: defined as "discouraged workers." They are typically not counted when characterizing unemployment, leading to an underestimation of the true level of lack of access to jobs.
3. *Under employment when people do not work full time* due to seasonal unemployment or to part-time work, measured at 15 percent.
4. *Underemployment when people are working in low-productivity jobs* relative to their skills and effort level, measured at 13 percent.

Using these employment indicators, total un- and underemployment in Colombia was as much as 33 percent, when open unemployment was only 5 percent.

Employment in the formal and informal sectors

The formal and informal sectors are interrelated. As Hernando de Soto (1989) argued, excessive regulation in the formal sector can push economic activity into the informal sector; and high wages paid in the formal sector, above the full-employment equilibrium, can push employment into the informal economy. These high wages can be due to feather-bedding in public-sector employment, minimum-wage legislation, labor unions effectively lobbying for higher wages for their members, and "efficiency wages," whereby employers pay wages above the full-employment equilibrium wage as a way of increasing worker productivity or efficiency (Akerlof and Yellen, 1986). We analyze these in the next section.

The impact on informality of formal-sector wages set above the market-clearing equilibrium can be seen in Figure 12.1. Workers who cannot find employment in the formal sector at the set high wage $\bar{W}_M$ crowd into the informal economy (shifting the supply curve of labor from S to S'), depressing wages W_I in the informal sector, which then becomes a refuge for the formally unemployed. The higher the formal-sector wage relative to the full-employment equilibrium wage, the lower the equilibrium wage in the informal sector.

Surveys conducted by the ILO (International Labor Office, 2002) have shown the enormous magnitude that the informal economy can reach. Informal employment is defined as not receiving social-security benefits through employment. Recent estimates are that informal employment makes up 48 percent of non-agricultural employment in North Africa, 51 percent in Latin America, 65 percent in Asia, and 72 percent in

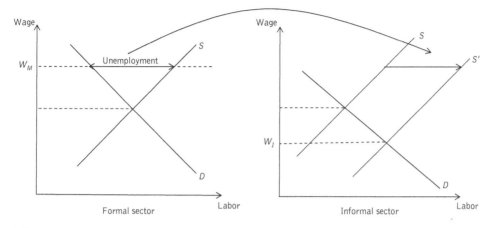

Figure 12.1 *Link between wages in the formal and informal sectors*

Sub-Saharan Africa. Some 70 percent of informal-sector workers are self-employed. ILO studies have also shown that the informal economy is highly heterogeneous (Tokman, 1989). Part of it is disguised unemployment, a large refuge sector for workers unable to find employment in the formal sector. This segment of the informal sector tends to be *counter-cyclical* to formal-sector employment: when formal-sector employment contracts due to a recession or to rising formal-sector wages, employment in the informal sector expands. But part of the informal economy is complementary to the formal sector, in particular subcontracting with formal-sector firms. This segment of the informal economy is *pro-cyclical* to formal-sector employment.

Empirical results for Colombia (Mondragón *et al.*, 2010) show that the counter-cyclical effect is supported empirically. An increase in non-wage costs and in the minimum wage in the formal sector had a large positive effect on informal employment and a negative effect on informal wages. Tracking the strategy used by households which lost formal-sector employment, Gaviria and Henao (2001) find that they compensated by participating in informal-sector employment.

An influx of rural migrants, pushed into urban labor markets by bad-weather shocks, can crowd out local residents in the formal-sector labor market and push them into informal employment. Using data for Indonesia, Kleemans and Magruder (2014) instrument rural–urban migration by excess rainfall (Figure 12.2). Bad weather is a good instrument as it has strong predictive power for migration, and yet no direct effect on urban labor markets (satisfying the exclusion restriction).

Results show that rural migrants pushed by adversity are detrimental to labor-market outcomes for local residents: for the latter, employment declines, especially in the formal sector, and income falls, especially in the informal sector. The impact is largest on low-skill resident workers (and also on women and young workers): their formal-sector employment declines, they switch to informal-sector employment, and there is a decline in informal-sector income. Kleemans and Magruder's study is important as it offers rigorous support for the link between formal- and informal-sector employment.

The expansion of social-assistance programs, with access to non-contributory health and pension benefits, may induce more firms and workers to remain in the

435

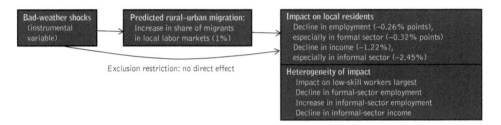

Figure 12.2 *Impact of rural–urban migration on labor market for local residents*

Source: Based on results in Kleemans and Magruder, 2014.

informal sector. Given the existence of these programs, workers may prefer a higher informal-sector wage with no contribution to these programs to a lower wage with social benefits, particularly if they have high discount rates and little confidence in the permanence of the programs (Maloney, 2004). In Latin America, the rise in informality coincided with the expansion of non-contributory public health insurance. Improved provision of social-assistance programs may thus have a perverse effect on informality, with associated losses in economies of scale and productivity gains for firms, and in fiscal revenues for governments (Levy, 2008). There can thus exist a complex trade-off between equity and efficiency gains when introducing social-assistance programs such as pension funds in Bolivia and South Africa, and free health services in Mexico, Colombia, and Bolivia. These programs are good for welfare but, by encouraging informality, impose an efficiency cost on the economy.

Recent studies have tried to estimate the efficiency cost of increased informality induced by expansion of coverage of non-contributory social-assistance programs. In Colombia, coverage of the subsidized public health-insurance program increased from 30 percent to 90 percent of the population. Camacho *et al.* (2014) estimate that this induced an increase in informal-sector employment of 8 percent, with workers accepting a 12 percent decline in wages as they could forego payment of social-security benefits. The government's public health budget increased by 11 percent as a consequence of this shift in employment to the informal sector. Because labor productivity is lower in informal- than in formal-sector employment, the authors estimate that it led to a 3.8 percent loss in GDP. Working in the informal sector was a strategic choice, and had a high aggregate efficiency cost.

RURAL–URBAN MIGRATION

Migration is a huge phenomenon, both domestically and internationally. Domestic migration is mainly rural–rural and rural–urban, and only urban–rural when unemployment or adversity strikes in the urban environment. Domestic migration can be seasonal, short-term, long-term, or permanent. It can be pushed by adversity, or driven by opportunity. And it can be at the initiative of the migrant, or part of a household strategy focused on the role of remittances for household welfare. We discuss here rural–urban migration, and consider international migration later.

Structural transformation and urbanization

Migration from rural to urban environments is a huge phenomenon, involving millions of people every year. More than half a billion people are estimated to have migrated from rural to urban areas in developing countries over the past 25 years (World Bank, 2007). Rural–urban migration contributed to the increase in urban population from 29 percent of world population in 1950, to 49 percent in 2005, and a predicted 60 percent in 2030. Urbanization increases with GDPpc (Table 12.1), rising from 29 percent in low-income countries to 80 percent in high-income countries. The rate of growth of the urban population is highest in low-income countries, rising at an average annual growth rate of 3.8 percent over the 1990–2013 period. In low- and middle-income countries, the rate is the highest in Sub-Saharan Africa (4.6 percent), followed by East Asia and the Pacific (3.6 percent), South Asia, the Middle East, and North Africa (2.8 percent), and Latin America and the Caribbean (2.1 percent). Rapid urbanization is clearly a problem that can be associated with convergence (rapid growth and structural transformation of poor countries), but also with failure to retain populations in rural areas, and urban poverty.

The world has become predominantly urban, with a prevalence of megacities, defined as having a population in excess of 10 million (Table 12.2). Of the 26 megacities in the world, 17 are located in developing countries. Many have explosive growth. If current growth rates continue unabated, Karachi will double in 14 years, Delhi in 15, and Dhaka and Guangzhou in 17.

Rural–urban migration is part of the normal process of structural transformation of an economy (Lewis, 1955; and see Chapter 8): as GDPpc rises, the labor force increasingly leaves agriculture and rural areas to move to urban environments and employment in industry and services. As can be seen in Figure 12.3, using cross-country data, the shares of agriculture in total employment (Figure 12.3a) and GDP (Figure 12.3b) fall, while the shares of industry and services rise (Kuznets, 1968; Chenery and Taylor, 1968). At high levels of GDPpc, the service sector is by far the largest employer in the economy and the largest contributor to GDP. It is also interesting to observe how these normal patterns have changed over time, comparing them in 1980–4 and in 2009–13. Industry is losing its capacity to generate employment with rising income, while services are gaining employment capacity, with the same pattern observed for

Table 12.1 Population and urbanization

Country category	GDPpc/year US$	Total population (millions)	Urban population (percent)	Average annual growth urban population 1990–2013 (percent)
Low-income	< $1,045	850	29	3.8
Lower middle-income	$1,045 to 4,125	2500	39	2.8
Upper middle-income	$4,125 to 12,745	2400	62	2.9
High-income	> $12,745	1300	80	0.9

Source: World Bank, *World Development Indicators.*

Table 12.2 *Megacities in developing countries, 2012*

Megacities	Country	Population (million)	Annual growth (%)	Time to double Years
Guangzhou	China	25.2	4.0	17
Seoul	South Korea	25.1	1.4	50
Shanghai	China	24.8	2.2	32
Delhi	India	23.3	4.6	15
Mumbai	India	23	2.9	24
Mexico City	Mexico	22.9	2	35
São Paulo	Brazil	20.9	1.4	50
Manila	Philippines	20.3	2.5	28
Jakarta	Indonesia	18.9	2.5	28
Karachi	Pakistan	17	4.9	14
Kolkata	India	16.6	2	35
Cairo	Egypt	15.3	2.6	27
Buenos Aires	Argentina	14.8	1	69
Dhaka	Bangladesh	14	4.1	17
Beijing	China	13.9	2.7	26
Rio de Janeiro	Brazil	12.5	1	69
Lagos	Nigeria	12.1	3.2	22

Source: Wikipedia, *Megacity.*

the share of GDP. This declining role of industry, which has been called premature deindustrialization (Rodrik, 2015), should be worrisome for countries that count on industrialization to help absorb rural–urban migrants in productive employment.

The decision to migrate from the rural to the urban sector responds to expected income differentials between rural and urban locations in excess of migration costs. Importantly, the comparison is not only about private income but also about the consumption of public goods and services. Typically much more accessible in the urban environment, they are referred to as the "lights of the city" and contribute to attracting migrants. Migration helps equilibrate the labor market, shifting labor toward higher-productivity urban employment. In this sense, migration is a "normal" and desirable phenomenon, contributing to both efficiency gains and poverty reduction (Ravallion *et al.*, 2007). However, things may not be that simple. Migration may be excessive if it adds to urban unemployment, contributes to the sprawl of urban slums, and creates congestion externalities in urban areas. As can be seen in Table 12.3, the share of the urban population that lives in slums is as high as 63 percent in Nigeria, 62 percent in Bangladesh, 53 percent in Iraq, and 47 percent in Pakistan. Migration may then displace poverty from the rural to the urban sector instead of contributing to rising levels of labor productivity and wellbeing. In this case, socially optimal migration may be less than privately optimal migration. A policy issue then emerges as to how to reconcile social and private optima by discouraging or constraining excess migration.

The reverse can also hold. Countries like India, Bangladesh, and Mexico have shares of their labor force in agriculture way in excess of normal patterns. Migration

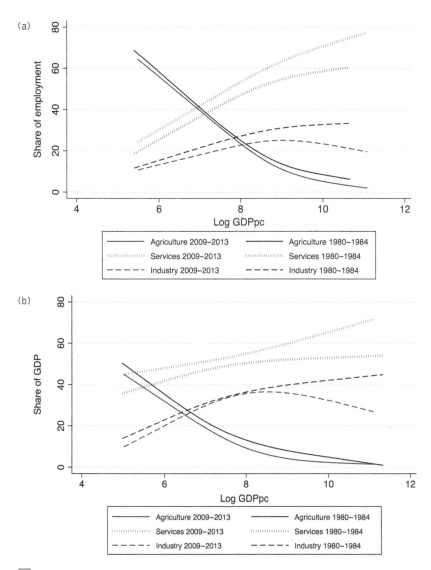

Figure 12.3 *Normal patterns of structural transformation of an economy as GDPpc rises, 1980–4 and 2009–13: Sectoral shares of employment (a) and GDP (b)*

Source: World Bank, *World Development Indicators.*

may be detained by lack of information, liquidity constraints, and excessive risk of migration failure given current poverty levels. We will see later that cash grants to potential migrants can help boost migration (Bryan *et al.*, 2014).

What induces people to migrate? There are two complementary theories. One is when migration is an individual decision, driven by self-interest. In this case, it is the expected gain for the migrant that makes him decide. The other is when migration is a household decision, where a household member migrates to improve conditions for the household as a whole. In this case, the key motivation in migration is the remittances that the migrant will send back home, driven by the household's collective interest.

Table 12.3 *Urban population living in slums, 2009*

Countries	Urban population living in slums	
	Millions	*% of urban population*
Nigeria	47.6	63
Bangladesh	27.5	62
Iraq	10.8	53
Pakistan	30.0	47
China	174.0	31
India	104.7	29
Brazil	44.9	27
Zimbabwe	1.1	24
South Africa	7.1	23
Indonesia	23.3	23
Egypt	6.1	17
Mexico	11.9	14
Colombia	4.9	14

Source: UN-Habitat, 2012.

Individual decision to migrate under urban labor-market failure: The Harris–Todaro model

The basic model

In this model, the unit of decision-making is the individual migrant (Harris and Todaro, 1970). A potential migrant has to decide whether to stay in the rural sector, where he gets a certain wage W_A or move to the urban sector, where he hopes to be employed in the modern sector and receive the high wage $\bar{W}_M$. He may be unlucky, and find himself unemployed. Todaro developed this model while working in East Africa, and he wanted to find an answer to a big puzzle he saw: why is there continuing, rapid rural–urban migration in spite of the fact that there is high urban unemployment? With a perfect labor market, economic theory predicts that, if there is unemployment, wages will fall until unemployment is eliminated. At this equilibrium, both wages will be equal, up to migration costs, and it will no longer be beneficial to migrate. In contrast, the Harris–Todaro model helps explain why migration continues even with high unemployment, but not forever. It does this by looking at how a distorted formal-sector urban wage held above the full-employment equilibrium (a labor-market failure) induces migrants to take a chance in the hope of getting the high wage, in spite of high unemployment.

The Harris–Todaro model is formulated as follows. Define the following variables:

W_A = current rural wage (rural income)
$\bar{W}_M$ = formal-sector urban wage
W_M^* = expected urban wage (urban income)

$m = 1$ if the individual decides to migrate, 0 otherwise

$P =$ probability of finding a job in the urban sector = urban employment rate

$1 - P =$ urban unemployment rate.

The structural form of the model has three equations:

Expected urban wage

$$W_M^* = P\bar{W}_M$$

In other words, the expected urban wage W_M^* is the urban wage $\bar{W}_M$ times the probability P of finding a job in the urban sector.

Probability of finding a job in the urban sector

This probability is equal to the urban employment rate, assuming that jobs are randomly allocated across the urban labor force in each period.

$$P = \frac{\text{Urban employment}}{\text{Total urban labor force}} = \text{Urban employment rate.}$$

By difference, $1 - P$ is the urban unemployment rate.

Decision to migrate

The individual will decide to migrate if the expected urban wage is higher than the current rural wage, i.e.

$$m = 1 \text{ if } W_M^* > W_A, m = 0 \text{ if } W_M^* \leq W_A.$$

The reduced form (solution) of the model consists in deriving the rate of unemployment that will stop migration:

$$m = 0 \text{ when } W_M^* = W_A, \text{ i.e., when } P\bar{W}_M = W_A \text{ or when } P = W_A / \bar{W}_M.$$

Hence the urban rate of employment that will stop migration is the ratio of the rural to the urban wage.

Two numerical examples will illustrate the power of this simple result.

If $W_A = 1$ and $\bar{W}_M = 2$: $P = 1/2$, and $1 - P$, the equilibrium urban unemployment rate, has to be as high as 50 percent to discourage rural people from migrating. Until then, it is incentive compatible for the potential rural migrant to decide to migrate.

If $W_A = 1$ and $\bar{W}_M = 4$: $P = 1/4$, migration will continue until there is a 75 percent urban unemployment rate.

The important message here is that migration is economically rational for rural migrants in spite of eventually extensive urban unemployment. Unemployment is provoked by a large urban labor-market failure, whereby the urban wage fails to adjust to unemployment. With a large rural–urban wage gap in the situations observed by Todaro in East Africa, it is no wonder that we find large and expanding urban informal sectors and slums.

Policy implications of the model

A labor-market equilibrium with urban unemployment is clearly highly inefficient, and it imposes a high welfare cost on the unemployed. It is also a source of exclusion and frustrations. The unlucky urban unemployed migrants would have been better off staying in the rural sector; yet it was incentive compatible for them to move. What can be done to reduce this inefficient outcome?

Create new jobs in the formal sector? Not the right solution

This policy response to urban unemployment has been extensively used, in particular creating public-sector jobs with the intention of mopping up the unemployed. The implication for unemployment is, however, perverse because new migrants vote with their feet. If government increases urban employment by one job at $\bar{W}_M$, more than one person will migrate to the city attracted by the higher employment rate. If, for example, one job is created when the formal-sector wage is four times the rural wage, four additional migrants will come to the city, of which three will be unemployed. The arithmetic is as follows:

Denote urban employment by UE, and the total urban labor force by $TULF$. The labor market equilibrium before job creation is:

$$P = \frac{UE}{TULF} = \frac{W_A}{\bar{W}_M} = \frac{1}{4}.$$

Hence $TULF = 4UE$.

If the government creates one new job at the same urban wage $\bar{W}_M$, P remains unchanged at ¼ since the wage ratio has not changed. Hence, after job creation, the new $TULF$ is $TULF'$ equal to:

$$\frac{UE + 1}{TULF'} = \frac{1}{4} \text{ or } TULF' = 4UE + 4.$$

The total urban labor force has increased by four migrants. Of these, one is employed and the other three are unemployed. Hence job creation at $\bar{W}_M$ is not the solution to urban unemployment. The policy backfires on good intentions, increasing both the number of migrants and the number of unemployed.

Reduce the gap between $\bar{W}_M$ and W_A? Two options

Creating jobs while maintaining the high fixed urban wage is not the answer. The model tells us to close the rural–urban wage gap to reduce incentives to migrate. How can this be done? There are two options.

Lower $\bar{W}_M$ These interventions are on the "pull" side of the wage gap. We need to understand, however, why the formal-sector wage is so high. There are two reasons.

The first is interventions by labor unions or by government for clientelistic purposes. The implication here is to resist excessive union power when there is still so much unemployment. The unions defend the wages of the employed, but create a backlash for the unemployed in the informal sector. We saw this for Colombia with the Mondragón *et al.* (2010) results. Another implication is to expose feather-bedding in the public sector by unscrupulous politicians who use it to build political support and enhance their chances of re-election. The social cost of these practices is high, taking the form of huge urban slums. To get a feel for life in these urban slums, take a moment to look at Kibera, the largest urban slum in Nairobi, with some 500,000 to a million inhabitants on a small piece of land (Wikipedia, *Kibera*). You can also visit the urban slum at the center of Mumbai, India by watching the video The Mumbai Makeover (Journeyman Pictures, *The Mumbai Makeover*). An interesting aspect of this visit is to see how the slum is both a crowded living environment and a place of bustling informal-sector enterprises.

The second reason for the existence of high formal-sector wages is because employers want to increase worker productivity or efficiency. This is the efficiency-wage theory referred to above, and developed by Akerlof and Yellen (1986). There are several versions of this theory. One is a nutritional theory, according to which higher wages allow workers to eat well enough to be able to work more productively. In this case, a high formal-sector wage is efficient for the employer, not a distortion, as above. The wage is set at $W*$ to maximize worker effort per dollar of wage paid along the S-shaped effort-response function in Figure 12.4a. Another influential version of the efficiency-wage theory is Shapiro and Stiglitz's (1984). The idea is that by paying wages higher than the equilibrium wage and creating unemployment, and threatening workers with dismissal for shirking on the job, unemployment creates a disciplinary device for workers to work hard. Other theories are that well paid workers are less likely to quit their jobs, thus decreasing turnover, and that higher wages attract more qualified workers and boost the morale of workers, increasing productivity. In all cases, the higher wages are paid to induce higher worker productivity, and hence are rational for the employer.

This efficiency wage may well be above the full-employment market-equilibrium wage W (Figure 12.4b), creating unemployment. This makes reducing the wage gap difficult to handle because it is incentive compatible for employers to pay above equilibrium wages. However, there are other options for employers to ensure hard work, including motivating workers by sharing the profits of the firm with them, i.e. making them residual claimants. As can be seen in Figure 12.4c, greater motivation shifts the effort-response function and helps reduce the incentive wage paid from $W*$ to $W*'$. Another option is to use a monitoring-enforcement approach to induce effort by direct supervision instead a wage incentive. These options have been extensively explored in the labor literature, in particular by Bowles and Gintis (1988).

443

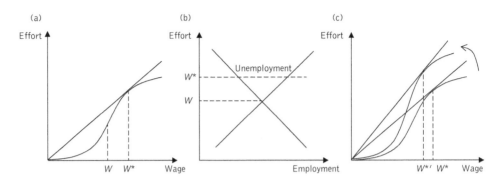

Figure 12.4 *Wage determination and labor-market failure under the efficiency wage theory*

Raise W_A These interventions are on the "push" side of the wage gap. They will induce more rural people to stay where they are. This calls for policies to improve living conditions in rural areas and make agriculture a more profitable and labor-intensive business. Interventions include rural development programs, land reform, better technology and institutions to improve productivity in agriculture, shifting to high-value crops, and decentralization of employment toward rural areas in order to create a thriving rural non-farm economy. The policy implication is, in a sense, somewhat counter intuitive: the solution to urban unemployment is not in the city, but in remote rural areas. We will explore these policies in Chapter 18.

Note, however, that in the context of other market failures, the impact of rising agricultural income on migration may be ambiguous. In the case of international migration, which is also applicable to rural–urban migration, Bazzi (2014) has shown that reducing the income gap through economic development in the emitting countries might have ambiguous effect on migration. Higher income at home narrows wage gaps with rich countries but also relaxes liquidity constraints that may have prevented migration among the poor. He tests for liquidity constraints in Indonesia using household-level land-holding heterogeneity, rainfall shocks, and a large exogenous increase in domestic rice prices with considerable spatial variation. He finds that the liquidity constraints are indeed binding and that positive agricultural income shocks are associated with significant increases in the share of village residents working abroad.

Regulate urban migration

A coercive solution also exists. Migration to the city may be restricted by requiring migrants to hold an urban residence permit, as in China under the Hukou system, introduced in 1952 and still partially in place today. Urban residents without a permit are not given access to local public services, including, for a long time, access to education for the children that may have migrated with them. This is of course very difficult to enforce. In 2003, it was estimated that there existed a floating population of 740 million migrants working without residence permits in urban areas. Lack of access to schooling for their children if they accompanied their parents imposed a huge welfare cost on the next generation.

Extensions of the model and empirical results

An attraction of the Harris–Todaro model is that its basic formulation is very simple, but it can incorporate a lot of modifications to capture particular situations. The model can be applied to domestic as well as to international migration, and we consider both here, as well as some of the extensions that have been introduced in the vast literature on the subject.

Migration costs and longer time horizon

Migration is expensive and should be thought of as a medium- to long-term decision. The decision to migrate can then be modeled by comparing the present value (PV) of the difference in income at the point of origin (y_{origin}) and income at the point of destination ($y_{destination}$) net of migration cost (Rosenzweig, 1988a):

Migrate if $PV(y_{destination} - y_{origin}) -$ Cost of migration > 0.

This model predicts that migration will increase with younger age (longer time horizon over which to benefit from migration) and lower migration cost (shorter distance to destination), in addition to greater income difference as in the Harris–Todaro model.

Model predictions are confirmed by descriptive statistics. The index of migration intensity between two regions, A (rural) and B (urban), is defined by the UNDP (Bell and Muhidin, 2009) as the ratio:

$$\frac{\text{Number of migrants from A to B over the period}}{\text{Number of inhabitants of A at the beginning of the period}}$$

The index of migration intensity can be measured by age. The age profile of five-year migration intensity for eight Latin American countries is shown in Figure 12.5. It confirms the prediction that there is a sharp peak between the ages of 20 and 30, with the highest intensity of migration at peak observed in Chile (15.6 percent), followed by Ecuador (10.3 percent) and Costa Rica (8.2 percent). In China, with restrictions on labor migration, the intensity of migration at peak is 6.2 percent, compared to 20.7 percent in Malaysia and 11.7 percent in Thailand. India also has a remarkably low intensity of migration, peaking at only 4.1 percent.

Role of social networks in finding a job

In the basic Harris–Todaro model, the probability of finding a job is the urban rate of employment, $P =$ Urban employment/Total urban labor force. It means that employment is determined by a random drawing of who will be employed in each period. This is evidently not realistic. More plausible specifications of the workings of the

445

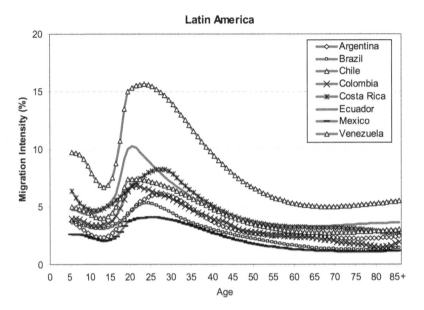

Figure 12.5 *Profile of five-year migration intensity by age, Latin American countries*

Source: Bell and Muhidin, 2009.

urban labor market for migrants can be explored. It is likely that migrants have a lower chance of being selected for employment than current residents who are already employed. In this case the equilibrium rate of unemployment to deter migration would be lower than in the Harris–Todaro model. But it may also be the opposite. Strong social networks of migrants from the same community may increase P for new migrants, raising the equilibrium-unemployment rate to stop migration. Empirical studies of the migration of Mexican workers have shown that migrant networks in the US play a large role as they help new migrants find employment through information and job referrals (Winters *et al.*, 2001). However, establishing the causal impact of networks on migration outcomes is challenging. Migrants with a large network may also share characteristics that are favorable to successful migration. These characteristics then create a spurious correlation between networks and migration that obscure the causal role of the network. To overcome this difficulty, Munshi (2003) used an instrumental variable approach (see Chapter 4) where migration is influenced by local weather shocks to show that a Mexican migrant in the US labor market is more likely to be employed and to hold a higher-paying non-agricultural job when his migrant network is larger.

The role of credit constraints and risk aversion

The cost of migration can be high: travel is expensive (for the 8–10 million Bangladeshi migrants working in the Gulf countries, for example), migrants have to rely on intermediaries who charge expensive fees to arrange visas and work permits, or pay fees to guides (*coyotes* on the Mexico–US border) that help them cross borders illegally. If migrants are poor and cannot borrow against future incomes, they will be constrained in their migration. Additionally, if migrants cannot take the risk of urban unemployment, either because they are poor and come to the city with no financial resources, or because they do not have access to credit, they will be constrained. A typical result from migration studies is that the poorest, who should have the greatest incentive to migrate, migrate less than less poor individuals. That migration is costly and risky, deterring many, has been applied to India to explain the surprisingly low rate of migration in spite of huge rural–urban wage disparities.

Bryan *et al.* (2014) ran an RCT in Bangladesh to show the role of cash constraints in the migration of the poor. They created incentives for rural inhabitants to migrate in the pre-harvest lean season (also called the hungry season) by giving an $8.50 cash grant to households, which covers the round trip travel cost. They found that the incentive induced 22 percent of the households to send a seasonal migrant. Their interpretation is that low migration was due to the risk of migration failure. Once households have sent a migrant and learn how well he can fare at the destination, in the following years they continue to do so at a higher rate than control households without a subsidy.

The role of skills in migration

Studies have shown that the return to education is generally higher in the urban than in the rural environment. As a consequence, it is rural residents with higher skills that are more likely to migrate (Rosenzweig, 1988a). Technological change in agriculture (for example, the Green Revolution, or the introduction of high-value crops using sophisticated production techniques) will increase the skill premium in the rural sector, and reduce the migration of skilled labor.

For international migration, the role of skills in migration may be different. The return to education obtained in Mexico is higher in Mexico than in the US due to different languages and institutions. As a consequence, economic logic tells us that it is the lower-skill workers who should migrate most to the US, implying negative selection. However, as Chiquiar and Hanson (2005) show, this is not the case. It is those men with intermediate levels of skills who migrate the most, and those women with the highest skill levels, implying positive selection. A possible explanation is the differential role of networks, credit constraints, and the ability to take risks.

McKenzie and Rapoport (2010) examined the role of migration networks in self-selection by skill levels in Mexico–US migration. They confirm that there is a lower return to education in the US than in Mexico (due in part to language differences), leading to negative selection by skills. High migration costs have an opposite, positive self-selection effect. However, the presence of strong migration networks reverses the role of cost and induces negative self-selection. Through the benefits of cost-reducing networks, it is lower-skill individuals who are most able to migrate.

The role of relative deprivation as a motivation to migrate

A powerful incentive to migrate is considering that your personal situation is inferior to a standard you aspire to. This is the theory of relative deprivation (Stark and Taylor,

1989). It implies that it is those whose educational and entrepreneurial potential is most unrewarded in the community who have the greatest urge to migrate. If this is the case, not only is low absolute income a determinant of migration, but also local inequality associated with relative deprivation. Policies to reduce migration must then focus on reducing both poverty and inequality (Quinn, 2006).

All these different reasons to migrate are of course not exclusive. This explains why correlations may not be consistent with theory, like seeing the most educated women migrate. One would have to properly control for the other determinants of migration to identify a causal relationship illustrating any one of these channels. So while these theories are intuitive, few have been empirically tested.

The household decision to send a migrant under local market failures: the new migration economics

In the Harris–Todaro model, it is the individual who decides whether or not to migrate based on the calculus of personal-income advantage. This is likely to be the most important determinant of migration. However, most individuals are members of households, and the decision to migrate may also be part of the household's overall income and security strategy. In this case, the decision to send a migrant is motivated by the household's objective of receiving remittances. This becomes a two-agent contract (the household and the migrant). We must look at their respective points of view to understand migration and the subsequent flow of remittances.

Household benefits: income from remittances

There are two interpretations of the rationale for a household to send a migrant. The first rationale is a direct extension of the Harris–Todaro argument, transposed from the individual to the household. From the perspective of the household, the contribution of a specific member to household income may be seen as higher if he is located in the urban sector or abroad rather than in the community. The incentive to send a migrant can be huge: for Mexican migrants to the US, the PPP-adjusted wage gap between destination and origin in jobs requiring identical skills in 2007 was 7 to 1. The household pays the cost and risk of migration for the designated member, and expects to receive remittances in exchange for this investment. The difference with the Harris–Todaro model is that the benefits of migrating are seen as not accruing exclusively to the migrant but at least in part to the household as a flow of remittances.

The second rationale, first introduced by Stark (1993) under the heading of the "new migration economics," consists in looking at the decision made by a household to sending a migrant who will send remittances to help overcome the market imperfections to which the household is subjected locally. Due to these market failures, the household is making sub-optimum use of the assets it controls. While under perfect local market conditions there may be no reason to send a migrant away, under market failures the migrant can help compensate for the market failure through the remittances sent back home. The market failures that can be relaxed through remittances are mainly for credit and insurance. The gains to the household are the remittances sent by the migrant (if successful, and if he or she agrees to remit) that will help relax the liquidity and risk constraints on productive household asset use. The cost to the household of sending a migrant is the loss of labor at home in using the assets controlled by the household. In this perspective, seasonal migration during the hungry season may have a zero opportunity cost, as in Bryan *et al.*'s (2014) study in Bangladesh. According to the theory, more local market failures induce more migration, and remittances are used to compensate for the market failures in generating more local autonomous income. Use of remittances is then specifically as follows.

1. *Credit constrained household.* A rural household will use remittances to spend on the farm as if it had access to local credit—buy inputs such as fertilizers and seeds, hire labor, pay for the services of work animals or a tractor, rent more land, etc.
2. *Risk constrained household.* When insurance is not available, a household has to engage in risk management and is less able to cope with shocks, both at a cost. Risk management requires choosing activities that yield lower expected income in exchange for lower risk. If the household knows that remittances will be transferred when there is a shock, serving as insurance, it can take more risk in generating autonomous incomes and achieve higher expected incomes. If hit by a shock (a harvest failure, an accident, sickness, unemployment, collapse in the price of coffee), and in need of risk-coping initiatives such as selling a productive asset or taking a child out of school, remittances sent by the migrant as insurance can prevent having to make these costly, and often irreversible, decisions. The empirical test here consists in verifying that the timing of the transfers follows the occurrence of shocks.

These rationales for migration are not mutually exclusive. It is likely that in most situations the flow of remittances more than compensates for the loss of local income associated with the departure of a household member, but that these remittances also compensate for market failures.

What motivates a migrant to remit?

Sending a migrant is a big gamble for the household as there is a time-consistency problem (between the time of paying the cost of migration and receiving remittances) with no corresponding commitment device (to force the migrant to remit to the household at least part of the income earned in the place where he migrated, if successful). This raises an interesting question: why do migrants remit instead of defaulting on family obligations? There are several reasons for this (Lucas and Stark, 1985). We discuss for each the corresponding empirical regularity associated with this particular motivation.

1. *Repayment.* For some migrants, remitting is part of a trade—they have received something from parents and must return remittances in exchange. From this perspective, remittances sent by a migrant can be seen as repaying parents for the

costs of rearing, feeding, and educating him or her. It can also be seen as repaying parents for the cost of migration. Controlling for other factors, the level of remittances should, in this interpretation, increase with the level of investment made by parents in the migrant. This includes the level of education achieved by the migrant and the migration distance travelled.

2. *Inheritance.* Several studies have shown that remittances may be motivated by securing a share of future inheritance from parents, especially when there is competition among siblings. A migrant sends remittances to compensate for the fact that he is away from the community, not able to help care for parents, and yet keep his share of the inheritance (Hoddinott, 1994). Migrants can even compete with each other in attracting the attention of parents and expecting to get a higher share of inheritance. In this case, remittances should increase with assets owned by parents and with the number of competing heirs. It may also increase with the migrant's intention to return, giving parents' land particular value to him. This is the case for boys more than for girls as the latter are more likely to return to the village of their husband rather than their village of origin (de la Brière *et al.*, 2002). The inheritance value of parents' land is all the more important to male migrants under two conditions. One is if local land markets are thin and land cannot be acquired through the migrant's earnings abroad. The other is that the migrant has acquired specific experience in cultivating the family land before migrating, and this land has, for this reason, more value to him than unknown land.

3. *Social security motive.* Migrants send remittances to support parents when they are old, particularly if there are no public social-assistance programs to provide free access to health services and to non-contributory pensions. The empirical test would consist in verifying that: (1) transfers respond to the stage of the life cycle parents are in and the conditions they are under, in particular increasing when parents stop working or are in need of special assistance in response to health and other shocks; (2) transfers decrease if the government introduces a formal rural social-security scheme (Cox and Jimenez, 1992). Mexico, Brazil, Bolivia, and South Africa have recently introduced non-contributory pensions and health coverage. The question is whether this will decrease private transfers from children to older parents. Research shows that it appears to be the case, which can be seen as a positive spillover effect of the program as it helps the working generation save more, and invest in productive activities and in the education of their own children. In studies of transfers in Peru, Cox *et al.* (1998) find that transfers would have been 20 percent higher without public social-security benefits. The social-security motive is revealed by the importance of parents' age and income position in determining remittances.

4. *Insurance motive.* With a lack of insurance markets, households will send a migrant who can remit when adversity strikes at home. This can be when harvests fail, an earthquake or a tornado damages parents' assets, an economic crisis raises the level of unemployment, or ill health or accidents require high medical expenses. In this case, we should see remittances flowing in an anti-cyclical fashion relative to fluctuations in household income. This is extensively supported by research results. Stark and Lucas (1988) have shown that remittances sent by migrants from Botswana

respond to the severity of the drought that has afflicted their parents. Cox and Jimenez (1998) found that the total transfer received by households in Colombia is a function of their income risk. And using panel data on Indian rural households, Rosenzweig (1988b) related remittances to the size of parents' income shocks, although remittances only compensate for a small fraction of the income loss.

5. *Altruism vs. trade.* Altruism is selfless concern for the welfare of others, in this case sending remittances back home without regard to personal benefits (Altonji *et al.*, 1998). In utility theory, it means that, if I am an altruist, your utility enters into my utility function: making you happier will increase my own happiness. The motivation is strictly the welfare of others, and altruism is expected to prevail among members of a household, especially toward parents, siblings, and close kin.

    Altruism would suggest that transfers increase either when parents become poorer and/or migrants become richer. It is, however, almost impossible to assert whether observed transfers are altruistic or part of a trade. This is because migrants providing insurance for their parents could be motivated by pure altruism or by trade either for earlier payments or later compensation by parents. Migrants could be paying back their education in the form of insurance. Migrants could expect to reinforce their claim to inheritance by providing insurance, either because it allows parents to maintain their assets, or because it strengthens their competitive position *vis-à-vis* their siblings.

Conclusion

Several empirical studies have found patterns that suggest heterogeneity in dominant motives. For example, a study of remittance patterns in the Dominican Republic shows that female migrants are more likely to remit to insure parents when affected by a negative shock and to help educate younger siblings, while male migrants are, by contrast, more likely to help parents invest and secure a flow of autonomous income (de la Brière *et al.*, 2002).

Focusing the decision to migrate on the household instead of on the individual is a realistic extension of the Harris–Todaro model. Households are indeed an important locus of decision-making and of assistance in migrating. The huge flow of remittances from migrants to their communities of origin is to a significant extent likely to be directed at the remaining members of the household.

IMPACTS OF MIGRATION

In both the Harris–Todaro and the household approaches to migration, we did not distinguish between national migration (largely rural–urban, but also rural–rural, often as intermediate stages toward an ultimate urban destination) and international migration. The migrant's decision-making process may largely be the same. On the other hand, the implications of migration for both the emitting community and the receiving location may be quite different across the two types of migration. We need to distinguish between the two in analyzing the impacts of migration.

Importance of international migration

In spite of severe restrictions to international labor movements (as opposed to the movements of goods and capital that are increasingly free with trade liberalization and globalization), migration is a hugely important phenomenon. Three percent (191 million people) of world population is composed of migrants, with 82 percent coming from developing countries. In the US, 14 percent of the population is composed of migrants.

Remittance flows at a world scale amount to US$350 billion annually (in 2012), with three quarters of these transfers going to developing countries (World Bank, 2014). These flows are exceeded only by foreign direct investment (US$665 billion) and private capital flows (US$315 billion), and are about three times larger than net official foreign-aid flows (US$133 billion) (Figure 12.6). 22 countries derive more than 10 percent of their GDP from remittances. Highest GDP percentages are 25 percent for Nepal, 20 percent for Haiti, 16 percent for El Salvador, Lebanon, and Honduras, 10 percent for the Philippines and Nicaragua, and 7 percent for the Dominican Republic (Table 12.4). This is a large underestimation of the true remittances flow as formal remittances are considered to be only about half of the total flow of remittances.

Impacts of migration on the emitting community and country

Migration has both positive and negative effects on the emitting community and country. Some of the best-known positive effects include the following.

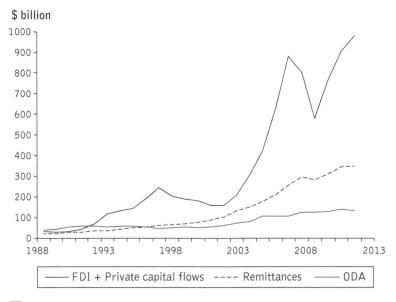

Figure 12.6 *Relative importance of remittances in international capital flows to developing countries, 1988–2012*

Source: World Bank, *Global Development Finance.*

Table 12.4 *Flows of remittances into developing countries: top recipients in dollar value and percent of GDP, 2012*

Remittances

In billion US$		In % of GDP	
India	69	Nepal	25
China	39	Haiti	20
Philippines	25	El Salvador	16
Mexico	23	Lebanon	16
Egypt	19	Honduras	16
Bangladesh	14	Philippines	10
Pakistan	14	Nicaragua	10
Morocco	7	Dominican Rep	7
Brazil	3	Nigeria	4

Source: World Bank, *World Development Indicators.*

Migration enhances the return to education

Most rural communities offer only a low return to education because local opportunities to use what has been learned at school are quite limited. As T.W. Schultz famously observed, the return to education increases with opportunities to use it productively (Schultz, 1975). Following this idea, Foster and Rosenzweig (1996) show that the returns to primary education increased in areas of India where the new technologies of the Green Revolution became (exogenously) available, thus creating a natural experiment. Higher returns to education in turn induced more private investment in schooling as well as more public investment in the availability of schools.

Rural education often has higher returns outside the community. In Mexico, the return to education obtained through *Progresa* in poor rural communities (measured as the present value of lifetime earnings) is very low inside the community (in agricultural wage work, non-agricultural wage work, and self-employment), but substantial outside the community through migration (Figure 12.7). By increasing the return to rural education, migration creates a strong incentive for rural children to seek education.

Other examples include returns to education received in Kerala (India) and in the Philippines (for women) through international migration. Kerala is the Indian state with the highest level of education, and, in the Philippines, it is notable that the average level of education is higher for women than for men as they are the ones who can migrate and derive a high return from education.

Income and consumption effects

Studies of the impact of international migration on development in the emitting countries suffer from a double self-selection bias. As a consequence, simple comparisons of the welfare of households with and without migrants give biased results: households self-select migration, and households also self-select either sending a subset of members as migrants with the rest remaining, or migrating as a whole. Countries like

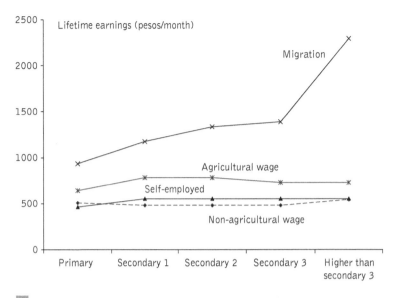

Figure 12.7 *Return to education obtained under* Progresa *in rural communities*

Source: de Janvry et al., 2005.

New Zealand (and also the US) have introduced migration quotas and a lottery system to randomly select winners from among the pool of applicants. This provides a natural experiment, where households with winners serve as migration treatments and households with non-winner applicants as controls. Gibson *et al.* (2011) analyze this for migrants from Tonga. They find the surprising result that the impact of migration of a family member on the income and consumption of household members left behind is largely negative. This implies that the loss of labor and local income earning for these households was larger than the benefits derived from remittances. This may be a special case, but the point is well made that non-controlled comparisons of households with and without migrants can give fallacious results.

Role of local financial institutions in facilitating local investment by non-migrants

It is difficult to expect migrants or their families to have the entrepreneurial talents to invest the remittances they receive in productive activities. As a consequence, remittances are most often spent on consumption goods, construction, and the buying of land, limiting the growth value of remittances. But this does not have to be the case. If local financial institutions (such as village banks and local savings and loans associations, as we will see in Chapter 13) use the remittances deposited by migrants to make loans to local entrepreneurs based on reputation (i.e. following the principles of proximity lending), they will be invested in productive activities that create local value-added and employment opportunities. If capital constraints limit local development, remittances that flow right to the heart of poor communities offer a unique opportunity to break this constraint. In some of the poorest areas of the Dominican Republic, from which large numbers of migrants were pushed by poverty to New York (perhaps half of the people born in the Dominican Sierra), we see remarkable examples of local development financed by the large flow of remittances through local savings-and-loan associations.

Experience gained in migration is used in communities of origin and transferred to non-migrants

Migrants come back home with experiences gained abroad that can be applied in the community and transmitted to others. Experience can be in entrepreneurship, leadership, use of advanced technology, and new institutions. This is how experience gained in Silicon Valley by Indian migrants spread back to Bengalore and Hyderabad, helping fuel a local software boom (Chacko, 2007). This reverse brain drain—turned into a brain gain—has made a major contribution to the acceleration of growth in India. Military service in Vietnam has been identified as a source of local innovations based on what conscripts have learned from their urban experiences.

Impact on wages in the local labor market

As President Porfirio Díaz once said, "Poor Mexico, so far from God and so close to the United States." Proximity has the extraordinary consequence that 16 percent of Mexico's labor force lives in the US. Mishra (2007) estimated that, by reducing the labor supply in the communities of origin, the wage of workers on Mexican labor markets increased by 7 percent. Through this labor-market effect, the benefits of migration are spilling over to non-migrants.

There are also negative effects of migration on emitting communities. One is the loss of direct benefits from investments in education, the well known brain drain. An example is the emigration of doctors and nurses from English-speaking African countries to England, the US, Canada, and Australia: in Ghana and Zimbabwe, 75 percent of all doctors emigrate within a few years of completing medical school. As we saw, this may not be true in the longer run if migration leads to remittances and also to investments by returning migrants, the reverse brain drain. Other negative changes that have been associated with migration are an increase in local inequality (with a class of new rich benefiting from remittances), land abandonment (if migrants are afraid of renting their lands while away as they may not be returned by tenants), rising land values as migrants invest their earnings in land (making access to land more expensive for local residents), the loss of traditional values as migrants bring back new patterns of behavior and sometimes gang warfare and criminality (for example, the Mara Salvatrucha gang that originated in Los Angeles and spread to Central America), broken families as migrants settle in other places and abandon their original families (resulting in many female-headed households), and the spread of HIV/AIDS through returning migrants.

Spending vs. investing remittances

Remittances tend to be spent on consumption (including the construction of housing) or safely invested in land. A lament from a development standpoint is that remittances are not more frequently invested in either education or new enterprises, but this is not always the case. Yang (2008) used the impact of the 1997 Asian financial crisis on the Philippines' exchange rate with countries that have large diasporas of Filipino migrants to see what happens when remittances gain value as the exchange rate depreciates. This is a natural experiment where migrants who send remittances get more "bang for their buck," and where a US dollar received by a migrant buys more Philippine pesos. The magnitude and timing of the exchange-rate effect was exogenous and different for migrants located in different countries, giving a good treatment effect for quantitative analysis. As can be seen in Figure 12.8, remittances coming from countries not affected by the Asian financial crisis gained in value as the Philippine peso depreciated against them. This was the case for remittances coming from countries such as Saudi Arabia, Hong Kong, Japan, Singapore, and Taiwan. By contrast, remittances lost value as the Philippine peso appreciated relative to Malaysia and Korea's currencies. This change in value is an exogenous shock that can be used to measure the corresponding changes in the use of remittances. Yang observed two effects. First, migrants send more remittances back home when the local currency depreciates, indicating a positive and significant elasticity of supply response of 0.6 of remittances to price. Second, recipients' consumption did not increase much compared to two types of investment: (1) investment in child education, with less child labor, more child schooling, and higher expenditures on education; and (2) investment in entrepreneurial activities with more self-employment, and more capital-intensive start-ups. This result is important in using a rigorous impact analysis to show that remittances can indeed be invested. This suggests that programs to enhance the development value of remittances could be quite effective for growth in the home country.

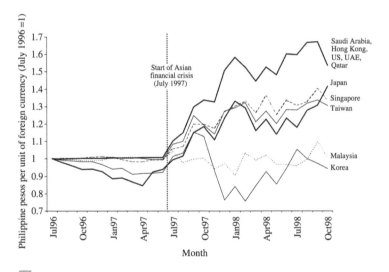

Figure 12.8 *Exchange rates in selected locations with overseas Filipinos, July 1996–October 1998*

Source: Yang, 2008.

456

Remittances have the unique feature of going directly to poor communities as this is where many of the migrants came from (though, as we have seen, not usually the poorest and most unskilled people in the community). They clearly make major direct contributions to poverty reduction among the recipient households. But they can also be a potentially important source of autonomous income if channeled toward productive investments and social projects. The *Tres-por-Uno* (three-for-one) program in Mexico matches every dollar invested in social projects by migrants' clubs in the US with a three-dollar contribution from the municipal, state, and federal governments. This public–private partnership is also used to support joint business ventures between migrants and residents in the communities of origin. The program has, however, been exposed for being regressive across communities, benefiting more the relatively richer communities, and for being used for political advantage, favoring municipalities supportive of the presidential party (Aparicio and Meseguer, 2008). Another astute initiative is helping to channel remittances toward the capitalization of local microfinance institutions. This was done in Mexico under President Salinas' Solidarity Program.

Given the extraordinary magnitude of remittance flows, it is no surprise that governments and development agencies are starting to experiment with ways of channeling remittances toward social infrastructure and local investments that can help create jobs and reduce poverty.

Impact of international migration on receiving countries

International migration is one of the most sensitive political issues, for both receiving and emitting countries. International migration was far less restrictive in the 1800s and up to World War One (during the first liberal period, also called the age of empire (Chapter 3)) than it is today. Then, migration flowed from more to less developed countries with vast open territories, inducing, through the transfer of institutions, a subsequent "reversal of fortune" (Acemoglu *et al.*, 2001). Today, the desired flows are mainly from less to more developed countries, and migration is severely restricted.

Free international labor movements, as advocated for instance by Pritchett (2007), would equalize opportunities and be efficient at a world scale, but would also result in massive relocation of populations and increased downward pressures on unskilled wages in MDC labor markets. This pressure on unskilled wages in industrialized countries is already felt as a consequence of trade (Chapter 7) and of outsourcing jobs to cheaper labor abroad. At the same time, unauthorized migration is increasingly difficult to contain, with more than 12 million undocumented persons in the US, who live, in many ways, at the margin of society and do not receive the full benefit of their work. Attempts to control migration with stronger borders have not proved effective. Restricted legal migration and increased undocumented migration also tends to shift the composition of migrants toward lower educational levels, increasing downward pressure on unskilled wages in the receiving country and making social integration more difficult.

There undoubtedly are important positive effects of migration for industrialized countries. Immigrants bring labor, ideas, and entrepreneurship. Migrants create jobs for others. They bring youth to an aging population, which helps maintain the solvency of social-security systems based on the pay-as-you-go principle (namely, where current contributions fund current transfers, as opposed to a system where contributions toward retirement are capitalized in income-earning investments). Contrary to frequent perceptions, undocumented migrants make positive contributions to the local welfare system as the taxes they pay tend to exceed the cost of their use of public services. Migrants help decrease labor shortages, especially high-skill workers given priority admission through H1-B temporary visas in the US. And they keep wages low in the service sector, which benefits the consumers of these services, which are broadly distributed across the population.

Negative effects include anti-immigrant responses in the resident population, based on the belief that immigrants add to crime, unemployment, and welfare fraud. And it can create a backlash against domestic low-skill workers when unskilled wages decline. A rapid increase in the number of undocumented immigrants in the context of a stagnant economy with high unemployment makes integration more difficult for all migrants and fuels discrimination.

Beaman (2012) analyzes the role of the size of social networks on labor-market outcomes for refugees newly arrived in the US. She uses exogeneity of location of refugees across cities as it is determined by resettlement agencies and not by refugee choice, avoiding placement bias. She shows that the labor-market outcome for newly arrived refugees in a community is negatively affected by the number of refugees already resettled in the community in the short run (current year and previous year). In the longer run, however, newly arrived refugees benefit from a larger network of long-tenured network members (refugees resettled three and four years ago).

Reforming immigration policy is politically explosive, and has for this reason not been adequately addressed. The current Graham–Schumer framework for US immigration reform is based on three main components: stricter border enforcement, a guest-worker program to manage the future flow of workers into the labor market, especially agriculture, and a path to citizenship for the 12 million undocumented immigrants currently living in the US. However, chances of rapid progress on immigration reform remain low.

A solution to illegal entries to industrialized countries—think of overloaded boats of the desperately poor reaching Lampedusa in Italy and the coast of Southern Spain, or illegal crossings into the US with the risks of exposure to the Arizona desert—will not involve stricter border controls and enforced legislation against hiring undocumented aliens (on the pull side) so much as reducing the pressures to migrate toward industrialized countries (on the push side). This requires improved living standards for the poor in developing countries. This includes not only higher per capita incomes, but also better provision of basic needs and improved quality of life, the other dimensions of development. Raising living standards in developing countries to reduce migratory pressures in industrialized countries is a powerful motivation for foreign aid, as explored in Chapter 19. If potential migrants are liquidity constrained, improved living standards may increase migration (Bazzi, 2014). Migration driven by opportunity will continue, and can create win–win opportunities if properly legislated and managed. However, migration pushed by adversity would decline, reducing illegal entries to industrialized countries.

CONCLUSION

Migration is part and parcel of a normal pattern of sectoral and geographical resource reallocation in the process of development. As such, it can be a source of efficiency gains. Domestically, it is the essence of structural transformation and internationally it is part of the globalization of a labor market. It can be an important force for development, with the potential for extensive benefits for both developing and industrialized countries. Remittances, in particular, create an extraordinary opportunity to finance development projects in some of the poorest emitting regions, if these regions have development potential and can channel the transfers toward productive investments. Yet migration is a difficult process to manage, both nationally and internationally, with a tendency for excessively rapid displacement of populations that are too often inadequately prepared to be absorbed productively in the receiving areas, and toward areas that are often not prepared to absorb them productively and culturally.

CONCEPTS SEEN IN THIS CHAPTER

Open unemployment, hidden unemployment, underemployment
Informal sector
Labor-market failure
Efficiency wage hypothesis
Harris–Todaro hypothesis in migration
Altruism vs. trade in remitting
Migration network
New migration economics
Role of credit and insurance-market failures on migration
Brain drain and brain gain
Remittances
Migrant motivation to remit
Immigration reform
Social networks and refugee resettlement

REVIEW QUESTIONS: LABOR AND MIGRATION

1. Define the concepts of open unemployment and underemployment. Define the relationship between formal- and informal-sector wages.
2. Explain why the efficiency wage hypothesis leads to unemployment, and hence market failure, even though it is incentive compatible for employers.
3. What is the Harris–Todaro hypothesis in migration? How does it explain continued migration in spite of urban unemployment? How does this relate to labor-market failure? Will creating

more jobs in the modern sector (e.g. in government employment) help reduce migration? What are the policy implications of the model to reduce rural–urban migration?

4. How does the new economics of migration analyze the decision to migrate? According to this approach, what are the main reasons for a household to send a migrant? Clearly identify the role of market failures in credit and insurance. How do policy implications to reduce migration under this theory differ from those of the Harris–Todaro model?

5. Why do migrants remit? Analyze the different motives that may apply.

6. What are the potential gains and losses from migration at the community level? What are the potential gains and losses from international migration for the emitting country?

REFERENCES

Acemoglu, Daron, Simon Johnson, and James Robinson. 2001. "Reversal of Fortune: Geography and Institutions in the Making of the Modern World Income Distribution." *Quarterly Journal of Economics* 117(4): 1231–94.

Akerlof, George, and Janet Yellen (eds.). 1986. *Efficiency Wage Models of the Labor Market.* Orlando, Florida: Academic Press.

Altonji, H., F. Hayashi, and L. Kotlikoff. 1998. "Parental Altruism and Inter Vivos Transfers: Theory and Evidence." *Journal of Political Economy* 105(6): 1121–66.

Aparicio, Francisco, and Covadonga Meseguer. 2008. "Collective Remittances and the State: The 3x1 Program in Mexican Municipalities." *World Development* 40(1): 206–22.

Bazzi, Samuel. 2014. "Wealth Heterogeneity and the Income Elasticity of Migration." Working paper, Department of Economics, Boston University.

Beaman, Lori. 2012. "Social Networks and the Dynamics of Labour Market Outcomes: Evidence from Refugees Resettled in the U.S." *Review of Economic Studies* 79(1): 128–61.

Bell, Martin, and Salut Muhidin. 2009. "Cross-national Comparisons of Internal Migration." UNDP: Human Development Research Paper 2009/30.

Bowles, Samuel, and Herbert Gintis. 1988. "Contested Exchange: Political Economy and Modern Economic Theory." *American Economic Review* 78(2): 145–50.

Bryan, Gharad, Shyamal Chowdhury, and Mushfiq Mobarak. 2014. "Underinvestment in a Profitable Technology: The Case of Seasonal Migration in Bangladesh." *Econometrica* 82(5): 1671–748.

Camacho, Adriana, Emily Conover, and Alejandro Hoyos. 2014. "Effects of Colombia's Social Protection System on Workers' Choice between Formal and Informal Employment." *World Bank Economic Review* 28(3): 446–66.

Chacko, Elizabeth. 2007. "From Brain Drain to Brain Gain: Reverse Migration to Bangalore and Hyderabad, India's Globalizing High Tech Cities." *GeoJournal* 68: 131–40.

Chenery, Hollis, and Lance Taylor. 1968. "Development Patterns: Among Countries and Over Time." *Review of Economics and Statistics* 50(3): 391–416.

Chiquiar, Daniel, and Gordon Hanson. 2005. "International Migration, Self-Selection, and the Distribution of Wages: Evidence from Mexico and the United States." *Journal of Political Economy* 113(2): 239–81.

Cox, Donald, and Emmanuel Jimenez. 1992. "Social Security and Private Transfers in a Developing Country: The Case of Peru." *World Bank Economic Review* 6(1): 155–69.

460

Cox, Donald, and Emmanuel Jimenez. 1998. "Risk Sharing and Private Transfers: What about Urban Households?" *Economic Developmentand Cultural Change* 46(3): 621–37.

Cox, Donald, Zekeriya Eser, and Emmanuel Jimenez. 1998. "Motives for Private Transfers over the Life Cycle: An Analytical Framework and Evidence from Peru." *Journal of Development Economics* 55(1): 57–81.

de Janvry, Alain, Frederico Finan, and Elisabeth Sadoulet. 2005. "Using a Structural Model of Educational Choice to Improve Program Efficiency." Working paper, Department of Agricultural and Resource Economics, University of California at Berkeley.

de la Brière, Bénédicte, Elisabeth Sadoulet, Alain de Janvry, and Sylvie Lambert. 2002. "The Roles of Destination, Gender, and Household Composition in Explaining Remittances: An Analysis for the Dominican Sierra." *Journal of Development Economics* 68(2): 309–28.

De Soto, Hernando. 1989. *The Other Path: The Economic Answer to Terrorism.* New York: Harper Collins.

Foster, Andrew, and Mark Rosenzweig. 1996. "Technical Change and Human Capital Returns and Investments: Evidence from the Green Revolution." *American Economic Review* 86(4): 931–53.

Gaviria, Alejandro, and Martha Luz Henao. 2001. "Comportamiento del desempleo en los últimos años y estrategias de los hogares para enfrentarlo." *Coyuntura Social de Fedesarrollo* 24: 23–38.

Gibson, John, David McKenzie, and Steven Stillman. 2011. "The Impacts of International Migration on Remaining Household Members: Omnibus Results from a Migration Lottery Program." *Review of Economics and Statistics* 93(4): 1297–1318.

Harris, John, and Michael Todaro. 1970. "Migration, Unemployment and Development: A Two-Sector Analysis." *American Economic Review* 60(1): 126–42.

Hoddinott, John. 1994. "A Model of Migration and Remittances Applied to Western Kenya." *Oxford Economic Papers* 46(3): 459–76.

International Labor Office. 2002. *Men and Women in the Informal Economy.* Geneva: International Labor Office.

Journeyman Pictures. *The Mumbai Makeover.* https://www.youtube.com/watch?v=9iC71S3o-4U&feature=related (accessed 2015).

Kleemans, Marieke, and Jeremy Magruder. 2014. "Labor Market Changes in Response to Immigration: Evidence from Internal Migration Driven by Weather Shocks." Working paper, Department of Agricultural and Resource Economics, University of California at Berkeley.

Kuznets, Simon. 1968. *Toward a Theory of Economic Growth.* New York: W.W. Norton and Co.

Levy, Santiago. 2008. *Good Intentions, Bad Outcomes.* Washington, DC: Brookings Institution Press.

Lewis, Arthur. 1955. *The Theory of Economic Growth.* Homewood, IL: Irwin.

Lucas, Robert, and Oded Stark. 1985. "Motivations to Remit: Evidence from Botswana." *Journal of Political Economy* 93(5): 901–18.

Maloney, William. 2004. "Informality Revisited." *World Development* 32(7): 1159–78.

McKenzie, David, and Hillel Rapoport. 2010. "Self-Selection Patterns in Mexico–U.S. Migration: The Role of Migration Networks." *Review of Economic and Statistics* 92(4): 811–21.

Mishra, Prachi. 2007. "Emigration and Wages in Source Countries: Evidence from Mexico." *Journal of Development Economics* 82(1): 180–99.

Mondragón, Camilo, Ximena Peña, and Daniel Wills. 2010. "Labor Market Rigidities and Informality in Colombia," *Economía* 11(1): 65–101.

Munshi, Kaivan. 2003. "Networks in the Modern Economy: Mexican Migrants in the U.S. Labor Market." *Quarterly Journal of Economics* 118(2): 549–99.

Pritchett, Lant. 2007. "Let Their People Come." New Economist http://neweconomist.blogs.com/new_economist/2007/06/lant_pritchard.html (accessed 2015).

Quinn, Michael. 2006. "Relative Deprivation, Wage Differentials, and Mexican Migration." *Review of Development Economics* 10(1): 135–53.

Ravallion, Martin, Shaohua Chen, and Prem Sangraula. 2007. "New Evidence on the Urbanization of Global Poverty." *Population and Development Review* 33(4): 667–701.

Rodrik, Dani. 2015. "Premature Deindustrialization." Working Paper No. 107, Institute of Advanced Studies: Princeton University.

Rosenzweig, Mark. 1988a. "Labor Markets in Low-income Countries." In H. Chenery and T.N. Srinivasan (eds.), *Handbook of Development Economics* 1(1): 713–62.

Rosenzweig, Mark. 1988b. "Risk, Implicit Contracts and the Family in Rural Areas of Low-income Countries." *Economic Journal* 98 (393): 1148–70.

Schultz, Theodore W. 1975. "The Value of the Ability to Deal with Disequilibria." *Journal of Economic Literature* 13 (September): 827–46.

Shapiro, Carl, and Joseph Stiglitz. 1984. "Equilibrium Unemployment as a Worker Discipline Device." *American Economic Review* 74(3): 433–44.

Stark, Oded. 1993. *The Migration of Labor*. Cambridge, MA: Blackwell Publishers.

Stark, Oded, and Robert Lucas. 1988. "Migration, Remittances, and the Family." *Economic Development and Cultural Change* 36(3): 465–81.

Stark, Oded, and J. Edward Taylor. 1989. "Relative Deprivation and Migration: Theory, Evidence, and Policy Implications." *Demography* 26(1):1–14.

Tokman, Victor. 1989. "Policies for a Heterogeneous Informal Sector in Latin America." *World Development* 17(7): 1067–76.

Trading Economics. www.trading economics.com (accessed 2014).

UN-Habitat. 2012. http://unhabitat.org/un-habitat-annual-report-2012/

Wikipedia. *Kibera*. http://en.wikipedia.org/wiki/Kibera (accessed 2015).

Wikipedia. *Megacity*. https://en.wikipedia.org/wiki/Megacity (accessed 2012).

Winters, Paul, Alain de Janvry, and Elisabeth Sadoulet. 2001. "Family and Community Networks in Mexico–U.S. Migration." *Journal of Human Resources* 36(1): 159–84.

World Bank. 2014. *Global Development Finance*. Washington, DC.

World Bank. 2007. *World Development Report 2008: Agriculture for Development*. Washington, DC.

World Bank, *Global Development Finance*. http://data.worldbank.org/indicator/BX.TRF.PWKR.CD.DT/countries (accessed 2013).

World Bank. *World Development Indicators*. http://data.worldbank.org/indicator (accessed 2015).

Yang, Dean. 2008. "International Migration, Remittances, and Household Investment: Evidence from Philippine Migrants' Exchange Rate Shocks." *Economic Journal* 118(528): 591–630.

Financial services for the poor

TAKE-HOME MESSAGES FOR CHAPTER 13

1. Because of asymmetrical information in time-delayed transactions, capital markets fail the poor who do not have collateral to pledge in seeking loans. The "microfinance revolution" is an effort at creating new institutions that can solve this problem without reliance on collateral.

2. In the absence of collateral, the lender problem to be solved has four components: avoiding adverse selection (AS) of potential borrowers, effective monitoring to reduce moral hazard (MH) in project implementation, providing some form of limited-liability insurance, and preventing MH in the repayment of loans.

3. Institutional alternatives to help the poor access lump sums of cash when needed while overcoming (at least partially) the lender problem include: moneylenders, ROSCAS, group lending, village banks, interlinked credit in value-chain contracts, and individual proximity lending.

4. Group lending has been the most successful innovation of microfinance institutions (MFIs) in overcoming the lender problem. It relies on self-selection by members, joint liability (inducing social sanctions and mutual insurance), and dynamic incentives.

5. Group lending is increasingly giving way to individual lending with the entry of for-profit lenders, rising competition among microfinance lenders, and "mission drift" away from poorer borrowers. Dynamic incentives and informed and motivated credit officers engaging in intensive screening and monitoring of clients are key for the success of individual lending without collateral.

6. Pervasive exposure to uninsured risks is a major source of poverty among smallholder farmers due to highly costly ex-ante risk management, and decapitalization and irreversibilities due to ex-post risk coping. Index-based weather insurance is a promising institutional innovation to give them access to formal insurance products. Uptake has, however, been low, and the product is in need of further improvement to become viable without large subsidies.

7. Safe and remunerative saving opportunities are one of the most essential financial services for the poor to help them manage liquidity and cope with risks. However, even when available, the discipline to save and to resist the temptation of dis-saving is often lacking. Innovative schemes have been put into place to help poor people help themselves in avoiding procrastination in saving and contain temptations to dis-save.

THE MICROFINANCE REVOLUTION

Credit is necessary whenever there is a time delay between an upfront investment and a pay-off that will only materialize later. The investment may be in education or in starting a new business. Credit is also necessary when incomes are discontinuous (a harvest, a pay day), while consumption expenditures are a continuous flow. Credit allows vitally important consumption smoothing. MFIs are institutional innovations designed to overcome a market failure in capital markets that is particularly detrimental to the poor. Because of asymmetrical information that induces AS and MH in borrowing, lenders require borrowers to provide collateral as a guarantee that the loan will be repaid.

For the poor, the implication is stark: even a good entrepreneur with a brilliant business idea will not qualify for a loan for lack of ownership of collateralizable assets (i.e. of assets that can serve as collateral with the lender). Capital markets selectively fail the poor as they are wealth-constrained by the collateral requirement. Lack of access to capital markets for the poor is then part of a vicious circle whereby poverty reproduces poverty through capital-market exclusion.

MFIs consist of a broad range of institutions that seek ways around this problem. Typically they will offer mechanisms by which lending can happen with minimal risk to the lender in spite of lack of formal collateral to secure the transaction. This is the microfinance revolution, a set of major institutional breakthroughs, pioneered by the Grameen Bank in Bangladesh, created in 1970 by Professor Yunus, who received the Nobel Peace Prize in 2006. Many other institutions have followed suit such as Banco Sol in Bolivia, BRAC in Bangladesh, with 4.2 million borrowers, 5.8 million depositors, and offices in 14 countries, Compartamos in Mexico (Table 13.1), and Bank Rakyat in Indonesia with 2 million borrowers and 16 million depositors. Progress in the microfinance sector has been continuously monitored and informed annually since 1997 by the Microcredit Summit Campaign accessible at www.microcreditsummit.org/ (accessed 2015). The Campaign says that microfinance currently reaches 175 million poor households through some 2500 institutions in 100 countries, with some $25 billion lent.

Table 13.1 Characteristics of selected MFIs

	Grameen Bank, Bangladesh	Banco Sol, Bolivia	Compartamos, Mexico
Year established	1983	1992	1990
Membership	6,950,000	104,000	617,000
Average loan balance (US$)	69	1571	440
Percent female	97	46	98
Legal status	Non-profit	Commercial bank	Commercial bank
Services offered	Loans	Savings and loans	Savings and loans
Group lending contracts?	Yes	Yes	Yes
Collateral required?	No	No	No
Portfolio at risk > 30 days (%)	1.9	2.9	1.1
Return on equity (%)	2.0	22.8	57.4

Source: Based on information in Sengupta and Aubuchon, 2008.

While MFIs in developing countries originated with the Grameen Bank extending small loans to poor women—loans which now number over 7 million—the movement has expanded as a worldwide phenomenon. MFIs increasingly go beyond credit to provide a broader range of financial services to the poor: savings, insurance (mostly for health with attempts at covering weather shocks), and the transfer of funds, including through SMS messages (Sengupta and Aubuchon, 2008). These services are complementary. Insurance is, for instance, important to help poor people avoid asset decapitalization when adversity strikes and assume more risks in developing profitable businesses and take more loans. Lump-sum expenditures can be met through saving, borrowing, and any combination of the two. It is interesting to note, in Table 13.1, that providers of MFI services can have the legal status of non-profit or commercial banks, that they can have high levels of performance (with very low shares of their lending portfolio at risk), and be quite profitable for the lender, making seeking "fortune at the bottom of the pyramid" in lending to the poor potentially quite attractive to large commercial banks (Prahalad, 2006).

Lump sums of money are needed by households to (1) meet life cycle needs such as dowries, school fees, and burial costs, (2) face emergencies such as doctor fees and hospital costs, (3) acquire indivisible assets such as livestock, land, housing, and durable goods, and (4) invest in business activities requiring capital goods and inventories (Rutherford, 2000). MFIs thus have the function of helping poor people transform a current or future flow of earnings into these discontinuous lump sums of money through credit and savings instruments.

In this chapter, we first analyze the generic-lending problem and explain how commercial banks respond and why poor people are excluded from formal financial institutions. We then look at the traditional institutions for access to loans and savings: moneylenders and ROSCAS (Rotating Saving and Credit Associations). We then analyze microfinance institutions practicing group lending, mobilizing savings in village banks and self-help groups, engaging in proximity lending for individual loans, and relying on interlinked transactions. We finish with recent institutional innovations to expand financial services for the poor such as mobile-phone banking, credit bureaus, index-based insurance, incentives to save, and internet-based lenders.

THE GENERIC-LENDER PROBLEM

Financial transactions are particularly complex because they involve a delay between the two sides of the transaction: a loan is given now, but will only be repaid later; a saving is deposited now and will be withdrawn later; an insurance premium is paid now and will become effective later when disaster strikes. Much of the difficulty in these deferred-payment transactions comes from asymmetric information among the parties involved, inviting opportunistic behavior, i.e. AS and MH. Institutional innovations such as MFIs have the purpose of defeating these sources of market failure (Williamson, 1985). AS and MH are defined as follows (Perloff, 2008):

> **Adverse selection (AS)** corresponds to *hidden information* about the characteristics of a person or a product that gives room for opportunistic behavior. In lending,

there is an AS problem when the lender cannot fully know the quality of a potential borrower, and thus cannot properly select only good borrowers (or adjust the interest rate to the borrower's riskiness). In insuring, more risky people will tend to seek insurance, raising the cost of payments for the insurance company that cannot recognize them ex-ante. This creates a market failure by reducing the size of the market for lending and insurance transactions, eventually completely eliminating the market as explained by Akerlof (1990) in his theory of the market for "lemons." Owners of good cars will not place their cars on the used car market as they will only receive the average price for cars on the market, which includes many lemons, and is thus inferior to the value of their car. As a consequence, on a market with products of uncertain quality, bad products will be driving out good products until the market eventually disappears.

Moral hazard (MH) corresponds to asymmetrical information allowing opportunism under the form of *hidden actions*. In lending, there is MH when the lender cannot observe or cannot enforce the proper use of funds and repayment by the borrower. In insuring, there is MH when the insurer cannot prevent the insured from behaving more recklessly and increasing the likelihood of accidents, knowing that he is now insured. Here again, this creates market failures by reducing transactions opportunities and eventually preventing any market activity.

Why are the poor excluded from formal financial institutions such as commercial banks and public development banks? Why do financial markets fail for them? There are four problems that a lender needs to solve in order to successfully obtain repayment of a loan made to a borrower. They are summarized in Figure 13.1.

1. Selection problem: avoid AS of borrower. The lender has difficulty in screening ex-ante good from bad borrowers due to incomplete and asymmetrical information. Hence he cannot fully know if the borrower will be able and willing to repay the loan.
2. Monitoring problem: avoid MH in project implementation. The lender cannot closely monitor (even if he could observe) the borrower's behavior. Hence he

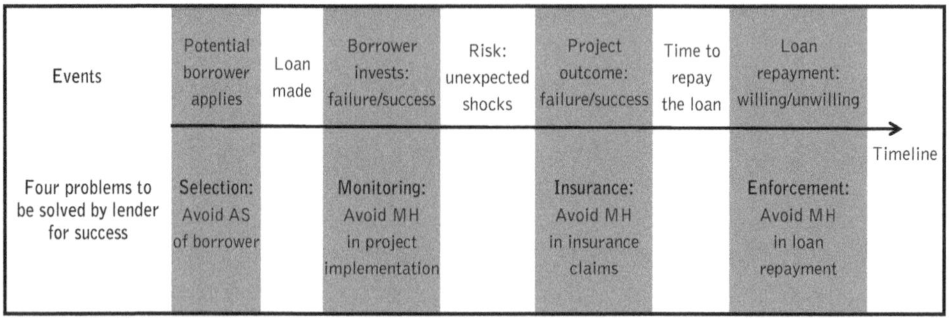

Events	Potential borrower applies	Loan made	Borrower invests: failure/success	Risk: unexpected shocks	Project outcome: failure/success	Time to repay the loan	Loan repayment: willing/unwilling	
								Timeline
Four problems to be solved by lender for success	Selection: Avoid AS of borrower		Monitoring: Avoid MH in project implementation		Insurance: Avoid MH in insurance claims		Enforcement: Avoid MH in loan repayment	

Figure 13.1 *The generic-lender problem*

cannot be certain that the borrower will make good use of the loan so that she will be able to repay.

3. Insurance problem: provide insurance and avoid MH in insurance claims. Poor borrowers need some form of insurance against unexpected shocks (i.e. limited liability in repaying the loan or rescheduling of the loan at some cost to the lender), otherwise even loans for good projects will not be repaid in bad years. But the lender cannot easily provide insurance as he cannot distinguish genuine failures from false claims due to imperfect information.

4. Enforcement problem: avoid MH in loan repayment. The lender cannot easily force the borrower to repay. He does not know if the borrower will be willing to repay, even if he is able to do so having made successful use of the loan.

We now analyze the different types of financial institution that operate in most developing countries, each with particular advantages and shortcomings in addressing the selection, monitoring, insurance, and enforcement dimensions of the lender problem. They are summarized in Table 13.2.

COMMERCIAL BANKS

The solution for a formal lender is to require collateral from the borrower in order to overcome the problems of selection, monitoring, and enforcement. Collaterals are assets that the borrower owns such as real estate, valuables, vehicles, investments, and cash accounts that the lender can take and sell in case of default. Hence access to credit is restricted to those with collateral. This creates a market failure as credit is provided in a wealth-constrained market. This has two costs:

1. An efficiency cost: the allocation of credit is unrelated to the marginal productivity of capital. Many good projects are not funded simply because the entrepreneur is poor and unable to pledge collateral. Note that even poor entrepreneurs with collateral may not be able to take loans as they cannot afford to put their collaterals (land, house) at risk (Boucher *et al.*, 2008). Hence formal asset ownership by the poor, as championed by Hernando de Soto (2000), is necessary but not sufficient to access commercial loans. The borrower needs to be able to self-insure or to access other sources of insurance in order to take a loan. Financial services for the poor thus need to provide not only access to loans, but also to insurance.

2. An equity cost: the poor with no collateralizable assets are excluded, creating sharp inequities across potential borrowers (World Bank, 2005). Allocation of credit to the wealthy thus contributes to reinforcing and reproducing inequality. Exclusion of the poor contributes to reproducing poverty.

The formal lender's collateral solution to the lender problem thus tends to exclude most of the poor from access to bank loans. By leaving unresolved the insurance problem, it also excludes the poor with collateral who cannot take the risk of losing it. This is a serious problem in development if we believe that entrepreneurship

Table 13.2 *Financial institutions and their ability to overcome capital-market failures for the poor*

Financial institutions	Selection AS in participant selection	Monitoring MH in project implementation	Insurance MH limited liability	Enforcement MH in repayment	Remaining problems
1. Formal lender (Formal collateral)	+	+	No Some limited liability	+	Wealth-constrained market No insurance for borrower
2. Money lender (Local information & social capital)	+	+	Not for covariate risk "Dilemma of the agrarian community"	+	Very high interest rates
3. ROSCAs (Local information & social capital)	+	+	No	+	Not useful for insurance. Small lump sums of money. No interest on money handed out
4. MFI with group lending (Self-selection, joint liability, dynamic incentives, frequent installments, mutual insurance, peer monitoring, interlinkages, collective sanction)	+	+ Small groups better	Not for covariate risk Large groups better	+	Risk of group default No insurance for covariate shocks Graduation to private loans?
5. Village banks (Savings, proximity lending)	+	+	Not for covariate risk	+	Risk of loss of savings (regulation) Weak management capacity
6. MFI with individual loans (Reputation, dynamic incentives, co-signataries)	Partial	Partial	Partial	Partial	Risk of double-dipping Imperfect information for credit officers
7. Interlinked transactions (Value chains, interlinked contracts)	+	+	+	+	Specific transactions only
8. Credit bureau (Information sharing among lenders)	+	NA	NA	+	Accuracy of information No information on new clients
9. Index-based weather insurance (Weather-based covariate risks)	+	+	+ Re-insurance	NA	Only insures weather-based covariate risks Leaves large "basis risk" uninsured Need build trust in provider

+ sign indicates that the institution has the ability to solve the corresponding problem. NA indicates not applicable.

can be an important pathway out of poverty. Banerjee and Duflo (2011) find that less than 5 percent of the poor have a loan from a bank in a data set covering 18 countries. As a consequence, the poor must turn to the informal sources of credit that tend to dominate in the developing world. For instance, in Udaipur, India, they find that two-thirds of poor households had a loan at survey time: 23 percent from a relative, 18 percent from a moneylender, 37 percent from a shopkeeper, and only 6 percent from a formal source.

LOCAL MONEYLENDERS, OR "USURERS"

Because there are profits to be made, local moneylenders are present in all contexts where people need to make expected or unexpected lump-sum payments but are left without access to formal lenders. Moneylenders are present in remote agrarian communities of Bangladesh, waiting to be repaid when the harvest comes. They are watching on the beach when fishermen return with their catch on the Malabar Coast of Kerala. As opposed to commercial lenders, they are able to lend money to the poor because they have found a solution to the four problems faced by any lender. How have they done this?

The comparative advantage of moneylenders is that they live in the community, where they have access to information about potential borrowers, information not available to commercial lenders. They typically are farmers or shopkeepers themselves, or have a steady job with a local employer and often interact with their clients outside of the lending relationship as well. They know who is who, who does what, what reputation each person has for hard work and honesty, and who is connected with whom. This allows them to defeat the problems of AS and MH in selection, monitoring, insurance (partially), and enforcement. Informal lenders typically lend to a fixed clientele—people with whom they have a repeated relationship and history—and are unwilling to lend outside their circle. Aleem (1990) found that in rural Pakistan over 75 percent of loans made by moneylenders were to existing clients. Beyond local information, moneylenders have access to local social capital in that they can ostracize someone who does not repay, diminishing the reputation a person has, with costs to him or her in terms of future transactions with other community members such as landlords, employers, and merchants. They can take some forms of collateral that a commercial bank cannot take such as animals, small durable goods (as pawnbrokers do), and use of the client's land for a season (so-called land pawning, which is frequent in the Philippines); and if there is limited competition among moneylenders, they can play repeated games with a clientele that wants to keep access to future loans. So local money lending seems to work pretty well in meeting the financial needs of the poor. What are the drawbacks? Why do moneylenders have such a poor reputation (typically given the unflattering name of usurers)?

The main problem is the high cost of credit. Interest rates are typically 1 percent per day in the Dominican Republic and 400 to 500 percent per year in South Africa. This may be due to monopoly power, but interest rates are high even when there is competition among moneylenders. This is for several reasons. One is that they need to be highly liquid to be able to make emergency loans. This is what they are there for. A child is sick in the middle of the night and a taxi is needed to take him to the hospital. A quick visit to wake up the moneylender enables parents to have the cash needed for the trip. A second reason is that by nature of a small market with short-term and irregular needs, as well as of heavy cyclical/seasonal demand (more frequently in the months that precede harvest in rural communities, in the weeks that precede wage payments in urban environments, in periods of exceptional expenses such as school fees, etc.), resources held by moneylenders often remain idle.

The very high cost of loans clearly limits their use by households to cash needs to cope with shocks, short-run liquidity needs to make payments (for example, for food at the local store until pay day, or to an MFI to make interest payments on a loan instead of defaulting), and high-return operations such as buying and selling animals and goods with a quick turnover.

At the same time, the moneylender is not well placed to deal with covariate shocks. If everyone in the community is affected by a drought or a plague, the moneylender has difficulty providing resources to all of them and securing repayment for his loans. A broader financial institution with a lending portfolio going beyond the community would be needed for this. Since knowledge of his clientele is limited to the community where he lives, this is a service the moneylender cannot offer. This is the so-called dilemma of the agrarian community: local information is quite perfect (the universal pastime of gossiping takes care of this), but local information is insufficient for some transactions such as insuring covariate risks.

Hence moneylenders provide extremely useful services to the poor, which is the reason why they exist, but their services are extraordinarily expensive, calling on alternative institutional innovations that can service the poor. Microfinance institutions have learned from them—for example, in using credit agents from the community, who benefit from the same informational advantage as a local moneylender—yet try to provide similar services at a much lower cost.

INFORMAL MICROFINANCE INSTITUTIONS: ROSCAS

Can poor people without access to formal loans and in need of lump sums of cash to meet particular expenditures do better than using loans from moneylenders? If these expenditures can be planned or their timing is not too important, one option is membership in a Rotating Saving and Credit Association (ROSCA). These are spontaneous associations that generally exist without any formal by-laws. They serve both to promote savings and to gain access to lump sums of cash. They are part of the extraordinary diversity of institutional innovations that one encounters at the grassroots level. We find them from Haiti (where they are called *tontines*) to African villages (called *susus* in West Africa), Mexico (called *tandas*), and among undocumented immigrant workers in East Oakland. Here is how they work.

A group of people who trust each other constitute a ROSCA. They are typically people who live in the same village or neighborhood, migrated from the same village, or work together—for instance, in a meat-packing plant in East Oakland. The association has N members who meet at regular intervals, typically monthly. At each meeting they all make an equal deposit d. One member takes home the lump-sum Nd

contributed at one meeting. Different ROSCAs have different rules of attribution: there can be a pre-assigned turn often decided by an initial random draw, or there can be bidding on turns, with the highest bidder coming first.

These associations are able to solve the problems of selection and enforcement. Because they perform irrespective of the use members make of the cash lump sums, they are not concerned with monitoring project implementation. Limited liability is also of lesser concern because deposits are usually small.

Consider the following example where ten members meet monthly and each member puts $10 on the table. The first winner gets $100 immediately, interest free. He will repay the others at zero interest through his $10 contribution at each of the nine subsequent meetings. The tenth winner gets $100, having made payments for nine months. He could have saved alone just the same—and he has lost interest earnings on his money during the nine months when he made his $100 contributions. So why did he participate?

The advantages of membership to a ROSCA are the following:

- If the ROSCA is a repeated game, being last, which is a random draw, is only for the first round. Subsequent rounds come with the same regularity for all.
- Loss of interest for those with higher turns is zero if money cannot be deposited in interest-bearing accounts or used for business.
- The ROSCA is largely able to defeat the selection and enforcement problems as members self-select and know each other well. They are usually tied by some form of social capital that serves as a guarantee that a member who receives the pot of money will not abstain from participating in subsequent meetings.
- One of the most important functions of ROSCA membership is that it provides a disciplinary device, i.e. a nudge to save via the routine of contributions at regularly scheduled meetings (Thaler and Sunstein, 2008). This helps resist spending on temptation goods (Banerjee and Mullainathan, 2010), withstand social pressures to help others in the family or the community, and defeat the well known human tendency of procrastinating with such activities as savings that can forever be postponed to tomorrow, and thus never happen. It is effective for lumpy expenditures such as a business investment, the purchase of a durable good, or a life cycle expenditure known ahead of time such as a dowry.
- Anderson and Baland (2002) studied the functions of ROSCAs in the Kibera slum of Nairobi, one of the largest in the world. They observed that 84 percent of ROSCA members were women, 40 percent of all women in the slum were members, 53 percent of all women in a couple were members, and 75 percent of all women in a couple who were earning an independent income were members. Their interpretation for this high rate of membership is based on conflict between genders in the household. Wives participate in ROSCAs as a strategy to protect their savings against claims by their husband for immediate consumption. This is consistent with a study by De Mel et al. (2009), which showed a husband's capture of women's savings within the household contributing to women being more credit-constrained and engaging in less profitable savings practices activities such as purchasing too much physical capital.

471

■ ROSCA membership often has other benefits such as information sharing among group members, organizing other business deals, allowing women to be away from home, and organizing social functions.

Disadvantages of ROSCA membership include the following:

■ Rigidity in the timing and amount of access to a lump sum of money. This rigidity makes the lump sum ineffective for insurance: you only get the lump sum when the group meets and when it is your turn.
■ Residual risk of MH since a member who had an early turn can decide to stop coming to meetings, effectively defaulting on others. This is particularly tempting if the amounts of money contributed at each meeting are large and if social capital among members is a weak enforcement mechanism.
■ Thus ROSCAs are quite useful, highly prevalent, but not infallible. As formal microfinance institutions seek ways of helping people discipline themselves in saving, ROSCAs have much to teach. Institutional innovations that emerged in the informal sector have generated ideas that are useful for the design of formal institutions.

MICROFINANCE WITH GROUP LENDING

The heart of the microfinance revolution consists in replacing the use of assets as collateral, which the poor do not have, by social collateral, which the poor can provide (Armendáriz de Aghion and Morduch, 2005). This is the idea of using solidarity groups where members are jointly liable for the loans taken by individual members. The approach was pioneered by the Grameen Bank in 1970.

MFIs were initially mainly non-profit organizations, motivated by providing access to capital to the poor. Because rates of repayment tend to be high, interest rates are high, and the poor are hundreds of millions of potential clients, MFIs are increasingly commercial banks that seek fortune at the bottom of the pyramid, with profit-making as the motive (Prahalad, 2006). Increasing competition among MFIs for good borrowers has created a rapid "mission drift" away from serving the poorest to finding viable clients among the poor (poor is here defined as households without assets that can serve as collateral, i.e. people who are asset poor), usually the least poor, who may be the best potential entrepreneurs. For donors who pour aid money into MFIs, mission drift creates a dilemma in using microfinance as an instrument for poverty reduction.

Group lending has been effective in solving the four lender problems, including, at least partially, the insurance problem. Here is how it works.

The MFI asks potential borrowers to self-select into groups of five to 30 members. Members typically choose to associate with others they know well. Loans are individual, but all group members are jointly liable for the repayment of all loans taken by group members. This means that each member is responsible for repaying the loans of those who default—and the whole group loses access to future loans if all loans are not repaid. In this fashion, the group serves as social collateral, acting as a substitute for the collateralizable assets that poor members do not own (Ghatak and Guinnane, 1999). The loans made by the MFI are small and inferior to the amounts each member would like to borrow, and most often for short terms of three months. Loans are gradually increased to reward good repayment behavior. This creates dynamic incentives that induce borrowers to repay their current loans in hopes of getting larger loans in the future.

Another feature of group lending by MFIs is that frequent installments (partial repayments of the loan) are required, typically on a weekly or bi-weekly basis. While this is a huge transaction cost for the borrower, it may in fact be desired by both the MFI and the client. On the MFI side, the advantages of frequent installments are that they allow officers to better monitor their clients and help screen borrowers who have a steady income flow—in addition to an expected return from the investment project funded by the loan—sufficient to cover the cost of the loan, thus reducing the risk of default. On the client side, frequent installments are a disciplinary device. In a way, taking an expensive loan to cover an expenditure such as house repairs when the money could have been saved appears irrational. The rationality for this decision is the disciplinary device of the frequent installments, the borrower saving more than she could have done by herself, at a very high cost (Banerjee and Duflo, 2011). In this sense, the client effectively borrows to save!

How does group lending help solve lender problems? Self-selection by group members helps solve the AS problem. Because members are jointly liable, they have a strong incentive to select other members likely to perform well, and to expel non-performing members. They are more effective at doing this than the lender as they have extensive private information on each other. They also have a strong incentive to monitor and help each other's projects using local information and direct assistance, in what is referred to as peer monitoring. For this, groups that are more homogenous in terms of people's occupations (they may, for instance, all be in the informal restaurant business) are more effective for monitoring than heterogeneous groups. The group can enforce payment on its members based on social capital (ostracism in the community if a member misbehaves), interlinkages among members (based on interlinked transactions, which will be explained later), seizure of petty collateral (e.g. personal belongings), and the threat of being expelled from the group (in a repeated-game perspective). Analyzing group lending by FINCA in Peru, Karlan (2007) finds that monitoring and enforcement activities by group members do improve group-lending outcomes, and that social connections (i.e. groups that are culturally similar and geographically concentrated) facilitate group members' monitoring and enforcement of each other. Finally, the group can mutually insure against idiosyncratic risks (but not against global shocks): successful members can repay the loan of a member with a true involuntary failure due, for example, to illness. For insurance purposes, large heterogeneous groups that do not suffer from covariate shocks are more effective as they diversify risks. How large and homogenous a group should be thus responds to a trade-off: small and homogenous is better for monitoring free-riding (MH); large and heterogeneous is better for mutual insurance. The Grameen Bank requires groups to have no fewer than five members. Members usually prefer smaller over larger groups, suggesting that the MH problem is of greater concern to them than the insurance benefit.

Finally, the MFI can enforce repayment by using dynamic incentives (gradually larger loans based on a good repayment performance) and collective sanctions (the whole group loses access to future loans if one loan is not repaid).

So what are some of the potential disadvantages of the MFI group-lending approach? One is that credit remains expensive. The MFI will typically charge a 7 to 10 percent interest mark-up as a management fee over the 15–20 percent interest rate charged by the bank that provides the capital, thus reaching interest rates in the range of 22–30 percent. Those are of course much lower than the rates charged by money-lenders (400–500 percent). Yet investment opportunities must be good in order to perform with loans that expensive. For that reason, MFI loans have been more successful in commerce and in rapid-turnover micro-enterprises activities such as retailing, than in agriculture with longer cycles, lower profitability, and higher risks.

Another disadvantage for the lender is that the whole group could potentially default if those who would not have defaulted individually cannot repay for defaulters, even though they could have paid for themselves (Besley and Coate, 1995). However, experience shows that repayment rates are high when MFIs have good credit officers working closely with their clients. Data in Table 13.1 show that repayment rates within 30 days of the due date were 98 percent for the Grameen Bank, 97 percent for Banco Sol, and 99 percent for Compartamos.

Group lending can also be interpreted as a transitory learning stage toward obtaining individual loans. Over time, as members are unequally successful in their investments, they can become increasingly different from each other, making joint liability and mutual insurance difficult to sustain. The more successful members should then switch to individual loans, capitalizing on their good borrower reputation established under group lending.

Practitioners and researchers have joined forces in designing randomized evaluations of certain features of MFI lending in order to improve its performance and efficiency. For example, an MFI from the Philippines working with Giné and Karlan (2011) removed the joint-liability clause on loans in a selected subset of its branches using an RCT design. Comparing default rates across branches, they found that the removal of the joint-liability clause did not induce any increase in default rates for groups that have been in existence for some time. They also found no difference in repayment rates across new clients that were offered individual-liability loans rather than joint-liability loans. However, this change of selection rule attracted a different type of client and was compensated for by a different level of effort by credit agents, making it impossible to attribute the result to anyone of these features.

Field and Pande (2008) designed a field experiment in Calcutta, India, in which clients were randomly assigned to a weekly or monthly repayment schedule in an otherwise classical MFI group-loan structure. To insure that the effect was solely due to the frequency of repayment, all other features were kept identical for the time of the experiment, including the weekly meetings, even among the groups selected for monthly repayment. US$100 loans were made to groups of ten women with joint liability to be repaid with a US$10 interest fee over 44 weeks. These women were all first-time borrowers without access to any other loan. They found no significant effect of type of repayment schedule on client delinquency or default. The results thus suggest that more flexible repayment schedules can allow MFIs to significantly lower their transaction costs without increasing client default.

So while the practice of group lending has led to a multiplicity of characteristics for these loans, the jury is still out as to which of these features are important, where, and for whom. The world of MFI clients is diverse and not all features are equally important everywhere. MFIs may want to test features that are particularly time-consuming and expensive for their agents or their clients in order to make sure that they are worthwhile maintaining.

To conclude, *group lending* is the core innovation in microfinance lending. The key design features of group lending are the following:

- *Joint liability* providing social collateral for individual loans: all members are jointly liable for the repayment of all loans taken by group members.
- *Self-selection* by group members into groups of five to 30 members based on private information.
- *Frequent installments* as a disciplinary device for self-control and supervision, typically on a weekly or bi-weekly basis.
- *Dynamic incentives*: loans are gradually increased to reward good repayment behavior.
- *Collective sanction* in case of default: the whole group loses access to future loans if all loans are not repaid.

These design features induce the following behavioral responses, which help solve the lender problem:

- *Assortative matching* in group formation, helping solve the AS problem among borrowers.
- *Peer monitoring*, helping solve the MH problem in project implementation.
- *Mutual insurance*, helping solve the MH problem in providing insurance for idiosyncratic shocks. This leaves unresolved the insurance problem for covariate shocks.
- *Social capital and interlinkages* among group members, helping solve the MH problem in enforcing repayment.

VILLAGE BANKS AND SELF-HELP GROUPS

A major lesson derived from detailed analyses of their finances is that the poor need access to financial services that go beyond loans to include savings, insurance, and financial transfers (Collins *et al.*, 2009). Poor people need in particular safe and profitable savings instruments for lump-sum payments (purchase of a durable good), self-insurance (risk coping), and life cycle expenditures (dowries, retirement). Institutional innovations for this include village banks, promoted in particular by FINCA (a Washington-based organization), credit cooperatives, local savings-and-loans associations, credit unions, and self-help groups in India, also called Accumulating Saving and Credit Associations (ASCAs). While the main challenge of lending to poor people was to find a substitute for formal collateral, the main challenge in offering savings services to the poor is guaranteeing security of deposits in an institutional context that is weakly regulated at best and highly decentralized. The worst savings service that could be offered to poor people (as a substitute for their use of animals, grain stocks, and jewelry as savings instruments) is savings accounts from which money will be lost or stolen, not altogether uncommon events.

A FINCA-type village bank usually has some 200–400 members and formal by-laws (Figure 13.2). It mobilizes savings from members (internal account) and also receives loans and grants from outsiders (external account). This equity can in turn be lent to members in the form of individual or group loans. Loans are relatively safe as they benefit from proximity lending: they are made on the basis of extensive personal information among members. The village bank can thus manage the problems of AS and MH based on local information. It can insure borrowers against idiosyncratic shocks by making use of local information and social capital, offering limited liability on loans (the option to reschedule loans) if there is genuine inability to repay.

Self-help groups (SHG) are usually composed of 10–20 local women. Members make small regular savings contributions over a few months until there is enough capital accumulated in the group's bank account to begin lending. Funds may then be lent back to the members of the SHG or to others in the village for any purpose. Having established a record of saving and repayment, the group can gain access to commercial bank loans, generally in fixed proportion (commonly 4 to 1) to its equity capital. In this way, the SHG acts as a local window to the commercial bank that could not otherwise reach this large and profitable "bottom of the pyramid" clientele. The SHG concept has emerged as one of the world's largest microfinance networks. In India, it reaches over 103 million poor households, members of nearly 8 million SHGs (NABARD, 2012). SHGs are associated in multiple federations. Membership of an SHG not only helps provide access to financial services to women formerly marginalized from such services, but also serves as an empowerment tool for them to participate in an organized fashion in social life and local affairs. The Self Employed Women's Association (SEWA), a membership-based organization of poor self-employed women workers with 1.2 million members in nine states of India, organizes its members in SHGs, effectively providing them with access to financial services.

Village banking is, however, not free from difficulties. The approach assumes that members have sufficient management capacity to self-manage the village bank. This is a big assumption. The risk of loss of savings through mismanagement and theft is a stark reality. For that reason, it is important that local MFIs that engage in savings mobilization be part of a legal regulatory framework. But the risk is that regulation is too rigid and demanding (e.g. in Mexico), making the mobilization of savings by village banks difficult. As the group gets larger, which is necessary to cover fixed management

Figure 13.2 *Village bank*

costs, AS and MH may creep in as shared information about members becomes more tenuous. Yet village banks are very important in providing access to more complete financial services to millions of poor people, often with the strong support of formal banks, as in India.

MFIs WITH INDIVIDUAL LOANS: PROXIMITY LENDING

MFIs have also developed methodologies that allow them to make individual loans, still without collateral. These loans are generally made by profit-oriented MFIs, which are in the business of microfinance to capture a market niche which commercial banks are unable to penetrate. They are opening a huge market for small loans to the micro-enterprise sector, which can be very profitable as long as interest rates are high, repayment rates are also high, and there is little competition. Kim and Mauborgne (2005) describe this as a "blue ocean" strategy, consisting of opening up new markets where competition is absent, as opposed to competing in markets that already have a lot of competitors, the "red oceans." How do they obtain high repayment rates from individuals without collateral?

Three instruments are used for this. One is dynamic incentives: make small loans, inferior to the size demanded by clients, with a steep increase in loan size over time to reward good performance, and loss of access to credit otherwise. This requires the MFI to have monopoly power, preventing the client from borrowing elsewhere. The second is to require co-signers to the loan who serve as personal collateral. The problem with this is that if there is default on the loan, it will be difficult to enforce payment on the co-signer when loans are made without collateral. And the third is proximity lending as the MFI makes intensive use of well informed credit agents for the selection and monitoring of clients. These agents are typically from the community, which gives them access to information about potential borrowers, somewhat similar to moneylenders (Fuentes, 1996), a lesson learned from the informal sector. Agents are given incentive contracts whereby they benefit from high repayment rates through bonuses. With motivated and skilled credit agents, success (for example, as achieved by Bank Rakyat in Indonesia and by Susu Collectors providing small loans for Barclays Bank in Ghana) shows that individual lending without collateral can also work with clients that have acquired the discipline of making payments, sometimes acquired through a previous phase of group lending. Client credit scoring is important. Credit bureaus are useful for this, allowing information about clients to be shared among lenders when competition rises and dynamic incentives are weakened, and they are emerging rapidly across developing countries.

LOCAL SOURCES OF CREDIT BASED ON INTERLINKAGES IN VALUE CHAINS

When there are market failures, interlinkages between two transactions often allow each transaction to perform better than it would alone. This is the theory of interlinked transactions (Bardhan, 2003). The two transactions have greater value together than the sum of the value of each transaction separately because each transaction improves the value of the other. Interlinkages can help solve the problems of AS, MH, and insurance in credit transactions. Consider the following examples:

- A local merchant gives credit to a farmer and will buy his products at harvest time under favorable conditions.
- A local landlord gives credit to a worker and also regularly rents land to him when there is a lot of competition among potential tenants to get access to land.
- A local moneylender gives credit and also provides insurance to his client when hit by a shock with no other insurance option for the client.

In all cases, the interlinkage of credit with a second transaction is used to put pressure on the recipient of the loan to repay: the borrower will be cut-off from the benefits of the other transaction if he does not repay the loan, creating an incentive to repay. In a sense, the other transaction serves as "collateral" for the credit transaction.

This form of lending happens increasingly within value chains. A value chain is the sequence of transactions that run from accessing inputs, to the production, processing, marketing, and consumption of a particular commodity. Transactions in these value chains are commonly interlinked. A provider of inputs will provide credit to a farmer and get paid in product at harvest time. A supermarket will finance the production of its providers, and impose strict quality and timing requirements on product delivery. Value chains increasingly serve as instruments where financial transactions occur along with transactions of inputs and products. The nature of the transaction can be quite complex. Casaburi and Reed (2015) ran an RCT experiment in Sierra Leone where traders received a per-unit bonus for delivery of cocoa to wholesalers. These traders buy cocoa from producers and provide them with credit. The question was how much price pass-through there is to farmers when prices rise for traders? They found that there is limited price pass-though but that there is a large increase in credit provision, both in the intensive margin (more credit to existing client farmers) and in the extensive margin (credit is extended to additional farmers). Credit is given under the form of paying the producer in advance for the good. The credit is paid back in the form of a lower output price. With credit boosting the capacity to produce of credit-constrained famers, both farmer and trader gain from using the credit channel as a pass-through channel, rather than just the price mechanism.

OTHER ISSUES IN MICROFINANCE LENDING

Some other issues in microfinance lending worth mentioning are the following.

Charity vs. business

NGOs engaged in lending activities sometimes have difficulty in enforcing repayment as they are seen by their clients as soft-hearted charitable institutions. The lesson learned is that it is better to clearly separate charitable activities from lending operations. NGOs engaged in eventually successful welfare activities should set up separate branches for their micro finance operations.

Access to financial markets for sustainability

Group lending is sustainable and replicable only if the MFI is linked to financial markets to access capital, as opposed to being dependent on donations for funds. Donations can be used to cover the start-up costs and learning phase of new MFIs until they become competitive, as done by Boston-based Acción International (www. accion.org). Unitus (www.unitus.com) channels internet donations specifically to assist MFI start-ups. This is another example where "smart" subsidies can be effective if designed to be transitory in helping the emergence of self-sustainable institutions.

Internet-based microlenders

Kiva (www.kiva.org), MYC4 (www.myc4.com), Prosper (www.prosper.com), Vittana (www.vittana.org), and other internet-based microlending institutions allow face-to-face relations between dispersed lenders and dispersed borrowers, under the oversight of the managing MFI. This approach to MFI lending has seen extraordinarily rapid growth, with contractual innovations and generally successful repayment rates.

Different business models are used by different internet lenders, some registered as non-profit and others as for-profit with competitive lending. Kiva.org is a non-profit operation where internet lenders can lend as little as US$25 to poor people around the world for projects presented on the Kiva website. Lenders do not receive interest, but can recuperate the principal lent when the project is over, unless they decide to donate it to Kiva for further lending. Adverse selection is addressed by using local field partners, typically trusted local MFIs, who are responsible for screening borrowers, sending loan requests to Kiva, disbursing loans, monitoring borrowers, and collecting repayments. MH is addressed by close monitoring by the field partner's loan officers and asking the borrower to start saving upon receiving the loan, ensuring that he will have money available when the time comes to repay the loan. Group lending with joint liability is also an option. While lenders are motivated by the "warm glow" (Andreoni, 1990) effect of a personal relation to a particular poor person to whom the loan is directed, money is in fact fungible at the level of the field partner and a specific donation may not necessarily go to the specific project that may, in fact, already have been funded. The Kiva business model is highly successful, with a repayment rate of 98.9 percent.

MYC4.com connects for-profit internet lenders to small entrepreneurs in Africa. Lenders participate in loan auctions after picking the project they feel has potential. The lenders who offer the lowest interest rates are the ones who will lend to the borrower when the auction is over, up to the amount requested. Investors earn money through the interest they collect once the loan is repaid. As with Kiva, adverse selection is addressed by working with local partners who make a thorough evaluation of the business projects of borrowers to assess their growth potential and repayment ability. To deal with MH, the borrower most of the time has to put up some form of collateral that can be collected by the local partner in case of default. The MYC4 business model is sustainable without dependency on donations and can be scaled up competitively.

Information sharing through credit bureaus under rising competition

Rising competition among MFIs reduces the power of dynamic incentives to repay loans as alternative sources of loans become available to individual borrowers. This can increase the default rate (McIntosh and Wydick, 2005). As clients can now take multiple loans without the knowledge of lenders, the rate of default can increase for the incumbent lender, a phenomenon seen in Uganda (McIntosh *et al.*, 2005). This is when the introduction of a credit bureau that provides competing lenders with information on the past repayment performance of potential clients and their total levels of indebtedness becomes truly important to lenders. The introduction of a credit bureau in Guatemala allowing MFI lenders to share information (about both past defaults and current levels of indebtedness) about their clients has been shown to help reduce AS and MH, significantly improving the repayment performance for participating institutions. This was analyzed by de Janvry *et al.* (2010) in two steps. First, they used the roll-out of the credit bureau to the different branches of the MFI as a natural experiment to identify a strong positive impact of its use on the quality of selected clients. Because clients were not initially told that the MFI was using the credit bureau to select them, this observed result is strictly the effect of the agents using the credit bureau for improved selection. Then, in the second step, researchers told clients about the existence and functions of the credit bureau as part of an RCT experiment, reducing MH as expected as clients understand that defaults will now be known by all lenders. Results show that clients concerned about their reputation beyond their current lenders responded by selecting out some members of their group that had relatively lower repayment performance. Hence the credit bureau re-establishes the informational environment that allows MFIs to function without requesting collateral. It can also serve to build borrowers' reputations for good repayment performance, and allows them to qualify for more flexible and larger individual loans at other institutions. Through this, MFIs can serve as a step on a credit ladder, incorporating unbanked people into group loans until their internal or external reputations give them access to more formal and cheaper loans.

Credit-agent incentives to counteract mission drift

International donors supporting non-profit MFIs through grants for their role in helping the poor gain access to capital are increasingly concerned with mission drift away from poorer potential clients. This is especially the case as commercial-bank entrants into microfinance (lending without collateral) take the better clients away from the non-profit pro-poor lenders. This prevents the pro-poor MFIs from using the profits made on the better (less poor) clients to cross-subsidize the weaker (poorer) clients, while maintaining overall profitability. The issue of achieving profitability (which is necessary for a sustainable operation with a high rate of loan repayment) while at the same time serving the relatively poorer potential borrowers remains an unresolved problem. MFIs have introduced payment incentives with credit agents, giving them bonuses proportional to their portfolio performance, the number of new members they bring in, and the average loan size. This improves their performance, but does not induce them to work with poorer potential clients when the less-poor are better clients. If incentive contracts do not suffice, coercion may be necessary. One option is to require credit agents to have a certain percentage of poor borrowers in their portfolio of clients, and to periodically verify this through random audits of the wealth status of their clients (Aubert *et al.*, 2009).

Impact evaluations on microfinance lending

There has been much enthusiasm about the microfinance revolution (Robinson, 2001). This can be appreciated by visiting the websites of the Consultative Group to Assist the Poor (CGAP) (http://www.cgap.org/), the Microfinance Gateway (www.micro financegateway.org/), and the Microfinance Summit Campaign (www.microcredit summit.org/). The approach has been praised by donors as a highly effective way of helping the poor become entrepreneurs and rise out of poverty. But does it work? Rigorous impact evaluations of benefits for clients are for this essential. Yet few are available.

In an early study, Pitt and Khandker (1998) conducted an evaluation of the impact of the Grameen Bank and two other group-based microcredit programs in Bangladesh on labor supply, schooling, household expenditures, and assets. They used a cross-sectional survey, including villages with and without branches. Village-level fixed effects are used to control for village-level placement bias. Within villages, they instrumented household loan size by the discontinuity rule, according to which households must own less than 0.5 hectares of land to qualify for a loan, a regression discontinuity design with a fuzzy discontinuity. They find large effects on household consumption, especially when women are the borrowers. They also observe increases in schooling for both girls and boys, and in women's labor supply when credit is provided to women but not to men.

In another early study, Brett Coleman (1999) used an ingenious roll-out (pipeline) design to construct a control group. He analyzed a CARE MFI program in Thailand, comparing beneficiaries in treated villages to households in villages pre-selected for future expansion of the program. In these pre-selected villages, households were asked if they were interested in receiving credit, and, if so, to self-select into groups that could then be compared to groups in the treated villages. His results showed no impact. This may be due to the fact that members of the control group changed their behavior knowing that they would be given access to credit in the near future, in accordance with the NGO's roll-out plan.

More recently, Cotler and Woodruff (2008) used the geographical roll-out of a credit program to small food retail enterprises offered by a large agribusiness company in two neighborhoods of Mexico City. Four-month loans were given and enterprises were surveyed at the start and after four and eight months. They found that inventories and assets increased in the smallest firms, but not their profits, and not in the larger enterprises. The authors interpreted these results as consistent with the hypotheses that smaller firms have higher marginal returns to capital and face greater credit constraints.

Working with Spandana, one of the fastest growing microfinance organizations in India, with over 2 million clients in eight states, Banerjee *et al.* (2015b) designed an

RCT in 104 slums of Hyderabad to evaluate the impact of access to MFI loans on the expansion of existing businesses, start-ups, and household consumption expenditures. Spandana uses group lending, organizing groups of ten women with joint liability, requesting weekly payments, and charging an interest rate of 24 percent per year. MFI branches were placed in a randomly selected half of the slums. By the end of the three-year experiment, 38 percent of households in the neighborhood were borrowing from the MFI, a much lower number than expected. This suggests that women have difficulty finding projects with a rate of return of at least 24 percent or that they prefer to borrow from family, friends, and moneylenders with greater repayment flexibility despite higher costs. Because there is self-selection in taking a loan, the RCT measured an intention-to-treat (ITT) impact by comparing the average outcomes for everyone in the T slums against those for everyone in the C slums. Banerjee *et al.* found that results fall somewhat short of expectations. Investment in durable goods increased among households with existing businesses, but there was no impact on new business creation, on measures of average monthly per capita consumption of non-durables, on health and education expenditures, and on women's empowerment in household decision-making.

Kaboski and Townsend (2012) used a pre- and post-program panel of households and quasi-experimental cross-village variation in credit per household. This was due to the fact that each of the 70,000 villages received a US\$24,000 allocation irrespective of population size, making credit availability exogenously heterogeneous across households in different villages. They found that Thailand's Million Baht Village Fund had positive effects on consumption, investment in agriculture and existing businesses, and local wages, creating benefits for non-borrowers as well. There was a decline in savings, possibly because precautionary savings are needed less when there is access to credit for emergencies, and this dis-saving allowed consumption to increase. There was an increase in borrowing for consumption but no impact of increased borrowing on start-ups.

Banerjee *et al.* (2015a) summarized the results obtained in six RCTs on microfinance lending runs in Bosnia-Herzegovina, Ethiopia, India, Mexico, Mongolia, and Morocco. They noticed that uptake of credit had been modest among entrepreneurs in response to experiments using encouragement designs, creating a difficulty with the power of tests to identify impacts. The measured effects were modestly positive, but not "transformative" on social indicators for the average borrower, in spite of investment effectively occurring in businesses, as intended by the loans. There was no evidence of disastrous outcomes such as falling into debt traps. Impacts were highly heterogeneous, with good outcomes for some and bad for others. The results were a call for more experimentation with new designs to improve impacts on the poor.

These results indicate that the jury is still out on a final verdict on the role of microfinance for development. There is considerable heterogeneity across potential users and many more experiments and impact evaluation studies will be needed before we can conclude. Early results show that positive income effects cannot be assumed simply because loans are taken and repaid. Quick results on poverty reduction are generally elusive, and conditional on additional assistance to the poor beyond access to a loan. However, positive impacts on investment suggest that future benefits for household welfare may follow in due time for these investments to yield income and welfare effects.

CAN THE POOR BE INSURED? THE PROMISE OF INDEX-BASED WEATHER INSURANCE

The cost of exposure to uninsured risks

An important dimension of financial services is the provision of insurance. Lack of access to insurance reduces the ability of the poor (who are particularly risk averse as exposure to an uninsured shock can have devastating consequences on survival) to take on risks that would be rewarded by higher expected incomes. As we saw in Chapter 1, exposure to risk requires the poor to engage in costly behavior of two types: (1) risk management strategies, e.g. non-adoption of more productive but more risky technologies, diversification of production away from comparative advantage, and accumulation of liquid assets such as animals as precautionary savings, even though they have a lower return than fixed investments such as pumps for irrigation (Rosenzweig and Wolpin, 1993); and (2) risk-coping (better called shock-coping) strategies, e.g. taking children out of school to make them work and earn income while knowing that once away from school they are unlikely ever to return; consuming next year's seeds that will compromise the ability to plant in the next season; selling productive assets such as land and draft animals that will be hard to re-accumulate after the shock has passed; and compromising long-term child development with short-run reductions in nutrition and health expenditures. Coping with large shocks can push households into poverty traps.

Exposure to risk also reduces the ability to take loans, as projects may fail and collateral that may have been pledged may be lost (Boucher et al., 2008). Lack of insurance thus acts as a major constraint on the development of financial markets. Yet traditional forms of insurance, which indemnify the insured based on verifiable individual losses, have largely failed the poor because of AS and MH. Insurance coverage works for verifiable events such as loss of life or pregnancy, but it has failed to insure business activities, and especially farming, because of the prohibitive cost of loss verification. The result is that the poor are largely unable to reduce the risks to which they are exposed, perpetuating poverty, and creating a source of new poor when they are exposed to shocks.

Index-based weather insurance

An interesting institutional innovation that is being tried in several countries such as Mongolia (IBLIP), India (BASIX), and Mexico (Agroasemex), is index-based weather insurance (Skees, 2008). In this case, indemnity payments for weather shocks are not based on an assessment of individual losses made by an adjuster from the insurance company, but on a single, easy-to-observe indicator such as local rainfall relative to a threshold level (also called a trigger). The basic principle is represented in Figure 13.3. In the background (scale not represented) is the historical distribution of rainfall at a

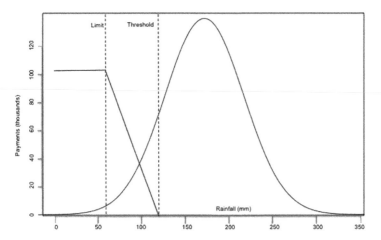

Figure 13.3 *Index-based drought insurance: payments under different rainfall scenarios*

location, centered around 150–200mm/year, with some probability of low extremes at 0–50mm/year, and some high extremes at 300–350mm/year. The payout from an index-based drought insurance is represented by the dark line: payments are triggered when rainfall falls below 120mm/year and rise to a maximum indemnity payment of $100 when rainfall reaches the lower limit of 60 mm/year.

Figure 13.4 illustrates how the insurance works in Mexican municipalities for drought affecting corn (Fuchs and Wolff, 2011). There are three critical periods: one for planting, one for growing, and one for maturing the crop. A threshold level of rainfall is defined for each period (horizontal blue line). When cumulative rainfall (dotted line) during a period exceeds the threshold, no payment is made, as in Figure 13.4a for the municipality of Apaseo el Alto in 2005. When cumulative rainfall during a period falls below the threshold, drought is declared and payments are made. This is the case for the first period in Figure 13.4b for the municipality of León in 2005.

Under an index-based insurance scheme, insurance contracts are issued to farmers for a premium, and indemnity payments are determined by the level of the single selected index (rainfall deficits in India, a temperature index in Mongolia, an average area yield level in Peru). The approach thus overcomes the classical insurance problems of AS and MH (since premium and indemnity payments are unrelated to behavior of the insured), as well as of costly assessment of individual losses (since they are not needed), that have made traditional insurance markets fail for small farmers. The expectation is that these insurance schemes, while eventually imperfect, can be much cheaper than the traditional indemnity-based schemes.

Imperfection comes from the fact that the insurance value of such an index-based scheme depends on how closely the weather index tracks the loss incurred by producers, i.e. how rainfall deficits predict low yields in India, how a temperature index for cold spells predicts livestock mortality in Mongolia, and how a low average yield in an area predicts yield events for particular farmers in that area. Several elements contribute to a potential disparity between the two.

484

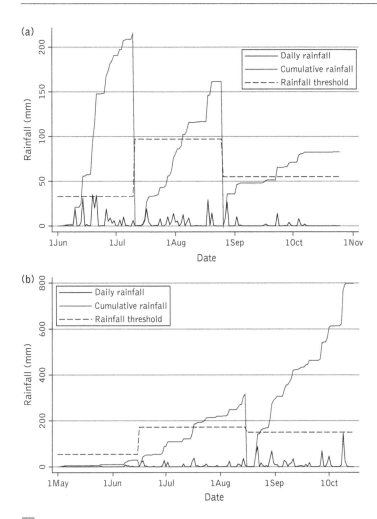

Figure 13.4 *Index-based drought insurance for corn in the municipalities of Villanueva in the state of Zacatecas (a) and Xiutetelco in the state of Puebla (b), 2007: rainfall thresholds, daily rainfall, and cumulative rainfall within each culti-vation sub-period. Payouts are triggered by drought in the planting season in Xiutetelco, but not in Villanueva*

Drawn by analogy with Fuchs and Wolff, 2011.

1. For weather events that are local, the indicator measured at the level of the nearest weather station may not correspond to what the farmers experience in their fields. The farther the producer is from the weather station and the more localized weather events are, the larger the possible discrepancy, with the risk that the trigger is not set off at the station while the farmer experiences losses. Increasing the density of stations can alleviate the problem.
2. The link between rainfall and yield loss may be complex. The Mexican drought index has three phases with one strike point (a cumulative rainfall threshold) for each. One scheme for rice in India has a dynamic adjustment of the timing of the

485

critical period, linking it to the start of the monsoon. But these schemes may still not capture the effective average loss of production. One solution to this problem is to have weather-index insurance triggered by either a rigid or a soft declaration of disaster, with payout defined on the average yield in a small area, as with the rice-insurance product in the Jiangxi Province of China (Cai *et al.*, 2015).

3. Incurred losses vary across farmers even for a given measured index. Excess rainfall produces localized mudslides in Central America; local winds amplify the negative effect of a cold spell in Mongolia. Some variation reflects genuine heterogeneity across farmers (some have sloping land subject to mudslides, others not), but variation is also just the luck of the draw (the specific trail of the mudslide, or the wind pattern), making an average index a poor predictor of the incurred damage.

4. Finally, the index insurance most often offers protection against a single risk based on the corresponding weather indicator. The insurance is then vastly incomplete, and the more incomplete the less attractive as a product. This need not be the case, however, if the payout is based on average loss as seen in 2. above. The Jiangxi-province insurance covers a multiplicity of natural disasters, including heavy rain, flood, wind storm, extremely high or low temperatures, and drought. If any of these pre-specified natural disasters happens and leads to a 30 percent or more average loss in yield in the area, farmers are eligible to receive payouts from the insurance company.

Index-based insurance is thus only partial: it protects individuals against covariate risks (average weather/loss in the area) and not against idiosyncratic risks (plot-specific weather events or loss). "Basis risk" (the remaining uninsured residual risk) can thus be high. This basis risk needs to be absorbed by the farmer, or potentially covered through other mechanisms such as mutual insurance among members of a community (when these basis risks are not covariate among them) or social-safety nets (such as the National Rural Employment Guarantee Scheme in India). Interesting index-insurance programs are in place for livestock in Mongolia, crops in India and Mexico, and groundnuts in Malawi (UN, 2007). The reality, however, is that, in spite of the appealing design of this new insurance product, uptake remains quite low, and only seems to work out where it is highly subsidized. This is a disappointing outcome that still needs to be better understood.

Impact of insurance provision on household behavior and welfare

The encouraging result is that index-based insurance tends to fulfill its intended purpose where it is used. Impact evaluations can focus on changes in ex-post shock coping or in ex-ante risk management. Focusing on ex-post shock coping, Janzen and Carter (2014) show that access to IBLI (Index Based Livestock Insurance), an index-based drought insurance for livestock in Northern Kenya, helps farmers reduce both asset smoothing and consumption smoothing, two key dimensions of self-insurance. Impact on smoothing is selective according to wealth position. When insured, poor households are less likely to have to destabilize their consumption in response to drought: they achieve better consumption smoothing. Rich households, by contrast, are less likely to have to decapitalize their accumulated assets when insured: they achieve better asset smoothing. Insured households, poor and rich, are observed to be less dependent on food aid and other forms of assistance when droughts occur, confirming their ability to cope with shocks.

Impact is also achieved on ex-ante investment behavior. Evaluations show that insurance encourages investment in higher-risk activities with higher expected profits. Mobarak and Rosenzweig (2014) use an RCT experiment where rainfall-index insurance was offered to Indian cultivators. Results show that insurance helps cultivators reduce self-insurance and switch to riskier, higher-yield production techniques. More risky production, however, destabilizes the labor market and hurts agricultural workers. When the same insurance is offered to farm workers, they respond less to changes in labor demand associated with weather shocks than the uninsured who increase labor supply when wages fall in an effort to protect income. This helps smooth wages across rainfall conditions. The policy implication is that weather insurance should be offered not only to cultivators, but also to farm workers in order to avoid the negative spillover effects of insurance for the first without insurance coverage for the second.

In another experiment, Mobarak and Rosenzweig (2013) showed that the existence of informal risk-sharing networks among members of a sub-caste increases demand for index insurance when informal risk sharing covers idiosyncratic losses. This is because informal insurance reduces basis risk and enhances the value of the formal insurance product. This is an interesting example of complementarity between formal and informal institutions. In this case as well, formal index insurance enables farmers to take on more risk in production and achieve higher expected incomes.

Cai et al. (2015) find that insurance for sows significantly increases farmers' tendency to raise sows in South Western China. Sow production is considered an activity with high potential returns but a high level of risk. Insurance helps risk-averse farmers enter this profitable activity.

Karlan et al. (2013) randomized access to both insurance and cash grants. They showed that lack of access to insurance is the limiting factor to investment for maize farmers in Ghana, not lack of access to liquidity. Farmers who purchased rainfall-index insurance increased agricultural investment by 13 percent. Importantly, demand for insurance remained strong even when a full market price was charged, equal to the fair price plus a 50 percent premium. At that price, some 50 percent of farmers still demanded insurance, insuring 60 percent of their cultivated area. This is, at this stage of experimentation with index insurance, a rare case of insurance demand holding at market prices. They also found that experiencing insurance payouts either oneself or through others is important for demand, indicating the importance of learning and trust. It also suggests fragility of uptake when a series of good years (when premiums are paid and no payouts are received) easily discourage sustained demand.

Cai (2013) uses as a natural experiment the roll-out of a weather-insurance policy for tobacco farmers offered by the People's Insurance Company of China. She uses the variation in provision of this compulsory insurance across both regions and household types (tobacco households vs. other households) to estimate the effect of being insured on household behavior with a double-difference approach. She finds that weather insurance induces Chinese tobacco farmers to increase the land devoted to this risky crop by 20 percent. This area expansion implies reduced crop diversification among tobacco farmers, consistent with less self-insurance. She also finds that insurance causes households to increase demand for credit by 25 percent and decrease savings by more than 30 percent, suggesting that households were holding large levels of precautionary savings in order to better smooth consumption in case of a shock. The benefits of insurance are greater for larger farmers with more capacity to reallocate land to tobacco and for households with less self-insurance (and hence more exposure to risk) through remittances from migrants.

Cole *et al.* (2014) used an RCT approach to provide free rainfall insurance to selected farmers in India. They found that the insurance induced farmers to shift their production toward higher-return and higher-risk cash crops, particularly among the more educated farmers. Finally, Vargas-Hill and Viceisza (2012) used experimental methods to show in a game-setting framework that insurance induces farmers in rural Ethiopia to take greater, yet profitable risks, by increasing their intended purchase of fertilizer.

At the institutional level, CADENA in Mexico provides insurance against catastrophic drought to smallholder farmers (cultivating less than 20 ha of rainfed land) through a state-level index-based insurance that is fully free to beneficiaries. Insurance payouts are triggered by cumulative rainfall falling below a threshold in any of three critical stages of corn cultivation (as described in Figure 13.4), with rainfall observed at the municipal meteorological station. Fuchs and Wolff (2011) used the roll-out of the program across 15 states between 2002 and 2008 as a natural experiment to identify impact on corn yields, area cultivated in corn, and per capita income and expenditures. The unit of analysis is the municipality. They found that insurance coverage induced ex-ante risk management responses with an 8 percent increase in corn yields where coverage is available, along with gains in income and expenditures. The latter suggest that behavioral responses extend to agents beyond the farm through spillover effects.

Fuchs and Rodriguéz-Chamussy (2011) also used the CADENA program to analyze the impact of insurance payouts on voter behavior in the 2006 presidential election. The unit of analysis is the electoral section, and the question is whether insurance payouts received by farmers in 2005 affected voting behavior toward the incumbent political party in the 2006 election. The identification strategy is a regression-discontinuity design based on the threshold rainfall levels that trigger payments of the index-based insurance. They found that disaster relief buys votes. The incumbent party is estimated to have garnered 8 percent more votes where indemnity payments had been made prior to the election, a gain attributed to voters switching political party rather than to increased electoral turnout.

The conclusion of this review of evidence is that, where available and affordable, index-based insurance does work for the intended purposes: it helps achieve more effective shock coping and less costly risk management. The outcome can be more growth and less poverty.

488

Difficulties with insurance uptake

In spite of its design's theoretical appeal, and its success in use, the uptake of index-based insurance has been largely disappointing. Major issues still need to be addressed with weather-insurance schemes in order to refine the product and increase uptake.

Understanding insurance

Farmers have difficulty understanding the concept of insurance. It is not a trivial thing to agree that if a shock did not happen in a particular year, the insurance company should not simply return the money to the farmer. To help farmers learn the concept of insurance, Chinese insurance programs start with some years of heavy smart subsidies, which allow farmers to observe payments made to themselves (learning-by-doing) and to others (learning-from-others) when adversity strikes. Once learning has occurred, initial heavy subsidies are rapidly descaled. Understanding index-based insurance is even more difficult, since payouts are not related to what happened on one's own or one's neighbors' farms, but at a distant location, often out of reach for an individual farmer.

Overcoming a tendency to under-insure and to ill insure

There is a well known tendency in the psychology of risk for people to under-insure. People tend to underestimate risk (perceived risk is inferior to actual risk) and to believe that misfortune will spare them. They pay disproportionate attention to recent events, creating a recency bias, with fluctuations in demand for insurance. And there is a tendency to engage in "narrow bracketing," whereby some risks are highly insured while others are not, instead of insuring the whole portfolio of sources of income (Rabin, 1998).

Reducing basis risk

"Basis risk" can be reduced by collecting more geographically fine-grained observations on climatic events. In addition to more weather stations, a promising new option is to use satellite-based observations of biomass as an indicator of weather condition (Carter, 2012). The Normalized Difference Vegetation Index (NDVI) is a freely available satellite-based measure of vegetation density measured every ten days at a resolution of 8 kilometres by 8 kilometres. The NDVI is transformed into a Vegetation Condition Index (VCI) like the HDI in Chapter 1:

$$VCI = 100 \times (NDVI - NDVI_{min})/(NDVI_{max} - NDVI_{min}).$$

For a given village, the VCI uses long-term series of NDVI to relate present NDVI to the extreme values observed since 1982 at each particular time of the year.

Developing trust in the insurance provider

Trust that the insurance company will indeed make payments when a disaster covered by the contract occurs needs to be established. Relatively frequent payments of insurance claims, and circulation of information on payments that have been made, is a way of building confidence. Clients can also be given formal or informal recourse in case the insurer does not deliver on promises (think of Hurricane Katrina in 2005 in New Orleans and the large share of insurance claims still not settled in 2012). Group insurance, giving more bargaining power to each member, is a way of obtaining greater security that insurance payments will be made.

Reducing the cost of insurance

Insurance premiums are expensive: not only must they cover the "fair price" (the price at which the premium equals the cost of the risk) but also the "loading" which allows the insurance company to cover its operational costs and derive a profit, typically a 30-40 percent margin over the fair price. How is this price calculated?

If p is the probability of loss, x the amount insured, and r the fair price, the expected profit for the insurance company is

$$p(rx - x) + (1 - p)\ rx.$$

The fair price corresponds to a zero expected profit: namely, cancelling x,

$$pr - p + r - rp = 0, \text{i.e.,}\ p = r.$$

Thus if a dollar is insured with a risk of loss every five years, the fair price of the insurance contract is $r = p = 1/5 = 20$ cents per year. With a 40 percent loading, the market price is 28 cents per dollar insured.

The need for re-insurance

To reduce their risks, and hence their loading, local insurance companies must be able to re-insure in order to protect their portfolios from local covariate risks. There are several international re-insurance companies such as SwissRe headquartered in Zurich, Switzerland, and MunichRe in Germany that offer this service. Obtaining re-insurance is difficult as companies want long-time series of weather data, collected close to the fields to be insured, that allow them to calculate a fair price. In developing countries, these data are typically missing. There is room here for public–private partnerships, whereby public subsidies can be used to absorb the data risk until enough data have been accumulated to establish the market price of insurance coverage (Carter, 2013).

CAN THE POOR SAVE? OFFERING SAVINGS OPPORTUNITIES AND INCENTIVES

In spite of their low-income condition, poor people need to save just like the non-poor do. It is consequently wrong to believe, as Keynes famously did, that only the non-poor save, while the poor consume. We do see high rates of savings in poor

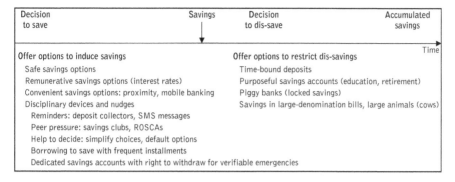

Decision to save		Savings	Decision to dis-save	Accumulated savings

Offer options to induce savings
  Safe savings options
  Remunerative savings options (interest rates)
  Convenient savings options: proximity, mobile banking
  Disciplinary devices and nudges
    Reminders: deposit collectors, SMS messages
    Peer pressure: savings clubs, ROSCAs
    Help to decide: simplify choices, default options
    Borrowing to save with frequent installments
    Dedicated savings accounts with right to withdraw for verifiable emergencies

Offer options to restrict dis-savings
  Time-bound deposits
  Purposeful savings accounts (education, retirement)
  Piggy banks (locked savings)
  Savings in large-denomination bills, large animals (cows)

Time

Figure 13.5 *Helping the poor accumulate savings*

countries and among poor people. This was the case in South Korea, Taiwan, and China, where rates of savings were typically 20-30 percent of national income even though they were still poor countries. In their detailed accounting of poor people's portfolios in India, Bangladesh, and South Africa, Collins, *et al.* (2009) show that rates of saving in the order of 30 percent are the norm rather than the exception.

The poor have three main reasons to save: (1) they accumulate precautionary savings so they can cope with shocks and smooth consumption by dis-saving when hit by an income or an expenditure shock, particularly if they do not have access to emergency loans or loans from local moneylenders are extraordinarily expensive; (2) they save to accumulate lump sums of money to purchase indivisible goods such as a large animal, a piece of equipment like a plow or a loom, a means of transportation, or pay school fees; and (3) they save to meet life cycle expenditures, such as a dowry and subsistence after they become too old to work. They can save using traditional means of savings, typically animals, food stocks, and jewelry. They are, however, risky as animals can die, food can rot, and jewelry can be stolen. They are also low yield in the case of food stocks and jewelry.

To accumulate savings the poor need options to increase savings and options to restrict dis-saving (Figure 13.5).

Offering options to induce savings

Most importantly, savings options to the poor must be safe, remunerative, and convenient. Safety from theft or bankruptcy of the depository institution is not easy to achieve. Informal institutions such as savings clubs and ROSCAs are based on trust, but are not immune from the defaults of members who collected other members' savings. Formal institutions can be regulated, but excessively stringent regulation will provide better protection at the cost of reduced convenience in terms of proximity. Mobile banking like M-PESA in Kenya offers new ways of reconciling convenience and safety as deposits can be made from anywhere into formal banking institutions.

A well known behavioral regularity across humanity is the tendency for people to under-save relative to what they themselves recognize to be best for them. This is due to procrastination (hyperbolic discounting), according to which we agree to save but only starting tomorrow, while we still enjoy high consumption today. Since tomorrow will be like today, the decision to save will be postponed forever (Rabin, 1998). A "sophisticated procrastinator" who knows that he will postpone his decision again tomorrow requires a commitment device or a nudge to help him save by overcoming time-inconsistent behavior (Thaler and Sunstein, 2008). There are fascinating institutional innovations that have emerged to offer disciplinary devices and nudges to willing savers, and they are being experimented with to verify their effectiveness (Karlan and Morduch, 2009).

The first type of intervention consists in encouraging savings through information and promotion campaigns, providing some means to save (a safe box, a savings account), and sending periodic reminders such as SMS messages.

Deposit collectors who go door-to-door can help meet good intentions to save. In Ghana, Susu deposit collectors travel to homes and businesses at regular intervals to collect savings, and the fee they charge for this service is frequently higher than the interest rate on savings deposits (Aryeetey and Steel, 1995). In this case, the saver anticipates her own weaknesses in implementing savings plans, and willingly signs on to be provided with this assistance at the cost of a fee. Peer pressure is also a disciplinary device—for example, at a savings club or a ROSCA.

Individuals also seek discipline to protect savings from pressures to spend from spouses, kin, and villagers. Pressures to share are very high in agrarian communities, particularly in Sub-Saharan Africa, where formal social-safety nets are largely missing and consumption needs to be protected from a multiplicity of shocks (this was explored by Scott (1976) for Southeast Asia). Frequent deposits are a way of sheltering money from these pressures. The most extreme is borrowing as a way of saving: the discipline of repayments, including high-frequency installments with associated penalties if payments are not made, can be a highly costly (the interest rate paid on the loan) way of seeking protection from others and from oneself in securing the discipline of savings (Banerjee and Duflo, 2011). Thus we often see something that otherwise appears irrational: people take loans at very high interest rates when they could be earning interest from savings to achieve the same asset-accumulation objective.

Deciding how much to save can also be a source of procrastination. As an example, using an RCT approach, Duflo et al. (2011) show that procrastination and impatience lead to suboptimal liquidity management for fertilizer purchases and that a small nudge (fertilizer delivery and commitment services in the form of advance purchase) can go a long way toward helping farmers make the right decisions. Simplifying choices and offering default options can help avoid postponing decisions and falling into the procrastination trap. This too is contradictory since we usually consider having more options to be better than having fewer. This is why 401k tax-deferred contributions toward retirement tied to wage payments are typically offered with a default option to avoid postponing the decision of how much to contribute, with postponement eventually extended forever. In an experiment in Guatemala, Atkinson et al. (2013) offered microfinance borrowers from the largest public bank, Crédito Hipotecario Nacional, the chance to deposit 10 percent of their monthly loan payments in a savings account as a default option. Where the 10 percent default option was offered, as opposed to simply the opportunity to save, the uptake in opening savings accounts was much higher.

Offering options to restrict dis-saving

In the same way as temptations to postpone saving exist, temptations to withdraw from accumulated savings also lurk hard. Sophisticated savers may thus want to limit the liquidity of their savings to make it harder to dis-save. This can be done by saving in larger denomination bills that cannot easily be broken for small expenses. Piggy banks are another option that most of us have used as a child, and still works for adults: it is hard to decide to break the porcelain to take money for a small expense, however tempting it may be. Time-bound and dedicated savings accounts have this function: the money is saved for withdrawal at a future date (with penalties for early withdrawal) and for specific purposes such as child education or a pension for retirement. It is hence a case where willingly limiting one's freedom can help us achieve the savings-accumulation objectives we have set for ourselves (Karlan, 2010). Less freedom, willingly surrendered, may be better than more.

Trade-offs between inducing savings and restricting dis-saving

While inducing savings requires offering more liquid options, with the guarantee that savings can be withdrawn easily at any time, protecting savings may require limiting liquidity. Innovations such as mobile banking may thus have contradictory effects. It facilitates transactions, inducing savings, but may also open the door to greater temptations to withdraw on impulse, exposing accumulated savings to depletion. The jury is still out as to which effect it may have on savings.

An interesting example is given by Dupas and Robinson (2013). They ran an RCT in Kenya that offered members of 113 ROSCAs different options to help them save for health expenditures. All participating individuals, including those in the control group, were encouraged to save for health and were asked at the beginning of the study to set a specific goal for themselves, such as the purchase of a preventive health product (like an insecticide-treated bed net) or putting aside cash for an emergency. One treatment group simply received a safe box in which to accumulate savings; the second group received the same safe box but the key was left with the project agent who ensured that the box was not opened until enough cash was available and that expenses were made for the earmarked purpose. The third group was offered a health-savings account that could only be used for the earmarked purpose; and the fourth group served as control. The amount that people saved and spent on health is interesting. Simply providing a safe place to keep money was sufficient to increase preventive health investment by 66 percent, and reduce vulnerability (not being able to meet an emergency need) by 25 percent, over the control. Enforcing the earmarking feature in the other two treatments had a contrasting effect: this rigidity increased savings for those whose objective was coping with emergencies, but reduced the investment for those that had a preventive goal, precisely because the rigidity prevents them from accessing their savings for emergencies. This shows the importance of maintaining escape options in the design of dedicated savings for investment to allow withdrawal for emergencies. The next step in this research should be to test the value of such a product and confirm this conclusion.

FACILITATING MONEY TRANSFERS

Beyond credit, insurance, and savings, important progress has been made facilitating cash transactions. Lack of cheap and safe ways of making payments or sending money can have major efficiency costs. Beaman *et al.* (2014) noted that small change is often unavailable to merchants, who lose business as a result. They estimate that small firms in Kenya lose, on average, 5 to 8 percent of total profits because change is unavailable at the right time. Remittances from abroad are transferred securely through the post office or Western Union, but the cost is often prohibitive, typically 8 percent of the transfer. Money is also sent through intermediaries such as bus drivers, or through friends and relatives, with a high risk of theft—so the recent introduction of money transfers through mobile phones is a major advance (Aker and Mbiti, 2010). In Kenya, M-PESA has 11 million registered users. Users do not need a bank account. They open an M-PESA account with Safaricom, the local subsidiary of Vodafone, the world's largest mobile-phone operator. They bring cash to one of 19,000 authorized M-PESA agents, typically a local shopkeeper who sells phone cards, who credits the M-PESA account with the amount of cash received. Users can then use their mobile phones to make transfers to others (typically to pay for a service, transfer money home, or reimburse debts), purchase Safaricom airtime, and pay bills using a PIN code. Money can also be stored in the M-PESA account, serving as a pseudo bank account. An app on the user's SIM card instantaneously transfers the balance from the sender's M-PESA account to the recipient's M-PESA account. These transfers can improve the effectiveness of mutual-insurance networks. Using millions of records on person-to-person transfers of mobile airtime in Rwanda, Blumenstock *et al.* (2014) showed that transfers were used to mobilize distant support on behalf of victims of the 2008 Lake Kivu earthquake. They found that these transfers were motivated by reciprocal risk sharing rather than pure charity or altruism. Electronic payments can also be used by informal savings groups to transfer money into group accounts (Jack *et al.*, 2013). The system's limitations are no interest paid on cash deposits, lack of insurance for the value stored in the mobile account, and lack of access to credit from formal financial institutions. For this, access to formal bank accounts would be needed.

CONCLUSIONS ON MFIS: HOW USEFUL ARE THEY FOR POVERTY REDUCTION?

MFIs are institutional innovations that help provide access to financial services for the poor. While they initially emphasized access to loans, following the lead of the Grameen Bank, services have been gradually broadened to include savings, insurance, and money transfers. The much heralded microfinance revolution has helped reduce credit-market failures for millions of poor people, principally women, who constitute 97 percent of the Grameen Bank's clients and 98 percent of those of Compartamos (Table 13.1). Can we say that this has helped reduce poverty? Many are convinced the answer is yes. Yet surprisingly few solid evaluations of this desirable impact are available—and solid evaluations (with proper counterfactuals) tend to show more modest results than are claimed by the advocates of microfinance (Banerjee *et al.*, 2015b). In spite of this, we make five preliminary conclusions.

1. *Good projects needed.*
   Successful use of loans by the poor requires access to good projects. Too many projects are very small (almost none have an employee), in highly competitive fields with very low entry costs, and difficult to expand given competition and the skills and life conditions of their entrepreneurs. Success necessitates a favorable investment climate: a reliable policy context, supportive public goods and institutions for investment, and help from NGOs to prepare projects. Hence the development of MFIs is complementary to these contextual determinants of success, not a substitute. MFIs without profitable investment opportunities for the poor will not reduce poverty.
2. *Not the poorest of the poor.*
   Loans will tend to be most useful for the most entrepreneurial among the poor, not the poorest of the poor. The MFI approach is a complement to social assistance that targets the poorest, not a substitute.
3. *Microlending can work.*
   Yet there have been remarkable success stories in taking people out of poverty through microfinance, particularly in creating income opportunities for women.
4. *Not the magic bullet.*
   MFIs are, however, not *the* magic bullet for poverty reduction. They cannot replace the many traditional approaches to poverty reduction that we will see in Chapter 14. But they offer important partial solutions that deserve improvement and expansion.
5. *Additional institutional innovations needed.*
   Further institutional innovations are needed to expand financial services in content (savings, insurance, transfers), in coverage (avoiding mission drift away from poorer people as commercial providers enter the field and competition rises), and in quality (containing costs to reduce interest rates, avoiding destructive competition, customizing products to individual needs and capacities, and making savings accounts safer and more accessible) (CSFI, 2012). In this sense, it is an ongoing "revolution" with much creative thinking and entrepreneurship yet to happen. It is indeed an exciting and promising field for development economists to work on.

CONCEPTS SEEN IN THIS CHAPTER

Imperfect information
Adverse selection and moral hazard
Institutional innovation and new institutional economics
Collateralizable assets
Wealth-constrained markets
Idiosyncratic risk vs. covariate risk

Limited liability
Dynamic incentives
Moneylender
Ostracization
Land pawning
Dilemma of the agrarian community
ROSCA (Rotating Saving and Credit Association)
Group lending
Self-selection and assortative matching
Joint liability
Social collateral
Mutual insurance
Interlinked transactions
Village bank
Proximity lending
Credit bureau
Reputation as collateral
Mission drift
Incentives for credit officers
Mobile banking
Index-based weather insurance
Warm glow in giving
Basis risk
Fair price and loading
Time inconsistency and procrastination
Sophisticated procrastinator
Commitment device
Precautionary savings
Dedicated savings
Default option in saving
Temptation goods
Borrowing to save
M-PESA money transfers

REVIEW QUESTIONS: FINANCIAL SERVICES FOR THE POOR

1. Why do capital markets fail, particularly for the poor? Explain why capital markets are wealth-constrained for them.
2. Explain why successful lending to the poor requires institutional innovations that can solve the following four problems: adverse selection (AS) in choosing borrowers; monitoring of project choice and implementation to prevent moral hazard (MH); providing insurance in spite of the risk of MH; enforcement in repayment to avoid MH (strategic default).

3. Moneylenders: why are they able to extend loans to the poor where the formal sector fails? Explain why interest rates charged by moneylenders are so high.

4. How do ROSCAs work? Why are they useful in helping the poor access lump sums of liquidity when they do not have access to credit?

5. Why is group lending as practiced by the Grameen Bank a potential solution to credit market failures for poor people? What does the joint-liability rule imply for group members? Discuss the roles of local information and social capital among group members to overcome AS in selection, prevent MH in project choice and implementation, induce mutual insurance among group members, and prevent MH in repayments.

6. What is meant by dynamic incentives and why is this instrument weakened by rising competition among microfinance lenders?

7. Why could index-based insurance schemes work where other insurance schemes fail?

8. Why do people tend to under-save and what can be done to help them acquire the necessary self-discipline to save? Explain the concepts of hyperbolic discounting and sophisticated procrastinator.

9. How can mobile phones improve access to financial services for the poor? How do internet-based microfinance lenders such as Kiva and myc4 work?

REFERENCES

Aker, Jenny, and Isaac Mbiti. 2010. "Mobile Phones and Economic Development in Africa." *Journal of Economic Perspectives* 24(3): 207–32.

Akerlof, George. 1990. "The Market for 'Lemons': Quality Uncertainty and Market Mechanisms." *Quarterly Journal of Economics* 84 (August): 488–500.

Aleem, Irfan. 1990. "Imperfect Information, Screening, and the Costs of Informal Lending: Study of a Rural Credit Market in Pakistan." *World Bank Economic Review* 4(3): 329–49.

Anderson, Siwan, and Jean-Marie Baland. 2002. "The Economics of Roscas and Intra-household Resource Allocation." *Quarterly Journal of Economics* 117(3): 963–95.

Andreoni, James. 1990. "Impure Altruism and Donations to Public Goods: A Theory of Warm-Glow Giving." *Economic Journal* 100(401): 464–77.

Armendáriz de Aghion, Beatriz, and Jonathan Morduch. 2005. *The Economics of Microfinance*. Cambridge, MA: MIT Press.

Aryeetey, Ernest and W.F. Steel. 1995. "Informal Savings Collectors in Ghana: Can they Intermediate?" *Finance and Development* 31: 36–7.

Atkinson, Jesse, Alain de Janvry, Craig McIntosh, and Elisabeth Sadoulet. 2013. "Prompting Microfinance Borrowers to Save: A Behavioral Experiment from Guatemala." *Economic Development and Cultural Change*, 62(1): 21–64.

Aubert, Cécile, Alain de Janvry, and Elisabeth Sadoulet. 2009. "Designing Credit Agent Incentives to Prevent Mission Drift in Pro-poor Microfinance Institutions." *Journal of Development Economics* 90(1): 153–62.

Banerjee, Abhijit, and Sendhil Mullainathan. 2010. "The Shape of Temptation: Implications for the Economic Lives of the Poor." Working Paper No. 10–9, Department of Economics, MIT.

497

Banerjee, Abhijit, and Esther Duflo. 2011. *Poor Economics: A Radical Rethinking of the Way to Fight Global Poverty*. New York: Public Affairs Books.

Banerjee, Abhijit, Dean Karlan, and Jonathan Zinman. 2015a. "Six Randomized Evaluations of Microcredit: Introduction and Further Steps." *American Economic Journal: Applied Economics* 7(1): 1–21.

Banerjee, Abhijit, Esther Duflo, Rachel Glennerster, and Cynthia Kinnan. 2015b. "The Miracle of Microfinance? Evidence from a Randomized Evaluation." *American Economic Journal: Applied Economics* 7(1): 22–53.

Bardhan, Pranab. 2003. *Poverty, Agrarian Structure, and Political Economy in India: Selected Essays*. New Delhi: Oxford University Press.

Beaman, Lori, Jeremy Magruder, and Jonathan Robinson. 2014. "Minding Small Change Among Small Firms in Kenya." *Journal of Development Economics* 108(C): 69–86.

Besley, Timothy, and Stephen Coate. 1995. "Group Lending, Repayment Incentives, and Social Collateral." *Journal of Development Economics* 46(1): 1–18.

Blumenstock, Joshua, Nathan Eagle, and Marcel Fafchamps. 2014. "Risk and Reciprocity Over the Mobile Phone Network: Evidence from Rwanda." Working paper, The Information School, University of Washington.

Boucher, Stephen, Michael Carter, and Catherine Guirkinger. 2008. "Risk Rationing and Wealth Effects in Credit Markets: Theory and Implications for Agricultural Development." *American Journal of Agricultural Economics* 90(2): 409–23.

Cai, Jing. 2013. "The Impact of Insurance Provision on Households' Production and Financial Decisions." *American Economic Journal: Economic Policy* forthcoming.

Cai, Jing, Alain de Janvry, and Elisabeth Sadoulet. 2015. "Social Networks and the Decision to Insure." *American Economic Journal: Applied Economics* 7(2): 81–108.

Carter, Michael. 2012. "Designed for Development: Next Generation Approaches to Index Insurance for Smallholder Farmers." Geneva: ILO/MunichRe Microinsurance Compendium, Volume 2.

Carter, Michael. 2013. "Sharing the Risk and the Uncertainty: Public–Private Reinsurance Partnerships for Viable Agricultural Insurance Markets." I4 Index Insurance Innovation Initiative Brief 2013-01 and FERDI Policy Brief B78.

Casaburi, Lorenzo, and Tristan Reed. 2015. "Interlinked Transactions and Pass-through: Experimental Evidence from Sierra Leone." Working paper, Economics Department, Harvard University.

Cole, Shawn, Xavier Giné, and James Vickery. 2014. "How Does Risk Management Influence Production Decisions? Evidence from a Field Experiment." Working paper, Harvard Business School, Harvard University.

Coleman, Brett. 1999. "The Impact of Group Lending in Northeast Thailand." *Journal of Development Economics* 60(1): 105–41.

Collins, Daryl, Jonathan Morduch, Stuart Rutherford, and Orlanda Ruthven. 2009. *Portfolios of the Poor: How the World's Poor Live on $2 a Day*. Princeton, NJ: Princeton University Press.

Cotler, Pablo, and Christopher Woodruff. 2008. "The Impact of Short-Term Credit on Microenterprises: Evidence from the Fincomun-Bimbo Program in Mexico." *Economic Development and Cultural Change* 56(4): 829–49.

CSFI (Center for the Study of Financial Innovation). 2012. "Microfinance Banana Skins 2012: Staying Relevant." New York: www.csfi.org (accessed 2015).

de Janvry, Alain, Craig McIntosh, and Elisabeth Sadoulet. 2010. "The Supply- and Demand-Side Impacts of Credit Market Information." *Journal of Development Economics* 93(2): 173–88.

De Mel, Suresh, David McKenzie, and Christopher Woodruff. 2009. "Are Women More Credit Constrained? Experimental Evidence on Gender and Microenterprise Returns." *American Economic Journal: Applied Economics* 1(3): 1–32.

de Soto, Hernando. 2000. *The Mystery of Capital: Why Capitalism Triumphs in the West and Fails Everywhere Else.* New York: Basic Books

Duflo, Esther, Michael Kremer, and Jonathan Robinson. 2011. "Nudging Farmers to Use Fertilizer: Theory and Experimental Evidence from Kenya." *American Economic Review* 101(6): 2350–90.

Dupas, Pascaline, and Jonathan Robinson. 2013. "Why Don't the Poor Save More? Evidence from Health Savings Experiments." *American Economic Review* 103(4): 1138–71.

Field, Erica, and Rohini Pande. 2008. "Repayment Frequency and Default in Micro-Finance: Evidence from India." *Journal of European Economic Association. Papers and Proceedings* 6(2–3): 501–50.

Fuchs, Alan, and Hendrik Wolff. 2011. "Drought and Retribution: Evidence from a Large Scale Rainfall-Indexed Insurance Program in Mexico." Working paper, Department of Agricultural and Resource Economics, University of California at Berkeley.

Fuchs, Alan, and Lourdes Rodriguéz-Chamussy. 2011. "Voters Response to Natural Disasters Aid: Quasi-Experimental Evidence from Drought Relief Payment in Mexico." Working paper, Department of Agricultural and Resource Economics, University of California at Berkeley.

Fuentes, Gabriel. 1996. "The Use of Village Agents in Rural Credit Delivery." *Journal of Development Studies* 33: 188–209.

Ghatak, Maitreesh, and Timothy Guinnane. 1999. "The Economics of Lending with Joint Liability: A Review of Theory and Practice." *Journal of Development Economics* 60: 195–228.

Giné, Xavier, and Dean Karlan. 2011. "Group versus Individual Liability: Long Term Evidence from Philippine Microcredit Lending Groups." Working Paper 970, Economic Growth Center, Yale University.

Jack, William, Adam Ray, and Tavneet Suri. 2013. "Transaction Networks: Evidence from Mobile Money in Kenya." *American Economic Review* 103(3): 356–61.

Janzen, Sarah, and Michael R. Carter. 2014. "After the Drought: The Impact of Microinsurance on Consumption Smoothing and Asset Protection." Working paper, Department of Agricultural and Resource Economics, University of California at Davis.

Kaboski, Joseph, and Robert Townsend. 2012. "The Impact of Credit on Village Economies." *American Economic Journal: Applied Economics* 4(2): 98–133.

Karlan, Dean. 2007. "Social Connections and Group Banking." *Economic Journal* 117(February): F52–F84

Karlan, Dean. 2010. "Helping the Poor Save More." *Stanford Social Investment Review* January.

Karlan, Dean, and Jonathan Morduch. 2009. "Access to Finance." In Dani Rodrik and Mark Rosenzweig (eds.), *Handbook of Development Economics,* Vol 5, Chapter 2. Amsterdam: Elsevier.

Karlan, Dean, Robert Darko Osei, Isaac Osei-Akoto, and Christopher Udry. 2013. "Agricultural Decisions after Relaxing Credit and Risk Constraints." *Quarterly Journal of Economics* 129(2): 597–652.

Kim, Chan, and Renée Mauborgne. 2005. *Blue Ocean Strategy: How to Create Uncontested Market Space and Make Competition Irrelevant.* Cambridge, MA: Harvard Business School Publishing Corporation.

McIntosh, Craig, and Bruce Wydick. 2005. "Competition and Microfinance." *Journal of Development Economics* 78: 271–98.

499

McIntosh, Craig, Alain de Janvry, and Elisabeth Sadoulet. 2005. "How Rising Competition among Microfinance Institutions Affects Incumbent Lenders." *Economic Journal* 115(506): 987–1004.

Mobarak, Mushfiq, and Mark Rosenzweig. 2013. "Informal Risk Sharing, Index Insurance, and Risk Taking in Developing Countries." *American Economic Review* 103(3): 375–80.

Mobarak, Mushfiq, and Mark Rosenzweig. 2014. "Risk, Insurance, and Wages in General Equilibrium. " Working paper, Department of Economics, Yale University.

NABARD (National Bank for Agriculture and Rural Development). 2012. "Status of Micro Finance in India 2011–12." Mumbai.

Perloff, Jeffrey. 2008. *Microeconomics*. New York: Addison-Wesley.

Pitt, Mark, and Shahidur Khandker. 1998. "The Impact of Group-based Credit Programs on Poor Households in Bangladesh: Does the Gender of Participants Matter?" *Journal of Political Economy* 106(5): 958–96.

Prahalad, C.K. 2006. *The Fortune at the Bottom of the Pyramid: Eradicating Poverty Through Profits*. Philadelphia: Wharton School Publishing.

Rabin, Matthew. 1998. "Psychology and Economics." *Journal of Economic Literature* 36(March): 11–46.

Robinson, Marguerite. 2001. *The Microfinance Revolution: Sustainable Finance for the Poor*. Washington, DC: World Bank.

Rosenzweig, Mark, and Kenneth Wolpin. 1993. "Credit Market Constraints, Consumption Smoothing, and the Accumulation of Durable Production Assets in Low-income Countries: Investment in Bullocks in India." *Journal of Political Economy* 101(2): 223–44.

Rutherford, Stuart. 2000. *The Poor and Their Money*. Delhi: Oxford University Press.

Scott, James. 1976. *The Moral Economy of the Peasant: Rebellion and Subsistence in Southeast Asia*. New Haven, CT: Yale University Press.

Sengupta, Rajdeep, and Craig Aubuchon. 2008. "The Microfinance Revolution: An Overview." *Federal Reserve Bank of St. Louis Review* (January–February): 9–30.

Skees, Jerry. 2008. "Innovations in Index Insurance for the Poor in Lower Income Countries." *Agricultural and Resource Economics Review* 37(1): 1–15.

Thaler, Richard, and Cass Sunstein. 2008. *Nudge: Improving Decisions about Health, Wealth, and Happiness*. New Haven, CT: Yale University Press.

UN. 2007. "Developing Index-Based Insurance for Agriculture in Developing Countries." *Sustainable Development Innovation Briefs*. New York: UN Department of Economic and Social Affairs.

Vargas-Hill, Ruth, and Angelino Viceisza. 2012. "A Field Experiment on the Impact of Weather Shocks and Insurance on Risky Investment." *Experimental Economics* 15(2): 341–71.

Williamson, Oliver. 1985. *The Economic Institutions of Capitalism: Firms, Markets, Relational Contracting*. New York: The Free Press.

World Bank. 2005. *World Development Report 2006: Equity and Development*. Washington, DC.

Social-assistance programs and targeting

TAKE-HOME MESSAGES FOR CHAPTER 14

1. Social programs can be aimed at reducing chronic poverty (either by creating income generation opportunities for the poor or by transferring resources to them in non-contributory social-assistance programs), at reducing the vulnerability to shocks of the non-poor so they do not fall into poverty when exposed to a shock (resilience through at least partially contributory social-protection programs), and at enhancing the risk-coping capacity of the poor to protect either their consumption or their assets when shocks occur so they do not fall into destitution and poverty traps.

2. An interesting "smart" design to social-assistance programs is the twin-track approach: it reduces poverty in the short run through transfers, but it also provides an escape to continued support by building assets to help beneficiaries generate autonomous incomes in the longer run and move out of poverty.

3. Social-assistance programs need to be targeted because budgets are limited. Targeting must be done to minimize both errors of exclusion (Type I) and of inclusion (Type II).

4. Targeting most often requires identifying specific individuals or households in poverty. Approaches include means tests, proxy means tests, community targeting, and conditional targeting.

5. Targeting can alternatively seek to identify categories of individuals or of households in poverty. Approaches include geographical and demographic targeting. The effectiveness of these approaches depends on homogeneity within the targeted category.

6. An appealing approach is self-targeting achieved by introducing a participation cost that only the poor will be willing to incur. This includes queuing, stigma, inferior goods, and work requirements at low levels of wages.

7. Targeting implies many difficult trade-offs that need to be addressed, including between accuracy and effective budgets, conditionality or not, low inclusion errors and political support, gender roles and effectiveness, community participation and risks of capture, and the incidence of program benefits and costs across social classes.

8. Social assistance is important not only for household welfare, but also as a source of growth in providing income opportunities when limited by market failures, inducing more risk-taking in investment by making risk management less costly, and protecting

assets from excessive decapitalization when shocks occur by making risk coping more effective.

9. Making social protection into a legally enforced right, like the guaranteed employment scheme in India and the right to food in Brazil, is a way of enhancing the risk management and risk-coping value of social programs if properly managed.

10. There exists a rich literature on impact evaluation of social-assistance programs that serves to achieve accountability to donors and improve the design of programs on such issues as conditioning or not, and using or not using community members' own perception of poverty in selecting program beneficiaries.

SOCIAL ASSISTANCE IN POVERTY-REDUCTION STRATEGIES

Reducing poverty requires raising the incomes of the currently poor above the poverty line. This can originate in either an enhanced capacity of the poor to generate earned incomes ("teaching them how to fish") or in targeted transfers to the poor in cash or in kind ("giving them fish"). In the following discussion, we categorize the determinants of income into five categories: household characteristics, asset endowments, the context in which the assets are used, transfers, and behavior.

For given characteristics of a poor household such as gender, age, and ethnicity, the first channel out of poverty (enhanced income–earning capacity) can be implemented through three types of intervention.

1. An increased control over productive assets by the poor. Assets consist of five types of capital: natural capital (land, water, animals), physical capital (tools, implements, constructions), human capital (health, education, skills), financial capital (liquid assets, savings, jewelry), and social capital (network membership, social status). A sixth type of capital, moral capital (a set of beliefs and principles), also helps in decision-making, particularly when "thinking fast" is necessary (Kahneman, 2011).

2. An improvement in the quality of the context in which these assets are used to allow efficiency and productivity gains. An efficiency gain is a move along the production function to the point where factors of production are optimally used for profit maximization given prevailing market prices. A productivity gain is a shift in the production function such as TFP growth in the Solow model. An improvement in the quality of context includes improved opportunities created by growth (employment and investment opportunities), improved access to markets (infrastructure, competition, information), new or better institutions (property rights, the enforcement of contracts, and financial services for savings, credit, insurance, and transactions), and more public goods (technology, public services).

3. Changes in behavior due to interventions that affect preferences such as high risk aversion or that help the poor overcome suboptimal actions such as procrastination (time inconsistency) and the purchase of temptation goods (goods that

create utility when they are consumed but not in other period—see Banerjee and Mullainathan, 2010), low take-up of small but high return investments, and lack of coordination and cooperation. Preferences can also be altered by information circulating in social networks or by public campaigns.

The second channel consists in social-assistance programs with income or consumption transfers to the poor and with instruments to cope with shocks. Because public budgets are scarce, and non-deserving households will strategically mimic poverty to qualify for an always-welcome transfer, targeting is essential. When targeting a program, it is important to avoid both excluding the deserving poor (exclusion errors) and wasting money in including the non-deserving non-poor (inclusion errors). A key issue that we will explore in detail is whether transfers, especially if conditional on education or work, can be used not only to reduce poverty, but also to help recipients generate earned incomes and contribute to growth.

The conceptual framework we use in identifying public anti-poverty interventions is shown in Figure 14.1. For given household characteristics, policies and programs can be aimed at increasing the household's assets, improving the context in which the assets are used, increasing transfers, and altering behavior. Changes in assets, context, transfers, and behavior will alter the household's livelihood strategies: namely, what they do with what they have to achieve better outcomes. These policies and programs in turn originate in a closed-loop political-economy process influenced by the state apparatus and by the social actors concerned with the definition and the implementation of these policies and programs (a process we will study in Chapter 21).

There is a third very important dimension to poverty reduction: to prevent the vulnerable non-poor from falling into poverty. In the long run, sheltering the vulnerable non-poor from income shocks that will take them below the poverty line may be the most important poverty-reduction strategy, yet it has been much misunderstood and neglected. Building their resilience to shocks and providing them with access to contributory social-protection programs is thus an additional fundamental dimension of long-term poverty reduction.

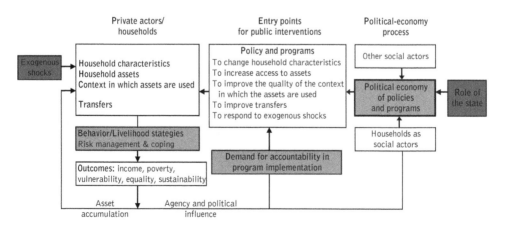

Figure 14.1 Conceptual framework for the definition of social-protection policies and programs

This tells us that a long-term poverty-reduction strategy will need to walk on three legs: (1) income-generation programs for the poor, creating opportunities, (2) social-assistance programs for the poor, creating equity, and (3) social-protection programs for the vulnerable non-poor, creating resilience. This tripartite approach has been used as the organizing principle for the World Bank (2012) report on social protection. We build on it in what follows.

A TYPOLOGY OF SOCIAL-ASSISTANCE PROGRAMS

We have seen (Chapter 5) that there are two types of poverty: chronic and transitory. The first consists of households on average below the poverty line, the second of normally non-poor households that are vulnerable to poverty and can fall into it as a consequence of a shock. Once in poverty, they may bounce back out of poverty, as transitory poor are expected to do, or they may remain in poverty as they join the ranks of the chronic and "always poor." The always poor may be in a poverty trap if they cannot escape poverty unless they reach a certain threshold of asset endowments, or slowly improve their asset positions to move out of poverty. Carter and Barrett (2006) have argued for the existence of poverty traps—for example, when pastoralists in Kenya fall below a minimum asset threshold, in this case a viable herd size. This corresponds to a low-level equilibrium in a multiple-equilibrium framework (Chapter 9). Antman and McKenzie (2007), by contrast, have shown with Mexican data that it is the slow processes of recapitalization after a shock that keeps people in poverty for a long time. These two contrasted poverty worlds are illustrated in Figure 14.2. The first (Figure 14.2a) is a multiple-equilibrium framework where getting out of poverty requires a big push to reach the critical asset threshold needed to generate income and rise above the poverty line. The second (Figure 14.2b) is a decreasing-returns framework where it takes time to accumulate productive assets and gradually increase income to reach the poverty line.

In Figure 14.3, we categorize social-protection and assistance programs based on what we have learned in previous chapters. We distinguish three types of program

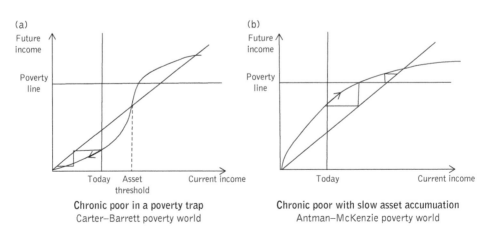

Chronic poor in a poverty trap
Carter–Barrett poverty world

Chronic poor with slow asset accumuation
Antman–McKenzie poverty world

Figure 14.2 *Two roads out of poverty*

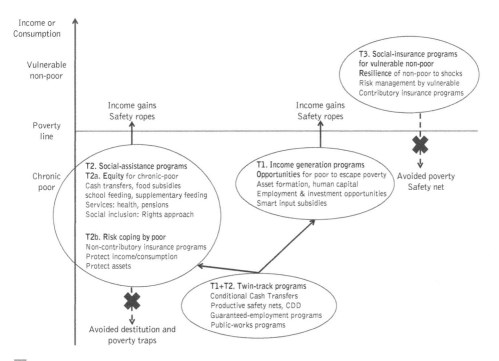

Figure 14.3 *A typology of social-protection and assistance programs*

according to their objectives (income opportunities for the poor, transfers to the poor through social assistance, and protection of the vulnerable non-poor through social insurance) and the category of people to whom they apply (the chronic poor, and the vulnerable non-poor who may fall into transitory or chronic poverty):

1. Programs to reduce chronic poverty and vulnerability:

   Type 1 (T1). Programs to reduce chronic poverty via income-generation opportunities for the poor, i.e. provide "safety ropes" out of poverty, to use the terminology proposed by Barrett *et al.* (2008).

   Type 2 (T2a). Non-contributory social-assistance programs to reduce chronic poverty via transfers and achieve social inclusion—for example, by targeting youth at risk. These programs aim at improving equity for the chronic poor. They are non-contributory in that the benefits can be obtained without having made contributions to the program. Non-contributory social-protection programs are called social assistance.

2. Programs to mitigate the effects of shocks (risk management and risk coping):

   Type 2 (T2b). Risk-coping programs to protect the income and consumption of the poor from negative shocks and/or to protect or replace their assets. The objective is to help the poor stay out of destitution and poverty traps.

   Type 3 (T3). Risk-management programs to reduce vulnerability to poverty of the currently non-poor by increasing resilience: contributory social-insurance programs. These programs are contributory in the sense that access to benefits is restricted to people who have made at least some payments to the program, even if only a fraction of cost. Contributory social-protection programs are called social insurance.

3. Combined types (T1+T2). Programs to both reduce immediate chronic poverty through transfers and wage payments (Type 2) and enhance future income-generating capacity through investment in productive assets (Type 1): the increasingly popular twin-track approach to social assistance.

Returning to Figure 14.1, the instruments that these programs use are:

1. Asset creation or asset protection/replacement.
2. Improvement of the context in which the assets are used.
3. Transfers to improve income, reduce vulnerability, protect income, or protect assets.
4. Changes in behavior to help the poor overcome suboptimal actions and improve their decision-making capacity.

In terms of specific programs, this gives the two-way typology of social programs in Table 14.1 that combines the T1, T2, T3 typology with the four instruments to be used: assets, context, transfers, and behavior. It allows us to recognize well known anti-poverty interventions such as (indicating in parentheses their location in the typology):

- Land-reform programs, as, for example, in Brazil through expropriations of large underused farms or subsidized land-purchase transactions (T1, asset).
- Input subsidies such as to fertilizers and seeds, as in Malawi, and to fertilizers, water, and electricity in India (T1, context).
- Index-based weather-insurance programs for crops, as in Mexico and India, and for livestock as in Mongolia (T3, assets and context).
- Community-driven development (CDD) for local public goods, as in Zambia and Sierra Leone (T1, context). These programs make funds competitively available to communities to invest in local public goods of their own choice.
- CCT or conditional food-transfer (CFT) programs for both immediate poverty and hunger relief and for longer-term human-capital formation conditional on school attendance and on basic health practices such as vaccination and maternal-health monitoring (T2, transfers).
- Public-works programs offering demand-driven and self-targeted guaranteed employment under "right to work" legislation extending to 100 days per year, as under the Mahatma Gandhi National Rural Employment Guarantee Act (NREGA) in India (T2b, context).
- Workfare programs and productive safety-net programs, as in Ethiopia and Yemen for both immediate wage income targeted to poor households and infrastructure construction to enhance future food-production capacity (T2b, context).
- Food-aid programs, including supplementary feeding for mothers, infants, and youth (the critical first 1,000 days after conception), and school-feeding programs to assist learning (T2b, assets).

Table 14.1 Two-way typology of social programs

Instruments	Programs to reduce chronic poverty and vulnerability to shocks (ex-ante)		Response to shocks: risk coping (ex-post)	
	Programs to reduce chronic poverty (T1, T2a)	Programs to reduce vulnerability to poverty: risk management (T3)	Programs to protect consumption (T2b)	Programs to protect assets (T2b)
Assets	Natural capital: land reform Human capital: education, health (CCT conditionalities) Physical capital Financial capital Social capital		Subsistence farming: production for home consumption	Education: stay-at-school programs Health: school feeding programs Livestock: fodder subsidies Asset reconstruction post-disaster, post-conflict
Context	Policies: growth, employment opportunities Markets: infrastructure Input subsidies Local public goods: CDD Institutions: financial services Local governance	Reduce sources of risk Risk management: irrigation, resilience Financial services: savings Social protection: contributory health and pensions Index-based weather insurance	Social-safety-nets programs Workfare Public works Productive safety nets Emergency loans	
Transfers	Food and cash transfers Non-contributory health and pensions Conditional cash transfers (CCT)	Subsidies to contributory health and pensions	Food aid Cash transfers CCT for vulnerable: quick response	
Behavior	CCT with strategy out of poverty	Right to social protection affecting risk-management behavior	Information on rights	

- Emergency stay-at-school programs and animal-feeding programs to protect households from asset decapitalization when hit by a shock (T2b, assets).
- Chile's CCT in which transfers are conditional on behavior following an agreed-upon strategy to get out of poverty using existing social programs and public services, with milestones to be respected by the beneficiary (T1, behavior).
- Taking the ultra-poor out of extreme poverty requires more than cash transfers (T2) or asset endowments (T1): it requires a sequential and coordinated strategy that combines the two, another example of a twin-track approach. This is because the ultra-poor need first to be freed from the daily struggle of survival so they can successfully focus on accumulating assets and their productive use. In their studies of the psychology of poverty, Mullainathan and Shafir (2013) have shown that people struggling to survive have difficulty focusing on other things. Attention is exclusively concentrated in the very short run on access to what is missing for survival, particularly money for food, by whatever means are available. Stress must be reduced to free the mind to focus on longer-term initiatives, such as asset accumulation and effective entrepreneurship. BRAC in Bangladesh has designed an approach to help the ultra-poor graduate out of poverty. It consists in giving the ultra-poor "breathing space" to focus on building new livelihoods, along with the opportunity to accumulate assets. This starts with support for consumption and health, access to savings instruments, and the building of confidence. It is followed by asset transfers and training in entrepreneurship for the management of these assets. The presumption is that support for consumption without asset building will not take the ultra-poor out of poverty, but neither will asset building without first securing consumption, and reducing the stress of survival will be effective in using assets for income generation. Using a large-scale and long-term RCT approach, Bandiera et al. (2013) find that the BRAC approach was successful in graduating ultra-poor women out of poverty. Support for survival, asset transfers, and skills development allowed the poorest women to shift out of agricultural labor and start small businesses, typically in animal raising, fish farming, embroidery, and carpentry. After assistance was removed, beneficiary women on average achieved a 38 percent increase in earnings. The approach is being piloted in a number of other countries, particularly in Sub-Saharan Africa.

What is impressive in Table 14.1 is the large number of types of intervention that exist. It is important to clearly distinguish what objectives each has and what instruments each is using—the purpose of the typology. Because there are complementarities between these different social-protection instruments, countries need to have comprehensive strategies that optimally combine their use, as, for example, in the Zero Hunger strategy in Brazil or USAID's Millennium Challenge Account. This is what the donor-assisted PRSP (Poverty Reduction Strategy Papers) helps countries design to qualify for development assistance. The key is to achieve not only complementarities among instruments, but also consistency across them in an effort to rationalize spending and have a coherent targeting framework. The challenges of coordination and consistency of social programs are typically made more difficult by the fact that they are under the authority of both central and local governments, and funded by different donors, each with their own criteria and demands. When states fail or are recovering from conflict, coordination is particularly challenging, necessitating the use of specially designed approaches to deliver "aid in hard places" that we explore in Chapter 18.

THE TARGETING OF SOCIAL PROGRAMS: BENEFITS AND COSTS

Targeting is an instrument to make social programs more effective for their intended purposes under a budget constraint. It is particularly important for cash-transfer programs (e.g. child allowances, fertilizer vouchers in Malawi), CCT programs (e.g. *Progresa-Oportunidades* in Mexico, *Bolsa Família* in Brazil), social-safety-nets programs (food aid), and subsidized or free education, health, nutrition, housing, and utilities programs because, for these programs, demand for transfers is always in excess of budgets. Targeting must consequently be done in terms of the program objectives. If the objective is poverty reduction, targeting requires identification of the currently poor. If the objective of the program is something else (e.g. increasing education, health, nutrition), targeting requires identification not of people meeting this objective (i.e. not going to school, being in poor health, being malnourished), but who would meet the objective if given a transfer. In a proactive perspective, targeting can also anticipate and prevent future undesirable behavior. A child going to school may be targeted for fellowship support if he is at risk of dropping out of school without the transfer, with irreversible consequences. A vulnerable non-poor household may be targeted for guaranteed employment benefits if a shock may take it below the poverty line. Meeting the program objective can be achieved through the income effect of the transfer, or through the conditionality effect of the transfer (which is equivalent to a price effect on the condition, as we will see later). For example, if the objective is to increase school achievement among the children of the poor through a CCT, with school attendance the conditionality, then targeting requires identification of children in poor households who are not going to school but would go if they received a conditional transfer. In a proactive sense, it could also identify children going to school but at high risk of dropping out, which is the objective of Brazil's *Bolsa Família* program.

Good targeting has both benefits and costs. The benefits of good targeting are decreased errors of exclusion of poor people and of inclusion of non-poor people. The costs are several, in particular (van de Walle, 1998):

Administrative costs. This is the cost of identifying who is poor and who is non-poor. There are increasing marginal costs of doing this as it becomes more and more difficult to find the remaining poor.

Private costs on the poor. These are the individual costs that the poor may have to incur to get the transfer (e.g. self-targeting imposes a purposeful cost on program participation to discourage the non-poor from seeking access). One such cost to program participation is the stigma associated with waiting in line publicly for free food handouts.

Incentive costs. Transfers change beneficiary behavior (an MH problem). The main issues of concern are that public transfers can: (1) decrease the labor supply of beneficiaries and increase their preference for leisure, thus decreasing earned incomes;

(2) decrease private transfers from family and friends to beneficiaries (in Peru, for example, Cox *et al.* (1998) found that the introduction of social-security benefits "crowded out" the incidence of private transfers); and (3) increase beneficiaries' dependency on public programs as opposed to seeking to raise earned incomes, a major concern for the non-poor in footing the bill of social-assistance programs. These behavioral changes contribute to raising the cost of the programs or to making them less effective.

Political costs. This is the case when less leakage as a result of more accurate targeting leads to loss of political support for the program budget from the non-poor. In Sri Lanka, for example, the food-subsidies program lost political support, and budget, when it targeted the poor more accurately, reducing leakages to politically influential non-poor.

Note that some of the incentive costs mentioned above must be interpreted with caution. When a beneficiary mother reduces labor-market participation to spend more "leisure" time at home raising her young children, this may be a significant positive spillover benefit of the program. When private transfers from working adults to retired parents are "crowded out" by social-security benefits, the income freed up may be invested in productive activities, again a potentially important positive spillover effect of the program. Positive spillover effects of a social-assistance program must be clearly identified and credited to the program.

Targeting is very difficult due to hidden/asymmetrical/strategic information for the implementation agency about the income status of potential beneficiaries, leading to an AS problem. Non-qualifying individuals will mimic qualifying individuals in an attempt to receive program benefits. This problem becomes particularly severe when targeting must be repeated over time—for example, with periodic re-certification, as people learn how to game the selection criteria. Good targeting thus consists in devising methods to address this information problem.

ERRORS IN TARGETING: EXCLUSION (TYPE I) AND INCLUSION (TYPE II) ERRORS

To target a subset of a relevant population, we start from the information we have from a population census. It gives us an approximate measure $\hat{y}$ of the indicator y (income or consumption) that we want to use to classify the population into two groups relative to a qualification threshold such as the poverty line z:

poor to be included in the program if $y \leq z$,
non-poor to be excluded from the program if $y > z$.

We use $\hat{y}$ to classify our population into two groups:

presumed poor if $\hat{y} \leq z$,
presumed non-poor if $\hat{y} > z$.

The problem is that there are people with a true $y > z$ among those whom we classify as poor; and there are people with a true $y \leq z$ among those whom we classify as non-poor. The true distribution of y among those classified as poor is $f(y \mid \hat{y} \leq z)$ and the true distribution of y among those classified as non-poor is $f(y \mid \hat{y} > z)$. This is represented in Figure 14.4. We can see that the approximate knowledge of y creates two types of error:

An exclusion error (Type I error) when we categorize a poor person as non-poor. The excluded poor will bear the cost of not benefiting from a program of which s/he is deserving, potentially at a huge personal cost—for example, a poor household excluded from income and educational support under a CCT program.

An inclusion error (Type II error) when we categorize a non-poor person as poor. This is a drain on the program's budget as resources are being wasted on non-qualifying individuals. This may lead indirectly to exclusion of qualifying poor if the budget constraint is binding.

This result is summarized in Table 14.2.

Type I and II errors are present in all statistical hypothesis testing when we use an approximate measure $\hat{y}$ derived from a sample (instead of the population) to test the hypothesis that $y < z$.

A Type I error is an incorrect rejection of a true null hypothesis, in this case the hypothesis that a particular person is poor (strictly speaking, not non-poor). We observe $\hat{y} > z$ and wrongly conclude that the person is not poor. We commit an exclusion error also called a false positive (a false hit). The size of the Type I error is α, the size of the test. It is the probability of committing a Type I error.

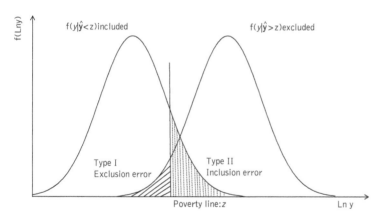

Figure 14.4 *Exclusion and inclusion errors in targeting*

Table 14.2 *Type I and Type II errors in targeting*

		Classification on the basis of approximate measure $\hat{y}$	
		"Poor": included	"Non-poor": excluded
Classification on the basis of true y	Poor	OK	Type I: exclusion error
	Non-poor	Type II: inclusion error	OK

A Type II error is the failure to reject a false null hypothesis, namely the hypothesis that this person is poor. We observe $\hat{y} \leq z$ and wrongly conclude that the person is poor. We commit an inclusion error also called a false negative (a miss).

Note that we can decrease Type I errors by raising the bar (call it $\hat{z}$) in classifying people as poor (which increases the number of people classified as poor), but this increases Type II errors. Hence there is a trade-off between the two losses: less Type I is achieved at the cost of more Type II. It means that we can use a loss function to choose the optimum $\hat{z}$ to minimize the aggregate cost of Type I and Type II errors. The loss function could weight Type I errors more than Type II errors if we are more concerned with the welfare losses of exclusion than we are with the budgetary costs of inclusion.

TARGETING METHODS

There are three approaches to targeting, none of which is perfect (Coady *et al.*, 2004). The art of targeting consists in choosing the most appropriate method for the particular problem at hand. The three approaches are:

> Target individual people or households
>> Means tests
>> Proxy means tests
>> Community-based targeting
>> Targeting on a conditionality
>
> Target categories of people or households
>> Geographical targeting
>> Demographic targeting
>
> Self-targeting

Target individual people or households

Means tests

The procedure consists in having an official directly assess each applicant's (household or individual) income and compare it to a poverty line to determine eligibility. There are three ways in which this assessment can be achieved. One is asking the applicant to declare a level of income and calling on a third party to verify the income declaration. This is the approach used in the US to qualify for welfare programs such as food stamps. The second is asking the applicant to provide proof of income through trustworthy documents such as income tax records and wage information from employment payrolls. The third is based on a simple interview by a program officer, typically at the applicant's home to have some visual verification of living conditions. This last method is used where there are no written records that can help verify income status. Brazil uses this to classify people as poor under the Cadastro Único (single registry) that gives them access to social programs such as *Bolsa Família*.

These methods work better when income taxes are paid and formal employment is the norm. This is how Piketty and Saez (2006) measured gross income before tax in 22 countries with long income-tax records. Income data are unlikely to be accurate in poor countries and for poor people. Home visits are costly if the poor are numerous, and it is exposed to MH as there is a wide margin for interpretation. Means testing, which should in principle be the best approach, is thus rarely feasible for developing-country programs. Other approaches need to be found to successfully target social-assistance programs.

Proxy means tests

This approach uses correlates of poverty to calculate an individual score that can be compared to a threshold for program eligibility. The idea is to identify a small number of characteristics X_i for individual or household i that are: (1) strongly correlated with income or expenditure y, (2) easy to observe, (3) verifiable by others, and (4) cannot be easily manipulated by the applicant. Typical candidate variables are demographic characteristics (age, gender, education, family size and composition), geographical location, characteristics of the house, ownership of durables, sector of work, and type of occupation. Constructing a score S is done using a household survey that measures both y and these X variables. This allows to use regression analysis to estimate the coefficients in a function:

$$y = f(X).$$

Estimation of the parameters in the function f assigns a weight to each X variable. The program officer then fills in a form with information on these Xs for every program applicant, often as part of a home visit to elicit more truthful answers. Applying the weights to the observed Xs gives a score (a predicted y) for the household that can be compared to a threshold value z for inclusion in the program. It is important to make sure that all potential beneficiaries apply to the program. Public information campaigns about the program's existence are useful for this. This was done for the urban arm of *Oportunidades* in Mexico. An alternative approach, used, for instance, for the rural arm of *Oportunidades*, is to run a census that exhaustively covers all potential participants in the selected localities and to subsequently notify the households that have been found to be eligible for the program.

Prediction of y will be accurate if there exist some Xs with a very strong correlation to y—for example, if most poor tend to be indigenous or female-headed households. The reality is usually more sobering, with a lot of heterogeneity among the poor and very large prediction errors at the individual level.

Oportunidades in Mexico uses seven correlates of poverty in a formula that is kept secret to avoid cheating. The ingredients of the formula are such items as ownership of particular consumer durable goods and indicators of the quality of the dwelling. The inconvenience of secrecy is that it does not allow for appeals by households that feel they have been unfairly excluded since they do not know why, and cannot be told why, they were rejected.

The Grameen Bank uses only one well publicized indicator, land ownership, which has to be less than 0.5 hectares to qualify for inclusion. The problem is that there are many determinants of income other than land, including intensity of land use, and other sources of income in the household. Simplicity is thus achieved at the cost of substantial imprecision in targeting.

By relying on correlates of poverty such as education, housing, and ownership of durable goods, proxy means tests are better at identifying the chronically poor than the transitory poor. For transitory poverty, other approaches to targeting are needed. Periodic re-certification, and certification on demand, are needed to lift successful households out of the program, and to incorporate the new chronic poor. Incorporating the new poor who fell into poverty as a consequence of a shock requires that they be allowed to ask to be considered for inclusion at any time when they have been hit by a shock, with the guarantee of a quick response. This is the way the Chilean CCT, *Chile Solidario*, operates.

Community-based targeting

Community-based targeting consists in delegating the selection of beneficiaries to the community. Delegation may be to elected officials, traditional leaders, or an ad hoc committee of local authorities and personalities. This is the case with Brazil's CCT, *Bolsa Família*, where selection is delegated to the municipality. In a first stage, a block grant is allocated to a municipality based on municipal poverty indicators derived from the population census. In a second stage, the mayor, assisted by an appointed social council, selects which households in the municipality will receive a CCT. Because the number of grants allocated to the mayor is less than the number of qualifying poor, this gives him power in selecting who will be targeted, opening the door to effectively select households most in need, or to use the fellowships for clientelistic purposes. CDDs also proceed in two stages, first assigning block grants to districts, and then making communities within the district compete for projects that they define in accordance with their own perceptions of unmet needs (Mansuri and Rao, 2013).

There are four presumed advantages to community-based targeting (Conning and Kevane, 2002). The first is that the community can access information about individuals in poverty at a much lower cost than the central welfare agency. Indeed, a special feature of community life is that information that would be private in a larger city tends to be locally public in small communities. The second is that the community can use local social capital and interlinked transactions to ostracize cheaters (Bardhan, 1991). This means that the community can punish a cheater by excluding him from other community benefits such as mutual insurance and job referrals. The third is that local officials can use a definition of deprivation that is adjusted to local conditions, and not necessarily the same definition as used in another community or by the central agency. For example, pastoralists will typically have a definition of poverty (e.g. insufficient ownership of animals) that differs from that of agriculturalists (lack of access to land) or town dwellers (un-employment, low productivity in self-employment). Households in need can be identified through heuristic ranking techniques with broad community participation—for instance, publicly placing cards with household names in three piles by poverty status: very poor, poor, non-poor. Finally, administrative costs may be lower because information is more readily available and local administrator salaries are lower than in the capital city. Faguet (2004) found that decentralization to the municipal level in Bolivia led to better identification of needs for local public investments and that accountability to local citizens was greatest in the smallest and poorest communities where transparency was higher. Alderman (2002) found that local authorities in Albania do a much better job at targeting social-assistance programs than central government because they have direct access to information that cannot be captured in household surveys. Galasso and Ravallion (2005) analyzed the Bangladesh Food for Education program that distributes fixed food rations to selected poor households, conditional on their school-aged children attending at least 85 percent of classes, targeting proceeds in two stages. In the first stage, central government assigns program resources across local government areas, typically villages. In the second, it relies on community groups to select beneficiaries within these villages. They found that pro-poor targeting was achieved through within-village targeting by local officials, not by inter-village targeting by central-government officials.

The disadvantage of community-based targeting is that local agents may have different objectives from those of the national program in targeting beneficiaries. These range from local elites who want to consolidate their power, elected officials who seek clients for re-election, and corrupt administrators who appropriate project resources. Local preferences in targeting may be less pro-poor and more growth-oriented than program objectives. Selection of a small number of beneficiaries in a cohesive community may also be divisive, fueling resentments and undermining local cooperation. And local administrative capacity may be quite weak and unable to organize data collection to implement targeting.

Empirical evidence supports the importance of elite capture in the definition and targeting of decentralized programs. Galasso and Ravallion (2005) show that the targeting of Food for Education-program benefits in Bangladesh is worse in communities where land is more unequally distributed. They attribute this outcome to greater capture of benefits by the elite where the poor are less powerful. Foster and Rosenzweig (2001) find that democracy helps hold in check elite capture of village projects in India. Where *panchayats* (local governments) are elected, as opposed to led, by traditional elites and where the poor represent a higher share of the population, villages have a higher likelihood of receiving pro-poor projects such as roads. Araujo *et al.* (2008) find that, in Ecuador, poorer and more equal villages are more likely to have community-driven-development projects of direct benefit to the poor such as private latrines, as opposed to public goods projects such as schools. Latrines are more pro-poor because the poor do not have them, while the rich already do. They use the statistical techniques of poverty mapping seen in Chapter 5 to estimate a poverty rate and a measure of inequality (the expenditure shares at the top of the distribution) for each community. They then correlate the choice of project with these community characteristics. They attribute the role of greater equality in project choice to a lesser degree of elite capture.

The existence of a well defined community where members know each other and interact in a long-run (repeated-game) perspective is key for the success of community targeting. The existence of a structure of social accountability (through local elections, social capital, or interlinked transactions in a long-term perspective) is also important so abuses can be exposed and reprimanded. de Janvry *et al.* (2012) thus find that the decentralized allocation of *Bolsa Família*'s CCTs by elected mayors in the North East of Brazil was more accurate when mayors were in their first term, and up for re-election, than when they were in their second term, with no right to run for re-election. First-term mayors with good program performance were in turn much more likely to be reelected. Local electoral incentives were thus effective in achieving social accountability by elected mayors. This measurement was identified by the fact that mayors were randomly into their first or second terms in the year *Bolsa Família* was introduced. The observed difference in program achievement between first- and second-term mayors thus reflects the role of electoral incentives on local politicians' accountability in community-based targeting.

Other methods of community targeting include (Rai, 2002):

1. *Cross-reporting.* If qualifying households have full information about the endowments of everyone in the village, and can thus identify the non-qualifying households, a scheme of cross-reporting can be put in place. In this scheme, the qualifying households are asked to identify the illegitimate participants, and gain a higher share of the program benefits as a consequence of weeding out the non-qualifying households. This contract is incentive compatible if the qualifying participants collectively share the budget that had been allocated to the non-qualifying participants; but cross-reporting without anonymity (in contrast to whistle-blowers in formal enterprises or in public administrations, where anonymity can be guaranteed) in a community where everyone knows each other may be difficult to achieve.

2. *Group targeting and random audits.* Community targeting can be achieved when agents are informed, not necessarily about everyone in the community, but at least about a subset of others in their own surroundings. In this case, potential beneficiaries are asked to self-select into sub-coalitions. Screening is thus delegated to the group members, who guarantee that the coalition does not include any non-qualifying members. Compliance is achieved by threatening the group with complete loss of benefits if any cheater is found in random audits. This is the way certification agencies—for organic coffee, for example—tend to proceed.

Targeting on a conditionality for education and health

CCT programs such as *Progresa-Oportunidades* in Mexico and *Bolsa Família* in Brazil are targeted at the poor. However, these programs have a double objective: reduce poverty in the short run (by targeting transfers to the poor) and increase school enrollment among the children of the poor in order to reduce the inheritance of poverty, and hence poverty in the long run. If budgets are tight, this requires a double targeting: not only on poverty, but also on children on whom the conditionality could be most effective. This means targeting the children of the poor who would not go to school without the transfer, and who will go to school if they benefit from a transfer. Targeting CCTs at parents who already meet the conditionality will not generate educational gains. In Mexico, 98 percent of the children of the poor go to primary school. Hence there is no need to use conditionality on them. The critical age in terms of dropping out of school is entry into secondary school. The key here is to identify correlates of dropping out at the end of primary school that can be used to target the conditionality. To be used, these correlates must be immune to manipulation by parents. For this, effective correlates are distance to school, education of the parents, and employment as farm workers (de Janvry and Sadoulet, 2006). The benefits from *Progresa* are measured by the difference between the proportion of children that quits school without *Progresa* and the proportion that quits school with *Progresa*, classified according to two criteria: distance from a secondary school (Figure 14.5) and the sum of years of education for the two parents (Figure 14.6). The figures show that the greatest benefits from the program are derived by children located around 3 km away from a secondary school and with parents with the highest combined level of education.

Targeting categories of people or households

Geographical targeting

Geographical targeting is typically associated with the construction of poverty maps (Hetschel and Lanjouw, 1998), as seen in Chapter 5. These maps can use different criteria to classify small areas, such as per capita consumption, nutritional status

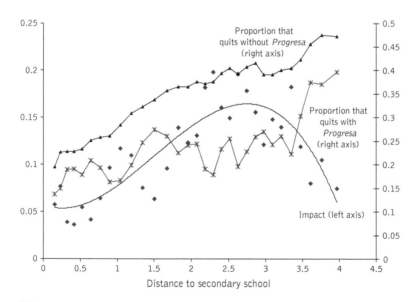

Figure 14.5 Progresa's impact according to distance to secondary school

Source: authors.

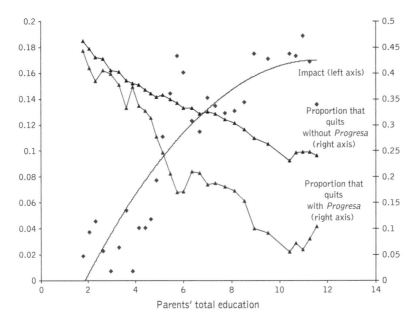

Figure 14.6 Progresa's *impact according to parents' education. The horizontal axis measures the combined years of education of husband and wife*

Source: authors.

based on z-scores, or a composite of correlates of poverty such as in Mexico's CONAPO (National Population Council) marginality index. The CONAPO index combines seven variables available in the population census: adult illiteracy, five indicators of housing quality, and the percentage of the labor force working in agriculture. To target social programs, the geographical area chosen will typically correspond to an administrative unit—for instance, a municipality or a community. Geographical targeting is extensively used as it is relatively easy to implement, but there are large Type I and II errors if intra-geographical unit heterogeneity is high, and precision will tend to decline with size of the area. In Egypt and India, fair-price shops (selling subsidized foods) are located in poor neighborhoods, but rich people can send their servants to shop in these neighborhoods. PRAF (Family Allowance Program) in Honduras (the national CCT equivalent to Mexico's *Oportunidades*) targets poor communities, with all households offered program benefits. This is a good targeting strategy when poverty is very high in a community and the (monetary or social) cost of excluding the non-poor is high. In Latin America, intra-geographical unit heterogeneity tends to be high, making geographical targeting less effective. In Ecuador, for instance, 86 percent of total inequality is explained by intra-parish income differences and only 14 percent by inter-parish differences (Elbers *et al.*, 2007). In this case, geographical targeting using a poverty map would need to be combined with within-community targeting mechanisms. In China, by contrast, disparities tend to be low within and high between communities, making geographical targeting much more effective.

Geographical targeting may be best used as the first stage of a two-stage procedure. In the first stage, budgets are allocated to poor geographical areas such as municipalities. In the second, proxy means tests are used to allocate the budget to households within the area. In Mexico, the CONAPO marginality index is used by *Progresa* to target communities, followed by proxy means testing to separate poor from non-poor. In Brazil, *Bolsa Família* allocates budgets to municipalities based on a marginality index calculated from the population census. The municipality is then given the responsibility of allocating the budget to beneficiaries.

Geographical targeting of social programs is thus best used where poverty is highly spatially correlated, where benefits are consumed in person with high frequency (to avoid traveling by the non-poor), and where other methods are either not feasible or used as complements.

Demographic targeting

Demographic targeting of poverty uses indicators such as age (young children and elderly people) and gender (female-headed households). Again, the method is simple, but precision depends on the strength of correlation of the indicator with poverty. If there is poverty heterogeneity within the demographic category, targeting the category will result in large errors. There are also situations where demographic characteristics such as age are not well established and parenthood is difficult to verify, as many unions are not officially registered and unstable. Yet many programs use demographic targeting because it is easy, because targeting the young and the elderly is politically well supported, and because it is often combined with other criteria such as proxy means testing or community-based methods.

Self-targeting

Self-targeted programs impose a cost on participation that the poor are willing to incur, but not the non-poor. Instead of trying to guess the type of a person (poor or non-poor), self-targeting seeks to have each person willingly reveal their type. The approach can thus potentially be effective. However, even if self-selection is effective, it imposes a cost on the poor (they have to pay it to reveal their type). Hence net benefit is diminished by the size of this cost. At the individual level, costs are typically of two types: transaction costs and work requirements. At the community level, projects may require co-participation.

Transaction costs

Transaction costs imposed for self-selection include having to wait in line, incurring a stigma associated with participation, and being offered low quality food. Long lines at food-distribution centers should thus not be interpreted as a symptom of poor program management, but as a necessary cost to deter participation of the non-poor. It assumes that the opportunity cost of time is less for the poor than for the

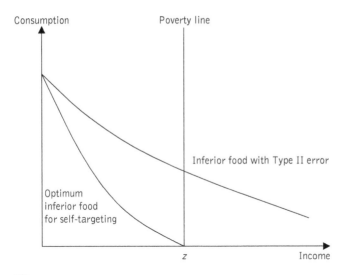

Figure 14.7 *Self-targeting with inferior food*

non-poor, meaning the poor are willing to wait. Transaction costs can also consist in locating the service at a distance from non-poor neighborhoods, requiring more travel time for the non-poor than for the poor. Stigma can be attached to participation depending on how the program is presented to the public. In the US, payment with clumsy food stamps was visible to all consumers waiting in line at the cash register of a supermarket, and a source of humiliation, with less than 50 percent of beneficiaries using the Food Stamps program (this has now been replaced by a debit card that resembles any other electronic payment card). As seen in Figure 14.7, the optimum inferior food for self-targeting would be one whose demand falls to zero at and above the poverty line z. Inferior foods for which there is demand among the non-poor will have a Type II error. Inferior foods with equivalent nutritional value would typically be sorghum as opposed to corn, broken rice as opposed to whole-grain rice, and yellow corn as opposed to white corn as, in many countries such as Mozambique (Dorosh *et al.*, 1992) and Mexico, yellow corn is considered animal feed and only white corn human food.

Work requirements: workfare programs

The self-targeting instrument used in workfare programs is a work requirement remunerated at a wage level that makes it attractive to the poor who choose to participate, but not to the non-poor (Besley and Coate, 1992). Examples of workfare programs include India's National Rural Employment Guarantee Program, enacted in 2005, and the World Food Program's food-for-work programs in Bangladesh and many other countries. Another example is the Trabajar program in Argentina, analyzed by Jalan and Ravallion (2003) using PSM and reviewed in Chapter 4.

520

Consider the situation where there are two types of worker:

Low-skill workers (L) can get a wage w_L on the labor market. If they work full time ($l_L = 8$ hours), their income is $w_L\, l_L < z$ the poverty line. They are poor.

High-skill workers (H) can get a wage w_H on the labor market. If they work full time ($l_H = 8$), their income is $w_H\, l_H > z$. They are non-poor.

The workfare contract consists in a wage offer w for a required time worked $\overline{l}$.

The contract can be written as a principal–agent contract between the workfare agency and the workers consisting of three constraints:

1. *An incentive compatibility constraint.* The non-poor are not willing to participate since:

   $$w_L < w < w_H.$$

2. *A participation constraint.* The poor are willing to participate since:

   $$\text{income with workfare} = w\,\overline{l} + w_L\, l_L' > \text{income without workfare} = w_L\, l_L,$$

   where $\overline{l} + l_L' = 8$. l_L' is residual time, after meeting the workfare obligation, that they can use to work on the labor market at their going wage.

3. *A poverty elimination constraint.* Participation in the program takes the poor out of poverty since:

   $$\text{income with workfare} = w\,\overline{l} + w_L\, l_L' > z.$$

Responses of the two types of worker to the program are as follows:

> *H*-types. The $(w, \overline{l})$ offer induces them to self-screen out of the workfare program as private work is more profitable to them (due to the separating work requirement).
>
> *L*-types. The program requires from them a fixed public-sector work contribution $\overline{l}$. They receive, for the work they do for the program, a flat transfer: $w\overline{l}$. They self-screen into the program since it gives them an income which is above their opportunity cost on the labor market.

For the poor, the effects of the workfare program on time worked and income received are summarized in Figure 14.8.

There are many innovative ways of using workfare programs so they immediately take beneficiaries out of poverty through the income earned, and contribute local public goods that can enhance future community incomes and food security. This is the twin-track approach referred to in Figure 14.3. This is how Ethiopia and Yemen run their Productive Safety Net Programs: work opportunities are offered for a wage to households with a food deficit (in Yemen, the number of days of work offered to each household is proportional to the size of its deficit), and the work contributed under workfare is applied to the provision of local public goods such as water- and soil-management programs defined on a CDD basis that help boost the community's

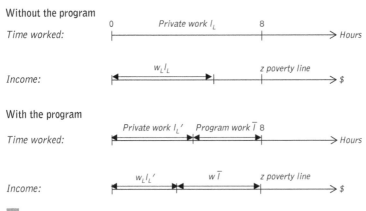

Figure 14.8 *Welfare effects of a workfare program*

Source: authors.

food-production capacity. Public-works programs used as safety nets that provide both emergency relief and economic development are widespread in Africa—for example, in Botswana, Niger, Zimbabwe, and South Africa (Adato *et al.*, 2004). These programs can be operated seasonally, when alternative sources of income are scarce—for example, during the hungry season in the months before the harvest starts. In Bangladesh, the Vulnerable Group Development Program pays work in food, making it a food-for-work program (Ahmed *et al.*, 2009). Argentina introduced a workfare program, Trabajar, to target transfers to the unemployed during the debt crisis (Jalan and Ravallion, 2003). The program worked well, but it attracted a much larger number of workers than the formal unemployment created by the crisis because scores of people employed in the informal sector found the workfare offer more attractive than informal work. This shows that it is quite difficult to calibrate a workfare program when there is a large informal economy. Similarly, the Bolivian Emergency Social Fund created employment in the construction sector to help the unemployed escape poverty (Newman *et al.*, 1991).

QUALITY OF TARGETING

We can compare the relative effectiveness of these various targeting methods by observing how pro-poor the anti-poverty interventions have been according to the method used. This was done by Coady *et al.* (2004), who examined 122 targeted anti-poverty interventions in 48 countries. The targeting-performance indicator is the percentage of program benefits accruing to the poorest 40 percent in the population relative to a random assignment that would have given them 40 percent of the benefits. A value greater then one indicates progressive targeting, with a maximum of $100/40 = 2.5$. Results in Table 14.3 show that categorical methods are the most frequently used, especially geographical targeting. These methods are, however, less accurate than individual assessments: namely, means tests, proxy means tests, and community assessments. Self-selection methods are overall the least accurate. However, self-selection

Table 14.3 *Targeting performance by method*

Targeting method	Frequency of method		Targeting performance indicator	
Individual assessment	22.1		1.5	
Means test		13.4		1.55
Proxy means test		3.2		1.5
Community assessment		5.5		1.4
Categorical methods	58.1		1.32	
Geographical		20.6		1.33
Demographic				
Age elderly		9.5		1.16
Age young		14.2		1.53
Other categorical		13.8		1.35
Self-selection method	19.8		1.1	
Workfare		5.1		1.89
Inferior goods		10.7		1
Community-level		4		1.1
All methods	100		1.25	

Source: Coady *et al.,* 2004.

based on work requirements is exceptionally accurate, with the poor getting 75.6 percent of the benefits. Weakest of all is self-selection based on consumption of inferior goods, with the poor only getting 40 percent of the benefits. However, there is also considerable variation across programs for a given method, suggesting that differences in context and in implementation are very important in determining the success of targeting poor individuals. In terms of context, the authors found that countries with greater government accountability (based on an index that accounts for political participation, civil liberties, and political rights) achieve better targeting performance.

TRADE-OFFS IN TARGETING

We discuss in what follows a number of issues in targeting social programs. Targeting is not a simple affair as there are many trade-offs involved, about which difficult decisions need to be made. We consider six such trade-offs.

Accuracy of targeting vs. effective program budget

Targeting is a costly enterprise. Achieving greater accuracy in reducing Type I and II errors becomes increasingly costly as the remaining errors are small. Hence for a given overall budget, there is an optimum trade-off between targeting accuracy (cost) and effective budget left for transfer to beneficiaries after the cost of targeting has been deducted (per capita benefit). How accurate the program should be in targeting is thus an economic optimum between the number of poor to benefit and the level of benefits to be given to those included.

Political economy of budget size

Precise targeting may erode political support for the program. This was the case in Sri Lanka in 1977, when targeted food subsidies were introduced to replace generalized price subsidies (Edirisinghe, 1987). Political support for the program diminished sharply, reducing budgetary support. Leakage to the non-poor thus has a political function in securing budgetary support. Here again, optimum targeting for project effectiveness balances political support (increase in Type II errors) and benefits to the poor (size of the program). With better targeting, the poor may get a larger share of a smaller budget and be absolutely worse-off. If political support affects program size via leakage of benefits to the non-poor, then there is an optimum leakage to maximize benefits to the poor.

Targeting transfers at women vs. men

Most CCT programs, where conditionality is on child education and health, target the transfers at women. The expectation is that women will make more effective use of the transfer for child welfare than men. The preference that men presumably have for alcohol and tobacco is frequently advocated as concern for child welfare. This may be partially true. However, transfers to men may be more effective for investment and to generate income-multiplier effects: for each dollar transferred, several dollars of income may be generated, helping in turn to increase future household expenditures. This was the case for the PROCAMPO cash transfers introduced in Mexico to compensate farmers for expected losses due to NAFTA, the free-trade agreement with the US and Canada, which depressed the price of corn in Mexico. In fact, what we observed is that every dollar transferred to men under the program generated a second dollar of income because it was used to enhance the household's production capacity by buying fertilizers and other agricultural inputs (Sadoulet *et al.*, 2001). Income effects can in turn feed into child welfare. The targeting of men or women must look carefully at short-run welfare gains for children (greater when targeting transfers at women) vs. longer-term welfare gains for the household including children through income multipliers (greater when targeting transfers at men). Careful impact evaluation of each form of transfer is needed to answer this question, something that can be done with an RCT approach.

Targeting community programs

In targeting resources at communities for local public goods under the CDD approach, communities have to compete by formulating projects and making direct contributions by sharing part of the cost of the project (Mansuri and Rao, 2004). This can be done in the form of cash, materials, or unpaid labor time. The approach has the advantage of giving communities the power to set their own priorities about which projects to invest in. The outcome is, however, not neutral for the targeting of beneficiary communities. It may favor communities with greater capacity in formulating projects and in making direct contributions to project costs. Political biases

524

may also favor communities with greater regional clout. In analyzing the PNIR (National Program for Rural Infrastructure) in Senegal, Arcand and Bassole (2006) found that inequality in capturing project benefits was not so much intra-community as inter-community, based on the relative political experience and weight of community representatives participating in the regional councils that allocate resources across projects.

Trade-offs in welfare effects across social classes

There are many unexpected general equilibrium effects that follow the introduction of a food-subsidy scheme, if it is large enough. Large food-subsidy programs are common, with notable examples in Egypt, Sri Lanka, Mozambique, and India. In India today, 800 million people benefit from food subsidies out of a population of 1.27 billion people—two out of three. Binswanger and Quizon (1984) analyzed the general equilibrium effects of food subsidies in India using a multi-market model. Distributional effects depend on three critical features of the program:

■ How the program is targeted: to the urban poor or to all the poor.
■ The origin of the food distributed through the program: domestic or foreign.
■ How the program is financed: through forced procurement from large farmers, an excise tax on urban households, or foreign aid.

The results are shown in Table 14.4.

Table 14.4 *Distributional effects of targeted food-subsidy programs in India. Signs indicate whether the corresponding changes induced by the program are positive or negative*

	Welfare effects of targeted food subsidies in India			
Targeting of program	Urban poor	Urban poor	Urban poor	All poor
Origin of food for program	Domestic	Domestic	Foreign	Foreign
Financing of program	Procurement	Excise tax	Foreign aid	Foreign aid
Changes induced by the food-subsidy program				
Food prices	+	+	−	−
Rural wage bill	+	−	−	−
Farm profits	+	+	−	−
Real income per capita				
Rural households				
Poorest 25%	−	−	+	+
Richest 25%	−	+	−	−
Urban households				
Poorest 25%	+	+	+	+
Richest 25%	+	−	+	+

Source: Binswanger and Quizon, 1984.

With an inelastic domestic supply of food, fair-price shops that target the urban poor (columns 1 and 2) impose a backlash effect on the excluded poor through rising food prices. In this case, the rural poor who do not have access to fair-price shops lose. The rural rich lose if they have to procure subsidized food at low prices (column 1). By contrast, it is the urban rich who lose (while the rural rich gain) if the food-subsidy program is financed through an urban excise tax (column 2). If food supply is obtained through foreign aid and imports are sufficiently large to depress the domestic price of food (columns 3 and 4), then all the poor gain either through targeting or through a decline in the price of food (the rural poor are net buyers even if small farmers). Rich rural households, who are net-seller farmers, lose as the price of food declines. The urban rich gain through real income effects from falling food prices.

This study shows that the design of targeted food-subsidy programs needs to be carefully assessed in a multi-market or general-equilibrium framework. This is because there are second-round effects via price changes that can be quite perverse for the welfare of poor people and yet will have been missed in a partial equilibrium analysis of targeting.

The economics of transfers: better food or cash?

Is it better to transfer food or cash to maximize the welfare of the recipient? The Food Stamp Program in the US and food coupons redeemed at fair-price shops in India are cases where food is transferred instead of cash to help the poor feed themselves better. We analyze this problem in Figure 14.9.

Before the food transfer, the consumer is at point A with a utility level U_1. The food transfer is equal to AB. The size of this transfer may be infra- or extra-marginal. We consider each in turn.

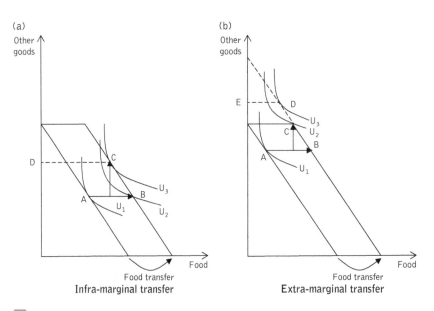

Figure 14.9 Effect of an infra- (a) and extra- (b) marginal food transfer on welfare

Infra-marginal transfer (Figure 14.9a): the food transfer is less than the optimal level of food consumption after the transfer

The food transfer brings him from A to B with a utility level U_2 higher than U_1. The consumer, however, can save on spending food and move to C with a higher utility level U_3. At C he spends DC on food which is more than the AB transfer received, hence the transfer was infra-marginal. He can save DC − AB and spend this amount on other goods. He can then reach C with the higher level of utility U_3. At C, he spends more on food than at A, but less than A plus the transfer (i.e. B). Part of the food transfer has thus leaked through fungibility of money to an increase in the consumption of other goods.

In this case, food is identical to cash as the consumer can simply save from spending part of the amount received in food and spend it on other goods. He could have reached U_3 with either a food or a cash transfer.

Extra-marginal transfer (Figure 14.9b): the food transfer is more than the optimal level of food consumption after the transfer

The food transfer brings him from A to B and then to C with a level of utility U_2. At C, he spends on food exactly the amount transferred. To maximize utility at U_3, he would need to consume less food (ED) than the amount transferred (AB), and more of the other goods than at C. He can only do this if there is a secondary market for food where excess food equal to AB − ED can be sold for cash, and then use the cash to buy more of the other goods to reach U_3 at D.

In this case, food is only identical to cash if there is a perfect secondary market for food, with no transaction costs. If there is no such market, or a market with transaction costs, then the food transfer is inferior to a cash transfer in terms of utility maximization.

The conclusion is that a cash transfer is generally better than a food transfer for the recipient to maximize utility. Only if the food transfer is infra-marginal does it make no difference to receive cash or food due to fungibility of money. If the food transfer is extra-marginal, then in general this is inferior to cash for maximizing utility, unless there is a secondary market where excess food can be transformed into cash, and then used to buy other goods.

General-equilibrium price effects of cash vs. food transfers

While infra-marginal food transfers may be identical to cash transfers for recipient households, the influx of cash vs. food in isolated rural villages, where most of the world poor live, can affect market prices and create indirect benefits or costs. The Mexican government used an RCT approach in 300 villages to test the relative value of cash vs. food transfers when it rolled out its Programa de Apoyo Alimentario. The poor in some of these villages received monthly in-kind food transfers, those in other villages cash transfers of equivalent value, and a third group of villages was used as control. Cunha *et al.* (2011) analyzed this experiment and found that cash transfers induced an increase in local prices that reduced the direct benefits of the program to consumers by 6 percent. Food transfers, by contrast, induced a decline in local prices that increased the direct benefits of the program to consumers by 5 percent. The indirect gain from in-kind above in-cash transfers for consumers was thus an extra 11 percent over the direct gain from the transfer. The welfare implications for producers were the reverse. Agricultural profits rose in cash villages as higher prices both increased the price of goods sold and induced farmers to produce more. In the longer run, this price increase may be dampened by increasing supply, raising benefits to consumers, and inducing local economic growth. Cash transfers combined with supply-side policies to enhance supply response may thus be the most appealing long-term policy even if food transfers may be the most appealing for consumers.

USING SOCIAL-SAFETY-NET (SSN) PROGRAMS FOR EFFICIENCY GAINS AND GROWTH

SSN programs (which include social-assistance programs and subsidized social-protection programs) are often seen as transfers to reduce current poverty, with all the risks they imply of perverse behavioral responses by beneficiaries and leakages to the non-poor. As such, they may have lukewarm political support. Are there situations where SSN programs can be sources of efficiency gains that will stimulate growth and contribute through growth to further poverty reduction? If there are, then political support to SSN programs will be easier to garner. This is the approach followed in a new wave of such programs (Ravallion, 2003). So how can SSN increase efficiency and growth?

1. *Efficiency wage*. Reducing malnutrition through food transfers can increase labor productivity and learning at school. This is what the efficiency-wage theory argues: namely, that effort increases with intake for a malnourished worker, justifying higher levels of pay (Akerlof and Yellen, 1990). School feeding programs may be the most effective way of improving learning among malnourished children. Both are sources of efficiency gains and of immediate or future growth.

2. *Market failures for the poor*. SSN can compensate for market failures that impede investment and growth. This is the case for cash transfers to entrepreneurs that allow them to start new businesses in spite of lack of access to credit. Often, a minimum threshold of capital endowment is necessary to get started, and qualify for loans (Eswaran and Kotwal, 1985). Targeting transfers to socially excluded groups such as minority ethnic groups may similarly compensate for lack of minimal capital endowments and credit-market failures. Sadoulet *et al.* (2001) find that the PROCAMPO transfers targeted at Mexican smallholder farmers in compensation for NAFTA led to a net increase in income that was nearly twice the value of the transfer. Gertler *et al.* (2012) find that recipients of CCTs under *Oportunidades* invested 26 percent of every peso received and increased income by 2 percent. Ardington *et al.* (2009) find that part of the transfers received through the non-contributory old-age-pension program in South Africa were used by the

household to finance migration and job search by younger members, contributing to future household income.

3. *Inequality and growth.* We have seen that inequality can act negatively on growth (Chapter 6). Cash transfers that reduce inequality and, as such, reduce crime that deters investment, or reduce social differences that limit cooperation and the provision of public goods supportive of private investment, can be effective for growth. *Bolsa Família* has been identified as one of the causes of falling inequality in Brazil, with a Gini coefficient that declined from 0.60 in 2001 to 0.54 in 2009. The growth value of reduced inequality and enhanced equity was the main theme of the World Development Report *Equity and Development* (World Bank, 2005).

4. *Risk reduction.* Uninsured risks reduce investment through the need for individuals and enterprises to engage in ex-ante risk management and by biasing asset portfolios toward less-productive liquid assets as opposed to more-productive fixed investments (Rosenzweig and Wolpin, 1993). They also lead to the decapitalization of assets when there is a shock through ex-post risk-coping responses. Insurance can be effective in helping poor farmers invest in more-profitable but riskier cash crops, but the track record of insurance take-up among poor households without heavy subsidies has repeatedly been shown to be very poor (Giné *et al.*, 2008). SSNs can thus be effective as a substitute for formal insurance in investing in risky activities when insurance markets fail. Large and reliable SSN programs such as India's National Rural Employment Guarantee Scheme (NREGS) not only have welfare value, but also insurance value in helping beneficiaries reduce costly self-insurance and invest more in higher-expected-return, higher-risk activities. Morten (2013) finds that NREGS reduces risk for rural residents, which in turn helps them engage less in migration as an element of risk response, and less in informal risk-sharing. Bianchi and Bobba (2013) observed the same for *Progresa* in Mexico, helping beneficiary households make more risky occupational choices.

   SSNs also have value for risk coping, helping households not to decapitalize productive assets and engage into irreversible strategies such as taking children out of school and reducing nutritional intake at critical ages, with the risk of falling into poverty traps (Carter and Barrett, 2006). Beneficiaries of the Ethiopian productive safety net had fewer distress sales and accumulated more capital over time (Berhane *et al.*, 2011). Children of *Progresa* recipients were less likely to drop out of school when an adult in the family was hit by unemployment (de Janvry *et al.*, 2006).

5. *Access to productive assets.* SSNs that help increase the private assets of the poor and those that build local public goods can contribute to growth. The first includes CCT programs such as Mexico's *Oportunidades*, Brazil's *Bolsa Família*, and Bangladesh's Food for Education program that help build human capital. The second includes productive safety nets and other workfare programs, as organized in Ethiopia's Productive Safety Net Project and Yemen's Labor Intensive Work Program (Subbarao *et al.*, 2013). These projects build the community's productive capacity and enhance the return from private investment.

529

6. *Safety nets to achieve political feasibility of growth-oriented reforms.* SSN programs can be targeted to compensate the losers in growth-oriented reforms such as stabilization and adjustment policies, or trade liberalization. In doing so, they can help achieve Pareto optimality after compensation, and make reforms politically feasible. PROCAMPO was introduced to make the NAFTA reforms more politically acceptable for the farm population, benefiting both poor and rich farmers hurt by the reform. Social programs to achieve "adjustment with a human face" (Cornia *et al.*, 1987) were essential in making policy reforms possible in response to the 1980s' debt crisis.

In conclusion, we see that many SSN programs have not only welfare but also growth effects (Alderman and Yemtsov, 2014). While the main purpose of these programs remains their direct contribution to poverty reduction, they can be designed in such a fashion that their contribution to growth can be increased, making them more politically acceptable. Returning to the typology of programs presented in Figure 14.3, it is likely that opportunity (income-generation) programs have relatively more growth value than equity (transfer) programs. The twin-track approach can be seen as an effort at increasing the growth value of transfer programs.

IMPACT EVALUATION OF SOCIAL PROGRAMS: SOME EXAMPLES

To condition or not to condition cash transfers?

There has been substantial controversy, with insufficient empirical evidence, about whether cash transfers should be conditional (CCT) or unconditional (CT). It depends on the objective sought. If the objective is to maximize the educational value of the transfer, with a conditional school attendance, then a CCT should be superior. This can be seen in Figure 14.10. A CT is an income effect that increases the demand for education and the demand for other goods from 1 to 2. A CCT is restricted to the demand for education, and has a price effect on education, cheapening the cost of education by the amount of subsidy received. The budget constraint thus pivots around the intercept on the other goods axis (when all income goes to the demand for other goods). It cuts the CT budget line at 2 to indicate that the cost of the CCT is identical to the cost of the CT. With the CCT price line, the demand for education has now risen to 3. The increase in demand for education under CCT (from 1 to 3) is larger than the demand under CT (from 1 to 2).

Labeling or social marketing can, however, be used to induce beneficiary households to use CTs for purposes intended by the program, such as child education. This is the flypaper effect, according to which the fungibility of money is reduced by labeling the money received. Since monitoring and enforcing compliance with a conditionality can be very costly, finding ways to induce fulfillment of the condition by inducing behavioral change can be an effective approach. In Ecuador, social marketing was used to induce beneficiaries of the *Bono Solidario* program to spend a CT on child schooling, even though no condition was enforced. Schady and Araujo

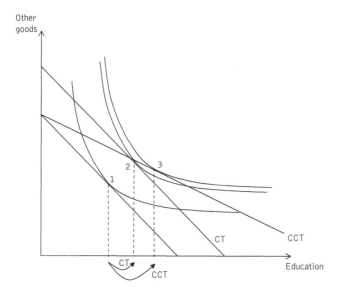

Figure 14.10 *Demand for education under CT and CCT*

(2008) find that households who believed that there were co-responsibilities in using the cash for education had higher school enrollments than other cash recipients. Channeling transfers through women can also increase household expenditures on child schooling without conditionality. This was observed by Attanasio *et al.* (2012) in a CT program in Colombia.

Baird *et al.* (2011) ran an RCT with CTs to girls ages 13–22 in Malawi. In 48 schools transfers were conditional on school attendance, in 27 schools unconditional, and 88 schools served as controls, with a total of 2907 recipients of transfers. The unconditional CT induced a small decline in the dropout rate, but it was only 43 percent as large as the CCT effect over a two-year period. CCT was also more effective at increasing school attendance and at improving performance in school tests. CCT is thus superior at enhancing school outcomes. However, the CT had a much larger effect in reducing the teenage-pregnancy rate by 27 percent and the marriage rate by 44 percent, while the CCT had no effect. This was entirely due to the income effect of CT on these outcomes among girls who dropped out of school, a group that was much larger among CT than CCT recipients. This result thus shows that there can be a trade-off in outcomes in using CCT vs. CT according to the objectives sought. The success of conditionality in promoting the formation of human capital among compliers (stayers at school) was achieved at the cost of denying transfers to non-compliers (dropouts), who are particularly "at risk" for early marriage and teenage pregnancy. For them, it is the income transfer that helped delay marriage and pregnancy. The policy lesson is that transfer programs must carefully decide the objective they want to achieve in the target population, with the choice of conditionality (for improved schooling) or not (for delayed marriage and childbearing) dependent on the objective pursued.

531

Other studies have confirmed the general result that CTs do produce results, but that CCTs are more effective at affecting education and health outcomes if they are used as the conditions for the transfers. In a review of 26 CCT programs, five CT programs, and four that directly compare CCTs with CTs, all of which were assessed using an RCT approach for their impact on school-enrollment rates, Baird *et al.* (2012) confirm the superiority of CCTs. The interesting result of this review is that the superiority of the CCT approach depends on the rigor of the enforcement of the conditionality. CTs increase enrollment on average by 23 percent compared to 41 percent for CCTs. When CCTs' conditionalities are weakly enforced, school enrollment increases by 25 percent and by 60 percent when strongly monitored and enforced.

The fact that direct cash transfers with no conditions attached produce an impact on poverty has come as a surprise to those concerned that poor people would waste these resources on futile pursuits or on leisure. Using an RCT in Kenya, Haushofer and Shapiro (2013) find that a CT reduced child hunger, increased livestock holdings, raised incomes, and reduced stress according to tests of cortisol level. Blattman *et al.* (2014) find that randomly allocated unsupervised CTs to groups of 20 young people in Uganda induced them to learn a trade, buy tools, increase enterprise start-ups, and raise average earnings by almost 50 percent in four years. The transfer had on average a 35 percent real annual return on capital. In assessing the welfare value of CTs, the important metric should be what income multiplier they ultimately had, as discussed above in the case of PROCAMPO.

How to best target the poor?

Alatas *et al.* (2012) organized an RCT to target a CT to people below the poverty line in Indonesia. The three targeting methods were: (1) a proxy means test (PMT) where the government collected information on assets and demographics of proxy household consumption, (2) community methods (CM) where the community chose beneficiaries in an interactive process, and (3) a hybrid (H) between the two where a community ranking is done but beneficiaries must be confirmed by a PMT score. The PMT uses a predictor of consumption based on 49 indicators collected in a baseline household survey. The CM approach consists of community meetings where participants first brainstorm on the characteristics that indicate poverty, and then rank all households in the village, based on participants' responses, by ordering cards representing each on a string across the room. The expectation is that there is a trade-off in accuracy because assets are harder to hide from the government (giving an advantage to PMT), while consumption is harder to hide from neighbors (giving an advantage to CM). CM targeting may not correspond to government objectives because community definitions of poverty may not match the government's goal of identifying people below a PPP$2/day poverty line, and because there are opportunities for elite capture. The authors used 640 Indonesian villages that they divided into PMT, CM, and H treatments. Results show that CM performs worse in identifying the poor than PMT, particularly around the poverty threshold set at PPP$2/day. The discrepancy does not come from elite capture, but from the community using a different concept of poverty, influenced in particular by how individual community members rank each other (including in earnings capacity) rather than how they assess current per capita expenditure. With this discrepancy, CM and H methods result in higher community satisfaction with the targeting outcome. This is because CM and H use information that is not observable using the PMT method and give importance to self- and peer rankings as opposed to simply per capita consumption ranking. There is thus a trade-off between government objectives in targeting the poor, better achieved through PMT, and community satisfaction in selecting poor beneficiaries, better achieved through CM and H.

CONCEPTS SEEN IN THIS CHAPTER

Opportunity, equity, and resilience in social programs
Type I exclusion and Type II inclusion errors in targeting
Proxy means tests
Self-targeting
Inferior goods
Workfare program
Conditional Cash Transfer (CCT) program
Productive safety-net program
Community-driven development (CDD) program
Ultra-poor graduation programs
Infra-marginal and extra-marginal transfers
Labeling and social marketing
Price effect of a CCT vs. income effect of a CT

REVIEW QUESTIONS: SOCIAL-ASSISTANCE PROGRAMS AND TARGETING

1. How do social programs to reduce chronic poverty and to reduce vulnerability to poverty eventually differ?
2. How do social programs to protect consumption from exposure to shocks eventually differ from programs directed at the protection of assets?
3. Can programs that reduce vulnerability to poverty be good for growth?
4. Why can short-run shocks eventually create irreversibilities on child education and health, with long-run consequences for future poverty. What could be done to avoid these irreversibilities? Give some examples.
5. In targeting, what are errors of exclusion (Type I) and of inclusion (Type II)? Why should we be concerned with each of these errors?
6. If we do not know people's income levels (means tests), and want to target program interventions at the poor, what options do we have?
7. Explain how a workfare program can be designed to achieve self-targeting.

8. Is it true that self-targeting always has a cost for beneficiaries? Why would this be? Give several examples of self-targeting and the associated costs.

9. Since the poor often know each other, while the social-welfare agency does not know them, how could this be used to target program interventions?

REFERENCES

Adato, Michelle, Akhter Ahmed, and Francie Lund. 2004. *Linking Safety Nets, Social Protection, and Poverty Reduction–Directions for Africa*. Washington, DC: International Food Policy Research Institute.

Ahmed, Akhter, Agnes Quisumbing, Mahbuba Nasreen, John Hoddinott, and Elizabeth Bryan. 2009. *Comparing Food and Cash Transfers to the Ultra Poor in Bangladesh*. Research Monograph No. 163. Washington, DC: International Food Policy Research Institute.

Akerlof, George, and Janet Yellen. 1990. "The Fair Wage-Effort Hypothesis and Unemployment." *Quarterly Journal of Economics* 105(2): 255–83.

Alatas, Vivi, Abhijit Banerjee, Rema Hanna, Benjamin Olken, and Julia Tobias. 2012. "Targeting the Poor: Evidence from a Field Experiment in Indonesia." *American Economic Review* 104(2): 1206–40.

Alderman, Harold. 2002. "Do Local Officials Know Something We Don't? Decentralization of Targeted Transfers in Albania." *Journal of Public Economics* 83(3): 375–404.

Alderman, Harold, and Ruslan Yemtsov. 2014. "How Can Safety Nets Contribute to Economic Growth?" *World Bank Economic Review* 28(1): 1–20.

Antman, Francisca, and David McKenzie. 2007. "Poverty Traps and Nonlinear Income Dynamics with Measurement Error and Individual Heterogeneity." *Journal of Development Studies* 43(6): 1057–83.

Araujo, Caridad, Francisco Ferreira, Peter Lanjouw, and Berk Özler. 2008. "Local Inequality and Project Choice: Theory and Evidence from Ecuador." *Journal of Public Economics* 92(5–6): 1022–46.

Arcand, Jean-Louis, and Léandre Bassole. 2006. "Does Community Driven Development Work? Evidence from Senegal." Clermont-Ferrand, France: CERDI Working Papers 200606.

Ardington, Cally, Anne Case, and Victoria Hosegood. 2009. "Labor Supply Responses to Large Social Transfers: Longitudinal Evidence from South Africa." *American Economic Journal: Applied Economics* 1(1): 22–48.

Attanasio, Orazio, Erich Battistin, and Alice Mesnard. 2012. "Food and Cash Transfers: Evidence from Colombia." *Economic Journal* 122(559): 92–124.

Baird, Sarah, Craig McIntosh, and Berk Özler. 2011. "Cash or Condition? Evidence from a Cash Transfer Experiment." *Quarterly Journal of Economics* 126(4): 1709–53.

Baird, Sarah, Francisco Ferreira, Berk Özler, and Michael Woolcock. 2012. "Relative Effectiveness and Cost-effectiveness of Conditional and Unconditional Cash Transfers for Schooling Outcomes in Developing Countries: A Systematic Review." The Campbell Collaboration, www.campbellcollaboration.org (accessed 2015).

Bandiera, Oriana, Robin Burgess, Narayan Das, Selim Gulesci, Imran Rasul, and Munshi Sulaiman. 2013. "Can Basic Entrepreneurship Transform the Economic Lives of the Poor?" Bonn: IZA Discussion Paper No. 7386, Institute for the Study of Labor (IZA).

Banerjee, Abhijit, and Sendhil Mullainathan. 2010. "The Shape of Temptation: Implications for the Economic Lives of the Poor." NBER Working Paper No. 15973.

Bardhan, Pranab. 1991. *The Economic Theory of Agrarian Institutions*. Oxford: Oxford University Press.

Barrett, Christopher, Michael Carter, and Munenobu Ikegami. 2008. "Poverty Traps and Social Protection." Washington, DC: World Bank Social Protection Discussion Paper #804.

Berhane, Guush, John Hoddinott, Neha Kumar, Alemayehu Seyoum Taffesse. 2011. "The Impact of Ethiopia's Productive Safety Nets and Household Asset Building Programme: 2006–2010." Washington, DC: International Food Policy Research Institute Working Paper.

Besley, Timothy, and Stephen Coate. 1992. "Workfare Versus Welfare: Incentive Arguments for Work Requirements in Poverty Alleviation Programs." *American Economic Review* 82(1): 249–61.

Bianchi, Milo, and Matteo Bobba. 2013. "Liquidity, Risk, and Occupational Choice." *Review of Economic Studies* 80(2): 491–511.

Binswanger, Hans, and Jaime Quizon, 1984. "Distributional Consequences of Alternative Food Policies in India." Washington, DC: World Bank, Agriculture and Rural Development Department.

Blattman, Christopher, Nathan Fiala, and Sebastian Martinez. 2014. "Generating Skilled Self-Employment in Developing Counties: Experimental Evidence from Uganda." *Quarterly Journal of Economics* 129(2): 697–752.

Carter, Michael, and Christopher Barrett. 2006. "The Economics of Poverty Traps and Persistent Poverty: An Asset-based Approach." *Journal of Development Studies* 42(2): 178–99.

Coady, David, Margaret Grosh, and John Hoddinott. 2004. *Targeting of Transfers in Developing Countries: Review of Lessons and Experience*. Washington, DC: World Bank and IFPRI.

Conning, Jonathan, and Michael Kevane. 2002. "Community-based Targeting Mechanisms for Social Safety Nets: A Critical Review." *World Development* 30(3): 375–94.

Cornia, Giovanni Andrea, Richard Jolly, and Frances Stewart (eds). 1987. *Adjustment with a Human Face. Volume I: Protecting the Vulnerable and Promoting Growth*. Oxford: Oxford University Press.

Cox, Donald, Zekeriya Eser, and Emmanuel Jimenez. 1998. "Motives for Private Transfers over the Life Cycle: An Analytical Framework and Evidence for Peru." *Journal of Development Economics* 55(1): 57–80.

Cunha, Jesse, Giacomo De Giorgi, and Seema Jayachandran. 2011. "The Price Effects of Cash Versus In-Kind Transfers." Working paper, Department of Economics, Northwestern University, IL.

Dorosh, Paul, René Bernier, and David Sahn. 1992. "Food Aid and Poverty Alleviation in Mozambique: The Potential for Self-targeting with Yellow Maize." Cornell Food and Nutrition Policy Program Working Paper 50, Cornell University.

de Janvry, Alain, and Elisabeth Sadoulet. 2006. "Making Conditional Cash Transfers More Efficient: Designing for Maximum Effect of the Conditionality." *World Bank Economic Review* 20(1): 1–29.

de Janvry, Alain, Frederico Finan, Elisabeth Sadoulet. 2012. "Local Electoral Incentives and Decentralized Program Performance." *Review of Economics and Statistics* 94(3): 672–85.

de Janvry, Alain, Frederico Finan, Elisabeth Sadoulet, and Renos Vakis. 2006. "Can Conditional Cash Transfer Programs Serve as Safety Nets in Keeping Children at School and from Working when Exposed to Shocks?" *Journal of Development Economics* 79(2): 349–73.

Edirisinghe, Neville. 1987. *The Food Stamps Scheme in Sri Lanka: Costs, Benefits, and Options for Modification*. Research Report No. 58. Washington, DC: International Food Policy Research Institute.

Elbers, Chris, Tomoki Fujii, Peter Lanjouw, Berk Özler, and Wesley Yin. 2007. "Poverty Alleviation through Geographic Targeting: How Much Does Disaggregation Help?" *Journal of Development Economics* 83(1): 198–213.

Eswaran, Mukesh, and Ashok Kotwal. 1985. "A Theory of Two-Tier Labor Markets in Agrarian Economies." *American Economic Review* 75(1): 162–77.

Faguet, Jean-Paul. 2004. "Does Decentralization Increase Responsiveness to Local Needs? Evidence from Bolivia." *Journal of Public Economics* 88(3–4): 867–94.

Foster, Andrew, and Mark Rosenzweig. 2001. "Democratization, Decentralization, and the Distribution of Local Public Goods in a Poor Rural Economy." Working Paper No. 01-056, Penn Institute for Economic Research.

Galasso, Emanuela, and Martin Ravallion. 2005. "Decentralized Targeting of an Antipoverty Program." *Journal of Public Economics* 89(4): 705–27.

Gertler, Paul, Sebastian Martinez, and Marta Rubio-Codina. 2012. "Investing Cash Transfers to Raise Long-Term Living Standards." *American Economic Journal: Applied Economics* 4(1): 1–32.

Giné, Xavier, Robert Townsend, and James Vickery. 2008. "Patterns of Rainfall Insurance Participation in Rural India." *World Bank Economic Review* 22(3): 539–66.

Haushofer, Johannes, and Jeremy Shapiro. 2013. "Household Response to Income Changes: Evidence from an Unconditional Cash Transfer Program in Kenya." Working paper, Department of Psychology and Public Affairs, Princeton University.

Hetschel, Jesko, and Peter Lanjouw. 1998. "Using Disaggregated Poverty Maps to Plan Sectoral Investments." *PREM Notes*. Washington, DC: World Bank.

Jalan, Jyotsna, and Martin Ravallion. 2003. "Estimating the Benefit Incidence of an Anti-Poverty Program by Propensity 'Score Matching'." *Journal of Business and Economic Statistics* 21(1): 19–30.

Kahneman, Daniel. 2011. *Thinking, Fast and Slow*. London: Penguin Group.

Mansuri, Ghazala, and Vijayendra Rao. 2004. "Community-Based and -Driven Development: A Critical Review." *World Bank Research Observer* 19(1): 1–39.

Mansuri, Ghazala, and Vijayendra Rao. 2013. *Localizing Development: Does Participation Work?* Washington, DC: World Bank.

Morten, Melanie. 2013. "Temporary Migration and Endogenous Risk Sharing in Village India." Working paper, Economics Department, Stanford University.

Mullainathan, Sendhil, and Eldar Shafir. 2013. *Scarcity: Why Having Too Little Means So Much.* New York: Times Books.

Newman, John, Steen Jorgensen, and Menno Pradhan. 1991. "How Did Workers Benefit from Bolivia's Emergency Social Fund?" *World Bank Economic Review* 5(2): 367–93.

Piketty, Thomas, and Emmanuel Saez. 2006. "The Evolution of Top Incomes: A Historical and International Perspective." *American Economic Review* 96(2): 200–5.

Rai, Ashok. 2002. "Targeting the Poor Using Community Information." *Journal of Development Economics* 69(1): 71–84.

Ravallion, Martin. 2003. "Targeted Transfers in Poor Countries: Revisiting the Trade-offs and Policy Options." Washington, DC: World Bank Social Protection Discussion Paper Series No. 314.

Rosenzweig, Mark, and Kenneth Wolpin. 1993. "Credit Market Constraints, Consumption Smoothing, and the Accumulation of Durable Production Assets in Low-Income Countries: Investment in Bullocks in India." Journal of Political Economy 101(2): 223–44.

Sadoulet, Elisabeth, Alain de Janvry, and Benjamin Davis. 2001. "Cash Transfer Programs with Income Multipliers: Procampo in Mexico." *World Development* 29(6): 1043–56.

Schady, Norbert, and Maria Caridad Araujo. 2008. "Cash Transfers, Conditions, and School Enrollment in Ecuador." *Economía* 8(2): 43–77.

Subbarao, Kalanidhi, Carlo del Ninno, Colin Andrews, and Claudia Rodríguez-Alas. 2013. *Public Works as a Safety Net: Design, Evidence, and Implementation.* Washington, DC: World Bank.

van de Walle, Dominique. 1998. "Targeting Revisited." *World Bank Research Observer* 13(2): 231–48.

World Bank. 2005. *World Development Report 2006: Equity and Development.* Washington, DC: Oxford University Press.

World Bank. 2012. *Resilience, Equity, and Opportunity: The World Bank's Social Protection and Labor Strategy, 2012–2022.* Washington, DC.

Sustainable development and the environment

TAKE-HOME MESSAGES FOR CHAPTER 15

1. Managing resource use and environmental sustainability are hugely important for successful development, particularly for long-term poverty reduction. Discrepancies between private incentives and the social optimum in resource use are created by market failures—externalities, public goods, sustainability considerations, missing markets for environmental services—by incomplete property rights, and by high and time-inconsistent discount rates.

2. Negative externalities induce over-production of a polluting good relative to the social optimum. Policy instruments to attack this problem include tax, subsidies, quotas, cap-and-trade, and assigning property rights to allow Coasian-type private bargains. The choice of instrument must pay close attention to property rights of the polluter and pollutee, and to the incidence of costs and benefits.

3. Incomplete property rights (open access, common property resources (CPR) without cooperation) induce over-extraction from the resource leading to exhaustion. Cooperation in the use of a CPR can, however, be socially efficient.

4. If an environmental activity is a public good, there is under-provision by the market and by the community if its members do not cooperate.

5. High private discount rates reduce the value of future incomes derived from conservation and accelerate depletion.

6. If a social goal is sustainability (intergenerational equity), market forces (with future generations absent from the market place) will generally induce overuse relative to the sustainability objective.

7. The Kuznets Environmental Curve links GDPpc and pollution as an inverted-U relationship. It holds for some forms of pollution and not others, and cannot claim causality.

8. Introducing payments for environmental services is a way of achieving a win–win situation for resource owners and society if properly calibrated and implemented.

LINKS BETWEEN DEVELOPMENT, RESOURCE CONSERVATION, AND ENVIRONMENTAL SUSTAINABILITY

Development, natural-resource use, and the environment have become so inextricably linked that they need to be jointly managed. This is a relatively recent phenomenon. It used to be that we could design industrialization strategies without too much concern for resource depletion, pollution, and climate change; or unleash a Green Revolution in agriculture without immediate concern for chemicals flowing into water tables and loss of biodiversity. Today's industrialized countries achieved their current levels of development largely without the burden of environmental constraints and certainly of the threats of climate change. This is no longer the case. The synergies have become so large that the very success of development is conditional on its impact on resource availability and environmental sustainability (see, for example, Al Gore's *An Inconvenient Truth*, 2009). Here are some examples.

Water use for irrigation in agriculture contributes to a global water shortage and deterioration of potable water quality. Eighty to ninety percent of the world's captured fresh water is used by agriculture, at a time when rapid urbanization and industrialization place new claims on water. Overdraft of underground water aquifers, often enhanced by farmers' electricity subsidies for pumping, as in India, leads to falling water tables. Water shortages in the major food-producing regions of the world are frequent enough to affect aggregate food supplies and prices. In most parts of the world, this will be made more critical by climate change. Declining water quality either requires expensive treatment or imposes threats on the health of consumers. The extensive pollution of China's rivers and the associated incidence of diseases are a case in point (Kahn and Yardley, 2007). What are some of the causes? They include unregulated negative externalities caused by use of chemical fertilizers and pesticides in agriculture and by factory effluents; ill defined property rights over water, often an open-access resource, inviting overuse; lack of use of efficient technologies—for instance, to meter water flows or apply water through drip irrigation; lack of markets for environmental services to reward upstream watershed management that can improve water flows for downstream regions; lack of direct control over water management by water users; and the incapacity of the public sector to regulate water use.

Deforestation, especially in tropical environments, leads to local changes in rainfall patterns and greenhouse-gas (GHG) emissions that contribute to global climate change, the flooding of lowlands and silting of dams and irrigation infrastructure, desertification if the use of cleared lands for agriculture is unsustainable, and loss of biodiversity. With a deforestation rate of 7 percent per decade in Africa, forested area is reduced by half every 100 years. For the world, the rate of deforestation was 2.4 percent in the 1990s. Deforestation still continues unabated in Latin America and the Caribbean, and is accelerating in Sub-Saharan Africa (Table 15.1). The main reason for deforestation is expansion of land area for agriculture and livestock. Some of the causes are profitable farming, poverty pushing the poor into the extensive margins of agriculture, unassigned or incomplete property rights (where deforestation is sometimes used as a signal to establish property rights), and lack of rewards to conserve forests for their social functions through payments for environmental services.

539

Table 15.1 *Rates of deforestation by region*

Regions	Average annual rate of change in forest area (%)				
	1990–4	*1995–9*	*2000–4*	*2005–9*	*2010–11*
East Asia and Pacific	−0.10	−0.10	0.30	0.06	0.06
South Asia	0.02	−0.01	0.44	0.12	0.12
Latin America and Caribbean	−0.47	−0.46	−0.49	−0.41	−0.42
Sub-Saharan Africa	−0.51	−0.57	−0.50	−0.51	−2.74

Source: World Bank, *World Development Indicators.*

Air pollution originates principally in the burning of coal and petroleum for transport, heating, and industrial production. Air pollution contributes to depletion of the ozone layer and the emission of particulate matters that in turn contribute to global warming and the melting of the icecaps and glaciers. Indoor air pollution and urban air quality are the most toxic forms of air pollution. The World Health Organization estimates that in 2012 air pollution caused the premature death of 7 million people worldwide. In India, more than half the population lives in places with such polluted air that they lose on average 3.2 years of life expectancy. Air pollution causing brown clouds that block sunrays has been blamed for the stagnation and even decline of rice yields in India (Auffhammer *et al.*, 2006).

Air pollution can also be due to forest fires. Jayachandran (2009) analyzed the health costs of air pollution for Indonesia, where there were massive forest fires in 1997, set off by commercial logging companies in the context of drought in an El Niño year. Smoke implied a level of particulate matter in the air far in excess of safe levels and for extended periods of time. Monthly satellite images give a time series of levels of smoke that vary with time and space, allowing for the identification of health impacts. Jayachandran measured the impact on "missing children" according to cohort size for a sub-district, calculated from the 2000 population census. Children in utero (exposed to pre-natal smoke) are more vulnerable to smoke than children already born (exposed to post-natal smoke). Using panel data for sub-districts, the estimated equation is:

$$\ln(Cohortsize)_{jt} = \alpha_j + \delta_t + \beta_1 Smoke_{jt} + \beta_2 PrenatalSmoke_{jt} + \beta_3 PostnatalSmoke_{jt} + \varepsilon_{jt},$$

where *Cohortsize$_{jt}$* is the number of people born in month *t* who are alive and residing in sub-district *j* at the time of the 2000 census, α_j is a sub-district fixed effect, δ_t a month fixed effect, *Smoke$_{jt}$* is the pollution level in the month of birth, and *Prenatal Smoke* and *PostnatalSmoke* specify the timing of exposure relative to birth. Results show that exposure to pre- and post-natal smoke explains 16,000 excess fetal and infant deaths, with an effect nearly twice as large for pre-natal compared to post-natal exposure. Valuing life at $1 million/person implies a loss of $16 billion compared to revenues for the timber and palm oil industry of $7 billion per year.

540

Global climate change due to GHG emissions results in exponentially rising temperatures and in the destabilization of rainfall patterns, with cycles of droughts and floods. The main sources of GHG emissions are energy consumption (63 percent), agriculture (15 percent), deforestation (11 percent), industrial processes (7 percent), and waste (4 percent) (World Bank, 2007). Since most of the deforestation is to expand the area cultivated, agriculture overall contributes no less than one quarter of total GHG, more than the world's fleet of cars. The issue of climate change for agriculture is consequently not only adaptation of farming systems to the new climate conditions, but also mitigation of emissions to reduce climate change. Climate change threatens world food supplies, and hurts poor people the most. Economic determinants of climate change include a massive market failure as air is a common property resource with no possibility of taxing its abuse or charging for improvements without an international agreement (Stern, 2007); negative externalities as polluters are allowed to externalize part of their costs; private discount rates that are too high to reflect in current economic decisions the distant consequences of rising temperatures; and lack of public research in clean technologies.

Other well known examples of resource depletion and environmental deterioration include the widespread decline in capture fisheries, soil degradation and fertility decline, mismanagement of irrigation leading to the salinization and water logging of soils, and overgrazing of pasture lands and desertification.

The link between resources, the environment, and development comes from the fact that resource depletion and environmental degradation reduce growth or make it unsustainable, and that poor people are the ones most negatively affected, while rarely being the major contributors, except at the local level in highly populated and fragile regions. This relationship is summarized in Figure 15.1.

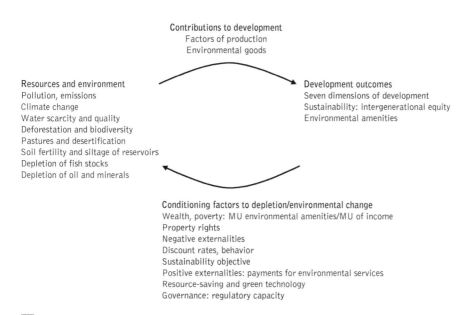

Figure 15.1 *Relation between environment and development, and mediating factors*

In this chapter, we analyze the origins of environmental problems and their bearings on development through seven basic economic concepts: (1) market failures due to externalities, (2) incomplete property rights and difficulties in sustaining collective action in managing common property resources, (3) under-provision of public goods, (4) private discount rates in excess of social discount rates, (5) society not recognizing sustainability objectives in decisions regarding resource use, (6) differential valuation of income and environmental amenities in poor and rich countries, and (7) missing markets for environmental services. These concepts help us design policy interventions to remedy resource and environmental problems such as the overproduction of a polluting activity, the underprovision of an environmental service, over-extraction of a renewable resource, and underprovision in the maintenance of a resource leading to its destruction.

NEGATIVE EXTERNALITIES

Market failures

There are many reasons why markets fail. They include positive and negative externalities, public goods, imperfect information, increasing returns to scale (natural monopoly), and non-competitive behavior. We know from welfare economics that, with perfect markets, a competitive equilibrium is efficient (Pareto optimal): it maximizes social welfare as measured by the sum of producer and consumer surpluses. Under market failures, by contrast, markets do not achieve an efficient allocation of resources. To correct for this, several options are available. One is government regulation, another is bargaining among private agents to arrive at better outcomes (the Coase (1937) theorem), and another is to make markets work or to introduce new markets—for instance, for environmental services.

Negative production externalities

There is a negative production externality when the production decision of an individual imposes costs on others. In this case, market prices do not reflect the true marginal cost or benefit of the goods and services traded in the market, incentives are distorted, and markets fail.

We consider here the case of a good whose production creates pollution that imposes a cost on others. Production and pollution are joint products.

This is represented in Figure 15.2 where:

> demand = MSB = marginal social benefit
> private supply = MPC = marginal private cost
> externality = MEC = marginal externality cost
> social supply = MSC = marginal social cost = $MPC + MEC$
> private (competitive) optimum output level: q^c where $MSB = MPC$
> social optimum output level: $q*$ where $MSB = MSC$.

Price signals to individual producers result in a level of production $q^c > q*$ when $MEC > 0$. Hence price signals are inefficient and the market is failing: there is excess

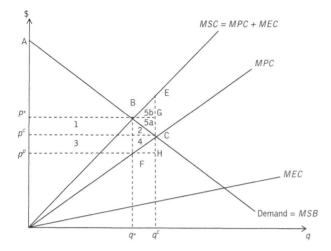

Figure 15.2 *Negative production externality*

production and excess pollution relative to the social optimum. The policy problem consists in designing an intervention that will help return the economy to the social optimum, i.e. obtain $q^c = q*$. There are several alternative policy instruments that can help achieve the desired outcome. They are:

1. An output or externality tax following the polluter-pays principle.
2. An output-reduction subsidy if the polluter has the right to pollute.
3. An output or pollution quota following the command-and-control approach.
4. Use of tradable pollution permits following the cap-and-trade approach.
5. Institutional changes in the organization of production: unitization or cooperation.
6. Private negotiations among parties in accordance with the Coase theorem.

Each policy instrument can reduce pollution to the social optimum, but has different efficiency and welfare/redistributive implications. The instrument to use to achieve the given desired outcome thus depends on property rights over pollution, on the relative importance of the efficiency and welfare effects, and on the incidence of gains and losses across economic agents.

Policy instrument 1: output or externality tax following the polluter-pays principle

If the polluter does not have the right to produce the externality, i.e. does not have property rights over pollution, he can be subjected to the polluter-pays principle with imposition of a tax on production. A tax equal to the segment BF (i.e. $p* - p^p$) changes the solution from C to B, with producers now at F and consumers at B. We can analyze the incidence of costs and benefits of this policy using the changes it implies in producer surplus (PS), consumer surplus (CS), government budget (B), pollution, and the resulting net social gain (NSG), which is the sum of the changes

543

in CS, PS, B, and pollution. As can be seen in Figure 15.2, they are equal to the following:

> change in CS = −1 −2 < 0
> change in PS = −3 −4 < 0
> change in B = +1 +3 > 0
> change (reduction) in pollution = +2 +4 +5
> NSG =5.

Note that the tax eliminates overproduction of the polluting good, but does not eliminate pollution. It only reduces pollution to its optimal level. This is because the good generates positive benefits (as represented by the demand function), and the good cannot be produced without the associated pollution. Clearly, the big gainer here is the government, which collects a pollution tax, while both producers and consumers lose. This tax on a negative externality is often referred to as a Pigouvian tax in reference to Arthur Pigou, the British economist who analyzed its logic.

Policy instrument 2: output-reduction subsidy if the polluter has the right to pollute

If the polluter owns the right to pollute, then he cannot be taxed but must be subsidized to reduce production to the socially optimum level. This may be the case when the polluter was the first occupant in an area that is now being settled by others suffering from his pollution. In Figure 15.2, the subsidy is (2+ 4+ 5a+ 6) which changes the solution from C to B, with producers at F and consumers at B. The incidence of gains and benefits is:

> change in CS = −1 −2
> change in PS = (1 −4) + (2 + 4 +5a +6) > 0
> change in B = −2 −4 −5a −6 < 0
> change in pollution = +2 +4 +5
> NSG = 5.

Reducing pollution requires paying a subsidy $p* - p^p$ for each unit of output not produced. This solution is very costly for government and highly attractive to firms that have the property right over pollution: they gain a rent equal to area 1 and receive a net subsidy equal to (2 +5a +6). The cost for government may increase in the long run if the subsidy attracts new firms with pollution rights into the industry.

Policy instrument 3: Output or pollution quota following the command-and-control approach

The coercive command-and-control approach consists in restricting q to a quota (or standard) $q*$. In Figure 15.2, the market equilibrium changes from C to B, with producers and consumers both at B. The incidence of gains and benefits is:

> change in CS = −1 −2 < 0
> change in PS = 1 −4, generally > 0

544

change in B = 0
change in pollution = +2 +4 +5
NSG = 5.

Note that the producer surplus under a production quota is greater than the producer surplus under an externality tax. This is because producers now capture the rent from regulation through a higher price instead of government through tax revenues. Thus, while consumers and pollution reduction are indifferent to a tax vs. a quota, government prefers a tax over a quota, while producers prefer a quota over a tax. This is somewhat counterintuitive as it means that producers prefer coercion over incentives, while government prefers incentives over coercion. Note also that producers, like monopolists, gain more when demand is more inelastic, as the price-increase effect is greater. Producers of an inelastic good such as gasoline love to be regulated by output standards. Note, however, that the government could capture this price rent by auctioning the quota to producers, who would bid a price to have the right to produce the quota until the price cancels the rent.

Policy instrument 4: tradable pollution permits following the cap-and-trade approach

When there are many firms contributing to pollution, the regulator needs to know the MPC and MEC curves for each firm to optimally set taxes or quotas—an impossible task. An alternative is to let firms decide for themselves. This is done by allocating pollution permits to firms and letting them trade these permits so they go to the most efficient users. This is the cap-and-trade approach used, for example, in the Kyoto Protocol on CO_2 emissions. It works as follows:

- The regulator sets the total output (or pollution) level $Q*$.
- The regulator allocates pollution permits to each of the N firms—say, for simplicity, an equal pollution quota $Q*/N$ to each firm.
- Firms can then trade pollution permits, and the market for permits establishes a price λ per unit of pollution. By being the market price for pollution, λ is the marginal social cost (MSC) of pollution for all N firms together.
- Firms with a marginal benefit (MB) derived from pollution below λ should sell excess permits: for firm i, if $MB_i < \lambda$, it should sell permits and decrease production to increase the MB from pollution to λ (Figure 15.3). It is more profitable for the firm to make money selling permits in excess of the production level where $MB_i = \lambda$ than using them for its own production.
- Firms with a MB derived from pollution above λ should buy permits: For firm i, if $MB_i > \lambda$, it should buy permits to increase production and reduce the MB from pollution to λ.
- At equilibrium, all firms equalize the MB from pollution to the market price λ, so the allocation of pollution permits is maximally efficient whatever the initial allocation of permits.

For all firms together, MB_i (all i) = λ = MSC.

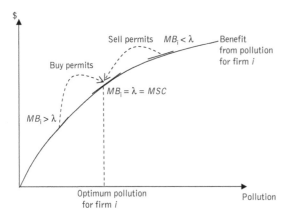

Figure 15.3 *Optimum trading of pollution permits by firm i*

Note that this is another application of the separability theorem, according to which asset ownership (here the distribution of pollution permits across firms) does not affect market efficiency when all markets are perfect. Note, too, that:

■ The regulator must keep track of who owns how many permits and verify that no firm pollutes more than it has permits for. Hence implementation of a cap-and-trade system requires a degree of capacity to govern (monitor and enforce) that may be missing in many developing countries as well as in setting up an international agreement.

■ Rents are captured by the firms that were allocated pollution permits in excess of their equilibrium use. New entrants have to acquire permits to have the right to produce, making entry quite difficult. Hence, while there are no efficiency issues in the allocation of permits, there are serious distributional implications through rent creation.

■ The approach is attractive because it leads to an efficient use of a given total level of pollution. It works in spite of the heterogeneity of firms and asymmetrical information on their marginal benefits from pollution. However, there are the following difficulties.

Allocating pollution rights

Under the Kyoto Protocol, which only included industrialized countries (but not the US), pollution quotas were allocated to countries on a grandfathering basis, i.e. based on current pollution levels. The Protocol ended in 2012. Today, the largest three polluters that account for 50 percent of world CO_2 emissions are not signatories of the Kyoto Protocol: China with 25 percent of world emissions, the US with 18 percent, and India with 7 percent. Including industrializing countries such as China and India in a new protocol cannot be done on a grandfathering basis. On a cumulative basis for the period 1850 to 2008, the US contributed 29 percent of the world total, China 9 percent, and India 3 percent. On a per capita basis, these contributions to the

1850–2008 stock of emissions are 1133 tons of CO_2 for the US, 85 for China, and 27 for India. Defining pollution rights for emerging economies is a major point of contention in post-Kyoto negotiations, as seen in the failure to agree on an allocation formula at the 2009 Copenhagen Conference on Climate Change.

The current IPCC (Intergovernmental Panel on Climate Change) estimate is that the global stock of emissions should be capped at 1 billion tons of CO_2 in order not to exceed a temperature increase of 2° centigrade, beyond which climate change would be catastrophic. The current stock of emissions is estimated at 550 million tons, leaving an unassigned quota of 450 million tons. Should it be allocated proportional to population, proportional to GDPpc, or should the share of industrialized countries be less, given that they are responsible for a majority of the existing stock, emitted when they had the opportunity to industrialize without concern for emissions?

Measuring and monitoring the emissions of each firm

Note that, if it is difficult to monitor pollution, permits can be allocated instead to the polluting activity. This has the inconvenience of reducing incentives to develop new technologies to reduce pollution per unit of output. The initial overall pollution quota $Q*$ and the corresponding allocations to firms can be gradually reduced over time, following a pre-announced schedule in order to create incentives for firms to innovate in reducing emissions per unit of output.

Insuring that pollution by a particular firm does not exceed its permits

Enforcement requires a mechanism for the regulator to fine firms that emit more than they have permits for. Under the Kyoto Protocol, the Clean Development Mechanism (CDM) allows countries' signatories to the Protocol to acquire marketable Certified Emission Reduction (CER) credits by reducing pollution in developing countries. This has led to more than 1,650 emission-reduction projects in developing countries such as more energy-efficient power plants. CDM is making important contributions to enhance sustainable development in developing countries.

Policy instrument 5: institutional changes in the organization of production — unitization or cooperation

One way of internalizing the externality between a polluting agent (e.g. a paper mill that dumps chemical solvents in a river) and a polluted agent suffering from the negative externality (a downstream agribusiness that needs clean water to process vegetables) is to bring the two interests into a single decision-making process. In this case, the joint business is managed in order to achieve the (local) social optimum. This can be done by unitization or merger of the two businesses, or by cooperation to optimally manage the externality as in the Coase theorem presented below. The social optimum is local in the sense that it applies to the two partners but does not consider other parties that may be affected by residual pollution.

Policy instrument 6: private negotiations among parties in accordance with the Coase theorem

The government is not always needed to bring pollution to its socially optimum level. This can be done by setting up private parties to negotiate a system of transfers to reduce pollution to its optimum level. This is the Coase theorem.

1. There are two parties: a polluter (a cement factory) and a pollutee (a neighboring farmer). The polluter has an *MB* from pollution, and the pollutee a *MC* from pollution.
2. Both polluter and pollutee have full information over the *MB* and *MC* of pollution so they can negotiate an agreement over pollution.
3. Property rights over pollution (also called entitlements) are clearly allocated between the two parties, either to the polluter (right to emit smoke) or to the pollutee (right to clean air). Rights to pollute can be sold by the owner of the property right to the other party for a fee.
4. There are low or no transactions costs in the bargaining process.

Under these conditions, the solution to the bargain will be maximally (locally) efficient, irrespective of who has property rights, creating an NSG relative to the pre-bargain outcome. Who captures the NSG is determined by who has the property rights. The solution is described in Figure 15.4.

Consider the following two cases where the owner of property rights over pollution differs.

Case 1: the polluter has the right to pollute

Initial situation:

> pollution occurs until *MB* of pollution for the polluter = 0 (i.e., equal to OA)
> polluter welfare = 1 +2 +3 +4
> pollutee welfare = −3 −4 −5 −6
> social welfare before = (1 +2) − (5 +6).

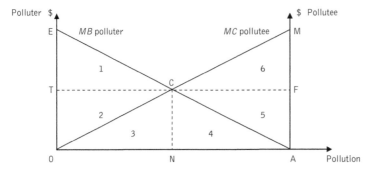

Figure 15.4 *Private bargaining over pollution: the Coase theorem*

Outcome after negotiation: the pollutee pays the polluter OT per unit of pollution reduction until $MC = MB$.

Pollution = ON
polluter welfare = $(1 +2 +3) + (4 +5) > 1 +2 +3 +4$, hence gains 5
pollutee welfare = $-3 -(4 +5) > -3 -4 -5 -6$, hence gains 6
social welfare after = $1 + 2 > 0$
NSG of the bargain = social welfare after − social welfare before = $5 +6 > 0$.

While OT is the minimum price that the polluter would accept to reduce pollution to ON, the owner of the right to pollute could appropriate the full NSG.

Case 2: the pollutee has the right to clean air

Initial situation:

pollution = 0
polluter welfare = 0
pollutee welfare = 0
social welfare before = 0.

Outcome after negotiation: the polluter pays the pollutee OT per unit of pollution emitted until $MC = MB$.

Pollution = ON
polluter welfare = $(1 +2 +3) - (2 +3) > 0$, hence gains 1
pollutee welfare = $-3 + (2 +3) > 0$, hence gains 2
social welfare after = $1 + 2$
NSG of the bargain = $1 +2 > 0$.

This NSG can be appropriated by the owner of the right to clean air, i.e. the pollutee.

The importance of the Coase theorem (Ronald Coase, who worked at University of Chicago Law School, received the 1991 Nobel Prize in economics for this achievement) is that it shows how, if property rights over pollution are clearly assigned, if there is full information about MB and MC for the two parties, and if transaction costs in negotiating are low, *private arrangements* (i.e. bargaining among parties without government intervention) can help reduce pollution, and create win–win, or Pareto optimum, gains. Pigouvian taxes are thus not the only way of internalizing an externality. Government is still needed to establish property rights and to enforce contracts, but not to manage the new market equilibrium. The agreement is locally optimal for the parties concerned. Here again, separability prevails: the solution is the same (equally (locally) socially efficient) regardless of the initial allocation of property rights. Who benefits from the bargain depends, however, on who has the property rights over pollution: whoever owns the right to pollute/the right to clean air can appropriate the net social gain from the agreement as he is ultimately the one who has to agree to the bargain. Hence, as with tradable permits, efficiency is not affected by the allocation of property rights, but welfare certainly is.

The Coase theorem will fail if the transaction cost in bargaining is larger than the NSG generated by bargaining. A policy implication is that government should create institutions that minimize transaction costs. Private property rights are one such institution. Individuals can also create institutions that minimize transaction costs, such as organizations that can negotiate on behalf of their members, with the ability to counteract individual incentives to free-ride in supporting the organization. The theorem has found important applications in contract law (the bargaining over the terms of contracts) and in tort law (the assignment of liability over damages).

INCOMPLETE PROPERTY RIGHTS

Property rights over an asset such as land have different degrees of completeness. Following Ostrom (2001), they include the following five dimensions:

    right to access
    right to extract
    right to manage
    right to exclude others
    right to alienate, i.e. to sell or transfer the asset to another person.

Right to access is the most incomplete form of property right. This would be, for instance, the right to enter a national park, to sail the open seas, or to breathe air. Having all five dimensions makes property rights complete. Private ownership including the right to alienate, with rights well enforced, is thus the most complete form of property right. Incomplete property rights may lead to mismanagement of the resource. This shows that the allocation of property rights and the nature of these rights is a fundamental determinant of how resources are used. This is the reason why Acemoglu and Robinson (2012), in their sweeping historical analysis of the role of institutions in development, typically place property rights enforced by the rule of law as the most important institution. But it does not mean that property rights have to consist in individual ownership, nor that they have to be complete for efficient use. Community ownership (that does not include the right to alienate, but does include the other four rights) backed by strong ability to cooperate can result in optimum resource use (as we will show in Chapter 16). The key for good use is security of rights (to access, extract, manage, and exclude others) and ability to manage if ownership is not individual. We consider here three types of property right— private ownership, open access, and common property— and their implications for resource use.

In Figure 15.5, we see extraction from a resource (e.g. fish catch) when the level of effort (number of boats) increases. Both total revenue (*TR*) and total cost (*TC*) initially increase with effort (*X*). As the resource is being depleted by extraction, total revenue rises and then falls, eventually to the point of total extinction. The optimum level of extraction by users depends on their property rights over the resource.

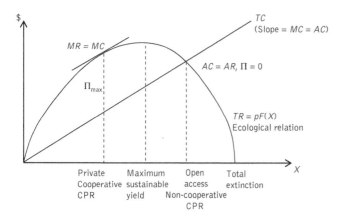

Figure 15.5 *Use of a resource according to property rights*

Private ownership

With complete and secure property rights, the resource is used to maximize profits, i.e. to the point at which MR equals MC, as seen in Figure 15.4. This is the benchmark level for comparing levels of resource use under other types of property right. If there are no externalities, private use is socially optimum.

Open-access resource

An open-access resource is one which everybody has the right to access and to extract. Clearly, under these conditions, users cannot manage the resource, exclude others, and sell the resource. Examples include the atmosphere, the open sea, and other resources with unassigned or unenforced property rights such as large expanses of tropical forest in the Amazon, the Congo DR, and Indonesia. Users of open-access resources only consider the harvesting cost—not the loss of future benefits—when making decisions on effort. They will continue to extract from the resource for as long as there are positive profits to be made, i.e. until $AC = AR$ (or $TC = TR$). There is a market failure as private parties fail to consider the impact of their activities on others. This is the "tragedy of the commons" (Hardin, 1968). It leads to over-extraction from the resource compared to the private (social) optimum, and to its eventual total exhaustion if AC is low.

Common property resource (CPR)

In this case, the property right is assigned to a community, with well defined membership and boundaries. Members have rights of access, extraction, and exclusion of non-members. This form of property right is prevalent across the world, particularly for land in most of Africa, but also for community forestry in India, and agrarian communities created by 1930s' land reform in Mexico. It will lead to overuse of the resource if the community members who own the resource (and can exclude

551

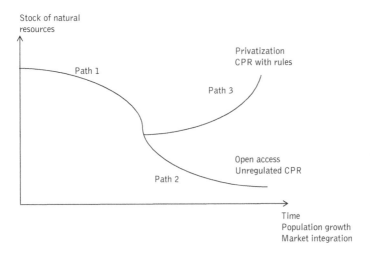

Figure 15.6 *Boserup's view of institutional responses to rising resource scarcity*

others) fail to cooperate in managing the resource, i.e. if each member extracts as with an open-access resource, approximating the tragedy of the commons, particularly if the number of community members is large. But this does not have to be the case. The community can define and enforce rules to manage the resource, codifying and regulating how each member is allowed to use the resource (Ostrom, 1990; Baland and Platteau, 1996). In this case, the outcome can be the same as under private ownership. The community either jointly manages the resource and maximizes profits, which are distributed among members, or each member works separately but under rules that mean the total effort does not exceed what would be the private optimum.

Ester Boserup (1965) was optimistic about communities introducing rules to engage in good resource husbandry. Her long view of history was that population pressure, increasing market integration, and economic development in general lead to increased demand for better resource management. This is because these changes increase $\Pi_{\max}$ in Figure 15.5, creating incentives to better manage the resource. This may lead to changes in property rights toward privatization or to emergence of rules of cooperation in the management of the CPR, helping to maintain the stock of natural resources, as illustrated by the choice of path 3 over path 2 in Figure 15.6.

PUBLIC GOODS

Many environmental amenities and resources have the character of public goods, and thus depend for their maintenance on the provision of public monies and collective effort. Examples of public goods are air quality, rivers, public forests, and infrastructure such as large-scale irrigation canals. Public goods are defined as goods with two characteristics:

> non-rivalry in use—use by one does not prevent use by others
> non-excludability in use—there is no barrier to use.

These two features imply that public goods suffer from market failure: they cannot be provided privately as individual suppliers cannot charge for their use. No one likes paying for the public good above his/her marginal benefits, but everybody would like to be a free-rider. There is, as a result, underprovision of public goods by the market.

If the market fails to provide environmental services, on whom can we rely to deliver these public goods? There are three options.

1. One is government, as it can use tax revenues to deliver public goods. Examples are scientific research, public parks, reforestation, and infrastructure such as roads and sanitation.
2. Other providers of public goods are the church, the rich, foundations, and philanthropic organizations.
3. Public goods can also be provided by collective action: citizens can collaborate in volunteer organizations to finance and support projects and share the benefits, especially for local public goods. Collective action can originate in institutions such as water-user associations, which share the maintenance costs of pumps and conveyance canals, and village associations and neighborhood associations for the delivery of local public goods such as infrastructure and social services.

However, collective action is not easy and can fail. Establishing organizations for collective action is a political challenge due to free-riding. Organizations that control public resources (e.g. waterways) may be managed by leaders, but this may be to serve the interests of particular subgroups, resulting in local capture, often by elites. Successful collective action requires four conditions (see Chapter 16):

positive expected individual benefits from cooperating
ability to monitor the behavior of others
ability to enforce the rules by punishing those who do not comply
time to learn to cooperate, as cooperation can be"habit-forming" (Seabright, 1997).

There are, fortunately, many examples of successful cooperation in the provision of local public goods. One case extensively studied is the management of irrigation systems to deliver water to members of communities, in South India (Wade, 1988) and the Dominican Republic (Ostrom, 1990).

DISCOUNTING: PRIVATE VS. SOCIAL, AND EXPONENTIAL VS. HYPERBOLIC

The decision to postpone or to accelerate extraction from a resource such as a forest depends on the present value (PV) of the net benefits of doing so. The present value of a revenue y_T that will accrue T periods from now is determined by the discount rate $r \geq 0$:

$$PV(y_T) = \frac{y_T}{(1+r)^T}.$$

PV is how much you can borrow today against the future revenue y received T periods in the future when the interest rate is r per year. The ratio $\delta = 1/(1 + r) \leq 1$ is the discount factor. The present value of an infinite stream of annual revenues y_t is thus:

$$PV(y_t, t = 0, \ldots, \infty) = \sum_{t=0}^{\infty} \frac{y_t}{(1+r)^t} = y_0 + \sum_{t=1}^{\infty} \frac{y_t}{(1+r)^t},$$

where y_0 is revenue today. This is exponential discounting. Someone with a greater concern for future incomes (more patient, more conservationist, more altruistic with future generations) will have a lower discount rate, a correspondingly higher discount factor, and a higher present value for future revenues than the reverse.

The tremendous importance of the discount rate on the PV of a future revenue is illustrated in Table 15.2, which gives the present value of $100 of future revenue for values of r that increase from 0 (the environmentalist ideal), to 2 percent (a social discount rate), 10 percent (a moderate private discount rate set by the financial market), and 25 percent (a not infrequent discount rate in contexts where capital is scarce, as in developing countries, for example, as dispensed by the MFI sector or for speculative capital).

These figures reveal a clear conflict between capital and nature. As soon as the discount rate rises above the social discount rate, there are private incentives to accelerate the depletion of nature relative to the social optimum. At a 25 percent discount rate, any forest stock has very little value beyond a ten-year horizon, falling to 10 cents for $100 of future revenue 30 years down the road. No wonder, then, that there is no incentive to conserve at these high discount rates.

Choice of a discount rate is key to decision-making regarding investment in mitigation for climate change (Karp and Traeger, 2013). A higher discount rate implies that we are willing to sacrifice fewer units of revenue today to obtain one more unit of revenue in the future, and, as a consequence, that we are willing to spend less today on emission-abatement activities to prevent future climate change. An illustration of the importance of the choice of a discount rate for optimal investment in abatement is the contrasting results in the equally influential reports on climate change prepared by Stern (2006) and Nordhaus (2008). The Stern report uses a 0 percent discount rate compared to 1.5 percent in the Nordhaus report. The same DICE (dynamic integrated climate-economy) model developed by Nordhaus and Boyer (2000) run with the two

Table 15.2 *Present value of a future revenue at different discount rates*

Discount rate r (%)	Year 0	Year 1	Year 2	Year 5	Year 10	Year 30	Present value of stream of $100 over 30 years
0 (environmentalist)	100	100	100	100	100	100	3,000
2 (social)	100	98	96	91	82	55	2,240
10 (private)	100	91	83	62	39	6	941
25 (MFI, speculative)	100	80	64	33	11	0.1 = 10¢	400

alternative discount rates gives sharply different results. The model integrates the economics, carbon cycle, climate science, and impacts of GHG emissions on climate change to measure the costs and benefits of investment in abatement activities. With the zero discount rate, the present value of cost of carbon emissions is ten times higher than with the 1.5 percent option, and the socially optimum investment in abatement is four times higher. The choice of a zero discount rate is motivated by a concern for intergenerational equity, and has been endorsed by influential economists such as Ramsey, Pigou, Harrod, Koopmans, and Solow.

Discounting at a constant rate per unit of delay regardless of the length of the delay (i.e. exponential discounting), while widely practiced in project evaluation, does not correspond to commonly observed behavior. A common observation in psychology is that valuation of the future falls rapidly for small delays, but slowly for longer delays. When offered $1 today or $3 in a month's time, most people prefer $1 today. However, when they are asked whether they would prefer $1 a year from now or $3 a year and a month from now, they agree to wait one more month for the higher transfer. This means that discounting for a one-month delay is not constant over time: it depends when it happens. This implies a time inconsistency or a "present bias" relative to exponential discounting. People are impatient today, and more willing to wait in the future. If the one-month delay were one generation, it means that we make less of a distinction between two contiguous generations in the distant future than between two generations close to us. In terms of abatement to reduce climate change, we are willing to make smaller sacrifices for our children than we would like them, and all subsequent generations, to make for their own children. This is hyperbolic as opposed to exponential discounting. It is typical of procrastination, where we value the present more in terms of smoking, eating junk food, spending instead of saving, not exercising, and not investing in abatement activities while postponing the decision to initiate these actions to a later date. This bias toward the present can explain low demand for health and education, and the prevalence of poverty traps (Banerjee and Mullainathan, 2010). It also explains the demand for commitment devices for decisions such as savings, and the demand for health-protecting technologies to help people help themselves in making the right choices.

Hyperbolic discounting is written as a the "beta-delta" or "$\beta\delta$" model, as follows:

$$PV(\gamma_t, t = 0, \ldots, \infty) = \gamma_0 + \beta\delta\gamma_1 + \beta\delta^2\gamma_2 + \ldots = \gamma_0 + \beta\sum_{t=1}^{\infty}\delta^t\gamma_t,$$

where $\delta \leq 1$ is the standard exponential discount factor, as above, and $\beta \leq 1$ measures the degree of time inconsistency. If $\beta = 1$, we have exponential discounting. As β falls away from 1 toward 0, time inconsistency increases. Procrastination happens when $\beta < 1$.

The problem is that, for "naïve" procrastinators, tomorrow will be like today, and $\beta\delta$ remains low forever, belittling the future. "Sophisticated" procrastinators will anticipate future bad behavior and hence the need for a nudge such as a commitment device that will prevent them from procrastinating again in the next period. This could be provided by a paternalistic government, for instance, for saving and smoking

555

(Thaler and Sunstein, 2008). It could also be obtained by signing in with a private commitment-assistance service such as Dean Karlan's Stickk (www.stickk.com). But it can apply, too, to the policy trade-off between generating income by extracting from a resource (a forest) vs. conservation, where hyperbolic discounting always lowers the present value of conservation. A legally binding agreement will serve as a commitment device that cancels future delays in investing in conservation and abatement.

THE SUSTAINABILITY OBJECTIVE

We saw in Chapter 1 that the Brundtland Commission (World Commission on Environment and Development, 1987) defined sustainability in the use of a resource as allowing a level of welfare (W) for the next generation that is not inferior to the welfare of this generation as a consequence of the level of use this generation makes of the resource. Sustainability is thus a concern with intergenerational equity in resource use. There is, however, market failure in securing sustainability since the next generation is not here to bid for conservation of the resource. For sustainability to happen, then, it has to be a goal that this generation sets itself, i.e. a social choice.

In using the concept of sustainability, we need to decide how to define welfare and what it is that should be sustained. We can think of three answers, explored in Figure 15.7:

1. *Sustainability of extraction from a renewable resource* (e.g. fish). In this case, as shown in Figure 15.7a, sustainability requires constant yield since there is no technological change and there are no substitutions in achieving welfare:

    $W = f(\text{Resource})$.

    The current generation cannot extract from the resource more than what will reproduce in the future the current yield.
2. *Sustainability of yield* (e.g. corn). In this case, as shown in Figure 15.7b, the current generation can deplete the resource (soil fertility) as it can use successive waves of technological change (TFP) to sustain yields on declining soil quality:

    $W = \text{TFP } f(\text{Resource})$.

    All it takes is optimism that waves of technological change will continue in due time to compensate for the decline in soil fertility. Many technological pessimists

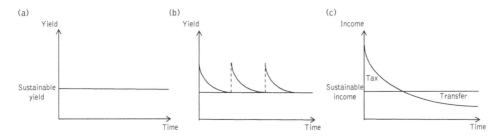

Figure 15.7 *Sustainability according to different concepts of welfare*

would not count on this, and prefer more conservation, invoking the "precautionary principle."[1]

3. *Sustainability of income.* In this case, as shown in Figure 15.7c, the current generation can deplete the resource but tax part of the benefits derived from use of the resource to invest in other activities that will secure substitute future incomes. One can say that the US cut trees in the Midwest and invested in industry, with activity substitution allowing income to be sustained. Sustainability of income was achieved via tax and investment in other productive assets able to maintain W:

$$W = f \text{ (Resource, Other assets)}.$$

Considerations of irreversibility and uncertainty are also important in achieving sustainability. Irreversibility concerns situations in which future effort cannot correct for current or past damage. Ciriacy-Wantrup (1969) introduced the concept of a "safe minimum standard" of conservation corresponding to the threshold below which loss is catastrophic. For instance, ecosystems have thresholds of irreversibility that limit the possibility of restoration. Sustainability cannot be achieved if ecosystems are pushed beyond the brink. Uncertainty concerns lack of knowledge about the performance of economic and ecological systems. Uncertainty requires (1) learning and (2) caution in applying the precautionary principle to resource use. If we are not sure, better play it safe. Ambiguity aversion, i.e. aversion to risky outcomes with unknown probability distribution, will lead us to choose bets with known probabilities over eventually more favorable but unknown bets.

In deciding how to achieve sustainability, it is thus fundamental to decide on what is to be sustained. Many development processes may be fueled by excessive extraction, while sustainable development aims at combining development and long-run survival, i.e. "treating the earth as if we intended to stay." In this perspective, sustainability may imply a trade-off between the pace of growth and securing the welfare of future generations.

DILEMMAS IN THE ENVIRONMENT–DEVELOPMENT RELATION

Environmental regulation

Environmental regulation may not exist or may not be enforced in poor countries, simply because little value is attached to the environment compared to income gains and poverty reduction. People in poor countries tend to value additional income more than gains in environmental amenities such as pollution abatement, while rich countries tend to value improvements in pollution abatement more than additional income. Comparing the marginal utility (MU) of income (y) and of environmental amenities (e) in MDCs and LDCs, we thus have:

LDC: $MUy > MUe$;
MDC: $MUy < MUe$.

Preferring income growth to conservation in LDCs is optimal given the current level of income, and concerns with conservation at the cost of lesser income will only come once GDPpc has risen sufficiently. This implies that environmental standards as they apply in industrialized countries simply cannot be transposed to developing countries. This is a big issue in international trade agreements. Industrialized countries would like to erase what they consider to be developing countries' unfair cost advantage of producing for exports with the lower environmental standards that correspond to their current income–environmental amenities trade-off.

The environmental Kuznets curve

Developing countries with medium levels of per capita income (between US$2,000 and $5,000/year) have the most severe pollution problems. Levels of pollution tend to decline—for instance, sulfur-dioxide (SO_2) emissions that are responsible for the acid rain that destroys forests and kills fish in lakes—as per capita income rises. SO_2 emissions thus first rise and then fall, creating a Kuznets inverted-U curve. This is shown in Figure 15.8a for the US (Ausubel and Waggoner, 2009). Even if this inverted-U is frequently observed, it does not mean that any one particular country will automatically follow this path over time. It also does not seem to apply to GHG emissions such as CO_2 (Figure 15.8b). As a consequence, income growth alone cannot be relied upon to reduce environmental degradation; it has to be an explicit policy choice.

The poverty–environment dilemma: is there a vicious circle?

There exists a two-way relationship between poverty and the environment. Does this create a vicious circle? The causal relation running from degradation to poverty is clear: as the poor are more dependent on natural resources, they are more affected by environmental degradation (for example, clean surface water for human consumption), and they are more exposed to environmental risks (for example, the impact of climate change on farming systems, rising waters in Bangladesh, and an increasing number of environmental refugees) than the non-poor. Even natural disasters that are temporary may have long-lasting debilitating effects on the economy of the poor as they can become decapitalized and fall into poverty traps (Carter *et al.*, 2007). But the causal relation between poverty and degradation that could lead to a vicious circle is far less clear. Poverty does contribute to degradation as it raises the discount rate and limits access to resources necessary for maintenance. However, degradation is mainly caused by intervening factors other than poverty such as high discount rates associated with high-priced capital, liquidity constraints due to capital-market failures, risk aversion and insurance-market failures, farms that are too small to sustain a family, leading to mining of the soil, ill defined property rights, and agribusiness deforesting for short-run gains in large-scale extensive ranching operations. Most of the deforestation in Brazil is due to large-scale cattle ranching driven by export demand and over-exploitation of fisheries by mechanized trawlers, not by poor farmers and artisanal fishermen. The poor themselves can be good

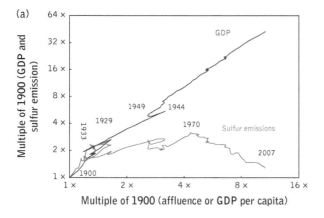

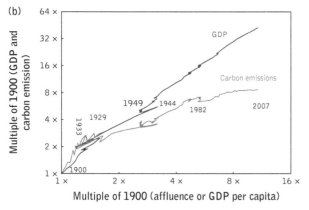

Figure 15.8 *The environmental Kuznets curve for SO_2 (a) and CO_2 (b) emissions in the US. 1900 = 1*

Sources: Ausubel and Waggoner, 2009; Carbon Dioxide Information Analysis Center (CDIAC), US Energy Information Administration (EIA), and US Environmental Protection Agency (EPA).

stewards of the environment when they are in a position to be so. This is exemplified by intricate terrace maintenance in Yemen, extensive reforestation for soil-fixing in Niger, and agro-ecological production systems resilient to hurricanes in Central America (Holt-Giménez, 2002). It is not because degradation contributes to poverty that it necessarily induces a dynamic sequence of further degradation caused by rising poverty (Nadkarni, 2000). There are too many spurious correlations between poverty and environmental degradation to easily establish a simple causality that would lead to a vicious circle.

Income growth can induce the rise of forests

Analyzing what happened to the forested area in 250 Indian villages over the period 1971–99 when the Green Revolution was being rolled out, Foster and Rosenzweig (2003) found that it increased. This was not because higher cereal yields allowed

559

reduction of the area planted, but because the income gain from productivity growth in agriculture (higher farm incomes and rural wages) induced an increase in demand for forest products, a normal good, in particular for firewood. Because forest products are non-tradable in India, the rise in demand induced a price increase, which in turn induced a supply response with an expansion of the forest area. This positive link between income growth and afforestation may not occur when forest products are tradable and when property rights do not give security that investment in forestry will lead to appropriable benefits. Extensive illegal logging of fine-grained lumber such as rosewood and ebony in Madagascar driven by extreme poverty and corruption is a case in point (Schuurman and Lowry, 2009). As the India study shows, non-tradability and well defined property rights may make economic growth and the rise of forests compatible.

INTRODUCING NEW MARKETS: PAYMENTS FOR ENVIRONMENTAL SERVICES

Consider a forest that produces two outputs: wood for which there is a market and an environmental service (ES) such as carbon capture for which there is not. Because there is a missing market for the environmental service, the private reward for forest maintenance is inferior to its social value. Market incentives result in underinvestment in maintenance of the resource and under-provision of the environmental service. If the provider has property rights over the resource (i.e. cannot be forced to deliver more of the ES), an attractive solution consists in introducing a market (or a contract) for the service. This is the novel concept of payments for environmental services, or PES (Pagiola, 2006).

Examples of environmental services for which markets (or contracts) can be introduced are the *in situ* conservation of biodiversity (e.g. forest habitat for wild species such as Monarch butterflies in the Sierra Madre of Mexico), carbon sequestration (planting forests to capture CO_2 or maintaining the current stock of CO_2 in mature trees by avoiding deforestation), soil conservation (zero tillage to maintain CO_2 stored in soils as opposed to ploughing), conservation of wetlands that are hotspots of biodiversity, protection of watersheds (to reduce soil erosion, reduce reservoir siltage and hence extend the useful life of dams, increase water quality, increase the regularity of water flows and hence reservoirs' effective capacity), and protection of landscapes and of open spaces. Examples of PES programs are the US Conservation Reserve Program (that pays farmers to take land out of production and into conservation activities such as prairie and forestation), the US Wetland Reserve Program (that pays owners US$2,600/ha to preserve wetlands), the private Nature Conservancy Program (that purchases land or development rights for conservation), and Costa Rica's payments to forest owners for conservation ($64/ha/year for 5 years) and new plantings ($96/ha/year for 5 years), funded by a tax on gasoline. China runs the largest PES in the world with its Sloping Land Conversion Program that has reforested vast areas of environmentally sensitive farmland since 1999 through payments to millions of poor farmers in mountainous western China. Introduction of a REDD (Reducing Emissions from Deforestation and Degradation) initiative to cut GHG emissions associated with forest clearing by including "avoided deforestation" in carbon market mechanisms was the only tangible agreement reached at the 2009 Copenhagen Climate Change Conference of the Parties. Note that the benefits of environmental services may be captured locally (water), nationally (biodiversity), or globally (climate change), requiring the PES scheme to be organized locally, nationally, or internationally. Payments that combine carbon sequestration, hydrological benefits (electricity generation, clean water, watershed management), ecotourism, and bio-prospection can easily reach US$200/ha, a significant sum compared to the earnings of people who live in extreme poverty (less than US$1/day).

In Figure 15.9, a PES can be analyzed as a positive externality. A forest produces wood as both a private good and an environmental service, which is initially unpaid. The market equilibrium for wood is at B (q^c, p^c), where the supply and demand for wood intersect.

Introduction of a PES adds an effective demand and shifts total demand for the forest to MSB that includes the demand for wood (MPB) and the demand for the environmental service (MEB). The private demand for wood after introduction of the PES is at C while the social demand for forest is at A. Calculation of the changes in economic surplus are as follows:

change in CS = 1 + 2 > 0
change in PS = 3 + 4 > 0
environmental gain = 4 + 5 + 6 > 0
PES = −1 −2 −3 −4 −6 < 0
NSG = 4 + 5 > 0.

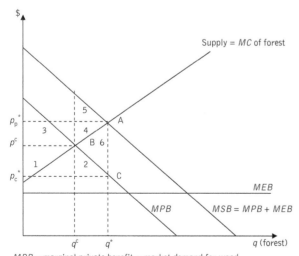

MPB = marginal private benefit = market demand for wood
MEB = marginal external benefit = unpaid environmental service
MSB = marginal social benefit = social demand for wood and environmental service

Figure 15.9 PES as a positive externality

Note that the PES is expensive, but it is not a subsidy. It is a correction for a market failure that creates a net social gain.

How much to pay for an environmental service is difficult to establish when there is no market to set a price for the service. This is the case for wildlife conservation and biodiversity. In this case, the price has to be established as willingness to pay through contingency-valuation techniques that ask people how much they would be willing to pay for the service to be provided instead of discontinued. In some cases, there are markets—for example, for CO_2 capture under the Kyoto Protocol and for water that is metered and sold to local water users. For a PES scheme to work, the payment must induce the provider to continue the service by offering him no less than his opportunity cost under deforestation.

In Figure 15.10, the forest owner could earn C by deforesting and shifting to the pasture option, which is larger than profits from the sale of forest products equal to A. The PES will offer F in exchange for preservation of the forest so that $D + F = C > A$ (Table 15.3). Society is better off paying F in environmental services and keeping E in environmental externalities than under the deforestation option, where the environmental externality is reduced to 0. Under this condition, PES is a Pareto optimal proposition: the forest owner does not lose from conservation relative to the opportunity cost of transforming the land into pasture, and society gains E from preservation of the environmental service through avoided deforestation.

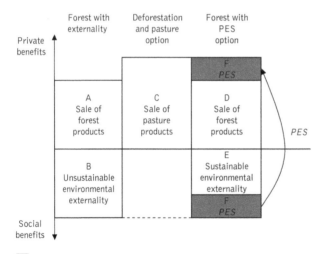

Figure 15.10 *Economics of a PES scheme for avoided deforestation*

Table 15.3 *Welfare effects of a PES scheme*

	Before	Option	PES	Net gain
Private	A	C > A	D + F > = C	win
Social	B	0	E = B - F > 0	win

Because deforestation contributes such a large share of annual CO_2 emissions at a world scale (some 20 percent), introducing PES for avoided deforestation (REDD) was a major achievement of the Copenhagen Climate Change Conference.

CONCEPTS SEEN IN THIS CHAPTER

Mitigation and adaptation to climate change
Externality: positive and negative
Internalization of externality
Tax, quota, tradable permit, Coase theorem
Cap-and-trade and Kyoto Protocol
Clean Development Mechanism
Complete property right
Open-access resource and tragedy of the commons
Public good
Sustainability
Discount rate, discount factor, and exponential discounting
Present value of a future revenue
Private and social present value
Hyperbolic discounting, procrastination, and $\beta\delta$ model
Sustainability as intergenerational equity
Precautionary principle
Irreversibility and "safe minimum standard"
Uncertainty and ambiguity aversion
Environmental Kuznets curve
Vicious circle between poverty and environmental degradation
Payment for environmental service and REDD

REVIEW QUESTIONS: SUSTAINABLE DEVELOPMENT AND THE ENVIRONMENT

1. Externality problem: define the concept of a negative externality. What are the different policy instruments that can be used to solve the externality problem? When can we use a tax vs. a subsidy? Taxes and quotas: which is preferred by government and which by industry? Why is a cap-and-trade approach efficient, but difficult to implement?

2. What are the conditions necessary for the Coase theorem to apply? Why can we say that the outcome is efficient but not necessarily equitable (separability theorem)?

3. Property rights: why are open-access resources prone to overuse? How are common property resources defined and when are they potentially well managed?

4. Public goods: why is there a tendency to the under-provision of public goods? How would you achieve the socially optimal delivery of public goods?

5. Define the discount rate and the present value of a future income. How would you calculate the present value of a stream of future benefits? Why do high interest rates undermine conservation?

6. The growth–environment dilemma: what is the environmental Kuznets curve? Why is it important if it holds true?

7. Payments for environmental services (PES, REDD): how can they be justified? How can they be calibrated? Why can they be win–win?

NOTES

1 The precautionary principle states that if an action (here soil depletion) is suspected of causing harm to the public (here lower yields for the next generation), in the absence of scientific consensus that the action is not harmful (here that TFP will be available to restore yield) the burden of proof that it is *not* harmful falls on those taking the action.

REFERENCES

Acemoglu, Daron, and James Robinson. 2012. *Why Nations Fail: The Origins of Power, Prosperity, and Poverty.* New York: Crown Business.

Auffhammer, Maximilian, V. Ramanathan, and Jeffrey Vincent. 2006. "Integrated Model Shows that Atmospheric Brown Clouds and Greenhouse Gases Have Reduced Rice Harvests in India." *Proceedings of the National Academy of Sciences* 103: 19668–72.

Ausubel, Jesse, and Paul Waggoner, 2009. "Is Green Greener?" The Rockefeller University Program for the Human Environment. New York: The Rockefeller University.

Baland, Jean-Marie, and Jean-Philippe Platteau. 1996. *Halting Degradation of Natural Resources: Is There a Role for Rural Communities?* Cambridge: Cambridge University Press.

Banerjee, Abhijit, and Sendhil Mullainathan. 2010. "The Shape of Temptation: Implications for the Economic Lives of the Poor." Working paper, Department of Economics, MIT.

Boserup, Ester. 1965. *The Conditions of Agricultural Growth: The Economics of Agrarian Change under Population Pressure.* Chicago: Aldine.

Carter, Michael, Peter Little, Tewodaj Mogues, and W. Negatu. 2007. "Poverty Traps and the Long-term Consequences of Natural Disasters in Ethiopia and Honduras." *World Development* 35(5): 835–56.

Ciriacy-Wantrup, Siegfried von. 1969. "Natural Resources in Economic Growth: The Role of Institutions and Policies." *American Journal of Agricultural Economics* 51(5): 1314–24.

Coase, Ronald. 1937. "The Nature of the Firm." *Econometrica* 4(16): 386–405.

Foster, Andrew, and Mark Rosenzweig. 2003. "Economic Growth and the Rise of Forests." *Quarterly Journal of Economics* 118(2): 601–37.

Gore, Al. 2009. *An Inconvenient Truth.* https://en.wikipedia.org/wiki/An_Inconvenient_Truth (accessed 2015).

Hardin, Garrett. 1968. "The Tragedy of the Commons." *Science* 162(3859): 1243–8.

Holt-Giménez, Eric. 2002. "Measuring Farmers' Agroecological Resistance after Hurricane Mitch in Nicaragua: A Case Study in Participatory, Sustainable Land Management Impact Monitoring."*Agriculture, Ecosystems, and Environment* 93(1–3): 87–105.

Jayachandran, Seema. 2009. "Air Quality and Early-life Mortality: Evidence from Indonesia's Wildfires." *Journal of Human Resources* 44(4): 916–54.

Kahn, Joseph, and Jim Yardley. 2007. "As China Roars, Pollution Reaches Deadly Extremes."*The New York Times*, August 26.

Karp, Larry, and Christian Traeger. 2013. "Discounting." *Encyclopedia of Energy, Natural Resources, and Environmental Economics* 2: 286–92.

Nadkarni, M. V. 2000. "Poverty, Environment, Development: A Many-Patterned Nexus." *Economic and Political Weekly* 35(14): 1184–90.

Nordhaus, William. 2008. *A Question of Balance: Economic Modeling of Global Warming*. New Haven, CT: Yale University Press.

Nordhaus, William, and Joseph Boyer. 2000. *Warming the World: Economic Models of Global Warming*. Cambridge, MA: MIT Press.

Ostrom, Elinor. 1990. *Governing the Commons: The Evolution of Institutions for Collective Action.* New York: Cambridge University Press.

Ostrom, Elinor. 2001. "The Puzzle of Counterproductive Property Rights Reforms: A Conceptual Analysis." In A. de Janvry *et al.* (eds.), *Access to Land, Rural Poverty, and Public Action,* Chapter 5. Oxford: Oxford University Press.

Pagiola, Stefano. 2006. *Payments for Environmental Services: An Introduction*. Washington, DC: World Bank Environment Department.

Schuurman, Derek, and Porter Lowry. 2009. "The Madagascar Rosewood Massacre."*Madagascar Conservation and Development* 4(2): 98–102.

Seabright, Paul. 1997. "Is Cooperation Habit-Forming?" In P. Dasgupta and K-G. Mäler (eds.), *The Environment and Emerging Development Issues*, Chapter 11. Oxford: Clarendon Press.

Stern, Nicholas. 2007. *Stern Review on The Economics of Climate Change. Executive Summary.* London: HM Treasury.

Thaler, Richard, and Cass Sunstein. 2008.*Nudge: Improving Decisions About Health, Wealth, and Happiness.* New York: Penguin Books.

Wade, Robert. 1988. *Village Republics: Economic Conditions for Collective Action in South India.* Cambridge: Cambridge University Press.

World Bank. 2007. *World Development Report 2008: Agriculture for Development.* Washington, DC.

World Bank. *World Development Indicators*. http://data.worldbank.org/indicator (accessed 2015).

World Commission on Environment and Development. 1987. *Our Common Future.* New York: Oxford University Press.

Common property resources and determinants of cooperation

TAKE-HOME MESSAGES FOR CHAPTER 16

1. Common property resources (CPR) yield products or services that are collectively excludable in access and rival in use. They can suffer from over-extraction from the resource and under-provision of maintenance services if there is no effective cooperation in use among members or management authority. Effective cooperation is necessary to avoid the tragedy of the commons that characterizes open-access resources.

2. Several potential advantages of CPR compensate for the risks of over-extraction and under-provision: economies of scale, geographical risk spreading, avoidance of costs and risks in dividing, and preservation of community relations.

3. Pessimism in effective management of a CPR is conceptualized in the prisoner's dilemma, where non-cooperation is the dominant strategy.

4. Optimism is derived from observing that many communities make effective use of CPR. Without formal cooperation, this can be explained by the chicken game, the assurance game, and repeated games such as the folk theorem and tit-for-tat.

5. Successful formal cooperation requires the definition and enforcement of rules that codify extraction from the resource and provision of services by individual members. Five conditions are necessary for successful cooperation: (1) well defined property rights and group membership, (2) positive expected gains from cooperation, (3) the capacity to observe and monitor the behavior of others, (4) the capacity to enforce rules, and (5) time to learn to cooperate.

6. Secure property rights over land are important for two reasons. One is to reduce the risk of expropriation, reducing the need for protective labor and increasing incentives to invest. The other is to facilitate land transactions through rentals and sales, concentrating the land in the hands of the more efficient farmers.

7. Behavioral games implemented in the lab or in the field are useful for revealing individual preferences toward norms such as altruism, trust, reciprocity, cooperation, aversion to inequity, and fairness. These norms can make a big difference in communities' differential ability to manage common property resources and deliver local public goods.

WHY ARE THERE COMMON PROPERTY RESOURCES?

As we saw in Chapter 15, property rights are defined in terms of five cumulative rights (Ostrom, 2001). They are the rights to:

access
extract
manage
exclude others
alienate (sell or transfer).

For these rights to matter, they have to be enforced. Open-access resources offer users only two rights: access and extraction. Common property resources (CPR), also called common pool resources, give community members the rights of access, extraction, management, and exclusion. Under CPR, the services of a resource such as fishing, grazing of animals, and the extraction of firewood or lumber from a forest are (1) collectively excludable (non-members are excluded, while members cannot be excluded), and (2) rival in use (the fish, forage, or lumber disappears with appropriation by one member). As can be seen in Figure 16.1, CPR can be compared to private and open-access resources in that they are rival; and they can be compared to club goods in that they are collectively excludable.

There are many CPRs in the world (Baland and Platteau, 1996). Examples include community grazing lands for cattle (Mexican *ejido* communities, Sahelian village communities), community forestry (village forests in India), community-run irrigation systems (as in Mexico, Nepal, and the Dominican Republic, but not in Egypt or Pakistan, where they are centrally managed), fishing grounds (as in Chile, where artisanal fisherfolk communities have exclusive rights over fishing in designated bays), and soil fertility under itinerant farming (slash-and-burn or swidden farming systems in West Africa, where plots of community fallow land are assigned to individual households by the village chief, cleared of trees by burning, cultivated for two to three years, and returned to fallow for as many as 30 to 50 years if there is enough land to be cultivated again before being slashed and burned).

A CPR has been defined by Ostrom (1990) as a resource with the following four characteristics:

1. *Well delineated boundaries and a well defined group of right holders* (*N* potential users). These two conditions are necessary to be able to exclude non-members from use of the resource.

Definition of types of good	Use rules	
	Rival	Non-rival
Access rules		
Excludable		
Individually	Private good	
Collectively	Common property resource	Club good
Non-excludable	Open-access resource	Public good

Figure 16.1 *Definition of types of good: use and access rules*

2. *Users cannot choose others and cannot exclude others.* All community members have an inherent right to use the resource, provided they follow the rules for extraction from the resource and provision of services for maintenance of the resource.

3. *The CPR is rival.* Each user appropriates the full benefit from his extraction from the resource, but only takes into account $1/N$th of the external cost he imposes on others when extracting (i.e. only that part of the total externality that he imposes on himself). As a result, individual users impose negative externalities on each other, leading to overuse. Unless the community is able to impose rules to limit individual levels of extraction, there is a tendency to over-extraction from the resource compared to the socially optimum level.

4. *In providing effort to maintain the resource (cleaning irrigation canals, removing weeds on pastures, fixing fences to keep animals enclosed, planting seedlings in the forest), each member pays the full cost of his contribution, but only appropriates $1/N$th of the benefits it creates.* As a result, unless the community is able to impose rules on individual contributions to maintenance, there is a tendency for under-provision of maintenance services compared to the socially optimum level of provision.

If there are so many resources held under common property around the world, it is evidently because there are advantages to this form of property right that more than compensate for its disadvantages for extraction and provision (Ostrom, 1990; Baland and Platteau, 1996).

Advantages of CPR over individual ownership include the following (Baland and Platteau, 1998):

1. *Economies of scale*—for example, in access to waterholes for cattle, in the management of watersheds for irrigation water, in fencing grazing lands, in building roads to access forest resources, and in constructing processing facilities such as a sawmill.

2. *Geographical risk spreading*—for example, in semi-arid grazing lands and catch fisheries. Rainfall is uncertain in a particular location. With CPR, pastoralists can freely move animals to areas where there has been more rainfall. This is one of the reasons for CPR in *ejidos* in Northwestern Mexico (Wilson and Thompson, 1993) and in the Sudan (Nugent and Sanchez, 1999). In artisanal fisheries, schools of fish move around, and fleets can freely follow them in the undivided waters of the bay over which the community has property rights.

3. *Resources are sometimes impossible to assign individually* (the sea, underground water aquifers), or too costly to divide (fencing of each plot), or the cost of enforcing individual property rights would be too high (the distance is too large for monitoring resource use by individual community members).

4. *Individualization may have negative equity effects* among community members. Thus allocation of individual plots when the quality of the resource is heterogeneous and uncertain may be seen as unfair.

5. *Interlinked advantages.* Division of the CPR into individual plots would lead to individualistic behavior and loss of advantages offered by the community such as mutual insurance, information sharing, interlinked transactions, common defense,

market power, and lobbying the state for privileges. Members of collective farms in Russia and of *ejido* communities in Mexico have for this last reason over-whelmingly refused the offer of dividing the commons into individual land plots.

CPR is not free from disadvantages compared to individual ownership. They are:

1. *CPR induces over-extraction from the resource* (negative externality) if group members are unable to cooperate due to moral hazard or coordination failures, leading to degradation and exhaustion of the resource. The result may be overgrazing, desertification, excessive deforestation, exhaustion of fisheries, soil-fertility depletion under slash-and-burn, over-pumping in community aquifers, and theft of water from irrigation canals (Ostrom, 1990).
2. *CPR induces under-provision of maintenance services* (positive externality) if group members fail to cooperate in providing the local public good. This includes poorly maintained irrigation systems with leaks and siltage of canals (Wade, 1987), poorly maintained pastures (unchecked weed infestations, lack of rotation of animals, no seeding of grasses), and extraction of trees without reforestation (planting of seedlings, protection of young trees from animals).

ECONOMICS OF CPR USE

Under CPR (Figure 16.2), effort in extracting from the resource can range from $q*$, the social optimum achieved under private profit maximization with MR = MC, to q^0, the level of extraction under open access with AR = AC and zero profits. To be achieved, $q*$ requires cooperation among community members so all agree to exercise restraint in their effort to extract from the resource; q^0 is achieved if cooperation fails. The reason why q is above $q*$ under CPR without cooperation is that each has the incentive to continue to extract from the resource for as long as there are positive

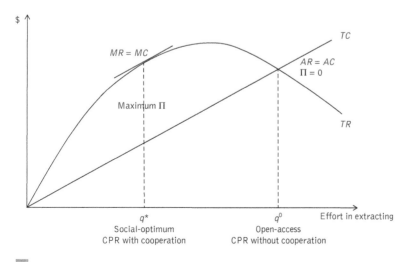

Figure 16.2 *Extraction from a CPR*

profits to be made, just as in an open-access resource. Each member imposes on others a negative externality in extracting from the resource (leading to depletion) that he does not take into account.

Hence the policy instruments used by a community social planner to force members to internalize this negative externality and reduce q to $q*$ are similar to those seen in Chapter 15 for a negative externality in general. They are (in the case of grazing):

1. *Impose a tax per animal (modify individual incentives).* The tax is calibrated to raise the TC to where the private optimum q^0 is equal to the social optimum $q*$. This leaves zero profit after tax. The tax revenue is captured by the social planner who can eventually redistribute it among community members.
2. *Impose a quota on the number of animals (coercion).* A production quota equal to $q*$ divided by the number of members is imposed on each member. The maximum profit thus reached is kept by community members who prefer this approach to taxation.
3. *Create a market for grazing permits (cap-and-trade).* The social planner issues $q*$ grazing permits, equal to $q*/N$ per member if distributed equally. Community members can trade permits for a price. When demand = supply for permits, the equilibrium price is equal to the optimum tax. For this to work, the social planner must enforce the rule that no member can graze more animals than he has grazing permits for after exchange. The solution is efficient as the members with higher productivity per animal buy permits from those with lower productivity.
4. *Change property rights.* The CPR can be transformed into a private resource (by division if there are no economies of scale, or by unitization under a single manager if there are). Under individual or centralized management, profits are maximized and the optimum extraction is at $q*$.
5. *Cooperation in management of the CPR.* This is the solution we are interested in exploring here. If community members cooperate in defining and enforcing rules that codify effort in extraction, they can reach the social optimum. How can this be achieved?

GROUNDS FOR PESSIMISM ABOUT COOPERATIVE BEHAVIOR

The story about use of CPRs starts with considerable pessimism about what can be achieved when property rights are incomplete. It then evolves toward more optimism in observing that many communities are in fact able to achieve a cooperative outcome, sometimes without explicitly cooperating, and sometimes through true cooperation.

Tragedy of the commons in open-access resources

Garrett Hardin (1968) argued that resources held in common were doomed to exhaustion: the tragedy of the commons. Because property rights are not assigned, cooperation is impossible. For each user, with the right to access and extract, the logic is to extract from the resource as fast as possible before others do so, to the point where $AR = AC$, and $\Pi = 0$ in Figure 16.2. Because Hardin did not clearly distinguish between open-access and common-property forms of commons, his results have been used to advocate the privatization or the nationalization of the commons in order to "protect" such resources from destructive use. The positive contribution of Hardin's work was to show that no solution to destruction and extinction can be found without assigning property rights either to individuals (privatization) or to the state (nationalization). However, there are alternatives to privatization and nationalization, such as the common-property regime, whereby property rights—going from access to exclusion in Ostrom's list above—are assigned to a community. Hardin's argument remains in full force for open-access resources that cannot be privatized or allocated in CPR, such as the earth's atmosphere, groundwater aquifers with undefined boundaries, and the oceans beyond territorial waters. It also applies to situations where a CPR remains unregulated due to cooperation failure.

Prisoner's dilemma

The prisoner's dilemma (PD) is the theoretical foundation to explain the tragedy of the commons, or the non-cooperative use of a CPR (Baland and Platteau, 1996; Wydick, 2008). It is a symmetric one-shot game where communication among players is not possible or, even if it was, they would not be able to credibly commit to behave for the common good as opposed to self-interest. Each player thus follows his own one-time self-interest. The outcome is that it is in the best interest of each player not to cooperate.

Consider the following game between two community members who can either cooperate (C) by agreeing to each graze ten animals, which maximizes profit, or refuse to cooperate and choose the default option (D), consisting in grazing 20 animals each, pushing extraction to zero profit, the tragedy of the commons. Under C, the maximum total profit is 200. If one member cooperates (ten animals), and the other defaults (20 animals), the total profit is 100, with the one who defaults benefiting from the fact that the one who cooperated only grazed ten animals, leaving more forage for the defaulter's 20 animals: the sucker (gullible cooperator) loses 100 while the opportunist (non-cooperator) earns 200 (Figure 16.3).

The solution to the game is found as follows:

> Player A considers first the case where Player B may choose C: in this case D (200) is better for him than C (−100).

	Player B		
Pay-offs		C	D
Player A	C	a = 100, 100	c = −100, 200
	D	b = 200, −100	d = 0, 0

Figure 16.3 Pay-off matrix for the prisoner's dilemma. Condition: $b(200) > a(100) > d(0) > c(-100)$. I gain more from defaulting (b) than from cooperating (a) if other cooperates. Solution is (D, D)

Player A next considers the case where Player B may choose D: in this case D (0) is better for him than C (–100).

Thus, in both cases, Player A should choose D. Player B goes through the same routine, and also concludes that D is the superior option, whatever A does. Hence, the solution to the game is the tragedy of the commons, an incentive compatible (0, 0) pay-off. This is clearly a second best outcome relative to the cooperative outcome (100, 100) had they been able to agree to select that strategy. However, for them, the default option (D, D) is the "dominant strategy" in that it is optimal for each player whatever the other player decides to do. Clearly, cooperation without the support of institutions to facilitate communication and commitment is difficult to achieve.

COOPERATIVE OUTCOMES IN NON-COOPERATIVE GAMES

The story, fortunately, does not end here. A number of scholars who looked into Hardin's tragedy of the commons observed that many communities are in fact able to manage their resources quite effectively in spite of common-property status. Most notable are cases of community management of irrigation systems (Ostrom, 1992; Wade, 1987; Meinzen-Dick and Di Gregorio, 2004) and fisheries (Platteau and Seki, 2000). They found two reasons why this could happen. The first is that there can be cooperative-like outcomes without formal cooperation; the other is when the community effectively cooperates. The first can be conceptualized in the chicken game, the assurance game, and two non-cooperative repeated games: the folk theorem and tit-for-tat. The second requires identifying the conditions that help members of a community cooperate.

The chicken game

This game was inspired by the James Dean movie *Rebel without a Cause*, in which two drivers drive full speed toward each other on a collision course. The chicken is the one who blinks first and sways off course to avoid a crash. While no driver prefers to yield, yielding is in the end so important that at least one of them will do so, averting the catastrophe of a collision. Thus there is the equivalent of cooperation (the task— doing what it takes to avoid a collision—is done by one party) even though there is no formal cooperation. This behavior is frequently observed in communities for important tasks that end up being done even without cooperation.

The pay-off for the chicken game is the same as for the PD for the symmetric actions: (100, 100) for (C, C) and (0, 0) for default (D, D) (Figure 16.4). However, everybody gains from the task being done (a pay-off of 200, equal to what is achieved under cooperation), even though the one who pays the cost of doing it gains less (50) than the one who defaults in contributing and benefits freely from the work of the other (150). There are positive gains from cooperation (50) even if the other defaults.

The solution is found through the same reasoning as used for the PD. If Player B chooses C, Player A chooses D since B is doing the task. If Player B chooses D, then Player A has no option but to choose C and to do the task himself as it is so important,

Pay-offs	C	D
C	$a = 100, 100$	$c = 50, 150$
D	$b = 150, 50$	$d = 0, 0$

Player A (row labels to the left: C, D)

Figure 16.4 *Pay-off matrix for the chicken game. Condition: b(150) > a(100) > c(50) > d(0). I gain more from cooperating (c) than defaulting (d) when the other defaults. Solution is (D, C) or (C, D), hence, C is always part of the outcome*

and better than D. Hence the game cannot predict who will do the job, but the job will certainly get done by one of the players. There was no cooperation, but the outcome is the same as if there had been.

This behavioral pattern applies to vital tasks that could be done cooperatively, but get done anyway, even if there is no cooperation. An example is community-managed irrigation schemes in Nepal, where canals have to be cleaned of silt and vegetation growth at the beginning of each cropping season. Everybody in the community is supposed to participate in cleaning on a particular day, but only a few community members show up with their shovels. Those who come curse the absent, but they will do the job without them as they otherwise will not be able to plant their fields, grow rice, and feed their children. Another example is fixing fences to contain animals in Mexican *ejido*. After the corn harvest, fences are removed to let animals graze collectively on the crop residues. However, when the time comes to plant corn again, the fence has to be put back up around the fields of community members located next to each other and (because it is cheaper) protected by only one common fence. Again, the suckers who show up to do the job may curse the opportunism of the absent, but they will do the job without waiting for them as the corn season will otherwise be delayed and possibly lost. We thus observe cooperation-like outcomes without cooperation.

Games of influence can of course be played in the chicken game if decision-making is sequential. The one who decides first always wins since he knows that the other will do the job if he does not. Perhaps the rich can decide first that they have better things to do, and let the poor with no choice do the canal cleaning and fence fixing—or the poor can claim that they are so poor that there is no way they will do it, forcing the rich to do the job. When visiting communities with CPR, it is always important to look for chicken games being played if you want to understand why things get done even though there may be no formal cooperation.

The assurance game

We have met this game several times before, from coordination in endogenous growth (the multi-industry investment game in Chapter 9) to multiple equilibria in investing. This also applies to using CPR resources when coordination matters and it is in everybody's best interest to do as the others do. Players know that they prefer to do things together (with an important role for social norms in deciding to do so), but do not agree on which of the two alternatives, C1 or C2, they will participate in. This needs to be decided outside the game.

	Player B		
Pay-offs		C_1	C_2
Player A	C_1	$a = 100, 100$	$c = -100, 50$
	C_2	$b = 50, -100$	$d = 0, 0$

Figure 16.5 *Pay-off matrix for the assurance game. Condition: a(100) > b(50) > d(0) > c(−100). I gain less from C2 (b) if the other chooses C1 (a). Solution (C1, C1) or (C2, C2)*

The pay-off is, again, the same as for the PD for the symmetric actions: agreeing on C1 yielding a pay-off (100, 100) better than the pay-off (0, 0) from agreeing on C2 (Figure 16.5). However, agreement with the other is always better than choosing the opposite option, which yields (50 − 100 = −50) collectively as well as a worse outcome for each player.

In finding the solution, we see that Player A chooses C1 if Player B chooses C1, and C2 if Player B chooses C2. Hence there are multiple cooperative equilibria without coordination to select the best outcome. The solution chosen, (C1, C1) or (C2, C2), depends on the probability that A attributes to the choice that B will make. There is no dominant strategy, as in the PD, since what is optimum for one depends on the choice of the other. Choosing the better solution, C1, thus requires something external to the game. Shifting from one solution to the other may be difficult as it requires a collective effort. It can come from the following:

1. *Pre-game communication* (coordination) to exchange information and coordinate choices so (C1, C1) is chosen over (C2, C2).
2. *Leadership*. If Player A acts as the leader and chooses C1, then Player B will choose C1. There is consequently a key role for a charismatic and trusted leader who can coordinate players so they choose the best option.
3. *Legal constraints and regulation*. Legislation and regulation will help people coordinate over the better equilibrium. There is here a role for the rule of law, whereby legal constraints on behavior will be enforced.
4. *Social norms* provide *focal points* that help coordination without the need for communication. They offer broadly shared conventions that option C1 is better than option C2 in doing things together. Conventions on norms of behavior may be specific to a particular society, and can be misunderstood by people in other societies. Generalized morality also guides individual choices, helping to anticipate the behavior of others. Grief (1994) and Platteau (2000) have explored the role of social norms in facilitating coordination and thus the shift from one equilibrium point to another in achieving economic development. Social norms create habits and reflexes that guide people toward choosing the better outcome. They include trust, honesty, respect for gender equality, and the exercise of decentralized peer pressure.

There are many examples in the management of CPR where the assurance game applies in both appropriation from the resource and provision of services to maintain the resource. In appropriation, C1 is self-restraint from using destructive practices such as dynamite fishing in lakes, polluting with farm chemicals the local fish-breeding grounds, excessive extraction of underground water leading to depletion of aquifers, and excess levels of irrigation resulting in soil salinization and water logging (Baland and Platteau, 1996). In provision, C1 is maintenance of terraces in Yemen and Nepal to prevent soil erosion and destruction of the terraces below, use of integrated pest management that relies on biological control as opposed to pesticides, and maintenance of tree cover.

Repeated PD games

Repeated games can also lead to cooperative outcomes without explicit cooperation. This is because it is incentive compatible for every player to play the cooperative outcome. It can be represented by a PD game that continues if there is cooperation and stops if there is default. If the game can be sustained over a sufficiently long period of time, then the present value of the cooperative outcome can be higher for every player than the short-run benefit from defaulting. If, however, the termination date is known, then the PD solution applies to that last period and recursively to all years before. Cooperation will fail. Cooperation thus requires games repeated over a sufficiently long period of time or games with an uncertain termination date. In stable rural communities, with little migration and few outside options, inhabitants play repeated games. This is a favorable setting for cooperative outcomes without explicit cooperation. There are two games that give this outcome.

1. *Folk theorem.* Each player cooperates if the present value (PV) of future gains from cooperation exceeds the immediate gain from defaulting, i.e.

    PV (Repeated 100) > One-time 200 now.

   Clearly, this will be more likely to hold when time horizons are longer, discount rates are lower, and one-time gains from defaulting (here 200) are not too superior to the annual sustained gains from cooperating (here 100). Stable agrarian communities where people act together in a long-term perspective, such as for water management in the Asian rice-producing communities studied by Hayami and Kikuchi (1981), are thus more likely to achieve cooperative behavior. By contrast, in communities where exit is an option, such as migrating to the city for residents of rural communities in the Sierra of the Dominican Republic, or where there is a lot of population turnover, as in the frontier settlements of Guatemala, repeated games are less likely to prevail and induce cooperation. A celebrated example of the collapse of a repeated game into a one-time PD with dire consequences is given by Lin (1990) in his interpretation of the 1959–61 agricultural crisis in China, which resulted in 30 million extra deaths. The collectivization of agriculture had met with initial success, based in part on the right for members to withdraw, leaving in the collective only those who wanted to cooperate and play a self-enforcing repeated game of hard work. The elimination in 1958 of the right to withdraw removed this escape valve, trapping in the collective system those who wanted to exit and introducing one-time opportunism that led to a collapse in productivity and to famine.

2. *Tit-for-tat*. This is a repeated game that was developed by Schelling (1960) to explain why a nuclear war didn't start during the Cold War period. Because default is so costly (nuclear war), Player A gives the benefit of the doubt to the other and starts by cooperating (C). Player A thus has a preference for cooperating if only the other will cooperate. Player B responds by doing the same. Hence there is a sequence of C–C–C ... if the probability that the game continues in the next period is high enough. Players need to allow for mistakes by the other or misinformation that could be interpreted as defaulting (D) to give the other party a second chance and avoid a breakdown of the sequence. Some system of warning or graduated sanctions in response to what may be interpreted as a D is useful for this. A handshake before engaging in a conversation can be interpreted as signal that cooperation is preferred, inviting a tit-for-tat response. Cooperation in animal communities has been conceptualized as an application of tit-for-tat behavior, resulting in expressions of reciprocal altruism toward, for example, sharing access to feeding or nesting grounds.

These two games ask the interesting question of what will help communities play repeated games, thus achieving cooperative outcomes without formal cooperation. Conditions favorable to this include:

1. Communities with a long history of cooperation and trust, a strong stock of social capital (well established individual reputations and social networks), shared social norms, and limited exit options. Hirschman (1970), for instance, analyzed how an exit option (e.g. migration) reduces cooperation, while commitment to finding a solution within the community or the organization increases "voice and loyalty."

2. Imposition of graduated sanctions for violation of rules to allow for one-time mistakes in repeated games. Ostrom (1990) analyzes how sanctions imposed on defaulting community members should be proportional to the estimated size of the offense.

3. Repeated games may lead to conservative behavior and to communities falling behind in taking advantage of new opportunities. If this is the case, strong community ties can become a hurdle for development, instead of an asset (Hayami, 1988). In rural African communities, strong social ties that are essential to support a system of mutual insurance when the community is exposed to weather shocks can also breed social conservatism and opposition to entrepreneurship among some community members, which is seen by others as a potential threat to the reproduction of existing social ties (Bernard *et al.*, 2010). Social conservatism, in defense of the vested interest that some have in the status quo, can thus be a serious obstacle to net gains for the community as a whole and to income growth. To avoid this, a community must have the ability to accept behavioral changes

and adapt the rules of the game to seize new opportunities. Such changes and adaptations should neither be too costly for opportunities to be seized (e.g. an adaptation of the rules to changes in market opportunities or in technologies without making it look like a default), nor too easy, as they may undermine the credibility of the rules—a delicate balance to achieve.

DETERMINANTS OF COOPERATION AND COLLECTIVE ACTION

What does it take for a group to cooperate effectively? Cooperation is needed to defeat PD outcomes, and to go beyond achieving cooperative outcomes without formal cooperation under the chicken game, the assurance game, and repeated games. Cooperation requires defining rules and being able to enforce respect of these rules through the imposition of sanctions. Successful cooperation is important for collective action in many aspects of development besides the management of CPR. This includes effective management of a producers' organization, lobbying by an interest group, coordination across economic sectors in investment decisions, coordination among donors in assisting a country and negotiating conditionalities, and selecting the most favorable among multiple equilibria.

Cooperation under the leadership of an appointed manager

Cooperation must be such that it enables the defeat of the non-cooperative outcome of the PD. This can be achieved through fines imposed by an authority (say, a community committee or a manager) appointed by the community to monitor members' behavior. Monitoring and sanctions induce the players to choose the cooperative outcome. This is shown in Figure 16.6, where a fine of 150 is levied in the case of default in the PD game analyzed in Figure 16.3. For this to work, the size of the fine must be larger than the gain from defaulting on cooperating in the PD game, equal to 100 in the current set-up. With a fine of 150 on D, player A prefers C with a pay-off of 100 to defaulting and paying a fine with a net gain of 50. Cooperation is thus achieved by agreeing to set C as a rule, and delegating to an authority the responsibility of credibly enforcing that rule through the imposition of fines. Introducing a structure of authority in a community and endowing this authority with the power to punish when rules are violated is thus a way of solving the PD problem.

	Player B		
Pay-offs		C	D
Player A	C	$a = 100, 100$	$c = -100, 200-150$
	D	$b = 200-150, -100$	$d = -150, -150$

Figure 16.6 *Cooperation under the leadership of a manager. Rule is C. The manager imposes a fine f = 150 if a player is found breaking the rule (D). Condition: a(100) > b-f (50) > c(−100) > d = -f(−150). Solution is (C, C)*

Conditions for successful cooperation

There are five broad conditions that all need to be satisfied for successful cooperation to occur. They can be met by following many different pathways, offering a broad array of options and much room for innovations.

1. The resource must have well defined property rights and group membership.
2. There must be positive individual expected gains from successful cooperation.
3. Members' actions must be observable by others, and others must be able to monitor them.
4. Sanctions must be enforceable in case of default.
5. There must be time to learn to cooperate.

Property rights and group membership

To allow cooperation in managing a CPR, the resource must have well defined boundaries and well defined group membership, and the group must have well defined property rights (authority) over the resource (Ostrom, 1990). This is necessary for the group to be able to restrict entry and extraction by others. Failure to establish clear property rights over the resource will turn it into an open-access resource. Assigning property rights is thus key to cooperation. In Mexico, some *ejido* community resources are seen by neighbors as public goods, giving them the "right" to encroach and extract resources (logging trees, grazing animals, fishing), which decreases incentives for community members to invest in management of the resource. In Sub-Saharan Africa, traditional community property rights were in general expropriated under colonization, and not returned after de-colonization. This creates disincentives for the community to manage resources, leading, for instance, to recurrent conflicts between agriculturalists and pastoralists. Global commons with property rights that cannot be assigned, such as the atmosphere, will require global cooperation as under the Kyoto Protocol to regulate CO_2 emissions.

The group with ownership over the CPR must have sufficient technical knowledge of the total-revenue and total-cost curves (represented in Figure 16.2) in using the resource. This is needed to establish the optimal level of use of the resource, to establish rules for extraction and provision, and to know what profit to expect from reducing overuse.

Expected gains from cooperation

For cooperative behavior to be incentive compatible for community members, it must be rewarded by individually profitable outcomes. This requires the following:

1. *Pay-off from cooperation.* Cooperation has to have a sufficiently high pay-off (200 in the current example) over the non-cooperative outcome (0) for the effort and cost of cooperation to be worth it for group members. The larger the expected profit under optimum use, the greater the incentive to cooperate.

578

2. *Triggers.* There is a role for triggers to cooperation. Cooperative behavior may be postponed because change via collective action seems too hard to achieve. This was analyzed by Hirschman (1984) in a number of case studies of communities and grassroots organizations that succeeded in "getting ahead collectively." He identified the role of crises, catastrophes, injustices, and distress in inducing collective action. A community destroyed by a flood organizes collective action to move to higher ground in a large landlord's property. Once cooperative behavior has been triggered, success can breed sustained cooperation and its extension to new areas of action. The community that successfully collaborated in moving the village to a new location can now use its capacity to engage in collective action to address other needs such as the provision of local public goods. In this sense, triggers can unlock cooperation that becomes self-sustaining as gains are realized and learning about cooperation progresses, unleashing a virtuous cycle of collective action.

3. *Number of members.* The number of members of the organization also matters. Smaller groups may allow for larger per capita gains from cooperation, but larger groups could have more electoral clout or achieve economies of scale in servicing their members. This "logic of collective action" is a famous paradox, analyzed by Mancur Olson (1971). He found that smaller groups can actually be more effective in collective action than larger groups. A small producer lobby can defeat a large consumer lobby in influencing farm-policy legislation that will raise food prices. This has been used to explain how highly inefficient and regressive OECD farm subsidies, estimated at 1 billion dollars a day, can be sustained politically even though they only benefit a small minority of producers and are costly to a large majority of consumers and taxpayers (Peterson, 2009).

4. *Legal right to cooperate.* Finally, collective action to succeed must be a right recognized by government authorities. Community members have to have the freedom to meet and to democratically decide how to manage the resource. Repressive governments that ban the right to meet and to act collectively—for instance, during the years of terror in Guatemala, where groups of more than five people were not permitted to gather—will not allow successful cooperative outcomes. In many African countries, farmers' cooperatives remain strongly restricted and are used by governments to achieve clientelistic gains, preventing members from using the organizations to pursue their own economic and social objectives (World Bank, 2007).

Cooperation in spite of selfishness

Can there be cooperation in spite of selfishness? Gary Becker's (1974) "rotten kid" theorem addresses this question at the level of the household. His answer is yes, if interests are linked. Assume that a benevolent parent (or a paternalistic state) with a given wealth endowment will transfer gifts of money income to children to make them happy, i.e. proportional to each child's level of unhappiness. In this case, a child's transfer is reduced by the level of unhappiness (poverty) of the other children. Even

579

if a child is a rotten kid who takes pleasure in harming his siblings, he will refrain from doing so because any utility taken away from a sibling is compensated for by a transfer from the parent, reducing the transfer to the rotten kid. Thus all family members will act in the family's best interest. Personal incentives are aligned so everybody cooperates in helping one another, not only refraining from doing harm but also improving others' welfare.

The implication for policy to induce cooperation is to delay gifts of money to children until they are older and have exercised their full capacity to help one another earn more income. In this two-stage game, children choose their actions and hence determine total family income in the first stage. In the second stage, the household head determines the transfers that will maximize aggregate happiness. Delaying the second stage will extend the period of cooperative behavior. Another implication is preference for equality in income-earning outcomes. If there is more inequality, the successful child will be taxed more heavily (or receive less from the parent) to compensate through transfers for the less successful income status of others.

There are, however, conditions under which Becker's optimistic rotten-kid theorem can fail. Bergstrom (1989) argued that if a child derives happiness from both leisure and consumption, then he might choose to consume more immediate leisure in the knowledge that lower current consumption will be compensated for by a higher transfer, at the cost of a lower family income. This applies in general to situations where individuals can choose between current and future consumption, with a future transfer compensating for lower current consumption.

Capacity to observe and monitor

To enforce rules, the behavior of individual members must be observable and be able to be monitored by others. This has implications for the characteristics of groups that are more likely to succeed in collective action. Some of these characteristics are the same as those identified for successful group lending by MFIs (Chapter 13). They are:

1. *Number of members*. Smaller groups have lower costs of communication among members, allow greater observability of others' behavior, and are consequently in a better condition to defeat free-riding and PD behavior.
2. *Peer monitoring*. The group can appoint accountable monitors, such as a vigilance committee (an important institution in the Mexican *ejido*), which is entrusted with observing and monitoring the behavior of group members.
3. *Group homogeneity*. Greater homogeneity of activities or wealth levels across members allows better understanding of what the others are doing, and hence greater capacity to monitor behavior.
4. *Physical ease of monitoring*. Greater proximity of members facilitates observability. In this sense, dispersed rural habitats make collective action more difficult, compared to urban settings or rural areas with greater population density.
5. *Organization based on nested enterprises instead of a single large organization*. Decentralization (local governance) and the formation of sub-coalitions of members

can facilitate access to individual information, and hence monitoring. This is the reason why many organizations use a nested system, where the center delegates authority over monitoring to local groups or local appointed officials, and the local groups or officials in turn monitor their members. An MFI typically uses local branches with credit officers who are part of the community. Each branch is accountable for its own performance. In the case of large CPRs, subgroups of the community (sub-coalitions) may be given exclusive rights over grazing in particular subsets of the common territory, improving the capacity to observe and monitor the behavior of members (Wilson and Thompson, 1993). Another example of decentralization for more effective collective action is a community-based natural-resources-management approach that pursues the dual goals of biodiversity conservation and poverty reduction through collective action in the management of CPR—for example, for the development of eco-tourism or the implementation of conservation contracts. In Madagascar, their approach consists in creating participatory village associations that can manage the collective action needed to implement such projects. While there have been success stories, these organizations are prey to elite capture and corruption (Gezon, 1997).

Enforcement of rules

Rules only have value if they can be enforced. There are several aspects of member behavior and group characteristics that facilitate the enforcement of rules.

1. *Individual enforcement of collective norms.* This is a very interesting pattern of behavior, where members of the group feel individually responsible for enforcing the rules on other members, personally bearing the cost of doing so. This has been analyzed by Grief (1994) for business groups (e.g. Venetians trading along the Silk Route) where members individually imposed a collective punishment on local trading partners who engaged in opportunistic behavior, defaulting on contracts (moral hazard), or delivering shoddy goods (adverse selection). Platteau (2000) also observed situations of "generalized morality," allowing anonymous market exchange to be sustained with little risk of non-fulfillment of contracts. This behavior has been conceptualized in the contagion game, where everybody voluntarily enforces the rules on others for fear that the overall social order will degenerate and collapse.

2. *Ease of applying sanctions.* Sanctions are easier to apply if:
    i.   The cost of an *exit option* (Hirschman, 1970) is high for members—for example, if there are limited opportunities for migration or for participation to the labor market outside the community.
    ii. There are shared *social norms*, and members are afraid of being ostracized for misbehavior and of losing their social capital (reputation) in the community (Fafchamps, 1992). Loss of reputation is more costly if there are extensive

581

interlinked transactions among community members. A member who defaults on rules will lose access to other community advantages such as mutual insurance, access to loans, access to land, access to employment opportunities, and the benefits of patron–client relations (Bardhan, 1984).

iii. There is greater *perception of fairness* in the distribution of gains and costs from cooperative behavior. A rule that is seen as fair, for instance, is one in which individual participation to costs (provision of services) is proportional to the benefits of participation (extraction from the resource). If the rule is seen as fair, so is the application of sanctions when the rules are violated (Ostrom, 1992).

iv. Threats that sanctions will be applied to defaulters are more credible if there are *commitment devices* to make these sanctions kick in automatically. This is one of the benefits of strongly institutionalized and respected leadership, under which the enforcement of rules and sanctions gains credibility, as opposed to personalized and discretionary leadership.

v. The community has *conflict-resolution mechanisms* for the enforcement of rules. These conflict-resolution mechanisms can be managed by the elders or the chief in the community, by traditional court systems, or by formal alternative dispute-resolution mechanisms that can help to avoid costly litigation.

3. *Meta-punishment.* If the punisher does not punish, who will punish the punisher for failing to punish? This is the meta-punishment problem. The enforcement authorities must be accountable to their constituencies. The leaders' electoral accountability and local exercise of democracy are important for this purpose. Local communities often do not have ways by which traditional authorities— for example, the elders—can be held accountable to the members for their actions. Like the market and the state, local communities can also fail (Platteau and Abraham, 2002).

Time to learn and the culture of cooperation

Cooperation is a behavioral practice that takes time to learn and establish. Cooperation can thus be habit forming (Seabright, 1997), translating itself into cultural norms. It takes some time for a community to evolve rules and behavioral patterns that support effective cooperation in CPR management.

In Guatemala, Katz (2000) observed that cooperation is typically less developed in recent frontier settlements than in long-established traditional village communities. The contrast in the technical conditions for growing rice and wheat has been used by anthropologists to explain differences in cooperative behavior across societies. In rice-growing communities, irrigation systems need to be carefully coordinated among farmers, creating strong interdependencies across individuals. In wheat-growing communities, where access to water only depends on rainfall, there is, by contrast, much more room for independence. This has been used to explain the existence of a long-established culture of individualism in the West and a culture of interdependencies in East Asia. Interdependencies created by the need to manage vast integrated irrigation systems, as in China, ancient Mexico, and Egypt can give rise to strong central states and "hydraulic despotism," as argued by Wittfogel (1957); but it can also lead to a culture of cooperation. Within China, Talhelm *et al.* (2014) used the contrast between rice-growing regions (in the South) and wheat-growing regions (in the North) as a natural experiment. They organized experimental games that revealed attitudes toward cooperation in counties on the two sides of the borderline between these regions. They found evidence of behavior that revealed the cultural traits of greater interdependence in rice-growing regions and of greater individualism in wheat growing regions. Hayami (1996) argued that, in Japan, long-established rural communities have built relations of trust that allowed for the establishment of the just-in-time system in industry, which requires high cooperative discipline in the timing of deliveries to minimize stock holding. Toyota, which championed this approach, had its roots in the cooperative discipline of the agrarian community that evolved over centuries in the management of irrigation systems for rice cultivation.

WHY SECURE PROPERTY RIGHTS OVER LAND MATTER FOR ECONOMIC DEVELOPMENT

We have seen that well defined property rights are a precondition for the efficient performance of markets and for successful Coasian bargains. More specifically, well defined property rights create efficiency gains by (1) eliminating the risk of expropriation from the land, thus securing the appropriation of benefits from investment, and (2) facilitating land-market transactions (Besley and Ghatak, 2010).

Property rights limit the risk of expropriation

Cultivating the land under pervasive risks of expropriation because property rights are not well established or not enforced has two efficiency costs. The first is the need to incur costs to defend the property from being seized by others. This requires paying guards or engaging in self-defense, limiting in particular mobility away from the asset such as participating in the labor market or migrating. One of the important impacts of granting complete property rights to Mexican *ejidatarios* under the 1993 Procede (land-certification) program, with farmers who previously only had contestable user rights over the land they cultivated, was to induce large-scale migration to the US (de Janvry *et al.*, 2015). Using the roll-out of the land-titling program across states and over a 13-year period to identify the impact on migration, this study shows that households obtaining land certificates were subsequently 28 percent more likely to have a migrant member. In an urban setting, too, Field (2007) found that granting property rights to slum dwellers in Lima allowed them to participate much more extensively in the labor market, without fear that their homes would be invaded while they were away (we reviewed this paper as an example of the diff-in-diffs approach in Chapter 4).

The second cost of uncertain property rights is a limit on investment incentives since the delay between investing and reaping the benefits from the investment exposes the investor to potential expropriation. Secure property rights are thus widely recognized as a precondition to long-term investments in agriculture. Jacoby *et al.* (2002) show that tenure insecurity induced by China's system of village-level land reallocation significantly reduces application of organic fertilizer which has long-lasting benefits for soil quality. They show no effect on the use of short-lasting chemical fertilizers. There may be situations, however, where insecurity increases investment incentives. This is the case if the threat of expropriation is related to underuse. Tree planting in Ghana, as in much of Sub-Saharan Africa, is thus a way of asserting property rights over the land (Besley, 1995). In Brazil, demonstration of land use may be done through deforestation. Thus secure property can be good and bad for the permanence of forests depending on the institutional context.

Property rights facilitate land-market transactions

There are two important trades that property rights support. The first is in the land itself, which can be for rentals or sales. In land rental, sharecropping contracts (studied in Chapter 20) can be designed to overcome market failures in risk, in non-tradable factors of production such as management and supervision functions, and in capital. They offer an easy entry into agriculture for young farmers still short of access to capital and of management expertise. Land-sales markets are important sources of efficiency gains as they allow land to get into the hands of the most efficient farmers, a phenomenon abundantly evidenced by Deininger (2003).

Land can also be used as collateral in accessing credit. This is an argument forcefully made by De Soto (2000), who claims that lack of formalization of assets owned by the poor prevents them from using to full advantage even the few assets they control. Land titling of informally occupied urban or agricultural lands is important for this purpose. This may not be sufficient, however. We see that farmers are reticent to pledge their land title as collateral for a loan if the harvest may fail, and the asset may thus be lost to the bank. As argued by Boucher *et al.* (2008), what is missing here is an insurance product to allow the farmer to pledge the land as collateral without risk of losing it.

BEHAVIORAL GAMES IN DEVELOPMENT ECONOMICS

There are situations in which we would like to characterize and measure the individual preferences of agents toward behavioral norms such as altruism, trust, reciprocity, cooperation, aversion to inequity, and preference for fairness. This could be to assess the likelihood of them respecting contracts even though they are incomplete and unenforceable by law, or to predict their willingness to participate in collective action even though others may default. This is all the more important in developing-country settings, where formal institutions (laws most particularly) are incomplete or not enforced, and where informal norms dominate in codifying behavior. Differences in behavioral norms can be a reason why some countries have been more successful than others in achieving growth, reducing poverty, and delivering public goods. We can set up experimental behavioral games to measure individual preferences, including altruism (dictator game), trust and reciprocity (trust game), cooperation (public-goods game), and fairness (ultimatum game).

Behavioral games can be implemented in laboratory settings, typically done with a population of students, or in lab-in-the-field experiments that can be done with a population that has experience of the issue studied, such as being poor, being engaged in farming, being a member of a ROSCA, or having been exposed to violence. Lab-based games tend to be more tightly controlled and replicable. Lab-in-the-field experiments are more difficult and costly to run but have the advantage of addressing issues to which a student population may not be sensitive or with which it may not be knowledgeable. An obvious difficulty with lab-in-the-field experiments is knowing which population the recruited players represent. This is important for characterizing the external validity of the results obtained in an experiment. Another difficulty is making sure that players understand the game without framing the answers, a difficult balance to achieve.

Dictator game: measuring altruism

The objective here is to characterize an individual's degree of altruism. The "dictator" (so named because he is the only decision-maker) receives a one-time endowment and must decide how to split it between himself and another player (this is not strictly a game since the other player is just a passive recipient). If the dictator is a "homo economicus," he should allocate the entire endowment to himself. The share donated to the other is a measure of altruism, as it suggests that the dictator derives utility from the benefit derived by the other from the transfer. The game may be polluted if the dictator makes a transfer in order not to appear greedy to the experimenter. Dictator games typically show that people like to make transfers to others in spite of the lack of economic rationality for doing so. In Sub-Saharan Africa and Latin America, mean allocations to others typically run between 25 and 40 percent (Henrich et al., 2006). The game can be extended into a taking game, where the dictator can not only give money to another person but also take it from them. The outcome tends to show less altruism than under the pure-giving dictator game. This suggests that framing affects behavior: namely, that behavior (giving or not giving in the dictator game) depends on alternative options such as the possibility of taking from others (List, 2007). As an example, willingness to help the poor and to engage in philanthropic acts is affected by how deserving the poor appear to the potential donor. For instance, identifying the poor with attempts to "pull herself up by her bootstraps," industriousness, and school enrollment are strong predictors of higher levels of donations. CCTs, where the poor display their deserve by sending their children to school, are for this reason more appealing to donors than pure cash transfers.

Trust game: measuring trust and reciprocity

In this game, the second player plays an active role upon receiving a transfer. As in the dictator game, the first player receives an endowment and must decide how to split it between himself and the second player. Whatever is given away is multiplied by the experimenter, with the multiplier known to the first player. The second player then decides how to split what has been received between himself and the first player. The fraction given by the first player measures trust, that by the second player altruism and reciprocity. The prediction for the game is that the second player has no incentive to send any money back—and, anticipating this, the first player should not give any money to the second. In spite of this, results show a tendency to share and to reciprocate. First players send on average 50 percent of their endowments, and second players return 30 percent of what they receive (Cárdenas and Carpenter, 2008). Reciprocity is found to increase with smaller and more homogenous groups. Countries with higher growth rates, less poverty, more equality in the division of gains from growth, and lower unemployment are correlated with more trust.

Because the first transfer may be motivated by both altruism and trust, some experimenters start with the dictator game to measure altruism. The transfer made by the first player in the trust game, net of the dictator-game transfer, can then be interpreted as "pure trust."

Finan and Schechter (2012) used a trust game to characterize the degree of intrinsic reciprocity that characterizes an individual. They analyze the people a politician targets in buying votes (in the expectation that they will vote for him in a secret-ballot election). Since the vote is not enforceable, the transfers only make sense if they are made to individuals with strong norms of intrinsic reciprocity. Finan and Schechter knew from a household survey the people who had been offered a transfer in exchange for a vote. Playing a trust game with these people allowed them to measure each individual's degree of intrinsic reciprocity. They measure altruism on a base transfer and reciprocity by the fraction returned on larger sums received net of the altruistic transfer. They found that politicians do target people with intrinsic reciprocal behavior. This is possible because political middlemen in small communities know villagers quite intimately, i.e. how much they can be trusted. To validate their proposition, Finan and Schechter showed that these middlemen are indeed able to predict each villager's degree of intrinsic reciprocity as measured in the trust game.

Public-goods game: measuring cooperation

The public-goods game takes as a theoretical basis the PD, with a choice for each player to cooperate C or defect D in contributing to the public good. While the social optimum is (C, C), the dominant strategy is for each individual to rationally prefer D, with (D, D) the game outcome. In the public-goods game, Player 1 secretly allocates a private endowment between a public pot for investment in a public good and keeps the rest for himself. The public pot is multiplied by less than N, the number of players, and is allocated equally across players as the pay-off from the public good. Player 1 thus receives 1/Nth of the multiplied deposit in the public pot, representing the benefit from the public good. The total pay-off would be maximized if all agents allocated all of their endowment to the public pot; however, a rational agent would allocate zero to the public pot, expecting that he can free-ride on the others. The share of the endowment contributed to the public pot measures preference toward cooperation. In spite of the PD prediction, results show that one third of players are willing to contribute to the public pot, that contributions of half of the endowment are common, and that willingness to cooperate tends to increase with the size of the multiplication factor (Cárdenas and Carpenter, 2008). Heterogeneity shows that older people are more cooperative. Cooperation is also higher in traditional societies. The game can be extended to a repeated public-goods game. When trusting contributors observe that free-riders have been rewarded without contributing, inequity aversion induces them to reduce their contributions. The public pot thus gradually shrinks to the contribution made by the hardcore givers who are not deterred by others' lack of cooperative behavior. In an open public-goods game, individual contributions are known to others. This induces each player to contribute more. Social sanctions such as making public information on contributions (resulting in ostracization and public shaming of free-riders) and allowing discussions between rounds of contributions significantly increase cooperation. Repeated open public-goods games thus predict that well informed and stable local communities are better able to sustain cooperation, an outcome that corresponds to Ostrom's (1990) field observations of the determinants of cooperation quality in managing CPR.

Ashraf (2009) used a public-goods game to study gender roles in managing household savings. The husband and wife in a household are allocated money and must decide to deposit it in either an account that only the depositor controls or in one that benefits the whole family. When wives know what men contribute to the family account, men contribute as much as women. When men can hide their choices, they allocate much more to their own account. This shows that, with incomplete information, household bargaining is incomplete. An implication of this result is that cash transfers allocated to a household to benefit children, such as CCTs, are more effective when allocated to mothers if there is incomplete information, or that the transfer should be fully transparent to both the man and the woman.

Ultimatum game: measuring preference for fairness

In this game, Player 1 receives an endowment and offers a share to Player 2, who either accepts or rejects it. If Player 2 rejects the split, neither player receives any money. If Player 1 knows that Player 2 plays rationally (i.e. will just accept whatever is transferred rather than losing it), he should offer Player 2 the smallest non-zero amount possible. Rejection should thus be an empty threat. However, Player 2 may reject the split if he deems it to be unfair. Player 2 can use his power to reject the split as leverage on Player 1 to be fair and make a significant transfer. This shows the power of social norms in codifying individual behavior. Ultimatum games played among people who belong to tight social groups such as small village communities typically find that offers of less than 30–40 percent will be rejected. High splits can be motivated by reputation, social status, inequity aversion, preference for fairness, empathy, and generosity. Higher stakes tend to increase preference for fairness.

Henrich *et al.* (2001) found that norms of fairness are more pervasive in communities where there are high pay-offs from cooperation (such as rice-producing communities with elaborate irrigation systems, as opposed to dispersed nomad societies). They also found that norms of fairness increase with the degree of market integration that creates experiences in dealing with strangers. In a follow-up study, Henrich *et al.* (2006) found that fairness is much more affected by community-level than by individual-level preferences, stressing the role of social norms in individual behavior toward fairness. Rejection of the split by Player 2 can be motivated by aversion to stinginess, unwillingness to accept injustice, and defense of honor in refusing what is perceived as an unfair offer. Adding costly punishments to a failure to share further reinforces distributive norms.

We conclude by observing that informal institutions are of considerable importance in the developing-country context, where formal institutions are typically incomplete and often dysfunctional. There are also many situations where informal institutions (such as the extended family, a ROSCA, or a self-help group) complement formal institutions (such as a courts-for-conflict resolution or commercial banks for access to credit). The performance of these informal institutions hinges on the individual preferences of participants and on the prevailing social norms. An important field of research is the identification of instruments that can crowd-in norms of altruism, trust and reciprocity, cooperation, and fairness that are expected to improve the development performance of informal institutions. Experimental games can help in this research, where much is left to be discovered.

CONCEPTS SEEN IN THIS CHAPTER

Excludable good, rival good
Five dimensions of property rights
Common Property Resource (CPR)
Open-access resource
Tragedy of the commons
Prisoner's dilemma (PD)
Chicken game
Assurance game
Multiple equilibria
Coordination problem
Folk theorem
Tit-for-tat game
Prisoner's dilemma with a manager
Determinants of cooperation
Olson's logic of collective action
Cooperation in spite of selfishness: Becker's "rotten kid" theorem
Generalized morality and the contagion game

Meta-punishment problem
Monitoring
Enforcement
Behavioral games
Dictator game
Trust game
Public-goods game
Ultimatum game

REVIEW QUESTIONS: MANAGEMENT OF CPR AND DETERMINANTS OF COOPERATION

1. Define the concepts of rival and excludable goods, and use them to classify goods as private, CPR, open-access, club, and public. Explain why a CPR is an "incomplete property right."
2. Identify the equilibrium in the extraction rate for an open-access resource and a CPR without cooperation. Why is there an individual incentive toward over-extraction? How can this create a tragedy of the commons?
3. Management of CPRs: why is there reason for pessimism? Explain and solve the prisoner's dilemma. Why does it lead to (D, D) as the dominant strategy?
4. Management of CPRs: how can there be ground for optimism even when there is no coopera-tion? Explain and solve the chicken game and the assurance game. Explain the folk theorem and the tit-for-tat strategy.
5. Determinants of cooperation: how can the introduction of rules (fines) change the outcome of the prisoner's dilemma? How can a community achieve cooperation in managing CPRs? Iden-tify for this the roles of: (1) well defined property rights and group membership, (2) positive expected gains from cooperation, (3) the capacity to observe and monitor the behavior of others, (4) the capacity to enforce rules, and (5) the time to learn to cooperate.

REFERENCES

Ashraf, Nava. 2009. "Spousal Control and Intra-Household Decision Making: An Experimental Study in the Philippines." *American Economic Review* 99(4): 1245–77.

Baland, Jean-Marie, and Jean-Philippe Platteau. 1996. *Halting Degradation of Natural Resources: Is There a Role for Rural Communities?* Cambridge: Cambridge University Press.

Baland, Jean-Marie, and Jean-Philippe Platteau. 1998. "Division of the Commons: A Partial Assessment of the New Institutional Economics of Land Rights."*American Journal of Agricultural Economics* 80(3): 644–50.

Bardhan, Pranab. 1984. *Land, Labor and Rural Poverty.* New York: Columbia University Press.

Becker, Gary. 1974. "A Theory of Social Interactions." *Journal of Political Economy* 82(6): 1063–93.

Bergstrom, Theodore. 1989. "A Fresh Look at the Rotten Kid Theorem." *Journal of Political Economy* 97(5): 1138–59.

Bernard, Tanguy, Alain de Janvry, and Elisabeth Sadoulet. 2010. "When Does Community Conservatism Constrain Village Organizations?" *Economic Development and Cultural Change* 58(4): 609–41.

Besley, Timothy. 1995. "Property Rights and Investment Incentives: Theory and Evidence from Ghana." *Journal of Political Economy* 103(5): 903–37.

Besley, Timothy, and Maitreesh Ghatak. 2010. "Property Rights and Economic Development." *Handbook of Development Economics* Vol. 5, 4525–95. Amsterdam: Elsevier.

Boucher, Steve, Michael Carter, and Catherine Guirkinger. 2008. "Risk Rationing and Wealth Effects in Credit Markets: Theory and Implications for Agricultural Development." *American Journal of Agricultural Economics* 90(2): 409–423.

Cárdenas, Juan Camilo, and Jeffey Carpenter. 2008. "Behavioral Development Economics: Lessons from Field Labs in the Developing World." *Journal of Development Studies* 44(3): 337–64.

Deininger, Klaus. 2003. "Land Markets in Developing and Transition Economies: Impact of Liberalization and Implications for Future Reform." *American Journal of Agricultural Economics* 85(5): 1217–22.

de Janvry, Alain, Kyle Emerick, Marco Gonzalez-Navarro, and Elisabeth Sadoulet. 2015. "Delinking Land Rights from Land Use: Certification and Migration in Mexico." *The American Economic Review* 105(10):3125–49.

De Soto, Hernando. 2000. *The Mystery of Capital: Why Capitalism Triumphs in the West and Fails Everywhere Else*. New York: Basic Books.

Fafchamps, Marcel. 1992. "Solidarity Networks in Pre-industrial Societies: Rational Peasants With a Moral Economy." *Economic Development and Cultural Change* 41(1): 147–76.

Field, Erica. 2007. "Entitled to Work: Urban Property Rights and Labor Supply in Peru." *Quarterly Journal of Economics* 122(4): 1561–602.

Finan, Frederico, and Laura Schechter. 2012. "Vote-Buying and Reciprocity." *Econometrica* 80(2): 863–81.

Gezon, Lisa. 1997. "Institutional Structure and the Effectiveness of Integrated Conservation and Development Projects: Case Study from Madagascar." *Human Organization* 56(4): 462–70.

Grief, Avner. 1994. "Cultural Beliefs and the Organization of Society: A Historical and Theoretical Reflection on Collectivist and Individualistic Societies." *Journal of Political Economy* 102(1): 912–50.

Hardin, Garrett. 1968. "Tragedy of the Commons." *Science* 162(December): 1243–48.

Hayami, Yujiro. 1988. "Elmhirst Memorial Lecture: Community, Market, and State." In A. Maunder and A. Valdés (eds.), *Agriculture and Governments in an Interdependent World*, 3–14. Dartmouth: Dartmouth Publishing Company.

Hayami, Yujiro. 1996. "The Peasant in Economic Modernization." *American Journal of Agricultural Economics* 78(5): 1157–67.

Hayami, Yujiro, and Masao Kikuchi. 1981. *Asian Village Economy at the Crossroads*. Baltimore: Johns Hopkins University Press.

Henrich, J., R. Boyd, S. Bowles, C. Camerer, E. Fehr, H. Gintis, and R. McElreath. 2001. "In Search of Homo Economics: Behavioral Experiments in 15 Small-scale Societies." *American Economic Review* 91(2): 73–8.

Henrich, J., R. McElreath, A. Barr, J. Ensminger, C. Barrett, A. Bolyanatz, J.C. Cárdenas, M. Gurven, E. Gwako, N. Henrich, C. Lesorogol, F. Marlowe, D. Tracer, and J. Ziker. 2006. "Costly Punishment across Human Societies." *Science* 312(5781): 1767–70.

Hirschman, Albert. 1970. *Exit, Voice, and Loyalty*. Cambridge, MA: Harvard University Press.

Hirschman, Albert. 1984. *Getting Ahead Collectively: Grassroots Experiences in Latin America*. New York: Pergamon Press.

Jacoby, Hanan, Guo Li, and Scott Rozelle. 2002. "Hazards of Expropriation: Tenure Insecurity and Investment in Rural China." *American Economic Review* 92(5): 1420–47.

Katz, Elizabeth. 2000. "Social Capital and Natural Capital: A Comparative Analysis of Land Tenure and Natural Resource Management in Guatemala." *Land Economics* 76(1): 114–32.

Lin, Justin. 1990. "Collectivization and China's Agricultural Crisis in 1959–1961." *Journal of Political Economy* 98(6): 1228–52.

List, John. 2007. "On the Interpretation of Giving in Dictator Games." *Journal of Political Economy* 115(3): 482–93.

Meinzen-Dick, Ruth, and Monica Di Gregorio. 2004. *Collective Action and Property Rights for Sustainable Development*. Washington, DC: International Food Policy Research Institute Brief 1.

Nugent, Jeffrey, and Nicolas Sanchez. 1999. "The Local Variability of Rainfall and Tribal Institutions: The Case of Sudan." *Journal of Economic Behavior and Organization* 39(3): 263–91.

Olson, Mancur. 1971. *The Logic of Collective Action: Public Goods and the Theory of Groups*. Cambridge, MA: Harvard University Press.

Ostrom, Elinor. 1990. *Governing the Commons: The Evolution of Institutions for Collective Action*. New York: Cambridge University Press.

Ostrom, Elinor. 1992. *Crafting Institutions for Self-Governing Irrigation Systems*. San Francisco: ICS Press.

Ostrom, Elinor. 2001. "The Puzzle of Counterproductive Property Rights Reforms: A Conceptual Analysis." In A. de Janvry, G. Gordillo, E. Sadoulet, and J.-P. Platteau (eds.), *Access to Land, Rural Poverty, and Public Action*, 129–50. Oxford: Oxford University Press.

Peterson, Wesley. 2009. *A Billion Dollars a Day: The Economics and Politics of Agricultural Subsidies*. New York: Wiley-Blackwell Publishing.

Platteau, Jean-Philippe. 2000. *Institutions, Social Norms, and Economic Development*. Amsterdam: Harwood Academic Publishers.

Platteau, Jean-Philippe, and Anita Abraham. 2002. "Participatory Development in the Presence of Endogenous Community Imperfections." *Journal of Development Studies* 32(2): 104–36.

Platteau, Jean-Philippe, and Erika Seki. 2000. "Coordination and Pooling Arrangements in Japanese Fisheries." In M. Aoki and Y. Hayami (eds.), *Market, Community, and Economic Development*. Oxford: Clarendon Press.

Schelling, Thomas. 1960. *The Strategy of Conflict*. Cambridge, MA: Harvard University Press.

Seabright, Paul. 1997. "Is Cooperation Habit-Forming?" In P. Dasgupta and K-G. Mäler (eds.), *The Environment and Emerging Development Issues*. Oxford: Clarendon Press.

Talhelm, T., X. Zhang, S. Oishi, C. Shimin, D. Duan, X. Lan, and S. Kitayama. 2014. "Large-scale Psychological Differences within China Explained by Rice versus Wheat Agriculture." *Science* 344(9 May): 603–8.

Wade, Robert. 1987. *Village Republics: Economic Conditions for Collective Action in South India*. Cambridge: Cambridge University Press.

Wilson, Paul, and Gary Thompson. 1993. "Common Property and Uncertainty: Compensating Coalitions by Mexico's Pastoral 'Ejidatarios'." *Economic Development and Cultural Change* 41(2): 299–318.

Wittfogel, Karl. 1957. *Oriental Despotism, A Comparative Study of Total Power*. New Haven, CT: Yale University Press.

World Bank. 2007. *World Development Report 2008: Agriculture for Development*. Washington, DC.

Wydick, Bruce. 2008. *Games in Economic Development*. New York: Cambridge University Press.

Human capital

Education and health

TAKE-HOME MESSAGES FOR CHAPTER 17

1. Health and education are both ends and means in development. Better health and education are sources of income and growth; and higher incomes induce more supply and more demand for health and education. Both health and education create large positive social externalities, and supporting services are largely public goods, resulting in under-investment coming from both the demand and the supply sides.

2. The demand for schooling by a household depends on the intrinsic value of schooling, the expected return from schooling, the direct cost and the opportunity cost of schooling, and the discount rate. Poor people tend to underinvest more in the schooling of their children as they tend to have a lower intrinsic value for education, liquidity constraints in meeting costs, and higher discount rates, contributing to the intergenerational transfer of poverty.

3. CCTs impose conditions on school attendance and health practices with the objective of reducing both current poverty through the transfers and future poverty through human-capital formation. These programs have been effective in increasing the demand for education among the poor by transforming the income effect of a transfer into a price effect on education.

4. The supply of health services is reduced by public underinvestment and weak intellectual property rights on pharmaceutical products that favor access to generics for global diseases, but lead to underinvestment in research into diseases specific to developing countries.

5. The demand for health services is reduced by the culture of poverty, liquidity constraints, high discount rates, coordination problems to confront externalities, misuse of pharmaceuticals, and strong information asymmetries. A general result is that there is low willingness among the poor to pay for health services, raising the issue of the use of subsidies to induce learning, either directly through learning-by-doing or indirectly through learning-from-others, usually trusted people in the same own social networks.

6. In spite of this, there are many opportunities for quick gains in health through simple interventions such as improved delivery of pharmaceuticals and local services that can have very large returns on development per dollar spent.

7. The low quality of services in health and education remains a major problem. It has been shown that it can be improved by using community workers and providing adequate incentives to providers.

WHY ARE EDUCATION AND HEALTH IMPORTANT FOR DEVELOPMENT?

Education and health/nutrition, which we called "basic needs" in characterizing the dimensions of development in Chapter 1, are both essential development outcomes and essential instruments for development: they are simultaneously ends and means. Because education and health are intrinsically valuable to individuals for their wellbeing, they are development objectives in themselves. For this reason, the Human Development Index gives salience not only to per capita income, but also to levels of achievement in education and health in characterizing a country's level of development. But education and health are also major sources of economic growth, a key dimension of development. This is because better education and health contribute to raising the productivity of labor and the quality of entrepreneurship, and hence the levels of wage and income. On the labor market, education serves as a signal for unobservable ability in helping employers select workers.

From a development-policy perspective, education and health pose special problems because of two important features. The first is that there are strong positive social externalities associated with individual education and health achievements. Your education will not only benefit you personally through access to better jobs, higher incomes, and a better partner, it will also benefit others as it helps generate more jobs, improve the human capital of your children, and create a better citizenship in political participation. If you are in better health, carrying fewer infectious diseases, you will reduce the risk of disease for others. Think, for example, of the de-worming of school children in Kenya; if some are not treated, they will reinfect the ones that were (Miguel and Kremer, 2004). Treatment should thus be applied at the school, not the individual level, to internalize the positive externalities of being treated. The same applies to vaccination against a communicable disease as it benefits not only the recipient but also others in his or her vicinity. As always when there are positive externalities, individual incentives to invest in the service are incomplete. As a result, everyone underinvests in education and health, requiring government intervention to compensate for market failure in the form of subsidies or free delivery of the service, especially in developing countries. The second feature is that many education and health services are public goods. This is because they are non-rival and non-excludable in their uses. This will be the case for a mosquito-eradication campaign to control malaria in a particular region. Here again, public goods tend to be under-provided as there is free-riding in assuming their cost: you would like everyone else to contribute, but preferably not you. Hence public intervention or effective collective action is needed for adequate provision.

This poses in a stark fashion the problems of education and health for development. They are both ends and means and thus fundamental to development. Yet there tends to be both private underinvestment in and public under-provision of these basic needs. Poor parents may in addition underinvest in child education and health because they have a low appreciation of the benefits of these investments from which they did not benefit themselves. Private underinvestment can also be due to liquidity constraints created in particular by capital-market failures and income shocks. In education, income shocks can induce parents to take children out of school because they need the child's labor this year or because they cannot afford to cover school costs. In health, income shocks can reduce child nutrition during the critical first 1,000 days of life, compromising future child health and development. In both cases, short-run shocks can have long-term consequences as irreversibilities are created: a child out of school for six months or a year may never return to school; a child undernourished in the womb or in the first three years of life may fall behind in physical and mental development and never catch up again, even with expensive remedial programs. Social-safety nets for health and education may thus be good public investments to prevent short-run shocks from having costly long-term consequences. Yet, here again, the public-good nature of these social-safety-net programs tends to result in under-provision.

We analyze in this chapter both the positive and normative aspects of education and health for development: why they are important and under-provided, and what could be done to improve the level, quality, and equity in the provision of these essential basic needs.

INDICATORS AND STATUS OF EDUCATION

Gross enrollment rate (GER)

The GER is the ratio of the number of children enrolled in a given school category (primary, secondary, or tertiary) to the number of children in the age group that officially corresponds to that level of schooling. For primary school, this would be children 6 to 11 years' old. The gross enrollment rate can be greater than 100 percent if children repeat grades and fall behind in their schooling relative to the official age for the category. A GER greater than 100 percent is thus not a good sign. As can be seen in Table 17.1, the GER for males is 105 percent in Sub-Saharan Africa, 110 percent in South Asia, and 118 percent in East Asia and the Pacific, compared to 101 percent in high-income OECD countries. Gross enrollment rates are only 8 percent for tertiary school in Sub-Saharan Africa, and 21 percent in South Asia, compared to 78 percent in high-income OECD countries. While enrollment rates have increased across the world, large gaps remain across regions and countries, and between rich and poor, rural and urban areas, and males and females (Orazem and King, 2008).

It is notable that there are huge disparities in educational outcomes across countries, genders, income levels, and rural/urban residence. This can be seen in Table 17.2 for some countries ranging from low- to middle-income and for men vs. women.

Primary-school enrollment ranges from 76 percent in Burkina Faso and 87 percent in Yemen to 115 percent in Colombia. Secondary-school enrollment ranges from 21 percent in Burkina Faso and 32 percent in Tanzania to 100 percent in Sri Lanka. At the secondary and tertiary levels, enrollment rises sharply with GDPpc. Gender disparities are large as well. In Yemen, primary-school enrollment is 96 percent

Table 17.1 *State of world education, 2012*

Regions	Gross school enrollment: males, primary (%)	Gross school enrollment: females, primary (%)	Gross school enrollment: secondary (%)	Gross school enrollment: tertiary (%)	Children out of school: primary (million)	Children out of school: primary (% of world total)
Sub-Saharan Africa	105	96	41	8	33	56
South Asia	110	111	63	21	10	17
East Asia and Pacific	118	116	85	31	7	12
Middle East and North Africa	112	106	81	34	1	2
Latin America and Caribbean	110	107	88	43	4	7
Europe and Central Asia	102	102	99	63	1	2
High-income OECD	101	101	100	78	3	4

Source: World Bank, World Development Indicators.

Table 17.2 *Percentage gross enrollment by countries and gender, 2010*

Country name	GDPpc 2005 US$	Gross school enrollment (%), 2010								
		Primary			Secondary			Tertiary		
		All	Female	Male	All	Female	Male	All	Female	Male
Ehtiopia	231	102	97	106	36	32	39	7	4	10
Tanzania	452	102	103	101	32	28	35	2	2	2
Burkina Faso	457	76	72	79	21	18	23	3	2	4
Yemen	910	87	78	96	44	34	54	10	7	15
India	1034	112	112	112	63	60	66	18	15	21
Sri Lanka	1610	99	99	99	100	102	99	15	20	11
China	2869	111	113	110	81	83	80	26	27	25
Colombia	3938	115	114	116	96	101	92	39	41	37
Mexico	7834	114	113	115	89	92	86	28	28	28
Korea, Rep.	20625	106	105	106	97	96	98	103	86	119

Source: World Bank, *World Development Indicators.*

for boys and 78 percent for girls. At the secondary level, it is 54 percent for boys and 34 percent for girls.

Net enrollment rates (NER)

The NER is the percentage of children of a given age group that are enrolled in a given school category (primary, secondary, or tertiary). NERs are always less than 100 percent. They can be represented in school-enrollment pyramids by age and proportion of the population in each level of schooling. Figure 17.1 shows the enrollment pyramid for Nepal in 2001. It reveals a large gender disparity, with 79 percent of seven-year-old boys enrolled in primary school, as opposed to 66 percent of girls. It also shows lags in educational achievements, with 42 percent of boys still in primary school at 14 years of age and only 33 percent in secondary school.

Out of school children (OOS) of primary-school age

OOS is the number of children of primary-school age not in school. The largest number is in Sub-Saharan Africa, where it reaches 33 million children and accounts for 56 percent of world OOS (Table 17.1).

Grade-completion rate

The grade-completion rate is the share of children who actually complete a certain grade level. The primary-completion rate (six years of schooling) in 2008 was 64 percent in Sub-Saharan Africa, 79 percent in South Asia, and 99 percent in East Asia and the Pacific.

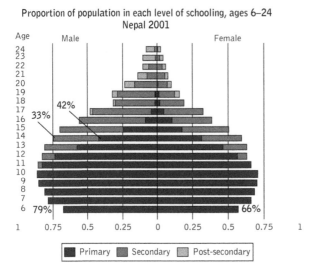

Figure 17.1 *School-enrollment pyramid for Nepal*

Source: World Bank, *Education Statistics Database.*

Grade-retention rate

The grade-retention rate is the percentage of children that do not pass into the next grade at the end of the school year. This can be due to dropping out of school during the year or failure to make the grade. In Northeast Brazil, for instance, grade retention in primary school is 25 percent, with a 15 percent dropout rate and a 12 percent grade-failure rate. The *Bolsa Família* program in Brazil is a CCT that pays mothers to keep their children at school in an attempt to reduce this high grade-retention rate. It was effective in reducing the dropout rate by half, a major success (de Janvry *et al.*, 2011).

Educational attainment

The educational attainment of a population is measured by completed years of schooling per adult in the population aged 25 years or older. It is four years in Sub-Saharan Africa, compared to six in Latin America and the Caribbean and more than ten in the high-income OECD countries. It can also be measured by the percentage distribution of the population across the following four categories of educational attainments: less than primary school, primary, secondary, and tertiary.

Learning achievements

Educational achievements depend on learning, not only on years of schooling. In the end, this is what matters. Measuring quality of schooling requires the use of standardized test procedures. One such test is the OECD's PISA (Program for International Student Assessment) in math, sciences, and reading. The highest-ranking countries in

2009 in math were Singapore, Hong Kong, South Korea, Taiwan, Finland, Switzerland, Japan, and Canada, with the US ranking 30th. But PISA does not cover most of the low-income countries. For these countries, comparative studies of learning achievements have to be interpreted with caution because scores are not easily comparable, based as they are on different tests and different samples (Caselli, 2005).

WHAT DETERMINES THE LEVELS OF SCHOOLING?

Education and growth

Based on cross-country panel data, there exists a strong correlation between a country's average level of schooling and GDPpc. The estimated equation is:

$$\ln Y_{it} = \alpha + \beta S_{it} + \varepsilon_{it},$$

where Y_{it} is GDPpc in country i and year t, and S_{it} the level of educational attainment in country i and year t. Because Y is measured in logs, the coefficient β measures the percentage increase in GDPpc due to an increase of one year in the average number of years of schooling. It is typically estimated at 0.04, implying that every one-year increase in the average level of schooling increases GDPpc by 4 percent (Barro, 1991). Both the level and the quality of education matter in explaining the contribution of education to growth, and quality is not taken into account in these estimations (Hanushek and Woessman, 2009). This implies that the role of education in accounting for differences in income growth may be understated. Schoellman (2012), for example, estimates that the role of quality may be as important as the role of years of schooling in explaining the contribution of education to differences in output per worker in the US. If this is the case, the contribution of education to growth could be double what years of education suggest.

Causality is also difficult to establish, as there is simultaneity between education and growth, with education affecting growth as much as growth affects education, and many omitted variables affecting both. However, the estimation of the relation between education and growth is highly stable across specifications and data sets, meaning we can be confident that education is likely to have a first-order-of-importance role in explaining growth.

Descriptive statistics show that there are large disparities in educational outcomes by country, income level, gender, and residence. With educational achievements being an important determinant of future income for individuals, understanding why there are such large disparities is the main question to be addressed here. The decision that parents make in sending their children to school has both supply- and demand-side determinants.

Supply side

On the supply side, both the quantity and the quality of schools and schooling services matter. Indicators of quantity are distance to school and hours of instruction.

599

Indicators of quality are teachers' attendance (19 percent of teachers are absent on a given day in Indian rural schools; see Chaudhury *et al.*, 2006), teachers' level of training, school resources (such as availability of textbooks and blackboards, and class size), and peer-quality effects (with important spillover effects across children, as analyzed by Akerlof and Kranton, 2002). Due to underinvestment and poor incentives for teachers, the supply side of schooling can be highly deficient, which may explain why motivation to go to school is so low. This was, for instance, evidenced for India in the PROBE report authored by De and Drèze (1999), which revealed the extent of teacher absenteeism and mistreatment of children in rural schools, creating strong incentives for children to miss or drop out of school.

Duflo (2001) analyzed the return from improving the supply side of schooling on years of educational achievement and on labor earnings 20 years later. She studied a large primary-school-construction program in Indonesia between 1974 and 1979 as the country was experiencing an oil boom. One primary school was added for every 500 children aged 5–14, resulting in the construction of 61,000 additional schools. School enrollment increased from 69 percent to 83 percent. Comparing the years of educational achievement and the wages earned 20 years later of children young enough (Y) to have benefited from the new schools with those of children too old (O) to have benefited, in areas with high (H) and low (L) school construction (a diff-in-diffs method), she found the following: years of education increased on average by 0.12 years for beneficiary (Y) children in high-program-intensity regions (H) (Figure 17.2a); and income earned on the labor market in 1995 was lower for younger (Y) than for older (O) children, but the gap was 3 percent less for children in high-program-intensity regions (H) than for children in low-program-intensity regions (L) (Figure 17.2b). These results are rigorous evidence that there were high educational pay-offs from investing in the supply side of primary education in Indonesia at that particular time, materializing in large income gains on the labor market 20 years later. For the sample of wage earners, gains in years of education were 0.26 years and the hourly wage gain 2.7 percent, implying a rate of return to schooling of 10 percent per year.

In another experiment on the supply side, Duflo *et al.* (2015) combine monitoring and incentives to reduce teacher absenteeism and assess what impact this has on students' educational achievements. Absenteeism is a serious problem in India among regular teachers as they have no reward for good performance. They have tenure, and their salary is not related to performance. The authors worked with para-teachers in non-formal education centers in Rajasthan. Monitoring consisted of asking teachers to take pictures of themselves with their students twice a day, in the morning and in the afternoon. The incentive payment was calculated as a function of attendance. The intervention was randomized with 57 treatment schools and 56 control schools. Results show that absenteeism fell by 21 percentage points relative to the control group, and that children's test scores increased by 0.17 standard deviations. The conclusion is that monitoring and incentives do work in improving teacher performance and that this has positive effects on learning. The huge problem of teacher absenteeism can be addressed with educational reforms that combine observability with monetary incentives.

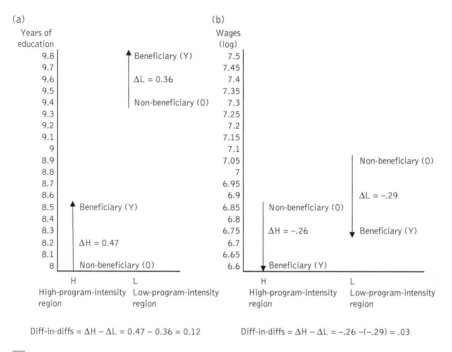

Figure 17.2 *Impact of primary-school-construction program in Indonesia on years of education (a) and wages (b)*

Source: based on Duflo, 2001.

Demand side

Schooling is a private decision, especially when a compulsory minimum number of years of school attendance is not enforced. A simple model that explains the demand for schooling by a student or their parents is as follows (Magruder, 2009). Since education is both an end and a means, it has both an intrinsic value and a value in enhancing future labor-market incomes. Assume that individuals live in two periods. In period 1, they decide whether they will go to school or work. In period 2, everyone works. People with schooling will earn w_1 when they work in period 2, while people without schooling earn w_0 in both periods, 1 and 2, with $w_1 > w_0$. Going to school has an intrinsic value equal to i. It has a double cost: a cash expenditure c to attend school and an opportunity cost w_0, which is the wage from work forgone by attending school. Future incomes are valued less than current incomes, as measured by a discount factor $\partial = 1/(1 + r) \leq 1$ (where r is the discount rate) so that the present value of future income w in period 2 is ∂w. An individual will then prefer to go to school in period 1 instead of working if benefits are larger than costs: namely,

$$i + \partial(w_1 - w_0) > c + w_0.$$

The private decision to go to school has five determinants.

601

Intrinsic value of schooling: i

Education has value as a consumption good: its so-called intrinsic value *i*. Parents derive pride from having their children at school and children can also be interested in school if it is of adequate quality. The value of *i* depends on parents' own education and on the child's ability; it also depends on the child's identification with others at school who have different levels of interest in studying, creating important peer effects (Akerlof and Kranton, 2002). The intrinsic value derived from school thus affects positively both the decision to stay in school (represented by *i* in the model) and performance at school (this could be added to the model by making w_1 a function of *i*).

Expected economic return from schooling: w_1-w_0

The return from schooling is the future gain in income in the labor market, $w_1 - w_0$. In developed countries, the income gain from schooling is estimated to be in the order of 9 percent additional income per year of school. In developing countries, returns from schooling can be even higher (Orazem and King, 2008). The private rate of return from education depends on:

1. The availability of employment opportunities for educated labor in the labor market. This could be represented, as in the Harris–Todaro model, by replacing w_1 by $w_1^* = Pw_1$, where P is the rate of employment. If there are differential employment opportunities for educated labor by gender, this will result in differential educational achievements between boys and girls. In places like the Philippines and Kerala, it is women who get a higher return from education, and investment in education will favor them. In Yemen, it is clearly the other way around, and investment in girls' education is correspondingly low.

2. Opportunities to use education for income generation, as reflected by w_1. A classical study by T.W. Schultz (1964) reasoned that education has little value in traditional agriculture, but that it does have value when there are opportunities to adopt new agricultural technologies that require skills. Foster and Rosenzweig (1996) confirmed this proposition for India, showing that there are high returns to education in agriculture where Green Revolution technology has become available, but not otherwise. Returns to education are typically higher in manufacturing and services than in agriculture. This is the reason why rural education is often principally a "passport" to successful migration to the urban economy. Because of migration, the return to rural education can be high even though it is low in rural areas. Figure 12.7 (in Chapter 12) shows the returns to rural education in Mexico by activity, with income earned in the rural community from agricultural wages, self-employment, and non-agricultural wages proving unresponsive to education, while migration offers a high return to education outside the rural community, especially for secondary and higher levels (Sadoulet *et al.*, 2001). Education is also an important signaling device of ability in the labor market, adding to its value for income generation (Spence, 1973). This is because the

employer assumes that schooling achievement is positively correlated with ability, even if the specific education acquired is not of direct value to the employer.

3. School quality affects $w_1 - w_0$ since what has been learned at school will determine the income achieved through education. The supply side of education (school quality) thus also influences parents' school choices, and children's willingness to go to school, as shown in the De and Drèze (1999) report. School quality typically depends on school resources, especially teacher quality (as shown, for example, by Lai *et al.*, 2011, for China). As we saw in the Duflo *et al.* (2011) study, teacher quality also depends on incentives for teachers to turn up for school and to exert effort in teaching. In many school systems, teachers are underpaid, and performance is not rewarded by level of pay. Designing incentive systems for teachers is thus a key determinant of school quality and of expected returns from education.

4. Returns to education typically depend on ownership of complementary assets A, such as your own health, parents' wealth, land ownership, and social capital (which is very important for referrals in finding a job). For this reason, better-off households will typically derive higher expected returns from education, with the result that schooling decisions may contribute to reinforcing existing inequalities, even if access to school is equal for all. This would be represented by replacing w_1 by $w_1^* = w_1(A)$ in our model, with w_1^* an increasing function of A. We saw in Figure 14.6 (in Chapter 14) that the impact of *Progresa* transfers on pupil continuing into secondary school increases with parents' own education. The de-worming study of Miguel and Kremer (2004) showed that improved health increases enrollment and educational achievements. School feeding programs are based on the presumption that better nutrition is fundamental for learning.

5. There may be considerable misinformation about the expected return from schooling, $w_1 - w_0$, especially among the poor, who tend to be surrounded by people either with low educational attainments, or who failed to take advantage of education. The latter is important as it can easily convey the wrong information, based on selection of failed cases, that education has no pay-off. Using an RCT in the Dominican Republic, Jensen (2010) showed that providing information about the return to secondary education (which was significantly above the perceived return in the case under study) increases the demand for education, resulting in 0.2 to 0.35 additional years of education over the next four years for those who were informed compared to those who were not.

6. At the primary and secondary level, it is parents who decide on child education. It may be that parents undervalue the benefits of education for their children, perhaps because they are uninformed themselves about the value of education. After all, they managed to survive in the context where they live, mainly rural, without education, and they do not see local people benefiting from education. Say that $m, 0 \leq m \leq 1$ is the parents' valuation of children's earnings through education. The school-decision equation is then:

$$i + m\partial \, (w_1 - w_0) > c + w_0.$$

If $m = 1$, parents value education as much as children will do. But there are many situations where $m < 1$ and parents consequently underinvest in education. Parents may also expect m to be less for girls than for boys, underinvesting in girls more than in boys. Jayachandran and Lleras-Muney (2009) showed that when parents learn that the return to investing in girls' education increases, in this case as a consequence of reduced maternal mortality, they respond positively by making a greater investment.

Direct costs of schooling: c

School is costly: there are tuition fees and costs of supplies such as uniforms and materials to be paid. Elimination of school fees in Uganda in 1997, and Kenya in 2003 led to a massive increase in school enrollment, with class size frequently doubling or increasing even more (Deininger, 2003). A major cost of going to secondary school in rural areas is transportation. In Duflo's (2001) study of primary-school construction in Indonesia, the densification of schools impacted on enrollment through reduced distance. In most countries, while rural communities of a sufficient size have a primary school, secondary schools are few and distant for most students. In Mexico, the transportation cost to go to secondary school for those without one in their community is typically \$1/day, which compares to income on the extreme poverty line, a prohibitive cost for many poor parents. Cost is thus affected by school availability, the supply side of schooling, discussed above. School vouchers and cash transfers conditional on school attendance are ways in which governments attempt to reduce the cost of schooling on parents, effectively lowering its price.

Opportunity cost of schooling: w_0

The opportunity cost of schooling is not working, forgoing w_0. In developing countries, child labor is valuable to the household. It can be used in agriculture on the home plot, to perform household chores, substituting for valuable parent time in producing z-goods (such as fetching water, collecting firewood, and taking care of younger siblings), or in the labor market in the many activities that legally or illegally employ children. The most notable are carpet weaving, working in brick factories, menial tasks in sweatshops, and herding animals for others. Child labor increases with parents' poverty, child-employment opportunities, and low enforcement of labor regulations (Basu, 1999). Lack of a credit market and of social-safety nets implies that child labor may be vital to the family for risk coping when there is an income shock. Indeed, well intentioned bans on child labor, as in India under the 1986 Child Labor Prohibition and Regulation Act prohibiting employment of children under the age of 14, may make things worse for households. The ban is thought to have induced a decline in child wages and, as a consequence, an increase in child labor, an outcome predicted by Basu and Van (1998). This is because poor families needing to make use of child labor to reach a subsistence constraint (Bharadwaj et al., 2013) have a backward-bending supply curve of child labor. The ban is thought, too, to have decreased children's school enrollment, and household welfare as measured by consumption expenditures, calorie intake, and asset holdings.

As Basu (2005) observed, well intentioned but poorly enforced legislation can have unintended perverse effects through the incentives it creates for behavior.

Time dimension: discount factor ∂

The cost of schooling (the direct cost c and the opportunity cost w_0) has to be paid now, while the benefits from education $(w_1 - w_0)$ will accrue later. The higher the discount rate r (i.e. the lower the discount factor ∂), the lower the present value of future benefits $\partial(w_1 - w_0)$ against which costs are compared. It is well known that poor people have a higher discount rate dictated by a higher cost of capital (they are more likely to be failed by capital markets due to lack of collateral) and the need to survive today. Hunger and the stress of poverty also contribute to raising discount rates (Haushofer *et al.*, 2013). There is also an intergenerational issue in that the cost of schooling is paid by parents, while the benefits go to children. Because the time dimension is so long (and capital markets fail the poor), parents cannot borrow now and have children repay the loan later with their educational benefits. Hence it is parents who decide the value of time and the present value of benefits from education; and they have shorter time horizons than their children, leading to underinvestment in education and excess child labor (Baland and Robinson, 2000). Gender differences in schooling may be affected by whether mothers or fathers make the education decisions. Duflo (2003) finds that pensions going to maternal grandmothers differentially increase the education of granddaughters in South Africa. There is also a great deal of evidence that children benefit from the education of women, as opposed to men. This includes more education for children (Currie and Moretti, 2003), improved family health, lower fertility, and gender empowerment. Orazem and King (2008) estimate the private return from schooling in 49 developing countries over the 1991–2004 period at 9.7 percent for females, higher than the value of 6.7 percent for males.

Figure 17.3 shows two earning profiles associated with primary- and secondary-school educational achievements that help us to understand the role of the discount rate in educational decisions. Child maintenance and education are costly, and increasingly so as a child ages and their education advances, implying negative earnings until work starts. Following primary education, work starts at ten years old; it starts at 16 following secondary education. Wage earning is flat with primary education at w_0 and higher with secondary at w_1. Calculating the internal rate of return (IRR, i.e. the discount rate that equates the present value of costs to the present value of benefits), we find with the data in Figure 17.3 that IRR is higher for primary education (30 percent) than for secondary education (20 percent). A poor household with a higher discount rate will choose primary over secondary education simply because it cannot afford the higher costs and cannot wait for the future higher returns. Say that the non-poor household has a discount rate of 10 percent (corresponding to the cost of borrowing from a commercial bank), while the poor household has a discount rate of 25 percent (corresponding to the cost of borrowing from a microfinance lender). For the poor household, the IIR for primary education (30 percent) is above its discount rate (25 percent) and primary education is affordable; but it cannot afford secondary

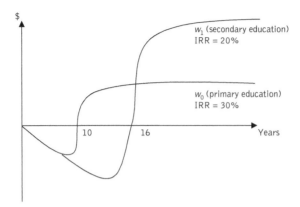

Figure 17.3 *Earning profiles by level of education*

education because the IRR is 20 percent, while the discount rate is 25 percent. For the non-poor, by contrast, secondary education is affordable as the IRR (20 percent) is above the discount rate (10 percent).

Note that a household with a longer life expectancy will benefit more from secondary over primary education. Health reforms that extend life expectancy will consequently increase the return from education and raise the optimum levels of investment in education (Jayachandran and Lleras-Muney, 2009).

Empirical validations of the model

Empirical studies have validated the negative impact on education of raising the opportunity cost of education w_0, and the positive impact on education of raising the return to education w_1.

Atkin (2012) studied the impact on schooling of the growth of low-skill employment in export manufacturing in Mexico over the period 1986–2000, which spans the introduction of NAFTA in 1994 and expansion throughout the country of the *maquila* sector. He used a roll-out design of the timing of factory openings across municipalities to measure impact on schooling. Identification was achieved by comparing the school attainments of cohorts of youths within a municipality who reached their key school-leaving age at the time of substantial factory openings with the school attainments of slightly younger and slightly older cohorts for whom this was not the case. Exogeneity of the roll-out was based on the argument that the opening, closing, expansion, or contraction of large firms in a municipality is associated with fixed costs, not with changes in the labor supply of a single cohort of youths. Two thirds of the local employment effect was created by these large firms. Results showed that raising the opportunity cost of schooling through the greater opportunity of wage earning in low-skill manufacturing employment (i.e. raising w_0) induced more dropouts. Specifically, Atkin found that for every 20 new jobs, one student dropped out of school at grade 9 rather than continuing on through grade 12.

This result can be contrasted with the impact on education of increased employment opportunities in high-skill jobs. In India, Munshi and Rosenzweig (2006) showed that creation of employment opportunities in IT service industries, raising the return to education w_1, increased educational achievements. Similarly, Oster and Steinberg (2013) found that local employment opportunities at call centers in India prompted more school enrollment, particularly in English-language schools. Finally, Atkin (2012) found that when job creation was in high-skill manufacturing, educational acquisition by Mexican youth increased.

Social externalities and underinvestment

The private decision to invest in education is always short of the social optimum because of the strong positive externalities that education generates. This includes such benefits for others as creating jobs, a better-functioning democracy, less crime, and better childcare with intergenerational benefits. To reconcile private and social optimum levels of education, either educational subsidies need to be transferred, as, for example, through CCTs, fellowships, or subsidized student loans, or the cost of education should be reduced, as, for example, through public education. Subsidies to education can thus be efficient, directed at overcoming an important market failure.

RETURN TO EDUCATION

Estimating the return to education

Returns to education are typically estimated econometrically using a methodology proposed by Mincer (1974). It consists in estimating a wage (w) equation for an individual i such as:

$$\ln(w_i) = \alpha + \beta(\textit{Years of schooling}_i) + \gamma(\textit{Years of experience}_i) + \varepsilon_i.$$

β measures the return to education: namely, the percentage increase in wage associated with one more year of schooling. The difficulty in estimating this equation is the endogeneity of the schooling decision that can be affected by omitted variables such as skills and ambitions that also affect the wage achievement. Some of these omitted variables are unobservable individual and household characteristics—not an easy problem to solve. This creates an upward bias in the estimated return to schooling β. As with impact analysis, this requires situations where there have been exogenous shifts in years of schooling that only affected a subset of the population and not another, which can serve as control, giving us a LATE for the population affected by the shift. The estimated return to schooling is usually in the range 0.05 to 0.15, meaning that one additional year of schooling induces a 5 to 15 percent gain in wage. In the Duflo (2001) study reviewed above, we saw that one extra year of education increased wage earnings in Indonesia, in a period of rapid economic growth, by 10 percent. In a review of papers on return to education, Psacharopoulos (1994) finds that the return to education is typically higher for girls than boys. He also finds that primary education exhibits the highest social return among all levels of education in all regions of the world. In a more recent collection of estimates of the Mincerian β coefficient for years of schooling across countries, Psacharopoulos and Patrinos (2002) find a world average of 9.7 percent, with 7.5 percent for the OECD countries, 9.9 percent for Asia, 11.7 percent for Sub-Saharan Africa, and 12 percent for Latin America and the Caribbean. The return to education is highest for low-income countries (10.9 percent), followed by middle-income countries (10.9 percent), and high-income countries (7.4 percent).

There are also indications that schooling improves health status—for example, as measured by life expectancy. Lleras-Muney (2005) uses as a natural experiment differences in the year of introduction of compulsory schooling laws across states in the US in the 1915–39 period. Introduction of these laws is a good predictor of completed education for individuals. At the same time, compulsory laws are not expected to influence health outcomes except through their impact on years of completed education. Instrumental variable results show that in 1960 an additional year of education increased life expectancy at age 35 by as much as 1.7 years.

Currie and Moretti (2003) find that higher maternal education improves infant health. They control for endogeneity of education by instrumenting a mother's education by the availability of colleges in her county of residence at 17 years old. They show that the channels through which a mother's education increases infant health are an increase in the probability that a new mother is married (as opposed to unwed), an increase in the likelihood of marrying a higher-earning man, an increased use of pre-natal care, and better health behavior such as reduced smoking during pregnancy.

Education has also been shown to reduce a woman's fertility rate. This is because education increases the opportunity cost of a woman's time and induces a trade-off between quantity and quality of children in favor of the latter. Using panel data at the district level for India, Drèze and Murthi (2001) find that a 10-percentage-point increase in female literacy is associated with an expected decline in the total fertility rate by 0.2 children.

One way of partially controlling for omitted variable biases in estimating the return to education is to use data on the educational achievement of twins. This allows us to control for common unobservable household characteristics. Li *et al.* (2012) do this for China. Results that do not control for the twin effect (and hence include omitted household characteristics among the determinants of earnings) find that one additional year of schooling increases an individual's earnings by 8.4 percent. Controlling for the twin effect, this return is reduced to 3.8 percent. This still leaves unobserved individual characteristics that contribute to overestimating the return to education.

Policy instruments to enhance the return from investment in education

There are numerous empirical studies of the determinants of educational achievement and of returns from education in terms of higher future incomes. The typical estimated equation is an education production function where test score (H) for student i in school j is a function of student characteristics (e.g. the student's family background such as income and parents' education), peer characteristics (e.g. the socio-economic background of other students), and school characteristics (e.g. the student–teacher ratio, teacher qualifications, and teacher salaries):

$$H_{ij} = \alpha + \beta(\textit{Student characteristics}_{ij}) + \gamma(\textit{Peer characteristics}_{ij}) + \delta(\textit{School characteristics}_j) + \varepsilon_{ij}.$$

Here again, there are issues of endogeneity since students may choose the school they attend, requiring RCTs or natural experiments such as a lottery for school assignment under open-enrollment programs.

On the supply side (school and peer characteristics), there are some notable results. In her study of school construction in Indonesia, Duflo (2001) observed positive effects on educational achievements of greater proximity to a primary school. Using class-size discontinuity imposed by a rule on maximum class size in Israel, Angrist and Lavy (1999) find that a smaller class size improves average reading scores. Using an RCT approach, Duflo *et al.* (2011) find that student tracking in primary schools in Kenya, by regrouping students in classes organized by levels of performance, improves test scores. This is attributed to the fact that tracking allows teachers to better tailor their instruction to the level of achievement of students in their class. Using RCTs, Banerjee *et al.* (2007) analyze the impacts of remedial teaching for students lagging in reading and numeracy skills and of computer-assisted learning for math. They find that both have positive short-run effects on test scores but small or no effects one year after the programs ended. Finally, Muralidharan and Sundararaman (2011) use an RCT approach to assess the relative effectiveness of spending more on class inputs and spending the same amount on improved teacher incentives to reduce absenteeism and induce effort. Teacher incentives were provided in the form of a bonus payment based on the average improvement of their students' test scores in math and languages. The program was implemented in 300 government-run rural primary schools in Andhra Pradesh, India. They find that individual teacher incentives are nearly three times more effective than an equal monetary value of class inputs. They also find positive spillover effects on test scores in non-incentivized subjects such as science and social studies.

On the demand side (student and family characteristics), the most notable results are the role of CTs (Ecuador), CCTs (Mexico, Brazil), merit awards for performance at school (Kremer *et al.* (2009) for Kenya, using an RCT in giving merit awards to students), vouchers giving parents a choice of school (Lai *et al.* (2011) for China, using admissions with random drawing of school assignment based on expressed preferences), food-for-school programs (Bangladesh), school feeding programs (Kenya), and complementary health programs (India).

CCT PROGRAMS: OPORTUNIDADES AS A CASE STUDY

Most school interventions focus on the supply side of education such as more schools, smaller classes, and better-trained teachers. Mexico's *Progresa* program (renamed *Oportunidades* in 2000 and *Prospera* in 2014) is a demand-side intervention that pays poor rural mothers to send their children to school (without missing more than three days per month, as certified by the teacher) and meet health requirements (vaccinations and regular health check-ups). The cash transfer is thus conditional on behavior. The stipend is larger for girls and for secondary school, reaching two thirds of a child's wage for that category. The design of this program is consistent with the predictions of the behavioral model developed above:

- The opportunity cost of schooling is highest for secondary-school children (w_0 is larger), hence transfers increase with the grade.
- Poor people are more constrained by school costs c and have higher discount rates r, hence the program targets households below the poverty line.
- The benefits of schooling ($w_1 - w_0$) tend to be lower in rural areas, hence the program is targeted on rural areas to induce more schooling.
- Parents may value boys' education over girls' (either because of boy preference or because boys are more likely to participate in the formal-sector labor force), hence a larger transfer is offered to girls to induce parents to send them to school just as they would boys.

Oportunidades has become a \$3.2 billion/year program that covers 25 percent of the Mexican population. The conditionality means that the cash transfer is tied to the demand for school services, thus creating a school-price effect (as opposed to an unconditional income effect). The program is highly innovative and has been extensively studied, in part because it involved a pilot study on 506 communities with randomized incorporation of 320 communities in the first wave of its roll out and 186 communities in the last wave, allowing the latter to serve as controls.

Here are some of the results from these evaluations for the rural population.

- The *main effect* of the transfer is not to increase primary-school attendance (which is already 98 percent without the transfer), but to significantly increase enrollment in secondary school (Figure 17.4). The percentage of children who enrolled in the first year of secondary school rose from 67 percent in the control villages to 76 percent in the *Progresa* villages, a 14 percent gain.
- The impact of the cash transfer on schooling is *heterogeneous* across the population. We observe a stronger effect with closeness to school (lower c), the educational level of parents (higher i), and the job experience of the father in valuing education (low response among farm workers for whom education has little relevance, and hence have a low expected $w_1 - w_0$ gain for their children).
- The *rate of return* to money spent on the program has been estimated to be 8 percent per year, making it competitive with other social investments (Schultz, 2004). An important achievement of the program is that, thanks to the transfers, the educational achievement of poor beneficiaries rose to the same level as that of the non-poor. The program has also been effective in keeping children at school when their parents are hit by an income shock (de Janvry *et al.*, 2006b). The transfers prevent parents from using child labor as an instrument for risk coping as they would lose the benefit from the program precisely when they need it most. The program is thus effective in *avoiding the irreversibilities* created by an income shock as children would be pulled out of school were it not for the transfer.

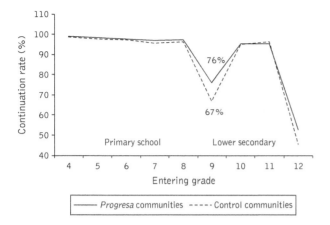

Figure 17.4 *School continuation rates in poor rural Mexico. Dotted line: no* Progresa *(control village); solid line:* Progresa *(treatment village)*

Source: de Janvry and Sadoulet, 2006a.

- A puzzling outcome of the program is that, as can be seen in Figure 17.4, 24 percent of the children who could benefit from the transfer and enter secondary school still do not do so. Why is this the case? It is likely that this has to do with the motivation to study (expected returns) and the quality of schools. This stresses the obvious fact that the demand side of education requires more than a cash transfer, but also expectations that the education received will result in *higher incomes*. It also stresses the fact that the *supply side* of schooling remains problematic and in need of attention. The Mexican government has recently been addressing these two issues by helping Oportunidades graduates to find a job, and investing in improving the quality of schools, in particular through greater parent participation in school management (PARE: *Programa para Abatir el Rezago Educativo*).

- CCT programs are quite expensive, so it is important to learn how to make them *more cost effective*. Two obvious lessons are: (1) paying mothers to do what they already do, e.g. send their children to primary school, is not necessary (it is more important to focus resources on what the transfer can do to change their behavior so they send their children to secondary school); and (2) cost savings can be achieved by targeting the transfers at children at risk of not going to school, such as those far away from a secondary school (with high transportation costs), and at those with parents who are not educated and have little appreciation for the expected benefits of schooling for their children.

- *To condition or not to condition?* There has been a huge debate as to whether conditions should be imposed on the poor when they are already struggling with survival: is it better (and more ethical) to offer CCTs or simple CTs? It could be that a CT, with a good understanding by parents that the transfer is to help children go to school, is enough. This is the flypaper effect, whereby the money transferred becomes non-fungible if it is recognized as having a specific function. This requires effective framing of the transfer in terms of an expected purpose.

611

Bono Solidario in Ecuador, a CT intended to keep children at school, apparently achieved this result (Fiszbein and Schady, 2009). In general, however, imposing conditionality has been considered much more effective for achieving the educational objective of the transfer. This is because the condition transforms the transfer from a general income effect into a specific price effect for education. There are several reasons why imposition of a constraint may be justified, in spite of the fact that it infringes on individual freedoms:

1. Poor parents *may not be fully informed* about the benefits of education for their children, in part because they are not educated themselves, in part because they live in agrarian communities where the return to education is very low, and they ignore the higher urban returns that could benefit their children through migration.
2. Parents *may not decide optimally* for their children because they have higher discount rates than them, the mother does not have sufficient bargaining power to represent her child's interest in household resource allocation, and there is social conservatism by parents who are afraid that their children will abandon them if they are educated.
3. Parents *underinvest in education* because there are positive externalities that they do not internalize. In this case, the conditionality reconciles private and social optima in the use of public transfers. From a social standpoint, it may also be cheaper to invest in education today than in welfare protection in the future.

INDICATORS AND STATUS OF HEALTH

Health indicators

Health is a form of human capital that is complex because it is multidimensional and full of unknowns. The definition of good health is itself controversial. The World Health Organization (2015) defines it as "a state of complete physical, mental, and social well-being and not merely the absence of disease and infirmity." It emphasizes not only a long life, but also quality of life. For this reason, multiple indicators are needed to characterize the health status of a population, and they are difficult to measure with accuracy (Strauss and Thomas, 2008). Health indicators include the following.

Life expectancy at birth

This is the most commonly used indicator of the overall health status of a population. It differs greatly across regions and countries. While there had been no gain over the 1985–2005 period in Sub-Saharan Africa, with life expectancy remaining at only 50 years, it rose to 56 over the 2005–12 period (Table 17.3). It is still far short of achievements in other regions, with life expectancy reaching 75 in East Asia and the Pacific and in Latin America and the Caribbean. Life expectancy at birth has fallen in a number of Sub-Saharan Africa countries due to the HIV/AIDS pandemic. In South Africa, it rose from 49 years in 1960 to 62 in 1990, to fall to 52 in 2005 and 56 in

2012. In Zambia, it rose from 45 in 1960 to 51 in 1980, to fall to 41 in 1956 and 57 in 2012. This indicator falls short of the WTO definition of health as it does not measure the level of wellbeing achieved during these years, unlike the burden-of-disease indicator, discussed below.

Infant mortality rate

This is a good indicator of health status as it characterizes the population most at risk of ill health, and is quite responsive to changes in health conditions. Significant progress was made over the 1985–2012 period, but rates remain high in Sub-Saharan Africa, where 6.4 in 100 infants die at birth, a rate 13 times higher than in high-income OECD countries (Table 17.3).

Burden of disease

The burden of disease attempts to measure the health status of a population by combining life expectancy with quality of life. It measures years of "good" life lost due to both premature death and disability (Figure 17.5). Health-adjusted life expectancy (HALE) is equal to the ideal life expectancy minus the years lost due to premature death and disability. Each disability is given a score that curtails years lived into a disability-adjusted life year (DALY). The global burden of disease in a population is the sum of the DALYs. The burden of disease differs between poor and rich nations. In the developing world, two thirds of the DALYs lost are due to premature deaths and the other third to disabilities, while it is the reverse in the rich countries. Causes of death also differ: communicable diseases (such as HIV/AIDS, diarrhea, tuberculosis, and malaria) account for 36 percent of deaths in poor countries and only 7 percent in rich ones; non-communicable diseases (such as cardiovascular, malignant, respiratory, digestive, and diabetes) account for 87 percent of deaths in rich countries and 54 percent in poor ones.

Table 17.3 *State of world health in 1985, 2005, and 2012*

Regions	Life expectancy at birth, total Years			Mortality rate, infant Per 1,000 live births		
	1985	2005	2012	1985	2005	2012
Sub-Saharan Africa	50	50	56	111	95	64
South Asia	56	64	67	101	63	47
East Asia and Pacific	66	71	75	45	25	16
Middle East and North Africa	61	69	72	73	35	20
Latin America and Caribbean	67	73	75	52	23	16
Europe and Central Asia	68	69	77	45	24	10
High income OECD	75	79	79	9	5	5

Source: World Bank, *World Development Indicators.*

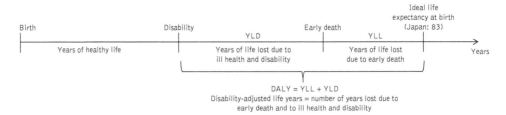

Figure 17.5 *Global burden of disease measured as DALY: disability-adjusted life years (from Chapter 1)*

Hunger and malnutrition

Malnutrition can be due to insufficient calorie consumption or to missing micronutrients in the local diet. Several indicators are used to measure malnutrition.

1. *Daily calorie intake.* This is based on information on consumption from memory or diaries. Daily intakes can vary widely from day to day without consequences for health or behavior. However, average daily calorie intake over a week or a month is a meaningful indicator of nutritional status.
2. *Micronutrient deficiencies.* These can be established by blood tests to measure micronutrients deficiencies in iron (anemia), zinc (decreased immunity), and vitamin A (resistance to infections, vision troubles). Because micronutrient deficiencies are hard to diagnose, they are referred to as hidden hunger. They are estimated to kill 1 million children under the age of five each year (see Global Alliance for Improved Nutrition, GAIN, online).
3. *Anthropometrics measures* of malnutrition are given by the *z*-scores for stunting and wasting (see Chapter 1). Stunting: height-for-age ratio, is an indicator of long-term health that reflects early malnutrition. Wasting: weight-for-height ratio, is an indicator of current nutritional status, rapidly responsive to change.
4. *Body-mass index* (BMI). It is the ratio of weight (in kilograms) to the square of height (in meters). It is easy to measure in surveys and is a widely used indicator of health status for adults. Individuals can be categorized by their BMI into the following categories: underweight < 18.5, normal 18.5 to 25, overweight 25 to 30, and obese > 30. An alternative measure is the BMI Prime ratio, measured as the actual BMI divided by 25, the upper limit BMI for a non–obese person. Obese people thus have a BMI Prime ratio above 1. Obesity is frequently associated with hypertension, diabetes, coronary heart disease, and stroke, health conditions increasingly associated with poverty in developing countries. However, the relation between BMI and any health condition is only very weakly established. Thus while easy to measure, it is a poor predictor of health status.

Self-reported health and morbidity

Morbidity is the incidence of ill health. It can be characterized by self-reported illnesses such as fevers, diarrhea, and respiratory problems, and by reporting activities of daily living (ADLs) such as "can walk a certain distance," "can lift a certain weight," "can sweep the floor," etc. Self-reporting of symptoms is, however, strongly biased as different people perceive health differently. In particular, richer individuals tend to rate their symptoms as more serious than poor people who are used and resigned to being in ill health (Strauss and Thomas, 2008). People who lose their jobs and become poor may exaggerate symptoms compared to equally poor people who have never been better off.

Major health issues in developing countries

While important progress has been made, indicators of health show the immensity of the health deficiencies to be addressed. The main issues that need attention are:

- *Hunger and malnutrition.* An estimated 791 million people were undernourished (below the minimum level of daily calorie intake, also called in chronic hunger) worldwide in 2013, showing a modest decline from 1 billion in 1990. Hunger affects one in every six people in LDCs, one in three in Sub-Saharan Africa, and two in three in the poorest countries such as Burundi. Hunger affects children disproportionately, with 26 percent undernourished in LDCs, 28 percent in Africa, 48 percent in South Asia, and 50 percent in Guatemala. One third of deaths of children under the age of 5 are due to child and maternal malnutrition (3.4 million/year). About 6 million children die of hunger-related causes every year— 16,000 per day—of which 2 million are in India. Worldwide, hunger is the largest killer and it has not been given the attention it deserves (Gross and Webb, 2006). There are irreversible consequences for physical and mental development associated with nutritional deficits in the first two years of life.

   As we saw in Figure 2.9 (in Chapter 2), it is notable that while the number of extreme poor (US$1/day) has fallen sharply, the number of hungry has declined only modestly. This may be due to mismeasurement as poverty is estimated from household surveys, while the number of hungry in a country is measured by the UN Food and Agriculture Organization (FAO) through a formula that deducts the aggregate food deficit in a country from production, trade, and consumption data. But it indicates that hunger is a complex phenomenon, much harder to attack than poverty, which can be addressed through cash transfers. Brazil has been successful at reducing not only poverty but also hunger because it has attacked the latter through a comprehensive program called Zero Hunger. Few countries have been able to organize such complex programs.
- *Malaria.* At least 1 million deaths occur every year due to malaria, mainly children. About 60 percent of the cases of malaria worldwide and more than 80 percent of the malaria deaths occur in Sub-Saharan Africa.
- *HIV/AIDS.* In spite of progress, the problem is of extraordinary magnitude. 35 million people lived with HIV/AIDS in 2012, of whom 70 percent are in Sub-Saharan Africa, and this number is still increasing, up from 30 million in 2001. Of the 35 million infected, 9.7 million received life-extending drugs in 2012, a 20 percent increase over 2011. 1.6 million people died of AIDS in 2012, down from 2.3 million in 2005. 2.4 million people were newly infected in

2012, down from 3.4 million in 2001. A total of more than 25 million people have died of AIDS since 1981. Africa has 11.6 million AIDS orphans. The percentage of the population with HIV/AIDS aged 15 to 49 in 2011 was 13.1 percent for males and 22.5 percent for females in South Africa, reaching 21 percent and 30 percent in Botswana and Swaziland respectively (Population Reference Bureau, www.prb.org).

■ *Diarrhea.* 1.8 million people die of diarrhea every year, mainly children. 707 million of deaths from diarrhea are in Sub-Saharan Africa and 604 million in South Asia. 17 percent of the 10 million children who die every year under the age of five do so from diarrhea.

■ *Tuberculosis.* 1.6 million people die from tuberculosis every year, of whom 544 million are in Sub-Saharan Africa and 512 million in South Asia.

WHAT DETERMINES HEALTH ACHIEVEMENTS?

Determinants of health are found on both the supply and the demand sides of health services. The supply side is linked to public goods and policy, while the demand side is linked to income and poverty.

Supply-side determinants

Under-provision and low quality of health services

There is a tendency for under-provision of health services due to their public-goods nature and large positive externalities, making markets fail. This is exacerbated in poor countries by weak fiscal resources and low availability and quality of medical personnel. The main healthcare supply problems in developing countries are: (1) the difficulty of inducing qualified doctors and health personnel to work in public clinics and health centers, and (2) the difficulty of targeting the poor for the free delivery of health services.

In a survey of health facilities in rural Rajasthan, Banerjee *et al.* (2004) found that 45 percent of medical personnel were absent from their posts at a particular time and that 41 percent of those who call themselves doctors did not have a medical degree. It is also important to remember that favorable health outcomes require participation of both the provider and the patient (Leonard, 2003). It is the patient who must seek assistance, choose a hospital and a doctor, and comply with requirements in implementing the treatment. Because medical treatments are incompletely understood by patients, in particular when illiteracy prevents them from reading prescriptions, there is an important role for providers to proactively engage in service delivery and in preventive measures. This was well understood by Paul Farmer, a medical anthropologist at Harvard University, who organized through his NGO, Partners In Health (PIH), a system of "barefoot nurses," or *accompagnateurs*, in Haiti to help patients comply with the discipline of taking medicines such as antibiotics and HIV antiretroviral pills (Kidder, 2004). His focus was on the delivery and use of drugs, not only on their availability. And because asymmetrical information can invite opportunistic behavior by providers (over-medication when the provider is on a percentage deal with the pharmaceutical company, as is frequently the case—for example, in the "Avon ladies" model), it is important for the state to regulate (i.e. license and monitor) health providers in order to protect patients. The high frequency of "quacks" among health personnel in rural India suggests that state capacity to regulate the provision of health services and protect patients from abuse can be highly deficient.

Constraints on the development of pharmaceuticals for LDC-specific diseases

There is a deficit of private investment in research on diseases specific to poor/ tropical countries such as malaria, tuberculosis, and AIDS (a vaccine for which would be better adapted to developing countries than HIV antiretroviral (ARV) treatments, which are expensive and hard to administer). Lack of investment is due to:

- *Small markets*, even when there may be large populations in need. This is because poverty shrinks effective demand. Because there are large economies of scale in pharmaceutical research, small markets do not provide adequate incentives for investment.
- *Lack of intellectual property rights* (IPR) and lack of enforcement of IPR in developing countries. India, for instance, does not enforce IPR on pharmaceuticals that can be copied cheaply as generics. Lack of IPR protection implies low private returns to investment in research on LDC-specific diseases. Pharmaceutical products are also widely counterfeited, creating competition from fakes at an eventually huge cost to human life.
- *Time inconsistency for governments* in enforcing IPR. The cost of developing a new drug is very high, but the drug has a very low marginal cost once it has been developed. It is consequently difficult for governments to credibly commit to enforcing IPR once the drug has been developed and there will be strong humanitarian and political pressures to provide access to the drug at low cost.

Availability of pharmaceuticals for global diseases

For diseases that are not specific to developing countries—for example, diabetes, cardiovascular diseases, cancer, and HIV antiretroviral treatments—private research finds profitable large markets in MDCs protected by IPR. Private pharmaceutical companies have an incentive to invest huge sums of money in research on new drugs for these markets. How could access to these drugs be granted to the poor in developing countries? An attractive possibility proposed by Jean Lanjouw (2005) would be to segment the world market between a high-price MDC market with patent protection and a low-price LDC market with no patent protection and access to generics. The difficulty is enforcing market segmentation without an international agreement and a regulatory facility, neither of which is in place. Private pharmaceutical companies are under pressure to allow the production of generics in developing countries due to the human sufferings associated with the lack of access to and the high cost of drugs. This is the case with antiretroviral treatment in Sub-Saharan Africa, which has

25 million out of a world total of 39 million people infected with HIV. Reputation effects for pharmaceutical companies operating in MDC markets can induce them to make concessions in developing-country markets (as, for example, in Brazil for antiretroviral drugs) for as long as they can keep markets separate. This is important for new diseases such as HIV/AIDS that require new drugs. For older diseases, many generic drugs are available once patents have expired, and their effectiveness may not be that different from drugs currently under patent protection if counterfeits can be kept under control.

Demand-side determinants

Income effects: poverty

Many studies have shown that the main determinant of effective demand for healthcare is income level. Calorie intake increases with income. Subramanian and Deaton (1996) show that the income elasticity of calorie consumption decreases slowly with income in rural India, starting from 0.6 at low levels of per capita expenditures and falling to 0.4 at high levels of expenditures. There has long been controversy as to why the income elasticity of demand for calories is not closer to one at low levels of income where malnutrition is extensive (Strauss and Thomas, 1998). An elasticity of less than one suggests that even the poor prefer to increase the quality of food as opposed to calorie intake when income rises.

An important result regarding income effects is that money in the hands of a mother or a grandmother is more effective at improving the health status of children than in the hands of a father or grandfather. A natural experiment to measure this differential effect was provided by the introduction of a non-contributory pension fund in South Africa in the early 1990s. Eighty percent of women over the age of 60 and 77 percent of men over 65 received this transfer. More than 25 percent of children under the age of five live in a household with a pension recipient. Duflo (2003) analyzed the impact of this transfer on child nutrition using the weight-for-height ratio as it responds quickly to a change in nutrition. The identification strategy was to use a regression discontinuity design around the cut-off age, within the population eligible for the pension. Children living with a pension recipient are different from the average child as they tend to be relatively disadvantaged; however, they are comparable on the two sides of the discontinuity. Result shows that pensions received by women increased the weight of girls by 1.19 standard deviations, with no impact on the nutritional status of boys. Pensions received by men had no impact on the health status of children of either gender.

A mother's empowerment through greater control over household income, which increases her bargaining power within the household, can thus be a powerful instrument in improving child health. It is the reason why CCTs that seek to improve child welfare have channeled the cash through the mother.

Price effects

As for other goods, the demand for health products is affected by not only income, but also price. A specific feature of demand for health products, however, is that consumers typically have difficulty assessing the expected benefits. As a consequence, these health products may be very price sensitive until they are better understood.

To explore this idea, Cohen and Dupas (2010) analyze whether price subsidies to anti-malarial insecticide-treated bed nets (ITN) has a large impact on demand. They conduct an RCT in Kenya randomizing the price at which ITNs are offered to pregnant women across pre-natal clinics. They find that demand for ITNs has a high price elasticity of demand, meaning that a small decline in price will induce a large increase in uptake. Conversely, even charging a small price, i.e. cost sharing, induces a large drop in demand: reducing the subsidy from 100 percent to 90 percent induces a 60-percentage-point drop in demand. An explanation is that as people do not know much about what the benefits from ITNs are, they are willing to acquire them if they do not cost anything, but are discouraged by even a small cost. From a health-policy perspective, the expectation is that the short-term subsidy will induce learning about the value of ITN, and induce longer-term WTP. In support of this, they also find that subsidies do not induce lesser use of the ITN (a phenomenon referred to as salience, whereby you may pay less attention to a product that was handed out for free instead of purchased) and do not deter future WTP (a phenomenon referred to as price anchoring, whereby a product subsidized at one time may induce future unwillingness to pay). Their conclusion is that short-term subsidies can be effective in inducing future long-term demand for a preventive health product such as ITN through the learning effect that they allow when information about its benefits is initially limited.

Other results confirm that there is low WTP for health products among the poor. We saw that increasing the cost of de-worming from free to not more than some 10 percent of cost decreases take-up by 80 percent (Miguel and Kremer, 2004). While externalities decrease private demand, this is not enough to explain such low WTP. Kremer *et al.* (2011) find that there is low WTP for clean water that would reduce child diarrhea in Kenya. Thornton (2008) in Malawi finds that even with free HIV testing, only 34 percent of people retrieved their results. However, an incentive as small as US$1 doubled this number. This conclusion is puzzling. Demand for health services is very sensitive to price, and demand disappears even at prices far removed from market level. Subsidies are needed, and can have large effects on behavior. However, informational and behavioral changes are needed to achieve demand without continued subsidies. How to induce these changes is yet to be determined.

Externalities and coordination

Because health expenditures create large positive externalities, especially with infectious diseases, there is a tendency for individual patients to underinvestment in treatment. Internalizing these externalities requires coordination among patients, e.g. in organizing de-worming campaigns at the level of the school for children in Africa, rather than promoting individual demand at the level of parents (Miguel and Kremer, 2004).

619

Misuse of pharmaceuticals

Effective use of pharmaceuticals such as antibiotics and antiretroviral treatments requires steady availability and discipline in use as prescribed. Irregular use due to discontinuous availability, low-quality health personnel, and extensive self-prescription leads to greater disease resistance and lower effectiveness. A high cost for poor people induces discontinuation of use (and possibly sharing with others) as soon as the patient feels better, contributing to antibiotic and malaria resistance. Use of barefoot nurses by Partners in Health has been an effective way of assisting patient discipline for better use of drugs for tuberculosis and HIV/AIDS.

Credit constraints

Expenditures on health services require lump sums of cash that may not be available when needed. Savings or credit is needed to meet these expenditures. Lack of access to affordable liquidity is thus an important constraint on meeting health expenditures in a timely fashion, suggesting potentially important health benefits from the microfinance revolution and other ways of bringing financial services to the poor.

Dupas and Robinson (2013) use an RCT in Kenya to show that simply providing individuals with a secure place to save for health expenditures (a safe box for which they have the key) together with a savings objective (health emergencies) increased savings by as much as 66 percent. They infer from this that the mental accounting of saving for a specific purpose can make a big difference in the discipline to save. For more present-biased individuals (i.e. people more inclined to procrastination), savings can be further increased by earmarking savings for health emergencies: that is, by restricting dis-saving to verifiable health emergencies with authorization given by a program officer who has the key to the safe box. Savings were also enhanced by disciplining depositors through membership of a ROSCA. Thus the conclusion is that existing informal mechanisms are insufficient to induce savings for health expenditures, but that simple methods can be quite effective in helping people discipline themselves to save for health emergencies.

Information asymmetries

Information is typically missing about the quality of health services: patient are ill-informed about alternative suppliers, quacks in India often pretend to be doctors (Banerjee *et al.*, 2004), and traditional healers are believed to be effective beyond their true competencies (Leonard, 2003). Patients are unable to fulfill their part of the treatment because of lack of knowledge about contagion and drug effectiveness, and because of a desire to minimize cost or to share medicines with others in need. For these reasons, even though supply is limited, there can be considerable under- and misuse of the available health services and treatments among low-income and low-education populations.

IMPACT OF HEALTH ON DEVELOPMENT OUTCOMES

Measuring the causal impact of health on development outcomes is difficult because, as we have seen, causality runs both ways: not only from health to development (i.e. as a means), but also from development to health (i.e. as an end). Health and nutrition affect economic growth, educational achievements, labor productivity, and income. Higher incomes increase the demand for health and nutrition. This is the so-called identification problem in econometrics. A correlation between health and development indicators does not tell us which way causality runs.

We can see this more precisely by thinking of a production function for health outcomes such as child educational achievement like the following:

$$E_t = f(H_t, H_{t-1}, PS_t, PS_{t-1}, X_t, \gamma),$$

where E_t is educational achievement (for example, test scores), H_t and H_{t-1} is child health at t and $t-1$, PS_t and PS_{t-1} is parental support for child education at t and $t-1$, X_t are school characteristics and other contextual features, and γ is the child's innate ability. This specification suffers from omitted variables and endogeneity, making a direct estimation impossible. γ is largely unobserved and as such typically omitted. H and PS are parent-decision variables affected by the expected return from health and parental support on educational achievement, itself a function of the child's innate ability. Measuring the impact of health on educational achievement (and other development indicators) needs an identification strategy that will help make health exogenous to the development outcomes of interest. This can be done using natural experiments (such as an exogenous health shock) or experimental approaches where health treatments (such as pharmaceuticals) are randomly made accessible to some and not to others, with due respect for the rights of human subjects.

Negative effect of health on per capita income

Acemoglu and Johnson (2007) use the 1940s external shock of the health revolution on developing countries as an instrument for the increase in life expectancy (and hence population growth) in the 1940–80 period, which in turn affected per capita income growth during that period. The health revolution was the discovery of antibiotics, new vaccines, and DDT treatment of mosquitoes. Specifically, the instrument is the country level of mortality from 15 leading (later eradicated) diseases in the 1940s. Using cross-country data, they find that each 1 percent increase in life expectancy led to a 1.7 to 2 percent increase in population. However, over the 1940–80 period, the gain in life expectancy had no corresponding impact on aggregate income (largely determined by fixed land and capital, not by population), with the result that per capita income fell. Exogenous health improvements inducing a demographic transition thus had a negative impact on per capita income during that particular period.

Young (2005) reasons similarly for a negative health and population shock caused by the effect of the recent HIV/AIDS epidemic in Africa. Using microdata for South

Africa, he shows that the decline in population may help increase income per capita despite the significant disruptions and human suffering caused by the disease.

Positive effects of health on development outcomes

RCTs have been used to test the effect of health interventions on development outcomes. One example is the Miguel and Kremer (2004) study on de-worming school children in Kenya (see Chapter 4). In the production function of health outcomes, randomizing H_{t-1} will not only directly affect the educational outcome E_t, but also indirectly through later health levels H_t and through behavioral changes such as parental support for education PS_t, which is now more profitable if children are in better condition to learn. The RCT thus helps measure the overall impact of the health intervention H_{t-1} on educational achievement E_t, which is the policy outcome of interest. If there are spillover effects (positive externalities) across schools, part of the gain from treatment is also its effect on non-treated schools.

Different types of worm infection are hugely prevalent, affecting more than 2 billion people in the world and accounting for over 40 percent of the global tropical burden of disease. Children are particularly vulnerable, with 400 million school children infected with intestinal worms. In rural Kenya where the RCT was implemented, 90 percent of children were infected. The expected impact is that worm infections reduce school participation rates and learning as measured by test scores.

Schools were randomly assigned to three groups:

T_1: treated in 1998 and 1999
T_2: no treatment in 1998, treated in 1999
C: no treatment in 1998 and 1999.

Because there are spillover effects that depend on distance between schools, the impact on health or education outcomes is estimated as a function of distance to treated schools (positive spillovers) and non-treated schools (negative spillovers). The estimated equation is thus as follows:

$$Y_{ijt} = \alpha + \beta_1 T_{1it} + \beta_2 T_{2it} + X'_{ijt}\delta + \sum_d \gamma_d N^T_{dit} + \sum_d \phi_d N_{dit} + u_i + \varepsilon_{ijt},$$

where Y_{ijt} is the health or educational outcome for school i, student j, and t the year of the program; T_{1it} and T_{2it} are indicators of de-worming treatment in year 1 or 2; X_{ijt} are school and student characteristics; N^T_{dit} is the number of students in treated schools at a distance d; N_{dit} is the number of students in schools treated and non-treated at a distance d; and u_i is a school fixed effect.

Results of the RCT on school de-worming in rural Kenya are as follows:

■ De-worming induced a 7-percentage-point average gain in primary-school attendance. This corresponds to a 25 percent reduction in school absenteeism.

Since de-worming is very cheap, the benefit–cost ratio in terms of future income gains associated with higher educational achievements is estimated to be of the order of three to one.

■ It is surprising that there was no gain in learning as indicated by test scores. This may be due to increased congestion in classrooms or simply to the fact that schools are of poor quality, with few learning benefits irrespective of children's health status.

■ Worms transmit from one person to another through exposure to fecal matter. This creates large positive externalities of treated on non-treated children. Students in treated schools who did not take de-worming pills had rates of infection 12 percent lower than in non-treated schools. With treatment at the school level, spillover effects occur across schools within a two-mile radius, accounting for some 20 percent of treatment gains. This implies that simple treatment-control differences underestimate the impact of de-worming as controls benefit from the treatment. Controlling for these externalities to measure the treatment effect was done by staggering the entry of schools into treatment.

■ Willingness to pay for the treatment is very low. Take-up where treatment is free was 75 percent, falling to 18 percent with cost sharing as low as 10 percent. This implies that school eradication campaigns need to be offered for free, with the justification of large positive externalities and low-cost gains in human capital for young children.

Other studies of the impact of health on development outcomes

Indicators of health used in quantitative analyses of the health–development relationship include worker height, BMI, calorie intake, and the incidence of specific diseases such as bilharzia among rice farmers (a waterborne disease where worms cycle between snails and people, damaging internal organs, also called schisto-somiasis). Indicators of development include labor-force participation (probability of working, number of hours worked), piece-rate wages, and farm profits from self-employment in agriculture. Results show that height and BMI (which signals a worker's health status to employers) determine higher wages in many countries. This relationship tends to be stronger in developing-country labor markets such as Brazil, rather than in the US (Schultz, 2002). This is because height is less variable in the US, where nutritional status is uniformly better, and because there are more white-collar jobs in which a worker's physical strength does not concern the employer.

An interesting result in family farming is that the health of a family member (e.g. a HIV-positive diagnosis or even a death in the family) does not affect farm production if labor and credit markets work, but does if they do not (Pitt *et al.*, 1990). This is another application of the separability theorem. If labor and credit markets work, a family member can be replaced by a hired worker when ill. By contrast, in subsistence agriculture where hired labor is not used (i.e. where the labor market fails), illness of a family member reduces farm output. This negative effect of health on farm output in subsistence agriculture has been observed to hold for bilharzia among rice farmers in Cameroon, HIV/AIDS in Kenya, and calorie intake in Sierra Leone.

HEALTH POLICIES

Supply side

Health services

Providing an adequate supply of health services in developing countries remains a critical issue in improving health outcomes. Public budgets are typically insufficient, quality of services is generally deficient, and attempts at introducing user fees have often increased the quality of services but left the poor unattended. The good news, however, is that many significant improvements in healthcare can be made in developing countries with simple and remarkably cheap interventions: there are a lot of low-hanging fruits offering opportunities for impact. Many of the health RCTs conducted by NGOs and research universities have sought to identify these opportunities. They include the provision of basic health services through community health workers, small incentives for the vaccination of children, subsidies to the acquisition of bed nets, improved sanitation through cheap water-purification methods, supplementation of normal household diets with micronutrients, de-worming of school children, preventive care with services such as family-planning education and use of condoms, and focusing on delivery to reduce, through barefoot supervision, the misuse of pharmaceuticals such as antibiotics and antiretroviral AIDS medicine (Mwabu, 2008). These simple health interventions can have very large returns on development per dollar spent.

IPR on pharmaceuticals

Policy options include seeking market segmentation and differential pricing of pharmaceuticals on MDC and LDC markets for diseases common to both groups of country (Lanjouw, 2005). Pharmaceutical companies can be encouraged to donate drug licenses to LDCs so they can be produced as generics. This can be rewarded by tax deductions on MDC markets if access is granted on LDC markets, enhancing the humanitarian reputation of pharmaceutical companies in MDCs. IPR protection can be introduced in LDCs for tropical and low-income-specific diseases in order to attract private research.

Research on LDC diseases can be encouraged by:

- Competitive availability of research grants, such as those made by the Bill & Melinda Gates Foundation for the development of a malaria vaccine.
- Using donor money to create a guaranteed purchase fund for new drugs in order to provide private research investors with a large market in developing countries in spite of poverty (Kremer, 2002). Alternatively, prizes can be offered for a medical

innovation applicable to markets in developing-countries (Stiglitz and Jayadev, 2010).

■ Public research on "orphan diseases," where markets are too small to attract private investment.

Public-goods provision

The key challenge on the supply side is how to overcome under-provision of health services and low quality in delivery. This is a political-economy issue, where public expenditures on health compete with other expenditures. Lobbying by interest groups rarely favors health consumers, who constitute large and heterogeneous constituencies, the opposite of what it takes for collective action to be successful.

User fees, privatization

The objective is to introduce a price to make the market work and create incentives on the provider side. There is an issue of monopoly power in local provision, and hence under-provision in quantity and quality. Another is poverty that requires giving vouchers to the poor, raising the difficult problem of targeting. However, payment of user fees can help improve delivery. It has been shown to be effective for the provision of potable water in Argentina, leading to a significant decline in child mortality (8 percent), especially in the poorest municipalities (26 percent) (Galiani *et al.*, 2005).

Pay for performance incentives

The objective is to introduce incentives where providers are rewarded for performance. In 2005, the Ministry of Health in Rwanda introduced a scheme of payments for performance (P4P), awarding bonuses to primary-healthcare facilities based on the provision of various types of service and their quality. Performance indicators included the percentage of children vaccinated, the percentage of birth deliveries in the facility, and the incidence of appropriate emergency transfers to hospital during delivery. On average, 77 percent of P4P funds were awarded to personnel, resulting in an increase of 38 percent in staff compensation. Introduction of the P4P scheme was randomized to measure impact, with treatment and comparison facilities given the same budgets (used as fixed payments in the comparison groups and as P4P in the treatment facilities). Gertler and Vermeersch (2013) find that the incentives led to a 20 percent increase in the provision of services and to significant improvements in child health.

Because performance cannot be measured in health outcomes (these occur long after provision and it is difficult to establish causality), P4P tend to be for medical procedures such as referrals and treatments. The risk is creating incentives to over-provide treatments in which the providers have special interest, as is common in the industrialized countries. This is less of an issue in poor countries such as Rwanda, where under-provision is the more pervasive issue.

Citizen report cards and links to rewards

Report cards on users' satisfaction with health services can serve to determine rewards for providers. The key here is establishing a link between consumer satisfaction and providers' budgets and salaries. This is what the World Bank called the "short route of accountability," whereby poor beneficiaries can voice their satisfaction with service providers, in contrast with the "long route of accountability" that goes through the electoral process, with poor people voting for policy-makers who in turn can exercise demands on service providers (World Bank, 2003).

Levels of pay and incentives to resist the brain drain

With the globalization of the market for health services, it is difficult for developing countries to retain trained doctors, who can move abroad to more lucrative markets. A key issue is thus to develop the right level of skills that will find rewards on the local market rather than be tempted to migrate.

Demand side

The puzzle of low effective demand

A repeated observation of the poor's use of essential health products is that, in spite of availability and potentially high benefits, there is very low effective demand at market prices. It has been estimated that two thirds of child deaths could be avoided with increased use of simple practices such as vaccination, point-of-use water treatment like water filters, insecticide-treated bed nets, iron fortification, and de-worming (Dupas, 2014). Yet while there are high uptakes when these services are provided for free, demand rapidly collapses as soon as prices rise: it is highly price-elastic near a zero price. In Ghana, the take-up for water filters fell from 89 percent when subsidized at 90 percent to 21 percent when subsidized at 70 percent, still only one third of the market price. In Kenya, the take-up of bed nets fell from near 100 percent when 100 percent subsidized to 10 percent when subsidized at 64 percent, again still only one third of the market price. In Kenya, the take-up of de-worming pills fell from 75 percent when free to 19 percent when subsidized at 50 percent, half of the market price. This has opened a huge debate as to whether these health products should be distributed for free to the poor, or whether subsidies are detrimental to future demand at market price.

The justification for price subsidies

There are three good reasons why essential health products should be heavily subsidized for the poor. The first is that there are strong positive externalities to reducing communicable diseases among the poor: it lowers transmission and thus has social benefits in addition to obvious private benefits. The second is that these products are experiential goods: demand requires learning, which can be done through self-use (learning-by-doing) or through witnessing the benefits accrued by other users (learning-from-others). Subsidies helps unleash this learning phase, leading to subsequent market demand. China heavily subsidized health insurance when it was first introduced, to rapidly bring it to market price. The third is that the poor are income-constrained in purchasing these products, resulting in over-exclusion: many of the poor who would benefit from the health product cannot afford to buy it. This would require effective targeting of subsidies to the selected poor.

Arguments against price subsidies

There is always suspicion that subsidies may induce perverse behavior that negates the subsequent possibility of removing them and of converging to market prices for the products offered. Specifically, this takes three forms in the case of health products. The first is that products made available may be used ineffectively or not at all. The argument is often made that something received for free does not receive as much attention as something at least partially purchased—and free allocations may go to people who do not need the product. Bed nets may be received, for example, but people may not sleep under them. This argument may not have so much weight if the product is essential. In Kenya, only 20 percent of the subsidized water filters and in Ghana only 10 percent of the free bed nets received were not used. The second argument is called price anchoring: people who receive something for less than the market price may get used to the low price and subsequently be less willing to pay the full price. This has been dismissed by a detailed RCT on the subject: Dupas (2010) showed that short-term subsidies to bed nets do not diminish long-term demand. Finally, overuse associated with subsidized access to, for example, malaria suppressants such as Artemisinin may contribute to the build-up of resistance. Here again, Cohen et al. (2015) showed with an RCT that over-treatment is associated not with subsidies but with lack of access to reliable diagnostics and to drugs without prescriptions. Thus the solution is to provide the poor with accurate diagnostics where they live and to enforce prescriptions-only access through adequate incentives to, and the monitoring of, providers.

How to use subsidies

If subsidies are to be used, then they should be used smartly, meaning that they should be well targeted, not create bad habits, not displace suppliers in the private sector, and be phased out when they have achieved their purpose. Vouchers that can be redeemed with private providers avoid private-sector displacement by public provision. The careful and credible announcement of a declining rate of subsidization can focus the learning period. Links to CCTs can create incentives to good behavior. And small gifts, like the kilogram of lentils in an RCT run by Banerjee et al. (2010) in India, can be effective in inducing parents to take their children to immunization camps, doubling the participation rate.

627

Eradication campaigns vs. individual choice

When there are strong externalities, as with de-worming (where children infect each others through bodily contact and the sharing of space and objects) or malaria (where mosquitoes carry infected blood from person to person), coordinated eradication campaigns may be more effective than incentives to individual uptake. This is how pin worms and malaria were eradicated in the US. Bleakley (2010) shows that the roll-out of malaria eradication campaigns in the US (in the 1920s) and in Brazil, Colombia, and Mexico (in the 1950s) is associated with cohorts of adults with higher incomes than the preceding generation. These campaigns are more effective because asking for individual discipline in using bed nets, putting chlorine in water at home (point-of-use behavior), and deciding to administer ill tasting de-worming pills at home may be self-defeating.

Changing behavior

Will HIV testing and people finding out their HIV status lead to more or less responsible behavior by those who discover that they are HIV-positive? Evidence suggests that information that reinforces beliefs leads to no change in behavior, but that information that contradicts beliefs leads to the reverse, including greater risk-taking. Recent research with data for Tanzania shows that people who discover they are, unexpectedly, HIV-positive may engage in more risky sex than before, putting others at risk of infection (Gong, 2015). In a CCT experiment where payment to young adults is conditional on remaining HIV negative, Kohler and Thornton (2012) found, unexpectedly, that at the end of the program, when beneficiaries had accumulated cash transfers through good behavior, girls used the cash to reduce risky sexual behavior while boys used it to engage in more risky sex. This says that programs have to be carefully designed, not only in terms of what they achieve while they last, but also in terms of the behavior they will induce when they finish.

CONCEPTS SEEN IN THIS CHAPTER

Education

Human capital
Intrinsic value of schooling
Gross and net enrollment ratios
Private benefits of education
Social benefits of education
Opportunity cost of education
Discount rate and hyperbolic discounting
Net Present Value (NPV) of investment in education
Internal Rate of Return (IRR)
Conditional cash transfer (CCT) program

Health

Burden of disease and disability-adjusted life years (DALY)

z-scores: stunting and wasting

Intellectual property rights (IPR) for pharmaceuticals

Health delivery and "barefoot" supervision

Payment for performance

Citizen report cards

Eradication campaigns

Externalities in de-worming

Price anchoring

REVIEW QUESTIONS. HUMAN CAPITAL: EDUCATION AND HEALTH

Education

1. Define the gross and net enrollment ratio.
2. On the demand side of education, explain why the decision to go to school instead of working is determined by the inequality:

$$i + \partial(w_1 - w_0) > c + w_0.$$

    Explain the meaning of each term.
3. Why is w_0 added to the direct cost of schooling in deciding to study instead of work?
4. How would you use the concept of internal rate of return (IRR) to assess the value of an educational plan that has short-run costs and long-term benefits?
5. Explain why poor people with high discount rates eventually decide to limit the education of their children to primary school compared to better-off people with lower discount rates?
6. In analyzing the supply side of education in Indonesia, how does Esther Duflo use a diff-in-diffs approach to measure the impact of a school-construction program on educational achievements and wages earned?
7. What would justify a country like Mexico offering $3.2 billion/year to poor mothers in the rural sector conditional on sending their children to school and to medical visits (CCT program)? Discuss both short-term and long-term effects.

Health

1. Define DALY (disability-adjusted life years) and HALE (health-adjusted life expectancy)
2. In developing countries, why is there a tendency for under-provision of health services on the supply side, and under- or misuse of health services on the demand side?
3. Why should developing countries uphold IPR on pharmaceuticals for LDC diseases but not for global diseases?
4. Why does Paul Farmer stress the importance of delivery (role of *accompagnateurs*) in helping improve health among the poor?
5. If health is a means to development, what indicators of impact would you use to characterize the relationship between health and development?

629

REFERENCES

Acemoglu, Daron, and Simon Johnson. 2007. "Disease and Development: The Effect of Life Expectancy on Economic Growth." *Journal of Political Economy* 115(6): 925–85.

Akerlof, George, and Rachel Kranton. 2002. "Identity and Schooling: Some Lessons for the Economics of Education." *Journal of Economic Literature* 40(4): 1167–201.

Angrist, Joshua, and Victor Lavy. 1999. "Using Maimonides' Rule to Estimate the Effect of Class Size on Student Achievement." *Quarterly Journal of Economics,* 114(2): 533–75.

Atkin, David. 2012. "Endogenous Skill Acquisition and Export Manufacturing in Mexico." Working paper, Economics Department, Yale University.

Baland, Jean-Marie, and James Robinson. 2000. "Is Child Labor Inefficient?" *Journal of Political Economy* 108(4): 663–79.

Banerjee, Abhijit, Angus Deaton, and Esther Duflo. 2004. "Wealth, Health, and Health Services in Rural Rajasthan." *American Economic Review* 94 (2): 326–30.

Banerjee, Abhijit, Shawn Cole, Esther Duflo and Leigh Linden. 2007. "Remedying Education: Evidence from Two Randomized Experiments in India." *Quarterly Journal of Economics* 122(3): 1235–64.

Banerjee, Abhijit, Esther Duflo, Rachel Glennerster, and Dhruva Kothari. 2010. "Improving Immunization Coverage in Rural India: Clustered Randomised Controlled Evaluation of Immunization Campaigns with and without Incentives." *British Medical Journal* 340(June): 2220.

Barro, Robert. 1991. "Economic Growth in a Cross Section of Countries." *Quarterly Journal of Economics* 106(2): 407–43.

Basu, Kaushik. 1999. "Child Labor: Causes, Consequences, and Cure." *Journal of Economic Literature* 37(3): 1083–120.

Basu, Kaushik. 2005. "Child Labor and the Law: Notes on Possible Pathologies." *Economic Letters* 87(2): 169–74.

Basu, Kaushik, and P.H. Van. 1998. "The Economics of Child Labor." *American Economic Review* 88(3): 412–27.

Bharadwaj, Prashant, Leah Lakdawala, and Nicholas Li. 2013. "Perverse Consequences of Well-intentioned Regulation: Evidence from India's Labor Ban." Working paper, Economics Department, University of California at San Diego.

Bleakley, Hoyt. 2010. "Malaria Eradication in the Americas: A Retrospective Analysis of Childhood Exposure." *American Economic Journal: Applied Economics* 2(2): 1–45.

Caselli, Francesco. 2005. "Accounting for Cross-Country Income Differences." In P. Aghion and S. Durlauf (eds.), *Handbook of Economic Growth,* Volume 1A, 679–741. Amsterdam: Elsevier Science, North-Holland Publishers.

Chaudhury, Nazmul, Jeffrey Hammer, Michael Kremer, Karthink Muralidharan, and F. Halsey Rogers. 2006. "Missing in Action: Teacher and Health Worker Absence in Developing Countries." *Journal of Economic Perspectives* 20(1): 91–116.

Cohen, Jessica, and Pascaline Dupas. 2010. "Free Distribution or Cost-Sharing? Evidence from a Randomized Malaria Prevention Experiment." *Quarterly Journal of Economics* 125(1): 1–45.

Cohen, Jessica, Pascaline Dupas, and Simone Schaner. 2015. "Price Subsidies, Diagnostic Tests, and Targeting of Malaria Treatment: Evidence from a Randomized Controlled Trial." *American Economic Review* 105(2): 609–45.

630

Currie, Janet, and Enrico Moretti. 2003. "Mother's Education and the Intergenerational Transmission of Human Capital: Evidence from College Openings." *Quarterly Journal of Economics* 118(4): 1495–532.

Deininger, Klaus. 2003. "Does Cost of Schooling Affect Enrollment by the Poor? Universal Primary Education in Uganda." *Economics of Education Review* 22(3): 291–305.

de Janvry, Alain, and Elisabeth Sadoulet. 2006a. "Making Conditional Cash Transfer Programs More Efficient: Designing for Maximum Effect of the Conditionality." *World Bank Economic Review* 20(1): 1–29.

de Janvry, Alain, Frederico Finan, Elisabeth Sadoulet, and Renos Vakis. 2006b. "Can Conditional Cash Transfer Programs Serve as Safety Nets in Keeping Children at School and from Working when Exposed to Shocks?" *Journal of Development Economics* 79(2): 349–73.

de Janvry, Alain, Frederico Finan, Elisabeth Sadoulet. 2011. "Local Electoral Incentives and Decentralized Program Performance." *Review of Economics and Statistics* 94(3): 672–85.

De, Anuradha, and Jean Drèze. 1999. *Public Report on Basic Education in India. The PROBE Report.* Oxford: Oxford University Press.

Drèze, Jean, and Mamta Murthi. 2001. "Fertility, Education, and Development: Evidence from India." *Population and Development Review* 27(1): 33–63.

Duflo, Esther. 2001. "Schooling and Labor Market Consequences of School Construction in Indonesia: Evidence from an Unusual Policy Experiment." *American Economic Review* 91(4): 795–813.

Duflo, Esther. 2003. "Grandmothers and Granddaughters: Old Age Pension and Intra-household Allocation in South Africa." *World Bank Economic Review* 17(1): 1–25.

Duflo, Esther, Pascaline Dupas, and Michael Kremer. 2011. "Peer Effects and the Impact of Tracking: Evidence from a Randomized Evaluation in Kenya." *American Economic Review* 101(5): 1739–74.

Duflo, Esther, Pascaline Dupas, and Michael Kremer. 2015. "School Governance, Teacher Incentives, and Pupil–Teacher Ratios: Experimental Evidence from Kenyan Primary Schools." *Journal of Public Economics* 123: 92–110.

Dupas, Pascaline. 2010. "Free Distribution or Cost-Sharing? Evidence from a Randomized Malaria Prevention Experiment." *Quarterly Journal of Economics* 125(1): 1–45.

Dupas, Pascaline. 2014. "Getting Essential Health Products to Their End Users: Subsidize, but How Much?" *Science* 345(6202): 1279–81.

Dupas, Pascaline, and Jonathan Robinson. 2013. "Why Don't the Poor Save More? Evidence from Health Savings Experiments." *American Economic Review* 103(4): 1138–71.

Fiszbein, Ariel, and Norbert Schady. 2009. *Conditional Cash Transfers: Reducing Present and Future Poverty.* Washington, DC: World Bank.

Foster, Andrew, and Mark Rosenzweig. 1996. "Technical Change and Human Capital Returns and Investments: Evidence from the Green Revolution." *American Economic Review* 86(3): 931–53.

GAIN (Global Alliance for Improved Nutrition). http://www.gainhealth.org/ (accessed 2015).

Galiani, Sebastian, Paul Gertler, and Ernesto Shargrodsky. 2005. "Water for Life: The Impact of Water Supply Privatization on Child Mortality." *Journal of Political Economy* 113(1): 83–120.

Gertler, Paul, and Christel Vermeersch. 2013. "Using Performance Incentives to Improve Medical Care Productivity and Health Outcomes." Working paper, Haas Business School, University of California at Berkeley.

Gong, Erick. 2015. "HIV Testing and Risky Sexual Behavior." *The Economic Journal* 125(582): 32–60.

Gross, Rainer, and Patrick Webb. 2006. "Wasting Time for Wasted Children: Severe Child Under Nutrition Must Be Resolved in Non-emergency Settings." *The Lancet* 367(April): 1209–11.

Hanushek Eric, and Ludger Woessman. 2009. "Do Better Schools Lead to More Growth? Cognitive Skills, Economic Outcomes, and Causation." NBER Working Paper No. 14633, Economics Department, Stanford University.

Haushofer, Johannes, Daniel Schunk, and Ernst Fehr. 2013. "Negative Income Shocks Increase Discount Rates." Working paper, Department of Psychology, Princeton University.

Jayachandran, Seema, and Adriana Lleras-Muney. 2009. "Life Expectancy and Human Capital Investments: Evidence from Maternal Mortality Declines." *Quarterly Journal of Economics* 124(1): 349–97.

Jensen, Robert. 2010. "The (Perceived) Returns to Education and the Demand for Schooling." *Quarterly Journal of Economics* 125(2): 515–48.

Kidder, Tracy. 2004. *Mountains Beyond Mountains: The Quest of Dr. Paul Farmer, a Man Who Would Cure the World*. New York: Random House.

Kohler, Hans-Peter, and Rebecca Thornton. 2012. "Conditional Cash Transfers and HIV/AIDS Prevention: Unconditionally Promising?" *World Bank Economic Review* 26(2): 165–90.

Kremer, Michael. 2002. "Pharmaceuticals and the Developing World." *Journal of Economic Perspectives* 16(4): 67–90.

Kremer, Michael, Edward Miguel, and Rebecca Thornton. 2009. "Incentives to Learn." *Review of Economics and Statistics* 91(3): 437–56.

Kremer, Michael, Jessica Leino, Edward Miguel, and Alix Peterson Zwane. 2011. "Spring Cleaning: Rural Water Impacts, Valuation, and Property Rights Institutions." *Quarterly Journal of Economics* 126(1): 145–205.

Lai, Fang, Elisabeth Sadoulet, and Alain de Janvry. 2011. "The Contributions of School Quality and Teacher Qualifications to Student Performance: Evidence from a Natural Experiment in Beijing Middle Schools." *Journal of Human Resources* 46(1): 123–53.

Lanjouw, Jean. 2005. "Intellectual Property and the Availability of Pharmaceuticals in Poor Countries." Working Paper #5, ARE, University of California at Berkeley.

Leonard, Kenneth. 2003. "African Traditional Healers and Outcome-Contingent Contracts for Health Care." *Journal of Development Economics* 71(1): 1–22.

Li, Hongbin, Pak Wai Liu, and Junsen Zhang. 2012. "Estimating Returns to Education Using Twins in Urban China." *Journal of Development Economics* 97(2): 494–504.

Lleras-Muney, Adriana. 2005. "The Relationship between Education and Adult Mortality in the U.S." *Review of Economic Studies* 72(1): 189–221.

Magruder, Jeremy. 2009. *Class notes EEP 152*. Working paper, Department of Agricultural and Resource Economics, University of California at Berkeley.

Miguel, Edward, and Michael Kremer. 2004. "Worms: Identifying Impacts on Education and Health in the Presence of Treatment Externalities." *Econometrica* 72(1): 159–217.

Mincer, Jacob. 1974. *Schooling, Earnings, and Experience.* New York: Columbia University Press.

Munshi, Kaivan, and Mark Rosenzweig. 2006. "Traditional Institutions Meet the Modern World: Caste, Gender, and Schooling Choice in a Globalizing Economy." *American Economic Review* 96(4): 1225–52.

Muralidharan, Karthik, and Venkatesh Sundararaman. 2011. "Teacher Performance Pay: Experimental Evidence from India." *Journal of Political Economy* 119(1): 39–77.

Mwabu, Germano. 2008. "Health Economics for Low-Income Countries." *Handbook of Development Economics*, Vol. 4. Amsterdam: Elsevier.

Orazem, Peter, and Elizabeth King. 2008. "Schooling in Developing Countries: The Roles of Supply, Demand, and Government Policy." *Handbook of Development Economics*, Vol. 4, Chapter 55. Amsterdam: Elsevier.

Oster, Emily, and Bryce Millett Steinberg. 2013. "Do IT Service Centers Promote School Enrollment? Evidence from India." *Journal of Development Economics* 104(September): 123–35.

Pitt, Mark, Mark Rosenzweig, and Md Nazmul Hassan. 1990. "Productivity, Health and Inequality in the Intrahousehold Distribution of Food in Low-Income Countries." *American Economic Review* 80(5): 1139–56.

Psacharopoulos, George. 1994. "Returns to Investment in Education: A Global Update." *World Development* 22(9): 1325–43.

Psacharopoulos, George, and Harry Patrinos. 2002. "Returns to Investment in Education: A Further Update." Washington, DC: World Bank Policy Research Working Paper No. 2881.

Sadoulet, Elisabeth, Frederico Finan, and Alain de Janvry. 2001. "How Effective Are Educational Subsidies Programs for the Rural Poor? Progresa in Mexico." Working paper, Department of Agricultural and Resource Economics, University of California at Berkeley.

Schoellman, Todd. 2012. "Education Quality and Development Accounting." *Review of Economic Studies* 79(1): 388–417.

Schultz, T. Paul. 2002. "Wage Gains Associated With Height as a Form of Human Capital." *American Economic Review* 92(2): 349–53.

Schultz, T. Paul. 2004. "School Subsidies for the Poor: Evaluating the Mexican Progresa Poverty Program." *Journal of Development Economics* 74(1): 199–250.

Schultz, Theodore W. 1964. *Transforming Traditional Agriculture*. New Haven, CT: Yale University Press.

Spence, Michael. 1973. "Job Market Signaling." *Quarterly Journal of Economics* 87(3): 355–74.

Stiglitz, Joseph, and Arjun Jayadev. 2010. "Medicine for Tomorrow: Some Alternative Proposals to Promote Socially Beneficial Research and Development in Pharmaceuticals." *Journal of Generic Medicines* 7(3): 217–26.

Strauss, John, and Duncan Thomas. 1998. "Health, Nutrition and Economic Development." *Journal of Economic Literature* 36(2): 766–817.

Strauss, John, and Duncan Thomas. 2008. "Health Over the Life Course." *Handbook of Development Economics*, Vol. 4, Chapter 54. Amsterdam: Elsevier.

Subramanian, Shankar, and Angus Deaton. 1996. "The Demand for Food and Calories." *Journal of Political Economy* 104(1): 133–62.

Thornton, Rebecca. 2008. "The Demand for, and Impact of, Learning HIV Status." *American Economic Review* 98(5): 1829–63.

World Bank. 2003. *World Development Report 2004: Making Services Work for Poor People*. Washington, DC.

World Bank. *Education Statistics Database*. http://data.worldbank.org (accessed 2005).

World Bank. *World Development Indicators*. http://data.worldbank.org/indicator (accessed 2005).

World Health Organization. 2015. *Health*. http://www.who.int/trade/glossary/story046/en/ (accessed 2015).

Young, Alwyn. 2005. "The Gift of the Dying: The Tragedy of AIDS and the Welfare of Future African Generations." *Quarterly Journal of Economics* 120(2): 423–66.

633

Chapter 18

Agriculture for development

TAKE-HOME MESSAGES FOR CHAPTER 18

1. Agriculture is a key sector for development at low levels of GDPpc, with the capacity to make important contributions to aggregate economic growth—through product, factor, and market contributions—poverty and hunger reduction, and the provision of environmental services.

2. The state of world agriculture shows that many countries have achieved success using agriculture for development, ranging from the Western experience to the Asian experience, and more recently China and Vietnam. Yet hunger is still with us, close to the billion-people mark, and many countries have failed to use agriculture for development to its potential, most particularly Sub-Saharan Africa and India in the last 15 years.

3. This neglect of agriculture has been due to a variety of causes, but important among them have been a focus on macro fundamentals with few sectoral concerns, descaling of the role of the state, and the use of transfers for poverty reduction as opposed to higher rural autonomous incomes. The recent food crisis and the continuing dominance of rural poverty in aggregate poverty are outcomes of this neglect.

4. Looking forward, agriculture has to face major challenges. Production will have to increase by 70 percent over the period 2005–50 in a context of competition for land with urban sprawl, falling agricultural productivity gains, demand for biofuels, climate change, and rising water scarcity. This has unleashed a competition for access to land at a world scale with potential high returns to investment in farming.

5. The theory of induced technological innovations explains the land-saving or labor-saving bias of technology in terms of changes in relative factor prices affecting public research priorities.

6. The gains from technological change accrue to consumers if food is non-tradable and to producers if tradable, with a corresponding product or land-market treadmill inducing the demand for new technologies.

7. Food security requires not only the availability of food but also continuous access to food, and proper use of food for nutritional achievements. Like poverty, food insecurity can be chronic or transitory. Governments can attack food insecurity through a vast array of market instruments and direct interventions.

AGRICULTURE FOR DEVELOPMENT

Seen from a long historical perspective, agriculture has been a (if not the initial) major development instrument for humanity. The Neolithic period, some 10,000 years ago, saw the birth of agriculture, which supported the first boom in world population. The dominance of Eurasian civilizations over others originated, according to Diamond (1998), in environmental endowments and technological advances supporting differentially high rates of productivity growth in agriculture. An agricultural revolution freeing labor from agriculture and providing food for a growing urban population was a precondition to almost every single successful industrial revolution (Bairoch, 1973). The recent accelerated-growth successes in India, China, Vietnam, Brazil, and Chile were importantly derived from the rapid growth of agriculture. Current difficulties in industrializing and accelerating growth in many parts of the world, from Sub-Saharan Africa to Yemen and Haiti, are in large part due to failure of these countries to achieve significant gains in productivity in agriculture, what has been called a Green Revolution. Two observations underscore the heavy costs of the failure of agriculture to grow. One is that 75 percent of the 1.2 billion people with incomes of less than a dollar a day are located in rural areas and are dependent for their livelihoods principally on access to land and the performance of agriculture. The other is the periodic return of global food crises that reflect the recurrent failure of agriculture to deliver enough produce to meet rising effective demand and to adjust to new production challenges. Growth failures in agriculture, and what it takes to induce successful agricultural growth, need to be better understood. This is all the more important given that the conditions for successful agricultural growth are both increasingly precarious (with rising land and water scarcity, as well as climate change) and markedly different today than they were in the past, as a consequence of globalization, the emergence of integrated food-value chains, new technological and institutional innovations, and environmental stress. Not only does better use need to be made of agriculture for development, but ways to do this in the current context need to be uncovered, and they will be different from those in the past, and for Africa compared to Asia. This poses a huge and fascinating challenge.

The role of agriculture for development is multidimensional: it can be an important source of growth in low-income countries, it is a source of livelihoods for half of humanity and can be a powerful instrument for poverty reduction, and it can be a source of resource saving for the other sectors of the economy and of environmental services such as carbon capture and biodiversity conservation (World Bank, 2007). We analyze each of these roles in turn. These multiple functions of agriculture for development imply that there will likely be trade-offs among them, as opposed to straight win–wins, and managing trade-offs implies the need to set priorities at the national level for how to best use agriculture for development in each particular country.

Agriculture as a source of growth

Agriculture can be a key source of growth for the rest of the economy at early stages of development, when the agricultural sector still looms large in employment of the labor force and in GDP (Mellor, 1966). The way in which agriculture helps the other sectors of the economy grow can be decomposed into the product, factor (capital, foreign exchange, and labor), and market contributions of agriculture. Agricultural growth can in turn have large multiplier effects in inducing industrial growth. Low-income countries typically have comparative advantage in agriculture more than in other, more institutionally demanding sectors.

Product contributions

The rise of labor productivity in agriculture allows farm producers to deliver a "marketed surplus" (defined as production above their own retention of product for consumption and factor use) to the urban environment where it can feed a labor force engaged in other activities. Hence it is the productivity of labor in agriculture that determines how large the urban population can be. An alternative way of seeing this is that greater productivity in agriculture helps lower the price of food, which in turn lowers the urban nominal wage (the cost of labor for industry) for a given real wage (the standard of living). This is particularly the case when food is largely non-tradable, as in India due to policy restrictions on trade, and in many Sub-Saharan Africa countries due to high transactions costs in reaching international markets. A lower urban nominal wage in turn raises the return to investment in industry and favors economic growth. This is the logic captured in the neoclassical dual-economy growth models seen in Chapter 8. Another product contribution is through forward linkages between agriculture and industry, whereby agriculture makes raw materials available to agro-processing and food value chains, allowing the expansion of these sectors (Hirschman, 1958).

Capital contributions

This is the so-called financial surplus of agriculture: namely, a monetary transfer out of agriculture that can be invested in other sectors of the economy, supporting their growth. The policy instruments through which these monetary transfers have taken place have differed by country and period of history.

Tax on agriculture, including a land tax

Imposing a land tax is how Japan mobilized a financial surplus to invest in industry following the Meiji restoration (1878–1917), fueling its industrial revolution (Ohkawa and Rosovsky, 1960). Rapid productivity gains had occurred in agriculture with the use of irrigation, fertilizers, and improved seeds. This allowed the state to raise a land tax on landlords, who in turn collected higher rents from the tenants working their lands. This land tax was so hefty that it contributed 85 percent of government revenues in the 1880s. These public revenues allowed the state to invest in infrastructure, technology development, and industry, prompting the emergence of a class of private industrial entrepreneurs. Clearly, productivity growth in agriculture was the mother of Japanese industry.

Imposing a tax on the raw value of the land (i.e. without improvements that would be deterred by taxation) has been a favorite of economists for a long time, in particular Henry George (1839–97) in the US. It has been called by Milton Friedman the "least bad tax" because it does not distort resource allocation as land is inelastic in supply, and it induces intensification of underused land to cover the tax. Yet, politically, raising a tax on land has proven difficult because of the power of the landlord class and because costs are immediate, while benefits are spread over a long period of time.

Confiscation of product and forced deliveries at a low price

Under Stalin, Russia in the 1930's collectivized agriculture, fundamentally as a way of gaining control over agricultural output and forcing collective farms to deliver a pre-determined quota of production to the state, for subsequent sale as cheap food to urban workers. Forced deliveries, low prices to producers, and cheap food for urban consumers was how agriculture generated a financial surplus to support cheap labor for accelerated heavy industrialization. This model was implemented by Nasser in Egypt and Nehru in India, with cheap food obtained through forced deliveries sold in government-run fair-price shops.

"Invisible transfers" through the terms of trade turned against agriculture

Low food prices allowed the provision of cheap food to the urban sector and hence cheap labor to industry. This is how an agricultural surplus was extracted from agriculture in Latin America. Food prices were kept low through export taxes (e.g. in Argentina), eventual price controls, export bans, and mainly overvalued exchange rates under the import-substitution industrialization (ISI) strategy (see Chapter 10). Low food prices were the equivalent of a tax on agriculture, except that the transfer was "invisible" as it occurred through market transactions.

Foreign-exchange contributions

Foreign-exchange earnings are essential for industrialization as many capital goods, intermediate goods, and raw materials need to be imported. Agriculture has for most countries been the main source of foreign-exchange earnings. This was the case with coffee in Brazil, sugar in Cuba, cereals and beef in Argentina, fruit in Chile, tobacco in Malawi, cocoa in Ghana and Côte d'Ivoire, tea in Kenya, and rubber in Malaysia. Foreign-currency earnings must be channeled through the central bank, which can give low (overvalued) exchange rates to agricultural exporters to favor industrial importers of raw materials and capital goods. Export taxes on agricultural commodities have also been a major source of foreign-currency earnings for governments as they are easy to levy when commodities transit through harbors. Raising income taxes on individuals or value-added taxes on enterprises is much more institutionally demanding.

Labor and welfare contributions

The dual-economy models, both classical and neoclassical, stressed the contribution made by agriculture to industrialization in releasing labor from agriculture for

637

industrial employment. This rural–urban migration of the labor force can originate in surplus agricultural labor (classical model), or in gains in labor productivity in agriculture, with a key role for technological change in achieving this result (neoclassical model). In Russia, the mechanization of agriculture (allowed by economies of scale in large collective farms, or *kolkhoz*) had the explicit purpose of substituting capital for labor in production, allowing especially young male labor to move to factories. Hence much of Russian agriculture was left in the hands of the male machinery operators and middle-aged female workers who remained in the *kolkhoz*.

There are two other less visible, but important, contributions of agricultural labor to industrialization. One is the human capital embodied in rural–urban migrants, with the cost of rearing, feeding, educating, and training the migrants paid by agriculture, while the benefits are captured by the receiving non-agricultural sector, a phenomenon identical to the cost of the brain drain for emitting countries in international migration. The other is "farm-financed social welfare" (Owen, 1966), where agriculture pays the cost of maintaining surplus labor and of providing safety nets to unemployed and aged households. A common phenomenon, for instance, is reverse migration during economic downturns, with rising urban unemployment and lack of safety nets for idle workers. An estimated 20 million unemployed Chinese urban workers returned to their villages during the financial crisis of 2008. With agriculture (and the urban informal sector) providing this safety-net function, urban employers and governments can save on the provision of social protection to the urban labor force, and maintain political stability in spite of the heavy social costs of a downturn.

Market contributions

Industry needs to find a domestic market for its products, either non-tradables or potentially tradables, until economies of scale and learning-by-doing reduce average costs to the level of the border price and enable entry to the international market. For this reason, the size of the domestic market has been key to the success of ISI strategies (as we saw in Chapter 8), and the market for industrial goods can be created by agriculture. This occurs through two types of linkage between agriculture and the other sectors of the economy (Hirschman, 1958). The first is backward linkages, whereby agriculture demands industrial products as intermediate goods for agricultural production. This includes factors of production such as fertilizers, tools, and machinery. The second is final-demand linkages, where incomes earned in agriculture and spent on non-agricultural consumption goods create a market for industry. This is the strategy of ADLI (agriculture demand-led industrialization) advocated by Adelman (1984). Rising expenditures from agricultural incomes drive industrialization by expanding the size of the domestic market for industry. This has been a powerful motive for redistributive land-reform policies and technological change for smallholder farmers. Mellor (1998) largely credited the mid 1960s Green Revolution in India with the subsequent growth of industry. China's current interest in land reform (allocating property rights over land to its current users) can be interpreted as an effort to expand the domestic market for industry among its 800 million rural households at a time when export demand is expected to decline due to slow growth in OECD countries.

Growth multipliers

Because of the numerous relations between agriculture and the other sectors of the economy, growth in agriculture can induce growth elsewhere. This is measured as growth multipliers. For instance, for China during the 1980–2001 period, estimated multipliers show that a US$1 growth originating in agriculture induced a US$1 growth in the rest of the economy, while a US$1 growth in the rest of the economy induced only a US$0.18 growth in agriculture (de Janvry and Sadoulet, 2010). Investing in agriculture thus has growth spillover effects in the rest of the economy. These growth multipliers of agriculture are believed to be larger in low-income countries, Sub-Saharan Africa in particular, because much of the industrial (agro-processing) and services (food-marketing) sectors are linked to the performance of agriculture (Christiaensen and Demery, 2007). Successful agricultural growth is thus seen as a potentially effective trigger of growth for the rest of the economy at the initial stages of industrialization.

Comparative advantage in agriculture

Many low-income countries have their comparative advantage in agriculture, making agriculture the priority sector for growth in an open economy (World Bank, 2007). There are three reasons why this is the case for most Sub-Saharan Africa countries. The first is factor endowments, due to the fact that many of these countries are rich in natural resources, with much growth potential in agriculture still to be captured, in part because of previous underinvestment. Sub-Saharan Africa has some of the lowest yields in the world, indicating both a huge challenge—namely, how to get yields to increase—but also a huge opportunity as there is probably no place in the world where current yields are further away from potential. The second reason is a weak business climate, with infrastructure and institutions that limit competitiveness in more complex manufacturing and high-value services, but are less constraining on agriculture and agro-industry. The third is the existence of large economies of scale in manufacturing that make it difficult for newcomers to enter the international market and which, again, are less binding on agriculture. Agriculture and its associated agro-industries thus offer comparative advantages in the short run, and a path toward industrialization via agro-industry in the longer run. For these countries, investing in agriculture can be the most cost-effective growth strategy toward industrialization and successful structural transformation (Mellor, 1998).

Agriculture as an effective instrument for poverty reduction

There is strong empirical evidence that growth in agriculture is particularly effective for poverty reduction. This is for the simple reason that most of the world's poor are in rural areas, where they are engaged in, or dependent upon, agriculture for their livelihoods. As we saw in Chapter 2, 78 percent of the world's extreme poor are rural and 63 percent of them work in agriculture. Its effectiveness in reducing poverty is an advantage that agriculture has over growth in other sectors; but agriculture has two disadvantages for poverty reduction. One is that it typically has a smaller share of GDP, meaning that growth in agriculture will have a lower weight in aggregate poverty reduction than that of a larger sector. The other is that growth in agriculture is typically lower than growth in non-agriculture. Even in China and India, countries with relatively good agricultural performance over a recent ten-year period (2003–13), average annual growth in agriculture was 4.5 percent and 4.1 percent respectively, compared with 11.1 percent and 7.2 percent in industry, and 10.7 percent and 8.9 percent in services. Whether agricultural growth is better for poverty reduction is thus an empirical issue. To address it, it is necessary to carefully account for the channels through which agricultural growth affects poverty.

Christiaensen *et al.* (2011) distinguish four channels through which agricultural growth may result in poverty reduction. Let P be a poverty index that can be P_0, P_1, or P_2. The rate of change in poverty can be written as an identity as follows:

$$\frac{dP}{P} = \left(\frac{dP}{P} \frac{Y}{dY} \right) \frac{dY}{Y}.$$

In this expression, Y is GDPpc and dY/Y is the rate of growth in GDPpc. The term in brackets is the elasticity of poverty with respect to income: namely,

$$E_P^Y = \frac{dP}{P} \frac{Y}{dY} = \frac{dP/P}{dY/Y},$$

which measures the degree of the pro-poorness of growth, what Christiaensen *et al.* call "participation." Poverty reduction is thus the product of a participation and a growth component as follows:

$$\frac{dP}{P} = E_P^Y \frac{dY}{Y} = \text{Participation component} \times \text{Growth component}.$$

Decomposing GDP into agriculture (Y_A) and non-agriculture (Y_N) gives

$$\frac{dP}{P} = s_A E_P^{Y_A} \frac{dY_A}{Y_A} + s_N E_P^{Y_N} \frac{dY_N}{Y_N},$$

where s_A and s_N are the shares of agriculture and non-agriculture in GDP respectively.

Agricultural growth also contributes to growth in non-agriculture, and, reciprocally, what we can call indirect growth effects.

The channels through which agriculture and non-agriculture growth affect poverty can then be summarized in Figure 18.1.

There are four channels:

1. The direct growth effect of agriculture.
2. The indirect growth effect of agriculture on non-agriculture growth.

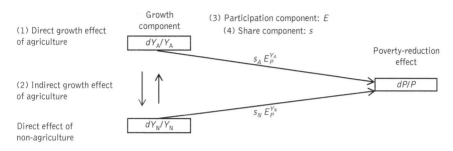

Figure 18.1 *Channels through which agriculture growth affects poverty*

Source: based on Christiaensen *et al.,* 2011.

3. The participation component measured by the elasticity of poverty with respect to growth.
4. The share component measured by the importance of agriculture in GDP.

Results show that agriculture has a larger indirect growth-multiplier effect than non-agriculture, ranging from 1.6 to 1.8 for Asia and 1.3 to 1.5 for Sub-Saharan Africa and Latin America and the Caribbean. This means that every one dollar of growth in agriculture induces another 60 to 80 cents of growth in non-agriculture in Asia and 30 to 50 cents in Sub-Saharan Africa and Latin America and the Caribbean. In low-income countries (mainly Sub-Saharan Africa), 1 percent GDP growth in agriculture induces three times more extreme-poverty reduction than a 1 percent GDP growth in non-agriculture. This result is driven by the much larger participation of poorer households in growth from agriculture. When the poverty line is at US$2 a day instead of US$1 for extreme poverty, it is the growth of non-agriculture that becomes more effective for poverty reduction. In middle-income countries, too, it is non-agriculture growth that is more effective for poverty reduction. In all cases, the degree of pro-poorness of growth increases with the degree of equality in the distribution of income. Thus the conclusion is that the growth of agriculture is very effective for poverty reduction at early stages of development, when income is low and poverty extreme, and this all the more so when inequality is low.

At higher levels of income, away from extreme poverty, other sectors become more instrumental for poverty reduction. Datt and Ravallion (2011) find that, while agriculture was most effective for poverty reduction in India until 1991, the growth of the service sector and urbanization, which pull people out of agriculture, have been the main drivers of poverty reduction since then. In Indonesia, Suryahadi *et al.* (2009) find that the service sector is the most effective, followed by agriculture, with no contribution coming from manufacturing growth.

Agriculture for resource saving and environmental services

Agriculture is a major user and frequent misuser of natural resources. For instance, while water is increasingly scarce for urban users, worldwide 80 percent of captured

641

fresh water is used in agriculture, often profligately. Polluting drinking water with agricultural chemicals can have serious health consequences, as in China and Northern India. LDC agriculture and the associated deforestation contribute an estimated 25 percent of world greenhouse gas emissions that are the source of global climate change—and expansion of agriculture is a cause of deforestation as new lands are opened for cultivation and cattle raising, resulting in loss of biodiversity, local climate change, and soil erosion in watersheds. This does not have to be the case. With an adequate definition of property rights, incentives to conserve, availability of resource-saving technology, and effective collective action in using CPR, agriculture can be a major source of resource saving and of the provision of environmental services (Chapter 15). The farming systems of the rural poor can also be made more resilient to climate change, which is increasingly essential to their food security. Managing the connections among agriculture, natural-resource conservation, and environmental sustainability has become an integral dimension of how agriculture can be used for development. Productivity gains in agriculture for growth and poverty reduction, i.e. future Green Revolutions, particularly in Africa, need to be compatible with the rising constraints of resource saving and environmental sustainability. In other words, future Green Revolutions need to be "doubly green" (Conway, 1999), achieving yield gains in an environmentally sustainable fashion, a major constraint given that world food production will have to increase by another 70 percent over the next 40 years to feed a population projected to reach at least 9 billion in 2050 (FAO, 2008).

THE STATE OF WORLD AGRICULTURE

Hunger is still with us, even if large-scale famines have declined

The world food situation remains both unsatisfactory and precarious, in spite of the extraordinary successes of agriculture in keeping up with a growing population. The world food system is rapidly being transformed by deep structural forces, including globalization of the sources of food, the emergence of integrated food-value chains and supermarkets, rapid urbanization and income growth that lead to changes in diets toward high-value products, major technological and institutional innovations in production, rising energy prices (except in the recent period), and climate change (von Braun, 2007). With food prices rising sharply from 2006, access to food has become increasingly precarious for millions of poor people. Close to 1 billion people remain chronically undernourished, and this number has been rising in the context of the food and financial crises (FAO, 2008). This is one out of every six people in developing countries (17 percent), one out of three in Sub-Saharan Africa, and two out of three in the poorest countries such as Burundi. Undernourishment is particularly high, and devastating, for children (Gross and Webb, 2006): 26 percent of children in the world, 28 percent in Sub-Saharan Africa, 48 percent in South Asia, and 50 percent in Guatemala suffer from wasting. One third of deaths of children under the age of five, totaling some 3–5 million/year, is due to malnutrition, a human cost that could be avoided. Beyond death, malnutrition of children under the age of two has irreversible consequences for growth, health, and mental development. While the MDG 1 of halving poverty by the year 2015 will be met for the world, this is not the case for that of halving undernourishment and child wasting, especially in Sub-Saharan Africa and in South Asia (78 percent of the world's wasted children are in South Asia, in spite of successful economic growth).

The incidence of hunger is more highly correlated with poverty and food entitlements (access to food) than with food availability. Markets can be used to make food available, but countries need foreign exchange and people need income to access it. Famines recur in the Horn of Africa and Niger, but the incidence of large-scale famines has been curtailed, in part thanks to greater political competition and freedom of the press in exposing these events to national and world attention. Sen (1982) observed that large-scale famines could occur in pre-independence India (such as the 1943 Bengal famine, which killed between 1.5 and 3 million people) and in China during the Great Leap Forward (1957–62), which killed between 10 and 30 million people. However, there were no famines in post-independence India once freedom of the press and democracy could expose famines and make politicians accountable. This hypothesis was tested by Besley and Burgess (2002) using a panel of 16 Indian states over the 1958–92 period. They found that states with more active local media and more competitive local politics were more effective at responding to natural disasters (drought and floods) by organizing public food distribution.

While large-scale, geographically concentrated famines are increasingly rare, undernourishment still affects millions of dispersed people who may live next door to people who are not necessarily malnourished. Progress in reducing undernourishment has been uneven across regions. Figure 18.2 characterizes three dimensions of the problem: the percentage change in the prevalence of undernourishment between 1992 and 2012 (horizontal axis), the prevalence of undernourishment in the total

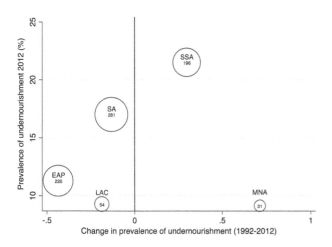

Figure 18.2 *Changing prevalence of undernourishment by region, 1992–2012 (percentage change), prevalence (percentage) and numbers (million) in 2012. Size of bubbles is proportional to millions of undernourished people in 2012*

Source: World Bank, *World Development Indicators.*

643

population in 2012 (vertical axis), and the number of undernourished in millions in 2012 (size of the bubbles). While the prevalence of undernourishment fell in East Asia and the Pacific, South Asia, and Latin America and the Caribbean, it increased in Sub-Saharan Africa and the Middle East and North Africa. The incidence of malnourishment remains high in Sub-Saharan Africa (22 percent) and South Asia (17 percent). The largest numbers of malnourished people are in South Asia (281 million), East Asia and the Pacific (225 million), and Sub-Saharan Africa (196 million). Malnutrition and hunger thus remain a huge problem, with inadequate progress relative to accepted goals and with high welfare and efficiency costs.

Productivity growth in agriculture, but uneven performances

The best indicator of the ability of agriculture to feed humanity is the real price of food grains. Remarkably, it has declined by 55 percent over the last century, from a smoothed index of 2.2 in 1900 to 1 in 2000 (Figure 18.3). This long decline was interrupted by price spikes during three cataclysmic world events: World War One, World War Two, and the Cold War, when Russia invaded Afghanistan in 1973 and the US imposed a trade embargo to use "food as a weapon." But this long-term decline notably came to an end in 2000, precipitating a food crisis in 2008, and a new era of rising prices and increased price volatility. As can be seen in Figure 18.4, these recent price events are closely associated with rising and highly unstable energy prices.

The performance of agriculture has been quite uneven across regions, with rapid growth in per capita food production in East Asia and stagnation or decline in Sub-Saharan Africa. Sub-Saharan Africa remains the only region in the world where food production barely keeps up with population growth (Figure 18.5).

With the availability of new land becoming rapidly exhausted, even in Africa where past output growth has basically been achieved via area expansion, the main source of agricultural output growth is rising yields. Yet two phenomena are worth noticing. The first is that cereal yields have been growing rapidly in OECD countries and in East Asia and the Pacific, and also, if more modestly, in Latin America and Caribbean and in South Asia; but they have been stagnant in Sub-Saharan Africa (Figure 18.6). This clearly shows that Sub-Saharan Africa has not had a Green Revolution, a major challenge to be addressed to achieve growth and poverty

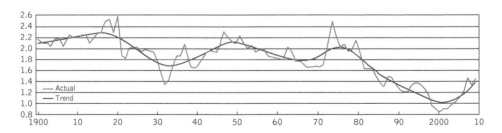

Figure 18.3 *International food real-price index, 1900–2010, 1997=100*

Source: IMF, *Commodity Price System* database.

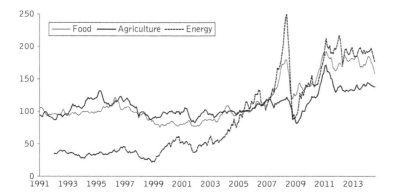

Figure 18.4 *Food-price spikes in 2008 and 2011 and increasing volatility. Monthly prices, 1/1991–9/2014, 6/2005=100*

Source: World Bank, *Global Monitoring Report.*

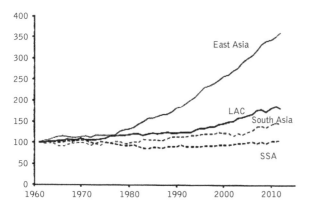

Figure 18.5 *Food production per capita, 1961–2012, 1961=100*

Source: FAO, FAOSTAT.

reduction. The second is that growth in yields has been declining since 1963 in developing countries, signaling the neglect of agriculture and explaining in part the recent recurrence of food crises (Figure 18.7).

The neglect of agriculture by governments and donors

The main message conveyed by the World Development Report 2008, *Agriculture for Development*, was the neglect of agriculture by governments and donors, starting with the stabilization and adjustment policies put in place by the Washington Consensus in response to the debt crisis of 1982. This happened in spite of evidence that agriculture can be a key source of growth for poor countries (see Chapters 3 and 8) (while growth was stagnating in Sub-Saharan Africa); that agriculture can be an effective

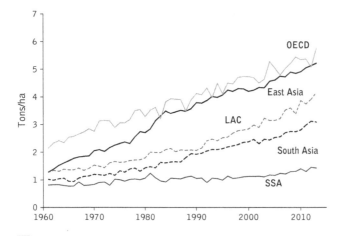

Figure 18.6 *Cereal yields across regions (ton/ha)*

Source: FAO, FAOSTAT.

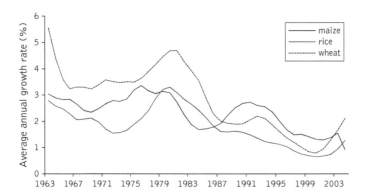

Figure 18.7 *Growth rates (percent) in yields for major cereals in developing countries, 1963–2004*

Source: World Bank, 2007.

instrument to reduce rural poverty (while MDG 1 was failing in Sub-Saharan Africa); and that agriculture can be a source of resource savings and environmental services (while it was absorbing 80 percent of captured water and contributing 20 percent of GHG emissions). The two most evident indicators of neglect are: (1) a declining share of agriculture in public expenditures (illustrated here by Uganda and Nigeria, where it is 4 percent of public expenditures) when African governments have agreed under NEPAD (New Partnership for Africa's Development, an African Union program) that some 10 percent of public expenditures should go to agriculture (Figure 18.8), which corresponds to the general level of expenditure in successful Asian countries when they were at a similar level of development; and (2) a declining share of agriculture in

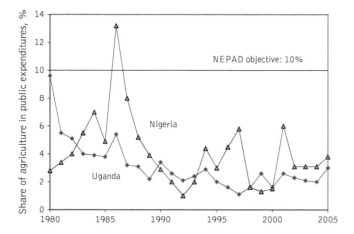

Figure 18.8 *The neglect of agriculture: share of agriculture in public expenditures in Nigeria and Uganda compared to the NEPAD 10-percent objective*

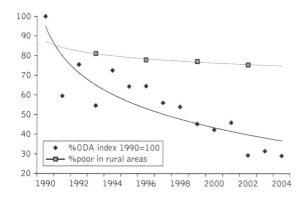

Figure 18.9 *The neglect of agriculture: share of agriculture in overseas development assistance (black line) compared to the share of rural areas in poverty*

Sources: OECD, ODA; World Bank, *PovcalNet*.

overseas development assistance, falling from 12 to 4 percent over the last 15 years, in spite of a steady 75 percent of world poverty being located in rural areas (Figure 18.9).

Why has agriculture been neglected by governments and donors over the last 25 years, with such heavy economic, social, and environmental costs? This is a heatedly debated issue, with much finger pointing. The following seven reasons make a compelling case.

1. Low and falling international commodity prices—due in part to extensive OECD farm subsidies (reaching the extravagant level of US$1 billion/day; see Peterson, 2009) leading to excess production and subsidized exports—discouraged investment in developing-country agriculture.

2. The 1982 debt crisis led to the implementation of stabilization and adjustment policies under the Washington Consensus, promoting a descaling of the role of the state in agriculture in spite of extensive market failures and the need for strong state support for agriculture to grow.

3. Because they are more expedient to implement, poverty-reduction strategies stressed the use of cash and food transfers as opposed to income generation by the poor, diverting attention away from the need to promote the competitiveness of smallholder farmers.

4. Environmental damage caused by adverse practices in agriculture (use of chemical fertilizers, pesticides, forest clearance for land expansion, animal residues) induced donors and environmentalists to distance themselves from investments in agriculture.

5. Misconceived development theory in pursuing industrialization looked at agriculture as a backward, sunset sector instead of a source of growth and an instrument for poverty reduction.

6. Ill defined roles for the state, the market, and civil society in agricultural development led to contradictions and inefficiencies, strongly constraining private sector investment in agriculture that was expected to replace declining public investment.

7. The rate of success of agriculture-for-development projects was low, as designing and implementing them required multidisciplinary approaches that are demanding in skills and time. Many projects had poor outcomes, discouraging investment and foreign-aid support for agriculture, most notably at the World Bank.

The neglect of agriculture for development has had extraordinary costs, now visible in the high contribution of rural areas to world poverty, the recurrence of food crises, and the unabated contributions of agriculture to water scarcity, loss of biodiversity, and climate change.

Why a food crisis in 2008?

It is shocking that there are food crises, with sharply rising and volatile prices, in our world today, in spite of globalization, integrated food-value chains, and remarkable technological and institutional innovations in agriculture. Why do they happen? A feature of food markets is that both supply and demand are quite inelastic in the short run: demand because food is an essential good, supply because it takes another season or two to respond to price incentives. As a consequence, relatively small movements in either supply or demand can have large price effects, especially if world stocks are low, as they were in 2007. This can be seen in Figure 18.10: between 2004 and 2007, world production of maize, rice, and wheat increased by 4.5 percent (from 1969 to 2058 million metric tons), while prices increased by 84 percent. The burden of food-price movements is largely borne by the poor. The food budget shares of poor people tend to be quite high, reaching 60–70 percent for the poorest, and rising prices can have very large welfare costs for them. In addition, the poor have a more price-elastic demand for food (say, −0.5) than the rich (near zero). They absorb a larger proportion of the quantity adjustment necessary for the market to balance supply and demand. The same happens between poor and rich countries, with the burden of imbalance in

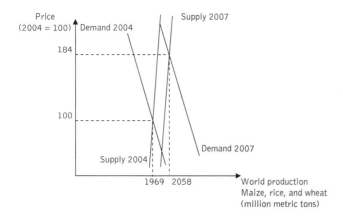

Figure 18.10 *World supply and demand for cereals, 2004 and 2007*

Source: FAO, FAOSTAT.

world supply and demand borne by the poor countries with more-elastic import demand. In countries highly dependent on food imports and with weak fiscal and administrative capacity to protect their poor, the consequences can be socially costly and politically destabilizing.

The main causes of the 2006–8 food crisis were factors that increased demand, decreased supply, and were amplified by short-run speculation and opportunistic policy responses.

Structural shifts on the demand side

1. OECD biofuel policies. In response to the energy crisis, with sharp increases in the price of oil, the US and Europe introduced mandates according to which 10 percent of fuel consumption has to be met by ethanol, while restricting imports of cheap sugarcane-based ethanol from Brazil. As a consequence, ethanol production absorbed 30 percent of US corn production, contributing importantly to the rise in price on the international market.
2. Rapidly rising incomes in large emerging countries such as China and India, inducing changes in diets toward meat and dairy products, and sharply increasing import demand for animal feed, particularly soybeans and corn from Brazil and the US.
3. Continued population growth.

Structural shifts on the supply side

1. High oil and fertilizer prices following the upsurge in petroleum prices pushed production costs upward in agriculture, as we saw in Figure 18.4.
2. A strong US dollar (weak domestic currencies), implying high prices in local currency units for countries that must acquire dollars to import commodities on the world market.

649

3. The long-term neglect of agriculture, with a fall in public investment and foreign aid going to agriculture, led to declining growth in crop yields, as we saw in Figures 18.8 and 18.9.
4. Climate change and greater frequency of extreme weather events, in particular droughts in Australia and crop diseases in Vietnam in the years of the food crisis.

Short-run responses amplifying price shocks

Low food stocks prevented any dampening of the impact on prices of shifts in supply and demand. Adverse policy responses to rising prices in countries such as India and Egypt, which imposed export bans, and Argentina, which imposed export taxes, also contributed to destabilizing international markets. And low interest rates induced speculative capital to move into commodity markets.

While prices have declined from their mid 2008 peaks, due in part to a global economic slowdown that contracted incomes and demand, prices are expected to remain high and volatile for the next 10–15 years. In October 2010, international rice and maize prices were respectively 80 percent and 100 percent above their 2005 prices. High and volatile food prices signal a continuing food crisis that governments need to address both through short-term policy responses (reduced import tariffs on food, social-safety nets to protect the poor) and medium/long-term investments in agriculture to supply the domestic market and generate incomes for the rural poor. Clearly, more attention needs to be given to the determinants of agricultural growth and to access to food for the poor if future food crises are to be avoided.

DETERMINANTS OF AGRICULTURAL GROWTH

Agricultural production responds to three determinants: price and market incentives, availability of sources of growth (technology, inputs, institutions, and public goods), and sustainability in resource use. We briefly review each, stressing in each case the development dilemmas involved and the corresponding policy implications.

Market and price incentives

Price policies

Empirical studies have shown that farmers are responsive to price incentives. This was a major contribution made by T.W. Schultz (1965), who showed that developing-country smallholder farmers are "poor but efficient." What he meant by this is that they are poor because they have little land, few other assets, and use a low-productivity traditional technology, but that they efficiently allocate the meager resources they control in response to price signals. For this reason, "getting the prices right" has been a concern in inducing agriculture to grow (Timmer, 1986). Yet in the short run, higher producer prices imply higher consumer prices, so there is a fundamental redistributive political-economy dilemma in setting the price of food. The historical outcome of this dilemma has been an "urban bias" in price setting against agriculture (Lipton, 1977). Krueger *et al.* (1991) have shown that, in 1980, agricultural taxation was often 40–50 percent for exportables in low-income countries, lowering the domestic price of food correspondingly. Today, agricultural taxation (on commodities such as sugar, cotton, cocoa, coffee, and tobacco) has declined to 19 percent in these countries, while importables (typically rice, maize) tend to be lightly protected, on average 10 percent above the world market price (Anderson and Martin, 2005). However, while developing countries have liberalized their agricultural markets, OECD countries have maintained high protection for their producers (30 percent above the international market price). This induces surplus production in these countries, depressing international prices, and hurting LDC exporters of commodities such as cotton and oilseeds. The Doha round of trade negotiations, under the leadership of the WTO, was expected to press the OECD countries to liberalize their agricultural markets, but they have to this day failed to progress. To reduce the negative impact of their farm policies on developing countries, OECD countries have "decoupled" support for their farmers from production by replacing commodity-price support by direct income transfers. In theory, income effects, as opposed to commodity-price support, should be neutral on production; but it isn't, as it reduces risk and liquidity constraints on producers when there are insurance- and capital-market failures (which there always are), creating incentives to produce more. Clearly, progress needs to be made in the Doha trade negotiations to open OECD agricultural markets to developing-country farmers if prices are to create undistorted incentives to invest in agriculture.

Agricultural markets

In recent years, food markets have been deeply transformed by the development of integrated value chains and the "supermarket revolution" (Reardon and Berdegué, 2002). As can be seen in Figure 18.11, food value chains integrate input producers, farmers, intermediaries (traders, wholesalers), agro-processors, retailers, and consumers into complex relations that allow exchange of information, support contracts, provide financing, define and enforce sanitary and phytosanitary standards, encourage risk sharing, and finance research among private actors. These relations are facilitated along the value chain by business enablers that provide financial services, telecommunications, transport, and energy sources to actors in the value chain. Supermarkets are rapidly becoming the main channel through which urban consumers access their food, even in poor countries, because there are such large economies of scale in food retailing and because they offer guarantees of food safety through privately enforced quality standards.

Atkin *et al.* (2015) use an event-analysis approach to analyze the impact on prices and employment of the entry into Mexico of foreign supermarkets. They use precise information on the location and date of the opening of the supermarkets, and relate this to high-frequency data on store prices, consumption, and employment in the same locations over the period 2002–14. They find that supermarkets create large welfare gains through a decline in the local cost-of-living index, not only by introducing cheaper commodities, but also by enhancing local competition. There is some adverse

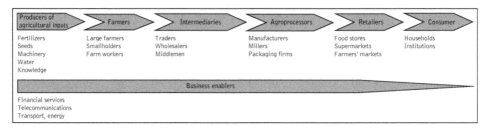

Figure 18.11 *Structure of integrated food value chains*

effect on traditional retail stores, with closures and loss of employment, but overall all income groups gain from the lower prices. The effect is, however, quite regressive, with a welfare gain twice as large for the highest income groups compared to the poorest.

Food export markets are also changing. They are increasingly shifting away from cereals toward non-traditional exports of high-value activities such as fruit (Chile), vegetables (Senegal, Kenya, Guatemala, Peru), fish (Vietnam), and meat (Brazil). These activities can provide sources of income for the rural poor because they tend to be highly labor intensive. They can also be produced by smallholders if they can organize (joining in cooperatives or producer organizations) and link to the value chains. However, there are also risks that smallholder farmers become excluded because it is easier for supermarkets to contract with large farmers, increasingly cutting off small-holders from access to domestic consumers. Family farms can sell directly at local farmers' markets, but their struggle for competitiveness and survival is very much dependent on their success in integrating into modern food value chains through which an increasingly large share of food supply reaches consumers.

Technological change

Because there are strict geographical limits to horizontal expansion (i.e. to the incorporation of new lands in production, also called growth on the extensive margin), future growth in agricultural output will have to come mainly from vertical expansion (gains in TFP, also called growth on the intensive margin). As can be seen in Figure 18.12, most of the growth in cereal production since 1961 has been achieved through yield gains in East Asia, and more recently in South Asia and Latin America as well. This is in sharp contrast with Sub-Saharan Africa, where growth is still being achieved through area expansion. However, even in Africa, area expansion is now severely limited and yield gains will have to become the major source of growth. For this reason, concerns with the growth of agriculture have emphasized technological and institutional innovations that can raise TFP. We focus here on the role of techno-logical innovations in agricultural growth.

To be used and have an impact on output growth, technology needs to meet three requirements:

> *Generation.* It must be generated, be socially profitable, and locally available.
> *Adoption.* It must be adopted by individual farmers for whom it is fit.

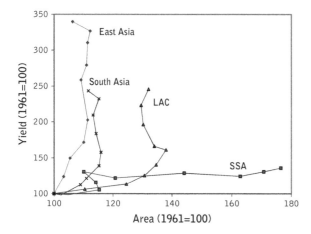

Figure 18.12 *Roles of area and yield in the growth of cereal production over the 1961–2005 period. Each point is a five year average*

Diffusion. It must diffuse across farmers, creating partial- and general-equilibrium effects on prices and on producer and consumer welfare.

We analyze these below.

Generation of technological change: theory of induced technological innovations

Types of technology

Technology can consist in an overall shift in the production function, as in the Solow model, where a TFP gain will help increase output for a given combination of inputs, or equivalently reduce input cost in achieving a given level of output. More specifically, however, technology is aimed at achieving specific gains that will be attractive to the adopter, with a variety of benefits or costs to others as a consequence of adoption. We can distinguish the following five categories of technologies:

- *Land-saving/yield-increasing*: they include high-yielding seed varieties (HYV), fertilizers, insecticides and pesticides, and irrigation. These are the technologies of the Green Revolution.
- *Labor-saving/cost-reducing*: they include animal draft for plowing and hauling, and mechanization such as tractors and harvesters. Labor-saving can be for low-skill labor (desirable in MDCs, where labor costs are high) or for high-skill labor (desirable in LDCs, where they are in short supply).
- *Risk-reducing*: this includes crops tolerant to flood, drought, and heat (abiotic resistance) and to pests and diseases (biotic resistance), and farming systems that provide diversification and resilience to shocks.

653

- *Quality-improving*: examples include more nutritious crops such as orange-fleshed sweet potatoes, high-lysine corn and sorghum, organic farming, and crops with enhanced storage or shelf life.
- *Externality-reducing or enhancing*: externality-reducing technologies include reduced water pollution (less need for fertilizers), reduced pesticide use (Bt corn and cotton (crops genetically modified to be resistant to many harmful insects)), reduced soil erosion (zero tillage, terracing); externality-enhancing technologies include carbon sequestration, agroecology, agroforestry, and biodiversity preservation in traditional farming systems.

Theory of induced technological innovations

What are the mechanisms through which appropriate technologies are generated that respond to farmers' needs? In the theory of induced technological innovations, Hayami and Ruttan (1985) show that this is driven by relative factor scarcity. Technology can be used to substitute for the most constraining factors, i.e. the factors with the greatest rise in relative prices. Where land is scarce and labor plentiful, the price of land will rise relative to that of labor, and innovations should be land-saving, seeking to raise yields (output per unit of land) through technological changes in seeds, farming systems, chemicals, and water management. Historically, this was the technological path pursued in Asia (especially Japan) and Europe (Figure 18.13). The Green Revolution, based on improved water control, high-yielding seed varieties, fertilizers, and chemicals for pest control, is part of this effort. By contrast, where land is plentiful and labor is scarce, the wage will rise relative to the price of land, and innovations should be labor-saving, seeking to raise the productivity of labor through innovations in mechanization (harvesters, tractors) and labor-saving chemicals

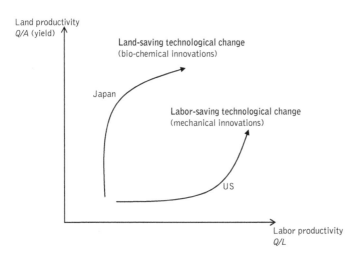

Figure 18.13 *Induced technological innovations to respond to relative factor scarcity. (Q = agricultural output, A = land area, L = labor force in agriculture)*

(e.g. Roundup Ready to weed genetically modified (GMO) crops). This has been the technological path followed in the US, Australia, and Canada. The bias of innovations in agriculture (land-saving or labor-saving) is thus "induced" by price signals that guide the allocation of resources to research priorities in public agricultural-research stations.

The theory of induced technological innovations can be formalized as follows. In the Solow tradition, the generic production function for agriculture would be:

$$q = tf(K, L, A),$$

where q is output, K is capital, L is labor, A is land, and t is TFP. In this case, technological change is factor neutral as it is not tied to any particular factor of production, and it shifts upward the whole production function. In the theory of induced technological innovations, by contrast, technological change is embedded in capital and it can be land-saving or labor-saving. The production function is represented as a two-level function where output is function of a labor index f_L and of a land index f_A as follows:

$$q = q \left[f_L \left(\overbrace{\underbrace{t_L K_L}_{\text{High substitution}}, L}^{\text{Low substitution}} \right), f_A \left(\underbrace{t_A K_A}_{\text{High substitution}}, A \right) \right],$$

where:

f_L = labor index,
f_A = land index,

with low substitution between the two indices,

t_L = labor-saving technological change,
K_L = capital goods that substitute for labor,
t_A = land-saving technological change,
K_A = capital goods that substitute for land (i.e., raise yields),

with high substitution between the labor-saving input $t_L K_L$ and labor, and between the land-saving input $t_A K_A$ and land.

This specification of the production function for agriculture helps contrast two technological paths depending on which factors become relatively more expensive. In the US, as the country was industrializing, labor in agriculture was increasingly scarce relative to land. As a consequence, the wage–price-of-land ratio (w/p_A) was rising. This induced technological change to save on labor, the factor becoming relatively more expensive. As a consequence, labor productivity (q/L) has been rising. In Japan, by contrast, land was increasingly scarce relative to labor due to population growth.

Change in relative resource scarcity (labor vs. land)
↓
Change in relative factor prices (w/p_A)
↓
Political economy: public-research response to rising relative factor scarcities
Research priorities
↓
Technological change toward saving the factor becoming relatively more expensive
↓
Bias of technological change: US/large farms: labor-saving; Japan/small farms: land-saving

Figure 18.14 *Logical sequence in induced technological innovations*

As a consequence, the wage–price-of-land ratio was declining. This induced techno-logical change to save on land, the factor becoming relatively more expensive. As a consequence, land productivity (q/A) has been rising.

The logical sequence in the Hayami and Ruttan theory of induced technological innovations is shown in Figure 18.14.

This theory of technological bias can also be applied to the contrast between large and small farms when there are labor- and land-market failures. On small farms, effective labor costs are low while effective land costs are high. Small farms are thus identical to Japan: they need land-saving technological change to be more competi-tive. By contrast, on large farms, effective labor costs are high and effective land costs are low. Large farms are thus identical to the US: they need labor-saving technological change to be more competitive.

Political economy of technological biases

If technological change is a public good (especially land-saving biological innovations that tend to be non-rival, while labor-saving mechanical innovations can more easily be produced by the private sector) with a budget constraint, the technology that prevails depends on the relative power of large vs. small farmers in the political arena. These farmers engage in lobbying and collective action to pressure public research to allocate budgets to land-saving or labor-saving technological change. If large farmers dominate the political process, then the course of technological change may starve small farmers of land-saving technological change. Small farmers will only acquire technology biased in correspondence with their factor price ratios if they can muster political support, which they typically lack. This was used to explain the lack of public research in Green Revolution technology in Argentina, as demanded by small farmers operating under land constraints, while large farmers, who dominated the allocation of public funds to research, were more interested in labor-saving technological change (de Janvry, 1973).

We can also return to the analysis of international transfers of technology and factor biases we analyzed in Figure 8.4 (in Chapter 8). There, using an Innovation Possibility Frontier, we showed that technology generated in MDCs with high labor/capital price ratios may not be optimum for LDCs with the opposite relative factor prices. This can be applied to the contrast between skilled-labor-saving vs.

unskilled-labor-saving technological change. Since most of the international agricultural research is done in MDCs, it is oriented to reducing the use of low-skill labor (for example, Roundup Ready herbicide used on GMO crops) instead of high-skill labor (Acemoglu and Zilibotti, 2001). LDCs would need research that reduces the need for scarce high-skill labor (e.g. with difficult management techniques such as integrated pest management and precision farming). Yet the technology available as an international public good is driven by factor scarcity in MDCs as opposed to that prevailing in LDCs, creating a second-best option for the LDCs. New technology is not as appropriate as it could be. The success of Bt crops in India, Brazil, and Argentina may be precisely due to the fact that it substitutes for high-skill labor in simplifying pest-control decisions (Qaim and Zilberman, 2003).

Adoption of technological change: farmers' decisions

Once available, technology must be adopted to have an impact on output growth. We saw that adoption of yield-increasing technology has been successful in East and South Asia and in Latin America, but that it is lagging in Sub-Saharan Africa. While 90 percent of the maize area harvested in East and South East Asia is planted with high-yielding varieties, and 57 percent in Latin America and the Caribbean, it is only 17 percent in Sub-Saharan Africa (Gollin *et al.*, 2005). Fertilizer consumption in kilograms per hectare of arable land in 2012 was 372 in East Asia and the Pacific, 161 in South Asia, 125 in Latin America and the Caribbean, 89 in the Middle East and North Africa, and only 15 in Sub-Saharan Africa (World Bank, *World Development Indicators*). Even where technology is successfully adopted, there exist categories of farmers that are constrained in adoption, typically smallholder farmers. A fundamental question, then, is to understand the barriers to technology adoption for Sub-Saharan Africa's smallholder farmers (Foster and Rosenzweig, 2010). A broadly held perception is that, while more new technologies need to be developed especially for Africa and for smallholders, there are many already existing, nationally available, and socially profitable technologies that remain unadopted. Why is this the case? Significant research efforts have been devoted to answering this question (see, for example, the Agricultural Technology Adoption Initiative, ATAI, 2015; Jack, 2011). The array of potential barriers is huge, and all barriers must ultimately be removed for adoption to occur. They fall into five categories.

Profitability

Technology may not be sufficiently profitable for many categories of farmer to adopt it. This is expected to be a first-order-of-importance barrier in Africa due to distorted prices (trade policies with high import tariffs), high transaction costs (poor infrastructure, lack of market facilities such as storage), lack of adaptation to heterogeneous local conditions, local unavailability as private-sector agro-dealers may not be in place, and high prices due to economies of scale (for instance, in importing fertilizers by bags instead of full shipping containers).

Foster and Rosenzweig (2010) discuss the fact that profitability is difficult to measure. At what wage should labor be valued when it is largely provided by the family?

657

With large weather fluctuations affecting yields in rain-fed farming, profitability varies from year to year, yet long series are not available. It is consequently difficult to accurately discount profitability for risk. Production conditions are highly differentiated across space, with prices affected by distance to market, with the result that profitability may decline sharply as soon as one gets to a certain distance from major markets.

Duflo *et al.* (2008) used an RCT with randomly assigned levels of fertilizer applied as "top-dressing" (i.e. two months into the growing season, after the plant has germinated and once the probability that it will grow to fruition is high) to maize in Kenya. The results are for one place in one year, and hence have limited external validity. In addition, the level of use of other inputs may not be adapted to the assigned level of fertilizer, raising questions about the internal validity of experimental conditions. The results they obtained suggest that there is a large heterogeneity in returns across farmers. While potential returns appear high, what matters is getting the amounts of fertilizer applied right. Hence the issue of adoption is not only whether to adopt or not, but, importantly, how to adopt, for which information and learning are essential, as we will see below.

Using historical data on hybrid maize cultivation in Kenya, Suri (2009) shows that there is considerable heterogeneity in profitability and adoption across categories of farmer. Marginal farmers have low net gains from adoption, and do not adopt. Many farmers with high expected returns from adoption do not adopt because of the high cost of adopting, due especially to poor infrastructure. For this reason, she observes that adoption is most intense for a middle group of farmers with both positive expected gains and low costs in adopting. Most important in this study is the emphasis on heterogeneity, explaining both uneven adoption across farmers and the need for customized adaptations to overcome idiosyncratic obstacles to adoption.

Finally, lack of private profitability (while the technology is socially profitable) may be due to positive externalities not captured by the adopter. A mechanism to internalize externalities is missing, transferring to the adopter the full benefit of his decision. Externalities may happen in learning, where farmers benefit from experimentation done by others. In this case, subsidies should be given to early adopters to induce full adoption by the more entrepreneurial farmers (Besley and Case, 1994). Externalities also occur in adopting soil-conservation and biodiversity-preservation techniques. Payments for environmental services (as explored in Chapter 15) have the purpose of implementing transfers when positive externalities limit adoption and induce underprovision of a privately delivered environmental service (Zilberman *et al.*, 2008).

Information and learning

Information about the existence, use, and expected benefits of adoption may be missing, particularly when the technology is new. A key proposition here is that the value of a given agricultural technology depends on local conditions, hence farmers need to learn how to use the technology in their own particular location. This information could be obtained from demonstration plots, through learning-by-doing, or through learning-from-others.

In their pioneering study of farmers' adoption of Green Revolution technology in India, Foster and Rosenzweig (1995) show that learning a new technology is essential for adoption as optimal use of technology depends on local conditions. Farmers can learn from their own experiments with the new technology, or from the experience of their neighbors. Using data for a panel of households, and tracking the roll-out of the Green Revolution across time and space, they find that imperfect knowledge about how to use new varieties is indeed a significant barrier to the adoption of these varieties. Learning-from-others (i.e. learning spillovers) increases adoption. For farmers with experienced neighbors, the new technology is significantly more profitable than for those with inexperienced neighbors. A given increase in average experience of a farmer's neighbors increases profitability by almost twice as much as the same increase in his own experience. However, the opportunity to learn from others slows down adoption as farmers would rather wait to assess their neighbors' experience with the new technology. The existence of positive learning spillovers implies that there is underinvestment in learning. Subsidies to early adopters are then justified to increase the level of adoption.

Conley and Udry (2010) improved on the learning-from-others idea by looking at the role of social networks in adoption. They studied the use of fertilizers on a new crop, pineapples, in Ghana. Again, technology is local and there is a need to learn by oneself or from neighbors in deciding to adopt. They used detailed survey data on who talks to whom about agricultural practices within social networks, and on what each farmer's neighbors do. They found that social learning is important. People adjust their fertilizer use based on their neighbors' experiences, paying particular attention to bad news. The effect is largest for inexperienced farmers. They also found that people pay more attention to farmers with similar wealth and with more experience than them.

These results show that learning how to use a technology, not just whether to use it or not, is important for adoption. There are high returns to experience (learning-by-doing) and to spillovers (learning-from-others). The extent of communication through social networks, and the type of information exchanged, are evidently context specific. Cai et al. (2015) show that farmers in traditional Chinese communities communicate to peers what they know about a new technology—weather insurance in this particular case. They are, however, not willing to tell others what decision they have taken regarding adoption for fear of being wrong and losing face with others as a consequence of bad judgment.

Credit and insurance market failures

In agriculture, there typically exists a long lag between planting and harvesting, implying that money is tied up in production for a long period of time. Lags are typically four to six months for cereals, but more than one year for cassava, and four to five years for tree crops such as coffee and cacao. Many technologies have large upfront costs, requiring credit, yet credit for smallholder farmers is largely unavailable. The microfinance revolution has sought collateral substitutes to provide access to credit to the poor, but the cost of microfinance loans remains too high for most agricultural activities. Other forms of access to credit have been explored, including using standing crops as collateral. Savings can also be promoted as an alternative to loans. For capital goods, such as KickStart irrigation pumps, rental-with-option-to-buy is a way of supporting adoption without formal lending arrangements.

Risk is also a major factor preventing the adoption of new technologies. Lack of access to insurance implies the need for risk management, maintaining farmers in the use of traditional crops. But even where insurance products are available, including index-based products that can overcome AS and MH problems in insurance, uptake has been very low. Cole *et al.* (2013) show that this is due to lack of trust in the insurance provider, high cost, and poor quality of the insurance product.

In general, progress in lifting credit and insurance market constraints has been insufficient. Agriculture has not benefited from the microfinance revolution. New credit and insurance products that can meet the cost requirements of agriculture are needed.

If insurance fails, technology itself can be a response to risk and insurance market failures. New rice varieties that are tolerant to extensive periods of flooding or of drought have recently been released. Dar *et al.* (2013) used an RCT approach to distribute 5kg minikits of flood-tolerant seeds to farmers in Odisha, India. They found that adoption of these varieties not only helped farmers cope better with floods, but also allowed them to engage less in risk management, using in particular better planting practices and early fertilizers. Farmers do this because they know that the risk of losing their investment in the crops due to flooding has now been reduced. The remarkable result is that the risk-reducing technology is good not only in bad years (through improved shock coping) but also in good years (through reduced risk management) (Emerick *et al.*, 2014). Specifically, yield losses avoided in a flood year are on average 682 kg/ha. The average gain in normal years due to ex-ante behavioral response is 283 kg/ha. Since there is one flood year for every three to four normal years, the expected gain in normal years for every flood year is between 566 kg/ha and 849 kg/ha—say, 700 kg/ha. Over time, the gain from risk management (achieved through behavioral response) thus approximately doubles the gain from improved shock coping (achieved through agronomic research).

Lack of secure property rights

In Sub-Saharan Africa, property rights over land are typically vested with the state, as opposed to users. Lack of secure property rights prevents farmers from investing in agricultural technologies that have lasting value. There is very little investment in irrigation and soil conservation as even fertilizers tend to have residual value on soil fertility over several years. Goldstein and Udry (2008) show that cocoa farmers in Ghana are unwilling to invest in soil fertility because of insecurity of continued access to land. Lack of formal titles also prevents farmers from using land as collateral in accessing commercial bank loans.

Behavior

Farmers' decisions about new technologies may not be consistent with profit maximization. The field of psychology and economics, pioneered by economists such as Thaler (1980), Kahneman and Tversky (1979), and Rabin (1998) has opened new perspectives on the behavior of poor people in developing countries. This has been applied by Duflo *et al.* (2011) to farmers' behavior toward adoption of new technologies such as fertilizers for maize production in Kenya. The question is: why do farmers not keep part of the cash earned from the harvest sale to buy fertilizers when they know that they are subject to credit constraints and that the use of fertilizers on the following year's crop will be highly profitable? A hypothesis is that it may be due to present-biased preferences (also called hyperbolic discounting), whereby farmers procrastinate in putting money aside for the future purchase of fertilizers.

Hyperbolic discounting is a situation in which people discount the entire future more than they discount any future period relative to the previous one. Normal discounting is written as: $U_t = \sum_{k=t}^{T} \delta^{k-t} v(c_k)$, where δ is the discount factor. By contrast, hyperbolic discounting is written as: $U_t = v(c_t) + \beta \sum_{k=t+1}^{T} \delta^{k-t} v(c_k)$. There is present bias if $\beta < 1$. For someone with present bias, \$100 now may be preferred to \$110 in one month even though \$110 in two months is preferred to \$100 in one month. There is time inconsistency in preferences. Sophisticated procrastinators, knowing that they will fail to set money aside at harvest time for future purchase, will seek commitment devices to place restraint on their future behavior.

Duflo *et al.* (2011) set up an RCT to test this proposition and to identify the types of farmer to whom this applies. Farmers were randomly allocated to two treatment arms and a control: T1 were visited by an agent at harvest time and, as a nudge, offered the opportunity to buy fertilizer then, with free delivery at planting time (called the SAFI: Saving and Fertilizer Initiative); T2 were visited by the agent before harvest, and asked when he should return to sell fertilizer, providing an opportunity for procrastination, although the sale offer was the same as in T1. A third group served as control. A fourth group was offered a large subsidy to measure the effect of price incentives. The results showed that the SAFI was taken by 30–40 percent of the farmers and increased fertilizer use by 10 to 12 percent. The effect of visiting early was comparable to a 50 percent reduction in price as measured in the fourth group. Many farmers in T2, offered the ex-ante choice of deciding when the agent should come back, chose to have the person come back immediately after harvest as opposed to later. This suggests that many farmers are sophisticated procrastinators, i.e. they know they need help in setting aside cash for the purchase of fertilizers. The conclusion is that behavior matters, that procrastination may be important in explaining low adoption, that many farmers know that they have a time-consistency problem and are interested in the availability of commitment devices, and hence that new incentive schemes should be put in place to help people discipline themselves in technology adoption.

661

*Diffusion of technological change: market effects
and incidence of benefits*

The diffusion of a technological change is the aggregate outcome of adoption decisions. It is driven by both the supply (availability) of technology and by farmers' decisions to adopt, making up the demand side. Griliches (1957) was the first to recognize the existence of a logistic pattern in his classical study of the diffusion of hybrid corn across the US (Figure 18.15). Seed companies made the hybrid seeds available first in states with larger potential effective demand (Iowa, Wisconsin, etc.). Once available, farmers would initially slowly adopt, then adoption would accelerate, and finally converge to a potential 100 percent, the logistic pattern. The new technology came later to states with less potential effective demand (Texas, Alabama), and diffusion was slower and eventually incomplete.

Ultimately, as markets re-equilibrate following a technological change, who benefits among producers and consumers depends on how prices adjust, which in turn depends on the elasticity of demand for the good. If it is a non-tradable good, demand is inelastic. As supply shifts, prices fall, benefiting consumers. The diffusion of innovations is propelled by the "product-market treadmill" of falling average costs and falling prices (Cochrane, 1958). As prices fall, early adopters' profits are erased. Schumpeterian farmers demand more new technology which, when innovated and adopted, will again increase supply and lower prices. There is in this fashion a continuing race between falling costs and falling prices, the so-called technological treadmill on which farmers always run after new technology, to find themselves at a standstill in terms of long-term profits.

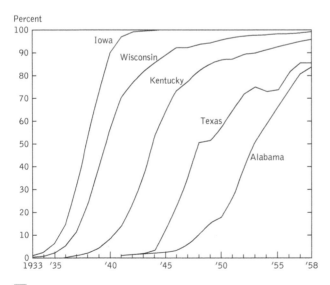

Figure 18.15 *Logistic diffusion pattern for hybrid corn seeds in the US*

Source: Griliches, 1957.

If, by contrast, the good is tradable, then demand is infinitely elastic. Supply shifts without a decline in prices and producers gain. The gain in producer surplus is capitalized into land values. The treadmill thus occurs via the land market, forming a "land-market treadmill." As technology diffuses across farmers, average costs fall and land prices and land rents rise. These rising costs eventually push farmers to seek new technological innovations in a technological treadmill.

These contrasted partial-equilibrium effects are represented in Figure 18.16. With a non-tradable good (a), the net social gain from technological change is absorbed by the rise in consumer surplus, all the more so when demand is more inelastic. With a tradable or price-supported good (b), the net social gain is absorbed by farmers in the form of a rising producer surplus. There are evidently stronger long-term incentives for farmers to adopt a yield-increasing technological change when it is used to produce a tradable or price-supported good.

This result about non-tradable goods has something to say about adoption of technological innovations in shallow markets, where demand is inelastic. In Sub-Saharan Africa, poor infrastructure and high transportation costs imply that markets tend to be isolated and shallow. A new technology, such as fertilizers or improved seeds, will shift local supply and quickly depress prices on local markets, choking further adoption. Unless a technological treadmill is in place to reduce production costs further, adoption will be limited. The key to sustained adoption, then, is to connect local to global markets to make demand more elastic, allowing farmers to capture the gains from the technological innovations they adopt in their operations. Limited

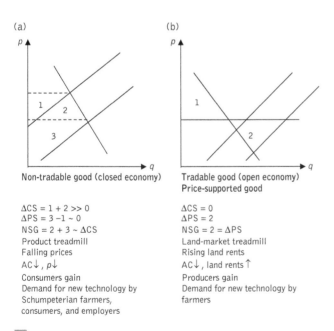

(a)

Non-tradable good (closed economy)

$\Delta CS = 1 + 2 >> 0$
$\Delta PS = 3 - 1 \sim 0$
$NSG = 2 + 3 \sim \Delta CS$
Product treadmill
Falling prices
$AC\downarrow, p\downarrow$
Consumers gain
Demand for new technology by
Schumpeterian farmers,
consumers, and employers

(b)

Tradable good (open economy)
Price-supported good

$\Delta CS = 0$
$\Delta PS = 2$
$NSG = 2 = \Delta PS$
Land-market treadmill
Rising land rents
$AC\downarrow$, land rents $\uparrow$
Producers gain
Demand for new technology by
farmers

Figure 18.16 Welfare gains from technological change for a non-tradable good (product-market treadmill) (a) and a tradable good (land-market treadmill) (b)

profitability of technological innovations is not an issue of the technology, but of the market conditions in which the technology diffuses. Linking farmers to deep markets through infrastructure investments is thus essential to a Green Revolution for Africa.

Role of the state in R&D

One of the important public goods for agriculture is investment in agricultural research. The reason why it is a public good is that many innovations have benefits that are non-rival and non-excludable such as better agronomic practices and improved farming systems. This research also has large positive externalities across countries. As such, agricultural research is an international public good. Estimates of the internal rate of return to investment in agricultural research have repeatedly been found to be very large, of the order of 40 percent (Alston *et al.*, 2000). This is higher than the rate of return in alternative public-goods investments, indicating that there is underinvestment in agricultural research. Why is this the case?

The most obvious answer is the positive externalities of research and the tendency for governments to under-provide public goods. There are also large economies of scale, favoring large over small countries. For this reason, the world's strongest public agricultural-research systems are found in Brazil (*Embrapa*), China, India, and the US (USDA and the Land Grant College System). The CGIAR (Consultative Group for International Agricultural Research) is an international non-profit alliance supporting 15 research centers across the globe that aims at remedying national-level underinvestment. It was at the heart of the 1960s Green Revolution, which doubled or tripled yields in the major cereals (wheat, corn, and rice). In spite of high returns to its spending on research, it too has had relatively stagnant budgets.

The tendency to underinvest in agricultural research, which is particularly notable in Sub-Saharan Africa, is another symptom of the neglect of agriculture. Private research (e.g. Monsanto, Novartis) is increasingly important, thanks to patent protection on biological innovations. However, more than 90 percent of this investment is located in industrialized countries. In developing countries, with a great deal of heterogeneity of farming systems, decentralized and participatory approaches to research are important. This has been quite effective in adapting seeds to local conditions, and is part of the institutional innovations needed to complement technological innovations. Introduction of GMO can make important contributions, but this technology has been used mainly for commercial crops in industrialized countries, with the exception of Bt cotton in India and South America. Bio-safety issues and public research for smallholder farming need to be addressed to make this technology effective for development and available in Africa, where it is badly needed, in part to address the rapidly rising threats of climate change with drought-, flood-, and heat-resistant seed varieties. Agroecology is another promising technological path as it addresses constraints on complete farming systems and seeks to find solutions that limit the use of external inputs, making the approach particularly useful in contexts and for farmers failed by markets. These two approaches—GMO and agroecology—should be seen as complementary, as opposed to ideological fortresses, as has been the case.

Sustainability in resource use and environmental services

Agriculture and the environment are closely interrelated. Agriculture intensification is reducing biodiversity and creating agrochemical pollution, overuse of scarce water, and health costs from pesticide poisoning. Animal diseases can affect humans, such as avian flu. Agriculture in fragile environments is contributing to deforestation and climate change. Climate change is probably the greatest challenge to the sustainability of farming systems, particularly in tropical and mountainous environments. Agriculture needs to help mitigate emissions, and it needs to adapt to climate change. Solutions include better technology (drought and flood resistance, precision farming aided by GPS observations), water management (larger reservoirs), payment for environmental services (carbon-trading schemes with payment for zero tillage and avoided deforestation), and devolution of resource management (irrigation schemes, watershed management) to local communities. Approaches to farming systems such as conservation agriculture and agro-ecology seek to achieve sustainability by enhancing the productivity of natural systems, as opposed to using mechanical and chemical technologies. There has been much underinvestment in these lines of research as well.

FOOD SECURITY IN DEVELOPING COUNTRIES

The state of malnutrition and hunger

The MDG 1 aimed at reducing by half the incidence of both extreme poverty and hunger between 1990 and 2015. Yet while substantial progress has been made in reducing poverty, this has not been the case for hunger. The incidence of hunger has fallen from 18.9 percent in 1990–2 to 12 percent in 2011–13, short of the MDG goal (FAO, IFAD, and WFP, 2013). There were 1 billion hungry people in 1990–2, 878 million during the food crisis in 2008–10, and 802 million in 2011–13. Qualitative deficiencies in diets exceed quantitative deficits. Inadequate diets, so-called hidden hunger, result in micronutrient deficiencies (particularly lack of iodine, Vitamin A, and iron) that affect 2 billion people globally. Quantitative and qualitative malnutrition is particularly devastating for children in the 1,000 days after conception. 165 million children in the world are stunted, preventing them from reaching their full physical and cognitive potential.

Inadequate diets also include overweight and obesity. Using the BMI as the indicator (equal to height in cm over weight in kg), 34 percent of world population is overweight, with a BMI in excess of 25, a number equal to 2.4 billion people. The number of overweight people has risen faster in developing than in industrialized countries: it rose from 321 million in 1980 to 557 million in 2008 in industrialized countries (a 174 percent increase), while it rose from 204 million to 904 million in developing countries over the same period (a 443 percent increase). Being overweight, and especially obese (a BMI of 30 and above, affecting 700 million people, or

665

29 percent of the overweight population), is associated with Type 2 diabetes, cardiovascular diseases, and some types of cancer. The WHO estimates that 2.8 million people die from obesity every year. Shockingly, the number of overweight people is now almost three times the number of people in hunger, and 62 percent of them are in developing countries.

Determinants of food insecurity and national policy approaches

How do we explain food insecurity? The commonly accepted definition of food security is "when all people, at all times, have physical, social, and economic access to sufficient, safe, and nutritious food to meet their dietary needs and food preferences for an active and healthy life" (FAO, 2008). As for poverty, it is useful to distinguish between two types of insecurity: chronic and transitory (Staatz et al., 2009). And it is useful to recognize three causes of food insecurity: availability, access, and use (adequacy). Each has particular determinants, and each can be addressed with specific policy options. Policy instruments in turn can consist in interventions through markets, or in direct state interventions (Galtier, 2011). This combination of types, causes, and instruments gives us a typology of policies and programs that can be used to reduce food insecurity (Table 18.1).

The entries in the table show the tremendous complexity of food insecurity, and the multiple policy and program instruments that can be mobilized to address it at the national level. Interventions concern the supply side (availability), the demand side (access), and the use of food (behavior, culture).

- *Supply side: increasing production.* The FAO (2009) estimated that global agricultural production will need to increase by 70 percent between 2005 and 2050 to accommodate population growth, higher incomes, and shifting diets linked to urbanization. We have seen that this increase will have to come from productivity improvements since horizontal expansion has largely reached its limits. This is made all the more challenging by climate change, soil degradation, water scarcity, and rising energy prices. Investment in agricultural research will be important for this, yet we know that there is a tendency for underinvestment in agricultural research, particularly when it is a public good (Alston et al., 2009). There are important debates between an agroecology approach, which minimizes the use of external inputs, and promotion of a "doubly Green Revolution," which balances the use of chemical technology (fertilizers, pesticides) with concerns for sustainability and a reduced agricultural contribution to GHG emissions and environmental degradation (de Schutter, 2010).
- *Supply side: availability to consumers.* Three important areas of debate must be considered here: livestock, biofuels, and waste. The first is whether the shift to meat-based diets that accompanies rising incomes and urbanization can be contained. Livestock production occupies 26 percent of agricultural land in pasture and 33 percent for the production of animal feed, mainly maize and soybeans, or a total of some 60 percent of world agricultural land. The expansion of pasture is a major source of deforestation, and livestock production contributes to 18 percent

Table 18.1 Food insecurity in developing countries: policy instruments

Type of food insecurity	Type of policy instrument	Causes of food insecurity			
		Lack of availability of food (supply-side)	Lack of access to food (demand-side, entitlements, direct access)		Misuse of food (household)
Chronic insecurity	Interventions through markets	Make markets work better in time and space	Aggregate economic growth		
	Direct state interventions	Invest in agriculture for productivity gains	Income-generation programs		Home economics and nutrition training
		Long-term food aid	Social-assistance programs for the chronic poor		
		Biofortification of staple foods	Enhance productivity in smallholder farming		
			Risk coping (ex-ante relative to shocks)	Risk management (ex-post relative to shocks)	
Transitory insecurity	Interventions through markets	Make markets work better in time and space	New financial products		
	Direct state interventions	Intervene in markets to stabilize prices	Enhance production in smallholder farming	Emergency loan programs	Emergency feeding practices
				Social assistance for vulnerable individuals (quick-response programs)	

of world GHG emissions, a larger share than transport. The second is the demand for biofuels. Biofuel mandates in transport in the US and EU were one of the most important factors explaining the global food-price increase in 2008. Biofuel mandates and food security currently lack coordination. The third is the magnitude of food waste. The FAO (Gustavsson *et al.*, 2011) estimated that one third of total food production is lost or wasted. Waste per capita is estimated at 95 to 115kg/year in Europe and North America, and 6 to 11kg/year in Sub-Saharan Africa and South/Southeast Asia. In developing countries, waste is principally a result of inadequate storage and packaging/processing facilities, as well as to poor connections between farmers to markets.

■ *Demand side: poverty*. Even if world supply has been overall adequate, with generally falling real food prices from the 1950s to the 2008 price spike, large groups of world population remain too poor to satisfy their basic nutritional needs. Largest among them is smallholder farmers, who, paradoxically, are a majority of the world's poor and malnourished (World Bank, 2007). Yet, as we will see in Chapter 22, there has been a lack of support for smallholder farmers, both for their own food production and to help them integrate into food markets to achieve competitiveness with larger commercial farmers. An important area of intervention to promote food security is thus the development of efficient local food systems, in which smallholder farmers can play a major role.

National food-security strategies

Implementing a food-security strategy, as described in Table 18.1, requires the ability to formulate comprehensive national strategies, as Brazil did in its Zero Hunger program. Piecemeal approaches will not work. However, formulating comprehensive strategies is demanding. It requires data collection, the analytical capacity to diagnose and establish causalities, broad consultations in defining medium-term strategies, sustained access to financial resources, and coordination across sectors, something that governments are notably bad at doing. No wonder that reducing malnutrition and hunger has been so difficult to achieve.

International coordination for food security

Due to the importance of international trade in food, domestic food prices are strongly affected by international prices. This was a major lesson of the 2008 food crisis, during which exporting countries responded to rising international prices with export bans or higher export taxes to protect their domestic consumers. Avoiding this requires greater international coordination. Yet world governance for food security is seriously lacking. The international community has begun to address this issue by reconstituting a Committee on World Food Security (CFS) with a membership of nation states, international organizations, NGOs and philanthropic foundations, and the private sector. This is a unique, ongoing experiment that may yet succeed or fail. Its achievements to this point have been limited to providing voluntary guidelines on such issues as the management of food-price volatility, access to land, biofuel mandates, climate change, social protection for food security, and investment in smallholder farming (CFS, High Level Panel of Experts on Food Security and Nutrition).

THE POLITICAL ECONOMY OF AGRICULTURE FOR DEVELOPMENT

Why is it so difficult to make good agricultural and food-security policies? There may be political-economy specificities to agriculture and food that explain the persistence of underuse and misuse of agriculture for development. Indeed, there are many dilemmas that stand in the way of good policy.

1. *There is a basic dilemma in "getting the prices right" for food products.* Prices should be set low for consumers to reduce hunger and increase their real incomes, but they should be set high to give incentives to farmers to invest in agriculture (Streeten, 1987). The price of food will always be politically charged, as it is a cost for some and a benefit for others, with both parties always dissatisfied and struggling for price gains. An alternative to the use of low-food prices for food security would be to use targeted social-assistance programs to protect the poorest groups. Yet, today, the International Labor Office (ILO, 2011) estimates that some 75 percent of world population does not have access to social protection against unemployment, illness, disability, crop failures, and spikes in food prices.

2. *There is a key aspect of heterogeneity among poor farmers that creates a price-policy dilemma.* Some are net sellers who benefit from higher prices, while others are net buyers who, like consumers, benefit from lower prices. Since many of the world's poor (possibly a majority) are net buying farmers, it is difficult to use prices to raise the income of net selling smallholders, many of whom are also poor, without creating a serious conflict of poor against poor (World Bank, 2007).

3. *There is a basic short-term–long-term policy dilemma in allocating scarce fiscal resources to respond to a food crisis that originates in rising food price.* Should fiscal resources be used to ease the short-run food problem for consumers (e.g. through food-aid programs) or should they be used to invest in agriculture and address the long-term productivity problem (thus increasing supply and reducing future upward pressures on prices)? The political economy of crisis response tends to favor consumers over producers, eventually reproducing the neglect of agriculture that may have caused (or at least contributed to) the crisis.

4. *There is a basic policy dilemma in seeking to achieve food security between reliance on comparative advantage and trade, and reliance on national food self-sufficiency.* Should food security be sought through greater domestic self-sufficiency or should a country use its comparative advantages and trade for food? This debate runs deep through the development community. The International Assessment of Agricultural Knowledge, Science, and Technology for Development (IAASTD, 2009), an intergovernmental process sponsored by the UN, took the position that food security should be achieved through food self-sufficiency. This position was also endorsed by the UN Special Rapporteur on the Right to Food (de Schutter, 2010). The World Bank (2007) and the International Food Policy Research Institute of the CGIAR take the position that countries should capitalize on

669

comparative advantage and trade for food security, with due account given to various sources of risk. Domestic prices of non-tradable foods are typically more unstable than international prices due to more variable local climate and smaller market size; but this was briefly reversed during the 2008 global food crisis. The choice of domestic self-sufficiency vs. food dependency to achieve food security depends on the origins of food shocks (international price shocks, domestic weather shocks, or employment and income shocks). It also depends on how well international and domestic food markets work, and whether a country can access international loans (e.g. through the IMF) to purchase food in case of emergency.

5. *There may exist a dilemma in achieving the multiple objectives of development through agriculture.* Agriculture is important not only as a sector producing a particular product (say, a pile of rice) but also as a process that involves households, communities, and the environment. The process of agricultural production is important in achieving a country's development objectives: smallholder farming will likely be more effective for poverty reduction, but large farms may be better for productivity gains and to access sophisticated markets through integrated value chains. This may lead to a trade-off between poverty and productivity (growth) that feeds into the policy debate on the relative merits of small vs. large farms, and to concern with the current "land grab" by large farmers, often through foreign direct investment (Deininger and Byerlee, 2011).

6. *There may, similarly, exist trade-offs,* and hence the need for difficult policy choices, between productivity gains using agro-chemicals (pesticides, antibiotics) and the health of farmers and farmworkers; intensification of farming and environmental degradation; irrigation for higher yields and breeding grounds for mosquitoes; and land expansion for agricultural growth and deforestation (e.g. expansion of soybean and cotton production in the Brazilian Cerrado region).

To conclude, we note that agriculture has, overall, been highly successful in feeding a rapidly rising world population and in inducing industrial growth in agrarian economies and in helping reduce poverty, with India, China, and Vietnam recent examples. Yet it has also been underused and misused, and nowhere is this more obvious than in Sub-Saharan Africa, where it still has a large unrealized potential role to play. The food crisis, failure to meet the MDG on hunger, and climate change make seizing this opportunity all the more urgent. In the end, however, whether agriculture is used for development or not is a political decision. The neglect of agriculture is not a mistake, but a social choice. Remedying this situation will require: (1) greater public awareness of what agriculture can do for development, (2) identification of more effective approaches in using agriculture for development, as opposed to relying on cash transfers and migration to reduce rural poverty, (3) the development of skills to use agriculture effectively for development, from producers' organizations to national governments and international organizations, and (4) commitments by governments and donors that they will give more importance to agriculture in their development plans and budgets. The current failures of agriculture have increased popular support for increased investment in agriculture. But support needs to be translated into sustainable action for the potential developmental role of agriculture to be more fully captured.

CONCEPTS SEEN IN THIS CHAPTER

Marketed surplus

Multiple functions of agriculture

Capital contributions

Forced deliveries

"Invisible transfers"

Market contribution

Green Revolution

Land-saving and labor-saving technology

Induced technological innovations

Logistic diffusion pattern

Barriers to adoption

Underinvestment in agricultural research

Food insecurity: availability, access, and use of food

REVIEW QUESTIONS: AGRICULTURE FOR DEVELOPMENT

1. What is meant by the "contributions of agriculture to development": product, factor (capital, foreign exchange, labor), and market contributions to growth; contributions to poverty reduction; contributions to the provision of environmental services?

2. If agriculture is good for growth and poverty reduction, why has it been neglected by governments and aid donors over the last 25 years?

3. What is the theory of "induced technological innovations," and why are innovations biased to respond to relative factor scarcity? Why was technological change in agriculture labor-saving in the US and land-saving in Japan?

4. How are the benefits from technological change differentially appropriated by producers and consumers depending on whether the commodity is tradable or non-tradable? When demand is inelastic, why are farmers on a technological treadmill?

5. How is a household's food insecurity related to the availability, access, and use of food?

REFERENCES

Acemoglu, Daron, and Fabrizio Zilibotti. 2001. "Productivity Differences." *Quarterly Journal of Economics* 116(2): 563–606.

Adelman, Irma. 1984. "Beyond Export-Led Growth." *World Development* 19(2): 937–49.

Alston, Julian, Michele Marra, Philip Pardey, and T.J. Wyatt. 2000. "Research Returns Redux: A Meta-analysis of the Returns to Agricultural R&D." *Australian Journal of Agricultural and Resource Economics* 44(2): 185–215.

Alston, Julian, Philip Pardey, Jennifer James, and Matthew Andersen. 2009. "A Review of Research on the Economics of Agricultural R&D." *Annual Reviews of Resource Economics* 1(1): 537–65.

Anderson, Kym, and Will Martin. 2005. *Agricultural Trade Reform and the Doha Development Agenda*. New York: Palgrave McMillan.

ATAI. 2015. Agricultural Technology Adoption Initiative. http://www.atai-research.org/ (accessed 2015).

Atkin, David, Benjamin Faber, and Marco Gonzalez-Navarro. 2015. "Retail Globalization and Household Welfare: Evidence from Mexico." Working paper, University of California at Berkeley.

Bairoch, Paul. 1973. "Agriculture and the Industrial Revolution, 1700–1914." In Carlo Cipolla (ed.), *The Fontana Economic History of Europe: The Industrial Revolution,* Vol. 3, 452–506. London: Collins/Fontana Books.

Besley, Timothy, and Ann Case. 1994. "Diffusion as a Learning Process: Evidence from HYV Cotton." Working paper, Development Studies, Princeton University.

Besley, Timothy, and Robin Burgess. 2002. "The Political Economy of Government Responsiveness: Theory and Evidence from India." *Quarterly Journal of Economics* 117(4): 1415–51.

Cai, Jing, Alain de Janvry and Elizabeth Sadoulet. 2015. "Social Networks and the Decision to Insure." *American Economic Journal: Applied Economics* 7(2): 81–108.

CFS. High Level Panel of Experts on Food Security and Nutrition. http://www.fao.org/cfs/cfs-hlpe (accessed 2015).

Christiaensen, Luc, and Lionel Demery. 2007. *Down to Earth: Agriculture and Poverty Reduction in Africa*. Washington, DC: World Bank.

Christiaensen, Luc, Lionel Demery, and Jesper Kuhl. 2011. "The (Evolving) Role of Agriculture in Poverty Reduction—An Empirical Perspective." *Journal of Development Economics* 96(2): 239–54.

Cochrane, Willard. 1958. *Farm Prices: Myth and Reality*. St. Paul: University of Minnesota Press.

Cole, Shawn, Xavier Giné, Jeremy Tobacman, Petia Topalova, Robert Townsend, and James Vickery. 2013. "Barriers to Household Risk Management: Evidence from India." *American Economic Journal: Applied Economics* 5(1): 104–35.

Conley, Timothy, and Christopher Udry. 2010. "Learning about a New Technology: Pineapple in Ghana." *American Economic Review* 100(1): 35–69.

Conway, Gordon. 1999. *The Doubly Green Revolution: Food for All in the Twenty-First Century*. Ithaca, NY: Cornell University Press.

Dar, Manzoor, Alain de Janvry, Kyle Emerick, David Raitzer, and Elisabeth Sadoulet. 2013. "Flood-tolerant Rice Reduces Yield Variability and Raises Expected Yield, Differentially Benefitting Socially Disadvantaged Groups." *Scientific Reports* 3, Article number 3315, November 22.

Datt, Gaurav, and Martin Ravallion. 2011. "Has India's Economic Growth Become More Pro-poor in the Wake of Economic Reforms?" *World Bank Economic Review* 25(2): 157–89.

Deininger, Klaus, and Derek Byerlee. 2011. *Rising Global Interest in Farmland: Can It Yield Sustainable and Equitable Benefits?* Washington, DC: World Bank.

de Janvry, Alain. 1973. "A Socio-economic Model of Induced Innovation for Argentine Agricultural Development." *Quarterly Journal of Economics* 87(3): 410–35.

de Janvry, Alain, and Elisabeth Sadoulet. 2010. "Agricultural Growth and Poverty Reduction: Additional Evidence." *World Bank Research Observer* 25(1): 1–20.

de Schutter, Olivier. 2010. "Agroecology and the Right to Food." Geneva: United Nations Human Rights Council.

Diamond, Jared. 1998. *Guns, Germs, and Steel: The Fates of Human Societies*. New York: W.W. Norton and Co.

Duflo, Esther, Michael Kremer, and Jonathan Robinson. 2008. "How High Are Rates of Return to Fertilizer? Evidence from Field Experiments in Kenya." *American Economic Review* 98(2): 482–8.

Duflo, Esther, Michael Kremer, and Jonathan Robinson. 2011. "Nudging Farmers to Use Fertilizer: Theory and Experimental Evidence from Kenya." *American Economic Review* 101(6): 2350–90.

Emerick, Kyle, Alain de Janvry, Elisabeth Sadoulet, and Manzoor Dar. 2014. "Risk and the Modernization of Agriculture." Working paper, Department of Economics, Tufts University.

FAO (Food and Agriculture Organization). 2008. *The State of Food Insecurity in the World 2008*. Rome: FAO.

FAO. 2009. *How to Feed the World in 2050*. Rome: FAO.

FAO, IFAD (International Fund for Agricultural Development), and WFP (World Food Program). 2013. *The State of Food Insecurity in the World 2013: The Multiple Dimensions of Food Insecurity*. Rome: FAO.

FAO. FAOSTAT. http://faostat3.fao.org/browse/Q/QI/E (accessed 2015).

Foster, Andrew, and Mark Rosenzweig. 1995. "Learning by Doing and Learning from Others: Human Capital and Technical Change in Agriculture." *Journal of Political Economy* 103(6): 1176–209.

Foster, Andrew, and Mark Rosenzweig. 2010. "Microeconomics of Technology Adoption." *Annual Review of Economics* 2(1): 395–424.

Galtier, Franck. 2011. "What Can the International Community Do to Help Developing Countries Manage Food Price Instability?" Working paper, CIRAD (Centre de coopération Internationale en Recherche Agronomique pour le Développement), Montpellier.

Goldstein, Markus, and Chris Udry. 2008. "The Profits of Power: Land Rights and Agricultural Investment in Ghana." *Journal of Political Economy* 116(6): 981–1022.

Gollin, Douglas, Michael Morris, and Derek Byerlee. 2005. "Technology Adoption in Intensive Post-Green Revolution Systems." *American Journal of Agricultural Economics* 87(5): 1310–16.

Griliches, Zvi. 1957. "Hybrid Corn: An Exploration of the Economics of Technological Change." *Econometrica* 25(4): 501–22.

Gross, Rainer, and Patrick Webb. 2006. "Wasting Time for Wasted Children: Severe Child Under-nutrition Must Be Resolved in Non-emergency Settings." *The Lancet* 367(April 8): 1209–11.

Gustavsson, Jenny, Christel Cederberg, Ulf Sonesson, Robert van Otterdijk, and Alexandre Meybeck. 2011. "Global Food Losses and Food Waste: Extent, Causes, and Prevention." Rome: FAO. www.fao.org/fileadmin/user_upload/suistainability/pdf/Global_Food_Losses_and_Food_Waste.pdf (accessed 2015).

Hayami, Yujiro, and Vernon Ruttan. 1985. *Agricultural Development: An International Perspective*. Baltimore: Johns Hopkins University Press.

Hirschman, Albert. 1958. *The Strategy of Economic Development*. New Haven, CT: Yale University Press.

IAASTD (International Assessment of Agricultural Knowledge, Science, and Technology for Development). 2009. *Agriculture at a Crossroads*. UNEP: www.unep.org/dewa/assessments/ecosystems/iaastd/tabid/105853/default.aspx (accessed 2015).

ILO (International Labor Office). 2011. *Social Protection Floor for a Fair and Inclusive Globalization*. Geneva: Report from the Advisory Group.

Jack, Kelsey. 2011. "Market Inefficiencies and the Adoption of Agricultural Technologies in Developing Countries." White paper prepared for the Agricultural Technology Adoption Initiative, J-PAL (MIT)/CEGA (UC Berkeley).

Kahneman, Daniel, and Amos Tversky. 1979. "Prospect Theory: An Analysis of Decision under Risk." *Econometrica* 47(2): 263–91.

Krueger, Anne, Maurice Schiff, and Alberto Valdés. 1991. *The Political Economy of Agricultural Pricing Policy*. Washington, DC: World Bank.

Lipton, Michael. 1977. *Why Poor People Stay Poor: A Study of Urban Bias in World Development*. London: Temple Smith.

Mellor, John. 1966. *The Economics of Agricultural Development*. Ithaca, NY: Cornell University Press.

Mellor, John. 1998. "Agriculture on the Road to Industrialization." In Carl Eicher and John Staatz (eds.), *International Agricultural Development*, 136–54. Baltimore: Johns Hopkins University Press.

OECD. ODA. www.oecd.org/dac/ (accessed 2015).

Ohkawa, Kazushi, and Henry Rosovsky. 1960. "The Role of Agriculture in Modern Japanese Economic Development." *Economic Development and Cultural Change* 9(1): 43–67.

Owen, Wyn. 1966. "The Double Developmental Squeeze on Agriculture." *American Economic Review* 56(1): 43–70.

Peterson, Wesley. 2009. *A Billion Dollars a Day: The Economics and Politics of Agricultural Subsidies*. Oxford: John Wiley and Sons.

Qaim, Matin, and David Zilberman. 2003. "Yield Effects of Genetically Modified Crops in Developing Countries." *Science* 299 (5608): 900–2.

Rabin, Matthew. 1998. "Psychology and Economics." *Journal of Economic Literature* 36(1): 11–46.

Reardon, Thomas, and Julio Berdegué. 2002. "The Rapid Rise of Supermarkets in Latin America: Challenges and Opportunities for Development." *Development Policy Review* 20(4): 371–88.

Schultz, T.W. 1965. *Transforming Traditional Agriculture*. New Haven, CT: Yale University Press.

Sen, Amartya. 1982. *Poverty and Famines: An Essay on Entitlements and Deprivation*. Oxford: Clarendon Press.

Staatz, John, Duncan Boughton, and Cynthia Donovan. 2009. "Food Security in Developing Countries." Staff Paper Series 2009–03, Department of Agricultural, Food, and Resource Economics, Michigan State University.

Streeten, Paul. 1987. *What Price Food? Agricultural Price Policies in Developing Countries*. London: Macmillan Press.

Suri, Tavneet. 2009. "Selection and Comparative Advantage in Technology Adoption." *Econometrica* 79(1): 159–209.

Suryahadi, Asep, Daniel Suryadarma, and Sudarno Sumarto. 2009. "The Effect of Location and Sectoral Components of Economic Growth on Poverty: Evidence from Indonesia." *Journal of Development Economics* 89(1): 109–17.

Thaler, Richard. 1980. "Toward a Positive Theory of Consumer Choice." *Journal of Economic Behavior and Organization* 1(1): 39–60.

Timmer, Peter. 1986. *Getting Prices Right: The Scope and Limits of Agricultural Price Policy*. Ithaca, NY: Cornell University Press.

von Braun, Joachim. 2007. *The World Food Situation: New Driving Forces and Required Actions*. Washington, DC: International Food Policy Research Institute.

World Bank. 2007. *World Development Report 2008*: *Agriculture for Development*. Washington, DC.

World Bank, *Global Monitoring Report*. www.worldbank.org/en/publication/global-monitoring-report (accessed 2015).

World Bank. *PovcalNet*. http://iresearch.worldbank.org/PovcalNet/index.htm (accessed 2015).

World Bank. *World Development Indicators*. http://data.worldbank.org/indicator (accessed 2015).

Zilberman, David, Leslie Lipper, and Nancy McCarthy. 2008. "When Could Payments for Environmental Services Benefit the Poor?" *Environment and Development Economics* 13(03): 255–78.

Chapter 19

Development aid and its effectiveness

TAKE-HOME MESSAGES FOR CHAPTER 19

1. Current development aid is the outcome of a long historical process, but its main characteristics evolved from post-World War Two reconstruction assistance to Europe under the Marshall Plan. Aid to developing countries is more complex as it may be motivated by altruism, access to markets and resources, geopolitics, and colonial legacy.

2. There is a micro–macro paradox in the effectiveness of foreign aid, with eventual micro successes not matched by visible macro growth effects. Macro growth effects are both harder to achieve because the magnitude of aid may not be sufficient to affect recipient countries' macro variables, and harder to observe because causality is difficult to establish in cross-country regressions.

3. Micro effects are easier to observe and can be quantified through rigorous impact-evaluation methods. Results from rigorous evaluations often deflate expectations built on partisan information. Project-level micro successes must meet the challenges of scalability and sustainability to be effective for development and achieve eventual macro effects.

4. Policy conditionality in seeking to achieve greater aid effectiveness has been hampered by fungibility of infra-marginal transfers and lack of commitment devices for enforceability.

5. The new economics of aid stresses instead the importance of good governance and good institutions for the successful use of aid in achieving growth. This has led to creation by the US of the Millennium Challenge Account, with transfers targeted at countries passing the good-policy test. Aid has thus moved away from project-based lending toward country selectivity and policy-based lending.

6. Focusing on countries with high Country Policy and Institutional Assessment (CPIA) scores leaves open the problems of building a developmental state that can qualify for aid, and of reaching the poor in countries with failed states and in post-conflict societies. This gives a particular role to social development funds, local governments, and NGOs that can help bypass the central government in spending aid monies while capacity building for improved governance goes on.

7. There are sharp controversies about what to do with foreign aid, ranging from strong advocates of increased aid to governments such as Sachs, to deep skeptics such as Easterly, pragmatists like Collier, opponents such as Moyo and Deaton, and advocates of the role of small- and medium-enterprise development for job creation as proposed by Karnani.

8. New contributors to foreign aid are creating competing models with relative effective-
    ness that is still incompletely understood. The new aid-effectiveness paradigm pursued
    by OECD governments and multilateral organizations seeking comprehensive develop-
    ment competes with the South–South aid paradigm, which is more concerned with infra-
    structure investment, access to natural resources, and economic growth.

OVERVIEW[1]

Foreign aid is the primary means by which industrialized countries have attempted
to promote economic development in poor countries. And it is big business. Sums
spent in Overseas Development Assistance (ODA) by OECD countries have been
considerable, amounting to some US$3 trillion since 1970 and an annual flow of
US$151 billion in 2012. Over the last five decades, development aid has evolved
in response to a dramatically changing global, political, and economic landscape. In
this chapter, we examine this evolution and discuss what seems to determine the
effectiveness of aid as seen by donors, intended beneficiaries, and outside observers
(positive analysis), and what could be done to make aid more effective (normative
analysis). We shall see that the heterogeneity of means, needs, and actors makes aid
an extremely complex institutional universe, with both dismal failures and exciting
successful initiatives.

A major difficulty in improving the effectiveness of aid is in assessing the causal links
between aid and its development outcomes. We will see that there is here a major
contrast between aid achievements at the micro and macro levels, with greater difficulties in establishing causalities at the macro/country level than at the micro/project
level. As a consequence, the effectiveness of aid in promoting development is often
uncertain and controversial, and opinions about it can be deeply ideological. For that
reason, there are ongoing heated controversies about how best to provide foreign aid,
with protagonists such as Jeffrey Sachs (2005), William Easterly (2006), Paul Collier
(2007), Dambisa Moyo (2009), Aneel Karnani (2011), and Angus Deaton (2013)
taking sharply contrasted positions, with recommendations ranging from expanding
aid massively to simply cancelling it. There are also important new players in foreign
aid such as large specialized global funds, well endowed philanthropic organizations
like the Bill & Melinda Gates Foundation, the private sector pursuing corporate
social-responsibility objectives, and developing country South–South aid initiatives
such as China's in Sub-Saharan Africa and Brazil's in tropical agriculture. This is creating competing models, especially between the traditional OECD government-to-
government aid and concessional lending for infrastructure projects in exchange for
access to natural resources, as offered by China. Which model works better for development is a huge issue affecting the welfare of millions of people, with as yet incomplete evidence to respond conclusively. The chapter begins with a historical survey of
aid, which will help introduce many basic aid-related concepts. With this background
in place, we go on to discuss aid effectiveness, assessments of aid impacts, and the
ongoing controversies about the level and practice of foreign aid.

AID IN A HISTORICAL PERSPECTIVE

A major achievement of economic development since the 1950s is to have shown that it can be done. There are many examples of development successes. "Basket case" countries in the 1950s such as South Korea and Taiwan have rapidly emerged from poverty and achieved high-income-country status. A large group of countries have been converging in GDPpc with high-income OECD countries. But there is also evidence of widening divergence between the most and the least successful. Foreign aid may have had a role to play in helping poor countries raise growth rates in per capita income to achieve convergence, and in helping bring large numbers of poor people out of poverty, but this is difficult to establish unequivocally. Aid effectiveness has thus been widely questioned, not only in long-time donor countries, but also among beneficiaries. Writers such as Moyo (2009), an economist writing from the perspective of aid recipients, have simply called for an end to foreign aid, other than for disaster relief and charities, exposing it as a source of government corruption and lack of accountability, and as an intervention detrimental to developing countries' long-term welfare. Perhaps because the effectiveness of aid is so difficult to establish, "aid fatigue" has set in and foreign aid has declined as a share of donor countries' Gross National Incomes (GNI) from half of 1 percent in 1960 to one third of 1 percent in 2010.

The roots of foreign aid can be traced back to at least the nineteenth century, but the economic and social development of the colonies, for its own sake, was clearly not a policy objective of the Western colonial powers before World War Two. Such an objective—as argued by Thorbecke (2000)—would have been inconsistent with the underlying division of labor and trading patterns within and among colonial blocks.

In the aftermath of World War Two, Europe faced an acute need for reconstruction and a critical shortage of capital. The response was the Marshall Plan, implemented from 1948 to 1953 and driven in part by fear of the spread of communism and the desire of the US to secure its dominance in global trade and investment. The plan was massive, even by today's standards. It transferred to 16 European countries the equivalent of what in 1997 would have been US$88 billion. Capital transfers were complemented with technical assistance to raise productivity in local industry. And it came with conditionalities on currency convertibility, trade openness toward the US, and reductions in public spending. The plan helped mitigate an acute scarcity of investment funds and foreign exchange in Europe, allowing first the import of critically missing food and fuel, and later capital and intermediate goods for infrastructure and industry. It was very successful, with the economy of every country surpassing its prewar level by 1952.

The Marshall Plan gave rise to many of the elements of the existing system of aid delivery. However, the needs of the developing areas of the world *per se* were not yet in focus. The International Bank for Reconstruction and Development (IBRD, also known as the World Bank), established at the 1944 Bretton Woods Conference, was originally concerned with postwar reconstruction in Europe and Japan. The International Development Association (IDA, a branch of the World Bank) was only created in 1960 to channel resources to the poorest countries on 'soft' conditions (grants, concessional loans). Developing regions did receive support from the colonial powers before 1960, notably from the UK and France, and the volume of French aid as a share of GDP actually reached more than 1 percent by the early 1960s. A major part of the rapidly increasing bilateral flows during the 1950s came from the US, whose aid/GDP share grew to well above 0.5 percent; but there was substantial continuity in the transition from colonial to post-colonial institutions, and colonial ties remained strong and influential in determining bilateral aid flows.

It is because of the success of the Marshall Plan that the idea of using foreign aid as an instrument to help poor countries catch up in development came into existence. How foreign aid was to be used for development closely matched the evolution of thought in development economics, as outlined in Chapter 3 and summarized in Table 19.1.

With the turmoil of the two world wars, many countries were becoming independent from colonial rule such as Egypt in 1922, Lebanon in 1943, and India in

Table 19.1 History of development objectives and role of foreign aid

Period	Development objectives	Role of foreign aid and instruments
1950s	GDP growth	Aid for growth
		Resource transfers (Harrod–Domar)
		Industrialization
		Standard support to the role of the state
1960s	GDP growth, employment	Aid for growth and employment creation
		Big Push and two-gap models
		Project lending rather than policy reforms
		Investment in human capital
1970s	Poverty and basic needs	Aid for development with a proactive role for the state
		Redistribution with and before growth
		Poverty reduction and basic needs
		Agriculture and rural development
1980–95	Stabilization and adjustment	Aid for macro-adjustments and to support market forces
		Washington Consensus priorities
		Conditionality for policy reforms
		Support for private sector and NGOs
1995–	Growth and development	Aid for growth and development with state intervention
		Good governance and aid-effectiveness paradigm
		Country-led development strategies (PRSP)
		Results-based management

Source: Based on information in Thorbecke (2000) and Dethier (2008).

1947. In this context, the first meeting of the nonaligned movement in 1955 gave voice to these countries, as did the various branches of the UN, notably the United Conference on Trade and Development (UNCTAD). The transition toward somewhat more independent, multilateral relations, as opposed to the traditional bilateralism inherited from colonialism, was underway. The objective of aid was to accelerate GDP growth and support convergence. The 1960s saw a distinct increase in the share of multilateral aid, and the role of aid started shifting toward a broader agenda of development goals, especially employment creation, which clearly went beyond the exclusive focus on promoting economic growth, characteristic of the 1950s. The Economic Commission for Africa (ECA) came into being in 1958, and the first of the three regional development banks, the Inter-American Development Bank (IADB), was established in 1959. The multilateralism of aid became even more pronounced in the 1970s, which saw an increased focus on poverty reduction, income distribution, and the satisfaction of basic needs as essential objectives of both development and aid, consistent with the emerging school of development economics and giving an important proactive role to the state in promoting a multidimensional development agenda.

Economic progress was visible across many LDCs during the 1960s and 1970s. Adelman (1991) refers to this era as the "golden age" of development economics, but it came to an abrupt end when the debt crisis exploded in the mid 1980s. It soon became evident that the downturn was persistent, not temporary as in 1973 during the oil and food crisis associated with political turmoil on the Russian front; and it was gradually recognized that the development strategies of the previous decades were no longer sustainable. Economic circumstances in developing countries and relations between North and South had changed radically, so adjustments were needed in economic policies. Achieving macroeconomic balance (externally and internally) appeared as an essential prerequisite for renewed development. Macroeconomic stabilization and adjustment thus became important, and, in much of the discourse of the Washington Consensus, virtually synonymous with economic transformation and development. Reliance on market forces, outward orientation, and the role of the private sector, including NGOs, were emphasized and became the drivers of foreign aid until the mid 1990s.

In parallel, bilateral donors and international agencies such as the World Bank grappled with how to channel resources to the developing world. Net aid flows were seriously undermined by counter flows related to recurrent indebtedness, and by the late 1970s it had become increasingly difficult to channel fresh resources to many developing countries. The various kinds of macroeconomic program assistance (such as balance-of-payments support and sector budget support), which were not tied to particular investment projects, and which could be justified under the headings of stabilization and adjustment programs, appeared an ideal solution to this dilemma. Financial program aid and adjustment loans became fashionable and policy conditionality more widespread. Conditionality refers to a set of economic or policy-performance standards imposed by the donor for the developing country to qualify for loans or grants, binding the aid recipient to reforms deemed necessary for effective use of development assistance. Maintaining a North–South flow of resources found a

679

new rationale, which corresponded well with the major tenets of the guidelines for "good policy" summarized under the banner of the Washington Consensus. Overall, aid continued to grow in real terms until the early 1990s, representing a constant share of the growing GDP of the donor community, and more than doubling during the period 1970–90 (Figure 19.1). However, after 1990, total aid flows started to decline both in absolute terms and as a share of donor country GNI. In spite of growth recovery since 2000, in both total value and share of donor countries GNI across OECD countries, ODA in 2013 was only 0.3 percent of GNI, well below the 0.7 percent UN target level. Of total ODA disbursements, 72 percent is through bilateral aid and 28 percent through multilateral organizations (OECD, 2014).

There are many reasons for the decline in foreign aid as a share of donor country GNI. One is the demise of communism and the end of the Cold War, epitomized by the fall of the Berlin Wall in 1989. Weakening patron–client relations between the developing countries and their former colonial rulers also played a role, and the traditional support for development aid from vocal interest groups in developed countries receded. Other concerns including environmental deterioration, community action, and distrust of domestic and foreign aid agencies also played a role. These latter institutions have been subjected to sharp criticism (Easterly, 2001) and were at times characterized as blunt instruments of commercial interests in the developed world, or as self-interested, rent-seeking bureaucracies with no accountability to the beneficiary countries. Also, a growing perception that aid is ineffective in fostering growth

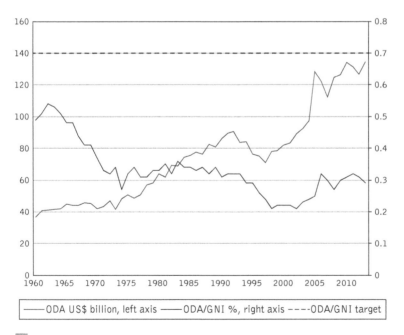

Figure 19.1 *Overseas Development Assistance (ODA): total value in billions of US$ (left axis) and as a percentage share of donor countries' GNI (right axis), 1960–2013. The horizontal dashed line is the UN target of 0.7 percent of GNI*

Source: OECD, International Development Statistics.

at the macro level emerged. Indeed, data suggested that aid is ineffective in promoting aggregate growth, and anecdotes about failed projects at the micro level contributed to an increasing sense of "aid fatigue" in donor countries. Finally, the acute awareness of cases of bad governance, corruption, and crony capitalism led during the 1990s to skepticism about the sincerity and credibility of aid-receiving governments and the potential role aid might be playing in underpinning corrupt and repressive regimes.

Foreign aid has throughout its history been subjected to close scrutiny both by academic researchers and others (Dethier, 2008). A large literature extending over several decades bears witness to this, and the boundary between policy advocacy and research has not always been clearly delineated. Be that as it may, most development economists and aid practitioners have at one stage or the other come across the so-called "micro–macro paradox," formulated by Mosley (1987). This thesis suggested that while aid seems effective at the micro level (with many demonstrably successful local projects), it is harder—or even impossible—to identify any positive impact of aid on the macroeconomy. Much interest in evidencing a macro impact arose from a desire among donors in the 1980s to ascertain the value of the expensive stabilization and structural-adjustment packages. In concert with adjustment programs in many countries, the use of a wider variety of analytical tools in aid-impact assessments became common. Evaluation methods such as the internal rate of return (IRR) of projects came under severe criticism as the perception of aid fungibility spread. The concept of fungibility, or additionality, means, for example, that giving governments money to build schools may simply liberate funds from their own education budgets to be spent on other things, when they might have built some or all of the schools anyway. Thus fungible aid can have the unintended consequence of financing unrelated or even undesirable activities like luxury projects and warfare. Rate-of-return metrics ignore more complex opportunity-cost issues like this. The IRR approach also became problematic as donors started to embrace broader goals for aid, such as environmental sustainability and multiple social goals, with benefits that are difficult to quantify.[2] In parallel, the weaknesses of impact evaluation, summarized under headings such as "before-and-after" and "with-and-without," were the topic for many debates, with the result that methodological issues gradually came to play an important role in the aid-effectiveness debate (see below).

THE EVOLUTION OF FOREIGN AID

Aid and foreign direct investment

While ODA was an important source of access to capital and foreign exchange for developing countries in the mid 1970s, representing 6 percent of GDP, its importance had fallen to 0.6 percent of GDP in 2012 (Figure 19.2). The main source of international capital transfers has become FDI, which rose from 0.6 percent of GDP in 1975 to 3 percent in 2012.

Aid effectiveness in this changing international environment clearly requires strong complementarity between public and private investment. Of particular importance is the role of the investment climate in attracting private investment with features such

681

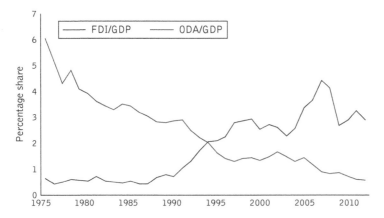

Figure 19.2 *Relative importance of FDI and ODA in percentage share of GDP in low- and middle-income countries, 1975–2012*

Sources: OECD Development Assistance Committee (DAC); World Bank, *World Development Indicators.*

Table 19.2 *Regional allocation of Overseas Development Assistance, 1960 to 2012, in percentage of total*

Regions	1960–69	1970–79	1980–89	1990–99	2000–09	2010–12
Africa North of Sahara	10	9	10	9	4	3
Europe and Oceania	9	9	8	9	7	7
Far East Asia	19	20	15	19	11	7
Middle East	4	8	9	7	16	8
Latin America and Caribbean	13	9	12	13	10	11
South and Central Asia	27	21	14	11	14	22
Sub-Saharan Africa	17	24	32	32	38	43

Source: OECD, *International Development Statistics.*

as property rights, public goods, and the rule of law, which are all public goods that may depend on foreign aid flows and the associated provision of technical assistance (World Bank, 1998). While losing its importance as a source of capital and foreign exchange, foreign aid may thus remain a key determinant of growth, and assessing aid effectiveness will become more indirect in its role attracting and enhancing the effectiveness of private capital transfers.

Destinations and sectoral contents of foreign aid

There are two other notable changes in the evolution of foreign aid. The first is that it has increasingly moved away from destinations in South, Central, and Far East Asia toward Sub-Saharan Africa (Table 19.2). The share of Asia declined from 46 to 29 percent of total ODA between 1960–9 and 2010–12, while that of Sub-Saharan Africa increased from 17 to 43 percent, becoming by far the largest share.

The second is that it has moved away from productive investments toward social expenditures (Table 19.3). The first declined from 31 to 11 percent of total ODA between 1970–9 and 2010–12 as private investment flowed in, while the second rose from 37 to 48 percent over the same period. Infrastructure, an important complement to private investment, remained constant at 21 to 24 percent.

FUNGIBILITY OF FOREIGN AID

The concept of *fungibility*, with aid coming in the form of food, is illustrated in Figures 19.3 and 19.4. With aid in kind equal to CD in Figure 19.3, the utility gain is from U_0 to U_1 at D. With fungibility of its own resources, the country uses part of what it was spending on food (to get C) to obtain other goods. In the case represented in Figure 19.3 and Table 19.4, the utility gain of this reallocation is from U_1 to U_2 at E. The food-aid transfers are *infra-marginal* in the sense that the country was always going to spend more on food than the aid received (AD'>CD): it simply saves what does not need to be spent and spends the money saved on other goods. The

Table 19.3 *Sectoral allocation of Overseas Development Assistance, 1970 to 2012, in percentage of total*

Sector	1970–9	1980–9	1990–9	2000–9	2010–12
Humanitarian	7	2	11	14	3
Production	31	35	16	10	11
Infrastructure	21	29	29	20	24
Social sectors	37	31	37	47	48

Source: OECD, *International Development Statistics.*

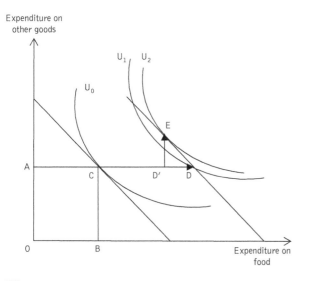

Figure 19.3 *Fungibility of aid in consumption with infra-marginal food transfer*

Table 19.4 *Fungibility of aid in consumption with infra-marginal food transfer*

	Food	Other goods	Utility reached
Expenditure without aid transfer	OB = AC	OA = BC	U_0
Aid transfer	CD	0	
Desired expenditure with transfer	AD′	OA + D′E	U_2
With infra-marginal transfer	AD′ > CD		
Save/reallocate	Save AD′ − CD > 0	Reallocate to D′E	

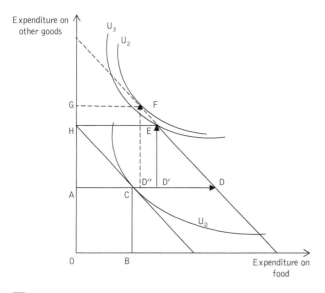

Figure 19.4 *Fungibility of aid in consumption with extra-marginal food transfer*

transfer is *extra-marginal* when the country receives more aid in kind than it was going to spend on that good—for example, in Figure 19.4 and Table 19.5 the optimal consumption of food (after aid) AD" is smaller than the food received CD. The country can only move from U_0 to U_2 if there exists a secondary market on which some of the food received can be sold, and the cash earned from the sale used to buy the other good. If a secondary market does not exist, then the recipient of the extra-marginal transfer must consume more food and fewer other goods than desired, and can only reach U_3 at E. Both situations are possible, but the infra-marginal transfer is more likely to happen. Note that in both cases, there is *incomplete additionality*: CD', the increase in food consumption, is less than CD, the amount of aid received.

Aid can also come in the form of investment goods, affecting the allocation of productive resources between the production of investment goods and the production of consumption goods. With fungibility of its own resources, the recipient country will shift some resources to the production of consumption goods to achieve its desired balance between the two types of good. So here again, there will be incomplete additionality as the increase in investment will be lower than the received aid.

Table 19.5 *Fungibility of aid in consumption with extra-marginal food transfer*

	Food	Other goods	Utility reached
Expenditure without aid transfer	OB = AC	OA = BC	U_0
Aid transfer	CD	0	
Desired expenditure with transfer	GF	OA + D″F	
With extra-marginal transfer	CD = AD′ > GF		
Sell/buy	Sell CD − GF > 0	Buy D″F	U_2
Or consume more food than optimum	HE > GF	OA + D′E	U_3

At the extreme, if the amount of in-kind aid is below current consumption of the targeted good, the country could fully substitute the received goods for domestic goods, not increasing its consumption at all, if it so desires. The saved resources could then be used for any other purpose. Aid, even in kind, would be equivalent to a cash transfer with no strings attached. Fungibility can therefore undo the purpose of the in-kind aid, leading to the frustration of intended purposes in the aid community.

AID EFFECTIVENESS FROM A MACRO PERSPECTIVE

Aid and growth

As we saw in the historical overview, public and private perceptions of aid effectiveness have deteriorated in recent decades. This aid fatigue has been reinforced by a growing faith in markets and skepticism of governments, both by recipients and donors. Perceptions, of course, depend on perspective, and outside observers are more likely to judge development assistance by its macroeconomic effects because these are more visible to them. This macro focus is compounded by the way aid is executed, more along official and large-NGO channels than as an extension of grass-roots relationships.[3] Indeed, foreign aid has to a large extent been principally a state-to-state relationship. Fatigue was also influenced by the fear that foreign aid has generated dependency relationships and is susceptible to adverse incentive effects. At the same time, there has been a growing perception that conditionality has failed to promote policy reform.

Conditionality in the 1980s was linked to the policies of the Washington Consensus (Williamson, 1989): liberalization, privatization, fiscal discipline, openness to trade, protection of property rights, market-determined exchange and interest rates, and redirection of public spending toward education, health, and public infrastructure. The Consensus ignored other policies such as governance, country ownership of policy reforms, democratic representation, and compensation for the social costs of the reforms.

Ravi Kanbur (2000) documents many accounts of failure, and notes that while there is reason to view the donor–recipient relationship as one of unequal power, the political economy of conditionality is much more subtle. Conditionality was no doubt 'imposed' on unwilling recipients at the time they signed adjustment documents, but "the recipients know, the donors know, and in fact everybody knows, that these are paper conditions; the outcome will be driven by the needs of both sides to maintain normal relations and the flow of aid" (Kanbur, 2000). The fundamental issue is that conditionality lacks commitment to be credible.

That conditionality did not work in improving aid effectiveness has been supported empirically. Dollar and Svensson (2000) find that donor-controlled policy instruments had no impact on the success of World Bank adjustment programs. Similar conclusions were obtained in a broad range of research projects sponsored by the World Bank (Devarajan *et al.* 2001).

This awareness has motivated a renewed interest in new kinds of donor–recipient relationships and the effectiveness of aid. In response, calls were made for increased national ownership of aid programs, and both World Bank researchers and others started analyzing the aid–growth relationship. This was facilitated in part by the availability of better data and in part by insights emerging from new growth theory and the rapidly increasing number of empirical studies of growth. Using cross-country data to correlate macroeconomic indicators with aid receipts, Boone (1996) suggested that aid does not work: it does not significantly increase investment and growth, nor does it benefit the poor; but it increases the size of government. This was followed by a very influential analysis by Burnside and Dollar (2000) looking at 56 countries for the period 1970 to 1993. Their results show that some aid does work, and they identify the conditions under which it works, providing an attractive and seemingly self-evident solution to the micro–macro paradox: aid promotes growth, but only in countries with "good policy." They base this on an aid–policy interaction term that emerged as statistically significant in their macroeconometric analysis of the aid–growth relationship in cross-country regressions. Good policy consists in balanced budgets, low inflation, and trade openness.

The Burnside and Dollar result was questioned by others. Easterly *et al.* (2004) show that the aid–policy relation is not robust enough for the expansion of the database in years and countries. As typical with cross-country regressions, causality of the relationship running from aid to growth cannot be rigorously established. The observed correlation can be due to aid fostering growth as well as to fast-growing, low-income countries being targeted by donors to receive higher levels of foreign aid. Aid is thus endogenous to growth, invalidating the claim of causal results. Rajan and Subramanian (2005) corrected for the bias of aid going to poorer countries, or to countries after an episode of poor performance, and found little empirical support for the proposition that aid induces growth, and that aid works better in better policy environments.

In spite of this, Burnside and Dollar, and subsequently Collier and Dollar (2002), used the above framework as a basis for suggesting that aid should be directed to "good policy" countries to improve aid's impact on poverty reduction. While these policy recommendations were considerably toned down in the Bank's Monterrey Document (World Bank, 2002), the basic thrust somehow remains that macroeconomic performance-evaluation and policy criteria (established by the World Bank) should play a key role in allocating aid. This introduced the concept of country selectivity in targeting foreign aid.

Heated debates about what constitutes good policy ensued from the work of Burnside and Dollar, and Collier and Dollar. They are in many ways extensions of more general debates and views about development strategy and policy, and meanwhile the concept of good policy has been gradually expanded by the World Bank to include a much wider and much more complex set of characteristics than originally considered. It is this concept that underlies the US government's approach to foreign aid through the Millennium Challenge Account, introduced under President George W. Bush. The funds in the Millennium Challenge Account (MCA) are to be allocated to developing countries that demonstrate a strong commitment to good governance, investment in the health and education of their people, and economic policies that foster enterprises and entrepreneurship. Countries are scored on 17 indicators (civil liberties, political rights, voice and accountability, government effectiveness, rule of law, control of corruption, immunization rate, public expenditure on health, girls' primary-education-completion rate, public expenditure on primary education, natural-resource management, inflation rate, trade policy, land rights and access index, regulatory quality, fiscal policy, and days to start a business). A country is eligible for an aid grant if its MCA score on these 17 indicators exceeds the median score of all potentially eligible countries, without political considerations. The score is meant to recognize policies that promote economic growth.

While the relationship between aid and growth is difficult to establish causally, there exists a category of countries for which it can be done with a rigorous identification strategy (Galiani *et al.*, 2014). They are the poor countries that graduate from the World Bank's GDPpc condition to qualify for IDA (International Development Association, the World Bank Group's fund for the world's poorest countries) grants and concessionary loans. This qualification condition is used by many other donors, making graduation into a potentially large public liquidity shock as access to IDA grants is lost. The qualification threshold is defined in current GDPpc dollars and is adjusted annually. It increased from $580 in 1987 to $1175 in 2010. Over this period, 35 countries crossed the threshold from below, suffering as a consequence a sudden sharp drop in aid. This exogenous threshold allows for a regression discontinuity design to identify the cost in GDPpc growth associated with the corresponding loss in aid. Assuming that the effect of aid as a share of GNI is symmetrical as it falls or rises, and that countries just above and below the cut-off are similar to each other, the result predicts that a 1 percent gain in aid/GNI induces a short term gain in GDPpc growth of 0.35 percentage points. The authors find that the main channel through which this effect operates is physical investment. Increasing the aid/GNI ratio by 1 percent increases the investment to GDP ratio by 0.54 percentage points. Graduating countries are typically poor countries where public liquidity is seriously constrained and where aid is a large source of government funding. In this particular case, at least, we can show that aid causally affects the growth performance. From a policy standpoint, this result suggests that the drop in aid associated with graduation should be mitigated by better credit worthiness to avoid a liquidity shock on public budgets and a drop in investment.

Aid and political outcomes

Historians have linked the rise of representative forms of governance to "revenue bargaining" (Moore, 2008). An autocratic government in need of tax revenues can be forced to exchange institutionalized influence over public policy by citizens for tax revenues collected by the state. The most famous historical examples of this principle of "no taxation without representation" are the 1689 English Bill of Rights that required parliament to authorize taxes, limiting the power of the king; and the 1773 Boston Tea Party, where British colonists refused to pay taxes on trade imposed by the British Parliament, where they had no representation, leading to the American Revolution and ultimately the United States Declaration of Independence in 1776 (Acemoglu and Robinson, 2012).

Those in control of economic assets generating taxable revenues can thus acquire significant leverage over government, which they can use to demand more account-ability, representation, and inclusiveness. It is this role of revenue bargaining in achieving democracy that can be broken by foreign aid, undermining the leverage that civil society has over public revenues. In many Sub-Saharan countries, foreign aid accounts for more than 50 percent of government expenditures, reaching up to 75 percent in some. The question, then, is whether foreign aid can undermine democracy, postpone political reforms, and reproduce autocratic regimes.

Here again, causality is difficult to establish. Using data for 108 recipient countries in the period 1960 to 1999, Djankov et al. (2008) find that foreign aid has a negative impact on democracy. They also find that, dollar for dollar, aid is a worse curse on democracy than oil rents. In their analysis, aid is instrumented with historical income and population levels, which creates doubt on the validity of this analysis, i.e. that the exclusion restriction is effectively met. Case studies are also useful. Eubank (2012) shows that Somaliland, which was ineligible for foreign aid, had to bargain with civil society to extract local tax revenues. This provided those outside government with leverage to obtain political concessions, leading to the emergence of inclusive, representative, and accountable political institutions. By contrast, Brautigam and Knack (2004) find that Sub-Saharan countries with easy-to-control natural-resource endowments—reducing government dependency on taxation and hence weakening the bargaining power of citizens—are associated with more autocratic and less effective forms of governance, suffering from the "resource curse."

Aid and conflicts

The other potential negative outcome of foreign aid is fueling conflict. Nunn and Qian (2014) find that greater food aid from the US increases the incidence and duration of small-scale civil conflicts. They instrument food aid by weather events in the US that affect wheat production and as a consequence the level of aid shipments. The main effect of food aid is in prolonging the duration of conflicts, rather than initiating new conflicts. The way this happens is that food shipments are fought over and a large fraction is appropriated by armed factions during transportation.

Crost et al. (2014) also associate aid with armed conflicts, but through another mechanism. They studied the onset of aid-funded development projects intended to win hearts and minds in conflict-affected regions of the Philippines. They use a regression-discontinuity design based on the eligibility requirement that qualifying municipalities be restricted to the poorest 25 percent of municipalities. Around the 25 percent threshold, municipalities with and without targeted aid should be identical in the factors that determine conflict. They show that the strategy to win hearts and minds can backfire. Local combatants try to block initiation of the programs for fear that their success will undermine future support for the insurgency. For the authors, avoiding that aid would induce violence implies that government should either carefully enforce security at the time of project installment, or negotiate a role for insurgent forces in the project rather than challenge their existence.

EVALUATING THE IMPACT OF FOREIGN AID FROM A MICRO PERSPECTIVE

The debate on aid effectiveness is in the end an empirical question, which calls for rigorous impact evaluation of what has been done. What protagonists advocate in the debate should be evidence-based. USAID and the World Bank are attempting to shift their allocation of aid budgets to a results-based management approach.

From the perspective of results-based management, we now have evaluation results for a large number of projects, many of which received funding through foreign aid. We have seen such impact evaluations throughout the chapters of this book. These results are useful in improving the design and implementation of projects. What we tend not to have is a comparative analysis of aid-funded projects across countries and across project types to show what determines success. In particular, is the macro-institutional context as strong a determinant of outcomes, as presumed by the new donor policies targeting aid to countries with better policy/governance contexts, as that measured by the CPIA? Or is there a lot of variation in project outcomes within countries due to micro-management determinants that could help projects to succeed even when the macro conditions do not necessarily hold, or fail even though they hold? A lot more research is needed, and it is difficult to do in controlling for endogeneity between determinants and outcomes.

The World Bank recently compiled information on 6,000 of its projects evaluated between 1983 and 2009 (Denizer et al., 2013). The degree of success (satisfactory/unsatisfactory) of each project in reaching its development objective is characterized on a scale of 1 to 6 in the corresponding Implementation Completion Report prepared by the task manager. Starting in 1995, this score had to be validated by the World Bank's Independent Evaluation Group, adding credibility to the evaluation. Determinants contrast macro country-level variables (such as macro stability, CPIA score for good policy, GDP growth, and democracy) and micro project-level variables (size in dollars, length in years, preparation and supervision costs as a share of total project size, and quality of the task manager). Decomposing the explanatory power of these variables between macro and micro shows that macro variables contribute 60 percent of explanatory power, and micro variables 40 percent. This can be taken to validate the importance given to macro determinants of success in the CPIA formula. Among macro correlates, macro-stability, good policy, and GDP growth correlate positively with project success, but not political rights. Among the micro-level variables, larger and longer projects as well as higher preparation and supervision costs correlate negatively with project success, with obvious unresolved causality issues (bad projects take longer, need more attention, etc.). Most important for outcome is task-manager

689

quality. Comparing the relative contributions of CPIA and task-manager quality shows a roughly equal contribution. This suggests that context does indeed matter, but that there is a lot of scope for within-country project improvement that can be handled by the task manager. What is missing is an interaction between CPIA and the task manager to see if the latter can compensate for deficiencies in the former, a million-dollar research question. Across sectors, transportation and education projects seem to have a greater likelihood of success.

THE PRACTICE OF FOREIGN AID

Official aid relationships originate between nation states on the recipient side and aid organizations on the donor side such as country bilateral agencies (e.g. USAID for the US, JICA for Japan, and DFID for the UK) and multilateral agencies (e.g. the World Bank, the regional development banks, and UN specialized agencies such as the UNDP). Each party to an aid relationship has its own domestic political agenda, motivating and regulating its engagements. While it is extremely difficult to generalize about the motives of these actors, several salient factors influence their behavior. We consider sovereign donors, aid agencies, and aid recipients separately. We then look in the next section at some of the strategies that have been introduced to enhance aid effectiveness.

Sovereign donor objectives

Countries that contribute to development grants or concessional loans can do this directly or though delegated institutions like NGOs or development banks. The UN sets a target for OECD countries to give as aid 0.7 percent of their GDP (or GNI). As can be seen in Table 19.6, among the top eleven donors, in 2012 only Sweden, Norway,

Table 19.6 *Top eleven aid donors by share in Gross National Income and in dollar amount, 2012*

	Aid/GNI %	*Aid millions US$*
Sweden	1.00	5240
Norway	0.96	4753
Denmark	0.87	2693
Netherlands	0.75	5523
UK	0.58	13891
France	0.41	12028
Australia	0.36	5403
Germany	0.34	12939
Canada	0.32	5650
US	0.28	30687
Japan	0.19	10605

Source: OECD, *Development Co-operation Directorate.*

Denmark, and the Netherlands reached this target. While the US and Japan are among the largest donors in magnitude, they only give as aid 0.28 percent and 0.19 percent of their GNIs respectively. Table 19.7 is suggestive of what motivates the choice of recipient countries by particular donors, here the US, the UK, and France, with clear roles for economic interests, colonial heritage, and geopolitics. The US focuses on geopolitical concerns and security issues, the UK and France on their former colonies. Japan and especially China are more motivated by economic interests.

In all cases, a few primary considerations influence their engagements.

1. *Altruism.* This in a sense is the simplest motive: the pure desire of bettering the economic performance of developing countries and the wellbeing of their people. This can consist in helping the economic "take-off" of recently decolonized countries, reducing countries' savings or foreign-exchange deficits (two-gap models), dampening balance-of-payments or debt shocks (stabilization and structural-adjustment policies), relieving distress originating in natural disasters and social conflict, and facilitating technological and institutional upgrading through technical assistance and improved absorptive capacity. While easy to invoke, altruism as a motive is difficult to prove. There can always exist hidden interests (i.e. trade and expected reciprocities) behind the observed aid transfers.

    Qian (2015) analyzes the determinants of the allocation of ODA across countries using a cross-country panel approach for the period 1960 to 2013 with country and year fixed effects. She finds that receiving ODA is not correlated with past-year low growth, past-year large conflicts, and current large natural disasters. Current small natural disasters receive some attention. The main correlates of cross-country ODA flows are population size with a negative sign (hence smaller countries receive more aid) and past-year GDP (hence larger economies receive more aid). Together, the population and GDP results indicate that countries with lower GDPpc receive less aid and hence that richer countries receive more aid. These results thus cast significant doubt on the poverty-reduction objectives of foreign aid. Indeed, the poorest 20 countries only received 2 to 5 percent of all foreign-aid flows in a given year (OECD, 2012).

2. *Economic interests.* Many donor countries seek to strengthen ties with a developing country because they want to advance the commercial interests of their own enterprise community with the country. Aid can be a powerful instrument for this purpose. This can take many forms, such as tied aid that requires use of domestic contractors (e.g. road building by US or Japanese construction companies, mine opening by Chinese corporations), joint ventures with credit and business-development services, export preferences, resource development cooperation, etc. Economic interests may be contracts and foreign-market expansion for domestic enterprises, or secure access to resources such as land, petroleum products, and minerals. They may also use aid to promote trade, simply by raising incomes in the recipient country to induce more aggregate demand for imports from the donor country. Aid for trade can thus be win–win in the aggregate for both countries, even though the growth sectors in the recipient country (perhaps agriculture promoted by transfers of agricultural technology, such as the Green Revolution) may

691

Table 19.7 Top 10 ODA recipients by donor, 2011

US			UK			France		
Recipients	Millions US$	% of total	Recipients	Millions US$	% of total	Recipients	Millions US$	% of total
Afghanistan	2951	10.5	India	632	7.3	Congo DR	594	6.3
Iraq	1445	5.1	Ethiopia	480	5.5	Morocco	510	5.4
Pakistan	1237	4.4	Afghanistan	331	3.8	Congo Rep	504	5.3
Congo DR	1053	3.7	Congo DR	317	3.7	China	366	3.9
Haiti	864	3.1	Pakistan	316	3.6	Cote d'Ivoire	358	3.8
Ethiopia	791	2.8	Nigeria	299	3.5	Mexico	357	3.8
West Bank and Gaza	673	2.4	Bangladesh	299	3.5	Mayotte	305	3.2
Kenya	642	2.3	Tanzania	219	2.5	Tunisia	299	3.2
South Africa	547	1.9	Uganda	163	1.9	Vietnam	290	3.1
Colombia	513	1.8	Ghana	149	1.7	Turkey	212	2.2
Total top 10	10716	38.0	Total top 10	3205	37.0	Total top 10	3795	40.0

Source: OECD, Development Co-operation Directorate.

Table 19.8 *Military and development assistance: top ten US recipients in 2013*

	Military aid million US$		Development aid million US$
Israel	9095	Iraq	2286
Egypt	6025	Congo, Dem Rep	804
Pakistan	4683	Egypt	767
Jordan	2670	Russia	737
Afghanistan	2664	Jordan	666
Colombia	2049	Afghanistan	632
Turkey	1325	Pakistan	590
Peru	446	Colombia	536
Bolivia	321	Israel	525
Poland	313	Ethiopia	500

Note: Iraq is absent from the left group because the cost of military activity is accounted for elsewhere in US government balance sheets.

reduce food imports from the donor country, antagonizing farm lobbies in that country. In this case, aggregate gains for the donor country are obtained at the cost of losses for specific sectors. The politics of aid for trade can thus be a contentious issue, with farm lobbies eventually opposing aid to food importing countries.

3. *Geopolitical and strategic interests.* Some donors may want to use aid to strengthen economic ties because beneficiary countries are important to their geopolitical interests. An example of potential discord between aid for development and aid for strategic (military) priorities can be seen in Table 19.8 in the US allocation of assistance to recipient countries for these two purposes. Military aid to Israel, Egypt, Pakistan, Jordan, and Afghanistan dwarfs development aid. Military aid to Colombia is related to drug control.

4. *Legacy relationships.* Examining historical patterns of colonial influence can provide reliable rationales for many of today's bilateral aid relationships. To an extent, the latter are a path dependent outcome of the former, but they persist for many practical reasons, including historical migration in both directions, established business partnerships, and residual geopolitical interests. Finally, in this category we can include religious and cultural affinities, which drive significant aid flows between higher-income Catholic, Protestant, and Muslim groups in MDC economies and LDCs with significant counterpart populations.

Aid agencies

As agents of particular donors, aid organizations such as the World Bank, regional development banks, relief agencies such as CARE, etc. are motivated in what they do by both the perceived objectives of the donors they represent and by their own self-interests in perpetuating themselves and expanding their specific missions. Here are some of the objectives of aid agencies.

693

1. *Donor service.* Because of their status as agents, these agencies must service their donors, and hence internalize their complex ecosystem perspectives into their work programs, in addition to potentially conflicting aims among donors. For example, the US may want the World Bank to shift its aid to post-conflict countries like Iraq and Afghanistan, while other member countries may resist this on behalf of their own traditional aid recipients and specific motives. The donor agency will thus be accountable to its donors, as opposed to its beneficiaries, creating a serious incentive dilemma, exposed by Easterly (2006) for the development effectiveness of foreign aid.

2. *Substitutability.* As long as an aid agency can credit itself with a project, there is limited risk that the additionality of its development contribution will be challenged. In this case, agencies may commit to deliver assistance, public goods, or other development resources. This is, however, not the case if there is substitutability of aid across donors. In this case, it is difficult for donors to establish causal links between their own contribution and specific outcomes. Because of the need to be accountable to their donors, aid agencies will prefer to select areas of intervention where their contributions can be easily recognized and outcomes credited to them. They will, for example, prefer to have exclusive jurisdiction over particular geographical areas of a country so that their roles are clearly visible. This tends to lead to an atomization of foreign-aid projects, as opposed to seeking complementarities and economies of scale in projects funded by multiple donors.

3. *Growth, donor competition, and conditionalities.* Like most organizations, aid agencies have natural incentives to enlarge their scope, authority, and budgets, in part to better achieve their donor objectives and in part to expand employment and secure stable jobs for themselves. This can lead to a variety of problems, including overlapping commitments, diminishing returns to core expertise, and competition that may strengthen the hand of opportunistic borrowers or recipient governments. In Sub-Saharan Africa, China's generally unconditional aid (however effective it is in promoting economic activity and growth) is providing competition for generally conditional assistance coming from Europe and the US, undermining conditionalities and arousing controversy among donors.

4. *Self-promotion, perpetuation, and mission creep.* The business of development assistance relies on a combination of addressing developing-country needs and seeking the means to meet those needs. The former are in plain sight in the global economy, but mobilizing the latter often requires active marketing for what is essentially a major global service industry. Looking more deeply into the aid industry, we can expect to see incentive problems, including, among other things, self-promotion and reporting biases that may overstate the importance of these services over time (Hancock, 1994). Independent reviews of the World Bank and other institutions have evidenced the existence of biases of this kind, and many leading agencies have established watchdog facilities to limit them. Rigorous impact evaluations of aid projects—for example, in the field of microfinance—thus have a tendency to deflate presumed results, creating ambiguity among aid agencies about the desirability of such evaluations. To a significant extent, individual or national aid projects

may also be captured by their local missions (the so-called mission-creep effect), and seek perpetuity even though global priorities may be shifting.

Aid recipients

Some countries are highly dependent on foreign aid. In 2012, measured as a share of GNI, ODA reached 35 percent in Liberia, 28 percent in Malawi, 21 percent in Burundi, 18 percent in the Congo DR, 16 percent in Haiti, and 14 percent in Mozambique and Niger. For Sub-Saharan Africa overall, aid as a share of GNI peaked at 7 percent in 1994 and declined to 3 percent in 2012.

In most cases, aid relationships are not managed by the intended beneficiaries, principally the country's poor, but by leadership systems at the national or community level. These systems have their own political economy, including vested interests in particular economic assets and activities. This political abstraction presents many challenges to the effective targeting and implementation of aid, including but by no means limited to the following.

1. *Domestic political processes.* Even the most monolithic dictatorship has a diversity of interests within the political and economic coalitions supporting it. In more openly factionalized political systems, this diversity will be more apparent, but in either case public decision-makers have to be mindful of economic interests when they allocate or manage public resources, including aid. The use of foreign aid thus needs to be interpreted in terms of the political-economy configuration of the interests to which it flows. These interests begin with individual decision-makers, often including their families, and then radiate outward to the social networks and stakeholders who influence them. The latter can include business interests, labor organizations, communities, and, perhaps last of all, the general public. Understanding the determinants of the effectiveness of foreign aid thus requires a careful and complex understanding of the political economy of the domestic context, of which foreign donors tend to be quite ignorant. This implies that aid will often be politically appropriated and/or made ineffective by a lack of understanding of the relevant political processes.

2. *Corruption and rent-seeking.* The phenomenon of corruption is one of the most intriguing, complex, and imperfectly understood forms of economic behavior. Generally speaking, corruption occurs when an individual diverts public resources for a private gain. It results in the diversion of governance benefits from the population to a few special interests (Kaufmann and Vicente, 2005). In an environment with ill defined property rights and weak surveillance and enforcement systems, the risk of corruption is very high, and for this reason corruption can be pervasive in developing countries. This behavior exists across a bewildering spectrum of economic activity, from arbitrary policy fines to massive looting of state assets. Often it involves conspiracy and delegation, leading to complex schemes of public–private misallocation and exploitation of resources. Corruption is usually seen as a net loss to society because it is generally believed that transparency and market mechanisms allocate resources more efficiently. In the context of aid,

695

the main problem with corruption is that it can decouple aid intentions from their impacts, as resources are diverted from initial objectives to satisfy other, private interests. This intermediate loss can be compounded if aid strengthens corrupt institutions or regimes, perpetuating them and amplifying their power to exploit their own populations. Because most international aid recognizes sovereign authority, even weak or compromised governments, corruption and the reproduction of corruption through aid transfers is a serious challenge to aid effectiveness. Corruption is a major criterion for the World Bank in assessing a country's adequacy for receiving foreign aid, as measured by its Country Policy and Institutional Assessment (CPIA) rating (Governance Assessment Portal, 2015).

3. *Aid as domestic interference.* Aid that sustains corrupt institutions is one example of a larger problem: aid as domestic interference (Moyo, 2009). Countries that receive higher levels of foreign aid show a deterioration in the quality of their governance (Knack, 2001). Necessary reforms are postponed; the presence of dysfunctional institutions is prolonged. This is the main reason why sustained government-to-government aid has been opposed by mainstream economists such as Deaton (2013).

4. *Dependence on experts.* For a variety of reasons, including weak fiscal resources, limited average education and skill levels, developing-country counterparts can be at a practical disadvantage in aid relationships. Particularly when aid has a strong technology component, such as infrastructure engineering, public health, or institutional transfers, these countries must often accept external expertise for decisions regarding adoption and the attendant financial obligations. This may take the form of experts working for the recipient, the donor, or even private-sector players, with conflicting interests regarding public commitments to growth or market-facilitating investment. It should be recalled that even development finance is a technology, and these financial instruments and obligations require significant expertise for prudent use.

AID STRATEGIES FOR GREATER EFFECTIVENESS: WHAT CAN BE DONE?

With all these challenges in mind, it is hardly surprising that the concept of aid strategy has gained importance over time. To make their work more effective, donors and agencies have developed a number of ideas and practices that can promote appropriate incentives and greater discipline linking intentions to outcomes. The main examples of these are as follows.

1. *MDGs as a disciplinary device.* Although the MDGs are merely numbers, they exert important informational discipline on the development-policy agenda and dialogue. As an agreed set of objective indicators of progress, they represent broad consensus among donors about what constitutes real development, and for this reason they can limit opportunistic use of aid and unproductive aid competition. Moreover, these indicators promote transparent public awareness of development progress, and thereby stand as metrics for assessing domestic government commitment and attainment.

696

2. *From project-based to policy-based lending and country selectivity.* Policy conditionality in seeking to achieve greater aid effectiveness has been hampered by fungibility of infra-marginal transfers and lack of enforceability. The new economics of aid thus stresses the importance of good governance for successful use of aid in achieving growth. This led to creation by the US in 2004 of the Millennium Challenge Corporation (MCC), with transfers targeted at countries passing the good-policy test, leading to country selectivity. For countries certified with good governance, aid is shifted from project to budget financing, giving them greater flexibility in setting their own priorities for use of the funds transferred. Aid has thus moved away from project-based lending toward policy-based lending. For the World Bank, countries qualify for aid based on their CPIA score. The CPIA rates the performance of poor countries and, since 1980, has been used to determine the allocation of zero-interest financing under the IDA. The CPIA rates 16 key development indicators, covering four areas: economic management (macro, fiscal, and debt), structural policies (trade, finance, and business-regulatory environment), policies for social inclusion and equity (gender, equity of public-resource use, building human resources, social protection of labor, environmental sustainability), and public-sector management and institutions (property rights, budgetary and financial management, revenue mobilization, public administration, and transparency, accountability, and corruption in the public sector). Countries are rated on a scale of 1 to 5 for each indicator. The overall CPIA score gives a weight of .24 to the first three areas combined and a weight of .68 to the public sector management and institutions area, with a weight of .08 reserved for the quality of management of IDA projects. Focusing on countries with high CPIA scores leaves open the problem of reaching the poor in countries with failed states and in post-conflict societies, with a particular role for social development funds and NGOs that help bypass the central government at the same time as capacity building for improved governance goes on.

   Country selectivity based on good policy and institution scores has become an important determinant of aid allocation. Dollar and Levin (2004) find that 75 percent of aid agencies, including Denmark, Norway, Sweden, the UK, Ireland, and the Netherlands, have a positive relationship between their aid allocations and a measure of good policies and institutions. The US Millennium Challenge Account automatically links aid to governance indicators. The IDA almost completely targets grant funds based on the CPIA index. Countries with high CPIA scores receive six to seven times the per capita IDA allocation of low-scoring countries.

3. *Country ownership.* As mentioned earlier in this chapter, conditionality was an imperfect instrument of policy discipline, largely because it rested on narrow and short-term criteria and because of fungibility and lack of commitment devices. An alternative that emerged at the same time was "country ownership," which required deeper bilateral consultations, joint announcements of development goals, joint monitoring of progress, and, sometimes, matching financial commitments. The basic idea is to more deeply embed reforms and development commitments in the domestic political economy, and this approach is increasingly practiced. The PRSP process described in Chapter 5 is an example.

697

4. *Diminishing returns to aid and absorptive capacity.* How much aid can a country usefully receive depends on its absorptive capacity, which depends on the quality of
   its policies. Cross-country analysis provided the following two important results.
   (1) Aid resources are typically infra-marginal and fungible, so that it is impossible
   for donors to target them at particular objectives or use them to alter the distribution of income (Pack and Pack, 1993). Since conditionality does not work, it is
   better to target countries with good policies. (2) The impact of aid on growth
   depends on the quality of the recipient country's economic policies, and is subject to diminishing returns (Burnside and Dollar, 2000). If this is the case, we can
   determine the maximum level of aid that a country can absorb based on the
   quality of its policies, as measured by the CPIA score between 1 and 5. Collier
   and Dollar (2002) use a cross-country regression with 349 growth episodes of
   four years each to estimate the relation between growth and aid with diminishing
   returns, helping to quantify the saturation point beyond which aid becomes ineffective in raising growth. The saturation point depends upon policy—the better
   the policy, the greater the amount of aid that can be productively absorbed. The
   growth regression they use takes the form:

$$\dot{GDP} = a + b_1 X + b_2 P + b_3 A + b_4 A^2 + b_5 AP + \varepsilon,$$

where $\dot{GDP}$ is the growth rate over the episode, X exogenous country characteristics, P the CPIA score, and A aid as a share of GDP. With this quadratic relation, the saturation point is achieved at $A^* = -(b_3 + b_5 P) / 2b_4$. Collier and
Dollar estimate the following values for the coefficients: $b_3 = 0$, $b_4 = -0.04$
(confirming decreasing returns to aid), and $b_5 = 0.2$ (confirming the good-
governance hypothesis) so that $A* = 2.5P$. Hence if $P = $ CPIA $= 3$ for a
good-governance country, the absorptive capacity for aid has a limit of around
7.5 percent of GDP (Figure 19.5). If CPIA $= 5$, the maximum absorptive
capacity is 12.5 percent of GDP. In this analysis, aid is measured at PPP prices.
If aid is measured at the official exchange rate, this would translate to around
20 percent of GDP for a CPIA of 3. Beyond this saturation point, the growth
effect of aid starts to decline. This result gives a useful rule of thumb that has
been influential in allocating aid, in particular to difficult post-conflict societies
(Collier and Hoeffler, 2004).

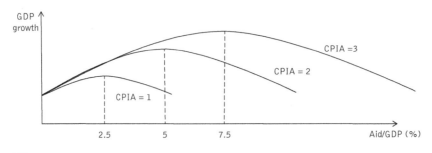

Figure 19.5 *Aid absorptive capacity for GDP growth by CPIA level*

5. *Coordination/pooling/harmonization.* All these measures require coordinated efforts on the donor side, with higher levels of communication to achieve shared donor objectives and limit donor competition. By pooling funds, they can achieve administrative and transaction-costs economies. With strategic coordination, they can reduce the risk of fragmenting local capacity and redundancy. The latest major effort at donor coordination was the 2005 Paris Declaration on Aid Effectiveness, whereby over 100 ministers, heads of agencies, and other senior officials from OECD countries committed their countries and organizations to continue to increase efforts at harmonization, alignment, and results-based management of aid with a set of actions and indicators that can be monitored (OECD, 2005). The Declaration rests on five principles of aid presumed to improve its impact on development.

- Ownership: developing countries exercise leadership over their development policies and plans.
- Alignment: donors base their support on countries' development strategies and systems.
- Harmonization: donors coordinate their activities and minimize the cost of delivering aid.
- Managing for results: donors and developing counties orient their activities to achieve the desired results.
- Mutual accountability: donors and developing countries are accountable to each other for progress in managing aid better and in achieving development results.

THE DEBATE ON FOREIGN AID

Because of the large amounts of money involved and the high stakes in achieving development, aid is a subject that has aroused heated debates. This can be seen in the confrontation between six major authors:

Jeffrey Sachs (2005), *The End of Poverty*
William Easterly (2006), *The White Man's Burden*
Paul Collier (2007), *The Bottom Billion*
Dambisa Moyo (2009), *Dead Aid*
Aneel Karnani (2011), *Fighting Poverty Together*
Angus Deaton (2013), *The Great Escape.*

Sachs is a strong believer in the potential effectiveness of foreign aid and, along with charismatic supporters like U2 singer Bono and actress Angelina Jolie, has been calling for a major increase in expenditure levels. The underlying theory is one of multiple equilibria, where only a coordinated big push in foreign aid can help poor countries take-off toward sustained growth. His role has been fundamental in working with the UN and its former General Secretary Kofi Annan in promoting the Millennium Project and the Millennium Development Villages. Easterly is, by contrast, deeply skeptical about the current practice of foreign aid and recommends experimentation and learning from past mistakes, while calling for a major overhaul of the aid industry to achieve accountability to beneficiaries. His role has been important in prodding the development community toward a results-based management approach and in supporting impact evaluations of development projects. Collier stresses the need for peace and the use of a broad set of instruments focused on the poorest billion— basically the population of extreme poor living on less than a dollar a day. His role has been important in stressing the potential role of aid in reducing conflict and in focus-ing on growth policy instruments, especially as head of the Research Division at the World Bank. Moyo looks at the perverting effects of official foreign aid on local governance, and calls for an end to aid other than emergency relief. As a developing-country researcher with a background in corporate finance, her role has been impor-tant in exposing the frequent corrosive influence of aid on governance, with dire consequences for the poor.

In spite of the frequently high-flying rhetoric, there are quite a few elements across the four positions summarized in Table 19.9 that are compatible. For instance, planning aid to achieve coordination across sectors and agencies, as advocated by Sachs, does not prevent experimenting and learning for institutional change and project improve-ment as recommended by Easterly. And, evidently, aid will not succeed without giving priority to peace and security, and should target the bottom billion as recommended by Collier. Corruption can be a major by-product of foreign aid, and there is broad agreement, not necessarily to cut foreign aid to quell corruption, as advocated by Moyo, but in placing anticorruption practices at the core of strategies to increase aid effectiveness. At the same time, we are still missing a pragmatic and effective set of guidelines to design specific approaches to aid for particular countries, based on received experiences and structured around rigorous impact evaluations and learning processes.

Karnani (2011) has recently rejoined the debate, adding a pragmatic note. He starts by observing that what poor people desire first and foremost is a good job, not the opportunity for self-employment. It is thus important to promote the competi-tiveness of small- and medium-size enterprises (SMEs), where the greatest poten-tial for job creation exists. This requires technical assistance that can be delivered by NGOs such as TechnoServe, which specializes in business development. There is a strong role for the state in three aspects. The first is to improve the investment climate for SMEs through public goods, the rule of law, and a favorable macroeconomic context; the second is to make poor people more employable through improved health, education, and skills, especially targeted at the youth; and the third is to help connect supply and demand on the labor market through employment services and job-creation programs. Civil society has an important role to play as catalyst, watch-dog, and advocate, to ensure that both business and government do their jobs prop-erly. This brings up the very important proposition that the main purpose of foreign aid should be to help poor people generate autonomous income through participa-tion in the formal sector of the economy, with self-employment in the informal sector seen as a temporary social-safety net and a stepping stone toward the formal economy.

Table 19.9 Contrasting positions in the debate on foreign aid: Sachs, Easterly, Collier, and Moyo

Aspects of aid	Jeffrey Sachs The End of Poverty	William Easterly The White Man's Burden	Paul Collier The Bottom Billion	Dambisa Moyo Dead Aid
Focus	Aid shoud be part of a national plan and be guided by the MDG.	Aid projects should be small and piecemeal, not part of a national plan.	Aid should be targeted at the bottom billion for effective use.	Government-to-government aid is detrimental and should be phased out over the next five years.
Scope	Aid should be part of a big-push effort (doubled or tripled) to overcome poverty traps (multiple equilibria).	Large scale aid does not work. Small scale projects are more effective.	Peace and security are key: use aid to reduce conflicts and manage post-conflict situations.	Successful countries did not use aid. Marshall Plan was short and one-time.
Role of government	African governments have the capacity to manage aid and a key role to play for success.	Aid should bypass governments. "Searchers" should be the main agents. Bottom-up solutions preferred.	Good governance (democracy, transparency) is essential to guide development and can be assisted.	Aid undermines governments: perpetuates dysfunctional regimes, postpones reforms, contributes to corruption, civil unrest, Dutch disease, debt, dependency.
Instruments	Technology is a major instrument: Green Revolution, vaccines, bed nets, safe water, etc.	Implementation is the main issue, not budgets.	Use a broad set of instruments. Trade is important but does not work for the bottom billion without aid.	Replace aid by trade, borrowing through capital markets, FDI, MFI.
Approach	Subsidies should be used to promote adoption: bed nets, fertilizers.	Experimentation, impact evaluation, and learning from mistakes are key for success. Scaling up of successes.		Favors Chinese approach to Africa: investments and contracts instead of handouts.
Donors	Donor coordination is essential. MDG are useful guidelines for priorities and achievements.	The aid industry is deeply flawed. Incentives for the aid bureaucracy need to be redesigned for accountability to recipients.	Military intervention may be needed for peace.	Governments, not donors should lead development. End OECD farm subsidies.
Overall message	Aid can be successful. Increase aid. Multiple equilibria. Coordinate donors. Develop national plan. Faith in donors and governments.	Deeply skeptical, except locally. Experiment, evaluate, small local projects, bottom up. Distrusts aid establishment and governments.	Believes in aid, but no details on implementation. Need peace and improved governance. Reliance on markets: trade, investment.	Deeply opposed to public aid. Transit out of aid. Causality problem between aid and development? How to manage the transition out of aid?

Most recently, Deaton (2013) has addressed the impact of aid on governance and institutions, two critical factors for development. In his book *The Great Escape*, he praises the enormous gains that have been achieved in health, wealth, and wellbeing in many parts of the world over the last 250 years, but also notes that there has been a sharp rise in inequality as many have been left behind. This raises the question of the potential role of foreign aid in helping them catch up with those who have achieved success. He notes that, while billions of dollars have been spent on government-to-government aid, it is an "illusion" to believe that money can solve the development problem. According to Deaton, this form of aid has not only been ineffective but has made poor countries worse-off. It benefits donors' commercial and geopolitical interests rather than recipients. Most aid transfers in fact do not reach the poor: half of the world's poor receive only one fortieth of official world aid—and what does reach them is ineffective because it is tied to the use of donor products and services, excessively fragmented, and comes with conditionalities that do not work due to fungibility and lack of commitment devices. He argues that the problem of underdevelopment is not due to lack of money but to weak institutions, lack of state capacity, and poor policies. Large inflows of foreign aid, accounting for more that 75 percent of public resources in many poor African countries, help reinforce these conditions. They undermine good governance, fuel corruption, postpone the need for institutional reforms, support authoritarian regimes, undermine democracy, and sustain Dutch diseases that are damaging to domestic agriculture and industry. He also believes that the evaluation of aid programs is flawed, including the use of an RCT approach that is too limited in scope and has insufficient external validity to scale up results, and that we have failed to learn from experience. Help for developing countries should instead be sought through other instruments, such as reducing damaging OECD trade policies in agriculture; technical advice on institution building; increased investment in research on pharmaceuticals for developing-country diseases and on agricultural technology for tropical environments; support for institutional reforms such as property rights and the rule of law; and a decline in arms sales to developing countries.

CONCLUSION: TOWARD A NEW AID ARCHITECTURE

We have seen that the aggregate growth effects of aid are not always obvious, creating the micro–macro paradox of foreign aid. This is perhaps because aggregate aid transfers are too small to have a macro-level impact, as Sachs would argue, or perhaps because the perverse institutional effects of aid cancel the positive micro effects, as Moyo and Deaton would argue. This can occur through the influence of aid in postponing necessary reforms, perpetuating dysfunctional institutions, facilitating non-democratic forms of governance, feeding corruption and clientelism, and unleashing Dutch diseases. The micro effects of foreign aid have been widely heralded, but rigorous evaluations are still scarce, while self-reported results are inflated and with limited credibility. Rigorous RCT evaluations of aid are more appropriate for small projects than for large policy reforms that are difficult to experiment on (Rosenzweig, 2012). Impact evaluations of foreign-aid projects based on natural experiments are scarce, with the recent work of Galiani *et al.* (2014), using the GDPpc discontinuity in qualifying for IDA grants, being an exception, showing that aid can affect growth in very poor countries through public investment.

New approaches to foreign aid have been introduced, based in part on the recognition that policy conditionality does not work due to the fungibility of infra-marginal transfers and to lack of commitment devices. Aid has shifted from conditionality to country selectivity based on good governance and good institutions. Project-based disbursements have evolved to government budgetary support for qualifying countries, where qualification is established by the comprehensive MCA or CPIA scoring schemes, immune to political considerations. Sustained aid increasingly depends on results-based management, giving an important role to impact evaluations. But rigorous evaluations often deflate expectations relative to results reported by donors or implementing agencies. Impact evaluation is thus eventually resisted at the level of each particular project, making it into an international public good with funding that needs to be external to projects.

This is why a new foreign-aid architecture has emerged in recent years (Gore, 2013). It has led to a proliferation of sources of aid and a lack of coordination. New sources include emerging countries' bilateral programs (especially from China, India, and Brazil), global funds (such as the Global Fund to Fight AIDS, Tuberculosis, and Malaria; the Global Alliance on Vaccines and Immunizations; the Global Environmental Facility; the Consultative Group for International Agricultural Research), foundations (such as the Bill & Melinda Gates Foundation, the Ford Foundation), corporate social responsibility (such as Danone in Bangladesh), social enterprises (such as the Grameen Bank), and large international NGOs (such as World Vision International, Save the Children, CARE, the Catholic Relief Service, Oxfam, *Médecins Sans Frontières*). There is an attempt at greater coordination among these multiple sources of aid, with the 2005 Paris Declaration on Aid Effectiveness a step in this direction, pursuing the principles of ownership, alignment, harmonization, managing for results, and mutual accountability. With the rapid rise of FDI and international bonds to access foreign capital, aid is shifting from a source of funds to the transfer of knowledge, policy advice, aid for trade, and building capacity, hence the World Bank aiming to become a knowledge bank, as opposed to a source of loanable funds.

The emergence of South–South donors is significant. Principal among them are China, India, and Brazil. Their aid offers developing countries an alternative to OECD–Development Advisory Committee (DAC) aid. In the case of China, it consists principally of heavily subsidized concessional loans made by the country's Eximbank in support of direct investment, generally the acquisition of rights to develop and import natural resources. Chinese aid assists large infrastructure projects, particularly access roads, airports, government buildings, and health facilities, often built directly by Chinese construction companies. This aid is typically not conditional on policy and not concerned with poverty reduction and respect for human rights. It is aimed at investments driven by market, FDI, and trade opportunities to accelerate growth and achieve GDPpc convergence. According to *The Economist* (2012), the provision of schools, hospitals, and infrastructure is financed by soft loans in return for a guaranteed supply of oil or other raw materials. Eximbank contributed a US$2 billion low-interest loan to help China's oil companies build infrastructure in

Angola. While there are no official data on the total amount of Chinese foreign aid, it has likely been significant in contributing to the recent growth spurt in Sub-Saharan Africa (Robertson, 2012).

Attempts were made to formalize the principles of the South–South approach at the 2011 meeting—the fourth—of the High Level Forum on Aid Effectiveness in Busan, Korea. The objective was to go from *aid effectiveness* for donors, as announced in the Paris Declaration, to *development effectiveness* in a global partnership between donors and recipient countries, as enunciated in the Busan Declaration. Four important principles emerged:

1. Development priorities pursued with the support of foreign aid should be owned by the recipient country, based on its own definition of the development model it wants to implement.
2. Aid should be driven by a focus on results.
3. Aid should be based on a partnership between parties, as opposed to a principal–agent model, where the donor imposes conditionalities on recipient behavior.
4. Cooperation for development should be accountable to all citizens, as opposed to only aid agencies and their donors.

These deep rearrangements of the aid business create two competing models. On one side, the updated DAC model with renewed emphasis on the PRSP process for poverty reduction, the MDGs, the post-2015 Sustainable Development Goals, and an effort at coordination for aid effectiveness. On the other, the new South–South aid model with emphasis on growth, investment opportunities, and partnerships for development effectiveness. This new architecture is very much work in progress. In spite of active quests for new approaches in redefining aid, it continues to be largely uncoordinated, unaccountable to recipients, and of limited effectiveness.

Future success of the updated DAC model may depend on meeting two major challenges. The first is the provision of assistance to improve governance so poor countries can qualify for selective aid. How to transform a failed state into a developmental state? How to use aid to build state capacity? State building is clearly a huge challenge. This is all the more important given that middle-income countries are eradicating extreme poverty, meaning a majority of the extreme poor will, by 2030, be located in fragile states such as Yemen, the Democratic Republic of the Congo, and Somalia, states that cannot use aid according to the good governance–good institutions–selectivity principle. How to deliver "good aid in hard places" while at the same time building state capacity needs further exploration (Al-Iryani *et al.*, 2015).

One way of thinking about aid to countries that have failing CPIA scores is in a multiple-equilibrium framework, as illustrated in Figure 19.6. This is the perspective used by Sachs (2005) in arguing for larger aid commitments and by Ravallion (2014) in questioning Deaton's (2013) skepticism of aid as not only ineffective for poverty reduction but harmful for the quality of governance. Say that, to qualify for aid, a country needs a threshold level of institutional quality represented by $CPIA_{min}$. Beyond this minimum, institutions will gradually improve to reach the desirable maximum score that corresponds to institutions in a developing-country framework.

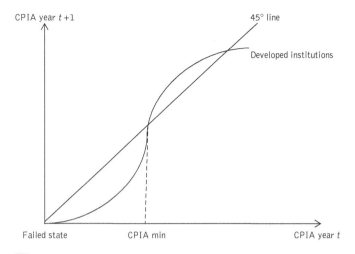

Figure 19.6 *Aid threshold in a multiple-equilibrium framework*

Countries with a CPIA score below the minimum will collapse into failing states at a zero score. The question is whether aid should be discontinued when the CPIA falls below the minimum threshold, as advocated by the pro-good-policy aid advocates. Say that aid can contribute to improving the CPIA score if properly targeted at institutional improvement—a reasonable assumption. As argued by Collier (2007) and Ravallion (2014), aid can be expected to help improve peace and security, the rule of law, sound fiscal policy, and better and more accountable public services, even if this is recognizably difficult, requires innovations in design, and takes a long time. In this case, international donors should make every effort to help countries reach the $CPIA_{min}$ score, even if the CPIA currently falls below this level. Most importantly, donors should not discontinue support if a country slips below $CPIA_{min}$ as this will drive it toward failing-state status, with catastrophic implications for the poor. Donors should commit sustained and sufficiently large aid to guarantee the $CPIA_{min}$ threshold, and take the long-term view that aid is needed for institutional development.

The second challenge is success in pursuing a comprehensive "beyond-aid" development agenda that links the aid instrument to other sources of development (Gore, 2013). This includes (1) linking aid to the mobilization of other sources of external finance such as commercial loans, FDI, and remittances for development, especially when countries graduate from concessional aid; (2) achieving greater policy coherence in donor countries so that national policies that affect developing countries (especially their trade, finance, technology-transfer, and migration policies) are consistent with and supportive of development-cooperation objectives; and (3) providing developing countries with an international development architecture that is more supportive of growth and poverty reduction, including progress on currently stalled multilateral trade agreements, a more effective international financial architecture, more open international transfers of knowledge, increased availability of international public goods, a more favorable international migration regime, and support for adaptation to climate change.

CONCEPTS SEEN IN THIS CHAPTER

Micro–macro paradox of foreign aid
Bilateral aid agency
Multilateral aid agency
Aid effectiveness
Aid fatigue
Aid for trade
Policy conditionality
Fungibility
Infra- and extra-marginal transfer
Additionality
Good policy for effective use of aid
Millennium Challenge Account
Selectivity
CPIA score and IDA aid allocation
Absorptive capacity for growth
Investment climate
Results-based management
New aid architecture
DAC vs. South–South aid modalities
"Beyond-aid" development agenda

REVIEW QUESTIONS: DEVELOPMENT AID AND ITS EFFECTIVENESS

1. Explain the concept of fungibility in aid. Why is aid in kind fungible if the transfer is infra-marginal?
2. Explain the concept of conditionality. Why does fungibility weaken the case for conditionality?
3. Why is there a micro–macro paradox in aid and how has the lack of macro effects been established?
4. How did research on the effectiveness of foreign aid lead to the result that "good policy" is the key to success?
5. How did this result affect the way aid is implemented and the creation of the Millennium Challenge Account? How is the CPIA score used to determine the optimum level of foreign aid?
6. What are the positions of Sachs, Easterly, Collier, Moyo, and Deaton on the scope of foreign aid, the role of government in foreign aid, and the instruments to be used?
7. Why does Karnani emphasize the role of employment creation in the SME sector, and what aid policies does this call for?

NOTES

1   In writing this chapter, we made extensive use of review papers by Roland-Holst and Tarp (2002) and Dethier (2008).

2   If analysts cannot value, for example, environmental costs and benefits, it is difficult to account for them in calculations of rates of return. The same goes for such approaches as participation by communities in the design of projects at the local level, an important objective of the CDD (community-driven development) approach.

3   There are many exceptions to this, particularly in humanitarian and religious development work, but the majority of aid flows pass between large institutions.

REFERENCES

Acemoglu, Daron, and James Robinson. 2012. *Why Nations Fail: The Origins of Power, Prosperity, and Poverty.* New York: Crown Business.

Adelman, Irma. 1991. "Long Term Economic Development." Working paper, Department of Agricultural and Resource Economics, University of California at Berkeley.

Al-Iryani, Lamis, Alain de Janvry, and Elisabeth Sadoulet. 2015. "The Yemen Social Fund for Development: An Effective Community-Based Approach amid Political Instability." *International Peacekeeping* 22(4): 321–36.

Boone, Peter. 1996. "Politics and the Effectiveness of Foreign Aid." *European Economic Review* 40(2): 289–329.

Brautigam, Deborah, and Stephen Knack. 2004. "Foreign Aid, Institutions, and Governance in Sub-Saharan Africa." *Economic Development and Cultural Change* 52(2): 255–85.

Burnside, Craig, and David Dollar. 2000. "Aid, Policies, and Growth." *American Economic Review* 90(4): 847–68.

Collier, Paul. 2007. *The Bottom Billion: Why the Poorest Countries are Failing and What Can Be Done About It.* Oxford: Oxford University Press.

Collier, Paul, and David Dollar. 2002. "Aid Allocation and Poverty Reduction." *European Economic Review* 46(8): 1475–500.

Collier, Paul, and Anke Hoeffler. 2004. "Aid, Policy, and Growth in Post-conflict Societies." *European Economic Review* 48(5): 1125–45.

Crost, Benjamin, Joseph Felter, and Patrick Johnston. 2014. "Aid under Fire: Development Projects and Civil Conflict." *American Economic Review* 104(6): 1833–56.

Deaton, Angus. 2013. *The Great Escape: Health, Wealth, and the Origins of Inequality.* Princeton, NJ: Princeton University Press.

Denizer, Cevdet, Daniel Kaufmann, and Art Kraay. 2013. "Good Countries or Good Projects? Macro and Micro Correlates of World Bank Project Performance." *Journal of Development Economics* 105(November): 288–302.

Dethier, Jean-Jacques. 2008. "Aid Effectiveness: What Can We Know? What Should We Know? What May We Hope?" Washington, DC: World Bank.

Devarajan, Shantayanan, David Dollar, and Torgny Holmgren (eds.). 2001. *Aid and Reform in Africa: Lessons from Ten Case Studies.* Washington, DC: World Bank.

Djankov, Simeon, José Montalvo, and Marta Reynal-Querol. 2008. "The Curse of Aid." *Journal of Economic Growth* 13(3): 169–94.

Dollar, David, and Jakob Svensson. 2000. "What Explains the Success or Failure of Structural Adjustment Programs?" *Economic Journal* 110(466): 894–917.

Dollar, David, and Victoria Levin. 2004. "The Increasing Selectivity of Foreign Aid, 1984-2002." Washington, DC: World Bank Policy Research Working Paper No. 3299.

Easterly, William. 2001. *The Elusive Quest for Growth: Economists' Adventures and Misadventures in the Tropics.* Cambridge, MA: MIT Press.

Easterly, William. 2006. *The White Man's Burden,* New York: Penguin Press.

Easterly, William, Ross Levine, and David Roodman. 2004. "New Data, New Doubts: A Comment on Burnside and Dollar's 'Aid, Policies, and Growth' (2000)." *American Economic Review* 94(3): 774–80.

The Economist (2012) "Going Abroad: The World in their Hands." January 21. www.economist.com/node/21542930 (accessed 2014).

Eubank, Nicholas. 2012. "Taxation, Political Accountability, and Foreign Aid: Lessons from Somaliland." *Journal of Development Studies* 48(4): 465–80.

Galiani, Sebastian, Stephen Knack, Lixin Xu, and Ben Zou. 2014. "The Effect of Aid on Growth: Evidence from a Quasi-experiment." Washington, DC: World Bank Policy Research Working Paper No. 6865.

Gore, Charles. 2013. "The New Development Cooperation Landscape: Actors, Approaches, Architecture." *Journal of International Development* 25(6): 769–86.

Governance Assessment Portal. 2015. *Country Policy and Institutional Assessment.* www.gaportal.org/global-indicators/country-policy-and-institutional-assessment (accessed 2015).

Hancock, Graham. 1994. *The Lords of Poverty: The Freewheeling Lifestyles, Power, Prestige, and Corruption of the Multibillion Dollar Aid Business.* New York: Grove/Atlantic, Inc.

Kanbur, Ravi. 2000. "Aid, Conditionality and Debt in Africa." In Finn Tarp (ed.), *Foreign Aid and Development: Lessons Learnt and Directions for the Future,* 409–22. New York: Routledge.

Karnani, Aneel. 2011. *Fighting Poverty Together: Rethinking Strategies for Business, Governments, and Civil Society to Reduce Poverty.* New York: Palgrave Macmillan.

Kaufmann, Daniel, and Pedro Vicente. 2005. *Legal Corruption.* Washington, DC: World Bank.

Knack, Stephen. 2001. "Aid Dependence and the Quality of Governance: Cross-Country Empirical Tests." *Southern Economic Journal* 68(2): 310–29.

Moore, Mick. 2008. "Between Coercion and Contract: Competing Narratives around Taxation and Governance." In Deborah Bräutigam, Odd-Helge Fjeldstad, and Mick Moore (eds.), *Taxation and State-Building in Developing Countries: Capacity and Consent,* 34–63. New York: Cambridge University Press.

Mosley, Paul. 1987. *Foreign Aid: Its Defense and Reform.* Lexington, KY: University Press of Kentucky.

Moyo, Dambisa. 2009. *Dead Aid: Why Aid Is Not Working and How There is a Better Way for Africa.* New York: Farrar, Straus and Giroux.

Nunn, Nathan, and Nancy Qian. 2014. "US Food Aid and Civil Conflict." *American Economic Review* 104(6): 1630–66.

OECD (Organization for Economic Co-operation and Development). 2005. "Paris Declaration on Aid Effectiveness." Document issued by participants at the Paris High-Level Forum. www.oecd.org/development/effectiveness/34428351.pdf (accessed 2015).

OECD. 2012. *Development Assistance Committee Online Database.* www.oecd.org/dac/ (accessed 2015).

OECD. 2014. *Multilateral Aid Report.* www.oecd.org/dac/aid-architecture/Multilateral%20Report%20N%201_2014.pdf (accessed 2015).

OECD. *Development Co-operation Directorate.* www.oecd.org/dac/stats/data.htm (accessed 2015).

OECD. *International Development Statistics*. http://stats.oecd.org/qwids/ (accessed 2015).

Pack, Howard, and Janet Rothenberg Pack. 1993. "Foreign Aid and the Question of Fungibility." *Review of Economics and Statistics* 75(2): 258–65.

Qian, Nancy. 2015. "Making Progress on Foreign Aid." *The Annual Review of Economics* 7(August): 277–308.

Rajan, Raghuram, and Arvind Subramanian. 2005. "Aid and Growth: What Does the Cross-Country Evidence Really Show?" Washington, DC: IMF Working Paper 05-127.

Ravallion, Martin. 2014. "On the Role of Aid in the Great Escape." *Review of Income and Wealth* 60(4): 967–84.

Robertson, Charles. 2012. *The Fastest Billion: The Story Behind Africa's Economic Revolution*. London: Renaissance Capital.

Roland-Holst, David, and Finn Tarp. 2002. "New Perspectives on Aid Effectiveness." World Bank, ABCDE conference, Oslo, Norway.

Rosenzweig, Mark. 2012. "Thinking Small: A Review of Poor Economics: A Radical Rethinking of the Way to Fight Global Poverty." *Journal of Economic Literature* 50(1): 115–27.

Sachs, Jeffrey. 2005. *The End of Poverty: Economic Possibilities for Our Time*. New York: Penguin Press.

Thorbecke, Erik. 2000. "The Evolution of the Development Doctrine and the Role of Foreign Aid, 1950–2000." In F. Tarp and P. Hjertholm (eds.), *Foreign Aid and Development—Lessons Learnt and Directions for the Future*, 17–47. London and New York: Routledge.

Williamson, John. 1989. "What Washington Means by Policy Reform." In John Williamson (ed.), *Latin American Readjustment: How Much has Happened*, 7–40. Washington, DC: Institute for International Economics.

World Bank. 1998. *Assessing Aid: What Works, What Doesn't, and Why*. Washington, DC.

World Bank. 2002. *The Role and Effectiveness of Development Assistance: Lessons from World Bank Experience*. Washington, DC.

World Bank. *World Development Indicators*. http://data.worldbank.org/indicator (accessed 2015).

Chapter 20

Institutional innovations and development

TAKE-HOME MESSAGES FOR CHAPTER 20

1. Institutions are rules that govern human behavior and the structure of social interactions. As such, they are enormously important for development, contributing to explanations for its successes and failures.

2. The New Institutional Economics (NIE) explains the emergence of institutions as innovations to reduce market failures and transaction costs that originate in adverse selection, moral hazard, and cooperation failures. The institution that is selected should be the most efficient among alternative institutions for the partners involved. This institution is locally efficient, but not necessarily socially efficient nor equitable.

3. Institutional change may fail to occur due to path dependency, time-consistency problems and lack of commitment devices, uncertain distribution of gains and losses, and coordination failures. Many good institutions thus fail to emerge and many dysfunctional institutions remain in existence.

4. An example of NIE reasoning is the choice of contracts for land rental, including wages for owner-operated enterprises, fixed rent, and sharecropping. Sharecropping suffers from the "Marshallian inefficiency" due to output sharing without corresponding input sharing. However, it may be the relatively most efficient contract in helping mitigate market failures for risk, credit, and/or non-contractible inputs.

5. Linking local/traditional institutions to national/modern institutions offers interesting possibilities for combining access to local information with links to broader markets, as used, for instance, in microfinance. Preserving local/traditional institutions can thus be efficient for development.

INSTITUTIONS AND DEVELOPMENT

Institutions matter enormously for development. While some development economists have emphasized the roles of resource endowments affecting specialization and trade (the "vent for surplus theories" in Myint, 1971), of geography affecting health and access to the sea for trading (Gallup and Sachs, 1999; Krugman, 1995), and of technological innovations for productivity growth adapted to relative factor scarcities

(Solow, 1956; Hayami and Ruttan, 1985), all would agree that institutions matter. Controversies over their roles are often overblown by building paper tigers. The roles of resources, geography, technology, and institutions are more a matter of balance and complementarities than of substitutions. Recognizing the role of institutions in development is certainly not new, but greater emphasis and better understanding have recently been given to the subject with theoretical developments in the "New Institutional Economics" (NIE) (North, 1990) and empirical analyses trying to more rigorously identify the direction of causalities between institutional choices and development outcomes (as, for example, in Acemoglu *et al.*, 2002).

The objective of the NIE is to explain the emergence, logic, transformation, and disappearance of institutions. Like technology, institutions are an outcome of development, and they in turn strongly determine developmental outcomes. Establishing causality between institutions and development is thus particularly difficult, and still the object of much controversy.

Institutions are defined as the rules and conventions that codify social interactions and, in so doing, constrain individual behavior. They exist because of the uncertainties involved in human interactions and the need to structure and guide these interactions to reduce uncertainties (North, 1990). As such, institutions are multiple and varied, ranging from the macro to the micro level, from economic to social and political, and from formal to informal. Examples of formal institutions include laws, the constitution, written contracts, recorded property rights, the market, the family, the church, the firm, and the school. Organizations such as General Electric, the Rotary Club, or the Peace Corps are specific groups of people and their corresponding governance arrangements (i.e. institutions) to coordinate team actions. Organizations are thus particular institutions. Examples of informal institutions include shared values, social norms, customs, implicit codes of conduct shared among the members of a community, ideology, ethical principles, verbal contracts, "palavers" to resolve differences, and informal property rights. Institutions have a strong impact on economic performance: they can be factors of growth and development, or of stagnation and exploitation. In previous chapters, we have met many types of institution: trade rules (e.g. NAFTA), educational and health systems, property rights such as common property or individual titles, financial institutions such as commercial banks and microfinance institutions, and international development agencies and NGOs in foreign aid. So how can such a vast array of institutions have a common body of theory? This is what the NIE tries to provide. The design of new institutions, i.e. institutional innovations, is a central aspect of development.

The reason why the NIE is so important for development is that institutions have a large role to play in enabling transactions and collective action to succeed: many markets fail—a signature feature of underdevelopment—but institutional innovations can help make markets work or can provide substitutes for markets in allowing transactions to happen—for instance, through contracts or trades among members of a social network. Institutions effective for development are not easy to put into place, and the failure of effective institutions to emerge is part and parcel of underdevelopment. But an interesting possibility emerges: developing countries are typically rich in social capital and traditional culture. Can these local/traditional institutions provide

711

the basis on which to construct modern institutions that will help markets perform or transactions to occur outside the market? Can traditional and modern institutions be coordinated, capitalizing on the advantages that each has to offer to the other in raising efficiency? There are many positive stories showing that this can indeed happen. Hayami (1998), for instance, reminds us that Toyota's just-in-time production system originated in the discipline of water management for rice farming in a peasant community. The coordination between traditional and modern institutions provides a fertile background for constructing new institutions that can be effective for development. It also highlights the role of disciplines such as anthropology and sociology in helping us, economists, better understand the structure, inner logic, and performance of these institutions.

ASSUMPTIONS UNDERLYING THE NEW INSTITUTIONAL ECONOMICS

There are two assumptions on which the NIE is built (Bardhan, 1992).

Assumption 1: imperfect information

Information is asymmetrically available to agents in a potential transaction, and is costly to acquire. This asymmetry has two consequences for behavior.

1. *Adverse selection (AS).* AS derives from the fact that there is hidden information about people or goods in a transaction, and that acquiring this information is costly. The quality of people, products, and projects is typically better known to one of the transacting parties than it is to the other. The result is that the market may fail. Bad cars (lemons) drive away good cars on used-car markets, to the point that the market may simply disappear (Akerlof, 1970). Potentially good borrowers cannot be distinguished from bad borrowers by a lender, with the result that the transaction cannot happen without collateral attached, imposing a wealth constraint on participants in financial markets that excludes the poor. High-risk people pretend to be safe to the insurance company, with the result that they create unexpected costs and drive up insurance premiums for safe clients. Prior medical conditions are not revealed to the insurer and are impossible to detect, or only at a very high cost, increasing the cost of insurance premiums. Non-poor households plead poverty to qualify for a cash- or food-transfer program, with the result that the aid agency incurs Type II (inclusion) errors and may run out of money to cover the poor in need. Because of AS, many markets fail or perform highly inefficiently.
2. *Moral hazard (MH).* MH derives from the fact that people engage in hidden actions that cannot be specified in contracts. You can hire someone and write a contract that specifies a wage to be paid and a time to be worked, but it does not indicate how hard the person is expected to work and/or how creative she is expected to be. The contract is incomplete. This gives the worker an opportunity to shirk and cheat. Or, alternatively, the contract does not fully specify the expected product to be delivered, giving the employer the possibility of abusing

the worker by demanding more. For the employer, the risk of MH means that costs must be incurred in seeking information, screening, selecting, negotiating, supervising, enforcing, litigating, etc. At the limit, MH may prevent the transaction from happening if the cost of preventing it is higher than the benefit created by the transaction.

AS and MH thus impose *transaction costs (TC)* on markets, eventually to the point that a transaction is too costly or too risky for the benefits it could provide, making markets fail. Institutions have as a purpose the search for ways to reduce transaction costs on markets, i.e. to economize and reduce risk in transactions (Williamson, 1985).

Assumption 2: methodological individualism

The NIE assumes that agents exercise choice. They can pursue "self-interest with guile," taking advantage of imperfect information to engage in opportunistic behavior. According to Williamson, they can lie, cheat, shirk, confuse, obfuscate, and play strategic games to their best interest. The pursuit of advantage does not mean that it is only done individually, and that advantage only concerns monetary rewards. The pursuit of advantage can be collective, as in lobbying for rents that create individual gains at a social cost. Individuals participate in collective action voluntarily in pursuit of perceived personal advantage. Individual advantage can include non-monetary rewards such as altruism (where one's own utility is a function of the utility of others, meaning that we can derive pleasure from the satisfaction of others, even at a cost to us), the perception of identity (one's sense of self), honor, and other non-materialistic purposes. Choice can also go beyond simple rationality, as explored in the fields of psychology and economics, with such determinants of behavior as time-inconsistency (procrastination), preference reversals, and anchoring effects.

MARKET FAILURES INDUCED BY TRANSACTION COSTS

AS and MH create high transaction costs on markets, eventually resulting in market failures and incomplete markets. Examples include the following:

■ *Credit.* A bank requires collateral from clients since it does not have the information needed to distinguish good from bad borrowers in extending loans. Hence market transactions are wealth constrained, creating inefficiencies in allocating loanable funds among borrowers. Banks also protect themselves from the more risky clients (gamblers who are willing to borrow at very high interest rates) by keeping the interest rate (r) below the market equilibrium level (r^*) (Figure 20.1). This avoids catering only to the more risky clients, but it also means that there will be excess demand for loans at $r < r^*$. The bank must consequently introduce a rationing scheme to allocate loans to a subset of the clients demanding loans at r (Greenwald et al., 1984).

713

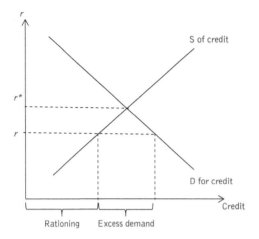

Figure 20.1 *Credit rationing under imperfect information*

- *Insurance.* With asymmetrical information, it is difficult for the insurance company to verify the veracity of claims: is the declared loss due to a genuine shock or to MH? Is the low crop yield shown to the adjuster due to low rainfall or to lack of effort in caring for plants—or perhaps part of the harvest was already collected and sold? If claims of loss are difficult to verify, many abusive claims for indemnification will be placed on the insurance company. The insurance premium must consequently increase for everybody, excluding good clients, who will prefer to self-insure, further driving up the insurance premium and creating a classical lemons problem. A government can avoid this adverse selection behavior by making insurance mandatory for all, as, for example, with car insurance. Lack of third-party verifiability of claims severely restricts the existence of an insurance market in agriculture. If farmers are risk averse, and cannot reduce their individual exposure to risk through access to insurance, they will self-insure by engaging in risk management and underinvest relative to the social optimum.

- *Labor.* With transaction costs on labor markets, and the need to motivate workers to work hard by offering a wage that maximizes effort per unit of pay, the "efficiency wage" w offered may have to be in excess of the full-employment equilibrium wage w^* (Shapiro and Stiglitz, 1984) (see Figure 12.4 in Chapter 12). In this case, the labor market is in equilibrium with unemployment. The line of workers waiting for employment outside the factory gate at this privileged level of wage serves as a "disciplinary device" for the employed (Bowles and Gintis, 1988): MH in work can lead to dismissal and replacement by a candidate in the long waiting line. Here again, the labor market fails in that it leaves workers unemployed as supply is in excess of demand.

- *Transaction costs create price bands* for product and factor transactions, with farm-gate prices received below market price for sellers, and farm-gate prices paid above market price for buyers. This results in selective market integration across households, some as net sellers and some as net buyers, and also selective market failures as many households remain in self-sufficiency, neither selling on nor buying from the market (Figure 20.2). When prices rise, as during the 2008 world food crisis, some self-sufficient households will become net sellers (as it now pays to sell), and some net buyers will become self-sufficient (as they can no longer afford to buy) (de Janvry *et al.*, 1991) (see Chapter 22).

■ *Land rental markets when risk or credit markets fail.* Many potential tenants are unable to assume the risk of production because there is no market on which they could share part of the production risk. Many other potential tenants are unable to mobilize the liquidity necessary to rent land because there is no market on which they could acquire the necessary liquidity. Weak property rights may also prevent a landlord from renting out for fear that the land will not be vacated by the tenant at the end of the contract. If landlords feel more secure renting to someone from the same social class, then the poor will be excluded from renting land from rich landlords who control most of the land, reproducing local inequalities (Macours *et al.*, 2010). For these various reasons, potentially profitable rental transactions that could satisfy workers, or small farmers with insufficient access to land, and landlords with excess land are prevented from occurring.

Market failures due to AS, MH, and TC create inefficiencies in market transactions, and sometimes missing markets. If it is the poor who are excluded, they also create inequities, reproducing inequalities: the poor are selectively excluded from access to capital, insurance, land, good jobs, etc. These market failures create non-separability between efficiency and equity. Asset ownership thus becomes an important determinant of efficiency. A well known example is the inverse relation between total factor productivity and farm size due to labor- and credit-market failures that we saw in Chapter 6. Transaction costs due to imperfect information can also create cooperation failures in collective action as there is imperfect monitoring and costly enforcement. Collective action will either be abandoned, or pursued at a level less than the social optimum. Common property resources that need cooperation in order to be managed at the social optimum will be mismanaged, with over-extraction of resources and under-provision of services, as we saw in Chapter 16.

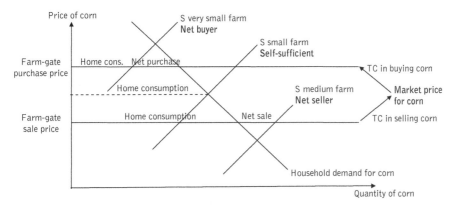

Figure 20.2 *Transaction costs create market failures*

INSTITUTIONAL RESPONSES TO MARKET FAILURES

Market failures leave money on the table, but this is fortunately not the end of the story. These failures can induce institutional innovations to overcome the hurdles to the transaction, or to collective action, and capture the unrealized gains. New institutions such as contracts, organizations, laws, regulations, and redefinitions of property rights may emerge to:

> Reduce the information problem and the associated transaction costs.
> Provide incentives to agents to:
>> reduce AS
>> reduce MH
>> i.e. reduce incentives to behave opportunistically.

Institutional innovations' functions are to:

- *Increase efficiency (economize).* Institutional innovations may be able to make markets work, reduce transaction costs, internalize externalities, avoid the tragedy of the commons, increase specialization, and redistribute assets to increase productivity.
- *Decrease risk.* Institutional innovations may permit risk sharing—for instance, among members of an extended family, in a mutual insurance network, or through sharecropping contracts where the rent paid is proportional to the level of output, allowing tenant and landlord to share the production risk.

If successful, the consequences of these institutional innovations will be:

- To *allow transactions to occur through the market* by reducing transaction costs, if the value of the transaction is greater than its cost.
- To *allow transactions to occur outside the market* via new institutions, if the cost of institutional change is less than the benefits from the transaction (e.g. contracts, Coase bargains and agreements, intra-household transactions, and intra-firm transactions).
- To *allow cooperation to succeed* by increasing the gains from cooperation, improving members' ability to monitor the behavior of others, and increasing the ability to enforce rules.

MECHANISMS OF INSTITUTIONAL CHANGE

There exist many alternative institutional innovations that can help to overcome a particular market failure or reduce a cost in a particular market transaction. Among these alternatives, the most efficient institution should in principle be the one that dominates and eliminates the others. This has been called institutional Darwinism—an analogy with the theory of evolution of species by natural selection, with the survival of the fittest among competing institutions. But the world of institutions is not that simple. First, the institution that dominates may not be socially efficient, even though it is the best option for the partners involved. Second, this institution may not be equitable in the way it shares the efficiency gains achieved among partners. And, third, many potentially efficient institutional innovations may fail to occur, with underdevelopment an unwelcome consequence of this failure.

These three outcomes can be explained as follows:

1. *The institution that dominates is the best option for the partners involved, but it may not be socially efficient.* We will say that it is "second-best efficient" or "locally efficient," but not "first-best efficient" or "socially efficient." An example is sharecropping (or franchising) contracts which are good for sharing risk among partners, but achieve this at the cost of an inefficiency due to the sharing rule that discourages effort (see below). If there existed a separate insurance market to achieve the same level of risk reduction, a more efficient (first-best) contract (such as fixed-rent or wage) could be used without having to sacrifice efficiency.

2. *The institution that dominates is the best option for the partners involved, but it may not be equitable.* This is the case for a *principal–agent contract* that allows the principal to extract from the agent all the efficiency gains created by the contract beyond the agent's participation constraint. This may also be the case if one partner has property rights over the resource that is the object of contracting (as in the Coase theorem, seen in Chapter 15, where the bargaining party with property rights over pollution can extract from the other all the efficiency gains generated by the contract). More generally, this is the case when there is unequal bargaining power among the contracting partners over sharing the efficiency gains from the institutional innovation.

3. *There are many reasons why efficient institutions may fail to emerge, or existing institutions may fail to adjust to achieve greater efficiency, or dysfunctional institutions may remain in existence.*

   ■ *Path dependency.* Consider the case of the disposition of the letters of the alphabet on the keyboard of a typewriter. Instead of concentrating at the center of the keyboard the most frequently used letters to achieve gains in speed, these letters are spread widely across the keyboard. When the keyboard was first designed, this was done to slow down secretaries at a time when typewriters could not handle a rapid succession of finger touches on keys because their levers would tangle up. Spreading widely the most commonly used letters across the keyboard allowed for the pacing of secretaries' speed to that which the technology could handle. Here, the institution (the rule) is the disposition of the letters on the keyboard following the QWERTY system. Today, with electronic keyboards, it would be more efficient to relocate the letters to maximize speed. But generations of users have already invested in learning the QWERTY system in high school, and it would be costly to change. The letter set-up thus has a huge sunken cost that would be lost with change. A superior institution fails to emerge due to path dependency: past investments block change and efficiency gains. Path dependency is thus an institutional lock-in where, once a path has been taken, the costs of switching to a new institution mean one is locked in to the original, less efficient institution.

■ *Lack of commitment device for credible compensation of losers by winners.* Institutional change often involves a *time-consistency problem* with no credible commitment that losers will be compensated by winners when benefits from the change occur. The institutional change happens now—for instance, with trade liberalization—net social gains (NSG) are expected to result, but we also know that there will be winners and losers. Because there are NSGs, the winners can compensate the losers; but how do the losers know that the winners will compensate them when the benefits from trade materialize? If there is no *commitment device* available to the policy-maker, losers will oppose the institutional change. If the number of losers is larger than the number of winners, the median voter will carry the vote against the change. Many socially beneficial institutional changes thus fail to materialize due to lack of commitment devices. "Read my lips," President George H. W. Bush's promise not to raise taxes, was not credible enough. Putting in escrow the money needed to compensate the losers is not feasible if credit against future NSG is not available. Redistributing land (i.e. land reform) when there is an inverse relation between TFP and farm size would fall into this category: smallholder beneficiaries could compensate expropriated large farmers for their losses, but what guarantee can be given that compensation will be paid when benefits materialize for the new owners? If this cannot be done, these beneficial institutional changes will not happen. Land reform will remain a promise, not a reality.

■ *Uncertain distribution of benefits from change.* Opposition to an institutional change will be stronger if the winners and losers are not known ex-ante, even if it is known that a majority will win, i.e. that the change will generate positive NSG in the aggregate and for the median voter. Not knowing who will gain makes ex-post compensatory transfers even less credible, as nobody can personally commit to the compensation. As we saw in Chapter 7, this reasoning has been applied by Fernández and Rodrik (1991) to opposition to free-trade agreements. Reforms that would receive adequate popular support once enacted may fail to attract sufficient support in advance to ensure their implementation. This creates a bias toward the status quo, limiting beneficial institutional change.

■ *Resistance to loss of relative status.* If there is utility in holding a dominant position in society, beyond the income difference attached to it, compensation of losers by winners will be all the more difficult. This will be the case if land is a source of prestige and social status, as it was in Tsarist Russian society (as explored in Anton Chekhov's play *The Cherry Orchard*). In this case, Pareto optimality after compensation would not be sufficient. Compensation would need to preserve status, requiring perhaps larger transfers to the losers, or preventing institutional change.

■ *Coordination failure.* Many institutional changes correspond to multiple equilibria, with the need to achieve coordination in order to move from a less desirable to a more desirable institution (as we saw in Chapters 9 and 16). Repeated failures to abolish the caste system in India, in spite of it being officially illegal after the constitutional reform of 1950, can be interpreted in this fashion. Castes were introduced at a time when they corresponded to a division of labor, with high castes specializing in the priesthood, middle castes in farming and commerce, and lower castes (untouchables) in the processing of dead animals and sanitation. With deep economic changes, castes no longer correspond to this ancient division of labor and have become dysfunctional and a hurdle to efficient labor use and market exchanges. Yet no individual can oppose the caste system without being accused of opportunism. And coordination to collectively agree to move to a casteless society has to this day failed (Akerlof, 1976). This dysfunctional social system has both heavy efficiency and equity costs, remaining a burden on progress in Indian society.

■ *Procrastination.* Certain types of institutional change are known to be important for the future, but implementation is delayed. This is due to time inconsistency, whereby discount rates would be low starting tomorrow but are high today (also called hyperbolic discounting or present bias), with the problem that tomorrow will in turn become today and discount rates always remain high (O'Donoghue and Rabin, 1999). Failure to introduce institutions to deal with climate change is one example (Gore, 2006). Like individuals, governments can suffer from procrastination, looking at the future with a hyperbolic discount rate. Like getting rid of bad habits (stop smoking, start dieting, go to the gym to exercise, start making progress on your homework early on, save for retirement while you are young), these institutional reforms are postponed to tomorrow. If the costs of inaction accumulate in an exponential fashion, as with climate change, implementing these reforms will be more costly tomorrow than they would have been today. Political action may thus be needed to defeat procrastination and trigger institutional change.

■ *Hold-up problem in contracting.* There are situations where a potentially lucrative contract will fail to emerge between two parties because one party can hold up the other. This is the case when there is a time-consistency problem between an investment made by one party to the contract and the timing of the payment for the product of the investment by the other party. Party A makes an investment specific to a transaction with B based on an agreement about a payment condition. After A has invested and produced the product, party B can renegotiate the contract and offer a lower price. If the lower price still covers the variable cost of production after the investment has been made, it is still in the best interest of party A to deliver the product, even though the lower price does not cover the fixed cost of the investment. The practice of holding-up will be all the easier for party B if A's investment only has value for a transaction with B. A's asset specificity is what allows B to engage in opportunistic behavior.

An example of this risk is in the "productive alliances" promoted by the World Bank between a group of smallholder farmers and a commercial partner such as an agro-industry or a supermarket. This is a widespread model

719

with some 3,000 partnerships in a dozen Latin American countries and many success stories (World Bank, 2014). The commercial partner agrees to buy a high-value crop from the farmers such as tomatoes for canning at a given price. The farmers invest in greenhouses and produce the tomatoes. There is, however, a risk of hold-up. When they deliver the tomatoes to the plant, the industrialist may offer a lower price, often claiming that quality is lower than expected because the contract was incomplete in precisely specifying quality. What can the farmers do? There is no other processing facility in the region. If the price covers at least some of the variable costs such as harvesting, they are better off selling at the lower price. The market will subsequently fail as the farmers will not invest again to produce a crop for a transaction that can be held up.

What are the solutions to the hold-up problem? The ideal is to have the contract legally drawn and to have a legal system that will enforce it. This is often missing in developing countries. Another option is to have vertical integration, whereby the firm pays the cost of the investment as a commitment device. Social norms can also be used, especially if the defaulting party can be punished through social ostracization or loss of opportunity in interlinked transactions with members of the community to which the group of farmers belongs. This enforcement mechanism has to be sufficiently credible that farmers will be willing to invest at the risk of hold-up.

- *Side-selling in group-contracts*. In the example of a contract between a group of producers (organized as a cooperative or a producers' organization) and a commercial partner, there is also a risk that the producers' side will default. The group commits to deliver a quantity of produce agreed upon in the contract at a certain price. If, as the time to deliver approaches, the price rises on the market, there is a great temptation for individual producers to default on the contract and side-sell directly to market agents. The group then falls short of produce to deliver to the commercial partner to meet the contractual obligation. How can this be avoided? One way is by imposing fines on defaulting members, perhaps by excluding them from other services that the group provides such as credit (for example, in coffee cooperatives in Guatemala) or mutual insurance. This is particularly easy in a repeated game. Another is social norms, whereby defaulting members will be ostracized. Yet imposing sanctions or pressuring poor people with whom one has close personal relationships is quite difficult. Side-selling is an important cause of contracting failure in cooperatives and producer organizations (Fulton, 1999).

AN EXAMPLE OF INSTITUTIONAL CHOICE: SHARECROPPING CONTRACTS

The principal–agent framework

A principal–agent framework is a game in which the principal designs the contract (i.e. the institution) to maximize his own objective. All benefits from the contract will be captured by the principal. The agent responds to the contract by adjusting his behavior to take maximum advantage of the offer. These changes in behavior are anticipated by the agent who takes them into account in designing the contract. The principal secures the agent's participation to the contract by setting the contract in such a way that it offers the agent a maximum level of welfare that is not inferior to his opportunity cost.

In a principal–agent model the principal chooses the terms of the contract that maximize his objective function (e.g. profit), subject to two constraints:

1. *The agent's incentive-compatibility constraint*
   The agent will choose the behavior that maximizes his welfare for the given terms of the contract.
2. *The agent's participation constraint*
   The contract must be such that the maximum welfare that the agent can reach is not inferior to his opportunity cost (e.g. the going wage in the labor market).

Sharecropping contracts

An illustration of institutional choice in a principal–agent framework is the choice of a contract between a principal (landlord) and an agent (tenant) for the rental of a plot of land. The landlord owns the plot of land and wants to rent it out; the tenant owns labor and would like to rent land. One of the contract options is sharecropping.

In this model:

r = share rent (the landlord's output share)
R = fixed rent
L = labor (effort) applied by the tenant.

The puzzle of sharecropping

Sharecropping is a contract where output is shared between a landlord and a tenant, but where some of the inputs are not correspondingly shared—for instance, labor (L), which is fully contributed by the tenant. The key feature is that, for such an input, the share in appropriation (equal to $1 - r$ for the tenant) is different from the share in provision (equal to 1 for the tenant). The cost of purchased inputs is, by contrast, usually shared proportionally to provision. Why does this contract exist? What are its advantages and disadvantages? Who gains what from the contract between landlord and tenant?

Share contracts are very frequent, both in traditional and in highly advanced agriculture, and also in activities other than agriculture. We find them in strawberry production in California (Wells, 1996). In Asia, 14 percent of farms use rented land and 85 percent of the rental contracts are sharecropping (Hayami and Otsuka, 1993). In the US, 37 percent of the farms have rented land and 32 percent of the rental contracts are sharecropping. Share contracts are also found in fishing in Senegal (Platteau and Nugent, 1992), in taxi driving in the Philippines (Otsuka *et al.*, 1986), and in franchising in industrialized countries (McDonald's fast-food restaurants, Subway sandwich shops, Starbucks coffee shops, and gas stations), where payment for the franchise is a share of gross receipts.

While frequent, there is a "puzzle of sharecropping" that was noted by Alfred Marshall in 1880 and needs to be explained: output sharing without corresponding input sharing creates a disincentive to provide the input. If you must surrender to the landlord half of what you produce in exchange for access to a plot of land, you clearly will not work as hard as you would if the land were yours (or if you were paying a fixed rent) and you were the residual claimant on your efforts. If the contract is inefficient in input provision, creating the so-called "Marshallian inefficiency of sharecropping," why is it chosen over contracts such as fixed-rent or wage that do not contain this inefficiency? This appears to violate the Darwinian logic of survival of the fittest institution.

A model of labor use under sharecropping

Consider a landlord who owns a plot of land. He can produce a product q with a labor input L using the production function:

$$q = q(L).$$

Say that the product price is p and the labor cost is the wage w.

The landlord has three options to derive a profit from the land: a wage contract, a fixed-rent contract, and a sharecropping contract.

1. *Wage contract.* In this case, he is the entrepreneur and he hires labor for a wage. His objective function is to maximize profit with respect to the choice of level of L:

   $$Max_L \; pq(L) - wL.$$

   This is obtained by choosing the level of L for which: $pMP_L = w$, where MP_L is the marginal product of labor. This is the usual efficient profit-maximizing condition on input use.

2. *Fixed-rent contract.* In this case, he rents his land to a tenant who pays a fixed rent R before using the land. The tenant's objective function is to maximize profit with respect to the choice of level of L:

   $$Max_L \; pq(L) - wL - R.$$

   This is obtained by choosing the level of L for which: $pMP_L = w$, which is the same efficient solution as before.

3. *Sharecropping contract.* In this case, he rents his land to a tenant who pays a share r of the output as rent. The landlord cannot force the tenant to apply a certain amount of labor to the land. We say that labor is "not contractible," meaning that there is a labor-market failure for the landlord. It is the tenant who decides this. The tenant's objective function is to maximize profit with respect to the choice of level of L:

$$Max_L (1-r)\, pq(L) - wL\cdot$$

This is obtained by choosing the level of L for which: $pMP_L = \dfrac{w}{1-r} > w$.

Hence, as shown in Figure 20.3, the sharecropper applies less labor (L^s) to the plot of land than the owner-operator with hired labor or the fixed-rent tenant (L^*). This is the Marshallian inefficiency of sharecropping.

Note that there is no inefficiency in the use of a purchased input X with a price p_X if the cost of the input is shared in the same proportion as the product is shared. In this case, the tenant's objective function is to maximize profit with respect to the choice of levels of L and X:

$$Max_{L,X}(1-r)pq(L,X) - wL - (1-r)p_X X\cdot$$

As $(1 - r)$ cancels out when applied to both product and input X, optimum use is given by

$$pMP_X = p_X,$$

which is the efficient solution. This cost sharing is achieved simply by deducting the factor cost from gross revenue before sharing, i.e. defining sharing as $r(pq - p_X X)$.

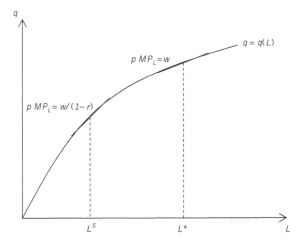

Figure 20.3 *The Marshallian inefficiency of sharecropping*

Shaban's test of the inefficiency of sharecropping

A precise test of the Marshallian inefficiency of sharecropping was made by Shaban (1987). He analyzed farmers from the ICRISAT-India data set who cultivate both a plot in ownership and a plot in rental, either fixed-rent or sharecropping. Comparing input intensity on the two plots provides a natural experiment to control for unobserved household characteristics. Data are at the plot level, with information on input intensity and plot characteristics such as soil fertility. The main defect of the study is that there may exist unobservable plot characteristics between the plots in ownership and rental.

The results show the following:

- Yields on owned land are 33 percent higher than on sharecropped land.
- After controlling for differences in irrigation, plot value, and soil quality between the plots owned and sharecropped, the difference is still 16 percent.
- Use of inputs for which provision is not shared (different categories of household labor, bullocks) is between 19 and 55 percent higher on owned land compared to sharecropped land.
- Use of inputs for which provision is shared (seeds, fertilizers, other inputs) shows no difference in provision between owned and sharecropped plots.
- There is no difference in yields and input use between owned and fixed-rent plots. Hence differences in yield and input are not due to tenancy in general, but specifically to incentive problems associated with sharecropping.

Shaban thus concludes his research by not rejecting the Marshallian inefficiency of sharecropping hypothesis.

Why Marshall did not solve the puzzle of sharecropping

Sharecropping is both a widespread and an inefficient contract for labor effort when the tenant is the sole supplier of labor compared to the other two contracts: wage and fixed-rent. Why does it exist? Marshall proposed the following analysis represented in Figure 20.4 (Hayami and Otsuka, 1993).

In this figure, we see, for a given plot size, the marginal product of labor MP_L, and the tenant's share of this marginal product, $(1 - r) MP_L$. Under both a wage and a fixed-rent contract, the optimum effort is L^* where $MP_L = w$. Under sharecropping, the optimum effort is L where $(1 - r) MP_L = w$.

We can compare the three contracts from the standpoint of the landlord:

> The landlord's rent under a fixed-rent contract or wage contract is area 1+2+3.
> The landlord's rent under a sharecropping contract is area 1.

Hence the landlord loses area 2+3 in a sharecropping contract compared to the other two efficient contracts, wage and fixed-rent: 2 is lost to the tenant and 3 is a deadweight loss, the Marshallian inefficiency of sharecropping.

724

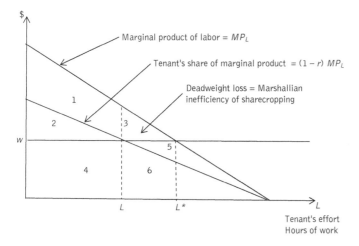

Figure 20.4 *Marshall's puzzle of sharecropping unexplained*

From the standpoint of the sharecropper:

The sharecropper's income is area 2+4.
His opportunity cost is area 4 on the labor market (working L at the wage w).

Hence the sharecropper's income exceeds his opportunity cost wL by area 2.

The result will be an excess supply of tenants. The landlord can thus charge an additional fixed rent $R = 2$ to capture the surplus from the tenant and reduce him to his reservation income 4. However, the landlord could do even better by decreasing his share r to zero and shifting to a fixed-rent contract, eliminating the deadweight loss 3 and increasing his rent to 1+2+3. Hence, while Marshall was right that sharecropping implies an inefficiency, the contract should never be observed under the first-best conditions (all markets performing perfectly, except for the eventual non-contractibility of labor leading the landlord to choose a fixed-rent as opposed to a wage contract) that he postulated. Only fixed-rent or wage contracts should be observed. This implies the need to look for other reasons why a sharecropping contract may prevail.

The answer to the puzzle consists in looking for the existence of other market failures beyond the non-contractibility of labor that rental helps remedy. Specifically, there can be an insurance-market failure (Stiglitz, 1974), a credit-market failure (Laffont and Matoussi, 1995), or market failures for non-contractible inputs in production such as management and labor supervision (Eswaran and Kotwal, 1985). In all cases, if sharecropping helps overcome these market failures, it may be the best option in spite of Marshallian inefficiency, because the other contracts would be even more inefficient. We say that sharecropping is "second-best efficient."

Sharecropping as a risk-sharing contract

Say that output q is risky because of climatic variations, and that both the landlord and the tenant are risk averse (Stiglitz, 1974). If there is no insurance market, sharecropping provides an institutional alternative to what the market does not offer. By sharing output as a form of rent payment, sharecropping allows for shared risk between the landlord and the tenant: the rent paid varies with the level of output achieved. If the tenant is risk-averse, reducing his risk will increase effort. Hence a sharecropping contract may be the preferred contract as it is better than:

> A *fixed-rent contract* for the tenant if he is risk averse.
> A *wage contract* for the landlord if he is risk averse.

This comparison is represented in Table 20.1. Say that the tenant pays both a share rent rpq and a fixed rent R. Risk is reduced for the tenant by increasing the landlord's share r (he absorbs more risk) and reducing R. But reducing the tenant's share increases the Marshallian disincentive. Hence there is a trade-off: a higher r reduces risk (which increases the level of L for the risk-averse tenant), but also increases the Marshallian disincentive (which reduces the level of L). There will consequently exist an optimal level of r that strikes a compromise between these two effects of r. If the landlord increases r to absorb more risk, he must decrease R to satisfy the tenant's participation constraint.

Sharecropping when the tenant is liquidity-constrained

Again, labor is non-contractible and sharecropping induces a Marshallian inefficiency. Say that production requires not only labor but also a purchased input X:

$$q = q(L, X).$$

Table 20.1 *Choice of contracts under risk*

Agent income y	Worker or tenant	Landlord	When chosen
Wage contract	Hires out $y = wL^*$ Certain	Hires in $y = pq(L^*) - wL^*$ Risky	Landlord is risk-neutral Efficient
Fixed-rent contract	Rents land $y = pq(L^*) - wL^* - R$ Risky	Leases land $y = R$ Certain	Tenant is risk-neutral Efficient
Sharecropping contract	Rents land $y = (1-r)\,pq(L) - wL - R$ Risky, but less than under a fixed-rent contract	Sharecrops land $y = r\,pq(L) + R$ Risky, but less than under a wage contract	Both are risk-averse Marshallian inefficiency on L

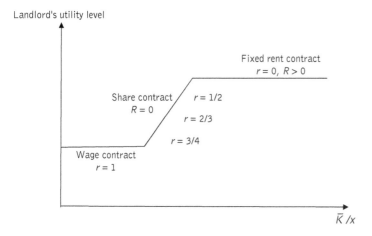

Figure 20.5 *Choice of contract under liquidity constraint*

If there is another market failure, this time for credit, sharecropping can help relax the tenant's liquidity constraint in buying the input X by sharing not only output, but also the cost of X (Laffont and Matoussi, 1995). Let $\bar{K}$ be the tenant's availability of working capital. The optimal contract is thus the following (Figure 20.5):

1. *Wage contract.* If the tenant has no liquidity at all to buy X, the landlord gives him a wage contract. The landlord's output share is thus $r = 1$.
2. *Share contract.* If the tenant has some but not enough liquidity to buy X, the landlord gives him a sharecropping contract (r, R), where they share both output and the cost of the purchased input. The landlord's share can decrease from, say, three quarters, to two thirds, and to half as the tenant's availability of working capital rises. The contract has a Marshallian inefficiency on labor but helps the tenant produce more by buying more of X.
3. *Fixed-rent contract.* If the tenant has no liquidity constraint in buying X, the landlord gives him a fixed-rent contract that avoids the Marshallian inefficiency. The contract is thus $(r = 0, R)$.

Sharecropping when there are market failures for two non-contractible inputs

Say that production requires not only labor (which can be hired), but also two other inputs: management (t) and labor supervision (s) (Eswaran and Kotwal, 1985). The production function is:

$$q = q(t, s, L).$$

Say that there are no markets for either management or labor supervision: they have to be provided by either the landlord or the tenant. Say also that the landlord is better

727

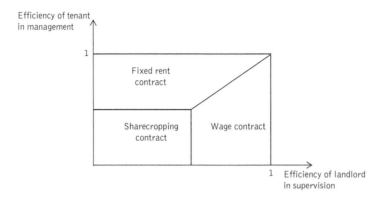

Figure 20.6 *Choice of contact with two non-contractible inputs*

than the tenant at management, and the tenant is better than the landlord at labor supervision. There will be three alternative contracts (Figure 20.6):

1. *Wage contract.* If labor supervision is not important (for example, in mechanized farming), then the landlord is able to assume supervision efficiently. In this case, the best contract for the landlord is to manage the farm himself and to hire labor.
2. *Fixed-rent contract.* If management is not important (for example, in producing a staple crop like corn with traditional technology), then the tenant is able to manage production efficiently. The best contract for the landlord is a fixed-rent. The tenant can supervise labor and there will be no Marshallian inefficiency.
3. *Sharecropping contract.* If both management and supervision matter, then sharecropping is the best option. The landlord manages, the tenant supervises, and they share output. There is a double Marshallian disincentive in providing management (the landlord provides the full management but only gets a share of output) and supervision (the tenant provides the full supervision but only gets a share of output), but, in spite of this, sharecropping is more efficient than having each party do what it does not do well: the landlord having to supervise under a wage contract, and the tenant having to manage under a fixed-rent contract. Share-cropping is, in this case, the relatively most efficient contract.

Conclusion

This analysis of optimal contracts for land use—wage, fixed-rent, or share rent—is a good illustration of what the NIE has to offer. It endogenizes the choice of an institution (here, a contract) to minimize the loss of profit for the landlord due to existing market failures.

Can a tenancy reform be effective in increasing land productivity? Operation Barga in West Bengal

In the 1970s, the left-leaning government of West Bengal implemented a large-scale tenancy reform called Operation Barga. The reform did not expropriate land, but offered both security of tenure and higher crop shares to registered sharecroppers. Specifically, a registered tenant could no longer be evicted by a landlord if he paid no less than 25 percent of output as rent, which was inferior to the pre-reform 50 percent share. The productivity effect is a priori ambiguous. Security of tenure may reduce effort as the landlord can no longer use the threat of expropriation to elicit effort from the tenant. Eighty percent of the sharecroppers said that landlords used threats of eviction before the reform, while 96 percent said that eviction became impossible after the reform. At the same time, security of tenure can induce greater investment and productivity gains. A higher share for the tenant can also induce greater effort and higher productivity, but at the cost of higher risk, with again an ambiguous net effect.

Identification of impact was done using both a diff-in-diffs methodology and a roll-out design with district-level panel data (Banerjee *et al.*, 2002). The diff-in-diffs approach consisted in comparing yields in sharecropper fields before and after the reform in West Bengal (treated) and in neighboring Bangladesh (control) with similar production conditions (and parallel trends in yields before the Barga reforms) and no tenancy reform. Results in Table 20.2 show a 5.85 percent gain in yield attributable to the reform.

The roll-out approach used the intensity of treatment across districts in West Bengal between 1979 and 1987, with some districts gaining higher numbers of registered tenants than others. The data are a panel on districts over the period. In this case, the estimation equation is:

$$y_{dt} = \alpha_d + \lambda_t + \beta B_{dt} + \gamma X_{dt} + \varepsilon_{dt},$$

where α_d is a district fixed effect, λ_t a year fixed effect, B_{dt} the number of registered tenants in district d and year t, and X_{dt} other district–time varying variables influencing productivity such as real wages, the price of rice, rainfall, public irrigation, and roads. Results show that yield increased by 28 percent due to the reform, indicating that there is no necessary trade-off between efficiency and equity in tenancy reform. The authors argue that tenancy reforms are easier to implement than land reforms that redistribute land ownership. However, it is likely that landlords will look for ways of not renewing sharecropper contracts now that they are less profitable.

Table 20.2 *Gain in rice yield due to tenancy reform, Operation Barga in West Bengal*

Rice yield in tons/ha	Before	After	Difference
West Bengal (T)	1.31	1.65	0.34
Bangladesh (C)	1.30	1.56	0.26
Difference	0.011	0.088	0.08
Percentage gain			5.85

Source: Banerjee *et al.*, 2002.

OTHER EXAMPLES OF INSTITUTIONAL INNOVATIONS THAT HELP REDUCE TRANSACTION COSTS AND/OR COMPENSATE FOR MARKET FAILURES

Redefinition of property rights

Incomplete property rights can lead to accelerated resource depletion. Institutional change would be needed to reverse depletion, moving from open access or CPR without cooperation to private property or CPR with cooperation. According to Boserup (1965), this institutional change may be induced by an increase in the profitability of the asset that may happen in response to population pressure, market integration, and technical change (see Chapter 15). In this perspective, and by analogy with the theory of induced technological innovations (Hayami and Ruttan, 1985), functioning markets that reflect resource scarcity can guide institutional innovations toward saving on resources that become relatively scarce.

Social capital

Producers' organizations, service cooperatives, and vertical integration across firms in the value chain are all institutions that help reduce transaction costs on markets and increase efficiency. These forms of institutional innovation build relational social capital. Putnam (2000) distinguished two types of social capital. *Bonding social capital* is links between socially homogenous groups of people such as members of an association or a community. *Bridging social capital* is links between socially heterogeneous groups of people such as a bowling club or subscribers to Facebook. In *Bowling Alone*, Putnam laments the decline of bridging social capital in the US. Social capital can help reduce transaction costs, facilitate collective action, and support democracy. Declining social capital and weakening or disappearance of the corresponding institutions can lead to insulation and exclusion.

Lobbies

Lobbies are institutions with the objective of achieving redistributive gains for the benefit of their members, eventually at a social-efficiency cost. This is the theory of *rent-seeking* (Krueger, 1974) that we will see in Chapter 21. An example is tariffs or subsidies in trade applied to particular commodities in response to demands of the corresponding interest groups: they create redistributive gains at an efficiency cost. Lobbies, and the institutional changes they induce, have thus been seen as sources of social costs. Lobbying can create net social gains if they militate for socially useful public goods about which policy-makers are otherwise poorly informed. But the door is also open to use the power of lobbies, such as pork barrel politics in allocating public budgets and introducing market distortions for purely redistributive gains.

Extended-family systems and tribal governance

Relations of trust in a kinship network help keep transaction costs low for exchanges within the network when they may be quite high with the rest of the world

(North *et al.*, 2009). Early forms of governance tend to be kinship-based, with strict enforcement of codes of conduct, in particular for women. Risk sharing can also happen within kinship networks with no AS and no MH. Hence clans can be an effective institution for risk reduction, even though they can only insure risks that are not covariate to the group as a whole. They thus suffer from the "dilemma of the agrarian community," a phenomenon we analyzed for moneylenders in Chapter 13. Agreements across warlords, with strict eye-for-an-eye codes of retaliation for justice in inter-tribal relationships (an application of the tit-for-tat principle we saw in Chapter 16), allow groups to broaden the territorial coverage of exchange. As we see in tribal areas like Afghanistan, Iraq, and Yemen, these forms of governance precede the introduction of democracy. Rushing into democracy and centralized governance may be counter to prevailing social norms and both illusory and dangerous.

Linkage between local/traditional institutions and regional/national/modern institutions

Developing societies have the advantage of institutional richness in that they contain many local/traditional institutions with two important advantages: they provide access to information (observability, gossip, face-to-face relations) and they have means of enforcement (based on social capital, reputation and ostracization, shared social norms, trust, and interlinked transactions). However, they suffer from the dilemma of the agrarian community and can only sustain exchange over narrow social circles. This severely limits the diversification of risk, access to broader labor pools, access to broader sources of money deposits and capital, and access to deeper markets with more stable prices. By contrast, regional/national/modern institutions do not provide access to local information and local social capital, but they have the advantage of accessing broader markets. Linking traditional and modern institutions can thus offer effective institutional constructs that have promise for development but remain underexplored. Examples include the following:

- *National commercial banks using local village agents to select loan recipients (information) and enforce repayment (social capital).* By using local financial officers, commercial banks can engage in microfinance lending, while benefiting from access to national and international financial markets to expand the size of their operations at the bottom of the pyramid. Commercial banks attracted by high repayment rates in microlending operations thus staff their operations in local branches with experienced credit officers who come from the communities where they want to lend, and who typically learned their trades working for local NGOs (Fuentes, 1996).
- *Global certification agencies using local producer organizations to observe and enforce quality.* This is done, for example, to lower the cost of certifying fair-trade or organic products for MDC markets (e.g. coffee). Members of a cooperative can observe the use of chemicals by other members who live and work near them. As an enforcement device, the certification agency does random spot checks and stops buying from all group members if it uncovers misbehavior by any

731

producer. Collective sanctions thus induce each group member to monitor the behavior of others and help enforce the rule to qualify for certification (Rai, 2002).

■ *Labor contractors delivering a workforce to large commercial farms.* The labor contractor plays a repeated game with the workers he delivers to commercial farmers, with the workers building their reputation for subsequent work contracts. In contrast, the workers only have a one-time contract with a grower, exposing the latter to AS and MH. The worker may shirk if hired directly by the grower, but not when hired for the same task by the labor contractor. Labor contractors are typically present in places like California, the coast of Peru, and the Central Valley of Chile, where farmers need large numbers of workers for short periods of time to harvest seasonal fruits and vegetables (Vandeman *et al.*, 1991).

These examples show the importance of preserving traditional institutions and of linking them to modern institutions. Local culture, folklore, local festivals, shared faith, attachment to place, stable community relations—often better understood by anthropologists and sociologists than economists (see Cochrane, 1971, for the role of anthropology in development)—can thus be an asset for the construction of effective modern institutions.

Role of decentralization in the provision of local public goods

Decentralization implies the devolution by central government of administrative, political, and/or economic functions to local (e.g. municipal) governments. In recent years, many countries have sought gains in performance by decentralizing the implementation of public programs to locally elected governments (Bardhan, 2002). The presumed advantages of decentralization are that it helps: (1) gain access to local information (preferences) about the demand for public goods, and (2) make decision-makers more accountable to the population through local elections or local social capital. If this is the case, decentralization can improve the use efficiency of public budgets to meet local demands. Local demands should reflect the objective needs of people in the locality, such as deficits in primary education, primary healthcare, water and sanitation, and infrastructure. However, decentralization also has potential drawbacks. The main two are: (1) the possibility of capture by local elites and local-interest groups, clientelism by local politicians using public budgets to mobilize votes, and corruption in using public resources for private gains; and (2) weak local administrative capacity that may make the management of public budgets not cost-effective. The balance between advantages and drawbacks is an empirical question. Like cooperation, decentralization is a learning process that can have rocky starts but can improve over time through learning-by-doing.

In an empirical analysis of decentralization of fiscal expenditures in Bolivia (the 1994 Law on Decentralization), Faguet (2004) found the following results.

1. Decentralization increased the allocation of public expenditures toward unmet local needs. The increase in investment in primary education was greatest in

municipalities where there was more illiteracy; the increase in investment in water and sanitation was greatest where water and sewage connection rates were lower; and the increase in investment in agriculture was greatest where there was more risk of malnutrition.

2. It was the smallest and poorest municipalities that changed the most. The increase in investment in human capital and social services was higher in these municipalities due to greater transparency in the availability of public resources, resulting in more effective cooperation.

3. Weak local administrative capacity did not prevent better satisfaction of local needs.

The benefits of decentralization do not always benefit the poorest geographical units more. Galiani *et al.* (2008) analyzed the decentralization of secondary schools in Argentina from central government to provincial administration. Of 3,456 public schools, 2,360 remained under central control and 1,096 were transferred to provinces at some point during a period of staggered implementation over the 1992–4 period. Using panel data across schools, they found that average test scores in math increased by 3.5 percent and in Spanish by 5.4 percent after five years of decentralization. However, this overall positive impact eluded the schools in poor communities, suggesting that better ability to manage and be heard is important in the decentralized management of public services. Similarly, Bardhan and Mookherjee (2006) found that poorer communities benefited less from the decentralization of credit, agricultural services, and employment programs in West Bengal.

The conclusion of these case studies is that decentralization of public expenditures to the municipal level can be more effective in meeting local social needs and public-goods priorities (social programs, infrastructure) than centralized public expenditures. This principle of delegating to municipalities the allocation of public budgets to better meet local needs underscores the growing practice of Community-Driven Development (CDD) in international development agencies. In the CDD approach, budgets are allocated to regional institutions, and municipalities compete to access these resources with projects that they themselves formulate and implement (Mansuri and Rao, 2004). It is a good example of the potential benefits of linking local and regional/national institutions in search of greater efficiency.

CDD can be more efficiently run when grants are related to performance. Olken *et al.* (2014) experimented in Indonesia with a CDD approach that rewarded good village performance by sustained support. A random subset of one third of 3,000 villages was allocated to a treatment where block grants were provided to improve maternal and child health and education indicators. Subsequent years' block grants depended on past performance relative to other villages in the same sub-district, implementing a yardstick competition. They found that rewarding performance helped increase the efficiency of block grants. This effect was visible in health, where providers are paid on a fee-for-service basis, but not in education, where teachers' salaries are unrelated to performance. For health, the impact was large: 50 to 75 percent of the impact of block grants on health indicators across villages was due to performance incentives.

CONCEPTS USED IN THIS CHAPTER

Institutions and organizations

Dysfunctional institutions

Path dependency

Bonding and bridging social capital

Decentralization of fiscal expenditures

Labor contractors

Hold-up problem in contracting

Side-selling in group contracts

Community-driven development (CDD)

Fixed-rent and share-rent contracts

Marshallian inefficiency of sharecropping

The puzzle of sharecropping

Sharecropping with risk-market failure: Stiglitz

Sharecropping with credit-market failure: Laffont and Matoussi

Sharecropping with factor-market failure: Eswaran and Kotwal

Tenancy reforms: Operation Barga

Yardstick competition

REFERENCES

Acemoglu, Daron, Simon Johnson, and James Robinson. 2002. "Reversal of Fortune: Geography and Institutions in the Making of the Modern World Income Distribution." *Quarterly Journal of Economics* 117(4): 1231–94.

Akerlof, George. 1970. "The Market for 'Lemons': Quality Uncertainty and the Market Mechanism." *Quarterly Journal of Economics* 84(3): 488–500.

Akerlof, George. 1976. "The Economics of Caste and of the Rat Race and Other Woeful Tales." *Quarterly Journal of Economics* 90(4): 599–617.

Banerjee, Abhijit, Paul Gertler, and Maitreesh Ghatak. 2002. "Empowerment and Efficiency: Tenancy Reform in West Bengal." *Journal of Political Economy* 110(2): 239–80.

Bardhan, Pranab. 1992. *The Economic Theory of Agrarian Institutions.* New York: Oxford University Press.

Bardhan, Pranab. 2002. "Decentralization of Governance and Development." *Journal of Economic Perspectives* 16(4): 185–205.

Bardhan, Pranab, and Dilip Mookherjee. 2006. "Pro-poor Targeting and Accountability of Local Governments in West Bengal." *Journal of Development Economics* 79(2): 303–27

Boserup, Ester. 1965. *The Conditions of Agricultural Growth: The Economics of Agrarian Change under Population Pressure.* Chicago: Aldine.

Bowles, Samuel, and Herbert Gintis, 1988. "Contested Exchange: Political Economy and Modern Economic Theory." *American Economic Review* 78(2): 145–50.

Cochrane, Glynn. 1971. *Development Anthropology.* New York: Oxford University Press.

de Janvry, Alain, Marcel Fafchamps, and Elisabeth Sadoulet. 1991. "Peasant Household Behavior with Missing Markets: Some Paradoxes Explained." *Economic Journal* 101(409): 1400–18.

Eswaran, Mukesh, and Ashok Kotwal. 1985. "A Theory of Contractual Structure in Agriculture." *American Economic Review* 75(3): 352–67.

Faguet, Jean-Paul. 2004. "Does Decentralization Increase Responsiveness to Local Needs? Evidence from Bolivia." *Journal of Public Economics* 88(3–4): 867–94.

Fernández, Raquel, and Dani Rodrik. 1991. "Resistance to Reform: Status Quo Bias in the Presence of Individual-Specific Uncertainty." *American Economic Review* 81(5): 1146–55.

Fuentes, Gabriel. 1996. "The Use of Village Agents in Rural Credit Delivery." *Journal of Development Studies* 33(2): 188–209.

Fulton, Murray. 1999. "Cooperatives and Member Commitment." *Finnish Journal of Business Economics* 48(4): 418–37.

Galiani, Sebastian, Paul Gertler, and Ernesto Schargrodsky. 2008. "School Decentralization: Helping the Good Get Better, but Leaving the Poor Behind." *Journal of Public Economics* 92(10–11): 2106–20.

Gallup, John, and Jeffrey Sachs. 1999. "Geography and Economic Development." *International Regional Science Review* 22(2): 179–232.

Gore, Al. 2006. *An Inconvenient Truth.* www.bing.com/videos/search?q=Gore%2c+Al.+2006.+An+Inconvenient+Truth&FORM=VIRE7#view=detail&mid=0FE21E27B59C5FB0E1720FE21E27B59C5FB0E172 (accessed 2015).

Greenwald, Bruce, Joseph Stiglitz, and Andrew Weiss. 1984. "Informational Imperfections in the Capital Markets and Macro-economic Fluctuations." *American Economic Review* 74(2): 194–9.

Hayami, Yujiro. 1998. "The Formation of Toyota's Relationship with Suppliers: A Modern Application of the Community Mechanism." In Y. Hayami, (ed.), *Towards the Rural-based Development of Commerce and Industry: Selected Experiences from East Asia,* Washington, DC: World Bank.

Hayami, Yujiro, and Vernon Ruttan. 1985. *Agricultural Development: An International Perspective.* Baltimore: Johns Hopkins University Press.

Hayami, Yujiro, and Keijiro Otsuka. 1993. *The Economics of Contract Choice: An Agrarian Perspective.* New York: Oxford University Press.

Krueger, Anne (1974). "The Political Economy of the Rent-Seeking Society." *American Economic Review* 64(3): 291–303.

Krugman, Paul. 1995. *Development, Geography, and Economic Theory.* Cambridge, MA: MIT Press.

Laffont, Jean-Jacques, and Mohamed Salah Matoussi. 1995. "Moral Hazard, Financial Constraints, and Sharecropping in El Oulja." *Review of Economic Studies* 62(3): 381–99.

Macours, Karen, Alain de Janvry, and Elisabeth Sadoulet. 2010. "Insecurity of Property Rights and Social Matching in the Tenancy Market." *European Economic Review* 54(7): 880–99.

Mansuri, Ghazala, and Vijayendra Rao. 2004. "Community-Based and -Driven Development: A Critical Review." *World Bank Research Observer* 19(1): 1–39.

Myint, Hla. 1971. *Economic Theory and the Underdeveloped Countries.* New York: Oxford University Press.

North, Douglas. 1990. *Institutions, Institutional Change and Economic Performance.* Cambridge: Cambridge University Press.

North, Douglas. 1991. "Institutions." *Journal of Economic Perspectives* 5(1): 97–112.

North, Douglas, John Joseph Wallis, and Barry Weingast. 2009. *Violence and Social Orders: A Conceptual Framework for Interpreting Recorded Human History*. Cambridge, MA: Cambridge University Press.

O'Donoghue, Ted, and Matthew Rabin. 1999. "Doing It Now or Doing it Later?" *American Economic Review* 89(1): 103–24.

Olken, Benjamin, Junko Onishi, and Susan Wong. 2014. "Should Aid Reward Performance? Evidence from a Field Experiment on Health and Education in Indonesia." *American Economic Journal: Applied Economics* 6(4): 1–34.

Otsuka, Keijiro, Masao Kikuchi, and Yujiro Hayami. 1986. "Community and Market in Contract Choice: The Jeepney in the Philippines." *Economic Development and Cultural Change* 34(2): 279–98.

Platteau, Jean-Philippe, and Jeff Nugent. 1992. "Share Contracts and their Rationale: Lessons from Marine Fishing." *Journal of Development Studies* 28(3): 386–422.

Putnam, Robert. 2000. *Bowling Alone: The Collapse and Revival of American Community*. New York: Simon and Schuster.

Rai, Ashok. 2002. "Targeting the Poor Using Community Information." *Journal of Development Economics* 69(1): 71–84.

Shaban, R.A. 1987. "Testing between Competing Models of Sharecropping." *Journal of Political Economy* 85(5): 893–920.

Shapiro, Carl, and Joseph Stiglitz. 1984. "Equilibrium Unemployment as a Worker Discipline Device." *American Economic Review* 74(3): 433–44.

Solow, Robert. 1956. "A Contribution to the Theory of Economic Growth." *Quarterly Journal of Economics* 70(1): 65–94.

Stiglitz, Joseph. 1974. "Incentives and Risk-Sharing in Sharecropping." *Review of Economics and Statistics* 41(2): 219–55.

Vandeman, Ann, Elisabeth Sadoulet, and Alain de Janvry. 1991. "Labor Contracting and a Theory of Contract Choice in California Agriculture." *American Journal of Agricultural Economics* 73(3): 681–92.

Wells, Miriam. 1996. *Strawberry Fields: Politics, Class, and Work in California Agriculture*. Ithaca, NY: Cornell University Press.

Williamson, Oliver. 1985. *The Economic Institutions of Capitalism*. New York: Free Press.

World Bank. 2014. "Small-scale Colombian Farmers Do Business with Industry Giants." http://www.worldbank.org/en/news/feature/2014/08/28/productive-alliances-small-producers-colombia (accessed 2015).

Political economy and the role of the state

INTRODUCTION

Development outcomes depend on the interactions between the state, the market, and civil society—the fundamental development triangle (Figure 21.1) we presented in the Introduction. Each of these three institutions has intrinsic functions to fulfill and unique instruments at its disposal to act in pursuing this purpose. The state has the responsibility of protecting individuals, enforcing rights and preventing abuse,

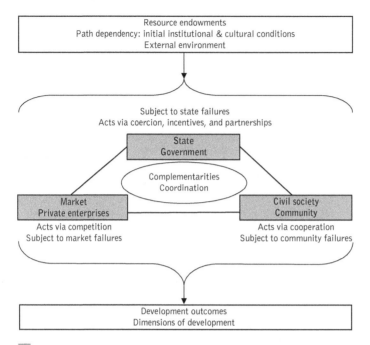

Figure 21.1 *Development triangle and role of the state*

coordinating for social gains, and delivering public goods and services. Important among these are public works, public education, public charity and social assistance, and public health. It acts via coercion, incentives, and partnerships. The market has the function of providing opportunities for the exchange of goods and services, and guiding the allocation of resources to their highest-valued uses. It acts via a set of institutions that favor competition and reduce transaction costs and risks. Civil society has the function of allowing individuals to coordinate in the pursuit of collective action and the provision of local public goods. It acts via cooperation (Hayami, 2009; Karnani, 2011). Each of these institutions can fail in its functions, calling on the others to compensate for what it does not do. The state in particular has a fundamental role to play in compensating for market and civil-society failures. If the state is effective in both its intrinsic functions and in its compensatory roles, development outcomes are more likely to be achieved; but the state can also fail. In this case, inefficiencies and deficits in development outcomes will result. Many potentially good policies will not be implemented and many bad policies and bad practices such as abuse of power and corruption will be. Clearly, a well-functioning state is key for development, especially if market and community failures are pervasive as is typically the case at early stages of development. However, a well-functioning state is itself a product of development. We thus face a fundamental development paradox: the state is most prone to failure precisely where it is most needed. The role of the state in development must thus be clearly understood, and making the state fulfill its functions is essential for successful development outcomes.

There are also fundamental philosophical disagreements as to how far the state can go in substituting for what the market and civil society do for development or in compensating for what they do not do. Libertarians, including Milton Friedman and the Tea Party movement, are skeptical of state authority and of state infringement on individual liberties. They advocate laissez-faire capitalism, strong private property rights, and a minimal state, restricted to the administration of defense, police, and justice. Because administering money is a function of the state, they advocate the use of monetary over fiscal policy in managing economic growth. Keynesians and neo-Keynesians, by contrast, including Paul Samuelson and Paul Krugman, advocate an active role for the state in managing economic growth, both to smooth economic cycles and to help developing countries accelerate growth and converge. Because taxation and public spending is an important function of the state, they advocate the use of fiscal policy in managing economic cycles and combating inequality if it is detrimental to growth. Social liberals, including many development economists such as Joseph Stiglitz and Amartya Sen, seek to achieve a balance between individual liberties and social justice. They endorse a market economy, but also a state that has the right to appropriate private wealth through taxation and distribution to protect the disadvantaged and redress inequities. Indeed, while there is general agreement among development economists that a strong and proactive state is necessary for catching-up and development, how far the state should go in relation to the market and civil society, and how to manage state roles to avoid corruption and abuse, remain fundamental points of contention in the development profession.

As in previous chapters, we set out the basic issue for analysis from a positive perspective and then appraise its normative implications. In particular, we examine theories of state behavior and then look into the consequences of policies and programs arising from that behavior. Seeking to reconcile the two in the context of observed outcomes, we see that many "good" development policies are not implemented, while many "bad" policies are in place. An economic equilibrium, with particular market and community failures that set the conditions for the state to perform, corresponds to a political equilibrium (Acemoglu and Robinson, 2012). Policy recommendations for the state to overcome these failures will need to correspond to a new political equilibrium, with new benefits and costs resulting from the policy changes. This new economic equilibrium, and its associated political equilibrium, must be politically feasible for the policy recommendation to be meaningful. *There is no policy without political economy.* This is why taking a policy recommendation to the level of political analysis is essential for implementation. An analysis of the state will thus proceed at two levels:

- *Positive analysis.* Analysis of the policy-making process: Why do governments do what they do?
- *Normative analysis.* What should governments do for development? What is the political feasibility of the new political equilibrium implied by the policy recommendation?

THEORIES OF THE STATE

In developing a theory of the state, we link the political process of policy-making with the economic process of policy implementation and impact. The two are related in a closed loop, whereby politics feeds into economics, and economics into politics (Figure 21.2). The state responds to demands for policy coming from a constituency of specific interest groups related to the policy issue. It responds by supplying policies and programs that affect what we have seen to be the determinants of development outcomes (Figure I.2 in Introduction): household characteristics, household assets, the context in which the assets are used, transfers, behavioral responses, and responses to exogenous shocks. These development outcomes in turn feed back to household behavior through adjustments in their livelihood strategies and to political demands for accountability in program implementation and for new policies.

There are two broad bodies of theory that we can call upon to understand the role of the state in development. One is the functionalist theory of the state that looks at what the state should be doing in development according to different schools of thought—a normative approach. The other is the pluralist theory of the state that looks at how the state effectively performs its functions, again as seen from the angle of different bodies of thought—a positive approach. In each of these cases, we have a multiplicity of interpretations that can be seen as largely complementary, each contributing useful insights about the role of the state in development.

THE FUNCTIONALIST STATE

The functionalist view of state behavior is a normative approach that assumes that government acts as a largely autonomous agent, actively pursuing its role as a social planner, and acting on behalf of society. From an economic perspective, state economic intervention is assumed to aim at generating efficiency gains (NSG > 0), compensating for market and civil-society failures. From a social-welfare perspective, it may remedy economic outcomes such as poverty, inequality, and inequity that do not correspond to national social objectives. Functionalist theories of the state are present in several bodies of thought seen in Chapter 3: namely, neoclassical theory, the Relative Economic Backwardness perspective on Western history, Keynesian economics, and development economics.

Neoclassical theory of the state

In neoclassical economics, state interventions are motivated by market failures. Using state intervention to overcome market failures can thus be a source of efficiency gains. The main market failures that motivate state intervention are the following:

- *Public goods* such as property rights, the rule of law, infrastructure, and basic health and education. Because public goods are non-rival and non-excludable, they cannot be provided privately in response to market incentives. Public goods are typically under-provided not only privately and but also publicly.
- *Negative and positive externalities*, with a role for the state in internalizing externalities to align market incentives with the social optimum. Negative externalities induce over-provision of the corresponding good, since part of the cost is not

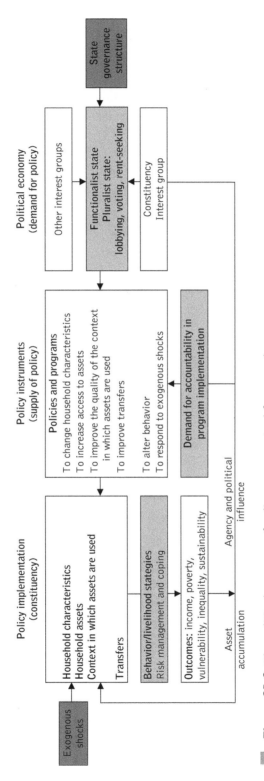

Figure 21.2 *The political economy of policy: a conceptual framework*

paid by the private provider, while positive externalities induce under-provision, since part of the benefit is not captured by the provider. The state has a key role to play in internalizing externalities to reconcile private and social optima (as we saw in Chapter 15).

■ *Economies of scale*, natural monopoly, and imperfect competition all lead to under-production and overpricing relative to the social optimum. Imperfect competition is not self-correcting via market forces. The state thus has a fundamental role to play in fomenting competition and regulating the emergence of monopolies—for instance, through anti-trust legislation.

■ *Asymmetrical information* induces adverse selection (hidden information) and moral hazards (hidden actions), both of which result in market failures. While the state may not be better informed than private parties, there are policy interventions that can help the generation and sharing of information.

■ *Coordination failures* that prevent the move from a lower to a higher multiple equilibrium. This includes the sectoral coordination of complementary investments. Coordination is not the product of market forces. State leadership can provide the necessary coordination capacity.

■ Wealth-constrained *capital markets* create selective market failures for the poor. Institutional innovations can help provide market access—for instance, through microfinance. While these institutions are private, the state can play a key role in facilitating and regulating their emergence.

■ Because of *market failures for insurance*, levels of uninsured risks may be too high, resulting in costly risk-management and risk-coping strategies. State interventions to make insurance markets work can thus have important efficiency and welfare gains.

■ *High transactions costs* may prevail on markets—for example, due to incomplete property rights or deficient infrastructure. State intervention to reduce transactions costs on markets can thus have large efficiency gains.

In each of these cases, neoclassical theory generally, and the new institutional economics in particular, predict that market outcomes will not be socially efficient. State interventions can thus be a source of efficiency gains. State intervention may also be motivated by welfare concerns when market outcomes are not socially desirable. For instance, the social planner may decide that market forces result in too much poverty or too much inequality. This assessment justifies corrective state interventions (e.g. through taxes and transfers or the redistribution of assets, as in land reform) to redistribute welfare. There will frequently exist trade-offs between efficiency and equity that lead the state to implement second-best interventions to support a social agenda.

Recalling that the state is a political institution, neoclassical theory recognizes that some Pareto criterion may be applied to secure the political feasibility of a policy. This kind of approach needs to be supported with incidence analysis to assess the distributional consequences of a policy (changes in consumer surplus ΔCS, in producer surplus ΔPS, and in budget revenues ΔB), with potential inclusion of a stakeholder weighting scheme (w). In cases like this, we have to consider some socio-politically contextual objective function for a hypothetical social planner. For example, this could take a utilitarian form like the following:

$$Max_{w.r.t.policy} \sum_i w_i \Delta u_i = \sum_i w_i (\Delta CS_i + \Delta PS_i) + \Delta B, \quad \sum_i w_i = 1,$$

where the weights w_i indictate the relative political importance of each stakeholder group.

Relative economic backwardness (Gerschenkron)

The functionalist role of the state in promoting development was important in Gerschenkron's (1962) theory of relative economic backwardness (REB), providing an interpretation of how Western nations were able to catch up with England in the nineteenth century. The state had a key role to play in providing protection, enhancing savings, and fomenting entrepreneurship for infant industries. Examples include the following:

- Tariff protection for infant industry to emerge, grow, and compete, from France in 1820 to Japan in 1880. Due to economies of scale, infant industries require temporary protection. The US Civil War of 1861–5 was in part fought over imposition of protective tariffs for industry in the North as opposed to free trade for Southern agriculture. A proactive role for the state was thus essential in promoting industrialization.
- Forced savings to support investment—for instance, via a land tax. In Japan, early investment in industry came from public revenues, 80 percent of which derived from imposing a land tax on landlords, who in turn extracted rents from their tenants.
- Entrepreneurship fomented by the state, as, for example, in Germany and Japan to accelerate industrialization, in part for military defense.

Keynesian state (Samuelson)

In the industrialized countries, Keynesian policies had the objective of stimulating aggregate demand in a context of economic crisis (the Great Depression of the 1930s) due to underconsumption and labor-market failures that prevented the economy from recovering under the drive of market forces. This was done by using fiscal expenditures to create public employment in infrastructure—as, for example, under the New Deal policies of the 1933–8 period—and redistribute income toward the poor, who have a relatively higher marginal propensity to consume than the rich. In the developing-country context, lack of investment (viz. the Harrod–Domar and Solow models in Chapter 8) is typically due to more than lack of effective demand. Keynesian thought has, however, been very influential in development economics as it legitimized using the state in response to market failures, and demonstrated the potential for success. It was particularly instrumental in the design of industrialization strategies. It was also key in coordinating investment across sectors to achieve a higher outcome among multiple equilibria, helping implement Big Push strategies to capture positive industrial investment externalities in both production and market creation.

Developmental state (Hirschman)

Development economics emphasizes the role of the state in counteracting market failures that limit growth, and in securing more socially desirable growth outcomes.

- *Industrialization strategies.* Market failures such as economies of scale prevent the onset of industrialization for latecomers. As we saw when analyzing growth in Chapter 7, there are different categories of industrialization strategy that can be used. These include ISI (tariff protection on selected sectors of industry), EOI (subsidies targeted at firms which promise to become competitive exporters), and OEI (managing the investment climate in order to attract foreign direct investment). In all cases, a proactive role for the state was key in the design and implementation of these policies.
- *Developmental state.* In the last half century, Asia provided examples of a new development paradigm, with state-led, rapid industrialization in an environment of relative paternalism and aggressive but largely temporary interventions giving competitive advantage to emerging domestic industries. In successful cases (Hong Kong, Singapore, Taiwan, South Korea), the role of state institutions had important shared characteristics:

  - A role for state-led planning to coordinate public investment and set collective goals for the private sector. South Korea was transformed from a "sinkhole for foreign assistance" in 1962 to a member of the OECD in 1996 through a rigorous planning exercise. The first five-year plan, from 1962–7, focused on infrastructure development and ISI. The second five-year plan, from 1967–72, emphasized export-oriented industrialization. Not only was growth rapid, it also led to quick poverty reduction with no increase in inequality, in part due to a highly egalitarian distribution of land and human capital. Adelman (1999) concludes her analysis of the South Korean experience by saying that, "It was only with the birth of a strong developmental state and the adoption of a coherent development program that the South Korean economic miracle was born."
  - A relatively autonomous and service-motivated bureaucracy with high administrative skills and close relations to the private sector. Evans (1995) calls this relation between bureaucracy and private sector "embedded autonomy." It has the advantage of access to information about the competitive potential of firms, which is essential for "picking winners" in an EOI strategy, but also opens the door to cronyism and corruption in the use of public subsidies, a factor that contributed to the 1997 Asian financial crisis.

Modernizing elites (sociological theories)

Another important dimension of the developmental state is the existence of leading socio-economic groups that help facilitate reform and social change. In modernization theory, formulated by Lipset (1959) and Rostow (1960), they consisted of Western-educated elites whose modern socio-political and cultural norms were the source of domestic social innovations and provided role models. The theory of modernizing elites has been criticized as Eurocentric, confusing the history of the Western experience with the necessary conditions for development and failing to anticipate the success of the Asian experience, discussed in Chapter 3.

Functionalist theories of the state are useful in that they give us a benchmark for what the state could be doing to assist a country achieve its vision of development. According to these theories, state interventions are efficiency-driven, generating a NSG>0, and welfare-driven in correcting market outcomes toward socially desirable ones. Logic of function does not, however, imply existence, otherwise all institutions would be efficient or welfare-enhancing, creating a functionalist fallacy. On the contrary, many inefficient and welfare-reducing public institutions exist, and their existence is, as we have seen, a major cause of underdevelopment. Reforming them is thus central to successful development. For this, we need to understand how the state operates and why it is not able to fulfill the functions expected of it for development. This is what the theories of the pluralist state give us. They help us understand how the problems of public choice and collective action can be solved in achieving development-enhancing reforms. This takes us toward understanding issues such as rent-seeking, lobbying, and corruption that limit the developmental functions of the state.

THE PLURALIST STATE: PUBLIC CHOICE

Taking the state from a functionalist perspective, where it is presumed to act as an autonomous agent in fulfilling its developmental roles, to the reality of what the state does, requires placing it within particular systems of governance. The actions of the state will be conditioned by relationships to stakeholder groups such as clients, voters, and special-interest coalitions. The nature of this relationship depends on the type of political regime.

In small kinship or tribal groups, cooperation can easily emerge to achieve a peaceful order and provide collective goods to the members of the group. This is because individual gains from the provision of collective goods are large enough compared to the cost for each provider for there to be no incentive to free-ride. There is a logic for voluntary collective action (Olson, 1971). Decisions can be made by consensus and a scheme of authority may not even be needed. However, this becomes impossible to sustain when groups become large. Incentives for voluntary collective action disappear as the individual gain from provision of a collective good (one n^{th} if group size is n) is small compared to the individual cost, which is not shared. Formalized systems of governance need to emerge to enforce cooperation. The simplest form of governance is to give authority to a single person under an autocratic regime. However, as society becomes more complex and citizens more educated, democratic forms of governance tend to emerge that are more efficient, giving power to the people. This began with direct democracy in the Greek *polis* and with representative democracy in the Roman Republic. In a democracy, citizens have the right to vote in free, fair, and competitive elections, and political leaders are elected to and out of office.

745

Autocratic regimes and development

While industrialized countries tend to have democratic forms of governance, many developing countries have autocratic regimes. These include those of China, Russia, most of the Middle Eastern countries, and many of the Sub-Saharan countries (see Freedom House, online). In an autocracy, state power resides in a single person or institution such as a dictator, king, warlord, supreme religious leader, or one-party system. While this person or institution may act as a benevolent social planner, promoting aggregate welfare, the reality tends to be the opposite. The theory of autocracy thus assumes that the one who holds power will use it to maximize his or her own self-interest.

Autocracy does not have to be incompatible with economic growth, as long as growth supports the self-interest of the ruler. With the uniquely successful growth performance of China, which has an autocratic form of governance under the rule of the Communist Party, there is considerable interest in understanding how autocracy can deliver growth—perhaps more successfully than democracy, eventually—especially in countries where institutions and culture are not ready to support electoral democracy. State capitalism, where market freedoms coexist with authoritarian forms of governance, can offer successful growth. A hard-learned lesson in countries such as Iraq and Afghanistan is that imposing transitions to democracy in countries that are not culturally and institutionally ready for this form of governance may be detrimental to social stability and growth.

The answer is that autocracy can exploit citizens in the best interest of the ruler without the need for economic growth or it can be exploitative with growth as the instrument to generate a surplus that can be extracted by the ruler. Olson (1993) helps us understand this difference in autocratic regime performance by contrasting two forms of governance, what he calls "roving" bandits and "stationary" bandits. In both cases, the ruler's objective is to pursue self-interest by maximizing tax revenue. The model uses the concept of the Laffer (2004) Curve that relates tax rate to tax revenue through an inverse-U shape relationship, as shown in Figure 21.3.

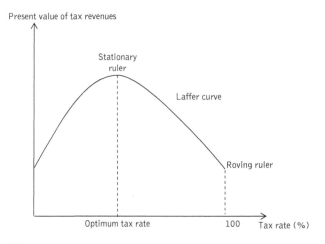

Figure 21.3 *Optimum taxation under roving and stationary rulers*

The roving ruler does not play repeated games: he moves from place to place, maximizing tax revenue by imposing a 100 percent tax rate, practicing one-time exhaustive plunder. The present value of tax revenues is consequently low. This is good for the ruler, but bad for growth. The stationary ruler is, by contrast, forward-looking, setting a tax rate that will maximize the present value of a sustained flow of future tax revenues. His optimum tax rate is inferior to that of the roving ruler. Key here is the ruler's expected length of tenure in office, which determines his discount rate. If the ruler's tenure is long and secure, he will maximize future economic growth with a low discount rate. If it is brief and uncertain, his discount rate rises and he will increase the tax rate at the cost of economic growth, approximating roving-ruler behavior. Note that maximum growth under the stationary ruler is not the same as development. He will only invest to generate income growth that can be taxed away. The investments can include public goods that raise future taxable revenues or contribute to his longevity in office, but not the other dimensions of development that correspond to people's preferences.

In this perspective, democracy is seen as an institution introduced to reduce predatory taxes and to broaden the dimensions of development delivered by growth. Because the political representatives in a democracy are members of the economy, the optimal tax rate will be lower than under autocracy (Olson, 1993). Democracy serves as a commitment device to secure private-property rights, transactions, and the enforcement of contracts, i.e. the institutions that are good for sustained growth, as shown by Acemoglu et al. (2001) (see Chapter 3). The dictator can never guarantee that his tenure is secure. The inherent uncertainty of succession in autocratic regimes (for example, at the death of a king) implies that they will not sustain economic performance. The long-term economic superiority of electoral democracy over autocracy is thus in the commitment value that elections provide for the respect of property rights and the enforcement of contracts. For democracy to be lasting, it must guarantee free speech, property rights, contract enforcement, the rule of law, individual rights, and an independent judiciary. In the short run, a secure stationary ruler can successfully deliver economic growth as it is in his self-interest to extract future rents from the people, but this is unlikely to be sustained without a political transformation that offers inclusive economic institutions. For Acemoglu and Robinson (2012), China has been able to achieve a breakneck pace of economic growth without inclusive political institutions, but lack of democratic rights is the biggest threat to sustained growth.

Democratic regimes and development

Electoral rules can vary widely, affecting what governments do. They include the following:

- *Unanimity rule*—for example, in EU foreign-policy decisions and in some UN committees such as the Committee on World Food Security.
- *Majority rule*, requiring more than 50 percent of the votes, for example in US Supreme Court decisions, in US presidential elections when there are only two

candidates, and in the second round of elections where a first turn eliminates all candidates but two.

■ *Super-majority rule*, where more than 50 percent is required to win. This typically applies to important decisions such as amending the constitution.

■ *Plurality rule*, where whoever gets the most votes wins. This is different from majority rule if there are more than two candidates.

■ *Committee rule*, where decisions are delegated to a small group that decides on behalf of the larger population, usually by majority rule within the committee. This is typically how bureaucracies make decisions.

Voting rules can be of the one-person-one-vote type, where each person's vote is counted the same, but can also be modified to assign different rights to voters. They include the following:

■ *Threshold requirements*, where everybody gets the same vote, but not everybody can vote. Voting may be limited by property, gender, and birth requirements, resulting in the disenfranchisement of non-qualifying citizens. In the US, women were disenfranchised from voting until 1920.

■ *Weighted voting*, where all stakeholders can vote, but the vote is proportional to the stake held. Corporate voting assigns weights proportional to the number of shares held. IMF country voting is weighted by financial contributions to the institution.

■ *Approval voting*, where citizens can decide to vote on anything they like, but are often limited by veto on specific issues and by a threshold number of signatures to place an issue on the ballot.

■ *Exhausted voting*, where multiple sequential votes are taken, each time eliminating an option. This is how the Olympics Committee selects a host country and how the winner is chosen in beauty pageants.

The median-voter theorem

When governments are subject to popular elections, their behavior is significantly influenced by voters' responses to their proposed policy platforms. Governments must make policy to win elections. The *median-voter model* is the most widely used interpretation of how elections influence policy-making. This model was initially developed by Hotelling (1929), who made an analogy between competing firms and competing politicians. Just as the products of different firms tend to be similar as they compete in the marketplace for the same majority of consumers, the political platforms of politicians tend to converge at election time as they compete for the same majority of voters. The model is based on the following assumptions (Congleton, 2002):

■ All voters are fully informed and rational.

■ All voters will vote for the politician with the platform closest to their preferred position.

■ There is equal disutility in voting for a platform that deviates positively or negatively along a single criterion from the preferred level.

- The politician that gets the most votes wins the election following the plurality rule.
- Everybody votes for his/her immediate interests, with no strategic voting.

The electoral outcome can be seen in Figure 21.4. The horizontal axis represents the policy preferences of voters from left to right on a single scale. The frequency distribution of voters across policy preferences is single peaked. In Figure 21.4a, politician A offers a platform closer to the preference of the median voter. He captures all votes to his left, plus half of the votes between A and B, reaching to point c. Politician B attracts all votes to his right and half of those between A and B up to c. Politician A is winning in the polls. Since political platforms can be adjusted to compete for votes, this is not a political equilibrium. Politician B adjusts his platform to the left, and an equilibrium is reached at election time when both platforms converge toward the policy preference of the median voter (Figure 21.4b). At that time, the outcome of the election is fully determined by the vote cast by the median voter. The outcome is a toss. Hence the model does not predict the electoral outcome, it only predicts the convergence of political platforms at election time. These platforms can of course diverge after the election; but the politicians responsible for this will be accountable to the electorate if they are candidates at the next election.

In most countries, the majority of the population (including the decisive median voter) has incomes below the economy-wide average (see Figure 6.11, in Chapter 6). The more unequal the distribution of income, the larger the gap between average and median voter incomes. A prediction of the median-voter model is thus that the political platform favored by the median voter should demand progressive income redistribution, with heavier taxation the greater the level of inequality.

There are other implications of the median-voter model. (1) Extremism is not an issue since the opinions of the extremes have no influence on the preference of the

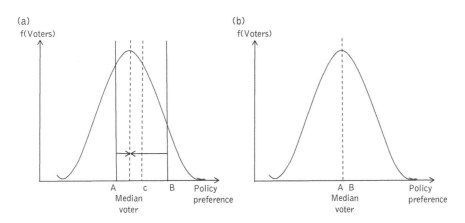

Figure 21.4 *Policy convergence under the median-voter model. In (a), c is the mid point between the policy platforms of politicians A and B. Politician A captures votes to the left of c and politician B votes to the right of c. In (b), politicians have adjusted their platforms to converge to the policy preference of the median voter*

median voter. (2) If the policy preference of the median voter changes, so does the policy. (3) The only time the policy preferences of other voters matter is when one of them changes from one side of the median voter to the other. This redefines who the median voter is. The policy that will prevail is that of the new median voter. (4) Changes of policy preference by other voters do not matter, as long as they do not cross over the median-voter policy preference. (5) Emergence of a third-party alternative—say, to the extreme left—robs politician A of votes in his left-wing tail of the distribution of opinions. This forces politician A to move to the right, seeking to reach the median voter in the rest of the distribution of votes. (6) Competition in primaries tends to force competing politicians to cater to tail voters; competition in the election between the remaining two candidates tends to cater to centrist voters. For these two candidates, the more extremist commitments they may have made to compete in the primaries can become a liability in adjusting their platforms toward the median voter.

Representative democracy

If instead of directly voting for a political position, each voter votes for a candidate who will represent his position in parliament, the median-voter model applies to representative democracy. With proportional representation, candidates have votes in parliament proportionate to the number of votes they received from the public. If there is a threshold percentage of votes that a candidate must reach to be allowed into parliament, this will induce the existence of a multiplicity of parties, each with the minimum threshold of votes. Parties will then be quite unstable, with large parties subject to splits to better represent their constituencies. With a multiplicity of parties to chose from, voters practice "exit" strategies, instead of Hirschman's (1970) "voice and loyalty" under a two-party system. To achieve a majority in parliament, and reach the median voter, parties need to form coalitions. Some of the extremist parties may then become swing voters, determining who will be the median voter. Extreme views will then be represented in parliament, and can gain considerable weight in policy-making. Predictions of the median voter under representative democracy are thus quite opposite to those of the median voter under direct democracy. The latter is typically illustrated by the US, the first by countries such as Italy and Israel.

An interesting question is whether government spending is higher under direct or under representative democracy. A natural experiment in Sweden allowed for the testing of this (Pettersson-Lidbom and Tyrefors, 2007). Direct democracy had historically prevailed, with citizens regularly deciding on public affairs at town meetings. In 1919, localities with a population of more than 1,500 were required to have representative democracy with proportional representation. In 1938, the threshold was lowered to 700. The threshold can be used as a regression discontinuity design (RDD). The change in threshold can be used to estimate a diff-in-diffs for the localities that had to switch. Both show that localities with direct democracy had much lower government spending. The RDD estimate is 30–50 percent less, representing a long-run policy effect, while the diff-in-diffs estimate is 10–13 percent less, representing a short-term adjustment to the switch. An interpretation of this result, which has been observed in other contexts, is that voters tend to be fiscal conservatives (Peltzman, 1992), with direct democracy giving them more direct control over government budgets.

The relationship between public expenditures and votes

How are voters rewarded by politicians for their votes through the delivery of public goods, and how do voters reward politicians for the delivery of public goods through the delivery of votes? Targeted public expenditures such as transfers and subsidies can have political objectives, with large opportunity costs in terms of forgone growth or poverty reduction. Examples include fertilizer subsidies in Zambia, Malawi, and Zimbabwe that can absorb a large share of government budgets. In Zambia, an average of 30 percent of the agricultural-sector budget was spent on targeted input subsidies in 2004–11 (Mason and Ricker-Gilbert, 2013). The questions are how political-economy objectives affect the allocation of subsidies, and whether subsidies are important in buying votes for the subsequent election. There is a useful contrast for this between two competing electoral models: the core-supporter model and the swing-voter model (Figure 21.5).

In the core-supporter model, projects follow votes (Cox and McCubbins, 1986). The winning politician allocates projects to the constituencies from which he has received the strongest electoral support as rewards for their loyalty. Core supporters are typically a tribe, an ethnic group, a caste, a religious group, or a region. This is the politics of patronage or neo-patrimonialism (van de Walle, 2001, for Africa; Finan, 2005, for Brazil). In neo-patrimonialism, politicians, as patrons, use state resources to secure the loyalty of clients in the population. In this case, politicians tend to be representatives of their own core (ethnic, tribal) group, and there is little electoral competition across core-supporter groups.

In the swing-voter model, votes follow projects. The incumbent politician or party targets communities with swing or opposition voters whose electoral behavior could be swayed by the provision of public projects. This is the politics of populism (Dixit and Londregan, 1996; Robinson and Verdier, 2013). If the politician is a challenger, the projects are in the form of promises, a well known feature of populist discourse in electoral campaigns. In this case, there is more electoral competition as projects are not locked into core-supporter groups. Political debates and information about the political platform of a candidate can influence electoral outcomes. Delivery against promises

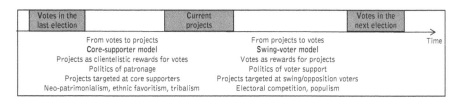

Figure 21.5 *Core-supporter model for elected politician and swing-voter model for incumbent candidate or party*

for challengers, and effective project management for incumbents help achieve electoral accountability. There are interesting empirical questions about whether projects do effectively buy votes, and whether more information on candidates can help reduce voting along core-supporter lines and induce more electoral competition.

Mason *et al.* (2013) addressed the issue of the allocation of fertilizer subsidies in Zambia in terms of core- vs. swing-voter models. Using household panel data, they found that the government systematically targeted subsidies to farmers in the constituencies that it won at the last election, and that per capita transfers increased with the margin of victory, supporting the core-supporter model of redistributive politics. They found, by contrast, that the government did not obtain more votes in subsequent elections in the districts where it had allocated more subsidies, rejecting the swing-voter model. Instead, reduced unemployment, a decline in poverty, and reduced inequality bought votes. In a study of voters' responses to the targeted allocation of benefits from development programs in West Bengal, Bardhan *et al.* (2015) found that there was strong response to short-term benefit programs but not to infrastructure benefits nor to more substantial one-time benefits such as receiving a land title. This suggests that recurrent transfers that can be revoked are more effective at buying votes than one-time irreversible transfers. This was confirmed in a study of the allocation of land certificates to Mexican farmers. Using the gradual roll-out of the certification program as an identification strategy, de Janvry *et al.* (2014) found that the asset transfer did not buy votes for the left-wing government in power. On the contrary, it induced a shift to the right among beneficiaries after they became asset owners, backfiring on the donating government. Certain types of government handout—short-term and repeated—are thus better than others—one-time and irreversible—in the exercise of populist politics.

Using an RCT in Sierra Leone, Casey (2014) tests whether increased information about candidates helps switch votes from an ethnic-based core model to more open electoral competition cutting across ethnic lines, corresponding to a swing-voter model. She organized debates among candidates broadcast by local radio stations in selected highly contested regions to inform the electorate about candidates' competence and political platforms. She found that information increases votes across ethnic-party lines, helping the better politicians attract more votes. Neo-patrimonial politics can thus be undermined by a better-informed electorate.

Democracy and development

Following the sedentary-ruler argument, autocracy can deliver growth, but not necessarily development. Democracy is likely to have a high intrinsic value for development, but is it good for growth? If in the end both growth and democracy are to be achieved, as in OECD countries, is it better to pursue economic liberalization (market reforms) first, or to pursue political liberalization (democracy) first? There has been a lot of debate on this. China is pursuing economic liberalization ahead of political liberalization. India has pursued political liberalization ahead of economic liberalization. There has been a strong wave of democratization across the developing world, particularly after the fall of the Berlin wall in 1989 and the descaling of the

Cold War. According to Freedom House (Freedom House, online), the percentage of countries with electoral democracies increased from 41 percent (69 of 167 countries) in 1989 to 63 percent (120 of 192 countries) in 2000. However, this gain has stagnated since then, reaching 61 percent (118 out of 195 countries) in 2012. Empirical evidence remains mixed on the benefits of democratization for growth, in part because of the difficulty of breaking the endogeneity between democracy and growth.

Papaioannou and Siourounis (2008) counted 67 countries that had a permanent transition to democracy over the 1960–2000 period. In Figure 21.6, they show that democratization has been good for growth, contributing to an increase of 0.5 percent to 1 percent in GDPpc growth over a period of five to ten years after the reform. The transition to democracy is, however, usually achieved at a cost in terms of growth. Using cross-country panel data, they show that the contribution to growth takes a U shape. The policy lesson is thus that democracy can be good for growth, but that it takes time for the political reform to have an impact on economic performance, and that reform is costly for growth during the transition period. These results should, however, be interpreted as descriptive of a regularity, not causal, because the event of democracy is itself an endogenous outcome.

Acemoglu *et al.* (2008) use cross-country data for 147 countries in the 1990s to show that there is a strong positive correlation between GDPpc and democracy. This confirms the well known observation that OECD countries have both high incomes and are democratic, while many of poor countries are non-democracies. But correlation does not imply causality. The correlation between change in income and change in democracy over the 1970–95 period is not significant. This is confirmed by a cross-country regression with country-fixed effects to track the relation within each country. Use of instruments for income, such as the lagged savings rate and growth rates in trading partners (while raising questions about the validity of the exclusion restriction), also finds no significant relation. Causality between income per capita and democracy is thus unsupported by the data, against conventional wisdom. In the end, high incomes and democracy converge as joint outcomes of development, but

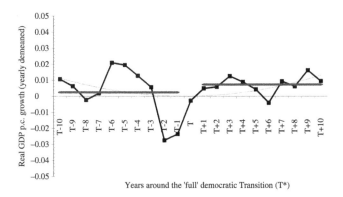

Figure 21.6 *Impact of permanent democratization (event year) on GDPpc growth (vertical axis)*

Source: Papaioannou and Siourounis, 2008.

the trajectory to this outcome is not causal. We need to look at more specific aspects of how democracy influences growth, or at specific dimensions of development.

One such aspect of development is the incidence of famines. In a celebrated study of the history of mass famines, Sen (1981) argued that large hidden famines cannot occur under democracy because freedom of the press makes information available to policy-makers and voters, and because elections create accountability in responding to famines. He looked at famines in India before independence, such as the 1943 Bengal famine that left between 1.5 and 3 million people dead, and at the fact that there has been no major famine since independence and the transition to democracy. Famine in communist China during the Great Leap Forward of 1957–62 left between 10 and 30 million people dead without political response. This relationship between democracy and the elimination of large-scale famines was empirically supported by Besley and Burgess (2002). Using panel data for 16 Indian states over the 1958–92 period, they show that there is greater government responsiveness to natural disasters that threaten food security where there is a greater role for the media and greater political competition, as measured by closer elections. Information and electoral accountability combine in inducing more public responsiveness in the form on food distribution and calamity-relief expenditures.

Failed developmental states

In extreme cases, states in developing countries can fail politically, losing their legitimacy as public agents and as stewards of national economic institutions and resources. Examples of this include extreme military dictatorships, like that in Zaire or today's Myanmar, which so completely exploited and/or manipulated their economies that up to 40 percent of GDP was eventually traded on black markets, and the Democratic Republic of the Congo, where governance itself is contestable and natural resources and other economic assets are appropriated to finance military action or simply taken as spoils of war. Finally, transition situations, like the early market liberalizations of Russia and some former Soviet Republics, are vulnerable to opportunism such as looting state assets and acquiring market power via political patronage. In all these cases, the state becomes the ultimate rent-seeker, and is commonly referred to as a predatory state.

In such circumstances, citizen resignation tends to prevail domestically, and corruption goes from being an exception to an endemic and epidemic competition for a perceived commons of appropriable assets. Disciplined authority structures such as military juntas (Indonesia, Myanmar, etc.) can maintain order even when public trust has evaporated, but rivalry within such regimes usually compromises their stability. For Acemoglu and Robinson (2012), it is this rivalry in the appropriation of public rents that undermines the sustainability of growth under non-inclusive political regimes. Working with such regimes is extremely challenging for international development organizations, since the leadership tends to be preoccupied with short-term gains/survival, as in the roving-ruler model, and has no real interest in the long-term opportunities offered by development, poverty alleviation, and sustainable growth.

In addition to more predatory and kleptocratic states, there are cases where more passive institutional evolution has led to development traps. For example, in India a de facto alliance exists between *kulaks* (relatively wealthy landowning rural dwellers), urban industrial elites, and state bureaucracies at all levels. In Bardhan's (1997) terminology, this had created—over the long period between independence in 1947 and economic liberalization in 1991—a "black hole state" which absorbed all surplus resources, keeping public and private investment low, rural and urban wages at subsistence level, and pursuing elaborate protectionist policies that created rents for incumbent interests to the detriment of competitive forces.

The issue of how to promote development and deliver aid under failed states is becoming increasingly relevant as poverty is reduced in emerging nations, and failed states increasingly become the geographical location of extreme poverty. Delivering "good aid in hard places" such as Yemen is thus a theme of increasing relevance for the international development community (see Chapter 19).

Violence and development

We saw in Chapter 2 that there has been a decline in the number of ongoing armed conflicts in the world since the end of the Cold War. The number remains large, however, and the recent period suggests an increase in the number of terrorist attacks. According to the Global Terrorism Database at the University of Maryland, the number of attacks by groups connected with Al-Qaeda and Islamic State increased from 200 per year over the period 2007–10 to 600 in 2013. It is well recognized that armed conflicts can be devastating for populations and on economic development. They involve loss of life, significant destruction of assets, losses in human capital, and displacement of populations; and they can induce major changes in governance, possibly for the better but typically for the worse. Development economists have thus addressed two questions: can we explain what causes armed conflicts and violence, with the idea that this understanding may help us do something to prevent their occurrence? And can we measure not only the short-run costs of conflicts, but also their long-term consequences, so we are better informed about the magnitude and nature of their individual and social consequences?

Causes of conflicts

Collier and Hoeffler's (1998) empirical work at the World Bank has been seminal in establishing correlates for two potential categories of determinants of violence: greed and grievances. With greed, violence is induced by the private economic gains offered by the opportunity of gaining control over sources of wealth and looting. Control over these resources in turn serves to finance armed conflict. Well known examples are plundered petroleum in Nigeria and Angola, river diamonds in Sierra Leone, coltan mined in the Kivu region of the Democratic Republic of the Congo, and drugs produced in Colombia. Poverty facilitates the exercise of greed. It lowers the opportunity cost of fighting, facilitates the recruitment of combatants, and makes easier the capture of child soldiers. The Naxalites prevail in the poorest states of India, from Bihar to Andhra Pradesh. Child soldiers are most prevalent in Liberia, Uganda, and Sierra Leone, all very poor countries. In cross-country regressions, Collier and Hoeffler find that low per capita income, a high share of primary exports in GDP, low levels of education, and less ethnic fractionalization (making it easier to recruit)—all symptomatic of the greed motive—are strongly associated with the occurrence of civil war.

Grievances could be associated with ideological principles, religious hatred, ethnic fragmentation, inequality, social exclusion and alienation, and the desire for retaliation and revenge. Examples include the civil war between Tamil Tiger separatists and the government in Sri Lanka, Fidel Castro's anti-imperialist revolutionary movement in Cuba, the Sandinista rebellion in Nicaragua, and Eritrea's ideological separatist movement. Collier and Hoeffler, however, find that variables symptomizing grievances are weak correlates of the broad range of armed conflicts. It is notable in particular that they find no role for social fragmentation, ethnic dominance by a minority, income inequality, or land concentration.

Economic determinants (greed) thus seem to dominate over grievances in correlating with conflict. This was established causally by Miguel *et al.* (2004) for Sub-Saharan Africa (a paper we reviewed in Chapter 4). Instrumenting negative shocks in GDPpc by adverse weather events (measured by deficits in rainfall), they find that a fall in GDPpc induces an increase in the likelihood of civil war. Brückner and Ciccone (2010) find similar results using international commodity-price shocks as an instrument for income shocks. Their results also confirm the lack of a significant role for grievance-type variables such as ethno-linguistic fragmentation. Protecting individuals from negative income shocks should thus be a major factor contributing to the decline in violence. This is a case where short-run responses by governments and foreign-aid agencies to economic shocks originating in weather or commodity-price declines could avoid very high long-term costs associated with violence.

Violence can also be induced by the opportunity of economic gains when these activities are illicit. Dell (2014) analyzed the impact of crackdowns on drug trafficking in Mexico on the incidence of homicides. Drug trafficking is a huge business: traffickers earn some $25 billion a year and the Mexican government spends some $9 billion in attempting to combat trafficking, as much as it spends on social programs. Dell used a regression discontinuity design to control for endogeneity of drug enforcement. In Mexico, drug enforcement was spearheaded by the PAN, the conservative political party. Using as a discontinuity mayoral elections narrowly won by the PAN in 2007–10, she shows that the subsequent crackdown on drug trafficking by the elected mayor sharply increased violence and homicides. This was due to the fact that the weakening of incumbent criminals opened the opportunity for rival traffickers to appropriate territory. An estimated 90 percent of the homicides were traffickers killing each other. Disrupting established power relations thus invites competition and violence, and also creates violence spillovers on alternative drug-trade routes that are open for control. The outcome is self-defeating as the magnitude of the overall drug trade remains unaffected.

Consequences of conflict

There is a large literature documenting the short-run costs of violence and armed conflict. Akresh and de Walque (2008) show how the Rwandan genocide reduced the school attainment of children exposed to conflict. Similar work was done for health in Rwanda, Burundi, and Angola, showing a negative impact on height-for-age z-scores for children exposed to conflict. The question, however, is whether these short-term impacts translate into long-term consequences, or whether there can be subsequent compensation and recovery. At a regional level, Davis and Weinstein (2002) for Hiroshima and Nagasaki, and Miguel and Roland (2011) for Vietnam have shown that the large short-term economic losses caused by severe bombing could be erased over a period of 20 to 30 years. Fewer studies are available at the individual level.

Blattman and Annan (2010) studied the long-term impact of having been kidnapped to become a child soldier in Uganda. They used as a counterfactual siblings who had escaped kidnapping by hiding in the jungle. They found that the psychological effects were generally not as important for child soldiers' achievements, once released, as the lost years of schooling. Lower educational achievements led to more low-skill jobs and wages 30 percent lower. Irreversibilities were more likely to be found in school achievements than in psychological traumas, suggesting the need for special schooling programs to help these children compensate for lost years rather than programs of social reinsertion.

León (2012) analyzed the long-term consequences of civil conflict in Peru involving the *Sendero Luminoso* (Shining Path), a Maoist insurgent organization. Using the time–space roll out of violence as an identification strategy (and, to validate this approach, showing that the variation in temporal and geographical violence is not correlated with any of the determinants of educational achievement), he found that children exposed to violence before starting school had lower educational achievements and worse labor-market outcomes. On the supply side of schooling, the channels included deaths of teachers delaying school attendance; on the demand side, a decline in a mother's health following a violent attack led to worse health for her children. The results point to vulnerability during early years of life to shocks that can create long-term irreversible consequences for human welfare.

Resource curse and political outcomes

Finally, there is the interesting question of the role of natural-resource wealth (the "resource curse") on political outcomes. Does natural-resource wealth undermine democracy? In general, the empirical literature observes a positive correlation between resource wealth and good outcomes (growth, non-violence) in democracies such as Norway and the US, and negative correlation in non-democracies such as the Democratic Republic of Congo and the Sudan (Arezki and Brückner, 2012). But does natural-resource wealth affect political outcomes? Causality is difficult to establish because resources are geographically fixed and thus spuriously correlated with many other local characteristics that affect outcomes.

Analyzing the election of mayors in Brazil, Brollo *et al.* (2013) use federal transfers to municipal governments to study the effect of local-government revenues (in this case unrelated to local natural-resource extraction) on political outcomes. Transfers change at given population thresholds, allowing them to use a regression discontinuity design. They find a "political resource curse": larger transfers increase corruption and lower the education of candidates for mayor. Asher and Novosad (2014) use exogenous variations in international mineral-resource prices to measure changes in natural-resource wealth across time and states in India. They analyze how this affects the outcomes of state legislative-assembly elections. They find that an increase in natural-resource wealth raises the electoral success of criminal politicians, thus increasing their presence in office. This happens in particular by giving corrupt incumbent candidates a political advantage. The resource curse thus makes elections less competitive and undermines institutional quality.

ECONOMICS OF PUBLIC AUTHORITY: RENT-SEEKING, POLITICAL INFLUENCE, AND CORRUPTION

Campaign spending to influence electoral outcomes can be very large. In the US, it reached $2.6 billion in the 2012 presidential election and $3.7 billion in the 2014 mid-term congressional elections. Concerned that money can be decisive in buying votes, many governments have attempted to restrict such spending, though this restriction was largely eliminated by the US Supreme Court in the 2010 Citizens United case. But how effective are campaign contributions in influencing who gets elected? Levitt (1994) used as a natural experiment elections in the US in which the same two candidates face one another on more than one occasion. Measuring the difference in campaign spending between the same two candidates eliminates the influence of any fixed candidate or district attributes. He found that campaign spending has an extremely small impact on election outcomes. In fact, companies have learned that it is more effective to influence politicians through rent-seeking expenditures once they are in power than to try to influence the selection of policy-makers by the median voter. As a consequence, they spend about ten times more on lobbying than they do in campaign contributions.

Rent-seeking refers to the search for private gain from an exercise of public authority (Krueger, 1974). It can occur through lobbying for a policy that will benefit a particular group, eventually at the cost of a net social loss. An example is obtaining imposition of a protective tariff that will benefit producers, tax consumers, and create an efficiency loss. This lobbying is perfectly legal, even though the rent captured is at the cost of others. Rent-seeking can also occur through corruption. This happens when a public agent accepts private compensation for exercising authority over a policy instrument that will create a rent transfer to the bribing agent.

Rent-seeking through political influence: lobbying

When the exercise of public authority has the potential to create private rents, the potential rents motivate resource transfers to influence policy decisions. We refer generically to this activity as lobbying, although it takes many forms and has many other names. As a social and economic behavioral problem, political influence implicates three generic groups of stakeholders, each with its own vested interests and objectives: lobbyists, the state, and civil society.

1. *Industry and lobbyists.* The basic motive is individual gain for the industry and the lobbyist it employs. To achieve this, the industry will maximize a combination of returns from private and public agency (Figure 21.7). Assume that the lobbyist represents an industry hoping for price support. In this case, the industry will make an optimal individual allocation of resources (*B*) between investment to increase production (Δ*q*) and expenditures on lobbying to obtain a better price (Δ*p*) through a government intervention such as a protective tariff. The optimum allocation of *B* between these two actions equates marginal revenue (Δ*pq*) from resources invested in production to marginal revenue from resources invested in lobbying, $(\Delta pq/\Delta q)(\Delta q/\Delta B) = (\Delta pq/\Delta p)(\Delta p/\Delta B) > 0$. Hence spending money on lobbying is incentive compatible for individuals if marginal revenue can be favorably influenced by policies affecting prices.

2. *The state.* As an aggregated public authority, we can just think of the state as acting selfishly in this context, maximizing the transfer of resources to government. Everyday examples of this are campaign contributions, endorsements from industry groups and organized labor, and "facilitating" industry behavior such as providing jobs for outgoing officials. More malign examples include bribery, nepotism, etc. In reality, state institutions are diverse and complex, and it is not uncommon to see intra-governmental competition for the use of influence. In any case, seeking the political or economic rewards offered by lobbyists is incentive compatible for the state.

3. *Society.* Taken again as an aggregate, society loses from lobbying in two ways. First, these activities generally induce economic distortions that create economic inefficiency as they lead to transfers. Second, resources used for lobbying are wasted from an aggregate social perspective, representing a deadweight loss (DWL) (NSG < 0) through Directly Unproductive (DUP) activities (Bhagwati, 1982).

For these reasons, lobbying may be unavoidable because it is incentive compatible with individual and state logic, while creating a double loss. To overcome these losses, society must see these as significant enough for itself (individually and collectively) to decide to reduce lobbying, and it must have a viable means of action for this at its disposal.

Note that not all lobbying is a source of NSG < 0. In the event that government faces uncertainty, while lobbies are informed, lobbying can convey useful information

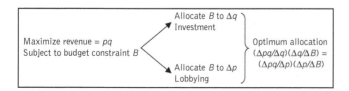

Figure 21.7 *Optimum allocation of resources to investment and rent-seeking*

to policy-makers (e.g. on the demand for public goods, on expected policy impacts) and help improve policy-making. In this case, lobbying can create redistributive gains with a NSG > 0.

Rent-seeking with malfeasance: corruption

When political influence leads to malfeasance, or abuse of public authority/trust, the result is usually called corruption. Following Transparency International, we define corruption as "the abuse of public office for private gain." It can take many forms, including bribes, theft, and nepotism. The risk of corruption exists anywhere that public authority can be used to create private wealth. Whether this risk leads to active corruption depends on a complex set of interacting conditions, including financial incentives and institutional uncertainties. While it is sometimes tempting to characterize some cultures, societies, or geographic regions as more corruption prone, the necessary conditions for this problem exist everywhere and sufficient conditions are more common than is generally acknowledged (see a variety of examples in Fisman and Miguel, 2008). Forensic economics is a branch of economics that specializes in fraud detection and the assessment of legitimate pecuniary damages associated with resulting litigations.

The aggregate cost of corruption

Corruption can have aggregate costs in reducing investment and growth. Using data for 70 countries, Mauro (1995) finds that countries with less corruption and red tape (more bureaucratic efficiency) had more investment and a higher GDPpc growth over the 1960–85 period. If Bangladesh had levels of bureaucratic integrity and efficiency comparable to those of Uruguay, its annual GDP growth would rise by half a percentage point. Because there is an issue with the endogeneity of corruption relative to growth due to omitted variable biases in cross-country analysis, a possible approach is to instrument corruption with a determinant that does not directly affect the growth performance. Mauro (1995) used ethno-linguistic fractionalization (defined in Chapter 6) to instrument corruption. He finds that corruption, as instrumented, reduces growth. The likelihood that fractionalization has a direct effect on growth (thus violating the exclusion restriction) is, however, an issue in the validity of the instrumentation. Subsequent work by Easterly and Levine (1997), for instance, shows that ethno-linguistic fractionalization is associated with low schooling, insufficient infrastructure, underdeveloped financial systems, distorted foreign-exchange markets, and political instability, all of which are in turn associated with slower growth.

Bribery and law enforcement: a corruption/compliance game

To better understand the basic determinants of corruption, and what can be done to reduce corruption, consider a generic corruption/compliance game involving two players: an official with authority in enforcing a rule, and a private agent whose actions are governed by some enforceable rule (Mookherjee and Png, 1995; Wydick, 2008).

Most corruption situations can be stated in this way, where the official has a salary S received in recognition of office and is expected to enforce the rule by levying a fine F in the event of violation (Figure 21.8). Assume further that the official receives as a bonus a share $1 \geq \lambda \geq 0$ of the fine levied, and that the private agent captures a gain V from violating the rule. We also assume that the private agent can offer a bribe B to the official, who risks with probability $1 \geq \mu \geq 0$ of getting caught and dismissed for corruption. Finally, note that we must have $V > B$ for the agent to have an incentive to bribe, and $V < F$ for the agent to have an incentive to comply.

This relatively simple example reveals much about the dilemma of official corruption and what can be done to deter it. The private agent may chose to either Comply or Violate. In both cases, we want the official to respond by enforcing the rule. Hence the incentives for the agent to resist the temptation of corruption (Ignore) must be set up in such a fashion that the equilibriums that prevail are either (Enforce, Comply) or (Enforce, Violate).

When the private agent chooses to Comply, (Enforce, Comply) will be the dominant strategy if $S > B/\mu$, i.e. if the official's direct salary exceeds the risk-adjusted value of the bribe. This reveals three fundamental determinants of rampant corruption: low official salaries, high potential bribes, and low vigilance in deterring bribe-taking. Imagine a Cambodian wildlife officer, making \$30/month, who is protecting a local tiger worth \$30,000 from trophy hunters and traditional-medicine collectors. Even with certain dismissal, the official could recover many multiples of annual income by making the tiger available to the collectors. Looked at from the opposite perspective, high wages and anti-corruption vigilance deter bribery, particularly in stable societies where (tenured) public salaries have high net present value.

When the private agent chooses to Violate, (Enforce, Violate) will be the dominant strategy if $S > (B-\lambda F)/\mu$. In this case, the salary must be sufficiently high that it exceeds the risk-adjusted value of the bribe net of the bonus λF. Enforcement can, however, fail. If public officials have relative impunity (μ low), bribes B do not have to be very high to invite corruption and in any case are de-coupled from V. Note that there exists an intermediate case when $B/\mu > S > (B-\lambda F)/\mu$. When this condition prevails, behavior cycles because there is no pure Nash equilibrium strategy. If the official enforces, the private agent complies. When the private agent complies, however, the official is better off ignoring, but that drives the private agent to violate. The ensuing rat race is typical of the so-called "trembling hand" enforcement systems in weak institutional settings.

		Private agent	
		Comply	Violate
Official	Enforce	$S, 0$	$S+\lambda F, V-F$
	Ignore	$(1-\mu)S+B, -B$	$(1-\mu)S+B, V-B$

Figure 21.8 *Generic corruption/compliance game*

S = salary, F = fine, λ = bonus on fine, V = gain from violating the rule, B = bribe, μ = probability of getting caught.

How extensive is corruption?

The extent of diversion of public funds to corrupt appropriations can be very large. Reinikka and Svensson (2004) calculated the fraction of public budgets allocated to education that actually reaches schools in Uganda. Using the World Bank's Public Expenditure Tracking Survey method, they found that district governments received the money allocated to their schools; but from then on only 13 percent of these funds reached the schools, and the median school received nothing. The degree of theft was larger on average for poorer communities.

Another way of measuring the pervasiveness of corruption is to use event analysis to identify a very short-term causal effect of corruption on economic outcomes. The identification idea is that, in the very short run, no other cause could have induced the observed outcome. This was done by Fisman (2001), who looked at whether episodes of bad news about the health of Suharto in Indonesia affected the stock market valuation of 79 large firms that were highly dependent on ties to Suharto and his family. He found that this was indeed the case, with Suharto-connected firms losing more market value the closer their political connection.

How to control corruption?

How to control corruption in public expenditures? Using an RCT approach, Olken (2007) compared two alternative approaches to reducing corruption in 608 village road-construction projects in Indonesia: a top-down approach using external monitoring by government auditors, and a bottom-up approach using community monitoring. In the top-down treatment, audits by Jakarta accountants were increased from 4 percent to 100 percent of the projects. In the bottom-up treatment, increased grassroots participation was induced by sending invitations to village meetings and distributing anonymous comment forms to collect villagers' opinions. The measure of corruption was very precise, taking samples of construction materials to detect the use of cheap sand in place of expensive rock and estimating the cost of the discrepancy. Comparing construction costs with the two materials showed that on average 29 percent of funds were stolen in control projects. The top-down audits approach proved to be much more effective at controlling corruption, reducing the discrepancy between official project costs and actual spending by 8 percentage points, or 28 percent—a large effect. Increasing grassroots participation in monitoring had, by contrast, little average impact, reducing missing expenditures only in villages with good cooperation and no elite capture. Olken concluded that traditional top-down monitoring can play an important role in reducing the cost of corruption, even in a highly corrupt environment.

Using a natural experiment, Reinikka and Svensson (2004) traced the influence of public information on leakages in the transfer of public funds in Uganda. In 1998, the government started to publish information on the monthly transfers made to school districts. Differential local availability of the newspapers circulating this information created a natural experiment for the transmission of the information shock. The authors found that transfers increased more where there was more access to newspapers. In line with Sen's argument (1981) on famines, the circulation of information exposing corruption can be a powerful instrument to increase political and bureaucratic accountability.

SEVEN STRATEGIES TO LIMIT RENT-SEEKING

Rent-seeking through lobbying or corruption is incentive compatible for individuals and governments, at a social cost. Hence it is reasonable to ask how countries can limit rent-seeking. The following seven approaches can be effective.

Increase state autonomy

Assuming that the state is not predatory, rent-seeking can be reduced by strengthening the autonomy of the state in decision-making, and in particular by reducing its dependency on funds obtained from lobbies. A variety of measures can limit state exposure to economic influence by special interests:

- Increase the strength of presidential leadership, with clearly delineated constitutional powers.
- Develop a professional bureaucracy with continuous service and a transparent, merit-based incentive structure.
- Define a clear contingent authority in times of crisis, making reforms easier to implement if they are seen as unavoidable and fair—for instance, in imposing adjustment policies to respond to a financial crisis.

Limit lobbying activities by regulation and exposure

Most modern states have so-called "influence-peddling" laws that explicitly restrict lobbying practices within socially acceptable boundaries. Of course, this is part of a process of institutional co-evolution, and lobbyists adapt very quickly to such regimes, including infiltration into the rule-making process itself. Nonetheless, states are usually better off articulating standards to establish the principle of deterrence. Beyond rule-making, there are indirect ways to limit these activities, including public information that exposes them and their perpetrators. These tactics can leverage popular sentiment against both lobbyists and unscrupulous office holders, even in countries not considered to be democratic. In China, for example, the most common cause of dismissal from senior offices is compromising public trust.

Strategies to circumscribe lobbying in this way include:

- Limit the role of private funds in office-seeking through campaign reforms and caps on political contributions. These efforts are not usually effective as lobbies find ways to circumvent the restrictive rules.
- Impose term limits on elected officials to increase competition.
- Introduce "revolving-door" policies to limit movements between enterprises and the agencies that regulate them.

763

■ Require public disclosure of financial support and personal financial interests.

■ Provide public records or open "transcripts" for all non-classified official communications.

■ Protect freedom of the press, exposing lobbying to public scrutiny. Ferraz and Finan (2008) find that municipal audits in Brazil are more effective in influencing electoral outcomes where there are more local media.

Scale down the predatory state

If we begin from the assumption that the state can succumb to bad intentions, from without or from within, it makes sense to limit the scope of its authority. This is the approach proposed by Bates (1981) to limit the scope for intervention by African states. This is particularly important in areas where economic stakes are large and mutable, i.e. when there are valuable public-domain resources and ill defined property rights.

■ Introduce transparent and enforceable rules for use/exploitation of public resources, including mineral rights, radio frequencies, public land transfers, etc.

■ Limit public ownership of commercial enterprises.

■ Introduce transparent and enforceable public-interest standards in regulation, contracting, and trade policy.

■ Impose fiscal and monetary discipline, with explicit pre-commitments, accounting targets, and conflict-of-interest rules (to limit the exercise of pork-barrel politics) where these are feasible.

■ Shift to greater reliance on market forces (trade liberalization, deregulation, privatizations) and correspondingly reduce state interventions that are sources of rents for lobbies and the state itself.

Use policy instruments less prone to lobbying, even if they are second-best in terms of efficiency

Policy-makers and economists know that there often are many policy instruments to achieve a desired economic objective (such as raising revenues, promoting a given industry, etc.), but they may each be inclined to choose different ones. Policy-makers have political-economy considerations in mind, while economists usually focus on efficiency gains. For example, infant industries can be promoted by tariff protection to sectors (ISI) or by start-up subsidies to firms (EOI). We have seen (Chapter 7) that tariffs impose a double distortion, with a DWL in both production and consumption, while subsidies impose a single distortion, with a DWL only in production. Tariffs are thus more inefficient than subsidies. There may, however, exist a trade-off between efficiency and exposure to lobbying that will guide a politician to choose a second-best instrument in terms of efficiency only because of reduced exposure to lobbying.

This can explain the political preference for tariffs over subsidies (Figure 21.9). Because they target sectors of economic activity (i.e. product categories) rather than individual firms, tariffs induce less lobbying activity. The tariff is essentially a

	Efficiency	Lobbying
Tariffs (ISI)	Double efficiency loss	Less exposed to lobbying
Subsidies (EOI)	Single efficiency loss	More exposed to lobbying

Figure 21.9 *Policy dilemma (double arrow) between efficiency and lobbying in trade-policy instruments. ISI = import-substitution industrialization, EOI = export-oriented industrialization*

public good to all producers of import substitutes in the industry, and they will simply free-ride on this rather than invest significant resources in sustained political influence. In the case of producer subsidies, however, firms are individually targeted and prone to bilateral client relationships with state regulators. They will invest in lobbying to attempt to reproduce the subsidy even once competitiveness has been achieved.

Promote cooperative over redistributive solutions

A perennial challenge of governance is sustaining the collective interest over throngs of individual claims on public resources and administrative capacity. Of course, most constitutions begin with a clear enunciation of collective interest as national identity. From this point onward, decentralization of political and economic reality exerts a bewildering array of narrower interests, from state/provincial competition down to individual households and citizens.

There are few rules of thumb in seeking cooperative solutions, but perhaps the most important is for members of policy institutions to recognize the importance for cooperation of the repeated nature of strategic interactions (conceptualized in the Folk theorem that we saw in Chapter 16). This repetition makes reputation and commitment more important, helping to avert destructive competition and prisoner's-dilemma outcomes in the use of public resources and authority. Such an approach would, for example, discourage single-term office holding in favor of incumbent eligibility. This principle then needs to be balanced against the risk of entrenched interest that justifies term limits. Ferraz and Finan (2011) and de Janvry *et al.* (2012) show that first-term mayors in Brazil are less prone to corruption and do a better job managing social programs than second-term mayors, who are not allowed to run for office again. Another important dynamic principle is promotion of party interests over individual personalities. Thus in Mexico, incumbency is not allowed, but strong political parties interested in remaining in power are the ones that seek cooperative over opportunistic (pork-barrel) solutions. Both individual and party incumbency improve prospects for continuity and reduce uncertainties associated with redistributive interests.

Finally, a variety of institutional "ethos" issues appear to promote collective interest, including charismatic leadership (such statesmen as Atatürk, Castro, Kennedy, and many others), shared hardship (the UK in World War Two, and solidarity in crises), nationalism (Swiss plebiscites), and "getting ahead collectively" (Hirschman, 1984).

Increase the effectiveness of policy-making

A primary source of political vulnerability comes from state ineffectiveness. A major difficulty for the state in policy-making is the time-consistency problem, and lack of commitment devices to overcome this problem. The time-consistency problem arises when government can arbitrarily change policy, and when instruments to guarantee that such change will not occur are missing, undermining government credibility in policy-making. This is the case with trade policy (Fernández and Rodrik, 1991): we know that trade will create NSG, but we also know that there will be winners and losers who are not easily identified today. The time-consistency problem arises in that the trade agreement has to be signed today, while compensation will be paid later, after the benefits from the trade agreement materialize. Lack of commitment devices whereby guarantees can be given to future losers that they will be compensated, implies that voters will oppose the agreement. This is a generic and pervasive policy problem, perhaps one of the main hurdles that governments face in making policy. What are the commitment devices available to governments to guarantee that policy will not change, and that promised compensations will indeed be paid?

1. *Commitment through set rules*. Rules diminish state flexibility in policy-making, but in so doing serve as commitment devices. Rules can be fixed, contingent, or have escape clauses. They include legal and administrative rules as well as membership to international organizations or agreements such as IMF and WTO membership, NAFTA, and introducing a currency board, as in the Argentine constitution.

2. *Commitment through delegation* to a policy-maker with a mandate different from that of government. This has been the main reason for guaranteeing the independence of the central bank, thus preventing elected governments from expanding the monetary base and engaging in populist expenditures before an election. It also prevents a government from negotiating a nominal minimum wage and subsequently undermining its real value by manipulating the rate of inflation. Delegation of environmental policy to specialized agencies such as the Environmental Protection Agency in the US has the same logic, as does Mexico agreeing to ISO 2000 certification of public administrations and Brazil to random audits of municipalities, with information publicly available on the internet. The fascinating aspect of this delegation strategy is that the government in fact gains policy-making credibility by voluntarily restricting its freedom to alter policy.

3. *Commitment through state variables*. In this case, time consistency is guaranteed by raising the cost of policy change due to sunken costs, creating policy irreversibility. High sunken costs reduce future incentives for government to change policy, making them into a credible commitment device. A government that wants to commit to not devaluing its currency in the future may thus hold its public foreign debt in domestic currency, making prohibitive the cost of a devaluation.

4. *Commitment through reputation* in a repeated game. In democracies, re-election can be used as a commitment device for sustained policy. President George H.W. Bush

committed not to raise taxes by saying, "read my lips." He subsequently raised taxes, and this contributed to his failure to be re-elected. For elections to serve as a commitment device, the government must be "office motivated," i.e. it must want to stay in office, and to have a high chance of re-election. Another necessary condition to achieve time consistency through the electoral process is an informed and educated population with access to historical evidence on government behavior and the capacity to interpret it without being manipulated by propaganda.

5. *Reducing flexibility to gain political influence.* It is perhaps ironic that inflexibility can be an asset in policy negotiation. This is because the more inflexible agent can more credibly commit, and will be seen as less vulnerable to political influence. The best way to do this is to reduce perceived individual discretion by articulating rigid, external (party, nationalist) principles. Thus, in policy-making, more effective leadership can be achieved by introducing rules that reduce the exercise of individual authority.

Citizen empowerment

Citizen empowerment to hold service providers accountable can occur through two alternative channels (World Bank, 2003). One is through the electoral process, the "long route" to social accountability (Figure 21.10). It is long because elections only occur every few years, and because a large number of issues are considered when making a judgment on the performance of politicians or political parties. The "short route" is through the exercise of direct pressures on service providers—for instance, through citizen report cards or representation on local social councils that have an evaluation function. Decentralization has an important role to play here as citizens will be better informed locally, and can mobilize local social capital to enforce rules. The potential risks of decentralization include elite capture, electoral clientelism, and limited administrative capacity. Experimentation with alternative accountability mechanisms is still needed, and trade-offs are involved. This applies to CCT programs. *Progresa* in Mexico is centralized, with less exposure to lobbying, but more targeting errors. Bolsa Família in Brazil is decentralized at the municipal level, with fewer targeting errors, but more exposure to lobbying and local political capture.

Figure 21.10 *Short and long routes to social accountability*

Source: Based on World Bank, 2003.

PUBLIC EXPENDITURES AND DEVELOPMENT: THE ROLE OF INFRASTRUCTURE

Infrastructure is one of the most important public goods entrusted to governments. Establishing causality between infrastructure and development outcomes is particularly difficult because of endogeneity of project placement. Projects are logically placed in regions with the greatest development potential (projects and outcomes are thus jointly determined by development potential). As we know, correlation between project and development does not imply causality. Identification strategies are necessary to overcome the endogeneity of projects. We review here several studies of infrastructure-investment projects where causality has been rigorously identified. RCTs are difficult to implement, and other identification strategies have been followed such as instrumentation and diff-in-diffs with natural experiments.

Impact of large-scale infrastructure: dams in India using an IV approach

Large dams are big investments with potential economic gains and also significant adjustment burdens, in particular in terms of resettlement of displaced populations. The World Bank has been the single biggest source of funds for the construction of large dams, and the management of resettlement programs has been controversial (Cernea, 1999). Dams offer flood control, irrigation services, electricity generation, and even transport facilitation. Even when they work as intended, however, their aggregate contribution can mask significant welfare redistribution. There is typically a conflict between the aggregate productivity benefits of dams that occur downstream from the site and the social costs that occur upstream through displacement of populations. Duflo and Pande (2007) attempted to account for both the economic and social consequences of dam building in India. The identification strategy they used consisted of instrumenting for dam placement by using the river gradient, which should be low for irrigation dams and very steep for hydroelectric dams. The results show that large dams generally have a positive net social benefit, but that they have significantly different effects in downstream districts compared to the district where the dam is located. In downstream areas, agricultural production increases and poverty declines. In the district where the dam is located, agricultural production becomes more volatile and poverty increases. This shows that efforts to compensate the losers from dam construction have not been fully effective. Opposition to large dams is in part due to the difficulty in designing effective compensation mechanisms. Displacement and relocation to other areas has rarely proven satisfactory. Cash compensation tends to dissipate rapidly, leaving targeted populations in disarray and longer-term poverty. The World Commission on Dams (2000) has proposed guidelines to more effectively manage compensation schemes.

Electrification in Brazil, India, and South Africa using IV methods

What is the benefit of connecting a previously unconnected person to a power grid, and how does this benefit materialize? Because of program placement, electrification is endogenous. Identification of impacts uses IV techniques to exogenize electrification. Lipscomb *et al.* (2013) assessed the impact of electrification across Brazil between 1960 and 2000 and the channels through which impacts occur. They developed a national electricity-grid-construction model to predict the time and place where electrification investments would have been made had they been guided strictly by cost considerations. Using these predicted values as instrumented variables, they find that electrification has large growth effects. The main channel through which this occurs is through improvements in labor productivity. Rud (2012) estimated the impact of electrification on industrial development across Indian states in the 1965–84 period. He used the spread of the Green Revolution as a natural experiment. Electrification is predicted to expand more where there is a greater deficit in availability of groundwater irrigation (and hence a greater demand for electric pumps) at the start of the Green Revolution. He finds that electrification has a large impact on state-level manufacturing output. Finally, Dinkelman (2011) estimates the impact of rural electrification on employment growth in South Africa. Project placement in a community is instrumented by land gradient. Assuming that the land gradient does not directly affect economic outcomes, she finds that electrification raises employment, principally by releasing women from home production and boosting micro-enterprise start-ups.

Road and railway construction in China using IV methods

Do roads and railroads contribute to local industrial growth and to economic decentralization? Or is it decentralized local growth that creates profitable conditions for investment in infrastructure, with construction responding to economic opportunities? Over the long term, there is clear coincidence between infrastructure and growth, but which way does causality run? Can infrastructure investment be used to induce economic growth? Establishing causality is evidently essential in deciding on investment in infrastructure. With construction placement endogenous to outcomes, IV methods are used to predict placement. Banerjee *et al.* (2012) use road connections between historical cities as exogenous predictors of current proximity to modern transportation networks. They analyze distance to these transportation networks (using the so-called "straight line instrument," i.e. the distance to a straight line between cities) to estimate a causal effect on income and growth during the 1986–2006 period of rapid overall economic growth. They find that proximity to transportation infrastructure had a small causal effect on a locality's level of GDPpc but no effect on its growth. Places close to the road network grew exactly as fast as places further away! Infrastructure does not induce growth, unless there is a demand for it, a result found by historians such as Fogel (1962). Why is this the case? Banerjee *et al.* rationalize that lack of labor mobility due to government control (the Hukou system restricting free rural–urban migration by requiring residence permits for urban settlement) and low mobility of capital relative to goods imply that GDPpc differences between well and poorly connected areas are small (they all benefit from transportation of goods) and that there may be no difference in growth rates between these areas. This shows that infrastructure investment without factor mobility may be of limited growth value. The result has implications for infrastructure investment in other developing countries such as India where labor has notably low geographical mobility (Munshi and Rosenzweig, 2009).

Baum-Snow *et al.* (2012) use the same IV approach to look at the impact of road- and railroad-network expansion on the decentralization of economic activity over the last 20 years in China. They find that radial railroads and highways induced a displacement of both population and industrial GDP away from the center of cities toward their urban peripheries. In this sense, infrastructure investment helped cities decentralize population and economic activity to surrounding areas, if not toward distant places.

Impact of rural roads in Vietnam and India using a diff-in-diffs approach

Because they provide such important infrastructure services, roads are often thought of as having strong growth-multiplier effects. Mu and van de Walle (2011) study the impact on market development of Vietnam's road-rehabilitation program, financed by the World Bank. Identification is achieved by difference in differences between the periods before and after road rehabilitation, using matching methods to identify comparable counterfactual communes. The results show that roads have strong effects on the development of local markets, and that it is the poorer communes that are most impacted due to initially lower levels of market development.

A diff-in-diffs approach has also been used to analyze the impact of transportation infrastructure on the performance of manufacturing firms in India. The country implemented its Golden Quadrilateral Highway program to improve transportation between the country's four largest cities. A diff-in-diffs approach can be used to compare the performance of non-nodal districts based upon their distance from the highway system. Using the World Bank Enterprise Surveys for India, Datta (2012) finds that firms in cities with improved transportation reduced their input inventories between 6 and 12 days' worth of production, the more so the closer their location to an improved highway. Ghani *et al.* (2013) also find positive effects on non-nodal firms. Gains were both at the intensive margin, in the form of increases in plant productivity, and at the extensive margin, in the form of a spread of economic activity toward intermediate cities.

Analyzing the benefits of urban infrastructure through an RCT

It is notably difficult to randomize the placement of construction projects. As a result, most impact evaluations of infrastructure projects have been done through natural experiments or IV methods. Gonzalez-Navarro and Quintana-Domeque (2012) were able to randomize the implementation of street-paving projects in the residential neighborhoods of a Mexican city by drawing randomly from a list of 56 candidate projects. Due to budget constraints, the city government could not pave all the streets deemed suitable at the same time, and agreed to randomize for the sake of fairness. The authors conducted a baseline and a follow-up survey of resident households, with street pavement happening in the intervening period. They found that street paving had a large effect on house values (+16 percent), on land value (+54 percent), and on rents paid (+31 percent) compared to the non-paved streets. This led to an increase in the consumption of durable goods, especially motor vehicles. The increase came about through two channels: one was the increase in real-estate wealth, which allowed access to collateralized borrowing and through this to finance for durable-goods purchases; the other was a direct increase in the marginal utility of vehicles due to greater ease of use. In the end, the benefit/cost ratio of construction was estimated at 1.09, justifying investment in the project.

CONCEPTS SEEN IN THIS CHAPTER

Development triangle
Functionalist theory of the state
Social planner
Pluralist theory of the state
Collective choice: interest-group competition
Public choice: median-voter theorem
Hirschman's exit vs. voice and loyalty strategies
Core-supporter vs. swing-voter models
Rent-seeking competition
Directly unproductive activities
Failed state
Predatory state
Lobbying
Corruption and patronage
Forensic economics
Instruments to limit rent-seeking
Democracy and autocracy
State autonomy
Electoral accountability
Time inconsistency and commitment device

REFERENCES

Acemoglu, Daron, and James Robinson. 2012. *Why Nations Fail: The Origins of Power, Prosperity, and Poverty.* New York: Crown Business.

Acemoglu, Daron, Simon Johnson, and James Robinson. 2001. "The Colonial Origins of Comparative Development: An Empirical Investigation." *American Economic Review* 91(5): 1369–401.

Acemoglu, Daron, Simon Johnson, James Robinson, and Pierre Yared. 2008. "Income and Democracy." *American Economic Review* 98(3): 808–42.

Adelman, Irma. 1999. "Lessons from (S) Korea." *Zagreb International Review of Economics and Business* 2(2): 57–71.

Akresh, Richard, and Damien de Walque. 2008. "Armed Conflict and Schooling: Evidence from the 1994 Rwandan Genocide." Working paper, Department of Economics, University of Illinois at Urbana-Champaign.

Arezki, Rabah, and Markus Brückner. 2012. "Commodity Windfalls, Democracy and External Debt." *Economic Journal* 122(561): 848–66.

Asher, Sam, and Paul Novosad. 2014. "Dirty Politics: Natural Resource Wealth and Politics in India." Working paper, Department of Economics, Oxford University.

Banerjee, Abhijit, Esther Duflo, and Nancy Qian. 2012. "On the Road: Transportation Infrastructure and Economic Growth in China." NBER Working Paper No. 17897, Economics Department, MIT.

Bardhan, Pranab, Sandip Mitra, Dilip Mookherjee, and Abhirup Sarkar. 2015. "Political Participation, Clientelism, and Targeting of Local Government Programs: Analysis of Survey Results from Rural West Bengal, India." In Jean-Paul Faguet and Caroline Pöschi (eds.), *Is Decentralization Good for Development?* Oxford: Oxford University Press.

Bardhan, Pranab. 1997. "Corruption and Development: A Review of Issues." *Journal of Economic Literature* 35(September): 1320–46

Bates, Robert. 1981. *Markets and States in Tropical Africa: The Political Basis of Agricultural Policy.* Berkeley, CA: University of California Press.

Baum-Snow, Nathanial, Vernon Henderson, Matthew Turner, and Qinghua Zhang. 2012. "Roads, Railroads and Decentralization of Chinese Cities." Working paper, Department of Economics, University of Toronto.

Besley, Timothy, and Robin Burgess. 2002. "The Political Economy of Government Responsiveness: Theory and Evidence from India." *Quarterly Journal of Economics* 117(4): 1415–51.

Bhagwati, N.J. 1982. "Directly Unproductive, Profit Seeking (DUP) Activities." *Journal of Political Economy* 90(5): 988–1002.

Blattman, Christopher, and Jeannie Annan. 2010. "The Consequences of Child Soldiering." *Review of Economics and Statistics* 93(4): 882–98.

Brollo, Fernanda, Tommaso Nannicini, Roberto Perotti, and Guido Tabellini. 2013. "The Political Resource Curse." *American Economic Review* 103(5): 1759–96.

Brückner, Markus, and Antonio Ciccone. 2010. "International Commodity Prices, Growth and the Outbreak of Civil War in Sub-Saharan Africa." *Economic Journal* 120(544): 519–34.

Casey, Katherine. 2014. "Crossing Party Lines: The Effects of Information on Redistributive Politics." Working paper, Stanford Graduate School of Business, Stanford University.

Cernea, Michael. 1999. *The Economics of Involuntary Resettlement: Questions and Challenges.* Washington, DC: World Bank.

Collier, Paul, and Anke Hoeffler. 1998. "On Economic Causes of Civil War." *Oxford Economic Papers* 50(4): 563–73.

Congleton, Roger. 2002. "The Median Voter Model." In C.K. Rowley and F. Schneider (eds.), *The Encyclopedia of Public Choice*, 707–12. Dordrecht: Kluwer Academic Press.

Cox, Gary, and Matthew McCubbins. 1986. "Electoral Politics as a Redistributive Game." *Journal of Politics* 48(2): 370–89.

Datta, Saugato. 2012. "The Impact of Improved Highways on Indian Firms." *Journal of Development Economics* 99(1): 46–57.

Davis, Donald, and David Weinstein. 2002. "Bones, Bombs, and Breakpoints: The Geography of Economic Activity." *American Economic Review* 92(5): 1269–89.

de Janvry, Alain, Frederico Finan, Elisabeth Sadoulet. 2012. "Local Electoral Incentives and Decentralized Program Performance." *Review of Economics and Statistics* 94(3): 672–85.

de Janvry, Alain, Marco Gonzalez-Navarro, and Elisabeth Sadoulet. 2014. "Are Land Reforms Granting Complete Property Rights Politically Risky? Electoral Outcomes of Mexico's Certification Program." *Journal of Development Economics* 110(September): 216–25.

Dell, Melissa. 2014. "Trafficking Networks and the Mexican Drug War." Working paper, Department of Economics, Harvard University.

Dinkelman, Taryn 2011. "The Effects of Rural Electrification on Employment: New Evidence from South Africa." *American Economic Review* 101(7): 3078–108.

Dixit, Avinash, and John Londregan. 1996. "The Determinants of Success of Special Interests in Redistributive Politics." *Journal of Politics* 58(4): 1132–55.

Duflo, Esther, and Rohini Pande. 2007. "Dams." *Quarterly Journal of Economics* 122(2): 601–46.

Easterly, William, and Ross Levine. 1997. "Africa's Growth Tragedy: Policies and Ethnic Divisions." *Quarterly Journal of Economics* 112(4): 1203–50.

Evans, Peter. 1995. *Embedded Autonomy: States and Industrial Transformation*. Princeton: Princeton University Press.

Fernández, Raquel, and Dani Rodrik. 1991. "Resistance to Reform: Status Quo Bias in the Presence of Individual-Specific Uncertainty." *American Economic Review* 81(5): 1146–55.

Ferraz, Claudio, and Frederico Finan. 2008. "Exposing Corrupt Politicians: The Effects of Brazil's Publicly Released Audits on Electoral Outcomes." *Quarterly Journal of Economics* 123(2): 703–45.

Ferraz, Claudio, and Frederico Finan. 2011. "Electoral Accountability and Corruption in Local Governments: Evidence from Audit Reports." *American Economic Review* 101(4): 1274–311.

Finan, Frederico. 2005. "Political Patronage and Local Development: Evidence from Brazil." Working paper, Department of Economics, University of California.

Fisman, Raymond. 2001. "Estimating the Value of Political Connections." *American Economic Review* 91(4): 1095–102.

Fisman, Raymond, and Edward Miguel. 2008. *Economic Gangsters: Corruption, Violence, and the Poverty of Nations*. Princeton, NJ: Princeton University Press.

Fogel, Robert. 1962. "A Quantitative Approach to the Study of Railroads in American Economic Growth: A Report of Some Preliminary Findings." *Journal of Economic History* 22(2): 163–97.

Freedom House. www.freedomhouse.org (accessed 2015).

Gerschenkron, Alexander. 1962. *Economic Backwardness in Historical Perspective: A Book of Essays*. Cambridge, MA: Harvard University Press.

Ghani, Ejaz, Arti Goswami, and William Kerr. 2013. "Highway to Success in India: The Impact of the Golden Quadrilateral Project for the Location and Performance of Manufacturing." Washington, DC: World Bank Policy Research Working Paper No. 6320.

Gonzalez-Navarro, Marco, and Climent Quintana-Domeque. 2012. "Paving Streets for the Poor: Experimental Analysis of Infrastructure Effects." Department of Economics, University of Toronto.

Hayami, Yujiro. 2009. "Social Capital, Human Capital and the Community Mechanism: Toward a Conceptual Framework for Economists." *Journal of Development Studies* 45(1): 96–123.

Hirschman, Albert. 1970. *Exit, Voice, and Loyalty: Responses to Decline in Firms, Organizations, and States*. Cambridge, MA: Harvard University Press.

Hirschman, Albert. 1984. *Getting Ahead Collectively: Grassroots Experiences in Latin America*. New York: Pergamon Press.

Hotelling, Harold. 1929. "Stability in Competition." *Economic Journal* 39(153): 41–57.

Karnani, Aneel. 2011. *Fighting Poverty Together: Rethinking Strategies for Business, Governments, and Civil Society to Reduce Poverty*. New York: Palgrave Macmillan.

Krueger, Anne (1974). "The Political Economy of the Rent-Seeking Society." *American Economic Review* 64(3): 291–303.

Laffer, Arthur. 2004. "The Laffer Curve: Past, Present, and Future." Washington, DC: The Heritage Foundation, Backgrounder #1765 on Taxes.

León, Gianmarco. 2012. "Civil Conflict and Human Capital Accumulation: The Long-term Effects of Political Violence in Peru." *Journal of Human Resources* 47(4): 991–1022.

Levitt, Steven. 1994. "Using Repeat Challengers to Estimate the Effect of Campaign Spending on Election Outcomes in the U.S. House." *Journal of Political Economy* 102(4): 777–98.

Lipscomb, Molly, Mushfiq Mobarak, and Tania Barham. 2013. "Development Effects of Electrification: Evidence from the Topographic Placement of Hydropower Plants in Brazil." *American Economic Journal: Applied* 5(2): 200–31.

Lipset, Seymour. 1959. "Some Social Requisites of Democracy: Economic Development and Political Legitimacy." *The American Political Science Review* 53(1): 69–105.

Mason, Nicole, and Jacob Ricker-Gilbert. 2013. "Disrupting Demand for Commercial Seed: Input Subsidies in Malawi and Zambia." *World Development* 45(C): 203–16.

Mason, Nicole, T.S. Jayne, and Nicolas van de Walle. 2013. "Fertilizer Subsidies and Voting Patterns: Political Economy Dimensions of Input Subsidy Programs." Working paper, Department of Agricultural, Food, and Resource Economics, Michigan State University.

Mauro, Paolo. 1995. "Corruption and Growth." *Quarterly Journal of Economics* 110(3): 681–712.

Miguel, Edward, and Gérard Roland. 2011. "The Long-run Impact of Bombing Vietnam." *Journal of Development Economics* 96(1): 1–15.

Miguel, Edward, Shanker Satyanath, and Ernest Sergenti. 2004. "Economic Shocks and Civil Conflict: An Instrumental Variables Approach." *Journal of Political Economy* 112(4): 725–53.

Mookherjee, Dilip, and I.P.L. Png. 1995. "Corruptible Law Enforcers: How Should They Be Compensated?" *Economic Journal* 105(428): 145–59.

Mu, Ren, and Dominique van de Walle. 2011. "Rural Roads and Local Market Development in Vietnam." *Journal of Development Studies* 47(5): 709–34.

Munshi, Kaivan, and Mark Rosenzweig. 2009. "Why is Mobility in India so Low? Social Insurance, Inequality, and Growth." Working paper, Department of Economics, Brown University.

Olken, Benjamin. 2007. "Monitoring Corruption: Evidence from a Field Experiment in Indonesia." *Journal of Political Economy* 115(2): 200–49.

Olson, Mancur. 1971. *The Logic of Collective Action: Public Goods and the Theory of Groups*. Cambridge, MA: Harvard University Press.

Olson, Mancur. 1993. "Dictatorship, Democracy, and Development." *American Political Science Review* 87(3): 567–76.

Papaioannou, Elias, and Gregorios Siourounis. 2008. "Democratisation and Growth." *Economic Journal* 118(2008): 1520–51.

Peltzman, Sam. 1992. "Voters as Fiscal Conservatives." *Quarterly Journal of Economics* 107(2): 327–61.

Pettersson-Lidbom, Per, and Björn Tyrefors. 2007. "The Policy Consequences of Direct versus Representative Democracy: A Regression-Discontinuity Approach." Working paper, Department of Economics, Stockholm University.

Reinikka, Ritva, and Jakob Svensson. 2004. "Local Capture: Evidence from a Central Government Transfer Program in Uganda." *Quarterly Journal of Economics* 119(2): 678–704.

Robinson, James, and Thierry Verdier. 2013. "The Political Economy of Clientelism." *Scandinavian Journal of Economics* 115(2): 260–91.

Rostow, Walt. 1960. *The Stages of Economic Growth: A Non-Communist Manifesto.* London: Cambridge University Press.

Rud, Juan Pablo. 2012. "Electricity Provision and Industrial Development: Evidence from India." *Journal of Development Economics* 97(2): 352–67.

Sen, Amartya. 1981. *Poverty and Famines: An Essay on Entitlements and Deprivation.* Oxford: Oxford University Press.

van de Walle, Nicholas. 2001. *African Economies and the Politics of Permanent Crisis, 1979–1999.* Cambridge: Cambridge University Press.

World Bank. 2003. *World Development Report 2004: Making Services Work for Poor People.* Washington, DC.

World Commission on Dams. 2000. *The Report of the World Commission on Dams.* www.unep.org/dams/WCD/report.asp (accessed 2015).

Wydick, Bruce. 2008. *Games in Economic Development.* Cambridge, MA: Cambridge University Press.

The economics of farm households

TAKE-HOME MESSAGES FOR CHAPTER 22

1. Farm households (also called family farmers, smallholders, or peasants) can be defined by Ellis' six conditions (activity, labor use, market integration, imperfect markets, role of the community, and position in society) or by their asset positions and corresponding labor-use strategies (sub-family farms with labor on- and off-farm, family farm with only on-farm labor, and small commercial farms with on-farm and hired labor).

2. When all markets work perfectly, production and consumption decisions are taken separately, with farm profits entering into the consumer budget constraint as the only link between the two decisions. When markets fail, production and consumption decisions are non-separable and taken jointly. A food-market failure forces the household to produce what it wants to consume; a labor-market failure forces it to adjust its production goals to its labor availability.

3. Transaction costs on food markets create categories of farm households that are net sellers, self-sufficient, and net buyers. A rise in food prices will benefit the first, leave the second unaffected, and hurt the last. A majority of smallholders are net buyers who were consequently hurt by the food crisis. In all cases, household food security importantly depends on production for home consumption.

4. A redistributive land reform can achieve both efficiency and equity gains if there is an inverse relation between total factor productivity and farm size. This inverse relation is more likely to hold if farming is labor-intensive with no economies of scale, giving residual claimant family labor a cost advantage over hired labor used on large farms. Efficiency gains allow for making the reform Pareto optimal after compensation.

5. The survival of the family farm depends on technological, institutional, political, and strategic innovations that attempt at compensating for the low asset endowments, the market failures, and the policy biases that are detrimental to its competitiveness, and on taking advantage of its unique labor-cost advantage and potential for community support.

6. With high risks in agriculture and risk aversion associated with poverty, risk-management and risk-coping strategies are important parts of rural household behavior. Both are costly for expected incomes and there are trade-offs between the two strategies.

Policy interventions such as weather insurance, flexible credit lines, and social-safety nets that help family farmers cope better with shocks and reduce the need for self-insurance can make major contributions to rural poverty reduction.

7. The intra-household decision-making process affects efficiency of the farm operation and welfare of each of the household members. In a bargaining (as opposed to unitary) set-up, the fallback option of women outside the household affects the level of influence they have over-production and consumption decisions, with strong implications for the welfare of children.

IMPORTANCE OF FARM HOUSEHOLDS

Farm households, also called family farmers, smallholders, and peasants, are one of the most important social categories in the world. Their numerical importance in developing countries is estimated to be some 400 million households, accounting for about 1.6 billion people, 30 percent of the LDC population, and nearly one quarter of humanity (World Bank, 2007). China alone has 200 million smallholder farmers, accounting for almost all the farmers in the country. As can be seen in Table 22.1, at a world scale, 73 percent of all farms have an area inferior to 1 ha and 85 percent under 2 ha. In China, 93 percent of all farms are under 1 ha, as are 62 percent in India and 53 percent in Africa. In Europe, 30 percent of all farms are less than 1 ha. Even in South America, where farms can be very large, 54 percent of all farms are less than 10 ha, which is considered small there (Bélières *et al.*, 2013). Clearly, at a world scale, smallholder farming dominates agriculture.

The evolution of farm size over time reflects the stage of the structural transformation countries are at. As can be seen in Figure 22.1, the number of holdings in India increased (from 62 million in 1950 to 120 million in 2000) under the pressure of population growth and insufficiently rapid urban migration. As a consequence, mean farm size continues to fall, from 2.2 to 1.3 ha, a dramatic decline. In Brazil, the number

Table 22.1 *Percentage distribution of farms by size, by region, and for the world. Based on 81 countries that account for two thirds of world population*

	Farm size (ha)					
	< 1	1–2	2–5	5–10	10–20	> 20
China	93	5	2	0	0	0
India	62	19	13	3	2	1
Africa	53	22	16	5	3	1
Europe	30	20	20	11	8	11
South America	13	12	18	11	12	34
World	73	12	9	3	1	2

Source: FAO, 2012.

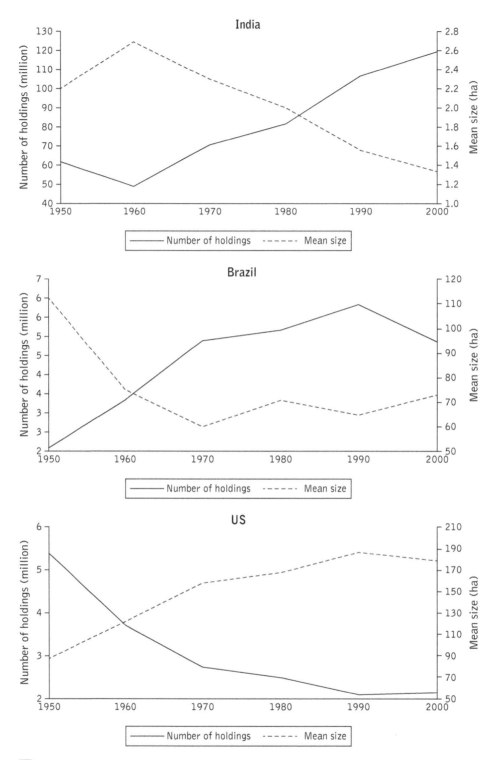

Figure 22.1 *Change in the number of holdings (left axis) and mean farm size (right axis) in India, Brazil, and the US, 1950 to 2000*

Source: FAO, 2012.

of holdings, which was rising until 1970, has stabilized around 5 million, with a mean size of 70 ha. In the US, where the structural transformation is complete, the number of holdings declined from 5.4 million in 1950 to 2 million in 2000, while farm size rose from 87 to 180 ha over that period.

In Sub-Saharan Africa, too, where the concept of farm is less well defined (land area per person in the rural population), land per person has been falling as structural transformation is delayed by lack of productivity growth in agriculture and insufficient labor-absorption capacity in the urban sector relative to population pressures in the rural sector (Figure 22.2).

The importance of smallholders is not only numerical, but also economic, social, and political.

In terms of economics, smallholders have a fundamental role to play in national agricultural production in most developing countries. In Sub-Saharan Africa and South Asia, the vast majority of farmers are smallholders. Successful agricultural growth thus depends on their entrepreneurship and competitiveness. Even in the US and Europe, where farmers can cultivate large farms, the vast majority of them are family farmers, with the family providing most of the labor and acting as residual claimant on farm profits.

In terms of social welfare, these households comprise the bulk of world poverty, and include the poorest of the poor. An estimated 75 percent of world poverty is rural, and a majority of these rural poor are smallholders, typically with insufficient land to feed themselves. Reducing rural poverty and improving food security among smallholders has thus been a *sine qua non* in successfully meeting the first MDG of halving poverty and hunger by 2015. Improving smallholders' welfare also benefits

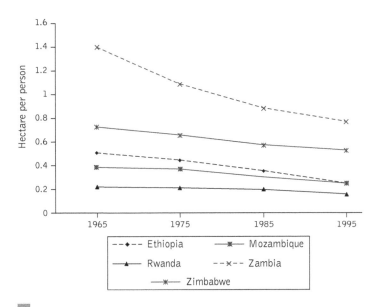

Figure 22.2 *Land area per person in Sub-Saharan Africa, selected countries, 1965–95*

Source: Jayne *et al.* (2005).

urban workers: the bulk of urban migrants are members of farm households who leave the land because of demographic pressures, lack of sufficient access to land or opportunities to raise yields, and lack of access to rural non-farm employment to secure their subsistence in the rural sector. These migrants, pushed by rural poverty, cram urban environments, lower unskilled-labor wages, and fill urban slums.

In terms of politics, farm households tend to be dominated by and subservient to other social classes (landlords, merchants, political and religious elites, urban dwellers), but they can have major roles to play, often in sporadic and unpredictable fashions (Wolf, 1965). The Mexican, Chinese, Cuban, and Vietnamese revolutions were all fought by peasants, even if rarely led by a peasant, with Mexico's Emiliano Zapata a notable exception. In Europe and Japan, the rural vote has a significant influence on electoral outcomes, and it is disproportionately represented in the US Senate, in spite of the low share of the population engaged in farming.

Given their economic, social, and political importance, it is fundamental for development to understand who these rural households are, what motivates their behavior, what determines their competitiveness as entrepreneurs and their welfare as consumers, and how their competitiveness and welfare can be improved. While smallholders are the main investors in their own farm operations, their incentives to invest depend on public and foreign-aid investments that complement their own. In addition, farm households do not act alone, but as members of communities. It is consequently also important to understand community behavior and how development agents can work with community organizations to support collective action. These questions are the subject of this chapter.

DEFINITIONS OF FARM HOUSEHOLDS

How do we define a household? While we have a general sense of what it means, there is no single accepted definition. For economists, a household is a group of people who jointly make decisions regarding production (or income generation), consumption, and reproduction (through demographic and investment decisions). Conceptualizing household behavior thus requires integrating the theory of consumer (and worker) behavior, with the theory of producer behavior (theory of the firm), and the theory of investment and demographic decisions with the determination of livelihood strategies. For anthropologists, the most commonly accepted definition of household is a group of people who eat together. This group can be quite small such as a nuclear family in Latin America, or very large such as an extended family in India, or a polygamous man with his several wives and their children in West Africa. Eating together means that members of a household do not have to be from the same family or be kin-related, although they most often are. It also means that family members who have migrated, but send remittances to the household, are not considered as household members. There are, however, cases, as in the new economics of migration (see Chapter 12), where household members who have migrated and send remittances need to be considered part of the household's livelihood strategy. So there is no rigid definition of the concept of household. The definition needs to be adjusted to the question analyzed and made explicit each time.

780

Having defined a household in general, there are characteristics that will specifically apply to farm households. There are two sets of characteristics that have been identified as defining a farm household: one is Ellis' six conditions, the other is a household's position in the labor market.

Peasant households according to Ellis

The term "peasant" (literally, country dweller) may sound pejorative in English, but it is not so in other languages, where family farmers proudly declare "peasant" as their profession when asked: *paysans* in France, *campesinos* in Mexico, *camponês* in Brazil, etc. Ellis (1994), in his book *Peasant Economics*, identifies six conditions that define a peasant household. Specifically, peasants households:

1. *Live mainly from agriculture*, broadly conceived to include pastoralism, forestry, and fishing. They all have access to natural capital (land, water, animals, trees) and use natural capital as the main asset for their livelihoods. They also engage in complementary activities in the rural non-farm economy (RNFE), the labor market, and migration. These off-farm engagements are often crucial to the survival of the family farm as an economically viable entity.
2. *Use mainly family labor* in production, hence the "family farm" connotation. Hired labor may be present, but it is a minority relative to family labor and is supervised by the family.
3. *Are partially integrated into markets* where they engage in multiple transactions, but they also have a certain degree of self-sufficiency in consumption (with production for home consumption) and in the self-provision of inputs (most particularly family labor for the farm, but also home-produced inputs such as open-pollinated seeds, animal manure for fertilizer, etc.).
4. *Participate in markets that are notably imperfect.* These markets have high transaction costs, imperfect and asymmetrical information, and lack competitiveness, typically with monopoly or monopsony power among merchants, money-lenders, and landlords. Markets where they sell surplus production are notably shallow, meaning that prices have a strong seasonal cycle and tend to fall sharply when there is a good harvest. Devising strategies to compensate for or bypass market imperfections is a central aspect of farm households' livelihood strategies.
5. *Are members of communities* that give them access to common property resources (forests, grazing lands, water, fishing grounds), mutual insurance (Scott, 1977), land and labor contracts, interlinked transactions (Bardhan, 2003), patron–client relations, the provision of local public goods, and voice in political affairs. The community can assist development but can also be a hurdle to entrepreneurship and individual success as a source of extraction by others, thereby diminishing investment and competitiveness, and of social conservatism, whereby net social-gain-creating innovations (such as new crops or the formation of producers' organizations) may be resisted to preserve the community's social cohesion (Hayami, 1996).

781

6. *Are part of a larger non-peasant society where they are dominated by other social classes.* According to Wolf (1965), no society has ever been dominated by peasants. Because they are dominated by other social classes, they typically suffer from surplus extraction (through taxation, forced labor, unfavorable terms of trade on markets, usurious interest rates), political domination (especially by the landlord class), religious credulity (hence the importance of cosmology, superstition, witchcraft, and myths in peasant folklore), and poverty (they account for the majority of the world poor). In this dominated position, peasant resistance to state control tends to use the "weapons of the weak," namely evasion, subterfuge, and foot dragging rather than voice and direct confrontation (Scott, 1985).

Family farmers based on labor-market participation: a price-band model

Family farmers can also be defined by the labor strategy they use in production relative to other types of rural household (Figure 22.3) (Eswaran and Kotwal, 1986). The labor strategy is determined by the household's asset endowment and transaction costs on the labor market (Sadoulet and de Janvry, 1995; see a formal model in the next section). The labor market offers a wage w, but the household incurs transaction costs when selling or hiring labor. When selling labor, the wage received is $w - TCs$, where TCs is the unit transaction cost in taking labor from the farm to the market. TCs will thus include such costs as transportation, search for an employer, interviewing, and failed attempts at finding a job. When hiring labor, the wage paid is $w + TCh$, where TCh is the unit transaction cost in taking labor from the market to the farm. TCh will include such costs as screening workers, paying for their transportation, supervising their work, and litigating in case of conflict.

In this model, there is a population of rural households with differentiated land endowments ranging from $A1$ (small farm) to $A6$ (large farm). The corresponding households demand an amount of labor to cultivate their land that rises from $D1(A1)$ to $D6(A6)$ as farm size A increases (Figure 22.3). The labor supply of all households is represented by the upward sloping line. A household with farm $A2$ and a demand for labor for that farm equal to $D2(A2)$ will work "on" the farm until its value marginal product of labor equals the wage it can earn on the labor market (where the labor-demand line intersects the horizontal wage-paid-in-selling line), and sell the excess supply of family labor on the labor market as "off" farm labor. A household with demand $D4(A4)$ will neither sell nor buy labor because, at the wage it could receive on the labor market, its demand is higher than the supply, and, at the wage it would have to offer a hired worker, its demand is lower than its supply. It is self-sufficient in labor and its shadow wage (implicit wage) for family labor is higher than when selling labor, and lower than when hiring labor. A household with demand $D6(A6)$ will work "on" the farm and meet the remaining demand for labor by "hiring in." Family time is also used to supervise these hired workers. These labor strategies according to asset positions are summarized in Table 22.2, enabling us to identify five categories of household. The asset position (farm size) thus defines the household's social-class position based on the labor-market strategy it uses (Roemer, 1998).

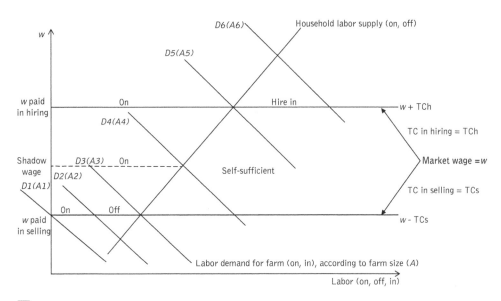

Figure 22.3 *Categories of farm household according to land endowments*

Table 22.2 *Social classes and family farms: sub-family, family, and small commercial*

| Social class | Family labor use | | | | |
	Farm size (assets)	Farm labor demand	Off-farm	On-farm	Hire in and supervise
Landless worker	< A1	< D1	++	0	0
Sub-family farm	A1 to A3	D1 to D3	+	+	0
Pure family farm	A3 to A5	D3 to D5	0	+	0
Small commercial farm	A5 to A6	D5 to D6	0	+	+
Large commercial farm	> A6	> D6	0	+	++

Among these five categories of household, there are three (shaded in Table 22.2) that can be considered family farms:

- *Sub-family farms*: household members work both on and off farm.
- *Pure family farms*: the household is self-sufficient in labor.
- *Small commercial farms*: household members work on the farm and also hire in labor, with the number of hired workers less than the number of working family members. This last rule on hired labor relative to family labor is somewhat arbitrary, and is used to place an upper limit on the small commercial farm category.

There are two categories of non–family farm:

- *Landless workers*: they own an insufficient amount of land (generally none) to make it worthwhile to produce, and only work off-farm on the labor market.

■ *Large commercial farms*: they hire in more labor than they use of family labor. Family labor is increasingly supervisory of hired labor as opposed to being directly engaged in farm labor.

This labor-based definition of family farm corresponds with Ellis' definition of peasants in that Ellis' first four features are satisfied: (1) live mainly from agriculture, (2) use mainly family labor, (3) are partially integrated into labor markets, with at least some labor used for home production, and (4) these markets are imperfect as they have transaction costs and completely fail for self-sufficient farmers.

Differentiated labor-allocation responses to an increase in wage

We can use this price-band model to predict the labor reallocation that will occur in response to an increase in the market wage. The wage increase shifts the wage band upward as shown in Figure 22.4. The labor reallocation that this induces is given in Table 22.3.

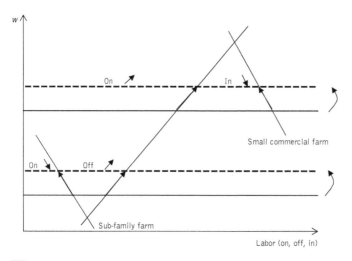

Figure 22.4 *Differentiated responses to a rise in the market wage*

Table 22.3 *Labor reallocation in response to a rise in the market wage*

	Off-farm	On-farm	Hire in and supervise	Total work by the household	Total labor applied to the farm
Sub-family farm	+	−	0	+	−
Family farm	0	0	0	0	0
Small commercial farm	0	+	−	+	−

Note: Signs indicate whether the corresponding labor category increases (+), decreases (−), or does not change (0).

■ **784**

As the wage rises, the sub-family farm delivers more off-farm work, and absorbs less on-farm labor. For these farm households, a higher wage is an income opportunity. The change in on-farm work is the opposite for the small commercial farm: this household works more on-farm and hires fewer workers because they have become more expensive. For them, a higher wage is a cost. Households within the wage band are unaffected by the change in wage. It is thus important to take into account household heterogeneity in analyzing the response to a change in wage as sub-family and small commercial farm households respond in opposite ways.

FARM-HOUSEHOLD-BEHAVIOR MODELS

The labor supply and demand functions used above for defining categories of household derive from a structural model of household behavior that we will now develop. The farm household is an economic unit that must make both production and consumption decisions (leaving the dynamics of reproduction decisions aside for the moment). We therefore combine the theory of the firm in deciding on labor allocation to the farm and the theory of consumer behavior in deciding how to allocate time between work and leisure. The household maximizes a utility function where both income Y and leisure T_Z contribute to utility, $U(Y, T_Z)$. It has a fixed land endowment $\bar{A}$ and a total time endowment T. This total time can be allocated to work L_S or to leisure T_Z. Time allocated to work in turn can be allocated to the farm (T_F) or to the labor market (T_W). On the farm, family labor may be complemented by hired labor (L_{IN}) to reach a total labor input L. The return to labor is given by the production function for given technology and land endowment, $Q(L, \bar{A})$. On the labor market, we consider the general case where the wage received by family labor w_S is possibly lower than the wage w_H paid to hired labor. This is a simplified way of accounting for transaction costs in finding and commuting to work, or of the disutility that working for others may inflict, or, on the hiring side, the need to supervise hired workers that are less self-motivated than family labor. In a perfectly functioning labor market these two wages are equal. Income for the household derives from the sale of farm output Q at a price p and from the sale of labor T_W at the going wage w_S, net of the cost of hiring in outside labor,

$$Y = pQ + w_S T_W - w_H L_{IN}.$$

The decision tree in using household time and hired labor is thus as shown in Figure 22.5.

The farm household behavior model can thus be formulated as follows:

$$Max_{T_F, T_W, T_Z, L_{IN}} U(Y, T_Z),$$

where

$$Y = pQ + w_S T_W - w_H L_{IN}, \quad \text{income equation}$$

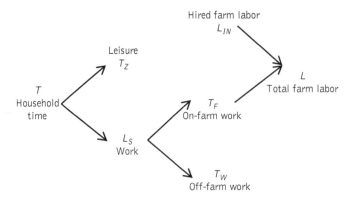

Figure 22.5 *Allocation of household time and hired farm labor*

$$Q = Q(L, \bar{A}), \quad \text{production function,}$$

subject to an accounting identity

$$L = T_F + L_{IN}, \quad \text{total farm labor use}$$

and a constraint

$$T_F + T_W + T_Z = T, \quad \text{household time constraint.}$$

Solving this model leads to the five categories of household we saw in the previous section, defined by a household's relative endowments of land and labor. Because hiring workers is more expensive than the wage that family members can get on the labor market (this is assuming all workers are identical and perfectly substitutable), the solution will never lead to simultaneous working off-farm and hiring workers. The different categories correspond to different endowments of land relative to family labor. The solutions are represented in Figure 22.6.

1. *Consumer–worker household* (Figure 22.6.1). This is a landless household with no land endowment. The model corresponds to the theory of consumer behavior.
    The behavioral model for this household is:

    $$Max_{T_W, T_Z} U(Y, T_Z),$$

    subject to: $T_W + T_Z = T$,   time constraint

    $\qquad\qquad\qquad Y = w_s T_W$,   income equation.

2. *Pure producer* (Figure 22.6.2). This is the case of a farmer who only uses hired labor. His own family's labor is entirely allocated to leisure (or activities not considered

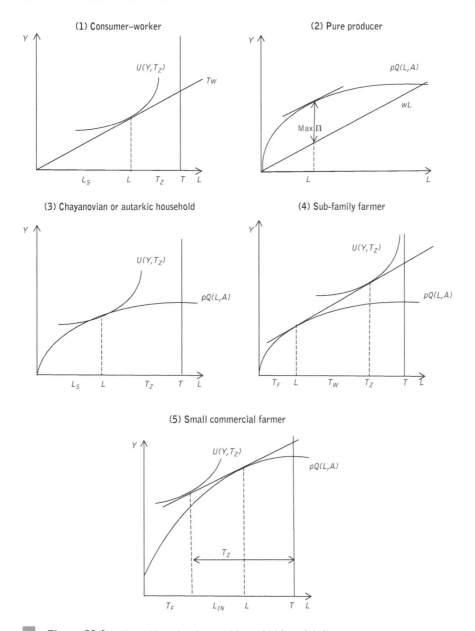

Figure 22.6 *Labor allocation in rural household models by type*

in this simple model). Maximizing utility is thus equivalent to maximizing restricted profit Π. The model corresponds to the theory of the firm:

$$Max_L \Pi = pQ - w_H L,$$

subject to: $Q = Q(L, \bar{A})$, production function.

3. *Chayanovian pure family farmer* (Figure 22.6.3). This is the case of a family farm with no labor market, or within the price band for a labor market with transaction costs. It has enough land that the marginal productivity of its family labor on the farm is above the opportunity cost w_S of going to the labor market, but not quite as high as the cost w_H of hiring additional workers. Thus the household must be self-sufficient in labor use. This is the model described by Alexander Chayanov (1966) in his interpretation of the behavior of the Russian peasantry that is "self-exploiting" family labor.

$$Max_{T_F, T_Z} U(Y, T_Z),$$

subject to: $Q = Q(T_F, \bar{A}),$ production function
$Y = pQ,$ income equation
$T_F + T_Z = T,$ time constraint.

4. *Sub-family farmer* (Figure 22.6.4). This is the case of a household with a large number of working-age members and a small land endowment. It will allocate surplus farm labor to the labor market in the following behavioral model:

$$Max_{T_F, T_W, T_Z} U(Y, T_Z),$$

subject to: $Q = Q(T_F, \bar{A}),$ production function
$Y = pQ + w_S T_W,$ income equation
$T_F + T_W + T_Z = T,$ time constraint.

5. *Small commercial farmer* (Figure 22.6.5). This household has a large land endowment relative to its number of working-age members. It will hire in labor to compensate for the deficit in family labor:

$$Max_{T_F, T_Z, L_{IN}} U(Y, T_Z),$$

subject to: $Q = Q(L, \bar{A}),$ production function
$Y = pQ - w_H L_{IN},$ income equation
$L = T_F + L_{IN},$ total farm labor use
$T_F + T_Z = T,$ time constraint.

RESPONSES TO MARKET SIGNALS: SEPARABILITY

In all the categories above, except for the pure family farmer, the household uses the labor market, either to sell its own labor or to hire workers, meaning that the opportunity cost of its labor is a market wage. And we have assumed the existence of a perfect market for its production, allowing the producer to sell all its output and purchase whatever it wants to consume with its income at the going market price. In these cases, where all markets work for the household, there is *separability* between production and consumption decisions. This means that the household behaves as if it was first a producer who maximizes profits and then a consumer who maximizes utility under a budget constraint. Consumption decisions include both the consumption of goods under the budget constraint, and the consumption of leisure (time not worked). The only link between production and consumption decisions is through farm profits that enter into the budget constraint that limits consumption decisions (Figure 22.7a) (Singh *et al.*, 1986). If in addition there is no transaction cost on labor, the land is *efficiently* used (as always when there are perfect markets). The level of assets owned by the household does not affect efficiency, but it does affect *equity*: the level of profit derived from farm production depends on the size of the farm.

When markets fail or are not used by a household, as in the case of the pure Chayanovian farmer household, production, and consumption decisions become one single interrelated problem (Figure 22.7b). If there is no market for labor, the level of leisure that the household decides to enjoy determines the amount of labor that will be available for production on the farm. This would also be the case if, for example, there is no market for food, and the food that the household decides to produce is what it will be able to consume. In this case, there is *non-separability* between production and consumption decisions. The household behaves as if it had an internal market for the food that it cannot purchase or for the labor that it cannot trade on the market and made decisions based on a shadow price that equates its marginal utility in consumption to its marginal productivity in production.

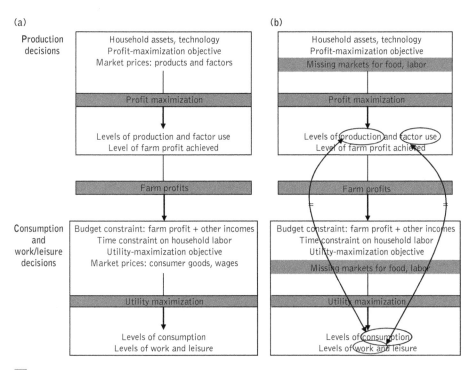

Figure 22.7 *Household production and consumption decisions under separability (a) and non-separability (b)*

What are the implications of non-separability on how the household responds to market-price signals? Say that the household produces both a food and a cash crop, and that the price of the cash crop rises, perhaps due to trade liberalization or a depreciation of the real exchange rate. If there is no market for food (or there are very high transaction costs on the food market), the household will be restrained in specializing in cash-crop production to take advantage of the higher price as it must continue to dedicate a significant amount of its resources to food production in order to eat. As a result, the elasticity of its cash-crop-supply response will be lower than if it could use the food market to buy food, allowing it to specialize in production. To the policy-maker, the farm household may appear unresponsive to price, but this is not due to non-economic behavior, it is due to the food-market failure. Similarly, if there is no labor market, the household's response to a higher cash-crop price will be muted: it can only increase labor applied to production of the cash crop by sacrificing its own leisure, precisely at a time when it is better off due to a higher cash-crop price. Again, the household appears unresponsive to price incentives, but this is due to market failure, not to lack of desire to respond to market signals. Whether peasants are *homo economicus* or not has been a subject of intense controversy in anthropology, between the *formalists* (who claimed that they are) and the *substantivists* (who claimed that they are not) (Forman, 1970). The result reported here shows that one can be a formalist (yes, peasants are motivated by price incentives) and yet agree with the substantivist observation that these households do not respond much to price (but not as a consequence of their presumed non-economic behavior). It is not lack of response to market signals that keeps supply response low, but the fact that markets notably fail smallholders in enabling them to respond to prices (de Janvry *et al.*, 1991).

NET BUYERS, NET SELLERS, AND FOOD SECURITY

The 2008 food crisis was due to a sharp increase in the price of food. The logical presumption is that farm households, as producers of food, should benefit. This, however, may not be true. Some farm households are net sellers who will benefit from a higher price of food, others are self-sufficient and not affected by a change in price if they remain in self-sufficiency, and yet others are net buyers and will lose from a higher food price. It is surprising that a majority of smallholders are net buyers of cereals, the price of which rose during the food crisis. As can be seen in Table 22.4, more than half of smallholders tend to be net buyers, reaching 73 percent in Ethiopia, 74 percent in India, 93 percent in the Peruvian Sierra, and 97 percent in Guatemala, with an unweighted average across the 11 countries covered of 64 percent. As a consequence, a majority of smallholders were hurt by rising prices. We estimated that, among the poor who lost from rising food prices, as many as 44 percent were farmers in India, 65 percent in Guatemala, and 73 percent in the Peruvian Sierra (de Janvry and Sadoulet, 2009, 2010).

Another example of differentiated price response is the case of NAFTA (North American Free Trade Agreement) between Canada, the US, and Mexico that lowered the price of corn for Mexican farmers as cheap corn was imported freely from the US. To compensate farmers for this negative price shock, Mexico introduced the PROCAMPO program, consisting of direct cash transfers decoupled from current

Table 22.4 *Net-buyer smallholders: percentage in the corresponding category*

Country	Category	Commodity	Net buyers %	Source
Sub-Saharan Africa				
Zambia	Smallholders	Staples	46	World Bank (2007)
Mozambique	Smallholders	Maize	63	Jayne et al. (2006)
Kenya	Smallholders	Maize	62	Jayne et al. (2006)
Ethiopia	Smallholders	Maize & teff	73	Jayne et al. (2006)
Latin America				
Guatemala	Smallholders	Maize	97	de Janvry and Sadoulet (2010)
Bolivia	Smallholders	Staples	70	World Bank (2007)
Peru Sierra	Farmers	Maize	93	de Janvry and Sadoulet (2009)
Asia				
India	Smallholders	Rice	74	de Janvry and Sadoulet (2009)
Bangladesh	Smallholders	Staples	59	World Bank (2007)
Vietnam	Smallholders	Staples	40	World Bank (2007)
Cambodia	Smallholders	Staples	32	World Bank (2007)
All above				
Unweighted average			64	

Staples include rice, wheat, maize, and beans.

production and proportional to the area previously planted with basic crops, particularly corn, before the trade agreement. Who gained and lost from the combination of NAFTA and PROCAMPO? We analyze this second case as follows.

In Figure 22.8, the corn market has price bands as there are transaction costs in bringing corn from the farm to the market as a net seller (TCs) and from the market to the farm as a net buyer (TCb). We represent a demand curve for home consumption of corn. Households have corn-supply curves that depend on their farm size, making them either net buyers, self-sufficient, or net sellers of corn. When the market price of corn falls, net sellers produce less and sell less; net buyers produce less and buy more. The income effect of NAFTA is thus positive on net buyers and negative on net sellers. All farmers receive a PROCAMPO transfer, even if they are not selling corn. As can be seen in Table 22.5, the net effect of NAFTA and PROCAMPO is thus a double net gain for net buyers, a gain for self-sufficient farmers, and a loss for net sellers (although mitigated by PROCAMPO). If net buyers and self-sufficient farmers are the poor, the joint NAFTA–PROCAMPO policy package both reduced poverty and increased equity across farm households. While the impact of NAFTA on Mexican farm households has been much vilified, a detailed analysis shows that impacts have been quite differentiated across categories of household and that the poor may have gained. The key to this more balanced assessment is to recognize that not all farmers are net sellers, but that many of them are either net buyers or self-sufficient. Recognizing heterogeneity and looking at the corresponding incidence of gains and losses from a policy reform can thus yield useful surprises.

It is notable that all farm households, be they net sellers, net buyers, or self-sufficient in food, rely importantly on production for their home food consumption. This is

791

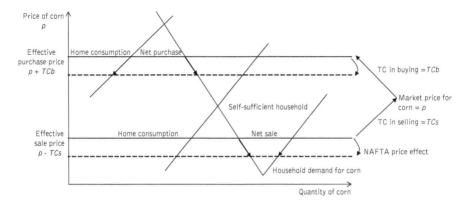

Figure 22.8 *Farm-household responses to a decline in the price of corn under NAFTA*

Table 22.5 *Real income effects of NAFTA and PROCAMPO on Mexican farm households*

Farm-household category		NAFTA: decline in the price of corn	PROCAMPO: cash transfer proportional to area	Incidence analysis: real income effect of NAFTA and PROCAMPO
Poor	Net buyers	+	+	+ +
	Self-sufficient	0	+	+
Non-poor	Net sellers	−	+	−

because transaction costs in selling and buying make it more advantageous to meet the household's demand for food out of their own production. Smallholders' food security thus depends on their capacity to produce food. As we saw in Chapter 14, production for home consumption offers an important social-safety net for this population, which includes a majority of the hungry in the world. Investing public resources in smallholder farming, even at the cost of a subsidy to private investment, thus has an important social justification: it saves on other more costly forms of social assistance in reducing hunger. This role of investment in smallholder farming has, for this reason, been stressed by the United Nations Committee on World Food Security (HLPE, 2013) as an important policy instrument in reducing hunger.

ACCESS TO LAND: THE ROLE OF LAND REFORM

Smallholder farmers largely define themselves by lack of sufficient access to land to need to hire farm labor. For many of them, this implies incapacity to generate a marketed surplus, of achieving food security, and of escaping poverty. We saw in Table 22.1 that 94 percent of landholders have less than 5 ha of land. In China, 93 percent of holdings have less than 1 ha, as do 62 percent in India, and farm size is declining in these countries. While access to land cannot be used to classify farmers because of heterogeneity of land quality, insufficient access to land is a clear feature common to the majority of smallholder farmers.

Redistributing land currently in large farms to a large number of family farms has the objective not only of achieving gains in *equity*, but also potentially in *efficiency*. This is a highly controversial issue, and reform has rarely occurred peacefully. The Mexican land reform that distributed large *haciendas* to *ejidos*, where community members each had usufruct over a small plot of land, was an outcome of the revolution of 1910 that left 1 million people dead. In Peru, the military regime expropriated *haciendas* (Albertus, 2015). Massive redistributive land reforms in Taiwan and South Korea that broke large farms into family farms were undertaken after World War Two under US military occupation. What is the theory behind expecting gains from this? Under what conditions will redistributing land toward the poor in family farms create not only equity gains, but also efficiency gains? It depends on whether or not an inverse relation between total factor productivity (TFP) (or, more simply, yield) and farm size holds (see Chapter 6). This in turn depends on the nature of the market failures that affect agriculture.

If there is an inverse relation between farm size and land productivity, as claimed, for example, by Lipton (2009) in his rationalization for land reform, the reform is win–win, as can be seen in Figure 22.9: family farms have higher productivity than large farms, and equality in the distribution of assets has been increased. The reform can also be Pareto optimal after compensation, as small farmers could compensate large farmers for their losses and keep for themselves the productivity gains achieved. When will such an inverse relation prevail?

Hired labor suffers from problems of adverse selection and moral hazard, a problem that does not affect family labor, where members are residual claimants on the fruits of their work efforts. Large farms are thus at a disadvantage in the labor market, as they have to resort to expensive mechanisms for inducing hard work such as supervision, high wages, and the threat of laying off workers who are found shirking. On the other

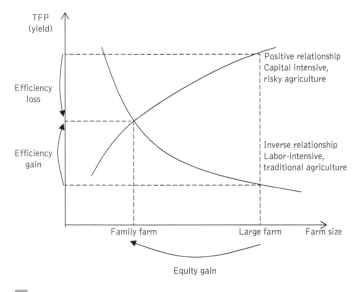

Figure 22.9 *Efficiency and equity effects of a redistributive land reform*

hand, large farms are typically at an advantage on the capital and insurance markets. There may also exist economies of scale in farming due to the existence of large indivisible factors such as management in, for example, precision farming.

Which of these factors dominates determines whether there is a positive relationship or an inverse relationship between farm size and TFP (Figure 22.9). The inverse relationship is more likely to hold if agriculture is labor-intensive and traditional (low-risk), so that other factor market failures such as for credit and insurance do not differentially hurt family farmers, and there are no economies of scale in production. Under these circumstances, there is complementarity (win–win) between efficiency (yield increase) and equity (more egalitarian distribution of the land). Land reform that redistributes land from large to family farms can achieve both efficiency and equity gains.

Note that if the land market is working perfectly for all households, it should achieve the same outcome of concentrating land at the most efficient farm size through freely decided land-market transactions. An approach to land reform would thus consist in making the land market work, and channeling real-estate credit to the poor so they can bid on land. This is the essence of the *land-market-assisted land reform* approach. If land is overpriced because it fulfills functions other than income generation (such as providing social status, offering a shelter for wealth against inflation, and providing tax breaks in agriculture), a subsidy is also needed to help the poor pay the extra value of the land not beneficial to them (Deininger, 2003). This approach has been extensively pursued in Brazil in the *Credito Fundiário* program. It was introduced with support from the World Bank to complement the redistributive land-reform program implemented by the Brazilian Land Reform Agency (INCRA), which expropriates underused large farms following land invasions organized by the Landless Workers' Movement (MST).

South Africa implemented a land-market-assisted land reform in its Land Redistribution for Agricultural Development program. The welfare effect of this program is analyzed by Keswell and Carter (2014). They identify the impact of access to land by using (exogenous) administrative delays in being granted access to land, creating the equivalent of a roll-out with variation in the duration of time over which beneficiaries had been using the land by the time of the study. They find that there is an initial drop in living standards, but that after 3–4 years they rise to 50 percent above the pre-transfer level. Lags in gains are attributed to the time needed for beneficiaries to invest and learn.

If, however, agriculture is capital-intensive and risky, and the capital- and insurance-market advantages of large farms dominate over their labor-cost disadvantage (Figure 22.9), a redistributive land reform will create equity gains but at an efficiency cost: there is a trade-off between efficiency and equity. Since this is likely to be the case in many situations today, a redistributive land reform must be *complete*, complementing land redistribution with institutional reforms in credit, insurance, marketing, and producer organizations in order to make the beneficiary family farmers competitive. A successful complete land reform is thus difficult to implement (Warriner, 1969). Access to land may be the relatively easy part, while securing the competitiveness of beneficiaries—a *sine qua non* for the land reform to be sustainable—requires multiple institutional reforms that are difficult to achieve.

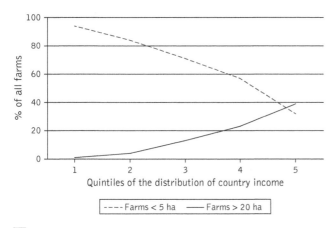

Figure 22.10 *Share of small (< 5ha) and large (> 20ha) farms across quintiles of the distribution of countries by per capita income level in the 2000 World Census of Agriculture*

Source: Based on data from Adamopoulos and Restuccia, 2011.

It is also important to note that, while an inverse relation between TFP and farm size may exist, per capita income tends to rise with farm size. Enlarging farm size is thus essential for reducing poverty and bridging the income gap between rural and urban environments. Using data from the World Census of Agriculture, Adamopoulos and Restuccia (2011) show in Figure 22.10 that countries in the lowest GDPpc quintile have a farm-size distribution dominated by small farms (94 percent of their farms are less than 5 ha), while countries in the highest GDPpc quintile have a distribution dominated by large farms (39 percent of their farms are more than 20 ha). For countries like India, allowing land concentration requires overcoming two fundamental challenges: reducing rural demographic growth and enhancing successful migration out of agriculture. China has overcome these two challenges and should see farm size increase, helping reduce the rural–urban income gap. Land concentration allows mechanization and rising labor productivity, the main source of gains in per capita farm incomes. Foster and Rosenzweig (2010) thus argue that farm size in India should rise to 20 acres, implying that 20 percent of the current farm labor force is surplus and would need to be relocated elsewhere.

CAN THE FAMILY FARM BE COMPETITIVE AND SURVIVE

One of the oldest and most politically charged controversies on the social structure of agriculture is whether the family farm will compete and survive, or whether it will be displaced by large-scale commercial farms making use of hired labor. This is the debate on the future of the family farm (see for example Hazell *et al.*, 2006). If large farms prevail, then a few family farmers may become large commercial farmers, but the majority of today's family farmers will become landless farm workers, work in the RNFE, or migrate to the city. Given urban overcrowding, and the difficulty of absorbing enough workers in the formal urban sector (see Chapter 12), this is a debate of fundamental importance. Ultimately, the structural transformation of the economy has to prevail, with a sharply declining share of the labor force in agriculture, and concentration of the land in the hands of the better farmers, allowing economies of scale in production and marketing, rising labor productivity through mechanization, and higher incomes in agriculture. However, key to social welfare is the pace at which land concentration may occur relative to the labor-absorption capacity of the non-agricultural sectors. If it is too rapid, displaced farm labor will accumulate in urban slums; if it is too slow, rural poverty will be reproduced and rural–urban income disparities will grow. Securing the competitiveness of the family farm without excessively rapid land concentration in relation to employment creation in the non-farm economy is thus a necessity for both efficiency and rural welfare (World Bank, 2007). Countries like Brazil have been quite successful at managing a balance between the emergence of very large commercial farms and the preservation of a large number of smallholder farmers. This large farm–small farm coexistence or competition is a hotly debated issue for Sub-Saharan Africa today, where extensive tracks of land are still underused relative to potential (Deininger and Byerlee, 2011). Many of these areas are currently being made accessible and linked to markets by roads constructed to access mining sites (Weng *et al.*, 2013). Large land concessions are eventually made to domestic and foreign investors in what has often been referred to as a land grab. Does this threaten the future of the family farm, or does the Brazilian example suggest ways to achieve efficient complementarities between small and large farms?

The differential advantage of the family farm is its lower labor cost. However, the competitiveness of the family farm is compromised by a host of market failures that differentially affect family farmers compared to larger commercial farmers. Few smallholders have access to financial services, and they face high transaction costs on markets. Governments can also fail the family farm, providing public services such as research and extension that are biased toward large farmers (as we have seen, for example, in the theory of induced technological innovations in Chapter 18). Playing fields are typically not level for the family farm, even when there may be no economies of scale in farming (Carter and Barham, 1996). There are also structural changes in food-value chains that threaten the competitiveness of the family farm in the domestic market. The rise of supermarkets in food retailing has changed conditions of access to markets for smallholders (Reardon *et al.*, 2003). Supermarkets demand large volumes in delivery, strict sanitary and quality standards, and traceability in production, all of which may be difficult for smallholders to achieve without strong producers' organizations. The survival of the family farm is thus an exercise in ingeniousness in devising solutions to the extensive and differential market and government failures that compromise its competitiveness, and to the rapidly changing context in which they have to compete for their existence.

The high cost of displaced distortions

To be competitive and survive, family farmers need to devise effective strategies to compensate for market, government, and coordination failures. These responses displace distortions on to other product and factor markets and lead to patterns of behavior and asset use that may appear totally irrational if assessed against a context of perfect markets and level playing fields (Barrett, 2005). We give here two examples of displaced distortions, when family farmers face credit-market failures, leading to second-best behavior in product markets. The first is selling at low price and buying at high price on the grain market: the opposite of standard economic arbitrage. The second is farming for others at the peak of planting and harvesting season, reducing labor allocation to and yields on one's own farm.

Selling low and buying high

In local food markets, due to high transaction costs in linking local to global markets, prices vary considerably with seasonality. In Kenya (Burke, 2014), prices are low at harvest time in August–September, and farmers expect them to rise by 100 percent over the next nine months, peaking in June–July during the hungry season, before any harvesting starts again in August (Figure 22.11). Similarly, Kaminski *et al.* (2014) report that national wholesale maize prices increased on average over the period 2000–2012 by 25 percent in Uganda and Tanzania and 50 percent in Malawi in the three to five months following harvest. This suggests that there are opportunities for inter-temporal arbitrage, storing grains (even buying at low price for additional storage) at harvest time and selling later at high prices. This is not what we see, creating an arbitrage puzzle: why do farmers sell at low price at harvest time to buy back six to nine months later at a very high price? This may be due to lack of access to credit, and

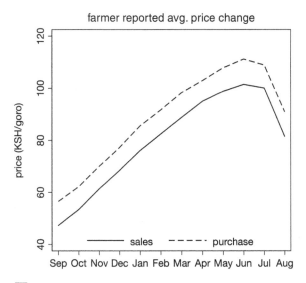

Figure 22.11 *Farmers' expected price variation on local market for sales and purchases of corn. August–September is the main harvest season. June–July is the hungry season*

Source: Burke, 2014.

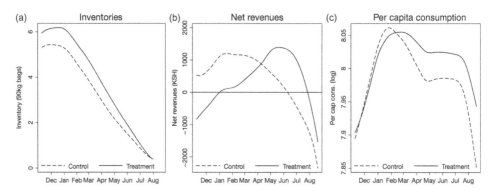

Figure 22.12 *Behavioral responses to price variations with (treatment) and without (control) access to credit. a: inventories. b: net revenues. c: per capita consumption*

Source: Burke, 2014.

the need to sell to meet urgent cash needs at harvest time, such as payment of school fees. Credit-market failure, and the displacement of this distortion on the product market, can thus be extremely costly for farm households, contributing to the reproduction of poverty and to family-farm failures. This sell low–buy high transaction is equivalent to a self-provided credit to gain access to post-harvest liquidity, at a very high implicit interest rate.

Burke (2014) together with the One Acre Fund, an NGO engaged in farmer service in Kenya, used an RCT to explore the benefits of access to post-harvest credit. Results suggest that it helps treated farmers store more after harvest in December–January (Figure 22.12a), sell less and even buy at harvest time (a negative net revenue in Figure 22.12b), sell later in June-July when prices are high, and postpone buying to the very end of the hungry season when inventories are driven to zero. The welfare effect, captured by per capita consumption, is convincing (Fig 22.12c). Instead of collapsing during the hungry season, consumption is maintained as a consequence of both more buying and destocking. If this storage activity is sufficiently prevalent in the community (which depends on the percentage of treated farmers, itself randomized), it has general equilibrium effects on local prices: prices fall less at harvest time and rise less later, spreading benefits through price smoothing to all farm households in the community. Overcoming the credit-market failure can thus have high efficiency and welfare benefits, contributing to the survival of the family farm.

Working for others at peak labor-demand time

With credit-market failures, and no harvest to sell during planting, weeding, and harvesting periods, liquidity can be obtained by selling labor to other farmers when demand for labor is high. This, however, competes with labor practices and yields on one's own farm. Takahashi and Barrett (2014) use this to explain lack of adoption of the labor-intensive System of Rice Intensification (SRI) by credit-constrained smallholders in Madagascar, at the cost of forgoing a potential 80 percent gain in yields.

Famers need to use off-farm wage labor in order to get the cash they need to buy food for their families during the hungry season, precisely when their own farms need labor allocation to adopt SRI.

Policy options to enhance the competitiveness of the family farm

Solutions may be technological, institutional, political, or strategic. They include the following.

1. *Land-saving technological innovations favoring smallholder farming*
    Because they have little land, smallholder farmers need access to land-saving technological change. This includes Green Revolution-type technologies, farming systems for high-value crops, and agro-ecological production techniques, with low use of purchased inputs if they have liquidity constraints (Altieri, 2009). Agroecological principles may be better adapted to the needs of small farmers than chemical-intensive agriculture, and this may increasingly be the case as petroleum resources become increasingly costly (IAASTD, 2008). However, like any other farmer, smallholder farmers need the benefits of modern science, including the contributions of Genetically Modified Organisms (GMOs) and other biological innovations (e.g. drought- and flood-resistant seed varieties) to their competitive advantage. In general, there is much underinvestment in the use of modern science to help smallholder farmers improve their resilience and competitiveness. These investments have to be largely in public research as smallholders tend not to offer an attractive market for private firms to invest in researching their production conditions. This is to a significant extent the strategy followed by the Gates and Rockefeller Foundations in their AGRA (a Green Revolution for Africa) program.

    There may exist constraints to adoption on the demand side as well. Farm households may have difficulty with the discipline of managing liquidity when there are so many unmet demands on the scarce cash available after harvest. We saw above that this may lead them to sell at low price to buy later at high price. It may also be due to behavior. Using an RCT approach, Duflo *et al.* (2011) show that farmers in Kenya tend to procrastinate in deciding on fertilizer purchases until later periods, when they may be too liquidity-constrained to purchase fertilizer, even though investing in fertilizer may be highly profitable. A solution consists in nudging these farmers to set aside at harvest time the necessary liquidity to buy fertilizers later in the season when they are needed. This can be done through small time-limited discounts such as the free delivery of fertilizers. These discounts can have higher welfare benefits than subsequent fertilizer subsidies, as practiced, for example, in Malawi.

2. *Institutional innovations to reduce credit-market failures*
    Because agriculture is seasonal, smallholders need liquidity-management strategies to have cash in hand when the time comes to plant again. Managing liquidity requires combining savings, access to credit with limited collateral, and other sources of income that provide monetary flows (such as remittances, wages earned

on the labor market, and income from rural non-farm employment). With interest rates in the 25 percent range, microfinance credit remains generally too expensive for traditional agriculture, leaving the problem of access to credit for smallholder farming largely unresolved. This deficit in accessing credit is symptomatic of the problem of the "missing middle" in enterprise finance: credit is available for very small financial transactions through microfinance, and for large transactions through commercial banks, but is still very much missing for small enterprises in agriculture and in other sectors to which these two options do not apply. Using a randomized grants approach, de Mel *et al.* (2008) show that there are high returns to capital investment in micro-enterprises in Sri Lanka, well in excess of market interest rates, which are not met through market mechanisms. This suggests that the supply side of credit is still highly deficient in serving the needs of small entrepreneurs in agriculture and in the RNFE.

3. *Institutional innovations to reduce insurance-market failures*
    Agriculture is highly risky, and poor smallholder farmers are highly risk-averse, creating a major dilemma for investment in family farming and the survival of the family farm. Mutual-insurance systems based on trust and reciprocity provide some protection for consumption against idiosyncratic shocks, but are insufficient to insure covariate production risks. New forms of risk management and risk coping are needed (see below). These include self-insurance (through savings and food stocks), diversification of sources of income, sharecropping contracts to share risk (as we saw in Chapter 20), and new index-based schemes insuring against climatic shocks. While progress has been made, uninsured risks remain pervasive, sharply limiting investment in smallholder farming.

4. *Institutional innovations to reduce transaction costs*
    Because agriculture is geographically dispersed, transaction costs in reaching markets can be huge, as illustrated in the price-band models. If farmers are located at some distance from markets, transaction costs become prohibitive and investment is not profitable. At the same time, local markets are shallow, and prices collapse in these markets as soon as there is success in production. Transaction costs can be reduced and market depth increased by better public infrastructure and better information systems. Market facilities such as warehouses with receipts that can be used as collateral for accessing loans can help farmers wait for prices better than those at harvest time. For smallholders, producers' organizations are key to servicing their members collectively, achieving scale in trading and market power, and contracting with supermarkets and agroindustry.

5. *Institutional innovations for the delivery of local public goods*
    When national governments fail to deliver public goods that are adequate to the needs of smallholders, local governments and communities can fill the gap. Local governments and community organizations have the advantage of accessing local information and social capital to help defeat opportunism in the provision of public goods. The community-driven development (CDD) approach has been developed for this purpose, allowing rural communities to prioritize the local public goods they need (Mansuri and Rao, 2004). Using an RCT across 49 Indonesian

villages, Olken (2010) compared decision-making mechanisms for local development projects, contrasting decisions taken in meetings led by representatives with direct democracy (decisions taken by votes). He found that choosing projects by direct democracy leads to higher satisfaction and greater willingness to participate, while making little difference to the actual projects selected (except for women's projects, which are favored more by direct democracy). But a community can also fail, in particular if it falls prey to capture by local elites (Platteau and Abraham, 2002) or suffers from excessive social conservatism, as it fears the risks of change (Bernard et al., 2010). Governments can also offer services specialized to the needs of smallholders. This is the case in Brazil, where the Ministry of Agriculture caters to medium–large commercial farmers, while the Ministry of Agrarian Development caters specifically to the needs of smallholders.

6. *Diversification of sources of income toward the RNFE*

Successful family farming relies on complementarity between on-farm activities and incomes derived from off-farm activities (Figure 22.13). Particularly important is self-employment in the RNFE. In Japan, Europe, and Taiwan, farm incomes are typically less than half the total income earned by smallholder households. For this, the local economy has to offer investment opportunities in formal or informal activities. Territorial development, supporting a vibrant local economy either linked to agriculture or based on decentralized economic activities, is thus an important factor for the survival of the family farm (Schejtman and Berdegué, 2004). The concept of clusters of economic activity, analyzed in Chapter 11, can be quite effective for this purpose.

7. *Economies of scale in farming, or marketing through organizations*

There are economies of scale in production due to the indivisibility of machinery, and in marketing due to the emergence of integrated value chains and supermarket contracts rewarding delivery of large product volumes with high quality standards. However, there exist institutional arrangements that allow smallholders to take advantage of these economies of scale, in spite of their small farm sizes (Reardon et al., 2009). Organizations for machine services can help break indivisibilities in capital goods. In Europe, the US, and Japan, most family farmers are members of cooperatives that help with marketing contracts. In India, Operation

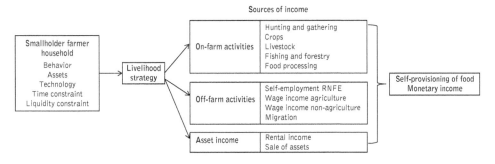

Figure 22.13 *Sources of income for a diversified smallholder household. RNFE = rural non-farm economy*

Flood, with 70,000 dairy cooperatives and 9 million members, has been a major success in linking smallholder producers, often landless dairy-cattle owners, to remunerative markets (Cunningham, 2009). Success in capturing economies of scale is essential for the competitiveness and permanence of smallholder farming. It can be done, but it requires a proactive role for family farmers and their organizations, and a supportive role for government and international donors (Hayami, 1996).

RISK AND SELF-INSURANCE IN HOUSEHOLD BEHAVIOR

Farming is a highly risky business. Poor people are risk-averse because a negative shock can have devastating consequences for them, operating as they are at the margin of survival. Recall the television scenes of dying children when smallholders and pastoralists are affected by drought in the Horn of Africa. At the same time, formal insurance is generally not available to these households. The combination of risk, risk aversion, and insurance-market failures implies that farm households must devise self-insurance strategies to reduce their income and consumption risks. This is done by risk management ex-ante relative to income realizations, and by risk-coping ex-post relative to income realizations. We have seen these strategies before and only briefly review here how they apply to farm households. For the household, the objective is to smooth consumption so it meets its consumption needs in both good and bad years. The timeline for risk-management and risk-coping initiatives is shown in Figure 22.14.

Risk management

Risk management refers to actions with the objective of reducing income risks for a given expected exposure to shocks. It includes the following actions:

1. *Income strategies*
   i. *Crop diversification.* Choose to specialize less than for maximum expected income. This is corroborated by the observation that smallholders have complex farming systems, in spite of their very small farms, while commercial farmers, with more land, tend to specialize more.
   ii. *Plant less risky traditional seeds* as opposed to high-yielding varieties (HYV) if the latter have higher expected yields but also higher exposure to climatic risk.
   iii. *Use a portfolio of activities to diversify sources of income.* Participate more in the labor market, in self-employment in the RNFE, and in migration to reduce

Figure 22.14 *Risk management and risk coping by farm households*

802

dependence on risky income from agriculture. Send a migrant to receive remittances, as in the new economics of migration (Chapter 12). Choose activities with incomes that have low correlation so that they will not all fail at the same time.

2. *Choice of contracts*

   i. *Use risk-sharing contracts* such as sharecropping, where the rent paid is proportional to output (Chapter 20), and forward-sales contracts that reduce price risks at harvest time. Both contracts help reduce risk at a cost. In sharecropping, risk reduction is obtained at the cost of reduced incentive for effort: the Marshallian inefficiency. In forward sales, more secure prices are obtained at the cost of a reduced price.

   ii. *Use insurance contracts.* An insurance contract, such as for index-based weather insurance, can be taken when available and affordable. It has, however, been widely observed that demand for formal insurance is low, even when potentially profitable. Successful weather-insurance schemes in India and Mexico are heavily subsidized. Cole *et al.* (2010) show that, in India, non-price factors also limit demand, in particular lack of trust in the insurance provider, liquidity constraints among poor households, and limited awareness of the importance of being insured.

3. *Mutual insurance.* Formal insurance is rarely available to farm households due to moral hazard and adverse selection creating market failures. Mutual insurance, where risk is shared among members of a social network, offers an alternative, although it only covers idiosyncratic shocks (that can be insured by others in the community) and shocks that are not too large (otherwise others will default in providing insurance coverage) (Townsend, 1994; Ligon *et al.*, 2002). The network can be the extended family system, the community (as in Scott's (1977) "moral economy of peasants"), or patron–client relations, where the patron helps the client in bad times in exchange for other services in normal times such as un-remunerated labor or political support. In mutual insurance, individual members share gains and losses with others in deviation from the long-term average. With perfect risk sharing, consumption at the household level should be insured against idiosyncratic risks and thus depend solely on the realization of community-level aggregate risk. Townsend (1994) tests this implication of perfect intra-village risk sharing using household panel data on consumption and income for three villages in India. He finds that the full-insurance hypothesis provides a good benchmark in that households' consumption levels move up and down together and do not appear to be much influenced by contemporaneous own income. The hypothesis has been tested by a number of others such as Morduch (1995) for India, Alderman and Garcia (1993) for Pakistan, Deaton (1992) for Côte d'Ivoire, and Udry (1990) for Nigeria. These studies reject the full-insurance model, but find that results are generally consistent with some degree of risk sharing.

4. *Precautionary savings.* Precautionary savings can take the form of cash, jewelry, animals, food stocks, and money in a savings account. Precautionary savings held in the form of productive assets imply choosing to accumulate more of the liquid

assets (e.g. bullocks in Pakistan) that can easily be sold in case of income shock, and fewer of the fixed assets (e.g. irrigation pumps) than needed for profit maximization (Rosenzweig and Wolpin, 1993). Precautionary savings in the form of liquid assets thus have an opportunity cost in terms of optimum investment for growth.

5. *Marriage of girls in other agroecological zones.* Rosenzweig and Stark (1989) showed that by marrying girls in other agroecological zones, a practice observed in South India, the extended family can assist in the event of covariate shocks that affect an entire agroecological zone.

Risk coping

Risk coping refers to actions that reduce consumption risks for given income realizations. It includes the following actions:

1. *Postpone non-essential consumption.* This is the easiest way of managing the deficit in liquidity to accommodate essential consumption expenditures and will typically be the first line of defense in responding to a liquidity shortage. This would apply most particularly to the acquisition of durable goods that can be postponed such as means of transportation and house furniture.

2. *Dis-save and borrow*

   i. *Dis-save productive assets.* Because productive assets are future sources of income—for instance, livestock for pastoralists in Ethiopia and Northern Kenya— there is an optimum balance between asset smoothing in response to a shock (letting household consumption fall to avoid selling too many animals when there is a shock) and consumption smoothing (selling animals when there is a shock to protect household consumption) (Carter and Barrett, 2006). Pastoralists are consequently willing to absorb considerable consumption hardship when there is a drought in order to shelter their livestock and secure future consumption. Fafchamps *et al.* (1998) show that, in drought-prone regions of Burkina Faso, farmers keep livestock as a buffer stock to protect their consumption from agricultural income fluctuations. They find, however, that livestock compensates for less than 30 percent of income shortfalls due to village-level rainfall shocks because farmers want to protect their productive investment in cattle for post-drought income recovery.

   ii. *Use credit.* To cope with a shock, households can take emergency loans from moneylenders or microfinance institutions (MFI). For risk coping, loans need to be flexible and quick. This is a desirable feature of loans made by moneylenders, at a high cost. An effective form of loan for risk-coping is quasi-credit, observed by Udry (1994) in northern Nigeria: the loan is taken when needed and repaid flexibly according to the mutual liquidity needs of the lender and the borrower. MFI loans (see Chapter 13) are often inadequate for risk coping because they have rigid rules and times of access, as, for instance, with ROSCAs and group lending. Much is left to do to adapt MFI lending for risk reduction—for instance, through access to pre-approved flexible lines of credit that can be used immediately when adversity strikes.

804

3. *Reallocate labor toward off-farm work.* Smallholder farmers typically balance on- and off-farm work as sources of income. When there is a weather shock, they seek greater off-farm employment. Income protection is reduced, however, if labor is locally non-tradable. Jayachandran (2006) shows that when there is a negative agricultural productivity shock due to lack of rainfall in India, more small farmers seek employment as farm workers, precisely when landlords demand less labor due to the drought. Higher supply and lower demand contribute to depress the farm wage, limiting the risk-coping value of the labor market. For landlords, by contrast, pro-cyclical wages serve as an effective insurance mechanism, providing them with cheaper labor just when they have lower yields.

4. *Take children out of school and send them to work.* There is, however, a high risk of irreversibility in doing this, as a child taken out of school is unlikely to return to school once the shock is over (de Janvry *et al.*, 2006). Risk coping through child labor thus provides a short-run solution to a household's income shortfall, at the risk of a long-run cost for the child (inheritance of poverty) in terms of lower schooling attainment. Saving on the nutrition and health needs of children is likely to have similarly long-term irreversible consequences. Using long-term panel data and differences in pre-school nutritional status across siblings for Zimbabwe, Alderman *et al.* (2006) show that drought and civil-war shocks that create pre-school malnutrition have large subsequent human-capital costs. Reduced height-for-age in pre-schoolers due to these shocks are associated with decreased height as young adults and a lower level of school achievement. This shows the large gains that social-safety-net programs can offer in helping to avoid these irreversibilities (Dercon, 2005).

5. *Rely on public social-safety nets.* This includes guaranteed-employment schemes in public works programs such as India's National Rural Employment Guarantee Act (NREGA) and food-for-work programs in Bangladesh. Other programs consist in CT or CCT programs such as the *Chile's Solidario* program that offers a quick response to those affected by a negative shock. However, as discussed in Chapter 14, few programs are yet designed to provide risk-coping protection to the vulnerable non-poor.

Note that risk management and risk coping are related since access to more risk-coping instruments allows for reduction of risk management. This in turn allows beneficiaries to take more risks in production and achieve higher expected incomes (Morduch, 1995). Because both risk management and risk coping are costly, there is an optimum balance to be decided in the use of each instrument.

INTRA-HOUSEHOLD ALLOCATION OF RESOURCES AND GENDER ROLES

A household is composed of several members who make production, consumption, and reproduction decisions. How these decisions are made can have deep implications for the efficient use of household resources, and for the welfare of the different household members, in particular men vs. women, and adults vs. children. Again, here we apply the separability theorem.

We analyze the role of gender in decision-making and the resulting consequences for efficiency and equity. Say that a household is composed of a man M and a woman F. Each member has their own utility function: $U_M(q, a)$ for the man and $U_F(q, a)$ for the woman, where:

> q is household consumption
> a is the household's set of actions such as labor supply.

The budget constraint for the household is:

> $pq = Y_M(a) + Y_F(a) + T_M + T_F,$
>
> where
> p is the price of the consumption good
> $Y_M(a)$ is the income earned by the man
> $Y_F(a)$ is the income earned by the woman
> T_M and T_F are unearned income transfers received by the man and the woman respectively.

There are two ways in which the household may decide on consumption q and actions a.

> *Unitary model.* In this case, one person decides on behalf of the household (this person could be a patriarch, a matriarch, or an elder), or both cooperate in deciding jointly on behalf of the household, or they have identical utility functions. In this case,

> $U_M(q, a) = U_F(q, a) = U(q, a).$

> The household's decision on q and a is thus given by the following unitary model:

> $\text{Max}_{q, a}\ U(q, a)$ subject to $pq = Y_M(a) + Y_F(a) + T_M + T_F.$

> In this case, there is separability between production and consumption decisions. Income is maximized and then allocated to the various members to maximize utility. The household is efficient. It is Pareto optimal. There is income pooling between the two genders before it is allocated to each for consumption.

> *Bargaining model.* In this case, the two genders have different utility functions (McElroy, 1990). The household will consequently maximize a weighted function of the two utilities, with the weight μ reflecting the bargaining power between the two genders:

> $\text{Max}_{q, a}\ U_M(q, a) + \mu U_F(q, a)$ subject to $pq = Y_M(a) + Y_F(a) + T_M + T_F.$

There are two possible situations regarding the specification of μ.

1. *When μ is exogenous to decisions regarding q and a.* In this case, the bargaining weight was established before household formation. Separability still holds. The household maximizes efficiency (Pareto-efficient, income-pooling), and then allocates

806

consumption according to the bargaining weight. This weight is thus important for equity. As in bargaining models, it is determined by each member's outside options. The woman's bargaining weight is increased by her opportunities outside the household, depending on her education, the opportunities she has in the labor market, and assets that she directly controls such as a dowry brought to the household over which she maintains jurisdiction in case of divorce. Fafchamps *et al.* (2009) showed that, among rural households in Ethiopia, the woman's bargaining power is associated with her cognitive ability, her level of independent income, and her control over assets in case of divorce.

2. *When μ is endogenous to household decisions on q and a.* In this case, separability breaks down. Bargaining is determined by:

$$\mu = \mu(Y_M(a), Y_F(a), T_M, T_F, p).$$

Efficiency and equity are related. Unless the two utility functions happen to be identical, resources are inefficiently allocated in the household because they affect the bargained outcome. There is no income pooling. Fafchamps *et al.* (2009) find that, among rural households in Ethiopia, the woman's bargaining power is associated not only with her cognitive ability and asset devolution upon divorce, but also with her current level of independent income. An unearned income transfer affects the bargaining position of the recipient, and consequently what the household does. The household is not Pareto-efficient. Distributional gains within the household are achieved at the cost of an efficiency loss (Bourguignon and Chiappori, 1992).

Implications for development outcomes

How the household makes decisions can have large consequences on outcomes such as the following:

- The allocation of land between food crops (typically prioritized by the woman) vs. cash crops (prioritized by the man).
- The allocation of fertilizer between the family plot under the authority of the man and the woman's own plot in West Africa.
- The allocation of CTs between investment (typically preferred by the man) and expenditures on children's health, nutrition, and education (preferred by the woman).
- The allocation of food among household members, most critically in periods of drought and food shortages, with implications for health and capacity to work.

Tests of income pooling

This important contrast between two outcomes—efficient under unitary and exogenous bargaining power, and inefficient under endogenous bargaining power—has motivated many empirical tests to find out which models holds best.

In a unitary household, the leader decides on resource allocation on behalf of the household's interest. S(he) acts as a household-level social planner. There could be unequal allocation of food across members in accordance with their unequal contributions to income and production. The objective of the decision-maker is to protect the food consumption of wage earners on behalf of the collective interest, resulting in gender-biased nutritional differences. However, studies of intra-household food allocation in India have shown that altruism prevails over efficiency rules to secure survival (Pitt *et al.*, 1990), implying a trade-off between equity and efficiency.

The use of income transfers that go directly to the man or to the woman give us a test of the income-pooling hypothesis. If there is pooling, the recipient of the transfer should not affect its use. The introduction of an old-age-pension program in South Africa allowed for such a test (Duflo, 2003). Non-contributory pensions were allocated to poor women above 60 years' old and poor men above 65 years' old. A regression discontinuity design can be used to contrast household expenditures in households with a grandmother who is just eligible vs. a grandmother who is not quite eligible, and the same for a grandfather. Results show a positive impact of grandmothers' pensions on the nutritional status of girls and no such effect of grandfathers' pensions. Income pooling is thus rejected.

In Burkina Faso, polygamous households cultivate a family plot and each woman cultivates her own plot. The family plot is used to feed the family, and each woman's plot is used to complement food allocations to her own children and to generate income for her personal expenditures such as clothing. Udry (1996) observed that fertilizer is over-allocated to the family plot and under-allocated to the woman's plot relative to the way it would be allocated to maximize the joint return from the two plots (i.e. to achieve the Pareto-efficient outcome). This suggests a bargaining household with male dominance of fertilizer-allocation decision-making, and Pareto inefficiency in using the household's resources.

Policy implications

The policy implications of a bargaining household with endogenous weight are clear for the design of programs to favor children. Oportunidades in Mexico and Bolsa Família in Brazil channel CCTs for child education, health, and nutrition through the woman. If the household were unitary, the gender of the recipient would make no difference. If households are of the bargaining type, transfers through the woman may have greater impact on child welfare. Evaluations of these programs (Quisumbing and McClafferty, 2006) show that giving mothers control over the transfer helps empower them and strengthen their bargaining positions in the household, with favorable outcomes for child welfare.

CONCEPTS SEEN IN THIS CHAPTER

Ellis' definition of peasants

Definition based on labor-market participation: net sellers, self-sufficient, net buyers

Residual claimant

Separability between production (efficiency) and consumption (equity) decisions

Net buyers and net sellers of food

Inverse relation between TFP and farm size

Incomplete land reform

Self-insurance

Mutual insurance

Patron–client relationship

Irreversibility in risk coping

Rural non-farm economy (RNFE)

Community-Driven Development (CDD)

Unitary household model

Bargaining household model

Income-pooling hypothesis or Pareto-efficient household

REFERENCES

Adamopoulos, Tasso, and Diego Restuccia. 2011. "The Size Distribution of Farms and International Productivity Differences." Working Paper 441, Department of Economics, University of Toronto.

Albertus, Michael. 2015. "Explaining Patterns of Redistribution Under Autocracy: The Case of Peru's Revolution from Above." *Latin American Research Review* 50(2): 107–34.

Alderman, Harold, and Marito Garcia. 1993. "Poverty, Household Food Security, and Nutrition in Rural Pakistan." Research Report No. 96. Washington, DC: International Food Policy Research Institute.

Alderman, Harold, John Hoddinott, and Bill Kinsey. 2006. "Long Term Consequences of Early Childhood Malnutrition." *Oxford Economic Papers* 58(3): 450–74.

Altieri, Miguel. 2009. "Agroecology, Small Farms and Food Sovereignty." *Monthly Review* 61(3): 102–13

Bardhan, Pranab. 2003. *Poverty, Agrarian Structure, and Political Economy in India: Selected Essays.* New Delhi: Oxford University Press.

Barrett, Christopher. 2005. "Displaced Distortions: Financial Market Failures and Seemingly Inefficient Resource Allocation in Low-Income Rural Communities." Working paper, Department of Economics, Cornell University.

Bélières, J-F., P. Bonnal, P-M. Bosc, B. Losch, J. Marzin, and J-M. Sourisseau. 2013. *Les agricultures familiales du monde. Définitions, contributions et politiques publiques.* Montpellier: CIRAD.

Bernard, Tanguy, Alain de Janvry, and Elisabeth Sadoulet. 2010. "When Does Community Conservatism Constrain Village Organizations?" *Economic Development and Cultural Change* 58(4): 609–41.

Bourguignon, François, and Pierre Chiappori. 1992. "Collective Models of Household Behavior: An Introduction." *European Economic Review* 36(2–3): 355–64.

Burke, Marshall. 2014. "Selling Low and Buying High: An Arbitrage Puzzle in Kenyan Villages." Working paper, Department of Agricultural and Resource Economics, University of California at Berkeley.

Carter, Michael, and Bradford Barham. 1996. "Level Playing Fields and Laissez Faire: Post-Liberal Development Strategies in Inegalitarian Agrarian Economies." *World Development* 24(7): 1133–50.

Carter, Michael, and Christopher Barrett. 2006. "The Economics of Poverty Traps and Persistent Poverty: An Asset-Based Approach." *Journal of Development Studies* 42(2): 178–99.

Chayanov, Alexander. 1966. *The Theory of Peasant Economy*. Madison, WI: University of Wisconsin Press.

Cole, Shawn, Xavier Giné, Jeremy Tobacman, Petia Topalova, Robert Townsend, and James Vickery. 2010. "Barriers to Household Risk Management: Evidence from India." Working Paper No. 09–116, Harvard Business School.

Cunningham, Kenda. 2009. "Rural and Urban Linkages: Operation Flood's Role in India's Dairy Development." Washington, DC: International Food Policy Research Institute Discussion Paper 00924.

Deaton, Angus. 1992. "Saving and Income Smoothing in Côte d'Ivoire." *Journal of African Economics* 1(1): 1–24.

Deininger, Klaus. 2003. *Land Policies for Growth and Poverty Reduction*. Washington, DC: World Bank.

Deininger, Klaus, and Derek Byerlee. 2011. "Rising Global Interest in Farmland: Can It Yield Sustainable and Equitable Benefits?" Washington, DC: Agriculture and Rural Development, World Bank.

de Janvry, Alain, and Elisabeth Sadoulet. 2009. "Subsistence Farming as a Safety Net for Food Price Shocks." *Development in Practice* 21(4–5): 449–56.

de Janvry, Alain, and Elisabeth Sadoulet. 2010. "The Global Food Crisis and Guatemala: What Crisis and For Whom?" *World Development* 38(9): 1328–39.

de Janvry, Alain, Marcel Fafchamps, and Elisabeth Sadoulet. 1991. "Peasant Household Behavior with Missing Markets: Some Paradoxes Explained." *Economic Journal* 101(409): 1400–17.

de Janvry, Alain, Frederico Finan, Elisabeth Sadoulet, and Renos Vakis. 2006. "Can Conditional Cash Transfer Programs Serve as Safety Nets in Keeping Children at School and from Working When Exposed to Shocks?" *Journal of Development Economics* 79(2): 349–73.

de Mel, Suresh, David McKenzie, and Christopher Woodruff. 2008. "Returns to Capital in Microenterprises: Evidence from a Field Experiment." *Quarterly Journal of Economics* 123(4): 1329–72.

Dercon, Stefan. 2005. "Risk, Growth, and Poverty: What Do We Know, What Do We Need to Know?" Washington, DC: World Bank.

Duflo, Esther. 2003. "Grandmothers and Granddaughters: Old-Age Pensions and Intra-household Allocation in South Africa." *World Bank Economic Review* 17(1): 1–25.

Duflo, Esther, Michael Kremer, and Jonathan Robinson. 2011. "Nudging Farmers to Use Fertilizer: Theory and Experimental Evidence from Kenya." *American Economic Review* 101(6): 2350–90.

Ellis, Frank. 1994. *Peasant Economics: Farm Households in Agrarian Development*. Cambridge: Cambridge University Press.

Eswaran, Mukesh, and Ashok Kotwal. 1986. "Access to Capital and Agrarian Production Organization." *Economic Journal* 96(382): 482–98.

Fafchamps, Marcel, Christopher Udry, and Katherine Czukas. 1998. "Drought and Saving in West Africa: Are Livestock a Buffer Stock?" *Journal of Development Economics* 55(2): 273–305.

Fafchamps, Marcel, Bereket Kebede, and Agnes Quisumbing. 2009. "Intra-household Welfare in Rural Ethiopia." *Oxford Bulletin of Economics and Statistics* 71(4): 567–99.

FAO (Food and Agricultural Organization of the United Nations). 2012. *2000 World Census of Agriculture: Analysis and International Comparison of the Results, 1996–2005*. FAO Statistical Development Series 12. Rome: FAO.

Forman, Shepard. 1970. *The Raft Fishermen: Tradition and Change in the Brazilian Peasant Economy*. Bloomington, IN: Indiana University Press.

Foster, Andrew, and Mark Rosenzweig. 2010. "Is There Surplus Labor in Rural India?" Working Paper #85, Economics Department, Yale University.

Hayami, Yujiro. 1996. "The Peasant in Economic Modernization." *American Journal of Agricultural Economics* 78(5): 1157–67.

Hazell, Peter, Colin Poulton, Steve Wiggins, and Andrew Dorward. 2006. "The Future of Small Farms: Synthesis Paper." Santiago: RIMISP background paper for the *World Development Report 2008*.

HLPE (High Level Panel of Experts on Food Security and Nutrition). 2013. *Investing in Smallholder Agriculture for Food Security*. A report by the HLPE of the Committee on World Food Security. Rome: HLPE.

IAASTD. 2008. *A Report of the International Assessment on Agricultural Science and Technology*. Washington, DC: World Bank.

Jayachandran, Seema. 2006. "Selling Labor Low: Wage Responses to Productivity Shocks in Developing Countries." *Journal of Political Economy* 114(3): 538–75.

Jayne, Thomas, G. Tembo and J.J. Nijhoff. 2005. "Experiences of Food Market Reform and Price Stabilization in Eastern and Southern Africa." Working paper, Department of Agricultural, Food, and Resource Economics, Michigan State University.

Jayne, Thomas, Ballard Zulu, and J.J. Nijhoff. 2006. "Stabilizing Food Markets in Eastern and Southern Africa." *Food Policy* 31(4): 328–41.

Kaminski, Jonathan, Luc Christiaensen, and Christopher Gilbert. 2014. "The End of Seasonality? New Insights from Sub-Saharan Africa." Washington, DC: World Bank.

Keswell, Malcolm, and Michael Carter. 2014. "Poverty and Land Redistribution." *Journal of Development Economics* 110(September): 250–61.

Ligon, Ethan, Jonathan Thomas, and Tim Worrall. 2002. "Informal Insurance Arrangements with Limited Commitment: Theory and Evidence from Village Economies." *Review of Economic Studies* 69(1): 209–44.

Lipton, Michael. 2009. *Land Reform in Developing Countries: Property Rights and Property Wrongs*. London: Routledge.

Mansuri, Ghazala, and Vijayendra Rao. 2004. "Community-Based and -Driven Development: A Critical Review." *World Bank Research Observer* 19(1): 1–39.

McElroy, Marjorie. 1990. "The Empirical Content of Nash-Bargained Household Behavior." *Journal of Human Resources* 25(4): 559–83.

Morduch, Jonathan. 1995. "Income Smoothing and Consumption Smoothing." *Journal of Economic Perspectives* 9(3): 103–14.

Olken, Benjamin. 2010. "Direct Democracy and Local Public Goods: Evidence from a Field Experiment in Indonesia." *American Political Science Review* 104(2): 243–67.

Pitt, Mark, Mark Rosenzweig, and Md Nazmul Hassan. 1990. "Productivity, Health, and Inequality in the Intra-household Distribution of Food in Low-Income Countries." *American Economic Review* 80(5): 1139–56.

811

Platteau, Jean-Philippe, and Anita Abraham. 2002. "Participatory Development in the Presence of Endogenous Community Imperfections." *Journal of Development Studies* 39(2): 104–36.

Quisumbing, Agnes, and Bonnie McClafferty. 2006. *Food Security in Practice: Using Gender Research in Development.* Washington, DC: International Food Policy Research Institute.

Reardon, Thomas, Peter Timmer, Christopher Barrett, and Julio Berdegué. 2003. "The Rise of Supermarkets in Africa, Asia, and Latin America," *American Journal of Agricultural Economics* 85(5): 1140–6.

Reardon, Thomas, Christopher Barrett, Julio Berdegué, and Johan Swinnen. 2009. "Agrifood Industry Transformation and Small Farmers in Developing Countries." *World Development* 37(11): 1717–27.

Roemer, John. 1998. *Equality of Opportunity.* Cambridge, MA: Harvard University Press.

Rosenzweig, Mark, and Kenneth Wolpin. 1993. "Credit Market Constraints, Consumption Smoothing, and the Accumulation of Durable Production Assets in Low-income Countries: Investment in Bullocks in India." *Journal of Political Economy* 101(2): 223–44.

Rosenzweig, Mark, and Odeth Stark. 1989. "Consumption Smoothing, Migration, and Marriage: Evidence from Rural India." *Journal of Political Economy* 97(4): 905–26.

Sadoulet, Elisabeth, and Alain de Janvry. 1995. *Quantitative Development Policy Analysis.* Baltimore: Johns Hopkins University Press.

Schejtman, Alejandro, and Julio Berdegué. 2004. *Rural Territorial Development.* Santiago: RIMISP.

Scott, James. 1977. *The Moral Economy of the Peasant: Rebellion and Subsistence in Southeast Asia.* New Haven, CT: Yale University Press.

Scott, James. 1985. *Weapons of the Weak: Everyday Forms of Peasant Resistance.* New Haven, CT: Yale University Press.

Singh, Inderjit, Lyn Squire, and John Strauss (eds.). 1986. *Agricultural Household Models: Extensions and Applications.* Baltimore: Johns Hopkins University Press.

Takahashi, Kazushi, and Christopher Barrett. 2014. "The System of Rice Intensification and its Impacts on Household Income and Child Schooling: Evidence from Rural Indonesia." *American Journal of Agricultural Economics* 96 (1): 269–89.

Townsend, Robert. 1994. "Risk and Insurance in Village India." *Econometrica* 62(3): 539–91.

Udry, Christopher. 1990. "Credit Markets in Northern Nigeria: Credit as Insurance in a Rural Economy." *World Bank Economic Review* 4(3): 251–69.

Udry, Christopher. 1994. "Risk and Insurance in a Rural Credit Market: An Empirical Investigation in Northern Nigeria." *Review of Economic Studies* 61(3): 495–526.

Udry, Christopher. 1996. "Gender, Agricultural Production, and the Theory of the Household." *Journal of Political Economy* 104(5): 1010–46.

Warriner, Doreen. 1969. *Land Reform in Principle and Practice.* New York: Oxford University Press.

Weng, Lingfei Agni Boedhihartono, Paul Dirks, John Dixon, Muhammad Lubis, and Jeffrey Sayer. 2013. "Mineral Industries, Growth Corridors, and Agricultural Development in Africa." *Global Food Security* 2(3): 195–202.

Wolf, Eric. 1965. *Peasants.* New York: Prentice Hall.

World Bank. 2007. *World Development Report 2008: Agriculture for Development.* Washington, DC.

Index